ConAmA	Contemporary American A...
ConAmL	Contemporary American Li...
ConAu	Contemporary Authors
ConDr	Contemporary Dramatists
ConLC	Contemporary Literary Criticism
ConNov	Contemporary Novelists
ConP	Contemporary Poets
CroCD	Crowell's Handbook of Contemporary Drama
CrtT	The Critical Temper
CurBio	Current Biography
CyAL	Cyclopaedia of American Literature
CyWA	Cyclopedia of World Authors
DcAmA	Dictionary of American Authors
DcAmB	Dictionary of American Biography
DcBiA	Dictionary of Biographies...Authors Digest Series
DcCAA	Dictionary of Contemporary American Artists
DcCLAA	Dictionary of Contemporary Latin American Authors
DcEnA	Dictionary of English Authors
DcEnL	Dictionary of English Literature
DcEuL	Dictionary of European Literature
DcLEL	Dictionary of Literature in the English Language
DcNAA	Dictionary of North American Authors Deceased before 1950
DcOrL	Dictionary of Oriental Literatures
DcRusL	Dictionary of Russian Literature
DcSpL	Dictionary of Spanish Literature
DrAF	Directory of American Fiction Writers (1976 edition)
DrAP	Directory of American Poets (1975 edition)
DrAS	Directory of American Scholars
EarABI	Early American Book Illustrators and Wood Engravers
EncAB	Encyclopedia of American Biography
EncMys	Encyclopedia of Mystery and Detection
EncWL	Encyclopedia of World Literature in the 20th Century
EuAu	European Authors, 1000-1900
EvEuW	Everyman's Dictionary of European Writers
EvLB	Everyman's Dictionary of Literary Biography, English & American
FamWC	Famous War Correspondents
FemPA	Female Poets of America
ForP	Foreign Press
ForWC	Foremost Women in Communications
HisAmM	History of American Magazines
HsB&A	House of Beadle and Adams and its Dime and Nickel Novels
IndAu	Indiana Authors and Their Books
IntMPA	International Motion Picture Almanac
IntWW	International Who's Who
InvJ	Investigative Journalist
JBA	Junior Book of Authors
LEduc	Leaders in Education
LiJA	Literary Journal in America
LivBAA	Living Black American Authors
LivFWS	Living Female Writers of the South
LongC	Longman Companion to Twentieth Century Literature
Lor&LP	Lords & Laborers of the Press
McGWD	McGraw-Hill Encyclopedia of World Drama
MnnWr	Minnesota Writers
ModAL	Modern American Literature
ModBL	Modern British Literature
ModGL	Modern German Literature
ModRL	Modern Romance Literatures
ModSL	Modern Slavic Literatures

(Continued on back end paper)

JOURNALIST
BIOGRAPHIES
MASTER INDEX

JOURNALIST BIOGRAPHIES MASTER INDEX

A Guide to 90,000 References to Historical and Contemporary Journalists in 200 Biographical Directories and Other Sources

Alan E. Abrams, Editor

FIRST EDITION

Gale Biographical Index Series
Number 4

Gale Research Company • Book Tower • Detroit, Michigan 48226

Editor: Alan E. Abrams
Assistant Editor: Elizabeth A. Scala
Editorial Associate: Margaret J. Mangold
Editorial Assistants: Barbara A. Brownell
Donna Willis
Robert Bruce Young, Jr.
Consultants: Dennis La Beau
Miranda Herbert
Barbara McNeil
Production Manager: Michaeline Nowinski
Cover Design: Arthur Chartow

Computerized photocomposition by
Computer Composition Corporation,
Madison Heights, Michigan

Library of Congress Cataloging in Publication Data

Main entry under title:

Journalist biographies master index.

(Gale biographical index series ; no. 4)
1. Journalists--Biography--Indexes. I. Abrams,
Alan E. II. Gale Research Company.
Z6940.J58 [PN4820] 016.070'92'2 [B] 77-9144
ISBN 0-8103-1086-4

Introduction

Journalist Biographies Master Index enables the user to locate, without tedious searching, biographical information on a single person from among the entries in over 200 standard biographical dictionaries and directories of journalists. An important feature of *JBMI* is that it also indexes textual references to individuals which appear in about 15 historical studies of the field of journalism.

JBMI tells the user which edition of which publication to consult or, almost equally as helpful, it reveals that there is no listing for a given individual in any of the publications indexed. In cases where *JBMI* has multiple listings for the same person, the searcher is able to choose the source which is most convenient to him, or to locate multiple sketches to compare with one another.

Compilation Procedures

Other volumes in Gale's Biographical Master Index Series are compiled strictly by citing only names listed in the biographical dictionaries indexed. In compiling *JBMI,* however, a reverse procedure has been followed in part, in that an attempt has been made to identify persons who have worked as journalists, and then to find sources of biographical information for them, if the source of the identification did not also contain personal data. This process has yielded some references to persons who have been of some importance in journalism, but the references have been too slight or oblique to justify citing the publication as a biographical source. The names of such individuals have been included in *JBMI,* however, marked *NF* (Not Found) to indicate the reason a biographical reference is not cited in the listing. The following are typical citations for such unidentified persons:

> **Belair,** Felix, Jr. 1908-1978 NF
> **Dalton,** David 1942- NF
> **Donaldson,** Sam NF
> **Frisch,** Leon NF
> **Fry,** William NF
> **Goldberg,** Abraham d1942 NF
> **Jarriel,** Tom NF
> **Kalb,** Bernard NF
> **Koppel,** Ted NF
> **Lewinson,** Minna NF
> **Perry,** Christopher J, Sr. d 1921 NF
> **Simon,** Bob NF

The editor would like to hear from users of the index who may be able to supply dates and biographical sources for names so marked.

How to Read a Citation

Each citation gives the journalist's name, followed by the years of birth and/or death. If there is no year of birth, the death date is preceded by a lower case *d*. After the dates are listed codes for the books indexed which include references to the individual, as in the following examples:

> **Parker,** George Frederick 1847-1926 *AmJnl,*
> *AmLY, BioIn 2, DcNAA, HisAmM XR, IndAu 1916,*
> *WhNAA*
> **Safire,** William L 1929- *BioIn 9, BioIn 10,*
> *ConAu 19R, CurBio XR, NewYTBE 4, WhoAm 1974*

The titles of works indexed in *JBMI* and the codes used to refer to them are printed on the endsheets, and a section of complete bibliographic citations for the indexed works follows this introduction.

Standards of Inclusion

A journalist, for purposes of selection for indexing in *JBMI,* has been defined as a person who has devoted a significant part of his or her career to work related to newspapers, magazines, or the broadcast media. Thus, major literary lights such as William Cullen Bryant, Edgar Allen Poe, Samuel L. Clemens, Ernest Hemingway, and Bret Harte, who are better known for their subsequent prose and poetry, qualify as journalists in this historic perspective.

In general, the definition has embraced newspaper and magazine reporters, editors, publishers, correspondents, cartoonists (both editorial and syndicated), broadcast news reporters and correspondents, network on-the-air and behind-the-scenes personalities, and news executives.

Special attention has been given to identifying, and finding biographical sources for, winners of journalism awards.

The emphasis on journalists suggests the focus of this publication, but perhaps it should be stated explicitly that *JBMI* is a *selective* compilation. Thus, not every name in a cited biographical source will appear here. This is especially true in the case of the two sources by Mott, which include many references to political, business, and other obviously non-journalistic personalities.

Editorial Practices

Spellings and birth and death dates have been standardized in accordance with common practice and the best information available. Although a listing may appear in *JBMI* in a somewhat different form than in the index of a cited source, care has been taken to assure that the user can still easily locate the indexed reference.

Cross indexes from and to variant forms of names appear with some frequency. Pseudonyms, however, are cited only if a writer used them for journalistic purposes; strictly literary nom-de-plumes do not appear in this work.

Biography Index, though not a biographical dictionary, has been included because it is a rich source of leads to obituraries, magazine articles, and other types of information concerning persons on whom information is often not available elsewhere.

Acknowledgments

As in any project of this size and scope, many people have made valuable contributions. In particular, however, the editor wishes to acknowledge the help of numerous people inside the major broadcast networks who made available internal personnel lists. It is only from such a source that it is possible to secure identifications for network television news correspondents whose names and faces enter our living rooms every night. Information about these correspondents is often even harder to find, and many of them are listed without references to biographical sources. (With the recent change in scope of Gale's *Contemporary Authors* series to include writers other than authors of books, biographical material on more and more journalists, including broadcast journalists, is becoming available.)

In addition, three antiquarian book dealers receive a special word of thanks for their assistance in providing the editor with primary research materials from which he drew heavily in the preparation of this work. The assistance of Marc Emery, of the City Lights Book Shop, London, Ontario, Canada; Jay Platt, of the West Side Book Shop, Ann Arbor, Michigan; and Ethel Claes, of the B. C. Claes Book Store, Detroit, Michigan, was invaluable.

Suggestions are Welcome

Journalist Biographies Master Index is to be used in conjunction with other biographical sources. Its primary purpose is to direct the user to sources of further information. The editor will welcome suggestions from users for additional works which could be indexed, or any other comments or suggestions.

Bibliographic Key to Publication Codes
for Use in Locating Sources

Unless otherwise noted, the books from which names were taken for *Journalist Biographies Master Index* provide biographical and bibliographical information.

Code	Source
AfA 1	*African Authors: A Companion to Black African Writing, Volume 1: 1300-1973.* By Donald E. Herdeck. Washington, D.C.: Black Orpheus Press, 1973.
Alli	Allibone, S. Austin. *A Critical Dictionary of English Literature and British and American Authors Living and Deceased from the Earliest Accounts to the Latter Half of the Nineteenth Century:* Containing Over Forty-six Thousand Articles (authors) with Forty Indexes of Subjects. 3 vols. Philadelphia: J.B. Lippincott & Co., 1858-1871. Reprinted, Detroit: Gale Research Company, 1965.
Alli Sup	*A Supplement to Allibone's Critical Dictionary of English Literature and British and American Authors:* Containing Over Thirty-seven Thousand Articles (authors), and Enumerating Over Ninety-three Thousand Titles. 2 vols. By John Foster Kirk. Philadelphia: J. B. Lippincott & Co., 1891. Reprinted, Detroit: Gale Research Company, 1965.
AmArch 1970	*American Architects Directory.* 3rd ed., 1970. Edited by John F. Gane. Published under the sponsorship of American Institute of Architects. New York: R. R. Bowker Company, 1970.
AmAu	*American Authors, 1600-1900: A Biographical Dictionary of American Literature.* Edited by Stanley J. Kunitz and Howard Haycraft. New York: H. W. Wilson Company, 1938.
AmAu&B	*American Authors and Books, 1640 to the Present Day.* 3rd rev. ed. By W. J. Burke and Will D. Howe. Revised by Irving Weiss and Anne Weiss. New York: Crown Publishers, 1972.
AmEA 1974	*American Economic Association 1974 Directory of Members.* Edited by Rendigs Fels. Published as Volume 54, Number 5, October, 1974 of *The American Economic Review.*
AmJnl	*American Journalism: A History, 1690-1960.* 3rd ed. By Frank Luther Mott. New York: Macmillan Company, 1962.
	The cornerstone of published works on the history of American journalism. This study succeeds in condensing 270 years of American journalistic history into one compact volume of facts and anecdotes. Textual references. Index begins on page 867.
AmLY	*The American Literary Yearbook: A Biographical and Bibliographical Dictionary of Living North American Authors; A Record of Contemporary Literary Activity; An Authors' Manual and Students' Text Book.* Vol. 1, 1919. Edited by Hamilton Traub. Henning, Minn.: Paul Traub, Publisher, 1919. Reprinted, Detroit: Gale Research Company, 1968.
	Biographical dictionary begins on page 57. A list of pen names and

pseudonyms begins on page 49, and is cited in this index by the code XR.

AmM&W 73   *American Men and Women of Science.* 12th ed. Edited by the Jaques Cattell Press. New York: R. R. Bowker Company, 1971-1973.

In two series:
The Physical and Biological Sciences, *indicated by code 73P.*
The Social and Behavioral Sciences, *indicated by code 73S.*

AmNov   *American Novelists of Today.* By Harry R. Warfel. New York: American Book Co., 1951. Reprinted, Westport, Conn.: Greenwood Press, 1976.

The Index of Married Names and Pseudonyms *begins on page 477, and is cited in this index by the code* XR.

AmRP   *The American Radical Press, 1880-1960.* 2 vols. Edited with an introduction by Joseph R. Conlin. Westport, Conn.: Greenwood Press, 1974.

One hundred essays on 119 different periodicals provide a comprehensive view of the radical press in America between 1880 and 1960 and, in effect, a history of American radicalism itself.

AmSCAP 1966   *The ASCAP Biographical Dictionary of Composers, Authors and Publishers.* 1966 ed. Compiled and edited by the Lynn Farnol Group. New York: American Society of Composers, Authors, and Publishers, 1966.

AmWr   *American Writers: A Collection of Literary Biographies.* 4 vols. Edited by Leonard Unger. New York: Charles Scribner's Sons, 1974.

Originally published as The University of Minnesota Pamphlets on American Writers.

AnCL   *Anthology of Children's Literature.* 4th ed. Compiled and edited by Edna Johnson, Evelyn R. Sickels and Frances Clarke Sayers. Boston: Houghton Mifflin Company, 1970.

AnMV 1926   *Anthology of Magazine Verse for 1926 and Yearbook of American Poetry.* Edited by William Stanley Braithwaite. 1926. Reprinted, Freeport, N.Y.: Books for Libraries Press, Granger Index Reprint Series, 1972.

A Biographical Dictionary of Poets in the United States is found in Part IV, at the back of this edition.

ArizL   *Arizona in Literature: A Collection of the Best Writings of Arizona Authors from Early Spanish Days to the Present Time.* By Mary G. Boyer. Glendale, Calif.: Arthur H. Clark Company, 1935. Reprinted, Ann Arbor: Gryphon Books, 1971. Also available from Gale Research Company on microfiche.

Use the Index that begins on page 569 to find any given journalist.

AtlBL   *Atlantic Brief Lives: A Biographical Companion to the Arts.* Edited by Louis Kronenberger. Boston: Little, Brown and Company, Atlantic Monthly Press, 1971.

Au&Wr   *The Author's and Writer's Who's Who.* 6th ed. Darien, Conn.: Hafner Publishing Company; London: Burke's Peerage, 1971.

AuBYP   *Authors of Books for Young People.* 2nd ed. By Martha E. Ward and Dorothy A. Marquardt. Metuchen, N.J.: Scarecrow Press, 1971.

AuNews 1   *Authors in the News:* A Compilation of News Stories and Feature Articles from American Newspapers and Magazines Covering Writers and Other Members of the Communications Media. Vol. 1. Edited by Barbara Nykoruk. Detroit: Gale Research Company, 1976.

Many of the articles give biographical information.

AuNews 2	*Authors in the News...* Vol. 2. Detroit: Gale Research Company, 1977.
	Many of the articles give biographical information.
BbD	*The Bibliophile Dictionary:* A Biographical Record of the Great Authors, with Bibliographical Notices of their Principal Works from the Beginning of History. Compiled and arranged by Nathan Haskell Dole, Forrest Morgan, and Caroline Ticknor. New York and London: The International Bibliophile Society, 1904. Reprinted, Detroit: Gale Research Company, 1966. Also available from Gale on microfiche.
	Originally published as volumes 29 and 30 of the Bibliophile Library of Literature, Art and Rare Manuscripts.
BbtC	*Bibliotheca Canadensis: or A Manual of Canadian Literature.* By Henry J. Morgan. Ottawa: G.E. Desbarats, 1867. Reprinted, Detroit: Gale Research Company, 1968. Also available from Gale on microfiche.
BiD&SB	*Biographical Dictionary and Synopsis of Books Ancient and Modern.* Edited by Charles Dudley Warner. Akron, Ohio: Werner Company, 1902. Reprinted, Detroit: Gale Research Company, 1965. Also available from Gale on microfiche.
BiDLA	*A Biographical Dictionary of the Living Authors of Great Britain and Ireland:* Comprising Literary Memoirs and Anecdotes of their Lives; and a Chronological Register of Their Publications, with the Number of Editions Printed; Including Notices of Some Foreign Writers Whose Works have been Occasionally published in England. London: Henry Colburn, Public Library, Conduit Street, Hanover Square, 1816. Reprinted, Detroit: Gale Research Company, 1966. Also available from Gale on microfiche.
	A supplemental listing of authors begins on page 407, and is indicated in this index by the code Sup.
BiDPara	*Biographical Dictionary of Parapsychology, with Directory and Glossary, 1964-1966.* Edited by Helene Pleasants. New York: Garrett Publications, Helix Press, 1964.
BiDSA	*Biographical Dictionary of Southern Authors.* By Lucian Lamar Knight. Originally published as *Library of Southern Literature, volume XV, Biographical Dictionary of Authors.* Atlanta, Ga.: Martin & Hoyt Company, 1929. Reprinted, Detroit: Gale Research Company, 1978. Also available from Gale on microfiche.
BiDrLUS	*A Biographical Directory of Librarians in the United States and Canada.* 5th ed. Edited by Lee Ash. Chicago: American Library Association, 1970.
BiE&WWA	*A Biographical Encyclopaedia & Who's Who of the American Theatre.* Edited by Walter Rigdon. New York: James H. Heineman, 1966.
BioIn	*Biography Index:* A Cumulative Index to Biographical Material in Books and Magazines. Volumes 1 through 10. New York: H.W. Wilson Company, 1949-1977.

BioIn 1	Volume 1:	January 1946-July 1949
BioIn 2	Volume 2:	August 1949-August 1952
BioIn 3	Volume 3:	September 1952-August 1955
BioIn 4	Volume 4:	September 1955-August 1958
BioIn 5	Volume 5:	September 1958-August 1961
BioIn 6	Volume 6:	September 1961-August 1964
BioIn 7	Volume 7:	September 1964-August 1967
BioIn 8	Volume 8:	September 1967-August 1970
BioIn 9	Volume 9:	September 1970-August 1973

BioIn 10	Volume 10: September 1973-August 1976
	Included because it is a rich source of leads to obituaries, magazine articles, and other types of information concerning persons on whom information is often not available elsewhere.
BioNews	*Biography News:* A Compilation of News Stories and Feature Articles from American News Media Covering Personalities of National Interest in All Fields. Edited by Frank E. Bair. Detroit: Gale Research Company, 1974-1975.
BioNews 1974	Volume 1, Number 1, January 1974 through Number 12, December, 1974.
BioNews 1975	Volume 2, Number 1, January-February 1975.
BkC	*The Book of Catholic Authors:* Informal Self-Portraits of Famous Modern Catholic Writers. Edited by Walter Romig. Detroit: Walter Romig & Company, 1942-?
BkC 1	First series, 1942
BkC 2	Second series, 1943
BkC 3	Third series, 1945
BkC 4	Fourth series, (n.d.)
BkC 5	Fifth series, (n.d.)
BkC 6	Sixth series, (n.d.)
BkCL	*A Book of Children's Literature.* 3rd ed. By Lillian Hollowell. New York and Chicago: Holt, Rinehart and Winston, 1966.
	Biographies of authors begin on page 553.
BlkAW	*Black American Writers Past and Present: A Biographical and Bibliographical Dictionary.* 2 vols. By Theressa Gunnels Rush, Carol Fairbanks Myers, Esther Spring Arata. Metuchen, New Jersey: Scarecrow Press, 1975.
BlkC	*Blacks in Communications, Journalism, Public Relations, and Advertising.* By M. L. Stein. New York: Julian Messner, 1972.
	Biographical sketches of blacks in all phases of journalism compiled by a veteran newsman. A retrospective study with greatest emphasis on post-civil rights accomplishments. Individual sketches and some textual references. Index begins on page 184.
Br&AmS	*British and American Sporting Authors: Their Writings and Biographies.* By A. Henry Higginson. London: Hutchinson & Company, 1951.
	Use index at back of book to locate journalists.
BrAu	*British Authors Before 1800: A Biographical Dictionary.* Edited by Stanley J. Kunitz and Howard Haycraft. New York: H.W. Wilson Company, 1952.
BrAu 19	*British Authors of the Nineteenth Century.* Edited by Stanley J. Kunitz. New York: H.W. Wilson Company, 1936.
CanNov	*Canadian Novelists, 1920-1945.* By Clara Thomas. Toronto: Longmans, Green & Company, 1946. Reprinted, Folcroft Library Editions, 1970.
CanWW 1972	*The Canadian Who's Who.* Vol. 12, 1970-1972. Toronto: Who's Who Canadian Publications, 1972.
CanWr	*Canadian Writers: A Biographical Dictionary.* New ed., rev. and enl. Edited by Guy Sylvestre, Brandon Conron, Carl F. Klinck. Toronto: Ryerson Press, 1966.
	Biographies of Quebec authors are in French.

CarSB   *The Carolyn Sherwin Bailey Historical Collection of Children's Books: A Catalogue.* Edited and compiled by Dorothy R. Davis. Southern Connecticut State College, 1966.

                  Some listings are not in strict alphabetical sequence. There is no index.

CasWL   *Cassell's Encyclopaedia of World Literature.* Edited by S. H. Steinberg in two volumes. Revised and enlarged in three volumes by J. Buchanan-Brown. New York: William Morrow & Company, 1973.

                  Biographies are found in volumes two and three.

CathA 1930   *Catholic Authors: Contemporary Biographical Sketches, 1930-1947.* Edited by Matthew Hoehn. Newark, N.J.: St. Mary's Abbey, 1948.

CathA 1952   *Catholic Authors: Contemporary Biographical Sketches.* Edited by Matthew Hoehn. Newark, N.J.: St. Mary's Abbey, 1952.

CelR 1973   *Celebrity Register.* 3rd ed. Edited by Earl Blackwell. New York: Simon and Schuster, 1973.

ChlLR 1   *Children's Literature Review:* Excerpts from Reviews, Criticism, and Commentary on Books for Children and Young People. Volume 1. Edited by Ann Block and Carolyn Riley. Detroit: Gale Research Company, 1976. Also available from Gale on microfiche.

                  A book of collected criticism.

ChlLR 2   *Children's Literature Review...* Volume 2. Edited by Carolyn Riley. Detroit: Gale Research Company, 1976. Also available from Gale on microfiche.

                  A book of collected criticism.

CIDMEL   *Columbia Dictionary of Modern European Literature.* Edited by Horatio Smith. New York and London: Columbia University Press, 1947. Also published as *A Dictionary of Modern European Literature.* London: Oxford University Press, 1947.

CnDAL   *Concise Dictionary of American Literature.* Edited by Robert Fulton Richards. Philosophical Library, 1955. Reprinted, New York: Greenwood Press, 1969.

CnE&AP   *The Concise Encyclopedia of English and American Poets and Poetry.* Edited by Stephen Spender and Donald Hall. New York: Hawthorn Books, 1963.

CnMD   *The Concise Encyclopedia of Modern Drama.* By Siegfried Melchinger. Translated from the German by George Wellwarth. Edited by Henry Popkin. New York: Horizon Press, 1964.

                  Biographies begin on page 159. A supplemental list of 21 playwrights with short biographical notices begins on page 287, and is cited in this index by the code SUP.

CnMWL   *The Concise Encyclopedia of Modern World Literature.* Edited by Geoffrey Grigson. London: Hutchinson of London, 1963.

                  Biographical entries begin on page 29.

CnThe   *A Concise Encyclopedia of the Theatre.* By Robin May. Reading, Berkshire, England: Osprey, 1974.

                  Use the index at the back of the book to locate biographies.

CngDr 1974   *Congressional Directory.* 93rd Congress, 2nd Session, convened January 21, 1974. Washington, D.C.: United States Government Printing Office, 1974.

                  To locate names use the Individual Index *at the back of the book.*

ConAmA   *Contemporary American Authors: A Critical Survey and 219 Bio-Bibliographies.* By Fred B. Millett. New York: Harcourt, Brace & World, 1940. Reprinted, New York: AMS Press, 1970.

Biographies begin on page 207.

ConAmL   *Contemporary American Literature: Bibliographies and Study Outlines.* By John Matthews Manly and Edith Rickert. Revised by Fred B. Millett. New York: Harcourt, Brace, 1929. Reprinted, New York: Haskell House Publishers, 1974.

Biographical section begins on page 101.

ConAu   *Contemporary Authors:* A Bio-Bibliographical Guide to Current Authors and their Works. Detroit: Gale Research Company, 1962-1978. Also available from Gale on microfiche.

ConAu 1	Volume 1, 1962
ConAu 1R	Volume 1-4, 1st revision, 1967
ConAu 2R	Volume 1-4, 1st revision, 1967
ConAu 3R	Volume 1-4, 1st revision, 1967
ConAu 4R	Volume 1-4, 1st revision, 1967
ConAu 5	Volume 5-6, 1963
ConAu 5R	Volume 5-8, 1st revision, 1969
ConAu 7R	Volume 5-8, 1st revision, 1969
ConAu 9	Volume 9-10, 1964
ConAu 9R	Volume 9-12, 1st revision, 1974
ConAu 11R	Volume 9-12, 1st revision, 1974
ConAu 13	Volume 13-14, 1965
ConAu 13R	Volume 13-16, 1st revision, 1975
ConAu 15	Volume 15-16, 1966
ConAu 15R	Volume 13-16, 1st revision, 1975
ConAu 17	Volume 17-18, 1967
ConAu 17R	Volume 17-20, 1st revision, 1976
ConAu 19	Volume 19-20, 1968
ConAu 19R	Volume 17-20, 1st revision, 1976
ConAu 21	Volume 21-22, 1969
ConAu 21R	Volume 21-24, 1st revision, 1977
ConAu 23	Volume 23-24, 1970
ConAu 23R	Volume 21-24, 1st revision, 1977
ConAu 25	Volume 25-28, 1971
ConAu 29	Volume 29-32, 1972
ConAu 33	Volume 33-36, 1973
ConAu 37	Volume 37-40, 1973
ConAu 41	Volume 41-44, 1974
ConAu 45	Volume 45-48, 1974
ConAu 49	Volume 49-52, 1975
ConAu 53	Volume 53-56, 1975
ConAu 57	Volume 57-60, 1976
ConAu 61	Volume 61-64, 1976
ConAu 65	Volume 65-68, 1978
ConAu 69	Volume 69-72, 1978
ConAu 73	Volume 73-76, 1978
ConAu XR	Index to volumes 1-80, *this code refers to pseudonym entries which appear only as cross references in the cumulative index to* Contemporary Authors.

ConAu P-1   *Contemporary Authors, Permanent Series:* A Bio-bibliographical Guide to Current Authors and their Works. Volume 1. Edited by Clare D. Kinsman. Detroit: Gale Research Company, 1975. Also available from Gale on microfiche.

ConDr *Contemporary Dramatists.* Edited by James Vinson. London: St. James Press; New York: St. Martin's Press, 1973.

> *Biographies are given in the following sections:* Contemporary Dramatists, *page 7;* Screen Writers, *page 847;* Radio Writers, *page 857;* Television Writers, *page 867;* Musical Librettists, *page 875;* The Theatre of Mixed Means, *page 889.*

ConLC *Contemporary Literary Criticism:* Excerpts from Criticism of the Works of Today's Novelists, Poets, Playwrights, and Other Creative Writers. Detroit: Gale Research Company, 1973-1976.

ConLC 1 Volume 1, 1973
ConLC 2 Volume 2, 1974
ConLC 3 Volume 3, 1975
ConLC 4 Volume 4, 1975
ConLC 5 Volume 5, 1976
ConLC 6 Volume 6, 1976

> *A series of collected criticism.*

ConNov 1972 *Contemporary Novelists.* Edited by James Vinson. London: St. James Press; New York: St. Martin's Press, 1972.

ConNov 1976 *Contemporary Novelists.* 2nd ed. Edited by James Vinson and D. L. Kirkpatrick. London: St. James Press; New York: St. Martin's Press, 1976.

> *Deceased authors are listed in the appendix, which begins on page 1565.*

ConP 1970 *Contemporary Poets.* Edited by Rosalie Murphie. London: St. James Press; New York: St. Martin's Press, 1970.

ConP 1975 *Contemporary Poets.* 2nd ed. Edited by James Vinson and D. L. Kirkpatrick. London: St. James Press; New York: St. Martin's Press, 1975.

> *Deceased poets are listed in the appendix, which begins on page 1745.*

CroCD *Crowell's Handbook of Contemporary Drama.* By Michael Anderson, Jacques Guicharnaud, Kristin Morrison, Jack D. Zipes, and others. New York: Thomas Y. Crowell Company, 1971.

CrtT *The Critical Temper:* A Survey of Modern Criticism on English and American Literature from the Beginnings to the Twentieth Century. 3 vols. Edited by Martin Tucker. New York: Frederick Ungar Publishing Company, 1969.

CrtT 1 Volume 1: From Old English to Shakespeare
CrtT 2 Volume 2: From Milton to Romantic Literature
CrtT 3 Volume 3: Victorian Literature, and American Literature

> *Authors are listed alphabetically within each period and division of literature.*

CurBio XR *Current Biography, 1940-1976.* New York: H.W. Wilson Company.

> *Use index to locate journalists.*

CyAL 1-2 *Cyclopaedia of American Literature:* Embracing Personal and Critical Notices of Authors, and Selections from their Writings, from the Earliest Period to the Present Day. 2 vols. By Evert A. Duyckinck and George L. Duyckinck. Philadelphia: Wm. Rutter & Company, 1875. Reprinted, Detroit: Gale Research Company, 1965. Also available from Gale on microfiche.

> *Use index at back of volume 2 to locate journalists.*

CyWA *Cyclopedia of World Authors.* Edited by Frank N. Magill and Dayton Kohler. New York: Harper & Row, 1958. (Originally published under title of *Masterplots Cyclopedia of World Authors.*)

DcAmA *A Dictionary of American Authors*. 5th ed., rev. and enl. By Oscar Fay Adams. Boston and New York: Houghton Mifflin Company, 1904. Reprinted, Detroit: Gale Research Company, 1969. Also available from Gale on microfiche.

DcAmB 1-20 *Dictionary of American Biography*. Volumes 1-20, A-Z. Under the auspices of the American Council of Learned Societies. New York: Charles Scribner's Sons, 1928-1936.

DcAmB S1 *Dictionary of American Biography*. Supplement 1. New York: Charles Scribner's Sons, 1944.

DcAmB S2 *Dictionary of American Biography*. Supplement 2. New York: Charles Scribner's Sons, 1958.

DcAmB S3 *Dictionary of American Biography*. Supplement 3. New York: Charles Scribner's Sons, 1973.

DcAmB S4 *Dictionary of American Biography*. Supplement 4. New York: Charles Scribner's Sons, 1974.

DcAmB S5 *Dictionary of American Biography*. Supplement 5. New York: Charles Scribner's Sons, 1977.

DcBiA *A Dictionary of Biographies of Authors Represented in the Authors Digest Series:* With a Supplemental List of Later Titles and a Supplementary Biographical Section. Edited by Rossiter Johnson. New York: The Authors Press, 1927. Reprinted, Detroit: Gale Research Company, 1974. Also available from Gale on microfiche.

DcCAA *A Dictionary of Contemporary American Artists*. 2nd ed. By Paul Cummings. New York: St. Martin's Press, 1971.

DcCLAA *A Dictionary of Contemporary Latin American Authors*. Compiled by David William Foster. Tempe: Center for Latin American Studies, Arizona State University, 1975.

DcEnA *A Dictionary of English Authors, Biographical and Bibliographical*. New ed., rev., and enl. By R. Farquharson Sharp. London: Kegan Paul, Trench, Trubner & Company, 1904. Reprinted, Detroit: Gale Research Company, 1978. Also available from Gale on microfiche.

   Biographies found in the Appendix are indicated by the code Ap.

DcEnL *Dictionary of English Literature:* Being a Comprehensive Guide to English Authors and Their Works. 2nd ed. By W. Davenport Adams. London: Cassell Petter & Galpin, (n.d.). Reprinted, Detroit: Gale Research Company, 1966. Also available from Gale on microfiche.

DcEuL *A Dictionary of European Literature:* Designed as a Companion to English Studies. 2nd rev. ed. By Laurie Magnus. London: George Routledge & Sons; New York: E.P. Dutton & Co., 1927. Reprinted, Detroit: Gale Research Company, 1974.

DcLEL *A Dictionary of Literature in the English Language, from Chaucer to 1940.* 2 vols. Compiled and edited by Robin Myers. Oxford and London: Pergamon Press, 1970.

   Biographical entries are found in volume 1. An author-title index is provided in volume 2.

DcNAA *A Dictionary of North American Authors Deceased before 1950.* Compiled by W. Stewart Wallace. Toronto: Ryerson Press, 1951. Reprinted, Detroit: Gale Research Company, 1968. Also available from Gale on microfiche.

DcOrL	Dictionary of Oriental Literatures. 3 vols. Jaroslav Prusek, General Editor. New York: Basic Books, 1974.
DcOrL 1	Volume 1, East Asia. Edited by Zbigniew Slupski.
DcOrL 2	Volume 2, South and South-East Asia. Edited by Dusan Zbavitel.
DcOrL 3	Volume 3, West Asia and North Africa. Edited by Jiri Becka.
DcRusL	Dictionary of Russian Literature. By William E. Harkins. New York: Philosophical Library, 1956. Reprinted, Westport, Conn.: Greenwood Press, 1971.
DcSpL	Dictionary of Spanish Literature. By Maxim Newmark. New York: Philosophical Library, 1956. Reprinted, Totowa, N.J.: Littlefield, Adams & Company, 1970.
DrAF 1976	A Directory of American Fiction Writers, 1976 Edition: Names and Addresses of More Than 800 Contemporary Fiction Writers Whose Work has been Published in the United States. New York: Poets & Writers, 1976.
	Provides addresses with mention of writer's latest published works. Use index, which begins on page 123, to find author listings.
DrAP 1975	A Directory of American Poets, 1975 Edition: Names and Addresses of More Than 1,500 Contemporary Poets Whose Work has been Published in the United States. New York: Poets & Writers, 1975.
	Provides addresses with mention of poet's latest work. Use index, which begins on page vii, to find listings.
DrAS 74E	Directory of American Scholars: English, Speech and Drama. 6th ed., volume 2. Edited by Jaques Cattell Press. New York: R. R. Bowker Company, 1974.
DrAS 74F	Directory of American Scholars: Foreign Languages, Linguistics and Philology. 6th ed., volume 3. Edited by Jaques Cattell Press. New York: R. R. Bowker Company, 1974.
DrAS 74H	Directory of American Scholars: History. 6th ed., volume 1. Edited by Jaques Cattell Press. New York: R. R. Bowker Company, 1974.
DrAS 74P	Directory of American Scholars: Philosophy, Religion and Law. 6th ed., volume 4. Edited by Jaques Cattell Press. New York: R. R. Bowker Company, 1974.
EarABI	Early American Book Illustrators and Wood Engravers 1670-1870: A Catalogue of a Collection of American Books Illustrated for the Most Part with Woodcuts and Wood Engravings in the Princeton University Library. Volume 1, Main Catalogue. By Sinclair Hamilton. Princeton, N.J.: Princeton University Press, 1968.
	Use the index at back of book to locate entries.
EarABI Sup	Early American Book Illustrators and Wood Engravers 1670-1870. Volume 2, Supplement. By Sinclair Hamilton. Princeton, N.J.: Princeton University Press, 1968.
	Use the index at back of book to locate entries.
EncAB	Encyclopedia of American Biography. Edited by John A. Garraty. New York: Harper & Row, 1974.
EncMys	Encyclopedia of Mystery and Detection. Edited by Chris Steinbrunner, Otto Penzler, Marvin Lachman and Charles Shibuk. New York: McGraw-Hill, 1976.
EncWL	Encyclopedia of World Literature in the 20th Century. 3 vols. Edited by Bernard Fleischmann. New York: Frederick Ungar Publishing Co., 1967. (An en-

larged and updated edition of the *Herder Lexikon der Weltliteratur in 20. Jahrhundert.)*

EuAu *European Authors, 1000-1900: A Biographical Dictionary of European Literature.* Edited by Stanley J. Kunitz and Vineta Colby. New York: H. W. Wilson Company, 1967.

EvEuW *Everyman's Dictionary of European Writers.* By W. N. Hargreaves-Mawdsley. London: J. M. Dent & Sons; New York: E. P. Dutton & Co., 1968.

EvLB *Everyman's Dictionary of Literary Biography, English & American.* Rev. ed. Compiled after John E. Cousin by D. C. Browning. London: J. M. Dent & Sons; New York: E. P. Dutton & Co., 1960.

FamWC *Famous War Correspondents.* By Frederick Lauriston Bullard. Boston: Little, Brown, 1914. Reprinted, New York: Beekman Publishers, 1974.

> *A famous Pulitzer Prize winning journalist compiles a collection of biographical sketches of representative pre-World War I war correspondents, including an incisive chapter on the young Winston Churchill. Textual references, index begins on page 425.*

FemPA *The Female Poets of America:* With Portraits, Biographical Notices, and Specimens of Their Writings. 7th ed., rev. By Thomas Buchanan Read. Philadelphia: E.H. Butler & Co., 1857. Reprinted, Detroit: Gale Research Company, 1978.

ForP *The Foreign Press: A Survey of the World's Journalism.* By John C. Merrill, Carter R. Bryan, Marvin Alisky. Baton Rouge: Louisiana State University Press, 1975.

> *A comparative study of the press systems of the world useful for its historical perspective on the newspaper press of the principal nations. Intended originally for journalism students, it provides a good insight into international journalism. Textual references, index begins on page 351.*

ForWC 1970 *Foremost Women in Communications.* New York: R. R. Bowker Company, Foremost Americans Publishing, 1970.

HisAmM XR *A History of American Magazines: 1741-1930.* 5 vols. By Frank Luther Mott. Cambridge: Harvard University Press, Belknap Press, 1930-1968.

> *A landmark historical study, well deserving of the Pulitzer Prize by which it was honored in 1939. Comprehensive to a fault, it is often the only available source of information on early periodical editors and publishers. Use index at back of volume five to locate journalists, textual references.*

HsB&A *The House of Beadle and Adams and its Dime and Nickel Novels: The Story of a Vanished Literature.* 2 vols. By Albert Johannsen. Norman: University of Oklahoma Press, 1950.

> *Biographical entries are found in volume 2, beginning on page 6.*

HsB&A Sup *The House of Beadle and Adams and its Dime and Nickel Novels...*Volume 3, Supplement, Addenda, Corrigenda. By Albert Johannsen. Norman: University of Oklahoma Press, 1962.

> *Corrections and additions to the biographies in volume 2 begin on page 15.*

IndAu 1816 *Indiana Authors and Their Books, 1816-1916:* Biographical Sketches of Authors Who Published during the First Century of Indiana Statehood with Lists of

Their Books. Compiled by R. E. Banta. Crawfordsville, Ind.: Wabash College, 1949.

IndAu 1917   *Indiana Authors and Their Books, 1917-1966:* A Continuation of *Indiana Authors and Their Books, 1816-1916,* and Containing Additional Names from the Earlier Period. Compiled by Donald E. Thompson. Crawfordsville, Ind.: Wabash College, 1974.

IntMPA 1975   *International Motion Picture Almanac, 1975.* Edited by Richard Gertner. New York: Quigley Publishing Company, 1975.

See the Who's Who in Motion Pictures and Television *section. The listings are identical with those in the* International Television Almanac.

IntWW 1974   *International Who's Who.* 38th ed., 1974-1975. London: Europa Publications, 1974. Distributed in the United States by Gale Research Company.

IntWW 1976   *International Who's Who.* 40th ed., 1976-1977. London: Europa Publications, 1976. Distributed in the United States by Gale Research Company.

InvJ   *The Investigative Journalist: Folk Heroes of a New Era.* By James H. Dygert. Englewood Cliffs, N. J.: Prentice-Hall, 1976.

A useful, post-Watergate compilation of outstanding performances by America's new folk heroes, written by a veteran journalist and one-time editor and publisher of the crusading Detroit Scope *magazine. Individual sketches and textual references, index begins on page 277.*

JBA 1934   *The Junior Book of Authors:* An Introduction to the Lives of Writers and Illustrators for Younger Readers from Lewis Carroll and Louisa Alcott to the Present Day. Edited by Stanley J. Kunitz and Howard Haycraft. New York: H.W. Wilson Company, 1934.

The 1934 edition contains many biographies that were not carried over into the second edition (see below).

JBA 1951   *The Junior Book of Authors.* 2nd ed., rev. Edited by Stanley J. Kunitz and Howard Haycraft. New York: H.W. Wilson Company, 1951.

LEduc 1974   *Leaders in Education.* 5th ed. Edited by Jaques Cattell Press. New York: R. R. Bowker Company, 1974.

LiJA   *The Literary Journal in America to 1900: A Guide to Information Sources.* The American Literature, English Literature, and World Literatures in English Information Guide Series, volume 3. Edited by Edward E. Chielens. Detroit: Gale Research Company, 1975.

A comprehensive bibliography providing leads to data sources for early American periodicals and their editors.

LivBAA   *Living Black American Authors: A Biographical Dictionary.* By Ann Allen Shockley and Sue P. Chandler. New York and London: R. R. Bowker Company, 1973.

LivFWS   *The Living Female Writers of the South.* Edited by the author of *Southland Writers.* Philadelphia: Claxton, Remsen & Haffelfinger, 1872. Reprinted, Detroit: Gale Research Company, 1978. Also available from Gale on microfiche.

LongC   *Longman Companion to Twentieth Century Literature.* By A. C. Ward. London: Longman, 1970.

Lor&LP   *Lords and Laborers of the Press: Men Who Fashioned the Modern British Newspaper.* By Linton Andrews and H.A. Taylor, with foreword by Howard Rush Long. Carbondale and Edwardsville: Southern Illinois University Press, 1970.

Useful as a source of biographical background material on the British Press Lords, from Northcliffe and Rothermere to Beaverbrook and Thomson of Fleet. Also includes hard to find data on their loyal, hard working, and often vastly underrated editors. Individual sketches and textual references, index begins on page 323.

McGWD   *McGraw-Hill Encyclopedia of World Drama:* An International Reference Work. 4 vols. New York: McGraw-Hill Book Company, 1972.

MnnWr   *Minnesota Writers:* A Collection of Autobiographical Stories by Minnesota Prose Writers. Edited and annotated by Carmen Nelson Richards. Minneapolis: T.S. Denison & Company, 1961.

Use the table of contents to locate authors.

ModAL   *Modern American Literature:* A Library of Literary Criticism. 4th enl. ed., 3 vols. Compiled and edited by Dorothy Nyren Curley, Maurice Kramer, and Elaine Fialka Kramer. New York: Frederick Ungar Publishing Company, 1969.

A book of collected criticism.

ModAL Sup   *Modern American Literature:* A Library of Literary Criticism. Volume 4, supplement to 4th ed. Compiled and edited by Dorothy Nyren Curley, Maurice Kramer, and Elaine Fialka Kramer. New York: Frederick Ungar Publishing Company, 1976.

A book of collected criticism.

ModBL   *Modern British Literature:* A Library of Literary Criticism. 3 vols. Compiled and edited by Ruth Z. Temple and Martin Tucker. New York: Frederick Ungar Publishing Company, 1966.

A book of collected criticism.

ModBL Sup   *Modern British Literature:* A Library of Literary Criticism. Volume 4, supplement to 4th ed. Compiled and edited by Martin Tucker and Rita Stein. New York: Frederick Ungar Publishing Company, 1975.

A book of collected criticism.

ModGL   *Modern German Literature:* A Library of Literary Criticism. 2 vols. Compiled and edited by Agnes Korner Domandi. New York: Frederick Ungar Publishing Company, 1972.

A book of collected criticism.

ModRL   *Modern Romance Literatures:* A Library of Literary Criticism. Compiled and edited by Dorothy Nyren Curley and Arthur Curley. New York: Frederick Ungar Publishing Company, 1967.

A book of collected criticism.

ModSL 1   *Modern Slavic Literatures, volume 1: Russian Literature;* A Library of Literary Criticism. Compiled and edited by Vasa D. Mihailovich. New York: Frederick Ungar Publishing Company, 1972.

A book of collected criticism.

ModSL 2   *Modern Slavic Literatures, volume 2: Bulgarian, Czechoslovak, Polish, Ukrainian and Yugoslav Literatures:* A Library of Literary Criticism. Compiled and edited by Vasa D. Mihailovich, Igor Hajek, Zbigniew Folejewski, Bogdan Czaykowski, Leo D. Rudnytzky and Thomas Butler. New York: Frederick Ungar Publishing Company, 1976.

A book of collected criticism. Authors listed alphabetically by country and language. Use the alphabetical listing on page vii to locate authors.

ModWD   *Modern World Drama: An Encyclopedia.* By Myron Matlaw. New York: E. P. Dutton & Company, 1972.

MorJA   *More Junior Authors.* Edited by Muriel Fuller. New York: H. W. Wilson Company, 1963.

MouLC   *Moulton's Library of Literary Criticism of English and American Authors, Through the Beginning of the Twentieth Century.* 4 vols., rev., abridged. By Martin Tucker. New York: Frederick Ungar Publishing Company, 1966.

MouLC 1   Volume 1, The beginnings to the Seventeenth Century.

Alphabetical listing of authors begins on page xv.

MouLC 2   Volume 2, Neo-Classicism to the Romantic Period.

Alphabetical listing of authors begins on page vii.

MouLC 3   Volume 3, The Romantic Period to the Victorian Age.

Alphabetical listing of authors begins on page vii.

MouLC 4   Volume 4, The Mid-Nineteenth Century to Edwardianism.

Alphabetical listing of authors begins on page vii.

NatCAB   *National Cyclopaedia of American Biography.* Volumes 1-51. New York: James T. White & Company, 1892-1969. Reprinted, Ann Arbor: University Microfilms, 1971.

Volume number will follow main code. Some references refer to the index and have the code XR.

NewC   *The New Century Handbook of English Literature.* Rev. ed. Edited by Clarence L. Barnhart and William D. Halsey. New York: Appleton, Century, Crofts, 1967.

NewMr   *The New Muckrakers.* By Leonard Downie, Jr. Washington, D.C.: New Republic Book Company, 1976.

An investigative reporter looks at his contemporaries, both Watergate and beyond. Includes reporters at the major metropolitan dailies as well as the smaller, semi-underground publications. Individual sketches as well as textual references. Index begins on page 867.

NewYTBE 1-4   *The New York Times Biographical Edition.* Volumes 1-4, 1970-1973. New York: Arno Press.

Continued by The New York Times Biographical Service.

NewYTBS 5   *The New York Times Biographical Service.* Volume 5, 1974. New York: Arno Press.

Continues The New York Times Biographical Edition.

NF   Not Found— References to this individual as being a journalist have been found in a source or sources checked for *Journalist Biographies Master Index.* No biographical references have been found, however. Please see the discussion of "NF" listings in the introduction to this volume (page v).

OhA&B   *Ohio Authors and Their Books:* Biographical Data and Selective Bibliographies for Ohio Authors, Native and Resident, 1796-1950. Edited by William Coyle. Cleveland and New York: World Publishing Company, 1962.

OvPC   *Overseas Press Club of America and American Correspondents Overseas 1975 Membership Directory.* New York: Overseas Press Club of America, 1975.

Biographies of journalists begin on page 32. The most current directory published as of our publication date.

OxAm   *The Oxford Companion to American Literature.* 4th ed. By James D. Hart. New York: Oxford University Press, 1965.

OxCan   *The Oxford Companion to Canadian History and Literature.* By Norah Story. Toronto: Oxford University Press, 1967.

Recipient of a well deserved Governor General's Award in 1967. One of the better volumes in the Oxford Companion Series.

OxCan Sup   *Supplement to the Oxford Companion to Canadian History and Literature.* Edited by William Toye. Toronto: Oxford University Press, 1973.

Most entries are biographical.

OxEng   *The Oxford Companion to English Literature.* Compiled and edited by Sir Paul Harvey. 4th ed., rev. By Dorothy Eagle. Oxford and New York: Oxford University Press, 1967.

OxFr   *The Oxford Companion to French Literature.* Compiled and edited by Sir Paul Harvey and J. E. Heseltine. Oxford: Clarendon Press, 1959.

OxGer   *The Oxford Companion to German Literature.* By Henry and Mary Garland. Oxford: Clarendon Press, 1976.

Pen Am   *The Penguin Companion to American Literature.* Edited by Malcolm Bradbury, Eric Mottram and Jean Franco. New York: McGraw-Hill Book Company, 1971. On spine: *The Penguin Companion to World Literature.*

In two alphabetical sections. One is for the USA, the other for Latin America.

Pen Cl   *The Penguin Companion to Classical, Oriental & African Literature.* Edited by D. M. Lang and D. R. Dudley. New York: McGraw-Hill Book Company, 1969. On spine: *The Penguin Companion to World Literature.*

In four alphabetical sections by period as well as region.

Pen Eng *The Penguin Companion to English Literature.* Edited by David Daiches. New York: McGraw-Hill Book Company, 1971. On spine: *The Penguin Companion to World Literature.*

Pen Eur *The Penguin Companion to European Literature.* Edited by Anthony Thorlby. New York: McGraw-Hill Book Company, 1969. On spine: *The Penguin Companion to World Literature.*

PoChrch *The Poets of the Church: A Series of Biographical Sketches of Hymn-Writers with Notes on Their Hymns.* By Edwin F. Hatfield. New York: Anson D. F. Randolph & Company, 1884. Reprinted, Detroit: Gale Research Company, 1978. Also available from Gale on microfiche.

PoIre   *The Poets of Ireland: A Biograpical and Bibliographical Dictionary of Irish Writers of English Verse.* By D.J. O'Donoghue. Dublin: Hodges Figgis & Company; London: Henry Frowde, Oxford University Press, 1912. Reprinted, Detroit: Gale Research Company, 1968. Also available from Gale on microfiche.

Has two biographical sections. The main section begins on page 5. The appendix starts on page 495.

PueRA   *Puerto Rican Authors: A Biobibliographic Handbook.* By Marnesba D. Hill and Harold B. Schleifer. Translations of entries into Spanish by Daniel Maratos. Metuchen, N.J.: Scarecrow Press, 1974.

A bilingual edition.

RAdv 1	*The Reader's Adviser: A Layman's Guide to Literature.* 12th ed., vol. 1. Edited by Sarah L. Prakken. New York and London: R. R. Bowker Company, 1974.
	See the index for locations of journalist biographies and bibliographies.
RComWL	*The Reader's Companion to World Literature.* 2nd ed., rev. Edited by Lillian Herlands Hornstein, Leon Edel and Horst Frenz. New York: New American Library, 1973.
REn	*The Reader's Encyclopedia.* By William Rose Benet. 2nd ed. New York: Thomas Y. Crowell Company, 1965.
REnAL	*The Reader's Encyclopedia of American Literature.* By Max J. Herzberg. New York: Thomas Y. Crowell Company, 1962.
REnWD	*The Reader's Encyclopedia of World Drama.* Edited by John Gassner and Edward Quinn. New York: Thomas Y. Crowell Company, 1969.
RGAfL	*A Reader's Guide to African Literature.* Compiled and edited by Hans M. Zell and Helene Silver. New York: Africana Publishing Corporation, 1971.
	Biographies begin on page 113.
RpN	*Reporting the News: Selections from Nieman Reports.* Edited by Louis M. Lyons. Cambridge, Mass.: Harvard University Press, Belknap Press, 1965.
	Names indexed are found in the following: Appendix I: List of Nieman Fellows through 1964-65. Appendix II: List of Associate Nieman Fellows through 1964-65.
SixAP	*Sixty American Poets, 1896-1944.* Selected, with preface and critical notes, by Allen Tate. Washington: Library of Congress, 1954. Reprinted, Detroit: Gale Research Company, 1969. Also available from Gale on microfiche.
	A bibliographical study of major American poets.
SmATA	*Something About the Author:* Facts and Pictures about Contemporary Authors and Illustrators of Books for Young People. Edited by Anne Commire. Detroit: Gale Research Company, 1971-1976. Also available from Gale on microfiche.
SmATA 1	Volume 1, 1971
SmATA 2	Volume 2, 1971
SmATA 3	Volume 3, 1972
SmATA 4	Volume 4, 1973
SmATA 5	Volume 5, 1973
SmATA 6	Volume 6, 1974
SmATA 7	Volume 7, 1975
SmATA 8	Volume 8, 1976
SmATA 9	Volume 9, 1976
SmATA 10	Volume 10, 1976
SmATA XR	Index to volume 1-10, *found in back of volume 10. This code refers to pseudonym entries which appear only as cross references in the cumulative index to* Something About the Author.
Str&VC	*Story and Verse for Children.* By Miriam Blanton Huber. 3rd ed. New York: Macmillan Company, 1965.
	Biographies are located on pages 793-856.
TexWr	*Texas Writers of Today.* By Florence Elberta Barns. 1935. Reprinted, Ann Arbor: Gryphon Books, 1971. Also available from Gale on microfiche.
ThrBJA	*Third Book of Junior Authors.* Edited by Doris De Montreville and Donna Hill. New York: H. W. Wilson Company, 1972.

TwCA *Twentieth Century Authors; A Biographical Dictionary of Modern Literature.* Edited by Stanley J. Kunitz and Howard Haycraft. New York: H. W. Wilson Company, 1942.

TwCA Sup *Twentieth Century Authors ... First Supplement.* Edited by Stanley J. Kunitz and Vineta Colby. New York: H. W. Wilson Company, 1955.

TwCW *Twentieth Century Writing: A Reader's Guide to Contemporary Literature.* Edited by Kenneth Richardson. Levittown, N.Y.: Transatlantic Arts, 1969.

USBiR 1974 *United States Department of State: The Biographic Register.* Washington, D.C.: United States Government Printing Office, July 1974.

WebBD *Webster's Biographical Dictionary.* Springfield, Mass.: G. & C. Merriam Company, 1974.

> *Although a few of the indexed names do not have individual sketches, they can be found under the family name.*

WebE&AL *Webster's New World Companion to English and American Literature.* Edited by Arthur Pollard. New York: World Publishing, 1973.

WhJnl *Who Was Who in Journalism, 1925-1928.* Gale Composite Biographical Dictionary Series, Number 4. Detroit: Gale Research Company, 1978. Also available from Gale on microfiche.

> *A consolidation of all material appearing in the 1928 edition of* Who's Who in Journalism, *with unduplicated biographical entries from the 1925 edition of* Who's Who in Journalism, *originally compiled by M. N. Ask (1925 and 1928 editions) and S. Gershanek (1925 edition.)*

WhJnl Sup *Names indexed from the 1925 Supplement found on colored stock at the back of* Who Was Who in Journalism, 1925-1928.

WhNAA *Who Was Who Among North American Authors, 1921-1939.* 2 vols. Gale Composite Biographical Dictionary Series, Number 1. Detroit: Gale Research Company, 1976. Also available from Gale on microfiche.

> *Originally published as* Who's Who Among North American Authors, *volumes 1-7. Los Angeles: Golden Syndicate Publishing Company, 1921-1939.*

Who 1974 *Who's Who.* London: A. & C. Black; New York: St. Martin's Press, 1974-1975.

WhoAdv 1972 *Who's Who in Advertising.* 2nd ed. Edited by Robert S. Morgan. Rye, N.Y.: Redfield Publishing Company, 1972.

WhoAm 1974 *Who's Who in America.* 38th ed., 1974-1975, 2 vols. Chicago: Marquis Who's Who, 1974.

WhoAmA 1973 *Who's Who in American Art.* Edited by the Jaques Cattell Press. New York: R. R. Bowker Company, 1973.

WhoAmP 1973 *Who's Who in American Politics.* 4th ed., 1973-1974. Edited by Paul A. Theis and Edmund L. Henshaw, Jr. Compiled by the Jaques Cattell Press. New York: R. R. Bowker Company, 1973.

WhoAmW 1974 *Who's Who of American Women.* 8th ed., 1974-1975. Chicago: Marquis Who's Who, 1974.

WhoCan 1973 *Who's Who in Canada,* 1973-1974. Toronto: International Press, 1973.

> *Use the index at the front of the book to locate biographies.*

Who ChL *The Who's Who of Children's Literature.* By Brian Doyle. New York: Schocken Books, 1968.

WhoCon 1973   *Who's Who in Consulting.* 2nd ed. Edited by Paul Wasserman. Detroit: Gale Research Company, 1973.

WhoE 1974   *Who's Who in the East.* 14th ed., 1974-1975. Chicago: Marquis Who's Who, 1973.

WhoF&I 1974   *Who's Who in Finance and Industry.* 18th ed., 1974-1975. Chicago: Marquis Who's Who, 1973.

WhoGov 1972   *Who's Who in Government.* 1st ed., 1972-1973. Chicago: Marquis Who's Who, 1972.

WhoGrA   *Who's Who in Graphic Art:* An Illustrated Book of Reference to the World's Leading Graphic Designers, Illustrators, Typographers and Cartoonists. Zurich: Amstutz & Herdeg Graphis Press, 1962.

Use the index, which begins on page 576, to locate citations.

WhoLA   *Who's Who Among Living Authors of Older Nations:* Covering the Literary Activities of Living Authors and Writers of All Countries of the World Except the United States of America, Canada, Mexico, Alaska, Hawaii, Newfoundland, the Philipine Islands, the West Indies, and Central America. Volume 1, 1931-1932. Edited by Alberta Lawrence. Los Angeles: Golden Syndicate Publishing Company, 1931. Reprinted, Detroit: Gale Research Company, 1966. Also available from Gale on microfiche.

WhoMW 1974   *Who's Who in the Midwest.* 14th ed., 1974-1975. Chicago: Marquis Who's Who, 1974.

WhoMus 1972   *Who's Who in Music and Musicians' International Directory.* 6th ed. London: Burke's Peerage; New York: Hafner Publishing Company, 1972.

WhoPNW   *Who's Who Among Pacific Northwest Authors.* 2nd ed. Edited by Frances Valentine Wright. Pacific Northwest Library Association, Reference Division, 1969.

WhoPubR 1972   *Who's Who in Public Relations (International).* 4th ed. Edited by Robert L. Barbour. Meriden, N.H.: PR Publishing Company, 1972.

Some names will be found in the Biographical Appendix on page 423.

WhoS&SW 1973   *Who's Who in the South and Southwest.* 13th ed., 1973-1974. Chicago: Marquis Who's Who, 1973.

WhoThe 1972   *Who's Who in the Theatre: A Biographical Record of the Contemporary Stage.* 15th ed. Edited by Ian Herbert. London: Pitman Publishing; Detroit: Gale Research Company, 1972.

WhoTwCL   *Who's Who in Twentieth Century Literature.* By Martin Seymour-Smith. New York: Holt, Rinehart and Winston, 1976.

WhoWest 1974   *Who's Who in the West.* 14th ed., 1974-1975. Chicago: Marquis Who's Who, 1974.

WhoWor 1974   *Who's Who in the World.* 2nd ed., 1974-1975. Chicago: Marquis Who's Who, 1973.

WhoWorJ 1972   *Who's Who in World Jewry.* Edited by I. J. Carmin Karpman. New York: Pitman Publishing, 1972.

WisWr   *Wisconsin Writers: Sketches and Studies.* By William A. Titus. 1930. Reprinted, Detroit: Gale Research Company, 1974. Also available from Gale on microfiche.

Use the table of contents to locate authors.

WorAu   *World Authors, 1950-1970:* A Companion Volume to *Twentieth Century Authors.* Edited by John Wakeman. New York: H. W. Wilson Company, 1975.

WrDr 1976   *The Writers Directory, 1976-78.* London: St. James Press; New York: St. Martin's Press, 1976.

YABC 1   *Yesterday's Authors of Books for Children:* Facts and Pictures about Authors and Illustrators of Books for Young People, from Early Times to 1960. Volume 1. Edited by Anne Commire. Detroit: Gale Research Company, 1977. Also available from Gale on microfiche.

A

A A 1897-1976 *ConAu XR, LongC*
A A *see also* Armstrong, Anthony
Aardema, Verna 1911- *ConAu 5, SmATA 4*
Aaron, Betsy *NF*
Aarons, George A *OvPC*
Aarvik, Egil 1912- *IntWW 1976*
Abbe, James 1882?-1973 *BioIn 10, NewYTBE 4*
Abbey, Edwin Austin 1852-1911 *OxAm, WebBD*
Abbey, Wallace W 1902?-1977 *NF*
Abbot, William Stickney 1886?-1958 *BioIn 3*
Abbot, Willis John 1863-1934 *Alli Sup, AmAu&B, AmJnl, BiD&SB, BioIn 3, DcAmA, DcAmB S1, DcNAA, HisAmM XR, NatCAB 32, REnAL, WhJnl 1928*
Abbott, Charles Howard 1880?-1954 *BioIn 3*
Abbott, Edward 1841-1908 *Alli Sup, AmAu&B, BiD&SB, DcAmA, DcNAA*
Abbott, Ernest Hamlin 1870-1931 *AmLY, DcAmA, DcNAA, HisAmM XR, WhNAA, WhJnl 1928*
Abbott, Francis Ellingwood *HisAmM XR*
Abbott, Frederic K 1892?-1957 *BioIn 4*
Abbott, Joseph Carter 1825-1882 *DcAmB 1, NatCAB 5*
Abbott, Keene 1876-1941 *AmAu&B, DcNAA, WhNAA*
Abbott, Lawrence Fraser 1859-1933 *DcNAA, HisAmM XR, WhJnl 1928*
Abbott, Leonard Dalton 1878-1953 *BioIn 3*
Abbott, Lyman 1835-1922 *Alli, Alli Sup, AmAu&B, AmLY, BbD, BiD&SB, BioIn 2, BioIn 3, BioIn 6, BioIn 9, CyAL 2, DcAmA, DcEnL, DcNAA, HisAmM XR, OxAm, REn, REnAL, TwCA, TwCA Sup, WebBD*
Abbott, Mabel *WhJnl 1928*
Abbott, May Laura 1916- *Au&Wr, ConAu 9R, WrDr 1976*
Abbott, Robert E *BioIn 9*
Abbott, Robert Sengstacke 1868-1940 *BioIn 3, BioIn 9, BlkC, CurBio XR, DcAmB S2*
Abbott, Walter Scott 1830- *DcNAA*
Abbott, Wenonah Stevens 1865-1950 *AmAu&B, BioIn 2, WhNAA*
A'Beckett, Arthur William 1844-1909 *Alli Sup, BiD&SB, DcEnA, DcEnA Ap, NewC, WebBD*
A'Beckett, Gilbert Abbott 1811-1856 *Alli, BbD, BiD&SB, BioIn 8, BrAu 19, CasWL, DcEnA, DcEnL, EvLB, NewC, OxEng, WebBD*
A'Beckett, Gilbert Arthur 1837-1891 *BioIn 8, DcEnA, DcEnA Ap, NewC, WebBD*
Abel, Bob 1931- *ConAu 65*
Abel, Deryck 1918-1965 *BioIn 7*

Abel, Elie 1920- *BioIn 8, CanWW 1972, ConAu 61, LEduc 1974, WhoAm 1974, WhoE 1974, WhoWor 1974, WhoWorJ 1972*
Abell, Arunah Shepherdson 1806-1888 *AmAu&B, AmJnl, DcAmB 1, NatCAB 21*
Abell, Charles Shepherdson 1876-1953 *BioIn 5, NatCAB 42*
Abell, Edwin Franklin 1840-1904 *AmJnl*
Abell, Walter W 1872-1941 *NatCAB 30*
Abelson, Alan 1925- *WhoAm 1974*
Abelson, Philip Hauge 1913- *AmM&W 73P, CurBio XR, IntWW 1974, NewYTBE 1, WhoAm 1974, WhoWor 1974*
Abend, Hallett Edward 1884-1955 *AmAu&B, BioIn 4, CurBio XR*
Abend, Jules *OvPC*
Abercrombie, Thomas J *NF*
Abern, Martin *AmRP*
Abernethy, Byron L 1899- *WhJnl 1928*
Abernethy, Robert Gordon 1927- *ConAu 21R, SmATA 5, WhoAm 1974*
Abert, Donald Byron 1907- *WhoAm 1974, WhoMW 1974*
Abner, David 1860- *BioIn 8*
Aboaf, Jack 1920- *NF*
About, Edmond Francois Valentin 1828-1885 *BbD, BiD&SB, CasWL, ClDMEL, CyWA, DcBiA, DcEuL, EvEuW, OxFr, Pen Eur, WebBD*
Abraham, George *NF*
Abraham, Molly *NF*
Abraham, Robert d1854 *BbtC, DcNAA*
Abraham, Willard 1916- *ConAu 13R, LEduc 1974, WhoAm 1974, WrDr 1976*
Abrahams, Alexander R 1888- *WhJnl 1928*
Abrahams, Peter 1919- *AfA 1, Au&Wr, CasWL, ConAu 57, ConLC 4, ConNov 1976, CurBio XR, Pen Eng, RGAfL, TwCW, WebE&AL, WhoWor 1974, WorAu, WrDr 1976*
Abramowitz, Barbara *NF*
Abrams, Earl Bernard 1911- *WhoAm 1974*
Abrams, Francis Basil 1898- *WhJnl 1928*
Abrams, Jane Brown *NF*
Abramson, Arnold Ernest 1914- *OvPC, WhoAdv 1972, WhoAm 1974*
Abramson, Harry 1888- *WhJnl 1928*
Abramson, Howard S *NF*
Abramson, Robert J *OvPC*
Abramson, Rudy P *NF*
Abu-Rish, M K *OvPC*
Ace *NF*
Acheson, Barclay 1887-1957 *BioIn 4*
Acheson, Cornell Wolley *OvPC*
Acheson, Samuel Hanna 1900- *WhJnl 1928*
Achilles, Theodore Carter 1905- *OvPC,*

WhoAm 1974
Achintre, Auguste 1834-1886 *DcNAA*
Achorn, Robert Comey 1922- *WhoAm 1974*
Achre, Paul H 1895- *WhJnl 1928*
Ackerley, Joe Randolph 1896-1967 *BioIn 10*
Ackerman, Carl William 1890-1970 *AmAu&B,*
　AmJnl, BioIn 4, BioIn 9, ConAu 29,
　ConAu 73, CurBio XR, IndAu 1917,
　NewYTBE 1, WhJnl 1928
Ackerman, Clara *BioIn 3*
Ackerman, Gordon *OvPC*
Ackerman, Henry S *OvPC*
Ackerman, Marshall *NF*
Ackerman, T *NF*
Acklin, Jessie M 1901- *NF*
Acton, Harry d1935 *NF*
Acton, Howard 1884?-1953 *BioIn 3*
Acuff, Lloyd Charles 1895?-1965 *BioIn 7*
Adachi, Barbara 1924- *ConAu 49*
Adachi, Kinnosuke 1871-1952 *BioIn 2*
Adair, Neal Gleghorn 1886-1952 *BioIn 2*
Adam, Madame 1836-1936 *BbD*
Adam, Madame *see also* Adam, Juliette Lamber
Adam, Edmond Antoine 1816-1877 *NF*
Adam, G S *NF*
Adam, Graeme Mercer 1839-1912 *Alli Sup,*
　DcLEL, DcNAA, HisAmM XR, OxCan
Adam, James 1898- *WhJnl 1928*
Adam, Juliette Lamber 1836-1936 *BiD&SB, OxFr,*
　REn, WebBD
Adam, Juliette Lamber *see also* Adam, Madame
Adamantios, Th Polyzoides 1885- *NF*
Adamic, Louis 1899-1951 *AmAu&B, CnDAL,*
　ConAmA, CurBio XR, DcAmB S5, DcLEL,
　OxAm, REn, REnAL, TwCA, TwCA Sup
Adams, A John 1931- *ConAu 33, OvPC*
Adams, A M *WhNAA, WhJnl 1928*
Adams, Abijah 1754-1816 *AmJnl, DcAmB 1*
Adams, Albertus M 1878?-1952 *BioIn 2*
Adams, Alton A *OvPC*
Adams, Anne *NF*
Adams, Betty *OvPC, WhoAmW 1974,*
　WhoE 1974
Adams, Braman Blanchard 1851-1944 *DcNAA*
Adams, Bristow 1875-1957 *BioIn 4*
Adams, Bruce T *NF*
Adams, Carlyle 1906- *WhoE 1974*
Adams, Caswell 1906?-1957 *BioIn 4*
Adams, Cedric M 1902-1961 *AmAu&B, BioIn 1,*
　BioIn 2, BioIn 5, BioIn 6, MnnWr
Adams, Chester W 1881- *WhJnl 1928*
Adams, Cindy *BioIn 8, ConAu 23*
Adams, Cyrus Cornelius 1849-1928 *AmLY,*
　DcAmA, DcAmB S1, DcNAA
Adams, Cyrus Field *NF*
Adams, Edward Francis 1839-1929 *AmLY,*
　DcNAA, WhNAA
Adams, Edward Thomas 1933- *WhoAm 1974,*
　WhoE 1974, WhoWor 1974
Adams, Elmer C 1885- *WhJnl 1928*
Adams, Elmer Ellsworth 1861-1950 *BioIn 6,*
　NatCAB 44
Adams, F B, Jr. *NF*
Adams, Franklin Pierce 1881-1960 *AmAu&B,*
　AmJnl, BioIn 1, BioIn 4, BioIn 6, BioIn 8,
　CnDAL, ConAmA, CurBio XR,
　HisAmM XR, OxAm, REn, REnAL,
　TwCA, TwCA Sup, WebBD, WhNAA
Adams, Frederick Upham 1859-1921 *AmAu&B,*
　DcAmA, DcNAA, WebBD
Adams, George Matthew 1878-1962 *AmAu&B,*
　BioIn 6, BioIn 7, NatCAB 47, REnAL
Adams, George Rodgers 1937- *WhoAm 1974*
Adams, George W 1838-1886 *NatCAB 15*

Adams, H Mat *OvPC*
Adams, Henry Austin 1861-1931 *AmAu&B,*
　DcNAA
Adams, Henry Brooks 1838-1918 *AmAu,*
　AmAu&B, AmWr, AtlBL, BbD, BiD&SB,
　CasWL, CnDAL, CyWA, DcAmA, DcBiA,
　DcLEL, DcNAA, EvLB, LiJA, LongC,
　ModAL, ModAL Sup, OxAm, OxEng,
　Pen Am, RAdv 1, RComWL, REn, REnAL,
　TwCW, WebBD, WebE&AL, WhoTwCL
Adams, James *AmJnl*
Adams, James Alonzo 1842-1925 *DcNAA,*
　HisAmM XR, OhA&B
Adams, James Barton 1843-1918 *DcAmA,*
　DcNAA, OhA&B
Adams, James Donald 1891-1968 *AmAu&B,*
　BioIn 5, BioIn 6, BioIn 7, BioIn 8,
　ConAu 2R, WhJnl 1928
Adams, James Edward 1941- *ConAu 73*
Adams, James H *NF*
Adams, Jean *NF*
Adams, Jean Prescott *NF*
Adams, Jim *NF*
Adams, John B 1909?-1968 *BioIn 8*
Adams, John Berry 1920- *AmM&W 73S, ForP,*
　WhoAm 1974
Adams, John Coleman *HisAmM XR*
Adams, John Hanly 1918- *WhoAm 1974,*
　WhoF&I 1974
Adams, John Haslup 1871- *BiDSA*
Adams, John M 1819- *NatCAB 1*
Adams, John Quincy *NF*
Adams, Joseph T *WhJnl 1928*
Adams, Kinlock Christy 1886?-1956 *BioIn 4*
Adams, Lester F 1895- *WhJnl Sup*
Adams, Malcolm Joseph 1911?-1964 *BioIn 6*
Adams, Maurice *NF*
Adams, Morley 1875?-1954 *BioIn 3*
Adams, Phelps Haviland 1902- *WhoAm 1974*
Adams, Phineas *HisAmM XR*
Adams, Phoebe-Lou 1918- *ForWC 1970,*
　WhoAm 1974, WhoAmW 1974, WhoE 1974
Adams, Robert *InvJ*
Adams, Robert Leroy 1937- *WhoAm 1974*
Adams, Sally *NF*
Adams, Samuel 1722-1803 *Alli, AmAu,*
　AmAu&B, AmJnl, DcAmA, DcNAA,
　OxAm, REn, REnAL
Adams, Samuel Ed 1876-1925 *WhJnl Sup*
Adams, Samuel Hopkins 1871-1958 *AmAu&B,*
　AmJnl, AmLY, AmNov, AuBYP, CnDAL,
　EncMys, HisAmM XR, OxAm, REn,
　REnAL, TwCA, TwCA Sup, WebBD,
　WhNAA
Adams, Thomas *AmJnl*
Adams, Thomas H 1860- *WhJnl 1928*
Adams, William Henry Davenport 1829-1891
　Alli Sup, BbD, NewC
Adams, William Lysander 1821-1906 *DcNAA,*
　OhA&B
Adams, William Taylor 1822-1897 *Alli Sup,*
　AmAu, AmAu&B, BbD, BiD&SB, CarSB,
　CnDAL, CyAL 2, DcAmA, DcEnL,
　DcNAA, HisAmM XR, HsB&A,
　HsB&A Sup, OxAm, REn, REnAL, WebBD
Adamson, David Grant 1927- *ConAu 15R*
Adamson, Hans Christian 1890-1968 *AmAu&B,*
　BioIn 8, ConAu 5
Adamson, Robert *NF*
Addams, Charles Samuel 1912- *AmAu&B,*
　BioIn 2, BioIn 3, BioIn 6, BioIn 7, BioIn 8,
　BioIn 10, ConAu 61, CurBio XR,
　IntWW 1976, WhoAm 1974,
　WhoAmA 1973, WhoWor 1974

Adde, Leo 1927?-1975 *ConAu 57*
Addington, Sarah 1891-1940 *AmAu&B,*
CurBio XR, DcNAA, OhA&B, WhNAA
Addis, Don *NF*
Addison, Joseph 1672-1719 *Alli, AmJnl, AtlBL,*
BbD, BiD&SB, BrAu, CasWL, CrtT 2,
CyWA, DcEnA, DcEnL, DcEuL, DcLEL,
EvLB, ForP, LiJA, McGWD, MouLC 2,
NewC, OxEng, Pen Eng, PoChrch, RAdv 1,
RComWL, REn, WebBD, WebE&AL
Addison, Walker *NF*
Ade, George 1866-1944 *AmAu&B, AmJnl,*
AmLY, BbD, BiD&SB, CasWL, CnDAL,
ConAmL, CurBio XR, DcAmA, DcNAA,
EvLB, HisAmM XR, IndAu 1816, McGWD,
ModWD, OxAm, Pen Am, REn, REnAL,
TwCA, TwCA Sup, TwCW, WebBD,
WhNAA
Ade, Ginny *NF*
Adeler, Max 1841-1915 *Alli Sup, AmAu,*
AmAu&B, DcAmA, DcNAA, EvLB, OxAm,
REnAL
Adeler, Max *see also* Clark, Charles Heber
Adels, Robert Mitchell 1948- *WhoAm 1974*
Aden, John *NF*
Adkins, Rose 1935- *NF*
Adkins, Sarah *NF*
Adlam, George Henry Joseph 1876-1946 *BioIn 1*
Adler, Elmer 1884-1962 *AmAu&B, BioIn 3,*
BioIn 5, BioIn 6
Adler, Emanuel Philip 1872-1949 *BioIn 1,*
BioIn 2, WhJnl 1928
Adler, Guido 1855-1941 *CurBio XR*
Adler, Harry Clay 1865-1940 *CurBio XR*
Adler, Jack *ConAu 73*
Adler, James B *BioIn 9*
Adler, Joseph *NF*
Adler, Julius Ochs 1892-1955 *AmAu&B, AmJnl,*
BioIn 1, BioIn 4, CurBio XR
Adler, Larry *NF*
Adler, Mortimer *NF*
Adler, Nathan *NF*
Adler, Philip David 1902-1947 *BioIn 2*
Adler, Renata 1938- *AmAu&B, ConAu 49,*
DrAF 1976, WhoAm 1974
Adler, Warren 1927- *ConAu 69*
Adler, Wendy *NF*
Adnerson, Nesl Ehlert 1890- *WhJnl 1928*
Adzhubei, Aleksei Ivanovich 1924- *BioIn 5,*
BioIn 6, BioIn 7, CurBio XR
AE *see* Russell, George William
Africano, Lillian 1935- *ConAu 69*
Agan, Patrick 1943- *ConAu 65*
Agar, Frank E 1888?- *BioIn 2*
Agar, Herbert Sebastian 1897- *BioIn 1, BioIn 4,*
ConAu 65, CurBio XR, IntWW 1974,
WebBD, Who 1974, WhoWor 1974
Agate, James Evershed 1877-1947 *DcLEL, EvLB,*
LongC, ModBL, NewC, Pen Eng, REn,
TwCA, TwCA Sup, TwCW, WebBD
Agee, James Rufus 1909-1955 *DcAmB S5*
Agee, Warren Kendall 1916- *ConAu 17R,*
DrAS 74E, LEduc 1974, WhoAm 1974,
WhoCon 1973, WhoS&SW 1973
Agel, Jerome 1930?- *BioIn 7*
Agen, Myer 1895- *OvPC, WhNAA,*
WhoWorJ 1972
Ager, Waldemar 1869- *WhJnl 1928*
Agnelli, Muriel *BioIn 2*
Agnew, Bruce Andras 1934- *WhoAm 1974*
Agnew, John Holmes 1804-1865 *AmAu&B*
Agniel, Lucien D 1919- *ConAu 29*
Agnus, Felix 1839-1925 *AmJnl, DcAmB 1*
Agron, Gershon 1893-1959 *BioIn 5*

Agron, Gershon *see also* Agronsky, Gershon
Agronsky, Gershon 1893-1959 *BioIn 1*
Agronsky, Gershon *see also* Agron, Gershon
Agronsky, Martin Zama 1915- *BioIn 3,*
WhoAm 1974, WhoS&SW 1973,
WhoWor 1974
Aguilera, Ventura Ruiz 1820-1881 *BiD&SB,*
WebBD
Ahearn, Francis T *OvPC, WhoE 1974*
Ahearn, James F 1932- *NF*
Ahern, Eugene Leslie 1895-1960 *BioIn 5*
Ahern, Margaret 1923- *WhoAmW 1974,*
WhoMW 1974
Ahern, Timothy 1951- *NF*
Ahlers, Conrad 1922- *IntWW 1976,*
WhoWor 1974
Ahlgren, Frank Richard 1903- *WhoAm 1974,*
WhoS&SW 1973
Ahlgren, Mrs. Oscar A 1902- *CurBio XR*
Ahlstrand, Franz A 1894- *WhJnl Sup*
Ahmed, Asrar *NF*
Ahnstrom, D N 1915- *ConAu 7R*
Ahrens, Charles 1905?-1978 *NF*
Aiken, David Wyatt 1828-1887 *BioIn 9*
Aiken, Scott *OvPC*
Aiken, William L 1873- *WhJnl 1928*
Aikens, Andrew Jackson 1830-1909 *BioIn 5,*
WebBD
Aikman, David 1944- *ConAu 65*
Aikman, Duncan 1889-1955 *AmAu&B,*
HisAmM XR, IndAu 1917, TexWr,
WhJnl 1928
Aikman, Leo 1908-1978 *WhoS&SW 1973*
Ailshire, Margaret Cobb 1886-1959 *BioIn 1*
Ainslie, Rosalynde 1932- *ConAu 25*
Ainsworth, Edward Maddin 1902-1968 *AmAu&B,*
BioIn 6, BioIn 8, ConAu 5R
Ainsworth, William Harrison 1805-1882 *Alli,*
Alli Sup, BbD, BiD&SB, BrAu 19, CasWL,
CyWA, DcBiA, DcEnA, DcEnA Ap,
DcEnL, DcEuL, DcLEL, EvLB, NewC,
OxEng, Pen Eng, REn, WebBD,
WebE&AL, WhoChL
Aird, Paul D 1896- *WhJnl 1928*
Aitken, Jonathan 1942- *ConAu 21R*
Aitken, Margaret 1908- *CanWW 1972*
Aitken, Robert 1734-1802 *Alli, AmAu&B,*
DcNAA, HisAmM XR, OxAm
Aitken, Sir William Traven 1905-1964 *BioIn 6*
Ajemian, Robert Myron 1925- *WhoAm 1974*
Akar, John 1927?-1975 *BioIn 10*
Akerman, John Camille 1880?-1950 *BioIn 2*
Akers, Berry H 1887- *WhJnl 1928*
Akers, Merton T 1898-1971 *BioIn 9, NewYTBE 2*
Akers, Milburn Peter 1900-1970 *BioIn 5, BioIn 7,*
BioIn 8, NewYTBE 1
Akerson, George Edward, Jr. 1918- *WhoAm 1974,*
WhoF&I 1974, WhoWor 1974
Akiyama, Ryoji 1943- *BioIn 10*
Aksakov, Ivan Sergeevich 1823-1886 *BioIn 7,*
CasWL, DcRusL, WebBD
Al, Li Ling *OvPC*
Al-Katib, Adnan A 1944- *NF*
Al-Yusuf, Rose Fatima *BioIn 4*
Alarcon, Pedro Antonio De 1833-1891 *BiD&SB,*
CasWL, CIDMEL, CyWA, EuAu, EvEuW,
Pen Eur, REn, WebBD
Alba, Pedro *ForP*
Albers, JoAnn *NF*
Albert, George *NF*
Albert, Jacob 1894- *WhJnl 1928*
Albert, John 1912- *WhoAm 1974, WhoGov 1972,*
WhoWor 1974
Albert, Robert Hartman 1924- *OvPC,*

WhoAdv 1972, WhoE 1974
Albertanti, Francis 1888-1958 *BioIn 4*
Albertini, Alberto 1879-1954 *BioIn 3*
Albertini, Luigi 1871-1941 *ForP, WebBD*
Albino, Joseph 1937- *NF*
Albitz, George 1947- *NF*
Albott, Frank L 1897- *WhJnl 1928*
Albrect, Wolfgang *NF*
Albrectsen, Bent *NF*
Albright, John Brannon 1930- *ConAu 65*
Albright, Joseph Medill Patterson 1937-
WhoAm 1974
Albright, William Edward 1873-1937 *BioIn 2*
Albright, William H 1875-1942 *NatCAB 32*
Albro, Frank 1932- *NF*
Alburn, Miriam Estelle *WhoAm 1974,*
WhoAmW 1974
Alcobre Ares, Manuel 1900- *IntWW 1976*
Alcock, J Curtis 1881- *WhNAA, WhJnl 1928*
Alcott, Carroll Duard 1901-1965 *BioIn 7*
Alcott, William 1868- *WhJnl 1928*
Alden, Cynthia May Westover 1861-1931
DcAmB S1, DcNAA
Alden, Henry Mills 1836-1919 *Alli Sup, AmAu,*
AmAu&B, BbD, BiD&SB, BioIn 5,
CnDAL, DcAmA, DcNAA, HisAmM XR,
LiJA, NatCAB 1, OxAm, REnAL
Alden, Isabella Macdonald 1841-1930 *Alli Sup,*
AmAu&B, AmLY, BbD, BiD&SB, CarSB,
DcAmA, DcAmB S1, DcNAA,
HisAmM XR, LongC, OhA&B, OxAm
Alden, John 1869-1934 *AmAu&B*
Alden, Joseph G 1876- *WhNAA, WhJnl 1928*
Alden, Robert 1922-1973 *BioIn 10, NewYTBE 4*
Alden, William Livingston 1837-1908 *Alli Sup,*
AmAu, AmAu&B, BbD, BiD&SB, CarSB,
DcAmA, DcAmB 1, DcNAA, HisAmM XR,
NatCAB 6
Aldenhoven, Franz Von d1875 *NF*
Alderman, Edith E 1905- *WhJnl 1928*
Alderson, Court *NF*
Alderson, Joanne Bartels 1930- *ConAu 65,*
WhoAmW 1974
Aldinger, Charles S *NF*
Aldouby, Zwy Herbert 1931- *ConAu 33*
Aldrich, Charles 1828-1908 *DcNAA, NatCAB 9*
Aldrich, Chester A 1874- *WhJnl 1928*
Aldrich, Mrs. E A *HisAmM XR*
Aldrich, Edward Burgess 1871-1957 *BioIn 4*
Aldrich, Edwin Burton 1879- *WhJnl 1928*
Aldrich, Nelson W, Jr. *NF*
Aldrich, Paul Irving 1870- *WhJnl 1928*
Aldrich, Richard 1863-1937 *AmAu&B, BioIn 1,*
DcAmB S2, DcNAA, NatCAB 33, WebBD,
WhNAA, WhJnl 1928
Aldrich, Thomas Bailey 1836-1907 *Alli, Alli Sup,*
AmAu, AmAu&B, BbD, BiD&SB, BioIn 1,
BioIn 2, BioIn 3, BioIn 5, BioIn 7, CarSB,
CasWL, CnDAL, CyAL 2, CyWA, DcAmA,
DcBiA, DcEnA Ap, DcEnL, DcLEL,
DcNAA, EncMys, EvLB, HisAmM XR,
JBA 1934, LiJA, OxAm, OxEng, Pen Am,
REn, REnAL, WebBD
Aldridge, Harold Edward James *see* Aldridge, James
Aldridge, James 1918- *Au&W Wr, BioIn 2,*
BioIn 4, ConAu 61, ConNov 1972,
ConNov 1976, CurBio XR, TwCA Sup,
Who 1974, WrDr 1976
Aldridge, Ron *NF*
Alessandrini, Jorge *ForP*
Alexander, Calvert Page 1900- *BioIn 1,*
CathA 1930
Alexander, Charles *AmJnl, HisAmM XR*
Alexander, Charles Thomas 1928- *WhoAm 1974*

Alexander, David C 1907-1973 *BioIn 9,*
NewYTBE 4
Alexander, Don *NF*
Alexander, Eben Roy 1899-1978 *BioIn 2,*
HisAmM XR
Alexander, Edgar d1970 *BioIn 7, BioIn 8*
Alexander, Edgar M 1879- *WhJnl 1928*
Alexander, F Russell 1902- *WhNAA, WhJnl 1928*
Alexander, Franklin Osborne 1897- *BioIn 2,*
ConAu 25
Alexander, George F *OvPC*
Alexander, Henry *NF*
Alexander, Holmes Moss 1906- *AmAu&B,*
BioIn 4, BioIn 8, ConAu 61, CurBio XR,
WhoAm 1974
Alexander, Hunter *NF*
Alexander, Jack 1904?- *BioIn 1, BioIn 5*
Alexander, James d1889 *NF*
Alexander, James 1691-1756 *AmJnl*
Alexander, James Eckert 1913- *ConAu 73,*
WhoAm 1974
Alexander, Jerry *NF*
Alexander, John White 1856-1915 *WebBD*
Alexander, Kenneth Lewis 1924- *WhoAm 1974*
Alexander, Lamar 1941?- *BioIn 10*
Alexander, M Bishop 1900- *WhJnl 1928*
Alexander, Mary D d1970 *BioIn 8*
Alexander, Robert C 1857-1899 *NatCAB 6*
Alexander, Roy *see* Alexander, Eben Roy
Alexander, Ruth Wilbur *WhoAm 1974,*
WhoAmW 1974, WhoWor 1974
Alexander, Shana 1925- *BioIn 2, BioIn 6,*
BioIn 8, ConAu 61, ForWC 1970,
WhoAm 1974, WhoAmW 1974,
WhoF&I 1974, WrDr 1976
Alexander, Truman Hudson 1891-1941 *AmAu&B*
Alexandrov, Victor 1908- *BioIn 1*
Alexandrovich, George 1930- *BioIn 10*
Alexeyev, Pyotr Fyodorovich 1913- *IntWW 1976*
Aley, Maxwell 1889- *BioIn 2, IndAu 1816,*
WhNAA
Alford, Eugene Samuel 1865- *WhJnl 1928*
Alford, Henry 1810-1871 *Alli, Alli Sup, BbD,*
BiD&SB, BrAu 19, CasWL, DcEnA,
DcEnL, EvLB, NewC, WebBD
Alford, Theodore Crandall 1885-1947 *BioIn 1,*
BioIn 4, NatCAB 40
Alfriend, Frank H *Alli Sup, BiDSA, DcNAA*
Alger, Edwin *NF*
Ali, Chaudri Iftikhar *NF*
Alicata, Mario 1918-1966 *BioIn 7*
Alisky, Marvin Howard 1923- *AmM&W 73S,*
ConAu 13R
Allan, Donald Aspinwall 1922- *WhoAm 1974*
Allan, Edwin *NF*
Allan, Mea 1909- *Au&Wr, ConAu 7R,*
WrDr 1976
Allan, William Alexander 1924- *WhoAm 1974*
Allard, Chester C *WhJnl 1928*
Allard, Leola *NF*
Allaway, Howard 1912- *WhoAm 1974*
Allbritton, Joe Lewis 1924- *BioIn 10,*
WhoAm 1974, WhoF&I 1974,
WhoS&SW 1973
Allees, Arnold Edward *WhJnl 1928*
Allen, A G *NF*
Allen, Alexander d1883 *NF*
Allen, Alice Towsley *OvPC*
Allen, Anne *NF*
Allen, Arthur Francis 1867-1949 *BioIn 2,*
WhNAA, WhJnl 1928
Allen, C Edmonds 1910- *WhoAm 1974*
Allen, C J *NF*
Allen, C Stanley 1916- *RpN, WhoPubR 1972*

Allen, Carl Beaty 1896?-1971 *BioIn 9*,
   NewYTBE 2
Allen, Clarence Edgar 1871-1951 *BioIn 2*, *BioIn 3*
Allen, Cleveland G 1887-1953 *BioIn 3*
Allen, Clifford 1889- *WhoLA*
Allen, David Donald 1931- *WhoAm 1974*,
   WhoF&I 1974
Allen, David H *NF*
Allen, Devere 1891-1955 *AmAu&B*, *BioIn 4*,
   HisAmM XR, *WhNAA*
Allen, Douglas *NF*
Allen, Douglass M 1918?-1966 *BioIn 7*
Allen, E C *AmJnl*, *HisAmM XR*
Allen, Edward Frank 1885- *AmAu&B*, *WhNAA*
Allen, Edward Lisle 1868- *WhNAA*, *WhJnl 1928*
Allen, Eliza C *HisAmM XR*
Allen, Elizabeth Ann Akers 1832-1911 *Alli Sup*,
   AmAu, *AmAu&B*, *BiD&SB*, *CyAL 2*,
   DcAmA, *DcNAA*
Allen, Eric William 1879-1944 *AmAu&B*,
   DcNAA, *WhNAA*, *WhJnl 1928*
Allen, Frederick James 1864-1927 *BioIn 1*
Allen, Frederick Lewis 1890-1954 *AmAu&B*,
   BioIn 1, *BioIn 3*, *BioIn 4*, *BioIn 5*, *BioIn 6*,
   CnDAL, *HisAmM XR*, *LiJA*, *OxAm*, *REn*,
   REnAL, *TwCA*, *TwCA Sup*, *WebBD*
Allen, George Howard 1914- *AmM&W 73S*,
   WhoAdv 1972, *WhoAm 1974*,
   WhoF&I 1974, *WhoWor 1974*
Allen, George M 1853- *NatCAB 5*
Allen, George Merritt 1876- *WhJnl 1928*
Allen, George N *NF*
Allen, Graham *see* Arnold, George
Allen, Gwenfread Elaine 1904- *ConAu 61*,
   ForWC 1970
Allen, H W 1890- *WhJnl 1928*
Allen, Mrs. Harland H *WhJnl Sup*
Allen, Harland Hill 1887- *WhoAm 1974*,
   WhJnl Sup
Allen, Henry Justin 1868-1950 *BioIn 2*, *BioIn 4*,
   BioIn 9, *DcAmB S4*, *WhNAA*, *WhJnl 1928*
Allen, Herbert F L 1874?-1950 *BioIn 2*
Allen, Herbert Warner 1881-1968 *BioIn 8*
Allen, Howard *OvPC*
Allen, Hugh 1882- *OhA&B*
Allen, Ida Bailey 1885-1973 *AmAu&B*,
   NewYTBE 4, *REnAL*, *WhNAA*,
   WhoAm 1974
Allen, Ira R 1948- *ConAu 65*
Allen, J Edward *RpN*
Allen, James Pryer 1871?-1951 *BioIn 2*
Allen, Jay Cooke 1900-1972 *BioIn 9*, *CurBio XR*,
   NewYTBE 3
Allen, Jean *NF*
Allen, Jerry 1911- *Au&Wr*, *ConAu 11R*,
   WhoE 1974
Allen, John Edward 1889-1947 *DcNAA*, *WhNAA*,
   WhJnl 1928
Allen, John Milton 1926- *WhoAm 1974*
Allen, Joseph Henry 1916- *WhoAdv 1972*,
   WhoAm 1974, *WhoF&I 1974*, *WhoWor 1974*
Allen, Kelcey 1875-1951 *DcAmB S5*
Allen, Kenneth R 1942- *NF*
Allen, Lafe Franklin 1914- *OvPC*, *USBiR 1974*,
   WhoAm 1974, *WhoGov 1972*
Allen, Laurence Edmund 1908-1975 *AmJnl*,
   CurBio XR, *WhoAm 1974*,
   WhoS&SW 1973, *WhoWor 1974*
Allen, Lee 1915-1969 *AuBYP*, *ConAu 1*,
   OhA&B
Allen, Lloyd E 1888?-1950 *BioIn 2*
Allen, Maryland d1927 *DcNAA*, *WhNAA*
Allen, Maryon Pittman 1925- *ForWC 1970*,
   WhoAm 1974, *WhoAmW 1974*,

   WhoF&I 1974, *WhoS&SW 1973*
Allen, Maury 1932- *ConAu 17R*
Allen, Mel 1913- *AuBYP*, *CurBio XR*,
   IntMPA 1975, *WhoAm 1974*,
   WhoWorJ 1972
Allen, Nancy O'Brien *NF*
Allen, Olive E *NF*
Allen, Patricia H *BioIn 7*
Allen, Paul 1775-1826 *Alli*, *AmAu*, *AmAu&B*,
   BiD&SB, *BiDSA*, *CyAL 1*, *DcAmA*,
   DcNAA, *HisAmM XR*, *OxAm*, *REnAL*
Allen, Ralph 1913-1966 *BioIn 4*, *BioIn 5*,
   BioIn 7, *BioIn 8*, *CanWr*, *CasWL*,
   CurBio XR, *OxCan*
Allen, Reginald Edgar 1931- *ConAu 33*,
   DrAS 74P, *WhoAm 1974*
Allen, Riley Harris 1884- *BioIn 5*, *WhNAA*,
   WhJnl 1928
Allen, Robert E *NF*
Allen, Robert J 1930- *ConAu 15R*
Allen, Robert Sharon 1900- *AmAu&B*, *AmJnl*,
   BioIn 1, *ConAu 57*, *CurBio XR*, *NewMr*,
   REnAL, *WhoAm 1974*, *WhoS&SW 1973*,
   WhoWor 1974
Allen, Stephen T 1810-1888 *DcNAA*,
   HisAmM XR
Allen, T Ernest *HisAmM XR*
Allen, Thomas Scott 1825-1905 *BioIn 5*
Allen, Victor Harvey 1910- *WhoAm 1974*
Allen, Wallace *NF*
Allen, Walter Dwight 1879- *WhNAA*,
   WhJnl 1928
Allen, William 1940- *ConAu 65*
Allen, William A 1859?-1954 *BioIn 3*
Allen, William Prescott 1896?-1965 *BioIn 7*
Allerup, Paul Richard 1912- *WhoAm 1974*,
   WhoWor 1974
Alless, Arnold Edward *NF*
Alley, Paul *OvPC*
Allingham, Garry 1900- *BioIn 1*
Allinson, Anne Crosby Emery 1871-1932 *AmAu&B*,
   DcAmB S1, *DcNAA*, *WhNAA*
Allison, Barbara *NF*
Allison, Bob F *OvPC*
Allison, Edward P d1901 *HisAmM XR*
Allison, Henry James 1879- *WhJnl 1928*
Allison, J H *NF*
Allison, James N 1902- *WhJnl 1928*
Allison, Marvin Lawrence 1934- *WhoAm 1974*,
   WhoWest 1974
Allison, Mary Lucille 1925- *BioIn 7*,
   ForWC 1970, *WhoAm 1974*, *WhoAmW 1974*
Allison, Noah Dwight 1899-1971 *TexWr*,
   WhNAA, *WhJnl 1928*, *WhoS&SW 1973*
Allison, Robert *NF*
Allison, Robert Burns 1916- *WhoAm 1974*
Allison, Ronald William Paul 1932- *Who 1974*
Allison, William O d1924 *HisAmM XR*
Allman, Martha *NF*
Allman, Norwood Francis 1893- *OvPC*, *WhNAA*
Alloway, Lawrence 1926- *AmAu&B*, *ConAu 41*,
   WhoAm 1974, *WhoAmA 1973*
Allsop, Kenneth 1920-1973 *Au&Wr*, *BioIn 9*,
   ConAu 3R, *WhoWor 1974*, *WorAu*
Allsopp, Frederick William 1868-1946 *AmAu&B*,
   WhNAA, *WhJnl 1928*
Allwell, Louis 1901-1956 *BioIn 4*
Almagro, Melchor F *ForP*
Almi, A Sheps 1893-1963 *NF*
Alnes, Ellis Stephen 1926- *WhoAm 1974*
Alonso-Fueyo, Sabino 1909- *IntWW 1976*
Alpern, David Mark 1942- *ConAu 73*
Alpert, Helen *OvPC*
Alpert, Hollis 1916- *AmAu&B*, *ConAu 3R*,

WhoAm 1974

Alsberg, Henry Garfield 1881-1970 *BioIn 2, BioIn 9, NewYTBE 1*

Alsop, Joseph Wright, Jr. 1910- *AmAu&B, AmJnl, BioIn 1, BioIn 2, BioIn 3, BioIn 4, BioIn 5, BioIn 6, BioIn 7, BioIn 8, BioIn 9, CurBio XR, ForP, HisAmM XR, IntWW 1976, NewMr, NewYTBS 5, REn, REnAL, WhoAm 1974, WhoS&SW 1973, WhoWor 1974, WorAu*

Alsop, Stewart Johonnot Oliver 1914-1974 *AmAu&B, BioIn 1, BioIn 2, BioIn 3, BioIn 4, ConAu 49, CurBio XR, ForP, HisAmM XR, IntWW 1974, NewMr, WhoAm 1974, WhoS&SW 1973, WhoWor 1974*

Alsterdal, Alvar *ForP*

Alston, Roland 1903?-1955 *BioIn 3*

Alt, James *NF*

Alter, A *NF*

Alterman, Loraine J 1942- *NF*

Altgens, James W 1919?- *BioIn 6*

Althouse, William E 1866- *WhJnl 1928*

Altiere, Fred 1952- *NF*

Altman, Frances 1937- *ConAu 65*

Altman, Henry *NF*

Altman, Irving 1884?-1954 *BioIn 3*

Altman, Jack 1938- *ConAu 21R, WhoMW 1974*

Altman, Peter Alexander 1943- *WhoAm 1974*

Altobello, Patricia *NF*

Altrincham, Edward William 1879-1955 *BioIn 4*

Altschul, Selig *OvPC*

Altsheler, Joseph Alexander 1862-1919 *AmAu&B, AuBYP, BiDSA, BioIn 7, DcAmA, DcNAA, HisAmM XR, REnAL, TwCA, TwCA Sup, YABC 1*

Altshul, Jack *NF*

Aluit, Alfonso J 1930- *WhoPubR 1972*

Alva, Violet 1908?-1969 *BioIn 8*

Alvah, Eastman 1858- *WhJnl 1928*

Alvarez, Alfred 1929- *Au&Wr, BioIn 10, ConLC 5, ConP 1970, ConP 1975, ModBL Sup, REn, Who 1974, WhoWor 1974, WorAu, WrDr 1976*

Alvarez, Casimir 1873- *WhJnl 1928*

Alvarez, Walter Clement 1884-1978 *AmAu&B, AmM&W 73P, ConAu 61, CurBio XR, MnnWr, WhNAA, WhoAm 1974, WhoWor 1974*

Alvarez DelCastillo, Jesus 1881?- *BioIn 4*

Alvarez DelVayo, Julio 1891-1975 *BioIn 2, ConAu 61*

Alvaro, Corrado 1895-1956 *BioIn 4, CasWL, CIDMEL, EncWL, ModRL, Pen Eur, REn, WorAu*

Alverson, Charles 1935- *ConAu 25*

Alvey, Murray *OvPC*

Alvord, Ned *BioIn 1*

Amann, Max 1891?-1957 *BioIn 4*

Amaury, Emilien 1909- *ForP, IntWW 1976, WhoWor 1974*

Amberg, Martin H 1913- *NF*

Amberg, Richard Hiller 1912-1967 *BioIn 2, BioIn 8*

Amberg, Richard Hiller, Jr. 1942- *NF*

Ambriere, Francis 1907- *IntWW 1976, WhoWor 1974*

Ambroz, Oton 1905- *ConAu 41*

Ament, Robert S *WhJnl 1928*

Americanus, Junius *see* Endicott, Charles Moses

Ameringer, Oscar 1870-1943 *AmRP, CurBio XR, DcAmB S3, DcNAA*

Amery, Leopold Charles Maurice Stennett 1873-1955 *WebBD*

Ames, Alfred Campbell 1916- *WhoAm 1974*

Ames, Knowlton Lyman 1893-1965 *BioIn 1, BioIn 7, BioIn 9*

Ames, Mary Clemmer 1839-1884 *Alli Sup, AmAu&B, BiD&SB, CyAL 2, DcAmA, DcNAA, HisAmM XR, WebBD*

Ames, Mary Clemmer *see also* Clemmer, Mary

Amfitheatrof, Erik *NF*

Amick, George Ellsworth, Jr. 1931?- *NF*

Amidon, Beulah 1895-1958 *BioIn 5*

Amidon, Donna *NF*

Amin, Ali 1914-1976 *BioIn 3, BioIn 5, ConAu 65*

Amin, Mostafa 1914- *BioIn 3, BioIn 5, BioIn 7, IntWW 1976*

Amis, John *NF*

Amman, Max *ForP*

Ammarell, Raymond Robert, Jr. 1917- *WhoAm 1974*

Ammon, Ralph E 1901- *WhJnl 1928*

Amoroso Lima, Alceu 1893- *BioIn 1*

Amory, Cleveland 1917- *AmAu&B, AuNews 1, BioIn 5, BioIn 7, BioNews 1975, CelR 1973, ConAu 69, REnAL, TwCA Sup, WhoAm 1974, WhoWor 1974, WrDr 1976*

Amos, Edgar McCall 1880- *WhJnl 1928*

Amos, Ernest Clarence 1872-1962 *BioIn 8*

Amos, Harry W 1876- *WhJnl 1928*

Amos, T E *WhJnl 1928*

Amper, Richard L 1915?-1960 *BioIn 5*

Amphlett, Horace W 1890- *WhJnl 1928*

Amster, Betty Lou 1925?- *BioIn 2*

Amussen, Robert Martin 1924- *WhoAm 1974*

Amy, George A 1870- *WhJnl 1928*

Amy, William Lacey *CanNov, OxCan*

An, Pham Xuan *NF*

Anable, David J *NF*

Anand, Mulk Raj 1905- *Au&Wr, CasWL, ConAu 65, ConNov 1972, ConNov 1976, DcOrL 2, IntWW 1976, Pen Eng, REn, WebBD, WebE&AL, WhoWor 1974, WorAu, WrDr 1976*

Ananian, Vakhtang Stepanovich 1905- *IntWW 1976, WhoWor 1974*

Anastasi, April *NF*

Andelman, David *NF*

Anderman, William E 1892-1966 *BioIn 7*

Anders, Clarice *NF*

Anders, Corrie M *NF*

Anders, Ronald *NF*

Andersen, Harold Wayne 1923- *WhoAm 1974, WhoF&I 1974, WhoMW 1974*

Anderson, Alexandra *NF*

Anderson, Andy 1892?- *BioIn 2*

Anderson, Barry C *NF*

Anderson, Bradley Jay 1924- *AmAu&B, BioIn 10, WhoAm 1974*

Anderson, Carl Thomas 1865-1948 *AmAu&B, AmJnl, BioIn 1, HisAmM XR, WebBD*

Anderson, Carolyn 1913- *NF*

Anderson, Chuck 1933- *ConAu 49*

Anderson, Curtiss Martin 1928- *WhoAm 1974*

Anderson, Dave *AuNews 2*

Anderson, David *OvPC*

Anderson, David 1875-1947 *DcNAA*

Anderson, David E *NF*

Anderson, Don 1900- *WhJnl 1928*

Anderson, Doris *OxCan Sup*

Anderson, Edwin Joseph Arthur 1900- *BioIn 7*

Anderson, F David 1905?-1969 *BioIn 8*

Anderson, Finley *AmJnl, FamWC*

Anderson, Floyd Edward 1906- *BkC 6, WhoAm 1974*

Anderson, Frederick Irving 1877-1947 *AmAu&B,*

*DcNAA, EncMys, TwCA, TwCA Sup,
WhNAA*
Anderson, George Everett 1869-1940 *BioIn 2,
CurBio XR, NatCAB 34*
Anderson, George Harding 1931- *WhoAm 1974,
WhoE 1974*
Anderson, Harold H 1901- *WhoAm 1974,
WhoF&I 1974*
Anderson, Harold MacDonald 1876-1940 *NF*
Anderson, Harry W *NF*
Anderson, Helen *NF*
Anderson, Henry James 1799-1875 *Alli, CyAL 1,
HisAmM XR*
Anderson, Howard 1944- *NF*
Anderson, J R L 1911- *ConAu 25*
Anderson, Jack 1935- *AmAu&B, ConAu 33,
DrAP 1975*
Anderson, Jack E *NF*
Anderson, Jack Northman 1922- *AuNews 1,
BioIn 8, BioIn 9, BioNews 1974, CelR 1973,
ConAu 57, CurBio XR, InvJ, NewMr,
NewYTBE 3, WhoAm 1974,
WhoS&SW 1973, WhoWor 1974,
WrDr 1976*
Anderson, James H *BlkC*
Anderson, Jean 1930- *ConAu 41, ForWC 1970*
Anderson, Jeanne *NF*
Anderson, Jennifer 1942- *ConAu 57*
Anderson, Jim *NF*
Anderson, Joe Holt *NF*
Anderson, John Hargis 1896-1943 *AmAu&B,
CurBio XR*
Anderson, John Weir 1928- *WhoAm 1974,
WhoS&SW 1973*
Anderson, John William 1897- *WhJnl 1928*
Anderson, Karl M 1893- *WhJnl 1928*
Anderson, Kenneth Norman 1921- *OvPC,
WhoAm 1974, WhoE 1974*
Anderson, Lee Stratton 1925- *WhoAm 1974,
WhoS&SW 1973*
Anderson, Leonard *NF*
Anderson, Malcolm E 1900?-1950 *BioIn 2*
Anderson, Margaret C 1886?-1973 *AmAu&B,
BioIn 2, BioIn 8, BioIn 9, BioIn 10,
HisAmM XR, IndAu 1917, NewYTBE 4,
REnAL*
Anderson, Maxwell 1888-1959 *AmAu&B,
AmSCAP 1966, CasWL, CnDAL, CnMD,
CnThe, ConAmA, ConAmL, CroCD,
CurBio XR, CyWA, DcLEL, EncWL,
EvLB, HisAmM XR, LongC, McGWD,
ModAL, ModWD, OxAm, Pen Am, REn,
REnAL, REnWD, TwCA, TwCA Sup,
TwCW, WebE&AL, WhJnl 1928*
Anderson, Nancy *NF*
Anderson, Patrick *NF*
Anderson, Patrick 1915- *Au&Wr, ConP 1970,
ConP 1975, OxCan, REnAL, WrDr 1976*
Anderson, Paul O 1916- *WhoAm 1974,
WhoWest 1974*
Anderson, Paul Y 1893-1938 *AmJnl, BioIn 4,
DcAmB S2, NewMr, WhNAA*
Anderson, Peyton Tooke 1873-1944 *BioIn 1,
BioIn 2*
Anderson, Peyton Tooke, Jr. 1907- *BioIn 1,
BioIn 2, WhoAm 1974*
Anderson, Prexy 1905- *WhJnl 1928*
Anderson, Ralph Alexander 1889?-1956 *BioIn 3,
BioIn 4*
Anderson, Ray F *NF*
Anderson, Raymond Harold 1926- *WhoAm 1974*
Anderson, Richard J 1901-1971 *BioIn 9*
Anderson, Robert Marion 1894- *WhJnl 1928*
Anderson, Roy 1905- *WhNAA*

Anderson, Roy 1936- *ConAu 15R, WrDr 1976*
Anderson, Russell F 1914- *BioIn 9, OvPC,
WhoF&I 1974*
Anderson, Ruth Nathan 1934- *ConAu 69*
Anderson, S S 1880- *WhJnl 1928*
Anderson, Sally A *NF*
Anderson, Scott *NF*
Anderson, Sherwood 1876-1941 *AmAu&B,
AmWr, AtlBL, CasWL, CnDAL, CnMWL,
ConAmA, ConAmL, CurBio XR, CyWA,
DcLEL, DcNAA, EncWL, EvLB, LongC,
ModAL, ModAL Sup, OhA&B, OxAm,
OxEng, Pen Am, RAdv 1, REn, REnAL,
TwCA, TwCA Sup, TwCW, WebBD,
WebE&AL, WhNAA, WhJnl 1928,
WhoTwCL*
Anderson, Shirley Lord 1934- *ConAu 65*
Anderson, Thomas Carl 1865-1948 *BioIn 5*
Anderson, Tom 1910- *ConAu 69*
Anderson, Walter V 1903- *WhNAA*
Anderson, William 1805?-1866? *Alli Sup*
Anderson, William E 1926?- *BioIn 10, InvJ*
Anderson, William Eugene, Jr. 1932-
WhoWest 1974
Anderson, William F 1927- *WhoAm 1974*
Anderson, William Gibson 1874- *WhNAA,
WhJnl 1928*
Anderson, William James 1813?-1873 *DcNAA*
Anderson, William Thomas 1871-1945 *BioIn 1*
Anderton, David Albin 1919- *ConAu 65, OvPC*
Anderton, Piers B *RpN*
Andes, Fred J *WhJnl 1928*
Andrade, Anne McIlhenney *OvPC*
Andrawes, Adib *NF*
Andree, Karl Theodor 1808-1875 *WebBD*
Andree, Richard 1835-1912 *WebBD*
Andrew, John J *AmJnl*
Andrew, Stanley 1894- *NF*
Andrews, Allen 1913- *ConAu 49, WrDr 1976*
Andrews, Bert 1901-1953 *BioIn 1, BioIn 2,
BioIn 3, CurBio XR, DcAmB S5*
Andrews, Byron 1852- *DcNAA*
Andrews, Charles Freer 1871-1940 *BioIn 1,
BioIn 2, BioIn 9*
Andrews, Charlton 1878-1939 *AmAu&B, BioIn 2,
DcNAA, WhNAA*
Andrews, Clarence N 1856- *WhNAA,
WhJnl 1928*
Andrews, Clinton Toms, Jr. 1933- *NF*
Andrews, Colman *NF*
Andrews, Dorothea Harris 1916-1976
WhoGov 1972
Andrews, Eamonn 1922- *BioIn 6, BioIn 9,
IntMPA 1975, IntWW 1976, Who 1974,
WhoWor 1974*
Andrews, Frank Edmund 1874-1947 *BioIn 5*
Andrews, George W 1878?-1955 *BioIn 3,
NewYTBE 2*
Andrews, Leonard E B *OvPC*
Andrews, Sir Linton 1886-1972 *Au&Wr, BioIn 7,
BioIn 9, ForP*
Andrews, Sir Linton *see also* Andrews, Sir William
Linton
Andrews, Lorenzo Frank 1828-1915 *DcNAA*
Andrews, Loring 1768-1805 *Alli, NatCAB 20*
Andrews, Marshall 1899?-1973 *ConAu 45*
Andrews, Oliver Burnside, Jr. 1904- *WhJnl 1928*
Andrews, Paul Benjamin 1901- *WhoAm 1974*
Andrews, Peter C 1931- *ConAu 17R*
Andrews, Robert Douglas 1908?- *AmAu&B,
BioIn 6, ConAu 9, ConAu P-1*
Andrews, Robert Douglas *see also* Andrews, Robert
Hardy
Andrews, Robert Hardy 1908?- *AmNov*

Andrews, Robert Hardy *see also* Andrews, Robert
Douglas
Andrews, Robert M 1932- *NF*
Andrews, Roger M 1874-1943 *NF*
Andrews, Roland Franklyn d1930 *WhJnl 1928*
Andrews, Sidney 1835-1880 *Alli Sup, DcAmA,*
DcAmB 1, DcNAA
Andrews, Siri Margreta 1894- *BioIn 1*
Andrews, Stanley 1894- *BioIn 2, BioIn 3,*
ConAu 45, CurBio XR, WhJnl 1928
Andrews, Steffan 1914-1953 *BioIn 3*
Andrews, Stephen Pearl 1812-1886 *Alli, Alli Sup,*
AmAu, AmRP, BbD, BiD&SB, BiDSA,
DcAmA, DcNAA, OxAm, REnAL
Andrews, Walter 1933- *NF*
Andrews, Sir William Linton 1886-1972 *ConAu 9,*
Lor&LP
Andrews, Sir William Linton *see also* Andrews, Sir
Linton
Andriadis, Dimitri H *OvPC*
Andrica, Theodore 1900?- *BioIn 1, BioIn 6,*
RpN
Andrieu, Rene Gabriel 1920- *IntWW 1976,*
WhoWor 1974
Andriola, Alfred *NF*
Angell, George Nelson 1887- *WhNAA,*
WhJnl 1928
Angell, George Thorndike 1823-1909 *DcNAA,*
WebBD
Angell, James Burrill 1829-1916 *Alli Sup,*
AmAu&B, BbD, BiD&SB, CyAL 1,
CyAL 2, DcAmA, DcAmB 1, DcNAA,
WebBD
Angell, Sir Norman 1872-1967 *BioIn 1, BioIn 2,*
BioIn 4, BioIn 5, BioIn 7, BioIn 8, BioIn 9,
ConAu 13, ConAu P-1, CurBio XR, DcLEL,
EvLB, HisAmM XR, LongC, NewC,
OxEng, TwCA, TwCA Sup, WebBD,
WhoLA
Angell, Roger 1920- *BioIn 9, ConAu 57,*
DrAF 1976, WhoAm 1974
Angelo, Bonnie *WhoAm 1974, WhoAmW 1974,*
WhoS&SW 1973
Angelo, Emidio 1903- *BioIn 2, BioIn 3,*
WhoAmA 1973
Angelo, Frank 1914- *ConAu 53, WhoAm 1974*
Angelopoulos, Alkaios *OvPC*
Angelou, Maya 1928- *BlkAW, ConAu 65,*
CurBio XR, DrAP 1975, LivBAA,
NewYTBE 2, WhoAm 1974, WrDr 1976
Angioli, Alex *NF*
Angle, Martha 1941- *NF*
Anglin, Timothy Warren 1822-1896 *WebBD*
Angly, Edward 1898-1951 *BioIn 2*
Angoff, Charles 1902- *AmAu&B, Au&Wr,*
BioIn 1, BioIn 3, BioIn 4, ConAu 5R,
CurBio XR, DrAF 1976, DrAP 1975,
DrAS 74E, HisAmM XR, REnAL,
WhNAA, WhoAm 1974, WhoWor 1974,
WhoWorJ 1972, WrDr 1976
Angrist, Stanley *NF*
Angus, Robert *NF*
Anker, Charlotte *NF*
Anker, Edward R 1881?-1950 *BioIn 2*
Anneke, Emil P 1823- *BioIn 2*
Anneke, Fritz 1818-1872 *BioIn 2, BioIn 5*
Anneke, Mathilde F 1817-1884 *NatCAB 4*
Annenberg, Ivan 1905?- *BioIn 3*
Annenberg, Max *NF*
Annenberg, Moses Louis 1878-1942 *DcAmB S3*
Annenberg, Walter Hubert 1908- *BioIn 3,*
BioIn 8, BioIn 9, CurBio XR, IntWW 1976,
NewMr, NewYTBS 5, USBiR 1974,
Who 1974, WhoAm 1974, WhoAmP 1973,

WhoE 1974, WhoGov 1972, WhoWor 1974,
WhoWorJ 1972
Annett, Fred Anzley 1879?-1959 *BioIn 2, BioIn 5*
Annin, Joseph Paddock 1889?-1956 *BioIn 4*
Ansbro, Mary Catharine *ForWC 1970, OvPC*
Ansell, Jack 1925-1976 *ConAu 17R, ConAu 69*
Anson, Robert Sam 1945?- *BioIn 9, InvJ*
Ansong, Roger *NF*
Anspacher, Carolyn *NF*
Anspacher, John M 1918- *OvPC*
Anstey, Frank 1865-1940 *BioIn 2*
Anstruther, George Elliot 1870-1940 *BioIn 1,*
CathA 1930, WhoLA
Antar, Elias *NF*
Antcliffe, Herbert, Jr. 1875- *BioIn 1, CathA 1930*
Antell, Len *NF*
Antelman, Leonard *NF*
Antes, Robert Manning 1863-1949 *BioIn 5*
Antevil, Jeffrey H *NF*
Anthan, George *InvJ*
Anthon, Miss Soester J 1890- *WhJnl 1928*
Anthony, Benjamin Harris 1863-1932 *WhJnl 1928*
Anthony, Daniel Read 1824-1904 *BioIn 2*
Anthony, Edmund 1889- *WhJnl 1928*
Anthony, Edward 1895-1971 *AmAu&B, AuBYP,*
BioIn 5, BioIn 8, BioIn 9, BkCL,
ConAu 33, ConAu 73, HisAmM XR,
NewYTBE 2, REnAL
Anthony, Fred Ahadd *OvPC*
Anthony, Henry Bowen 1815-1884 *Alli Sup,*
AmAu&B, DcAmB 1, DcNAA, NatCAB 9
Anthony, Joseph 1897- *AmAu&B, WebBD*
Anthony, Michael *NF*
Anthony, Michael 1932- *Au&Wr, CasWL,*
ConAu 17R, ConNov 1972, ConNov 1976,
LongC, WebE&AL, WrDr 1976
Anthony, Noel *NF*
Anthony, Norman 1889-1968 *BioIn 1, BioIn 8,*
HisAmM XR
Anthony, Susan B 1916?- *NewYTBE 2*
Anthony, Susan Brownell 1820-1906 *BbD,*
DcNAA, EncAB, HisAmM XR, OxAm,
REn, WebBD
Antoncich, Betty Kennedy *BioIn 8*
Antrobus, Edmund *OvPC*
Anzer, Richard C *WhJnl 1928*
Aoi, Katsui *NF*
Apenszlak, Jakob 1894-1950 *BioIn 2*
Apgar, Garry *NF*
Apone, Carl Anthony 1923- *WhoAm 1974*
Appel, David *AuBYP, BioIn 8*
Appel, J Phil 1876- *BioIn 2*
Appelius, Mario 1892-1946 *BioIn 1*
Appelman, Herman 1902-1960 *BioIn 5*
Apple, Raymond Walter, Jr. 1934- *WhoAm 1974*
Appleby, Frank B 1895- *WhJnl 1928*
Applegate, Albert Angelo 1889- *WhNAA,*
WhJnl 1928
Appleton, Jerry *NF*
Appleton, Lewis Wilson, Jr. *WhJnl 1928*
Appleyard, Thomas J 1850- *WhJnl 1928*
Apthorp, William Foster 1848-1913 *Alli Sup,*
AmAu, AmAu&B, BiD&SB, DcAmA,
DcNAA, HisAmM XR
Aragon, Louis 1897- *CasWL, ClDMEL,*
ConAu 69, ConLC 3, EncWL, EvEuW,
IntWW 1976, LongC, ModRL, ModWD,
OxEng, OxFr, Pen Eur, REn, TwCA,
TwCA Sup, TwCW, WebBD, Who 1974,
WhoTwCL, WhoWor 1974
Aramayo, Carlos Victor 1889- *BioIn 1*
Aranda, Gabriel 1939?- *BioIn 9, BioIn 10*
Araquistain, Luis 1866-1959 *BioIn 5*
Araujo Jorge, Arthur Guimaraes De 1884- *WebBD*

Arbasino, Alberto 1930- *BioIn 10, WorAu*
Arber, Myles *NF*
Arbocz, Jules R 1883- *WhJnl 1928*
Archambault, Gaston Hanet 1877-1951 *BioIn 2*
Archambault, Pierre 1912- *IntWW 1976, WhoWor 1974*
Archer, Benjamin Edgar 1898- *WhNAA, WhJnl 1928*
Archer, Frederic 1838-1901 *DcAmA, HisAmM XR*
Archer, Jules 1915- *AuBYP, BioIn 8, BioIn 9, ConAu 9, SmATA 4*
Archer, Nick *NF*
Archer, Richard Mather 1869- *WhJnl 1928*
Archer, W K *NF*
Archibald, Eldred J 1881?-1958 *BioIn 4*
Archibald, Fred Irwin 1893- *WhoAm 1974, WhJnl 1928*
Archibald, Fred J *OvPC*
Archibald, James Francis Jewell 1871-1934 *DcNAA, FamWC, HisAmM XR*
Archibald, John J 1925- *ConAu 5R*
Archibald, Joseph S 1898- *BioIn 7, BioIn 9, ConAu 9R, SmATA 3*
Archibald, Jules Francois 1856-1919 *BioIn 2, BioIn 3, BioIn 9*
Archinard, Paul *NF*
Arciniegas, German 1900- *ConAu 61, CurBio XR, DcCLAA, DcSpL, IntWW 1976, Pen Am, WhoWor 1974*
Ardenne DeTizac, Andree Francoise C D' 1878-1950 *BioIn 2*
Ardies, Tom 1931- *ConAu 33*
Ardoin, John Louis 1935- *ConAu 57, WhoAm 1974, WhoS&SW 1973*
Arenstein, Yetta 1912?-1965 *BioIn 7*
Argens, Jean Baptiste DeBoyer D' 1704-1771 *OxFr, WebBD*
Argus, M K 1900-1970 *BioIn 2, BioIn 9, NewYTBE 1*
Aria, Eliza *NF*
Arias, Roberto Emilio 1918- *BioIn 6, BioIn 7, IntWW 1974, Who 1974, WhoWor 1974*
Arikan, Ruchan *OvPC*
Arinos, Affonso 1868-1916 *BioIn 1, Pen Am*
Ariyoshi, Shoichiro *NF*
Arkell, Reginald 1882-1959 *LongC, NewC, WebBD, WorAu*
Arkell, Roderick 1892- *WhNAA, WhJnl 1928*
Arkell, William J. 1856-1930 *DcNAA*
Arkins, John 1842- *NatCAB 1*
Arkush, Arthur Spencer 1925- *WhoAm 1974*
Arledge, Roone Pinckney 1931- *WhoAm 1974*
Arlen, Michael J 1930- *AmAu&B, ConAu 61, WhoAm 1974, WhoE 1974*
Arlt, Paul *NF*
Arm, Walter 1907?- *BioIn 4*
Armagnac, Arthur S 1877- *WhNAA, WhJnl 1928*
Armat, Virginia *NF*
Armati, Leo Francis *NF*
Armbrister, Trevor *NF*
Armbruster, Willis Thien 1896- *WhJnl 1928*
Armenise, Giovanni 1897-1953 *BioIn 3*
Armentrout, Vance *BioIn 1*
Armero, Jose Mario *OvPC*
Armes, Oscar St. John 1880?-1952 *BioIn 2*
Armfield, Eugene Morehead 1905-1953 *BioIn 3, HisAmM XR*
Armijo, Isadoro *NF*
Armistead, George H 1861?-1950 *BioIn 2*
Armistead, Moss William, III 1915- *WhoAm 1974, WhoS&SW 1973*
Armitage, Charles H 1868?-1947 *BioIn 1*
Armitage, John 1885?- *BioIn 1*

Armitage, John 1910- *Who 1974*
Armour, Lloyd Rowland 1922- *ConAu 29, WhoAm 1974*
Armstead, George Brooks 1883-1950 *WhJnl 1928*
Armstrong, Anthony 1897-1976 *Au&Wr, ConAu XR, DcLEL, EncMys, EvLB, IntWW 1974, LongC, Who 1974, WhoWor 1974*
Armstrong, C C 1890- *NF*
Armstrong, Charles H 1890- *WhJnl 1928*
Armstrong, Charles Leland 1880- *NF*
Armstrong, Collin *NF*
Armstrong, Corwin C 1889- *WhJnl 1928*
Armstrong, Dale *BioIn 10*
Armstrong, Douglas Albert 1920- *Au&Wr, ConAu 9R*
Armstrong, Douglas Knox 1923- *OvPC, WhoAm 1974*
Armstrong, Dwight LeRoy 1854-1927 *BioIn 2, IndAu 1816*
Armstrong, Everhardt 1892- *WhJnl 1928*
Armstrong, Frank L 1878- *WhJnl 1928*
Armstrong, Hamilton Fish 1893-1973 *AmAu&B, BioIn 1, BioIn 2, BioIn 3, BioIn 4, BioIn 6, BioIn 9, BioIn 10, ConAu 41, CurBio XR, NewYTBE 4, TwCA, TwCA Sup, WebBD, WhNAA, WhoWor 1974*
Armstrong, Henry E *NF*
Armstrong, Henry M *NF*
Armstrong, John A *RpN*
Armstrong, John Byron 1917-1976 *ConAu 5R, ConAu 65*
Armstrong, Judith *NF*
Armstrong, LeRoy 1854-1927 *DcAmA, DcNAA*
Armstrong, Moses Kimball 1832-1906 *DcNAA, OhA&B*
Armstrong, O K 1893- *WhJnl 1928*
Armstrong, Paul 1869-1915 *AmAu&B, DcNAA, REnAL, TwCA, TwCA Sup*
Armstrong, Richard *NF*
Armstrong, Robert Burns 1873-1946 *BioIn 1*
Armstrong, Robert Burns 1903-1955 *BioIn 3*
Armstrong, Ruth *NF*
Armstrong, S J 1886- *WhJnl 1928*
Armstrong, T *NF*
Armstrong, Thomas Veigh 1878- *WhJnl 1928*
Armstrong, Voyle Neville 1891- *WhJnl 1928*
Armstrong, William W 1833-1905 *NatCAB 24*
Armstrong-Jones, Antony 1930- *CurBio XR, WebBD, WhoWor 1974*
Armstrong-Jones, Antony *see also* Snowdon, A A-J, Earl Of
Armstrong-Jones, Antony *see also* Snowdon, Lord
Arndt, Walter Tallmadge 1872-1932 *DcNAA*
Arne, Sigrid 1900- *CurBio XR, OhA&B*
Arneaux, J A 1855- *BioIn 8*
Arnesen, Sigurd J 1887?-1966 *BioIn 7*
Arnett, Judd 1911- *WhoAm 1974*
Arnett, Peter Gregg 1934- *BioIn 7, BioIn 9, OvPC, WhoAm 1974, WhoWor 1974*
Arno, Peter 1904-1968 *AmAu&B, BioIn 8, ConAu 25, ConAu 73, CurBio XR, LongC, WebBD*
Arnold, Sir Arthur 1833-1902 *Alli Sup, BiD&SB, BrAu 19, DcEnL, NewC*
Arnold, Birch *see* Bartlett, Alice Elinor
Arnold, Bob Lee *NF*
Arnold, Charles J 1879- *WhJnl 1928*
Arnold, Edmund Clarence 1913- *ConAu 4R, WhoCon 1973, WhoWor 1974, WrDr 1976*
Arnold, Sir Edwin 1832-1904 *Alli, Alli Sup, BbD, BiD&SB, BioIn 3, BioIn 6, BrAu 19, DcEnA, DcEnA Ap, DcEnL, DcEuL, DcLEL, EvLB, HisAmM XR, LongC,*

NewC, OxEng, REn, WebBD
Arnold, Edwin Vernon 1902- *WhJnl 1928*
Arnold, Elliott 1912- *AmAu&B, AmNov, Au&Wr, AuBYP, ConAu 19R, SmATA 5, TwCA Sup, WhoAm 1974, WhoWest 1974, WhoWor 1974, WrDr 1976*
Arnold, Gale H *NF*
Arnold, Gary Howard 1942- *WhoAm 1974*
Arnold, George 1834-1865 *Alli Sup, AmAu, AmAu&B, BiD&SB, CyAL 2, DcAmA, DcLEL, DcNAA, OxAm, REnAL, WebBD*
Arnold, Henri *NF*
Arnold, Jud *NF*
Arnold, Lynn John, Jr. 1891- *WhJnl 1928*
Arnold, Martin 1929- *WhoAm 1974*
Arnold, Ron L *OvPC*
Arnold, Russ *NF*
Arnold, Samuel George 1806-1891 *DcNAA, NatCAB 9*
Arnold, Tom M 1890?-1967 *BioIn 7*
Arnold, Waldo Robert 1896-1946 *BioIn 1*
Arnold, Wilbur G 1895- *WhJnl 1928*
Arnold-Forster, Mark 1920- *ConAu 65*
Arnolt, Jan *ForP*
Arnot, Charles P *OvPC*
Arnot, John Paul 1887-1951 *BioIn 2, WhJnl 1928*
Arnstein, Daniel *NF*
Arnstein, Joseph M 1913- *WhoAm 1974, WhoWorJ 1972*
Aron, Raymond Claude Ferdinand 1905- *Au&Wr, BioIn 3, BioIn 4, BioIn 7, BioIn 8, CasWL, CurBio XR, IntWW 1976, Who 1974, WhoWor 1974, WhoWorJ 1972, WorAu, WrDr 1976*
Aronhime, M F 1884- *WhJnl 1928*
Aronin, Bertha *NF*
Aronowitz, Alfred G 1928- *WhoWorJ 1972*
Aronson, Albert Y 1886-1957 *WhJnl 1928*
Aronson, James 1915- *AmRP, ConAu 29*
Aronson, Shlomo 1936- *ConAu 73*
Arp, Bill 1826-1903 *Alli Sup, AmAu, AmAu&B, BiDSA, CnDAL, DcAmA, DcLEL, DcNAA, OxAm, REnAL, WebBD*
Arp, Bill *see also* Smith, Charles Henry
Arran, Earl Arthur Kattendyke S D A Gore 1910- *BioIn 6*
Arrandale, Thomas J *NF*
Arries, Leslie Goodwin, Jr. 1924- *WhoAm 1974, WhoE 1974*
Arrington, Alfred W 1810-1867 *Alli Sup, AmAu, AmAu&B, BiD&SB, BiDSA, CnDAL, DcAmA, DcNAA, OxAm, REnAL*
Arrington, Alfred W *see also* Summerfield, Charles
Arriola, Gustavo Montano 1917?- *BioIn 1*
Arrowsmith, Marvin 1913- *WhoAm 1974*
Arter, Theodore *WhJnl 1928*
Arthur, Franklin Kilnore, Jr. 1910- *WhoAm 1974*
Arthur, Marv *NF*
Arthur, R J 1903- *WhJnl 1928*
Arthur, Robert James 1904- *WhoAm 1974*
Arthur, Timothy Shay 1809-1885 *Alli, Alli Sup, AmAu, AmAu&B, BbD, BiD&SB, BioIn 4, CarSB, CasWL, CyAL 2, DcAmA, DcBiA, DcEnL, DcNAA, HisAmM XR, OxAm, Pen Am, REn, REnAL, WebBD*
Arthur, William 1911?- *BioIn 2*
Artman, Lawrence P 1874?-1954 *BioIn 3*
Artom, Guido 1906- *ConAu 29*
Artz, Robert M *NF*
Arvidson, Cheryl R *NF*
Asbury, Herbert 1891-1963 *AmAu&B, REnAL, TwCA, TwCA Sup, WebBD, WhNAA*
Ascher, Saul 1767-1822 *BioIn 6*
Ascher, Sidney *NF*

Aschman, George *NF*
Ascoli, Max 1898-1978 *AmAu&B, CurBio XR, WhoAm 1974*
Ascroft, Eileen 1914-1962 *BioIn 6*
Ashbrook, John Milan 1928- *CngDr 1974, CurBio XR, WhoAm 1974, WhoAmP 1973, WhoGov 1972, WhoMW 1974*
Ashby, Babette *NF*
Ashby, Neal *NF*
Ashcroft, Thomas Calvin 1866-1935 *BioIn 1, NatCAB 33*
Ashe, Samuel A'Court 1840-1938 *AmAu&B, BiDSA, DcNAA, NatCAB 28, WhNAA*
Asher, Court 1893- *BioIn 1*
Asher, Robert L *NF*
Ashford, Gerald 1907- *ConAu 41*
Ashley, James David 1902- *WhJnl 1928*
Ashley, Keith *NF*
Ashley, Maurice 1907- *ConAu 41*
Ashley, Roberta *NF*
Ashley, Tom 1913- *NF*
Ashmead, Gordon Blane *BioIn 8*
Ashmore, Harry Scott 1916- *AmAu&B, BioIn 1, BioIn 4, BioIn 5, BioIn 8, ConAu 15, CurBio XR, RpN, WhoAm 1974, WhoWest 1974, WhoWor 1974*
Ashmore, Richard *NF*
Ashmore, Ruth 1857?-1898 *DcAmA, DcNAA*
Ashton, Donald 1897- *WhJnl 1928*
Ashworth, Maynard Richard, Sr. 1894- *WhoAdv 1972, WhoAm 1974, WhoS&SW 1973*
Asim-Ali, Yazid *NF*
Asimov, Stanley *NF*
Asimus, William 1881?-1951 *BioIn 2*
Ask, Mihran N 1886- *WhJnl 1928*
Aslakson, Arnold *NF*
Aspley, John Cameron 1888- *WhJnl 1928*
Assaf, Michael 1896- *WhoWorJ 1972*
Asselin, Joseph Francois Olivar 1874-1937 *BioIn 7, CanWr, DcNAA, OxCan*
Assis Chateaubriand Bandeira DeMelo, F 1891-1968 *BioIn 1, BioIn 2, BioIn 3, BioIn 4, BioIn 5, BioIn 6, BioIn 7, BioIn 8, ForP*
Ast, Genevieve *NF*
Astier DeLaVigerie, Emmanuel De 1900-1969 *BioIn 8, CasWL*
Astley, William 1854-1911 *BioIn 2*
Aston, Frank 1897- *WhJnl 1928*
Astor, Brooke *BioIn 8*
Astor, David 1912- *Au&Wr, BioIn 1, WhoWor 1974*
Astor, David *see also* Astor, Francis David Langhorne
Astor, Francis David Langhorne 1912- *IntWW 1976, Who 1974*
Astor, Francis David Langhorne *see also* Astor, David
Astor, Gavin, 2nd Baron Of Hever 1918- *ForP, Lor&LP, WhoWor 1974*
Astor, Gavin, 2nd Baron Of Hever *see also* Astor Of Hever, Gavin
Astor, John Jacob, Baron Of Hever 1886-1971 *BioIn 3, BioIn 6, BioIn 9, BioIn 10, CurBio XR, ForP, HisAmM XR, WebBD*
Astor, John Jacob, Baron Of Hever *see also* Astor Of Hever, Lord
Astor, Waldorf, Viscount Astor Of Hever 1879-1952 *BioIn 3, WebBD*
Astor, William W, Viscount Of Hever 1848-1919 *Alli Sup, AmAu, AmAu&B, BbD, BiD&SB, BioIn 6, CyAL 2, DcAmA, DcAmB 1, DcBiA, DcNAA, FamWC, Lor&LP, WebBD*

Astor Of Hever, Lord 1886-1971 *Lor&LP*

Astor Of Hever, Lord *see also* Astor, John Jacob, Baron Of Hever

Astor Of Hever, Baron Gavin Astor 1918- *IntWW 1976, Who 1974*

Astor Of Hever, Baron Gavin Astor *see also* Astor, Gavin, Baron

Astrachan, Anthony *NF*

Aswell, Edward Campbell 1900-1958 *BioIn 1, BioIn 4, BioIn 5*

Atcheson, Richard 1934- *ConAu 29*

Aten, Marion C 1904- *WhJnl 1928*

Athanassiades, George 1912- *IntWW 1976*

Athanassiades, Panos 1899- *IntWW 1976*

Atherton, Alexander Simpson 1913- *WhoAm 1974*

Atherton, Frank Cooke 1877-1945 *BioIn 3*

Atherton, James Kenneth Ward 1927- *WhoAm 1974*

Atholstan, Baron Hugh Graham 1848-1938 *BioIn 2, WebBD*

Atkin, William Wilson 1912?-1976 *ConAu 65*

Atkins, James G 1932- *ConAu 17, OvPC, WhoPubR 1972*

Atkins, James William 1880- *BioIn 2, WhJnl 1928*

Atkins, John Black 1871-1954 *BioIn 3, FamWC, WhoLA*

Atkins, Oliver Ollie F 1916-1977 *ConAu 73, WhoAm 1974, WhoS&SW 1973, WhoWor 1974*

Atkins, Stewart 1913- *BioIn 3*

Atkinson, Alex 1916-1962 *BioIn 6*

Atkinson, Brooks 1894- *BiE&WWA, BioIn 1, BioIn 8, CelR 1973, ConAu 61, CurBio XR, NewYTBE 4, OxAm, REnAL, TwCA, TwCA Sup, WebBD, WhNAA, Who 1974, WrDr 1976*

Atkinson, Brooks *see also* Atkinson, J Brooks

Atkinson, Brooks *see also* Atkinson, Justin Brooks

Atkinson, Charles D 1875- *WhJnl 1928*

Atkinson, Claude Malcolm 1862- *WhJnl 1928*

Atkinson, Clettus 1923- *WhoAm 1974*

Atkinson, Francis Blake d1930 *DcNAA*

Atkinson, J Brooks 1894- *WhoThe 1972*

Atkinson, J Brooks *see also* Atkinson, Brooks

Atkinson, J Brooks *see also* Atkinson, Justin Brooks

Atkinson, Joseph 1846-1924 *Alli Sup, DcNAA*

Atkinson, Joseph E 1865-1948 *BioIn 1, BioIn 4, BioIn 6*

Atkinson, Joseph Story 1904-1968 *BioIn 4, BioIn 8*

Atkinson, Justin Brooks 1894- *AmAu&B, CurBio XR, IntWW 1976, TwCA, TwCA Sup, Who 1974, WhoAm 1974, WhJnl 1928*

Atkinson, Justin Brooks *see also* Atkinson, Brooks

Atkinson, Justin Brooks *see also* Atkinson, J Brooks

Atkinson, Marc 1889- *WhJnl 1928*

Atkinson, Percy Christopherson 1867-1941 *BioIn 5*

Atkinson, Samuel Coate *AmJnl, HisAmM XR*

Atkinson, Thomas R 1884- *WhJnl 1928*

Atkinson, Vinnin Edward, Jr. 1902- *WhJnl 1928*

Atkinson, W P Bill *NF*

Atkinson, Wilmer 1840-1920 *AmAu&B, AmJnl, BioIn 10, DcAmB 1, DcNAA, HisAmM XR*

Atlas, Helen Vincent 1931- *WhoAm 1974, WhoAmW 1974*

Atree, William H *AmJnl*

Attaway, Douglas 1878-1957 *BioIn 7*

Attenborough, David Frederick 1926- *Au&Wr, ConAu 1, IntWW 1976, Who 1974, WrDr 1976*

Attiyate, Yvonne *NF*

Attwood, Frances G *HisAmM XR*

Attwood, William 1919- *AmAu&B, BioIn 5, BioIn 6, BioIn 7, BioIn 8, BioIn 9, ConAu 21R, CurBio XR, IntWW 1976, InvJ, NewMr, OvPC, WhoAm 1974, WhoF&I 1974*

Atwater, Helen Woodard 1876-1947 *BioIn 1, BioIn 6, WhNAA*

Atwater, James David 1928- *WhoAm 1974*

Atwater, Richard Tupper 1892-1948 *AmAu&B, AmJnl, BioIn 1, BioIn 6, BkCL, MorJA*

Atwell, Ben H 1876?-1951 *BioIn 2*

Atwood, Albert William 1879- *BioIn 1, HisAmM XR, WhoGov 1972*

Atwood, David 1815-1889 *BioIn 5, DcNAA*

Atwood, Millard VanMarter 1886-1941 *AmAu&B, DcNAA, WhNAA, WhJnl 1928*

Atwood, Robert Bruce 1907- *AuNews 2, BioIn 3, WhoAm 1974, WhoWest 1974*

Auberjonois, Fernand 1910- *NF*

Auble, Helen Lowe 1915- *ForWC 1970, OvPC*

Aubry, Lyla *NF*

Auchincloss, Douglas *BioIn 3*

Auchincloss, Kenneth 1937- *WhoAm 1974*

Audrain, Lawrence Alton 1910-1957 *BioIn 4*

Aue, D F John 1881- *WhJnl 1928*

Auer, Bernhard Machold 1915- *HisAmM XR, WhoAm 1974, WhoF&I 1974*

Auerbach, Stuart C 1935- *OvPC*

Auerbach-Levy, William 1889-1964 *CurBio XR*

Auerback, Bethami *NF*

Aug, Steve *NewMr*

Augstein, Rudolf 1923- *BioIn 8, CurBio XR, ForP, IntWW 1976, WhoWor 1974*

Augur, Robert Clayton 1866-1953 *BioIn 3*

August, Robert Olin 1921- *WhoAm 1974*

Augustin, John Alcee 1838-1888 *BiDSA, DcNAA*

Aukofer, Frank Alexander 1935- *ConAu 65*

Auld, Robert Campbell MacCombie 1857-1937 *DcNAA, NatCAB 15*

Auldridge, Lawrence R *OvPC*

Auletta, Ken 1942- *ConAu 69*

Aull, Arthur 1872?-1948 *BioIn 1, BioIn 3*

Ault, E B 1883- *WhJnl 1928*

Ault, Phillip H 1914- *BioIn 1, WhoAm 1974, WhoMW 1974*

Aultman, Merwyn L *BioIn 2*

Aultman, Richard Eugene 1933- *ConAu 65, WhoAm 1974*

Auman, William Richard 1902- *WhJnl 1928*

Aumente, Jerome Louis 1938?- *NF*

Aurandt, Paul Harvey 1918- *AmAu&B*

Aurandt, Paul Harvey *see also* Harvey, Paul

Aurner, Robert Ray 1898- *ConAu 5, WhNAA, WhoAm 1974, WhoCon 1973, WhJnl 1928, WrDr 1976*

Auslander, Joseph 1897-1965 *AmAu&B, CnDAL, HisAmM XR, OxAm, REn, REnAL, TwCA, TwCA Sup, WebBD, WhNAA, WhJnl 1928*

Austad, Mark *NF*

Austell, Robert Rhett, Jr. 1925- *WhoAm 1974, WhoF&I 1974*

Austen, Alice 1866-1952 *DcAmB S5*

Austin, Alfred 1835-1913 *Alli Sup, BbD, BiD&SB, BrAu 19, DcEnA, DcEnA Ap, DcEnL, DcEuL, DcLEL, EvLB, LongC, NewC, OxEng, Pen Eng, TwCW, WebBD*

Austin, Anthony 1919- *ConAu 33*

Austin, Carl M *WhJnl 1928*

Austin, Charles M 1941- *ConAu 69*

Austin, Edward Thompson 1897-1975 *BioIn 1, WhoWest 1974*

Austin, Grace 1872-1948 *BioIn 1*

Austin, Gwendolyn *NF*

Austin, H Russell 1920- *Bioln 2*
Austin, Henry Willard 1858-1912 *Alli Sup,*
  AmRP, BbD, BiD&SB, DcAmA, DcNAA
Austin, James A 1886- *WhJnl 1928*
Austin, James C 1906?-1955 *Bioln 4*
Austin, Jean 1900- *Bioln 4*
Austin, John 1922- *ConAu 61, IntMPA 1975*
Austin, Laurence H 1903- *WhJnl 1928*
Austin, Norman *NF*
Austin, Oscar Phelps 1848-1933 *AmLY, DcNAA,*
  WhNAA
Austin, Whitley 1910- *WhoAm 1974*
Austregesilo DeAthayde, Belarmino M 1898-
  IntWW 1976
Auth, Tony *NF*
Authier, George Francis 1876- *NF*
Autry, James A *NF*
Autry, Orvon Gene 1907- *WhoAm 1974*
Avedon, Richard 1923- *CelR 1973, CurBio XR,*
  IntWW 1976, WhoAm 1974, WhoWor 1974
Avellaneda, Nicolas 1836-1885 *WebBD*
Averill, John H 1923- *NF*
Avery, Benjamin Parke 1828?-1875 *Alli Sup,*
  AmAu, AmAu&B, BiD&SB, DcAmA,
  DcAmB 1, DcNAA, HisAmM XR,
  NatCAB 1
Avery, Carlos 1868- *WhNAA, WhJnl 1928*
Avery, Isaac Erwin 1871-1904 *BiDSA, Bioln 3,*
  DcNAA
Avery, Isaac Wheeler 1837-1897 *BiDSA, DcAmA,*
  DcAmB 1, DcNAA, NatCAB 3
Avery, Johnston 1900- *WhJnl 1928*
Avery, Samuel Putnam *HisAmM XR*
Avey, Dan M 1888- *WhJnl 1928*
Avirett, John W 1863-1914 *NatCAB 16*
Avnery, Uri 1923- *Bioln 7, WhoWor 1974,*
  WhoWorJ 1972
Aw, Boon-Haw 1883-1954 *Bioln 3*
Awbrey, Stuart *NF*
Awolowo, Obafemi Awo 1909- *AfA 1, ConAu 65*
Axelbank, Jay *NF*
Axelsson, George 1899?-1966 *Bioln 7*
Axen, Hermann 1916- *IntWW 1976,*
  WhoWor 1974
Axford, Clinton B 1898- *Bioln 3, HisAmM XR*
Axler, Bruce H *OvPC*
Axman, Clarence 1877- *Bioln 1, Bioln 6,*
  Bioln 8
Axthelm, Pete *NF*
Aycock, Perry *NF*
Aycock, William Frank, Jr. 1909- *WhoAdv 1972,*
  WhoAm 1974, WhoF&I 1974,
  WhoS&SW 1973
Ayer, Lady Alberta Constance *Bioln 10*
Ayer, Harriet 1854-1903 *DcAmA, DcNAA*
Ayers, Eben A 1890- *WhNAA, WhJnl 1928*
Ayers, Harry Brandt 1935- *WhoS&SW 1973*
Ayers, Harry Mell 1886- *WhJnl 1928*
Ayers, Hartwell F 1902- *WhJnl 1928*
Ayers, James Bellamy 1935?- *NF*
Ayers, Percy T *NF*
Ayers, William L 1898?-1950 *Bioln 2*
Ayerst, David *Lor&LP*
Aylesworth, Merlin Hall 1886-1952 *NF*
Ayling, Keith 1898-1976 *ConAu 69, ConAu 73*
Ayre, Robert 1900- *CanWW 1972, ConAu 4R*
Ayres, John Fearhake 1900- *WhoAm 1974*
Ayuso Valdivieso, Antonio 1899-1970 *Bioln 8*
Azarian, Martin Vartan 1927- *WhoAm 1974*
Azem, Antonio Carlos *NF*
Azikiwe, Nmadi 1904- *Bioln 1, CurBio XR*
Aznar, Camon *ForP*
Azrael, Louis *OvPC, WhoE 1974*
Azuaje, Luis *NF*

Azzi, Robert J *NF*

B

Baal-Teshuva, Jacob 1929- *ConAu 7R*
Baba, Tsunego 1875-1956 *BioIn 4*
Babb, Glen *NF*
Babb, Howard Kroger 1906- *WhJnl 1928*
Babb, Sanora 1907- *AmRP, Au&Wr, ConAu 15, WrDr 1976*
Babcock, Charles R *NF*
Babcock, Franklin Lawrence 1905-1960 *BioIn 5*
Babcock, Frederic 1896- *AmAu&B, Au&Wr, ConAu 5R, WhNAA, WhoAm 1974*
Babcock, H L *NF*
Babcock, Howard H *OvPC*
Babize, August C 1862- *NatCAB 18*
Babson, Roger Ward 1875-1967 *AmJnl, AmLY, CurBio XR, WhNAA*
Babson, Walter B *NF*
Bac, Ferdinand 1858?-1952 *BioIn 3*
Bacall, Aaron *NF*
Bacas, Harry A *NF*
Bach, Mickey *NF*
Bach, Milton Francis 1909- *WhoAm 1974, WhoE 1974, WhoWor 1974*
Bach, Ralph Edward 1903-1973 *NewYTBE 4, WhoAm 1974*
Bach, Richard David 1936- *AuNews 1, BioIn 9, BioNews 1974, ConAu 9R, CurBio XR, WrDr 1976*
Bacharach, Bert 1898- *CelR 1973, CurBio XR*
Bachay, George S *NF*
Bache, Benjamin Franklin 1769-1798 *AmAu&B, AmJnl, BioIn 8, DcAmB 1, OxAm, WebBD*
Bacheler, Origen *NF*
Bacheller, Irving 1859-1950 *AmAu&B, BiD&SB, ConAmL, DcAmA, DcAmB S4, DcBiA, DcLEL, JBA 1934, OxAm, REn, TwCA Sup, WebBD, WhNAA*
Bachinski, Eugene *InvJ, NewMr*
Bachmann, Kurt 1909- *IntWW 1976, WhoWor 1974*
Bachmann, Marcy *NF*
Bachmann, Max *HisAmM XR*
Bachmeyer, Karl H *OvPC*
Bachrach, Judith *NF*
Back, Jacques *HisAmM XR*
Backer, George 1903-1974 *AmJnl, NewYTBS 5*
Backer, Jack d1976 *NF*
Backlund, Ralph T 1918- *ConAu 73*
Backman, Jules 1910- *AmAu&B, AmEA 1974, AmM&W 73S, Au&Wr, ConAu 1, CurBio XR, WhoAm 1974, WhoCon 1973, WhoE 1974, WhoWor 1974, WhoWorJ 1972, WrDr 1976*
Backus, August Charles 1877-1952 *BioIn 2*
Bacon, Daisy Sarah *AmAu&B, WhoAm 1974, WhoAmW 1974, WhoE 1974*
Bacon, Edward L 1873?-1961 *BioIn 6*

Bacon, Edwin Munroe 1844-1916 *Alli Sup, AmAu, AmAu&B, DcAmA, DcAmB 1, DcNAA, HisAmM XR, NatCAB 13*
Bacon, James *NF*
Bacon, Julius F 1879- *WhJnl 1928*
Bacon, Kenneth H *NF*
Bacon, Leonard 1802-1881 *Alli, Alli Sup, AmAu&B, BiD&SB, DcAmA, DcEnL, DcNAA, OhA&B, PoChrch, WebBD*
Bacon, Paul Valentine 1876-1949 *BioIn 2*
Bacon, Richard Mackenzie 1775-1844 *BioIn 2*
Badger, Barker *NF*
Badhwar, Inderjit *InvJ*
Baehr, Harry William 1907- *WhoAm 1974*
Baensch, Emil 1857-1939 *BioIn 5*
Baer, Arthur 1886?-1969 *BioIn 5, BioIn 8, BioIn 9, REnAL*
Baer, Bugs *see* Baer, Arthur
Baer, Frederick H *OvPC*
Baer, Jean L 1926- *ConAu 15R, ForWC 1970, OvPC, WhoE 1974*
Baer, John M 1886-1970 *ConAu 29*
Baerlein, Henry 1875-1960 *NewC, WebBD, WhoLA*
Baermann, Arthur L 1899- *WhJnl 1928*
Bagby, George William 1828-1883 *Alli Sup, AmAu, AmAu&B, AmJnl, BiD&SB, BiDSA, CnDAL, DcAmA, DcLEL, DcNAA, HisAmM XR, LiJA, OxAm, WebBD*
Bagdikian, Ben Haig 1920- *AmAu&B, BioIn 7, ConAu 11R, WhoAm 1974, WhoS&SW 1973, WhoWor 1974, WrDr 1976*
Bagehot, Walter 1826-1877 *Alli Sup, AtlBL, BbD, BiD&SB, BioIn 1, BioIn 4, BioIn 5, BioIn 6, BioIn 8, BioIn 9, BrAu 19, CasWL, CrtT 3, DcEnA, DcEnL, DcEuL, DcLEL, EvLB, NewC, OxEng, Pen Eng, REn, WebBD, WebE&AL*
Bagg, John S *NF*
Bagg, Lyman Hotchkiss 1846-1911 *Alli Sup, DcAmA, DcNAA*
Bagger, Eugene Szekeres 1892- *BioIn 1*
Baggs, William Calhoun 1922-1969 *BioIn 4, BioIn 6, BioIn 8*
Baginski, Frank *NF*
Bague, Don *NF*
Bahn, Chester B 1893- *WhJnl 1928*
Bahr, Hermann 1863-1934 *BiD&SB, CasWL, ClDMEL, CnMD, EncWL, EvEuW, McGWD, ModGL, ModWD, OxGer, Pen Eur, REn, WebBD*
Bahr, Robert 1940- *ConAu 65*
Bahree, Bhushan *NF*
Bailby, Leon 1867?-1954 *BioIn 3*
Bailey, A Purnell *NF*

Bailey, Anthony 1933- *ConAu 3R*
Bailey, Bill *NF*
Bailey, Charles Waldo, II 1929- *BioIn 7,*
  ConAu 1R, WhoAm 1974, WrDr 1976
Bailey, E Prentiss 1834-1913 *NatCAB 16*
Bailey, Edwin N 1849-1923 *NatCAB 21*
Bailey, Eric 1933- *Au&Wr, ConAu 33*
Bailey, Francis 1735-1815 *AmAu&B, DcAmB 1,*
  REnAL
Bailey, Gamaliel 1807-1859 *AmAu&B, AmJnl,*
  BiD&SB, DcAmB 1, HisAmM XR,
  NatCAB 2, WebBD
Bailey, George 1919- *ConAu 25*
Bailey, George McClellan 1864-1927 *WhJnl 1928*
Bailey, George Milroy 1862- *NatCAB 5*
Bailey, Gilbert E *NF*
Bailey, Henry Lloyd 1874-1961 *BioIn 7*
Bailey, J Edward, III *NF*
Bailey, James Martin 1929- *BioIn 5,*
  WhoAm 1974
Bailey, James Montgomery 1841-1894 *Alli Sup,*
  AmAu, AmAu&B, AmJnl, BiD&SB,
  BioIn 1, CnDAL, DcAmA, DcAmB 1,
  DcEnL, DcNAA, HisAmM XR, OxAm,
  REnAL, WebBD
Bailey, Janet D *NF*
Bailey, Joel Smith 1883- *WhJnl 1928*
Bailey, Melville Knox 1856-1948 *BioIn 1*
Bailey, Morton Shelley, III 1922- *WhoAm 1974*
Bailey, Prentiss 1873-1939 *DcNAA, WhNAA,*
  WhJnl 1928
Bailey, Ralph Edgar 1893- *ConAu 17,*
  ConAu P-1
Bailey, Ray *AmJnl*
Bailey, Roy F 1883- *WhNAA, WhJnl 1928*
Bailey, Seth T *WhJnl 1928*
Bailey, W A 1884- *WhJnl 1928*
Bailey, Warren Worth 1855-1928 *BioIn 4,*
  DcNAA, WhNAA, WhJnl 1928
Bailey, William *AmJnl*
Baillie, David G d1937 *NF*
Baillie, Hugh 1890-1966 *AmJnl, BioIn 1,*
  BioIn 5, BioIn 7, BioIn 9, CurBio XR
Bain, Brian *NF*
Bain, George *NF*
Bain, George Grantham 1865- *WhNAA,*
  WhJnl 1928
Bain, Leslie Balogh 1900-1962 *BioIn 6*
Bainbridge, John 1913- *AmAu&B, ConAu 13R,*
  WhoAm 1974, WhoWor 1974, WrDr 1976
Baines, Edward 1774-1848 *Alli, Alli Sup,*
  DcEnL, WebBD
Baines, Sir Edward 1800-1890 *Alli, Alli Sup,*
  DcEnL, WebBD
Bainville, Jacques 1879-1936 *BioIn 1, BioIn 2,*
  CasWL, ClDMEL, OxFr, WebBD
Bair, Edna F *BioIn 1, BioIn 2*
Bair, Ron *NF*
Baird, Irvin 1900?-1964 *BioIn 6*
Baird, K A *NF*
Baird, Russell Norman 1922- *ConAu 19R,*
  DrAS 74E, WrDr 1976
Bairnsfather, Bruce 1888-1959 *BioIn 5, LongC,*
  WebBD
Bajza, Jozsef 1804-1858 *WebBD*
Bakeless, John Edwin 1894- *AmAu&B, Au&Wr,*
  AuBYP, BioIn 4, BioIn 7, ConAu 5R,
  HisAmM XR, REnAL, SmATA 9, TwCA,
  TwCA Sup, WebBD, WhNAA, WrDr 1976
Baker, A T *NF*
Baker, Alton Fletcher 1894-1961 *BioIn 6*
Baker, Alton Fletcher 1919- *WhoWest 1974*
Baker, Arthur *NF*
Baker, Arthur, III 1923- *LEduc 1974*

Baker, Baldwin, Jr. *NF*
Baker, Bill 1919- *ConAu 57*
Baker, Charles B 1897- *WhJnl 1928*
Baker, Charles Whiting 1865-1941 *AmLY,*
  DcAmA, DcNAA, NatCAB 16, WhNAA
Baker, Charlotte Adele 1903- *WhJnl 1928*
Baker, Colgate d1940 *AmAu&B*
Baker, Colley S 1890- *WhJnl 1928*
Baker, David Dudrow 1897-1950 *BioIn 2*
Baker, Dean C *NF*
Baker, Donald P *NF*
Baker, Elbert Hall 1854-1933 *NatCAB XR,*
  WhJnl 1928
Baker, Elbert Hall, II 1910- *WhoAdv 1972,*
  WhoAm 1974, WhoF&I 1974,
  WhoWest 1974
Baker, Elizabeth Calhoun 1934- *WhoAm 1974*
Baker, Elmer J 1889-1964 *BioIn 7*
Baker, Frank Smith 1879-1960 *BioIn 9,*
  WhJnl 1928
Baker, Frank Tarkington 1878-1924 *BioIn 2,*
  IndAu 1816
Baker, George 1915-1975 *AmAu&B, AmJnl,*
  BioIn 2, ConAu 57, CurBio XR
Baker, George Barr 1870-1948 *AmAu&B,*
  BioIn 1, HisAmM XR
Baker, George L *NF*
Baker, Gilbert H *OvPC*
Baker, Gladys *BioIn 2, BioIn 3, CathA 1952*
Baker, Harry Babcock 1895-1956 *BioIn 4*
Baker, Harry M *NF*
Baker, Harry Torsey 1877- *WhNAA,*
  WhJnl 1928
Baker, Herman 1911- *WhoAm 1974*
Baker, Howard Gould 1893- *WhJnl 1928*
Baker, I Marsh 1888- *WhJnl 1928*
Baker, James Heaton 1829-1913 *DcAmB 1,*
  OhA&B
Baker, James Lawrence 1941- *ConAu 53*
Baker, James Loring d1886 *DcNAA*
Baker, Jehu 1822-1903 *Alli Sup, DcAmB S1*
Baker, Jim 1924- *NF*
Baker, Joan *NF*
Baker, John F 1931- *NF*
Baker, John Milton 1895- *WhNAA, WhJnl 1928*
Baker, John Q *WhJnl 1928*
Baker, John R 1893- *WhJnl 1928*
Baker, John Wellington 1869- *WhJnl 1928*
Baker, Joseph 1806-1873 *BioIn 5*
Baker, Leonard 1931- *ConAu 23R, WrDr 1976*
Baker, Leone 1892-1960 *BioIn 5*
Baker, Lewis 1832- *NatCAB 1*
Baker, Lisle, Jr. 1902- *WhoAm 1974,*
  WhoS&SW 1973
Baker, Marilyn 1929?- *BioIn 10, BioNews 1975,*
  InvJ, NewMr
Baker, Nathan Addison 1843-1934 *BioIn 7*
Baker, Orlando Harrison 1830-1913 *BioIn 2,*
  IndAu 1816
Baker, Page M 1840- *NatCAB 13*
Baker, Patrick C d1928 *NF*
Baker, Paul S 1900- *WhJnl 1928*
Baker, R Ray 1890- *WhJnl 1928*
Baker, Ray Stannard 1870-1946 *AmAu&B,*
  AmLY, BioIn 1, BioIn 2, BioIn 3, BioIn 4,
  BioIn 5, BioIn 6, BioIn 7, BioIn 8, CarSB,
  ConAmL, CurBio XR, DcAmA, DcAmB S4,
  DcLEL, DcNAA, EncAB, EvLB, FamWC,
  HisAmM XR, LongC, NewMr, OxAm,
  REn, REnAL, TwCA, TwCA Sup, TwCW,
  WebBD, WhNAA, WisWr
Baker, Richard Terrill 1913- *ConAu 3R,*
  DrAS 74E, WhoAm 1974, WhoE 1974
Baker, Robert E L *NF*

Bangor, Edward Henry H Wad, Viscount 1905- *BioIn 8, BioIn 9, Who 1974*

Bangs, John Kendrick 1862-1922 *AmAu&B, BbD, BiD&SB, CarSB, DcAmA, DcLEL, DcNAA, EncMys, HisAmM XR, OxAm, REnAL, Str&VC, TwCA, TwCA Sup, WebBD*

Bangs, Nathan 1778-1862 *Alli, AmAu&B, DcAmA, DcNAA, HisAmM XR*

Bangsberg, Cora M *WhJnl 1928*

Bangsberg, R L 1896- *WhJnl 1928*

Banigan, Leon F 1886?-1957 *BioIn 2, BioIn 4, WhNAA, WhJnl 1928*

Banker, Paul Albert 1921- *WhoAm 1974, WhoE 1974*

Banker, Paul J 1893- *WhJnl 1928*

Banks, Carolyn 1941- *NF*

Banks, Charles Eugene 1852-1932 *AmAu&B, DcAmA, DcNAA, WhNAA*

Banks, David *NF*

Banks, Eloise Hardison 1926- *WhoAm 1974*

Banks, Emanuel Simon 1900-1956 *BioIn 4*

Banks, George Linnaeus 1821-1881 *Alli Sup, NewC, WebBD*

Banks, Mrs. George Linnaeus 1821-1897 *WebBD*

Banks, Mrs. George Linnaeus *see also* Banks, Isabella Varley

Banks, Isabella Varley 1821-1897 *Alli Sup, NewC, WebBD*

Banks, Louis Layton 1916- *WhoAm 1974*

Banks, Richard 1910?-1965 *BioIn 7*

Banks, William d1920 *DcNAA*

Bankson, Russell Arden 1889- *AmAu&B, OxCan*

Bannerman, Norman M 1896- *WhJnl 1928*

Banning, Kendall 1879-1944 *AmAu&B, AnMV 1926, CurBio XR, DcNAA, NatCAB XR, WhNAA*

Bannister, Alla Ripley *NF*

Bannon, Barbara Anne 1928- *ForWC 1970, WhoAm 1974, WhoE 1974*

Banta, Albert Franklin 1843-1924 *BioIn 3, BioIn 4*

Banton, Thomas W *NF*

Banyon, Stanley R 1866- *WhJnl 1928*

Baquir, Muhammad *ForP*

Barach, Arnold B *NF*

Barach, Norma *NF*

Baranik, Gary *NF*

Baranyi, Eva Vertes *NF*

Barbash, Fred *NewMr*

Barbeau, Clayton Charles 1930- *ConAu 73, WhoWest 1974*

Barbee, David Rankin 1874-1958 *BioIn 4, WhNAA, WhJnl 1928*

Barber, Donald Herbert 1907- *BioIn 1*

Barber, Edith Michael 1892-1963 *BioIn 6*

Barber, George F *HisAmM XR*

Barber, Henry Hervey *HisAmM XR*

Barber, Jean *BioIn 8*

Barber, Joseph 1909- *HisAmM XR, WhoAm 1974, WhoWor 1974*

Barber, Mary *BioIn 1*

Barber, Noel 1911?- *BioIn 3, BioIn 4*

Barber, Rowland *NF*

Barber, Solon Ray 1896- *WhJnl 1928*

Barber, Stephen Guy 1921- *ConAu 69*

Barber, Will d1935 *AmJnl*

Barbi, Olga *NF*

Barbosa, Manuel Alfredo 1901- *WhJnl 1928*

Barbour, Beverly Anderson *NF*

Barbour, John *NF*

Barbour, Phillips T 1884-1952 *BioIn 2*

Barbour, Robert Leland 1910- *WhoPubR 1972*

Barbour, William Albert 1921- *WhoAdv 1972, WhoAm 1974*

Barcella, Ernest Lawrence 1910- *WhoAm 1974, WhoF&I 1974*

Barclay, Foster 1914?-1977 *NF*

Barclay, Hartley Wade 1903-1978 *WhoAm 1974, WhoE 1974, WhoF&I 1974, WhoWor 1974*

Barclay, Wade Crawford 1874-1965 *BioIn 7*

Barcs, Emery 1906- *BioIn 2*

Barcs, Sandor 1912- *IntWW 1976, WhoWor 1974*

Bard, Abby *NF*

Barde, C M 1876- *WhJnl 1928*

Bardeen, Charles William 1847-1924 *Alli Sup, AmAu&B, AmLY, DcAmA, DcNAA, HisAmM XR*

Barette, Paul *NF*

Barger, Floyd 1906-1975 *BioIn 10, WhoAm 1974, WhoE 1974, WhoF&I 1974*

Barger, Marilee 1897- *WhNAA, WhJnl 1928*

Bargeron, Carlisle 1895-1965 *AmAu&B, BioIn 7*

Barham, Frank Forrest 1879-1953 *BioIn 3*

Barilli, Bruno 1880-1952 *BioIn 3*

Baring, Maurice 1874-1945 *BkC 4, CasWL, CathA 1930, DcLEL, EncWL, EvLB, LongC, ModBL, NewC, OxEng, REn, TwCA, TwCA Sup, TwCW, WebBD, WebE&AL*

Baris, Behzat H *NF*

Barkdoll, Robert S *NF*

Barke, Robert 1892?-1956 *BioIn 4*

Barken, Lisa *OvPC*

Barker, Bill *ConAu 65*

Barker, Dennis 1929- *ConAu 25, WrDr 1976*

Barker, Dudley 1910- *Au&Wr, ConAu 2R, WrDr 1976*

Barker, Edmund Asa 1927- *BioIn 8*

Barker, George Frederick 1835-1910 *Alli Sup, DcAmA, DcNAA, HisAmM XR*

Barker, J Ellis 1870-1948 *WebBD*

Barker, Jane Valentine 1930- *ConAu 65*

Barker, Joseph *HisAmM XR*

Barker, LeBaron R, Jr. 1904-1973 *BioIn 10, NewYTBE 4, WhoAm 1974*

Barker, Myrtie Lillian 1910- *ConAu 7R, IndAu 1917*

Barker, Shirley *OvPC*

Barker, Wharton 1846-1921 *DcNAA, HisAmM XR*

Barker, William John *ConAu 65*

Barkham, John *NF*

Barkhorn, Jean Cook 1931- *WhoAm 1974, WhoAmW 1974*

Barkley, Frederick R 1892-1963 *BioIn 6, WhNAA*

Barkman, Elin *AmRP*

Barkow, Al 1932- *ConAu 53, WrDr 1976*

Barlett, Donald L *InvJ, NewMr*

Barlow, John H *NF*

Barlow, Perry 1892?-1977 *NF*

Barlow, Robert L 1911?-1966 *BioIn 7*

Barlow, Ruel R 1894- *WhJnl 1928*

Barman, Howard Henry *WhJnl 1928*

Barman, Thomas *BioIn 8*

Barmash, Isadore 1921- *ConAu 45*

Barnard, Charles 1838-1920 *Alli Sup, AmAu&B, AmLY, BiD&SB, DcAmA, DcNAA*

Barnard, Charles Inman 1850-1942 *DcNAA, HisAmM XR*

Barnard, Charles Nelson 1924- *ConAu 49, WhoAm 1974*

Barnard, Francine *NewMr*

Barnard, Harry 1906- *BioIn 4, ConAu 5, DrAS 74H, WhoAm 1974, WhoWorJ 1972*

Barnard, Henry 1811-1900 *Alli, Alli Sup, AmAu,*

BbD, BiD&SB, CyAL 1, CyAL 2, DcAmA, DcNAA, HisAmM XR, WebBD
Barnard, Ken *NF*
Barnard, Russell Duane 1937- *WhoAm 1974*
Barnard, William Calvert 1914- *WhoAm 1974, WhoF&I 1974*
Barnathan, Julius 1927- *WhoAm 1974, WhoF&I 1974, WhoWor 1974*
Barnd, Bert 1883- *WhJnl 1928*
Barnea, Nahum 1944- *NF*
Barnes, A Victor 1870-1944 *NatCAB 34*
Barnes, Albert 1798-1870 *Alli, Alli Sup, AmAu&B, BiD&SB, CyAL 2, DcAmA, DcEnL, DcNAA, HisAmM XR*
Barnes, Andrew Wallace 1878- *WhNAA, WhJnl 1928*
Barnes, Arthur M 1913- *BioIn 8*
Barnes, Arthur Seth 1871- *WhJnl 1928*
Barnes, Arthur Stapylton 1861-1936 *CathA 1930*
Barnes, Bernard 1909- *WhoAm 1974*
Barnes, Betty 1902?-1971 *BioIn 9*
Barnes, Mrs. Bob *NF*
Barnes, Clive Alexander 1927- *AmAu&B, BioIn 8, BioIn 9, BioIn 10, CurBio XR, IntWW 1976, WhoAm 1974, WhoE 1974*
Barnes, Demas 1827-1888 *Alli Sup, DcNAA*
Barnes, Dick *InvJ*
Barnes, Djuna Chappell 1892- *AmAu&B, Au&Wr, CasWL, CnMD, ConAu 9R, ConDr, ConLC 3, ConLC 4, ConNov 1972, ConNov 1976, DcLEL, EncWL, HisAmM XR, LongC, ModAL, ModAL Sup, OxAm, Pen Am, RAdv 1, REn, REnAL, TwCA, TwCA Sup, TwCW, WhoAm 1974, WhoTwCL, WrDr 1976*
Barnes, Frederic W *NF*
Barnes, George Anthony 1909-1965 *BioIn 7*
Barnes, Harry Elmer 1889-1968 *AmAu&B, AmRP, ConAu 25, HisAmM XR, OxAm, REnAL, TwCA, TwCA Sup, WebBD, WhNAA*
Barnes, Howard 1904-1968 *NF*
Barnes, Jack *NF*
Barnes, James 1866-1936 *AmAu&B, BiDSA, DcAmA, DcNAA*
Barnes, Jean 1926- *NF*
Barnes, John *NF*
Barnes, John Gorell 1848-1913 *WebBD*
Barnes, John K *HisAmM XR*
Barnes, Joseph 1907-1970 *BioIn 1, BioIn 3, BioIn 8, NewYTBE 1*
Barnes, Len R *NF*
Barnes, Leon Simeon 1894-1959 *BioIn 7, NatCAB 49*
Barnes, Melvin Wallace 1910- *AmM&W 73S, WhoAm 1974, WhoE 1974*
Barnes, Ralph *AmJnl*
Barnes, Richard L *NF*
Barnes, Russell 1897- *WhoAm 1974, WhoWor 1974*
Barnes, Ruth *NF*
Barnett, B G *HisAmM XR*
Barnett, C C 1870- *WhJnl 1928*
Barnett, Claude Albert 1889-1967 *BioIn 8, WhJnl 1928*
Barnett, David Leon 1922- *WhoAm 1974, WhoS&SW 1973*
Barnett, Ferdinand L *NF*
Barnett, Ida B Wells *see* Wells, Ida B
Barnett, John R 1938?-1975 *BioIn 10*
Barnett, Lincoln Kinnear 1909- *AmAu&B, BioIn 10, WorAu*
Barnett, Marvin Robert 1916- *BioIn 2, CurBio XR*

Barnett, Paul 1877?-1949 *BioIn 1*
Barnett, Stanley P 1892?-1969 *BioIn 8*
Barnett, Victor F 1893- *WhJnl 1928*
Barnhart, Dean Leffel 1889- *WhNAA, WhJnl 1928*
Barnhart, Hugh Arthur 1892- *WhoAm 1974, WhoAmP 1973, WhJnl 1928*
Barnhart, John W 1878-1970 *BioIn 8*
Barnhart, Thomas Frederick 1902-1955 *BioIn 3, BioIn 6*
Barnitz, Richard M 1891- *WhJnl 1928*
Barnouw, Adrian Jacob *HisAmM XR*
Barns, Charles Edward *HisAmM XR*
Barns, Florence Elberta *AmAu&B, TexWr, WhNAA*
Barns, William Eddy 1853-1915 *BioIn 2, DcNAA, IndAu 1816*
Barnum, H L *HisAmM XR*
Barnum, Jerome Dewitt 1888-1965 *BioIn 7, BioIn 8*
Barnwell, R Grant *Alli Sup, HisAmM XR*
Barodness, Joseph *AmRP*
Baroja, Pio 1872-1956 *CnMWL, DcSpL, ModRL, TwCW, WebBD, WhoTwCL*
Barolini, Antonio 1910-1971 *BioIn 9, ConAu 1*
Baron, Alan J *NF*
Baron, Harold *NF*
Baron, Theodore 1928- *OvPC, WhoPubR 1972*
Barondess, Sue Kaufman 1926-1977 *ConAu 1R, ConAu 69*
Barondess, Sue Kaufman *see also* Kaufman, Sue
Barone, Amico J 1899- *WhJnl 1928*
Baronian, Harry 1911?-1965 *BioIn 7*
Barr, Albert J 1851-1912 *NatCAB 5, NatCAB 30*
Barr, Edward H *NF*
Barr, James 1862-1923 *DcNAA, WhoLA*
Barr, Jean Beryl *BioIn 3*
Barr, Jeff 1941- *ConAu 69*
Barr, John 1927?-1971 *BioIn 9*
Barr, Robert 1850?-1912 *BbD, BiD&SB, EncMys, EvLB, NewC, OxCan, REn, TwCA, WebBD*
Barr, Robert M *NF*
Barrer, Lester *NF*
Barrer, Myra E *NF*
Barres, Auguste Maurice 1862-1923 *WebBD*
Barres, Auguste Maurice *see also* Barres, Maurice
Barres, Maurice 1862-1923 *BiD&SB, BioIn 1, BioIn 2, BioIn 5, BioIn 6, BioIn 9, BioIn 10, CasWL, CIDMEL, EvEuW, LongC, NewC, OxEng, OxFr, Pen Eur, REn, TwCA, TwCA Sup*
Barres, Maurice *see also* Barres, Auguste Maurice
Barres, Philippe 1896- *BioIn 7*
Barrett, Bill *NF*
Barrett, Bob 1925- *ConAu 73*
Barrett, Dean 1942- *ConAu 69*
Barrett, Edward Ware 1910- *BioIn 1, BioIn 2, BioIn 4, BioIn 8, CurBio XR, DrAS 74E, IntWW 1976, LEduc 1974, WhoAm 1974, WhoE 1974, WrDr 1976*
Barrett, George C *HisAmM XR*
Barrett, Howard 1901- *WhJnl 1928*
Barrett, J C *HisAmM XR*
Barrett, James Wyman *WhJnl 1928*
Barrett, John 1866-1938 *AmLY, BioIn 4, BioIn 6, DcAmA, DcAmB S2, DcNAA, HisAmM XR, WebBD*
Barrett, John Erigena 1849- *DcNAA, NatCAB 4, PoIre*
Barrett, Joseph Hartwell 1824-1907? *BioIn 5, DcNAA, OhA&B*
Barrett, Laurence Irwin 1935- *ConAu 69, WhoE 1974*

Bartlett, William O *AmJnl*
Bartlett, William Warren 1861-1893 *DcNAA*
Bartley, E Ross 1892-1969 *Bioln 8*
Bartley, Robert L 1938?- *Bioln 10*
Bartnett, Edmond *NF*
Barton, Bruce 1886-1967 *AmAu&B, CurBio XR, EncAB, HisAmM XR, OhA&B, WebBD, WhNAA*
Barton, Bruce 1921-1963 *Bioln 6*
Barton, Charles W 1887- *WhJnl 1928*
Barton, George 1866-1940 *AmAu&B, Bioln 1, CathA 1930, CurBio XR, DcNAA*
Barton, George Arthur 1885-1969 *Bioln 3, Bioln 4, Bioln 8, CurBio XR*
Barton, John F *NF*
Barton, Leslie Marsh 1885- *WhJnl 1928*
Barton, Ralph 1891-1931 *AmAu&B, DcNAA, HisAmM XR*
Barton, Roger Avery 1903-1976 *ConAu 65, WhoAm 1974*
Barton, Todd 1886- *WhJnl 1928*
Barton, William Sydney 1897?-1957 *Bioln 2, Bioln 4*
Bartruff, Dave *NF*
Barzini, Luigi 1874-1947 *Bioln 7, Bioln 9, Bioln 10*
Barzini, Luigi 1908- *ConAu 13, CurBio XR, ForP, IntWW 1976, WhoWor 1974*
Basch, Buddy 1922- *IntMPA 1975*
Basch, C J B, Jr. *NF*
Baschet, Rene 1860-1949 *Bioln 2*
Bascom, Henry Bidleman 1796-1850 *Alli, BiDSA, DcAmA, DcNAA, HisAmM XR, OhA&B*
Bascombe, W Radford, Jr. *OvPC*
Basford, George M *HisAmM XR*
Basham, Maud Ruby *Bioln 4*
Bashford, Herbert 1871-1928 *AmLY, DcAmA, DcNAA, HisAmM XR*
Basich, Pauline *AmRP*
Baskervill, William Malone 1888-1953 *Bioln 3*
Baskerville, Tim *OvPC*
Baskett, E Sebree 1889- *WhJnl 1928*
Baskett, Kirtley M 1905- *NF*
Baskette, Gideon Hicks 1845- *BiDSA, NatCAB 8*
Baskin, Robert Edward 1917- *WhoAm 1974*
Bass, Charlotta A *BlkC*
Bass, Frank Lyman 1884- *WhJnl 1928*
Bass, Jack 1934- *ConAu 29, InvJ, WrDr 1976*
Bass, John Foster 1866-1931 *DcNAA, HisAmM XR, NatCAB 23*
Bass, Leo 1878?-1951 *Bioln 2*
Bass, Mary Carson *WhoAm 1974, WhoAmW 1974*
Bass, Milton B 1923- *ConAu 25*
Bass, Ralph *NF*
Bassani, Giorgio 1916- *CasWL, ConAu 65, EncWL, EvEuW, IntWW 1976, ModRL, Pen Eur, REn, TwCW, WhoTwCL, WhoWor 1974, WorAu*
Basset, Abbot *HisAmM XR*
Basset, Gene 1927- *WhoAm 1974, WhoS&SW 1973*
Bassett, Allen Lee *HisAmM XR*
Bassett, Ben 1909- *WhoAm 1974, WhoWor 1974*
Bassett, Brian *NF*
Bassett, Gene *NF*
Bassett, George B *HisAmM XR*
Bassett, Grace 1927- *ConAu 73*
Bassett, H S *WhJnl 1928*
Bassett, James Elias 1912-1978 *ConAu 61, WhoAm 1974*
Bassett, John 1886-1958 *Bioln 4*
Bassett, John Alva 1886-1956 *Bioln 4*
Bassett, John White Hughes 1915- *CanWW 1972,*

WhoAm 1974, WhoCan 1973, WhoE 1974, WhoWor 1974
Bassett, Robert Cochem 1911- *Bioln 3, WhoAm 1974*
Bassett, Warren L 1898?-1950 *Bioln 2*
Bassett, William *HisAmM XR*
Bassin, Max 1889-1963 *Bioln 6*
Bassity, Matthew A R 1915- *OvPC, WhoPubR 1972*
Basso, Joseph Hamilton 1904-1964 *WebBD*
Bassow, Whitman 1921?- *Bioln 6*
Bastian, George Conrad 1875-1925 *DcNAA*
Bastien, G Harold 1901- *WhJnl 1928*
Batal, James *RpN*
Batchelder, Charles F 1853?-1947 *Bioln 1*
Batchelder, James Locke 1816-1909 *Alli Sup, DcNAA*
Batchelder, Roger 1897-1947 *AmAu&B, DcNAA*
Batchelor, Clarence Daniel 1888-1977 *Bioln 7, ConAu 73, WhoAm 1974*
Batchelor, Denzil Stanley 1906- *Bioln 6*
Batchelor, E A, Jr. *NF*
Batchelor, E A, Sr. d1968 *NF*
Batchelor, George 1836-1923 *Alli Sup, AmLY, Bioln 3, DcAmA, DcNAA*
Batdorff, Emerson *NF*
Bate, Henry 1745-1824 *Alli, BiDLA*
Bate, Lucy Neumark 1939- *ConAu 69, ForWC 1970, OvPC*
Bateman, Alan M *HisAmM XR, WhNAA*
Bateman, M B *HisAmM XR*
Bates, Arlo 1850-1918 *Alli Sup, AmAu, AmAu&B, BbD, BiD&SB, CarSB, DcAmA, DcBiA, DcNAA, HisAmM XR, OxAm, REnAL, WebBD*
Bates, Brainerd S *OvPC*
Bates, Daisy 1860?-1951 *WebBD*
Bates, Edward W 1883-1971 *Bioln 9, NewYTBE 2, WhJnl 1928*
Bates, Elisha 1779?-1861 *Alli, HisAmM XR, OhA&B*
Bates, Ernest Sutherland 1879-1939 *CurBio XR*
Bates, George *NF*
Bates, Harry Wakefield *HisAmM XR*
Bates, Jerome Paine 1837-1915 *DcNAA*
Bates, John Dickerman 1873- *WhJnl Sup*
Bates, Mary E *HisAmM XR*
Bates, Robert S 1910?- *Bioln 2*
Bates, Walter Irving 1873- *WhJnl 1928*
Bates, William Oscar 1852-1924 *AmLY, DcNAA, IndAu 1816*
Bateson, Tom 1930- *NF*
Bateta, Ramon d1965 *ForP*
Bath, Dane N *OvPC*
Batiuk, Thomas M 1947- *ConAu 69*
Batlin, Robert Alfred 1930- *WhoAm 1974*
Batlle Pacheco, Lorenzo 1897?-1954 *Bioln 3*
Batlle Y Ordonez, Jose 1856-1929 *ForP, WebBD*
Batman, Robert Gordon 1900- *WhJnl 1928*
Bator, Victor 1891-1967 *Bioln 8*
Batson, Charles Alvin 1916- *WhoAm 1974, WhoS&SW 1973*
Batte, Pryor H 1895- *WhJnl Sup*
Battelle, Phyllis Marie 1922- *ForWC 1970, WhoAm 1974, WhoAmW 1974*
Batten, Frank 1927- *WhoAdv 1972, WhoAm 1974, WhoS&SW 1973*
Batten, Jack 1932- *ConAu 49, OxCan Sup*
Batten, James Knox 1936- *WhoAm 1974*
Batterberry, Ariane 1935- *ConAu 69*
Batterberry, Michael *NF*
Battersby, Roy Joseph 1912- *OvPC, WhoPubR 1972*
Battison, John Henry 1915- *WhoAm 1974,*

WhoMW 1974
Battisti, Cesare 1875-1916 *WebBD*
Battle, William Robert 1927- *WhoAm 1974,*
  WhoS&SW 1973
Bauer, Carl Friedrich 1824-1889 *BioIn 2*
Bauer, Mrs. Erwin A *NF*
Bauer, Fred 1934- *ConAu 29*
Bauer, Gerard 1888-1967 *NF*
Bauer, Hambla *BioIn 1*
Bauer, Herbert 1884-1949 *WebBD*
Bauer, Malcolm Clair 1914- *RpN, WhoAm 1974*
Bauer, Otto *AmRP*
Bauer, Robert Albert 1910- *ConAu 69,*
  WhoGov 1972
Baughman, J Ross 1954?- *NF*
Baughman, William C *NF*
Baukhage, Hilmar Robert 1889-1976 *AuNews 2,*
  ConAu 65
Baulch, Jerry T 1913- *NF*
Baum, Allyn Zelton 1924- *ConAu 17R,*
  WhoE 1974
Baum, Arthur W *BioIn 1, BioIn 2*
Baum, Doris Doscher 1881?-1970 *BioIn 8,*
  NewYTBE 1
Baum, Henry Mason 1848- *Alli Sup, DcAmA,*
  HisAmM XR
Baum, Herman 1904- *NF*
Baum, Lyman Frank 1856-1919 *AmAu&B,*
  AuBYP, CarSB, CnDAL, DcAmA, DcNAA,
  LongC, OxAm, Pen Am, REn, REnAL,
  ThrBJA, TwCA, WebBD, WhoChL
Bauman, Everett *OvPC*
Bauman, George Duncan 1912- *WhoAm 1974,*
  WhoMW 1974
Bauman, Richard 1941- *NF*
Bauman, Steve *NF*
Baumel, Rachael B *OvPC*
Baumes, J R *HisAmM XR*
Baumfield, David L *RpN*
Baumgart, Carl Arthur 1888- *WhJnl 1928*
Baumgarth, Ernest A 1896- *WhJnl 1928*
Baumgartner, J P *WhJnl 1928*
Baumgartner, Stanwood Fulton 1894-1955 *BioIn 4*
Baumgold, Julie *NF*
Baur, Charles Samuel 1880- *WhJnl 1928*
Baur, Don *NF*
Bausman, John *OvPC*
Bavernschmid, Carl Edward *NF*
Bavier, Robert N, Jr. *NF*
Baxter, Sir Beverley 1891-1964 *BioIn 6, LongC,*
  Lor&LP
Baxter, Elmar 1924- *WhoPubR 1972*
Baxter, Ernie *NF*
Baxter, Katherine d1924 *DcNAA, HisAmM XR*
Baxter, Mike *InvJ, NewMr*
Baxter, Norman K *NF*
Baxter, Norman Washington 1891-1952 *BioIn 3*
Baxter, Sylvester 1850-1927 *AmAu&B, BiD&SB,*
  BioIn 6, DcAmA, DcNAA, HisAmM XR
Baxter, Victor 1880- *WhJnl 1928*
Bay, Ahmed Emin *NF*
Bay, Andre 1916?- *BioIn 8, BioIn 9*
Bayard, Mary Temple *NF*
Bayer, Charles Maxwell 1891?-1966 *BioIn 7*
Baylass, Charles O 1897- *WhJnl 1928*
Bayles, James Copper 1845-1913 *Alli Sup,*
  DcNAA, HisAmM XR, NatCAB 13
Bayless, Kenneth 1913?-1972 *BioIn 9*
Bayly, Charles 1897?-1954 *BioIn 3*
Bayne, Charles Joseph 1870- *BiDSA, BioIn 2*
Bayne, Reed Taft 1885-1951 *BioIn 3, WhNAA,*
  WhJnl 1928
Baynes, Ernest Harold 1868-1925 *AmLY,*
  DcNAA, HisAmM XR, JBA 1934,

JBA 1951, Str&VC
Beach, Alfred Ely 1826-1896 *Alli Sup, AmJnl,*
  BioIn 5, DcNAA, HisAmM XR, WebBD
Beach, Mrs. C Y *HisAmM XR*
Beach, Charles Fisk 1827-1908 *Alli Sup, DcAmA,*
  DcNAA, HisAmM XR
Beach, Clark Jackson 1888- *WhJnl 1928*
Beach, Edward P 1886- *WhJnl 1928*
Beach, Erasmus Darwin *NF*
Beach, Frederick Converse *HisAmM XR*
Beach, H D *HisAmM XR*
Beach, James S *HisAmM XR*
Beach, Moses Sperry 1822-1892 *AmJnl,*
  NatCAB 13, WebBD
Beach, Moses Yale 1800-1868 *AmAu&B,*
  DcAmB 2, DcNAA, HisAmM XR,
  NatCAB 1, WebBD
Beach, Robert King 1865- *WhJnl 1928*
Beach, Stewart Taft 1899- *AmAu&B, BioIn 7,*
  HisAmM XR
Beachy, Lucille 1935- *NF*
Beadle, Erastus Flavel 1821-1894 *AmAu&B,*
  DcAmB S1, DcNAA, HisAmM XR, OxAm,
  REnAL
Beadle, Irwin *HisAmM XR*
Beadle, John Hanson 1840-1897 *Alli Sup,*
  BioIn 2, DcNAA, IndAu 1816, OhA&B
Beadle, Muriel 1915- *ConAu 21R*
Beadle, Roy James 1912- *WhoAm 1974,*
  WhoWest 1974
Beal, Charles A 1891- *WhNAA, WhJnl 1928*
Beal, George Brinton 1887?-1957 *BioIn 4*
Beal, Junius Emery 1860-1942 *NF*
Beale, Betty 1912?- *BioIn 5, BioIn 6, BioIn 8,*
  CelR 1973, ConAu 73, ForWC 1970,
  WhoAm 1974, WhoAmW 1974,
  WhoS&SW 1973
Beale, Robert C 1877- *WhJnl 1928*
Beall, William Charles 1911- *WhoAm 1974*
Bealle, Alfred Battle 1879- *WhJnl 1928*
Beals, Carleton 1893- *AmAu&B, AmRP,*
  Au&Wr, AuBYP, ConAu 4R, CurBio XR,
  DcLEL, IntWW 1974, OxAm, REnAL,
  TwCA, TwCA Sup, WebBD, WhNAA,
  WhoAm 1974, WhoWor 1974, WrDr 1976
Beals, Clyde 1896?-1975 *BioIn 10*
Beals, Jessie Tarbox *WhNAA*
Beals, Thomas d1899 *NF*
Beam, Alvin Wesley 1912- *WhoAm 1974*
Beamish, Richard Joseph 1869-1945 *BioIn 2,*
  DcNAA, WhNAA
Bean, Alice Pearse 1919- *NF*
Bean, Edgar Rogers 1888- *WhJnl 1928*
Bean, Louis M *NF*
Bean, Mabel Greene 1898?-1977 *ConAu 73*
Bean, Mabel Greene *see also* Greene, Mabel
Bean, Rodney *NF*
Beane, Charles Everett *HisAmM XR*
Beane, Francis Stephen 1898- *WhJnl 1928*
Beane, Joseph A 1863- *WhJnl 1928*
Bear, Charles Benson 1919- *WhoAm 1974,*
  WhoE 1974
Beard, Annie E S d1930 *DcNAA*
Beard, Chris 1936- *WhoAm 1974*
Beard, Daniel Carter 1850-1941 *Alli Sup,*
  AmAu&B, AmLY, BiD&SB, CarSB,
  CurBio XR, DcAmA, DcAmB S3, DcNAA,
  JBA 1934, OhA&B, OxAm, REnAL,
  TwCA, TwCA Sup, WebBD, WhNAA
Beard, Frank 1939- *CurBio XR, WhoAm 1974*
Beard, James Andrews 1903- *AmAu&B,*
  WhoAm 1974, WrDr 1976
Beard, Oliver Thomas 1832- *Alli Sup, DcAmA,*
  DcNAA

Beard, Thomas Francis 1842-1905 *DcNAA*, *EarABI*, *OhA&B*, *WebBD*
Beard, William Ewing 1873-1950 *BioIn 2*
Beardsley, David D 1900- *WhJnl 1928*
Beardsley, Harry *NF*
Beardsley, William Waite 1885?-1965 *BioIn 7*
Beargie, C Anthony *NF*
Beary, Matthew W 1902- *WhJnl 1928*
Beasley, Delilah Leontium 1871-1934 *BioIn 8*
Beasley, Norman *NF*
Beason, Robert Gayle 1927- *WhoAm 1974*
Beatie, Paul *NF*
Beaton, Kenneth Carrol *HisAmM XR*
Beaton, Leonard 1929-1971 *BioIn 9*, *BioIn 10*, *ConAu 7R*, *ConAu 29*
Beaton, Philip Cuyler 1897- *WhNAA*, *WhJnl 1928*
Beaton, Roderick *NF*
Beattie, Charles M *NF*
Beattie, Edward William, Jr. 1909- *AmJnl*, *BioIn 1*
Beatty, A P *HisAmM XR*
Beatty, Bessie 1886-1947 *AmAu&B*, *AmJnl*, *BioIn 1*, *CurBio XR*, *DcNAA*, *HisAmM XR*, *WhNAA*
Beatty, Floy Ward 1908- *WhoAm 1974*, *WhoAmW 1974*, *WhoS&SW 1973*
Beatty, George *HisAmM XR*
Beatty, Jerome, Jr. 1918- *AuBYP*, *BioIn 2*, *BioIn 7*, *BioIn 8*, *BioIn 10*, *ConAu 9R*, *SmATA 5*
Beatty, Mary Lou *NF*
Beatty, Morgan 1902-1975 *BioIn 1*, *BioIn 2*, *ConAu 61*, *OvPC*
Beauchamp, Catherine W *BioIn 3*
Beaudette, Richard *NF*
Beaudoin, Mike *NF*
Beaudry, Yvonne *OvPC*
Beaufort, John 1912- *WhoThe 1972*
Beaugrand, Honore 1849-1906 *DcNAA*, *OxCan*
Beaumont, Cyril William 1891-1976 *Au&Wr*, *ConAu 65*, *Who 1974*, *WrDr 1976*
Beaumont DeLaBonniniere, Gustave De 1802-1866 *BioIn 8*
Beauregard, Joseph *NF*
Beautet, Gene *OvPC*
Beauwin, Polly *NF*
Beaverbrook, Lord William Maxwell Aitken 1879-1964 *BioIn 1*, *BioIn 2*, *BioIn 3*, *BioIn 4*, *BioIn 5*, *BioIn 6*, *BioIn 7*, *BioIn 8*, *BioIn 9*, *CurBio XR*, *HisAmM XR*, *LongC*, *Lor&LP*, *WebBD*
Beazell, William Preston 1877-1946 *BioIn 1*, *OhA&B*, *WhNAA*, *WhJnl 1928*
Bebb, Russ, Jr. 1930- *ConAu 49*
Becan, John 1890-1956 *BioIn 4*
Bechdolt, Jack *HisAmM XR*
Bechdolt, John Ernest 1884-1954 *BioIn 3*
Becher, Johannes Robert 1891-1958 *CasWL*, *CIDMEL*, *CnMD*, *EncWL*, *EvEuW*, *ForP*, *ModGL*, *ModWD*, *OxGer*, *Pen Eur*
Bechtel, Louise 1894- *BioIn 1*, *BioIn 9*
Bechtel, Welker George 1902- *WhoAm 1974*
Beck, Alan *BioIn 2*
Beck, Anthony J 1886- *WhNAA*, *WhJnl 1928*
Beck, Basse A 1896- *WhJnl 1928*
Beck, Burt 1918- *WhoAm 1974*
Beck, C C *NF*
Beck, Charlton T 1879?-1946 *BioIn 1*
Beck, Christian 1931?- *BioIn 2*
Beck, Clyde Byron 1884-1967 *WhJnl 1928*
Beck, Edward J 1890- *WhNAA*, *WhJnl 1928*
Beck, Edward S 1892-1964 *NatCAB 51*
Beck, Edward Scott 1868- *WhJnl 1928*

Beck, Jesse McFall 1873?- *WhNAA*, *WhJnl 1928*
Beck, Joan *NF*
Beck, Joel 1943- *BioIn 10*
Beck, Marilyn Mohr 1928- *BioIn 10*, *ConAu 65*, *ForWC 1970*, *WhoAmW 1974*
Beck, Thomas Hambly *HisAmM XR*
Beckenstein, Myron 1938- *WhoAm 1974*
Becker, A C, Jr. 1920- *ConAu 65*
Becker, August 1813-1872 *BioIn 2*
Becker, August 1828-1891 *BiD&SB*
Becker, B Jay 1904- *ConAu 65*
Becker, Hans Detlev 1921- *ForP*, *IntWW 1976*, *WhoWor 1974*
Becker, Howard S *NF*
Becker, Jim *NF*
Becker, Jim 1926- *WhoWest 1974*
Becker, John 1877- *WhJnl 1928*
Becker, John Leonard 1901- *AuBYP*, *BioIn 10*
Becker, Kenneth *NF*
Becker, Lazar *AmRP*
Becker, Leod D 1895- *WhJnl 1928*
Becker, Loraine Alfred 1897- *WhNAA*, *WhJnl 1928*
Becker, Marjory *NF*
Becker, Maurice *AmRP*
Becker, May Lamberton 1873-1958 *AmAu&B*, *BioIn 1*, *BioIn 4*, *BioIn 5*, *CurBio XR*, *HisAmM XR*, *REnAL*, *TwCA*, *TwCA Sup*, *WebBD*, *WhNAA*
Becker, Murray *NF*
Becker, Paul 1913?-1966 *BioIn 7*
Becker, Philip *NF*
Becker, Rudolf Zacharias 1751?-1822 *OxGer*, *WebBD*
Becker, Samuel Leo 1923- *ConAu 15R*, *DrAS 74E*, *WhoAm 1974*, *WhoWorJ 1972*
Becker, Thomas A *HisAmM XR*
Becker, Truman *NF*
Beckett, Harry *HisAmM XR*
Beckett, Henry 1884?-1969 *BioIn 10*
Beckett, Rupert *NF*
Beckhard, Arthur J *AuBYP*, *BioIn 8*
Beckles, Gordon 1901-1954 *BioIn 3*
Beckley, Zoe d1961 *AmJnl*, *HisAmM XR*
Beckman, Aldo Bruce 1934- *ConAu 73*
Beckman, Frederick W 1873- *WhJnl 1928*
Beckovic, Matija 1939- *ConAu 33*
Beckwith, George *HisAmM XR*
Beckwith, Nina *OvPC*
Bedacht, Max *AmRP*, *NewYTBE 3*
Bedard, I 1901- *WhJnl 1928*
Bedard, Patrick *NF*
Beddoes, Richard H 1926- *ConAu 37*
Beddow, Reid *NF*
Bedell, William E 1866?-1951 *BioIn 2*
Bedford, Emmett Gruner 1922- *ConAu 45*, *DrAS 74E*
Bedichek, Wendell H 1903- *WhJnl 1928*
Bednarek, David Isadore 1936- *WhoAm 1974*
Bee, Noah *NF*
Beebe, Frederick Sessions 1914-1973 *BioIn 5*, *BioIn 9*, *ConAu 41*, *NewYTBE 4*, *WhoE 1974*, *WhoF&I 1974*
Beebe, George Hollis 1910- *InvJ*, *WhoAm 1974*, *WhoS&SW 1973*
Beebe, Lucius Morris 1902-1966 *AmAu&B*, *BioIn 4*, *BioIn 6*, *BioIn 7*, *BioIn 8*, *ConAu 25*, *CurBio XR*, *REn*, *REnAL*, *WebBD*
Beebe, M A *HisAmM XR*
Beebe, Ralph A 1910?-1964 *BioIn 6*
Beebe, William *HisAmM XR*
Beeby, Nell V 1896-1957 *BioIn 4*, *BioIn 8*
Beech, Keyes 1913- *AmJnl*, *BioIn 3*, *BioIn 5*,

ConAu 33, RpN, WhoAm 1974,
  WhoWor 1974
Beecher, Catherine Esther *HisAmM XR*
Beecher, Edward 1803?-1895 *Alli, Alli Sup,*
  AmAu&B, BbD, BiD&SB, CyAL 2,
  DcAmA, DcNAA, HisAmM XR, REnAL
Beecher, Henry Ward 1813-1887 *Alli, Alli Sup,*
  AmAu, AmAu&B, AmJnl, BbD, BiD&SB,
  CasWL, CyAL 1, CyAL 2, DcAmA,
  DcBiA, DcEnL, DcNAA, EncAB, EvLB,
  HisAmM XR, OhA&B, OxAm, OxEng,
  Pen Am, REn, REnAL, WebBD
Beecher, J A *HisAmM XR*
Beecher, Lucas J *NF*
Beecher, Luther *HisAmM XR*
Beecher, Thomas Kinnicut 1824-1900 *Alli Sup,*
  CyAL 2, DcAmA, DcNAA, HisAmM XR
Beecher, William M 1933- *BioIn 10, ConAu 65*
Beecroft, Bill *NF*
Beecroft, Chester 1882?-1959 *NF*
Beecroft, David 1875- *WhJnl 1928*
Beede, Carl Greenleaf 1870?-1952 *BioIn 2*
Beedon, A Phillips *NF*
Beeler, Maxwell Newton 1888- *IndAu 1917,*
  WhNAA, WhJnl 1928
Beeman, Art *NF*
Beene, Wallace *BioIn 8*
Beer, Frank R 1868- *WhJnl 1928*
Beer, Israel J 1816-1899 *ForP*
Beer, Israel J *see also* Reuter, Baron Paul Julius Von
Beer, Max 1886?-1965 *BioIn 7*
Beer, Otto F 1910- *IntWW 1976, WhoWor 1974*
Beerbohm, Sir Max 1872-1956 *AtlBL, CasWL,*
  CnMD, CnMWL, CyWA, DcLEL, EvLB,
  HisAmM XR, LongC, ModBL, ModBL Sup,
  ModWD, NewC, OxEng, Pen Eng, RAdv 1,
  REn, TwCA, TwCA Sup, TwCW, WebBD,
  WebE&AL
Beery, William C 1879?-1949 *BioIn 2*
Beeston, Richard *NF*
Beetle, David Harold 1908-1972 *Au&Wr, BioIn 9*
Beevers, John 1911-1975 *ConAu 61*
Begbie, Harold 1871?-1929 *LongC, NewC,*
  WebBD
Beghtol, Vance Richards 1902- *WhJnl 1928*
Beguin, Bernard 1923- *IntWW 1976,*
  WhoWor 1974
Behr, Edward 1926- *ConAu 2R, NewYTBE 2*
Behr, Peter B 1941?- *NF*
Behre, Doris *NF*
Behrendt, David Frogner 1935- *WhoAm 1974*
Behrendt, Fritz Alfred 1925- *BioIn 6*
Behrens, E T 1866- *BioIn 1*
Behrens, John C 1933- *ConAu 37, WrDr 1976*
Behrman, Daniel 1923- *ConAu 65*
Behymer, Francis Albert 1870?- *BioIn 1, BioIn 2,*
  BioIn 4
Beichman, Arnold 1913- *ConAu 49*
Beirne, Francis F 1890?- *BioIn 2*
Beirne, Hugh J *NF*
Beirne, Richard Foulke 1882- *WhJnl 1928*
Beisel, Daniel Cunningham 1916- *WhoAm 1974*
Beith, Robert Bruce 1904- *WhoAm 1974,*
  WhoE 1974, WhoF&I 1974
Beitler, Brooks *NF*
Beitler, Stanley 1924- *AuBYP, BioIn 7,*
  ConAu 5
Beizer, James *OvPC*
Bejarano, Jose Miguel 1887?-1954 *BioIn 3*
Bekker, Paul 1882-1937 *NF*
Bel, Matej *ForP*
Belair, Felix, Jr. 1908?-1978 *NF*
Belaunde, Fernando *ForP*

Belcher, George Frederick Athur 1875-1947 *BioIn 1*
Belcher, Joshua *HisAmM XR*
Belcher, Robert W *HisAmM XR*
Belden, Henry Marvin *HisAmM XR*
Belden, Jack 1910- *NF*
Belden, Marva *NF*
Belding, Albert Martin 1859- *WhJnl 1928*
Belding, Anson Wood 1881-1970 *BioIn 10*
Belding, Everett Elijah 1879- *WhJnl 1928*
Belford, Barbara *NF*
Belford, Robert J *HisAmM XR*
Belfrage, Cedric 1904- *AmAu&B, AmNov,*
  AmRP, Au&Wr, ConAu 11R, TwCA,
  TwCA Sup, WrDr 1976
Belgin, Harvey *NF*
Belgion, H Montgomery 1892- *WhJnl Sup*
Belinski, Vissarion Grigorievich 1811-1848 *WebBD*
Belk, Henry 1898- *WhJnl Sup, WhoS&SW 1973*
Belkind, Myron *NF*
Belknap, Joseph *HisAmM XR*
Bell, Adrian Hanbury 1901- *DcLEL, EvLB,*
  LongC, TwCA, TwCA Sup, Who 1974
Bell, Brian 1926- *USBiR 1974, WhoGov 1972*
Bell, Charles Frederic Moberly 1847-1911 *FamWC,*
  NewC, WebBD
Bell, Clark 1832-1918 *HisAmM XR, WebBD*
Bell, Clive 1881-1964 *DcLEL, LongC, ModBL,*
  NewC, OxEng, Pen Eng, REn, TwCA,
  TwCA Sup, WebBD
Bell, Colin 1938- *ConAu 29*
Bell, Edgar T 1892- *WhJnl 1928*
Bell, Edward Price 1869-1943 *AmAu&B, AmJnl,*
  BioIn 1, BioIn 4, CurBio XR, DcNAA,
  HisAmM XR, IndAu 1917
Bell, Edwin Q *HisAmM XR*
Bell, Elliott Vallance 1902- *BioIn 2, BioIn 3,*
  CurBio XR, IntWW 1976, IntWW 1974,
  WhoAm 1974
Bell, F G *NF*
Bell, Henry Glassford 1803-1874 *Alli, Alli Sup,*
  BrAu 19, DcEnL, EvLB, NewC, WebBD
Bell, Hobart H *BioIn 7*
Bell, Horace *HisAmM XR*
Bell, Hunter 1901- *WhJnl 1928*
Bell, J D *HisAmM XR*
Bell, Jack L 1904-1975 *BioIn 8, ConAu 1R,*
  ConAu 61, WhoAm 1974, WhoS&SW 1973
Bell, Jacob 1810-1859 *WebBD*
Bell, James Adrian 1917- *ConAu 73,*
  WhoAm 1974
Bell, Jean M *NF*
Bell, Jesse G *OvPC*
Bell, John 1745-1831 *ForP*
Bell, John Joy 1871-1934 *EvLB, LongC, NewC,*
  Pen Eng, WebBD
Bell, John Keble 1875-1928 *WebBD*
Bell, Joseph Newton 1921- *AuBYP, ConAu 5,*
  IndAu 1917, WhoWest 1974
Bell, L H *HisAmM XR*
Bell, L Nelson 1894-1973 *BioIn 10, ConAu 19,*
  ConAu 45, ConAu P-1, NewYTBE 4
Bell, Lester M *NF*
Bell, Lillian *HisAmM XR*
Bell, Norman 1899- *ConAu 61*
Bell, Paul W 1901- *WhJnl 1928*
Bell, Phillip Alexander *NF*
Bell, R P 1883- *WhJnl 1928*
Bell, Rebecca *NF*
Bell, Sir Robert 1800-1867 *Alli, Alli Sup, BbD,*
  BiD&SB, BiDLA, DcEnL, NewC, PoIre,
  WebBD
Bell, Samuel W *NF*
Bell, Smith *WhJnl 1928*

Bell, Stephen Scott 1935- *ConAu 65*
Bell, T H *AmRP*
Bell, Ulric 1891-1960 *NatCAB 45*
Bell, William Dixon 1865-1951 *BioIn 10,*
   WhNAA
Bell, William M 1879- *WhJnl 1928*
Bellah, Hutton 1896- *WhJnl 1928*
Bellaigue, Camille 1858-1930 *WebBD*
Bellaire, Robert 1914-1945 *AmJnl, HisAmM XR*
Bellamy, Blanche 1852-1919 *DcNAA*
Bellamy, Charles Joseph 1852-1910 *AmAu&B,*
   DcAmA, DcNAA
Bellamy, Edward 1850-1898 *Alli Sup, AmAu,*
   AmAu&B, AmRP, BbD, BiD&SB,
   BioIn 10, CasWL, CnDAL, CyWA,
   DcAmA, DcBiA, DcEnA Ap, DcLEL,
   DcNAA, EncAB, EvLB, HisAmM XR,
   MouLC 4, OxAm, OxEng, Pen Am,
   RAdv 1, REn, REnAL, WebBD, WebE&AL
Bellamy, Francis *HisAmM XR*
Bellamy, Francis Rufus 1886-1972 *AmAu&B,*
   AmNov, BioIn 2, BioIn 7, BioIn 9,
   ConAu 33, HisAmM XR
Bellamy, Guy 1935- *ConAu 65*
Bellamy, Jeanne 1911- *AmAu&B, ForWC 1970,*
   WhoAmW 1974
Bellamy, Paul 1884-1956 *AmAu&B, BioIn 4,*
   WhJnl 1928
Bellamy, Peter 1914- *WhoAm 1974*
Bellamy, William Butler 1920- *WhoAm 1974*
Bellanger, Claude 1910- *IntWW 1976,*
   WhoWor 1974
Bellati, Robert C 1886- *WhJnl 1928*
Bellemy, Frank *NF*
Beller, Jacob 1896- *ConAu 25*
Bellew, Frank Henry Temple 1828-1888 *DcNAA,*
   EarABI, EarABI Sup, HisAmM XR
Bellew, Frank P W *Alli Sup, HisAmM XR*
Bellew, Thomas J 1882- *WhJnl 1928*
Bellinger, Martha Idell 1870-1960 *BioIn 5*
Bellis, Milton B 1924- *OvPC, WhoPubR 1972*
Bellnap, David *NF*
Bello, Francis Cesare 1917- *WhoAm 1974*
Belloc, Hilaire 1870-1953 *AnCL, AtlBL, AuBYP,*
   BkC 5, CarSB, CasWL, CathA 1930,
   CnE&AP, CnMWL, CyWA, DcLEL, EvLB,
   LongC, ModBL, ModBL Sup, NewC,
   OxEng, Pen Eng, RAdv 1, REn, TwCA,
   TwCA Sup, TwCW, WebBD, WebE&AL,
   WhoChL, WhoLA, YABC 1
Bellow, Frank H T 1828-1888 *AmAu&B*
Bellows, Henry Whitney 1814-1882 *Alli Sup,*
   AmAu&B, BiD&SB, CyAL 2, DcAmA,
   DcEnL, DcNAA, HisAmM XR, WebBD
Bellows, James Gilbert 1922- *BioIn 10,*
   Who 1974, WhoAm 1974
Belly, Felix 1816-1886 *BioIn 8*
Belmont, Georges 1909- *ConAu 29*
Belmont, Oliver Hazard Perry 1858-1908
   HisAmM XR
Belmont, Trixie *NF*
Belnap, David F *OvPC*
Belo, Alfred Horatio 1839-1901 *AmAu&B,*
   AmJnl, DcAmB 2, NatCAB 1
Belo, Alfred Horatio 1873-1906 *AmAu&B*
Belous, Richard S *NF*
Belser, Lee 1925- *ConAu 73*
Belshaw, Mortimer *NF*
Beltaire, Mark Anthony, III 1914- *WhoAm 1974*
Beltran, Miriam 1914- *ConAu 33*
Beltran, Pedro Gerardo 1897- *BioIn 9,*
   CurBio XR, ForP, IntWW 1974,
   WhoWor 1974
Beltran, Washington 1914- *IntWW 1976*

Bemis, Elizabeth P *HisAmM XR*
Ben, Philip 1913-1978 *WhoWor 1974*
Ben Baruch, Shalom 1886- *IntWW 1976*
Ben-Horin, Eliahu 1902?-1966 *BioIn 7*
Ben Yehuda, Eliezer 1858-1922 *CasWL, EuAu,*
   Pen Cl, Pen Eur, WebBD
Ben-Yehuda, Hemda *NF*
Ben-Zvi, Rachel 1886- *WhoWorJ 1972*
Benadon, Haim *NF*
Benagh, Jim 1937- *ConAu 57*
Benard, Pierre 1901?-1946 *BioIn 1*
Benarone, David *NF*
Benchley, Nathaniel 1915- *BiE&WWA,*
   CelR 1973, CurBio XR, SmATA 3
Benchley, Robert Charles 1889-1945 *AmAu&B,*
   ConAmA, CurBio XR, DcAmB S3, DcLEL,
   DcNAA, EvLB, HisAmM XR, LongC,
   ModAL, OxAm, Pen Am, RAdv 1, REn,
   REnAL, TwCA, TwCA Sup, TwCW,
   WebBD
Bend, Silas 1882- *WhJnl 1928*
Bendel, Peggy *NF*
Bender, Eric J 1893-1966 *AmAu&B, BioIn 7,*
   HisAmM XR, OhA&B
Bender, Marylin 1925- *ConAu 21R*
Bender, Rene J *BioIn 8*
Bender, Robert J 1890-1936 *AmJnl, NatCAB 28*
Bender, William Isett, Jr. 1930- *WhoAm 1974*
Bendigo, C W 1911- *BioIn 1*
Bendiner, Alfred 1899- *BioIn 2, BioIn 6,*
   BioIn 7, BioIn 8
Bendiner, Elmer 1916- *ConAu 57*
Bendiner, Robert 1909- *AmAu&B, Au&Wr,*
   ConAu 11R
Benedetti, Cipro Giovanni *OvPC*
Benedetti, Giulio De *ForP*
Benedetti, Mario 1920- *CasWL, DcCLAA,*
   IntWW 1976, Pen Am, WhoWor 1974
Benedict, Agnes Elizabeth 1889-1950 *BioIn 2,*
   OhA&B
Benedict, Frank Lee 1834-1910 *Alli Sup,*
   AmAu&B, BiD&SB, BiDSA, DcAmA,
   DcNAA, HisAmM XR
Benedict, George Grenville 1826-1907 *Alli Sup,*
   DcAmA, DcNAA
Benedict, Howard *NF*
Benedict, S W *HisAmM XR*
Benedict, Stanley Rossiter 1884-1936 *BioIn 3,*
   WhNAA
Benedict, Stewart Hurd 1924- *ConAu 13R,*
   WhoE 1974
Benedictsson, Sigfus B 1865- *BioIn 2*
Benefield, Barry 1877- *AmAu&B, AmNov,*
   BioIn 2, BioIn 4, ConAmL, DcLEL,
   HisAmM XR, OxAm, REnAL, TexWr,
   TwCA, TwCA Sup, WebBD
Benefield, June 1921- *ConAu 45,*
   WhoS&SW 1973
Benet, James 1914- *ConAu 61, WhoAm 1974,*
   WhoWest 1974
Benet, William Rose 1886-1950 *AmAu&B,*
   BioIn 1, BioIn 2, BioIn 3, BioIn 4, CnDAL,
   ConAmA, ConAmL, DcAmB S4, DcLEL,
   HisAmM XR, LongC, OxAm, OxEng,
   Pen Am, REn, REnAL, TwCA, TwCA Sup,
   WebBD, WhNAA
Benfield, Richard E *NF*
Benford, Timothy B 1941- *NF*
Bengelsdorf, Irving Swem 1922- *AmM&W 73P,*
   WhoAm 1974
Bengough, John Wilson 1851-1923 *DcLEL,*
   DcNAA, OxCan, WebBD
Benham, Frederick Darius 1892- *BioIn 2, BioIn 5,*
   WhJnl Sup

Benham, Joseph *NF*
Benham, P D *HisAmM XR*
Benington, Arthur *NF*
Benish, Allan *NF*
Benitez, Justo Pastor 1896- *WebBD*
Benjamin, Anna *NF*
Benjamin, Burton Richard 1917- *WhoAm 1974,*
 WhoWor 1974
Benjamin, Charles Love *HisAmM XR*
Benjamin, James *InvJ*
Benjamin, Louis 1883- *WhJnl 1928*
Benjamin, Milton R *NF*
Benjamin, Park 1809-1864 *Alli, AmAu,*
 AmAu&B, AmJnl, BiD&SB, BioIn 1,
 CyAL 2, DcAmA, DcEnL, DcNAA,
 HisAmM XR, OxAm, WebBD
Benjamin, Park, Jr. 1849-1922 *Alli Sup,*
 AmAu&B, BiD&SB, DcAmA, DcNAA,
 WebBD
Benjamin, Philip Robert 1922-1966 *BioIn 7*
Benjamin, Robert *NF*
Benjamin, Robert Spiers *OvPC*
Benjamin, Samuel Green Wheeler *HisAmM XR*
Benjamin, Stanford H *NF*
Benjamin, Walter Romeyn d1943 *HisAmM XR*
Benjamin, William Evarts d1940 *CurBio XR,*
 HisAmM XR
Benjaminson, Peter 1945- *ConAu 73*
Benn, Anthony Neil Wedgwood 1925- *BioIn 7,*
 BioIn 9, CurBio XR
Benn, R Davis *HisAmM XR*
Bennack, Frank Anthony, Jr. 1933- *WhoAm 1974,*
 WhoF&I 1974, WhoS&SW 1973
Benner, E Austin 1896- *WhJnl 1928*
Bennett, Charles Leo 1920- *WhoAm 1974*
Bennett, Estelline d1948 *DcNAA*
Bennett, Harry Wiggin, Jr. 1907- *WhoAm 1974*
Bennett, Harve 1930- *IntMPA 1975*
Bennett, Ira Elbert 1868-1957 *BioIn 4,*
 HisAmM XR
Bennett, James Gordon, Jr. 1841-1918 *AmAu&B,*
 AmJnl, BioIn 2, BioIn 3, BioIn 4, EncAB,
 FamWC, WebBD
Bennett, James Gordon, Sr. 1795-1872 *AmAu&B,*
 AmJnl, BioIn 1, BioIn 2, BioIn 3, BioIn 4,
 BioIn 6, BioIn 9, EncAB, ForP,
 HisAmM XR, OxAm, REn, REnAL,
 WebBD
Bennett, James O'Donnell 1870-1940 *AmAu&B,*
 AmJnl, CurBio XR, DcNAA, NatCAB 30
Bennett, Janet *NF*
Bennett, Jerry *NF*
Bennett, Jesse Lee 1885-1931 *DcNAA, WhNAA*
Bennett, Jessie 1927- *NF*
Bennett, Jim *NF*
Bennett, Jim 1921- *WhoAm 1974,*
 WhoWest 1974
Bennett, John *HisAmM XR*
Bennett, Joseph 1922-1972 *BioIn 9, ConAu 3R,*
 ConAu 33
Bennett, Lerone, Jr. 1928- *BlkAW, BlkC,*
 ConAu 45, LivBAA, WhoAm 1974,
 WhoMW 1974
Bennett, Mary Alice *NF*
Bennett, Orlando *HisAmM XR*
Bennett, Raine Edward *OvPC*
Bennett, Roscoe D 1894- *WhJnl 1928*
Bennett, Roy *NF*
Bennett, Roy Coleman 1889- *WhNAA,*
 WhJnl 1928
Bennett, Mrs. S R I *Alli Sup, HisAmM XR*
Bennett, Samuel 1902?-1955 *BioIn 3*
Bennett, Tiny *NF*
Bennett, Walter Edward 1921- *WhoAm 1974,*

WhoS&SW 1973
Bennett-England, Rodney Charles 1936-
 ConAu 61, WhoPubR 1972, WrDr 1976
Bennewitz, James Richard 1936- *WhoAm 1974*
Benoit, Richard 1898?-1970 *BioIn 8*
Bensley, Robert Russell 1930- *WhoAm 1974*
Bensley, Rus *NF*
Benson, Allan Louis 1871-1940 *AmAu&B, AmRP,*
 CurBio XR, DcNAA
Benson, Carl 1820-1874 *Alli Sup, AmAu&B,*
 BiD&SB, DcAmA, DcNAA
Benson, Carl *see also* Bristed, Charles Astor
Benson, Charles *NF*
Benson, Elizabeth English 1904-1972 *BioIn 9*
Benson, Eugene 1839?-1908 *Alli Sup, AmAu&B,*
 BiD&SB, DcAmA, DcNAA, EarABI,
 HisAmM XR
Benson, Frances M *HisAmM XR*
Benson, George Aaron 1889-1959 *BioIn 5*
Benson, Ivan 1896- *WhJnl 1928*
Benson, Mildred Wirt 1905- *AuBYP, BioIn 8,*
 OhA&B
Benson, Miles R *NF*
Benson, Stuart *HisAmM XR*
Bent, Andrew 1791-1851 *BioIn 2*
Bent, George *HisAmM XR*
Bent, Silas 1882-1945 *AmAu&B, AmJnl,*
 BioIn 2, BioIn 4, DcAmB S3, DcNAA,
 HisAmM XR, REnAL, TwCA, TwCA Sup,
 WhNAA
Bentham, Myron S 1867?-1946 *BioIn 1*
Benti, Joseph 1932?- *BioIn 8*
Bentley, Carole *NF*
Bentley, Edmund Clerihew 1875-1956 *BioIn 4,*
 BioIn 6, DcLEL, EncMys, EvLB, LongC,
 NewC, OxEng, REn, TwCA, TwCA Sup,
 TwCW
Bentley, Edwin R 1888- *WhNAA, WhJnl 1928*
Bentley, Eric Russel 1916- *AmAu&B,*
 HisAmM XR
Bentley, George 1828-1895 *WebBD*
Bentley, Helen Delich 1923- *BioIn 8, BioIn 9,*
 CurBio XR, ForWC 1970, IntWW 1974,
 WhoAmP 1973, WhoAmW 1974,
 WhoE 1974, WhoGov 1972
Bentley, James Luther 1937- *WhoAm 1974*
Bentley, Larry Dean 1943- *WhoAm 1974*
Bentley, Max 1888- *HisAmM XR, TexWr*
Bentley, Richard 1794-1871 *NewC, WebBD*
Bentley, William 1759-1819 *Alli, AmAu,*
 AmAu&B, AmJnl, DcNAA
Benton, Caroline French *HisAmM XR, WhNAA*
Benton, Joel 1832-1911 *Alli Sup, AmAu,*
 AmAu&B, BbD, BiD&SB, DcAmA,
 DcAmB 2, DcNAA, HisAmM XR
Benton, Myron *HisAmM XR*
Benton, Nelson *NF*
Benton, Robert 1932- *AmAu&B, BioIn 8,*
 ConAu 1, ConDr, IntMPA 1975
Benton, Thomas Hart 1782-1858 *Alli, AmAu&B,*
 AmJnl, BbD, BiD&SB, BiDSA, CyAL 1,
 DcAmA, DcNAA, OxAm, REn, REnAL,
 WebBD
Bentov, Mordechai 1900- *IntWW 1976,*
 WhoWor 1974, WhoWorJ 1972
Benvenisti, James Lincoln 1890- *BioIn 1, BkC 2,*
 CathA 1930
Benyon, John Foster *HisAmM XR*
Benz, Margaret 1898?-1967 *BioIn 7*
Beranek, Leo Leroy 1914- *AmM&W 73P,*
 ConAu 5, CurBio XR, WhoAm 1974,
 WhoE 1974, WhoF&I 1974, WhoWor 1974
Beraud, Henri 1885-1958 *BioIn 5*
Berck, Martin Gans 1928- *ConAu 65, OvPC*

Bercovici, Bernard S 1895?-1973 *BioIn 10*
Bercovici, Hyperion LeB 1902- *WhJnl Sup*
Bercovici, Joseph 1879?-1967 *BioIn 7*
Bercovici, Rion 1903?-1976 *ConAu 69, OvPC*
Bercowitz, Anna *AmRP*
Berdanier, Paul Frederick 1879-1961 *BioIn 5*
Berdes, George Raymond 1931- *ConAu 29,*
   WhoAmP 1973
Berdes, Jane L *NF*
Berdsall, Sidney S *WhJnl 1928*
Berenberg, David Paul 1890- *AmRP,*
   WhoWorJ 1972
Berendt, John *NF*
Beresford, James Alfred 1901-1977 *WhoAm 1974*
Berg, Albert Ellery *Alli Sup, HisAmM XR*
Berg, David 1920- *ConAu 21R*
Berg, Herbert N 1876- *WhJnl 1928*
Berg, Lewis d1977 *NF*
Berg, Mary Randolph *BioIn 9*
Berg, Roland Hobsbawn 1908- *WhoAm 1974,*
   WhoWorJ 1972
Berg, Susie *HisAmM XR*
Bergamini, David H 1928- *ConAu 1R*
Bergen, John Vanderveer 1934- *WhoAm 1974*
Bergengren, Anna 1865- *BioIn 2*
Bergenheim, Robert Carlton 1924- *RpN,*
   WhoAm 1974, WhoAm 1974
Berger, Daniel *RpN*
Berger, Doris *AmRP*
Berger, Eric 1906- *WhoAm 1974*
Berger, James R *NF*
Berger, Josef 1903-1971 *AmAu&B, BioIn 9,*
   ConAu 7R, ConAu 33, NewYTBE 2,
   WhJnl 1928
Berger, Joseph E *NF*
Berger, Lawrence Sherwin 1925- *WhoAdv 1972,*
   WhoAm 1974, WhoF&I 1974
Berger, Lisa 1947- *NF*
Berger, Marilyn *NF*
Berger, Meyer 1898-1959 *AmAu&B, BioIn 2,*
   BioIn 5, BioIn 6, CurBio XR, NatCAB 46
Berger, Oscar 1901- *BioIn 5, BioIn 6,*
   WhoAm 1974, WhoE 1974, WhoWor 1974
Berger, Phil 1942- *ConAu 61*
Berger, Sheila *NF*
Berger, Victor Louis 1860-1929 *AmJnl, AmRP,*
   BioIn 10, DcAmB S1, DcNAA, EncAB,
   WebBD, WhJnl 1928
Bergeret, Ida Treat 1889?-1978 *NF*
Berges, Marshall William *WhoAm 1974*
Bergh, Henry 1811?-1888 *Alli Sup, AmAu,*
   AmAu&B, BbD, BiD&SB, DcAmA,
   DcNAA, HisAmM XR, WebBD
Bergh, Keith David *BioIn 6, MnnWr*
Berghaus, V Hummel, Jr, 1879- *WhJnl 1928*
Bergholz, Richard Cady 1917- *WhoAm 1974*
Bergman, Bernard Aaron 1894- *WhoAm 1974,*
   WhoWorJ 1972
Bergman, Jules *InvJ*
Bergman, Lowell *InvJ*
Bergquist, Laura *NF*
Bergstresser, J C *HisAmM XR*
Beringer, George M *HisAmM XR*
Beringer, P N *NF*
Berk, Viola Greenhut 1900- *WhoAm 1974*
Berkand, Necdet *NF*
Berke, Anita Diamant *ForWC 1970, OvPC*
Berkeley, H J F 1865- *WhJnl 1928*
Berkman, Alexander 1870-1936 *AmRP, DcNAA,*
   WebBD
Berkman, Edward 1914- *ConAu 61*
Berkman, Jack Neville 1905- *OhA&B,*
   WhoAm 1974, WhoE 1974, WhoF&I 1974
Berkman, Louis 1909- *WhoAm 1974,*

WhoF&I 1974
Berkow, Ira 1939?- *BioIn 10*
Berkson, Seymour 1905-1959 *AmAu&B, BioIn 2,*
   BioIn 5, CurBio XR
Berland, Theodore 1929- *ConAu 5, OvPC,*
   WhoMW 1974
Berle, Gustav *NF*
Berlet, John F 1949- *NF*
Berlin, Ellin Mackay 1904- *ConAu 65*
Berlin, Michael Joseph 1938- *ConAu 69*
Berlin, Richard E 1894- *CelR 1973,*
   HisAmM XR, WhoAm 1974, WhoE 1974,
   WhoF&I 1974, WhoWest 1974
Berliner, Franz 1930- *ConAu 29*
Berling, Ernst Henrich *ForP*
Berlinrut, E B *OvPC*
Berman, Art *InvJ*
Berman, Audrey *NF*
Berman, Avis 1949- *NF*
Berman, Berel Vladimir 1896- *WhNAA,*
   WhJnl 1928
Berman, Connie *NF*
Berman, Harold 1878?-1949 *BioIn 1*
Berman, Keeve *NF*
Berman, L *AmRP*
Berman, N H *AmRP*
Berman, Susan 1945- *ConAu 65*
Bermingham, Donald M 1905?-1973 *BioIn 10*
Bernabei, Ettore 1921- *IntWW 1976*
Bernal, Antonio Arlas 1913?-1960 *BioIn 5*
Bernald, Eugene 1908- *OvPC, WhoE 1974,*
   WhoF&I 1974
Bernard, Alma *NF*
Bernard, Charles *NF*
Bernard, George 1939- *ConAu 73*
Bernard, George S 1837-1912 *BiDSA, DcNAA*
Bernard, Harry 1898- *BioIn 5, CanWW 1972,*
   CanWr, OxCan, WhNAA
Bernard, John I *HisAmM XR*
Bernard, Lawrence 1927- *OvPC, WhoE 1974,*
   WhoF&I 1974
Bernard, Peter D *HisAmM XR*
Bernard, Sidney 1918- *ConAu 29, WrDr 1976*
Bernays, Carl L 1815-1879 *BioIn 2*
Bernays, Edward L 1891- *AmAu&B,*
   ConAu 17R, CurBio XR, OvPC, REnAL,
   WhNAA, WhoAm 1974, WhoPubR 1972,
   WhoWor 1974, WhoWorJ 1972, WrDr 1976
Berndt, Walter *NF*
Bernet, Michael M 1930- *ConAu 25*
Bernhard, Clayton Valentine 1900- *WhJnl 1928*
Bernhard, Finley 1939- *NF*
Bernhard, Georg 1875-1944 *WebBD*
Bernhardsen, Christian 1923- *ConAu 29*
Bernhardt, Gene *NF*
Bernheimer, Martin 1936- *ConAu 69,*
   WhoAm 1974, WhoWest 1974
Bernier, Bob 1949- *NF*
Berns, Frederick *NF*
Bernstein, Aaron David 1812-1884 *NF*
Bernstein, Burton 1932- *ConAu 1R, WrDr 1976*
Bernstein, Carl 1944- *AuNews 1, BioNews 1974,*
   InvJ, NewMr, WhoAm 1974
Bernstein, David 1915-1974 *ConAu 53,*
   NewYTBS 5, WhoWorJ 1972
Bernstein, Elliot d1977 *NF*
Bernstein, Herman 1876-1935 *AmAu&B, BioIn 1,*
   DcAmA, DcAmB S1, DcNAA,
   NatCAB XR, WebBD, WhNAA,
   WhJnl 1928
Bernstein, Hillel 1892?-1977 *ConAu 69*
Bernstein, Kenneth *OvPC*
Bernstein, Paul *NF*
Bernstein, Peter J *NF*

Bernstein, Sidney Ralph 1907- *WhoAdv 1972,*
  WhoAm 1974, WhoF&I 1974,
  WhoWorJ 1972
Bernstein, Simon Gerson 1884- *BioIn 2, BioIn 6*
Bernstein, Theodore Menline 1904- *BioIn 6,*
  ConAu 1R, NewYTBE 3, WhNAA,
  WhoAm 1974, WhJnl 1928, WhoWorJ 1972
Bernstein, Walter *BioIn 1*
Bernstein, Z H *NF*
Bernus, Pierre 1881-1951 *BioIn 2*
Berr, Michel 1780-1843 *NF*
Berra, Franco 1875?-1955 *BioIn 3*
Berrigan, Darrell *BioIn 1, BioIn 5*
Berrigan, Thomas J 1904?-1970 *BioIn 9*
Berrill, Jack *NF*
Berry, Adrian M 1937- *ConAu 57, WrDr 1976*
Berry, Henry T *NF*
Berry, James Gomer 1883-1968 *CurBio XR*
Berry, James Gomer *see also* Kemsley, James Gomer
  Berry, Viscount
Berry, James O 1932- *BioIn 7, ConAu 23R*
Berry, James R *NF*
Berry, Jim *see* Berry, James O
Berry, John M 1938- *AmEA 1974*
Berry, John Nichols, III 1933- *BiDrLUS, BioIn 6,*
  BioIn 8
Berry, Philip C *NF*
Berry, Robert E *OvPC*
Berry, Watson B *NF*
Berry, Sir William *NF*
Berryman, Clifford Kennedy 1869-1949 *AmJnl,*
  BioIn 1, BioIn 2, BioIn 4, DcAmB S4
Berryman, James Thomas 1902-1971 *BioIn 2,*
  BioIn 9, CurBio XR, NewYTBE 2
Bertelson, Arthur Robards 1907- *WhoAm 1974*
Berthiaume, Eugene 1881?-1946 *BioIn 1*
Bertin, Francois Edouard 1797-1871 *WebBD*
Bertin, Louis Francois 1766-1841 *WebBD*
Bertin, Louis Francois DeVeaux 1771-1842 *WebBD*
Bertin, Louis Marie Armand 1801-1854 *WebBD*
Bertolini, Mario *NF*
Berton, Pierre 1920- *Au&Wr, BioIn 5,*
  CanWW 1972, CanWr, ConAu 3R, OxCan,
  OxCan Sup, WhoE 1974, WrDr 1976
Berwick, Adrian *BioIn 2*
Berzok, Robert M *OvPC*
Besant, Annie Wood 1847-1933 *Alli Sup, DcLEL,*
  EvLB, LongC, NewC, REn, TwCA,
  TwCA Sup, WebBD, WhoLA
Besas, Peter 1933- *NF*
Beshoar, Michael 1833-1907 *BioIn 10, DcNAA*
Besnard, Pierre *AmRP*
Bess, Demaree Caughey 1893-1962 *BioIn 2,*
  BioIn 4, BioIn 6, CurBio XR, HisAmM XR
Bess, Gordon *NF*
Bessalko, Pavel Karpovich 1880-1920 *BioIn 8*
Besser, Milton 1911-1976 *ConAu 65, ConAu 69,*
  DrAS 74E
Bessie, Simon Michael 1916- *WhoAm 1974,*
  WhoWor 1974
Bessom, Harold E *HisAmM XR*
Bessonette, Colin B *NF*
Best, Carol *BioIn 2*
Best, Gertrude 1869-1947 *BioIn 4*
Best, James A *NF*
Best, James B *HisAmM XR*
Best, Robert Henry 1896-1952 *BioIn 3*
Besterman, Walter M 1903-1974 *BioIn 10*
Bethea, Jack 1892-1928 *DcNAA, WhNAA*
Betocchi, Carlo 1899- *BioIn 10, CasWL,*
  ConAu 9, WorAu
Bettauer, Hugo *NF*
Bettey, Emily Verdery *AmJnl*
Bettleheim, Edward S *HisAmM XR*

Bettman, Iphigene Molony 1884?-1978 *NF*
Betts, Charles Dudley Ames 1920- *WhoAm 1974*
Betts, Charles Henry 1863- *AmLY, WhNAA,*
  WhJnl 1928
Betts, Lillian W *HisAmM XR*
Betz, Betty 1920- *AuBYP, BioIn 1, BioIn 6,*
  BioIn 7, ConAu 1, MorJA
Betz, Fred 1896?- *BioIn 5*
Betzina, Sandra *NF*
Beuick, Marshall D 1891- *WhJnl 1928*
Beumelburg, Werner 1899-1963 *OxGer, WebBD*
Beutel, Bill *BioIn 10*
Beuth, Philip Roy 1932- *WhoAdv 1972,*
  WhoAm 1974, WhoWest 1974
Beuve-Mery, Hubert 1902- *BioIn 8, ForP,*
  IntWW 1976, WhoWor 1974
Bever, Wendell 1917-1971 *BioIn 9*
Beveridge, George D, Jr. *NF*
Bevilacqua, Edward Martin 1920-1968 *BioIn 8*
Beyer, Andrew 1943- *BioIn 9, ConAu 69*
Beyers, Charlotte K *NF*
Beyle, Marie Henri 1783-1842 *BiD&SB, EuAu,*
  EvEuW, NewC, REn
Beyschlag, Carl 1816- *BioIn 2*
Bezencon, Marcel 1907- *IntWW 1976,*
  WhoWor 1974
Bhat, J N *OvPC*
Bhatia, Krishan 1926?-1974 *ConAu 53*
Bhatia, Prem Narain 1911- *IntWW 1976,*
  WhoWor 1974
Bhattacharya, Bhabani 1906- *CasWL,*
  ConAu 5R, ConNov 1972, ConNov 1976,
  DcLEL, IntWW 1976, REn, WebE&AL,
  WrDr 1976
Bhattacharyya, Birendra Kumar 1924-
  IntWW 1976, WhoWor 1974
Bialostotsky, B J 1893-1962 *NF*
Bianchi, Augusto Guido 1868-1951 *BioIn 2*
Biancolli, Louis Leopold 1907- *ConAu 65*
Biasetti, Mario *NF*
Bibaud, Michel 1782-1857 *Alli, BbtC, CanWr,*
  DcNAA, OxCan, OxCan Sup
Bibb, Henry *NF*
Bibb, J D *NF*
Bibb, Porter, III 1937- *ConAu 65*
Bibber, Max *NF*
Bible, Howard Wiswall 1872?-1951 *BioIn 2*
Bice, Max H 1916- *WhoAdv 1972, WhoAm 1974*
Bickel, Karl August 1882-1972 *AmJnl, BioIn 9,*
  NewYTBE 3, WhJnl 1928
Bickers, Dan G 1875- *WhJnl 1928*
Bickerstaff, Isaac 1672-1729 *WebBD*
Bickerstaff, Isaac *see also* Steele, Sir Richard
Bickham, Jack Miles 1930- *AmAu&B,*
  ConAu 7R, WhoAm 1974, WrDr 1976
Bicknell, Thomas Williams 1834-1925 *Alli Sup,*
  AmAu&B, AmLY, BioIn 2, DcAmA,
  DcNAA
Bidault, Georges 1899- *IntWW 1974, WebBD,*
  Who 1974, WhoWor 1974
Biddle, Charles John 1819-1873 *Alli, DcAmA,*
  NatCAB 25
Biddle, Margaret Thompson *HisAmM XR*
Biddle, Nicholas 1786-1844 *Alli, AmAu,*
  AmAu&B, BiD&SB, CyAL 1, DcAmA,
  DcNAA, HisAmM XR, OxAm, REn,
  WebBD
Bidwell, Walter Hilliard 1798-1881 *Alli Sup,*
  AmAu&B, HisAmM XR
Bie, Oscar 1864-1939 *NF*
Biebel, Frederick K, Jr. *OvPC*
Biedermann, Louis, Jr. 1873- *WhJnl Sup*
Biemiller, Ruth Cobbett 1914- *ConAu 37,*
  ForWC 1970, OvPC

Bien, Esther R 1899?-1978 *NF*
Bienstock, Victor Morris 1908- *WhoWorJ 1972*
Bierbauer, Charles *NF*
Bierce, Ambrose Gwinett 1842-1914? *AmAu&B,*
AmJnl, BioIn 1, DcAmB 2, DcNAA,
EncAB, HisAmM XR, LiJA, WebBD
Bierce, Harley *InvJ, NewMr*
Bigart, Homer 1907- *AmJnl, BioIn 2,*
CurBio XR, WhoAm 1974
Bigelow, David *HisAmM XR*
Bigelow, Frederick Southgate 1871-1954 *BioIn 3,*
HisAmM XR, WhNAA, WhJnl Sup
Bigelow, John 1817-1911 *Alli, Alli Sup, AmAu,*
AmAu&B, AmJnl, BbD, BiD&SB, BioIn 1,
BioIn 8, CyAL 2, DcAmA, DcNAA,
HisAmM XR, OxAm, REn, REnAL,
WebBD
Bigelow, Poultney 1855-1954 *AmAu&B, BbD,*
BiD&SB, BioIn 3, DcAmA, DcEnA Ap,
HisAmM XR, WebBD
Bigelow, William Frederick 1879-1966 *BioIn 7,*
HisAmM XR, WhJnl 1928
Bigg, John Stanyan 1828-1865 *Alli, Alli Sup,*
BrAu 19, DcEnL, NewC, WebBD,
WebE&AL
Biggar, Emerson Bristol 1853-1921 *DcNAA*
Biggers, George Clinton 1893- *BioIn 2, BioIn 6,*
BioIn 9
Biggs, Wellington Allen 1923- *WhoAm 1974,*
WhoF&I 1974, WhoS&SW 1973
Bigiaretti, Libero 1906- *ConAu 29*
Biglow, Horatio *AmJnl, HisAmM XR*
Biglow, William 1773-1844 *Alli, AmAu&B,*
CyAL 1, DcAmA, DcNAA
Bigney, Mark Frederick 1817-1886 *Alli Sup,*
AmAu&B, BbtC, BiDSA, DcNAA
Bigney, T O *NF*
Bigote *see* Reyes Mozo, Alberto
Bigsby, Carl M 1898- *WhJnl 1928*
Bihalji-Merin, Oto 1904- *IntWW 1976,*
WhoWor 1974, WhoWorJ 1972
Bikle, Philip Melancthon *HisAmM XR*
Bildersee, Barnett 1911- *OvPC, WhoAm 1974,*
WhoPubR 1972, WhoWorJ 1972
Bilkey, Paul *NF*
Bill, Edward Lyman 1862-1916 *DcNAA,*
NatCAB 12
Bille, Constance *NF*
Biller, David Wolfe 1912?-1966 *BioIn 7*
Billheimer, Thomas C *HisAmM XR*
Billing, Arthur H *NF*
Billinger, Lois *BioIn 3*
Billings, John Shaw 1898-1975 *BioIn 3,*
HisAmM XR, WhJnl 1928
Billings, Josh 1818-1885 *Alli Sup, AmAu,*
AmAu&B, BbD, BiD&SB, CasWL, CnDAL,
DcAmA, DcEnL, DcLEL, DcNAA, EvLB,
OhA&B, OxAm, OxEng, Pen Am, REn,
REnAL
Billings, Josh *see also* Shaw, Henry Wheeler
Billings, Robert *NewMr*
Billings, Victoria *NF*
Billington, Addie S *NF*
Billington, Cecil 1875?-1950 *BioIn 2*
Billington, D *NF*
Billington, Joy 1931- *NF*
Billy, Andre 1882-1971 *CasWL, ConAu 29,*
NewYTBE 2, Pen Eur
Bilsland, Ernest Charles, Jr. 1931- *ConAu 69*
Bimrose, Arthur Sylvanus, Jr. 1912- *WhoAm 1974,*
WhoWest 1974
Bims, Hamilton J *NF*
Binder, Carroll 1896-1956 *BioIn 2, BioIn 3,*
BioIn 4, CurBio XR, WhJnl 1928

Binder, David 1931- *ConAu 65*
Binder, Heinrich 1829- *BioIn 2*
Binder, Otto Oscar 1911-1974 *AuBYP, BioIn 8,*
ConAu 1, ConAu 53
Binet, Satane 1827-1899 *WebBD*
Binet, Satane *see also* Sarcey, Francisque
Bingay, Malcolm Wallace 1884-1953 *BioIn 1,*
BioIn 2, BioIn 3, DcAmB S5, WhJnl 1928
Bingenheimer, Rodney 1946- *BioIn 10*
Bingham, Alfred Mitchell 1905- *AmAu&B,*
AmRP, TwCA, TwCA Sup
Bingham, Barry (1906) *see also* Bingham, George
Barry
Bingham, Barry 1906- *AmJnl, CurBio XR,*
IntMPA 1975, IntWW 1974, WhoAm 1974,
WhoS&SW 1973, WhoWor 1974
Bingham, Barry, Jr. 1934?- *BioIn 2, BioIn 4,*
WhoS&SW 1973
Bingham, Colin William Hugh 1898- *Au&Wr,*
IntWW 1974
Bingham, Frederick d1883 *NF*
Bingham, George Barry 1906- *BioIn 7*
Bingham, George Barry *see also* Bingham, Barry
Bingham, Harry *NF*
Bingham, Mary Caperton 1904- *WhoAm 1974,*
WhoAmW 1974, WhoS&SW 1973
Bingham, Robert 1925- *WhoAm 1974*
Bingham, Robert Worth 1871-1937 *AmJnl,*
BiDSA, BioIn 4, BioIn 7, DcAmB S2,
WebBD, WhJnl 1928
Bingham, Stillman H 1873- *WhJnl 1928*
Binion, Willie Clayte, Jr. 1912- *WhoAm 1974,*
WhoS&SW 1973
Binkley, William Campbell 1889-1970 *AmAu&B,*
BioIn 9
Binkowski, Johannes Aloysius Joseph 1908-
IntWW 1976
Binnart, Martin *ForP*
Binns, Archie 1899-1971 *AmAu&B, AmNov,*
ConAu 73, OxAm, REnAL, TwCA,
TwCA Sup, WebBD, WhoPNW
Binns, John 1772-1860 *Alli, AmAu&B,*
DcAmB 2, DcNAA
Binns, John Robinson 1884-1959 *BioIn 7*
Binsse, Harry Lorin 1905-1971 *BioIn 9*
Bintliff, James 1824-1901 *BioIn 5*
Binyon, Claude 1905- *IntMPA 1975*
Binzen, Peter H *RpN*
Biondi, Shirley 1944- *NF*
Bioren, John *HisAmM XR*
Biossat, Bruce 1910?-1974 *BioIn 10*
Birchall, Frederick Thomas 1868?-1955 *AmJnl,*
BioIn 3, DcAmB S5
Birchansky, Leo 1887-1949 *BioIn 1*
Bird, Albert A *HisAmM XR*
Bird, Cyril Kenneth 1887-1965 *BioIn 1, BioIn 2,*
BioIn 3, ConAu P-1, LongC, WhoLA
Bird, Dillard E *BioIn 2*
Bird, E B *HisAmM XR*
Bird, Eric Leslie 1894-1965 *BioIn 7*
Bird, Frederic Mayer 1838-1908 *Alli Sup,*
AmAu&B, DcAmA, DcNAA, HisAmM XR
Bird, George Lloyd 1900- *AmM&W 73S,*
Au&Wr, ConAu 5R, IndAu 1917,
WhoAm 1974, WhoWor 1974
Bird, Hobart Stanley 1873-1960 *BioIn 5*
Bird, J *HisAmM XR*
Bird, J Malcolm *HisAmM XR*
Bird, John Alexander 1910- *WhoAm 1974*
Bird, Milton *HisAmM XR*
Bird, Robert Montgomery 1806-1854 *Alli, AmAu,*
AmAu&B, AmJnl, BiD&SB, CasWL,
CnDAL, CnThe, CyAL 2, CyWA, DcAmA,
DcBiA, DcEnL, DcLEL, DcNAA, EvLB,

HisAmM XR, McGWD, OxAm, Pen Am,
REn, REnAL, REnWD
Bird, Robert Stewart 1904-1970 *BioIn 8,*
NewYTBE 1
Bird, William 1889-1963 *BioIn 6, WhNAA,*
WhJnl 1928
Bird, William A *HisAmM XR*
Birdfeather, Barbara 1940- *BioIn 10*
Birdsall, Ruth *BioIn 2*
Birdsall, Timothy 1936?-1963 *BioIn 6*
Birdsong, Henry Ellis 1887- *BioIn 4, WhJnl 1928*
Birdwell, Russell 1903-1977 *CurBio XR, OvPC,*
WhoWest 1974
Birge, Benjamin *HisAmM XR*
Birke, Helen Morse *WhoAm 1974,*
WhoAmW 1974
Birke, William David 1911-1963 *BioIn 6*
Birmingham, Ernest F *HisAmM XR*
Birmingham, Frederic Alexander 1911?-
AmAu&B, BioIn 5, ConAu 17R,
WhoAm 1974
Birmingham, Lloyd *NF*
Birnbaum, Jesse *NF*
Birnbaum, Stephen *NF*
Birney, James Gillespie 1792-1857 *AmJnl, BbD,*
BiD&SB, BiDSA, DcAmA, DcNAA,
HisAmM XR, OxAm, WebBD
Birnie, William Alfred Hart 1910- *BioIn 3,*
CurBio XR, HisAmM XR, WhoAm 1974
Birns, Jack *OvPC*
Birrell, August *HisAmM XR*
Birsh, Arthur Thomas 1932- *WhoAm 1974*
Bisbee, Frank A *HisAmM XR*
Bisbee, Frederick Adelbert 1855-1923 *DcNAA,*
HisAmM XR
Bisco, Jack *BioIn 1*
Bisco, John *HisAmM XR*
Bisher, James Furman 1918- *ConAu 5R,*
WhoAm 1974, WhoS&SW 1973
Bishop, Barry *OvPC*
Bishop, Bob *NF*
Bishop, Carolyn Benkert 1939- *ForWC 1970,*
WhoAm 1974, WhoAmW 1974
Bishop, Freeman C *NF*
Bishop, Gerry *NF*
Bishop, Henry O 1875-1954 *BioIn 3*
Bishop, James Alonzo 1907- *AmAu&B,*
AuNews 1, BioIn 3, BioIn 4, BioIn 8,
BioNews 1974, ConAu 19R, CurBio XR
Bishop, John *HisAmM XR*
Bishop, Joseph Bucklin 1847-1928 *AmLY,*
DcAmA, DcNAA, HisAmM XR, WebBD,
WhNAA
Bishop, Leslie G 1908- *BioIn 1, CanNov*
Bishop, Robert Lee 1931- *ConAu 15R,*
DrAS 74E
Bishop, Stanley W 1878- *WhJnl 1928*
Bishop, Warren *NF*
Bishop, William D W 1889- *WhJnl 1928*
Bisland, Elizabeth 1862?-1929 *AmAu&B, BbD,*
BiD&SB, DcAmA, DcNAA, HisAmM XR
Bisland, Elizabeth *see also* Wetmore, Elizabeth
Bisland
Bisque, Anatole *see* Bosquet, Alain
Bissell, Charles Overman 1908- *WhoAm 1974,*
WhoS&SW 1973
Bissell, Jerry *OvPC*
Bissell, Phil 1926- *WhoAm 1974,*
WhoAmA 1973
Bisson, T A *AmRP*
Bitner, Henry M 1883-1960 *BioIn 2, BioIn 6*
Bittel, Lester Robert 1918- *ConAu 15, OvPC*
Bittencourt, Mrs. Paulo *ForP*
Bittencourt, Paulo 1895?-1963 *BioIn 6*

Bittinger, John L 1833- *NatCAB 1*
Bittner, A H *HisAmM XR*
Bivins, Joseph Francis *HisAmM XR*
Bixby, Ammi Leander 1856-1934 *AmLY,*
DcNAA, NatCAB 13, WhNAA
Bixby, Edson K 1887- *WhJnl 1928*
Bixby, George Stephenson 1861-1937 *DcNAA*
Bixby, Tams 1855-1921 *NatCAB 19*
Bixby, Tams, III 1918- *WhoS&SW 1973*
Bixler, Norma 1905- *ConAu 49*
Bixler, Paul Howard 1899- *BiDrLUS, BioIn 10,*
ConAu 69
Bizet, Jacques 1872-1922 *BioIn 8*
Bjerre, Jens 1921- *Au&Wr, ConAu 11R*
Bjorkman, Carol 1930?-1967 *BioIn 8*
Bjorkman, Edwin August 1866-1951 *AmAu&B,*
ConAmL, TwCA, TwCA Sup, WebBD,
WhNAA, WhJnl 1928
Bjornson, Bjornstjerne Martinius 1832-1910 *AtlBL,*
BbD, BiD&SB, CasWL, ClDMEL, CnMD,
CnThe, CyWA, DcBiA, DcEuL, EuAu,
EvEuW, HisAmM XR, LongC, McGWD,
ModWD, Pen Eur, REn, REnWD, WebBD
Bjornsson, Andres 1883-1916 *BioIn 2*
Black, Alexander 1859-1940 *Alli Sup, AmLY,*
CurBio XR, DcAmA, DcNAA, REnAL
Black, Brady Forrest 1908- *WhoAm 1974*
Black, Charles Lloyd 1922- *OvPC,*
WhoPubR 1972
Black, Christine M *NF*
Black, Creed Carter 1925- *ConAu 73,*
WhoAm 1974, WhoWor 1974
Black, Fischer Sheffey 1911- *BioIn 1,*
WhoAm 1974, WhoF&I 1974,
WhoS&SW 1973
Black, Frank 1894- *NF*
Black, Gary 1914- *BioIn 4*
Black, Harry C 1887-1956 *BioIn 4*
Black, John 1783-1855 *Alli, BiDLA, DcEnL,*
NewC
Black, John R d1880 *Alli Sup, ForP*
Black, Norman David 1887-1944 *BioIn 4*
Black, Robert Gordon 1929- *OvPC,*
WhoPubR 1972
Black, Roe Coddington 1926- *WhoAm 1974,*
WhoE 1974
Black, Roger *NF*
Black, Ruby Aurora 1896- *WhNAA, WhJnl 1928*
Black, Van-Lear *AmJnl*
Black, William 1841-1898 *Alli Sup, BbD,*
BiD&SB, BrAu 19, CasWL, DcBiA,
DcEnA, DcEnA Ap, DcEnL, DcLEL, EvLB,
HisAmM XR, HsB&A, NewC, OxEng,
WebBD
Black, William E *NF*
Black, Winifred 1869-1936 *AmJnl, BioIn 8,*
HisAmM XR, WhNAA
Black, Winifred *see also* Bonfils, Winifred Black
Blackburn, Arthur S d1935 *NF*
Blackburn, Bob *NF*
Blackburn, Henry 1830-1897 *Alli Sup, DcEnL*
Blackburn, Henry 1930- *NF*
Blackburn, John *NewMr*
Blackburn, Josiah 1823-1890 *NF*
Blackburn, Victoria Grace d1928 *BioIn 1,*
CanNov
Blackburn, Victoria Grace *see also* Fan-Fan
Blackburn, W E 1862- *WhJnl 1928*
Blackburn, Walter J d1920 *NF*
Blackburn, Walter Juxon 1914- *CanWW 1972*
Blackburn, William F 1916- *WhoAm 1974,*
WhoF&I 1974
Blackford, William Matthews 1801-1864 *BioIn 2,*
NatCAB 34

Blasingame, M D *NF*
Blatchford, Christie 1951- *ConAu 73*
Blatchford, Nicholas 1919- *WhoAm 1974,*
   WhoS&SW 1973
Blatt, John Frederick, Jr. 1900- *WhJnl 1928*
Blaushild, Babette 1927- *ConAu 29*
Blauss, John Lincoln 1865- *WhJnl 1928*
Blauvelt, Lee *NF*
Bledsoe, Albert Taylor 1809-1877 *Alli Sup,*
   AmAu, AmAu&B, BiD&SB, BiDSA,
   DcAmA, DcEnL, DcNAA, HisAmM XR,
   LiJA, OhA&B
Bleeker, Ann Eliza *HisAmM XR*
Bleeker, Anthony *HisAmM XR*
Bleiberg, Robert Marvin 1924- *WhoAm 1974,*
   WhoF&I 1974
Bless, Bertha 1889-1977 *NF*
Blessing, Gerald F *WhJnl 1928*
Blethen, Alden J 1846-1915 *NatCAB 17*
Blethen, Clarance Brettun 1879-1941 *BioIn 3*
Blethen, William Kingsley 1913-1967 *BioIn 7*
Blevins, Don *NF*
Blevins, Winfred 1938- *ConAu 45*
Blew, William Charles Arlington 1848- *Alli Sup,*
   BioIn 2, Br&AmS
Blewett, Jean 1862-1934 *DcLEL, DcNAA,*
   OxCan
Bley, Lou *OvPC*
Bleyer, Willard Grosvenor 1873-1935 *AmJnl,*
   AmLY, BioIn 5, DcAmB S1, DcNAA,
   ForP, WhNAA, WhJnl 1928
Blickensderfer, Joseph Patrick 1894-1960 *BioIn 5*
Blind, Karl *HisAmM XR*
Blinder, Abe Lionel 1909- *WhoAm 1974*
Blinkhorn, Thomas Ambrose 1936?- *NF*
Blinn, Johna *NF*
Bliss, Burton Thurston 1900- *WhJnl 1928*
Bliss, Charles H *HisAmM XR*
Bliss, Edward, Jr. 1912- *ConAu 41*
Bliss, Edward Munsell *HisAmM XR*
Bliss, George William 1918-1978 *InvJ,*
   WhoAm 1974
Bliss, Harriet *HisAmM XR*
Bliss, Harry Hayner 1871-1937 *BioIn 5*
Bliss, Howard Festes 1844-1919 *BioIn 5*
Bliss, Porter Cornelius 1838-1885 *Alli Sup,*
   DcAmA, DcAmB 2
Bliss, William Dwight Porter 1856-1926 *AmRP,*
   BiD&SB, DcAmA, DcNAA, HisAmM XR
Bliss, William T 1865- *WhJnl 1928*
Blitzer, Wolf I *NF*
Bliven, Bruce 1889-1977 *AmAu&B, Au&Wr,*
   AuBYP, BioIn 4, BioIn 8, ConAu 37,
   ConAu 69, CurBio XR, HisAmM XR,
   IntWW 1976, TwCA, TwCA Sup, WebBD,
   Who 1974, WhoAm 1974, WhJnl 1928,
   WhoWest 1974, WrDr 1976
Bliven, Bruce, Jr. 1916- *ConAu 19R, SmATA 2,*
   WhoAm 1974
Bliven, Naomi 1925- *ConAu 33, WhoAm 1974,*
   WhoAmW 1974
Blizzard, William C 1916- *NF*
Bloc, Andre 1896-1966 *BioIn 7, BioIn 8*
Blochman, Lawrence Goldtree 1900-1975 *BioIn 10,*
   ConAu 19, ConAu 53, EncMys, OvPC,
   WhNAA, WhoWorJ 1972, WrDr 1976
Block, Alex Ben *NF*
Block, Eugene B 1890- *ConAu 7R,*
   WhoWorJ 1972
Block, Gwendoline 1906-1956 *BioIn 4*
Block, Hal *OvPC*
Block, Herbert Lawrence 1909- *AmAu&B,*
   BioIn 1, BioIn 2, BioIn 3, BioIn 4, BioIn 5,
   BioIn 6, BioIn 9, CurBio XR, EncAB,

   WebBD, WhoAm 1974, WhoS&SW 1973,
   WhoWor 1974
Block, Jean Libman *ConAu 5, OvPC*
Block, Jerome W. *OvPC*
Block, Julian 1934- *NF*
Block, Lewis J *HisAmM XR*
Block, Marguerite 1889- *BioIn 4*
Block, Paul 1877-1941 *AmJnl, CurBio XR,*
   DcAmB S3
Block, Paul, Jr. 1911- *AmM&W 73P,*
   WhoAm 1974, WhoMW 1974
Block, Rudolph 1870-1940 *AmJnl, CurBio XR,*
   DcNAA
Block, Rudolph *see also* Lessing, Bruno
Block, Sharon *NF*
Block, Victor *NF*
Block, William 1915- *WhoAm 1974*
Blodgett, L *NF*
Blodgett, Richard 1940- *ConAu 49*
Blodgett, Thomas Harper *HisAmM XR*
Bloe, W C *HisAmM XR*
Bloede, Gustav 1814- *BioIn 2*
Bloeth, William B 1912?-1974 *BioIn 10*
Blondell, Joseph A 1889- *WhJnl 1928*
Blood, Clifford C 1888- *WhJnl 1928*
Blood, James H *HisAmM XR*
Bloodgood, John D 1931- *AmArch 1970*
Bloom, Lynn *OvPC*
Bloom, Lynn William 1882- *WhNAA,*
   WhJnl 1928
Bloom, Marshall *NF*
Bloom, Murray Teigh 1916- *BioIn 8, ConAu 19,*
   WhoAm 1974, WhoE 1974, WrDr 1976
Bloomer, Amelia Jenks 1818-1894 *DcAmA,*
   OxAm, REnAL, WebBD
Bloomer, Harvey M *HisAmM XR*
Bloomer, John Wellman 1912- *WhoAm 1974,*
   WhoS&SW 1973
Bloomer, Millard J 1870?-1949 *BioIn 2*
Bloomer, William J *HisAmM XR*
Bloomfield, Arthur John 1931- *ConAu 65,*
   WhoWest 1974
Bloomfield, Maurice 1855-1928 *DcNAA,*
   HisAmM XR, WhNAA
Bloomington, J S *HisAmM XR*
Blos, Wilhelm 1849-1927 *WebBD*
Blossom, Sumner Newton 1892- *AmAu&B,*
   HisAmM XR, WhJnl 1928
Blough, J A 1872- *WhJnl 1928*
Blount, Jonathan 1945- *WhoAm 1974*
Blow, Katharine Cooke 1896?-1965 *BioIn 7*
Blowitz, Henri Georges S A Opper De 1825-1903
   BioIn 6, BioIn 7, BioIn 10, ForP
Blue, Archibald 1840-1914 *BioIn 1*
Blue, E N *HisAmM XR*
Blum, Daniel 1900-1965 *BiE&WWA, BioIn 7*
Blum, Emil *HisAmM XR*
Blum, Ernest 1836-1907 *BiD&SB, WebBD*
Blum, Ethel Widlus 1921- *WhoAmW 1974,*
   WhoS&SW 1973
Blum, Sam *NF*
Blumberg, Leon J 1900?-1965 *BioIn 7*
Blumberg, Myrna 1932- *Au&Wr, ConAu 23R*
Blumberg, Nathan Bernard 1922- *Au&Wr,*
   BioIn 4, DrAS 74E, WhoAm 1974
Blumenberg, Marc A *HisAmM XR*
Blumenfeld, Harold 1908- *BioIn 6,*
   WhoWorJ 1972
Blumenfeld, Ralph David 1864-1948 *BioIn 1,*
   BioIn 5, LongC, Lor&LP, WhoLA
Blumenfeld, Yorick 1932- *ConAu 25*
Blumer, Herbert 1900- *HisAmM XR,*
   WhoAm 1974, WhoWor 1974
Blumley, Andrew *BioIn 8*

Blunden, Godfrey 1906- *BioIn 1*
Blunk, Frank M 1897?-1976 *ConAu 69*
Bly, Nellie 1867-1922 *AmAu, AmAu&B,
   CnDAL, DcNAA, OxAm, REn, REnAL,
   WebBD*
Bly, Nellie *see also* Cochrane, Elizabeth
Bly, Nellie *see also* Seaman, Elizabeth Cochrane
Blystone, Richard *NF*
Blyth, Alan 1929- *ConAu 49, WhoMus 1972*
Blyth, Henry 1910- *ConAu 21R, IntMPA 1975*
Blyth, Jeffrey 1926- *ConAu 65*
Blythe, LeGette 1900- *AmAu&B, BioIn 3,
   ConAu 3R*
Blythe, LeGette *see also* Blythe, William LeGette
Blythe, Samuel George 1868-1947 *AmAu&B,
   BioIn 1, DcNAA, HisAmM XR, REnAL*
Blythe, Stuart Oakes 1890- *AmAu&B,
   HisAmM XR*
Blythe, William LeGette 1900- *WhoAm 1974*
Blythe, William LeGette *see also* Blythe, LeGette
Blyton, William Joseph 1887-1944 *BioIn 1,
   CathA 1930*
Boaden, James 1762-1839 *Alli, BiDLA, DcEnL,
   NewC, WebBD*
Boal, Samuel Jeffrey 1913-1964 *BioIn 1, BioIn 7*
Boardman, E H *HisAmM XR*
Boardman, Kathryn *WhoAmW 1974*
Boardman, Samuel Lane 1836-1914 *Alli Sup,
   DcNAA*
Boardman, Thomas Leslie 1919- *WhoAm 1974*
Boas, Louis A 1900- *WhJnl 1928*
Boatner, Verne 1932- *WhoAm 1974*
Bobbe, Dorothie DeBear 1905-1975 *ConAu 57,
   SmATA 1*
Bobrow, Robert *NF*
Bocca, Geoffrey 1923- *BioIn 3, BioIn 7*
Boccasile, Gino 1900?-1952 *BioIn 2*
Bock, Eugene Reeves 1905- *WhJnl 1928*
Bock, Harold I 1939- *ConAu 29, SmATA 10*
Boddie, William W *OvPC*
Boddy, Elias Manchester 1891- *AmJnl, BioIn 2,
   BioIn 3, BioIn 6, BioIn 7*
Bode, Richard *NF*
Bode, Roy E 1948- *NF*
Bode, Vaughn 1941- *BioIn 10*
Bodenwein, Theodore 1864-1939 *NF*
Bodin, Thomas C *OvPC*
Bodine, Aldine Aubrey 1906-1970 *BioIn 10*
Bodmer, C H *HisAmM XR*
Bodmer, Johann Jakob 1698-1783 *BiD&SB,
   CasWL, DcEuL, EuAu, EvEuW, OxGer,
   Pen Eur, REn, WebBD*
Bodsworth, Fred 1918- *Au&Wr, ConAu 1R,
   ConNov 1972, ConNov 1976, OxCan,
   OxCan Sup, WrDr 1976*
Bodwell, J C *HisAmM XR*
Boehm, Richard 1888- *WhJnl 1928*
Boehringer, Cora Louise *BioIn 1*
Boelio, Robert C *NF*
Boenisch, Peter H 1927- *IntWW 1976*
Boenzi, Neal *NF*
Boerhaave, Hermann 1668-1738 *BioIn 10*
Boeschenstein, Charles 1862-1952 *BioIn 2*
Boesen, Victor 1908- *ConAu 37, IndAu 1917,
   OvPC*
Boeth, Richard *NF*
Boettiger, Anna Dall 1906- *BioIn 1, BioIn 7*
Boettiger, John 1900- *BioIn 1, BioIn 2*
Bogan, Louise 1897-1970 *AmAu&B, AuBYP,
   CnDAL, CnE&AP, ConAmA, ConAu 25,
   ConAu 73, ConLC 4, ConP 1970, DcLEL,
   EncWL, HisAmM XR, ModAL,
   ModAL Sup, NewYTBE 1, OxAm, Pen Am,
   RAdv 1, REn, REnAL, SixAP, TwCA,*

TwCA Sup, TwCW, WebBD
Bogardus, A *HisAmM XR*
Bogart, Florence S *WhJnl Sup*
Bogart, John B *AmJnl*
Bogart, Leo 1921- *AmM&W 73S, ConAu 41,
   OvPC, WhoE 1974*
Bogart, William Henry 1810-1888 *Alli Sup,
   AmAu&B, BiD&SB, Br&AmS, DcAmA,
   DcNAA*
Bogen, Ludwig 1810-1886 *BioIn 2*
Bogert, J A *HisAmM XR*
Boggs, Edward B *HisAmM XR*
Bogin, Benjamin 1900- *WhoAm 1974*
Bogran, Edmond *ForP*
Bogunovic, Branko 1920?- *BioIn 8*
Boguslav, David 1897?-1962 *BioIn 6*
Bohannan, John *OvPC*
Bohen, Fred *HisAmM XR*
Bohle, Bruce William 1918- *ConAu 21R,
   WhoAm 1974*
Bohn, Charles *HisAmM XR*
Bohn, Frank 1878-1975 *ConAu 57, OhA&B*
Bohn, William Edward 1877-1967 *BioIn 8*
Boileau, Albert D *AmJnl*
Boissevain, Natasha *HisAmM XR*
Boissonneault, Glen Alvin 1917- *WhoAm 1974*
Bok, Cary William 1905-1970 *AmJnl, ConAu 29,
   WhoE 1974*
Bok, Edward William 1863-1930 *Alli Sup,
   AmAu&B, AmJnl, BiD&SB, BioIn 1,
   BioIn 5, BioIn 6, BioIn 7, BioIn 8, BioIn 9,
   DcAmA, DcAmB S1, DcLEL, DcNAA,
   EncAB, HisAmM XR, OxAm, REn,
   REnAL, TwCA, TwCA Sup, WebBD,
   WhNAA, WhJnl 1928*
Bokum, Branko 1920- *BioIn 9*
Bokum, Fanny Butcher 1888- *ConAu 37*
Bokum, Fanny Butcher *see also* Butcher, Fanny
Bolam, Sylvester 1905?-1953 *BioIn 3, Lor&LP*
Bolce, Harold *HisAmM XR*
Boldizsar, Ivan 1912- *IntWW 1976,
   WhoWor 1974*
Boldt, Herbert M *NF*
Bolen, Lin L 1941- *WhoAm 1974*
Bolens, Harry Wilbur 1864-1944 *BioIn 5*
Boley, Forest Irving 1925- *BioIn 9*
Bolger, James F 1904- *WhJnl 1928*
Bolger, William M 1891?-1949 *BioIn 1*
Bolin, Luis 1894-1969 *BioIn 8, ConAu 23*
Bolintineanu, Dimitrie 1819-1872 *BiD&SB,
   CasWL, EvEuW, WebBD*
Bolitho, William 1891?-1930 *DcLEL,
   HisAmM XR, LongC, NewC, TwCA,
   WebBD*
Boll, Erwin *OvPC*
Bollen, Rog *NF*
Bolles, A S *HisAmM XR*
Bolles, Blair 1911- *AmAu&B, ConAu 9R,
   WrDr 1976*
Bolles, Donald F 1928-1976 *ConAu 65,
   ConAu 73, InvJ*
Bolles, Frank 1856-1894 *AmAu&B, BiD&SB,
   DcAmA, DcNAA*
Bolles, Frederick Duntn *NF*
Bolles, Stephen 1872-1941 *BioIn 5, CurBio XR,
   WhJnl 1928*
Bolles, William E *HisAmM XR*
Bologna, Sando *NF*
Bolser, Claude M 1891?- *WhJnl 1928*
Bolte, Gisela *NF*
Boltinoff, Henry *NF*
Bolton, Edwin L d1971 *NF*
Bolton, Kenneth 1914- *ConAu 9R*
Bolton, Lemuel D 1898-1926 *WhJnl Sup*

Bolton, Nathaniel 1803-1858 *BioIn 2,*
IndAu 1816
Bolton, Whitney 1900-1969 *BiE&WWA, BioIn 2,*
BioIn 8, ConAu 25
Boltwood, Edward 1870-1924 *DcNAA*
Bolwell, Ted *NF*
Bomar, Edward Earle 1897-1953 *BioIn 3*
Bombeck, Erma 1927- *AuNews 1, BioIn 8,*
BioIn 9, ConAu 23
Bomberger, Christian Martin Hess 1884-1950
BioIn 2, BioIn 5, WhNAA, WhJnl 1928
Bona, Frederick E 1939- *OvPC, WhoPubR 1972*
Bonafede, Dominic D *RpN*
Bonalumi, Arthur W 1905- *WhJnl 1928*
Bonar, Andrew *Alli Sup*
Bond, Alice Dixon *AmAu&B*
Bond, Anna *NF*
Bond, Benjamin F *AmJnl*
Bond, Dorothy Ann *AmAu&B, WhoAmW 1974,*
WhoMW 1974
Bond, Frank Fraser 1891-1965 *BioIn 7,*
WhJnl 1928
Bond, Mary Fanning Wickham 1898- *ConAu 23R,*
WrDr 1976
Bond, Merritt 1886- *WhJnl 1928*
Bond, Thomas Emerson 1782-1856 *BiDSA,*
DcNAA, HisAmM XR, NatCAB 11
Bondonno, Pauline *NF*
Bondurant, William *NF*
Bone, James 1872-1962 *BioIn 1, LongC*
Bone, John Herbert Aloysius 1830-1906 *Alli Sup,*
OhA&B
Bone, John Rainsford 1877- *WhJnl 1928*
Bone, Scott Cardelle 1860-1936 *AmJnl, DcNAA,*
IndAu 1917
Boner, John Henry 1845-1903 *Alli Sup, AmAu,*
AmAu&B, BiD&SB, BiDSA, BioIn 3,
CnDAL, DcAmA, DcNAA
Bonesteel, Chesley *HisAmM XR*
Bonetti, Pedro *NF*
Bonfante, Jordan *NF*
Bonfils, Charles Alden 1871-1955 *BioIn 6,*
NatCAB 45
Bonfils, Frederick Gilmer 1860-1933 *AmJnl,*
BioIn 2, DcAmB S1, NatCAB 27
Bonfils, Frederick W 1894-1958 *NatCAB 49*
Bonfils, Helen G 1889-1972 *BioIn 9, NewYTBE 3*
Bonfils, Winifred Black 1869-1936 *AmJnl,*
WhNAA
Bonfils, Winifred Black *see also* Black, Winifred
Bonham, Howard Bryan 1900- *WhoAm 1974*
Bonnard, Lucien *NF*
Bonner, Amy 1891-1955 *BioIn 5*
Bonner, Griffith 1885- *WhJnl 1928*
Bonner, John 1828-1899 *Alli, BbtC, CyAL 2,*
DcNAA, HisAmM XR, NatCAB 12
Bonner, Robert 1824-1899 *AmAu&B, AmJnl,*
BioIn 3, BioIn 5, HisAmM XR, LiJA
Bonner, Robert E *HisAmM XR*
Bonner, Robert Elliott 1938- *DrAS 74H*
Bonnet, Theodore Firmin 1865-1920 *DcNAA,*
HisAmM XR
Bonney, Mabel Therese 1897-1978 *ConAu 73,*
CurBio XR, HisAmM XR, OvPC
Bonnier, Tor *ForP*
Bonnin, Gertrude 1875-1914 *BioIn 10*
Bonsal, Stephen 1865-1951 *AmAu&B, AmJnl,*
BiD&SB, BiDSA, BioIn 1, CurBio XR,
DcAmA, DcAmB S5, FamWC,
HisAmM XR, OxAm, REnAL, TwCA Sup,
WebBD
Bonsall, Henry L 1834- *NatCAB 4*
Bonventre, Peter *NF*
Bonython, Sir John Langdon 1848-1939 *BioIn 2*

Bonython, Sir Lavington 1875-1960 *BioIn 5*
Boody, Shirley Bright *NF*
Booker, Edna Lee *CurBio XR*
Booker, Graham *NF*
Booker, Simeon Saunders 1918- *BioIn 10,*
ConAu 11R, LivBAA, RpN
Bookhout, Raymond G 1883- *WhJnl 1928*
Bookman, George *BioIn 3*
Bookman, George Baruch 1914- *OvPC,*
WhoAm 1974, WhoWor 1974
Bookman, W F *WhJnl 1928*
Bookspan, Martin 1926- *ConAu 41, WhoE 1974,*
WhoWorJ 1972
Boone, Buford *see* Boone, James Buford
Boone, Ivy *WhJnl 1928*
Boone, James Buford 1909- *WhoAm 1974*
Boone, Perley Howell 1887?-1948 *BioIn 1*
Boone, Richard Gause 1849-1923 *DcAmA,*
DcNAA, HisAmM XR, IndAu 1816,
OhA&B
Boorstein, Regula S *NF*
Boorstin, David *NF*
Booth, Alice Lynn *NF*
Booth, Charles Asa 1840-1913 *BioIn 5*
Booth, Edmund Wood 1866- *AmJnl, WhJnl Sup*
Booth, Edward Townsend *NF*
Booth, Ernest *HisAmM XR*
Booth, George Francis 1870-1955 *BioIn 4*
Booth, George Gough 1864-1949 *AmJnl, BioIn 1,*
BioIn 2, BioIn 7, WhJnl 1928
Booth, John Erlanger 1919- *BiE&WWA,*
ConAu 9R
Booth, John Lord *WhoAm 1974*
Booth, John N *OvPC*
Booth, John Nicholls 1912- *WhoAm 1974,*
WhoWor 1974
Booth, Mary Louise 1831-1889 *Alli Sup,*
AmAu&B, BiD&SB, BioIn 4, CyAL 2,
DcAmA, DcNAA, HisAmM XR
Booth, Ralph Harman 1873-1931 *AmJnl, BioIn 1*
Booth, Sherman Miller 1812-1904 *BioIn 5*
Booth, Warren Scripps 1894- *BioIn 5,*
WhoAm 1974, WhJnl 1928
Booth, Windsor Peyton 1912- *WhoAm 1974*
Boothe, Clare 1903- *AmAu&B, BiE&WWA,*
CurBio XR, IntWW 1974, LongC, McGWD,
ModWD, OxAm, REnAL, TwCA,
TwCA Sup, WebBD, Who 1974,
WhoAm 1974, WhoAmW 1974,
WhoWor 1974
Boothe, Clare *see also* Luce, Claire Boothe
Boothe, Clare *see also* Luce, Clare Boothe
Boothroyd, Basil 1910- *Au&Wr, ConAu 33,*
WrDr 1976
Borah, Leo Arthur 1889- *HisAmM XR,*
WhNAA, WhJnl 1928
Boraisho, Menakhem 1889-1949 *NF*
Borbee, Jack 1891- *WhJnl 1928*
Borchgrave, Arnaud De *NF*
Borcover, Alfred S *NF*
Borda, Carlos J Villar *NF*
Bordages, Asa *NF*
Borden, Gail, Jr. 1801-1874 *AmJnl, WebBD*
Borden, Thomas H *AmJnl*
Borders, William 1939- *NF*
Bordner, Robert *RpN*
Borg, Donald Gowen 1906- *WhoAm 1974,*
WhoE 1974
Borg, Flora Austin 1908?-1971 *BioIn 9,*
NewYTBE 2
Borg, John 1883-1956 *BioIn 4*
Borg, Malcolm Austin 1938- *BioIn 9,*
WhoAm 1974, WhoE 1974
Borgen, Chris 1933?- *BlkC*

Borgese, Giuseppe Antonio 1882-1952 *BioIn 1,*
   CasWL, ClDMEL, EncWL, Pen Eur, REn,
   TwCA, TwCA Sup, WebBD
Borglund, William Holt 1912- *WhoAm 1974*
Borgstedt, Douglas 1911- *WhoAm 1974,*
   WhoE 1974
Borgstedt, Jean *NF*
Borie, A J *HisAmM XR*
Boring, Edwin Garrigues 1886-1968 *AmAu&B,*
   ConAu 1, CurBio XR, WhNAA
Boring, Wayne *BioIn 3*
Boris, Joseph J *WhNAA, WhJnl 1928*
Borkenau, Franz 1900- *BioIn 3*
Borland, Hal 1900-1978 *AmAu&B, Au&Wr,*
   BioIn 6, ConAu 4R, REnAL, SmATA 5,
   WhoAm 1974, WhoWor 1974, WorAu
Borland, Harold Glen *see* Borland, Hal
Borland, James Brown 1861-1939 *DcNAA,*
   WhJnl 1928
Borne, Ludwig 1786-1837 *BbD, BiD&SB,*
   BioIn 3, CasWL, DcEuL, EvEuW, OxGer,
   REn, WebBD
Bornn, Jose, Jr. 1892- *WhJnl 1928*
Bornstein, Heinrich 1805-1892 *BioIn 2*
Bornstein, Joseph 1900?-1952 *BioIn 3*
Bornstein, Sam 1913- *WhoAm 1974, WhoE 1974*
Boroson, Warren 1935- *ConAu 23R*
Borovsky, Havel 1821-1856 *DcEuL, WebBD*
Borovsky, Havel *see also* Havlicek, Karel
Borowiec, Andrew C *NF*
Borowsky, Irvin J 1924- *WhoAdv 1972,*
   WhoE 1974
Borsa, Mario 1870-1952 *BioIn 3*
Borsky, Franklin *OvPC*
Borst, Raymond I 1894?-1969 *BioIn 8*
Borth, Christian C 1895?-1976 *ConAu 65*
Borthwick, Algernon *see* Glenesk, Lord
Borthwick, Oliver 1873?-1905 *NF*
Borthwick, Peter 1804-1852 *NF*
Bosanquet, Theodora 1887?-1961 *BioIn 9*
Bosch, Patricia *NF*
Bosdan, J J 1880- *WhJnl 1928*
Bosette, Skip *NF*
Boshier, Brian J 1883- *WhJnl Sup*
Boskovic, Boris *NF*
Bosquet, Alain 1919- *ConAu 13R, IntWW 1974,*
   OxCan, OxCan Sup, WhoWor 1974
Boss, Benjamin 1880-1970 *HisAmM XR,*
   NewYTBE 1
Boss, Lewis 1846-1912 *HisAmM XR, WebBD*
Boss, R P *NF*
Bosshard, Theodore 1876- *WhJnl 1928*
Bosshard, Walter 1892- *BioIn 10*
Bossu, Regis *NF*
Bostick, Benjamin S *NF*
Bostwick, Arthur Elmore 1860-1942 *AmAu&B,*
   AmLY, CurBio XR, DcAmB S3, DcNAA,
   HisAmM XR, WhNAA
Bostwick, Arthur S 1902- *WhJnl 1928*
Boswell, Peyton 1879-1936 *AmAu&B*
Boswell, Peyton 1904-1950 *BioIn 2*
Bosworth, J Allan *AuBYP, BioIn 8*
Bothwell, Angela *NF*
Bothwick, J D *HisAmM XR*
Botkin, Benjamin Albert 1901-1975 *AmAu&B,*
   Au&Wr, ConAu 57, ConAu P-1, DrAS 74E,
   REnAL, TwCA Sup, WhoAm 1974,
   WhoWorJ 1972
Botsford, Harry 1890?- *BioIn 4*
Bottel, Helen 1914- *BioIn 4, ConAu 25,*
   WhoAmW 1974, WrDr 1976
Botter, David E, Jr. *RpN*
Botthof, Walter *WhJnl 1928*
Bottolfsen, Clarence A 1891- *BioIn 3*

Bottom, Raymond Blanton 1893-1953 *BioIn 3*
Bottome, Margaret 1827-1906 *AmAu&B,*
   DcNAA, HisAmM XR
Bottomley, Horatio William 1860-1933 *BioIn 2,*
   BioIn 4, BioIn 9, BioIn 10, LongC, WebBD
Bottorff, Robert Ingram 1907-1978 *WhoAm 1974*
Botwin, Carol *OvPC*
Boubat, Edouard 1923- *BioIn 10*
Bouchard, Lucille *NF*
Boucher, Anthony 1911-1968 *AmAu&B,*
   CurBio XR, EncMys, TwCA Sup
Boucher, Anthony *see also* White, William Anthony
   Parker
Boughan, John P 1860?-1948 *BioIn 1*
Boughner, Genevieve Jackson 1884- *WhJnl 1928*
Boughton, VanTuyl 1888- *BioIn 4*
Boultwood, George *NF*
Bourassa, Henri 1868-1952 *AmLY, BioIn 8,*
   CanWr, OxCan, WebBD
Bourchier, James David 1920- *BioIn 7*
Bourdet, Claude 1909- *IntWW 1976,*
   WhoWor 1974
Bourdier, James Aaron 1929- *WhoAm 1974*
Bourdin, Henri 1882?-1949 *BioIn 2*
Bourdon, David 1934- *ConAu 37*
Bourgault, Pierre 1935?- *BioIn 8*
Bourgholtzer, Frank 1919- *BioIn 4, ConAu 25,*
   WhoWest 1974
Bourinot, Sir John George 1837-1902 *Alli Sup,*
   BbtC, BrAu 19, DcNAA, OxCan, WebBD
Bourjaily, Monte Ferris 1894- *AmAu&B, BioIn 1,*
   HisAmM XR, WhoAm 1974
Bourke, John T 1858- *WhJnl 1928*
Bourke-White, Margaret 1906-1971 *AmAu&B,*
   AmJnl, ConAu 15, ConAu 29, ConAu P-1,
   CurBio XR, HisAmM XR, NewYTBE 2,
   REn, REnAL, WebBD
Bourne, Edward Gaylord 1860-1908 *Alli Sup,*
   AmAu, DcAmA, DcNAA, HisAmM XR
Bourne, Henry Eldridge 1862-1946 *AmAu&B,*
   AmLY, HisAmM XR
Bourne, Randolph Silliman 1886-1918 *AmAu&B,*
   AmRP, AmWr, CasWL, CnDAL, DcLEL,
   DcNAA, EncAB, HisAmM XR, ModAL,
   OxAm, Pen Am, REn, REnAL, TwCA,
   TwCA Sup, WebE&AL
Bourne, St Clair 1943?- *BioIn 7*
Bourne, William C 1899?-1957 *BioIn 4*
Bouslog, Raymond W 1899- *WhJnl 1928*
Boussac, Marcel 1889- *NewYTBE 2, Who 1974,*
   WhoWor 1974, ForP
Boutell, Clarence Burley 1908- *AmAu&B,*
   BioIn 1, CurBio XR, WhoAm 1974
Boutelle, Charles Addison 1839-1901 *DcAmB 2*
Boutelle, DeWitt Clinton *HisAmM XR*
Bouton, John Bell 1830-1902 *Alli Sup, AmAu,*
   AmAu&B, BiD&SB, DcAmA, DcNAA,
   OhA&B
Bouton, S Miles *NF*
Boutwell, William Dow *BioIn 6*
Bouve, Pauline Carrington d1928 *DcAmA,*
   DcNAA
Bova, Benjamin William 1932- *WhoAm 1974,*
   WhoE 1974
Bovard, Oliver Kirby 1872-1945 *AmJnl, BioIn 3,*
   DcAmB S3, NatCAB 35
Bowden, H L *HisAmM XR*
Bowden, Jesse Earle 1928- *WhoAm 1974*
Bowditch, Henry Pickering 1840-1911 *BiDPara,*
   DcNAA, WebBD
Bowdoin, William Goodrich 1860-1947 *AmAu&B,*
   AmLY, DcAmA, DcNAA, WhNAA,
   WhJnl 1928
Bowell, Sir Mackenzie 1823-1917 *OxCan, WebBD*

Bowen, Abel 1790-1850 *AmAu&B, DcNAA,*
EarABI, EarABI Sup, HisAmM XR
Bowen, Charles *HisAmM XR*
Bowen, Charles W *HisAmM XR*
Bowen, Croswell 1905-1971 *BioIn 9, BioIn 10,*
ConAu 33, NewYTBE 2
Bowen, Francis 1811-1890 *Alli, Alli Sup, AmAu,*
AmAu&B, CyAL 2, DcAmA, DcEnL,
DcNAA, HisAmM XR, LiJA, WebBD
Bowen, Henry Chandler 1813- *HisAmM XR,*
NatCAB 1
Bowen, John Eliot 1858-1890 *Alli Sup, DcAmA,*
DcNAA
Bowen, Joshua David 1930- *AuBYP, BioIn 8*
Bowen, Lewis H 1939- *OvPC, WhoCon 1973*
Bowen, Robert A 1899?-1958 *BioIn 5*
Bowen, Robert Sidney 1900-1977 *AuBYP,*
BioIn 8, ConAu 69, ConAu 73
Bowen, T P *HisAmM XR*
Bowen, William Abraham 1856-1921 *AmLY,*
DcNAA
Bowen, William Henry 1836-1915 *DcNAA,*
HisAmM XR
Bowen, William S *NF*
Bower, Helen Carolyn 1896-1964 *NF*
Bower, John Keely 1877- *WhJnl 1928*
Bower, Richard John 1917- *WhoAm 1974*
Bower, Warren 1898- *DrAS 74E, IndAu 1917*
Bowers, Arthur *NF*
Bowers, Carolyn 1948?- *BlkC*
Bowers, Claude Gernade 1878-1958 *AmAu&B,*
CurBio XR, EncAB, HisAmM XR,
IndAu 1816, OxAm, REn, REnAL, TwCA,
TwCA Sup, WebBD, WhJnl 1928
Bowers, Nathan Abbott 1886- *BioIn 2*
Bowker, Frank C 1878- *WhJnl 1928*
Bowker, Richard Rogers 1848-1933 *Alli Sup,*
AmAu&B, BbD, BiD&SB, BioIn 2, BioIn 3,
DcAmA, DcAmB S1, DcNAA,
HisAmM XR, NatCAB 12, WebBD,
WhNAA
Bowkett, Gerald Edson 1926- *WhoAm 1974*
Bowler, Duane Wilson 1917- *WhoAm 1974,*
WhoWest 1974
Bowler, Leo *NF*
Bowler, Mae N *OvPC*
Bowles, Billy *NF*
Bowles, Heloise 1919-1977 *WhoAmW 1974,*
WhoE 1974
Bowles, Heloise see also Cruse, Heloise Bowles
Bowles, Heloise see also Reese, Heloise
Bowles, Jay C *OvPC*
Bowles, Leonard C *HisAmM XR*
Bowles, Pete *NF*
Bowles, Samuel, II 1797-1851 *AmAu&B, AmJnl,*
HisAmM XR, NatCAB 1, REnAL, WebBD
Bowles, Samuel, III 1826-1878 *Alli Sup,*
AmAu&B, AmJnl, BbD, BbtC, BiD&SB,
BioIn 3, BioIn 6, BioIn 8, DcAmA,
DcNAA, EncAB, NatCAB 1, OxAm,
REnAL, WebBD
Bowles, Samuel, IV 1851-1915 *AmAu&B, AmJnl,*
BioIn 5, NatCAB 1, WebBD
Bowles, Sherman Hoar 1890-1952 *AmJnl, BioIn 3*
Bowles, Thomas Gibson 1842- *BioIn 7*
Bowman, Charles Arthur 1883- *BioIn 7,*
OxCan Sup, WhJnl 1928
Bowman, Cynthia *NF*
Bowman, Elizabeth C *NF*
Bowman, George E 1903- *WhJnl 1928*
Bowman, George Ernest 1860-1941 *CurBio XR,*
HisAmM XR
Bowman, Harold 1904- *WhJnl 1928*
Bowman, James Henry 1931- *WhoAm 1974*

Bowman, La Barbara *NF*
Bowman, Lowry 1926?- *BioIn 7*
Bowman, Norman Howard 1919- *WhoAm 1974*
Bowman, Robert T 1910- *ConAu 73*
Bowman, Waldo G 1900- *BioIn 6*
Bowman, Will W 1901- *WhJnl 1928*
Bowman, Willard E 1890- *WhJnl 1928*
Bowman, William Stacey 1897- *WhJnl 1928*
Bowne, Borden Parker *HisAmM XR*
Bowser, Betty Ann 1944- *ForWC 1970,*
WhoAmW 1974
Bowser, Hallowell *NF*
Bowser, J D 1846- *BioIn 8*
Bowsfield, Colvin Cullen 1855-1940 *DcNAA*
Boyack, James E, Jr. *OvPC*
Boyarsky, Benjamin William 1934- *WhoAm 1974*
Boyarsky, Benjamin William see also Boyarsky, Bill
Boyarsky, Bill 1934- *ConAu 25*
Boyarsky, Bill see also Boyarsky, Benjamin William
Boyce, Frank M, Jr. 1879- *WhJnl 1928*
Boyce, Joseph N *NF*
Boyce, R H *NF*
Boyce, William Dickson 1860-1923 *DcNAA,*
HisAmM XR
Boyd, Andrew 1920- *ConAu 1R*
Boyd, Barbara *AmAu&B, WhNAA*
Boyd, Brendan *NF*
Boyd, Crosby Noyes 1903- *WhoAm 1974,*
WhoS&SW 1973, WhoWor 1974
Boyd, Elmer Beattie 1880-1955 *BioIn 3,*
WhJnl 1928
Boyd, Ernest 1887-1946 *HisAmM XR, WebBD*
Boyd, Harry Edwin 1904- *BioIn 1, WhoAm 1974*
Boyd, Hugh Newell 1911- *WhoAm 1974*
Boyd, J Andrew 1855- *WhJnl 1928*
Boyd, J Francis 1910- *ConAu 7R, ForP*
Boyd, James *NewMr*
Boyd, James 1888-1944 *AmAu&B, CnDAL,*
ConAmA, ConAmL, CurBio XR, CyWA,
DcAmB S3, DcLEL, DcNAA, LongC,
OxAm, Pen Am, REnAL, TwCA,
TwCA Sup, WebBD, WhNAA
Boyd, John *BioIn 7*
Boyd, John 1864-1933 *DcNAA*
Boyd, L M *NF*
Boyd, Robert *BioIn 2*
Boyd, Robert Hamilton 1891- *WhJnl Sup*
Boyd, Robert S 1928- *ConAu 15, InvJ,*
WhoAm 1974
Boyd, Robert Stewart 1908- *WhoAm 1974,*
WhoE 1974
Boyd, Robert Wright, Jr. 1911- *WhoAm 1974*
Boyd, Rosalyn *NF*
Boyd, Rutherford 1883?-1951 *BioIn 2*
Boyd, Thomas Alexander 1898-1935 *AmAu&B,*
ConAmA, ConAmL, DcAmB S1, DcLEL,
DcNAA, LongC, OhA&B, OxAm, REnAL,
TwCA, WebBD, WhNAA
Boyd, William *HisAmM XR*
Boyd, William Kenneth 1879-1938 *BiDSA,*
DcNAA, HisAmM XR
Boyden, Albert Augustus *HisAmM XR*
Boyden, Eddie 1882- *WhJnl 1928*
Boyer, Brian D 1939- *ConAu 45*
Boyer, Dwight 1912- *ConAu 65, WhoMW 1974*
Boyer, Edward J *NF*
Boyer, Helena M *NF*
Boyer, J Monroe 1873- *WhJnl 1928*
Boyer, Norman *HisAmM XR*
Boyer, Richard *AmRP*
Boyett, Don *NF*
Boykin, Elizabeth Macrae 1903- *WhoAmW 1974*
Boylan, Hoyt F 1882- *WhJnl 1928*
Boylan, James 1927- *ConAu 4R*

Boyle, Frederick 1841- *Alli Sup, FamWC*
Boyle, Hal 1911-1974 *NewYTBS 5*
Boyle, Hal *see also* Boyle, Harold Vincent
Boyle, Harold Vincent 1911-1974 *AmJnl, BioIn 4, BioIn 8, CurBio XR, HisAmM XR, WhoAm 1974, WhoWor 1974*
Boyle, Harold Vincent *see also* Boyle, Hal
Boyle, Harry Joseph 1915- *BioIn 10, CanWW 1972, ConAu 13*
Boyle, Jack *EncMys*
Boyle, James 1853-1939 *DcNAA, OhA&B*
Boyle, John 1855-1936 *WhJnl 1928*
Boyle, Joseph M *NF*
Boyle, P C *NF*
Boyle, Robert H 1928- *ConAu 19R*
Boyle, Samuel 1920- *WhoAm 1974, WhoE 1974*
Boyle, Vilas J *OvPC*
Boynton, Henry VanNess 1835-1905 *Alli Sup, DcAmA, DcNAA, HisAmM XR, OhA&B*
Boynton, Henry Walcott 1869-1947 *AmAu&B, AmLY, BioIn 1, DcAmA, DcNAA, HisAmM XR, REnAL, WebBD, WhNAA*
Boyo, Gene *OvPC*
Boys, Samuel Evan 1871-1966 *IndAu 1917, WhJnl 1928*
Braaten, David G *NF*
Bracco, Roberto 1861?-1943 *CasWL, CIDMEL, CnThe, CurBio XR, EncWL, McGWD, ModWD, REnWD, WebBD*
Brace, Irvine A *NF*
Brace, John Pierce 1793-1872 *Alli, AmAu&B, BioIn 4, DcAmA, DcNAA*
Bracken, Sir Brendan 1901-1958 *CurBio XR, WebBD*
Bracken, James Lucas 1913- *WhoAm 1974, WhoF&I 1974, WhoWest 1974*
Bracken, Thomas 1843-1898 *Alli Sup, PoIre*
Bracken, Thomas 1876-1959 *BioIn 5*
Brackenbury, Harry *FamWC*
Brackenridge, Hugh Henry 1748-1816 *Alli, AmAu, AmAu&B, AmJnl, BiD&SB, BiDSA, CasWL, CnDAL, CyAL 1, CyWA, DcAmA, DcLEL, DcNAA, HisAmM XR, OxAm, OxEng, Pen Am, REn, REnAL, WebE&AL*
Bracker, Milton 1909-1964 *BioIn 2*
Brackman, Arnold C 1923- *Au&Wr, AuNews 1, ConAu 5, OvPC*
Brackman, Henrietta 1917- *ForWC 1970, OvPC*
Bradbrooke, Joan *BioIn 8*
Braddon, Russell 1921- *BioIn 5*
Bradee, Richard W *NF*
Braden, Anne McCarty 1924- *AmAu&B, BioIn 8, WhoAmW 1974*
Braden, Charles Samuel 1887- *AmAu&B, ConAu 5, WhNAA*
Braden, Frank Wilson 1885?-1962 *BioIn 6*
Braden, Thomas Wardell 1918- *BioIn 8, NewMr, WhoAm 1974*
Braden, William 1930- *ConAu 23R*
Bradfield, Harriet 1898?-1953 *BioIn 3*
Bradford, Alden 1765-1843 *Alli, AmAu&B, BiD&SB, DcAmA, DcNAA*
Bradford, Amory Howe 1846-1911 *Alli Sup, AmAu&B, DcAmA, DcNAA, HisAmM XR*
Bradford, Amory Towe 1912- *BioIn 8*
Bradford, Andrew 1686-1742 *AmAu&B, AmJnl, HisAmM XR, NatCAB 19, REn, WebBD*
Bradford, Anna Mae 1871- *WhJnl 1928*
Bradford, Barbara Taylor 1933- *ForWC 1970*
Bradford, Charles Barker 1862-1917 *DcNAA*
Bradford, Christina *NF*
Bradford, Cornelia Smith d1755 *NF*
Bradford, Edward A 1851- *WhJnl 1928*
Bradford, Fielding *AmJnl*

Bradford, James *WhJnl 1928*
Bradford, James M *AmJnl*
Bradford, John 1749-1830 *AmAu&B, AmJnl, DcNAA, NatCAB 1, OxAm*
Bradford, Joseph 1843-1886 *AmAu, AmAu&B, BiD&SB, BiDSA, DcAmA, DcAmB 2, DcNAA*
Bradford, Roark 1896-1948 *AmAu&B, AmSCAP 1966, CnDAL, DcAmB S4, DcNAA, LongC, OxAm, REn, REnAL, TwCA, TwCA Sup, WebBD*
Bradford, Thomas 1745-1838 *AmAu&B, AmJnl, HisAmM XR, WebBD*
Bradford, William 1663-1752 *AmAu&B, AmJnl, OxAm, REnAL, WebBD*
Bradford, William, III 1722-1791 *AmAu&B, AmJnl, HisAmM XR, OxAm, REnAL, WebBD*
Bradlaugh, Charles 1833-1891 *Alli Sup, HisAmM XR, OxEng, REn*
Bradlee, Benjamin Crowninshield 1921- *AuNews 2, BioIn 3, ConAu 61, CurBio XR, ForP, NewMr, WhoAm 1974, WhoS&SW 1973, WhoWor 1974*
Bradlee, Frederic *NF*
Bradley, Alice 1875-1946 *HisAmM XR, WhNA/*
Bradley, Andrew F *NF*
Bradley, David Rall 1917- *WhoAdv 1972, WhoAm 1974*
Bradley, Ed *NF*
Bradley, Edward Sculley 1897- *AmAu&B, WhNAA, WhoAm 1974*
Bradley, George A 1898- *WhJnl 1928*
Bradley, Harold W 1929?- *BioIn 7*
Bradley, Hassell 1930- *ConAu 65*
Bradley, Henry D 1893- *WhoAm 1974, WhJnl 1928*
Bradley, Horace *HisAmM XR*
Bradley, Hugh 1900-1964 *BioIn 6*
Bradley, Ina *OvPC*
Bradley, Jack *NF*
Bradley, John A 1895?-1974 *BioIn 10*
Bradley, LaVerne *HisAmM XR*
Bradley, Luther D *NF*
Bradley, Marvin P *NF*
Bradley, Van Allen 1913- *AmAu&B, ConAu 37, WhoAm 1974, WhoMW 1974*
Bradley, Will H 1868-1962 *AmAu&B, HisAmM XR*
Bradley, William Aspenwall 1878-1939 *AmAu&B, AmLY, DcNAA, HisAmM XR*
Bradner, C C d1940 *NF*
Bradnick, Jean A *OvPC*
Bradshaw, Henry E *NF*
Bradshaw, Herbert Clarence 1908- *BioIn 2, WhoS&SW 1973*
Bradshaw, John *NF*
Bradshaw, Leslie Havergal 1892- *AmAu&B, WhNAA*
Bradshaw, Vera Foss *NF*
Bradsher, Henry St. Amant 1932?- *NF*
Bradwell, Baron Thomas E N Driberg 1905-1976 *IntWW 1976*
Bradwell, Baron Thomas E N Driberg *see also* Driberg, Thomas E N
Brady, Albert *HisAmM XR*
Brady, Frank 1934- *ConAu 61*
Brady, George Lewis 1905- *WhJnl 1928*
Brady, James 1928- *BioIn 9, CelR 1973*
Brady, Jane Ellen 1941?- *BioIn 7*
Brady, Joe *NF*
Brady, John 1942- *ConAu 65*
Brady, Kathleen *NF*
Brady, Mathew B 1823?-1896 *AmAu&B, EncAB,*

HisAmM XR, OxAm, REn, REnAL,
WebBD
Brady, Mildred 1906?-1965 BioIn 7
Brady, Phil NF
Brady, Raymond John OvPC, WhoAm 1974
Brady, Terence d1878 NF
Brady, Thomas Francis 1915?-1972 BioIn 9,
  BioIn 10, NewYTBE 3
Brady, William 1880-1972 BioIn 9
Braestrup, Angelica NF
Braestrup, Peter RpN
Braga, Jane Gray OvPC
Braga, Ruben 1913- IntWW 1976
Bragdon, E L NF
Bragdon, Joseph H 1887- WhJnl 1928
Brague, L Harry 1912-1968 BioIn 8
Braibanti, Ralph HisAmM XR
Brailsford, Henry Noel 1873-1958 BioIn 10,
  LongC, NewC, TwCA, TwCA Sup, WebBD
Brainard, Clinton T 1865-1935 AmJnl
Brainard, John Gardiner Calkins 1796-1828 Alli,
  AmAu, AmAu&B, BiD&SB, CyAL 1,
  DcAmA, DcEnL, DcLEL, DcNAA,
  HisAmM XR, OxAm, REnAL, WebBD
Brainerd, Chauncey Corey 1874-1922 DcNAA
Brainerd, Erastus 1855-1922 AmAu&B, DcNAA
Brainerd, Gretchen S NF
Brainerd, Thomas 1804-1866 Alli Sup, DcNAA,
  HisAmM XR, OhA&B
Brainin, Joseph 1896?-1970 BioIn 8,
  NewYTBE 1, WhNAA
Braithwaite, Dennis NF
Braken, Bishop NF
Braley, Berton 1882-1966 AmAu&B,
  AnMV 1926, BioIn 7, HisAmM XR, WisWr
Braley, Russell NF
Braman, Harold Pier 1901- WhJnl 1928
Brams, Stanley Howard 1910- ConAu 11R
Bramson, Betty NF
Bramstedt, Alvin Oscar 1917- WhoAdv 1972,
  WhoAm 1974, WhoAmP 1973
Branch, Edward Douglas 1905- AmAu&B
Branch, Harllee 1879?-1967 BioIn 7
Branch, Taylor NF
Brand, Joel 1906-1964 BioIn 7
Brand, Max 1892-1944 AmAu&B, CurBio XR,
  DcLEL, DcNAA, EncMys, LongC, REn,
  REnAL, TwCA, TwCA Sup
Brand, Max see also Faust, Frederick
Brand, Stewart 1938- AuNews 1, BioIn 8,
  WhoAm 1974
Brande, Dorothea Thompson 1893-1948 AmAu&B,
  BioIn 1, WebBD
Brandeberry, Carl NF
Brandel, Max OvPC
Brandenburg, Oscar Dalzella 1858-1930 BioIn 5
Brandes, Carl Edvard Cohen 1847-1931 CasWL,
  WebBD
Brandes, Georg Morris Cohen 1842-1927 BbD,
  BiD&SB, CasWL, CIDMEL, DcEuL,
  EncWL, EvEuW, HisAmM XR, LongC,
  OxGer, Pen Eur, REn, TwCA, TwCA Sup,
  TwCW, WebBD
Brandis, Werner N OvPC
Brandl, Alois HisAmM XR
Brandle, Lowell S RpN
Brandon, Albert Duff 1885- WhJnl 1928
Brandon, B S, Jr. NF
Brandon, Dorothy 1899?-1977 ConAu 69
Brandon, Gerald NF
Brandon, Henry Oscar 1916- BioIn 8, ConAu 49,
  ForP, IntWW 1976, WhoAm 1974
Brandreth, Gyles 1948- BioIn 9, ConAu 65,

WrDr 1976
Brandt, Albert HisAmM XR
Brandt, Bert AmJnl
Brandt, Erdmann Neumister 1890?-1966 BioIn 7,
  HisAmM XR
Brandt, Frank Erwin 1869- WhNAA,
  WhJnl 1928
Brandt, Henry J 1896?-1956 BioIn 4
Brandt, Joseph August 1899- AmAu&B,
  IndAu 1917, WhNAA
Brandt, Lillian HisAmM XR
Brandt, Nat NF
Brandt, Raymond Peter 1896-1974 BioIn 2,
  NewYTBS 5, WhoAm 1974, WhJnl 1928
Brandt, William E 1891?-1963 BioIn 6
Brandwein, Peter 1910-1956 BioIn 4
Brandys, Marian 1912- ConAu 57,
  WhoWor 1974
Branigan, Alan NF
Branigin, William NF
Brann, William Cowper 1855-1898 AmAu,
  AmAu&B, BioIn 4, BioIn 5, DcAmB S1,
  DcNAA, HisAmM XR, OxAm, REnAL,
  WebBD
Brannan, Dana 1884-1965 BioIn 7
Brannan, Samuel 1819-1889 WebBD
Branner, Martin Michael 1888-1970 BioIn 8,
  NewYTBE 1
Branner, Robert 1927-1973 BioIn 10,
  NewYTBE 4, WhoAm 1974, WhoAmA 1973
Brannigan, Bill 1936- ConAu 65
Brannigan, Bill see also Brannigan, William A
Brannigan, William A 1936- OvPC
Brannigan, William A see also Brannigan, Bill
Brannon, Hazel BioIn 1
Brannon, William T 1906- ConAu 15,
  ConAu P-1, OvPC, WrDr 1976
Branscomb, Harvey HisAmM XR
Branscome, James InvJ
Bransford, Audie NF
Branstetter, Otto F AmRP
Branstetter, Winnie AmRP
Brant, Irving Newton 1885-1976 AmAu&B,
  BioIn 2, ConAu 9R, ConAu 69, REnAL,
  TwCA Sup, WhoAm 1974
Brantley, Rabun Lee LiJA
Branyan, James 1918?-1949 BioIn 2
Branzburg, Paul Marshal 1941- ConAu 73
Bras, Harry L 1862- WhJnl 1928
Brasch, Walter Milton 1945- ConAu 57,
  DrAS 74F
Brasher, Christopher William 1928- ConAu 7R,
  WrDr 1976
Brastow, Virginia 1872?-1952 BioIn 2
Braucher, Howard S 1881-1949 BioIn 1
Braudy, Susan Orr 1941- ConAu 65,
  ForWC 1970
Brauff, Herbert Davenport 1891-1955 BioIn 3,
  WhJnl 1928
Braun, Arthur E 1876-1976 ConAu 69
Braun, Heinrich 1854-1927 WebBD
Braun, Lev 1913- ConAu 41, OvPC
Braun, Ruth NF
Braun, Will C HisAmM XR
Braunthal, Julius 1889?- ConAu 23,
  WhoWorJ 1972
Braverman, Harry 1920-1976 ConAu 53,
  ConAu 69
Braverman, Robert Paul 1929- WhoAm 1974
Brawley, E M 1851- BioIn 8
Brawley, Paul Leroy 1942- BiDrLUS, ConAu 73
Bray, Frank Chapin 1866-1949 AmAu&B,
  BioIn 1, DcNAA, HisAmM XR, OhA&B
Bray, Howard NewMr

Bray, James L 1894- *WhJnl 1928*
Bray, James M *HisAmM XR*
Bray, Ralph G 1897- *WhJnl 1928*
Brayley, Arthur Wellington 1863-1919 *DcNAA,*
HisAmM XR
Brayman, Harold 1900- *ConAu 23, ConAu 73,*
WhoAm 1974, WhoE 1974, WhoF&I 1974,
WhoPubR 1972
Brayman, J O *HisAmM XR*
Brayman, Mason 1813-1895 *BioIn 7, DcNAA*
Brayton, Aaron Martin 1872-1949 *BioIn 5*
Brayton, Arthur H 1891- *WhJnl 1928*
Brazaitis, Thomas J 1940- *NF*
Brazelton, Ethel M C *WhNAA, WhJnl 1928*
Brazelton, Ethel M C *see also* Colson, Ethel M
Brazier, Donald G *RpN*
Brazier, Edward Carl 1885- *WhJnl 1928*
Brazier, Marion Howard 1850-1925 *DcNAA,*
WhNAA
Brea, Mary *AmRP*
Breadnell, W L *HisAmM XR*
Bready, James Ely 1880- *WhJnl 1928*
Brean, Herbert 1907-1973 *BioIn 9, ConAu 41,*
EncMys, WhoE 1974, WorAu
Brearley, Harry Chase 1870-1940 *DcNAA*
Brearley, William Henry 1846-1909 *AmJnl,*
DcAmA, DcNAA
Breathnach, Sarah Ban *NF*
Breck, Joseph *HisAmM XR*
Breck, Robert L *HisAmM XR*
Breckinridge, Desha 1867-1935 *DcAmB S1,*
WhJnl 1928
Breckinridge, Robert Jefferson 1800-1871 *BiD&SB,*
BiDSA, DcAmA, DcNAA, HisAmM XR
Brede, William J 1887-1968 *BioIn 8*
Bredemeier, Kenneth H *NF*
Breece, Edward J 1896- *WhJnl 1928*
Breed, Jack *HisAmM XR*
Breed, Joseph B *HisAmM XR*
Breede, Adam 1879-1928 *DcNAA, WhJnl 1928*
Breen, Dan *NF*
Breen, Joseph I 1890-1965 *CurBio XR*
Breese, Frank *OvPC*
Breger, David 1908?-1970 *AmJnl, BioIn 8*
Bregg, Peter *NF*
Bregman, Adolph 1890- *WhNAA, WhJnl 1928*
Brehm, George *HisAmM XR*
Breig, Joseph Anthony 1905- *BioIn 4, BkC 6,*
CathA 1952, ConAu 5R
Breisky, William J 1928- *ConAu 53*
Breit, Harvey 1913-1968 *BiE&WWA, BioIn 8,*
ConAu 5R, ConAu 25, WorAu
Breitman, George 1916- *AmRP, ConAu 61*
Breitmeyer, Eleanor Amelia 1926- *ForWC 1970,*
WhoAm 1974, WhoAmW 1974
Brekkan, Friorik Asmundsson 1888- *BioIn 1*
Brelis, Dean 1924- *ConAu 11R, RpN*
Brem, Ralph *WhoE 1974*
Bremer, Gerald John 1904-1965 *BioIn 9*
Bremner, Archibald 1849-1901 *DcNAA*
Bremner, Malcolm d1910 *NF*
Bremner, Robert Gunn 1873-1914 *NF*
Brenan, Gerald 1894- *BioIn 6, ConAu 1, LongC,*
TwCA Sup, Who 1974, WrDr 1976
Brennan, Francis Edwin 1910- *BioIn 1,*
WhoAm 1974, WhoAmA 1973,
WhoWor 1974
Brennan, Frederick Hazlitt 1901-1962 *AmAu&B,*
BioIn 6, HisAmM XR, WebBD
Brennan, J F *HisAmM XR*
Brennan, James *NF*
Brennan, Jay *OvPC*
Brennan, John *NF*
Brennan, Joseph 1913- *IntWW 1974,*

WhoWor 1974
Brennan, Kathleen *NF*
Brennan, Philip J 1914?-1977 *NF*
Brennan, Ray 1908?-1972 *BioIn 9, ConAu 37,*
NewYTBE 3
Brennan, Richard P *NF*
Brennan, Wallace A 1896?-1967 *BioIn 8*
Brennecke, Ernest 1896-1969 *BioIn 10*
Brenner, Anita 1905-1974 *AnCL, ConAu 49,*
ConAu 53, NewYTBS 5, TexWr
Brenner, Bernard *NF*
Brenner, Leah 1915- *ForWC 1970, OvPC*
Brenner, Marie 1949- *ConAu 73*
Brenon, Aileen St. John *NF*
Brent, Henry Johnson 1811-1880 *Alli Sup,*
AmAu&B, BiDSA, DcAmA, DcNAA
Brentano, Lorenz 1813-1891 *BioIn 2, DcAmB 3*
Brentano, Lowell 1895-1950 *AmAu&B, BioIn 2,*
REnAL
Brenton, Myron *NF*
Bresette, James Edward 1945- *WhoAm 1974*
Breslauer, Bernard 1901?-1950 *BioIn 2*
Breslin, Edward 1926- *BioIn 1*
Breslin, Jimmy 1930- *AmAu&B, AuNews 1,*
BioIn 10, CelR 1973, ConAu 73, ConLC 4,
CurBio XR, NewMr, WhoAm 1974,
WhoE 1974, WhoWor 1974, WrDr 1976
Bressler, Harry S 1893- *WhJnl 1928*
Brethauer, Otto 1830-1882 *BioIn 2*
Breton, Andre 1896-1966 *AtlBL, CasWL,*
CIDMEL, ConAu 19, ConAu 25, ConLC 2,
EncWL, EvEuW, LongC, ModRL, ModWD,
OxFr, Pen Eur, RComWL, REn, REnWD,
TwCA Sup, TwCW, WebBD, WhoTwCL
Bretscher, Willy 1897- *IntWW 1976,*
WhoWor 1974
Brett, Carl *NF*
Brett-Smith, Richard 1923- *Au&Wr, ConAu 21R*
Brevik, J Albert 1920- *WhoAm 1974*
Brewer, Carson *InvJ*
Brewer, Fredric *OvPC*
Brewer, Jim *NF*
Brewer, Sam Pope 1909?-1976 *ConAu 65, OvPC*
Brewer, W Harrison *OvPC*
Brewer, William Miles 1889-1970 *BioIn 9*
Brewster, Charles Warren 1812-1868 *Alli Sup,*
DcAmA, DcNAA
Brewster, Eugene Valentine 1871-1939 *AmAu&B,*
DcNAA
Brewster, Frederick R *OvPC*
Brewster, Harold Pomeroy 1831-1906 *DcNAA,*
OhA&B
Briand, Aristide 1862-1932 *WebBD*
Brice, John A 1876-1946 *BioIn 2*
Brickell, Henry Herschel 1889-1952 *AmAu&B,*
DcAmB S5
Brickell, Henry Herschel *see also* Brickell, Herschel
Brickell, Herschel 1889-1952 *BioIn 2,*
HisAmM XR
Brickell, Herschel *see also* Brickell, Henry Herschel
Brickell, William D 1852- *NatCAB 1*
Brickhill, Paul Chester Jerome 1916- *Au&Wr,*
ConAu 11R, EvLB, TwCW, Who 1974
Brickhouse, John B 1916- *WhoAm 1974*
Brickley, Terry *NF*
Bricklin, Mark *NF*
Brickman, Arthur *NF*
Brickman, Morrie 1917- *BioIn 6, WhoAm 1974*
Bridenthal, Cyrus W 1884- *WhJnl 1928*
Bridge, Don 1894- *WhJnl 1928*
Bridge, James Howard 1856-1939 *AmAu&B,*
DcAmA, DcNAA, HisAmM XR, LiJA
Bridge, Nancy A *NF*
Bridge, Peter J 1936?- *BioIn 10*

Bridgeman, L H *HisAmM XR*
Bridges, Albert Fletcher 1853-1926 *BioIn 2,*
 IndAu 1816
Bridges, Herb *NF*
Bridges, Robert 1858-1941 *AmAu&B, AmLY,*
 BbD, BiD&SB, CurBio XR, DcAmA,
 DcNAA, HisAmM XR, WhNAA,
 WhJnl 1928
Bridges, Thomas A 1941- *NF*
Bridgman, Henry *HisAmM XR*
Bridgman, Herbert Lawrence 1844-1924 *DcNAA,*
 NatCAB 22, WebBD
Bridgman, Raymond Landon 1848-1925 *Alli Sup,*
 DcNAA
Bridgwater, William 1908-1966 *BioIn 7*
Bridle, Augustus 1869-1952 *CanNov, OxCan*
Brien, Alan 1925- *BioIn 7, WhoThe 1972*
Brier, Howard Maxwell 1903-1969 *AuBYP,*
 ConAu 13, ConAu P-1, CurBio XR, MorJA,
 SmATA 8, WhoPNW
Brier, Royce 1894-1975 *AmAu&B,*
 WhoAm 1974, WhoWest 1974
Brier, Warren Judson 1931- *ConAu 25,*
 DrAS 74E, LEduc 1974, WhoAm 1974,
 WhoWest 1974
Brieux, Eugene 1858-1932 *CasWL, ClDMEL,*
 CnMD, CnThe, EvEuW, LongC, McGWD,
 ModWD, NewC, OxEng, OxFr, Pen Eur,
 REn, REnWD, TwCA, TwCA Sup, WebBD
Briffault, Robert *HisAmM XR*
Briggs, Charles Augustus 1841-1913 *HisAmM XR*
Briggs, Charles Frederick 1804-1877 *Alli,*
 Alli Sup, AmAu, AmAu&B, BbD, BiD&SB,
 CyAL 2, DcAmA, DcAmB 3, DcEnL,
 DcNAA, HisAmM XR, LiJA, OxAm,
 REnAL
Briggs, Clare A 1875-1930 *DcAmB S1, WebBD*
Briggs, Emily Pomona Edson 1830-1910 *DcNAA*
Briggs, Frank Parks 1894- *BioIn 5,*
 WhoAm 1974, WhoAmP 1973
Briggs, Fred 1932- *ConAu 73*
Briggs, Henry Franco *Alli Sup*
Briggs, John Gurney, Jr. 1916- *WhoAm 1974*
Briggs, Kenneth Arthur 1941- *WhoAm 1974*
Briggs, Robert *HisAmM XR*
Briggs, Walter Ladd 1919- *ConAu 69,*
 WhoWest 1974
Briggs, Wenike Opurum 1918- *IntWW 1976*
Brigham, Amariah 1798-1849 *Alli, DcAmA,*
 DcNAA, WebBD
Brigham, Charles D 1819-1894 *NatCAB 9*
Brigham, Clarence Saunders 1877-1963 *AmAu&B,*
 CurBio XR, WhNAA
Brigham, Gertrude Richardson *AmAu&B,*
 AmLY, WhNAA
Brigham, Herbert O 1875- *WhJnl 1928*
Brigham, James H *HisAmM XR*
Brigham, Johnson 1846-1936 *AmLY, DcNAA,*
 HisAmM XR
Brigham, William E 1865- *WhJnl 1928*
Bright, Edward 1808-1894 *HisAmM XR*
Bright, F E W 1879- *WhJnl 1928*
Bright-Sagnier, Barbara *NF*
Bright-Sagnier, Thierry *see* Sagnier, Thierry
Brightbill, Dorothy *NF*
Brightbill, R A *NF*
Brightman, Samuel Charles 1911- *WhoAmP 1973,*
 WhoPubR 1972
Briles, Ernest Austin 1892- *WhJnl 1928*
Brill, Steve *NF*
Brilliant, Ashleigh 1933- *ConAu 65*
Brilliant, Moshe *NF*
Brin, Herb 1915- *ConAu 49*

Brinckerhoff, Drew Quackenbus 1921- *WhoAm 1974*
Brindel, Paul 1895- *OvPC, WhoWest 1974*
Brindle, Jeff *InvJ*
Brine, Ruth *NF*
Brinegar, David Franklin 1910- *WhoAm 1974,*
 WhoWest 1974
Brines, Russell 1911- *ConAu 69*
Briney, Nancy 1911- *BioIn 3, CurBio XR*
Bringmark, Gosta *ForP*
Brininstool, Earl Alonzo 1870-1957 *AmAu&B,*
 WhNAA
Brinitzer, Carl 1907-1974 *ConAu 7R, ConAu 53*
Brink, W J *NF*
Brink, Wellington 1895- *WhJnl Sup*
Brinkerhoff, Frederick Walter 1885?-1966 *BioIn 7*
Brinkerhoff, R A *NF*
Brinkerhoff, Robert Moore 1880-1958 *BioIn 4,*
 OhA&B, WhNAA, WhJnl 1928
Brinkley, David 1920- *BioIn 6, CelR 1973,*
 CurBio XR, ForP, WhoAm 1974,
 WhoS&SW 1973, WhoWor 1974
Brinkley, Nell 1888-1944 *CurBio XR*
Brinkley, William Clark 1917- *BioIn 4,*
 ConAu 21R, OvPC, WhoAm 1974
Brinkman, Grover 1903- *ConAu 73*
Brinsmade, Herman H *WhJnl 1928*
Brinton, Christian 1870-1942 *AmAu&B, DcNAA*
Brinton, Daniel Garrison 1837-1899 *Alli Sup,*
 AmAu, AmAu&B, BiD&SB, CyAL 2,
 DcAmA, DcNAA, HisAmM XR, OxAm
Brinton, Larry *NF*
Briordy, William J 1913?-1966 *BioIn 7*
Brisbane, Albert 1809-1890 *AmAu, AmAu&B,*
 AmJnl, DcNAA, HisAmM XR, OxAm,
 REnAL
Brisbane, Arthur 1864-1936 *AmAu&B, AmJnl,*
 BioIn 1, BioIn 3, BioIn 4, BioIn 9,
 DcAmB S2, DcNAA, NatCAB 27, OxAm,
 REnAL, TwCA, WebBD, WhJnl 1928
Brisk, James Mossman *BioIn 7*
Brislin, John Harold 1911-1973 *BioIn 9, BioIn 10,*
 NewYTBE 4
Brisson, Pierre 1896-1964 *BioIn 7, ForP*
Brissot, Jacques Pierre 1754-1793 *REn, WebBD*
Brissot, Jacques Pierre *see also* Brissot, Jean-Pierre
Brissot, Jacques Pierre *see also* Brissot DeWarville, J
 P
Brissot, Jean-Pierre 1754-1793 *OxFr*
Brissot, Jean-Pierre *see also* Brissot, Jacques Pierre
Brissot, Jean-Pierre *see also* Brissot DeWarville,
 Jacques P
Brissot DeWarville, Jacques Pierre 1754-1793
 BioIn 9
Brissot DeWarville, Jacques Pierre *see also* Brissot,
 Jacques P
Brissot DeWarville, Jacques Pierre *see also* Brissot,
 Jean-P
Bristed, Charles Astor 1820-1874 *Alli, Alli Sup,*
 AmAu&B, BiD&SB, CyAL 2, DcAmA,
 DcNAA, HisAmM XR, LiJA
Bristed, John 1778-1855 *Alli, AmAu, AmAu&B,*
 BiDLA, CyAL 1, DcAmA, DcNAA,
 HisAmM XR
Brister, Bob 1928?- *BioIn 9*
Bristol, Claude Myron 1891-1951 *BioIn 2*
Bristow, Nora *NF*
Britt, Albert 1874- *AmAu&B, ConAu 5R,*
 HisAmM XR
Britt, Bloys 1913?-1975 *BioIn 10*
Britt, George William Hughes 1895- *AmAu&B,*
 HisAmM XR
Britt, W W *HisAmM XR*
Brittain, Sir Harry Ernest 1873- *BioIn 2,*

Who 1974
Brittain, Vera 1893?-1970 *ConAu* 15, *ConAu* 25, *NewYTBE* 1, *WebBD*
Brittan, Belle *see* Fuller, Hiram
Brittan, S B *Alli Sup, HisAmM XR*
Brittan, Samuel 1933- *ConAu* 29, *Who* 1974
Britten, Clarence *HisAmM XR*
Britten, Emma Hardinge *HisAmM XR*
Britten, Milton Reese 1924- *WhoAm* 1974, *WhoS&SW* 1973
Brittenden, Arthur 1924- *ForP, Who* 1974
Britter, Eric V B 1906-1977 *ConAu* 73
Brittingham, Bettie S 1903?-1949 *BioIn* 1
Britton, Dennis A *NF*
Britton, Jack *NF*
Britton, Milton *NF*
Britton, Willard P 1923- *WhoAm* 1974
Britton, William W 1872- *WhJnl* 1928
Broackes, Nigel *NF*
Broad, Charles Lewis 1900- *ConAu* 7R
Broadhurst, George Howells 1866-1952 *AmAu&B, BiD&SB, DcNAA, ModWD, NewC, REnAL, TwCA, TwCA Sup*
Broadwater, Jim *NF*
Brobeck, Florence 1895- *OhA&B, OvPC, WhNAA*
Brock, Henry Irving 1876-1961 *BioIn* 5
Brock, Paul 1932- *NF*
Brock, Ray 1913-1968 *BioIn* 8
Brockhaven, Eugene F 1895?-1967 *BioIn* 7
Brockington, Leonard W 1885-1966 *NF*
Brockman, Zoe Kincaid 1893- *BioIn* 3
Brockway, Beman 1815-1892? *DcNAA*
Brockway, Fenner 1888- *ConAu P-1, IntWW* 1976, *WhoWor* 1974, *WrDr* 1976
Brockway, Wallace 1905-1972 *BioIn* 9, *ConAu* 37, *NewYTBE* 3
Brod, Ruth Hagy *ForWC* 1970, *OvPC*
Broder, David Salzer 1929- *BioIn* 8, *NewMr, WhoAm* 1974
Broderick, Peter *NF*
Brodeur, Albert S 1869?- *WhJnl* 1928
Brodeur, Paul 1931- *ConAu* 7R, *ConNov* 1972, *ConNov* 1976, *NewMr, WrDr* 1976
Brodfuehrer, O M 1889- *WhJnl* 1928
Brodhead, James E, III *OvPC*
Brodhead, Thornton F *NF*
Brodhecker, Andrew I 1869- *WhJnl* 1928
Brodhecker, Andrew J 1887- *NF*
Brodhecker, Rolland A 1898- *WhJnl* 1928
Brodie, Edward Everett 1876-1939 *BioIn* 6, *WhNAA, WhJnl* 1928
Brodie, Howard Joseph 1915- *BioIn* 1
Brodney, Spencer 1883-1973 *Au&Wr, BioIn* 9, *HisAmM XR, WhNAA, Who* 1974
Brodovitch, Alexey *HisAmM XR, NewYTBE* 2
Brodribb, Charles William 1878-1945 *BioIn* 5
Brodrick, George Charles 1831-1903 *Alli Sup, WebBD*
Brody, Charles M 1899?-1947 *BioIn* 1
Brody, Iles 1899?-1953 *BioIn* 3
Brody, Jane *NF*
Brody, Judith A *NF*
Brody, Rosalie *OvPC*
Broeg, Bob 1918- *ConAu* 13R, *WhoAm* 1974
Broening, Steve *NF*
Brogan, Colm 1902- *BioIn* 3, *CathA* 1952, *LongC, Who* 1974
Broiles, Barnes Hoover 1897- *TexWr, WhNAA, WhoF&I* 1974, *WhJnl* 1928
Brokaw, Roberta Miriam 1917- *BioIn* 10, *ForWC* 1970, *WhoAmW* 1974
Brokaw, Tom *BioIn* 10
Brokenshire, John Roberts 1896- *WhJnl* 1928

Brokenshire, Norman 1898-1965 *BioIn* 7, *CurBio XR*
Brokmeyer, H C *HisAmM XR*
Bromberger, Merry Marie Louis 1906- *IntWW* 1976
Bromberger, Serge Paul 1912- *ConAu* 29, *IntWW* 1976, *WhoWor* 1974
Bromfield, Louis 1896-1956 *AmAu&B, AmNov, CnDAL, ConAmA, ConAmL, CurBio XR, CyWA, DcBiA, DcLEL, EncWL, EvLB, LongC, OhA&B, OxAm, Pen Am, REn, REnAL, TwCA, TwCA Sup, TwCW, WebBD, WhNAA*
Bromley, Dorothy Dunbar 1896- *BioIn* 1, *CurBio XR*
Bromley, Isaac Hill 1833-1898 *AmAu&B, DcAmB* 3, *NatCAB* 12
Brondfield, Jerome 1913- *ConAu* 73, *IntMPA* 1975
Broniarek, Zygmunt 1925- *IntWW* 1976
Bronk, Mitchell 1862-1950 *BioIn* 2, *WhNAA*
Bronson, Enos *AmJnl, HisAmM XR*
Bronson, Harry G 1898- *WhNAA, WhJnl* 1928
Bronstrup, G A 1869- *WhJnl* 1928
Brook, Marina 1909?- *BioIn* 9
Brook-Shepherd, Gordon 1918- *Au&Wr, ConAu* 9R
Brooke, Albert Bushong, Jr. 1921- *BioIn* 8, *WhoAm* 1974, *WhoAmP* 1973, *WhoGov* 1972
Brooker, Bertram 1888-1955 *BioIn* 10, *CanNov, DcLEL, OxCan*
Brooker, William *AmJnl*
Brookhouser, Frank 1912?-1975 *ConAu* 4R
Brooks, Albert Neal Dow 1898?-1964 *BioIn* 7
Brooks, Alice *NF*
Brooks, Allen *HisAmM XR*
Brooks, Charles William Shirley 1816-1874 *Alli, Alli Sup, BbD, BiD&SB, CasWL, DcBiA, DcEnA Ap, DcEnL, DcLEL, EvLB, WebBD*
Brooks, Cleanth 1906- *AmAu&B, CasWL, ConAu* 17, *DcLEL, DrAS* 74E, *IntWW* 1974, *LongC, ModAL, OxAm, Pen Am, RAdv* 1, *REn, REnAL, TwCA Sup, Who* 1974, *WhoAm* 1974, *WhoTwCL, WhoWor* 1974, *WrDr* 1976
Brooks, Clifton C 1903- *WhJnl* 1928
Brooks, Dick 1930- *IntMPA* 1975
Brooks, Elbridge Streeter 1846-1902 *Alli Sup, AmAu, AmAu&B, BbD, BiD&SB, BioIn* 3, *CarSB, DcAmA, DcNAA, HisAmM XR, JBA* 1934, *REnAL*
Brooks, Elston 1930- *NF*
Brooks, Erastus 1815-1886 *AmJnl, DcAmB* 3, *DcNAA, NatCAB* 6
Brooks, Florence 1860-1948 *BioIn* 3
Brooks, George Sprague 1895-1961 *WhNAA, WhJnl* 1928
Brooks, Henry S 1830?-1910 *DcAmA, DcNAA*
Brooks, James 1810-1873 *Alli Sup, AmAu&B, AmJnl, DcAmB* 3, *DcNAA*
Brooks, James Gordon 1801-1841 *Alli, AmAu, AmAu&B, BioIn* 1, *CyAL* 2, *DcEnL, DcNAA, HisAmM XR*
Brooks, John *WhoE* 1974
Brooks, John 1920- *AmAu&B, Au&Wr, BioIn* 2, *BioIn* 4, *ConAu* 13R, *WhoAm* 1974
Brooks, Joseph W 1905-1972 *BioIn* 9
Brooks, Kate Neal 1862?-1962 *BioIn* 6
Brooks, Kenneth *OvPC*
Brooks, Louis J 1853- *NatCAB* 9
Brooks, Milton *NF*
Brooks, Nathan Covington 1819?-1898 *Alli, CyAL* 2, *DcAmA, DcNAA, HisAmM XR*

Brooks, Ned 1900-1969 *BioIn 8, WhJnl 1928*
Brooks, Noah 1830-1903 *Alli Sup, AmAu,*
AmAu&B, BbD, BiD&SB, CarSB, DcAmA,
DcAmB 3, DcNAA, HisAmM XR,
JBA 1934, NatCAB 7, OxAm, REnAL
Brooks, Olive *OvPC, WhoAmP 1973*
Brooks, S Raymond 1894- *WhJnl 1928*
Brooks, Sydney *HisAmM XR*
Brooks, Thomas Reed 1925- *ConAu 73*
Brooks, Van Wyck 1886-1963 *AmAu&B, AmLY,*
AmWr, AtlBL, CasWL, CnDAL, ConAmA,
ConAmL, ConAu 1R, DcLEL, EvLB,
LongC, ModAL, OxAm, Pen Am, RAdv 1,
REn, REnAL, TwCA, TwCA Sup, TwCW,
WebBD, WhNAA
Brooks, William E *HisAmM XR*
Brooks, William F *OvPC*
Brooks, Winfield Sears 1902-1963 *AmAu&B,*
BioIn 2, BioIn 6
Broom, William Wescott 1924- *WhoAm 1974*
Brophy, Charles George 1925- *OvPC, WhoE 1974*
Brosnan, James Patrick 1929- *BioIn 7, BioIn 8,*
ConAu 4R, CurBio XR, WhoMW 1974
Bross, William 1813-1890 *Alli Sup, AmAu&B,*
BiD&SB, BioIn 1, DcAmA, DcAmB 3,
DcNAA
Brossard, Chandler 1922- *AmAu&B, BioIn 2,*
ConAu 61, ConNov 1972, ConNov 1976,
DrAF 1976, Pen Am, WhoE 1974,
WrDr 1976
Brossier, Clem *NF*
Brossolette, Pierre 1944- *BioIn 8*
Brost, Erich Eduard 1903- *IntWW 1976,*
WhoWor 1974
Brothers, George Raleigh 1887-1957 *BioIn 6*
Broudhecker, John *NF*
Brough, Elizabeth *AmJnl*
Brough, Elizabeth *see also* Dare, Helen
Brougham, Lord Henry Peter 1778-1868 *Alli,*
Alli Sup, AmJnl, BbD, BiD&SB, BiDLA,
BrAu 19, CasWL, DcLEL, EvLB, NewC,
OxEng, Pen Eng, WebBD
Brougham, John 1810?-1880 *Alli, Alli Sup,*
AmAu, AmAu&B, BbD, BiD&SB, DcAmA,
DcEnL, DcNAA, HisAmM XR, OxAm,
PoIre, REnAL
Brougham, Royal 1894-1978 *BioIn 1, BioIn 7,*
WhoAm 1974, WhJnl 1928, WhoWest 1974
Broughan, Herbert *NF*
Broughton, Charles Elmer 1873-1956 *BioIn 5,*
WhJnl 1928
Broun, Aaron 1893- *WhJnl 1928*
Broun, Heywood Campbell 1888-1939 *AmAu&B,*
AmJnl, BioIn 1, BioIn 2, BioIn 3, BioIn 4,
BioIn 5, BioIn 6, CathA 1930, ConAmA,
CurBio XR, DcAmB S2, DcLEL, DcNAA,
HisAmM XR, NatCAB 30, NewMr, OxAm,
REn, REnAL, TwCA, TwCA Sup,
WhJnl 1928
Broun, Heywood Campbell *see also* Broun, Matthew
Heywood Campbell
Broun, Heywood Hale 1918- *BiE&WWA,*
BioIn 1, BioIn 3, BioIn 7, BioIn 8,
BioNews 1974, ConAu 17R
Broun, Matthew Heywood Campbell 1888-1939
WebBD
Broun, Matthew Heywood Campbell *see also* Broun,
Heywood Campbell
Browde, H *NF*
Browder, Earl Russell 1891-1973 *AmRP,*
ConAu 45, CurBio XR, NewYTBE 4,
WebBD
Brower, Ann *NF*
Brower, Brock 1931- *AmAu&B, ConAu 25,*

DrAF 1976
Brower, Bunny *NF*
Brown *see* Bromley, Isaac Hill
Brown, A E *HisAmM XR*
Brown, Amery *NF*
Brown, Andrew H *HisAmM XR*
Brown, Arthur W *HisAmM XR*
Brown, Ashmun 1872-1948 *BioIn 1, WhNAA*
Brown, Aubrey Neblett, Jr. 1908- *WhoAm 1974,*
WhoWor 1974
Brown, Barry 1914- *BioIn 2, IntMPA 1975,*
RpN, USBiR 1974
Brown, Beriah 1815-1900 *BioIn 5*
Brown, Bernard D *NF*
Brown, Bernice *HisAmM XR*
Brown, Bill *NF*
Brown, Bo 1906- *WhoAmA 1973*
Brown, Bob *WhoE 1974*
Brown, Bob 1886- *AmAu&B, WhNAA*
Brown, Brenda Lois 1934- *WhoAm 1974*
Brown, Britt 1927- *WhoAm 1974*
Brown, Buck 1936- *WhoAm 1974*
Brown, Buford Otis *WhNAA, WhJnl 1928*
Brown, Carleton Fairchild 1869-1941 *CurBio XR,*
HisAmM XR
Brown, Mrs. Caro *NF*
Brown, Cecil B *OvPC*
Brown, Charles Brockden 1771-1810 *Alli, AmAu,*
AmAu&B, AmJnl, AtlBL, BbD, BiD&SB,
CasWL, CnDAL, CrtT 3, CyAL 1, CyWA,
DcAmA, DcAmB 3, DcEnL, DcLEL,
DcNAA, EncMys, EvLB, HisAmM XR,
LiJA, MouLC 2, OxAm, OxEng, Pen Am,
RAdv 1, REn, REnAL, WebBD, WebE&AL
Brown, Charles Edward 1877- *WhJnl 1928*
Brown, Charles Farrar *HisAmM XR*
Brown, Charles H *OvPC*
Brown, Charles Henry 1910- *ConAu 23R,*
WhoAm 1974
Brown, Charles Kenneth 1893-1944 *BioIn 1*
Brown, Claude Adolphus 1887- *WhJnl Sup*
Brown, Constantine 1889-1966 *BioIn 2, BioIn 7,*
ConAu P-1
Brown, Cowley Stapleton *HisAmM XR*
Brown, Cyril 1887-1949 *AmJnl, BioIn 2,*
DcNAA, HisAmM XR
Brown, David 1916- *ConAu 15R, IntMPA 1975,*
OvPC, WhoAm 1974, WhoE 1974,
WhoF&I 1974, WhoWor 1974
Brown, Don Adair 1899- *WhJnl 1928*
Brown, Dorothy *NF*
Brown, Douglas 1907- *ConAu 25*
Brown, E C *HisAmM XR*
Brown, E Francis 1903- *HisAmM XR*
Brown, E Francis *see also* Brown, Francis
Brown, Earl Louis 1902- *BioIn 5*
Brown, Edmund Randolph 1888- *WhoAm 1974*
Brown, Edwin G 1882- *WhJnl 1928*
Brown, Frances Opie *WhJnl 1928*
Brown, Francis 1903- *AmAu&B, BioIn 9,*
ConAu 73, DrAS 74H, WhoAm 1974
Brown, Francis *see also* Brown, E Francis
Brown, Frank Chouteau 1876-1947 *AmAu&B,*
WhNAA
Brown, Frank W 1882- *WhJnl 1928*
Brown, G Stanley *WhJnl 1928*
Brown, G Stanley 1926- *USBiR 1974*
Brown, Gene Marvyn 1923- *OvPC,*
WhoF&I 1974
Brown, George 1818-1880 *BbtC, BioIn 6, OxCan,*
WebBD
Brown, George Pliny 1836-1910 *DcNAA,*
HisAmM XR
Brown, George Rothwell 1879-1960 *AmAu&B,*

Bioln 5, OvPC
Brown, George W Alli Sup, HisAmM XR
Brown, Gilbert Patten 1868- WhJnl 1928
Brown, Gwilym Slater 1928-1974 Bioln 10,
ConAu 11R, ConAu 53
Brown, H T HisAmM XR
Brown, Harris Bioln 1
Brown, Harry 1889- WhJnl 1928
Brown, Harry Leggett 1872-1954 Bioln 3,
WhJnl 1928
Brown, Helen E Alli Sup, HisAmM XR
Brown, Helen Gurley 1922- AmAu&B, Bioln 7,
Bioln 8, Bioln 9, CelR 1973, ConAu 7R,
CurBio XR, ForWC 1970, WhoAm 1974,
WhoAmW 1974, WhoE 1974,
WhoWor 1974, WrDr 1976
Brown, Mrs. Henry see West, Lillie
Brown, Herbert Ross 1902- ConAu 15,
DrAS 74E, WhoAm 1974
Brown, Herrick NF
Brown, Hilary NF
Brown, Hilton Ultimus 1859-1958 Bioln 2,
Bioln 5, IndAu 1816, WhJnl 1928
Brown, Holmes OvPC
Brown, Houston WhJnl 1928
Brown, Howard Hays 1884?-1953 Bioln 3
Brown, Innis 1884- WhJnl 1928
Brown, Iris NF
Brown, Irving 1905- WhJnl 1928
Brown, Ivor John Carnegie 1891-1974 Au&Wr,
Bioln 2, Bioln 3, Bioln 4, ConAu 11R,
ConAu 49, DcLEL, EvLB, LongC, ModBL,
NewC, Pen Eng, SmATA 5, TwCA Sup,
Who 1974, WhoWor 1974
Brown, J G L HisAmM XR
Brown, J Goddard 1879- WhJnl 1928
Brown, J Harry 1884?-1961 Bioln 5
Brown, James Allen 1821-1883 DcAmA,
HisAmM XR
Brown, James Nicholas 1889- WhJnl 1928
Brown, James P NF
Brown, James Patrick, Jr. 1921- WhoMW 1974
Brown, James Wright 1873-1959 HisAmM XR,
WhJnl 1928
Brown, James Wright, Jr. 1902- HisAmM XR,
WhJnl 1928
Brown, Jeff AuBYP
Brown, Jimmy 1936- Bioln 7, Bioln 8, Bioln 9
Brown, Joe David 1915-1976 AmAu&B, AmNov,
ConAu 13R, ConAu 65
Brown, John Howard 1840-1917 Bioln 2, DcAmA,
DcNAA
Brown, John Mason 1900-1969 AmAu&B,
BiE&WWA, CnDAL, ConAu 9R,
ConAu 25, CurBio XR, HisAmM XR,
LongC, OxAm, Pen Am, REnAL, TwCA,
TwCA Sup
Brown, Joseph HisAmM XR
Brown, Joseph E 1929- ConAu 53
Brown, Kenneth NF
Brown, Kenneth 1868- AmAu&B, BiDSA,
WhNAA
Brown, Kevin V NF
Brown, Les 1928- Bioln 9, ConAu 33,
WhoAm 1974
Brown, Lew Buford 1861-1944 Bioln 5
Brown, Llewellyn Chauncey 1887?-1978 NF
Brown, Mark H NF
Brown, Maynard Wilson 1896- WhJnl 1928
Brown, Merrill 1952- NF
Brown, Monte F 1880- WhJnl 1928
Brown, Nancy 1870-1948 AmAu&B, WhNAA
Brown, Nancy 1941?- Bioln 6
Brown, Nancy see also Leslie, Mrs. J E

Brown, Ned 1882?-1976 ConAu 65
Brown, Nella 1878?-1969 Bioln 8
Brown, Nona Baldwin NF
Brown, Oliver W, Jr. OvPC
Brown, Parke 1883-1943 NatCAB 32
Brown, Peter 1784-1863 BbtC, DcNAA, WebBD
Brown, Phil NF
Brown, Prudence Gruelle 1885- WhJnl 1928
Brown, Ray Andrews 1890- WhNAA,
WhJnl 1928
Brown, Ray C B 1880-1951 Bioln 2, WhNAA,
WhJnl 1928
Brown, Raymond J HisAmM XR
Brown, Raymond S 1885- WhJnl 1928
Brown, Robert NF
Brown, Robert Edward 1945- ConAu 65,
DrAS 74E
Brown, Robert L OvPC
Brown, Robert N Bioln 10
Brown, Robert Utting 1912- HisAmM XR,
WhoAdv 1972, WhoAm 1974
Brown, Robert Woodrow 1912-1974 Bioln 10,
NewYTBS 5, RpN, WhoAm 1974,
WhoS&SW 1973
Brown, Roscoe Conkling Ensign 1867-1946 Bioln 1,
Bioln 2, NatCAB 34, WhNAA, WhJnl 1928
Brown, Rose Z WhJnl 1928
Brown, Royal 1886?-1953 Bioln 3
Brown, Sevellon Ledyard 1886-1956 AmJnl,
Bioln 2, Bioln 3, Bioln 4, HisAmM XR
Brown, Stanley H 1927- ConAu 45
Brown, T Allston 1836-1918 Alli Sup,
HisAmM XR
Brown, T Allston see also Brown, Thomas Allston
Brown, Terry NF
Brown, Theron 1832-1914 Alli Sup, AmAu&B,
DcAmA, DcNAA, HisAmM XR
Brown, Thomas HisAmM XR
Brown, Thomas Allston 1836-1918 AmAu&B,
DcNAA
Brown, Thomas Allston see also Brown, T Allston
Brown, Thomas Storrow 1803-1888 BbtC,
DcNAA, OxCan
Brown, Thurlow Weed d1866 Alli Sup, DcAmA,
DcNAA
Brown, Vera 1897?-1976 Bioln 2
Brown, Vivian d1978 NF
Brown, W F NF

Brown, Warren 1894?-1978 NF
Brown, Warren 1948?- BlkC
Brown, Warren Wilmer 1880-1946 Bioln 2,
NatCAB 35, WhNAA
Brown, Willet Henry 1905- IntMPA 1975,
WhoAm 1974, WhoWest 1974
Brown, William 1738?-1789 OxCan
Brown, William 1939- Bioln 9
Brown, William F 1903- WhoAm 1974
Brown, William L AmJnl
Brown, William Orwell 1815-1884 Bioln 5
Brown, William Oswell 1876-1956 Bioln 3,
Bioln 4, WhJnl 1928
Brown-Buck, Lillie 1860-1939 DcNAA
Brown-Buck, Lillie see also West, Lillie
Browne, Charles Farrar 1834-1867 Alli Sup,
AmAu, AmAu&B, AmJnl, BbD, BiD&SB,
CnDAL, DcAmA, DcEnA Ap, DcEnL,
DcLEL, DcNAA, EvLB, HisAmM XR,
OhA&B, OxAm, OxEng, Pen Am, REn,
REnAL, WebBD, WebE&AL
Browne, Charles Farrar see also Ward, Artemus
Browne, Charles Herbert 1881- WhNAA,
WhJnl 1928
Browne, Dik 1917- AuNews 1

Browne, Francis Fisher 1843-1913 *Alli Sup,*
 AmAu, AmAu&B, BioIn 1, DcAmA,
 DcNAA, HisAmM XR, LiJA
Browne, George *OvPC*
Browne, George Waldo 1851-1930 *AmAu&B,*
 AmLY, DcAmA, DcNAA, HsB&A,
 WhNAA
Browne, George Waldo *see also* Saint Clair, Victor
Browne, Herbert J 1861-1963 *NatCAB 27*
Browne, Howard 1908- *ConAu 73, EncMys*
Browne, John Ross 1821?-1875 *Alli, Alli Sup,*
 AmAu&B, ArizL, BbD, BiD&SB, CnDAL,
 CyAL 2, DcAmA, DcEnL, DcNAA,
 EarABI, EarABI Sup, HisAmM XR, OxAm,
 REnAL
Browne, Junius Henri 1833-1902 *Alli Sup,*
 AmAu&B, AmJnl, BbD, BiD&SB, DcAmA,
 DcAmB 3, DcNAA, FamWC, HisAmM XR,
 NatCAB 13, OhA&B
Browne, Lewis Allen 1876-1937 *AmAu&B,*
 DcNAA, REnAL
Browne, Malcolm Wilde 1931- *ConAu 17R,*
 OvPC, WhoAm 1974
Browne, Millard Child 1915- *RpN, WhoAm 1974*
Browne, Morgan Trew 1919- *WhoAm 1974*
Browne, Stanley George 1907- *IntWW 1976,*
 Who 1974, WhoWor 1974, WrDr 1976
Browne, Waldo Ralph 1876-1954 *AmAu&B,*
 HisAmM XR
Browne, Walter L 1885- *WhJnl 1928*
Browne, William Hand 1828-1912 *Alli Sup,*
 AmAu&B, BiDSA, DcAmA, DcNAA,
 HisAmM XR
Brownell, Agnes Mary *HisAmM XR*
Brownell, Atherton 1866-1924 *DcNAA,*
 HisAmM XR
Brownell, Baker 1887-1965 *AmAu&B,*
 TwCA Sup, WhJnl 1928
Brownell, F C *HisAmM XR*
Brownell, Frederick Gwyn 1901- *WhoPubR 1972*
Brownell, James Garland 1933- *LEduc 1974,*
 WhoAm 1974
Brownell, William Crary 1851-1928 *AmAu&B,*
 AmLY, BiD&SB, CnDAL, ConAmL,
 DcAmA, DcLEL, DcNAA, HisAmM XR,
 NatCAB 22, OxAm, Pen Am, REnAL,
 TwCA, TwCA Sup, WebBD, WhNAA
Browning, Norma Lee 1914- *AmAu&B, BioIn 2,*
 ConAu 61, WhoAm 1974, WhoAmW 1974
Browning, Robert Marcellus 1911- *BioIn 7,*
 DrAS 74F
Brownlow, Cecil *NF*
Brownlow, Louis 1879-1963 *AmAu&B, BioIn 3,*
 BioIn 4, BioIn 6, BioIn 7
Brownlow, William Gannaway 1805-1877 *Alli Sup,*
 AmAu, AmJnl, BiD&SB, BiDSA, DcAmA,
 DcNAA, OhA&B, OxAm, WebBD
Brownson, Orestes Augustus 1803-1876 *Alli,*
 Alli Sup, AmAu, AmAu&B, BbD, BiD&SB,
 CasWL, CyAL 2, DcAmA, DcEnL, DcLEL,
 DcNAA, HisAmM XR, LiJA, OxAm,
 Pen Am, REn, REnAL, WebBD,
 WebE&AL
Brownstein, Cheryl *NF*
Brownstone, Cecily *NF*
Broxholme, John Franklin 1930- *ConAu 65*
Broxholme, John Franklin *see also* Kyle, Duncan
Broy, Anthony 1916- *NF*
Broyles, William Dodson, Jr. 1944- *BioIn 10,*
 ConAu 73
Brubaker, Herbert *NF*
Brubaker, Howard 1882-1957 *AmAu&B, AmRP,*
 BioIn 4, HisAmM XR, IndAu 1917
Bruce, A D, Jr. *NF*

Bruce, Arthur Loring 1872-1947 *AmAu&B,*
 DcNAA, WebBD
Bruce, Arthur Loring *see also* Crowninshield, Frank
Bruce, Arthur Loring *see also* Crowninshield, Francis
 Welsh
Bruce, B G *HisAmM XR*
Bruce, Bob T *NF*
Bruce, Campbell 1884- *WhJnl 1928*
Bruce, Charles T 1906?-1971 *BioIn 9, BioIn 10*
Bruce, David *AmJnl*
Bruce, H Addington 1874-1959 *AmAu&B,*
 BiDPara, HisAmM XR, WhNAA
Bruce, John Edward 1856-1924 *BioIn 9, BlkAW*
Bruce, L C *HisAmM XR*
Bruce, Philip Alexander 1856-1933 *AmAu&B,*
 BiDSA, DcAmA, DcNAA, HisAmM XR,
 OxAm, WhNAA
Bruce, Sir Robert 1871-1955 *BioIn 3*
Bruce, Saunders Dewees 1825-1902 *DcAmA,*
 HisAmM XR
Bruce, William George 1856-1949 *WhNAA,*
 WhJnl 1928
Bruce, William H *WhJnl 1928*
Bruce Lockhart, Sir Robert Hamilton 1887-1970
 Au&Wr, BioIn 8, BioIn 9, LongC
Bruce Lockhart, Sir Robert Hamilton *see also*
 Lockhart, Robert H
Bruce Lockhart, Robin 1920- *Au&Wr,*
 ConAu 25, WrDr 1976
Bruck, O S 1885- *WhJnl 1928*
Bruck, Paul *NF*
Bruckart, William d1940 *AmJnl*
Brucker, Herbert 1898-1977 *AmAu&B, BioIn 6,*
 ConAu 5R, DrAS 74E, WhoAm 1974,
 WrDr 1976
Bruckner, D J *NF*
Bruckner, R *NF*
Brudon, Lynn *BioIn 4*
Bruen, John J, Jr. *OvPC*
Bruestle, Beaumont 1905- *AmAu&B,*
 WhoAm 1974
Brugmann, Bruce *BioIn 9, NewMr*
Brumby, James R 1902- *WhJnl 1928*
Brumby, Robert M *OvPC*
Brumder, George 1839-1910 *BioIn 5*
Brumder, William Charles 1868-1929 *BioIn 5*
Brumley, Jayne *NF*
Brumm, John Lewis 1878-1958 *AmAu&B,*
 BioIn 5, WhJnl 1928
Brumwell, George Murray 1872-1963 *BioIn 6*
Brundidge, Harry T *AmJnl, HisAmM XR*
Bruneau, Alfred 1857-1934 *WebBD*
Bruner, Felix F 1898- *WhJnl 1928*
Bruner, Raymond A 1900-1970 *BioIn 8, BioIn 9*
Bruner, W Richard *OvPC*
Bruner, Wally 1931- *ConAu 49*
Brunini, John Gilland 1899- *AmAu&B, BioIn 1,*
 BkC 4, CathA 1930
Brunius, Teddy *ForP*
Brunk, Charlotte *WhoAm 1974*
Brunkhorst, Walter H 1893- *WhJnl 1928*
Brunn, Robert R *RpN*
Brunner, Bernard H 1895- *WhJnl 1928*
Brunner, Edward J 1888- *WhJnl 1928*
Brunner, William L 1875- *WhJnl 1928*
Bruno, Anne Turner *ForWC 1970, OvPC*
Bruno, Guido 1884- *AmAu&B, AmLY, REnAL*
Bruno, Harold Robinson, Jr. 1928- *WhoAm 1974,*
 WhoE 1974
Bruno, Harry A 1893-1978 *OvPC, WhNAA,*
 WhoAm 1974, WhoF&I 1974,
 WhoPubR 1972
Bruno, Jerry 1926- *BioIn 9, BioIn 10,*
 WhoAmP 1973

Bruns, Franklin Richard, Jr. 1912- *CurBio XR, WhoAm 1974*
Bruns, Ken *NF*
Bruns, Renee *NF*
Brunst, G Rudolph 1900?-1956 *BioIn 4*
Brunton, George 1900- *WhJnl 1928*
Brush, Edward Nathaniel 1852-1933 *WebBD, WhNAA*
Brush, Harlan Willis 1865-1942 *BioIn 2*
Brush, Isabel *HisAmM XR*
Brush, Louis Herbert 1872-1948 *AmJnl, BioIn 1, BioIn 2*
Brusic, Kenneth *NF*
Bruss, Robert 1940- *NF*
Brust, August T 1889- *WhJnl 1928*
Brustein, Robert Sanford 1927- *AmAu&B, ConAu 11R, WhoAm 1974, WhoE 1974, WhoWor 1974*
Bruun, Laurids *HisAmM XR*
Bryan, Carter S 1911- *ConAu 33*
Bryan, Charles Page *HisAmM XR*
Bryan, Charles Wayland 1867-1945 *CurBio XR, DcAmB S3, HisAmM XR, WebBD*
Bryan, Charlotte Augusta 1867-1948 *BioIn 2, BioIn 3, IndAu 1816*
Bryan, Clark W *HisAmM XR*
Bryan, Courtlandt Dixon Barnes 1936- *AmAu&B, ConAu 73, WhoAm 1974, WhoE 1974*
Bryan, David Tennant 1906- *BioIn 9, WhoAm 1974, WhoS&SW 1973*
Bryan, Diana *BioIn 10*
Bryan, Dorothy *BioIn 3*
Bryan, Ernst Rowlett 1906-1955 *CurBio XR*
Bryan, Isabel 1874?-1957 *BioIn 4*
Bryan, John Edward 1913- *WhoAm 1974, WhoF&I 1974*
Bryan, John Stewart 1871-1944 *AmAu&B, AmJnl, BioIn 2, DcAmB S3, WhJnl 1928*
Bryan, Joseph, III 1904- *AmAu&B, AuBYP, ConAu 61, HisAmM XR, REnAL, WhoAm 1974*
Bryan, Julien 1899-1974 *BioIn 3, ConAu 53, CurBio XR, WhoAm 1974*
Bryan, Lee *NF*
Bryan, Mary Edwards 1842?-1913 *Alli Sup, AmAu, AmAu&B, BiDSA, DcAmA, DcAmB 3, DcNAA, HisAmM XR, LivFWS, NatCAB 8*
Bryan, Thomas E *NF*
Bryan, Walter G 1878- *WhJnl 1928*
Bryan, William Jennings 1860-1925 *AmAu&B, AmJnl, DcAmA, DcNAA, EncAB, HisAmM XR, OxAm, REn, REnAL, WebBD*
Bryan, Wright 1905- *AmJnl, BioIn 3, IntWW 1976, OvPC, WhoAm 1974*
Bryant, G *NF*
Bryant, Gay 1945- *ConAu 73*
Bryant, Henry Edward Cowan 1873- *WhNAA, WhJnl 1928*
Bryant, Larry W *NF*
Bryant, Lawrence M 1939?- *BlkC*
Bryant, Louise 1890-1936 *AmRP, DcNAA*
Bryant, Samuel Wood, Jr. 1908- *AmAu&B*
Bryant, Vaughn 1888- *WhJnl 1928*
Bryant, William Bernard 1876- *WhJnl 1928*
Bryant, William Cullen 1794-1878 *Alli, Alli Sup, AmAu, AmAu&B, AmJnl, AtlBL, BbD, BiD&SB, BioIn 1, BioIn 2, BioIn 3, BioIn 4, BioIn 5, BioIn 6, BioIn 7, BioIn 8, BioIn 9, CarSB, CasWL, CnDAL, CnE&AP, CrtT 3, CyAL 1, CyWA, DcAmA, DcEnL, DcLEL, DcNAA, EncAB, EvLB, HisAmM XR, MouLC 3, OxAm,*

OxEng, Pen Am, PoChrch, RAdv 1, REn, REnAL, Str&VC, WebBD, WebE&AL
Bryce, C A *HisAmM XR*
Bryce, Frank A 1884- *WhJnl 1928*
Bryce, Lloyd Stephens 1851-1917 *AmAu&B, BiD&SB, DcAmA, DcNAA, HisAmM XR, NatCAB 1*
Bryden, Ronald 1927- *NF, WhoThe 1972, WhoWor 1974*
Bryer, James T 1828-1895 *BioIn 2, IndAu 1816*
Bryers, Paul 1945- *ConAu 73*
Bryson, Jack F *NF*
Bryson, Lyman 1889-1959 *AmAu&B, REnAL, TwCA Sup, WhNAA*
Buch, Vera *NF*
Buchan, Alastair Francis 1918-1976 *ConAu 65, ConAu 73, IntWW 1974, Who 1974, WhoWor 1974*
Buchanan, David Tarbell 1898- *WhJnl Sup*
Buchanan, George 1904- *Au&Wr, ConAu 11R, ConNov 1972, ConNov 1976, ConP 1970, ConP 1975, Who 1974, WrDr 1976*
Buchanan, Joseph Ray 1851-1924 *BioIn 9, DcNAA, HisAmM XR*
Buchanan, Mary E 1898-1970 *BioIn 8*
Buchanan, Patrick Joseph 1938- *BioIn 8, BioIn 9, WhoAm 1974, WhoAmP 1973, WhoGov 1972, WhoS&SW 1973*
Buchanan, Thompson 1877-1937 *AmAu&B, DcNAA*
Buchanan, William Asbury 1876-1954 *BioIn 3, BioIn 6*
Buchard, Robert 1931- *ConAu 33*
Bucher, Anthony 1911-1968 *NF*
Buchholz, Horst *OvPC*
Buchman, Larry d1977 *NF*
Buchner, Frank *OvPC*
Buchner, J K *NF*
Buchta, J William 1895-1906 *BioIn 9*
Buchwach, Buck *NF*
Buchwald, Art 1925- *AmAu&B, AmAu&B, AuNews 1, BioIn 3, BioIn 4, BioIn 5, BioIn 6, BioIn 7, BioIn 8, BioIn 9, BioNews 1974, CelR 1973, ConAu 5R, CurBio XR, IntWW 1976, NewYTBE 3, Pen Am, SmATA 10, Who 1974, WhoAm 1974, WhoS&SW 1973, WhoWor 1974, WorAu, WrDr 1976*
Buck, Axford Cleveland 1903-1967 *BioIn 7*
Buck, E A *HisAmM XR*
Buck, Sir Edward John 1862- *WhoLA*
Buck, Glenn A 1905- *WhJnl 1928*
Buck, Joan *NF*
Buck, Lillie 1860-1939 *DcNAA*
Buck, Lillie *see also* West, Lillie
Buck, Max E 1913- *WhoAm 1974*
Buck, Morris 1881- *WhJnl 1928*
Buck, Osborne T 1903- *WhJnl 1928*
Buck-Morss, Susan *NF*
Bucke, Emory Stevens 1913- *WhoAm 1974*
Buckingham, Edwin *HisAmM XR, LiJA*
Buckingham, James Silk 1786-1855 *Alli, BbtC, BrAu 19, DcEnL, EvLB, HisAmM XR, NewC, OxAm, OxCan, OxEng, WebBD*
Buckingham, Joseph Tinker 1779-1861 *Alli, AmAu&B, AmJnl, BioIn 1, BioIn 3, BioIn 9, CyAL 2, DcAmA, DcNAA, HisAmM XR, LiJA*
Buckingham, Rob Roy 1920- *OvPC, WhoAm 1974*
Buckingham, William 1832-1915 *BbtC, DcNAA, OxCan*
Buckland, Albert William James 1900-1960 *BioIn 5*
Buckle, George Earle 1854-1935 *LongC, NewC,*

WebBD
Buckle, Richard 1916- *Au&Wr, IntWW 1976, Who 1974, WhoWor 1974, WrDr 1976*
Buckler, Beatrice Gotthold 1933- *WhoAm 1974*
Buckler, Helen *OvPC*
Buckley, Aloise 1918-1967 *BioIn 2, BioIn 7, BioIn 9*
Buckley, Christopher 1905-1950 *BioIn 2*
Buckley, Christopher T *OvPC*
Buckley, Edmund 1855- *HisAmM XR*
Buckley, George D *HisAmM XR*
Buckley, Gerald d1930 *NF*
Buckley, James Monroe 1836-1920 *Alli Sup, AmAu&B, BbD, BiD&SB, DcAmA, DcNAA, HisAmM XR, WebBD*
Buckley, Jim 1944- *BioIn 10*
Buckley, Kevin P 1911?- *NF*
Buckley, Michael F 1880?-1977 *ConAu 69*
Buckley, Priscilla Langford 1921- *ForWC 1970, WhoAm 1974, WhoAmW 1974, WhoF&I 1974*
Buckley, William Elmhirst 1913- *WhoAm 1974*
Buckley, William Frank, Jr. 1925- *AmAu&B, AuNews 1, BioIn 3, BioIn 5, BioIn 6, BioIn 7, BioIn 8, BioIn 9, BioIn 10, BioNews 1974, CelR 1973, ConAu 4R, CurBio XR, IntWW 1976, NewYTBE 1, OvPC, WhoAm 1974, WhoAmP 1973, WhoE 1974, WhoF&I 1974, WhoGov 1972, WhoWor 1974, WorAu, WrDr 1976*
Buckmaster, Henrietta 1909- *AmAu&B, AmNov, Au&Wr, ConAu XR, CurBio XR, OhA&B, SmATA 6, WorAu*
Buckmaster, Richard Price 1872- *WhJnl 1928*
Bucknam, James Romeo 1911- *WhoAm 1974, WhoE 1974*
Buckner, Simon Bolivar 1823-1914 *WebBD*
Buckwalter, Izaac Z 1898- *WhJnl 1928*
Budd, James *ForP*
Budd, Montgomery R 1899- *WhJnl 1928*
Budd, Richard Wade 1934- *AmM&W 73S, ConAu 23R, WhoCon 1973*
Budde, Henry F 1873?-1951 *BioIn 2*
Buddy, Edward Carr 1907?-1953 *BioIn 3*
Budenz, Louis Francis 1891-1972 *AmAu&B, AmRP, BioIn 1, BioIn 2, BioIn 3, BioIn 9, BioIn 10, BkC 6, CathA 1952, CurBio XR, IndAu 1917, NewMr, NewYTBE 3*
Buder, Gustavus Adolphus 1877-1954 *BioIn 6, WhJnl 1928*
Budge, Dave *NF*
Budgell, Eustace 1686?-1737? *Alli, BioIn 4, CasWL, DcEnL, EvLB, NewC, OxEng, Pen Eng*
Budimir, Velimir 1926- *ConAu 65*
Budish, J M *AmRP*
Budlong, Ware Torrey 1905?-1967 *BioIn 8*
Buechler, A F 1869- *WhNAA, WhJnl 1928*
Buel, Arthur 1877?-1952 *BioIn 3*
Buel, Clarence Clough 1850-1933 *AmAu&B, BbD, BiD&SB, BioIn 8, DcAmA, HisAmM XR*
Buel, James William 1849-1920 *Alli Sup, AmAu&B, BiD&SB, DcAmA, DcNAA*
Buel, Jesse 1778-1839 *AmJnl, DcAmA, DcNAA, HisAmM XR*
Buel, Walker Shower 1890-1957 *BioIn 4, WhJnl 1928*
Buell, Ellen Lewis *AuBYP, BioIn 8, ForWC 1970*
Buell, George P *HisAmM XR*
Buell, Nellie L 1892- *WhJnl 1928*
Buell, Raymond Leslie 1896-1946 *AmAu&B, BioIn 2, CurBio XR, DcNAA, WebBD*
Bueno, Guy 1913- *NF*

Buero, Juan Antonio 1891-1950 *BioIn 2*
Buescher, Alfred J *NF*
Buffle, Martine 1947- *NF*
Buffum, Edward Gould 1820-1867 *Alli Sup, AmAu&B, DcNAA*
Bugbee, Emma *AuBYP, BioIn 7*
Bugg, Bob *NF*
Bugg, Ralph 1922- *ConAu 73*
Buies, Arthur 1840-1901 *CanWr, CasWL, DcNAA, OxCan*
Bujega, Vincent *NF*
Bukro, Casey *NF*
Bulatovic, Vukoje 1927- *IntWW 1976*
Bulgarin, Faddei Vonediktovich 1789-1859 *WebBD*
Bulkeley, Christy C 1941?- *AuNews 2, BioIn 10*
Bull, Alvin Fred 1925- *WhoAm 1974*
Bull, Bartle 1938- *BioIn 8*
Bull, Henry Adsit *HisAmM XR*
Bull, Jerome Case *HisAmM XR*
Bull, Johan 1893-1945 *CurBio XR*
Bull, Lois M 1900- *WhJnl 1928*
Bull, Louise *HisAmM XR*
Bullard, Arthur 1879-1929 *AmLY, DcNAA, HisAmM XR, NatCAB 21, WebBD, WhNAA*
Bullard, Frederic Lauriston 1866-1952 *AmAu&B, BioIn 3, OhA&B, REnAL, WhJnl 1928*
Bullard, Laura Curtis *Alli Sup, HisAmM XR*
Bullen, Dana Ripley 1931- *ConAu 73*
Bullen, Percy Sutherland 1867-1958 *BioIn 4*
Bullitt, William Christian 1891-1967 *CurBio XR, REn, REnAL, WebBD*
Bullitt, William S *HisAmM XR*
Bulloch, John Malcolm 1867- *WhoLA*
Bullock, Barry *BioIn 1*
Bullock, W F *NF*
Bullock, William *AmJnl*
Bullock, William H *HisAmM XR*
Bulmer, John 1938- *BioIn 6*
Buloz, Charles 1843-1905 *WebBD*
Buloz, Francois 1803-1877? *BiD&SB, OxFr, WebBD*
Bulwer-Lytton, Edward George E Lytton 1803-1873 *AtlBL, BiDLA, BrAu 19, CyWA, DcBiA, HsB&A, McGWD, MouLC 3, NewC, Pen Eng*
Bulwer-Lytton, Edward George E Lytton *see also* Lytton, Baron E G
Bumbarger, Paul R *NF*
Bump, Charles Weathers 1872-1908 *DcNAA*
Bump, Franklin E, Jr. 1898- *WhNAA, WhJnl 1928*
Bunce, Alan 1939- *BiE&WWA*
Bunce, George *NF*
Bunce, Harold R 1889-1969 *BioIn 8*
Bunce, Oliver Bell 1828-1890 *Alli Sup, AmAu, AmAu&B, BbD, BiD&SB, DcAmA, DcNAA, HisAmM XR, OxAm, REnAL*
Bunch, Ross E *NF*
Bundy, Jonas Mills 1835-1891 *Alli Sup, AmAu&B, BbD, BiD&SB, DcAmA, DcAmB 3, DcNAA, NatCAB 1*
Bundy, William Putnam 1917- *CurBio XR, IntWW 1976, WhoAm 1974, WhoAmP 1973, WhoE 1974*
Bungay, George Washington 1818?-1892 *Alli Sup, AmAu&B, BbD, BiD&SB, DcAmA, DcNAA, HisAmM XR*
Bunge, Alejandro 1880-1943 *WebBD*
Bunge, Charles Albert 1936- *BiDrLUS, WhoCon 1973, WhoMW 1974*
Bunker, Earle L d1975 *NF*
Bunker, Edmund Cason 1915- *WhoAdv 1972, WhoAm 1974, WhoWest 1974*

Bunker, Isabel Leighton *OvPC*
Bunnelle, Robert Ellsworth 1903- *OvPC,*
 WhoAm 1974, WhoS&SW 1973
Bunner, Henry Cuyler 1855-1896 *Alli Sup, AmAu,*
 AmAu&B, BbD, BiD&SB, CnDAL,
 DcAmA, DcLEL, DcNAA, EvLB,
 HisAmM XR, OxAm, REn, REnAL,
 WebBD
Bunny 1866-1939 *DcNAA, WebBD*
Bunny *see also* Schultze, Bunny
Bunny *see also* Schultze, Carl Emil
Buntin, William Harve 1902- *WhJnl 1928*
Bunting, Joe 1890- *WhJnl 1928*
Bunting, Oliver W 1870- *WhJnl 1928*
Bunting, Sir Percy William 1836-1911 *BioIn 5*
Buntline, Ned 1823-1886 *Alli Sup, AmAu,*
 AmAu&B, DcAmA, DcNAA, HsB&A,
 OhA&B. OxAm. REn. REnAL
Buntline, Ned *see also* Judson, Edward Zane C
Bunyan, Maureen *NF*
Burack, Abraham Saul 1908-1978 *AmAu&B,*
 BioIn 4, ConAu 9, WhoAdv 1972,
 WhoWorJ 1972
Burack, Sylvia Kammerman 1916- *ConAu 21,*
 FamWC, WhoAmW 1974
Buranelli, Prosper 1890- *WhJnl 1928*
Burba, Howard L *WhJnl 1928*
Burbach, George M 1883- *WhJnl 1928*
Burbee, David Rankin 1874?-1958 *BioIn 4*
Burby, John P *RpN*
Burch, A T *NF*
Burch, Charles Sumner 1855-1920 *HisAmM XR*
Burch, H Wendel 1908-1970 *BioIn 8*
Burch, Monte *NF*
Burchard, R B *HisAmM XR*
Burchardt, Bill *NF*
Burchell, Sam *NF*
Burchett, Wilfred Graham 1911- *Au&Wr,*
 BioIn 3, BioIn 7, BioIn 9, ConAu 49,
 WrDr 1976
Burck, Jacob 1904- *WhoAm 1974*
Burd, Frank J 1870-1962 *BioIn 6*
Burd, Lawrence *NF*
Burden, Grant *OvPC*
Burden, S Carter, Jr. 1941- *BioIn 8, BioIn 9,*
 NewYTBE 2
Burdett, Charles 1815- *Alli, Alli Sup, AmAu&B*
 BiD&SB, DcAmA, DcNAA, EncMys
Burdett, Winston M 1913- *ConAu 29,*
 CurBio XR
Burdette, Leah d1942 *AmJnl*
Burdette, Robert Jones 1844-1914 *Alli Sup,*
 AmAu, AmAu&B, AmJnl, BbD, BiD&SB,
 DcAmA, DcNAA, HisAmM XR, OhA&B,
 OxAm, REnAL, WebBD
Burdick, George *NF*
Burdick, George 1879?-1958 *BioIn 5*
Burdick, Henry Hagaman 1878?-1953 *BioIn 3*
Burdick, William *HisAmM XR*
Bure, Emile 1876-1952 *BioIn 2, BioIn 3*
Buresch, Joe E *NF*
Buresh, Berniece *InvJ*
Burg, Amos *HisAmM XR*
Burg, Copeland 1889-1961 *BioIn 7, NatCAB 47*
Burg, George Roscoe 1916- *WhoAm 1974,*
 WhoF&I 1974
Burg, Marcia *NF*
Burge, Ethel 1916- *ConAu 65*
Burger, Eric *OvPC*
Burger, Gottfried August 1747-1794 *BbD,*
 BiD&SB, CasWL, DcEuL, EuAu, EvEuW,
 OxGer, Pen Eur, REn, WebBD
Burger, Max *HisAmM XR*

Burger, Nash K 1908- *ConAu 23*
Burger, Robert S 1913- *ConAu 29*
Burgert, Theodore P *OvPC*
Burgess, Ernest Watson 1886-1966 *HisAmM XR,*
 WhNAA
Burgess, Frank Gelett 1866-1951 *DcAmB S5,*
 WebBD
Burgess, Frank Gelett *see also* Burgess, Gelett
Burgess, Frank H 1875-1939 *WhJnl 1928*
Burgess, Fred H *NF*
Burgess, Gelett 1866-1951 *AmAu&B, AmLY,*
 AnMV 1926, BiD&SB, CnDAL, ConAmL,
 DcAmA, EncMys, EvLB, HisAmM XR,
 LiJA, LongC, OxAm, REn, REnAL,
 TwCA, TwCA Sup, TwCW, WhNAA
Burgess, Gelett *see also* Burgess, Frank Gelett
Burgess, Sir John Lawie 1912- *IntWW 1976,*
 WhoWor 1974
Burgess, Thornton Waldo 1874-1965 *AmAu&B,*
 AuBYP, CarSB, ConAu 73, JBA 1934,
 JBA 1951, OxAm, REn, REnAL, WebBD,
 WhNAA, WhoChL
Burgheim, Richard *NF*
Burgin, C David 1939- *ConAu 73*
Burgin, F F *NF*
Burgner, Fred *NF*
Burgoyne, Arthur Gordon d1914 *DcNAA*
Burgoyne, Henry Bartlett 1885-1950 *BioIn 2*
Burhardt, Neil Wilbur 1889- *WhJnl 1928*
Burick, Si *NF*
Burk, Addison B 1847-1912 *NatCAB 28*
Burk, Bill Eugene 1932- *ConAu 65*
Burk, Dale A 1937?- *NF*
Burk, John Daly 1775?-1808 *AmAu, AmAu&B,*
 AmJnl, BiDSA, DcAmA, DcNAA,
 HisAmM XR, OxAm, PoIre, REnAL
Burkam, Elzey Gallatin 1872-1940 *AmAu&B*
Burke, Albert Edward *BioIn 5, BioIn 6*
Burke, Alice *NF*
Burke, Art 1914- *WhoAm 1974,*
 WhoS&SW 1973
Burke, Daniel Barnett 1929- *WhoAm 1974*
Burke, Donald *RpN*
Burke, Edward d1898 *NF*
Burke, Gene 1910- *USBiR 1974*
Burke, Harry 1912?-1974 *BioIn 10*
Burke, J W *HisAmM XR*
Burke, John Franklin 1873?-1966 *BioIn 7,*
 WhJnl 1928
Burke, John Joseph 1875-1936 *DcNAA,*
 HisAmM XR
Burke, Kenneth Duva 1897- *AmAu&B, AmWr,*
 Au&Wr, CasWL, CnDAL, ConAmA,
 ConAu 5R, ConLC 2, ConNov 1972,
 ConNov 1976, ConP 1970, ConP 1975,
 DcLEL, EvLB, HisAmM XR, ModAL,
 ModAL Sup, OxAm, Pen Am, RAdv 1,
 REn, REnAL, TwCA, TwCA Sup, WebBD,
 WebE&AL, WhoTwCL, WrDr 1976
Burke, Kenneth Karl 1910- *WhoAm 1974*
Burke, Merton *NF*
Burke, Mildred A *WhJnl 1928*
Burke, T A *HisAmM XR*
Burke, Ted 1933?-1977 *NF*
Burke, Tom *ConAu 73*
Burke, Veronica *NF*
Burke, Wally E *NF*
Burket, Harriet 1908- *ForWC 1970,*
 WhoAm 1974
Burkett, Charles William 1873-1962 *AmLY,*
 DcAmA, HisAmM XR, OhA&B, WhNAA
Burkett, David Young, III 1934- *ConAu 65*
Burkham, James Campbell 1918- *BioIn 2*
Burkhard, John P *HisAmM XR*

Burkhardt, Robert *NF*
Burkhardt, Wilbur Neil 1889- *WhNAA,*
WhJnl 1928
Burkhart, John 1908- *AmEA 1974,*
AmM&W 73S
Burkhart, Kathryn Watterson 1942- *ConAu 45*
Burkov, Boris Sergeevich 1908- *IntWW 1976*
Burleigh, Bennet *FamWC*
Burleigh, Charles A 1892- *WhJnl 1928*
Burleigh, Charles Calistus 1810-1878 *DcNAA,*
HisAmM XR
Burleigh, Clarence Blendon 1864-1910 *DcNAA,*
NatCAB 14
Burleigh, Edwin Clarence 1891- *WhNAA,*
WhJnl 1928
Burleigh, William Henry 1812-1871 *Alli, AmAu,*
AmAu&B, BiD&SB, CyAL 2, DcAmA,
DcAmB 3, DcNAA, HisAmM XR,
NatCAB 2
Burleson, Rufus Columbus *HisAmM XR*
Burlingame, Edward Livermore 1848-1922
Alli Sup, AmAu&B, BioIn 3, DcNAA,
WebBD
Burman, Ben Lucien 1895- *AmAu&B, AmNov,*
Au&Wr, ConAu 5R, OvPC, OxAm,
REnAL, SmATA 6, TwCA, TwCA Sup,
WebBD, WhNAA, WhoAm 1974,
WhoWor 1974, WrDr 1976
Burn, Walter P 1894- *WhJnl 1928*
Burnaby, Frederick Gustavus 1842-1885 *Alli Sup,*
BiD&SB, FamWC, NewC, OxEng, WebBD
Burnand, Sir Francis Cowley 1836-1917 *Alli Sup,*
BiD&SB, BrAu 19, DcEnL, EvLB, LongC,
NewC, OxEng, REn, WebBD
Burnes, Jim 1927?-1970 *BioIn 8*
Burness, Tad 1933- *ConAu 69*
Burness, Wallace B 1933- *ConAu 69*
Burnet, Alastair 1928- *BioIn 7, ForP,*
IntWW 1974, Who 1974
Burnet, Alastair *see also* Burnet, James William
Alexander
Burnet, James William Alexander 1928-
IntWW 1976, Who 1974, WhoWor 1974
Burnet, James William Alexander *see also* Burnet,
Alastair
Burnett, Constance 1893- *BioIn 1, BioIn 8*
Burnett, David Benjamin Foley 1932?-1971 *BioIn 9*
Burnett, Hallie Southgate 1908- *AmAu&B,*
BioIn 1, BioIn 3, ConAu 13, CurBio XR,
OvPC, TwCA Sup, WebBD, WhoAm 1974,
WhoAmW 1974, WhoWor 1974, WrDr 1976
Burnett, James *NF*
Burnett, Leon R *NF*
Burnett, Martha Foley *see* Foley, Martha
Burnett, Robert A 1927- *WhoAm 1974,*
WhoF&I 1974
Burnett, Sally K 1906?-1965 *BioIn 7*
Burnett, Vivian 1876-1937 *BioIn 8, DcNAA*
Burnett, W C *NF*
Burnett, Whit 1899-1973 *AmAu&B, BioIn 4,*
BioIn 9, BioIn 10, ConAu 13, ConAu 41,
CurBio XR, NewYTBE 4, REnAL, TwCA,
TwCA Sup, WebBD, WhoAm 1974
Burnett, Mrs. Whit 1908- *CurBio XR*
Burnett, Mrs. Whit *see also* Burnett, Hallie
Southgate
Burnett, William Clyde, Jr. 1928- *WhoAm 1974*
Burney, Elizabeth 1934- *ConAu 23R*
Burney, Mary Chase *HisAmM XR*
Burnham, David Bright 1933- *InvJ, NewMr,*
WhoAm 1974
Burnham, Baron Edward Frederick Lawson
1890-1963 *BioIn 6*

Burnham, Lord Edward Levy-awson 1833-1916
Lor&LP, WebBD
Burnham, Guy Miles 1860-1939 *BioIn 5*
Burnham, Harry *NF*
Burnham, Harry L W Lawson, Viscount 1862-1933
BioIn 2, BioIn 6, WebBD
Burnham, James 1905- *AmAu&B, CurBio XR,*
Pen Am, TwCA Sup, Who 1974,
WhoAm 1974, WhoWor 1974
Burnham, Mary 1881- *BioIn 1*
Burnham, Ruth 1928?-1966 *BioIn 7*
Burns, A L 1893- *WhJnl 1928*
Burns, Benjamin Joseph 1940- *WhoAm 1974*
Burns, Charles d1973 *BioIn 9*
Burns, Creighton *ForP*
Burns, Edward Harold 1891-1955 *BioIn 3*
Burns, Eugene *NF*
Burns, Frances 1894-1961 *BioIn 5*
Burns, George E *OvPC*
Burns, George R 1902?-1964 *BioIn 6*
Burns, John *NF*
Burns, Maxine Isaacs *NF*
Burns, Peter *NF*
Burns, Robert Edward 1919- *WhoAm 1974*
Burns, Walter Noble 1872-1932 *AmAu&B, ArizL,*
DcNAA
Burns, William *NF*
Burns, William 1912?- *BioIn 2*
Burr, Agnes Rush *AmAu&B, WhNAA*
Burr, Alfred Edmund 1815-1900 *AmAu&B,*
NatCAB 1, WebBD
Burr, Charles Chauncey 1817-1883 *Alli Sup,*
AmAu&B, DcNAA, HisAmM XR
Burr, Edwin Marcellus 1893- *WhJnl 1928*
Burr, Malcolm 1878-1954 *BioIn 3*
Burr, Willie Olcott 1843-1921 *NatCAB 19,*
WebBD
Burrell, Hedley *NF*
Burrelle, Frank A *NF*
Burrier, Dale G *NF*
Burrington, David E 1931- *ConAu 73, OvPC*
Burritt, Burton Turrell 1899- *WhNAA,*
WhJnl 1928
Burritt, Daniel Ernest 1907?-1951 *BioIn 2*
Burritt, Elihu 1810-1879 *Alli, Alli Sup, AmAu,*
AmAu&B, BbD, BiD&SB, CyAL 2,
DcAmA, DcEnL, DcNAA, OxAm, REnAL,
WebBD
Burros, Marian *NF*
Burroughs, Benjamin F 1918- *ConAu 65*
Burroughs, Elton 1870- *WhJnl 1928*
Burroughs, W B, Jr. *HisAmM XR*
Burrowes, Alonzo Moore 1887-1953 *BioIn 3*
Burrows, Edwin Grant 1891- *WhJnl 1928*
Burrows, Frank G 1880?-1949 *BioIn 2*
Burrows, Frederick M *HisAmM XR*
Burrows, Jay *HisAmM XR*
Burrows, Larry *NF*
Burrows, William E 1937- *ConAu 65*
Burruss, John C *HisAmM XR*
Bursk, Edward C 1907- *AmM&W 73S,*
ConAu 4R
Burslem, Alex Y d1946 *BioIn 1*
Burson, Elbert Eugene 1903- *WhNAA,*
WhJnl 1928
Burson, Harold 1921- *OvPC, WhoAdv 1972,*
WhoAm 1974, WhoF&I 1974,
WhoPubR 1972, WhoWor 1974
Burson, John H 1905- *WhJnl 1928*
Bursten, Martin A *OvPC*
Burt, Albert L *HisAmM XR*
Burt, Alvin Victor, Jr. 1927- *ConAu 25,*
WhoAm 1974, WhoS&SW 1973

Burt, Charles *HisAmM XR*
Burt, George Dole Wadley 1909- *WhoAm 1974,
WhoS&SW 1973*
Burt, Henry M *HisAmM XR*
Burt, Maxwell Struthers 1882-1954 *AmAu&B,
HisAmM XR, TwCA, TwCA Sup, WebBD,
WhJnl 1928*
Burt, Michael 1900- *BioIn 1, CathA 1930*
Burt, Richard *NF*
Burtis, Aleyn *NF*
Burtner, John C 1895- *WhJnl 1928*
Burton, Anthony *NF*
Burton, Earl 1916-1968 *BioIn 8*
Burton, Ernest DeWitt 1856-1925 *DcAmA,
DcNAA, HisAmM XR, OhA&B, WebBD*
Burton, Frederick Russell 1861-1909 *AmAu&B,
DcNAA*
Burton, Harold Bernard 1908- *WhoAm 1974,
WhoE 1974*
Burton, Harold R *NF*
Burton, Harry Payne *HisAmM XR*
Burton, Joe Wright 1907- *AmAu&B,
WhoAm 1974, WhoWor 1974*
Burton, Lewis 1905-1969 *BioIn 8*
Burton, Naomi *BioIn 7*
Burton, Sir Pomeroy 1868?-1947 *BioIn 1*
Burton, Richard *LiJA*
Burton, Richard Eugene 1861-1940 *AmAu&B,
AnMV 1926, BbD, BiD&SB, DcAmA,
DcAmB S2, DcNAA, REnAL, WebBD,
WhNAA*
Burton, Rush d1946 *BioIn 1*
Burton, Sandra *NF*
Burton, Scott *NF*
Burton, William Evans 1804-1860 *Alli, AmAu,
AmAu&B, DcAmA, DcNAA, HisAmM XR,
OxAm, REnAL*
Burwell, William MacCreary 1809-1888 *BiDSA,
DcNAA, HisAmM XR*
Busbey, Hamilton 1840-1924 *DcNAA,
HisAmM XR, OhA&B*
Busbey, L White 1852-1925 *DcNAA, OhA&B*
Busch, Gilbert E 1914- *OvPC, WhoPubR 1972*
Busch, Moritz 1821-1899 *WebBD*
Busch, N C *NF*
Busch, Niven 1903- *AmAu&B, AmNov,
Au&Wr, ConAu 13R, IntMPA 1975, REn,
REnAL, TwCA Sup, WhoAm 1974,
WhoWor 1974*
Busch, Noel Fairchild 1906- *AmAu&B,
ConAu 49, WhoAm 1974, WhoWor 1974*
Busche, J F *HisAmM XR*
Busenbark, Ross E 1894- *WhJnl 1928*
Bush, Asahel d1944 *AmJnl*
Bush, Asahel 1824-1913 *NF*
Bush, Charles G 1842-1909 *AmJnl, EarABI Sup,
HisAmM XR*
Bush, Chilton Rowlette 1896- *AmM&W 73S,
WhJnl 1928*
Bush, Gordon Kenner 1903- *WhNAA,
WhJnl 1928*
Bush, Gordon Kenner, Jr. 1934- *WhoF&I 1974,
WhoMW 1974*
Bush, Lew *BioIn 8*
Bush, Martin *NF*
Bush, Peter Birdsall 1924- *WhoAm 1974,
WhoS&SW 1973*
Bush, Rufus T *HisAmM XR*
Bush, Sam Stone *HisAmM XR*
Bushinsky, Jay 1932- *OvPC*
Bushmiller, Ernest Paul 1905- *AuNews 1,
BioIn 1, ConAu 29, WhoAm 1974*
Bushnell, Edward Rogers 1876?-1951 *BioIn 2*
Busino, Orlando Francis 1926- *WhoAm 1974*

Buskin, Martin 1930-1976 *ConAu 65,
WhoAm 1974*
Buss, Kate 1884- *WhNAA*
Bussard, Paul C 1904- *BioIn 1*
Bussenius, Luellen Cass 1868?-1968 *BioIn 8*
Bussing, Wilfrid Charles 1889- *WhoAm 1974,
WhJnl 1928*
Bustamante, Carlos Lopez 1886?-1950 *BioIn 2*
Butcher, Fanny 1888- *AmAu&B, BioIn 3,
BioIn 9, ForWC 1970, WhNAA,
WhoAm 1974, WhoAmW 1974*
Butcher, Fanny *see also* Bokum, Fanny Butcher
Butcher, Lee *NF*
Butler, Burridge Davenal 1868-1948 *DcAmB S4,
HisAmM XR*
Butler, Charles R 1879- *WhNAA, WhJnl 1928*
Butler, Mrs. Edward Hubert (D1974) *see also* Butler,
Kate
Butler, Mrs. Edward Hubert d1974 *WhoAm 1974,
WhoAmW 1974, WhoE 1974*
Butler, Edward Hubert 1883-1956 *BioIn 2,
BioIn 4, BioIn 5, WhJnl 1928*
Butler, Eugene 1894- *WhoAm 1974, WhJnl 1928*
Butler, Frank *BioIn 2*
Butler, G Paul 1900- *ConAu 17, WhoAm 1974*
Butler, George Vincent 1904- *WhNAA,
WhJnl 1928*
Butler, Hal 1913- *AuBYP, BioIn 8, ConAu 57*
Butler, J B *WhJnl 1928*
Butler, J H 1894- *WhJnl 1928*
Butler, Jack Lawrence 1917- *WhoAm 1974,
WhoS&SW 1973*
Butler, James J 1901?-1959 *BioIn 5*
Butler, James Thomas 1921- *WhoAdv 1972,
WhoAm 1974, WhoF&I 1974,
WhoMW 1974*
Butler, Jeffrey S *NF*
Butler, Kate d1974 *BioIn 10, BioNews 1974*
Butler, Kate *see also* Butler, Mrs. Edward Hubert
Butler, Merrill *HisAmM XR*
Butler, Ovid E 1880-1960 *BioIn 1, BioIn 4,
BioIn 5, BioIn 6, WhJnl 1928*
Butler, Robert Gordon 1860-1906 *BioIn 3*
Butler, Robert M *NF*
Butler, Roland 1887-1961 *BioIn 1, BioIn 3,
BioIn 4, BioIn 6*
Butler, Ron 1934- *ConAu 69*
Butler, Sheppard 1883-1962 *BioIn 6*
Butler, Susan L *NF*
Butler, Tait 1862-1939 *BioIn 2, WhJnl 1928*
Butler, William *NF*
Butler, William Mill 1857-1946 *AmAu&B,
DcNAA, HisAmM XR*
Butorac, Tomislav *NF*
Butsikares, S K *OvPC*
Buttedahl, Oscar *RpN*
Buttelman, Clifford V 1886?-1970 *BioIn 9*
Buttenheim, Edgar Marion 1922- *WhoAm 1974,
WhoF&I 1974*
Buttenheim, Harold Sinley 1876-1961 *BioIn 4,
WhNAA, WhJnl 1928*
Butter, Jack L *NF*
Butter, Nathaniel d1664 *NewC, WebBD*
Butterfield, Fox *NF*
Butterfield, Jan VanAlstine 1937- *WhoAm 1974*
Butterfield, Roger Place 1907- *AmAu&B,
BioIn 1, ConAu P-1, CurBio XR, REnAL*
Butterworth, Benjamin T 1870-1953 *BioIn 3,
WhJnl 1928*
Butterworth, Hezekiah 1839-1905 *Alli Sup,
AmAu, AmAu&B, BbD, BiD&SB, CarSB,
DcAmA, DcAmB 3, DcNAA*
Buttice, Alexander J *OvPC*
Buttre, John Chester *HisAmM XR*

Buttrill, Sidney Eugene 1920- *WhoAm 1974,*
  WhoF&I 1974
Butts, Asa K *HisAmM XR*
Butts, Isaac 1816-1874 *Alli Sup, DcNAA,*
  NatCAB 21
Butzgy, Helen *HisAmM XR*
Buxton, Bonnie 1948- *ConAu 69*
Buxton, Charles Roberts 1913- *ConAu 65,*
  WhoAdv 1972, WhoAm 1974,
  WhoF&I 1974, WhoWest 1974
Buxton, Frank W 1878?-1974 *BioIn 10,*
  NewYTBS 5, WhJnl 1928
Buxton, H W *NF*
Buxton, Henry James 1882-1939 *DcNAA*
Buys, Donna *NF*
Buzacott, Charles Hardie 1835-1918 *BioIn 2*
Buzzati, Dino 1906-1972 *BioIn 2, BioIn 5,*
  BioIn 9, BioIn 10, CnMD, ConAu 33,
  CroCD, EncWL, NewYTBE 3, Pen Eur,
  TwCW, WhoTwCL, WorAu
Byam, Guy *NF*
Byars, William Vincent 1857-1938 *AmAu&B,*
  AmLY, BiDSA, DcNAA
Byas, Hugh 1875-1945 *CurBio XR, DcNAA*
Bye, George Thurman 1887- *AmAu&B,*
  WhJnl 1928
Byerly, Kenneth Rhodes 1908- *AmM&W 73S,*
  ConAu 2R, WhoWest 1974
Byers, Margaretta 1901- *CurBio XR*
Byers, Mark Rhea 1892-1950 *BioIn 2, BioIn 5,*
  WhJnl 1928
Byers, Vincent 1892- *WhJnl 1928*
Byers, William Newton 1831-1903 *Alli Sup,*
  AmJnl, BioIn 8, DcNAA, OhA&B, WebBD
Byington, E H *FamWC*
Bykowsky, Germain *NF*
Byles, Matthew *NF*
Bylinsky, Gene Michael 1930- *WhoAm 1974*
Byng, Edward John 1894-1962 *BioIn 6*
Byoir, Carl 1888-1957 *AmJnl*
Byram, John 1901-1977 *BiE&WWA*
Byrd, Harry Flood 1887-1965 *CurBio XR,*
  WebBD
Byrd, Harry Flood, Jr. 1914- *BioIn 7, BioIn 8,*
  BioIn 9, CelR 1973, CngDr 1974,
  IntWW 1976, WhoAm 1974, WhoAmP 1973,
  WhoGov 1972, WhoS&SW 1973
Byrd, Lee *NF*
Byrne, Charles Alfred 1848-1909 *Alli Sup,*
  DcNAA, HisAmM XR
Byrne, Charles D 1895- *WhNAA, WhJnl 1928*
Byrne, Don *NF*
Byrne, John Francis 1880- *BioIn 3*
Byrne, Nicholas 1761-1833 *BioIn 4*
Byrne, Robert Eugene 1928- *WhoAm 1974*
Byrnes, C A *AmJnl*
Byrnes, Eugene F 1890?-1974 *BioIn 10,*
  ConAu 49
Byrod, Fred Jacob 1911- *WhoAm 1974,*
  WhoE 1974
Byron, Christopher 1944- *NF*
Byron, Florence Smith Vincent 1969- *BioIn 8*
Byron, John *ConAu XR*
Byron, Robert 1905-1941 *BioIn 5, DcLEL,*
  EvLB, LongC
Bywater, Hector Charles 1884-1940 *NewC,*
  WebBD

C

Cabaniss, Henry Harrison 1848-1934 *Alli Sup*
Cabell, James Branch 1879-1958 *AmAu&B,*
 AmLY, AmNov, BiDSA, CasWL, CnDAL,
 CnMWL, ConAmA, ConAmL, CyWA,
 DcAmA, DcBiA, DcLEL, EncWL, EvLB,
 HisAmM XR, LongC, ModAL, OxAm,
 OxEng, Pen Am, RAdv 1, REn, REnAL,
 TwCA, TwCA Sup, TwCW, WebBD,
 WebE&AL, WhNAA
Cabell, Nathaniel Francis 1807-1891 *AmAu&B,*
 DcNAA
Cabluck, Harry *NF*
Cabot, Charles M *HisAmM XR*
Cabot, James Elliot 1821-1903 *Alli, BioIn 6,*
 DcAmA, DcNAA, HisAmM XR, LiJA,
 OxCan
Cabrera, Alejandro *ForP*
Cacella, Joseph 1882- *BioIn 3, CathA 1952*
Cadbury, Edward 1873-1948 *BioIn 1*
Cadbury, Henry Tylor 1882-1952 *BioIn 3*
Caddell, Patrick 1950?- *BioIn 9, BioIn 10*
Cadden, Vivian *NF*
Caddick, William Andrew 1904- *WhoAm 1974*
Cade, J J *HisAmM XR*
Cadge, William Fleming 1924- *WhoAm 1974,*
 WhoE 1974
Cadieux, Leo 1908- *CanWW 1972,*
 IntWW 1976, Who 1974, WhoAm 1974,
 WhoCan 1973, WhoWor 1974
Cadigan, Robert James 1912- *WhoAm 1974*
Cadman, Anne Bradford *NF*
Cadman, Charles Wakefield 1881-1946
 AmSCAP 1966, OxAm, REnAL, WebBD
Cadwell, O H 1888- *WhJnl 1928*
Cady, Ernest Albert 1899- *WhoAm 1974*
Cady, Harrison 1877-1970 *BioIn 1, BioIn 2,*
 BioIn 3, BioIn 9, NewYTBE 1, WhNAA
Cady, Richard E 1940?- *BioIn 10, InvJ*
Cady, Steve 1927- *ConAu 45*
Caen, Herb 1916- *AuNews 1, BioIn 1, BioIn 2,*
 BioIn 4, BioIn 8, CelR 1973, ConAu 1R,
 WhoAm 1974, WhoWor 1974
Caesar, Irving 1895- *AmSCAP 1966, Au&Wr,*
 BiE&WWA, IntMPA 1975, REnAL,
 Who 1974, WhoAm 1974
Cafe Filho, Joao 1899-1970 *CurBio XR*
Caffi, Andrea *AmRP*
Caffie, Barbara J 1936?- *BlkC*
Caffin, Charles Henry 1854-1918 *AmAu&B,*
 AmLY, DcAmA, DcNAA, HisAmM XR
Cagnoni, Romano *NF*
Cahan, Abraham 1860-1951 *AmAu&B, AmJnl,*
 BbD, BiD&SB, BioIn 1, BioIn 2, BioIn 3,
 BioIn 4, BioIn 8, CasWL, ConAmL,
 DcAmA, DcAmB S5, EncWL,
 HisAmM XR, ModAL, OxAm, Pen Am,
 REn, REnAL, TwCA, TwCA Sup, WebBD,
 WhNAA, WhJnl 1928
Cahan, Samuel 1896- *WhJnl 1928*
Cahill, Harry Holmes 1901- *WhoAm 1974,*
 WhJnl 1928
Cahill, James E, Jr. 1918?-1971 *BioIn 9,*
 NewYTBE 2
Cahill, Jerome S *NF*
Cahill, Regina *NF*
Cahn, Robert 1917- *WhoAm 1974,*
 WhoGov 1972, WhoS&SW 1973
Cahn, William 1912-1976 *ConAu 23, ConAu 69,*
 WhoAdv 1972
Cahn, Zvi 1896- *ConAu 23*
Caillavet, Gaston Arman De 1869-1915 *CIDMEL,*
 EvEuW, McGWD, OxFr, WebBD
Cain, Bob 1934- *NF*
Cain, Charles Cornelius 1886-1971 *BioIn 10*
Cain, J Byron 1874- *WhJnl 1928*
Cain, James Mallahan 1892-1977 *AmAu&B,*
 AmNov, AuNews 1, BiE&WWA,
 CelR 1973, CnDAL, CnMWL, ConAu 17R,
 ConAu 73, ConLC 3, ConNov 1972,
 ConNov 1976, CurBio XR, DcLEL, EncMys,
 HisAmM XR, LongC, ModAL, OxAm,
 Pen Am, REn, REnAL, TwCA, TwCA Sup,
 TwCW, WebBD, WebE&AL, WhNAA,
 WhoAm 1974, WhoWor 1974, WrDr 1976
Cain, Mary 1904- *BioIn 4*
Cain, Robert Owen 1934- *ConAu 65*
Cain, Walter 1862- *WhJnl 1928*
Caine, Lynn *BioIn 10*
Caine, Sir Thomas Henry Hall 1853-1931 *Alli Sup,*
 BbD, BiD&SB, DcBiA, DcEnA, DcEnA Ap,
 DcLEL, EvLB, OxEng, WebBD
Caine, William Ralph Hall 1865-1939 *NewC,*
 WebBD, WhoLA
Cairncross, Frances 1944- *ConAu 57*
Cakars, Maris 1942- *BioIn 10*
Calamandrei, Mauro 1925- *ConAu 69*
Calcraft, Eric *AmJnl*
Calder, Iain *NF*
Calder, Ritchie 1906- *AmAu&B, Au&Wr,*
 BioIn 6, ConAu 1R, CurBio XR, LongC,
 OxCan, Who 1974, WorAu
Calder, Ritchie *see also* Ritchie-Calder, Baron Peter
Calderoni, Louis J *OvPC*
Caldwell, Douglas E *NF*
Caldwell, Earl 1938?- *BioIn 9, BlkC*
Caldwell, Edward 1861-1949 *NatCAB 38*
Caldwell, Erskine Preston 1903- *AmAu&B,*
 AmNov, AmWr, Au&Wr, AuNews 1,
 BioNews 1974, CasWL, CnDAL, ConAmA,
 ConAu 1, ConAu 3, ConAu 1R, ConLC 1,
 ConNov 1972, ConNov 1976, CurBio XR,
 CyWA, DcLEL, DrAF 1976, EncWL,

EvLB, IntWW 1974, LongC, ModAL,
ModAL Sup, OxAm, Pen Am, RAdv 1,
REn, REnAL, TwCA, TwCA Sup, TwCW,
WebBD, WebE&AL, WhNAA, Who 1974,
WhoAm 1974, WhoS&SW 1973, WhoTwCL,
WhoWor 1974, WrDr 1976
Caldwell, Evelyn 1908?- *BioIn 2*
Caldwell, George *NF*
Caldwell, John E *HisAmM XR*
Caldwell, Nathan Green 1912- *RpN,*
WhoS&SW 1973
Caldwell, O H 1888-1967 *WhJnl Sup*
Caldwell, Robert N 1908?-1973 *BioIn 9,*
NewYTBE 4
Caldwell, W F *NF*
Caldwell, William Anthony 1906- *NewYTBE 3,*
WhoAm 1974
Cale, Gladstone Hume 1890-1965 *BioIn 7*
Calhoun, Alfred R *Alli Sup*
Calhoun, Fillmore 1908?-1967 *BioIn 7*
Calhoun, John *AmJnl*
Calkins, Carroll Cecil 1918- *OvPC, WhoAm 1974*
Calkins, Charles Edward 1903- *WhJnl 1928*
Calkins, John Thiers 1889- *WhJnl 1928*
Calkins, Norman Allison 1822-1895 *AmAu,*
DcAmA, DcNAA, HisAmM XR
Call, Harvey A 1882- *WhJnl 1928*
Call, S Leigh 1872-1952 *WhJnl 1928*
Callaghan, Barry *OxCan Sup*
Callaghan, J Dorsey 1895-1975 *OhA&B*
Callaghan, Morley Edward 1903- *CanNov,*
CanWr, CasWL, CathA 1930, ConAu 9R,
ConLC 3, ConNov 1972, ConNov 1976,
DcLEL, EncWL Sup, LongC, NewC,
OxAm, OxCan, OxCan Sup, Pen Eng, REn,
REnAL, TwCA, TwCA Sup, TwCW,
WebBD, WebE&AL, WhoTwCL,
WrDr 1976
Callaham, John Robert 1911- *BioIn 2,*
WhoAm 1974, WhoF&I 1974
Callahan, Claire Wallis 1890- *AuBYP, BioIn 8,*
ConAu 5
Callahan, Daniel John 1930- *BioIn 10,*
WhoAm 1974, WhoE 1974, WhoWor 1974
Callahan, Jack 1889?-1954 *BioIn 3*
Callahan, John Peter 1914-1967 *BioIn 8*
Callahan, Michael J 1877- *WhJnl 1928*
Callahan, North 1908- *AmAu&B, Au&Wr,*
ConAu 1, DrAS 74H, WhoAm 1974,
WrDr 1976
Callahan, Ralph Wilson 1906- *WhoF&I 1974,*
WhJnl 1928, WhoS&SW 1973
Callahan, Rosellen *NF*
Callanan, Victor J 1883- *WhJnl 1928*
Callander, Douglas N 1890- *WhJnl 1928*
Callaway, Ben Anderson 1927- *WhoAm 1974*
Callaway, John Douglas 1936- *WhoAm 1974*
Callcott, J *NF*
Callender, A M *HisAmM XR*
Callender, Harold 1892-1959 *AmAu&B, BioIn 5,*
WhNAA, WhJnl 1928
Callender, James Thomson 1758-1803 *Alli, AmJnl,*
BiD&SB, BiDSA, BioIn 8, DcAmA,
DcNAA
Callender, Joseph *HisAmM XR*
Callihan, E L 1903- *ConAu 25, WhoAm 1974,*
WhoS&SW 1973, WrDr 1976
Callimahos, Demetrios 1879- *WhJnl 1928*
Callow, Lewis Chilberg 1895- *WhJnl 1928*
Calloway, Earl *WhoAm 1974*
Callum, Myles 1934- *ConAu 9R, WhoAm 1974*
Callvert, Ronald Glenn 1873-1955 *BioIn 3*
Calman, Mel *NF*
Calmer, Ned 1907- *BioIn 2, ConAu 69,*

WhoAm 1974, WhoWor 1974
Calmette, Gaston 1858-1914 *WebBD*
Calnon, William Lee *NF*
Calosso, Umberto 1895- *BioIn 2*
Calvert, George Henry 1803-1889 *Alli, Alli Sup,*
AmAu, AmAu&B, BbD, BiD&SB, BiDSA,
CyAL 2, DcAmA, DcEnL, DcLEL,
DcNAA, HisAmM XR, OxAm, REnAL
Calvert, William Robinson 1882-1949 *BioIn 2*
Calverton, Victor Francis 1900-1940 *AmAu&B,*
AmRP, DcAmB S2, DcLEL, DcNAA,
HisAmM XR, LiJA, OxAm, Pen Am,
REnAL, TwCA, WebBD
Calvin, Jack E 1906?- *BioIn 3*
Calvin, Joseph Floyd 1902- *WhJnl 1928*
Calvin, Roy L *OvPC*
Cam, Hubert *NF*
Camac, William *HisAmM XR*
Camacho, Mathilde *ForWC 1970*
Camara, Kaliphia *NF*
Came, Barry *NF*
Cameron, Andrew Carr 1836-1892 *HisAmM XR*
Cameron, Ann *HisAmM XR*
Cameron, Barney George 1911- *OvPC,*
WhoAdv 1972, WhoAm 1974
Cameron, Charles Duncan 1877- *WhJnl 1928*
Cameron, David *WhJnl 1928*
Cameron, Frank 1909- *NF*
Cameron, George C *HisAmM XR*
Cameron, George Toland 1873-1955 *BioIn 4,*
BioIn 6, NatCAB 44, WhJnl 1928
Cameron, James 1911- *Au&Wr, BioIn 8,*
ConAu 23R, IntWW 1976, Who 1974,
WrDr 1976
Cameron, John Alexander *FamWC*
Cameron, Julia *NewMr*
Cameron, Ludovick C R Duncombe-Jewell 1866-
BioIn 2, Br&AmS
Cameron, Robert *NF*
Cameron, Robert 1839- *BbtC*
Cameron, Robert Buchanan 1871-1955 *BioIn 7,*
NatCAB 49
Cameron, Ross 1898- *WhJnl 1928*
Cameron, Silver Donald *NF*
Cameron, Simon 1799-1889 *EncAB, WebBD*
Cameron, William Evelyn 1842-1927 *BiDSA,*
DcNAA
Cameron, William John 1878-1955 *NF*
Cameron-Emslie, George *WhJnl Sup*
Camfield, W H *AmRP*
Camille, Roussan 1915-1961 *BioIn 6*
Camp, Charles Wadsworth 1879-1936 *AmAu&B,*
DcNAA
Camp, Enoch E *HisAmM XR*
Camp, John *InvJ*
Camp, Kavanagh-Fletcher *NF*
Camp, Raymond R *NF*
Campaigne, Jameson Gilbert 1914- *ConAu 2R,*
IntWW 1976, WhoAm 1974
Campaigne, Jameson Gilbert, Jr. 1940-
WhoMW 1974
Campanile, Achille 1900-1977 *CIDMEL,*
ConAu 69
Campau, Joseph 1769-1863 *NF*
Campbell, A Bruce *OvPC*
Campbell, Alexander 1788-1866 *Alli, Alli Sup,*
AmAu&B, BbD, BiD&SB, DcAmA,
DcNAA, OxAm, WebBD
Campbell, Alexander 1912-1977 *BioIn 2,*
ConAu 61, HisAmM XR, WhoAm 1974
Campbell, Andrew 1848-1890 *HisAmM XR*
Campbell, Anne 1888- *REnAL, WhoAm 1974,*
WhoAmW 1974
Campbell, Barbara *BlkC*

Campbell, Bartley 1843-1888 *AmAu*, *AmAu&B*,
BiD&SB, *DcAmA*, *DcAmB 3*, *DcNAA*,
HisAmM XR, *HsB&A*, *OxAm*, *REnAL*
Campbell, Bland Hayden 1905- *WhoAmP 1973*,
WhJnl 1928
Campbell, Brewster P *BioIn 1*
Campbell, Bryn 1934?- *BioIn 6*
Campbell, Charles E, Jr. *OvPC*
Campbell, Charles Edwin 1885-1966 *WhJnl 1928*
Campbell, Charles Henry 1904?-1956 *BioIn 2*,
BioIn 3, *BioIn 4*
Campbell, Charles Milton 1852-1940 *DcNAA*
Campbell, Chesser M 1897-1960 *AmJnl*, *BioIn 5*
Campbell, Claude V 1882- *WhJnl 1928*
Campbell, Colin Clyde 1861?-1946 *BioIn 1*
Campbell, Delwin Morton 1880-1952 *BioIn 3*,
BioIn 5, *NatCAB 42*
Campbell, Donald Guy 1922- *ConAu 19R*,
IndAu 1917, *WhoAm 1974*
Campbell, Dortch 1880-1953 *BioIn 3*, *WhJnl 1928*
Campbell, E Simms 1906-1971 *BioIn 6*, *BioIn 7*,
BioIn 8, *BioIn 9*, *CurBio XR*, *NewYTBE 2*
Campbell, E Walter 1904- *WhJnl 1928*
Campbell, Gardner E 1886- *WhJnl 1928*
Campbell, Georgia May 1901- *WhJnl 1928*
Campbell, Hannah *ConAu 11R*
Campbell, Sir Harold Alfred Maurice 1892-1959
BioIn 5
Campbell, Helen Alexander *OvPC*
Campbell, Herbert Johnston 1882-1941
NatCAB 31, *WhJnl 1928*
Campbell, Heyworth *HisAmM XR*
Campbell, J *HisAmM XR*
Campbell, James *HisAmM XR*
Campbell, James 1920- *ConAu 57*
Campbell, James A 1853- *WhJnl 1928*
Campbell, James M *HisAmM XR*
Campbell, Lady Jeanne Louise 1928- *BioIn 6*
Campbell, Jeremy T *NF*
Campbell, John d1886 *NF*
Campbell, John 1653-1728? *AmJnl*, *DcAmB 3*,
REnAL, *WebBD*
Campbell, John 1810-1874 *AmAu&B*
Campbell, John Bayard Taylor 1880-1956 *BioIn 1*,
BioIn 4, *BioIn 6*, *NatCAB 45*, *WhNAA*
Campbell, John Evens 1895- *WhJnl 1928*
Campbell, John Franklin 1940?-1971 *BioIn 9*,
BioIn 10, *ConAu 33*
Campbell, John Wood 1910-1971 *AmAu&B*,
BioIn 5, *BioIn 9*, *ConAu 21*, *ConAu 29*,
NewYTBE 2, *WorAu*
Campbell, Leonel *AmJnl*
Campbell, Leonel *see also* Pry, Polly
Campbell, Louise *BioIn 5*
Campbell, Marion 1921- *WhoAm 1974*,
WhoAmW 1974
Campbell, Patrick Gordon 1913- *BioIn 2*, *BioIn 3*
Campbell, Petey *NF*
Campbell, Richard Rice 1923- *WhoAm 1974*
Campbell, Robert 1922-1977 *ConAu 53*
Campbell, Robert F *RpN*
Campbell, Roy 1901?-1957 *CathA 1930*,
CnE&AP, *CnMWL*, *EncWL*, *LongC*,
ModBL, *ModBL Sup*, *OxEng*, *Pen Eng*,
REn, *TwCA*, *TwCA Sup*, *TwCW*, *WebBD*,
WebE&AL, *WhoTwCL*
Campbell, Russell E 1901- *WhJnl 1928*
Campbell, Ruth 1891?- *BioIn 2*
Campbell, Shepherd 1931- *NF*
Campbell, Thomas 1777-1844 *Alli*, *BbD*,
BiD&SB, *BiDLA*, *BrAu 19*, *CasWL*,
CrtT 2, *DcEnA*, *DcEnA Ap*, *DcEnL*,
DcEuL, *DcLEL*, *EvLB*, *HisAmM XR*,
MouLC 3, *NewC*, *OxAm*, *OxEng*, *Pen Eng*,

PoChrch, *REn*, *WebBD*, *WebE&AL*
Campbell, Walter J *BioIn 10*
Campbell, William Alexander 1881-1938
HisAmM XR, *WhNAA*, *WhJnl 1928*
Campbell, William Steen 1919- *WhoAdv 1972*,
WhoAm 1974, *WhoE 1974*, *WhoWor 1974*
Campe, Louise *BioIn 1*
Camper, Diane *NF*
Campion, Donald Richard 1921- *WhoAm 1974*,
WhoE 1974, *WhoF&I 1974*
Campisteguy, Juan 1859-1937 *WebBD*
Campo, Tirso *NF*
Camprubi, Jose Aymar 1879-1942 *BioIn 4*,
WhJnl 1928
Camron, Roxy *NF*
Camrose, William Ewert Berry, Viscount 1879-1954
BioIn 2, *BioIn 3*, *CurBio XR*, *Lor&LP*
Camus, Paul 1897- *NF*
Canabate, D *ForP*
Canaday, John Edwin 1907- *AmAu&B*,
ConAu 13, *CurBio XR*, *DrAS 74H*,
EncMys, *InvJ*, *WhoAm 1974*,
WhoAmA 1973, *WhoE 1974*, *WorAu*
Canan, James William 1929- *ConAu 61*
Canary, Betty *BioIn 7*
Canavan, Joseph J 1887-1940 *CurBio XR*
Canby, Henry Seidel 1878-1961 *AmAu&B*,
AmLY, *BioIn 1*, *BioIn 2*, *CnDAL*,
ConAmA, *ConAmL*, *CurBio XR*, *DcLEL*,
HisAmM XR, *LiJA*, *LongC*, *OxAm*, *REn*,
REnAL, *TwCA*, *TwCA Sup*, *WebBD*,
WhNAA
Canby, Vincent 1924- *IntMPA 1975*
Candler, Julie 1919- *ConAu 65*
Candler, William Fulbright 1894- *WhNAA*,
WhJnl 1928
Canelas, Jorge *NF*
Canfield, Byron Hilton 1879-1932 *BioIn 4*,
NatCAB 41
Canfield, Henry S *HisAmM XR*
Canfield, Ola 1892- *WhJnl 1928*
Canfield, William Newton 1920- *WhoAm 1974*
Canfield, William Walker 1857-1937 *AmAu&B*,
DcNAA, *WhJnl 1928*
Cang, Joel 1899- *ConAu 29*
Canham, Erwin Dain 1904- *AmAu&B*, *AmJnl*,
BioIn 1, *BioIn 2*, *BioIn 3*, *BioIn 7*, *BioIn 9*,
ConAu 13, *ConAu P-1*, *CurBio XR*,
HisAmM XR, *IntWW 1976*, *Who 1974*,
WhoAm 1974, *WhoWor 1974*
Caniff, Milton Arthur 1907- *AmJnl*, *AuNews 1*,
BioIn 1, *BioIn 2*, *BioIn 4*, *BioIn 5*, *BioIn 8*,
BioIn 9, *CurBio XR*, *OhA&B*, *OvPC*,
REnAL, *WhoAm 1974*, *WhoAmA 1973*,
WhoE 1974, *WhoWor 1974*
Canisius, Theodor 1827?-1885 *BioIn 2*
Cannady, Edward D *WhJnl 1928*
Canning, Jeffrey Michael 1947- *ConAu 73*
Canning, Lee *NF*
Cannon, Fanny 1876- *AmAu&B*
Cannon, Frank J 1859-1933 *HisAmM XR*
Cannon, George *BioIn 4*
Cannon, George Quayle 1827-1901 *BioIn 4*,
HisAmM XR
Cannon, Grant G 1912?-1969 *BioIn 8*
Cannon, James J 1909-1973 *BioIn 2*, *BioIn 3*,
BioIn 5, *BioIn 10*
Cannon, James Monroe, III 1918- *ConAu 2R*
Cannon, James P 1890?-1974 *AmRP*, *ConAu 53*,
NewYTBS 5
Cannon, Lou 1933- *ConAu 29*, *NewMr*
Cannon, Orla M 1873- *WhJnl 1928*
Cannon, Poppy 1906?-1975 *ForWC 1970*, *OvPC*
Cannon, Poppy *see also* White, Poppy Cannon

Cannon, Sandra NF
Cannon, William J 1893?-1966 BioIn 7
Cano Villegas, Luis 1885-1950 BioIn 2
Canonge, Louis Placide 1822-1893 AmAu&B,
    BiDSA, BioIn 3, DcAmB 3, DcNAA
Cansler, Leslie Ervin 1920- WhoAm 1974
Cant, Arthur Rolleston 1910- WhoAm 1974
Cant, Gilbert 1909- WhoAm 1974
Cant, Stuart H 1900- WhJnl 1928
Cantelmo, Frank 1902?-1968 BioIn 8
Cantine, Holley, Jr. AmRP
Cantlon, R M NF
Canton, William 1845-1926 Alli Sup, NewC,
    WebBD
Cantor, George NF
Cantril, Albert Hadley 1906- AmAu&B
Cantwell, Charles Stanley 1896- WhJnl 1928
Cantwell, Mary ForWC 1970, WhoAm 1974
Cantwell, Robert Emmett 1908-1978 AmAu&B,
    Au&Wr, ConAu 5R, ConNov 1972,
    ConNov 1976, OxAm, REnAL, TwCA,
    TwCA Sup, TwCW, WebBD, WhoAm 1974,
    WhoE 1974, WrDr 1976
Canty, Donald James 1929- WhoAm 1974
Capa, Cornell 1918- BioIn 10, OvPC
Capa, Robert 1913-1954 BioIn 1, BioIn 3,
    BioIn 4, BioIn 6, BioIn 8, BioIn 10
Caparell, Basil A 1888?-1949 BioIn 2
Capdevielle, Armand 1851- NatCAB 10
Capek, Karel 1890-1938 CasWL, CIDMEL,
    CnMD, CnThe, CyWA, EncWL, EvEuW,
    LongC, McGWD, ModSL 2, ModWD,
    Pen Eur, REn, REnWD, TwCA,
    TwCA Sup, TwCW, WebBD, WhoTwCL
Capen, Oliver Bronson 1878-1953 AmAu&B,
    NatCAB 42
Capetillo, Luisa 1880?-1922 BioIn 10
Caplan, Samuel 1895-1969 BioIn 8,
    WhoWorJ 1972
Caplice, William Francis 1923- WhoAm 1974
Caplin, Alfred Gerald 1909- BioIn 1, BioIn 2,
    BioIn 3, BioIn 4, BioIn 5, BioIn 6, BioIn 8,
    BioIn 9, ConAu 57
Caplin, Alfred Gerald see also Capp, Al
Capouya, Emile AmAu&B, WhoAm 1974
Capp, Al 1909- AmAu&B, AmJnl, BioIn 2,
    CelR 1973, ConAu 57, CurBio XR,
    IntWW 1976, InvJ, REnAL, WhoAm 1974,
    WhoAmA 1973, WhoWor 1974
Capp, Al see also Caplin, Alfred Gerald
Cappelli, John NF
Capper, Arthur 1865-1951 AmAu&B, AmJnl,
    CurBio XR, DcAmB S5, HisAmM XR,
    NatCAB 41, WebBD, WhNAA, WhJnl 1928
Cappon, Alexander Patterson 1900- AmAu&B,
    DrAS 74E, WhoAm 1974
Cappon, Lester Jesse 1900- DrAS 74H,
    WhoAm 1974
Capps, Bob NF
Capps, Marvin Manly 1895- WhJnl Sup
Capra, Gianni 1907- NF
Caprile, Alberto 1871?-1951 BioIn 2
Capriles, Miguel A ForP
Capus, Alfred 1858-1922 BioIn 1, BioIn 6,
    CIDMEL, CnMD, EvEuW, McGWD,
    ModWD, OxFr, WebBD
Caputo, Philip Joseph 1941- ConAu 73, InvJ,
    WhoAm 1974
Caracappa, Michael 1913?-1971 BioIn 9
Caravello, James G 1918- USBiR 1974
Carberry, Clifton B 1876-1940 NatCAB 30
Carbine, Patricia Theresa 1931- BioIn 9,
    ForWC 1970, WhoAm 1974, WhoAmW 1974
Carden, Charles E NF

Carden, Ray E NF
Cardoso, J Seara ForP
Cardoza, Anthony 1930- NF
Cardoza, Norman F NF
Cardozo, Jacob Newton 1786-1873 BioIn 4,
    BioIn 7, DcNAA
Cardus, Sir Neville 1889-1975 Au&Wr,
    ConAu 57, ConAu 61, DcLEL, LongC,
    Who 1974, WhoMus 1972, WhoWor 1974
Carelman, Jacques 1930?- BioIn 9
Carens, Thomas Henry 1893-1960 AmAu&B,
    WhJnl 1928
Carew, Dorothy 1910?-1973 BioIn 9, ConAu 41,
    NewYTBE 4
Carew, Harold David 1890-1943 AmAu&B,
    WhNAA
Carew, Jan 1922- BioIn 9
Carey, Art NF
Carey, Francis E 1909- RpN, WhoAm 1974
Carey, Francis E see also Carey, Frank E
Carey, Frank E 1909- BioIn 7
Carey, Frank E see also Carey, Francis E
Carey, James AmJnl
Carey, John W 1877- WhJnl 1928
Carey, Mathew 1760-1839 Alli, AmAu,
    AmAu&B, BiD&SB, CyAL 1, DcLEL,
    EncAB, HisAmM XR, LiJA, OxAm, PoIre,
    REn, REnAL, WebBD
Carey, William HisAmM XR
Cargile, James Thomas 1880- WhJnl 1928
Cargill, A B 1877- WhNAA, WhJnl 1928
Cargill, Jesse Taylor 1892- WhJnl 1928
Carl, Frank Lee 1871- WhJnl 1928
Carlebach, Azriel 1908-1956 BioIn 4
Carlebach, Emil 1914?- BioIn 1
Carleton 1823-1896 AmAu, AmAu&B, DcNAA
Carleton see also Coffin, Charles Carleton
Carleton, Henry Guy 1856-1910 AmAu,
    AmAu&B, BbD, BiD&SB, BiDSA, DcAmA,
    DcNAA, OxAm, REnAL
Carleton, Monroe Guy 1833-1918 DcNAA
Carleton, R Milton 1899- BioIn 1, ConAu 69
Carleton, S B HisAmM XR
Carleton, Will 1845-1912 Alli Sup, AmAu,
    AmAu&B, BbD, BiD&SB, CyAL 2,
    DcNAA, EvLB, HisAmM XR, OxAm,
    REnAL, WebBD
Carley, Jane M NF
Carley, Walter F 1890?-1954 BioIn 3
Carley, William NF
Carlile, Richard 1790-1843 BrAu 19, ForP,
    NewC, WebBD
Carlin, Steven Roy 1917?- BioIn 1
Carlin, Thomas Leo 1921- WhoAm 1974,
    WhoF&I 1974
Carlisle, David, Jr. HisAmM XR, LiJA
Carlisle, Frank J 1865?-1950 BioIn 2
Carlisle, H I 1904?- BioIn 2
Carlisle, John C NF
Carlisle, John M NF
Carlisle, W B HisAmM XR
Carlisle, Walter Ewing 1877-1956 OhA&B
Carll, S Edwards 1895?-1967 BioIn 8
Carlova, John BioIn 4
Carlson, Avis Dungan 1896- ConAu 73
Carlson, Conwell 1900- WhJnl 1928
Carlson, Dale 1935- BioIn 9
Carlson, Eugene 1940- NF
Carlson, Harriet NF
Carlson, Jerry Alan 1936- WhoAm 1974
Carlson, John Roy 1909- AmAu&B, CurBio XR,
    HisAmM XR, TwCA Sup
Carlson, Stan W 1909- MnnWr
Carlson, Wally 1884-1967 BioIn 3

Carlsson, Leif 1930- *BioIn 8*
Carlton, William *AmJnl*
Carlton, Wright Miles 1884- *WhJnl 1928*
Carlyn, Jill *NF*
Carmack, George 1907- *WhoAm 1974,*
  WhoWest 1974
Carman, Albert Richardson 1865-1939 *DcNAA*
Carman, Bliss 1861-1929 *BbD, BiD&SB, CanWr,*
  CnDAL, ConAmL, DcAmA, DcEnA Ap,
  DcLEL, DcNAA, HisAmM XR, LongC,
  OxAm, OxCan, OxEng, Pen Am, Pen Eng,
  REn, REnAL, TwCA, TwCA Sup,
  WebE&AL, WhNAA
Carman, Bliss *see also* Carman, William Bliss
Carman, Elbert S *HisAmM XR*
Carman, Ian Douglas 1927- *WhoAm 1974*
Carman, Jan *NF*
Carman, William Bliss 1861-1929 *CasWL, EvLB,*
  WebBD
Carman, William Bliss *see also* Carmen, Bliss
Carmany, John H *HisAmM XR*
Carmer, Carl Lamson 1893-1976 *AmAu&B,*
  Au&Wr, AuBYP, ConAu 69, OxAm, REn,
  REnAL, Str&VC, TwCA, TwCA Sup,
  WebBD, WhoAm 1974, WhoWor 1974
Carmichael, Colin 1905- *BioIn 1, BioIn 5*
Carmichael, Joel 1915- *ConAu 1R*
Carmichael, Otto *NF*
Carmichael, Thomas N 1919- *ConAu 29*
Carmichael, Vernal H d1973 *BioIn 9*
Carmichael, Wilmer 1891?- *BioIn 2*
Carmody, Jay 1900?-1973 *BiE&WWA,*
  ConAu 41
Carmody, John *NF*
Carmody, John Michael 1882?-1963 *CurBio XR,*
  WebBD
Carmony, Clifford 1907- *WhJnl 1928*
Carnahan, William T *OvPC*
Carnegie, Robert Kenneth 1884?-1951 *BioIn 2*
Carnes, James *NF*
Carnese, Paul *NF*
Carnevali, Emanuel *HisAmM XR*
Carney, Edward M 1879- *WhJnl 1928*
Carney, Edward O 1931?-1966 *BioIn 7*
Carney, Otis 1922- *BioIn 4*
Carney, William P 1898-1972 *BioIn 9, BioIn 10,*
  NewYTBE 3
Carnot, Lazare Hippolyte 1801-1888 *WebBD*
Caro, Miguel Antonio 1843-1909 *BiD&SB,*
  WebBD
Caro, Robert A 1936?- *NewMr, WrDr 1976*
Carousso, Georges 1909- *WhoE 1974,*
  WhoPubR 1972
Carpeaux, Otto Maria 1900- *IntWW 1976*
Carpenter, Allyne V 1892- *WhJnl 1928*
Carpenter, Edmund H 1890- *WhJnl 1928*
Carpenter, Edmund Janes 1845-1924 *AmAu&B,*
  AmLY, DcAmA, DcAmB 2, DcNAA,
  OxCan
Carpenter, Edmund S 1900- *WhJnl 1928*
Carpenter, Edward Childs 1872-1950 *AmAu&B,*
  REnAL, WebBD, WhNAA
Carpenter, Elizabeth Sutherland 1920- *BioIn 6,*
  BioIn 7, ConAu 41, WhoAm 1974,
  WhoAmW 1974
Carpenter, Elizabeth Sutherland *see also* Carpenter,
  Liz
Carpenter, Frank George 1855-1924 *AmAu&B,*
  DcAmB 3, DcNAA, HisAmM XR, OhA&B
Carpenter, G H *NF*
Carpenter, George Hiram 1889?-1971 *BioIn 9*
Carpenter, Guy R 1885- *WhJnl 1928*
Carpenter, Henry C 1884- *WhJnl 1928*
Carpenter, Iris *BioIn 1*

Carpenter, James D 1854- *WhJnl 1928*
Carpenter, Leon A 1886- *WhJnl 1928*
Carpenter, Leslie 1922-1974 *BioIn 10,*
  NewYTBS 5
Carpenter, Liz 1920- *ConAu XR, WhoAmP 1973*
Carpenter, Liz *see also* Carpenter, Elizabeth
  Sutherland
Carpenter, Ralph S 1906- *WhJnl 1928*
Carpenter, Rene 1927?- *BioIn 7*
Carpenter, Richard M *OvPC*
Carpenter, S M *NF*
Carpenter, Stephen Cullen d1820 *Alli, AmAu&B,*
  BbD, BiD&SB, DcAmA, DcAmB 3,
  DcNAA, HisAmM XR
Carpenter, Stephen Decatur 1821-1906 *BioIn 5*
Carpentier, John *NF*
Carpentier Y Valmont, Alejo 1904- *ConAu 65,*
  IntWW 1974, WhoWor 1974
Carper, Elsie M *OvPC*
Carper, Jean Elinor 1932- *ConAu 17, InvJ*
Carpintero, Andres *NF*
Carpozi, George, Jr. 1920- *ConAu 13R*
Carr, Agnes *BioIn 2*
Carr, C C 1884- *WhJnl 1928*
Carr, Dabney Smith 1802-1854 *DcAmB 3*
Carr, Edward 1948?- *BioIn 10*
Carr, Edward Ellis *HisAmM XR*
Carr, Gene 1881-1959 *BioIn 5, BioIn 6,*
  NatCAB 43, REnAL, WebBD
Carr, Harry 1877-1936 *DcNAA*
Carr, J Roland 1903?-1971 *BioIn 9*
Carr, Jay Phillip 1936- *WhoAm 1974*
Carr, John Arthur 1911- *WhoAm 1974*
Carr, Leander K 1863- *WhJnl 1928*
Carr, Marsha E *NF*
Carr, Mary Jane 1899- *AuBYP, BioIn 9, BkC 1,*
  CathA 1952, ConAu P-1, JBA 1951,
  SmATA 2
Carr, Patrick William 1920- *OvPC,*
  WhoPubR 1972
Carr, Ralph L 1887-1950 *NF*
Carr, Willard Avery 1883- *WhJnl 1928*
Carr, William Bouvard 1905- *WhoAm 1974*
Carr, William Emsley 1912- *WhoAm 1974,*
  WhoWor 1974
Carr, William Henry Alexander 1924-
  ConAu 15R, WhoE 1974
Carrascal, Jose M 1930- *NF*
Carraway, Gertrude Sprague 1896- *BioIn 3,*
  CurBio XR, WhNAA, WhoAm 1974,
  WhoAmW 1974, WhJnl 1928
Carrel, Al *NF*
Carrel, Frank 1870-1940 *DcNAA, WhNAA*
Carrel, Nicolas Armand 1800-1836 *WebBD*
Carrere, Jean 1865-1932 *WebBD*
Carrick, Bruce 1937- *BioIn 10*
Carriell, Cruse *HisAmM XR*
Carrier, Cornelia B 1938?- *NF*
Carrier, Robert 1925?- *BioIn 8*
Carrillo, Adolfo 1885-1887 *BioIn 2*
Carrington, David L *NF*
Carrington, Frances Sedgwick 1894- *WhJnl 1928*
Carrington, John B *HisAmM XR*
Carrington, Richard Adams 1889-1960 *BioIn 5*
Carrol, Bartholomew R *HisAmM XR*
Carrol, Regina *NF*
Carroll, Alfred L *HisAmM XR*
Carroll, Charles *HisAmM XR*
Carroll, Dan 1887- *WhJnl 1928*
Carroll, Dana *NF*
Carroll, E Elmer 1901?-1951 *BioIn 2*
Carroll, Frank T 1881- *WhJnl 1928*
Carroll, George Anthony 1904?-1966 *BioIn 7*
Carroll, Gordon 1903-1978 *AmAu&B,*

HisAmM XR, WhoAm 1974
Carroll, Harrison *NF*
Carroll, Howard 1854-1916 *Alli Sup, AmAu&B, DcNAA, NatCAB 3, WebBD*
Carroll, John 1942?- *BioIn 8*
Carroll, John Charles 1885-1939 *DcNAA, WhJnl 1928*
Carroll, John Wallace 1906- *AmAu&B, WhoAm 1974*
Carroll, Kathleen *WhoAmW 1974*
Carroll, Les *NF*
Carroll, Loren 1904- *AmAu&B, WhoAm 1974, WhJnl 1928*
Carroll, Nan *NF*
Carroll, Patrick Joseph 1876-1959 *BioIn 1, BioIn 2, BioIn 5, BkC 1, CathA 1930, IndAu 1816, WhNAA*
Carroll, Paul 1927- *ConAu 25, ConP 1970, ConP 1975, DrAP 1975, WrDr 1976*
Carroll, Paul 1933- *WhoS&SW 1973*
Carroll, Pete *NF*
Carroll, Raymond G d1945 *AmAu&B, AmJnl*
Carroll, Richard Augustine 1898-1959 *BioIn 5*
Carroll, Sidney *NF*
Carroll, V E 1872- *WhJnl 1928*
Carrozza, Bernadette Patricia 1944- *OvPC, WhoAm 1974*
Carruth, Arthur Jay, Jr. 1887-1962 *WhNAA, WhJnl 1928*
Carruth, Charles Weldon 1921- *WhoAm 1974, WhoE 1974*
Carruth, Fred Hayden 1862-1932 *DcAmA, DcAmB S1, DcNAA*
Carruth, Fred Hayden *see also* Carruth, Hayden
Carruth, Gorton Veeder 1888- *WhNAA, WhJnl 1928*
Carruth, Hayden (1862-1932) *see also* Carruth, Fred Hayden
Carruth, Hayden 1862-1932 *AmAu&B, AmLY, BioIn 10, CarSB, REnAL*
Carruth, Hayden 1921- *AmAu&B, ConAu 9, ConLC 4, ConP 1970, ConP 1975, DrAP 1975, HisAmM XR, RAdv 1, WhoAm 1974, WhoE 1974, WhoWor 1974, WorAu, WrDr 1976*
Carruthers, Arthur C 1876- *WhJnl 1928*
Carruthers, Ben F *NF*
Carruthers, Frank I 1868- *WhJnl 1928*
Carruthers, Robert 1799-1878 *Alli Sup, BrAu 19, DcEnL, EvLB, NewC, WebBD*
Carruthers, William Joseph 1906?-1977 *NF*
Carse, Matilda B d1917 *HisAmM XR*
Carsen, Robert A *NF*
Carson *FamWC*
Carson, Jerome S 1891?-1952 *BioIn 2*
Carson, John M *NF*
Carson, Joseph 1826-1876 *HisAmM XR*
Carson, Lee d1973 *NF*
Carson, Norman Bright *HisAmM XR*
Carson, Rachel Louise 1907-1964 *AmAu&B, AnCL, CurBio XR, EvLB, LongC, OxAm, REn, TwCA, TwCW, WebBD*
Carson, S L *NF*
Carson, Will *HisAmM XR*
Carstensen, Carl 1837-1932 *ForP*
Cart, Jo *NF*
Carter, Amon Giles 1879-1955 *BioIn 2, BioIn 3, BioIn 4, BioIn 5, BioIn 6*
Carter, Amon Giles, Jr. 1919- *WhoAm 1974, WhoGov 1972, WhoS&SW 1973*
Carter, Anthony *NF*
Carter, Augustus Daniels 1894?-1957 *BioIn 4*
Carter, Barbara Barclay 1900- *BioIn 1, BkC 3, CathA 1930, WhNAA*

Carter, Boake 1898-1944 *BioIn 1, BioIn 2, CurBio XR, DcAmB S3, DcNAA*
Carter, Don Earl 1917- *ConAu 73, WhoAm 1974, WhoE 1974, WhoWor 1974*
Carter, Edwin 1906?- *BioIn 1*
Carter, Ernestine *BioIn 9*
Carter, Frederick Roy 1877-1951 *BioIn 2*
Carter, George 1865-1948 *BioIn 2, NatCAB 34, WhJnl 1928*
Carter, George Edward 1910- *WhoAm 1974, WhoMW 1974*
Carter, Henry 1821-1880 *AmAu&B, HisAmM XR, WebBD*
Carter, Henry *see also* Leslie, Frank
Carter, Hodding, III *see* Carter, William Hodding, III
Carter, Hodding, Jr. 1907-1972 *AmAu&B, AmNov, AuBYP, BioIn 9, ConAu 13, ConAu 33, ConAu P-1, CurBio XR, NewMr, NewYTBE 3, RpN, SmATA 2, TwCA Sup, WhoS&SW 1973*
Carter, J Stanley *NF*
Carter, James *AmRP*
Carter, James Gordon 1795-1849 *DcAmA, DcNAA, HisAmM XR*
Carter, John 1745-1814 *AmAu&B, BioIn 9*
Carter, John Franklin, Jr. 1897-1967 *AmAu&B, BioIn 4, BioIn 8, ConAu 25, CurBio XR, EncMys, REnAL, TwCA, TwCA Sup, WhJnl 1928*
Carter, John H 1896-1959 *BioIn 5*
Carter, John Henton d1882 *DcNAA*
Carter, John Mack 1928- *AmAu&B, BioIn 6, WhoAm 1974, WhoE 1974*
Carter, Joseph *HisAmM XR*
Carter, Joseph 1912- *ConAu 49*
Carter, Luther J 1927- *ConAu 57*
Carter, Lydia G *OvPC*
Carter, Matilda P *HisAmM XR*
Carter, Nathaniel Hazeltine 1787-1830 *Alli, AmJnl, CyAL 1, DcAmA, DcNAA*
Carter, Ovie 1946?- *BlkC*
Carter, Philip *NewMr*
Carter, Robert 1819-1879 *Alli Sup, AmAu, AmAu&B, BiD&SB, BioIn 3, BioIn 5, DcAmA, DcNAA, HisAmM XR, LiJA*
Carter, Roy Ernest, Jr. 1922- *AmM&W 73S, ForP, WhoAm 1974*
Carter, S *NF*
Carter, William Hodding, III 1935- *WhoS&SW 1973*
Carter, William Hodding, Jr. 1907-1972 *CurBio XR*
Carter, William Hodding, Jr. *see also* Carter, Hodding, Jr.
Cartier-Bresson, Henri 1908- *CurBio XR, IntWW 1974, Who 1974, WhoWor 1974*
Cartlidge, Edward L 1901- *WhJnl 1928*
Cartmell, Van Henry 1896-1966 *BioIn 7*
Cartwell, Robert *NF*
Cartwright, Charles *NF*
Cartwright, Marguerite *OvPC*
Caruba, Alan 1937- *ConAu 65*
Caruba, Rebecca *NF*
Carus, Mary *HisAmM XR*
Carus, Paul 1852-1919 *Alli Sup, AmAu&B, CasWL, DcAmA, DcNAA, HisAmM XR, REnAL, TwCA, WebBD*
Caruso, Charles *NF*
Carvalho, Solomon Solis 1856-1942 *AmJnl, DcAmB S3, HisAmM XR*
Carver, Lawton 1903?-1973 *BioIn 9*
Carver, Wayne *NF*
Cary, Edward 1840-1917 *AmAu&B, BiD&SB,*

DcAmA, DcNAA, NatCAB 25, WebBD
Cary, Elisabeth Luther 1867-1936 AmAu&B,
DcAmB S2, DcNAA, LiJA, WebBD
Cary, F G HisAmM XR
Cary, James Donald 1919- ConAu 5R
Cary, Lucian 1886-1971 AmAu&B, BioIn 9,
ConAu 33, NewYTBE 2, WhNAA, WisWr
Cary, Mary Ann Shadd 1823-1893 NF
Cary, Richard L 1886- WhJnl 1928
Cary, Sturges F NF
Cary, Thomas 1751-1823 BbtC, DcNAA, OxCan
Casalengo, Carlo 1916?-1977 NF
Casamajor, George Holberton 1868- HisAmM XR
Cascio, Chuck NF
Case, Ann 1944- BioIn 10
Case, John Francis 1876-1966 WhNAA,
WhJnl 1928
Case, L S 1870- WhJnl 1928
Case, Leland Davidson 1900- AmAu&B,
ConAu 17, WhoAm 1974
Case, Margaret 1892-1971 BioIn 9
Case, May Lucy 1873- BioIn 5
Case, Rex Ronald 1874- WhJnl 1928
Case, Ron NF
Case, Theodore Spencer 1832-1900 DcNAA,
HisAmM XR
Case, Walter Hodgin 1882- WhJnl 1928
Casey, Amedee J 1883?-1950 BioIn 2
Casey, Charles Leon OvPC
Casey, Daniel Aloysius 1886- BioIn 1, BkC 4
Casey, Edward Dennis 1931- WhoAm 1974,
WhoE 1974
Casey, Eugene Ross 1910-1964 BioIn 6
Casey, F W Lor&LP
Casey, Francis DeSales 1882- HisAmM XR
Casey, John E 1875?- WhNAA, WhJnl 1928
Casey, John Harold 1897- WhNAA, WhJnl 1928
Casey, Kathleen Aston AmAu&B
Casey, Leo NF
Casey, Martin NF
Casey, Michael Vincent 1886-1948 BioIn 1
Casey, Ralph Droz 1890-1977 AmAu&B,
WhJnl 1928
Casey, Robert Joseph 1890-1962 AmAu&B,
BioIn 1, BioIn 3, BioIn 6, CathA 1930,
CurBio XR, REnAL
Casey, Sally NF
Casey, W J 1861- WhJnl 1928
Casey, William Francis 1884-1957 BioIn 1,
BioIn 4
Cash, J Allan 1901- ConAu 1R
Cash, Kevin 1926- NF
Cash, Wilbur Joseph 1901-1941 AmAu&B,
BioIn 3, BioIn 8, DcAmB S3, DcNAA,
EncAB, HisAmM XR, WorAu
Cashman, Cathy NF
Cashman, John R AmJnl
Cason, Clarence E 1896- WhJnl 1928
Cass, James 1915- BioIn 9
Cassandra 1909-1967 LongC, Lor&LP
Cassandra see also Connor, Sir William Neil
Cassell, John 1817-1865 Alli Sup, NewC,
WebBD
Cassels, Louis Welborn 1922-1974 BioIn 10,
ConAu 9R, WhoAm 1974, WhoWor 1974
Casserley, Henry Cyril 1903- ConAu 65
Casserly, John Joseph 1927- OvPC,
WhoAm 1974, WhoGov 1972, WhoWor 1974
Casses, Sidney 1939- BioIn 9
Cassidy, Claudia 1905?- AmAu&B, BiE&WWA,
CelR 1973, CurBio XR, WhoAm 1974,
WhoAmW 1974
Cassidy, George Livingston 1902-1962 BioIn 6
Cassidy, Henry Clarence 1910- AmAu&B,

CurBio XR, OvPC
Cassidy, James Joseph 1916- OvPC,
WhoAm 1974, WhoCon 1973, WhoE 1974,
WhoF&I 1974, WhoPubR 1972,
WhoWor 1974
Cassidy, Morley Franklin 1900-1968 AmAu&B,
BioIn 8
Cassidy, William 1815-1873 BioIn 9, DcAmB 3
Cassier, Louis HisAmM XR
Cassill, Harold E 1897-1957 BioIn 2
Cassill, Kay 1930- NF
Cassini, Austine 1920?- BioIn 1
Cassini, Igor Loiewski 1915- BioIn 2, BioIn 6
Cassino, Herman E HisAmM XR
Cassino, J Allen 1894- WhJnl Sup
Cassino, Samuel Edson 1856-1937 Alli Sup,
HisAmM XR
Cassirer, Henry Reinhard 1911- IntWW 1976,
WhoWor 1974
Casson, Herbert N 1869- HisAmM XR
Casson, Mel NF
Castaigne, Andre HisAmM XR
Castan, Sam 1935-1966 BioIn 7
Castel, Jack 1912- WhoAm 1974
Castellaneta, Carlo 1930- Au&Wr, ConAu 13R
Castelli, Ignaz Franz 1781-1862 BiD&SB, OxGer,
WebBD
Castelli, James J NF
Castillo, Graciela Levi OvPC
Castle, Egerton 1858-1920 Alli Sup, BbD,
BiD&SB, DcEnA Ap, EvLB, LongC, NewC,
REn, TwCA, WebBD
Castle, William Richards, Jr. 1878-1963
HisAmM XR
Castleberry, Vivian Lou Anderson 1922-
WhoAm 1974, WhoAmW 1974,
WhoS&SW 1973
Castlerosse, Viscount Lor&LP
Castleton, D R HisAmM XR
Castleton, Virginia 1925- ConAu 49, OvPC
Castonguay, Emile 1894-1956 BioIn 4
Castro, Augusto De 1883-1971 BioIn 9, BioIn 10,
ForP
Castro, Emilio BioIn 8
Castro, Tony 1946- ConAu XR, WrDr 1976
Catalano, Jim OvPC
Cate, Benjamin Wilson 1931- ConAu 73
Cater, Douglass 1923- AmAu&B, BioIn 8,
ConAu 1, IntWW 1976, WhoAm 1974,
WhoWor 1974, WrDr 1976
Cates, J Sidney 1877-1949 HisAmM XR
Cathcart, Noble Aydelotte 1898- AmAu&B
Cather, Willa Sibert 1873-1947 AmAu&B,
AmWr, AtlBL, CasWL, CnDAL, CyWA,
DcAmB S4, DcBiA, DcLEL, DcNAA,
EncAB, EncWL, EvLB, JBA 1934, LongC,
ModAL, ModAL Sup, OxAm, OxCan,
OxEng, Pen Am, RAdv 1, RComWL, REn,
REnAL, TwCA, TwCA Sup, TwCW,
WebBD, WebE&AL, WhNAA, WhoTwCL
Cathro, Morton NF
Catledge, Turner 1901- AmAu&B, AuNews 1,
BioIn 2, BioIn 5, BioIn 7, BioIn 8, BioIn 9,
ConAu 57, CurBio XR, IntWW 1976, InvJ,
NewYTBE 1, Who 1974, WhoAm 1974,
WhoWor 1974
Catlin, George Byron 1857-1934 BioIn 6,
NatCAB 30
Catlin, George Lynde 1840-1896 Alli Sup, AmJnl,
DcAmA, DcNAA
Catling, Thomas NF
Caton, Thomas George 1913- WhoAm 1974
Catt, Carrie Lane Chapman 1859-1947 EncAB
Cattell, Hettie Fithian WhJnl 1928

Cattell, Jacques 1904-1960 *AmAu&B*
Cattell, James McKeen 1860-1944 *AmAu&B,*
    BioIn 2, BioIn 6, BioIn 7, BioIn 9,
    DcNAA, HisAmM XR, WebBD
Cattell, Josephine Owen *HisAmM XR*
Catton, Bruce 1899-1978 *Alli Sup, AmAu&B,*
    AuNews 1, BioIn 3, BioIn 4, BioIn 5,
    BioIn 6, BioIn 7, BioIn 8, BioIn 9,
    BioIn 10, BioNews 1974, CelR 1973,
    ConAu 5R, CurBio XR, IntWW 1976,
    OxAm, Pen Am, REn, REnAL, SmATA 2,
    TwCA Sup, WebBD, Who 1974,
    WhoAm 1974, WhoWor 1974, WrDr 1976
Cau, Jean 1925- *CnMD, IntWW 1976, TwCW,*
    WhoWor 1974, WorAu
Caufield, John H 1889- *WhJnl 1928*
Cauldwell, William 1824- *HisAmM XR,*
    NatCAB 1
Cauley, John Rowan 1908-1976 *ConAu 65,*
    WhoAm 1974, WhoS&SW 1973
Causey, Mike *NF*
Cavagnaro, Robert John 1905-1969 *NF*
Cavaignac, Eleonore Louis Godefroy 1801-1845
    WebBD
Cavaliere, Angel Maria *BioIn 9*
Cavaliero, Eric *NF*
Cavallari, Alberto 1927- *ConAu 23R,*
    WhoWor 1974
Cavalli, Dick 1923- *WhoAmA 1973*
Cavanaugh, Dale *NF*
Cave, Edward 1691-1754 *Alli, CasWL, DcEnL,*
    DcEuL, DcLEL, EvLB, NewC, WebBD
Cave, Edward 1878-1951 *BioIn 2, HisAmM XR*
Cave, Ray *NF*
Cavin, Patty 1925- *BioIn 5, WhoAm 1974,*
    WhoAmW 1974
Cavling, Henrik 1858-1933 *ForP*
Cawley, Janet *NF*
Cawthorne, David M *NF*
Cazalas, Robert P *NF*
Cazenave, Rene 1906- *WhoAm 1974*
Ceaglio, Gina *NF*
Cecchi, Emilio 1884-1966 *BioIn 1, BioIn 7,*
    CasWL, CIDMEL, EncWL, EvEuW,
    Pen Eur
Cecil, Lord Richard Valentine 1948?-1978 *NF*
Cedrone, Louis Robert, Jr. 1923- *WhoAm 1974,*
    WhoE 1974
Cellario, Alberto R *OvPC*
Celliers, Peter Joubert 1920- *OvPC, WhoE 1974,*
    WhoF&I 1974, WhoPubR 1972
Center, Alfred *HisAmM XR*
Center, Harry Bryant 1877- *WhJnl 1928*
Cerf, Edward Owen 1918-1959 *BioIn 5*
Cermak, Emil 1864?-1949 *BioIn 2*
Cernick, Clifford 1918- *WhoAm 1974*
Cerruti, Eugene *NewMr*
Cerutti, Joseph *NF*
Cesare, Oscar Edward 1883-1948 *BioIn 1,*
    DcAmB S4
Cestare, Frank *AmRP*
Chabel, Bernard *NF*
Chace, Carleton 1882?-1965 *BioIn 7*
Chacko, George Kuttickal 1930- *ConAu 73,*
    WhoF&I 1974, WhoS&SW 1973
Chadbourne, John S *HisAmM XR*
Chadwick, Charles 1874-1953 *AmAu&B, BioIn 3,*
    WhNAA
Chadwick, H A *HisAmM XR*
Chadwick, Henry 1824-1908 *Alli Sup, AmAu&B,*
    AmJnl, BioIn 7, DcAmA, DcNAA,
    HisAmM XR, HsB&A, WebBD
Chadwick, John *NF*
Chaffee, Charles D 1890- *WhJnl 1928*

Chaikin, Joseph 1885?-1946 *BioIn 1*
Chakrapani, Raghavendra *NF*
Chalfant, Floyd 1889-1954 *BioIn 6, NatCAB 44,*
    WhJnl 1928
Chalifour, Joseph Onesime 1889-1956 *BioIn 4*
Chalk, Oscar Roy 1907- *BioIn 8, BioIn 9, OvPC*
Chalkley, Alfred Philip 1886-1959 *BioIn 5*
Challis, Luther C *HisAmM XR*
Chalmers, Alexander 1759-1834 *Alli, BiD&SB,*
    BiDLA, BiDLA Sup, DcEnL, NewC,
    WebBD
Chalmers, Floyd Sherman 1898- *CanWW 1972,*
    ConAu 25, IntWW 1976, OxCan Sup,
    WhNAA, WhoE 1974, WhJnl 1928
Chalmers, John S 1887?-1967 *BioIn 8*
Chamberlain, Alonzo 1846- *WhJnl 1928*
Chamberlain, Arthur *HisAmM XR*
Chamberlain, Arthur Henry 1872?-1942 *AmAu&B,*
    HisAmM XR, WhNAA
Chamberlain, Betty 1908- *ConAu 33,*
    WhoAm 1974, WhoAmA 1973,
    WhoAmW 1974, WrDr 1976
Chamberlain, Frank *NF*
Chamberlain, George D *HisAmM XR*
Chamberlain, Henry Richardson 1859-1911
    DcAmA, DcAmB 3, DcNAA
Chamberlain, Jerome *NF*
Chamberlain, Jo Hubbard *HisAmM XR*
Chamberlain, John Rensselaer 1903- *AmAu&B,*
    AmRP, ConAu 57, CurBio XR,
    HisAmM XR, OxAm, REnAL, TwCA,
    TwCA Sup, WebBD, WhoAm 1974,
    WhoWor 1974
Chamberlain, Joseph Perkins 1873-1951
    HisAmM XR
Chamberlain, Mary *HisAmM XR*
Chamberlain, Pye, Sr. *NF*
Chamberlain, Rudolph W 1891- *WhJnl 1928*
Chamberlain, Ruth Benson 1896- *WhJnl 1928*
Chamberlain, Samuel Selwyn 1851-1916 *AmJnl,*
    HisAmM XR
Chamberlain, Winthrop Burr 1864- *WhNAA,*
    WhJnl 1928
Chamberlin, Anne *BioIn 5*
Chamberlin, Brown 1827- *BbtC*
Chamberlin, Edward Hastings 1899- *AmAu&B*
Chamberlin, Ernest O *NF*
Chamberlin, Hope 1917?-1974 *BioIn 10*
Chamberlin, Joseph Edgar 1851-1935 *AmAu&B,*
    BiD&SB, DcAmA, DcNAA, HisAmM XR,
    NatCAB 25
Chamberlin, Joseph Webb 1913- *WhoAm 1974*
Chamberlin, Thomas Chrowder 1843-1928 *Alli Sup,*
    AmAu&B, DcAmA, DcNAA, HisAmM XR,
    WebBD
Chamberlin, Wilbur J *NF*
Chamberlin, William Henry 1897-1969 *AmAu&B,*
    BioIn 2, BioIn 4, BioIn 5, BioIn 8,
    ConAu 5R, HisAmM XR, OxAm, REnAL,
    TwCA, TwCA Sup, WebBD
Chambers, Anne Cox 1919- *NF*
Chambers, Edward Thomas Davies 1852-1931
    DcNAA
Chambers, Ernest John 1862-1925 *DcNAA,*
    OxCan, WebBD
Chambers, George *NF*
Chambers, Gretta *NF*
Chambers, James Floyd, Jr. 1913- *AmAu&B,*
    WhoAm 1974, WhoS&SW 1973
Chambers, James Julius 1850-1920 *AmJnl,*
    DcAmB 3, DcNAA, NatCAB 14, OhA&B
Chambers, James Julius see also Chambers, Julius
Chambers, Joseph M *HisAmM XR*
Chambers, Julius 1850-1920 *AmAu&B*

Chambers, Julius *see also* Chambers, James Julius
Chambers, Lenoir 1891-1970 *BioIn 8*
Chambers, Robert 1832-1888 *WebBD*
Chambers, Stuart Munson 1887-1960 *BioIn 5,*
   BioIn 7, NatCAB 49, WhJnl 1928
Chambers, Walter 1896-1953 *BioIn 3*
Chambers, Walter Scott 1870?-1951 *BioIn 2*
Chambers, Walter Scott, Jr. 1922- *WhoMW 1974*
Chambers, Whittaker 1901-1961 *AmAu&B,*
   BioIn 10, HisAmM XR, LongC, WorAu
Chambers, William 1800-1883 *Alli, Alli Sup,*
   BiD&SB, CasWL, DcEnA, DcEnL, DcEuL,
   EvLB, WebBD
Chamblin, Walter 1898?-1955 *BioIn 4*
Chambliss, H Darden, Jr. 1929- *OvPC,*
   WhoPubR 1972
Chambraud, Andre *NF*
Chamorro, Pedro Joaquin 1891-1952 *BioIn 3*
Chamorro, Xavier *NF*
Chamorro Cardenal, Pedro J 1924?-1977 *NF*
Champion, Fitz Roy 1878-1933 *WhJnl 1928*
Champion, Fred H *NF*
Champion, Hale 1922- *LEduc 1974, RpN*
Champion, Henry Hyde 1859-1928 *BioIn 2*
Champion, Thomas T *NF*
Champlin, Charles Davenport 1926- *ConAu 69,*
   IntMPA 1975, WhoAm 1974,
   WhoWest 1974, WhoWor 1974
Champlin, Edwin Ross 1854-1928 *Alli Sup,*
   AmAu&B, DcNAA, WhNAA
Champlin, John Denison 1834-1915 *Alli Sup,*
   AmAu&B, BiD&SB, DcAmA, DcNAA,
   HisAmM XR
Champney, James Wells 1843-1903 *AmAu&B,*
   HisAmM XR
Chamreun, Meas *NF*
Chan, Sou *OvPC*
Chancellor, Sir Christopher John 1904- *BioIn 2*
Chancellor, George *NF*
Chancellor, John William 1927- *BioIn 7, BioIn 8,*
   BioIn 9, CurBio XR, IntWW 1976,
   WhoAm 1974
Chandler, Al *NF*
Chandler, Charles Henry 1840-1885 *DcNAA*
Chandler, Charles Lyon 1883-1962 *BioIn 8*
Chandler, David Leon *ConAu 49*
Chandler, Dorothy Buffum 1901- *BioIn 4,*
   BioIn 5, BioIn 7, BioIn 8, BioIn 9,
   CurBio XR, WhoAm 1974, WhoAmW 1974,
   WhoF&I 1974, WhoWor 1974
Chandler, Dorothy Buffum *see also* Chandler, Mrs.
   Norman
Chandler, H P *HisAmM XR*
Chandler, Hannibal H *HisAmM XR*
Chandler, Harry 1864-1944 *BioIn 4, DcAmB S3,*
   NatCAB 40, WhJnl 1928
Chandler, John Paul 1887- *WhJnl 1928*
Chandler, Joseph Ripley 1792-1880 *Alli,*
   AmAu&B, DcAmA, DcAmB 3, DcNAA,
   HisAmM XR
Chandler, Julius 1899- *WhJnl 1928*
Chandler, Norman 1899-1973 *BioIn 2, BioIn 4,*
   BioIn 5, BioIn 10, CurBio XR,
   NewYTBE 4, WhoF&I 1974,
   WhoWest 1974, WhoWor 1974
Chandler, Mrs. Norman 1901- *CelR 1973*
Chandler, Mrs. Norman *see also* Chandler, Dorothy
   Buffum
Chandler, Otis 1927- *BioIn 5, BioIn 7, BioIn 8,*
   BioIn 9, CelR 1973, CurBio XR,
   IntWW 1976, WhoAm 1974, WhoF&I 1974,
   WhoWest 1974, WhoWor 1974
Chandler, Ralph Bradford 1891-1970 *WhJnl Sup*
Chandler, Russell 1932- *NF*

Chandler, Seth C 1846-1913 *HisAmM XR*
Chandley, John Stothers 1908- *WhoAm 1974*
Chang, Ch'un-Chi'ao 1911?- *BioIn 10*
Chang, Hai-Tao *NF*
Chang, Josephine *NF*
Chang, Sungyung *NF*
Chanin, Abe 1921- *WhoWest 1974*
Channing, Edward Bruce *HisAmM XR*
Channing, Edward Tyrrell 1790-1856 *Alli, AmAu,*
   AmAu&B, BioIn 3, CyAL 1, DcAmA,
   DcNAA, HisAmM XR, OxAm, Pen Am,
   REn, REnAL
Channing, Walter 1786-1876 *Alli, Alli Sup,*
   DcAmA, DcNAA, HisAmM XR, WebBD
Channing, William Henry 1810-1884 *Alli, AmAu,*
   AmAu&B, BiD&SB, CyAL 2, DcAmA,
   DcNAA, HisAmM XR, LiJA, OhA&B,
   OxAm, REnAL, WebBD
Chaparral *FamWC*
Chapelle, Dickey 1918?-1965 *BioIn 6, BioIn 7*
Chapin, Ben E 1867- *WhJnl 1928*
Chapin, Carl Mattison 1879-1938 *DcNAA,*
   WhNAA, WhJnl 1928
Chapin, Charles E 1858-1930 *AmAu&B, BioIn 2,*
   DcNAA
Chapin, Dwight Allan 1938- *ConAu 41, NewMr*
Chapin, Earl V *BioIn 3*
Chapin, Elden Stedman 1809- *BioIn 2,*
   IndAu 1816
Chapin, John *HisAmM XR*
Chapin, Kim 1942- *ConAu 53*
Chapin, Lon F 1862- *WhJnl 1928*
Chapin, Louis Le Bourgeois 1918- *WhoThe 1972*
Chapin, Nettie Sanford 1830-1901 *BioIn 8*
Chapin, S A *HisAmM XR*
Chapin, Samuel Austin 1858-1959 *BioIn 5*
Chapin, William 1918- *ConAu 37*
Chapin, William Wallace 1874-1957 *BioIn 1,*
   BioIn 4
Chapin, William Wisner *HisAmM XR*
Chapiro, Jose 1893-1962 *BioIn 6*
Chaplin, George 1914- *AuNews 2, BioIn 1,*
   ConAu 69, RpN, WhoAm 1974,
   WhoWest 1974, WhoWor 1974,
   WhoWorJ 1972
Chaplin, W W 1895?-1978 *OvPC*
Chaplin, William Edwards 1860-1948 *NF*
Chapman, Alfred F *HisAmM XR*
Chapman, Alvah Herman, Jr. 1921- *AuNews 2,*
   WhoAm 1974, WhoF&I 1974,
   WhoS&SW 1973
Chapman, Alvah Herman, Sr. d1961 *NF*
Chapman, Arthur 1873-1935 *AmAu&B, DcNAA,*
   HisAmM XR, WhNAA
Chapman, Arthur M *NF*
Chapman, Bertrand L *HisAmM XR*
Chapman, C C 1876-1956 *BioIn 4*
Chapman, Charles Frederic 1881-1976 *BioIn 5,*
   BioIn 6, BioIn 8, ConAu 65, CurBio XR
Chapman, Charles Henry 1879- *BioIn 8, WhoChL*
Chapman, Christine *NF*
Chapman, Colin 1937- *ConAu 29*
Chapman, Earl R 1886- *WhJnl 1928*
Chapman, Edmond Beaubien 1884-1954 *BioIn 3*
Chapman, Ethel *BioIn 1, CanNov, OxCan*
Chapman, Frank Michler 1864-1945 *CurBio XR*
Chapman, Frederick L *HisAmM XR*
Chapman, Henry Grafton *HisAmM XR*
Chapman, Henry Smith 1871-1936 *DcNAA*
Chapman, Irv *NF*
Chapman, Irwin M *OvPC*
Chapman, J C *FamWC*
Chapman, John 1822-1894 *Alli, Alli Sup,*
   WebBD

Chapman, John 1900-1972 *AmAu&B,*
  BiE&WWA, ConAu 33, NewYTBE 1,
  WhoThe 1972
Chapman, John F *OvPC*
Chapman, Joseph M *NF*
Chapman, Judson William 1900-1951 *BioIn 2*
Chapman, Michael Andrew 1884-1960 *BioIn 1,*
  CathA 1930, IndAu 1917
Chapman, Nathaniel 1780-1853 *Alli, BiDSA,*
  CyAL 1, DcAmA, DcNAA, HisAmM XR,
  HisAmM XR
Chapman, Ralph *NF*
Chapman, Reid Gillis 1920- *WhoAdv 1972,*
  WhoAm 1974
Chapman, Toni *NF*
Chapman, William Francis 1925- *WhoMW 1974*
Chapman, William T *NF*
Chappell, James Edward 1885-1960 *BioIn 4,*
  BioIn 5, WhJnl 1928
Chapple, Abby *NF*
Chapple, John Crockett 1876-1946 *BioIn 5*
Chapple, Joseph Mitchell 1867-1950 *AmAu&B,*
  BioIn 2, BioIn 6, DcAmA, HisAmM XR,
  NatCAB 46
Chaput, Girard Raoul 1896- *WhJnl 1928*
Charles, Dorothy 1906-1956 *BioIn 4*
Charles, Emily 1845- *BioIn 2*
Charles, Francis Eugene 1897- *WhJnl 1928*
Charles-Roux, Edmonde 1920- *IntWW 1976*
Charless, Joseph 1772-1834 *AmAu&B, BioIn 6*
Charlesworth, Hector Willoughby 1873-1945
  DcNAA, OxCan
Charlton, Alfred Evan 1912- *IntWW 1976,*
  WhoWor 1974
Charlton, Linda *NF*
Charmes, Francis 1848-1916 *WebBD*
Charnay, David B *OvPC*
Charnay, Desire *HisAmM XR*
Charney, Nicolas Herman 1941- *WhoAm 1974*
Charniak, Hyman *OvPC*
Charnley, Mitchell Vaughn 1898- *AmAu&B,*
  AmM&W 73S, ConAu 69, IndAu 1917,
  WhNAA, WhoAm 1974, WhJnl 1928
Charteris, Hugo Francis Guy 1922-1970 *BioIn 10*
Charters, Sam *NF*
Chartier, Emilio 1946- *ConAu XR*
Charton, Edouard Thomas 1807-1890 *WebBD*
Chartron, Charles *NF*
Charvet, Michael *OvPC*
Chase, Dennis *NF*
Chase, Edna Woolman 1877-1957 *BioIn 4,*
  CurBio XR, HisAmM XR, REnAL
Chase, Edward T *NF*
Chase, Edwin Percy 1879- *WhJnl 1928*
Chase, Francis *BioIn 1*
Chase, Frank H *HisAmM XR*
Chase, Franklin Henry 1864-1940 *DcNAA*
Chase, Frederick Augustus 1908- *WhoAm 1974*
Chase, Gilbert 1906- *ConAu 17, DrAS 74H,*
  WhoAm 1974
Chase, Harold T 1864-1935 *WhJnl 1928*
Chase, Julian 1878?-1974 *BioIn 10, WhJnl 1928*
Chase, Martyn *NF*
Chase, Sylvia 1942- *NF*
Chase, William Calvin 1854-1921 *AmJnl, BioIn 8,*
  BioIn 10
Chaseman, Joel 1926- *WhoAm 1974,*
  WhoE 1974, WhoF&I 1974
Chassler, Seymour Murray 1919- *WhoAm 1974,*
  WhoWorJ 1972
Chastel, Andre 1912- *Au&Wr, IntWW 1976*
Chastenet DeCastaing, Jacques 1893-1978
  IntWW 1976, Who 1974, WhoWor 1974
Chataway, Christopher John 1931- *BioIn 7,*

IntWW 1974, Who 1974, WhoWor 1974
Chatelain, Nicolas 1913-1976 *ConAu 65*
Chatfield-Taylor, Otis 1900?-1948 *BioIn 1*
Chattaway, Edward 1873-1956 *BioIn 4*
Chatterton, Edward Keble 1878-1944 *EvLB,*
  NewC, WebBD, WhoLA
Chauchat, Arsene Marie 1880?-1953 *BioIn 3*
Chaudhuri, Nirad Chandra 1897- *Au&Wr,*
  BioIn 2, BioIn 8, CasWL, DcOrL 2,
  IntWW 1976, NewC, Pen Eng,
  WhoWor 1974
Chaumeix, Jean Henri Andre 1874-1955 *BioIn 3,*
  WebBD
Chauncey, Tom 1913- *WhoAm 1974*
Chauvet, Ernest G 1888?-1958 *BioIn 4*
Chavez Franco, Modesto 1872- *WebBD*
Chawner, Mary Grove *HisAmM XR*
Chaze, William L *NF*
Chazin, Michael *NF*
Cheatham, Bertha M *NF*
Cheatham, Edgar *NF*
Cheatham, Patricia *NF*
Cheatham, T *NF*
Cheesman, Joseph R 1864- *WhJnl 1928*
Cheesman, William E 1891- *WhJnl 1928*
Cheetham, James 1772-1810 *Alli, AmAu,*
  CyAL 1, DcAmA, DcAmB 4, DcNAA,
  HisAmM XR, OxAm, REnAL
Cheetham, John *Alli Sup, AmJnl*
Cheever, George Barrell 1807-1890 *Alli, Alli Sup,*
  BbD, BiD&SB, DcAmA, DcEnL, DcNAA,
  HisAmM XR
Cheever, Henry Theodore 1814-1897 *Alli,*
  Alli Sup, AmAu&B, BiD&SB, CyAL 2,
  DcAmA, DcNAA
Chellas, Allen *OvPC, WhoPubR 1972*
Chelminski, Rudolph *OvPC*
Chen, Eugene 1878-1944 *CurBio XR, WebBD*
Chen, In *OvPC*
Chen, Jack 1908- *BioIn 9, ConAu 41*
Chenery, Thomas 1826-1884 *Alli Sup, WebBD*
Chenery, William Ludlow 1884-1974 *BioIn 2,*
  ConAu 53, HisAmM XR, LiJA,
  NewYTBS 5, REnAL, WhNAA
Cheney, Brainard 1900- *ConAu 25, CurBio XR,*
  WrDr 1976
Cheney, Charles Baldwin 1872-1955 *WhJnl 1928*
Cheney, Sheldon Warren 1886- *AmAu&B,*
  WebBD, WhoAm 1974, WhoWor 1974
Cheney, Warren 1855?-1921 *AmLY, DcNAA,*
  HisAmM XR
Cheney, William *NF*
Chennault, Anna Chan 1925- *AmAu&B,*
  ConAu 61, ForWC 1970, OvPC,
  WhoAm 1974, WhoAmP 1973,
  WhoAmW 1974, WhoS&SW 1973
Chequer, John D 1900?-1965 *BioIn 7*
Cherniavsky, Michael 1923?-1973 *ConAu 41*
Cherniss, Harold *HisAmM XR*
Cherniss, Norman Arnold 1926- *RpN,*
  WhoF&I 1974, WhoWest 1974
Chernoff, Howard Leonard 1907- *WhoAm 1974,*
  WhoGov 1972, WhoWest 1974
Chernofsky, Jacob L 1928- *ConAu 73*
Chernov, Viktor Mikhailovich 1876-1952 *WebBD*
Chernyshev, Vyacheslav Ivanovich 1914-
  IntWW 1976
Chernyshevski, Nikolai Gavrilovich 1828?-1889
  WebBD
Cherones, Joyce *NF*
Cherrier, James Fuller 1930- *WhoAm 1974*
Cherrington, Ernest Hurst 1877-1950 *DcAmB S4,*
  OhA&B
Cherry, Mary Boulware 1901- *WhJnl 1928*

Cherry, Rona *NF*
Cherry, Zena *NF*
Cheseborough, Caroline 1825-1873 *HisAmM XR*
Cheshire, Maxine 1930- *BioIn 8, BioIn 9,
CelR 1973, NewMr, WhoAm 1974,
WhoAmW 1974*
Chesney, Kellow 1914- *Au&Wr, ConAu 29,
WhoE 1974*
Chesnoff, Richard Z 1937- *ConAu 25*
Chesnutt, Edgar B 1906- *WhNAA*
Chesnutt, Edgar B *see also* Chestnut, Edgar B
Chess, Stanley 1947?- *BioIn 10*
Chessman, Merle Rowland 1886-1947 *BioIn 1,
WhJnl 1928*
Chessman, William O *HisAmM XR*
Chester, Edmund A *NF*
Chester, Jerome 1885?-1954 *BioIn 3*
Chester, Joseph Lemuel 1821-1882 *Alli Sup,
CyAL 2, DcAmA, DcNAA, WebBD*
Chester, Lewis *NF*
Chester, Stephen M *HisAmM XR*
Chesterfield, Ray *HisAmM XR*
Chesterton, Ada Elizabeth Jones 1888-1962 *NewC,
WebBD*
Chesterton, Gilbert Keith 1874-1936 *AnCL,
AtlBL, BkC 6, CasWL, CathA 1930,
DcLEL, EvLB, HisAmM XR, OxEng,
Pen Eng, TwCA, TwCA Sup, TwCW,
WebBD, WhoLA*
Chestnut, Edgar B 1906- *WhJnl 1928*
Chestnut, Edgar B *see also* Chesnutt, Edgar B
Cheval, Alfred *NF*
Chevalier, Lois R *NF*
Chevalier, Willard T 1886-1961 *NatCAB 46,
WhJnl 1928*
Chevrier, J H *NF*
Chew, Arthur Percy 1887- *WhJnl 1928*
Chew, James A 1882-1964 *NatCAB 50*
Chew, Peter 1924- *ConAu 57*
Cheyette, Herbert *OvPC*
Chi, Ch'ao-Ting *AmRP*
Chiang, Te-Cheng *RpN*
Chiaromonte, Nicola *AmRP*
Chickering, William 1917?-1945 *NF*
Chidsey, Donald Barr 1902- *AmAu&B, AmNov,
Au&Wr, ConAu 5R, REnAL, SmATA 3,
TwCA Sup*
Chifley, Joseph B 1885-1951 *CurBio XR*
Chigounis, Evans 1931- *ConAu 45, DrAP 1975*
Chilcote, Don 1892?-1948 *BioIn 1*
Child, David Lee 1794-1874 *DcAmB 4, DcNAA*
Child, Harold Hannyngton 1869-1945 *BioIn 5*
Child, Lydia Maria Francis 1802-1880 *Alli,
Alli Sup, AmAu, AmAu&B, BbD, BiD&SB,
CarSB, CasWL, CyAL 2, DcAmA, DcEnL,
DcLEL, DcNAA, EvLB, OxAm, REnAL,
Str&VC, WebBD*
Child, Morris *AmRP*
Child, Richard Washburn 1881-1935 *AmAu&B,
BioIn 9, DcAmB S1, DcNAA, EncMys,
WebBD, WhNAA*
Child, W Stanley 1865- *WhNAA, WhJnl 1928*
Childers, James Saxon 1899-1965 *AmAu&B,
REnAL, WhNAA*
Childress, Edmund Howard 1873- *WhNAA,
WhJnl 1928*
Childress, James *NF*
Childress, William F *NF*
Childs, Cephas Grier 1793-1871 *HisAmM XR*
Childs, Francis *AmJnl*
Childs, Francis James *HisAmM XR*
Childs, George William 1829-1894 *AmAu&B,
AmJnl, BbD, BiD&SB, BioIn 8, DcAmA,
DcNAA, HisAmM XR, WebBD*

Childs, Harwood Lawrence 1898-1972 *Au&Wr,
BioIn 9, ConAu 25, NewYTBE 3*
Childs, Henry E *HisAmM XR*
Childs, John Lewis 1856- *HisAmM XR*
Childs, Marquis William 1903- *AmAu&B, AmJnl,
BioIn 3, BioIn 4, BioIn 6, ConAu 61,
CurBio XR, HisAmM XR, IntWW 1976,
NewMr, OxAm, REn, REnAL, TwCA Sup,
WebBD, WhoAm 1974, WhoS&SW 1973*
Chilton, William Edwin 1893-1950 *BioIn 2,
WhJnl 1928*
Chilton, William Edwin, III 1921- *WhoAm 1974,
WhoAmP 1973, WhoE 1974, WhoWor 1974*
Chimes, Enisse 1918- *NF*
Chinnock, Frank W *OvPC*
Chipman, Herbert Lawrence 1866- *WhNAA,
WhJnl 1928*
Chipman, William J 1898?-1950 *BioIn 2*
Chirico, Andrea De 1891-1952 *BioIn 2, BioIn 3*
Chirol, Sir Ignatius Valentine 1852-1929 *WebBD*
Chirol, Sir Ignatius Valentine *see also* Chirol, Sir
Valentine
Chirol, Sir Valentine 1852-1929 *BioIn 7, LongC,
NewC*
Chirol, Sir Valentine *see also* Chirol, Sir Ignatius
Valentine
Chisholm, Hugh 1866-1924 *LongC, NewC,
WebBD*
Chisholm, James 1838-1903 *BioIn 5*
Chisholm, Samuel S *HisAmM XR*
Chisholme, David 1796?-1842 *BbtC, DcNAA*
Chism, Olin *WhoS&SW 1973*
Chisum, Melvin J d194-? *BioIn 10*
Chittenden, Simeon 1814-1889 *HisAmM XR*
Chitty, Fred Forrest 1897- *WhJnl 1928*
Chnoupek, Bohuslav 1925- *IntWW 1976*
Choate, Robert Burnett 1898-1963 *BioIn 6*
Chodorov, Frank 1887-1966 *BioIn 6, BioIn 7*
Choga, Kazuya *NF*
Chotzinoff, Samuel 1889-1964 *CurBio XR,
WebBD*
Chouinard, Ernest 1856-1924 *DcNAA*
Choukanoff, Boyan *OvPC*
Choyke, William Jeff *NF*
Christ, I H *NF*
Christen, Fred A 1884- *WhJnl 1928*
Christensen, Bente *NF*
Christensen, Frederick L *NF*
Christensen, Henry 1922- *IntWW 1976*
Christensen, Nephi C 1896- *WhJnl 1928*
Christenson, Walter E 1899-1969 *BioIn 8*
Christerson, Melbourne 1905?-1957 *BioIn 4*
Christgau, Robert Thomas 1942- *ConAu 65*
Christian, George Eastland 1927- *BioIn 7,
BioIn 8, ConAu 65, WhoAm 1974,
WhoAmP 1973*
Christian, Marcus Bruce 1900- *BlkAW,
ConAu 73, LivBAA*
Christian, Michelle *NF*
Christian, Roger Willis 1928- *OvPC,
WhoAdv 1972*
Christian, Shirley 1939?- *NF*
Christiansen, Arthur 1904-1963 *BioIn 1, BioIn 5,
BioIn 6, ConAu 2R, LongC, Lor&LP*
Christiansen, Ernst 1891- *BioIn 1, IntWW 1974,
WhoWor 1974*
Christiansen, Michael Robin 1927- *Who 1974*
Christiansen, Richard *NF*
Christianson, David *NF*
Christianson, K Scott *NF*
Christie, Alexander James d1843 *DcNAA*
Christie, Trevor L 1905-1969 *BioIn 8, ConAu 21*
Christman, Henry *HisAmM XR*
Christman, Paul 1918?-1970 *BioIn 8,*

New YTBE 1
Christman, Zoe 1908?-1968 *BioIn 8*
Christopher, Lawrence C *OvPC*
Christopher, Robert Collins 1924- *BioIn 5,*
   WhoAm 1974
Christopherson, Fred Carl 1896- *WhoAm 1974,*
   WhJnl 1928
Christy, Marian 1932- *ConAu 65, ForWC 1970*
Chrysler, K M *NF*
Chrzan, Nat *NF*
Chu, Daniel 1933- *ConAu 15R*
Chu, George *NF*
Chu, Mu-Chih *IntWW 1976*
Chu, Valentin 1919- *ConAu 9R*
Chuan, Ong Beng *NF*
Chuan, Wee Sin *NF*
Chubb, Lieutenant *see* Browne, Charles Farrar
Chubb, Lieutenant *see* Ward, Artemus
Chubb, Thomas Caldecot 1899-1972 *AmAu&B,*
   Au&Wr, ConAu 2R, ConAu 33,
   New YTBE 3, REn, REnAL, WhNAA
Chubbuck, Lawrence Stone 1887- *WhJnl 1928*
Chujoy, Anatole 1894-1969 *AmAu&B*
Chung, Connie *NF*
Chunn, Leona Hayes *BioIn 8*
Church, C A *HisAmM XR*
Church, Edward *NF*
Church, Foster *NF*
Church, Francis Pharcellus 1839-1906 *AmAu&B,*
   AmJnl, BiD&SB, DcNAA, HisAmM XR
Church, George J *NF*
Church, John Adams 1843-1917 *Alli Sup,*
   DcAmA, DcNAA, HisAmM XR
Church, Joseph M *HisAmM XR*
Church, Richard William 1815-1890 *Alli Sup,*
   BrAu 19, CasWL, DcEnL, DcLEL, EvLB,
   NewC, OxEng, WebBD
Church, Wells 1901?-1974 *BioIn 10, New YTBS 5*
Church, William Conant 1836-1917 *AmAu&B,*
   BiD&SB, BioIn 3, BioIn 9, DcAmA,
   DcNAA, HisAmM XR
Churcher, Sharon *NF*
Churchill, Allen 1911- *AmAu&B, BiE&WWA,*
   HisAmM XR
Churchill, Bonnie 1936?- *BioIn 6*
Churchill, Creighton 1912- *ConAu 69*
Churchill, Gail W *NF*
Churchill, John Wesley 1839-1900 *HisAmM XR*
Churchill, Lloyd *NF*
Churchill, Randolph Frederick Edward S 1911-1968
   BioIn 1, BioIn 4, BioIn 5, BioIn 6, BioIn 7,
   BioIn 8, BioIn 9, BioIn 10, CurBio XR,
   ForP
Churchill, Reba 1933?- *BioIn 6*
Churchill, Rhona Adelaide 1913- *Au&Wr,*
   ConAu 7R
Churchill, Winston 1871-1947 *AmAu&B,*
   BiD&SB, BiDSA, CarSB, CasWL, CnDAL,
   CyWA, DcAmA, DcBiA, DcLEL, DcNAA,
   EvLB, LongC, OxAm, OxEng, Pen Am,
   REn, REnAL, TwCA Sup, TwCW, WebBD,
   WebE&AL, WhNAA
Churchill, Sir Winston Leonard Spencer 1874-1965
   BioIn 8, BioIn 9, BioIn 10, CasWL,
   CurBio XR, CyWA, DcLEL, EvLB,
   FamWC, HisAmM XR, LongC, NewC,
   New YTBS 5, OxEng, Pen Eng, REn,
   TwCA, TwCA Sup, TwCW, WebBD,
   WebE&AL
Churchill, Winston Spencer 1940- *Who 1974*
Chusmir, Janet *NF*
Cianfarra, Camille Maximillian 1907-1956 *BioIn 4*
Ciardi, John Anthony 1916- *AmAu&B, AuBYP,*
   BkCL, CasWL, CnDAL, ConAu 5,

ConP 1970, ConP 1975, CurBio XR,
   DrAP 1975, ModAL, OxAm, RAdv 1, REn,
   REnAL, SmATA 1, Str&VC, ThrBJA,
   TwCA Sup, WebBD, WebE&AL,
   WhoAm 1974, WrDr 1976
Cidie 1886-1961 *WebBD*
Cieplinski, Michel 1906- *OvPC, USBiR 1974,*
   WhoAm 1974
Ciervo, Arthur *NF*
Cilley, Gordon Harper 1874-1938 *DcNAA,*
   WhJnl 1928
Cimons, Marlene *NF*
Cingoli, Guilio *BioIn 8*
Cioffi, Lou *NF*
Cioffi, Sam *NF*
Cipolletti, Emilio D 1898?-1948 *BioIn 1*
Cipriani, Frank Joseph 1898?-1955 *BioIn 3*
Cissell, Eldrew Donald *WhJnl 1928*
Cist, Charles 1738-1805 *AmAu&B, HisAmM XR*
Citron, Byron *AmRP*
Clabby, William Robert 1931- *WhoAm 1974*
Claessens, August *AmRP*
Claffey, Mike 1897?-1942 *NF*
Claflin, Tennessee Celeste 1846-1923 *AmAu,*
   OxAm, WebBD
Claflin, Tennessee Celeste *see also* Claflin, Tennie C
Claflin, Tennie C 1846-1923 *Alli Sup,*
   HisAmM XR, OhA&B
Claflin, Tennie C *see also* Claflin, Tennessee Celeste
Claflin, Victoria 1838-1927 *WebBD*
Claflin, Victoria *see also* Woodhull, Victoria Claflin
Clague, Stanley R 1895- *WhJnl 1928*
Claiborne, Craig 1920- *AmAu&B, BioIn 7,*
   BioIn 8, BioIn 9, BioIn 10, ConAu 2R,
   CurBio XR, WhoAm 1974, WhoE 1974
Claiborne, Robert 1919- *ConAu 29*
Claiborne, William L *NF*
Claire, Aileen *NF*
Clairejeune, Yvan S 1935- *NF*
Clancy, Eugene A 1882?-1952 *BioIn 2*
Clancy, Frank J 1891-1958 *BioIn 6, NatCAB 45*
Clancy, Harold Eugene 1920- *WhoAm 1974,*
   WhoE 1974, WhoF&I 1974
Clancy, Mike *InvJ*
Clancy, Robert Henry 1882-1962 *NF*
Clapp, Almon M 1811- *NatCAB 1*
Clapp, E B *HisAmM XR*
Clapp, Edward H *NF*
Clapp, Edwin Jones 1881-1930 *DcNAA*
Clapp, George E 1901- *WhJnl 1928*
Clapp, Henry, Jr. 1814-1875 *AmAu, AmAu&B,*
   HisAmM XR, OxAm, Pen Am
Clapp, Henry Austin 1841-1904 *AmAu,*
   AmAu&B, DcAmA, DcNAA, HisAmM XR
Clapp, J Milton *HisAmM XR*
Clapp, Robert P *HisAmM XR*
Clapp, Roger Howland 1928- *WhoAdv 1972,*
   WhoAm 1974
Clapp, William Warland, Jr. 1826-1891 *Alli Sup,*
   AmAu&B, AmJnl, DcAmB 4, DcNAA,
   HisAmM XR, NatCAB 2
Clapper, Olive Ewing 1896-1968 *CurBio XR*
Clapper, Raymond Lewis 1892-1944 *AmAu&B,*
   AmJnl, BioIn 1, BioIn 2, BioIn 6,
   CurBio XR, DcAmB S3, ForP,
   HisAmM XR, NatCAB 35, WhJnl 1928
Clare, Israel Smith 1847-1924 *Alli Sup,*
   AmAu&B, AmLY, DcNAA, HisAmM XR
Clarendon, J Hayden *HisAmM XR*
Claretie, Jules 1840-1913 *HisAmM XR, WebBD*
Clarey, John E, Jr. 1888- *WhJnl 1928*
Clarity, James *NF*
Clark, Albert Edwin 1915- *WhoAm 1974,*
   WhoS&SW 1973

Clark, Alexander 1826- *BioIn 8*
Clark, Alexander 1834-1879 *Alli Sup, AmAu&B, BiD&SB, DcAmA, DcNAA, OhA&B*
Clark, Allen W 1867- *WhJnl 1928*
Clark, Barrett Harper 1890-1953 *AmAu&B, BioIn 3, BioIn 4, OxAm, REnAL, TwCA, TwCA Sup, WebBD, WhNAA*
Clark, Blair 1917- *WhoAm 1974*
Clark, Blake 1908- *BioIn 2, WhoAm 1974*
Clark, Champ 1923- *WhoAm 1974*
Clark, Charles Heber 1841-1915 *Alli Sup, AmAu, AmAu&B, AmJnl, BiD&SB, BiDSA, BioIn 2, DcAmA, DcNAA, EvLB, NatCAB 35, OxAm, REnAL*
Clark, Charles Hopkins 1848-1926 *WhJnl Sup*
Clark, Charles S *NF*
Clark, Clinton R *NF*
Clark, Conrad *OvPC*
Clark, Cummings C 1901- *WhJnl 1928*
Clark, Daniel D, Jr. 1871- *WhJnl 1928*
Clark, David 1877- *WhJnl 1928*
Clark, David Gillis 1933- *ConAu 53, DrAS 74E, WhoCon 1973*
Clark, Davis Wasgatt 1812-1871 *Alli Sup, DcAmA, DcNAA, HisAmM XR, OhA&B*
Clark, Delbert 1900-1953 *BioIn 1, BioIn 3*
Clark, Donald Hugh 1896- *WhJnl 1928, WhoMW 1974*
Clark, Edward Brayton *HisAmM XR*
Clark, Edward Heermans 1885- *WhJnl 1928*
Clark, Edwin 1899?-1978 *NF*
Clark, Elmer Talmage 1886-1966 *AmAu&B, ConAu 5, WhNAA*
Clark, Emily 1893-1953 *Alli, AmAu&B, BiDLA*
Clark, Esther 1920?- *BioIn 7*
Clark, Evans 1888-1970 *BioIn 9, CurBio XR, NewYTBE 1*
Clark, Evert *InvJ*
Clark, Francis Edward 1851-1927 *AmLY, DcAmA, DcNAA, HisAmM XR, WebBD, WhNAA*
Clark, Frank 1921- *WhoPubR 1972*
Clark, Frank Atherton 1911- *WhoMW 1974*
Clark, Frank J 1884- *WhJnl 1928*
Clark, George *AmRP*
Clark, George 1903?- *BioIn 1, BioIn 3*
Clark, George Hartley *WhJnl 1928*
Clark, Gerald 1918- *ConAu 13R, OxCan*
Clark, Gregory 1892-1977 *CanWW 1972*
Clark, Grover 1891-1938 *DcNAA, WhNAA*
Clark, Harry Hayden 1901-1971 *AmAu&B, BioIn 9, ConAu 29, LiJA*
Clark, Herbert M 1907?-1964 *BioIn 7*
Clark, Herma Naomi 1871?-1959 *BioIn 3, BioIn 5*
Clark, Hubert Galbraith 1890- *WhJnl 1928*
Clark, James Anthony 1907- *BioIn 9, ConAu 65, WhoF&I 1974, WhoS&SW 1973*
Clark, James C 1939- *NF*
Clark, James F *NF*
Clark, John Maurice 1884-1963 *ConAu 5, HisAmM XR*
Clark, John McLane 1910-1950 *BioIn 2, BioIn 4, RpN*
Clark, Joseph *AmRP, BioIn 4*
Clark, Joseph Sylvester 1800-1861 *DcNAA, HisAmM XR*
Clark, Joseph Thomas *NF*
Clark, Kate Upson 1851-1935 *AmAu&B, AmLY, DcAmA, DcNAA, HisAmM XR, WhNAA*
Clark, Keith 1879-1951 *BioIn 2*
Clark, Ken *NF*
Clark, Kenneth 1899- *IntMPA 1975, WhJnl 1928*

Clark, Lewis Gaylord 1808-1873 *Alli, AmAu, AmAu&B, AmJnl, BbD, BiD&SB, BioIn 3, BioIn 4, BioIn 7, CyAL 2, DcAmA, DcEnL, DcNAA, HisAmM XR, LiJA, OxAm, REnAL, WebBD*
Clark, Lindley Hoag, Jr. 1920- *ConAu 65*
Clark, Lyman 1902- *WhJnl 1928*
Clark, Marguerite Sheridan 1900?- *AmAu&B, BioIn 3, ForWC 1970, WhoAm 1974, WhoAmW 1974*
Clark, Marion L 1942?-1977 *ConAu 73*
Clark, Martin *WhoAm 1974, WhoWest 1974*
Clark, Matt 1930- *WhoAm 1974, WhoE 1974*
Clark, Michele 1943?-1972 *BioIn 9*
Clark, Mizzell *NF*
Clark, P L 1870- *WhJnl 1928*
Clark, Paul 1930?- *BioIn 6*
Clark, Peter Bruce 1928- *WhoAm 1974, WhoF&I 1974, WhoMW 1974*
Clark, Reginald J *NF*
Clark, Robert Edward 1922- *WhoAm 1974*
Clark, Robert Phillips 1921- *RpN, WhoAm 1974, WhoS&SW 1973*
Clark, Ronald William 1916- *Au&Wr, AuBYP, ConAu 25, SmATA 2*
Clark, Rufus Reid 1864- *WhJnl 1928*
Clark, Shannon Kelley *NF*
Clark, Sonia Tomara *OvPC*
Clark, Sue C 1935- *ConAu 41*
Clark, T Edward *HisAmM XR*
Clark, Thomas Curtis 1877-1954 *AmAu&B, AnMV 1926, BioIn 2, BioIn 3, IndAu 1816, WhNAA*
Clark, Victor Selden 1868-1946 *AmLY, HisAmM XR, WhNAA*
Clark, W G C *HisAmM XR*
Clark, Walter Eli 1869-1950 *BioIn 2, BioIn 3, NatCAB 38*
Clark, Walter H 1846- *WhJnl 1928*
Clark, Willard *NF*
Clark, William A 1931- *ConAu 33*
Clark, William Donaldson 1916- *ConAu 29*
Clark, William H d1955 *RpN*
Clark, William Heermans 1848-1928 *WhJnl 1928*
Clark, William Newport 1919- *WhoAm 1974, WhoF&I 1974*
Clark, William R 1895?-1970 *BioIn 8*
Clark, Willis Gaylord 1808-1841 *Alli, AmAu, AmAu&B, BbD, BiD&SB, BioIn 4, BioIn 7, CyAL 2, DcAmA, DcNAA, HisAmM XR, REnAL, WebBD*
Clark, Z *HisAmM XR*
Clarke, Amy B 1903- *WhJnl 1928*
Clarke, Arthur C 1870?-1949 *BioIn 2*
Clarke, Arthur L 1869- *WhJnl 1928*
Clarke, Arthur M *AmJnl*
Clarke, Sir Basil *NF*
Clarke, Charles C 1928- *OvPC, WhoPubR 1972*
Clarke, Charles S *HisAmM XR*
Clarke, Donald Henderson 1887-1958 *AmAu&B, AmNov*
Clarke, Dorus 1797-1884 *Alli Sup, CyAL 2, DcAmA, DcNAA, HisAmM XR*
Clarke, Ernest Perley 1859-1933 *WhNAA, WhJnl 1928*
Clarke, George *AmRP*
Clarke, George Herbert 1873-1953 *BioIn 3, DcLEL, HisAmM XR, OxCan, REnAL, WebBD, WhNAA*
Clarke, Gerald *NF*
Clarke, Grace Giddings Julian 1865-1938 *BioIn 2, IndAu 1816*
Clarke, Helen Archibald 1860-1926 *AmAu&B, BiD&SB, DcNAA, HisAmM XR, WebBD,*

WhNAA
Clarke, Howard L 1882- *WhJnl 1928*
Clarke, Ida Clyde 1878-1956 *WhNAA*
Clarke, James Freeman 1810-1888 *Alli, Alli Sup,
  AmAu, AmAu&B, BbD, BbtC, BiD&SB,
  CyAL 2, DcAmA, DcLEL, DcNAA,
  HisAmM XR, LiJA, OxAm, REnAL,
  WebBD*
Clarke, James M 1903- *WhJnl 1928*
Clarke, James W *NF*
Clarke, Jay 1927- *WhoS&SW 1973*
Clarke, John Henrik 1915- *AmAu&B, AuNews 1,
  BioIn 10, BlkAW, ConAu 53, LivBAA,
  WhoAm 1974, WhoE 1974*
Clarke, John Smith 1885-1959 *BioIn 5*
Clarke, Joseph Ignatius Constantine 1846-1925
  *Alli Sup, AmAu&B, DcAmA, DcAmB 4,
  DcNAA, HisAmM XR, PoIre*
Clarke, Mary Bayard Devereux 1827?-1886
  *Alli Sup, AmAu, AmAu&B, BiD&SB,
  BiDSA, DcAmA, DcNAA, LivFWS*
Clarke, Mary G *HisAmM XR*
Clarke, Phil *NF*
Clarke, Richard Wilton 1896-1971 *BioIn 1,
  BioIn 9, NewYTBE 2*
Clarke, Robin Harwood 1937- *Au&Wr,
  ConAu 15R*
Clarke, S M *NF*
Clarke, Selah M *AmJnl*
Clarke, Thomas Cottrell *HisAmM XR*
Clarke, Tom 1884-1957 *BioIn 4*
Clarke, W Houghton 1894- *WhJnl 1928*
Clarke, Will F *WhJnl 1928*
Clarke, William 1825-1901 *BioIn 10*
Clarke, William Fayal 1855-1937 *AmAu&B,
  HisAmM XR, NatCAB 27*
Clarke, William Malpas 1922- *ConAu 41,
  Who 1974*
Clarke, William T *HisAmM XR*
Clarkin, Franklin 1868?-1960 *BioIn 5*
Clarkson, Grosvenor Blaine 1882-1937 *BioIn 4,
  NatCAB 39*
Clarkson, James S 1842-1918 *NatCAB 2*
Clarkson, Mary *NF*
Clarkson, Richard Blodgett 1910?-1949 *BioIn 2*
Claro, Ricardo *ForP*
Clary, C C Tennant *HisAmM XR*
Clary, Jack 1932- *ConAu 57*
Clary, Mike *NF*
Classen, Harold *AmJnl*
Clauber, Adolph *NF*
Claus, Henry Turner 1885-1966 *WhJnl 1928*
Clauser, Henry Ray *BioIn 9*
Clauson, James Earl 1873-1937 *AmAu&B,
  DcNAA, WhNAA, WhJnl 1928*
Clavel, Guy *NF*
Clavers, Mary *see* Kirkland, Caroline Matilda S
Clawson, Ken Wade 1937?- *BioIn 10,
  BioNews 1974, InvJ, NewMr, NewYTBS 5*
Claxton, Oliver 1900?-1959 *BioIn 5*
Clay, Cassius Marcellus 1810-1903 *Alli, Alli Sup,
  AmJnl, BiD&SB, BiDSA, DcAmA, DcNAA,
  WebBD*
Clay, George 1924?-1964 *BioIn 7*
Clay, Grady Edward 1916- *RpN, WhoAm 1974*
Clay, Thomas Hart *HisAmM XR*
Claypool, David C 1757-1849 *AmJnl, NatCAB 20*
Clayton, Charles Curtis 1902- *AmAu&B, BioIn 1,
  ConAu 23, ConAu 73, DrAS 74E,
  WhoAm 1974*
Clayton, Howard 1929- *BiDrLUS, ConAu 65*
Clayton, James Edwin 1929- *ConAu 11R,
  WhoAm 1974*
Clayton, John 1892- *ConAu 33*

Clayton, Lou 1887?-1950 *BioIn 2*
Clayton, William E *NF*
Clear, Claudius 1851-1923 *NewC, WebBD*
Clear, Claudius *see also* Nicoll, Sir William
  Robertson
Cleary, David J, Jr. *NF*
Cleary, Dennis 1940- *NF*
Cleaton, Allen 1903?-1958 *BioIn 4*
Cleave, Kit Van *NF*
Cleaver, Hylton Reginald 1891-1961 *ConAu 73,
  LongC, WhoChL*
Cleaves, Freeman 1904- *ConAu 4R*
Cleghorn, Reese 1930- *ConAu 25, WhoAm 1974,
  WhoS&SW 1973*
Cleland, Elizabeth *NF*
Cleland, John A *NF*
Clemenceau, Georges 1841-1929 *ClDMEL,
  HisAmM XR, REn, WebBD*
Clemens, Cyril 1902- *AuNews 2, BioIn 1,
  BkC 3, CathA 1930, LiJA, REnAL,
  WhNAA*
Clemens, Mazie E d1952 *BioIn 2, WhJnl 1928*
Clemens, Samuel Langhorne 1835-1910 *Alli Sup,
  AmAu, AmAu&B, AmJnl, AnCL, ArizL,
  AuBYP, BbD, BiD&SB, BiDPara, BiDSA,
  CarSB, CasWL, CnDAL, CyAL 2, DcAmA,
  DcEnA, DcEnL, DcLEL, DcNAA, EncAB,
  EncMys, EncWL, EvLB, JBA 1934, LongC,
  OxAm, OxEng, Pen Am, RComWL, REn,
  REnAL, TwCA, WebBD*
Clemens, Samuel Langhorne *see also* Twain, Mark
Clemens, Will M *HisAmM XR*
Clement, Edward Henry 1843-1920 *AmJnl,
  DcAmB 4, NatCAB 22*
Clement, J F 1895- *WhJnl 1928*
Clement, Jesse *HisAmM XR*
Clement, Travers *AmRP*
Clements, H Everest *NF*
Clements, Hazel Kane 1891?-1967 *BioIn 7*
Clements, John A 1901- *HisAmM XR,
  WhoPubR 1972, WhoS&SW 1973*
Clements, Traverse 1900?-1977 *ConAu 69*
Clements, William *NF*
Clemmer, Mary 1839-1884 *Alli Sup, AmAu,
  AmAu&B, DcAmA, DcNAA*
Clemmer, Mary *see also* Ames, Mary Clemmer
Clemons, Walter, Jr. 1929- *ConAu 1, DrAS 74E*
Clendenin, Henry Wilson 1837-1927 *BioIn 7,
  NatCAB 47*
Clendinen, James Augustus 1910- *WhoAm 1974,
  WhoS&SW 1973*
Clendinning, Katherine W 1893-1956 *BioIn 4*
Clerici, Gianni 1930- *ConAu 65*
Cleroux, Richard *NF*
Cleveland, Chester Wilson 1898-1961 *IndAu 1917,
  WhNAA, WhJnl 1928*
Cleveland, Harlan 1918- *AmM&W 73S, BioIn 3,
  ConAu 1, CurBio XR, IntWW 1974,
  LEduc 1974, WhoAm 1974, WhoAmP 1973,
  WhoWest 1974, WhoWor 1974, WrDr 1976*
Cleveland, Reginald M 1886?-1971 *BioIn 9,
  NewYTBE 2*
Cleveland, Robert *NF*
Clevenger, James *NF*
Clew, William Joseph 1904- *OvPC,
  WhoAm 1974, WhoF&I 1974*
Click, J W 1936- *ConAu 57*
Clifford, George E *NF*
Clifford, Jack Carl 1933- *WhoAdv 1972,
  WhoAm 1974*
Clifford, Josephine *HisAmM XR*
Clifford, Margaret Cort 1929- *BioIn 9, BioIn 10,
  ConAu 25, ForWC 1970, SmATA 1,
  WhoAmW 1974*

Clifford, Maurice Paul 1901- *WhJnl 1928*
Clifford, William *NF*
Clift, Betty 1881- *WhNAA, WhJnl 1928*
Clift, Charles A 1904- *WhJnl 1928*
Clift, Fred W 1889- *WhJnl 1928*
Clift, John *NF*
Clift, John W 1856- *WhJnl 1928*
Clift, William *Alli Sup, HisAmM XR*
Clifton, Thomas A 1859-1935 *BioIn 2, IndAu 1816*
Clifton, Tony *NF*
Clifton, W H *WhJnl 1928*
Clinch, Charles Powell 1797-1880 *AmAu, AmAu&B, BiD&SB, DcNAA*
Clinchy, Evans *RpN*
Cline, John H *NF*
Cline, Leonard *HisAmM XR*
Cline, Marjorie Ann 1920- *WhoAm 1974, WhoAmW 1974, WhoS&SW 1973*
Cline, Ned A 1939?- *NF*
Cline, Raymond H 1896- *WhJnl 1928*
Cline, Yandell C 1897?- *WhJnl 1928*
Clinton, John Hart 1905- *WhoAm 1974*
Clip *see* Boutell, Clarence Burley
Clippinger, Frank Warren 1895- *WhoAm 1974, WhJnl 1928*
Clippinger, Roy 1886-1962 *NatCAB 50*
Clissitt, William Cyrus 1898- *Who 1974*
Clissold, H R *HisAmM XR*
Clive, Madeleine *OvPC*
Cloherty, Jack *NewMr*
Cloke, H Walton 1919- *OvPC, WhoAdv 1972, WhoF&I 1974, WhoPubR 1972*
Close, Upton 1894-1960 *AmAu&B, CurBio XR, EvLB, HisAmM XR, TwCA, TwCA Sup, WebBD, WhNAA*
Close, Upton *see also* Hall, Josef Washington
Clot, Frederic DeT. d1901 *NF*
Clough, Arthur Hugh *HisAmM XR*
Clough, Desmond *ForP*
Clough-Leighter, Henry 1874-1956 *BioIn 1, BioIn 4*
Cloutier, Nancy *NF*
Clover, Samuel Travers 1859-1934 *AmAu&B, DcNAA*
Clowes, Ernest Seabury 1881-1957 *BioIn 4*
Clowes, Molly 1906- *WhoAmW 1974*
Clowes, Norris A *WhJnl 1928*
Clubb, Henry S *BioIn 10*
Cluett, John P 1900?-1965 *BioIn 7*
Clum, John P 1851-1923 *ArizL*
Clune, Henry W 1890- *BioIn 1, ConAu 2R, REnAL*
Clurman, Harold Edgar 1901- *AmAu&B, ConAu 4R, CurBio XR, IntWW 1976, WhoWor 1974*
Clurman, Irene *NF*
Clute, Willard Nelson 1869-1950 *AmAu&B, AmLY, DcAmA, HisAmM XR, WebBD, WhNAA*
Clutton-Brock, Arthur 1868-1924 *EvLB, LongC, NewC, REn, TwCA, WebBD*
Clutz, Jacob A 1848-1925 *HisAmM XR*
Clyde, Elbert Thornton 1879- *WhJnl 1928*
Clyman, Rhea *OvPC*
Clymer, Adam 1937- *NF*
Clymer, Ernest F *HisAmM XR*
Clymer, George E 1754-1834 *AmJnl, WebBD*
Clymer, Rolla *NF*
Coady, Michael F *NF*
Coakley, Daniel H 1864?-1952 *BioIn 3*
Coakley, John P 1881?-1950 *BioIn 2*
Coakley, LeBaron 1901?-1961 *BioIn 5*
Coan, Nonnee 1910- *NF*

Coan, Philip M 1881?-1968 *BioIn 8*
Coaten, Arthur W 1872-1939? *BioIn 2, Br&AmS*
Coates, Charles B 1908- *WhoAm 1974, WhoPubR 1972*
Coates, Foster d1914 *AmJnl, HisAmM XR*
Coates, Harold Wilson 1882- *WhJnl 1928*
Coates, James *NF*
Coates, Joseph Hornor 1849-1930 *DcNAA*
Coates, Paul 1920?-1968 *BioIn 4, BioIn 7, BioIn 8*
Coates, Reynell 1802-1886 *Alli, HisAmM XR*
Coates, Robert Myron 1897-1973 *AmAu&B, AmNov, Au&Wr, CnDAL, ConAu 5R, ConNov 1972, DcLEL, NewYTBE 4, OxAm, Pen Am, REn, REnAL, TwCA, TwCA Sup, WhoAmA 1973*
Cobb, Beatrice 1888-1959 *BioIn 5, BioIn 6, NatCAB 46*
Cobb, Carl M 1935?- *NF*
Cobb, Cully Alton 1884-1975 *WhoAm 1974*
Cobb, Cyril R 1904?-1950 *BioIn 2*
Cobb, David *NF*
Cobb, Frank Irving 1869-1923 *AmAu&B, AmJnl, BioIn 8, WebBD, WhJnl Sup*
Cobb, H *HisAmM XR*
Cobb, Hubbard Hanford 1917- *WhoAm 1974*
Cobb, Irvin Shrewsbury 1876-1944 *AmAu&B, AmJnl, CnDAL, ConAmL, CurBio XR, DcAmB S3, DcNAA, EncMys, EvLB, HisAmM XR, LongC, OxAm, REn, REnAL, TwCA, TwCA Sup, WebBD, WhNAA*
Cobb, Ron 1937- *BioIn 10*
Cobb, Samuel T *HisAmM XR*
Cobb, Sanford *HisAmM XR*
Cobb, Sylvanus 1799?-1866 *Alli Sup, DcAmA, DcNAA, HisAmM XR*
Cobb, Sylvanus, Jr. 1823-1887 *Alli, AmAu, AmAu&B, BiD&SB, CnDAL, DcAmA, DcBiA, DcNAA, EncMys, HisAmM XR, HsB&A, HsB&A Sup, OxAm, REnAL*
Cobbett, William 1762?-1835 *Alli, AmJnl, AtlBL, BbD, BbtC, BiD&SB, BiDLA, BiDLA Sup, BioIn 1, BioIn 2, BioIn 3, BioIn 4, BioIn 5, BioIn 6, BioIn 7, BioIn 8, BioIn 9, BioIn 10, BrAu 19, CarSB, CasWL, CnDAL, DcAmB 4, DcEnA, DcEnL, DcEuL, DcLEL, EvLB, ForP, HisAmM XR, MouLC 3, NewC, OxAm, OxEng, Pen Eng, REn, WebBD, WebE&AL*
Cobbs, John Lewis 1917- *WhoAm 1974, WhoWor 1974*
Cobean, Samuel E 1913-1951 *BioIn 1, BioIn 2*
Cobleigh, Nelson Simmons 1845-1927 *WhJnl Sup, WhJnl 1928*
Coblentz, Edmond David 1882-1959 *AmAu&B, BioIn 2, BioIn 5*
Coblentz, Gaston *OvPC*
Coblentz, Stanton Arthur 1896- *AmAu&B, AnMV 1926, Au&Wr, BioIn 3, BioIn 5, ConAu 5R, CurBio XR, REnAL, WhNAA, WhoAm 1974, WrDr 1976*
Coburn, Judith *NF*
Coccola, Richard A 1932- *NF*
Cochel, Wilber Andrew 1877- *WhJnl 1928*
Cochran, Bert 1917- *AmRP, ConAu 45*
Cochran, Frank C 1889- *WhJnl 1928*
Cochran, Nan *WhJnl 1928*
Cochran, Negley Dakin 1863-1941 *AmJnl, OhA&B*
Cochran, Robert E 1896- *WhJnl 1928*
Cochran, Thomas B 1845-1910 *NatCAB 6*
Cochrane, Charles Henry 1856-1940 *DcNAA*
Cochrane, Elizabeth 1867-1922 *AmAu, DcNAA,*

WhoAmW 1974
Colby, Clara Bewick *HisAmM XR*
Colby, Ethel 1908- *BiE&WWA, ForWC 1970, IntMPA 1975, WhoAm 1974, WhoAmW 1974, WhoWor 1974*
Colby, Frank 1892?-1951 *BioIn 2*
Colby, Frank Moore 1865-1925 *AmAu&B, BioIn 3, DcLEL, DcNAA, HisAmM XR, NatCAB 29, OxAm, REnAL, TwCA, TwCA Sup, WebBD*
Colby, Frederick Myron 1848- *Alli Sup, DcAmA, DcNAA*
Colby, Jean *BioIn 2*
Colby, Wayne *NF*
Colcord, Lincoln Ross 1883-1947 *AmAu&B, DcAmB S4, DcNAA, HisAmM XR, REnAL, WebBD, WhNAA*
Coldren, Philip 1882-1955 *WhJnl 1928*
Cole, Albert Leslie 1894- *WhoAm 1974, WhoF&I 1974*
Cole, Benjamin Richason 1916- *WhoAm 1974, WhoS&SW 1973*
Cole, Cyrenus 1863-1939 *AmAu&B, DcNAA*
Cole, Harry Ellsworth 1861-1928 *BioIn 5, IndAu 1917, WhNAA*
Cole, Sir Henry 1808-1882 *Alli Sup, BioIn 2, BrAu 19, DcEnL, WebBD*
Cole, Hubert 1908- *Au&Wr, ConAu 7R*
Cole, James Robert 1927- *WhoAm 1974*
Cole, Kenneth *NF*
Cole, Lee S 1901- *WhJnl 1928*
Cole, Martha *NF*
Cole, Paul Fremont 1880-1951 *BioIn 2*
Cole, R Taylor *HisAmM XR*
Cole, Verne H *NF*
Cole, Walton Adamson 1912-1963 *BioIn 6*
Cole, Willard Glover 1906-1965 *BioIn 7, BioIn 8, NatCAB 51*
Cole, William *NF*
Colebaugh, Charles Henry 1893?-1944 *HisAmM XR*
Colegrove, Arthur Dana 1891-1955 *BioIn 6*
Colegrove, Kenneth Wallace 1886-1975 *AmAu&B, BioIn 10, ConAu 5, ConAu 53, WhNAA, WhoAm 1974*
Coleman, Abe *AmRP*
Coleman, Albert Evander 1847- *WhNAA, WhJnl 1928*
Coleman, Alexander Wescott 1879?-1947 *BioIn 1*
Coleman, Charles M 1877- *WhJnl 1928*
Coleman, Fred W *NF*
Coleman, Harry 1872-1918 *NatCAB 17*
Coleman, Herbert *NF*
Coleman, James Alexander 1911- *BioIn 9, CanWW 1972*
Coleman, Kathleen Blake 1864-1915 *DcNAA*
Coleman, Lester L *NF*
Coleman, McAllister *AmRP*
Coleman, Oliver *HisAmM XR*
Coleman, Ralph Pallen, Jr. 1923- *WhoAm 1974*
Coleman, Terry 1931- *ConAu 15R, WrDr 1976*
Coleman, Valerie Dickerson *BlkC*
Coleman, William 1766-1829 *Alli Sup, AmAu&B, AmJnl, DcAmB 4, DcNAA, HisAmM XR, NatCAB 11*
Coleman, William Werner 1835-1888 *BioIn 5*
Colen, B D 1946- *ConAu 65*
Coleridge, Sir John Taylor 1790-1876 *Alli, Alli Sup, DcEnL, WebBD*
Coles, G *HisAmM XR*
Coles, Sydney Frederick Arthur 1896- *Au&Wr, ConAu 5, ConAu 7R*
Colesworthy, Daniel Clement 1810-1893 *Alli Sup, CyAL 2, DcAmA, DcNAA, HisAmM XR*

Colfax, Schuyler 1823-1885 *AmJnl, IndAu 1816, WebBD*
Colgan, Donald F 1920-1955 *BioIn 3*
Colgan, Susan *NF*
Colin, Paul Joseph Pierre Marie 1908- *WhoAm 1974*
Colister, Ron *NF*
Coll, Raymond S 1875-1962 *BioIn 6*
Collard, Edgar Andrew 1911- *CanWW 1972, OxCan*
Colledge, Charles Hopson 1911- *WhoAm 1974*
Colles, Henry Cope 1879-1943 *CurBio XR, WebBD*
Collett, Alec *NF*
Collier, Barnard L *NF*
Collier, Bert *BioIn 3*
Collier, Bryan *NF*
Collier, Ethel 1903- *AuBYP, ConAu 65*
Collier, Everett Dolton 1914- *BioIn 7, WhoAm 1974, WhoS&SW 1973*
Collier, Ezra *HisAmM XR*
Collier, John Payne 1789-1883 *Alli, Alli Sup, BiD&SB, CasWL, DcEnL, DcEuL, DcLEL, NewC, OxEng, WebBD*
Collier, Peter 1939- *ConAu 65*
Collier, Peter Fenelon 1849-1909 *AmAu&B, HisAmM XR, WebBD*
Collier, Rex *NF*
Collier, Robert Joseph 1876-1918 *HisAmM XR, WebBD*
Collier, William *HisAmM XR*
Colligan, Douglas *NF*
Collings, Anthony *NF*
Collingwood, Charles Cummings 1917- *ConAu 29, CurBio XR, IntWW 1976, WhoAm 1974*
Collingwood, Herbert Winslow 1857-1927 *Alli Sup, AmLY, HisAmM XR, WhNAA*
Collins, Alan C *HisAmM XR*
Collins, Albert T *NF*
Collins, Arnold Quint 1935- *ConAu 73*
Collins, B A 1884- *WhJnl 1928*
Collins, Beulah *NF*
Collins, Bud *NF*
Collins, Carmen *NF*
Collins, Charles D *NF*
Collins, Charles William 1880-1964 *AmAu&B, AmJnl, BioIn 2, IndAu 1816*
Collins, Dean 1887- *WhJnl 1928*
Collins, Douglas *BioIn 8*
Collins, Ed *NF*
Collins, Edward H 1892?-1961 *BioIn 5*
Collins, Edwin R 1876-1933 *WhNAA, WhJnl 1928*
Collins, Eugene R 1890- *WhJnl 1928*
Collins, Francis 1801-1834 *BbtC, BioIn 1, OxCan*
Collins, Francis Arnold 1873-1957 *AmAu&B, BioIn 4*
Collins, Francis M 1884- *WhJnl 1928*
Collins, Frank d1898 *FamWC*
Collins, Frederic William 1906- *BioIn 2, WhoAm 1974*
Collins, Frederick Lewis 1882-1950 *AmAu&B, BioIn 2, HisAmM XR*
Collins, George *NF*
Collins, Herman Leroy 1865-1940 *AmAu&B*
Collins, Howard *NF*
Collins, Isaac *NF*
Collins, J Edward 1886- *WhJnl 1928*
Collins, J Michael 1935- *WhoAm 1974, WhoE 1974*
Collins, James E 1915- *WhoAm 1974*
Collins, James H 1873- *HisAmM XR, WhNAA*
Collins, James Sullivan 1893?-1949 *BioIn 2*
Collins, John *CanWW 1972*

Collins, John L NF
Collins, John Martin 1892-1952 BioIn 2, BioIn 4, NatCAB 41
Collins, John Walter 1895-1956 BioIn 4
Collins, Joseph Edmund 1855-1892 Alli Sup, DcNAA, OxCan
Collins, Kreigh 1908- BioIn 2, WhoAmA 1973
Collins, Larry 1929- AmAu&B, CelR 1973, ConAu 65, WhoAm 1974, WhoWor 1974
Collins, Mark Francis 1913- WhoAm 1974, WhoE 1974
Collins, Michael Francis 1854-1928 WhJnl 1928
Collins, Nancy NF
Collins, Norman Richard 1907- Au&Wr, DcLEL, EvLB, IntWW 1974, LongC, NewC, TwCA Sup, WebBD, Who 1974, WhoAm 1974, WhoWor 1974, WrDr 1976
Collins, Pat NF
Collins, Paul Valorous 1860-1931 HisAmM XR, WhJnl 1928
Collins, Peter 1942- NF
Collins, Philip S 1864-1943 WhJnl 1928
Collins, Ralph A NF
Collins, Reid NF
Collins, Richard L NF
Collins, Robert InvJ
Collins, Robert Joseph 1927- WhoAm 1974
Collins, Seward B 1899?-1952 BioIn 3, HisAmM XR
Collins, Thomas Hightower 1910-1978 BioIn 4, WhoAm 1974
Collins, Tom 1899- WhNAA, WhJnl 1928
Collins, Treve H 1892- WhJnl 1928
Collins, Walton Robert 1930- WhoMW 1974
Collins, William French 1872?-1949 BioIn 1
Collitz, Hermann 1855-1935 HisAmM XR
Colman, Henry 1785-1849 Alli, CyAL 1, DcAmA, DcNAA, HisAmM XR
Colman, Norman Jay 1827-1911 BioIn 3, HisAmM XR, WebBD
Colmant, Clotilde A NF
Colombres, Juan Carlos 1923?- BioIn 5
Colson, Ethel M HisAmM XR
Colson, Ethel M see also Brazelton, Ethel M C
Colstello, Louis B 1876- WhJnl 1928
Coltart, James Milne 1903- IntMPA 1975, Lor&LP, Who 1974
Colton, Calvin 1789-1857 Alli, AmAu, AmAu&B, CyAL 1, DcAmA, DcAmB 4, DcNAA
Colton, Delia M HisAmM XR
Colton, Ferry Barrows 1903-1954 BioIn 3, HisAmM XR
Colton, George Hooker 1818-1847 Alli, AmAu&B, CyAL 2, DcAmA, DcNAA, HisAmM XR
Colton, Walter 1797-1851 Alli, AmAu, AmAu&B, BiD&SB, BioIn 2, CyAL 2, DcAmA, DcAmB 4, DcNAA, HisAmM XR, OxAm, REnAL, WebBD
Colton, Wendell P HisAmM XR
Colum, Mary Maguire 1887?-1957 AmAu&B, HisAmM XR, WebBD, WhNAA
Colum, Padraic 1881-1972 AmAu&B, AmSCAP 1966, AnCL, AuBYP, BkC 3, CarSB, CasWL, CathA 1930, CnMD, ConAu 33, ConAu 73, ConP 1970, DcLEL, EncWL, EvLB, HisAmM XR, JBA 1934, JBA 1951, LongC, McGWD, ModBL, ModBL Sup, ModWD, NewC, NewYTBE 2, NewYTBE 3, Pen Eng, RAdv 1, REn, REnWD, Str&VC, TwCA, TwCA Sup, TwCW, WebBD, WebE&AL
Colver, William B 1870-1926 NatCAB 28
Colvig, Fred d1949 BioIn 2

Colville, Robert 1909- BioIn 2, Br&AmS
Colvin, Fred Herbert 1867-1965 BioIn 1, BioIn 5, BioIn 7, BioIn 9, WhNAA, WhJnl 1928
Colvin, Ian Duncan 1877-1938 BioIn 2
Colvin, Ian G 1912-1975 ConAu 19, ConAu 57
Colvin, James E RpN
Coman, Martha d1959 BioIn 5
Coman, Thomas F 1902?- BioIn 2
Combes, Abbott NF
Combes, Charles L 1905-1972 BioIn 9
Combes, Helen Merritt 1864?-1949 BioIn 2
Combes, Willard Wetmore 1901- WhoAm 1974
Comer, Cornelia Atwood d1929 DcNAA
Comfort, Will Levington 1878-1932 AmAu&B, ConAmL, DcAmB S1, DcNAA, REnAL, TwCA, TwCA Sup, WebBD, WhNAA
Comings, A V 1878- WhJnl 1928
Cominsky, Jacob Robert 1899-1968 WhJnl 1928
Commodore, Chester NF
Como, William 1925- ConAu 69, NF
Compere, Tom 1907?-1973 BioIn 10, NewYTBE 4
Compton, Ann 1947?- BioIn 10
Compton, Denis Charles Scott 1918- IntWW 1976, Who 1974
Compton, Walter 1912-1959 BioIn 5
Comstock, Alzada 1888-1960 HisAmM XR
Comstock, Amy 1886- WhNAA, WhJnl 1928
Comstock, Helen 1893-1970 BioIn 9, ConAu 5
Comstock, Jim 1910?- BioIn 5
Comstock, William T HisAmM XR
Comte, George Richard 1913- WhoAdv 1972, WhoAm 1974
Conant, Charles Arthur 1861-1915 AmAu&B, DcAmA, DcAmB 4, DcNAA, WebBD
Conant, Francis A NF
Conant, Lawrence M HisAmM XR
Conant, Luther, Jr. 1911- OvPC, WhoPubR 1972
Conant, Samuel Stillman 1831-1885 Alli Sup, DcAmA, HisAmM XR
Conant, William Cowper HisAmM XR
Conard, Jesse BioIn 2, IndAu 1816
Conaway, James Bennett 1932?- BlkC
Conconi, Charles N 1938- NF
Conde, Carlos BioIn 9, BioIn 10
Condict, Fred G 1884?-1949 BioIn 2
Condie, Thomas HisAmM XR
Condie, Thomas G, Jr. HisAmM XR
Condit, Abbie Harrison 1883?-1948 BioIn 1
Condit, J B HisAmM XR
Condit, Kenneth Hamilton 1888-1974 WhNAA, WhJnl 1928
Condomitros, Solon NF
Condon, David NF
Condon, Frank 1882-1940 CurBio XR, DcNAA, HisAmM XR, OhA&B
Condon, George Edward 1916- ConAu 45, WhoMW 1974
Cone, Edwin F 1867?-1952 BioIn 2
Cone, Orello 1835-1905 AmAu, DcAmA, DcNAA, HisAmM XR, OhA&B
Cone, Spencer Wallace 1819-1888 DcNAA, HisAmM XR
Congdon, Charles H 1870-1933 NatCAB 26, WhJnl 1928
Congdon, Charles Taber 1821-1891 Alli Sup, AmAu, AmAu&B, BiD&SB, BioIn 1, DcAmA, DcNAA, HisAmM XR
Congdon, Clement Hillman 1868- WhNAA, WhJnl 1928
Congdon, Tom 1931?- BioIn 10
Conger, Beach 1912-1969 AmJnl, BioIn 8, BioIn 10
Conger-Kaneko, Josephine AmRP

Conine, Ernest 1925- *ConAu 69, WhoWest 1974*
Conklin, Edward D *WhJnl 1928*
Conklin, Gordon L *NF*
Conklin, Oscar Thompson 1879- *WhJnl 1928*
Conklin, William D *BioIn 2*
Conkling, Frank W *NF*
Conkling, Herbert 1879- *WhJnl 1928*
Conlan, Michael F *NF*
Conland, Henry Holton 1882-1944 *BioIn 2, NatCAB 34*
Conley, Clare Dean 1929- *WhoAm 1974, WhoE 1974*
Conley, Philip Mallory 1887- *AmAu&B, ConAu 69, WhoAm 1974*
Conley, Walter F 1905- *WhJnl 1928*
Conlon, Michael J *NF*
Conlon, Pat *NF*
Conlon, Scoop *BioIn 1*
Conly, Robert Leslie 1918?-1973 *ConAu 73*
Conn, Frederick James, Jr. 1908- *WhoAm 1974, WhoS&SW 1973*
Conn, Harry F *NF*
Conn, Kenneth Smith 1900- *WhoAm 1974, WhoWest 1974*
Connatty, Thomas J *NF*
Connell, Brian Reginald 1916- *Au&Wr, BioIn 4, ConAu 4R, WrDr 1976*
Connell, Evan Shelby, Jr. 1924- *AmAu&B, Au&Wr, BioIn 7, BioIn 8, ConAu 4R, ConLC 4, ConLC 6, ConNov 1972, ConNov 1976, DrAF 1976, ModAL Sup, OxAm, Pen Am, RAdv 1, REnAL, WhoAm 1974, WhoTwCL, WhoWor 1974, WorAu, WrDr 1976*
Connell, George S 1885- *WhJnl 1928*
Connelly, Celia Logan 1837-1904 *AmAu&B, BiD&SB, DcAmA, DcNAA*
Connelly, Celia Logan *see also* Fairfax, L
Connelly, Marc 1890- *AmAu&B, BiE&WWA, CnDAL, CnMD, CnThe, ConAmA, ConAmL, ConDr, CurBio XR, DcLEL, IntWW 1974, LongC, McGWD, ModAL, ModWD, OxAm, Pen Am, REn, REnAL, REnWD, WebBD, Who 1974, WhoAm 1974, WhoThe 1972, WhoWor 1974, WrDr 1976*
Connelly, Patrick d1894 *NF*
Connelly, William A *NF*
Connely, Willard 1888-1967 *AmAu&B, ConAu 17*
Conner, Ben *NF*
Conner, Charles *NF*
Conner, Harry W *OvPC*
Conners, William James 1857-1929 *WebBD*
Conners, William James, III 1922- *WhoAm 1974, WhoE 1974*
Conners, William James, Jr. 1895-1951 *BioIn 2, BioIn 6, NatCAB 45, WebBD, WhJnl 1928*
Connery, David Pugsley 1895- *WhNAA, WhJnl 1928*
Connery, Thomas Bernard Joseph 1838?- *BiD&SB, DcAmA, HisAmM XR*
Conniff, Frank 1914-1971 *BioIn 9, ForP, NewYTBE 2*
Connolly, Bruce *NF*
Connolly, Christopher Powell 1863-1933 *HisAmM XR*
Connolly, Cyril 1903-1974 *BioIn 1, BioIn 2, BioIn 3, BioIn 4, BioIn 10, ConAu 21, ConAu 53, CurBio XR, NewYTBS 5, Who 1974*
Connolly, James Brendan 1868-1957 *AmAu&B, AmLY, BkC 3, CathA 1930, HisAmM XR, REnAL, TwCA, TwCA Sup, WebBD*
Connolly, Joseph Vincent 1895-1945 *AmJnl, BioIn 2, NatCAB 36, WhJnl 1928*

Connolly, Margaret *HisAmM XR*
Connolly, Mary Joe 1924- *ForWC 1970, OvPC*
Connolly, Mike 1914?-1966 *BioIn 7*
Connolly, Olga 1926- *BioIn 9*
Connolly, Paul 1926- *BioIn 8, WrDr 1976*
Connolly, Paul *see also* Wicker, Thomas Grey
Connolly, Ray *WrDr 1976*
Connolly, Roger A 1901?-1953 *BioIn 3*
Connor, Francis J *NF*
Connor, John *NF*
Connor, Sir William Neil 1909-1967 *BioIn 3, BioIn 7, BioIn 8, BioIn 9, ConAu 25, LongC, Lor&LP*
Connors, Charles J 1884-1962 *BioIn 6*
Connors, Dorsey *ConAu 45, ForWC 1970, WhoAmW 1974*
Connors, John Stanley 1925- *WhoAm 1974, WhoF&I 1974*
Connors, Thomas J, Jr. *NF*
Conomos, William G 1931- *WhoAm 1974, WhoS&SW 1973*
Conot, Robert E 1929- *AmAu&B, ConAu 45, WrDr 1976*
Conover, Dick *NF*
Conover, Lynn *NF*
Conrad, Daniel B 1884- *WhJnl 1928*
Conrad, Harold *BioIn 6*
Conrad, Michael Georg 1846-1927 *BiD&SB, CIDMEL, OxGer, WebBD*
Conrad, Miles 1911?-1964 *BioIn 7*
Conrad, Paul Francis 1924- *BioIn 5, BioIn 6, WhoAm 1974, WhoWest 1974*
Conrad, Robert Taylor 1810-1858 *Alli, AmAu, AmAu&B, AmJnl, BiD&SB, CyAL 2, DcAmA, DcAmB 4, DcNAA, HisAmM XR, McGWD, OxAm, REnAL*
Conrad, William Harrison 1888-1951 *BioIn 5*
Conroy, Jack 1899- *AmAu&B, AmNov, AmRP, BioIn 2, BioIn 10, ConAu XR, ConNov 1972, ConNov 1976, OhA&B, OxAm, WhNAA, WhoAm 1974, WrDr 1976*
Conroy, John Wesley 1899- *ConAu 5R*
Conroy, John Wesley *see also* Conroy, Jack
Conroy, Sarah Booth 1927- *WhoAmW 1974*
Conroy, Thomas Francis 1897-1953 *BioIn 3*
Conselman, Bill *NF*
Considine, Bob 1906-1975 *AmAu&B, AuNews 2, CelR 1973, ConAu XR, OvPC, REnAL*
Considine, Bob *see also* Considine, Robert Bernard
Considine, James P 1863-1946 *NatCAB 37*
Considine, Robert Bernard 1906-1975 *AmAu&B, BioIn 1, BioIn 5, BioIn 7, BioIn 10, CathA 1930, ConAu 61, CurBio XR, ForP, HisAmM XR, WhoAm 1974, WhoWor 1974*
Considine, Robert Bernard *see also* Considine, Bob
Consolas, Richard B *OvPC*
Consoli, John P 1949- *NF*
Constable, Archibald 1774-1827 *WebBD*
Constantine, Arthur *NF*
Constantineau, Donald 1927- *NF*
Converse, Amasa 1795-1872 *NF*
Converse, Blair 1893- *WhJnl 1928*
Converse, Florence 1871- *AmAu&B, BiDSA, CarSB, DcAmA, WebBD, WhNAA*
Converse, Frank H *HisAmM XR*
Converse, Gordon Noble 1920- *WhoAm 1974*
Converse, Harry Pollard 1876-1960 *NF*
Conway, Faulkner 1860-1939 *AmAu&B, AmLY XR*
Conway, Harry Earl 1888?- *WhJnl 1928*
Conway, Hugh 1942- *AmEA 1974, OvPC*
Conway, Jack *NF*
Conway, Katherine Eleanor 1853-1927 *Alli Sup, AmAu&B, BiD&SB, DcAmA, DcNAA,*

HisAmM XR, PoIre
Conway, Moncure Daniel 1832-1907 Alli Sup,
　AmAu, AmAu&B, AmJnl, BbD, BiD&SB,
　BiDSA, CyAL 2, DcAmA, DcLEL,
　DcNAA, FamWC, HisAmM XR, LiJA,
　OhA&B, OxAm, Pen Am, REnAL, WebBD
Conway, Robert John 1899-1972 BioIn 10,
　NewYTBE 3
Conway, William NF
Conwell, Christopher Columbus AmJnl
Conwell, John NF
Conwell, Leon Martin 1870-1953 BioIn 5,
　NatCAB 42
Cony, Edward Roger 1923- WhoAm 1974,
　WhoE 1974
Conybeare, Fred C HisAmM XR
Conyngham FamWC
Conyngham, David Power 1840-1883 Alli Sup,
　AmAu&B, BbD, BiD&SB, DcAmA,
　DcNAA
Coogan, James Allan OvPC
Cook, Albert Stanburrough 1853-1927 Alli Sup,
　AmAu&B, DcAmA, DcNAA, HisAmM XR,
　WebBD
Cook, Alton 1905-1967 WhJnl 1928
Cook, Barbara C NF
Cook, Bill NF
Cook, Bruce 1932- ConAu 33
Cook, Charles B d1896 NF
Cook, Charles Emerson HisAmM XR
Cook, Clarence Chatham 1828-1900 Alli Sup,
　AmAu, AmAu&B, BbD, BiD&SB, DcAmA,
　DcAmB 4, DcNAA, HisAmM XR
Cook, David 1850-1927 HisAmM XR
Cook, David Charles, III 1912- WhoAm 1974
Cook, David T 1946- ConAu 65
Cook, Denis NF
Cook, Don 1920- ConAu 15R, WhoAm 1974,
　WhoWor 1974, WrDr 1976
Cook, Dorothy Elizabeth 1890-1959 BioIn 3,
　BioIn 5
Cook, E Fullerton 1879-1961 NatCAB 49,
　WhNAA
Cook, Eliza 1818-1889 Alli, Alli Sup, BbD,
　BiD&SB, BrAu 19, DcEnA, DcEnL,
　DcLEL, EvLB, NewC, OxEng, WebBD
Cook, F Rhodes NF
Cook, Fred James 1911- AmAu&B, AuBYP,
　BioIn 4, BioIn 5, BioIn 7, BioIn 9,
　ConAu 9R, DcAmA, NewMr, SmATA 2,
　WhoAm 1974, WhoWor 1974
Cook, George Thomas 1921- WhoAm 1974,
　WhoF&I 1974, WhoS&SW 1973
Cook, James 1926- ConAu 73
Cook, James Graham 1925- ConAu 2R
Cook, Jan 1900?-1972 BioIn 9
Cook, Jess NF
Cook, Joan Marble 1920- ConAu 57
Cook, Joe T BioIn 2
Cook, Joel 1842-1910 Alli Sup, DcAmA,
　DcNAA, FamWC
Cook, Joseph 1838-1901 Alli Sup, AmAu,
　AmAu&B, BbD, DcAmA, DcNAA,
　HisAmM XR, WebBD
Cook, Louis 1915- WhoAm 1974
Cook, Marc 1854-1882 Alli Sup, DcAmA,
　DcNAA
Cook, Marshall Lannis 1858-1955 BioIn 9,
　WhJnl 1928
Cook, Martha Elizabeth Duncan Walker 1806-1874
　Alli Sup, HisAmM XR
Cook, Philip S NF
Cook, Richard L BioIn 10
Cook, Robert Cecil 1903- LEduc 1974,

WhoAm 1974
Cook, Stanton Rufus 1925- WhoAm 1974
Cook, Terry 1942- ConAu 73
Cook, Sir Theodore Andrea 1867-1928 BioIn 2,
　Br&AmS
Cook, Theodore Pease 1844-1916 Alli Sup,
　DcAmA, DcNAA
Cook, Thomas M d1905 NF
Cook, Tom NF
Cook, Waldo Lincoln 1865-1951 BioIn 2
Cook, William NF
Cook, William I HisAmM XR
Cook, William Wallace 1867-1933 DcNAA
Cook, William Warner 1913- WhoAm 1974,
　WhoF&I 1974, WhoPubR 1972
Cooke, Alfred Alistair 1908- AmAu&B,
　Who 1974, WhoAm 1974, WhoWor 1974
Cooke, Alfred Alistair see also Cooke, Alistair
Cooke, Alistair 1908- AmAu&B, AuNews 1,
　BioIn 2, BioIn 3, BioIn 4, BioIn 8, BioIn 9,
　CelR 1973, ConAu 57, CurBio XR, ForP,
　IntMPA 1975, IntWW 1976, LongC,
　NewMr, OxAm, REnAL, TwCA Sup,
　WrDr 1976
Cooke, Alistair see also Cooke, Alfred Alistair
Cooke, Catherine Nixon NF
Cooke, Charles NF
Cooke, Charles Harris 1904?-1977 ConAu 73
Cooke, Clarence G WhJnl 1928
Cooke, Douglas Hageman 1885?-1948
　HisAmM XR, NatCAB 37, WhNAA
Cooke, Grace MacGowan 1863-1944 AmAu&B,
　BiDSA, DcAmA, HisAmM XR, OhA&B
Cooke, Henry David 1825-1881 DcAmB 4
Cooke, James Francis 1875-1960 AmAu&B,
　AmSCAP 1966, BioIn 1, BioIn 5,
　HisAmM XR, WebBD, WhNAA,
　WhJnl 1928
Cooke, Marjorie NF
Cooke, Morris Llewellyn 1872-1960 AmAu&B,
　CurBio XR
Cooke, Robert NF
Cooke, Russell NF
Cookridge, E H 1908- ConAu 25
Cooksley, Sidney Bert HisAmM XR
Coolbrith, Ina Donna 1842-1928 Alli Sup, AmAu,
　AmAu&B, AmLY, BbD, BiD&SB, DcAmA,
　DcNAA, HisAmM XR, OxAm, REnAL,
　WebBD
Cooley, Donald G OvPC
Cooley, John NF
Cooley, John Booth 1889- WhJnl 1928
Cooley, John Kent 1927- ConAu 15R, OvPC,
　WhoAm 1974, WhoWor 1974, WrDr 1976
Cooley, William O 1891- WhJnl 1928
Coolidge, Archibald Cary 1866-1928 AmAu&B,
　DcNAA, WebBD, WhNAA
Coolidge, Emelyn Lincoln 1873-1949 DcNAA,
　HisAmM XR, WhNAA
Cooling, Michael NF
Cools, G Victor 1892?-1952 BioIn 2, BioIn 3
Coombs, Orde LivBAA
Coon, Frederick William 1850-1919 BioIn 5
Cooney, Joan Ganz 1929- CelR 1973,
　CurBio XR, ForWC 1970, WhoAm 1974,
　WhoAmW 1974, WhoE 1974
Cooney, John NF
Cooney, Lloyd Everett 1923- WhoAm 1974
Cooney, Matthew T, Jr. NF
Coonradt, P T 1898- WhJnl 1928
Coons, Ron NF
Cooper, Alfred 1859- WhJnl 1928
Cooper, Allen Robert 1922- WhoAm 1974
Cooper, Ann K NF

Cooper, Arthur Darrah 1931- *WhoAm 1974*
Cooper, Brainerd 1904?-1967 *BioIn 1, BioIn 2,
  BioIn 3, BioIn 5, BioIn 6, BioIn 7*
Cooper, Charles Alfred 1829-1916 *NF*
Cooper, Charles Phillips 1866-1950 *WhJnl 1928*
Cooper, Clay C *WhJnl 1928*
Cooper, Courtney Ryley 1886-1940 *AmAu&B,
  CurBio XR, DcNAA, HisAmM XR,
  REnAL, TwCA, TwCA Sup, WebBD*
Cooper, Dallas *NF*
Cooper, David *NF*
Cooper, Douglas Edward 1902- *WhJnl 1928*
Cooper, Edward *HisAmM XR*
Cooper, Frederic G 1883-1961 *BioIn 1, BioIn 6*
Cooper, Frederick Taber 1864-1937 *AmAu&B,
  DcNAA, HisAmM XR*
Cooper, George L 1872-1937 *NatCAB 28*
Cooper, Gordon 1890- *WhJnl 1928*
Cooper, Harold R 1911?-1978 *NF*
Cooper, Harry 1880?-1957 *BioIn 4*
Cooper, Henry Spotswood Fenimore, Jr. 1933-
  ConAu 69
Cooper, J A *NF*
Cooper, Jacob 1830-1904 *DcNAA, HisAmM XR,
  OhA&B*
Cooper, James Lees 1907- *CanWW 1972,
  IntWW 1976, Who 1974, WhoAm 1974,
  WhoF&I 1974, WhoWor 1974*
Cooper, Julius 1921- *NF*
Cooper, Kent 1880-1965 *AmAu&B, AmJnl,
  AmSCAP 1966, BioIn 1, BioIn 5, BioIn 7,
  CurBio XR, DrAF 1976, IndAu 1917*
Cooper, Lester Irving 1919- *WhoAm 1974*
Cooper, Madison 1868?-1946 *BioIn 1*
Cooper, Martin DuPre 1910- *IntWW 1976,
  Who 1974, WhoMus 1972, WhoWor 1974,
  WrDr 1976*
Cooper, Nina *NF*
Cooper, Page 1891-1958 *BioIn 4*
Cooper, Richard Lee 1946- *WhoAm 1974,
  WhoE 1974*
Cooper, Richard T *NF*
Cooper, Sanford L *RpN*
Cooper, Susan 1935- *ConAu 29, SmATA 4*
Cooper, Thomas 1805-1892 *Alli Sup, BiD&SB,
  BrAu 19, CasWL, DcEnL, EvLB, NewC,
  WebBD*
Cooper, Thomas Yost 1884- *WhJnl 1928*
Cooper, Willard 1890- *WhNAA, WhJnl 1928*
Coote, Sir Colin Reith 1893- *BioIn 2, BioIn 7,
  IntWW 1976, WhoWor 1974*
Cope, Channing 1894?- *BioIn 2*
Cope, Edward Drinker 1840-1897 *Alli Sup,
  DcAmA, DcNAA, HisAmM XR, WebBD*
Cope, John *NF*
Cope, Millard Louis 1905-1964 *BioIn 6, TexWr,
  WhJnl 1928*
Cope, Myron 1929- *ConAu 57*
Cope, Porter Farquharson 1869-1950 *BioIn 2,
  BioIn 6, NatCAB 46*
Cope, Willard *NF*
Copeland, Al *NF*
Copeland, Edith *NF*
Copeland, Fayette, Jr. 1895- *WhJnl 1928*
Copeland, George H *OvPC*
Copeland, H G 1874- *WhJnl 1928*
Copeland, Paul William 1917- *ConAu 25,
  WhoS&SW 1973*
Copeland, Walter Scott 1856-1928 *WhJnl 1928*
Copeman, George Henry 1922- *Au&Wr,
  ConAu 7R, WrDr 1976*
Copley, Helen *BioIn 10*
Copley, Ira Clifton 1864-1947 *AmJnl, BioIn 1,
  BioIn 2, NatCAB 36*

Copley, James Strohn 1916- *WhoAm 1974*
Coppee, Henry 1821-1895 *Alli, Alli Sup, AmAu,
  AmAu&B, BiD&SB, BiDSA, CyAL 2,
  DcAmA, DcNAA, HisAmM XR*
Coppel, Alfred 1921- *ConAu 19R, DrAF 1976,
  WrDr 1976*
Coppenbarger, Howard Lee 1913- *WhoAm 1974*
Copperud, Roy Herman 1915- *ConAu 9,
  DrAS 74E, HisAmM XR, WrDr 1976*
Coppola, John F 1947- *USBiR 1974*
Copps, Edwin 1922?- *BioIn 3*
Copson, John *NF*
Corbett, David E 1931?- *NF*
Corbett, Mary Ellen Mohr 1941- *WhoAmW 1974,
  WhoWest 1974*
Corbett, Sidney 1891- *BioIn 1*
Corbett, W A 1902- *WhJnl 1928*
Corbin, Harold S 1887?-1947 *BioIn 1*
Corbin, John 1870-1959 *AmAu&B, BiD&SB,
  CarSB, DcAmA, HisAmM XR, WebBD,
  WhNAA*
Corbin, W T 1885- *WhJnl 1928*
Corbyn, Wardell *HisAmM XR*
Corcoran, Fred 1905?- *BioIn 2*
Corcoran, James A *HisAmM XR*
Corcoran, John H, Jr. *NF*
Corcoran, William *HisAmM XR*
Corcoran, William Warwick 1884-1962 *BioIn 3*
Corddry, Charles W *NF*
Cordier, Henri 1849-1925 *WebBD*
Cordingley, William Andrew 1917- *WhoAm 1974*
Cordray, Robert 1929- *NF*
Cordray, Ronald E *NF*
Cordtz, Dan 1927- *ConAu 73*
Corea, Ernest *NF*
Corea, Gene *NF*
Coren, Alan 1938- *ConAu 69, WrDr 1976*
Corey, Ben *NF*
Corey, Herbert 1872-1954 *BioIn 3, BioIn 5,
  OhA&B*
Corey, Lewis 1894?-1953 *AmAu&B, DcAmB S5,
  OhA&B, TwCA, TwCA Sup*
Corey, Lewis see also Fraina, Louis
Corey, N J *HisAmM XR*
Corina, Maurice 1936- *ConAu 57*
Corkery, John 1886- *WhJnl 1928*
Corkery, P J *NF*
Corley, William Angus *OvPC*
Corlin, Len 1928- *NF*
Cormier, Frank 1927- *ConAu 23R*
Corn, Herbert F 1896?-1966 *BioIn 7*
Corn, Ira George, Jr. 1921- *NewYTBE 1,
  WhoAm 1974, WhoF&I 1974*
Corn, Ralph B 1902- *WhJnl 1928*
Cornall, Barbara *BioIn 9*
Cornelius, Elias 1794-1832 *DcAmA, DcNAA,
  HisAmM XR*
Cornell, C E 1878- *WhJnl 1928*
Cornell, Doug *NF*
Cornell, George Washington, II 1920- *ConAu 9R,
  WhoAm 1974, WhoE 1974*
Cornell, Harry W 1866- *WhJnl 1928*
Cornell, John *NF*
Cornell, Thomas C 1880- *WhJnl 1928*
Cornfeld, Gaalyahu 1902- *ConAu 17, ConAu 73,
  WhoWorJ 1972*
Cornish, George Anthony 1901- *WhoWor 1974*
Cornish, Samuel E 1795- *AmJnl, BioIn 7,
  BioIn 8, BlkC*
Cornish, Worthen C 1901- *WhJnl 1928*
Cornwall, Barbara *BioIn 9*
Cornwall, George M 1867-1950 *NatCAB 38*
Cornwallis, Kinahan 1839-1917 *Alli Sup, AmAu,
  AmAu&B, BbtC, BiD&SB, DcAmA,*

DcNAA, OxCan
Cornwell, Mrs. Herbert J 1877- *WhJnl 1928*
Cornwell, John *RpN*
Cornwell, John Jacob 1867-1953 *BioIn 3*
Cornyn, John Hubert 1875-1941 *AmAu&B,*
  WhNAA
Corominas, Enrique V 1910- *BioIn 1*
Cororan, William Warwick 1884-1962 *BioIn 6*
Corpus, Chris *BioIn 6*
Corr, John Patrick 1934- *WhoAm 1974*
Corradini, Enrico 1865-1931 *BioIn 1, CIDMEL*
Corre, Max 1912- *BioIn 1, IntWW 1976,*
  WhoWor 1974
Corrick, Ann Marjorie *WhoAm 1974,*
  WhoAmW 1974
Corrigan, Edward B *OvPC*
Corrigan, John Thomas 1936- *ConAu 65*
Corrigan, Robert W *NF*
Corrigan, Robert Willoughby 1927- *BiE&WWA,*
  ConAu 5, DrAS 74E, WhoAm 1974,
  WhoWor 1974, WrDr 1976
Corrigan, William Thomas 1921- *WhoAm 1974,*
  WhoE 1974
Corry, John J *BioIn 7, RpN*
Corsi, Mario 1882-1954 *BioIn 3*
Cort, David 1904- *AmAu&B, ConAu 9R,*
  WhoAm 1974, WhoWor 1974
Cortambert, Louis Richard 1808-1881 *AmAu&B,*
  DcAmB 4, DcNAA
Cortese, A James 1917- *ConAu 65*
Cortesi, Arnaldo 1897-1966 *BioIn 7*
Cortesi, Salvatore 1864-1947 *BioIn 1,*
  HisAmM XR
Cortissoz, Ellen Mackay Hutchinson d1933
  AmAu&B, DcAmA, DcNAA, WebBD
Cortissoz, Royal 1869-1948 *AmAu&B,*
  DcAmB S4, DcNAA, HisAmM XR, TwCA,
  TwCA Sup, WebBD
Cortney, Don *NF*
Corum, Bill *NF*
Corum, Martene Windsor 1894-1958 *BioIn 1,*
  BioIn 2, BioIn 4, BioIn 5
Corvin Wiersbitzki, Otto Julius B Von 1812-1886
  BioIn 2
Corwin, Norman 1910- *AmAu&B,*
  AmSCAP 1966, AuNews 2, CnDAL,
  ConAu 4R, OxAm, TwCA Sup,
  WhoAm 1974, WrDr 1976
Cory, Fanny 1878?- *BioIn 2*
Cose, Ellis *NF*
Cosell, Howard 1920- *BioNews 1974, CelR 1973,*
  CurBio XR, NewYTBS 5, WhoE 1974
Coser, Lewis *AmRP*
Cosgrave, John O'Hara 1866-1947 *BioIn 1,*
  DcNAA, HisAmM XR, WhJnl Sup
Cosgrave, Mary 1914- *BioIn 4*
Cosgrave, Patrick 1941- *ConAu 33, WrDr 1976*
Cosgrove, Gerald 1894- *WhJnl 1928*
Cosgrove, John J 1861- *WhJnl 1928*
Cossette, Pierre *NF*
Cossio, Francisco De 1887- *BioIn 2*
Costa, Francis *BioIn 2*
Costa, Jean Charles *NF*
Costa, Joseph 1904- *AmJnl, WhoAm 1974*
Costa Rego, Pedro 1889-1954 *BioIn 3*
Costain, Thomas Bertram 1885-1965 *AmAu&B,*
  AmNov, AuBYP, CanWr, ConAu 5R,
  ConAu 25, CurBio XR, DcLEL,
  HisAmM XR, LongC, OxAm, OxCan, REn,
  REnAL, TwCA Sup, TwCW, WhJnl 1928
Costantini, Dario *NF*
Costello, Lovis B 1876- *WhJnl 1928*
Costello, Mary *NF*
Costello, Russell Hill 1904- *WhoAm 1974*

Costello, Thomas Francis *BioIn 2*
Costello, William Aloysious 1904-1969 *BioIn 8,*
  ConAu 4R
Costenla, Manuel 1882?-1952 *BioIn 2*
Coster, Morris *HisAmM XR*
Costigan, Peter *NF*
Costigan, Tom 1916?- *BioIn 6*
Cosulich, Bernice 1896- *WhJnl 1928*
Cosulich, Gilbert 1889- *WhNAA, WhJnl 1928*
Cote, Thomas 1869-1918 *DcNAA*
Cotes, Everard 1862-1944 *DcNAA, WebBD*
Cotes, Sara Jeannette Duncan 1862-1922 *BbD,*
  BiD&SB, NewC, WebBD
Cotes, Sara Jeannette Duncan *see also* Duncan, Sara
Cotlow, Lewis *OvPC*
Cotnam, Perry 1855-1914 *NatCAB 18*
Cotner, William G *NF*
Cott, Jonathan 1942- *ConAu 53*
Cott, Tom *NF*
Cotta, Johann *ForP*
Cotter, Arundel 1883-1952 *BioIn 3*
Cotter, William Donald 1921- *WhoAm 1974,*
  WhoF&I 1974
Cottey, Raymond R *NF*
Cottin, Lou *NF*
Cottingham, George W 1894-1948 *BioIn 1*
Cottle, Brooks 1897-1967 *WhJnl 1928*
Cottom, Charles W *BioIn 2, IndAu 1816*
Cotton, Dorothy Whyte 1915- *BioIn 7,*
  ForWC 1970, WhoAmW 1974
Cottrell, Florance E 1873?-1953 *BioIn 3*
Cottrell, Jesse Samuel 1878-1944 *BioIn 1,*
  NatCAB 33
Cottrell, Leonard 1913- *Au&Wr, AuBYP,*
  BioIn 10, ConAu 5, IntWW 1974, TwCW,
  Who 1974, WhoWor 1974, WorAu,
  WrDr 1976
Cottrell, Mary 1899-1952 *BioIn 3*
Couch, Frank Warre 1889- *WhJnl 1928*
Couch, Hilda Juanita *ForWC 1970, WhJnl 1928*
Couey, James Henry, Jr. 1923-1971 *BioIn 9,*
  NewYTBE 2
Coughlan, John Robert 1914- *AmAu&B,*
  ConAu 65, WhoAm 1974
Coughlin, Bill *NF*
Coughlin, Jack 1915?- *BioIn 1*
Coughlin, Joseph Leo *BioIn 1*
Coughlin, Peter 1917?- *BioIn 1*
Coulborn, Helen Marie 1903-1962 *BioIn 6*
Coulter, Ernest Kent 1871-1952 *DcAmB S5,*
  OhA&B, WhNAA
Coulter, John Merle 1851-1928 *Alli Sup, DcAmA,*
  DcNAA, HisAmM XR, IndAu 1816,
  WhNAA
Coulton, David T *NF*
Councill, William Hooper 1848-1909 *BiDSA,*
  BioIn 8
Counihan, Daniel F 1894?- *BioIn 4*
Counihan, Maureen *OvPC*
Countryman, Russell *BioIn 3*
Coupe, Henry Francis 1901- *WhJnl 1928*
Coursey, Oscar William 1873- *AmAu&B,*
  WhNAA, WhJnl 1928
Courtade, Roy J *NF*
Courtenay, Vincent *NF*
Courtenay, William 1895?-1960 *BioIn 5*
Courteville, Raphael d1772 *BioIn 2*
Courtial, Gabriel 1880?-1960 *BioIn 5*
Courtine, Robert 1910?- *BioIn 8*
Courtney, John F X 1895- *WhJnl 1928*
Courtney, Leonard Henry 1832-1918 *Alli Sup,*
  WebBD
Courtney, William Basil *HisAmM XR*
Courtney, William Leonard 1850-1928 *Alli Sup,*

Crabbe, Robert *NF*
Craddock, John *NF*
Craemer, Justus F 1886- *WhJnl 1928*
Craft, Carl C *NF*
Cragg, Kenneth C 1904-1948 *DcNAA*
Cragon, Rene Cleveland 1928?-1966 *BioIn 7*
Craib, Ralph Grant 1925- *WhoAm 1974*
Craig, Asa Hollister 1847-1934 *HisAmM XR,
    WhNAA*
Craig, Bill 1930- *ConAu 33*
Craig, Daniel H 1814-1895 *BbtC, DcAmB 4*
Craig, Donald Laurence 1946- *ConAu 73*
Craig, Elizabeth Josephine *ConAu 11R*
Craig, Elizabeth May 1889?-1975 *BioIn 1,
    BioIn 2, CurBio XR*
Craig, Elizabeth May *see also* Craig, May
Craig, Eugene W 1916- *WhoAm 1974*
Craig, F D *HisAmM XR*
Craig, Gordon 1922- *WhoAm 1974,
    WhoF&I 1974*
Craig, Hugh 1881- *BioIn 2*
Craig, James Barkley 1912- *WhoAm 1974,
    WhoS&SW 1973*
Craig, James Edward 1881-1970 *NF*
Craig, John 1887?-1950 *BioIn 2*
Craig, John C 1934?- *BioIn 9*
Craig, John Dixon 1887?-1953 *BioIn 3*
Craig, John Gilbert, Jr. 1933- *WhoAm 1974*
Craig, May 1889?-1975 *BioIn 3, BioIn 4,
    BioIn 6, NewYTBE 3*
Craig, May *see also* Craig, Elizabeth May
Craig, Nancy *BioIn 1*
Craig, Neville B 1847-1926 *Alli Sup, DcNAA,
    HisAmM XR*
Craig, Samuel G 1874-1960 *AmAu&B, WhNAA*
Craig, Thomas 1855-1900 *Alli Sup, DcNAA,
    HisAmM XR*
Craig, William Warren 1883-1952 *BioIn 3*
Craighead, Erwin 1852-1932 *DcNAA,
    NatCAB 24, WhNAA, WhJnl 1928*
Craigie, Chester F 1883?-1949 *BioIn 2*
Craik, James S 1890- *WhJnl 1928*
Crain, G D, Jr. *WhoAm 1974*
Crain, K E *NF*
Crain, Rance *NF*
Cram, George Franklin 1842-1928 *DcAmA,
    DcNAA, HisAmM XR, WhNAA*
Cram, Ralph Adams 1863-1942 *AmAu&B,
    AmLY, BiD&SB, CurBio XR, DcAmA,
    DcAmB S3, DcNAA, OxAm, REnAL,
    WebBD, WhNAA*
Cram, Ralph Warren 1869-1952 *BioIn 4,
    WhJnl 1928*
Cram, W Winston 1906?-1965 *BioIn 7*
Cramer, Harriet Laura 1848-1922 *BioIn 5*
Cramer, John F *NF*
Cramer, Polly 1903- *ForWC 1970,
    WhoAmW 1974*
Cramer, Robert S *OvPC*
Cramer, William Edward 1817-1905 *BioIn 5*
Cranch, Christopher Pearse 1813-1892 *Alli,
    Alli Sup, AmAu, AmAu&B, BbD, BiD&SB,
    BiDSA, CasWL, CyAL 2, DcAmA,
    DcNAA, EarABI, OxAm, REnAL, WebBD*
Crandall, Arthur Fitz James 1854-1951 *BioIn 2*
Crandall, Bruce Verne 1873-1945 *AmAu&B,
    DcNAA*
Crandall, C F *NF*
Crandall, George Strachen 1880-1959 *BioIn 7,
    NatCAB 48*
Crandall, Lee *HisAmM XR*
Crandall, Robert S *RpN*
Crandall, Roland Dimon 1892?-1972 *BioIn 9*
Crandell, Charles *NF*

Crandell, Richard F 1901-1974 *BioIn 10,
    ConAu 53, NewYTBS 5*
Crane, Albert Loyal 1893- *WhNAA, WhJnl 1928*
Crane, Burton 1900?-1963 *BioIn 6*
Crane, Charles Edward 1884-1960 *BioIn 5*
Crane, Charles R *HisAmM XR*
Crane, Evan Jay 1889-1966 *BioIn 1, BioIn 2,
    BioIn 3, BioIn 5, BioIn 7*
Crane, Frank 1861-1928 *AmAu&B, AmLY,
    DcAmA, DcAmB 4, DcNAA, HisAmM XR,
    NatCAB 22, REnAL, WebBD, WhNAA,
    WhJnl 1928*
Crane, Frank E 1884- *WhJnl 1928*
Crane, Frank Harrison 1912- *WhoAm 1974*
Crane, Frank Warren 1867?-1953 *BioIn 3*
Crane, Frederick Lea 1888-1949 *BioIn 2*
Crane, George Washington, III 1901- *AmAu&B,
    BioIn 2, WhNAA*
Crane, James M *NF*
Crane, Robert Clark 1920-1962 *BioIn 6*
Crane, Royston Campbell 1901-1977 *BioIn 2,
    WhoAm 1974, WhoWor 1974*
Crane, Stephen 1871-1900 *AmAu, AmAu&B,
    AmWr, AtlBL, BbD, BiD&SB, CasWL,
    CnDAL, CnE&AP, CrtT 3, CyWA,
    DcAmA, DcLEL, DcNAA, EncAB, EvLB,
    LongC, ModAL, OxAm, OxEng, Pen Am,
    RAdv 1, RComWL, REn, REnAL, WebBD,
    WebE&AL*
Crane, Winston Stephen *NF*
Craner, Lawrence M 1900?-1969 *BioIn 8*
Cranfield, Arthur Leslie 1892-1957 *BioIn 4*
Crankshaw, Edward 1909- *BioIn 2, BioIn 4,
    BioIn 5, ConAu 25, LongC, TwCA Sup,
    Who 1974, WhoWor 1974*
Cranston, Alan 1914- *BioIn 2, BioIn 8, BioIn 9,
    CngDr 1974, CurBio XR, IntWW 1974,
    WhoAm 1974, WhoWest 1974*
Cranston, Claudia 1892?-1947 *AmAu&B,
    BioIn 1, DcNAA, TexWr, WhNAA*
Cranston, Herbert *NF*
Cranston, James Herbert 1880-1952 *BioIn 3,
    WhJnl 1928*
Cranston, Paul F 1905?-1951 *BioIn 2*
Craper, Margaret *NF*
Crapo, George Swafford 1897- *WhJnl 1928*
Crary, John C 1880?-1961 *BioIn 6*
Crate, John S 1876- *WhJnl Sup*
Crater, Robert Winfield 1912- *WhoAm 1974*
Crater, Rufus *NF*
Craven, Bruce 1881- *WhNAA, WhJnl 1928*
Craven, H T 1879- *WhJnl 1928*
Cravens, Gwyneth *NF*
Cravens, Kathryn *BioIn 2, WhoAm 1974,
    WhoAmW 1974*
Crawford, Bill *NF*
Crawford, Claude K 1872- *WhJnl 1928*
Crawford, George 1849-1927 *BioIn 5*
Crawford, George Gaver 1898- *WhNAA,
    WhJnl 1928, WhoMW 1974*
Crawford, Iain 1922- *ConAu 3R*
Crawford, John A 1899- *WhJnl 1928*
Crawford, Judy *NF*
Crawford, Kenneth Gale 1902- *AmAu&B,
    WhoAm 1974, WhoWor 1974*
Crawford, Linda 1938- *ConAu 65*
Crawford, Marvin Howard 1894- *WhNAA,
    WhJnl 1928*
Crawford, Mary Caroline 1874-1932 *AmAu&B,
    AmLY, BiD&SB, DcAmA, DcNAA,
    REnAL, WebBD, WhNAA*
Crawford, Nelson Antrim 1888-1963 *AmAu&B,
    AnMV 1926, HisAmM XR, WebBD,
    WhNAA, WhJnl 1928*

Crawford, Oliver H *BioIn 3*
Crawford, Robert H *NF*
Crawford, Robert Lindsay 1868-1945 *BioIn 9,
  BioIn 10*
Crawford, Robert Moffett 1854-1921 *BioIn 5*
Crawford, Robert Platt 1893- *AmAu&B,
  ConAu 17, WhNAA, WhJnl 1928*
Crawford, Roy Virgel 1897- *WhNAA,
  WhJnl 1928*
Crawford, Stuart *NF*
Crawford, Will 1869?- *HisAmM XR*
Crawford, William *InvJ*
Crawford, William Hulfish 1913- *WhoAm 1974,
  WhoAmA 1973*
Crawford, William Sterling 1865-1948 *BioIn 1*
Crawley, James A *WhJnl 1928*
Crawley, John *NF*
Crawmer, Michael S *NF*
Crayhon, James W *OvPC*
Creager, Marvin H 1882-1954 *BioIn 3, BioIn 5,
  WhJnl 1928*
Creagh, Edward F 1918?-1959 *BioIn 5*
Creamer, Joseph *HisAmM XR*
Creamer, Robert 1922- *BioIn 10, ConAu 21*
Creamer, Thomas J *HisAmM XR*
Creecy, John *NF*
Creedy, John A *OvPC*
Creel, George 1876-1953 *AmAu&B, AmJnl,
  BioIn 1, BioIn 3, BioIn 4, CurBio XR,
  DcAmB S5, EncAB, HisAmM XR, REnAL,
  WebBD*
Creelman, Eileen *NF*
Creelman, James 1859-1915 *AmAu&B, AmJnl,
  BioIn 9, DcAmA, DcAmB 4, DcNAA,
  FamWC, HisAmM XR, WebBD*
Creery, Timothy W *RpN*
Creighton, James Edwin 1861-1924 *AmAu&B,
  DcNAA, HisAmM XR*
Creighton, John Douglas 1929- *WhoAm 1974*
Crellin, John 1916- *ConAu 69*
Cremer, Sir William Randal 1838-1908 *WebBD*
Cremony, John Carey 1815-1879 *ArizL, BioIn 10*
Crempton, Robert D *OvPC*
Crenshaw, Albert B *NF*
Crenshaw, Mary Ann *ConAu 57*
Crepeau, Frank *NF*
Crespi, Aldo 1885?-1978 *NF*
Crespi, Consuelo *NF*
Crespi, Mario 1879-1962 *BioIn 6*
Crespo-Ordonez, Manuel 1900?-1954 *BioIn 3*
Cressey, Kendall Brooks 1877- *WhJnl 1928*
Cresswell, Donald McCauley 1891- *BioIn 1*
Cresswell, Robert 1897-1943 *AmJnl, CurBio XR*
Crewdson, John M *NF*
Crewdson, Prudence *NF*
Crewe, Regina *NF*
Crews, Joseph Preston 1907- *WhJnl 1928*
Creyton, Paul 1827-1916 *AmAu, DcEnL,
  DcNAA*
Creyton, Paul *see also* Trowbridge, John Townsend
Crichton, Kyle Samuel 1896-1960 *AmAu&B,
  Au&Wr, BioIn 4, BioIn 5, BioIn 6,
  NatCAB 46, REnAL, TwCA, TwCA Sup*
Crichton, Robert *NF*
Crider, John Henshaw 1906-1966 *BioIn 1,
  BioIn 2, BioIn 7, CurBio XR, RpN*
Crile, George, III *NF*
Crim, Mort 1935- *ConAu 41*
Crimmins, James Custis 1935- *ConAu 5R*
Crinkle, Nym 1835-1903 *Alli Sup, BiD&SB,
  DcNAA*
Crinkle, Nym *see also* Wheeler, Andrew Carpenter
Crippen, William G 1820-1863 *Alli Sup, OhA&B*
Criscuolo, Luigi 1887-1957 *BioIn 4*

Crisman, Charles B *OvPC*
Crisp, Porter Lee 1927- *WhoAm 1974*
Crisp, Robert *ConAu 1R*
Crissan, Michael G *OvPC*
Crissey, Charles E 1895?-1975 *BioIn 10*
Crissey, Forrest 1864-1943 *AmAu&B, DcNAA,
  HisAmM XR*
Crist, Arthur H *HisAmM XR*
Crist, Harris McCabe 1874-1946 *BioIn 1,
  BioIn 2, NatCAB 34, WhJnl 1928*
Crist, Judith Klein 1922- *AmAu&B,
  WhoAm 1974*
Cristy, Terri K 1953- *NF*
Criswell, Charles d1960 *BioIn 5*
Criswell, John 1932?- *BioIn 8*
Criswell, R W *HisAmM XR*
Critchfield, Richard Patrick 1931- *ConAu 41,
  WhoAm 1974, WhoS&SW 1973*
Croasland, William T *HisAmM XR*
Croce, Benedetto 1866-1952 *AtlBL, BioIn 1,
  BioIn 2, BioIn 3, BioIn 4, BioIn 5, BioIn 9,
  CasWL, CIDMEL, CurBio XR, DcEuL,
  EncWL, EvEuW, LongC, NewC, OxEng,
  Pen Eur, REn, TwCA, TwCA Sup, TwCW,
  WhoLA, WebBD*
Crocker, Elvira *NF*
Crocker, Harry *BioIn 2*
Crocker, S R d1878 *Alli Sup, HisAmM XR*
Crocker, Thomas F 1892- *WhJnl 1928*
Crockett, Albert Stevens 1873-1969 *AmAu&B,
  BioIn 8, WhNAA*
Crockett, Edward H *NF*
Crockett, Gibson Milton 1912- *WhoAm 1974,
  WhoS&SW 1973*
Crockett, Harry E d1943 *AmJnl*
Crockett, Walter Hill 1870-1931 *DcNAA,
  WhNAA, WhJnl 1928*
Croffut, William Augustus 1835-1915 *Alli Sup,
  AmAu&B, BiD&SB, DcAmA, DcNAA*
Croft, Fred J 1880- *WhJnl 1928*
Crofton, Francis Blake 1841-1912 *Alli Sup,
  DcNAA, PoIre*
Croil, James 1821-1916 *BbtC, DcNAA*
Croker, John Wilson 1780-1857 *Alli, BiD&SB,
  BiDLA, BrAu 19, CasWL, DcEnA, DcEnL,
  DcEuL, DcLEL, EvLB, NewC, OxEng,
  Pen Eng, PoIre, WebBD, WebE&AL*
Croll, Edward Everett 1881- *WhNAA,
  WhJnl 1928*
Croly, David Goodman 1829-1889 *Alli Sup,
  AmAu, AmAu&B, BiD&SB, DcAmA,
  DcAmB 4, DcNAA, HisAmM XR,
  NatCAB 11, WebBD*
Croly, George 1780-1860 *Alli, BbD, BiD&SB,
  BrAu 19, DcBiA, DcEnL, DcLEL, EvLB,
  NewC, OxEng, PoIre, WebBD*
Croly, Herbert David 1869-1930 *AmAu&B,
  BioIn 1, BioIn 2, BioIn 3, BioIn 5,
  DcAmB S1, DcNAA, EncAB, OxAm,
  TwCA, TwCA Sup, WebBD*
Croly, Jane Cunningham 1829-1901 *Alli Sup,
  AmAu, AmAu&B, BbD, BiD&SB, DcAmA,
  DcAmB 4, DcNAA, HisAmM XR, OxAm,
  WebBD*
Croly, Jane Cunningham *see also* June, Jennie
Cromie, Alice *NF*
Cromie, Bill *NF*
Cromie, Donald *NF*
Cromie, Robert Allen 1909- *AmAu&B, BioIn 9,
  ConAu 2R, WhoAm 1974, WhoMW 1974*
Cromie, Robert James 1887- *WhJnl 1928*
Cromley, Allan Wray 1922- *WhoAm 1974*
Cromley, Raymond Avolon 1910- *WhoAm 1974,
  WhoWor 1974*

Crompton, Robert D *OvPC*
Cromwell, Oliver J 1864?-1949 *BioIn 1*
Cromwell, Ralph H 1896- *WhJnl Sup*
Cronan, Calvin Shaw 1917- *AmM&W 73P,*
  WhoAm 1974
Cronan, Carey *NF*
Crone, Ruth 1919- *AuBYP, ConAu 9R,*
  SmATA 4
Cronin, Mary *NF*
Cronin, Patrick 1835-1905 *HisAmM XR, PoIre*
Cronin, Ray *NF*
Cronin, Sylvia Ash *NF*
Cronin Hastings, Hubert De 1902- *BioIn 9*
Cronise, Ralph R 1886- *WhJnl 1928*
Cronkite, Walter Leland, Jr. 1916- *BioIn 4,*
  BioIn 6, BioIn 7, BioIn 8, BioIn 9,
  BioIn 10, ConAu 69, CurBio XR, ForP,
  IntWW 1976, NewMr, WhoAm 1974
Cronyn, Thoreau *HisAmM XR*
Crook, Dorothy 1911- *AmEA 1974,*
  WhoAm 1974, WhoAmW 1974
Crooks, Bill *NF*
Crooks, David H 1899- *WhJnl Sup*
Crooks, George Richard 1822-1897 *Alli, Alli Sup,*
  DcAmA, DcNAA, HisAmM XR
Croom, Joe N 1896- *WhNAA, WhJnl 1928*
Croop, Arthur Vernon 1904- *WhoAm 1974*
Crosby, Alexander L 1906- *AuBYP, ConAu 29,*
  SmATA 2
Crosby, Caresse 1892-1970 *ConAu 25,*
  NewYTBE 1
Crosby, Ed *NF*
Crosby, Ernest Howard 1856-1907 *AmAu&B,*
  DcAmA, DcNAA, HisAmM XR, WebBD
Crosby, Henry Grew 1898-1929 *DcNAA,*
  NatCAB 31
Crosby, Joan *NF*
Crosby, John Campbell 1867-1962 *BioIn 2,*
  BioIn 3, BioIn 6, BioIn 8
Crosby, John Campbell 1912- *AmAu&B, BioIn 1,*
  ConAu 1R, CurBio XR, IntWW 1976,
  REnAL, WhoAm 1974, WhoWor 1974,
  WrDr 1976
Crosby, Laurence E 1895- *WhJnl 1928*
Crosby, Margaret *HisAmM XR*
Crosby, Percy Leo 1891-1964 *AmAu&B, BioIn 7,*
  HisAmM XR
Crosby, Thomas R, Jr. 1942- *NF*
Crosby, Willard Barnhart 1904-1957 *BioIn 4*
Crosby, William Flower 1890-1953 *BioIn 3*
Croskill, John H 1810-1855 *BbtC, DcNAA*
Crosland, Thomas William Hodgson 1865-1924
  BioIn 2
Crosman, Ralph L 1887-1948 *BioIn 1,*
  WhJnl 1928
Cross, Colin 1928- *ConAu 9R*
Cross, Douglas 1920-1975 *BioIn 10*
Cross, Ian 1925- *Au&Wr, ConNov 1972,*
  ConNov 1976, Pen Eng, RpN, TwCW,
  WrDr 1976
Cross, Jennifer 1932- *ConAu 29*
Cross, L C 1918- *BioIn 9*
Cross, Leslie Frank 1909- *ConAu 65,*
  WhoAm 1974
Cross, Mary Ann Evans 1819-1880 *Alli Sup,*
  BrAu 19, EvLB, HisAmM XR, Pen Eng
Cross, Mary Ann Evans *see also* Eliot, George
Cross, Mercer *NF*
Cross, Milton John 1897-1975 *AmAu&B,*
  CurBio XR, WhoAm 1974
Cross, Robert Clark 1939- *WhoAm 1974*
Cross, Sidney *HisAmM XR*
Cross, Theodore Lamont 1924- *ConAu 45,*
  WhoAm 1974, WhoF&I 1974

Cross, Wilbur Lucius 1862-1948 *AmAu&B,*
  DcAmA, DcLEL, DcNAA, HisAmM XR,
  OxAm, REnAL, TwCA, TwCA Sup,
  WebBD
Cross, Wilbur Lucius, III 1918- *Au&Wr,*
  ConAu 1, SmATA 2, WhoE 1974,
  WrDr 1976
Crossman, Ann *NF*
Crossman, John C *HisAmM XR*
Crossman, Richard 1907-1974 *Au&Wr, BioIn 9,*
  BioIn 10, ConAu 49, ConAu 61,
  CurBio XR, REn, Who 1974, WorAu
Crosson, John 1900?-1953 *BioIn 3*
Croswell, Edwin 1797-1871 *Alli, AmJnl,*
  DcAmB 4, NatCAB 10
Croswell, Harry 1778-1858 *Alli, Alli Sup, AmJnl,*
  BioIn 8, CyAL 2, DcAmA, DcNAA
Crothers, Robert A 1853- *AmJnl, NatCAB XR*
Crouch, Bill *NF*
Crouch, Mary *NF*
Croudace, Glynn 1917- *Au&Wr, ConAu 29*
Crouse, Russel 1893-1966 *AmAu&B, AuBYP,*
  BiE&WWA, CnDAL, CnThe, ConAu 25,
  CurBio XR, McGWD, ModWD, OhA&B,
  OxAm, REn, REnAL, TwCA Sup, WebBD
Crouse, Timothy *NF*
Crow, Carl 1883-1945 *AmAu&B, BioIn 2,*
  BioIn 4, CurBio XR, DcNAA,
  HisAmM XR, TwCA, TwCA Sup, WebBD,
  WhNAA
Crow, Carl C 1882-1953 *NatCAB 42*
Crow, John T *NF*
Crow, Wendell C *NF*
Crowder, Bill *NF*
Crowder, Charles Allen 1900?- *BioIn 1*
Crowe, Cameron *NF*
Crowe, E R *HisAmM XR*
Crowe, Eugene F *HisAmM XR*
Crowe, Eyre Evans 1799-1868 *Alli, Alli Sup,*
  BiD&SB, EvLB, NewC, PoIre, WebBD
Crowe, John Finley *HisAmM XR*
Crowe, Sir Joseph Archer 1825-1896 *Alli Sup,*
  BiD&SB, EvLB, WebBD
Crowell, Chester Theodore 1888-1941 *DcNAA,*
  HisAmM XR, OhA&B, TexWr
Crowell, Francis J 1889- *WhJnl 1928*
Crowell, James R 1893-1948 *BioIn 1, DcNAA*
Crowell, John Franklin 1857-1931 *DcAmA,*
  DcNAA, WebBD
Crowell, John Stephen 1850-1921 *HisAmM XR*
Crowell, Merle 1888-1956 *AmAu&B, BioIn 4,*
  HisAmM XR, WhNAA, WhJnl 1928
Crowell, Paul 1891-1970 *BioIn 9, NewYTBE 1*
Crowley, B J *NF*
Crowley, John 1869-1949 *BioIn 2, BioIn 3*
Crowley, Raymond J 1902?-1970 *BioIn 9*
Crowley, Raymond L 1895- *BioIn 2*
Crowley, Thomas J 1894-1958 *NatCAB 44*
Crowninshield, Francis Welch 1872-1947
  DcAmB S4, DcNAA, WebBD
Crowninshield, Francis Welch *see also*
  Crowninshield, Frank
Crowninshield, Frank 1872-1947 *AmAu&B,*
  BioIn 1, BioIn 2, BioIn 3, BioIn 5,
  HisAmM XR, NatCAB 36, REn, REnAL
Crowninshield, Frank *see also* Crowninshield, Francis
  Welch
Crowther, Bosley 1905- *AmAu&B, ConAu 65,*
  CurBio XR, IntMPA 1975, WhoWor 1974
Crowther, Baron Geoffrey 1907-1972 *BioIn 1,*
  BioIn 2, BioIn 4, BioIn 7, BioIn 9,
  BioIn 10, ConAu 33
Crowther, James Gerald 1899- *Au&Wr, AuBYP,*
  ConAu 73, WrDr 1976

Crowther, Samuel 1880-1947 *AmAu&B, DcNAA, HisAmM XR, REnAL, WhNAA*
Crowther, Samuel 1917?-1966 *BioIn 1, BioIn 7*
Croy, Homer 1883-1965 *AmAu&B, AmNov, REnAL, TwCA, TwCA Sup*
Crozier, Brian 1918- *Au&Wr, ConAu 11R, WrDr 1976*
Crozier, Emmett *NF*
Crozier, William Percival 1879-1944 *BioIn 5*
Cruger, F R *HisAmM XR*
Cruger, Jacob W 1819-1864 *BioIn 4*
Cruickshank, Herbert W 1893-1965 *WhJnl 1928*
Cruikshank, John M 1865- *NatCAB 15*
Cruikshank, Robert James 1898-1956 *BioIn 4*
Crum, Bartley Cavanaugh 1900-1959 *AmAu&B, AmJnl, BioIn 1, BioIn 5, CurBio XR*
Crum, C W 1883- *WhJnl 1928*
Crume, Paul 1912- *WhoS&SW 1973*
Crump, James Irving 1887- *AmAu&B, ConAu 73, WhNAA*
Crump, Joseph G *NF*
Crump, Louise *BioIn 2*
Crump, Spencer 1923- *ConAu 23R, WhoF&I 1974, WhoWest 1974, WrDr 1976*
Crunden, Reginald *see* Cleaver, Hylton Reginald
Cruse, Heloise Bowles 1919-1977 *AmAu&B, BioIn 5, BioIn 6, BioIn 7, FamWC, WhoAmW 1974*
Cruse, Heloise Bowles *see also* Bowles, Heloise
Cruse, Heloise Bowles *see also* Reese, Heloise
Cruse, Peter Hoffman 1793?-1832 *Alli, BiDSA, HisAmM XR*
Crutcher, Anne *NF*
Crutcher, Marjorie *NF*
Cruz, Antonio *ForP*
Cruz, Ruben *NF*
Crymes, Mary Furey *NF*
Crysler, R Lindsay *NF*
Crystal, Les *NF*
Cuadra, Pablo Antonio 1912- *BioIn 8, DcCLAA, Pen Am*
Cubbison, Christopher *InvJ*
Cudahy, Raymond M *OvPC*
Cuddihy, H Lester 1896-1953 *NatCAB 42*
Cuddihy, Robert Joseph *HisAmM XR*
Cuddy, Jack 1898?-1975 *BioIn 10*
Cude, Jean 1906- *BioIn 8*
Cudhea, David W 1932?- *BioIn 9*
Cudlipp, Lord Hugh 1913- *Au&Wr, BioIn 3, BioIn 5, BioIn 6, BioIn 8, IntWW 1976, Lor&LP, Who 1974, WhoF&I 1974, WhoWor 1974*
Cudlipp, Percy 1905-1962 *BioIn 3, BioIn 6*
Cudlipp, Reginald 1910- *Au&Wr, BioIn 3, ForP, Who 1974*
Cue, Pedro 1896?-1950 *BioIn 2*
Cuevas, Clara 1933- *ConAu 57, WhoAmW 1974*
Cuhel, Frank J *AmJnl*
Culbertson, James Coe 1840-1908 *HisAmM XR, OhA&B*
Culhane, David *NF*
Cullen, George 1901- *WhoAm 1974*
Cullen, John E 1896?-1953 *BioIn 3*
Cullen, Joseph L 1903- *WhJnl 1928*
Cullen, Maurice Raymond, Jr. 1927- *ConAu 73, DrAS 74E*
Cullen, Susan *NF*
Cullen, Thomas Joseph Vincent 1892-1966 *BioIn 7*
Culligan, Glendy 1915- *ForWC 1970, WhoAm 1974, WhoAmW 1974*
Cullings, Emmett H 1876- *WhJnl 1928*
Cullings, Evan R *WhJnl 1928*
Cullison, Alvin E *OvPC*
Culmsee, Carlton Fordis 1904- *DrAS 74E, ForP,*

WhoAm 1974
Culver, D Jay 1902- *BiE&WWA, WhJnl Sup*
Cuming, Edward William Dirom 1862-1941 *BioIn 2, Br&AmS, WhoLA*
Cummings, Alexander *AmJnl*
Cummings, Amos Jay 1841-1902 *AmJnl, DcAmA, DcAmB 4, DcNAA, HisAmM XR*
Cummings, Arthur John 1885-1957 *BioIn 4, Lor&LP*
Cummings, Charles R *HisAmM XR*
Cummings, John M 1888?-1970 *BioIn 9*
Cummings, Michael *ForP*
Cummings, Patricia 1927- *BioIn 4*
Cummings, Pierce A 1899- *WhJnl 1928*
Cummings, Thomas Harrison *NF*
Cummings, Willis A 1927?-1972 *BioIn 9*
Cummings, Yvette *NF*
Cummins, Albert W 1867-1935 *WhJnl 1928*
Cummins, Henry *NF*
Cummiskey, Thomas L 1898-1952 *BioIn 2*
Cuneo, Ernest 1905- *WhoWor 1974*
Cunha, Euclydes Da 1866-1909 *BioIn 1, BioIn 3, Pen Am*
Cuniff, Al *NF*
Cunliffe, Guy S 1904-1959 *BioIn 5*
Cunliffe, John William 1865-1946 *AmAu&B, BioIn 1, DcNAA, TwCA, TwCA Sup, WebBD, WhNAA, WhJnl 1928*
Cunniff, Frank *NF*
Cunniff, John *NF*
Cunniff, Michael Glen 1875-1914 *HisAmM XR*
Cunningham, Alan 1864-1924 *NatCAB 6*
Cunningham, Barry 1940- *ConAu 73*
Cunningham, Christopher R 1910-1947 *BioIn 1*
Cunningham, Ed *OvPC*
Cunningham, Elijah William 1896-1960 *BioIn 5*
Cunningham, Elmer E 1897- *WhJnl 1928*
Cunningham, Gene *NF*
Cunningham, J Harry 1865-1946 *NatCAB 35*
Cunningham, Jack 1882- *WhJnl 1928*
Cunningham, Joe *BioIn 5*
Cunningham, John Ferguson 1877-1953 *WhJnl 1928*
Cunningham, Joseph Harry 1865-1946 *BioIn 2*
Cunningham, Lynn *NF*
Cunningham, Morris 1917- *WhoAm 1974, WhoS&SW 1973*
Cunningham, Paul James, Jr. 1917- *ConAu 73*
Cunningham, Paul Millard 1915- *WhoAm 1974*
Cunningham, Ralph E 1887- *WhJnl 1928*
Cunningham, Robert H *OvPC*
Cunningham, Ross Lee 1906- *WhoAm 1974, WhoWest 1974*
Cunningham, Thomas J, Jr. *OvPC*
Cunningham, Thomas Jefferson 1852-1941 *BioIn 5*
Cunningham, Walter W *NF*
Cunningham, William 1901-1967 *AmAu&B*
Cuppet, Charles *NF*
Cupples, Victor W 1863-1941 *NatCAB 31*
Cuppy, Hazlitt Alva 1863-1934 *BioIn 2, HisAmM XR, IndAu 1816, WhNAA*
Cuppy, William Jacob 1884-1949 *AmAu&B, DcAmB S4, DcNAA, IndAu 1816, REnAL, TwCA, TwCA Sup, WebBD*
Curcio, Dominic *NF*
Cure, Karen 1949- *ConAu 65*
Curfman, Greg *NF*
Curie, Eve 1904- *AmAu&B, AnCL, Au&Wr, ConAu P-1, SmATA 1, WebBD, Who 1974, WhoAm 1974, WhoAmW 1974, WhoWor 1974*
Curie, Eve *see also* Labouisse, Eve Denise
Curley, John J *NF*
Curley, William A 1875-1955 *BioIn 1, BioIn 4*

Curnow, Allen 1911- *BioIn 10, CasWL,*
  ConAu 69, ConDr, ConP 1970, ConP 1975,
  LongC, TwCW, WebE&AL, WorAu,
  WrDr 1976
Curran, Sir Charles John 1921- *IntWW 1976,*
  Who 1974
Curran, Dale 1898- *AmAu&B, AmNov*
Curran, Frederick R 1894?-1953 *BioIn 3*
Curran, James Watson 1865-1952 *BioIn 2*
Curran, Phil R 1911- *ConAu 73, OvPC*
Curran, Thomas Raphael 1901- *OvPC,*
  WhoAm 1974
Current, Wayne Gast 1912- *WhoAm 1974,*
  WhoF&I 1974
Currie, Barton Wood 1878-1962 *BioIn 6,*
  HisAmM XR, WhJnl 1928
Currie, Chester William Yerxa 1884-1948 *BioIn 1*
Currie, Gilbert Egleson *Alli Sup, HisAmM XR*
Currie, Hazel Shore *ForWC 1970, OvPC*
Currie, John Stewart 1877-1956 *BioIn 4*
Currie, William Richard 1941- *InvJ,*
  WhoAm 1974
Curros Enriquez, Manuel 1851-1908 *BioIn 1,*
  CIDMEL, Pen Eur
Curry, Bob *NF*
Curry, Brack *NF*
Curry, Daniel 1809-1887 *Alli Sup, DcAmA,*
  DcNAA, HisAmM XR
Curry, George E 1947- *BlkC, ConAu 69*
Curry, Leonard *NF*
Curry, Otway 1804-1855 *Alli, AmAu&B,*
  DcAmA, DcNAA, HisAmM XR, OhA&B
Curry, Richard Earl 1933- *WhoAm 1974,*
  WhoS&SW 1973
Curry, Walter Clyde 1887- *HisAmM XR,*
  WhNAA
Curtin, D Thomas 1886-1963 *AmAu&B*
Curtin, John 1885-1945 *WebBD*
Curtin, William *NF*
Curtis, C Michael *NF*
Curtis, Charles Henry 1869- *BioIn 1*
Curtis, Charlotte Murray 1931?- *BioIn 7,*
  BioIn 8, BioIn 9, BioIn 10, ConAu 9R,
  ForWC 1970, WhoAm 1974,
  WhoAmW 1974, WhoE 1974
Curtis, Christopher Michael 1934- *WhoAm 1974*
Curtis, Claude C *WhJnl 1928*
Curtis, Cyrus Hermann Kotzschmar 1850-1933
  AmAu&B, AmJnl, DcAmB S1,
  HisAmM XR, WebBD, WhJnl 1928
Curtis, David A 1846-1923 *Alli Sup, AmLY,*
  DcNAA
Curtis, Emma 1860-1918 *BioIn 2*
Curtis, F D *NF*
Curtis, F G B *HisAmM XR*
Curtis, Frank *NF*
Curtis, George Byron *NF*
Curtis, George William 1824-1892 *Alli, Alli Sup,*
  AmAu, AmAu&B, AmJnl, BbD, BiD&SB,
  BioIn 4, BioIn 6, BioIn 8, BioIn 9, CasWL,
  CyAL 2, DcAmA, DcBiA, DcEnL, DcLEL,
  DcNAA, EncAB, EvLB, HisAmM XR,
  LiJA, OxAm, REn, REnAL, WebBD
Curtis, Hugh Everett, Jr. 1907- *HisAmM XR,*
  WhoAm 1974, WhoMW 1974,
  WhoWor 1974
Curtis, J Harold *WhJnl 1928*
Curtis, Jean *NF*
Curtis, Josiah Montgomery 1905- *WhoAm 1974*
Curtis, Lionel George 1872-1955 *BioIn 2, BioIn 4*
Curtis, Louisa Knapp *HisAmM XR*
Curtis, Lucius Fisher 1879-1954 *BioIn 3,*
  WhJnl 1928
Curtis, Patrick *BioIn 8*

Curtis, Paul Allan, Jr. 1889-1943 *AmAu&B,*
  WhNAA
Curtis, Robert Edward *NF*
Curtis, William Eleroy 1850-1911 *Alli Sup,*
  AmAu&B, BbD, BiD&SB, DcAmA,
  DcAmB 4, DcNAA, HisAmM XR,
  NatCAB 5, OhA&B, OxCan
Curtiss, Frederic Haines 1869- *BioIn 2, Br&AmS*
Curtiss, Wendell *NF*
Curwen, M E *HisAmM XR*
Curwood, James Oliver 1878-1927 *AmAu&B,*
  DcNAA, LongC, OxAm, OxCan, REnAL,
  TwCA, TwCA Sup, WebBD, WhNAA
Cusacha, Philip G *HisAmM XR*
Cushendun, Ronald John McNeill 1861-1934
  BioIn 2
Cushing, Charles Phelps 1884-1973 *AmAu&B,*
  NewYTBE 4
Cushing, Christopher *HisAmM XR*
Cushing, Edward Thomas Francis 1902?-1956
  BioIn 4
Cushing, Frank d1975 *NF*
Cushing, George Holmes 1873-1953 *OhA&B,*
  WhNAA
Cushing, John T 1887-1938 *NatCAB 28*
Cushing, Luther Stearns 1803-1856 *Alli, AmAu,*
  DcAmA, DcNAA, HisAmM XR, WebBD
Cushing, Marshall Henry 1860-1915 *DcNAA*
Cushing, Mary W 1890?-1974 *ConAu 53*
Cushman, Elisha *HisAmM XR*
Cushman, Elton G 1879-1946 *NatCAB 35*
Cust, Henry John Cockayne 1861-1917 *NewC,*
  WebBD
Custer, Edgar A 1861-1937 *DcNAA*
Custer, Ellis H *WhJnl Sup*
Custis, John Trevor 1875-1944 *WhJnl 1928*
Cutforth, Rene *Au&Wr, BioIn 8*
Cuthriell, Robert E *NF*
Cutler, E *HisAmM XR*
Cutten, Theodore G *NF*
Cutter, Charles Ammi 1837-1903 *Alli Sup,*
  AmAu&B, DcNAA, HisAmM XR, WebBD
Cutter, William 1801-1867 *Alli, CyAL 2,*
  DcNAA
Cutting, Bronson 1888-1935 *WhJnl 1928*
Cutting, Elisabeth Brown 1871-1946 *AmAu&B,*
  BioIn 1, DcNAA, HisAmM XR
Cutting, Sewall Sylvester 1813-1882 *DcAmA,*
  DcNAA, HisAmM XR
Czarnecki, Anthony 1877?-1952 *BioIn 2*
Czermanski, Zdzislaw 1899?-1970 *BioIn 8*
Czerniejewski, Halina J *NF*

D

Dabkin, Edwin Franden 1898?-1976 *ConAu 65*
Dabney, Joseph Earl 1929- *ConAu 49,*
WrDr 1976
Dabney, Virginius 1835-1894 *Alli Sup, AmAu,*
AmAu&B, BiD&SB, BiDSA, DcAmA,
DcNAA
Dabney, Virginius 1901- *AmAu&B, BioIn 1,*
BioIn 3, BioIn 4, ConAu 45, CurBio XR,
DrAS 74H, REnAL, TwCA Sup,
WhoAm 1974, WhoWor 1974, WrDr 1976
Dabney, Wendell Phillips 1865-1952 *BioIn 1,*
BioIn 2, OhA&B
Dacey, C Joseph *HisAmM XR*
Dadswell, Jack 1895?- *BioIn 1*
Daffan, Katie *AmAu&B, BiDSA, TexWr*
Dafoe, John Wesley 1866-1944 *BioIn 1, BioIn 5,*
CurBio XR, DcLEL, DcNAA, OxCan,
WebBD, WhJnl 1928
Daggett, Nella I *HisAmM XR*
Daggett, Rollin Mallory 1831-1901 *DcNAA,*
HisAmM XR
Dagonet 1847-1922 *NewC, WebBD*
Dagonet *see also* Sims, George Robert
DaGrosa, John 1901?-1953 *BioIn 3*
Dahl, Francis Wellington 1907-1973 *AmAu&B,*
BioIn 1, BioIn 9, NewYTBE 4, REnAL,
WhoAmA 1973
Dahl, J O 1893-1942 *NatCAB 32*
Dahlberg, Edward 1900-1977 *AmAu&B,*
CelR 1973, ConAu 69, ConLC 1,
ConNov 1972, ConNov 1976, DrAF 1976,
ModAL, ModAL Sup, OxAm, Pen Am,
TwCA Sup, TwCW, WhoAm 1974,
WhoWor 1974, WrDr 1976
Dahlin, Robert *NF*
Dahlquist, Eric Eugene 1937- *WhoAm 1974*
Dahlqvist, Borje Gunnar 1929- *WhoAm 1974,*
WhoWor 1974
Daigh, Ralph Foster 1907- *WhoAm 1974*
Daigneault, Mike *NF*
Dailey, Alan Davis 1903- *WhJnl 1928*
D'Aillon, Paul Gros 1924- *CanWW 1972,*
WhoAm 1974
Dakin, Roger 1905-1978 *WhoAm 1974*
Dalby, Henry *NF*
Dale, Alan 1861-1928 *Alli Sup, AmAu&B,*
AmJnl, DcAmA, DcNAA, HisAmM XR
Dale, Alan *see also* Cohen, Alfred J
Dale, Albert Ennis 1890-1954 *BioIn 3, BioIn 6,*
BioIn 8, WhJnl 1928
Dale, Bruce Albert 1938- *WhoAm 1974*
Dale, Edwin L, Jr. 1923- *ConAu 69*
Dale, Francis L *NF*
Dale, Fred *NF*
Dale, Tom 1899-1965 *BioIn 7*
Dale, Walter Max 1894-1969 *BioIn 8*

Dalecki, Kenneth B *NF*
D'Alessio, Gregory 1904- *BioIn 1, WhoE 1974*
Daley, Arthur James 1916- *WhoAm 1974*
Daley, Arthur John 1904-1974 *AmAu&B,*
BioIn 10, ConAu 23, ConAu 45, CurBio XR
Daley, George Herbert 1869- *WhJnl 1928*
Daley, George William 1875-1952 *BioIn 3,*
WhJnl 1928
Daley, Robert 1930- *ConAu 2R, NewYTBE 3*
Daley, Roger A *WhoS&SW 1973*
Dalgleish, Oakley Hedley 1910-1963 *BioIn 6*
Dalgliesh, Alice 1893- *AmAu&B, AnCL,*
AuBYP, BioIn 1, BioIn 2, BioIn 5, BioIn 6,
BioIn 7, ConAu 73, JBA 1934, JBA 1951,
Str&VC, WhNAA
Dalla Torre, Giuseppe *NF*
Dallas, Eneas Sweetland 1828-1879 *Alli Sup,*
BioIn 7, BrAu 19, LongC
Dallas, Roland *NF*
Dallenbach, Karl M 1887-1971 *HisAmM XR*
Dalley, John Bede 1878-1935 *BioIn 2, DcLEL*
Dallin, David Julievich 1889-1962 *AmAu&B,*
Au&Wr, BioIn 2, BioIn 4, BioIn 6,
TwCA Sup
Dallis, Nicholas Peter 1911- *BioIn 6*
Dallman, Paul Jerald 1939- *WhoAm 1974*
Dallman, Vincent Y 1873-1964 *BioIn 2*
Dall'Ongaro, Francesco 1808-1873 *BbD, BiD&SB,*
CasWL, EvEuW, WebBD
Dallyn, Gordon M *BioIn 5*
Dalquist, Karl John 1894- *WhJnl 1928*
Dalrymple, Louis 1866-1905 *HisAmM XR*
Dalton, David 1942- *NF*
Dalton, James 1886?-1948 *BioIn 1*
Dalton, John A 1893-1954 *BioIn 3*
Dalton, Neil 1897- *WhJnl 1928*
Dalton, Susan Rossi 1942- *NF*
Dalva, Leon 1906?-1972 *BioIn 9*
Daly, Augustin 1838-1899 *Alli Sup, AmAu,*
AmAu&B, BbD, CnDAL, CnThe, DcNAA,
HsB&A, McGWD, ModWD, OxAm,
REnAL, REnWD, WebBD
Daly, James Jeremiah 1872-1953 *BioIn 1,*
BioIn 3, BkC 2, CathA 1930
Daly, James Joseph 1916- *WhoAm 1974,*
WhoF&I 1974, WhoS&SW 1973
Daly, John Charles, Jr. 1914- *BioIn 1, BioIn 2,*
IntWW 1976, OvPC, WhoAm 1974,
WhoE 1974
Daly, John J *HisAmM XR*
Daly, John Jay 1888?-1976 *ConAu 69*
Daly, John Joseph, Jr. 1931- *WhoAm 1974,*
WhoE 1974
Daly, Maggie Dorothea *WhoAm 1974,*
WhoAmW 1974
Daly, Maureen 1921- *AmAu&B, AmNov,*

*AuBYP, BioIn 1, BioIn 2, BioIn 6, BioIn 7,
BioIn 9, BkC 4, CathA 1930, ConAu XR,
CurBio XR, MorJA, REnAL, SmATA 2*
Daly, Sheila John 1927- *AuBYP, BioIn 2,
BioIn 3, BioIn 8, CathA 1952*
Daly, Thomas Augustine 1871-1948 *AmAu&B,
AmLY, BioIn 1, BioIn 4, BioIn 5, BioIn 6,
BkC 1, CathA 1930, CnDAL, ConAmL,
DcNAA, OxAm, REn, REnAL, TwCA,
TwCA Sup, WebBD, WhNAA*
Daly, Timothy W *NF*
Dalziel, Baron Davison Alexander 1854-1928
HisAmM XR, WebBD
Dalziel, Baron James Henry Dalziel 1868-1935
BioIn 2, WebBD
Dam, Hari Narayan 1921- *ConAu 57, DrAS 74E*
Dam, Henry Jackson Wells d1906 *HisAmM XR*
Dame, Jack *NF*
Dame, Lawrence 1898- *Au&Wr, ConAu P-1,
WhoAm 1974, WhoAmA 1973,
WhoS&SW 1973*
Damen, J *NF*
Dames, Joan Foster 1934- *WhoAmW 1974,
WhoMW 1974*
Damis, A W *NF*
Damon, W Ward *NF*
Dana, Arnold Guyot 1862-1947 *BioIn 1, BioIn 2,
DcNAA*
Dana, Bob *NF*
Dana, Charles Anderson 1819-1897 *Alli, Alli Sup,
AmAu, AmAu&B, AmJnl, BbD, BiD&SB,
BioIn 2, BioIn 4, BioIn 6, BioIn 8, CnDAL,
DcAmA, DcNAA, FamWC, ForP,
HisAmM XR, OxAm, REn, REnAL,
WebBD*
Dana, Edward Salisbury 1849-1935 *Alli Sup,
DcAmA, DcNAA, HisAmM XR, WebBD,
WhNAA*
Dana, Gus *NF*
Dana, James Dwight 1813-1895 *Alli, Alli Sup,
AmAu, BbD, BiD&SB, CyAL 1, DcAmA,
DcNAA, HisAmM XR, OxAm, REnAL,
WebBD*
Dana, James Henry *HisAmM XR*
Dana, John Cotton 1856-1929 *AmAu&B,
DcNAA, HisAmM XR, OxAm, WhNAA*
Dana, Margaret *BioIn 10, ForWC 1970*
Dana, Marshall Newport 1885-1966 *BioIn 2,
BioIn 9, WhoPNW*
Dana, Marvin 1867- *AmAu&B, DcAmA,
HisAmM XR*
Dana, Paul 1852-1930 *WebBD*
Dana, Richard Henry, Sr. 1787-1879 *Alli, AmAu,
AmAu&B, BbD, BiD&SB, CnDAL,
CyAL 1, DcAmA, DcEnL, DcLEL,
DcNAA, EvLB, OxAm, Pen Am, REn,
REnAL, WebBD*
Dana, William B *Alli Sup, HisAmM XR*
Danard, Jean *NF*
Danby, John Blench 1905- *OvPC, WhoAm 1974,
WhJnl 1928*
Dance, James *NF*
Dancey, Charles Lohman 1916- *WhoAm 1974*
Dancy, John *NF*
Dancy, John C 1857- *BioIn 8*
Danebarger, William Fowler 1910- *WhoAm 1974*
Danenberg, Elsie N *OvPC*
Danenberg, Leigh 1893-1976 *ConAu 69, OvPC,
WhoAm 1974, WhoWorJ 1972*
Danforth, Roy H *WhJnl 1928*
D'Angelo, Joseph F *OvPC*
Dangerfield, George 1904- *BioIn 10, CurBio XR,
DrAS 74H, WhoAm 1974, WhoWest 1974,
WhoWor 1974*

Daniel, Anita *AuBYP, BioIn 8, ForWC 1970*
Daniel, Charles Floyd 1901- *WhNAA,
WhJnl 1928*
Daniel, Clifton, Jr. 1912- *BioIn 4, BioIn 7,
BioIn 9, CurBio XR, IntWW 1976, InvJ,
NewMr, WhoE 1974, WhoWor 1974*
Daniel, Clifton, Jr. *see also* Daniel, Elbert Clifton, Jr.
Daniel, David R 1902?-1967 *BioIn 7*
Daniel, Elbert Clifton, Jr. 1912- *WhoAm 1974*
Daniel, Elbert Clifton, Jr. *see also* Daniel, Clifton, Jr.
Daniel, Harben Winfield 1906- *WhoAdv 1972,
WhoAm 1974, WhoF&I 1974*
Daniel, Hawthorne 1890- *AmAu&B, Au&Wr,
ConAu 5R, JBA 1934, JBA 1951,
SmATA 8, WhNAA, WhoAm 1974,
WhoWor 1974, WrDr 1976*
Daniel, James 1916- *ConAu 69, RpN,
WhoAm 1974, WhoE 1974*
Daniel, John Moncure 1825-1865 *Alli Sup, AmJnl,
BiDSA, DcAmA, DcAmB 5, DcNAA,
NatCAB 10, WebBD*
Daniel, Leon 1901- *WhoWorJ 1972*
Daniel, Royal 1870- *BiDSA*
Daniel, Walter Green 1905- *BioIn 10*
Daniel-Rops, Henry 1901-1965 *BkC 6,
CathA 1952, CurBio XR, EncWL*
Daniell, Francis Raymond 1901-1969 *WhJnl 1928*
Daniell, Francis Raymond *see also* Daniell, Raymond
Daniell, Raymond 1901-1969 *BioIn 8, CurBio XR*
Daniell, Raymond *see also* Daniell, F Raymond
Daniels, Derick January 1928- *WhoAm 1974*
Daniels, Dixie *HisAmM XR*
Daniels, Frank Arthur 1904- *WhoAm 1974,
WhoS&SW 1973*
Daniels, Frank Arthur, Jr. 1931- *WhoAdv 1972*
Daniels, George Goetz 1925- *WhoAm 1974,
WhoE 1974*
Daniels, George Henry 1842-1908 *HisAmM XR*
Daniels, George M 1927- *ConAu 29*
Daniels, Harold Griffith 1874-1952 *BioIn 2,
BioIn 3*
Daniels, Jonathan Worth 1902- *AmAu&B,
BioIn 2, BioIn 3, BioIn 4, BioIn 5, BioIn 7,
ConAu 49, WebBD, WhoAm 1974,
WhoAmP 1973*
Daniels, Josephus 1862-1948 *AmAu&B, BiDSA,
BioIn 10, CurBio XR, DcAmB S4, DcNAA,
EncAB, HisAmM XR, OxAm, REn,
REnAL, WebBD, WhJnl 1928*
Daniels, Randy 1949- *NF*
Daniels, Walter Machray 1898-1958 *BioIn 4*
Danielson, George W *NF*
Danielson, Richard Ely 1885-1957 *AmAu&B,
BioIn 2, BioIn 4, Br&AmS, HisAmM XR*
Danihy, John, S J *WhJnl 1928*
Daniloff, Nicholas 1934?- *NF*
Daniloff, Ruth *NF*
Daninos, Pierre 1913- *Au&Wr, BioIn 4,
BioIn 6, CasWL, IntWW 1976, REn,
TwCW, Who 1974, WhoWor 1974, WorAu*
Danish, Max D 1891-1964 *AmRP, BioIn 2,
BioIn 6*
Danish, Roy Bertram 1919- *WhoAm 1974,
WhoF&I 1974*
Danjou, Henri 1899?-1954 *BioIn 3*
Dankoler, Harry Edward 1863-1955 *BioIn 5*
Dann, Michael Harold 1921- *WhoAm 1974*
Dannenberg, Karl *AmRP*
Dannenhower, W W *HisAmM XR*
Dannheisser, Ralph *NF*
Dansereau, Dollard 1909- *CanWW 1972*
Dantas, Orlando Ribeiro 1896-1953 *BioIn 3*
Danzer, Carl 1818- *BioIn 2*
Danzig, Allison 1898- *ConAu 37, WrDr 1976*

Danzig, Fred Paul 1925- *ConAu 65,*
WhoAdv 1972
Danziger, Charles William *WhJnl 1928*
Danziger, Jerry 1924- *WhoAdv 1972,*
WhoAm 1974
Danzis, Mordecai 1887?-1952 *BioIn 3*
Daoust, Charles Roger 1865-1924 *DcNAA, OxCan*
Dapping, William Osborne 1880-1969 *BioIn 8,*
WhJnl 1928
Darack, Arthur J 1918- *WhoAm 1974*
Darby, Ada Claire 1883-1953 *AmAu&B, AuBYP*
Darby, Edwin Wheeler 1922- *WhoAm 1974,*
WhoF&I 1974
Darby, Rufus H *HisAmM XR*
Darby, William Dermot 1885-1947 *BioIn 1,*
DcNAA
D'Arcy, Ruth *NF*
Darcy, Tom Francis 1932- *WhoAm 1974*
Dare, Dorothy *AmJnl*
Dare, H Craig *HisAmM XR*
Dare, Helen *AmJnl*
Dare, Helen *see also* Brough, Elizabeth
Dareff, Hal 1920- *AmAu&B, AuBYP, BioIn 8,*
ConAu 65, WhoAm 1974, WhoE 1974
Dargan, Edwin Charles 1852-1930 *BiDSA,*
BioIn 3, DcNAA
Dargie, William *NF*
Dark, Sidney 1874-1947 *BioIn 1, LongC,*
Lor&LP
Darling, Jay Norwood 1876-1962 *AmAu&B,*
AmJnl, BioIn 1, BioIn 3, BioIn 5, BioIn 6,
CurBio XR, HisAmM XR, WebBD,
WhNAA, WhJnl 1928
Darling, Samuel Boyd 1873-1948 *BioIn 1,*
DcNAA
Darlington, William Aubrey 1890- *Au&Wr,*
BioIn 2, ConAu 15, ConAu P-1, DcLEL,
IntWW 1976, Who 1974, WhoThe 1972,
WhoWor 1974
D'Armand, Jacques 1890- *WhJnl 1928*
Darnton, Byron *AmJnl*
Darnton, Eleanor 1907-1968 *BioIn 8*
Darnton, John *NF*
DaRosa, J Pereira *ForP*
Darr, Bert Ernest 1920- *WhoWest 1974*
Darrah, David Harley 1894- *OhA&B*
Darrell, Robert Donaldson 1903- *AmAu&B,*
CurBio XR, WhoAm 1974, WhoMus 1972,
WhoWor 1974
Darrow, L B *HisAmM XR*
Darrow, Richard William 1915- *ConAu 21,*
OvPC, WhoAm 1974, WhoPubR 1972
Darrow, Whitney, Jr. 1909- *AmAu&B, BioIn 2,*
BioIn 5, ConAu 61, CurBio XR,
WhoAm 1974, WhoAmA 1973,
WhoWor 1974
Dart, Edward Nelson 1873?-1952 *BioIn 3*
Dart, Henry Plauche 1858-1934 *DcAmB S1*
Dart, Susan *NF*
Darveau, Louis Michel 1833-1875 *BbtC, DcNAA,*
OxCan
Dary, David Archie 1934- *ConAu 29,*
WhoMW 1974, WrDr 1976
Das, Durga 1900-1974 *BioIn 10, ConAu 29,*
ConAu 49, NewYTBS 5
Dasent, Sir George Webbe 1817-1896 *Alli Sup,*
AnCL, BbD, BiD&SB, BrAu 19, DcEnA,
DcEnL, DcEuL, EvLB, NewC, OxEng,
Str&VC, WebBD, WhoChL
Dash, Earl *NF*
Dash, Leon *NF*
Dash, Norman *NF*
Dash, Thomas Robert 1897- *AmAu&B*
Dashiell, Alfred Sheppard 1901-1970 *AmAu&B,*

BioIn 9, NewYTBE 1, WhNAA
DaSilva, Wladimir Pinto *NF*
Dassault, Marcel 1892- *CurBio XR,*
IntWW 1976, WhoWor 1974
Dater, John Grant *HisAmM XR*
Daubert, Harold E *NF*
Daudet, Ernest Louis Marie 1837-1921 *WebBD*
Daudet, Leon 1867-1942 *BioIn 1, CasWL,*
CIDMEL, CurBio XR, EncWL, NewC,
OxFr, REn, WebBD
Dauer, Malcolm *NF*
Daughen, Joseph R 1935- *ConAu 33*
Daugherty, Bob *NF*
Daumier, Honore 1808-1879 *AtlBL, BioIn 5,*
BioIn 6, BioIn 7, BioIn 8, BioIn 9, OxFr,
REn, WebBD
Davenport, Arthur C 1888- *WhJnl 1928*
Davenport, Basil 1905-1966 *BioIn 7*
Davenport, Benjamin Rush *HisAmM XR*
Davenport, Diana 1939- *NF*
Davenport, Dona Lee 1931- *ForWC 1970,*
WhoAm 1974
Davenport, Erwin R 1876?-1967 *BioIn 8*
Davenport, Homer Calvin 1867-1912 *AmAu&B,*
BioIn 6, BioIn 9, BioIn 10, DcAmA,
DcNAA, WebBD
Davenport, John 1904- *BioIn 2*
Davenport, Marcia 1903- *AmAu&B, AmNov,*
AuBYP, ConAu 9, CurBio XR, DcLEL,
LongC, OxAm, REn, REnAL, TwCA Sup,
WebBD, WhoAm 1974, WhoAmW 1974,
WhoWor 1974
Davenport, Reuben Briggs 1852-1932 *Alli Sup,*
DcNAA, WhNAA
Davenport, Russell Wheeler 1899-1954 *AmAu&B,*
BioIn 3, BioIn 4, CurBio XR, DcAmB S5,
HisAmM XR, NatCAB 40
Davenport, Walter 1889-1971 *BioIn 1, BioIn 9,*
HisAmM XR, NewYTBE 2
Daver, Abidin 1885?-1954 *BioIn 3*
Daves, Jessica 1898-1974 *BioIn 10, ConAu 53,*
HisAmM XR, NewYTBS 5, WhoAm 1974,
WhoAmW 1974
Davey, Clark William 1928- *WhoAm 1974*
Daviault, Pierre 1899-1964 *BioIn 7, CanWr,*
WhNAA
David, Barbara *NF*
David, Clyde Byron 1891- *WhJnl 1928*
David, E W *HisAmM XR*
David, Francis 1874- *WhJnl 1928*
David, Joseph B, III *NF*
David, Lester 1914- *ConAu 37*
David, Oren John 1883- *WhJnl 1928*
Davidoff, Henry 1879?-1951 *BioIn 2*
Davidow, Leonard S 1900- *WhoAm 1974*
Davidow, Mike 1913- *ConAu 57*
Davids, Georgina Bruce 1889- *WhJnl 1928*
Davidson, Basil Risbridger 1914- *AmAu&B,*
BioIn 10, ConAu 1R, Who 1974
Davidson, Bill 1918- *AuBYP, BiE&WWA,*
BioIn 8
Davidson, David 1908- *AmAu&B, AmNov,*
ConAu 49, TwCA Sup, WrDr 1976
Davidson, DeWitt S *OvPC*
Davidson, Donald Grady 1893-1968 *AmAu&B,*
HisAmM XR, WebBD, WhJnl 1928
Davidson, Ellis W 1890?-1948 *BioIn 1*
Davidson, Eugene 1902- *Au&Wr, ConAu 1,*
WrDr 1976
Davidson, Frank C *HisAmM XR*
Davidson, Georgia Marie 1907- *WhoAm 1974*
Davidson, Grace L *HisAmM XR*
Davidson, Herbert Marc 1895- *WhJnl 1928,*
WhoS&SW 1973

Davidson, James Wheeler 1872-1933 *AmLY,
DcAmA, DcNAA, WhNAA*
Davidson, James Wood 1829-1905 *Alli Sup,
AmAu, AmAu&B, BiDSA, DcAmA,
DcAmB 5, DcNAA, HisAmM XR*
Davidson, Marshall Bowman 1907- *AmAu&B,
Au&Wr, BioIn 2, ConAu 33, WhoAm 1974,
WhoAmA 1973*
Davidson, Michael Childers 1897- *Au&Wr,
ConAu 29*
Davidson, Ralph P 1927- *IntWW 1976*
Davidson, Sara 1943?- *BioIn 9, BioIn 10*
Davidson, Susan B *NF*
Davidson, Thomas 1840-1900 *Alli Sup, AmAu,
AmAu&B, BbD, BiD&SB, BrAu 19,
DcAmA, DcNAA, HisAmM XR, OxAm,
REnAL*
Davie, Michael 1924- *ConAu 57*
Davied, Camille 1893- *ConAu XR, ForWC 1970,
OvPC*
Davies, Acton 1870-1916 *DcNAA*
Davies, Colin 1925- *ConAu XR*
Davies, David Percy 1891-1946 *BioIn 1*
Davies, Ernest 1902- *CurBio XR*
Davies, Frederic *NF*
Davies, H Denny *OvPC*
Davies, Harry Donald 1892-1958 *BioIn 7*
Davies, Hubert Henry 1876-1917 *DcLEL WebBD*
Davies, Hunter 1936- *ConAu 57, WhoWor 1974,
WrDr 1976*
Davies, John O, Jr. *RpN*
Davies, Lawrence E 1900-1971 *BioIn 9,
NewYTBE 2*
Davies, Linton Lincoln 1895- *WhJnl 1928*
Davies, Michael J *NF*
Davies, Raymond Arthur 1908- *BioIn 1*
Davies, Robertson 1913- *Au&Wr, BioIn 6,
BioIn 9, BioIn 10, CanWW 1972, CanWr,
CasWL, CnThe, ConAu 33, ConDr,
ConLC 2, ConNov 1972, ConNov 1976,
CurBio XR, DcLEL, DrAS 74E, LongC,
McGWD, OxCan, OxCan Sup, Pen Eng,
REnAL, REnWD, TwCW, WhoAm 1974,
WhoWor 1974, WorAu, WrDr 1976*
Davies, Ruby Ellen 1892- *WhJnl 1928*
Davies, Stan Gebler 1943- *ConAu 65*
Davies, W Rupert *NF*
Davies, William Wills 1880?-1953 *BioIn 3*
Davila, Carlos Guillermo 1887-1955 *BioIn 1,
BioIn 3, BioIn 4*
Davin, Nicholas Flood 1843-1901 *Alli Sup,
BioIn 5, DcLEL, DcNAA, OxCan, PoIre*
Davis, A E *HisAmM XR*
Davis, Alvin 1925- *RpN, WhoAm 1974,
WhoE 1974*
Davis, Andrew Jackson 1826-1910 *Alli, Alli Sup,
BbD, BiD&SB, DcAmA, DcNAA,
HisAmM XR, OxAm*
Davis, Arthur W 1867?-1954 *BioIn 3*
Davis, B Dale 1922- *NF*
Davis, Bancroft C *HisAmM XR*
Davis, Belva *BlkC*
Davis, Ben Reeves 1927- *WhoAm 1974,
WhoS&SW 1973*
Davis, Burke 1913- *AmAu&B, AuBYP, BioIn 3,
BioIn 4, BioIn 5, BioIn 7, BioIn 9,
ConAu 1R, SmATA 4, WhoAm 1974,
WrDr 1976*
Davis, Charles Belmont 1868-1926 *DcAmA,
DcNAA, HisAmM XR*
Davis, Charles E 1916?-1968 *BioIn 8*
Davis, Charles Palmer 1859-1921 *HisAmM XR*
Davis, Christina Tree *NF*

Davis, Clara Ogden 1892- *WhJnl Sup*
Davis, Clyde Brion 1894-1962 *AmAu&B, AmNov,
CnDAL, ConAu 5R, OxAm, REn, REnAL,
TwCA, TwCA Sup*
Davis, Cornelius *HisAmM XR*
Davis, Curtis Wheeler 1928- *WhoAm 1974*
Davis, Daniel S 1936- *ConAu 45*
Davis, Daphne *ConAu 65*
Davis, Donald A *NF*
Davis, Donald Walter 1896- *WhJnl 1928*
Davis, Douglas *NF*
Davis, Edna Staats 1894?-1978 *NF*
Davis, Edward Parker 1856-1937 *DcNAA,
HisAmM XR*
Davis, Edward Wiker Closson 1902- *WhJnl 1928*
Davis, Elise Miller 1915- *ConAu 69,
WhoAmW 1974*
Davis, Elmer Holmes 1890-1958 *AmAu&B,
BioIn 2, BioIn 3, BioIn 4, BioIn 5, BioIn 6,
BioIn 8, CurBio XR, EncAB, HisAmM XR,
IndAu 1816, LiJA, OxAm, REn, REnAL,
TwCA, TwCA Sup, WhNAA*
Davis, Emily C 1898- *WhJnl 1928*
Davis, Flora 1934- *ConAu 65*
Davis, Forrest 1893-1962 *BioIn 6, HisAmM XR*
Davis, Foster S 1940?- *NF*
Davis, George 1906-1957 *BioIn 4*
Davis, George D *WhJnl 1928*
Davis, Glenmore Whitney *NF*
Davis, Harold Larue 1925- *AmM&W 73P,
WhoAm 1974*
Davis, Harold Lenoir 1896-1960 *AmAu&B,
DcLEL, TwCA, TwCA Sup, WebBD*
Davis, Harrie *NF*
Davis, Harriet Ide 1881?-1974 *BioIn 1, BioIn 10*
Davis, Harry M d1950 *RpN*
Davis, Harry Orville 1877-1964 *HisAmM XR*
Davis, Hartley C d1938 *NF*
Davis, Helen 1895-1957 *BioIn 4*
Davis, Henry P 1894?-1970 *BioIn 9, BioIn 10*
Davis, Horance Gibbs, Jr. 1924- *ConAu 65,
WhoAm 1974*
Davis, J Frank 1870-1942 *AmAu&B, DcNAA,
TexWr, WhNAA*
Davis, J Frank *see also* Davis, James Francis
Davis, Jack *NF*
Davis, James 1721-1785 *AmJnl, NatCAB 7*
Davis, James Francis 1870-1942 *CurBio XR,
DcNAA*
Davis, James Francis *see also* Davis, J Frank
Davis, Jessica *AmAu&B*
Davis, Jim 1945- *NF*
Davis, Joel 1934- *WhoAdv 1972, WhoAm 1974,
WhoE 1974, WhoF&I 1974*
Davis, Johanna 1937-1974 *ConAu 41, ConAu 53*
Davis, John Burton 1893- *WhJnl Sup*
Davis, John M *HisAmM XR*
Davis, John Preston 1905?-1973 *BioIn 10, BlkAW*
Davis, Joy Shannon *NF*
Davis, Mrs. L Clare *WhJnl 1928*
Davis, Lambert 1905- *BioIn 4, BioIn 7,
WhoAm 1974, WhoS&SW 1973*
Davis, Lemuel Clarke 1835-1904 *Alli Sup,
AmAu&B, DcAmA, DcNAA, HisAmM XR,
OhA&B*
Davis, Lou *NF*
Davis, Malcolm McTear 1920?-1973 *BioIn 9*
Davis, Marc 1934- *ConAu 29*
Davis, Marguerite *WhoAm 1974,
WhoAmW 1974, WhoS&SW 1973*
Davis, Mary Gould 1882-1956 *AmAu&B, AnCL,
AuBYP, JBA 1934, JBA 1951*
Davis, Matthew Livingston 1766-1850 *Alli, AmJnl,
DcAmA, DcAmB 5, DcNAA, NatCAB 5*

Davis, Maxine *AmAu&B, BioIn 1,*
  WhoAm 1974, WhoAmW 1974, WrDr 1976
Davis, Melton S 1910- *ConAu 41, WhoAm 1974*
Davis, Murray 1902?- *BioIn 2, BioIn 5*
Davis, Nathan Smith 1817-1904 *Alli Sup,*
  DcAmA, DcNAA, HisAmM XR, WebBD
Davis, Neil O *RpN*
Davis, Nolan 1942- *BlkAW, ConAu 49*
Davis, Norman Maurice 1936- *ConAu 69*
Davis, Oscar King 1866-1932 *DcAmA,*
  DcAmB S1, DcNAA, HisAmM XR
Davis, Paulina Kellogg Wright 1813-1867
  HisAmM XR
Davis, Paxton 1925- *ConAu 9R*
Davis, Peter Frank 1937- *WhoAm 1974,*
  WhoE 1974
Davis, Philip 1906?-1964 *BioIn 1, BioIn 7*
Davis, Preston *HisAmM XR*
Davis, Ralph Stuart 1882- *WhJnl 1928*
Davis, Regula 1922?-1973 *BioIn 10*
Davis, Richard Harding 1864-1916 *AmAu&B,*
  AmJnl, BbD, BiD&SB, BioIn 3, BioIn 4,
  BioIn 5, BioIn 6, BioIn 8, BioIn 9, CarSB,
  CasWL, CnDAL, DcAmA, DcAmB 5,
  DcBiA, DcEnA Ap, DcLEL, DcNAA,
  EncMys, EvLB, FamWC, HisAmM XR,
  JBA 1934, LongC, NewMr, OxAm,
  Pen Am, REn, REnAL, TwCA, TwCA Sup,
  WebBD, WebE&AL
Davis, Rick *NF*
Davis, Robert *BbtC*
Davis, Robert 1881-1949 *AmAu&B, AnCL,*
  BioIn 2, CurBio XR, DcNAA, JBA 1951,
  YABC 1
Davis, Robert Hobart 1869-1942 *AmAu&B,*
  BioIn 2, BioIn 4, DcNAA, HisAmM XR,
  NatCAB 34, REnAL, WhNAA
Davis, Robert S 1841-1911 *Alli Sup,*
  HisAmM XR, NatCAB 6
Davis, Royal Jenkins 1878-1934 *DcNAA,*
  WhNAA, WhJnl 1928
Davis, Sam 1909?-1949 *BioIn 2*
Davis, Samuel Harrison d1903 *HisAmM XR*
Davis, Saville Rogers 1909- *WhoAm 1974,*
  WhoS&SW 1973, WhoWor 1974
Davis, Shelden B *WhJnl 1928*
Davis, Sid 1927- *WhoAm 1974,*
  WhoS&SW 1973
Davis, Singleton Waters *HisAmM XR*
Davis, Sydney Charles Houghton 1887- *Au&Wr,*
  ConAu 7R
Davis, Theodore Russell 1840-1894 *HisAmM XR*
Davis, Thomas Osborne 1814-1845 *BbD, BiD&SB,*
  BrAu 19, CasWL, EvLB, NewC, Pen Eng,
  PoIre, REn, WebBD
Davis, Thurston N 1913- *AmAu&B,*
  WhoAm 1974
Davis, W H *NF*
Davis, Wallace McCroan, Jr. 1929- *NF*
Davis, Watson 1896-1967 *BioIn 7, BioIn 8,*
  CurBio XR, HisAmM XR, WhNAA,
  WhJnl 1928
Davis, William 1933- *Au&Wr, ConAu 65,*
  Who 1974, WhoWor 1974
Davis, William A *NF*
Davis, William E *FamWC*
Davis, William Hawley 1880-1962 *BioIn 6,*
  BioIn 8, HisAmM XR, NatCAB 50
Davis, William Watts Hart 1820-1910 *Alli Sup,*
  AmAu&B, DcAMA, DcNAA
Davison, Gideon Miner 1791?-1869 *DcNAA,*
  OxCan
Davison, Kensington *BioIn 8*
Davol, Ezra *NF*

Dawe, Grosvenor 1863-1948 *BioIn 1*
Dawes, Anna Laurens 1851-1938 *Alli Sup,*
  AmAu&B, BiD&SB, DcAmA, DcNAA,
  WhNAA
Dawley, Thomas Robinson, Jr. 1862-1930 *DcAmA,*
  DcNAA, WhNAA
Dawson, Alan 1942- *NF*
Dawson, Benjamin Franklin *HisAmM XR*
Dawson, Christopher Henry 1889-1970 *BioIn 1,*
  CathA 1930, ConAu 1, ConAu 29,
  TwCA Sup
Dawson, Francis Warrington 1840-1889 *BiDSA,*
  DcAmB 5
Dawson, Francis Warrington 1878-1962 *BioIn 6,*
  BioIn 7, BioIn 8
Dawson, G F *HisAmM XR*
Dawson, Geoffrey 1874-1944 *BioIn 4, BioIn 5,*
  LongC, Lor&LP, WebBD
Dawson, George 1813-1883 *Alli Sup, DcAmA,*
  DcNAA, NatCAB 2
Dawson, Henry Barton 1821-1889 *Alli, Alli Sup,*
  AmAu&B, CyAL 2, DcAmA, DcNAA,
  HisAmM XR
Dawson, Mrs. J Allan *NF*
Dawson, James Baxter 1876- *WhJnl 1928*
Dawson, James P 1895-1953 *BioIn 3*
Dawson, Mary d1922 *DcNAA*
Dawson, Thomas d1888 *NF*
Dawson, William Meredith, Jr. 1903- *WhJnl 1928*
Day, Anthony 1933?- *NF*
Day, Benjamin H, Jr. 1838-1916 *AmJnl, EarABI,*
  EarABI Sup, HisAmM XR
Day, Benjamin Henry 1810-1889 *AmAu&B,*
  AmJnl, BioIn 7, DcAmB 5, DcNAA,
  WebBD
Day, Charles Manley 1863-1945 *WhJnl 1928*
Day, Chon 1907- *AmAu&B, BioIn 3,*
  WhoAmA 1973
Day, Clifford Louis 1890-1964 *BioIn 6*
Day, Clive 1871-1951 *AmLY, HisAmM XR,*
  WebBD, WhNAA
Day, Crosby L 1935- *NF*
Day, David *AmAu&B*
Day, Donald *AmJnl*
Day, Dorothy 1897- *AmRP, BiE&WWA,*
  BioIn 1, BioIn 2, BioIn 3, BioIn 6, BioIn 8,
  BioIn 9, BioIn 10, BioNews 1974,
  CathA 1930, CelR 1973, ConAu 65,
  CurBio XR, NewYTBE 3, WhoAm 1974,
  WhoE 1974
Day, Ernest Hermitage 1866-1946 *BioIn 1*
Day, Mrs. F H *HisAmM XR*
Day, Frank A 1857- *WhJnl 1928*
Day, Frank Miles 1861-1918 *DcNAA,*
  HisAmM XR, WebBD
Day, George Edward 1815-1905 *Alli Sup,*
  DcNAA, HisAmM XR
Day, George Parmly 1876-1959 *AmAu&B,*
  NatCAB 48
Day, George Tiffany *Alli Sup, HisAmM XR*
Day, Helen Herries 1886?-1971 *BioIn 9,*
  NewYTBE 2
Day, Holman Francis 1865-1935 *AmAu&B,*
  BioIn 7, DcAmA, DcAmB S1, DcNAA,
  HisAmM XR, REnAL, TwCA, TwCA Sup,
  WebBD
Day, Ingeborg *NF*
Day, Irene F *OvPC*
Day, J Laurence 1934- *NF*
Day, James Francis Meagher 1900- *WhJnl 1928*
Day, James Wentworth 1899- *ConAu 13R,*
  Who 1974
Day, John F, Jr. *RpN*
Day, John Laurence 1934- *AmM&W 73S,*

Dee, Ted *NF*
Deeb, Gary *NF*
Deedes, William Francis 1913- *IntWW 1976,*
Who 1974, WhoWor 1974
Deedy, John Gerard, Jr. 1923- *ConAu 33,*
WhoAm 1974, WhoE 1974, WhoF&I 1974
Deemer, Samuel *HisAmM XR*
Deems, Charles Force 1820-1893 *Alli, Alli Sup,*
BiD&SB, BiDSA, DcAmA, DcNAA,
HisAmM XR, WebBD
Deems, Richard Emmet 1913- *AmJnl,*
WhoAm 1974, WhoF&I 1974
Deen, Edith Alderman 1905- *ConAu 7R,*
ForWC 1970
Deepe, Beverly 1935?- *BioIn 7*
Deering, Ferdie Jackson 1910- *WhoAm 1974,*
WhoF&I 1974, WhoS&SW 1973
Deering, William P 1878- *WhJnl 1928*
Deery, Robert H *NF*
Defferre, Gaston 1910- *CurBio XR,*
IntWW 1974, WhoWor 1974
Defoe, Daniel 1660?-1731 *Alli, AtlBL, BbD,*
BiD&SB, BrAu, CarSB, CasWL, CrtT 2,
CyWA, DcBiA, DcEnA, DcEnL, DcEuL,
DcLEL, EvLB, ForP, HsB&A, MouLC 2,
NewC, OxEng, Pen Eng, RAdv 1,
RComWL, REn, WebBD, WebE&AL,
WhoChL
DeFoe, Louis Vincent 1869-1922 *NF*
DeFonseka, Joseph Peter 1897-1948 *BioIn 1,*
CathA 1930
DeFontaine, Edward J *OvPC*
DeFontaine, Felix Gregory 1834-1896 *AmAu,*
AmAu&B, BiD&SB, DcAmA, DcAmB 5,
DcNAA
DeFontaine, Felix Gregory *see also* Personne
DeFontaine, Wade Hampton 1893-1969 *BioIn 8,*
ConAu 5
Deford, Frank 1938- *ConAu 33, WrDr 1976*
DeFord, Miriam Allen 1888-1975 *AmAu&B,*
ConAu 3R, EncMys, REnAL, TwCA,
TwCA Sup, WhNAA, WhoAm 1974,
WhoAmW 1974
DeForeest, Henry *AmJnl*
DeForest, Robert Weeks 1848-1931 *DcAmA,*
HisAmM XR
DeFornaro, Carlo 1871-1949 *BioIn 2*
Degan, Henry V *HisAmM XR*
DeGandt, John *NF*
DeGarmo, Charles 1849-1934 *DcAmA, DcNAA,*
HisAmM XR
DeGarmo, Kenneth Scott 1943- *NF*
DeGeer, I Vern 1902?- *WhNAA, WhJnl 1928*
DeGraffenreid, Claude C 1875-1918 *NatCAB 18*
DeGramont, Sanche 1932- *AmAu&B, ConAu 45*
Degras, Jane 1905-1973 *BioIn 10*
DeGraw, John L *HisAmM XR*
Degroot, Don Ferdinand 1911- *WhoAm 1974,*
WhoMW 1974
DeGroot, Roy Andries *NF*
DeGrouchy, William John 1889-1954 *BioIn 3*
DeHaan, Jacob Israel d1924 *NF*
DeHaas, Carl 1817-1875 *BioIn 5*
DeHaas, Carl *see also* Haas, Carl De
DeHaas, Jacob 1872-1937 *NF*
Dehlgren, Sten Fredrik 1881-1947 *BioIn 1*
Dehmel, Klaus *NF*
Dehmel, Peter *NF*
Dehn, Adolph 1895-1968 *AmRP, WebBD*
Dehn, Alfred *AmRP*
Dehn, Paul Edward 1912- *Au&Wr, ConP 1970,*
ConP 1975, DcLEL, LongC, WrDr 1976
Deiderich, Bernard *NF*

Deitch, Kim 1944- *BioIn 10*
Deitch, Mark *NF*
Deitchman, Carolyn *NF*
Deiter, Berthold *HisAmM XR*
Deitz, Gilbert A 1896- *WhJnl 1928*
Deitz, Marion Lawrance 1902- *WhJnl 1928*
Deitz, Robert Eugene 1940- *WhoS&SW 1973*
Deitz, Susan *NF*
DeJean, David L *NF*
DeKay, Charles Augustus 1848-1935 *DcNAA,*
HisAmM XR, WebBD
Dekobra, Maurice 1885-1973 *Au&Wr,*
ConAu 5R, ConAu 41, LongC,
NewYTBE 4, WhoLA
DeKock, Paul *HisAmM XR*
DeKock, Wilhelmina *OvPC*
Dekom, Otto *NF*
DeKoven, Reginald 1861-1920 *AmAu&B,*
AmSCAP 1966, OxAm, REn, REnAL
DeKruif, Paul 1890-1971 *AmAu&B, AmRP,*
BiE&WWA, ConAu 9, ConAu 29,
CurBio XR, JBA 1934, LongC, OxAm,
REn, REnAL, SmATA 5, TwCA,
TwCA Sup, WebBD
Dektar, Joan *NF*
DeLaBedoyere, Count Michael 1900- *Au&Wr,*
BioIn 1, CathA 1930, WhoWor 1974
Delacour, Jean Theodore 1890- *Au&Wr,*
WhoAm 1974
Delahay, Mark W 1828-1879 *NF*
DeLamar, W Curtis 1900- *WhJnl 1928*
DeLand, Charles V 1826-1903 *NatCAB 6*
DeLand, Fred *HisAmM XR*
Delane, John Thadeus 1817-1879 *Alli, BioIn 4,*
DcEnL, DcLEL, FamWC, ForP, Lor&LP,
NewC, OxEng, WebBD
Delaney, Charles W *WhJnl 1928*
Delaney, Joe *NF*
Delaney, Paul *NF*
Delaney, Steve *NF*
Delaney, William E, Jr. *NF*
Delano, Alonzo 1806?-1874 *AmAu, AmAu&B,*
DcNAA, OxAm, REnAL
Delano, Anthony *NF*
Delano, Arthur Hobart 1873?-1949 *BioIn 1*
Delano, Charles F 1877?-1964 *BioIn 7*
Delano, Edwin F 1891-1948 *BioIn 1*
Delano, Hugh 1933- *ConAu 65*
Delano Frederick, Jorge 1895- *BioIn 3*
Delany, Kevin F X 1927- *ConAu 73,*
WhoAm 1974, WhoWor 1974
Delany, Martin Robinson 1812-1885 *Alli Sup,*
AmAu, BlkAW, DcNAA, EncAB, WebBD
Delaplaine, Joseph 1777-1824 *AmAu&B,*
HisAmM XR
Delaplane, Stanton Hill 1907- *ConAu 25,*
WhoAm 1974, WhoWest 1974,
WhoWor 1974
DeLaVega, Santiago R *NF*
DelBoca, Angelo 1925- *ConAu 25*
DelCarpio, Pablo *NF*
DelDuca, Cino 1899-1967 *BioIn 7*
DeLeeuw, Hendrik 1891-1977 *AmAu&B,*
ConAu 73, WhoAm 1977
DeLemos, Pedro Joseph 1882- *BioIn 2*
DeLeon, Daniel 1852-1914 *AmRP, DcNAA,*
HisAmM XR, OxAm
DeLeon, Edward *HisAmM XR*
DeLeon, Edwin 1828-1891 *Alli Sup,' BbD,*
BiD&SB, BiDSA, BioIn 4, DcAmA,
DcNAA
DeLeon, Robert A d1977 *NF*
DeLeon, Solen *AmRP*
DeLeon, Thomas Cooper 1839-1914 *Alli Sup,*

AmAu, AmAu&B, BiDSA, DcAmA, DcNAA, NatCAB 19, REnAL
DeLestry, Edmond Louis 1860-1933 *DcNAA, WhNAA*
Delfico, Melchiorre 1835-1859 *BioIn 10*
Delforge, Marc 1909- *IntWW 1976, WhoWor 1974*
Delgado, Martin Morua 1856-1910 *BioIn 9*
Delgado Losano, Rafael 1908- *BioIn 1*
D'Elia, Andrew *NF*
Delich, Helen 1924?- *BioIn 2, BioIn 3*
DeLisser, Herbert George 1878-1944 *BioIn 3, BioIn 9, CasWL, DcLEL, WebE&AL*
Delker, Thomas Bancroft 1870-1949 *BioIn 2*
Dell, Floyd 1887-1969 *AmAu&B, AmRP, AnMV 1926, CnDAL, ConAmA, ConAmL, DcLEL, LongC, ModAL, OxAm, Pen Am, REn, REnAL, TwCA, TwCA Sup, WebBD, WhNAA*
Dellale, Dina *NF*
Dellinger, David T 1915- *AmRP, ConAu 65, WhoAm 1974*
Delmer, Denis Sefton 1904- *Au&Wr, BioIn 2, ConAu 5, ConAu 5R*
Delmer, Denis Sefton *see also* Delmer, Sefton
Delmer, Sefton 1904- *BioIn 6, IntWW 1974, Who 1974*
Delmer, Sefton *see also* Delmer, Denis Sefton
Delmerico, George *NF*
Delong, David A 1901- *WhJnl 1928*
DeLong, Edmund S 1900- *WhJnl 1928*
DeLong, Edward K 1942- *NF*
DeLorenzi, John 1921- *OvPC, WhoPubR 1972, WhoS&SW 1973*
DeLoss, Arnold 1897- *WhJnl 1928*
Delp, Alfred 1907-1945 *BioIn 2*
DeLuce, Daniel 1911- *CurBio XR, WhoAm 1974, WhoWor 1974*
Delugach, Albert Lawrence 1925- *InvJ, WhoAm 1974, WhoWest 1974*
DelVecchio, Tom *NF*
Demaree, Allan Thomas 1937?- *NF*
Demarest, Helen Moffatt 1917-1946 *BioIn 1*
Demarest, Lloyd 1883- *WhJnl 1928*
Demarest, Michael 1924?- *BioIn 4*
Demarteau, Joseph 1919- *IntWW 1976*
DeMartinau, Duarte *NF*
DeMasi, H Armand 1884- *WhJnl 1928*
DeMauny, Erik 1920- *ConAu 33*
Dembner, S Arthur 1920- *WhoAm 1974, WhoE 1974, WhoF&I 1974*
Dembo, Joseph T *NF*
Demby, Emanuel Harry 1919- *IntMPA 1975, OvPC, WhoE 1974*
DeMedici, Marino *NF*
DeMenil, Alexander Nicolas 1849-1928 *BiDSA, DcNAA, HisAmM XR, WhNAA*
Demers, Albert Fox 1863-1943 *AmAu&B, DcNAA*
Demetracopoulos, Elias P *OvPC*
Demetriadis, Phokion 1894- *ForP, IntWW 1976, WhoWor 1974*
Demicheal, Donald Anthony 1928- *WhoAm 1974*
DeMilt, James 1884?-1949 *BioIn 2*
Deming, Barbara 1917- *AmRP, ForWC 1970*
Deming, Clarence 1848-1913 *Alli Sup, DcAmA, NatCAB 12*
Deming, E D *HisAmM XR*
Deming, Henry Champion 1815-1872 *Alli Sup, DcAmA, DcNAA, HisAmM XR*
Deming, Philip *HisAmM XR*
Deming, William Chapin 1869-1949 *BioIn 1, BioIn 2, OhA&B, WhNAA*
Demma, Joe *InvJ*

Demme, Robert E *OvPC*
Demokan, Feridun *NF*
DeMontalvo, Marie 1886?-1950 *BioIn 2*
Demorest, Ellen Louise *AmAu&B, HisAmM XR*
Demorest, Henry C *HisAmM XR*
Demorest, William C *HisAmM XR*
Demorest, William Jennings *AmAu&B, HisAmM XR*
Demott, G Stuart 1896- *WhJnl 1928*
Dempewolff, Richard Frederic 1914- *ConAu 4R, OvPC, WhoAm 1974*
Dempsey, Lotta *CanWW 1972*
Dempster, Nigel *NF*
Demson, Edward J *NF*
Demulder, Francoise *NF*
Den, Yoshiyuki *NF*
Denberg, Jeffrey *NF*
Dench, Ernest Alfred 1895- *WhNAA, WhJnl 1928*
Denenberg, Herbert 1929- *NF*
Denham, Will S 1893- *WhJnl 1928*
Denhof, Miki 1912- *WhoAm 1974, WhoAmW 1974*
Denhoff, Alice *NF*
Denicke, George *AmRP*
Denious, Jess C 1879-1953 *BioIn 9, WhNAA, WhJnl 1928*
Denis, Paul 1909- *ConAu 21R*
Denison, Grace Elizabeth d1914 *DcNAA, HisAmM XR*
Denison, Jane K *NF*
Denison, Lindsay 1873-1934 *WhJnl 1928*
Denison, Merrill 1893- *BioIn 3, BioIn 10, CanWW 1972, CanWr, DcLEL, McGWD, OxCan, OxCan Sup, REnWD, WhNAA*
Denisov, Vladimir V *NF*
Denlinger, Sutherland 1900-1963 *BioIn 6*
Denman, Mack F 1901- *WhJnl 1928*
Denman, Robert A *NF*
Dennen, Grace Atherton 1874-1927 *AnMV 1926, DcNAA, WhNAA*
Dennen, Leon *OvPC*
Denner, Jerome *NF*
Dennett, Jim *NF*
Dennett, John Richard 1838-1874 *HisAmM XR, NatCAB 8*
Dennett, Raymond 1913-1961 *BioIn 4, BioIn 6*
Dennie, Joseph 1768-1812 *Alli, AmAu, AmAu&B, AmJnl, BiD&SB, BioIn 2, BioIn 5, BioIn 10, CasWL, CyAL 1, DcAmA, DcEnL, DcLEL, HisAmM XR, LiJA, NatCAB 7, OxAm, Pen Am, REnAL, REnAL*
Dennigan, M *NF*
Dennis, Albert N 1891- *WhJnl 1928*
Dennis, Charles 1844-1919 *BioIn 2, IndAu 1816*
Dennis, Charles Henry 1860-1943 *AmAu&B, CurBio XR, DcNAA, HisAmM XR, NatCAB 32*
Dennis, Clarence James 1876-1938 *BioIn 2, BioIn 3, BioIn 7*
Dennis, Everette E 1942- *ConAu 41*
Dennis, Frederic James 1888-1945 *BioIn 6*
Dennis, George Palmer 1877-1955 *BioIn 4, WhNAA, WhJnl 1928*
Dennis, Henry Arnold 1891- *WhNAA, WhJnl 1928*
Dennis, Landt 1937- *ConAu 65*
Dennis, Lawrence 1893-1977 *AmAu&B, CurBio XR, WhoAm 1974, WhoF&I 1974*
Dennis, Nigel 1912- *Au&Wr, CnMD, CnMWL, CnThe, ConAu 25, ConDr, ConNov 1972, ConNov 1976, CroCD, ModBL, ModBL Sup, ModWD, NewC, Pen Eng, RAdv 1, REn,*

TwCW, WebE&AL, WorAu, WrDr 1976
Dennis, Stanley Arthur 1882- *WhJnl 1928*
Dennis, William 1856- *NF*
Dennis, William Francis 1933- *WhoAm 1974*
Dennis, William Henry 1887-1954 *BioIn 3*
Denniston, Lyle William 1931- *ConAu 65*
Denny, Alma *NF*
Denny, George Vernon, Jr. 1899-1959 *CurBio XR, HisAmM XR*
Denny, Harold Norman 1889-1945 *AmAu&B, AmJnl, BioIn 2, DcNAA, NatCAB 34*
Denny, Ludwell 1894-1970 *AmAu&B, ConAu 29, IndAu 1917*
DeNormandie, James 1836-1924 *HisAmM XR*
Denoyer, Pierre 1901-1965 *BioIn 2, BioIn 7*
Denselow, Robin *NF*
Denslow, Ray Vaughn 1885- *WhNAA, WhJnl 1928*
Denslow, V B *HisAmM XR*
Denslow, William Wallace 1856-1915 *AmAu&B, DcNAA, HisAmM XR*
Densmore, James 1820-1889 *BioIn 1, BioIn 3, BioIn 5*
Denson, John Lee 1905- *AmAu&B, BioIn 5, HisAmM XR*
Dent, Alan 1905-1978 *ConAu 9R, WhoThe 1972*
Dent, John Charles 1841-1888 *DcNAA, OxCan*
Denton, Franklin Evert 1859-1947 *Alli Sup, DcAmA, OhA&B*
Denton, Herbert H *NF*
Denton, Patrick *NF*
Denver, James Edmund 1864- *WhJnl 1928*
Denver, Robert 1897-1961 *BioIn 5*
Denzer, Peter W 1921- *ConAu 7R*
Deon, Michel 1919- *ConAu 37*
Deonis, Juan *NF*
Depardon, Raymond *NF*
DePawlowski, G *NF*
Depretis, Agostino 1813-1887 *WebBD*
DePuy, Clifford 1886- *WhJnl 1928*
DeQuincey, Thomas 1785-1859 *Alli, AtlBL, BbD, BiD&SB, BrAu 19, CasWL, CrtT 2, CyWA, DcBiA, DcEnA, DcEnL, DcEuL, DcLEL, EvLB, MouLC 3, NewC, OxEng, Pen Eng, RAdv 1, RComWL, REn, WebBD, WebE&AL*
Derby, Chauncey H 1873- *WhJnl 1928*
Derby, George Horatio 1823-1861 *AmAu, AmAu&B, BiD&SB, CnDAL, DcAmA, DcLEL, DcNAA, EarABI, OxAm, REnAL, WebBD*
Derby, George Horatio *see also* Phoenix, John
DeReeder, Edward Louis 1899- *WhJnl 1928*
Dernburg, Bernhard 1865-1937 *HisAmM XR, WebBD*
Dernburg, Friedrich 1833-1911 *BiD&SB, WebBD*
Dero, Gertrude Don *OvPC*
DeRochemont, Richard 1903- *CurBio XR, IntMPA 1975, OvPC*
DeRohan, Pierre 1895- *WhJnl 1928*
DeRoin, Nancy 1934- *ConAu 65*
DeRoos, Robert 1912- *ConAu 11R, RpN*
DeRoquemaurel, Ithier 1914- *WhoAm 1974*
Derose, Harriet 1877?-1960 *BioIn 5*
Derounian, Arthur 1909- *BioIn 4*
Derounian, Arthur *see also* Carlson, John Roy
DeRoussy DeSales, Raoul 1896-1942 *BioIn 1, CurBio XR, DcNAA*
Derrick, Michael 1915-1961 *BioIn 3, BioIn 6, CathA 1952*
Derrickson, Marione Reinhard *HisAmM XR*
Derrig, John d1890 *NF*
Derso, Alois 1888-1964 *BioIn 2, BioIn 7*

Deruaz, G *NF*
Dervin, Brenda 1938- *ConAu 29*
DeSabatino, Gabriel *OvPC*
DeSaint Andre, Lucille *OvPC*
DeSalvo, Chris 1954- *NF*
DeSantis, Ann *InvJ*
DeSantis, Florence *NF*
DeSantis, Mary Allen 1930- *ConAu 9R*
Desatta, Katie *NF*
Desaulniers, Louise *NF*
Desaulniers, Lucien Lesieur 1875-1952 *BioIn 4, NatCAB 40*
Desbarats, Peter 1933- *ConAu 17R, OxCan*
Descarques, Pierre 1925- *ConAu 37*
Descaves, Lucien 1861-1949 *CIDMEL, EvEuW, McGWD, OxFr, WebBD*
Descaves, Pierre 1896-1966 *BioIn 7*
Desch, Kurt 1903- *IntWW 1976*
Deschamps, Emile 1791-1871 *CasWL, DcEuL, EuAu, EvEuW, OxFr, Pen Eur, WebBD*
Deschamps, Gaston 1861-1931 *WebBD*
DeSchauensee, Max 1899- *WhoAm 1974*
Deschodt, M Georges *NF*
DeSegonzac, Adalbert Rene DeBardon 1912- *WhoAm 1974, WhoS&SW 1973, WhoWor 1974*
Desfor, Irving 1907?- *BioIn 2*
Desfor, Max 1913- *AmJnl, WhoAm 1974*
Desguin, Georges Maurice 1913- *IntWW 1976, WhoWor 1974*
Desilva, Leo H 1880- *WhJnl 1928*
DeSilva, Ranjit *NF*
Desir, Hermann L, Sr. *OvPC*
Desjardins, Alphonse 1854-1920 *BioIn 2, OxCan*
Desjardins, Noella *NF*
DesJardins, Rene *NF*
Desmond, Henry W *HisAmM XR*
Desmond, Humphrey Joseph 1858-1932 *BioIn 5, DcAmA, DcNAA*
Desmond, James 1908-1968 *BioIn 8*
Desmond, John 1909?-1977 *ConAu 73*
Desmond, Robert William 1900- *Au&Wr, ConAu 73, DrAS 74E, WhoAm 1974*
Desmond, Shaw 1877-1960 *BiDPara, NewC, WebBD*
Desmond, Timothy J 1884- *WhJnl 1928*
Desmoulins, Camille 1760-1794 *BioIn 1, BioIn 2, BioIn 5, DcEuL, EvEuW, OxFr, REn, WebBD*
DesRoches, Monique Nuytemans *NF*
Dessauer, Phil *NF*
DeStefano, Ettore 1874?-1967 *BioIn 8*
Destree, Jacques 1905- *IntWW 1976*
Detjen, Gustav, Jr. 1905- *WhoAm 1974, WhoE 1974, WhoF&I 1974, WhoWor 1974*
DeToledano, Ralph 1916- *AmAu&B, AuNews 1, BioIn 3, BioIn 5, BioIn 6, CurBio XR, HisAmM XR, WhoAm 1974*
DeToledano, Ralph *see also* Toledano, Ralph De
Dettinger, Alma *BioIn 2*
Dettmer, Roger Christian 1927- *WhoAm 1974*
Detzer, Karl William 1891- *AmAu&B, OvPC, WhoAm 1974*
Deuel, Alanson Chase 1874-1954 *BioIn 3*
Deuel, Mrs. Harvey *AmJnl*
Deuel, Norman B *AmJnl*
Deuel, Wallace Rankin 1905- *CurBio XR, NewYTBS 5*
Deus Ramos, Joao De 1830-1896 *CIDMEL, WebBD*
Deusing, Murl 1908- *WhoAm 1974*
Deuss, Edward L 1897- *WhJnl 1928*
Deuster, Peter Victor 1831-1904 *BioIn 5*
Deutsch, Albert 1905-1961 *AmAu&B, BioIn 1,*

BioIn 5
Deutsch, Hermann Bacher 1889-1970 *BioIn 8,
WhoS&SW 1973*
Deutsch, Keith *NF*
Deutsch, Richard *NF*
Deutscher, Irwin 1923- *AmM&W 73S,
ConAu 25, WhoMW 1974, WrDr 1976*
Deutscher, Isaac 1907-1967 *BioIn 2, BioIn 6,
BioIn 8, BioIn 9, ConAu 5, ConAu 25,
WorAu*
Deutschkron, Inge 1922- *ConAu 29*
Deutschman, Paul *NF*
Deutzman, Lawrence F 1880-1952 *BioIn 2,
WhNAA, WhJnl 1928*
DeValera, Eamon 1882-1975 *CurBio XR, ForP,
IntWW 1974, NewYTBE 4, REn, WebBD,
Who 1974, WhoGov 1972, WhoWor 1974*
DeVane, William Clyde 1898-1965 *AmAu&B,
HisAmM XR*
Devaney, John 1926- *ConAu 19R*
Devaney, Mary A 1902- *WhJnl 1928*
Devau, Jean 1908?-1950 *BioIn 2*
Devaux, Paul 1801-1880 *WebBD*
Devel, Wallace R *NF*
Dever, Joseph 1919-1970 *CathA 1952, ConAu 19,
ConAu 29*
Dever, Joseph X 1919- *CelR 1973, WhoE 1974*
Devereaux, H L *NF*
Devereaux, Thomas *HisAmM XR*
Devereux, Mrs. C A R *HisAmM XR*
DeView, Lucille 1920- *ConAu 73*
DeVilleneuve, Justin 1940?- *BioIn 8, BioIn 9*
Devine, Edward Thomas 1867-1948 *DcAmA,
DcNAA, HisAmM XR, WebBD, WhNAA*
Devine, Janice Zeller 1908?-1973 *BioIn 9*
DeVine, Joseph Lawrence 1935- *ConAu 73,
WhoAm 1974*
Devine, Thomas *BioIn 1*
Devlin, James J 1908?-1965 *BioIn 7*
Devlin, John C, Sr. *OvPC*
Devoe, Alan 1909-1955 *AmAu&B, HisAmM XR*
Devoe, Fanchon *NF*
DeVore, Robert *HisAmM XR*
DeVoto, Bernard Augustine 1897-1955 *AmAu&B,
AmNov, AuNews 1, CnDAL, ConAmA,
CurBio XR, DcAmB S5, DcLEL, EncWL,
HisAmM XR, LongC, ModAL, OxAm,
Pen Am, RAdv 1, REn, REnAL, TwCA,
TwCA Sup, WebBD, WhNAA*
Devoy, John 1842-1928 *Alli Sup, DcAmB 5,
DcNAA, HisAmM XR*
Devree, Howard 1890-1966 *BioIn 7*
DeVries, Peter 1910- *AmAu&B, Au&Wr,
BiE&WWA, CelR 1973, CnDAL,
ConAu 17, ConLC 1, ConLC 2, ConLC 3,
ConNov 1972, ConNov 1976, CurBio XR,
DrAF 1976, EncWL, HisAmM XR,
IntWW 1974, ModAL, ModAL Sup, OxAm,
Pen Am, REnAL, Who 1974, WhoAm 1974,
WhoTwCL, WhoWor 1974, WorAu,
WrDr 1976*
Dewar, Helen *NF*
Dewart, Thomas W *NF*
Dewart, William Thompson 1875-1944 *AmAu&B,
AmJnl, CurBio XR, HisAmM XR,
WhJnl 1928*
Dewart, William Thompson 1910?-1946 *BioIn 1*
DeWatteville, Rowland A 1897- *WhJnl 1928*
DeWeerd, H A *HisAmM XR*
Dewees, William Potts 1768-1841 *Alli, DcAmA,
DcNAA, HisAmM XR*
DeWeese, Ennis McCuis 1899- *WhJnl 1928*
Dewel, Duane E 1901- *WhJnl 1928*
Dewey, A Peter 1916-1945 *BioIn 1*

Dewey, Melvil 1851-1931 *Alli Sup, AmAu&B,
AmLY, DcAmA, DcNAA, HisAmM XR,
OxAm, REn, REnAL, WebBD, WhNAA*
Dewey, Mike *NF*
Dewey, Phelps 1928- *WhoAm 1974*
Dewey, Stoddard 1853-1933 *HisAmM XR*
Dewhurst, Brian *NF*
DeWindt, Sandor A *OvPC*
DeWitt, George *NF*
DeWitt, R M *HisAmM XR*
DeWitt, William A 1907?-1968 *BioIn 8*
Dewolf, Rose 1934- *ConAu 29*
DeWolf, Townsend *HisAmM XR*
Dexter, Alexander Grant 1896-1961 *BioIn 6*
Dexter, Byron 1900-1973 *AmAu&B, BioIn 10,
WhoWor 1974*
Dexter, Daniel Sheehan 1890- *WhJnl 1928*
Dexter, Franklin *HisAmM XR*
Dexter, George *HisAmM XR*
Dexter, George T *HisAmM XR*
Dexter, Grant *NF*
Dey, Hattie Cahoon 1857-1950 *BioIn 2*
Deyell, Mossom John 1882?-1964 *BioIn 7*
DeYoung, Charles 1845-1880 *AmJnl, BioIn 1,
WebBD*
DeYoung, Michel Harry 1849-1925 *AmJnl,
NatCAB 1, WebBD*
DeYoung Thierot, Charles *NewMr*
Dezapp, Rudolphe 1873- *WhJnl 1928*
Diah, Burhanudin Mohamad 1917- *IntWW 1976,
WhoWor 1974*
Diah, Herawati 1917- *IntWW 1976,
WhoWor 1974*
Diamond, Edwin 1925- *ConAu 15, NewMr*
Diamond, H Louis 1904-1966 *NF*
Diamond, Nina *NF*
Diamond, Robert A *NF*
Diaz, Jaime *NF*
Dibble, Arnold *NF*
Dibble, Chester W 1872- *WhJnl 1928*
Dibble, Fred A *WhJnl 1928*
Dibble, Tony *NF*
Dibelka, Susan Shaffer 1895- *ForWC 1970,
WhJnl 1928*
DiBennedetto, William R 1950- *NF*
DiBlassi, Agostina *NF*
Dicey, Albert Venn 1835-1922 *Alli Sup, DcEuL,
HisAmM XR, NewC, OxEng*
Dicey, Edward James Stephen 1832-1911 *BioIn 6,
HisAmM XR, WebBD*
Dick, Archibald L *HisAmM XR*
Dick, David *NF*
Dick, Elsie d1949 *BioIn 2*
Dick, R McCulloch 1873?-1960 *BioIn 4, BioIn 5*
Dick, Ross Melvin 1912- *WhoAm 1974,
WhoF&I 1974*
Dick, William Ernest 1914-1960 *BioIn 3, BioIn 4,
BioIn 5*
Dickason, Deane H 1898- *WhJnl Sup*
Dickens, Charles 1812-1870 *Alli, Alli Sup,
AtlBL, AuBYP, BbD, BiD&SB, BrAu 19,
CarSB, CasWL, CrtT 3, CyWA, DcBiA,
DcEnA, DcEnA Ap, DcEnL, DcEuL,
DcLEL, EncMys, EvLB, HsB&A,
JBA 1934, MouLC 3, NewC, OxAm,
OxEng, Pen Am, Pen Eng, RAdv 1,
RComWL, REn, Str&VC, WebBD,
WebE&AL, WhoChL*
Dickens, Charles, Jr. 1837-1896 *Alli Sup, BbD,
BiD&SB, WebBD*
Dickenson, Fred 1909- *NF*
Dickenson, James R 1931- *ConAu 65*
Dickerman, Sherwood E *OvPC*
Dickerson, J A Spencer *HisAmM XR*

Dickerson, Nancy Hanschman 1930- *BioIn 8,*
ConAu 69, CurBio XR, ForWC 1970,
WhoAm 1974, WhoAmW 1974,
WhoS&SW 1973
Dickey, J W 1893?-1975 *BioIn 10*
Dickey, Carl C 1894- *HisAmM XR, OvPC,*
WhJnl 1928
Dickey, Fred *NF*
Dickey, John Wesley 1894- *WhJnl 1928*
Dickey, Maurice Woodburn 1878- *WhJnl 1928*
Dickey, Robert Livingston 1861-1944 *BioIn 2*
Dickey, W Laurence 1894- *WhNAA, WhJnl 1928*
Dickey, Walter Simpson 1862-1931 *AmJnl,*
BioIn 3
Dickie, John 1923- *ConAu 13R*
Dickins, Asbury *HisAmM XR*
Dickins, Elizabeth *HisAmM XR*
Dickins, John 1747-1798 *HisAmM XR*
Dickinson, A C 1864- *WhJnl 1928*
Dickinson, Albert Morton 1861?-1946 *BioIn 1*
Dickinson, Ashley Weed 1889?-1954 *BioIn 3*
Dickinson, Charles Monroe 1842-1924 *AmAu&B,*
DcAmA, DcAmB 5, DcNAA, WebBD
Dickinson, Clinton Roy 1888-1943 *AmAu&B,*
DcNAA
Dickinson, J J *HisAmM XR*
Dickinson, John 1732-1808 *Alli, AmAu,*
AmAu&B, AmJnl, BiD&SB, CyAL 1,
DcAmA, DcLEL, DcNAA, ForP,
HisAmM XR, OxAm, Pen Am, REnAL,
WebBD
Dickinson, Lois 1898?-1970 *BioIn 9*
Dickinson, Mabel *WhJnl Sup*
Dickinson, Porter 1906- *WhoAm 1974,*
WhoWest 1974
Dickinson, Richard William *HisAmM XR*
Dickinson, Samuel Henry *HisAmM XR*
Dickinson, Timothy *NF*
Dickinson, William Boyd 1908-1978 *RpN,*
WhoE 1974, WhoAm 1974
Dickinson, William Boyd, Jr. 1931- *WhoAm 1974,*
WhoS&SW 1973
Dickinson, William P *NF*
Dickman, Thelma *NF*
Dickson, Cecil B *NF*
Dickson, Dee *NF*
Dickson, Edward Augustus 1879-1956 *BioIn 1,*
BioIn 4, BioIn 6, WhJnl 1928
Dickson, Frazier 1906?-1978 *OvPC*
Dickson, Harris 1868- *AmAu&B, AmLY,*
BiDSA, DcAmA, WhNAA
Dickson, Paul 1939- *ConAu 33, WrDr 1976*
Dickson, Robert E 1900?-1947 *BioIn 1, RpN*
Didato, S V 1926- *NF*
Didier, Eugene Lemoine 1838-1913 *Alli Sup,*
AmAu, AmAu&B, BiD&SB, BiDSA,
DcAmA, DcNAA, HisAmM XR
Didier, John L *HisAmM XR*
Didion, Joan 1934- *AmAu&B, AuNews 1,*
ConAu 5R, ConLC 1, ConLC 3,
ConNov 1976, DrAF 1976, ModAL Sup,
WrDr 1976
Diebler, William *NF*
Dieck, Herman L 1873- *WhNAA, WhJnl 1928*
Diederich, Bernard 1926- *NF*
Dieffenbach, Albert Charles 1876-1963 *BioIn 6*
Diehl, Bill *NF*
Diehl, Charles Sanford 1854-1946 *AmAu&B,*
AmJnl, BioIn 1, TexWr
Diehl, Digby 1940- *ConAu 53*
Diehl, W W 1916- *ConAu 19R*
Diehm, Harold Frederic 1900- *WhJnl 1928*
Diehm, Victor Christian 1902- *OvPC,*
WhoAdv 1972, WhoAm 1974,

WhoAmP 1973, WhoE 1974, WhoF&I 1974
Dienstag, Eleanor 1938- *ConAu 65*
Dienstfrey, Harris David 1934- *WhoAm 1974*
Dierdorff, John Ainsworth 1928- *WhoAm 1974*
Dierks, Donald Arthur 1925- *WhoAm 1974*
Dieterich, George N 1860- *WhJnl 1928*
Dietrich, Frances *NF*
Dietrich, Harold *NF*
Dietrich, Otto 1897?-1952 *BioIn 3*
Dietsch, Robert William 1919- *WhoAm 1974*
Dietz, Cecil Eugene 1925- *WhoAm 1974,*
WhoF&I 1974
Dietz, David Henry 1897- *Au&Wr, BioIn 5,*
ConAu 1R, IntWW 1976, OhA&B, REnAL,
SmATA 10, WhoAm 1974, WhoWorJ 1972
Dietz, Lorna 1895?-1964 *BioIn 6*
Dietz, Peter Ernest 1878-1947 *BioIn 3*
Dietzgen, Eugene *AmRP*
Diez DeMedina, Raul 1914- *BioIn 1,*
IntWW 1974, WhoWor 1974
Digges, Jeremiah *see* Berger, Josef
Digges, Sam Cook 1916- *WhoAm 1974*
Diggs, Annie 1853-1916 *DcNAA*
Digilio, Don *NF*
DiIorio, Louis A *NF*
Dikshit, Umar Shankar 1901- *IntWW 1976*
Diles, Dave 1931- *ConAu 57*
Dilg, John *HisAmM XR*
Dilke, Sir Charles *HisAmM XR*
Dill, Alonzo Thomas 1914- *ConAu 37,*
DrAS 74H, WhoPubR 1972
Dill, Benjamin Franklin *AmJnl*
Dill, Clarence C 1884-1978 *WhoAmP 1973*
Dill, J B *AmJnl*
Dill, Leonard Carter, Jr. 1906-1974 *WhoAm 1974*
Dill, Robert *NF*
Dill, William A 1881- *WhJnl 1928*
Dillard, Annie 1945- *ConAu 49, DrAP 1975,*
SmATA 10, WrDr 1976
Dillard, Katherine Shannon Rawlings
WhoAm 1974, WhoAmW 1974,
WhoS&SW 1973
Dille, John Flint, Jr. 1913- *WhoAm 1974,*
WhoWor 1974
Dille, Robert Crabtree *WhoAm 1974,*
WhoF&I 1974
Dilliard, Irving 1904- *AmM&W 73S,*
ConAu 21R, HisAmM XR, RpN
Dillie, John M 1921?-1971 *BioIn 9*
Dillingham, Charles Bancroft 1868-1934 *AmAu&B,*
WebBD
Dillingham, John Hoag 1839-1910 *DcNAA,*
HisAmM XR
Dillman, Grant *NF*
Dillon, Charles 1873-1942 *AmAu&B, WhNAA*
Dillon, Donald 1914- *WhoAm 1974,*
WhoWor 1974
Dillon, Emile Joseph 1854-1933 *BioIn 2, WebBD*
Dillon, George 1906-1968 *AmAu&B,*
AnMV 1926, BioIn 4, BioIn 8, ConAmL,
DcLEL, HisAmM XR, OxAm, REn,
REnAL, TwCA, TwCA Sup, WebBD
Dillon, John A *NF*
Dillon, John Blake 1816-1866 *WebBD*
Dillon, John Irving 1870-1938 *HisAmM XR*
Dillon, John James 1856-1950 *BioIn 2*
Dillon, Philip Robert 1868- *AmAu&B,*
HisAmM XR
Dillon, Thomas Joseph 1878-1949 *AmAu&B,*
BioIn 3
Dillon, Walter Stanley 1893- *WhoAm 1974*
Dilnot, Frank 1875-1946 *BioIn 1*
Dilworth, Lloyd Lester 1900- *WhJnl 1928*
DiMaggio, Josie *BioIn 1*

Dimant, Abel *NF*
DiMaria, Gene *InvJ*
Dimbleby, David 1938?- *BioIn 8*
Dimbleby, Richard 1913-1965 *BioIn 6, BioIn 7*
Dimitry, Charles Patton J 1837-1910 *Alli Sup,
    AmAu&B, BbD, BiDSA, DcAmA,
    DcAmB 5, DcNAA, HisAmM XR*
Dimitry, John Bull Smith 1835-1901 *Alli Sup,
    BiDSA, DcAmA, DcNAA*
Dimmock, Frederick Hayden 1895-1955 *BioIn 8,
    WhoChL*
Dimon, William Bingham 1873- *WhJnl 1928*
Dimont, Madelon 1938- *ConAu 41*
D'Imperio, Dan *NF*
Dine, Joe *OvPC*
Dineen, Joseph Francis 1897-1964 *BioIn 6,
    WhNAA*
Dines, Alberto *ForP*
Ding *see* Darling, Jay Norwood
Ding, J N *see* Darling, Jay Norwood
Dingley, Edward Nelson 1862-1930 *DcNAA,
    NatCAB 21*
Dinh, LeKim *NF*
Dinhofer, A 1928- *ConAu 25*
Dininny, Paulette 1945- *NF*
Dinneen, Joseph Francis 1898- *BioIn 4*
Dinsmore, William Henry 1911- *WhoPubR 1972*
Dinwiddie, Donal 1919- *WhoAm 1974*
Dinwiddie, William 1867-1934 *DcNAA*
Dinwoodey, Dean 1899- *WhoAm 1974*
Dipman, Carl William 1889-1954 *BioIn 3*
Dippold, Mrs. J A 1881- *WhJnl 1928*
DiPreta, Tony *NF*
DiRaimondo, Gene *OvPC*
Direnberg, Suzanne 1929- *WhoAm 1974*
Dirks, Clarence 1903?- *BioIn 2*
Dirks, John 1916?- *BioIn 2*
Dirks, Rudolph 1877?-1968 *AmJnl, BioIn 2,
    BioIn 4, BioIn 8*
Disher, Leo S 1912?-1969 *BioIn 8*
Disney, Bud *NF*
Dissentshik, Aryeh 1907-1978 *WhoWor 1974*
Dithmar, Edward Augustus 1854-1917 *AmAu,
    AmAu&B, DcNAA, HisAmM XR*
Dittman, Marion Martha 1909- *BioIn 2,
    WhoAm 1974, WhoAmW 1974*
Dittmann, Laura L *BioIn 8*
Dittrick, Howard 1877-1954 *BioIn 3, OhA&B*
Ditzen, L Stuart *NF*
Diuguid, Lewis H *NF*
Divine, Arthur Durham 1904- *Au&Wr, DcLEL,
    Who 1974*
Divine, Charles 1889- *AmAu&B, AnMV 1926,
    WhNAA*
Divoire, Fernand 1883-1951 *OxFr, WebBD*
Divver, Patricia *NF*
Diwakar, Ranganath 1894- *IntWW 1976,
    WhoWor 1974*
Dix, Albert V *OvPC*
Dix, Dorothy 1870-1951 *AmAu&B, AmJnl,
    BiDSA, CurBio XR, DcAmB S5, OxAm,
    REn, REnAL, WebBD, WhNAA*
Dix, Dorothy *see also* Gilmer, Elizabeth Meriwether
Dix, Fred Keller 1891-1944 *OhA&B, WhNAA,
    WhJnl 1928*
Dix, John Ross *HisAmM XR*
Dix, Robert Clinton 1908- *WhoAm 1974,
    WhoMW 1974*
Dix, William Frederick 1867- *HisAmM XR*
Dixon, Bernard 1938- *ConAu 65, Who 1974*
Dixon, Campbell 1895-1960 *BioIn 5*
Dixon, Charles A *HisAmM XR*
Dixon, Franklin *NF*
Dixon, Frederick d1923 *AmJnl*

Dixon, Fritzie Williams *BioIn 3*
Dixon, George Hall 1900-1965 *BioIn 6, BioIn 7*
Dixon, Henry Hall 1822-1870 *Alli Sup, BioIn 2,
    Br&AmS, BrAu 19, NewC, WebBD*
Dixon, Jane 1882?-1960 *BioIn 5*
Dixon, Jeane L 1918- *ConAu 65, WhoAm 1974*
Dixon, John James 1910- *WhoAm 1974*
Dixon, John Morris 1933- *AmArch 1970,
    WhoAm 1974, WhoE 1974*
Dixon, Ken *NF*
Dixon, Margaret 1907?-1970 *BioIn 1, BioIn 8,
    NewYTBE 1*
Dixon, Willard J 1886- *WhJnl 1928*
Dixon, William Hepworth 1821-1879 *Alli,
    Alli Sup, BbD, BiD&SB, BrAu 19, CasWL,
    DcEnA, DcEnL, DcEuL, EvLB, NewC,
    WebBD*
Dixon, William J 1899?-1968 *BioIn 8*
Dixson, Owen *BioIn 7*
Djuric, N *NF*
Doak, Donn 1930- *ConAu 65*
Doan, Michael F 1942- *NF*
Doane, Augustus Sidney 1808-1852 *Alli,
    HisAmM XR*
Doane, Eugene *NF*
Doane, George Washington 1799-1859 *Alli,
    AmAu&B, BiD&SB, CyAL 2, DcAmA,
    DcNAA, HisAmM XR, PoChrch, REnAL,
    WebBD, WebE&AL*
Doane, William Croswell 1832-1913 *Alli Sup,
    AmAu&B, BiD&SB, DcAmA, DcNAA,
    HisAmM XR, WebBD*
Dobbin, Muriel *NF*
Dobbins, Charles Gordon 1908- *ConAu P-1,
    WhoAm 1974*
Dobbins, Del *NF*
Dobbins, Harry Thompson 1865- *WhNAA,
    WhJnl 1928*
Dobbins, James Joseph 1924- *WhoAm 1974,
    WhoWor 1974*
Dobbs, Farrell 1907- *AmRP, ConAu 49*
Dobbs, Greg 1946- *ConAu 65*
Dobbs, Kildare Robert Eric 1923- *CanWW 1972,
    WhoAm 1974*
Dobell, Byron Maxwell 1927- *AmAu&B,
    WhoAm 1974*
Dobie, Beatrice Tormey 1922- *OvPC,
    WhoAmW 1974*
Dobie, Charles Caldwell 1881-1943 *AmAu&B,
    DcNAA, HisAmM XR, OxAm, REnAL,
    TwCA, TwCA Sup, WebBD, WhNAA,
    WhJnl 1928*
Dobie, Wilma *ForWC 1970, OvPC*
Dobkin, Robert A *NF*
Dobler, William O 1926- *WhoAm 1974*
Dobrich, Walter 1945- *NF*
Dobrish, Cecelia M *NF*
Dobrolyubov, Nikolai Aleksandrovich 1836-1861
    *BiD&SB, CasWL, DcEuL, DcRusL, EuAu,
    EvEuW, Pen Eur, REn, WebBD*
Dobrowolski, Tomasz B 1914?-1976 *ConAu 65*
Dobson, George *NF*
Dobson, H *FamWC*
Dobyns, Lloyd *NF*
Dockery, Eva Hunt *WhNAA, WhJnl 1928*
Doclar, Ernest 1930- *NF*
Doctor, Powrie Vaux 1903-1971 *BioIn 9*
Dod, Charles Roger 1793-1855 *Alli, DcEnL*
Dodd, Allen R, Jr. *OvPC*
Dodd, Anna Bowman 1855-1929 *Alli Sup,
    BiD&SB, DcAmA, DcNAA*
Dodd, Edward Benton 1902- *BioIn 2, BioIn 5,
    BioIn 9, ConAu 25, ConAu 73,
    WhoAm 1974*

Dodd, Eugenia 1900- *WhJnl Sup*
Dodd, Frank Howard 1844-1916 *AmAu&B,*
  HisAmM XR, WebBD
Dodd, Frank S 1871- *WhJnl 1928*
Dodd, Moses S *HisAmM XR*
Dodd, Thomas *NewMr*
Dodd, William E, Jr. *AmRP*
Dodds, Alexander 1874-1920 *NF*
Dodds, Harold Willis 1889- *AmAu&B,*
  CurBio XR, IntWW 1974, WebBD,
  Who 1974, WhoAm 1974, WhoGov 1972
Doder, Dusko *NF*
Dodge, Clarence P 1877-1939 *NatCAB 30*
Dodge, Fred *NF*
Dodge, Homer Joseph 1891-1960 *OhA&B*
Dodge, Jacob Richards 1823-1902 *DcAmB 5,*
  OhA&B
Dodge, Joseph G 1898- *WhJnl Sup*
Dodge, Mary Abigail 1833-1896 *Alli Sup, AmAu,*
  AmAu&B, AmJnl, BbD, BiD&SB, DcAmA,
  DcEnL, DcNAA, HisAmM XR, OxAm,
  WebBD
Dodge, Mary Abigail see also Hamilton, Gail
Dodge, Mary Elizabeth Mapes 1831-1905 *Alli Sup,*
  AmAu, AmAu&B, BbD, BiD&SB, BioIn 5,
  BioIn 6, BioIn 8, CarSB, DcBiA,
  DcNAA, HisAmM XR, JBA 1934, LiJA,
  OxAm, REn, REnAL, WebBD, WhoChL
Dodge, Nathaniel Shatswell 1810-1874 *Alli Sup,*
  DcAmA, DcNAA
Dodge, Ossian E *HisAmM XR*
Dodge, Wendell Phillips 1883-1976 *AmAu&B,*
  ConAu 65, WhNAA, WhoAm 1974
Dodson, Angela 1951- *NF*
Dodson, Martha Ethel *WhJnl 1928*
Dodson, Reynolds *NF*
Doe, Charles Henry 1838-1900 *Alli Sup, DcAmA,*
  DcNAA
Doelling, Otto C *NF*
Doellken, Dieter E *NF*
Doerflinger, William Main 1910- *AmAu&B,*
  HisAmM XR, WhoAm 1974
Doerner, William R *NF*
Doesticks, Q K Philander 1831-1875 *AmAu,*
  AmAu&B, BiD&SB, DcAmA, DcEnL,
  DcNAA, WebBD
Doesticks, Q K Philander see also Thomson,
  Mortimer Neal
Doggett, Daniel Seth 1810-1880 *Alli Sup, BiDSA,*
  DcNAA, HisAmM XR
Doherty, Bill 1910- *BioIn 7*
Doherty, Daniel M *OvPC*
Doherty, Edward Joseph 1890-1975 *AmAu&B,*
  BioIn 1, BioIn 8, BkC 3, CathA 1930,
  ConAu 57, ConAu 65, WhoAm 1974
Doherty, Edward Joseph 1927- *WhoAm 1974*
Doherty, Frank *NF*
Doherty, Henry Latham 1870-1939 *AmJnl,*
  CurBio XR, OhA&B
Doherty, James F *NF*
Doherty, Jim *NF*
Doherty, Lawrence E *NF*
Doherty, Martin W 1899- *CathA 1930*
Doherty, Tom *NF*
Doherty, William H 1904?-1965 *BioIn 7*
Dohm, Ernst 1819-1883 *BiD&SB, WebBD*
Doidge, Sir Fredeick Widdowson 1884-1954 *BioIn 3*
Dokmo, Rolf Eugene 1904-1961 *NatCAB 49*
Dolan, Anthony R 1948- *ConAu 73*
Dolan, Daniel Leo 1895-1966 *BioIn 4, CurBio XR*
Dolan, Frank *NF*
Dolan, John Breed *OvPC*
Dolan, Peter A *NF*
Dolan, Thomas Paul 1919- *WhoAm 1974,*

WhoF&I 1974
Dolbeare, Harris M 1870-1938 *NatCAB 28*
Dolben, David 1935- *WhoAm 1974*
Dolbier, Maurice Wyman 1912- *AmAu&B,*
  AmAu&B, AuBYP, ConAu 65, CurBio XR,
  MorJA, WhoAm 1974
Dole, Jeremy H 1932- *BioIn 7, ConAu 17R*
Dole, Nathan Haskell 1852-1935 *Alli Sup,*
  AmAu&B, AmLY, BbD, BiD&SB, DcAmA,
  DcBiA, DcLEL, DcNAA, HisAmM XR,
  OxAm, REnAL, TwCA, TwCA Sup,
  WebBD, WhNAA
Doletsky, J G *NF*
Dolger, Jonathan 1938- *BioIn 8, WhoAm 1974*
Dolhenty, Edward D 1874- *WhJnl 1928*
Dolson, David *NF*
Dommen, Arthur John 1934- *ConAu 11R,*
  WhoAm 1974, WhoWor 1974
Domschcke, Bernhard 1827-1869 *BioIn 1,*
  BioIn 2, BioIn 5
Donaghey, Frederick 1865?-1937 *AmAu&B*
Donahey, James Harrison 1875-1949 *AmAu&B,*
  BioIn 1, BioIn 2, OhA&B
Donahey, William 1883-1970 *AuBYP, OhA&B,*
  WhNAA
Donahoe, Patrick 1811-1901 *AmAu&B, BioIn 1,*
  HisAmM XR
Donald, Sir Robert 1861-1933 *BioIn 2, Lor&LP*
Donald, William Henry 1875-1946 *BioIn 1,*
  CurBio XR, WebBD
Donaldson, Dorothy Mills 1900-1968 *BioIn 8*
Donaldson, Sam *NF*
Donaldson, Ulysses S *BioIn 2*
Donaldson, W H *NF*
Donas, Thalia *NF*
Donato, Andy *NF*
Donegal, Marquis *NF*
Donegan, Arthur Bruce *WhJnl 1928*
Donelson, Loren E 1903?-1965 *BioIn 7*
Doney, Thomas *HisAmM XR*
Doney, Walter Ferguson 1897- *WhJnl 1928*
Dong-Joon, Kim *NF*
Donhoff, Marion Grafin 1909- *BioIn 6, ForP,*
  WhoWor 1974
Donlevy, Harriet 1817-1907 *DcAmA, DcNAA*
Donley, Bettie Louis 1931- *NF*
Donlin, George Bernard *HisAmM XR*
Donlon, J Patrick *NF*
Donlon, Jack *NF*
Donnahoe, Alan Stanley 1916- *WhoAm 1974*
Donnell, Lloyd Hamilton 1895- *BioIn 6*
Donnelley, Dixon 1915- *BioIn 5, BioIn 7, OvPC,*
  WhoAm 1974, WhoGov 1972
Donnelly, Antoinette 1891?-1964 *BioIn 1,*
  BioIn 7, CurBio XR
Donnelly, Gerard B 1891-1950 *BioIn 2*
Donnelly, Harrison H *NF*
Donnelly, Ignatius 1831-1901 *Alli Sup, AmAu,*
  AmAu&B, BbD, BiD&SB, CasWL,
  DcAmA, DcEnA Ap, DcLEL, DcNAA,
  HisAmM XR, OxAm, Pen Am, PoIre,
  REnAL, WebBD, WebE&AL
Donnelly, J Louis *OvPC*
Donnelly, John B d1965 *NF*
Donnelly, Lucia Burbadge 1911-1975 *BioIn 10*
Donnelly, Tom *NF*
Donnelly, William d1885 *NF*
Donner, Frank J *NewMr*
Donner, Mrs. S A *HisAmM XR*
Donoho, William T, Jr. *OvPC*
Donohoe, Denis 1861-1924 *HisAmM XR*
Donohoe, Edward J *RpN*
Donohue, Edward F *WhJnl 1928*
Donohue, James Fitzgerald 1934- *ConAu 73*

Donovan, Hedley Williams 1914- *BioIn 6,*
BioIn 7, CurBio XR, HisAmM XR,
IntWW 1976, WhoAm 1974, WhoE 1974,
WhoWor 1974
Donovan, Leo 1903?-1957 *BioIn 4*
Donovan, Peter 1884- *BioIn 1, CanNov, OxCan*
Donovan, Robert John 1912- *AmAu&B, Au&Wr,*
BioIn 9, ConAu 1R, ForP, WhoAm 1974,
WhoWor 1974
Donovan-Tober, Barbara Maud 1934-
WhoAm 1974
Dooher, M Joseph 1913- *WhoAm 1974,*
WhoWor 1974
Dooley, A H d1903 *BioIn 2, IndAu 1816*
Dooley, Edmund James 1914- *WhoAm 1974*
Doolittle, Duane *NF*
Doolittle, Isaac *AmJnl*
Doolittle, Jerome 1933- *ConAu 53*
Doolittle, William *NF*
Dooly, Irma *NF*
Doorly, Edward 1873?-1952 *BioIn 2*
Doorly, Henry 1879-1961 *BioIn 1, BioIn 4,*
BioIn 5, BioIn 7, NatCAB 48, WhJnl 1928
Doorty, John C *OvPC*
Dopking, Al *NF*
Dopoulos, Philemon *NF*
Dopson, Roland *NF*
Dor-Ner, Zvi 1941?- *NF*
Doran, John 1807-1878 *Alli, Alli Sup, BbD,*
BiD&SB, BrAu 19, DcEnA, DcEnL, EvLB,
NewC, PoIre, WebBD
Dore, Arthur G 1891-1956 *BioIn 4*
Dorfman, Dan 1936- *WhoE 1974*
Dorfman, John 1947- *ConAu 69*
Dorfman, Nat N 1895-1977 *BiE&WWA,*
BiE&WWA, ConAu 73
Dorgan, Thomas Aloysius 1877-1929 *AmAu&B,*
BioIn 4, WebBD
Dorgan, Vincent N *WhJnl 1928*
Dorman, J Anderson *NF*
Dorman, Michael 1932- *ConAu 15R, SmATA 7,*
WrDr 1976
Dorman, Robert *NF*
Dorman, William K 1898- *WhJnl 1928*
Dornberg, John Robert 1931- *ConAu 3R,*
WrDr 1976
Dornfeld, Steven R *NF*
Dorr, Charles Henry *WhNAA, WhJnl 1928*
Dorr, Rheta Childe 1866-1948 *AmAu&B, AmJnl,*
HisAmM XR
Dorsett, Alton C *WhJnl 1928*
Dorsey, Charles Howard, Jr. 1904-1973 *BioIn 10,*
WhoAm 1974
Dorsey, Eugene Carroll 1927- *WhoAm 1974*
Dorsey, Thomas Brookshler 1928- *WhoAm 1974,*
WhoWor 1974
Dorsheimer, William Edward 1832-1888 *DcAmB 5*
Dorvillier, William Joseph 1908- *BioIn 5,*
WhoAm 1974
Dorweiler, Virgil Walter 1930- *DrAS 74E*
Dosch, Arno *AmJnl*
Dosch, Emmett A 1889- *WhJnl 1928*
Dosch-Fleurot, Arno Walter 1879-1951 *BioIn 2,*
HisAmM XR
Doss, Margot Patterson 1922- *SmATA 6,*
WrDr 1976
Dotson, John L, Jr. *BlkC*
Doty, Douglas Zabriskie 1874-1935 *AmAu&B,*
DcNAA, HisAmM XR
Doty, Laurence Lappin, Jr. 1912- *WhoAm 1974*
Doty, W L *HisAmM XR*
Douai, Adolf 1819-1888 *BioIn 2*
Doubleday, Frank Nelson 1862-1934 *AmAu&B,*
DcAmB S1, HisAmM XR, WebBD

Doucet, Cordelia *NF*
Dougall, John *HisAmM XR*
Dougall, John Redpath *NF*
Dougherty, Jocelyn *OvPC*
Dougherty, John L 1918- *RpN, WhoAm 1974,*
WhoE 1974
Dougherty, Philip H *NF*
Dougherty, Richard 1921- *AmAu&B, BioIn 9,*
ConAu 1R, WhoAm 1974
Dougherty, William *AmJnl*
Doughman, Margaret DeMille 1909?-1978 *NF*
Doughty, C Jack *NF*
Douglas, Carlyle C *NF*
Douglas, Charles Henry 1861-1954 *AmAu&B,*
BioIn 3, WhNAA
Douglas, Claude L 1901- *WhJnl 1928*
Douglas, Cy *NF*
Douglas, Frederick A 1860- *WhJnl 1928*
Douglas, George William 1863-1945 *AmAu&B,*
DcNAA, HisAmM XR, WhNAA,
WhJnl 1928
Douglas, John Harold 1931- *WhoAm 1974*
Douglas, Malcolm *HisAmM XR*
Douglas, Marjory Stoneman 1890- *AmAu&B,*
AuNews 2, ConAu 1R, CurBio XR,
ForWC 1970, SmATA 10
Douglas, Mary Stahlman *ForWC 1970*
Douglas, Robert *NF*
Douglas, Ted *NF*
Douglas, William Archer Sholto 1886-1951 *BioIn 2,*
WhNAA, WhJnl 1928
Douglass, Earl Leroy 1888-1972 *BioIn 9,*
WhoE 1974
Douglass, Elisha *NF*
Douglass, Ellwood *NF*
Douglass, Frederick 1817-1895 *Alli Sup, AmAu,*
AmAu&B, AmJnl, BbD, BiD&SB, BiDSA,
BlkAW, BlkC, DcAmA, DcAmB 5,
DcNAA, EncAB, HisAmM XR, OxAm,
REn, REnAL, WebBD, WebE&AL
Douglass, H Elwood 1900?-1969 *BioIn 8*
Douglass, Walter Raleigh 1893- *WhJnl 1928*
Doulens, Humphrey E 1907-1963 *BioIn 6*
Doumic, Rene 1860-1937 *CIDMEL,*
HisAmM XR, WebBD
Dounce, Harry Esty 1889-1957 *AmAu&B*
Dove, Alfred 1844-1916 *WebBD*
Dove, David James 1696?-1769 *AmAu&B,*
CyAL 1, DcNAA
Dove, Herschel 1869- *BioIn 2*
Dove, Ian *NF*
Dove, John 1872-1934 *BioIn 2*
Dovell, Ray C 1887?-1968 *BioIn 8*
Dover, N H *HisAmM XR*
Doviak, Robert F *OvPC*
Dovifat, Emil 1890- *BioIn 3*
Dow, Charles Henry 1851-1902 *BioIn 5, WebBD*
Dow, David *NF*
Dow, David McKenzie 1870-1953 *BioIn 3*
Dow, Harold 1947- *NF*
Dow, Harold B *OvPC*
Dow, Moses A 1810-1886 *AmAu&B,*
HisAmM XR
Dowd, Arthur Scott d1966 *BioIn 7*
Dowd, James Edward 1899-1966 *BioIn 7*
Dowd, Maxine E *NF*
Dowd, Merle E 1918- *NF*
Dowd, W C 1865-1927 *WhJnl 1928*
Dowd, William *NF*
Dowd, William Carey 1893-1949 *BioIn 3,*
NatCAB 38
Dowdey, Clifford Shirley, Jr. 1904- *ConAu 11R,*
WhoAm 1974
Dowdy, Earl *NF*

Dowe, Charles E d1904 *NF*
Dowell, Edwin E 1916- *OvPC, WhoPubR 1972*
Dower, Walter H 1884- *WhJnl 1928*
Dowling, Daniel Blair 1906- *BioIn 2, BioIn 3, WhoAm 1974, WhoAmA 1973*
Dowling, Ellen Condon 1905-1960 *BioIn 5*
Dowling, John Graham 1914-1955 *BioIn 3*
Dowling, Lyle R 1908?-1964 *BioIn 6*
Dowling, Robert J *NF*
Dowling, Thomas *NF*
Downe, Edward R, Jr. *WhoAm 1974, WhoF&I 1974*
Downer, George F 1885- *WhJnl 1928*
Downer, Henry E 1885?-1968 *BioIn 8*
Downes, Alfred Michael 1862-1907 *DcNAA*
Downes, Bruce 1899-1966 *BioIn 7*
Downes, Edmund William 1920- *WhoAm 1974, WhoE 1974*
Downes, Edwin Olin 1886-1955 *WebBD*
Downes, Edwin Olin *see also* Downes, Olin
Downes, Olin 1886-1955 *AmAu&B, CurBio XR, DcAmB S5*
Downes, Olin *see also* Downes, Edwin Olin
Downes, William Howe 1854-1941 *Alli Sup, AmAu&B, AmLY, BiD&SB, DcAmA, DcNAA, HisAmM XR, NatCAB 32, WhNAA*
Downey, Alan 1889- *BioIn 3, CathA 1952*
Downey, Barbara *NF*
Downey, Charles E 1944- *NF*
Downey, Fairfax Davis 1893- *AmAu&B, AmSCAP 1966, AuBYP, ConAu 1, OxCan, REnAL, SmATA 3, WebBD, WhNAA, WhoAm 1974, WrDr 1976*
Downey, Henry T *HisAmM XR*
Downey, Joseph Francis 1916- *WhoAm 1974*
Downie, Leonard, Jr. 1942- *ConAu 49, WrDr 1976*
Downing, Andrew Jackson 1815-1852 *Alli, AmAu, AmAu&B, BiD&SB, CyAL 2, DcAmA, DcNAA, HisAmM XR, WebBD*
Downing, Francis 1903?-1965 *BioIn 7*
Downing, Jack 1792-1868 *AmAu, CnDAL, DcAmA, DcNAA, WebBD*
Downing, Jack *see also* Downing, Major Jack
Downing, Jack *see also* Smith, Seba
Downing, Major Jack 1792-1868 *DcEnL, DcNAA, OxAm*
Downing, Major Jack *see also* Downing, Jack
Downing, Major Jack *see also* Smith, Seba
Downing, Robert *NF*
Downing, Robert 1914- *BiE&WWA*
Downs, Adam M *NF*
Downs, Christine *NF*
Downs, Frederick, Jr. *NF*
Downs, Kenneth T *OvPC*
Downs, Linda 1939- *NF*
Downs, William Randall, Jr. 1914-1978 *WhoAm 1974*
Downs, Winfield Scott 1895- *WhNAA, WhJnl 1928*
Dowst, Robert Saunders 1890-1959 *BioIn 5*
Doxey, William *HisAmM XR*
Doying, George Everett 1881?-1951 *BioIn 2*
Doyle, Alexander P 1857-1912 *HisAmM XR*
Doyle, Alvin D 1916?-1967 *BioIn 8*
Doyle, Bill *NF*
Doyle, Henry V 1897?-1952 *BioIn 3*
Doyle, James S *RpN*
Doyle, John *NF*
Doyle, Joseph Edward 1894?-1946 *BioIn 1*
Doyle, Mildred D *LiJA*
Doyle, Ray *NF*
Doyle, Richard 1824-1883 *Alli Sup, BioIn 10,*

DcEuL, NewC, WebBD
Doyle, Richard James 1923- *CanWW 1972, ConAu 65, WhoE 1974*
Doyle, Robert J 1918?-1950 *BioIn 2*
Doyle, T *FamWC*
Dr. Johnson 1709-1784 *WebBD*
Dragonwagon, Crescent 1952- *ConAu 65*
Drake, Alexander Wilson 1843-1916 *AmAu&B, DcNAA, HisAmM XR, WebBD*
Drake, Benjamin 1795?-1841 *Alli, AmAu, AmAu&B, BiD&SB, BiDSA, CyAL 1, DcAmA, DcNAA, OhA&B, WebBD*
Drake, Bruce *NF*
Drake, Charles *HisAmM XR*
Drake, Daniel 1785-1852 *Alli, AmAu&B, BiDSA, CyAL 1, DcAmA, DcNAA, HisAmM XR, OhA&B, OxAm, REnAL, WebBD*
Drake, Frances *NF*
Drake, Francis Vivian 1894-1971 *BioIn 2, BioIn 9, NewYTBE 2*
Drake, Frederic N 1887-1965 *NatCAB 51*
Drake, Galen *BioIn 1*
Drake, Harrington 1919- *WhoAm 1974*
Drake, J G *HisAmM XR*
Drake, John N *HisAmM XR*
Drake, Joseph Rodman 1795-1820 *Alli, AmAu, AmAu&B, BbD, BiD&SB, CnDAL, CyAL 1, DcAmA, DcLEL, DcNAA, EvLB, OxAm, Pen Am, REn, REnAL, WebBD*
Drake, Lee D 1882- *WhJnl 1928*
Drake, Samuel Gardner 1798-1875 *Alli, Alli Sup, AmAu, AmAu&B, BiD&SB, CyAL 1, DcAmA, DcNAA, HisAmM XR, OxCan, WebBD*
Drake, Stan *NF*
Drake, William A 1899-1965 *AmAu&B, OhA&B*
Drane, William L *AmJnl*
Drapeau, Stanislaus 1821-1893 *DcNAA*
Draper, Alfred 1924- *ConAu 33*
Draper, Arthur Stimson 1882-1963 *BioIn 6, HisAmM XR, WhNAA, WhJnl 1928*
Draper, Charles Hiram 1888- *WhNAA, WhJnl 1928*
Draper, E D *HisAmM XR*
Draper, George 1915?- *BioIn 5*
Draper, John 1702-1762 *AmAu&B, AmJnl, WebBD*
Draper, John Christopher 1835-1885 *Alli Sup, BiDSA, CyAL 2, DcAmA, DcNAA, HisAmM XR, WebBD*
Draper, Margaret Green 1750-1807 *WebBD*
Draper, Richard 1727-1774 *AmAu&B, AmJnl, WebBD*
Draper, Tom *NF*
Drath, Viola Herms 1926- *ConAu 65*
Draughon, Roland 1947- *BlkC*
Draut, George 1917?-1965 *BioIn 7*
Drawbell, James Wedgwood 1899- *Au&Wr, BioIn 5, BioIn 6, BioIn 8, ConAu 65, Who 1974*
Drayton, Grace Gebbie 1877-1936 *AmAu&B, AmLY, WhNAA*
Drebinger, John 1890- *BioIn 6*
Dreher, Carl 1896-1976 *ConAu 73, WhoWorJ 1972*
Dreier, Alex 1916- *BioIn 5, WhoAm 1974*
Dreier, Thomas 1884- *AmAu&B, WhNAA*
Dreiman, David B *RpN*
Dreiser, Theodore 1871-1945 *AmAu&B, AmLY, AmWr, AtlBL, CasWL, CnDAL, CnMD, CnMWL, ConAmA, ConAmL, CurBio XR, CyWA, DcAmA, DcAmB S3, DcBiA,*

DcLEL, DcNAA, EncMys, EncWL, EvLB,
HisAmM XR, IndAu 1816, LongC, ModAL,
ModAL Sup, ModWD, OxAm, OxEng,
Pen Am, RAdv 1, RComWL, REn, REnAL,
TwCA, TwCA Sup, TwCW, WebBD,
WebE&AL, WhNAA, WhoTwCL
Dresden, Donald *NF*
Dressel, Dick *NF*
Dresser, Clarence P *NF*
Dresser, Helen McCloy 1904- *Au&Wr,*
ConAu XR, ForWC 1970, OvPC
Dresser, Horatio Willis 1866-1954 *AmAu&B,*
AmLY, BiD&SB, DcAmA, HisAmM XR,
NatCAB 11
Dresser, Norm 1916- *NF*
Dressler, Louis Raphael 1861-1932 *BioIn 1*
Drew, Edwin C *HisAmM XR*
Drew, Elizabeth Brenner 1935- *BioIn 7, BioIn 9,*
BioIn 10, ForWC 1970, WhoAm 1974,
WhoS&SW 1973
Drew, Harris Eugene 1886- *WhJnl 1928*
Drew, Robert L *RpN*
Drewry, John Eldridge 1902- *AmAu&B,*
DrAS 74E, WhNAA, WhoAm 1974,
WhJnl 1928, WrDr 1976
Drews, Robert *NF*
Drexel, Anthony Joseph 1826-1893 *AmJnl,*
WebBD
Drexel, Constance 1888?-1956 *BioIn 4*
Drexel, Francis A d1885 *AmJnl*
Dreyer, Edward P 1910?-1950 *BioIn 2*
Dreyer, H Peter *OvPC*
Dreyer, Max 1862-1946 *CIDMEL, ModWD,*
OxGer, WebBD
Dreyfack, Raymond 1919- *ConAu 65*
Dreyfus, Carl *BioIn 2*
Dreyfus, John 1918- *BioIn 7*
Dreyfuss, John 1933- *NF*
Driberg, Thomas Edward Neil 1905-1976 *Au&Wr,*
BioIn 3, BioIn 7, ConAu 65, IntWW 1974,
Who 1974, WhoWor 1974, WrDr 1976
Driberg, Thomas Edward Neil *see also* Bradwell,
Baron Thomas E N
Drinkwater, Fred H 1871- *WhJnl 1928*
Drinkwater, Terry 1936- *ConAu 69*
Drips, William E 1890- *WhJnl 1928*
Driscoll, Charles Benedict 1885-1951 *AmAu&B,*
BioIn 1, BioIn 2, BioIn 3, REnAL,
WhNAA
Driscoll, Frederick 1830- *BbtC, DcNAA*
Driscoll, James Joseph 1870-1949 *BioIn 2*
Driscoll, Joseph 1902-1954 *AmAu&B, BioIn 3*
Driscoll, Peter 1942- *ConAu 49*
Driscoll, Ted *NF*
Driver, Archibald D 1879- *WhJnl 1928*
Driver, Christopher 1932- *ConAu 57*
Droch 1858-1941 *AmAu&B, AmLY XR,*
DcAmA, WhNAA
Droch *see also* Bridges, Robert
Drogheda, Earl Of 1910- *WhoAm 1974*
Drogin, Marc *NF*
Droit, Michel 1923- *ConAu 7R, IntWW 1976,*
WhoWor 1974
Droke, Maxwell 1896-1959 *BioIn 5, IndAu 1917*
Dromgoole, Fred H 1886- *WhJnl 1928*
Dromgoole, Joseph J 1898- *WhJnl 1928*
Dromgoole, Miss Will Allen 1860-1934 *AmAu&B,*
BiD&SB, BiDSA, DcAmA, DcNAA,
HisAmM XR, WhNAA
Dromgoole, Miss Will Allen *see also* Dromgoole,
William Allen
Dromgoole, William Allen 1860-1934 *DcAmB S1*
Dromgoole, William Allen *see also* Dromgoole, Miss
Will Allen

Drone, Eaton Sylvester 1842-1917 *Alli Sup,*
DcAmA, DcNAA
Drosnin, Michael *InvJ*
Drought, James William 1931- *WhoAm 1974*
Droz, Numa 1844-1899 *WebBD*
Drukker, Dow Henry 1872-1963 *BioIn 6, BioIn 7*
Drukker, Dow Henry, Jr. 1903- *WhoAm 1974*
Drukker, Hazel 1882-1949 *BioIn 1*
Drukker, Richard 1906-1973 *BioIn 9,*
NewYTBE 4
Drummie, T F *NF*
Drummond, Charlotte B d1977 *NF*
Drummond, Dorothy *see* Grafly, Dorothy
Drummond, Geoffrey 1930?-1971 *BioIn 9*
Drummond, John Milton 1880- *WhJnl 1928*
Drummond, Roscoe 1902- *AmJnl, BioIn 2,*
BioIn 3, CurBio XR, ForP, IntWW 1974,
WhoAm 1974, WhoS&SW 1973,
WhoWor 1974
Drummond, William J 1946?- *BlkC*
Drumont, Edouard 1844-1917 *BioIn 8, OxFr*
Drury, Allen Stuart 1918- *ConAu 57,*
IntWW 1974, Who 1974, WhoAm 1974,
WhoWor 1974
Drury, K C *NF*
Drury, Wells 1851-1932 *AmLY, BioIn 1,*
DcNAA
Dryansky, Gerald Y *ConAu 49*
Dryden, Harold A 1894- *WhJnl 1928*
Dryden, Helen *HisAmM XR*
Dryden, Ralph Waldo 1899- *WhJnl 1928*
Dryfoos, Orvil Eugene 1912-1963 *BioIn 5,*
BioIn 6, BioIn 7, CurBio XR, InvJ
Drysdale, Andrew P 1936?- *NF*
Drysdale, William 1852-1901 *Alli Sup, BiD&SB,*
BiDLA, CarSB, DcAmA, DcNAA
Duane, William 1760-1835 *Alli, AmAu&B,*
AmJnl, BioIn 7, CyAL 1, DcAmA,
DcAmB 5, DcNAA, HisAmM XR, OxAm,
WebBD
Dubas, Danielle 1949- *NF*
Dubin, Reggi Ann *OvPC*
DuBois, David Graham 1925- *ConAu 65*
DuBois, Eugene 1911- *OvPC, WhoPubR 1972*
DuBois, Guy Pene 1884-1958 *AmAu&B,*
CurBio XR, DcCAA, WebBD
DuBois, James T 1851-1920 *DcNAA,*
HisAmM XR
Dubois, Jules 1910-1966 *BioIn 4, BioIn 5,*
BioIn 7
DuBois, Patterson 1847-1917 *DcNAA*
DuBois, William Edward Burghardt 1868-1963
AmAu&B, BiDSA, BioIn 1, BioIn 2,
BioIn 3, BioIn 4, BioIn 5, BioIn 6, BioIn 7,
BioIn 8, BioIn 9, BioIn 10, BlkAW, BlkC,
CasWL, ConAmL, ConLC 1, ConLC 2,
DcAmA, DcLEL, HisAmM XR, LongC,
OxAm, Pen Am, REn, REnAL, TwCA,
TwCA Sup, WebBD, WebE&AL, WhNAA,
WhJnl 1928
DuBose, Horace Mellard 1858-1941 *BiDSA,*
CurBio XR, DcNAA, HisAmM XR
Duc, Mai Van *NF*
DuCamp, Maxime 1822-1894 *BiD&SB, BioIn 3,*
BioIn 7, OxFr, WebBD
Ducas, Dorothy 1905- *AuBYP, BioIn 8,*
ConAu 5R, ForWC 1970, OvPC,
WhoAmW 1974, WhoE 1974
Duche, Jean 1915- *Au&Wr, ConAu 9R*
Duchemin, Henry Pope 1874-1950 *BioIn 2,*
WhJnl 1928
Duchesne, Pere 1755-1794 *WebBD*
Duchesne, Pere *see also* Hebert, Jacques Rene
Duchovny, Moshe 1901?-1960 *BioIn 5*

DuCloe, Chester H 1902- *WhJnl 1928*
Duclot, Louis *NF*
Ducommun, Elie 1833-1906 *BioIn 9, WebBD*
Dudgeon, Farnham Francis 1912- *WhoAm 1974, WhoS&SW 1973*
Dudley, Bide 1877-1944 *AmAu&B, CurBio XR, WhNAA, WhJnl 1928*
Dudley, Bide *see also* Dudley, Walter Bronson
Dudley, Bruce 1894- *WhJnl 1928*
Dudley, Edith Sabra 1892?-1967 *BioIn 8*
Dudley, Helen *HisAmM XR*
Dudley, R L *WhJnl 1928*
Dudley, Walter Bronson 1877-1944 *AmAu&B, AmSCAP 1966, CurBio XR, WhNAA*
Dudley, Walter Bronson *see also* Dudley, Bide
Dudman, Richard Beebe 1918- *InvJ, RpN, WhoAm 1974, WhoS&SW 1973*
Duell, Wally *NF*
Duer, Caroline King 1865-1956 *BioIn 3, BioIn 4*
Duer, Carolyn *HisAmM XR*
Duer, Elizabeth *HisAmM XR*
Duerson, M K 1872- *WhJnl 1928*
Duff, Annis *BioIn 5*
Duff, Ashton d1923 *NF*
Duff, Jim *NF*
Duff, William Alexander 1872-1950 *OhA&B, WhJnl 1928*
Duffee, Warren Sadler 1917-1967 *BioIn 8*
Duffield, Eugene Schulte 1908-1974 *BioIn 10, WhoAm 1974, NewYTBDS 5*
Duffield, Marcus 1903?-1973 *BioIn 9*
Duffield, Pitts 1869-1938 *AmAu&B*
Duffus, Louis *BioIn 8*
Duffus, Robert Luther 1888-1972 *AmAu&B, AmNov, Au&Wr, ConAu 37, HisAmM XR, NewYTBE 3, REnAL, TwCA, TwCA Sup*
Duffus, Roy *OvPC*
Duffy, Charles G 1899?-1952 *BioIn 3*
Duffy, Sir Charles Gavan 1816-1903 *Alli Sup, BrAu 19, EvLB, NewC, OxEng, Pen Eng, PoIre, WebBD*
Duffy, Christopher Richard 1873-1949 *BioIn 1*
Duffy, E E 1900- *WhJnl 1928*
Duffy, Edmund 1899-1962 *AmAu&B, BioIn 1, BioIn 5, BioIn 6, CurBio XR, WebBD*
Duffy, Edward P *NF*
Duffy, James Edmund 1881-1969 *BioIn 8*
Duffy, John 1915- *ConAu 19, DrAS 74H*
Duffy, Martha M *NF*
Duffy, Martin *NF*
Duffy, Richard 1873-1949 *DcNAA, HisAmM XR*
Duffy, Ward Everett 1891-1961 *BioIn 5, BioIn 7, NatCAB 48*
Dufresne, Frank 1895?-1966 *BioIn 7, WhNAA*
Dufty, William 1916- *ConAu 65*
Dugan, George 1909- *OvPC, WhoAm 1974*
Dugan, Thomas J 1866-1926 *WhJnl Sup, WhJnl 1928*
Duganne, Augustine Joseph Hickey 1823-1884 *Alli, Alli Sup, AmAu, AmAu&B, BiD&SB, DcAmA, DcNAA, HisAmM XR, HsB&A, OxAm, REnAL*
Dugat, Gentry 1895- *TexWr, WhNAA, WhJnl 1928*
Dugdale, Blanche Elizabeth Campbell d1948 *BioIn 1, BioIn 10*
Dugdale, Robert Iliff 1868-1956? *BioIn 5*
Duggan, Eileen 1900?-1952 *BioIn 2*
Dugger, Ronnie 1930- *BioIn 7, ConAu 21R, NewMr*
Duhamel, P Albert 1920- *ConAu 5*
Dujardin, Edouard 1861-1949 *BioIn 1, BioIn 9, LongC, NewC, OxFr, REn, WebBD*

Duke, Basil Wilson 1838-1916 *Alli Sup, BiDSA, DcNAA, HisAmM XR*
Duke, Ellen 1911?-1969 *BioIn 8*
Duke, Forrest 1918- *NF*
Duke, John *see* Chalmers, Floyd Sherman
Duke, Maurice 1934- *DrAS 74E*
Duke, Robert *NF*
Duke, W Charles 1885- *WhJnl 1928*
Dukes, Ofield 1932- *WhoPubR 1972*
Dukes, Sir Paul 1889-1967 *BioIn 2, BioIn 8, WhoLA*
Dulles, Foster Rhea 1900-1970 *AmAu&B, ConAu 13, ConAu 29, ConAu P-1, NewYTBE 1, OhA&B, TwCA Sup*
Dulye, Raymond J *OvPC*
Dumas, Georges 1866-1946 *WebBD*
Dumas, Sir Lloyd 1891-1973 *BioIn 9*
DuMaurier, George Louis Palmella Busson 1834-1896 *BbD, BiD&SB, BrAu 19, CasWL, CyWA, DcBiA, DcEuL, DcLEL, EvLB, HisAmM XR, MouLC 4, NewC, OxEng, Pen Eng, RAdv 1, REn, WebBD*
Dumay, Henri *HisAmM XR*
DuMond, F V *HisAmM XR*
Dumont, Pierre Etienne Louis 1759-1829 *BioIn 2, EvEuW, WebBD*
Dumouriez, Charles *ForP*
Dun, John Davis 1891- *OhA&B*
Dun, Robert Graham 1826-1900 *HisAmM XR, WebBD*
Dunagin, Ralph *NF*
Dunaway, Phillip 1911?-1957 *BioIn 4*
Dunaway, Vic *NF*
Dunbar, C A *NF*
Dunbar, Charles Franklin 1830-1900 *AmJnl, DcAmA, DcNAA, HisAmM XR, WebBD*
Dunbar, Ernest 1927- *BioIn 9, BlkC, ConAu 25, WhoE 1974*
Dunbar, James 1833- *Alli, Alli Sup, BbtC*
Dunbar, Rudolph 1907- *BioIn 1, CurBio XR, WhoMus 1972*
Duncan, David Douglas 1916- *AmJnl, AuNews 1, BioIn 8, BioIn 9, CurBio XR, WhoAm 1974, WhoWor 1974*
Duncan, Donald 1914-1965 *BioIn 7*
Duncan, Gerald 1903-1970 *BioIn 8*
Duncan, Hall *BioIn 9*
Duncan, Hobert Edward 1927- *WhoAm 1974, WhoWest 1974*
Duncan, John *HisAmM XR*
Duncan, Kunigunde 1886- *AmAu&B, ConAu 7R, WhNAA*
Duncan, Marilyn I 1946?- *BlkC*
Duncan, Matthew *AmJnl*
Duncan, Norman 1871-1916 *AmAu&B, CanWr, DcAmA, DcLEL, DcNAA, JBA 1934, JBA 1951, OhA&B, OxCan, REnAL, YABC 1*
Duncan, Patrick B 1918-1967 *BioIn 7*
Duncan, Sara Jeannette 1862-1922 *CanWr, DcLEL, DcNAA, OxCan*
Duncan, Sara Jeannette *see also* Cotes, Sara Jeannette
Duncan, T C *Alli Sup, HisAmM XR*
Duncan, Thomas William 1905- *AmAu&B, AmNov, ConAu 1, CurBio XR, HisAmM XR, REnAL, WhoAm 1974*
Duncan-Clark, Samuel John 1875-1938 *DcNAA*
Duneka, Frederick A *NF*
Dungan, Hubert Leo 1878- *WhJnl 1928*
Dunham, Bert H 1887- *WhJnl 1928*
Dunham, Corydon Bushnell 1927- *WhoAm 1974*
Dunham, Curtis *HisAmM XR*
Dunham, Harold H 1903- *WhJnl 1928*

Dunham, Robert 1931- *ConAu 69*
Dunham, Samuel Clarke 1855-1920 *DcNAA*
Dunham, Stuart A 1920- *WhoE 1974*
Dunisveld, Johannus 1944-1970 *BioIn 9*
Duniway, Abigail Scott 1834-1915 *AmAu&B,*
   HisAmM XR
Dunkel, Courtney *NF*
Dunkel, Richard Hadley 1933- *ConAu 73*
Dunkleberger, Alvand C 1907- *WhoAm 1974,*
   WhoS&SW 1973
Dunkley, Charles Willis 1887-1957 *BioIn 3,*
   BioIn 4
Dunlap, John 1747-1812 *AmAu&B, AmJnl,*
   WebBD
Dunlap, John Robertson 1857-1937 *BioIn 7*
Dunlap, Laura 1855-1947 *DcNAA*
Dunlap, Orrin E 1861?-1953 *BioIn 3*
Dunlap, Orrin Elmer, Jr. 1896-1970 *AmAu&B,*
   ConAu P-1, NewYTBE 1
Dunlap, William 1766-1839 *Alli, AmAu,*
   AmAu&B, AmJnl, BbD, BiD&SB, BiDLA,
   CasWL, CnDAL, CnThe, CyAL 1, DcAmA,
   DcNAA, EvLB, HisAmM XR, LiJA,
   McGWD, OxAm, Pen Am, REnAL,
   REnWD, WebBD, WebE&AL
Dunleavy, Steve *NF*
Dunlop, Joseph R 1844- *NatCAB 1*
Dunlop, Laura 1855-1947 *BioIn 1*
Dunlop, Richard 1921- *ConAu 17, WrDr 1976*
Dunn, A M *HisAmM XR*
Dunn, Al M 1875-1957 *NatCAB 43*
Dunn, Alan Cantwell 1900-1974 *AmAu&B,*
   BioIn 10, ConAu 33, ConAu 49
Dunn, Arthur Wallace 1859-1926 *BioIn 9,*
   DcNAA
Dunn, Bob *NF*
Dunn, Byron Archibald 1842-1923? *AmAu&B,*
   AmLY, BioIn 4, DcAmA, DcNAA,
   NatCAB 39
Dunn, Charles, Jr. *HisAmM XR*
Dunn, Charles Gwyllym 1885?-1967 *BioIn 8*
Dunn, D D 1898- *WhJnl 1928*
Dunn, Donald H 1929- *ConAu 33*
Dunn, Elizabeth *BioIn 3*
Dunn, Hampton 1916- *ConAu 57*
Dunn, James Joseph 1920- *WhoAdv 1972,*
   WhoAm 1974, WhoF&I 1974, WhoWor 1974
Dunn, John *NF*
Dunn, John Francis 1926- *WhoAm 1974*
Dunn, John Howard 1894- *WhJnl 1928*
Dunn, Joseph Willcox 1899?- *BioIn 5*
Dunn, Joseph Willcox, Jr. 1937- *WhoAm 1974,*
   WhoS&SW 1973
Dunn, Martin T 1879?-1968 *BioIn 8*
Dunn, Oscar 1844-1885 *DcNAA, OxCan*
Dunn, Philip G *NF*
Dunn, Samuel Orace 1877-1958 *BioIn 1, BioIn 2,*
   BioIn 4, BioIn 6, HisAmM XR,
   NatCAB 43, WebBD
Dunn, Tom *OvPC*
Dunn, William J 1906- *ConAu 33, IndAu 1917*
Dunne, Finley Peter 1867-1936 *AmAu&B, AmJnl,*
   BiD&SB, CathA 1930, ConAmL, DcAmA,
   DcAmB S2, DcLEL, DcNAA, EncAB,
   EvLB, HisAmM XR, LongC, OxAm,
   OxEng, Pen Am, REn, REnAL, TwCA,
   TwCA Sup, WebBD
Dunne, Nancy *NF*
Dunnell, Milt *NF*
Dunnett, Alastair MacTavish 1908- *Au&Wr,*
   ConAu 65, IntWW 1976, Lor&LP,
   Who 1974, WhoWor 1974
Dunning, Abigail Scott *HisAmM XR*
Dunning, Albert Elijah 1844-1923 *Alli Sup,*

AmAu&B, DcAmA, DcNAA, HisAmM XR,
   NatCAB 13
Dunning, Bruce 1940- *NF*
Dunning, Bruce Gardner *OvPC*
Dunning, Silas W 1838-1924 *NatCAB 20*
Dunning, William Archibald 1857?-1922
   AmAu&B, DcAmA, DcNAA, HisAmM XR,
   WebBD
Dunningan, Alice 1906- *BioIn 6*
Dunphy, Harry *NF*
Dunraven, Wyndham T Wyndham-Quin, Earl
   1841-1926 *BioIn 7, BioIn 9, HisAmM XR*
Dunscomb, Charles Ellsworth 1868-1938
   WhJnl 1928
Dunsmore, Barrie *NF*
Dunstan, Reginald 1914- *ConAu 21R*
Dunster, Edward Swift *HisAmM XR*
Dunton, John 1659-1733 *Alli, BrAu, CyAL 1,*
   DcEnL, DcNAA, NewC, OxAm, OxEng,
   REnAL, WebBD
Dupee, F W 1904-1979 *AmRP, ConAu 13*
Dupont, Ewald Andre 1891-1956 *NF*
Dupont, Kedma *WhJnl 1928*
Dupuch, Sir Etienne 1899- *BioIn 8, Who 1974*
Dupuch, Etienne, Jr. 1931- *WhoWor 1974*
Dupuis, Paul *NF*
Dupuy, Frank Russell, Jr. 1907- *WhoAm 1974*
Dupuy, Helen d1951 *BioIn 2*
Dupuy, Jean 1844-1919 *WebBD*
DuPuy, William Atherton 1876-1941 *AmAu&B,*
   AmLY, CurBio XR, DcNAA, WhNAA,
   WhJnl 1928
Duquet, Joseph Norbert 1828-1891 *BbtC, DcNAA,*
   OxCan
Durand, John 1822-1908 *Alli Sup, DcNAA,*
   HisAmM XR
Durand, Lionel 1921-1961 *BioIn 5*
Durant, Kenneth 1889-1972 *BioIn 9,*
   NewYTBE 3
Durant, William d1903 *NF*
Durante, Albert Joseph 1915- *OvPC,*
   WhoAdv 1972, WhoPubR 1972
Duranty, Walter 1884-1957 *AmAu&B, AmJnl,*
   BioIn 4, BioIn 5, CurBio XR, HisAmM XR,
   OxAm, REnAL, TwCA, TwCA Sup,
   WebBD
Durbin, Karen *NF*
Durboraw, Raymond H *HisAmM XR*
Durden, Robert Franklin 1925- *ConAu 9,*
   HisAmM XR, WrDr 1976
Durdin, Frank Tillman 1907- *OvPC,*
   WhoAm 1974, WhoE 1974
Durdin, Frank Tillman *see also* Durdin, Tillman
Durdin, Tillman 1907- *RpN*
Durdin, Tillman *see also* Durdin, Frank Tillman
Durein, Ted 1909- *BioIn 9*
Durell, William *AmJnl*
Duren, William Larkin 1870- *AmAu&B*
Durgin, Don 1924- *IntMPA 1975, WhoAdv 1972,*
   WhoAm 1974
Durham, Howard *HisAmM XR*
Durham, Maynard Lee 1902- *WhJnl 1928,*
   WhoMW 1974
Durham, Michael *NF*
Durham, Richard 1922?- *BioIn 8*
Duricka, John *NF*
Durivage, Francis Alexander 1814-1881 *Alli,*
   Alli Sup, AmAu, AmAu&B, BiD&SB,
   DcAmA, DcAmB 5, DcNAA, HisAmM XR
Durivage, John E *NF*
Durkin, Jim *NF*
Durkin, Martin T 1881-1931 *NatCAB 23*
Durling, Edgar Vincent 1893-1957 *BioIn 4*
Durniak, John *NF*

Durno, George E 1902?-1957 *BioIn 4*
Durrah, Joseph F 1890- *WhJnl 1928*
Durrant, Digby 1926- *ConAu 21R*
Durrell, William *BioIn 4*
Durrenmatt, Peter Ulrich 1904- *IntWW 1976,*
WhoWor 1974
Durslag, Melvin 1921- *WhoAm 1974,*
WhoWest 1974
Durso, Joe *NF*
Durstine, Roy Sarles 1886-1962 *AmAu&B*
Durston, John Hurst 1848-1929 *NF*
Duscema, John *NF*
Duscha, Julius Carl 1924- *ConAu 73, RpN,*
WhoAm 1974, WhoS&SW 1973
DuShane, Graham 1910-1963 *BioIn 8,*
NatCAB 50
Dusky, Lorraine *NF*
DuSolle, John S *HisAmM XR*
Dusseck, Jacques *NF*
D'Utassy, George 1871?-1953 *BioIn 3,*
HisAmM XR
Dutkin, Howard L *NF*
Dutourd, Jean Hubert 1920- *ConAu 65*
DuTremblay, Pamphile-Real 1879-1955
WhJnl 1928
Dutriz, Jose *ForP*
Dutt, Romesh Chunder 1848-1909 *Alli Sup,*
BioIn 7, BioIn 9, BrAu 19, CasWL, DcLEL
Dutton, C P 1857- *WhJnl 1928*
Dutton, Davis M *NF*
Dutton, James R W *OvPC*
Dutton, Nan *BioIn 2*
Dutton, Samuel William Southmayd 1814-1866
DcNAA, HisAmM XR
Duus, Ole *NF*
Duvall, Jed *NF*
Duvergier DeHauranne, Prosper 1798-1881 *WebBD*
Duveyoung, Edward *NF*
Duwaerts, Leon-Louis 1905- *IntWW 1976,*
WhoWor 1974
Duyckinck, Evert Augustus 1816-1878 *Alli,*
Alli Sup, AmAu, AmAu&B, BbD, BiD&SB,
CyAL 2, DcAmA, DcEnL, DcNAA,
HisAmM XR, LiJA, OxAm, REnAL,
WebBD
Duyckinck, George Long 1823-1863 *Alli, Alli Sup,*
AmAu, AmAu&B, BbD, BiD&SB, CyAL 2,
DcAmA, DcNAA, HisAmM XR, Pen Am,
REnAL, WebBD
Dvorak, Bill *NF*
Dvorak, John 1948- *NF*
Dwiggins, Clare Victor 1874?-1958 *BioIn 5*
Dwight, Francis 1808-1845 *HisAmM XR*
Dwight, Harrison Griswold 1875-1959 *AmAu&B,*
HisAmM XR, WebBD, WhNAA
Dwight, Henry Otis 1843-1917 *Alli Sup,*
AmAu&B, DcAmA, DcNAA, WebBD
Dwight, James H *HisAmM XR*
Dwight, John Sullivan 1813-1893 *Alli, Alli Sup,*
AmAu, AmAu&B, BbD, BiD&SB, BioIn 1,
BioIn 2, BioIn 4, BioIn 6, BioIn 10,
DcAmA, DcNAA, HisAmM XR, OxAm,
REnAL, WebBD
Dwight, Marvin 1880- *WhJnl 1928*
Dwight, Minnie 1873-1957 *BioIn 4*
Dwight, Theodore 1764-1846 *Alli, AmAu,*
AmAu&B, BiD&SB, CyAL 1, DcAmA,
DcNAA, OxAm, REn, REnAL, WebBD
Dwight, Theodore 1796-1866 *AmAu&B,*
HisAmM XR, NatCAB 11, WebBD
Dwight, William 1903- *BioIn 4, WhoAm 1974*
Dwight, William, Jr. 1929- *WhoAm 1974,*
WhoE 1974
Dwinell, Harriet Douty *NF*

Dwinell, Melvin 1825-1887 *DcNAA*
Dwire, Henry Rudolph 1882-1944 *HisAmM XR*
Dworkin, Andrea *NF*
Dworshak, Henry C 1894-1962 *CurBio XR*
Dwyer, Charles d1916 *HisAmM XR*
Dwyer, Ed 1948?- *BioIn 10*
Dwyer, James Francis 1874- *AmAu&B,*
HisAmM XR
Dwyer, Michael T 1876- *WhJnl 1928*
Dwyer, Patrick 1875-1954 *BioIn 3, BioIn 5,*
WhJnl 1928
Dwyer, William Michael 1916- *OvPC,*
WhoE 1974
Dyar, Warren 1887- *WhJnl 1928*
Dyche, Russell 1884-1959 *BioIn 7, NatCAB 47*
Dyckman, Martin *InvJ*
Dye, Homer A, Jr. *WhJnl 1928*
Dye, John C 1888- *WhJnl 1928*
Dyer, George Bell 1903-1978 *AmAu&B,*
AmM&W 73S, WhNAA, WhoAm 1974,
WhoE 1974, WhoWor 1974
Dyer, George C *HisAmM XR*
Dyer, Herman d1900 *HisAmM XR*
Dyer, Louis 1851-1908 *AmAu, AmAu&B,*
DcAmA, DcNAA, HisAmM XR
Dyer, Oliver 1824-1907 *DcAmA, DcNAA,*
NatCAB 3
Dyer, Theresa E *HisAmM XR*
Dyer, W Earl, Jr. 1927- *NF*
Dyer, Walter Alden 1878-1943 *AmAu&B, AmLY,*
DcNAA, HisAmM XR, WhNAA
Dyer, William Allan, Jr. 1902- *WhoAm 1974,*
WhoF&I 1974
Dygert, James Herbert 1934- *ConAu 65*
Dykinga, Jack William 1943- *WhoAm 1974,*
WhoMW 1974
Dyment, Clifford 1914-1971 *Au&Wr, ConAu 33,*
ConAu P-1, ConP 1970
Dyment, Colin Victor 1879-1928 *BioIn 4,*
NatCAB 40
Dynan, Joseph E 1912?-1974 *NewYTBS 5, OvPC*
Dysart, Margaret *NF*
Dyson, Verne 1879- *AmAu&B*
Dyson, William Henry 1880-1938 *BioIn 2,*
WebBD
Dystel, Oscar 1912- *BioIn 1, OvPC,*
WhoAm 1974

E

Eade, Charles 1903-1964 *BioIn 7*
Eady, Allen *NF*
Eager, George T 1886-1957 *NatCAB 50*
Eagle, Dean 1920- *WhoAm 1974*
Eagle, Edward E *HisAmM XR*
Eagle, John 1875- *WhJnl 1928*
Eagle, Solomon 1884-1958 *LongC, NewC, WebBD*
Eagle, Solomon *see also* Squire, Sir John Collings
Eaker, Ira Clarence 1896- *AmAu&B, CurBio XR, WebBD, Who 1974*
Eakin, Wallace C 1893- *WhJnl 1928*
Eakins, Joseph J *NF*
Eales, Roy *NF*
Eames, Charles *HisAmM XR*
Eames, Hugh F 1890- *WhJnl 1928*
Earl, Edwin T d1919 *NF*
Earl, Johnrae 1919?-1978 *NF*
Earl, Lawrence 1915- *Au&Wr, ConAu 9R*
Earle, John M 1794-1874 *NatCAB 11*
Earle, L H *HisAmM XR*
Earley, E N *NF*
Early, Eleanor d1969 *AmAu&B, CathA 1952, TwCA Sup, WhNAA*
Early, Eugene E 1889-1956 *BioIn 4*
Early, John *NF*
Early, Joseph J 1881?-1949 *BioIn 2*
Early, Maurice 1889-1954 *BioIn 3*
Early, Robert Paul 1905- *WhoAm 1974*
Early, Robert R *NF*
Early, Stephen Tyree 1889-1951 *BioIn 2, BioIn 3, BioIn 4, BioIn 6, BioIn 8, CurBio XR, DcAmB S5, WebBD*
Earnshaw, Kirk Alfred 1909-1949 *BioIn 1, BioIn 2*
Earp, Thomas *NF*
Easley, John F 1872- *WhJnl 1928*
East, Ben 1898- *ConAu 33*
East, Clyde H 1899- *WhNAA, WhJnl 1928*
East, P D 1921- *BioIn 4, BioIn 5, ConAu 1*
East, Pearl M 1898- *WhJnl 1928*
East, William H 1906- *WhJnl 1928*
Easterline, Harry Dony 1901- *WhJnl 1928*
Eastham, Thomas 1923- *WhoAm 1974, WhoWest 1974*
Eastland, Warren Charles 1884- *WhJnl 1928*
Eastman, Charles Gamage 1816-1860 *Alli, AmAu&B, BbD, BiD&SB, CyAL 2, DcAmA, DcAmB 5, DcNAA, REnAL, WebBD*
Eastman, Crystal 1881-1928 *NF*
Eastman, Dave *NF*
Eastman, Edward Roe 1885- *ConAu 13, ConAu P-1, HisAmM XR, WhNAA, WhJnl 1928*
Eastman, Max Forrester 1883-1969 *AmAu&B,*

AmRP, BioIn 1, BioIn 2, BioIn 4, BioIn 5, BioIn 6, BioIn 8, BioIn 9, BioIn 10, ConAu 11R, ConAu 25, CurBio XR, HisAmM XR, WebBD
Eastman, Roe Stephenson 1885?-1956 *BioIn 4*
Easton, Carol 1933- *ConAu 65*
Easton, Edward 1907?-1964 *BioIn 7*
Eaton, Amherst *WhJnl 1928*
Eaton, Anne Thaxter 1881-1971 *AmAu&B, NewYTBE 2*
Eaton, Charles Aubrey 1868-1953 *CurBio XR, DcAmB S5*
Eaton, Earle Hooker 1865?-1950 *BioIn 2*
Eaton, Elton R 1881?-1952 *BioIn 3*
Eaton, G D 1894?-1930 *NF*
Eaton, Glenn 1899- *WhJnl 1928*
Eaton, Mary *HisAmM XR*
Eaton, Seymour 1859-1916 *DcNAA, HisAmM XR*
Eaton, Walter Prichard 1878-1957 *AmAu&B, CarSB, ConAmL, HisAmM XR, REnAL, TwCA, TwCA Sup, WebBD, WhNAA*
Eaton, William James 1930- *RpN, WhoAm 1974, WhoMW 1974*
Eaton, William O *HisAmM XR*
Ebach, Carl Alfred 1901?-1949 *BioIn 1*
Ebbutt, Norman 1894?-1968 *BioIn 8*
Ebener, Charlotte *BioIn 3, BioIn 8*
Eberhard, Wallace Beatty 1931- *AmM&W 73S*
Eberhardt, Charles *RpN*
Eberhart, Lloyd *NF*
Eberl, George *NF*
Eberle, James A *NF*
Eberle, Josef 1901- *EncWL, IntWW 1976, WhoWor 1974*
Ebert, Alan *NF*
Ebert, Friedrich 1894- *IntWW 1976*
Ebert, Justus 1869-1946 *AmRP, DcNAA*
Ebert, Roger Joseph 1942- *ConAu 69, WhoAm 1974, WhoMW 1974*
Ebsworth, Joseph Woodfall 1824-1908 *Alli Sup, BioIn 2*
Eby, Carl Laurence 1901- *WhJnl 1928*
Eccles, Mary A d1964 *BioIn 6*
Ecevit, Bulent 1925- *BioIn 10, CurBio XR, IntWW 1976, WhoWor 1974*
Echaniz, Jose *NF*
Echols, Evelyn 1915- *NF*
Echols, Marion P *AmJnl*
Eckardt, Felix Von 1903- *BioIn 3, BioIn 4, CurBio XR, IntWW 1974, WhoWor 1974*
Eckardt, Julius Von 1836-1908 *WebBD*
Eckel, George Leonard 1912?-1951 *BioIn 2*
Eckersall, Walter Herbert 1887-1930 *BioIn 6, WebBD*

Eckhardt, Fred *NF*
Eckman, Fern Marja *WhoAm 1974,*
  WhoAmW 1974
Eckman, James Russell 1908- *DrAS 74H,*
  WhoAm 1974
Eckstein, Ernst 1845-1900 *BbD, BiD&SB,*
  OxGer, WebBD
Eckstein, Louis *HisAmM XR*
Eckstrom, Frederick A 1870- *WhJnl 1928*
Economou, Rose 1946?- *BioIn 9*
Ed, Carl Frank Ludwig 1890-1959 *AmAu&B,*
  BioIn 5
Edberg, Rolf 1912- *ConAu 69, IntWW 1976,*
  WhoWor 1974
Eddy, Allen 1870-1957 *WhJnl 1928*
Eddy, Bob 1917- *RpN, WhoAm 1974,*
  WhoE 1974
Eddy, James *HisAmM XR*
Eddy, John L 1869?-1952 *BioIn 2*
Eddy, Mary Morse Baker Glover 1821-1910
  Alli Sup, AmAu, AmAu&B, BiD&SB,
  CasWL, DcAmA, DcLEL, DcNAA, EncAB,
  LongC, OxAm, OxEng, REn, REnAL,
  WebBD
Eddy, Paul 1944- *ConAu 73*
Eddy, Richard 1828-1906 *Alli Sup, CyAL 2,*
  DcAmA, DcNAA, HisAmM XR
Eddy, Walter Hollis 1877-1959 *HisAmM XR*
Edel, Leon 1907- *AmAu&B, BioIn 3, BioIn 6,*
  BioIn 9, BioIn 10, CanWW 1972, ConAu 1,
  CurBio XR, DrAS 74E, IntWW 1974,
  NewYTBE 3, OxAm, RAdv 1, REn,
  Who 1974, WhoWor 1974, WorAu,
  WrDr 1976
Edelman, Maurice 1911-1975 *Au&Wr, ConAu 65,*
  ConNov 1972, ConNov 1976, CurBio XR,
  LongC, TwCW, Who 1974, WhoWor 1974,
  WorAu, WrDr 1976
Edelmann, Heinz 1934- *BioIn 8, BioIn 10*
Edelson, Edward 1932- *ConAu 19R, WhoE 1974*
Edelstein, Julius C C *OvPC*
Edelstein, Morton A 1925- *ConAu 69*
Eder, Richard *NF*
Eder, Shirley *NF*
Edes, Benjamin 1732-1803 *AmAu&B, AmJnl,*
  BioIn 3, BioIn 7, DcAmB 6, HisAmM XR
Edes, Mary Elisabeth 1922-1962 *BioIn 6*
Edes, Richard W *AmJnl*
Edey, Kenneth S 1909- *CanWW 1972*
Edgar, Day *HisAmM XR*
Edgar, Joanne *NF*
Edgar, Randolph 1884-1931 *DcNAA, WhNAA*
Edgar, William Crowell 1856-1932 *DcNAA*
Edge, Walter Evans 1873-1956 *CurBio XR,*
  WebBD
Edgecomb, Frank O 1864?-1947 *BioIn 1*
Edgerton, Art 1927?- *BioIn 7*
Edgerton, Constance 1884- *WhJnl 1928*
Edgerton, James Arthur 1869-1938 *AmLY,*
  DcAmA, DcNAA, NatCAB XR, OhA&B
Edgett, Edwin Francis 1867-1946 *AmAu&B,*
  BioIn 1, DcAmA, DcNAA
Edgeworth, Francis Ysidro 1845-1926 *Alli Sup,*
  BioIn 2, BioIn 8, WebBD
Edgington, Frank *NF*
Edholm, Charles Lawrence *HisAmM XR*
Ediff, Sonia *OvPC*
Ediger, Don *NF*
Edinborough, Arnold 1922- *Au&Wr,*
  CanWW 1972, ConAu 73, WhoF&I 1974
Edinger, Ray William 1888- *WhNAA,*
  WhJnl 1928
Edldredge, C H 1879- *WhJnl 1928*
Edlin, William 1878-1947 *BioIn 1*

Edman, Louis E 1917- *NF*
Edmiston, Susan 1940- *ConAu 65*
Edmond, James 1859-1933 *BioIn 2, DcLEL*
Edmonds, Arthur Denis 1932- *ConAu 73*
Edmonds, Richard Hathaway 1857-1930 *BiDSA,*
  DcNAA, HisAmM XR, NatCAB 2,
  WhNAA, WhJnl 1928
Edmunds, Nora Caroe 1893?-1968 *BioIn 8*
Edmunds, Thomas Field 1889?-1953 *BioIn 3*
Edmundson, Charles *RpN*
Edom, Clifton Cederic 1908?- *BioIn 7*
Edsall, Thomas B *NF*
Edson, Bernard *OvPC*
Edson, Clement M *HisAmM XR*
Edson, Elie C 1882?-1971 *BioIn 9*
Edson, Gus 1901-1966 *AmAu&B, AmJnl,*
  BioIn 7
Edson, Lee *NF*
Edson, Peter 1896-1977 *AmJnl, BioIn 1, BioIn 2,*
  ConAu 73, WhoAm 1974
Edstrom, Edward *RpN*
Edwards, Agustin 1899-1956 *BioIn 4, ForP*
Edwards, Alanson William 1904- *WhJnl Sup*
Edwards, Albert 1879-1929 *AmLY XR, DcNAA*
Edwards, Albert *see also* Bullard, Arthur
Edwards, Alfred Shenstone 1849- *AmRP,*
  HisAmM XR
Edwards, Alicia Betsy *NF*
Edwards, Anne 1910?- *BioIn 5*
Edwards, Arthur 1834- *HisAmM XR, NatCAB 9*
Edwards, Bela Bates 1802-1852 *Alli, AmAu&B,*
  CyAL 2, DcAmA, DcNAA, HisAmM XR
Edwards, C S 1901- *WhJnl 1928*
Edwards, Deltus Malin 1874-1962 *NF*
Edwards, Donald Isaac 1904- *BioIn 8, ConAu 65,*
  Who 1974
Edwards, Douglas 1917- *BioIn 3, BioIn 4,*
  IntMPA 1975, WhoAm 1974
Edwards, Duncan *OvPC*
Edwards, E Theodore 1894- *WhJnl 1928*
Edwards, Edwin *NF*
Edwards, Elisha Jay 1847-1924 *DcNAA*
Edwards, Forrest *OvPC*
Edwards, Frank 1908-1967 *BioIn 2, BioIn 4,*
  BioIn 7, BioIn 8
Edwards, H Pierrepont 1871- *WhJnl 1928*
Edwards, Harry Stillwell 1855-1938 *AmAu&B,*
  BiD&SB, BiDSA, DcAmA, DcNAA,
  HisAmM XR, NatCAB 39, OxAm, REn,
  REnAL, WebBD, WhNAA
Edwards, Harvey 1929- *ConAu 25, OvPC,*
  SmATA 5, WrDr 1976
Edwards, Henry 1871- *TexWr, WhNAA,*
  WhJnl 1928
Edwards, Homer Floyd, Jr. 1918- *DrAS 74H*
Edwards, India *CurBio XR*
Edwards, James L *HisAmM XR*
Edwards, Jorge 1931- *DcCLAA*
Edwards, Julia Spalding 1920- *ConAu 37,*
  ForWC 1970, OvPC, WhoAm 1974,
  WhoAmW 1974, WhoWor 1974
Edwards, Louise Betts d1928 *DcNAA*
Edwards, Sir Owen Morgan 1858-1920 *BioIn 1,*
  CasWL, TwCA, TwCA Sup
Edwards, Pamela *NF*
Edwards, Paul *NF*
Edwards, Paul Carroll 1882-1962 *BioIn 4, BioIn 6*
Edwards, Phil *OvPC*
Edwards, Philip *AmJnl*
Edwards, Robert Chambers 1864-1922 *BioIn 5*
Edwards, Robert John 1884- *TexWr, WhNAA*
Edwards, Robert John 1925- *IntWW 1976,*
  IntWW 1974, Who 1974
Edwards, Russell 1909- *WhoAm 1974,*

WhoE 1974
Edwards, Ted *NF*
Edwards, Thomas E 1891- *WhJnl 1928*
Edwards, Verne Ervie, Jr. 1924- *AmM&W 73S, ConAu 33, WhoMW 1974*
Edwards, Walter Meayers 1908- *HisAmM XR, WhoAm 1974*
Edwards, Will C 1878- *WhJnl 1928*
Edwards, Willard 1902- *WhoAm 1974, WhoS&SW 1973*
Eeden, Frederik Willem Van 1860-1932 *BiD&SB, CasWL, CIDMEL, EncWL, Pen Eur, WebBD*
Eekhoud, Georges 1854-1927 *BbD, BiD&SB, CasWL, CIDMEL, WebBD*
Eells, George 1922- *ConAu 21R, WhoE 1974*
Efendi, Agah *ForP*
Effel, Jean *BioIn 2, WhoGrA*
Efron, Edith 1922?- *BioIn 2, NewMr*
Egan, Charles E 1902-1968 *BioIn 8*
Egan, Jack *NF*
Egan, James *NF*
Egan, Leo 1907-1962 *BioIn 6*
Egan, Maurice Francis 1852-1924 *Alli Sup, AmAu&B, AmLY, BbD, BiD&SB, BkC 4, DcAmA, DcNAA, HisAmM XR, PoIre, WebBD*
Egan, Pierce 1772-1849 *BbD, BiD&SB, BioIn 5, BioIn 9, Br&AmS, BrAu 19, CasWL, CyWA, DcEnA, DcEnL, DcEuL, DcLEL, EvLB, HisAmM XR, NewC, OxEng, PoIre, WebBD*
Egan, Vincent Joseph 1921- *WhoAm 1974*
Egerstrom, Lee *NF*
Egger, Charles *NF*
Eggleston, Arthur D 1899?-1959 *BioIn 5, RpN*
Eggleston, Charles *NF*
Eggleston, Edward 1837-1902 *Alli Sup, AmAu, AmAu&B, BbD, BiD&SB, CarSB, CasWL, CnDAL, CyAL 2, CyWA, DcAmA, DcBiA, DcNAA, DcRusL, EvLB, HisAmM XR, IndAu 1816, JBA 1934, LiJA, OxAm, OxEng, Pen Am, REn, REnAL, WebBD, WebE&AL*
Eggleston, George Cary 1839-1911 *Alli Sup, AmAu, AmAu&B, AmJnl, BbD, BiD&SB, BiDSA, BioIn 2, CyAL 2, DcAmA, DcAmB 6, DcBiA, DcLEL, DcNAA, HisAmM XR, IndAu 1816, LiJA, OxAm, REnAL, WebBD*
Eggleston, George T *HisAmM XR*
Eggleston, Wilfrid 1901- *CanNov, CanWW 1972, ConAu 23R, OxCan, OxCan Sup, WrDr 1976*
Egler, Daniel *NF*
Egner, Frank L 1892-1957 *NatCAB 46*
Egorov, Anatoli Grigorievich 1920- *IntWW 1976, WhoWor 1974*
Ehlert, Fred *NF*
Ehmann, John *HisAmM XR*
Ehrenburg, Ilya Grigoryevich 1891-1967 *BioIn 1, BioIn 2, BioIn 3, BioIn 4, BioIn 6, BioIn 7, BioIn 8, BioIn 9, CasWL, CIDMEL, CurBio XR, DcRusL, EncWL, EvEuW, LongC, ModSL 1, REn, TwCW, WebBD*
Ehrenhalt, Alan *NF*
Ehrhart, J *HisAmM XR*
Ehrlich, Arnold 1923- *ConAu 33, WhoAm 1974*
Ehrlich, Cindy *NF*
Ehrlich, Henry *HisAmM XR*
Ehrman, Riccardo *NF*
Ehrman, Robert W *OvPC*
Eichel, Leslie P 1890-1967 *BioIn 7, WhJnl 1928*
Eichelbaum, Frederick *OvPC*

Eichelbaum, Stanley 1926- *BiE&WWA, ConAu 73, WhoAm 1974, WhoWest 1974, WhoWorJ 1972*
Eichenauer, Charles Frederick 1882-1945 *WhJnl 1928*
Eichholz, Gerhard Carl 1930- *WhoAm 1974*
Eichhorn, Tom *NF*
Eid, Leif 1908?-1976 *ConAu 65*
Eidell, T Arden *OvPC*
Eidelsberg, David 1893-1963 *BioIn 6*
Eifert, Virginia 1911-1966 *BioIn 9*
Eiges, Sydney Hirsh 1909- *IntMPA 1975, WhoAm 1974, WhoPubR 1972*
Einarson, Susan *NF*
Einaudi, Luigi 1874-1961 *CurBio XR*
Einfrank, Aaron R *OvPC*
Einhorn, Arthur 1934- *WhoAm 1974*
Einhorn, Nathan 1906?-1969 *BioIn 8*
Einstoss, Ron 1930?-1977 *ConAu 69*
Einzig, Paul 1897- *Au&Wr, ConAu 11R, WhoWor 1974*
Eioesheim, Julie 1884-1972 *BioIn 9*
Eisele, Albert A 1936- *ConAu 41*
Eisen, Jack 1925- *ConAu 73*
Eisenberg, Arlene *NF*
Eisenberg, David 1907-1977 *WhoWorJ 1972*
Eisenberg, Dennis 1929- *ConAu 25*
Eisenberg, Howard *NF*
Eisenberg, Lee 1946- *ConAu 61*
Eisenberg, Sydney A 1910-1964 *BioIn 7*
Eisendrath, Cosman 1906- *WhJnl 1928*
Eisendrath, David B *BioIn 7*
Eisenhower, Julie Nixon 1948?- *BioNews 1974, NewYTBE 2*
Eisenstaedt, Alfred 1898- *BioIn 10, BioNews 1974, CurBio XR, IntWW 1976, WhoAm 1974, WhoWor 1974*
Eiserer, Leonard Arnold 1948- *ConAu 73*
Eisman, Hy 1927- *ConAu 65*
Eismann, Bernard N 1933- *ConAu 4R*
Eisner, Gil *NF*
Eisner, Kurt 1867-1919 *OxGer, WebBD*
Eisner, Will 1917- *AmAu&B, WhoAm 1974*
Ejbye-Ernst, Arne 1927- *IntWW 1976*
Ekblaw, Walter Elmer 1882-1949 *WhJnl 1928*
Ekins, Herbert Roslyn 1901-1963 *AmAu&B, BioIn 2, BioIn 4, BioIn 6*
Ekman, Carl Gustaf 1872-1945 *CurBio XR*
Elbaum, Harry *OvPC*
Elbaum, Moshe 1902?-1969 *BioIn 4, BioIn 7, BioIn 8*
Elder, A P T *HisAmM XR*
Elder, Eccles Duncan *WhJnl 1928*
Elder, Genevieve d1977 *NF*
Elder, Paul 1872-1948 *AmAu&B, HisAmM XR, WhNAA*
Elder, Paul 1906- *WhoAm 1974*
Elder, Shirley *InvJ*
Elderkin, John 1841- *Alli Sup, HisAmM XR*
Elderman, Roy *NF*
Eldridge, Frederick William 1877-1937 *AmAu&B, DcNAA, WhJnl 1928*
Elegant, Robert Sampson 1928- *AmAu&B, BioIn 4, BioIn 7, ConAu 4R, WhoAm 1974, WhoWest 1974, WhoWor 1974, WrDr 1976*
Elfenbein, Julien 1897- *Au&Wr, ConAu 2R, WhoAdv 1972, WhoE 1974, WhoWorJ 1972, WrDr 1976*
Elfin, Mel 1929- *WhoAm 1974, WhoS&SW 1973, WhoWorJ 1972*
Elfving, Gosta 1908- *IntWW 1976, WhoWor 1974*
Elias, Christopher 1925- *ConAu 33*
Elias, Donald S 1889- *WhJnl 1928*

Elias, Robert Henry 1914- *AmAu&B, ConAu 61, DrAS 74E, WhoAm 1974*
Eliason, Marcus *NF*
Elie 1929?- *BioIn 3*
Eliot, Alexander 1919- *AmAu&B, ConAu 49, WhoAm 1974*
Eliot, George 1819-1880 *Alli Sup, AtlBL, BbD, BiD&SB, BrAu 19, CasWL, CrtT 3, CyWA, DcBiA, DcEnA, DcEnA Ap, DcEnL, DcEuL, DcLEL, EvLB, HsB&A, MouLC 3, NewC, OxEng, Pen Eng, RAdv 1, RComWL, REn, WebBD, WebE&AL*
Eliot, George Fielding 1894-1971 *AmAu&B, BioIn 4, BioIn 9, BioIn 10, ConAu 29, CurBio XR, HisAmM XR, NewYTBE 2, REnAL, TwCA, TwCA Sup, WebBD*
Eliot, John *HisAmM XR*
Elisofon, Eliot 1911-1973 *AmAu&B, ConAu 41, CurBio XR, NewYTBE 4, WhoAmA 1973*
Elizabeth, Wilson Anne 1902- *WhJnl 1928*
Elkins, Frank 1910-1973 *BioIn 10, NewYTBE 4, WhoPubR 1972*
Elkins, Liston Dickson 1903- *WhJnl 1928*
Ellan, Patrick *OvPC*
Elland, Percy 1908-1960 *BioIn 5*
Ellard, Roscoe Brabazon 1899-1962 *BioIn 6, BioIn 8, ForP, HisAmM XR*
Ellefson, Dennis *NF*
Ellenberg, Albert *NF*
Ellenwood, Henry S *AmJnl*
Ellerbe, Rose Lucille 1861-1929 *DcNAA, WhNAA*
Ellerbee, Linda *NF*
Ellingson, Steve 1910- *WhoAm 1974, WhoWest 1974*
Ellington, Thomas W *OvPC*
Ellington, William *NF*
Ellinwood, Ralph Everett 1893-1930 *DcNAA, WhJnl 1928*
Elliot, Daniel 1927- *ConAu XR*
Elliot, Ian 1925- *ConAu 69*
Elliot, Karen *NF*
Elliot, Kathryn *NF*
Elliot, Levinia Scott *NF*
Elliot, Shirley *NF*
Elliott, Aaron Marshall 1844-1910 *HisAmM XR*
Elliott, Ashbel R *HisAmM XR*
Elliott, Ernest Eugene 1878-1941 *BioIn 2, DcNAA, IndAu 1816, WhNAA*
Elliott, Ernest L 1869-1948 *NatCAB 36*
Elliott, Francis Perry 1861-1924 *DcNAA, HisAmM XR*
Elliott, Frank R 1893- *WhJnl 1928*
Elliott, Fred J d1888 *NF*
Elliott, George *NF*
Elliott, George 1851-1930 *AmLY, DcNAA, OhA&B, WhNAA*
Elliott, George A, III *OvPC*
Elliott, J L *NF*
Elliott, Janice 1931- *ConAu 15R, WrDr 1976*
Elliott, Jesse M 1888?-1948 *BioIn 1*
Elliott, Joy *NF*
Elliott, Lawrence 1924- *ConAu 5, OvPC, WhoAm 1974, WhoE 1974*
Elliott, Nora Alice Kerr 1892?-1951 *BioIn 2*
Elliott, Osborn 1924- *AmAu&B, BioIn 9, ConAu 1R, ConAu 69, IntWW 1976, WhoAm 1974, WhoE 1974, WhoWor 1974*
Elliott, Robert 1903?- *BioIn 1*
Elliott, Robert C *RpN*
Elliott, Robert Charles Dunlop 1886-1950 *BioIn 2*
Elliott, Stephen 1771-1830 *Alli, CyAL 1, DcAmA, DcNAA, HisAmM XR, WebBD*

Elliott, W A *NF*
Elliott, Wayne 1879- *WhJnl 1928*
Elliott, William Yandell 1896- *AmAu&B, AmM&W 73S, HisAmM XR*
Ellis, Albert Gallatin 1800-1885 *BioIn 5*
Ellis, Benjamin 1798-1831 *Alli, DcNAA, HisAmM XR*
Ellis, Bertram 1860-1920 *NatCAB 18*
Ellis, Brian *NF*
Ellis, Donald 1888- *WhJnl 1928*
Ellis, Edward Robb 1911- *ConAu 25, WrDr 1976*
Ellis, F B *NF*
Ellis, Griffith Ogden 1869-1948 *AmAu&B, NatCAB 36, REnAL, WhNAA*
Ellis, Grover *NF*
Ellis, Harry Bearse 1921- *AmAu&B, AuBYP, BioIn 8, ConAu 1R, SmATA 9, WhoAm 1974, WhoWor 1974, WrDr 1976*
Ellis, J Ray 1888- *WhJnl 1928*
Ellis, Kenneth M 1890?-1950 *BioIn 2*
Ellis, Merle *NF*
Ellis, Paul Franklyn 1904- *WhNAA, WhJnl 1928*
Ellis, Ralph 1879- *WhJnl 1928*
Ellis, Reed Hobart 1918-1972 *BioIn 9*
Ellis, Robert C *OvPC*
Ellis, Theodore Thaddeus 1867-1934 *AmJnl*
Ellis, Wade Hampton 1866-1948 *BioIn 1, WhNAA*
Ellis, William Thomas 1873-1950 *BioIn 2, WhNAA*
Ellison, Jerome 1907- *AmAu&B, BioIn 2, BioIn 4, BioIn 5, ConAu 29, DrAS 74E, WhoAm 1974*
Elliston, Miss George 1883-1946 *AmAu&B, AnMV 1926, OhA&B, WhJnl 1928*
Elliston, Herbert Berridge 1895-1957 *BioIn 1, BioIn 2, BioIn 4, BioIn 6, CurBio XR, NatCAB 45*
Elliston, Thomas Ralph 1919-1977 *ConAu 73, USBiR 1974*
Ellithorpe, Harold 1925- *NF*
Ellmaker, Lee 1896-1951 *DcAmB S5, WhJnl 1928*
Ellmaker, Lee 1922- *BioIn 2, BioIn 3*
Ellsworth, Arthur Whitney 1936- *WhoAm 1974, WhoWor 1974*
Ellsworth, William Webster 1855-1936 *AmAu&B, DcNAA, LiJA, NatCAB 27*
Ellwood, Peter *NF*
Elmendorf, Roy C 1897-1949 *BioIn 2*
Elmlark, Harry Eugene 1909- *WhoAm 1974*
Eloesser, Arthur *NF*
Elon, Amos *NF*
Elrod, Jack *NF*
Elsasser, Glen Robert 1935- *ConAu 65*
Elser, Frank Ball 1885-1935 *AmAu&B, DcNAA, TexWr, WebBD*
Elsesser, Bernard 1876- *WhJnl 1928*
Elsila, David August 1939- *LEduc 1974, WhoAm 1974, WhoS&SW 1973*
Elsman, Max C *NF*
Elsner, Sidney Edgar 1919- *WhoAm 1974*
Elson, Arthur 1873-1940 *AmAu&B, AmLY, DcAmA, DcNAA, WebBD, WhNAA*
Elson, John Mebourne 1880?- *BioIn 1, CanNov, OxCan, WhNAA*
Elson, John T *NF*
Elson, Louis Charles 1848-1920 *Alli Sup, AmAu, AmAu&B, AmLY, BbD, BiD&SB, DcAmA, DcNAA, OxAm, WebBD*
Elson, Robert T 1906- *CanWW 1972*
Elston, E *AmRP*
Elston, Wilbur Evans 1913- *WhoAm 1974*
Elton, David Horton 1877- *NF*

Elverson, James 1838-1911 *AmJnl*
Elverson, James, Jr. d1929 *AmJnl*
Elwell, Edward Henry 1825-1890 *Alli Sup,*
DcAmA, DcNAA, NatCAB 9
Elwell, Hector *AmJnl*
Elwers, George 1921- *OvPC, WhoAdv 1972*
Elwin, Whitwell 1816-1900 *BrAu 19, DcEnL,*
EvLB, NewC, WebBD
Ely, Mary Lillian d1950 *BioIn 2*
Ely, William N 1896-1947 *NatCAB 37*
Emanuel, Guglielmo 1879- *BioIn 3*
Emanuelli, Enrico 1909-1967 *BioIn 8*
Embrey, George A *NF*
Emerson, Edwin 1869-1959 *AmAu&B, AmJnl,*
BiD&SB, BioIn 5, DcAmA, WhNAA
Emerson, Gloria 1929?- *BioIn 9, BioIn 10*
Emerson, Howard Foord 1875-1947 *BioIn 3,*
NatCAB 38
Emerson, Ralph Waldo 1803-1882 *Alli, Alli Sup,*
AmAu, AmAu&B, AmJnl, AmWr, AnCL,
AtlBL, BbD, BiD&SB, CasWL, CnDAL,
CnE&AP, CrtT 3, CyAL 2, CyWA,
DcAmA, DcEnA, DcEnA Ap, DcEnL,
DcLEL, DcNAA, EvLB, LiJA, MouLC 4,
OxAm, OxEng, Pen Am, RAdv 1,
RComWL, REn, REnAL, Str&VC, WebBD,
WebE&AL
Emerson, Walter Crane 1863-1929 *DcNAA*
Emerson, William 1769-1811 *NF*
Emerson, William Austin, Jr. 1923- *BioIn 3,*
WhoE 1974
Emery, Edwin 1914- *ConAu 69*
Emery, Frank 1927-1950 *AmJnl, BioIn 2*
Emery, Fred 1933- *ConAu 65*
Emery, Fred A 1875-1962 *BioIn 6, WhNAA*
Emery, George M 1884- *WhJnl 1928*
Emery, Michael 1940- *ConAu 73*
Emery, Sherman R *NF*
Emery, Susan L 1846-1917 *DcNAA*
Emery, William Morrell 1866-1951 *BioIn 2*
Emett, Rowland 1906- *BioIn 1, BioIn 3,*
BioIn 7, BioIn 9, WhoGrA
Emig, Elmer Jacob 1898-1957 *NF*
Emlen, S, Jr. *HisAmM XR*
Emme, Duane A *NF*
Emmerich, John O, Jr. *RpN*
Emmerich, John Oliver 1896-1978 *BioIn 2*
Emmett, Burton 1871-1935 *DcAmB S1*
Emmitt, Robert 1925- *ConAu 29*
Emmons, Earl H 1888- *WhJnl 1928*
Emmons, Nathaniel 1746-1840 *Alli, BiDLA,*
HisAmM XR
Emmwood *BioIn 6*
Emory, Alan S 1922- *ConAu 69*
Emory, Frederick 1853-1908 *DcAmA, DcNAA,*
HisAmM XR
Emory, John 1789-1835 *BiDSA, DcAmA,*
DcNAA, HisAmM XR
Emory, Percy McCarthy *HisAmM XR*
Enander, Johan Alfred 1842-1910 *DcNAA*
Ende, Alice Ankeney Von *HisAmM XR*
Ende, Lex 1901?-1951 *BioIn 3*
Enderis, Guido 1874-1948 *BioIn 1*
Endicott, Charles Moses 1793-1863 *Alli Sup,*
AmAu&B, BbD, BiD&SB, DcAmA,
DcNAA
Endicott, Robert Rantoul 1905- *AmAu&B, OvPC,*
WhoAm 1974
Endicott, William *InvJ*
Endroi, Bela 1886?-1956 *BioIn 4*
Endrst, Jeff *NF*
Eng, Veng *NF*
Engberg, Eric *NF*
Engdahl, J Louis *AmRP*

Engel, Carl 1883-1944 *AmSCAP 1966, BioIn 1,*
BioIn 5, BioIn 9, CurBio XR, WhNAA
Engel, Conrad, Jr. *HisAmM XR*
Engel, Gertrude *BioNews 1975*
Engel, Louis *Alli Sup, HisAmM XR*
Engel, Louis 1909- *ConAu 21R*
Engel, Mark *InvJ*
Engeldinger, Harvey Young 1912- *WhoAm 1974,*
WhoF&I 1974
Engelhard, G P *HisAmM XR*
Engelhardt, Thomas Alexander 1930-
WhoAm 1974, WhoMW 1974
Engh, Jeri *NF*
Engh, Rohn 1938- *ConAu 69*
Englade, Kenneth F *NF*
England, Isaac W *HisAmM XR*
Engle, George *NF*
Engle, Robert *NF*
Engle, Willis Darwin 1846-1925 *BioIn 2,*
IndAu 1816
Englebardt, Stanley L *NF*
Englehardt, George W *HisAmM XR*
Englehart, Bob *NF*
Engleman, Earl W 1927- *NF*
Engler, Faye *NF*
English, David 1931- *ConAu 69, ForP,*
Who 1974
English, E Schuyler 1899- *AmAu&B,*
WhoAm 1974
English, Earl 1905- *ConAu 37*
English, Eugene B *OvPC*
English, John *NF*
English, John Wesley 1940- *NF*
English, Pritch *NF*
English, Sandal *NF*
English, Thomas Dunn 1819-1902 *Alli, Alli Sup,*
AmAu, AmAu&B, BbD, BiD&SB, CnDAL,
CyAL 2, DcAmA, DcLEL, DcNAA,
HisAmM XR, OxAm, REnAL, WebBD
Englking, Lessing L *NF*
Enix, Lucille 1933- *WhoS&SW 1973*
Ennever, William Joseph 1869-1947 *WebBD*
Ennis, Jean 1916-1970 *BioIn 9*
Enright, Walter Joseph Pat 1879-1969 *AmAu&B,*
BioIn 8, HisAmM XR, WhJnl 1928
Enriquez, Roberto *NF*
Ensor, David B *NF*
Enstad, Robert *NF*
Ent, William H *WhJnl 1928*
Entenza, John Dymock 1905- *BioIn 5, BioIn 10,*
WhoAm 1974
Enwright, Frederick W 1886?-1964 *BioIn 6*
Enzer, Milton *OvPC*
Epes, Horace 1882?- *WhJnl 1928*
Ephron, Edith *NF*
Ephron, Nora 1941- *AuNews 2, ConAu 65,*
NewMr
Epley, Malcolm 1904- *WhoAm 1974*
Eppie *ConAu XR*
Eppinger, Josh, III 1940- *NF*
Epple, August 1880- *WhJnl 1928*
Eppstein, John 1895- *BioIn 1*
Epstein, Barbara 1928- *BioIn 9, WhoAm 1974,*
WhoAmW 1974
Epstein, Constance *BioIn 5*
Epstein, Edward Jay 1935- *ConAu 19, InvJ,*
WhoWorJ 1972
Epstein, Eleni Sakes 1925- *ForWC 1970,*
WhoAm 1974, WhoAmW 1974,
WhoS&SW 1973
Epstein, Helen *NF*
Epstein, Joseph *NF*
Epstein, Julius 1901-1975 *ConAu 57*
Epstein, Louis *OvPC*

Epstein, Louis 1895?-1954 *BioIn 3*
Epstein, Morris 1921-1973 *BioIn 10, ConAu 15,*
   ConAu 45, ConAu P-1, NewYTBE 4,
   WhoWorJ 1972
Epstein, Robert *NF*
Epstein, Sidney 1920- *WhoAm 1974,*
   WhoS&SW 1973
Erb, Hubert *NF*
Erbsen, Claude *NF*
Erburu, Robert F 1930- *WhoAm 1974*
Erhard, Raymond F 1895?-1949 *BioIn 1*
Erickson, Don 1932- *WhoAm 1974*
Ericson, Helen J *NF*
Erikson, Art *NF*
Erk, Cemil Tahir *NF*
Erkko, Eero *ForP*
Erkko, Juho Elijas 1895-1965 *BioIn 1, BioIn 4,*
   BioIn 7
Erlenkotter, Charles 1881?-1948 *BioIn 1*
Erlick, Everett Howard 1921- *WhoAm 1974,*
   WhoE 1974, WhoF&I 1974
Ernle, Baron *see* Prothero, Rowland Edmund
Ernst, Carl Wilhelm 1845-1919 *BioIn 3, DcNAA*
Ernst, Clayton Holt 1886-1945 *AmAu&B,*
   WhNAA
Ernst, Grant W 1895- *WhJnl 1928*
Ernst, Ken *BioIn 8*
Ernst, William A 1883- *WhJnl 1928*
Ernst, William E *HisAmM XR*
Errett, Isaac 1820-1888 *Alli Sup, AmAu&B,*
   DcAmA, DcNAA, HisAmM XR, OhA&B
Erskine, Albert Russel, Jr. 1911- *WhoAm 1974*
Ervin, Janet 1923- *BioIn 9*
Ervin, John, Jr. 1927- *WhoAm 1974*
Erwin, James L 1867- *WhJnl 1928*
Erwin, Ray *HisAmM XR*
Erwin, Roy 1905?-1968 *BioIn 8*
Esar, Evan *NF*
Escourido, Joe *NF*
Esenwein, Joseph Berg 1867-1946 *AmAu&B,*
   BioIn 1, DcNAA, HisAmM XR, REnAL,
   WhNAA
Eshelman, William Robert 1921- *BiDrLUS,*
   BioIn 8, WhoAm 1974, WhoE 1974
Eshenfelder, Alma *NF*
Eskenazi, Gerald 1936- *ConAu 61*
Eskenazi, Samuel I *NF*
Eskew, Rhea Taliaferro 1923- *WhoAm 1974,*
   WhoS&SW 1973
Eskey, Kenneth D 1930- *NF*
Esper, George *NF*
Espinosa, Robin *OvPC*
Espy, Willard Richardson 1910- *BioIn 2,*
   ConAu 49
Ess, I R *NF*
Essary, Helen 1886?-1951 *BioIn 2*
Essary, Jesse Frederick 1881-1942 *AmLY,*
   BioIn 2, DcNAA, NatCAB 34, WhNAA,
   WhJnl 1928
Esse, Peter J *NF*
Esselburne, George H *NF*
Esselen, Christian 1823-1859 *BioIn 2*
Esser, Charles H 1892-1959 *NatCAB 47*
Esser, Robin 1933- *ConAu 29*
Essman, Robert N *OvPC*
Essoyan, Roy *NF*
Estabrook, Robert Harley 1918- *ConAu 69,*
   WhoAm 1974, WhoWor 1974
Estang, Luc 1911- *ConAu 61, EncWL,*
   IntWW 1976, OxFr, Pen Eur,
   WhoWor 1974, WorAu
Estanislao, Jesus 1939- *NF*
Estenssoro, Hugo 1946- *ConAu 69*
Estep, H Cole 1886- *WhJnl 1928*

Esterly, Glenn 1942- *ConAu 33*
Esterow, Milton 1928- *ConAu 19R,*
   WhoAm 1974
Esters, Bernard E 1898?-1966 *BioIn 7*
Estes, Carl Lewis 1896?-1967 *BioIn 7*
Estes, Don Cameron *WhJnl 1928*
Estes, Jack 1888- *WhJnl 1928*
Estock, Anne 1923- *ConAu 4R*
Estrada, Frank *NF*
Estrada, Jose Manuel 1842-1894 *BioIn 2, BioIn 9*
Estrin, Michael 1907-1960 *BioIn 5*
Esty, Lucien Coy 1899-1929 *DcNAA*
Eswaran, V V *RpN*
Eszterhas, Joe *NF*
Etchison, William P 1878- *WhJnl 1928*
Etelson, N B *NF*
Etheredge, Sumpter Price 1883-1953 *BioIn 5,*
   NatCAB 42
Etheridge, James P, Jr. *RpN*
Ethridge, Mark, III *InvJ*
Ethridge, Mark Foster 1896- *BioIn 1, BioIn 2,*
   CurBio XR, IntWW 1976, WhoAm 1974
Ethridge, Mark Foster, Jr. 1924- *WhoAm 1974,*
   WhoMW 1974
Etienne, Charles Guillaume 1777?-1845 *BbD,*
   BiD&SB, OxFr, WebBD
Ettelson, Lee 1895- *WhJnl 1928*
Ettenson, Herb *NF*
Etter, Betty 1911?- *OvPC, WhoAm 1974,*
   WhoAmW 1974, WhJnl Sup
Etting, Gloria *NF*
Ettinghausen, Richard 1906- *ConAu 65,*
   DrAS 74H, IntWW 1974, WhoAm 1974,
   WhoAmA 1973, WhoWor 1974
Ettinger, Harold 1910?-1944 *DcNAA*
Eude, Louis-Marie *HisAmM XR*
Eula, Joe *NF*
Eulau, Heinz H F *HisAmM XR*
Euler, W D 1875- *WhJnl 1928*
Euler, W M 1896- *WhJnl 1928*
Eunson, Robert Charles Romaine 1912-1975
   ConAu 13R, ConAu 61, OvPC,
   WhoAm 1974, WhoE 1974
Eury, Clande A 1880- *WhJnl 1928*
Evan, John 1890- *BioIn 4*
Evangelides, A C *NF*
Evans, Albert O *WhJnl 1928*
Evans, Amon C *NF*
Evans, Austin Patterson 1883-1962 *BioIn 6*
Evans, B R *HisAmM XR*
Evans, Caradoc 1878-1945 *CasWL, CnMWL,*
   DcLEL, EvLB, LongC, ModBL, NewC,
   REn, TwCA, TwCA Sup, TwCW, WebBD,
   WebE&AL, WhoLA, WhoTwCL
Evans, Charles *Alli Sup, HisAmM XR*
Evans, Clifford *OvPC, WhoWorJ 1972*
Evans, Edith Brazwell 1912-1964 *BioIn 1,*
   BioIn 3, BioIn 6
Evans, Edward Andrew 1892-1951 *BioIn 2,*
   WhJnl 1928
Evans, Ernestine 1890?-1967 *BioIn 8*
Evans, Ewart D 1883- *WhJnl 1928*
Evans, Floyd *NF*
Evans, Frank S 1893- *WhJnl 1928*
Evans, Harold Matthew 1928- *ConAu 41, ForP,*
   IntWW 1976, NewMr, Who 1974,
   WhoWor 1974, WrDr 1976
Evans, Harry Carroll 1858-1932 *DcNAA,*
   WhNAA
Evans, Herndon *NF*
Evans, Homer C 1886- *WhJnl 1928*
Evans, Hugh Davy 1792-1868 *Alli, Alli Sup,*
   BiDSA, DcAmA, DcNAA, HisAmM XR
Evans, Idamay *NF*

Evans, Jack NF
Evans, John C W BioIn 9
Evans, John Crippen 1890-1965 BioIn 7
Evans, John J, Sr. 1861- WhNAA
Evans, John Wainwright 1883- BiDPara
Evans, Joseph Early 1919-1971 BioIn 9, BioIn 10,
    NewYTBE 2
Evans, Lanius Duane 1861?-1953 BioIn 3
Evans, Larry Melvyn 1932- WhoAm 1974
Evans, Les AmRP
Evans, Lynnette 1941- NF
Evans, Marian 1819-1880 WebBD
Evans, Marian see also Eliot, George
Evans, Marie HisAmM XR
Evans, Mary Ann 1819-1880 WebBD
Evans, Mary Ann see also Eliot, George
Evans, Maude Swalm NF
Evans, Medford Stanton 1934- BioIn 5, BioIn 7,
    BioIn 8, ConAu 65, WhoAm 1974
Evans, Newton Coulston 1889- WhJnl 1928
Evans, Orrin C 1903?-1971 BioIn 9, BioIn 10,
    NewYTBE 2
Evans, Paul Lewis 1914- RpN, WhoAm 1974,
    WhoGov 1972, WhoPubR 1972,
    WhoS&SW 1973
Evans, Phil NF
Evans, Ray O 1887-1954 BioIn 3, BioIn 6,
    NatCAB 43
Evans, Richard Louis 1906-1971 AmAu&B,
    BioIn 9, BioIn 10, ConAu 9, NewYTBE 2
Evans, Robert d1977 NF
Evans, Robert Mayer NF
Evans, Robert VanOrman 1920- WhoAm 1974
Evans, Rowland, Jr. 1921- BioIn 7, CelR 1973,
    ConAu 23R, WhoAm 1974,
    WhoS&SW 1973, WhoWor 1974,
    WrDr 1976
Evans, Ruby 1881-1968 BioIn 8
Evans, Silliman 1894-1955 BioIn 1, BioIn 3,
    BioIn 4, BioIn 6, NatCAB 43
Evans, Silliman 1925-1961 BioIn 6
Evans, Mrs. Silliman, Sr. WhoS&SW 1973
Evans, Sir Vincent 1851-1934 BioIn 2
Evans, W Leonard, Jr. 1914- BioIn 7,
    WhoMW 1974
Evans, Walker 1903-1975 AmAu&B, CurBio XR,
    EncAB, WhoAm 1974, WhoWor 1974
Evans, Webster 1908- ConAu 41
Evans, William Augustus 1865-1948 BioIn 1,
    BioIn 2, WhJnl 1928
Evans, William D, Jr. 1907-1969 WhJnl 1928
Evans, William David 1862-1955 BioIn 4
Evarts, Jeremiah 1781-1831 Alli, DcNAA,
    HisAmM XR
Evelyn, William HisAmM XR
Everett, Alexander Hill 1790-1847 Alli, AmAu,
    AmAu&B, BbD, BiD&SB, BioIn 6,
    CyAL 2, DcAmA, DcNAA, HisAmM XR,
    OxAm, Pen Am, REnAL, WebBD
Everett, Charles Carroll 1829-1900 Alli Sup,
    AmAu&B, BiD&SB, DcAmA, DcNAA,
    HisAmM XR, WebBD
Everett, Charles Horatio 1855-1936 WhJnl 1928
Everett, David 1770-1813 Alli, AmAu,
    AmAu&B, BiD&SB, CyAL 1, DcAmA,
    DcAmB 6, DcNAA
Everett, Edward 1794-1865 Alli, Alli Sup,
    AmAu, AmAu&B, BbD, BiD&SB, CyAL 1,
    DcAmA, DcEnL, DcNAA, HisAmM XR,
    LiJA, OxAm, Pen Am, REnAL, WebBD
Everett, Glenn D 1921- ConAu 69
Everett, M Wayne WhJnl 1928
Everett, Sir Percy NF
Everett, Richard Mather 1924?-1963 BioIn 6

Everett, Walter 1910- BioIn 8, WhoAm 1974
Everitt, Arthur F 1873- WhJnl 1928
Everitt, Helen 1901-1969 BioIn 8
Everitt, S A HisAmM XR
Everpoint DcNAA
Everpoint see also Field, Joseph M
Everritt, Tom NF
Everson, Ray D 1884- WhJnl 1928
Eves, Jesse Parvin 1894- WhoAm 1974
Evett, Robert 1922-1975 BioIn 10, HisAmM XR,
    WhoAm 1974
Evjue, William Theodore 1882-1970 BioIn 1,
    BioIn 4, BioIn 8, NewYTBE 1
Evoe 1881-1971 LongC, NewC, TwCA,
    TwCA Sup, WebBD
Evoe see also Knox, Edmund George Valpy
Ewald, William F NF
Ewan, Earl O NF
Ewart, Andrew 1911- ConAu 17R
Ewen, David 1907- AmAu&B, Au&Wr, AuBYP,
    BiE&WWA, BioIn 8, BioIn 9, ConAu 1,
    REnAL, SmATA 4, WhoAm 1974,
    WhoMus 1972, WhoS&SW 1973,
    WhoWor 1974, WhoWorJ 1972, WrDr 1976
Ewer, Ferdinand Cartwright 1826-1883 Alli Sup,
    DcAmA, DcNAA, HisAmM XR
Ewing, David Walkley 1923- ConAu 1R,
    WrDr 1976
Ewing, Donald M 1895?-1978 NF
Ewing, Elizabeth 1904- ConAu 41
Ewing, Fred R 1876- WhJnl 1928
Ewing, James Lindsay 1889- WhJnl 1928
Ewing, John Dunbrack 1892-1952 BioIn 2,
    BioIn 3, WhJnl 1928
Ewing, Robert 1859-1931 AmJnl
Ewing, Samuel HisAmM XR
Ewing, William H NF
Ewing, Wilson 1901-1952 BioIn 4, NatCAB 41
Eyes, Raymond 1925- WhoAdv 1972,
    WhoAm 1974, WhoF&I 1974
Eyler, Ervan Charles 1900- WhNAA,
    WhJnl 1928
Eynon, David Lewis OvPC
Eyraud, Emile 1890?-1954 BioIn 3
Eyre, Cynthia NF
Eyre, Lincoln NF
Eyre, Wilson, Jr. 1858-1944 HisAmM XR
Eyster, Clarence 1882- WhJnl 1928
Eyster, William Henry 1889-1968 BioIn 8
Ezcurra, Ignacio E d1968 NF

F

F P A 1881-1960 *WebBD*
F P A *see also* Adams, Franklin Pierce
Faas, Horst 1933- *WhoAm 1974, WhoWor 1974*
Faber, Doris 1924- *AuBYP, BioIn 7, ConAu 17, SmATA 3*
Faber, Jim *NF*
Fabian, Robert 1901- *CurBio XR*
Fabre, Hector 1834-1910 *BbtC, DcNAA, OxCan*
Fabrick, Jonathan *see* Holbrook, Silas Pinckney
Fabry, Jaro 1912-1952 *BioIn 2*
Fabry, Jean 1876-1968 *BioIn 8*
Fabry, Joseph *OvPC*
Facchinetti, Cipriano 1889-1952 *BioIn 2*
Fackenthal, Frank Diehl 1883-1968 *CurBio XR*
Factor, Harry *NF*
Fader, Shirley Sloan *NF*
Fadiman, Clifton Paul 1904- *AmAu&B, CelR 1973, ConAu 61, CurBio XR, HisAmM XR, IntMPA 1975, RAdv 1, REnAL, TwCA, TwCA Sup, WebBD, WhoAm 1974, WhoWest 1974, WhoWor 1974*
Fagan, Arthur Lawrence 1899-1946 *BioIn 2, NatCAB 36*
Fagerholm, Karl-August 1901- *CurBio XR, IntWW 1974*
Fago, Vincent 1915?- *BioIn 1*
Faherty, Justin L *NF*
Fahey, John H 1873-1950 *AmAu&B, BioIn 2*
Faichney, James B *IntMPA 1975, OvPC*
Fain, Jim 1920- *WhoAm 1974*
Fain, William 1917-1961 *AmAu&B, BioIn 3, BioIn 5*
Fairall, Herbert S 1858-1907 *Alli Sup, DcNAA*
Fairbairn, Don *NF*
Fairbairn, Garry 1947- *NF*
Fairbanks, C M *HisAmM XR*
Fairbanks, Charles M *NF*
Fairbanks, Frederick C 1881-1940 *NatCAB 30*
Fairbanks, Richard 1883-1944 *BioIn 1, NatCAB 33*
Fairbanks, Warren C 1878-1938 *NatCAB 35*
Fairbanks, Wilson Lincoln 1865-1953 *BioIn 1, BioIn 3*
Fairchild, Charles B 1878?-1950 *BioIn 2*
Fairchild, Clarence 1854-1928 *AmAu&B*
Fairchild, Clarence *see also* Champlin, Edwin Ross
Fairchild, Elisabeth E *NF*
Fairchild, Herbert Bigelow 1880- *WhJnl 1928*
Fairchild, John Burr 1927- *BioIn 6, BioIn 7, BioIn 8, BioIn 9, CurBio XR, WhoAm 1974, WhoE 1974*
Fairchild, Lee *HisAmM XR*
Fairchild, Wilma *BioIn 9*
Faircloth, E W *NF*

Fairfax, Beatrice (1873?-1945) *see also* Manning, Marie
Fairfax, Beatrice 1873?-1945 *AmAu&B, CurBio XR, DcNAA, REnAL*
Fairfax, Beatrice 1893?-1977 *ConAu XR*
Fairfax, John 1804-1877 *Alli Sup, BioIn 2*
Fairfax, John 1930- *ConP 1970, ConP 1975, WrDr 1976*
Fairfax, L 1837-1904 *Alli Sup, AmAu&B, DcNAA, OhA&B*
Fairfax, L *see also* Connelly, Celia Logan
Fairfax, Sir Warwick Oswald 1901?- *IntWW 1976, Who 1974*
Fairfield, Cicily Isabel *see* West, Rebecca
Fairfield, Edward George 1890-1933 *WhJnl 1928*
Fairfield, Flash *NF*
Fairfield, Francis Gerry 1844-1887 *Alli Sup, DcAmA, DcNAA*
Fairman, Charles George 1870- *WhJnl 1928*
Fairman, Henry Clay 1849- *BiDSA, HisAmM XR*
Fairman, Milton 1904- *OvPC, WhoAm 1974, WhoPubR 1972*
Fairweather, David Carnegy 1899- *WhoThe 1972*
Faith, George A 1872- *WhJnl 1928*
Fajon, Etienne 1906- *IntWW 1976*
Fake, John D *NF*
Falbo, Italo Carlo 1876-1946 *BioIn 1*
Falco, Thomas A 1910?-1949 *BioIn 2*
Falcon, Robert d1977 *NF*
Fales, Daniel C *NF*
Fales, Edward Daniel, Jr. 1906- *WhoE 1974*
Fales, Virginia B *NF*
Falk, Bernard *NF*
Falk, Carol H *NF*
Falk, Dorian *NF*
Falk, Lee *NF*
Falk-Roenne, Arne 1920- *ConAu 23R*
Falkenburg, Jinx 1919- *CurBio XR*
Falkenburg, Jinx *see also* McCrary, Jinx
Falklner, Leonard 1900- *ConAu 23R*
Falkner, Frank 1918- *AmM&W 73P*
Falkner, Roland Post 1866-1940 *CurBio XR, HisAmM XR*
Fall, Bernard B 1926-1967 *AmAu&B, BioIn 3, BioIn 5, BioIn 7, BioIn 8, ConAu 1, ConAu 25, WorAu*
Falla, F G *NF*
Fallaci, Oriana 1930?- *BioIn 7, BioIn 8, BioIn 9, BioIn 10, NewYTBE 4*
Faller, Kevin 1920- *ConAu 53, ConP 1970, WrDr 1976*
Fallow, Valentine A 1890?-1978 *NF*
Fallows, Samuel 1835-1922 *Alli Sup, AmAu&B, AmLY, DcAmA, DcNAA, HisAmM XR*
Falls, Joe *NF*

Fallucchi, Anne NF
Falstaff, Jake AmAu&B, DcNAA, OhA&B
Falstaff, Jake see also Fetzer, Herman
Falvey, Mary BioIn 6
Falzer, Gus A 1884?-1953 BioIn 3
Fan-Fan OxCan
Fan-Fan see also Blackburn, Victoria Grace
Fancher, Albert H 1895-1950 BioIn 2
Fancher, Edwin NewMr
Fang, Irving E 1929- ConAu 49
Fanning, Ambrose C d1893 NF
Fanning, Katherine Woodruff 1927- WhoAm 1974,
    WhoAmW 1974
Fanning, Lawrence Stanley 1914-1971
    NewYTBE 2
Fanning, Michael A HisAmM XR
Fanning, Neville O HisAmM XR
Fanning, Odom 1920- ConAu 53, WhoE 1974,
    WhoGov 1972, WhoPubR 1972, WrDr 1976
Fanning, Thomas BioIn 2
Fanning, Tolbert 1810-1874 BioIn 8
Fanning, Win 1918- BiE&WWA
Fanshaw, Daniel HisAmM XR
Farabee, Samuel Howard 1882-1939 WhJnl 1928
Farago, Ladislas 1906- AmAu&B, BioIn 9,
    BioNews 1975, CelR 1973, ConAu 65,
    WhoAm 1974, WhoWor 1974,
    WhoWorJ 1972
Farah, Adelaide Perry OvPC
Faran, James J, Jr. 1921- AmM&W 73P
Faran, James John 1808-1892 AmJnl
Farber, Barry NF
Farber, Myron A NF
Farge, Yves 1899-1953 BioIn 1, BioIn 3
Faria, Francisco Dutra 1910?-1978 NF
Faries, Belmont 1913- WhoAm 1974,
    WhoS&SW 1973
Farinacci, Roberto 1892-1945 WebBD
Faris, Barry 1889-1966 AmJnl, BioIn 7
Faris, Ellsworth 1874-1953 HisAmM XR
Faris, John Thomson 1871-1949 AmAu&B,
    BioIn 1, BioIn 5, CarSB, DcNAA, WebBD,
    WhNAA
Faris, Peter NF
Farjeon, Annabel 1919- ConAu 53
Farjeon, Benjamin Leopold 1838-1903 Alli Sup,
    BbD, BiD&SB, BrAu 19, DcBiA, DcEnL,
    DcLEL, EncMys, HisAmM XR, HsB&A,
    NewC, WebBD
Farkas, Marvin OvPC
Farley, Austin NF
Farley, Harriet 1817-1907 Alli, Alli Sup, AmAu,
    AmAu&B, BbD, BiD&SB, CarSB, CyAL 2,
    DcAmA, DcNAA, OxAm, REnAL
Farman, Ella 1843-1907 Alli Sup, AmAu&B,
    BiD&SB, CarSB, DcAmA, HisAmM XR
Farman, Ella see also Pratt, Ella Ann Farman
Farmer, Don 1938- ConAu 65
Farmer, Elihu Jerome 1836-1900 Alli Sup,
    DcAmA, DcNAA, OhA&B
Farmer, Eunice NF
Farmer, Gene 1919-1972 BioIn 9, ConAu 37,
    NewYTBE 3
Farmer, William L 1862- NatCAB 16
Farnell, George BioIn 1
Farneti, Milo OvPC
Farney, Dennis NF
Farnham, Charles W 1901- WhJnl 1928
Farnham, Henry Walcott HisAmM XR
Farnsworth, Clyde OvPC
Farnum, A M HisAmM XR
Farquhar, David Michael NF
Farquhar, Harold B 1879- WhJnl 1928
Farquhar, James Shaw 1890- WhNAA,

WhJnl 1928
Farquhar, Roger NewMr
Farquhar, Silas Edgar 1887-1948 BioIn 1
Farquhar, Walter S 1888- WhJnl 1928
Farr, William T 1934?- BioIn 9, BioIn 10
Farra, Charles Sheridan 1888- WhJnl 1928
Farrall, Saundra NF
Farrally, John HisAmM XR
Farrar, Clarence B 1873?-1970 BioIn 8
Farrar, John Chipman 1896-1974 AmAu&B,
    ConAu 65, ConAu 53, NewYTBS 5,
    REnAL, Str&VC, WebBD, WhoAm 1974,
    WhJnl Sup
Farrar, Larston Dawn 1915-1970 ConAu 2R
Farrar, Margaret 1897- CurBio XR
Farrar, Ronald Truman 1935- ConAu 33,
    DrAS 74H, WrDr 1976
Farrell, Adrienne NF
Farrell, Barry NF
Farrell, Dan NF
Farrell, David NF
Farrell, Eugene George 1905- WhoAm 1974
Farrell, Frank 1912- WhoF&I 1974
Farrell, John 1851-1904 BioIn 2, DcLEL, PoIre
Farrell, John Henry NF
Farrell, Mark 1913- CanWW 1972,
    WhoAm 1974
Farrell, Robert E RpN
Farrell, Robert W BioIn 9
Farrell, William E NF
Farrelly, R A AmJnl
Farrer, David NF
Farrington, Al NF
Farrington, Elizabeth Pruett 1898- CurBio XR,
    WhoAm 1974, WhoAmP 1973,
    WhoGov 1972
Farrington, Elizabeth Pruett see also Farrington,
    Mrs. Joseph R
Farrington, Helen OvPC
Farrington, Mrs. Joseph R 1898- CurBio XR,
    WhoAmW 1974
Farrington, Mrs. Joseph R see also Farrington,
    Elizabeth Pruett
Farrington, Joseph Rider 1897-1954 BioIn 1,
    BioIn 3, CurBio XR, DcAmB S5,
    WhJnl 1928
Farrington, Wallace Rider 1871-1933 BioIn 6,
    DcAmB S1, WhNAA
Farrior, John E LiJA
Farris, Frederick J NF
Farris, Grace 1895- WhJnl 1928
Farris, Joseph NF
Farrow, Suzanne NF
Farson, James Negley 1890-1960 WebBD
Farson, James Negley see also Farson, Negley
Farson, Negley 1890-1960 AmAu&B, BioIn 4,
    BioIn 5, BioIn 9, LongC, TwCA,
    TwCA Sup
Farson, Negley see also Farson, James Negley
Fassio, Virgil 1927- WhoMW 1974
Fat Contributor see Griswold, A Miner
Fatchen, Max 1920- Au&Wr, ConAu 25
Fatemi, Hossein 1918-1954 CurBio XR
Fates, Joseph Gilbert 1914- WhoAm 1974
Fath, Mahmoud Abul 1893?-1958 BioIn 5
Faubion, Bynum Burnan 1894- WhJnl 1928
Faubus, Orval Eugene 1910- BioIn 1, BioIn 5,
    BioIn 6, BioIn 7, BioIn 8, BioIn 9,
    CurBio XR, WhoAm 1974, WhoAmP 1973
Faucher DeSaint-Maurice, Narcisse H E 1844-1897
    BbtC, CanWr, DcNAA, OxCan
Fauconnier, Anna-Lena NF
Fauley, Wilbur Finley 1872-1942 AmAu&B,
    CurBio XR, DcNAA, OhA&B

Faulk, John Henry 1913- *AmAu&B,*
  WhoAm 1974, WhoS&SW 1973
Faulkes, Fred W 1855-1905 *NatCAB 16*
Faulkes, James Nelson 1888-1956 *BioIn 6,*
  NatCAB 44
Faulkner, Adele *NF*
Faulkner, Harry Charles 1866- *HisAmM XR*
Faulkner, Virginia Louise 1913- *AmAu&B,*
  ConAu 65, ForWC 1970
Faull, Robert W *OvPC*
Fauntleroy, Thomas 1888- *WhJnl 1928*
Faure, Lucie 1908-1977 *ConAu 73*
Faust, Frederick 1892-1944 *AmAu&B, AmJnl,*
  CurBio XR, DcLEL, DcNAA, EncMys,
  HisAmM XR, LongC, REn, REnAL,
  TwCA, TwCA Sup
Faust, Jan 1944- *BioIn 9*
Fauvet, Jacques 1914- *Au&Wr, BioIn 8,*
  IntWW 1976, WhoWor 1974
Faville, E E 1870- *WhJnl 1928*
Fawcett, Anthony *NF*
Fawcett, Denby 1941?- *BioIn 7*
Fawcett, Roger Knowlton 1909- *WhoAm 1974*
Fawcett, William 1902-1941 *BioIn 2*
Fawcette, Gene *NF*
Fawkner, John Pascoe 1792-1869 *BioIn 2,*
  BioIn 6, WebBD
Fawley, Wilbur *see* Fauley, Wilbur Finley
Faxon, Charles, Jr. *HisAmM XR*
Faxon, Frederick Winthrop 1866-1936 *AmLY,*
  DcNAA, HisAmM XR, LiJA, WhNAA
Faxon, James *NF*
Fay, Arthur S *OvPC*
Fay, Charles *NF*
Fay, Gerard 1913-1968 *BioIn 1, BioIn 6,*
  BioIn 8, ConAu 15, ConAu P-1, ForP
Fay, John Francis Xavier 1907?-1977 *NF*
Fay, S P, Jr. *OvPC*
Fay, Stephen 1938- *ConAu 25*
Fay, Theodore Sedgwick 1807-1898 *Alli, Alli Sup,*
  AmAu, AmAu&B, BbD, BiD&SB, CnDAL,
  CyAL 2, DcAmA, DcEnL, DcLEL,
  DcNAA, HisAmM XR, OxAm, REnAL,
  WebBD
Fayant, Frank H 1876?-1965 *BioIn 7*
Fayard, Jean 1902- *WebBD*
Fazy, James *see* Fazy, Jean Jacques
Fazy, Jean Jacques 1794-1878 *WebBD*
Fearon, Percy Hutton 1874-1948 *BioIn 1*
Fearn, Richard Lee 1862- *NF*
Feather, A G *HisAmM XR*
Featherstone, Joseph 1940- *ConAu 33,*
  HisAmM XR
Featherstonehaugh, George William *Alli,*
  HisAmM XR
Featherstonhaugh, Duane 1913?-1952 *BioIn 3*
Feck, Luke 1935- *ConAu 69*
Feder, Daniel 1898?-1956 *BioIn 4*
Feder, Sid 1909?-1960 *BioIn 5*
Federici, William Vito 1931- *WhoAm 1974*
Feders, Sid 1941- *NF*
Federzoni, Luigi 1878- *WebBD*
Fedin, Konstantin Alexandrovich 1892-1977
  CasWL, CIDMEL, ConAu 73, DcRusL,
  EncWL, EvEuW, IntWW 1974, ModSL 1,
  Pen Eur, REn, TwCW, WebBD,
  WhoWor 1974, WorAu
Fedler, Jon *NF*
Fedorov, Evgenil Konstantinovich *BioIn 1*
Fedou, R Eaton 1885- *WhJnl 1928*
Feeger, L M 1883- *WhJnl 1928*
Feehan, Gordon Francis 1919?- *BioIn 4*
Feehan, Richard P 1895?-1957 *BioIn 4*
Feeley, Mary 1915?-1969 *BioIn 8*

Feeney, Harry Thomas 1897?-1950 *BioIn 2*
Fegan, Lois J *NF*
Fehr, Louis White 1884?-1957 *BioIn 4,*
  WhJnl 1928
Feiffer, Jules 1929- *AmAu&B, Au&Wr,*
  BioIn 5, BioIn 6, BioIn 7, BioIn 8, BioIn 9,
  BioIn 10, CelR 1973, CnThe, ConAu 19,
  ConDr, ConLC 2, CroCD, CurBio XR,
  ForP, IntWW 1976, McGWD, SmATA 8,
  WhoAm 1974, WhoThe 1972, WhoWor 1974,
  WrDr 1976
Feigenbaum, William Morris 1886?-1949 *AmRP,*
  BioIn 1
Feigl, Fred *HisAmM XR*
Feil, Emanuel Monty 1895- *WhJnl 1928*
Fein, Georg 1803-1869 *BioIn 2*
Fein, Irving Ashley 1911- *ConAu 69,*
  IntMPA 1975, WhoAm 1974,
  WhoWest 1974, WhoWorJ 1972
Fein, Nathaniel 1914- *WhoAm 1974*
Feinberg, Lawrence W *NF*
Feinberg, Leon 1897?-1969 *BioIn 8*
Feinberg, Samuel *NF*
Feinen, Edward N d1976 *NF*
Feininger, Andreas 1906- *AmAu&B, CurBio XR,*
  WhoAm 1974, WhoWor 1974
Feininger, Lyonel 1871-1956 *AtlBL, CurBio XR,*
  DcCAA, OxGer, REn, WebBD
Feinsilber, Mike *NF*
Feinsilber, Myron *NF*
Feinstein, Phylis *NF*
Feitel, Donald G 1925?-1976 *ConAu 65*
Feito, Francois 1909- *ConAu 29*
Felberbaum, Harvey *OvPC*
Felch, W Farrand *HisAmM XR*
Feld, Rose Caroline 1895- *AmAu&B, WhNAA*
Feldman, Irving B 1902- *WhJnl 1928*
Feldman, Leonard 1927- *ConAu 69*
Feldman, Les 1948?- *BioIn 10, BioNews 1975*
Feldman, Marcia *NF*
Feldman, Trude B *NF*
Feldmann, Leonard G 1909?-1972 *BioIn 9,*
  NewYTBE 3, WhoE 1974
Feldmann, Markus 1897-1958? *CurBio XR*
Feldmeir, Daryle Matthew 1923- *ConAu 73,*
  WhoAm 1974
Felek, Burhan 1889- *IntWW 1976,*
  WhoWor 1974
Felgate, Edward 1888- *WhJnl 1928*
Felkel, Herbert 1889-1934 *WhNAA, WhJnl 1928*
Felker, Clay S 1928- *BioIn 8, BioIn 10,*
  CelR 1973, ConAu 73, CurBio XR, InvJ,
  NewMr, WhoAm 1974, WhoE 1974,
  WhoF&I 1974, WhoWor 1974
Fell, Charles Albert 1889-1969 *WhJnl 1928*
Fell, Herbert Granville 1872-1951 *BioIn 2*
Fellig, Arthur 1899-1968 *BioIn 8, BioIn 10*
Fellow, Henry Coffin 1856- *IndAu 1816,*
  WhNAA, WhJnl 1928
Fellowes, Pat *NF*
Fellows, Carl H 1894- *WhJnl Sup*
Fellows, Dexter William 1871-1937 *BioIn 4*
Fellows, James A *NF*
Fellows, John *HisAmM XR*
Fellows, Lawrence 1924- *ConAu 49*
Felt, Arthur Fairfield, Jr. 1914- *WhoAm 1974,*
  WhoS&SW 1973
Felt, Jack O 1904?-1953 *BioIn 3*
Felt, Joseph Barlow 1789-1869 *Alli, Alli Sup,*
  AmAu, AmAu&B, BiD&SB, DcAmA,
  DcNAA, HisAmM XR
Felter, Frederick C 1879-1948 *NatCAB 38*
Felton, Bruce 1946- *ConAu 65*
Felton, David *NF*

Felton, James Bruner 1927- *WhoAm 1974*
Felton, Rebecca Latimer 1835-1930 *AmAu&B,*
　BiDSA, BioIn 2, BioIn 4, BioIn 5, DcNAA,
　WebBD, WhNAA
Felts, C T *WhJnl 1928*
Felut, Maurice 1903?-1953 *BioIn 3*
Femling, Charles *NF*
Fendell, Bob 1925- *ConAu 57*
Fendell, Jack D *OvPC*
Fenderich, Charles *HisAmM XR*
Fenety, George Edward 1812-1899 *BbtC, DcNAA,*
　OxCan
Fenger, Austin B 1900- *WhJnl 1928*
Fenik, Omer Faruk *OvPC*
Fenn, Albert *OvPC*
Fenn, Alfred C d1893 *NF*
Fenn, Edward P *HisAmM XR*
Fenn, George Manville 1831-1909 *Alli Sup, BbD,*
　BiD&SB, BioIn 8, BrAu 19, DcBiA,
　DcEnL, EvLB, HisAmM XR, HsB&A,
　NewC, WebBD, WhoChL
Fenn, Ingemund 1907- *IntWW 1976,*
　WhoWor 1974
Fennelly, William A 1897?-1975 *BioIn 10*
Fenner, Mildred Sandison 1910- *ConAu 33,*
　LEduc 1974, WhoAm 1974, WhoAmW 1974,
　WhoS&SW 1973
Fenno, Harriet *HisAmM XR*
Fenno, John 1751-1798 *AmAu&B, AmJnl, ForP,*
　NatCAB 19, OxAm, WebBD
Fenno, John Ward *AmJnl*
Fenton, John H 1906?-1973 *BioIn 9, NewYTBE 4*
Fenton, Thomas Trail 1930- *WhoAm 1974,*
　WhoWor 1974
Fentress, E S 1876?-1951 *BioIn 2*
Fentress, J Simmons *RpN*
Fenwick, Benedict Joseph *HisAmM XR*
Fera, Adolph C *NF*
Ferber, Edna 1887-1968 *AmAu&B, AmNov,*
　AuNews 1, BiE&WWA, CnDAL, CnMD,
　CnThe, ConAmA, ConAmL, ConAu 5,
　ConAu 25, DcLEL, EncWL, EvLB,
　HisAmM XR, LongC, McGWD, ModAL,
　ModWD, OxAm, Pen Am, REn, REnAL,
　SmATA 7, TwCA, TwCA Sup, TwCW,
　WebBD, WhNAA, WisWr
Ferber, Nat Joseph 1889-1945 *AmAu&B,*
　DcNAA, WhJnl 1928
Ferber, Samuel *NF*
Ferdinand-Lop, Samuel 1891- *BioIn 1*
Ferguson, Charles Austin, Jr. 1937-
　WhoS&SW 1973
Ferguson, David *NF*
Ferguson, Elmer W 1885-1972 *BioIn 10*
Ferguson, Frank Currier 1898- *WhJnl 1928*
Ferguson, Fred E 1898- *WhJnl 1928*
Ferguson, Fred Swearengin 1887-1959 *AmJnl,*
　BioIn 5
Ferguson, George Victor 1897- *BioIn 1,*
　CanWW 1972, WhoAm 1974
Ferguson, Harry 1903- *WhoAm 1974*
Ferguson, J Halcro 1920- *ConAu 1R*
Ferguson, John Donald 1890?-1964 *BioIn 6,*
　BioIn 7, BioIn 9
Ferguson, Libby *NF*
Ferguson, Lucia 1887?-1962 *BioIn 6*
Ferguson, Melville Foster 1874-1968 *BioIn 4,*
　BioIn 8, BioIn 10
Ferguson, Oliver Watkins 1924- *ConAu 5,*
　DrAS 74E, HisAmM XR, WhoAm 1974
Ferguson, Robert Willi 1913- *OvPC, WhoE 1974,*
　WhoF&I 1974
Ferguson, Stanley 1912- *WhoAm 1974,*
　WhoF&I 1974

Ferguson, Ted 1936- *ConAu 65*
Ferguson, Thomas 1870?-1951 *BioIn 2*
Ferguson, William Porter Frisbee 1861-1929
　AmLY, DcNAA, WhNAA, WhJnl 1928
Fergusson, John W *HisAmM XR*
Feria, Benny F 1904- *BioIn 3*
Ferm, Alexis *AmRP*
Ferman, Joseph Wolfe 1906-1974 *AmAu&B,*
　HisAmM XR, WhoAm 1974,
　WhoWorJ 1972
Fern, Ben *NewMr*
Fern, Burton Hoffman 1925- *BioIn 5*
Fern, Fanny 1811-1872 *Alli, AmAu, AmAu&B,*
　BbD, BiD&SB, DcAmA, DcBiA, DcEnL,
　DcNAA, EncAB, OxAm, REnAL
Fern, Fanny see also Parton, Sara Payson Willis
Fern, Stewart Everson 1914?- *BioIn 6*
Fernald, Chester Bailey 1869-1938 *AmAu&B,*
　BiD&SB, DcAmA, DcNAA, HisAmM XR,
　OxAm, REnAL, WebBD, WhNAA
Fernandes, Helio *BioIn 6*
Fernandez, Genevieve *NF*
Fernandez, Juan L *NF*
Fernandez Guardia, Ricardo 1867-1950 *BioIn 2*
Fernandez Martinez, Jesse A 1923- *BioIn 1*
Ferniot, Jean 1918- *IntWW 1976*
Fernsworth, Lawrence A *RpN*
Feron, James Martin 1928- *WhoAm 1974*
Ferrand, G A d1900 *NF*
Ferrara, Fred *OvPC*
Ferraz, Austin T *NF*
Ferre, Luis Alberto 1904- *CurBio XR, ForP,*
　IntWW 1974, WhoAmP 1973,
　WhoGov 1972, WhoS&SW 1973,
　WhoWor 1974
Ferree, Mark 1905- *BioIn 5, BioIn 7*
Ferrer, Jose M, III *NF*
Ferrero, M P *ForP*
Ferri, Enrico 1856-1929 *WebBD*
Ferri, Luigi 1826-1895 *WebBD*
Ferril, Helen Ray 1897- *OhA&B*
Ferril, Thomas Hornsby 1896- *AmAu&B,*
　CnDAL, ConAu 65, ConP 1970, ConP 1975,
　OxAm, REnAL, TwCA Sup, WhoAm 1974,
　WrDr 1976
Ferril, William C 1855-1939 *NatCAB 18*
Ferrin, Augustin William 1875- *NatCAB 15*
Ferrin, Wesley W *HisAmM XR*
Ferris, Charles D *HisAmM XR*
Ferris, Clifford G 1903- *WhJnl 1928*
Ferris, Helen Josephine 1890-1969 *AmAu&B,*
　AuBYP, BioIn 2, BioIn 7, BioIn 8,
　JBA 1934, JBA 1951, REnAL, WhNAA
Ferris, John Orland 1893- *WhoAm 1974*
Ferris, Mary Lanman Douw 1855-1932 *AmLY,*
　HisAmM XR
Ferris, Paul 1929- *ConAu 7R, WhoWor 1974*
Ferris, Susan 1947- *NF*
Ferris, Timothy 1944- *ConAu 69*
Ferris, William H 1874- *WhJnl 1928*
Ferslew, Christian 1836-1910 *ForP*
Fertig, Lawrence 1898- *WhoAm 1974*
Fesperman, Tom *WhoS&SW 1973*
Fessenden, Thomas Green 1771-1837 *Alli, AmAu,*
　AmAu&B, AmJnl, BbD, BiD&SB, BiDLA,
　BiDLA Sup, BioIn 2, BioIn 3, CnDAL,
　CyAL 1, DcAmA, DcAmB 6, DcEnL,
　DcNAA, HisAmM XR, OxAm, REnAL,
　WebBD
Fessler, Loren W 1923- *ConAu 9R, OvPC*
Fest, Joachim C 1926- *ConAu 49*
Fetis, Francois Joseph 1784-1871 *BiD&SB,*
　WebBD
Fetridge, William Harrison 1906?- *ConAu 73,*

WhoAm 1974, WhoAmP 1973,
WhoF&I 1974, WhoMW 1974,
WhoWor 1974
Fett, Georne *NF*
Fetter, George Griffith *HisAmM XR*
Fetter, Theodore Henry *WhoAm 1974*
Fetterman, John Davis 1920-1975 *ConAu 61,
WhoAm 1974*
Fetzer, Herman 1899-1935 *AmAu&B, DcNAA,
OhA&B, REnAL*
Fetzer, John Earl 1901- *BioNews 1974,
IntMPA 1975, WhoAm 1974*
Few, William Preston 1867-1940 *BiDSA,
CurBio XR, HisAmM XR, WebBD*
Fewkes, Jesse Walter 1850-1930 *AmAu&B,
DcAmA, DcNAA, HisAmM XR, WebBD*
Fey, Harold Edward 1898- *BioIn 4, ConAu 19R,
IndAu 1917, WhoAm 1974*
Feyerick, Ada Pesin *OvPC*
Feyl, Albert John 1884- *WhJnl 1928*
Ffrench Blake, Neil 1940- *ConAu 69*
Fialka, John J *NF*
Fiarotta, Phyllis 1942- *ConAu 69*
Fichenberg, Robert Gordon 1920- *WhoAm 1974*
Fickertt, Earl 1885- *WhNAA, WhJnl 1928*
Ficklen, Herc *NF*
Ficklen, Jack Howells 1911- *WhoAm 1974,
WhoS&SW 1973*
Fidler, James M 1900- *BioIn 1, BioIn 9*
Fiebig, Jim 1941- *NF*
Fiehn, John *NF*
Field, Adelaide Anderson 1916- *WhoAm 1974,
WhoAmW 1974*
Field, Bryan 1900-1968 *BioIn 8*
Field, Carter *NF*
Field, Cathy Post *NF*
Field, Cecil 1905- *BioIn 1*
Field, Charles K *HisAmM XR*
Field, Dickey *see* Field, Eugene
Field, Edward Brenton 1903- *WhNAA,
WhJnl 1928*
Field, Edward S 1840-1927 *NatCAB 32*
Field, Eugene 1850-1895 *Alli Sup, AmAu,
AmAu&B, AmSCAP 1966, AuBYP, BbD,
BiD&SB, BiDSA, BioIn 1, BioIn 2, BioIn 3,
BioIn 4, BioIn 5, BioIn 6, BioIn 7, BioIn 8,
BioIn 9, BioIn 10, CarSB, CasWL, CnDAL,
DcAmA, DcLEL, DcNAA, EvLB,
HisAmM XR, JBA 1934, NatCAB 1,
OxAm, OxEng, Pen Am, RAdv 1, REn,
REnAL, Str&VC, WebBD*
Field, Frederic P *NF*
Field, Frederica Pisek *HisAmM XR*
Field, Frederick Vanderbilt 1905- *AmRP,
WhNAA*
Field, Henry Martyn 1822-1907 *Alli, Alli Sup,
AmAu&B, BbD, BiD&SB, DcAmA,
DcNAA, HisAmM XR, WebBD*
Field, James Alfred 1880-1927 *DcNAA,
HisAmM XR*
Field, John *NF*
Field, Joseph M 1810-1856 *AmAu&B, BiDSA,
DcAmA, DcAmB 6, DcNAA, OxAm, PoIre,
REnAL, WebBD*
Field, Kate 1838-1896 *Alli Sup, AmAu&B, BbD,
BiD&SB, BiDSA, BioIn 3, DcAmA,
DcNAA, HisAmM XR, NatCAB 6*
Field, Kate *see also* Field, Mary Katherine Keemle
Field, Marshall, III 1893-1956 *AmJnl, AmRP,
CurBio XR*
Field, Marshall, IV 1916-1965 *NF*
Field, Marshall, V 1941- *BioIn 1, BioIn 2,
BioIn 3, BioIn 4, BioIn 5, BioIn 6, BioIn 7,
BioIn 8, CelR 1973, WhoAm 1974,*

WhoF&I 1974, WhoMW 1974,
WhoWor 1974
Field, Marvin *NF*
Field, Mary Katherine Keemle 1838-1896 *DcAmA,
DcAmB 6, DcNAA, WebBD*
Field, Mary Katherine Keemle *see also* Field, Kate
Field, Richard Lane 1897- *WhoAm 1974,
WhoS&SW 1973*
Field, Roger *NF*
Field, Roswell Martin 1851-1919 *AmAu,
AmAu&B, BiD&SB, BiDSA, DcAmA,
DcNAA, HisAmM XR*
Field, Walter, Sr. *NF*
Field, William Henry 1877-1935 *WhJnl 1928*
Fielder, Wilson 1917?-1951 *AmJnl, BioIn 2*
Fielding, Nancy Parker *OvPC*
Fielding, Temple Hornaday 1913- *AmAu&B,
OvPC, WhoAm 1974, WhoWor 1974*
Fields, Dorothy *NF*
Fields, Howard K *NF*
Fields, Jack *NF*
Fields, James Thomas 1817?-1881 *Alli, Alli Sup,
AmAu, AmAu&B, BbD, BiD&SB, BioIn 2,
BioIn 3, CnDAL, CyAL 2, DcAmA,
DcEnL, DcLEL, DcNAA, LiJA, OxAm,
REnAL, WebBD*
Fields, Larry *NF*
Fields, Sidney *NF*
Fields, William 1898?-1961 *BioIn 5*
Fields, William Henry 1915- *WhoAm 1974,
WhoS&SW 1973*
Fiess, Robert G 1937?- *NF*
Fife, George Buchanan 1869-1939 *AmAu&B,
DcNAA, HisAmM XR, WhJnl 1928*
Fifer, Orien W, Jr. *NF*
Fiffick, William S 1900- *WhJnl 1928*
Figueroa, Anselmo *NF*
Fike, Pierre Hicks 1873-1943 *WhJnl 1928*
Filan, Frank *NF*
Fildes, Frank P 1895- *WhJnl Sup*
Filek, Karel *NF*
Filipacchi, Daniel *NF*
Fillmore, Charles 1854-1948 *HisAmM XR*
Fillmore, Hildegarde *OvPC*
Filo, John Paul 1948- *WhoAm 1974*
Filosa, Gary Fairmont Randolph, II 1931-
ConAu 65, WhoAm 1974, WhoWest 1974
Filteau, Jerome W *NF*
Finborud, Arne *NF*
Finch, Frank J 1879?-1950 *BioIn 2*
Finch, Jerald Allen 1927- *WhoS&SW 1973*
Finch, L Durwood *BioIn 7*
Finch, Sara *NF*
Finch, William George Harold 1895- *IntWW 1974,
WhoAm 1974*
Finch, William R 1847-1913 *NatCAB 15*
Fincher, J C *HisAmM XR*
Finck, Henry Theophilus 1854-1926 *Alli Sup,
AmAu&B, AmLY, BbD, BiD&SB, BiDSA,
DcAmA, DcNAA, HisAmM XR, REnAL,
WebBD*
Findeisen, Frederick *NF*
Finder, Leonard V 1910?-1969 *BioIn 8*
Findlay, Sir Edmund *NF*
Findlay, John Ritchie 1824-1898 *Alli Sup, NewC,
WebBD*
Findley, Earl Nelson 1877?-1956 *BioIn 4*
Findsen, Owen *NF*
Fine, Benjamin 1905-1975 *AmAu&B, BioIn 2,
BioIn 3, BioIn 4, BioIn 5, BioIn 6,
ConAu 5R, ConAu 57, CurBio XR, OvPC,
WhoAm 1974, WhoWorJ 1972*
Finely, Garry J 1896?-1948 *BioIn 1*
Fineman, Howard D *NF*

Finerty, John Frederick 1846-1908 *AmAu&B,*
DcAmA, DcNAA, NatCAB 13
Fineshriber, William H, Jr. 1909- *IntMPA 1975,*
WhoAm 1974
Finger, Charles Joseph 1869-1941 *AmAu&B,*
AnCL, AuBYP, BkCL, CurBio XR,
DcNAA, HisAmM XR, JBA 1934, OhA&B,
REnAL, TwCA, WebBD, WebE&AL
Fink, Arthur A *WhJnl 1928*
Fink, Bob *NF*
Fink, Donald Glen 1911- *AmM&W 73P,*
WhoAm 1974, WhoF&I 1974, WhoWor 1974
Fink, Herman *OvPC*
Fink, John 1926- *WhoAm 1974*
Fink, John Francis 1931- *WhoAm 1974*
Fink, Reuben 1889-1961 *BioIn 5*
Finke, Blythe Foote 1922- *ConAu 65, OvPC,*
USBiR 1974, WhoPubR 1972
Finkel, Benjamin Franklin 1865-1947
HisAmM XR, WhNAA
Finkelstein, Leonid Vladimirovitch 1924-
ConAu 23R
Finkelstein, Nina *NF*
Finlay, J W *HisAmM XR*
Finlay, Robert M d1977 *NF*
Finletter, June *NF*
Finley, Art *NF*
Finley, Emmet 1881-1950 *BioIn 2, BioIn 4,*
NatCAB 40
Finley, George T *NF*
Finley, John Huston 1863-1940 *AmAu&B, AmJnl,*
BioIn 1, BioIn 3, BioIn 8, BioIn 9,
BioIn 10, CurBio XR, DcAmB S2, DcNAA,
HisAmM XR, NatCAB 13, NatCAB 30,
WebBD, WhJnl 1928
Finley, Ruth Ebright 1884-1955 *AmAu&B,*
BioIn 4, LiJA, OhA&B
Finn, Allan *NF*
Finn, Ed *NF*
Finn, Edmund 1819-1898 *BioIn 2, DcLEL*
Finn, James 1924- *BioIn 8, IndAu 1917*
Finn, P J *NF*
Finn, Robert 1930- *WhoAm 1974*
Finne, Gabriel 1866-1899 *WebBD*
Finnegan, John R *NF*
Finnegan, Mike *NF*
Finnegan, Richard James 1884-1955 *BioIn 3,*
WhJnl 1928
Finneran, John A 1900- *WhJnl 1928*
Finney, Burnham 1899- *BioIn 7, OhA&B*
Finney, Charles Grandison 1905- *AmAu&B,*
ConAu 29, TwCA, TwCA Sup
Finney, Frank *NF*
Finney, James Imboden 1877-1931 *WhJnl 1928*
Finney, John Warren *NF*
Finney, Nathaniel Solon 1903?- *BioIn 1*
Finney, Paul Burnham 1929- *ConAu 73,*
WhoAm 1974
Finney, Ruth 1898- *WhoAm 1974,*
WhoAmW 1974
Finnigan, Joseph *NF*
Finot, Jean 1858-1922 *NF*
Fins, Alice *NF*
Finstad, William L *NF*
Fiore, Mary *NF, WhoAmW 1974*
Fiori, Pamela 1944- *NF*
Fireman, Peter *HisAmM XR*
Firestone, Clark Barnaby 1869-1957 *AmAu&B,*
BioIn 3, BioIn 4, OhA&B, REnAL,
WhJnl 1928
Firkins, Oscar W 1864-1932 *AmAu&B, DcNAA,*
HisAmM XR, LiJA, TwCA
First, Jean *HisAmM XR*
First, Wesley 1920- *WhoAm 1974*

Firth, Norman Charles 1895- *WhNAA,*
WhJnl 1928
Fisch, Anna 1875?-1966 *BioIn 7*
Fischbeck, Frank *NF*
Fischer, Adolph *AmJnl*
Fischer, Carl *HisAmM XR*
Fischer, Carl 1924- *WhoAm 1974, WhoE 1974*
Fischer, Ed *NF*
Fischer, Jo 1904- *BioIn 1, WhoAm 1974*
Fischer, John 1910-1978 *AmAu&B, BioIn 1,*
BioIn 3, ConAu 9R, CurBio XR,
IntWW 1976, LiJA, Who 1974,
WhoAm 1974, WhoWor 1974
Fischer, Leo 1897- *BioIn 1*
Fischer, Louis 1896-1970 *AmAu&B, Au&Wr,*
BioIn 1, BioIn 2, BioIn 3, BioIn 4, BioIn 8,
BioIn 9, ConAu 25, ConAu P-1,
CurBio XR, NewYTBE 1, REn, REnAL,
TwCA Sup, WebBD, WhoWorJ 1972
Fischer, Maurice Ritz 1903-1974 *BioIn 1,*
BioIn 4, WhoAm 1974
Fischer, Max 1893-1954 *BioIn 3*
Fischer, Paul 1946?- *BioIn 9*
Fischer, Peter W 1939- *NF*
Fischer, Richard *NF*
Fischer, Stephen M *RpN*
Fischer, Will H 1875?-1953 *BioIn 3*
Fischetti, John 1916- *BioIn 2, WhoAm 1974,*
WhoWor 1974
Fischler, Stan *OvPC*
Fish, Arthur Lyman 1878-1952 *BioIn 2, BioIn 3*
Fish, Byron 1908- *ConAu 45*
Fish, Hamilton, III *NF*
Fish, Herbert Henry 1870-1948 *BioIn 1, BioIn 2,*
NatCAB 36
Fish, Horace 1885-1929 *DcNAA, WhNAA*
Fish, Walter George 1874-1947 *BioIn 1*
Fishbein, Morris 1889-1976 *AmAu&B,*
AmM&W 73P, BioIn 1, BioIn 2, BioIn 8,
ConAu 5, ConAu 69, HisAmM XR,
IntWW 1976, WebBD, WhNAA,
WhoAm 1974, WhoWor 1974,
WhoWorJ 1972
Fishburn, Junius Blair 1865-1955 *BioIn 3,*
BioIn 4, NatCAB 41
Fishburn, Junius Parker 1895-1954 *BioIn 4,*
NatCAB 41
Fishenden, Richard Bertie 1880-1956 *BioIn 4*
Fisher, Allan Carroll, Jr. 1919- *WhoAm 1974,*
WhoS&SW 1973, WhoWor 1974
Fisher, Andrew 1862-1928 *WebBD*
Fisher, Andrew 1920- *NewYTBE 2,*
WhoAm 1974
Fisher, Bud 1884-1954 *AmAu&B, DcAmB S5,*
WhJnl 1928
Fisher, Bud *see also* Fisher, Harry Conway
Fisher, C J B *HisAmM XR*
Fisher, Charles Eugene 1900-1955 *BioIn 3*
Fisher, Craig Becker 1932- *OvPC, WhoAm 1974*
Fisher, Don *NF*
Fisher, Douglas *NF*
Fisher, Dudley 1890?-1951 *BioIn 2*
Fisher, E Burke 1799?-1859? *HisAmM XR,*
OhA&B
Fisher, E J O *NF*
Fisher, Ed *NF*
Fisher, Edwin Shelton 1911- *WhoAm 1974,*
WhoF&I 1974, WhoWor 1974
Fisher, Emily Ann d1976 *NF*
Fisher, Franklin L 1855-1953 *HisAmM XR*
Fisher, Galen Merriam 1873- *WhNAA*
Fisher, Galen Merriam, Jr. *WhJnl 1928*
Fisher, George Park 1827-1909 *Alli Sup, AmAu,*
AmAu&B, BbD, BiD&SB, DcAmA,

DcNAA, HisAmM XR, WebBD
Fisher, Graham *NF*
Fisher, H C *NF*
Fisher, Ham *see* Fisher, Hammond Edward
Fisher, Hammond Edward 1900-1955 *AmAu&B,*
 AmJnl, BioIn 3, BioIn 4, DcAmB S5
Fisher, Harrison 1875?-1934 *AmAu&B, DcNAA,*
 WebBD
Fisher, Harry Conway 1884-1954 *AmJnl, BioIn 3,*
 BioIn 6
Fisher, Harry Conway *see also* Fisher, Bud
Fisher, Heather *NF*
Fisher, Henry Conroy 1884-1954 *DcAmB S5*
Fisher, Henry Conroy *see also* Fisher, Bud
Fisher, Henry Conroy *see also* Fisher, Harry Conway
Fisher, Irene 1895- *WhNAA, WhJnl 1928*
Fisher, Jane O'Reilly *NF*
Fisher, John Wiggins 1913- *CanWW 1972*
Fisher, Jonathan *NF*
Fisher, Katharine Anderson d1958 *BioIn 3,*
 BioIn 4
Fisher, M E *BioIn 2*
Fisher, Mary Jane *NF*
Fisher, Max Henry 1922- *IntWW 1976,*
 Who 1974
Fisher, Paul *NF*
Fisher, Philip Sydney 1896- *CanWW 1972,*
 WhoAm 1974
Fisher, Robert William 1883- *WhNAA,*
 WhJnl 1928
Fisher, Roy Mac 1918- *RpN, WhoAm 1974*
Fisher, Shelton *see* Fisher, Edwin Shelton
Fisher, Thomas Henry 1879-1962 *BioIn 8*
Fisher, Walt M *HisAmM XR*
Fishler, Bennett Hill 1887-1969 *BioIn 8, BioIn 10*
Fishman, Jacob 1878-1946 *BioIn 1*
Fishman, Lew 1939- *ConAu 61*
Fisk, Wilbur M 1887- *WhJnl 1928*
Fiske, Amos Kidder 1842-1921 *AmAu&B, AmLY,*
 BiD&SB, DcAmA, DcNAA, NatCAB 20,
 WebBD
Fiske, DeLancey Walker d1948 *BioIn 1*
Fiske, Harrison Grey 1861-1942 *DcAmB S3,*
 HisAmM XR, NatCAB 10, WebBD
Fiske, Mary H *HisAmM XR*
Fiske, Mary H d1889 *DcNAA*
Fiske, Redington 1898?-1969 *BioIn 8*
Fiske, Stephen Ryder 1840-1916 *Alli Sup, AmAu,*
 AmAu&B, BiD&SB, DcAmA, DcAmB 6,
 DcNAA, HisAmM XR, WebBD
Fister, Gordon Brong 1911- *WhoAm 1974*
Fitch, Alva Revista 1907- *WhoAm 1974*
Fitch, Charles Elliott 1835-1918 *DcNAA*
Fitch, Charles W 1819-1899 *BioIn 5*
Fitch, Don Bradford 1894-1950 *BioIn 2*
Fitch, E H *HisAmM XR*
Fitch, George Hamlin 1852-1925 *AmAu&B,*
 DcNAA, HisAmM XR
Fitch, George Helgeson 1877-1915 *AmAu&B,*
 CarSB, DcNAA, REnAL
Fitch, Geraldine Townsend 1892?-1976 *ConAu 69,*
 ForWC 1970, OvPC
Fitch, Jack *NF*
Fitch, John Andrews 1881-1959 *HisAmM XR*
Fitchen, Allen Nelson 1936- *WhoAm 1974*
Fitchen, Richard *NF*
Fite, Jerry *NF*
Fithian, Robert Edward 1890- *WhJnl 1928*
Fitt, Arthur Percy 1869-1947 *BioIn 1*
Fitten, J H *HisAmM XR*
Fitts, James Franklin 1840-1890 *AmAu&B,*
 BiD&SB, CarSB, DcAmA, DcNAA,
 HisAmM XR
Fitz-Patrick, Hugh Louis 1861-1921 *DcNAA*

Fitzgerald, Anthony W 1911-1958 *NatCAB 43*
Fitzgerald, Charles *NF*
FitzGerald, Christopher J *NF*
Fitzgerald, Ed 1898- *CurBio XR*
Fitzgerald, Edward Earl 1919- *AmAu&B,*
 AuBYP, BioIn 1, BioIn 8, ConAu 73,
 WhoAm 1974, WhoF&I 1974
FitzGerald, Frances 1940- *BioIn 7, BioIn 8,*
 BioIn 9, ConAu 41, WhoAm 1974
FitzGerald, Francis V 1885?-1952 *BioIn 3*
FitzGerald, G J *NF*
Fitzgerald, Harold Alvin 1896- *WhoAm 1974,*
 WhoF&I 1974
Fitzgerald, James V 1889?-1976 *ConAu 69*
Fitzgerald, Jim *NF*
Fitzgerald, Oren Aram 1900- *WhJnl 1928*
Fitzgerald, Oscar Penn 1829-1911 *Alli Sup,*
 AmAu&B, BiDSA, DcAmA, DcNAA,
 HisAmM XR
Fitzgerald, Pegeen 1910- *BioIn 1, CurBio XR,*
 IntMPA 1975
Fitzgerald, Robert Stuart 1910- *AmAu&B,*
 BioIn 3, BioIn 4, BioIn 7, CathA 1952,
 ConAu 1, ConP 1970, ConP 1975,
 DrAP 1975, DrAS 74E, ModAL, OxAm,
 Pen Am, REnAL, TwCA Sup,
 WhoAm 1974, WrDr 1976
Fitzgerald, Scott *NF*
Fitzgerald, Stephen E d1964 *RpN*
Fitzgerald, Thomas 1819-1891 *AmAu, AmAu&B,*
 AmJnl, NatCAB 1
Fitzgibbon, John *NF*
FitzHenry, Charlotte L *RpN*
Fitzmorris, Thomas G *NF*
Fitznoodle 1843-1926 *AmAu*
Fitznoodle *see also* Vallentine, Benjamin Bennaton
Fitzpatrick, Daniel Robert 1891-1969 *BioIn 1,*
 BioIn 3, BioIn 4, BioIn 8, CurBio XR,
 WebBD
Fitzpatrick, John Clement 1876-1940 *AmAu&B,*
 DcAmB S2, DcNAA
Fitzpatrick, John Francis 1889-1960 *BioIn 5*
Fitzpatrick, Malachy Goodwin 1868-1952 *BioIn 3,*
 BioIn 5, NatCAB 42
Fitzpatrick, Richard S 1920?-1964 *BioIn 7*
Fitzpatrick, Ruth McDonough *NF*
Fitzpatrick, Thomas L 1880?-1948 *BioIn 1*
Fitzpatrick, Tom 1927- *BioIn 8, WhoMW 1974*
Fitzpatrick, William Henry Walter 1908-
 WhoAm 1974, WhoS&SW 1973
Fitzwater, Bonnie 1923- *WhoAm 1974,*
 WhoAmW 1974, WhoWest 1974
Fixx, James Fuller 1932- *ConAu 73,*
 WhoAm 1974
Flack, Harvey 1912-1966 *BioIn 7*
Flagg, Charles A *NF*
Flagg, Edmund 1815-1890 *Alli, Alli Sup, AmAu,*
 AmAu&B, BbD, BiD&SB, BiDSA, CyAL 2,
 DcAmA, DcEnL, DcNAA, NatCAB 13
Flagg, James Montgomery 1877-1960 *AmAu&B,*
 CurBio XR, OxAm, REnAL, WebBD
Flagg, Willard Cutting *HisAmM XR*
Flagler, John M 1922?-1972 *NewYTBE 3,*
 BioIn 9
Flaherty, Francis F 1900- *WhJnl 1928*
Flaherty, Frank 1903- *WhoAm 1974*
Flaherty, Joe *AmAu&B*
Flaherty, Robert Joseph 1933- *ConAu 73*
Flaherty, Vincent X 1908?-1977 *ConAu 73*
Flajano, Ennio 1910-1972 *BioIn 9*
Flambeau, Viktor *see* Brigham, Gertrude Richardson
Flanagan, Barbara *ForWC 1970, WhoAm 1974,*
 WhoAmW 1974
Flanagan, Dennis 1919- *BioIn 6, WhoAm 1974*

Flanagan, James W 1886-1949 *BioIn 2,*
WhJnl 1928
Flanagan, Mike D 1940?- *WhoS&SW 1973*
Flander, Judy *NF*
Flanders, Mrs. C W *HisAmM XR*
Flanders, Charles 1907-1973 *BioIn 9*
Flanders, Fred C 1883-1959 *WhJnl 1928*
Flanigan, James *NF*
Flannagan, Roy C 1938- *DrAS 74E*
Flannagan, Roy Catesby 1897?-1952 *BioIn 2*
Flanner, Janet 1892-1978 *AmAu&B, BioIn 1,*
BioIn 8, BioIn 9, BioIn 10, CelR 1973,
ConAu 65, CurBio XR, IndAu 1917, OxAm,
REnAL, WhoAm 1974, WhoAmW 1974,
WhoWor 1974, WorAu, WrDr 1976
Flannery, Harry William 1900-1975 *BioIn 1,*
ConAu 57, ConAu P-1, CurBio XR,
WhoAm 1974
Flannery, Henry W *NF*
Flannery, Thomas 1919- *BioIn 2, WhoAm 1974,*
WhoE 1974
Flashner, Amy *HisAmM XR*
Flattau, Edward 1937- *ConAu 65*
Flayer, Paul *NF*
Fleay, F G *HisAmM XR*
Fleeming, John *AmJnl*
Fleeson, Doris 1901-1970 *AmJnl, BioIn 2,*
BioIn 4, BioIn 5, BioIn 6, BioIn 7, BioIn 9,
CurBio XR, HisAmM XR, NewYTBE 1,
WhNAA, WhoAmW 1974
Fleet, Samuel *HisAmM XR*
Fleet, Thomas 1685-1758 *AmAu&B, AmJnl*
Fleetwood, Milton Luther 1892- *WhJnl 1928*
Fleischer, Charles 1871-1942 *WhNAA,*
WhJnl Sup
Fleischer, Nathaniel S 1887-1972 *BioIn 1,*
BioIn 5, BioIn 6, BioIn 9, ConAu 37
Fleischman, William John 1919- *WhoAm 1974*
Fleischmann, Peter Francis 1922- *WhoAm 1974,*
WhoF&I 1974, WhoWor 1974
Fleischmann, Raoul H 1885-1969 *AmAu&B,*
WhoE 1974
Fleisher, Benjamin Wilfrid 1870-1946 *BioIn 1,*
DcAmB S4, WhJnl 1928
Fleisher, Frederic 1933- *ConAu 21R, ForP*
Fleisher, Wilfried 1897?-1976 *ConAu 65,*
WhJnl 1928
Fleming, Dewey Lee 1898-1955 *BioIn 3*
Fleming, George H *NF*
Fleming, George James 1904- *BioIn 1, LivBAA*
Fleming, H K 1901- *Au&Wr, ConAu 33*
Fleming, Harold M 1900- *ConAu 21*
Fleming, Howard 1882?-1956 *BioIn 4*
Fleming, Ian 1908-1964 *AuBYP, ConAu 5,*
ConLC 3, CurBio XR, EncMys, LongC,
NewC, Pen Eng, REn, SmATA 9, TwCW,
WorAu
Fleming, James Roy 1881-1973 *BioIn 3, BioIn 9,*
WhoAm 1974
Fleming, John Rimer 1899- *WhJnl 1928*
Fleming, Joseph Benedict 1919- *WhoAm 1974*
Fleming, Lionel *BioIn 7*
Fleming, Robert Henry 1912- *BioIn 3, RpN,*
WhoAm 1974, WhoAmP 1973,
WhoGov 1972
Fleming, Shirley *NF*
Fleming, Thomas James 1927- *AmAu&B,*
ConAu 7R, SmATA 8, WhoAm 1974,
WhoWor 1974
Flemmons, Jerry *NF*
Flesch, Rudolph *AmJnl*
Flessel, Craig *NF*
Fletcher, Alan Mark 1928- *ConAu 73,*
WrDr 1976

Fletcher, Arthur 1908?-1964 *BioIn 7*
Fletcher, Elijah 1797-1858 *BioIn 7*
Fletcher, Frank *NF*
Fletcher, Herbert H 1855-1941 *NatCAB 30*
Fletcher, James E 1921- *WhoAm 1974,*
WhoF&I 1974, WhoMW 1974
Fletcher, Janet *NF*
Fletcher, Jefferson Butler 1865-1946 *AmAu&B,*
DcNAA, HisAmM XR, REnAL
Fletcher, Joseph Smith 1863-1935 *Alli Sup, BbD,*
EncMys, EvLB, LongC, NewC, TwCA,
WebBD, WhoLA
Fletcher, Leopold Raymond 1921- *Who 1974*
Fletcher, Martin 1904- *WhoAm 1974*
Fletcher, Vivian R *NF*
Fleurot, Arno Dosch *NF*
Flick, John Edmond 1922- *WhoAm 1974,*
WhoF&I 1974
Flicker, Edward 1869-1939 *NatCAB 29*
Flickinger, Samuel J 1848-1929 *NatCAB 2*
Flieger, Howard Wentworth 1909- *WhoAm 1974,*
WhoWor 1974
Fliegers, Serge *NF*
Fliess, Maurice R *NF*
Flinchum, James M, Jr. 1916- *WhoAm 1974*
Flinders-Petrie, William Matthew *HisAmM XR*
Fling, Karen J *NF*
Flinker, David 1897?-1978 *NF*
Flinn, John Joseph 1851-1929 *DcNAA*
Flinner, Charles E *NF*
Flint, Emily Pauline Riedinger 1909- *ForWC 1970,*
WhoAm 1974, WhoAmW 1974
Flint, Grover 1867-1909 *DcAmA, DcNAA,*
FamWC
Flint, Henry Martyn 1829-1868 *Alli Sup,*
DcAmA, DcNAA
Flint, John *NF*
Flint, Leon Nelson 1875-1955 *AmAu&B, AmJnl,*
BioIn 6, WhNAA, WhJnl 1928
Flint, Timothy 1780-1840 *Alli, AmAu,*
AmAu&B, BbD, BiD&SB, BiDSA, CnDAL,
CyAL 1, DcAmA, DcEnL, DcLEL,
DcNAA, HisAmM XR, LiJA, OhA&B,
OxAm, REnAL, WebBD
Floerscheim, Otto *HisAmM XR*
Flohil, Dick *NF*
Flohri, E *HisAmM XR*
Flood, A John 1891- *WhJnl 1928*
Flood, Patrick 1897?-1973 *BioIn 9*
Flood, Theodore L 1842- *Alli Sup, HisAmM XR*
Flora, Whitt *NF*
Florance, Howard 1885-1959 *HisAmM XR*
Florence, Thomas B 1812-1875 *HisAmM XR*
Flores-Banuet, Fernando 1908- *WhoAm 1974,*
WhoWor 1974
Florian, Tibor 1908- *ConAu 73*
Flory, Harry Russell 1899-1976 *ConAu 69,*
WhoAm 1974
Floto, Otto *AmJnl*
Flournoy, Harry Lightfoot 1878-1954 *WhJnl 1928*
Flower, Benjamin Orange 1858?-1918 *AmAu&B,*
AmJnl, BbD, BiD&SB, BioIn 2, BioIn 3,
BioIn 5, BioIn 6, DcAmA, DcNAA,
HisAmM XR, LiJA, WebBD
Flower, Elliott C 1863-1920 *DcNAA,*
HisAmM XR
Flower, Elsie *WhJnl 1928*
Flower, Frank Abial 1854-1911 *Alli Sup,*
BiD&SB, DcAmA, DcNAA
Flower, John H *RpN*
Flower, Richard G *HisAmM XR*
Flower, Sydney *HisAmM XR*
Flowers, Fred C *RpN*
Flowers, James Paul, Jr. 1918- *OvPC, WhoE 1974*

Flowers, John Garrison 1889- *WhJnl 1928*
Flowers, Paul *BioIn 2*
Floy, James 1806-1863 *Alli Sup, DcAmA,
DcNAA, HisAmM XR*
Floyd, William 1871-1943 *CurBio XR, DcNAA,
WhNAA, WhJnl 1928*
Fluharty, Irwin Adrian 1904?- *WhNAA,
WhJnl 1928*
Fluss, Felix F *NF*
Flusser, Martin 1947- *ConAu 73*
Flynn, Bernard F *OvPC*
Flynn, Bill *NF*
Flynn, Donald R 1928- *ConAu 29*
Flynn, Edward Patrick Dennis 1906-1947 *BioIn 1*
Flynn, Elizabeth Gurley 1890-1964 *AmRP,
CurBio XR*
Flynn, Eugene L 1890- *WhJnl 1928*
Flynn, Francis Marion 1903-1974 *OvPC,
WhoAm 1974, WhoE 1974, WhoWor 1974*
Flynn, George J *OvPC*
Flynn, J Walter 1910- *WhoAm 1974,
WhoWor 1974*
Flynn, Jack *NF*
Flynn, Jeremiah E *NF*
Flynn, John Thomas 1882-1964 *AmAu&B, AmRP,
BioIn 4, BioIn 6, HisAmM XR, TwCA,
TwCA Sup, WebBD*
Flynn, Lucinda *HisAmM XR*
Flynn, Maurice G *HisAmM XR*
Flynn, Thomas O'Brien 1892- *WhJnl 1928*
Flynt, Larry 1936- *AuNews 2, BioIn 10*
Flyth, William P 1893-1956 *NF*
Flythe, Starkey Sharp, Jr. 1935?- *ConAu 69,
WhoAm 1974*
Foa, Sylvana *NF*
Foard, J MacDonough *HisAmM XR*
Focht, Benjamin Kurtz 1863-1937 *NF*
Fockler, Shirley Maas 1934- *WhoAmW 1974*
Fodor, Denis *NF*
Fodor, Eugene 1905- *AmAu&B, BioIn 5,
ConAu 21, WhoAm 1974, WhoWor 1974*
Fodor, Marcel W 1890?-1977 *AmJnl, ConAu 69*
Foeldy, Charles 1880?-1954 *BioIn 3*
Foell, Earl William 1929- *ConAu 69,
WhoAm 1974*
Foellinger, Helene R 1910- *BioIn 3,
WhoAm 1974, WhoAmW 1974*
Foellinger, Oscar G 1885-1936 *WhJnl 1928*
Foerster, Friedrich Wilhelm 1869-1966
CurBio XR, HisAmM XR
Fogelman, Lazar 1891- *WhoWorJ 1972*
Fogelqvist, Torsten 1880-1941 *BioIn 1, ClDMEL*
Fogg, Lawrence Daniel 1879-1914 *DcNAA*
Fogg, Miller Moore 1868-1926 *WhJnl 1928,
WhJnl Sup*
Fogg, Sam *NF*
Fogg, Susan Ann *NF*
Fogo, William Montgomery 1841-1903 *BioIn 5*
Foisie, Jack 1919- *RpN, WhoAm 1974,
WhoWor 1974*
Foisie, Philip Manning 1922- *WhoAm 1974,
WhoS&SW 1973*
Foisy, J Albert 1887-1952 *BioIn 2*
Foldes, Margaret 1902- *WhJnl 1928*
Foley, Alan *NF*
Foley, Armund E *OvPC*
Foley, B *NF*
Foley, Charles 1908- *Au&Wr, BioIn 5,
ConAu 15, ConAu P-1*
Foley, George F 1879?-1949 *BioIn 1*
Foley, John *NF*
Foley, Martha 1897?-1977 *AmAu&B, ConAu 73,
CurBio XR, REnAL, WebBD,
WhoAmW 1974*

Foley, Raymond Michael 1890-1975 *CurBio XR*
Foley, Scott *ConAu XR*
Foley, Scott *see also* Dareff, Hal
Foley, William B 1872?-1951 *BioIn 2*
Folger, Franklin *NF*
Folkard, Charles *NF*
Folliard, Edward Thomas 1899-1976 *BioIn 1,
BioIn 2, BioIn 4, ConAu 69, CurBio XR*
Folmsbee, Beulah *BioIn 1*
Folsom, Charles 1794-1872 *Alli, AmAu&B,
HisAmM XR, WebBD*
Folsom, George 1802-1869 *Alli, AmAu&B,
DcAmA, DcNAA, HisAmM XR*
Folsom, Montgomery Morgan 1857-1898 *BiDSA,
DcNAA*
Folsom, William E, Jr. *NF*
Folts, Betty Hill *NF*
Foltz, Charles Steinman 1859-1941 *AmAu&B,
DcNAA*
Foltz, James Arthur 1903-1956 *BioIn 4*
Foltz, Moses A 1837-1915 *NatCAB 16*
Folwell, Amory Prescott 1865-1960 *BioIn 7*
Folwell, Arthur Hamilton 1877-1962 *AmAu&B,
BioIn 2, BioIn 6, HisAmM XR*
Folwell, Charles H *NF*
Fonblanque, Albany 1793-1872 *BioIn 4, WebBD*
Fong-Torres, Benson *NF*
Fonseca, Eleonora Pimentel, Marchesa Di 1768-1799
WebBD
Fontaina, Raul *ForP*
Fontaine, Andre 1910- *ConAu 65*
Fontaine, Andre 1921- *ConAu 25*
Fontaine, S S *WhJnl 1928*
Fontan, Louis Marie 1801-1839 *BbD, BiD&SB,
WebBD*
Fontane, Theodor 1819-1898 *BiD&SB, CasWL,
ClDMEL, CyWA, EuAu, EvEuW, OxGer,
Pen Eur, REn, WebBD*
Fontenay, Charles Louis 1917- *ConAu 25,
WrDr 1976*
Fonzi, Gaeton *NF*
Foord, John 1842-1922 *AmJnl, DcNAA,
HisAmM XR, NatCAB 13*
Foot, Michael Mackintosh 1913- *Au&Wr,
BioIn 1, BioIn 2, BioIn 4, BioIn 9,
BioIn 10, IntWW 1976, WrDr 1976*
Foot, Paul Mackintosh 1937- *BioIn 9,
ConAu 17R*
Foote, A E *HisAmM XR*
Foote, A Edward 1937- *ConAu 73*
Foote, Allen Ripley 1842-1921 *DcNAA,
HisAmM XR, OhA&B*
Foote, Henry Wilder 1838-1889 *Alli Sup,
DcAmA, DcNAA, HisAmM XR*
Foote, John Parsons 1783-1865 *Alli Sup, DcNAA,
HisAmM XR, OhA&B*
Foote, Joseph *NF*
Foote, Mark 1882-1957 *NF*
Foote, Nellie K 1872?-1950 *BioIn 2*
Foote, Thomas M 1808-1858 *NatCAB 7*
Foote, Timothy *NF*
Foote, Wilder 1905-1975 *BioIn 10, ConAu 57*
Foote, William Jenkins 1905- *WhoAm 1974*
Footlick, Jerold K *NF*
Foppens, Adrien *ForP*
Forain, Jean Louis 1852-1931 *OxFr, WebBD*
Forbath, Peter *BioIn 9*
Forbes, A Holland *HisAmM XR*
Forbes, Archibald 1838-1900 *Alli Sup, BbD,
BiD&SB, BrAu 19, DcEnL, FamWC,
HisAmM XR, WebBD*
Forbes, Bertie Charles 1880-1954 *BioIn 7,
BioIn 8, CurBio XR, WebBD*
Forbes, Charles B 1883- *WhJnl Sup*

Forbes, Charles Spooner *HisAmM XR*
Forbes, Christine 1903-1965 *BioIn 7*
Forbes, Claude M 1897- *WhJnl 1928*
Forbes, Edwin 1839-1895 *Alli Sup, AmAu&B,
DcNAA, EarABI, EarABI Sup,
HisAmM XR, WebBD*
Forbes, Elmer Severance 1860-1933 *BioIn 3*
Forbes, John *BioIn 2*
Forbes, Sir John 1787-1861 *Alli, DcEnL, WebBD*
Forbes, Leonard *HisAmM XR*
Forbes, Malcolm Stevenson 1919- *ConAu 69,
CurBio XR, WhoAm 1974, WhoF&I 1974,
WhoWor 1974*
Forbes, Richard E 1915- *WhoAm 1974,
WhoF&I 1974*
Forbes, Thomas Harold 1885?-1953 *BioIn 3*
Forcade, Thomas King 1943?-1978 *NF*
Force, Charles L *ForP*
Force, Kenneth O'Neil 1907-1969 *BioIn 8*
Force, Peter 1790-1868 *Alli, AmAu, AmAu&B,
AmJnl, BiD&SB, CyAL 2, DcAmA,
DcNAA, HisAmM XR, OxAm, REnAL,
WebBD*
Ford, Arthur Rutherford 1880-1968 *BioIn 2,
BioIn 8*
Ford, Arthur Younger 1861-1926 *NF*
Ford, Barbara *NF*
Ford, Sir Bertram 1869-1955 *BioIn 4*
Ford, Daniel Sharp 1822-1899 *AmAu&B,
HisAmM XR, LiJA, NatCAB 5*
Ford, Edward Lloyd *HisAmM XR*
Ford, George *NF*
Ford, Harvey Seabury 1915?-1978 *ConAu 73*
Ford, Isaac Nelson 1848-1912 *DcAmA, DcNAA,
HisAmM XR*
Ford, Jack *NF*
Ford, James Lauren 1854-1928 *AmAu&B, BbD,
BiD&SB, BiDSA, DcAmA, DcNAA,
HisAmM XR*
Ford, James Lawrence Collier 1907- *ConAu 29,
DrAS 74E, WhoAm 1974*
Ford, Mabel G *WhJnl 1928*
Ford, Patrick 1835-1913 *AmAu, AmAu&B,
BioIn 9, DcAmB 6, DcNAA, HisAmM XR*
Ford, Paul Leicester 1865-1902 *Alli Sup, AmAu,
AmAu&B, BbD, BiD&SB, CarSB, CnDAL,
DcAmA, DcBiA, DcLEL, DcNAA, EvLB,
JBA 1934, OxAm, REn, REnAL, WebBD*
Ford, Samuel Howard 1819-1905 *DcAmA,
DcNAA, HisAmM XR*
Ford, Sheridan d1922 *DcNAA*
Ford, Stephen 1949- *NF*
Ford, Stephen VanRensselaer 1836-1910 *DcNAA*
Ford, Thomas Francis 1873-1958 *BioIn 5*
Fore, Samuel Lane 1891-1966 *BioIn 8*
Foreman, Gene 1934- *NF*
Foresman, Bob 1912- *WhoAm 1974,
WhoF&I 1974, WhoS&SW 1973*
Forester, Frank 1807-1858 *AmAu, AmAu&B,
DcAmA, DcEnL, DcLEL, HsB&A, NewC,
OxAm, REnAL*
Forester, Frank *see also* Herbert, Henry William
Forgrave, Leslie L 1883?-1953 *BioIn 3*
Forker, Eugene 1888?-1948 *BioIn 1*
Forman, Allan 1860-1914 *AmJnl, HisAmM XR,
NatCAB 1*
Forman, Chandler *NF*
Forman, Ezekiel *HisAmM XR*
Forman, Harrison 1904-1978 *AmAu&B, Au&Wr,
AuBYP, ConAu 5R, WhoAm 1974,
WhoE 1974, WhoWor 1974, WrDr 1976*
Forman, Henry James 1879-1966 *AmAu&B,
ConAu 7R, WhNAA*
Forman, Stanley *NF*

Forman, Tom 1936- *NF*
Forney, John Weiss *see* Forney, John Wein
Forney, John Wien 1817-1881 *Alli Sup, AmAu,
AmAu&B, AmJnl, BiD&SB, CyAL 2,
DcAmA, DcAmB 6, DcNAA, HisAmM XR,
NatCAB 3*
Forney, Mathias N *HisAmM XR*
Fornof, John Renchin 1889-1978 *WhoAm 1974*
Forrest, Jane *NF*
Forrest, Joseph K C 1820-1896 *NatCAB 7*
Forrest, K C *NF*
Forrest, Wilbur Studley 1887-1977 *BioIn 1,
BioIn 2, ConAu 69, CurBio XR, WhNAA*
Forrester, Alfred Henry 1804-1872 *Alli, DcEnL,
NewC, WebBD*
Forrester, Francis *DcAmA, DcNAA,
HisAmM XR*
Forrester, Leland S 1905?-1978 *WhoS&SW 1973*
Forrey, Carl R 1901?-1954 *BioIn 3*
Forsberg, Franklin S 1905- *WhoAm 1974,
WhoWor 1974*
Forshey, Calib Goldsmith *HisAmM XR*
Forster, Dora *NF*
Forster, Friedrich Christoph 1791-1868 *BbD,
BiD&SB, OxGer, WebBD*
Forster, John 1812-1876 *Alli, Alli Sup, BbD,
BiD&SB, BrAu 19, CasWL, DcEnA,
DcEnL, DcEuL, DcLEL, EvLB, NewC,
OxEng, Pen Eng, WebBD*
Forster, Weidman Wallace 1895-1969 *BioIn 10*
Forsyth, David P 1930- *ConAu 9R*
Forsyth, Frederick 1938- *BioIn 9, BioIn 10,
ConLC 2, ConLC 5, WhoAm 1974,
WrDr 1976*
Forsyth, Gordon 1904?-1972 *BioIn 9*
Forsyth, John 1811-1877 *NatCAB 8*
Forsythe, Davis H *HisAmM XR*
Fort, Dancy 1870- *WhJnl 1928*
Fort, Paul 1872-1960 *CasWL, ClDMEL,
EncWL, EvEuW, OxFr, Pen Eur, REn,
WebBD, WorAu*
Forte, Angelo *NF*
Forte, Marjorie *NF*
Forte, Ralph E *OvPC*
Fortenberry, Thomas W *NF*
Fortescue, Granville Roland 1875-1952 *AmAu&B,
BioIn 2*
Forthingham, Paul Revere *LiJA*
Fortian, Florian 1885- *WhJnl 1928*
Fortuna, Michael *NF*
Fortune, Timothy Thomas 1856-1928 *Alli Sup,
AmAu&B, BioIn 5, BioIn 6, BioIn 8,
BioIn 9, BlkAW, BlkC, DcNAA, EncAB,
HisAmM XR*
Fortune, William 1863-1942 *HisAmM XR*
Fortune, William Lemcke 1912- *WhoAm 1974*
Forwood, Harry 1905?-1967 *BioIn 7*
Fosnot, Walter 1879-1950 *BioIn 4, NatCAB 41*
Foss, Kendall 1904?-1964 *BioIn 7, RpN*
Foss, Sam Walter 1858-1911 *AmAu, AmAu&B,
DcAmA, DcAmB 6, DcNAA, EvLB,
HisAmM XR, OxAm, REnAL, WebBD*
Foster, Alan Stephens 1892-1969 *BioIn 8*
Foster, Arthur R d1948 *BioIn 1*
Foster, Cedric 1900-1975 *WhoAm 1974*
Foster, Chapin D 1887- *WhNAA, WhJnl 1928*
Foster, Charles James 1820-1883 *Alli Sup,
AmAu&B, DcNAA, HisAmM XR, OhA&B*
Foster, Clifford J *NF*
Foster, Edgar M *NF*
Foster, Ellsworth Decatur 1869-1936 *DcNAA,
NatCAB 27*
Foster, Emory *NF*
Foster, Frances Middleton 1888-1951 *BioIn 2,*

BioIn 3
Foster, Francis Apthorp 1872- *HisAmM XR*
Foster, Frank Hugh 1851-1935 *Alli Sup, DcNAA,
   HisAmM XR, OhA&B, WhNAA*
Foster, Frank Pierce 1841-1911 *DcNAA,
   HisAmM XR, WebBD*
Foster, Freeling *HisAmM XR*
Foster, George G d1850 *Alli Sup, AmAu&B,
   DcNAA, HisAmM XR*
Foster, Glenn L *WhJnl 1928*
Foster, Harold Rudolph 1892- *BioIn 4, BioIn 5*
Foster, Jack *NF*
Foster, James E *NF*
Foster, Jeanne Robert 1884-1970 *AmAu&B,
   BioIn 9, WhNAA*
Foster, Jesse L 1883- *WhJnl 1928*
Foster, John B 1863- *WhNAA, WhJnl 1928*
Foster, Lawrence G 1925- *OvPC, WhoPubR 1972*
Foster, Lee 1923?-1977 *ConAu 69*
Foster, Marcellus Elliott 1870-1942 *NatCAB XR,
   WhJnl 1928*
Foster, Maximilian 1872-1943 *AmAu&B,
   CurBio XR, DcNAA*
Foster, Michael 1904- *NF*
Foster, Sir Michael 1836-1907 *Alli Sup, WebBD*
Foster, Mosley Stratton 1900- *WhNAA,
   WhJnl 1928*
Foster, Paul Pinkerton 1875- *HisAmM XR,
   WhJnl 1928*
Foster, Preston S 1893- *WhJnl 1928*
Foster, Robert D *NF*
Foster, Robert Frederick 1853-1945 *WebBD,
   WhNAA*
Foster, Solomon 1878- *WhJnl 1928*
Foster, Stephen Symonds 1809-1881 *DcAmA,
   DcNAA, HisAmM XR, WebBD*
Foster, Theodore A *HisAmM XR*
Foster, Thomas Jefferson 1843-1936 *DcAmB S2*
Foster, Virgil Elwood 1901- *BioIn 7*
Foster, William Garnett 1884-1946 *BioIn 1*
Foster, William S *OvPC*
Fougasse *see* Bird, Cyril Kenneth
Fougner, G Selmer 1884-1941 *AmAu&B,
   CurBio XR*
Fouhy, Ed 1934- *ConAu 69*
Foulke, Adrienne 1915- *ConAu 65*
Foulke, Edward D *NF*
Foulke, William Dudley 1848-1935 *Alli Sup,
   AmAu&B, AmLY, DcAmA, DcAmB S1,
   DcNAA, IndAu 1816, WebBD*
Fountain, Joseph H 1899- *WhJnl 1928*
Fourcade, Yvonne *NF*
Fournier, Jules 1884-1918 *BbtC, CanWr,
   DcNAA, OxCan*
Fowells, Harry A *BioIn 10*
Fowle, Daniel 1715-1787 *AmAu&B, AmJnl,
   DcNAA, NatCAB 23*
Fowle, Farnsworth *OvPC*
Fowle, Leonard M 1904?-1971 *BioIn 9*
Fowle, William Bentley 1795-1865 *DcNAA,
   HisAmM XR*
Fowle, Zechariah *AmJnl*
Fowler, Albert Vann 1904?-1968 *BioIn 8*
Fowler, Arthur H *NF*
Fowler, C H *HisAmM XR*
Fowler, Eltinge Alexander 1879-1916 *NF*
Fowler, Gene 1890-1960 *AmAu&B, CathA 1952,
   CurBio XR, REn, REnAL, TwCA,
   TwCA Sup, WebBD, WhJnl 1928*
Fowler, Giles Merrill 1934- *WhoAm 1974,
   WhoMW 1974*
Fowler, Hammond 1901- *WhNAA,
   WhoAmP 1973, WhJnl 1928,
   WhoS&SW 1973*

Fowler, Helen 1907?-1968 *BioIn 8*
Fowler, J A *Alli Sup, HisAmM XR*
Fowler, Jerry Scott 1891- *WhJnl 1928*
Fowler, Lorenzo Niles 1811-1896 *Alli Sup,
   DcAmA, DcNAA, HisAmM XR*
Fowler, Louise A 1898- *WhJnl 1928*
Fowler, Orson Squire 1809-1887 *Alli Sup,
   DcAmA, DcNAA, HisAmM XR*
Fowler, Richard Brosing 1902- *WhoAm 1974*
Fowler, Robert Howard 1926- *ConAu 73, OvPC,
   WhoAm 1974, WhoE 1974, WhoF&I 1974,
   WhoWor 1974*
Fowler, Virginie *BioIn 3*
Fowler, Volney B 1896- *WhJnl 1928*
Fowler, W H B *WhJnl 1928*
Fox, A Harry 1880- *WhJnl 1928*
Fox, Albert W *NF*
Fox, Arthur Joseph, Jr. 1923- *WhoAm 1974*
Fox, Barbara *NF*
Fox, Beauvais B 1876?-1955 *BioIn 4*
Fox, C Lyn *BioIn 1*
Fox, Charles Donald d1952 *BioIn 2*
Fox, Charles James *HisAmM XR*
Fox, Christy *ForWC 1970, WhoAmW 1974*
Fox, Dorus Martin 1817-1901 *DcNAA,
   HisAmM XR*
Fox, Ed *HisAmM XR*
Fox, Fontaine Talbot, Jr. 1884-1964 *AmAu&B,
   AmJnl, BioIn 3, BioIn 7, BioIn 8,
   NatCAB 51*
Fox, Frederick 1885- *WhJnl 1928*
Fox, Gilbert T 1915- *ConAu 69*
Fox, Hale Drury 1926- *WhoAm 1974,
   WhoF&I 1974*
Fox, Harry A 1880- *NF*
Fox, Jack Vernon 1918- *WhoAm 1974*
Fox, Jay *AmRP, CurBio XR*
Fox, John 1906- *BioIn 2, BioIn 3, BioIn 4,
   BioIn 5*
Fox, John, Jr. 1863-1919 *AmAu&B, AmJnl,
   BbD, BiD&SB, BiDSA, CarSB, CnDAL,
   ConAmL, DcAmA, DcBiA, DcLEL,
   DcNAA, EvLB, FamWC, HisAmM XR,
   OxAm, REn, REnAL, TwCA, TwCA Sup,
   TwCW, WebBD*
Fox, Kenneth Lee 1917- *WhoAm 1974*
Fox, Lester *OvPC*
Fox, Michael *NF*
Fox, Richard Kyle 1846-1922 *BioIn 5, BioIn 6,
   DcAmB 6, DcNAA, HisAmM XR*
Fox, Sylvan *BioIn 7*
Fox, Ted *ConAu XR*
Fox, Thomas B 1808-1876 *DcNAA, HisAmM XR*
Fox, Tom *NF*
Foxall, Raymond 1916- *Au&Wr, ConAu 9R,
   WrDr 1976*
Foxcroft, Frank 1850-1921 *Alli Sup, AmAu&B,
   DcNAA, HisAmM XR*
Foxhall, Mrs. Lewis *RpN*
Foy, Louis *NF*
Fradon, Dana 1922- *WhoAm 1974*
Fraenkel, Heinrich 1897- *Au&Wr, BioIn 5,
   ConAu 13R, ConAu 15, Who 1974,
   WrDr 1976*
Fraina, Louis 1894?-1953 *AmRP*
Fraina, Louis *see also* Corey, Lewis
Fraker, Susan *NF*
Fraley, Oscar 1914- *AmAu&B, BioIn 6*
France, Beulah Sanford 1891-1971 *BioIn 9,
   ConAu 33, NewYTBE 3*
France, Harry Clinton 1890-1972 *BioIn 5, BioIn 9*
Frances, Evan *NF*
Francis, Dale L 1917- *BioIn 2*
Francis, David Rowland 1850-1927 *AmJnl,*

BiDSA, DcNAA, WebBD
Francis, Devon 1901- *ConAu 61*
Francis, Fred *NF*
Francis, Frederick *HisAmM XR*
Francis, John Morgan 1823-1897 *NatCAB 1*
Francis, Susan M *HisAmM XR*
Francis-Williams, Baron Edward F W 1903-1970 *BioIn 8, BioIn 9, CurBio XR*
Francke, Linda *NF*
Franco, Harry 1804-1877 *AmAu, AmAu&B, DcEnL, OxAm, REnAL*
Franco, Harry *see also* Briggs, Charles Frederick
Francois-Poncet, Andre 1887-1978 *ConAu 73, CurBio XR, IntWW 1974, Who 1974, WhoWor 1974*
Frandsen, Julius, Jr. 1907-1976 *ConAu 69, WhoAm 1974*
Franjola, Matt *NF*
Frank, Bailey R *NF*
Frank, Ben G *OvPC*
Frank, E R *AmRP*
Frank, Gerold 1907- *Au&Wr, BioIn 5, BioIn 8, BioIn 9, OvPC, WhoAm 1974*
Frank, Glenn 1887-1940 *AmAu&B, BioIn 4, BioIn 5, BioIn 7, BioIn 8, CurBio XR, DcAmB S2, DcNAA, HisAmM XR, WebBD, WhJnl 1928, WisWr*
Frank, Herman 1893?-1952 *BioIn 3*
Frank, James Marshall *HisAmM XR*
Frank, Karolena May *WhJnl Sup*
Frank, May *WhNAA, WhJnl 1928*
Frank, Morris *WhoS&SW 1973*
Frank, Morton 1912- *OvPC, WhoAdv 1972, WhoE 1974, WhoF&I 1974*
Frank, Murray 1908- *ConAu 37, ConAu 73, WhoWorJ 1972*
Frank, Pat 1907-1964 *AmNov, ConAu 5R*
Frank, Reuven 1920- *BioIn 8, BioIn 9, CurBio XR, WhoAm 1974, WhoWor 1974, WhoWorJ 1972*
Frank, Stanley B 1908- *AmJnl, ConAu 7R, HisAmM XR*
Frank, Tenney 1876-1939 *AmAu&B, DcNAA, HisAmM XR, WebBD, WhNAA*
Frank, Waldo David 1889-1967 *BioIn 1, BioIn 2, ConAu 25, CurBio XR, HisAmM XR, WebBD*
Frank-Kamenetskii, David Al'Bertovich 1910-1970 *BioIn 9*
Franke, F R 1904- *BioIn 3*
Frankel, Eliot 1922- *NF*
Frankel, Herbert R *OvPC*
Frankel, James Andrew 1923- *WhoAm 1974*
Frankel, Joseph Wallace 1872?-1950 *BioIn 2*
Frankel, Lou 1911?-1974 *NewYTBS 5, OvPC*
Frankel, Max 1930- *BioIn 9, ConAu 65, NewMr, WhoAm 1974, WhoS&SW 1973, WhoWorJ 1972*
Frankel, Stanley Arthur 1918- *OvPC, WhoAm 1974, WhoF&I 1974, WhoPubR 1972*
Frankel, William 1917- *Who 1974, WhoWorJ 1972*
Frankenstein, Alfred Victor 1906- *AmAu&B, ConAu 3R, DrAS 74H, WhoAm 1974, WhoAmA 1973, WhoMus 1972*
Frankfurter, Alfred Moritz 1906-1965 *BioIn 7*
Frankish, John F *AmJnl*
Frankland, Mark 1934- *ConAu 69*
Franklin, Ann 1696-1763 *AmJnl, REnAL*
Franklin, Ben *NF*
Franklin, Benjamin 1706-1790 *Alli, AmAu, AmAu&B, AmJnl, AmWr, AtlBL, BbD, BiD&SB, CasWL, CnDAL, CrtT 3,*

CyAL 1, CyWA, DcAmA, DcEnL, DcLEL, DcNAA, EvLB, ForP, MouLC 2, NewC, OxAm, OxEng, Pen Am, RComWL, REn, REnAL, WebBD, WebE&AL
Franklin, Benjamin 1812-1876? *BioIn 2, DcNAA, IndAu 1816*
Franklin, Benjamin A 1927- *NF*
Franklin, Chester Arthur 1880-1955 *WhNAA, WhJnl 1928*
Franklin, Donald *BlkC*
Franklin, Fabian 1853-1939 *AmLY, BioIn 4, DcAmB S2, DcNAA, HisAmM XR, WebBD*
Franklin, James 1697-1735 *AmAu&B, AmJnl, CyAL 1, EarABI, ForP, NatCAB 8, OxAm, REnAL*
Franklin, Jay 1897-1967 *ConAu XR, CurBio XR, TwCA, TwCA Sup*
Franklin, Jay *see also* Carter, John Franklin, Jr.
Franklin, Jim 1945?- *BioIn 9*
Franklin, Olga Rose 1912- *BioIn 2, BioIn 4, BioIn 8*
Franklin, Rebecca *BioIn 1*
Franklin, Wade *NF*
Franklin-Bouillon, Henry 1872-1937 *WebBD*
Franks, Janice *NF*
Franks, L P *HisAmM XR*
Franks, Lucinda Laura 1946- *ConAu 53, WhoAm 1974, WhoAmW 1974*
Frantz, Dolph Griffin 1886-1953 *BioIn 3, WhJnl 1928*
Frantz, Harry Warner 1891- *HisAmM XR, WhoAm 1974, WhoWor 1974*
Frantz, N A 1882- *WhJnl 1928*
Frantz, Ralph Jules *OvPC*
Franzos, Karl Emil 1848-1904 *BiD&SB, EuAu, EvEuW, OxGer, WebBD*
Frapollo, Elizabeth *NF*
Frasca, John Anthony 1916- *WhoAm 1974*
Fraser, Alexander *Alli, BiDLA*
Fraser, Alexander 1860-1936 *AmLY, BioIn 1, DcNAA, OxCan*
Fraser, Blair 1909-1968 *BioIn 8, ConAu 23, OxCan Sup*
Fraser, Cedric Douglas 1891- *WhJnl Sup*
Fraser, George MacDonald 1925- *Au&Wr, ConAu 45, WrDr 1976*
Fraser, Gordon *NF*
Fraser, Hugh Russell 1901- *CurBio XR*
Fraser, J Gordon *OvPC*
Fraser, James K *HisAmM XR*
Fraser, John *HisAmM XR*
Fraser, John *NF*
Fraser, Sir John Malcolm 1868- *NF*
Fraser, Nicholas *NF*
Fraser, Sir Robert Brown 1904- *CurBio XR, IntWW 1976, Who 1974*
Fraser, Sylvia 1935- *ConAu 45*
Fraser, William Lewis *HisAmM XR*
Fratney, Frederick 1815-1855 *BioIn 5*
Frawley, Ernest David 1920- *WhoAm 1974*
Frayn, Michael 1933- *Au&Wr, BioIn 10, ConAu 5R, ConDr, ConNov 1972, ConNov 1976, ModBL Sup, NewC, Who 1974, WorAu, WrDr 1976*
Frazer, John Fries 1812-1872 *HisAmM XR*
Frazer, Persifor 1844-1909 *Alli Sup, DcAmA, DcNAA, WebBD*
Frazier, Edna M *NF*
Frazier, George 1911-1974 *BioIn 6, BioIn 10, ConAu 25, ConAu 49, NewYTBS 5, WhoE 1974*
Frazier, James H *HisAmM XR*
Frazier, Julius Leroy 1885-1966 *BioIn 7, HisAmM XR*

Frazier, Kendrick 1942- NF
Frazier, Robert B 1920?-1977 RpN
Freaner, James L AmJnl, FamWC
Frechette, Louis Honore 1839-1908 BbD, BbtC,
    BiD&SB, CanWr, CasWL, DcNAA, OxAm,
    OxCan, REn, REnAL, WebBD
Frederic, Harold 1856-1898 Alli Sup, AmAu,
    AmAu&B, AmJnl, AmWr, BbD, BiD&SB,
    BioIn 5, BioIn 7, BioIn 8, CasWL, CnDAL,
    CyWA, DcAmA, DcAmB 7, DcBiA,
    DcEnA Ap, DcLEL, DcNAA, EvLB,
    HisAmM XR, ModAL, ModAL Sup, OxAm,
    Pen Am, REn, REnAL, WebBD,
    WebE&AL
Frederick, Esther Paulus HisAmM XR
Frederick, Harriet I 1903- WhJnl Sup
Frederick, John Towner 1893- AmAu&B,
    CurBio XR, HisAmM XR
Frederick, Pauline 1908?- BioIn 1, BioIn 2,
    BioIn 3, BioIn 4, BioIn 5, BioIn 6, BioIn 7,
    BioNews 1974, CelR 1973, CurBio XR,
    ForWC 1970, WhoAm 1974,
    WhoAmW 1974, WhoWor 1974
Fredericks, Alan NF
Fredericks, Fred NF
Fredericks, Leonard H 1888- WhJnl 1928
Fredericks, Pierce 1921?- BioIn 2
Fredericks, Stephanie NF
Fredericks, Tina 1923?- BioIn 2
Frederiksen, Emil 1902- IntWW 1976,
    WhoWor 1974
Free, Ann Cottrell ConAu 9R, WhoS&SW 1973
Free, James 1908- WhoS&SW 1973
Free, Montague 1885-1963 BioIn 7
Free, Victor Ward 1903- WhJnl 1928
Freeburg, Victor Oscar 1882-1953 BioIn 3,
    WhNAA
Freed, Bruce NF
Freed, Fred 1920- NewYTBS 5, WhoAm 1974,
    WhoWor 1974
Freed, Josh NF
Freed, Kenneth J NF
Freedel, Anna E 1904?- WhJnl 1928
Freedland, Michael 1934- ConAu 65, WrDr 1976
Freedland, Nathaniel 1936- ConAu 65
Freedley, George Reynolds 1904-1967 AmAu&B,
    ConAu 5R
Freedman, Emanuel Ralph 1910-1971 BioIn 4,
    BioIn 9, NewYTBE 2, WhoWorJ 1972
Freedman, Max 1914- BioIn 7, WhoS&SW 1973
Freedman, Paul W OvPC
Freehoff, William F RpN
Freeland, Stephen L 1911?-1977 ConAu 69
Freeman, Alex 1928?-1967 BioIn 7
Freeman, Andrew A NF
Freeman, Charles 1890?-1977 NF
Freeman, Don NF
Freeman, Don 1908-1978 AuBYP, MorJA
Freeman, Douglas Southall 1886-1953 AmAu&B,
    AmJnl, CyWA, DcAmB S5, HisAmM XR,
    OxAm, REn, REnAL, TwCA, TwCA Sup,
    WebBD, WhJnl 1928
Freeman, Edward AmJnl
Freeman, Edward 1914- WhoAm 1974,
    WhoS&SW 1973
Freeman, Frederick K 1841-1928 NatCAB 24
Freeman, Gilbert 1893- WhNAA, WhJnl 1928
Freeman, Graydon Laverne 1904- WhoAm 1974
Freeman, Harry 1906-1978 WhoAm 1974,
    WhoWor 1974
Freeman, J B HisAmM XR
Freeman, James 1759-1835 Alli, DcAmA,
    HisAmM XR, WebBD
Freeman, James Leo 1908- WhoAm 1974

Freeman, Jim NF
Freeman, John 1915- BioIn 5, BioIn 7, BioIn 8,
    CurBio XR, IntWW 1976, Who 1974,
    WhoWor 1974
Freeman, John D, Jr. 1884-1974 WhNAA,
    WhoAm 1974, WhJnl 1928
Freeman, Joseph 1897-1965 AmAu&B, AmNov,
    BioIn 2, BioIn 4, BioIn 6, BioIn 7, OxAm,
    TwCA, TwCA Sup, WebBD, WhJnl 1928
Freeman, Joseph W 1863-1939 NatCAB 31
Freeman, Lucy 1916- AmAu&B, BioIn 2,
    BioIn 3, ConAu 5, CurBio XR,
    ForWC 1970, WhoAm 1974,
    WhoAmW 1974, WhoWorJ 1972,
    WrDr 1976
Freeman, Neal Blackwell 1940- WhoAm 1974,
    WhoE 1974
Freeman, Samuel AmJnl
Freeman, Siler 1901-1962 BioIn 6
Freeman, Tom 1899- WhJnl 1928
Freemantle, Brian Harry 1936- ConAu 65
Freene, F V HisAmM XR
Freer, Charles H AmJnl
Freese, Arthur S NF
Freeston, Charles Lincoln 1865- HisAmM XR,
    WhoLA
Frehm, Ron NF
Freiberger, Edward HisAmM XR
Freidin, Seymour Kenneth 1917- AmAu&B,
    BioIn 10, ConAu 4R, OvPC
Freilicher, Lila NF
Fremd, Mary Elizabeth BioIn 3
Fremes, Ruth NF
Fremont-Smith, Eliot 1929?- BioIn 9
French, Alvah P 1867-1927 DcNAA,
    HisAmM XR
French, Benjamin I, Jr. OvPC
French, Girard Hollingsworth 1906- WhJnl 1928
French, Henry Willard 1854?- Alli Sup, BiD&SB,
    DcAmA, DcNAA
French, Herbert NF
French, J Wymond d1952 BioIn 3
French, John A NF
French, Lewis Clark 1893- WhJnl 1928
French, Lillie Hamilton 1854-1939 AmAu&B,
    DcAmA, DcNAA
French, Peter 1918- Au&Wr, ConAu 1, OvPC
French, Roy LaVerne 1888-1968 WhJnl 1928
French, William D BioIn 8
French, William Harold 1926- ConAu 69, RpN,
    WhoAm 1974
Freneau, Peter 1757-1813 Alli, AmJnl, BioIn 1,
    CyAL 1
Freneau, Philip Morin 1752-1832 Alli, AmAu,
    AmAu&B, AmJnl, AtlBL, BiD&SB,
    BioIn 3, BioIn 4, BioIn 5, BioIn 7, BioIn 8,
    BioIn 9, CasWL, CnDAL, CrtT 3, CyAL 1,
    CyWA, DcAmA, DcLEL, DcNAA, EncAB,
    EvLB, ForP, HisAmM XR, LiJA,
    MouLC 3, OxAm, OxEng, Pen Am, REn,
    REnAL, WebBD, WebE&AL
Freniere, Emile F 1901- WhJnl 1928
Frentz, Edward Williston HisAmM XR
Frere, A NF
Frere, John Hookham 1769-1846 Alli, BbD,
    BiD&SB, BrAu 19, CasWL, DcEnL,
    DcEuL, EvLB, NewC, OxEng, Pen Eng,
    REn, WebBD, WebE&AL
Frere Sauvage see Wilde, William Charles K
Freron, Elie Catherine 1718-1776 DcEuL, OxFr,
    Pen Eur, WebBD
Freron, Louis Marie Stanislas 1754-1802 WebBD
Freshfield, Douglas William 1845-1934 Alli Sup,
    WebBD

Freson, Robert 1926?- *BioIn 6*
Freudeneau, William *HisAmM XR*
Freudenheim, Milton 1927- *OvPC, WhoAm 1974*
Freudenthal, Elsbeth Estelle 1902?-1953 *BioIn 3*
Freund, Gisele 1912- *BioIn 10, ConAu 49*
Freund, Harry E *HisAmM XR*
Freund, John C *HisAmM XR*
Freund, Mrs. John C *HisAmM XR*
Freund, Philip 1909- *AmAu&B, AmNov,*
  ConAu 13, CurBio XR, WhNAA,
  WrDr 1976
Freundlich, Irwin *BioIn 8*
Freundlich, Lawrence Stewart 1939- *WhoAm 1974*
Frey, Albert Romer 1858-1926 *Alli Sup, DcAmA,*
  DcNAA, HisAmM XR
Frey, Michael J 1898- *WhoAm 1974,*
  WhoWest 1974
Frey, Richard L *NF*
Freyse, William 1899?-1969 *BioIn 8*
Freytag, Gustav 1816-1895 *BbD, BiD&SB,*
  CasWL, CIDMEL, CyWA, DcBiA, DcEuL,
  EuAu, EvEuW, McGWD, OxGer, Pen Eur,
  REn, REnWD, WebBD
Friang, Elizabeth 1924- *BioIn 3*
Frick, Ford Christopher 1894-1978 *CurBio XR,*
  WhoAm 1974
Fried, Alexander 1902- *WhoAm 1974,*
  WhoAmA 1973, WhoMus 1972,
  WhoWest 1974, WhoWorJ 1972
Fried, Alfred Hermann 1864-1921 *WebBD*
Fried, Ida *NF*
Fried, Joseph *NF*
Fried, Phillip Paul 1933- *OvPC, WhoPubR 1972*
Friedan, Betty 1921- *AmAu&B, WrDr 1976*
Friedberg, Judith E *NF*
Friedenberg, Walter Drew 1928- *WhoAm 1974,*
  WhoMW 1974
Friedheim, Bette Sweeney *NF*
Friedheim, Eric *OvPC*
Friedlander, Gordon D *OvPC*
Friedlander, Paul Josef Crost 1910- *WhoAm 1974*
Friedman, A E Robert *OvPC*
Friedman, Arnold D'Arcy 1900- *WhoAdv 1972,*
  WhoAm 1974
Friedman, Edward Ludwig 1903- *ConAu 3R,*
  WhoAm 1974
Friedman, Esther Pauline *see* Landers, Ann
Friedman, Esther Pauline *see* Lederer, Esther Pauline
Friedman, Frieda 1905- *BioIn 6, MorJA*
Friedman, Gerry Gewirtz 1920- *ForWC 1970,*
  OvPC
Friedman, Isaac Kahn 1870-1931 *AmAu&B,*
  DcAmA, DcNAA
Friedman, Joseph H *OvPC*
Friedman, Milton 1912- *AmAu&B, AmEA 1974,*
  AmM&W 73S, Au&Wr, CelR 1973,
  ConAu 1, CurBio XR, EncAB,
  IntWW 1974, NewYTBE 1, Who 1974,
  WhoAm 1974, WhoWor 1974,
  WhoWorJ 1972, WrDr 1976
Friedman, Paul *NF*
Friedman, Ralph 1916- *ConAu 69*
Friedman, Saul 1929- *InvJ, NewMr, RpN*
Friedman, William S 1911?-1951 *BioIn 2*
Friedmann, Thomas D W *OvPC*
Friedrich, Dernburg 1833-1911 *NF*
Friedrich, Otto 1929- *ConAu 5R*
Friedwald, Eugene Marie *BioIn 1*
Friend, Emil 1863-1921 *NF*
Friend, Ted 1900?-1978 *NF*
Friendlich, Dick 1909- *AuBYP, BioIn 8,*
  ConAu XR
Friendly, Alfred 1911- *IntWW 1976,*
  WhoAm 1974

Friendly, Alfred, Jr. *NF*
Friendly, Edwin Samson 1884-1970 *BioIn 2,*
  BioIn 7, BioIn 9, CurBio XR, NewYTBE 1,
  WhNAA, WhJnl 1928, WhoWorJ 1972
Friendly, Fred W 1915- *AmAu&B, ConAu 23,*
  CurBio XR, IntMPA 1975, IntWW 1976,
  WhoAm 1974
Frierson, John W 1897-1959 *NatCAB 48*
Frierson, William V *HisAmM XR*
Fries, Elmer Plumas 1884-1949 *WhJnl 1928*
Fries, George 1881- *WhJnl 1928*
Friggens, Paul *NF*
Friis, Erik Johan 1913- *ConAu 69, DrAS 74H,*
  WhoAm 1974, WhoE 1974, WhoF&I 1974,
  WrDr 1976
Frimbo, Ernest Malcolm 1901?- *BioIn 10*
Frink, Maurice 1895-1972 *ConAu 25,*
  IndAu 1917
Fris, Henry H 1884-1950 *BioIn 2, WhJnl 1928*
Frisbee, Lucy Post *NF*
Frisbie, William Albert 1867- *AmAu&B*
Frisch, Efraim 1873-1942 *BioIn 6*
Frisch, Leon *NF*
Frischauer, Willi 1906- *Au&Wr, BioIn 7,*
  ConAu 7R
Frise, Jimmy 1890?-1948 *BioIn 1*
Frishauf, Peter *NF*
Friskey, Margaret 1901- *BioIn 2, BioIn 4,*
  BioIn 8, BioIn 10
Fritchey, Clayton *BioIn 2, BioIn 4, BioIn 5,*
  WhoAm 1974
Fritchman, Stephen Hole 1902- *BioIn 1, BioIn 3,*
  OhA&B, WhoAm 1974
Fritz, Bruce *NF*
Fritz, Sara Jane *NF*
Froggatt, Gordon *NF*
Froggett, Joseph *WhJnl 1928*
Frome, Michael 1920- *ConAu 1, WrDr 1976*
Frommer, Arthur B *NF*
Frommer, Lawrence J 1917- *NF*
Fromson, Murray *OvPC*
Frosch, Frank d1970 *BioIn 8, BioIn 9*
Frost, Andrew *HisAmM XR*
Frost, Arthur Burdett 1851-1928 *AmAu&B,*
  DcAmA, DcNAA, HisAmM XR, OxAm,
  REnAL, Str&VC, WebBD
Frost, Charles W *HisAmM XR*
Frost, David Paradine 1939- *BioIn 8, BioIn 9,*
  CelR 1973, ConAu 69, CurBio XR,
  IntMPA 1975, IntWW 1976, NewYTBE 2,
  WhoWor 1974, Who 1974
Frost, George Henry 1838-1917 *HisAmM XR,*
  NatCAB 18
Frost, Meigs Oliver 1882-1950 *BioIn 2, BioIn 7,*
  TexWr, WhNAA, WhJnl 1928
Frost, Russell Elwell 1900- *WhNAA, WhJnl 1928*
Frost, S Annie *HisAmM XR*
Frost, Stanley 1881-1942 *DcNAA, OhA&B*
Frost, Walter Archer 1876-1964 *AmAu&B,*
  BioIn 6, WhNAA
Frost, William Henry 1863-1902 *CarSB, DcNAA*
Frothingham, Arthur Lincoln 1859-1923 *AmAu&B,*
  DcAmA, DcNAA, HisAmM XR, WebBD
Frothingham, David 1765-1814? *AmJnl, BioIn 7,*
  HisAmM XR
Frothingham, Richard 1812-1880 *Alli, Alli Sup,*
  AmAu, AmAu&B, CyAL 2, DcAmA,
  DcNAA, WebBD
Frothingham, Robert 1865-1937 *AmAu&B,*
  DcNAA, HisAmM XR
Fruchtman, Helen *OvPC*
Frueh, Alfred Nee 1880-1968 *BioIn 6, BioIn 8,*
  WhJnl 1928
Frumkin, Gene 1928- *AmAu&B, ConAu 9,*

DrAP 1975, DrAS 74E, WrDr 1976
Frumkin, Paul 1914- *WhoAm 1974*
Frummer, Jack *OvPC*
Frutig, Judith *NF*
Fry, Benjamin St. James 1824-1892 *BiDSA, DcNAA, OhA&B*
Fry, Joseph Reese 1811-1865 *AmAu&B, DcNAA, HisAmM XR, OhA&B*
Fry, Kenneth D 1902- *CurBio XR*
Fry, Varian M 1907-1967 *AmRP, BioIn 8*
Fry, William Henry *NF*
Fry, William Henry 1815-1864 *AmAu&B, DcAmB 7, DcNAA, WebBD*
Fryatt, Norma R *AuBYP, BioIn 8, ConAu 57*
Fryd, Norbert 1913-1976 *ConAu 65, WhoWor 1974*
Frye, Helene *BioIn 1, BioIn 3*
Frye, John 1910- *ConAu 49*
Frye, Ralph Bridges 1878?-1955 *BioIn 4*
Frye, William Fenner 1908-1961 *BioIn 1, BioIn 5*
Frye, William Ruggles 1918- *ConAu 73, WhoAm 1974, WhoE 1974, WhoWor 1974*
Fu, Chien Chung *NF*
Fuad, Kim *NF*
Fuentes, Carlos 1928- *AuNews 2, CasWL, ConLC 3, CurBio XR, DcCLAA, EncWL, IntWW 1976, Pen Am, TwCW, WhoS&SW 1973, WhoTwCL, WorAu*
Fuerbringer, Otto 1910- *BioIn 2, HisAmM XR, WhoAm 1974*
Fuermann, George Melvin 1918- *WhoAm 1974*
Fuessle, Newton Augustus 1883-1924 *DcNAA*
Fugere, Peter John 1951- *NF*
Fugger, Jakob, II 1459-1525 *NewC, WebBD*
Fuhrman, Harold George 1921- *WhoAm 1974*
Fuhrman, Lee 1903?-1977 *ConAu 73*
Fujii, John *NF*
Fukuda, Ichihei 1887- *WhJnl Sup*
Fukushima, Shintaro 1907- *ForP, WhoWor 1974*
Fukuzawa, Sutejiro 1865-1926 *WebBD*
Fukuzawa, Yukichi 1834?-1901 *DcOrL 1, ForP, WebBD*
Fulbright, Freeman 1925-1978 *WhoAm 1974, WhoE 1974*
Fulbright, Newton H *OvPC*
Fulbright, Roberta W 1874-1953 *BioIn 3, BioIn 7, NatCAB 49*
Fuldheim, Dorothy 1893- *BioIn 7, ConAu 49*
Fulford, Robert L *NF*
Fulford, Roger Thomas Baldwin 1902- *Au&Wr, ConAu 65, DcLEL, LongC, Who 1974*
Fulkerson, Horace Smith 1818-1891 *DcNAA*
Fulkerson, Roe 1870-1949 *BioIn 1*
Fullen, Hiram 1900- *WhNAA, WhJnl 1928*
Fuller, Andrew Samuel 1828-1896 *Alli Sup, DcAmA, DcNAA, HisAmM XR*
Fuller, Anne *BioIn 8*
Fuller, Charles L 1877-1958 *BioIn 6, NatCAB 46*
Fuller, Curtis G 1912- *WhoAm 1974*
Fuller, DeWolf Harold 1874-1957 *WhJnl 1928*
Fuller, DeWolf Harold *see also* Fuller, Harold DeWolf
Fuller, Edward 1860-1938 *Alli Sup, DcAmA, DcNAA*
Fuller, Edwin Keith 1923- *WhoAm 1974*
Fuller, Ethel 1883-1965 *BioIn 7*
Fuller, Frank *NF*
Fuller, George Newman 1873- *BioIn 1, WhNAA*
Fuller, H S *HisAmM XR*
Fuller, Harold 1940- *ConAu 65*
Fuller, Harold DeWolf 1874-1957 *AmLY, BioIn 4, HisAmM XR*
Fuller, Harold DeWolf *see also* Fuller, DeWolf Harold

Fuller, Harrison 1892- *WhJnl 1928*
Fuller, Hector 1864-1934 *BioIn 2, IndAu 1816, WhNAA*
Fuller, Helen 1914?-1972 *BioIn 9, ConAu 37, HisAmM XR, WhoAmW 1974, WhoS&SW 1973*
Fuller, Henry Starkey 1852- *DcNAA*
Fuller, Hiram 1814?-1880 *Alli, Alli Sup, BiD&SB, DcAmA, DcAmB 7, DcNAA, HisAmM XR*
Fuller, Horace B *HisAmM XR*
Fuller, Horace W *Alli Sup, HisAmM XR*
Fuller, Hoyt 1927?- *BlkC, ConAu 53, LivBAA*
Fuller, John Grant 1913- *AmAu&B, BiE&WWA, ConAu 1, WhoAm 1974, WhoWor 1974*
Fuller, Lee N 1889- *WhJnl 1928*
Fuller, Margaret 1810-1850 *AmAu, AmAu&B, AmJnl, AtlBL, BbD, BiD&SB, CnDAL, CrtT 3, DcAmA, DcLEL, HisAmM XR, LiJA, OxAm, OxEng, Pen Am, REn, REnAL, WebBD, WebE&AL*
Fuller, Margaret *see also* Fuller, Sarah Margaret
Fuller, Margaret *see also* Ossoli, Margaret Fuller
Fuller, Melville Weston *HisAmM XR*
Fuller, Ralph Briggs 1890-1963 *BioIn 2, BioIn 6, HisAmM XR*
Fuller, Robert Higginson 1864-1927 *DcNAA*
Fuller, Sarah Margaret 1810-1850 *Alli, AmAu, CasWL, DcAmB 7, DcEnL, DcNAA, EncAB, EvLB, MouLC 3*
Fuller, Sarah Margaret *see also* Fuller, Margaret
Fuller, Sarah Margaret *see also* Ossoli, Margaret Fuller
Fuller, W M 1877- *WhJnl 1928*
Fuller, Walter Deane 1882-1964 *AmAu&B, CurBio XR, HisAmM XR*
Fuller, Walter G *HisAmM XR*
Fuller, Wesley 1912-1958 *BioIn 5, RpN*
Fuller, William Oliver 1856-1941 *AmAu&B, AmLY, BioIn 2, DcNAA, NatCAB 35, WhNAA*
Fullerton, Hugh Stuart 1873-1945 *BioIn 1, DcNAA, OhA&B*
Fullerton, Max *NF*
Fulop-Miller, Rene 1891-1963 *AmAu&B, BioIn 4, BioIn 6, TwCA, TwCA Sup, WebBD*
Fulton, Margret *NF*
Fulton, William John, Jr. 1907-1977 *WhoAm 1974*
Fultz, Walter J 1924?-1971 *BioIn 9*
Fulweiler, John H 1910?-1978 *NF*
Fumasoni Biondi, Leonte, Conte 1901?-1949 *BioIn 2*
Fumet, Stanislas 1896- *BioIn 1, CathA 1930*
Funabashi, Yoichi 1944?- *NF*
Funder, Friedrich 1872- *BioIn 3*
Funk, Charles Earle 1881-1957 *CurBio XR*
Funk, Erwin Charles 1876- *WhJnl 1928*
Funk, Isaac Kauffman 1839-1912 *AmAu&B, DcAmA, DcNAA, HisAmM XR, OhA&B*
Funk, John 1893?-1964 *BioIn 6*
Funk, Sherman *NF*
Funk, Walther 1890-1960 *CurBio XR, WebBD*
Funk, Wilfred John 1883-1965 *AmAu&B, CurBio XR, HisAmM XR*
Funke, Lewis 1912- *AmAu&B, BiE&WWA, ConAu 49, WhoAm 1974, WhoE 1974*
Funkhouser, Abram Paul 1853-1917 *BioIn 2*
Fuoss, Robert Martin 1912- *BioIn 5, CurBio XR, HisAmM XR, IntWW 1976, WhoF&I 1974*
Fuqua, Stephen Ogden 1874-1943 *CurBio XR, DcNAA*
Furay, James Henry 1879-1955 *BioIn 4*
Furbay, John Harvey 1903- *AmAu&B, OhA&B, WhoAm 1974*

Furgurson, Ernest Baker, Jr. 1929-   *ConAu 73,*
   WhoAm 1974, WhoE 1974
Furillo, Bud   *NF*
Furlong, James C   *OvPC*
Furlong, William Barry   *NF*
Furman, Bess 1894-1969   *AmAu&B, BioIn 1,*
   BioIn 3, BioIn 5, BioIn 8
Furness, Betty 1916-   *CelR 1973, CurBio XR,*
   ForWC 1970, WhoAm 1974,
   WhoAmW 1974, WhoE 1974,
   WhoS&SW 1973
Furniss, Edgar Stephenson 1890-1972   *ConAu 37,*
   HisAmM XR, NewYTBE 3, WhNAA
Furniss, Harry 1854-1925   *WebBD, WhoChL*
Furr, LaVonne Doden   *HisAmM XR*
Furth, Albert Lavenson 1902-1962   *BioIn 6*
Furukawa, Tsukasa   *NF*
Futch, Ladell Jefferson 1931-   *WhoAm 1974*
Fyfe, Hamilton 1869-1951   *Lor&LP*
Fyfe, Hamilton *see also* Fyfe, Henry Hamilton
Fyfe, Henry Hamilton 1869-1951   *BioIn 2,*
   CurBio XR, WebBD
Fyfe, Henry Hamilton *see also* Fyfe, Hamilton
Fyles, Franklin 1847-1911   *AmAu&B, DcAmA,*
   DcNAA, REnAL

G

Gaal, George *NF*
Gabel, Emile 1908- *BioIn 3*
Gabelle, James 1874-1940 *DcNAA*
Gable, D H *HisAmM XR*
Gable, Tom *NF*
Gabriel, Alexander *NF*
Gabriel, Gilbert Wolf 1890-1952 *AmAu&B,
    AmNov, REnAL, WhNAA*
Gabriel, Terry *NF*
Gaddis, J Wilson 1910?-1975 *ConAu 57*
Gaenzle, Walter C 1899- *WhJnl 1928*
Gaertner, Fred, Jr. 1891-1963 *BioIn 8,
    NatCAB 51, WhJnl 1928*
Gaffney, Fannie Humphreys *HisAmM XR*
Gagan, Bernard 1915- *NF*
Gage, Frances Dana Barker 1808-1884 *Alli Sup,
    AmAu, AmAu&B, DcAmA, DcNAA,
    HisAmM XR, OhA&B, REnAL*
Gage, George M *HisAmM XR*
Gage, Hy 1878- *WhNAA, WhJnl 1928*
Gage, Matilda Joslyn 1826-1898 *DcAmA,
    DcNAA, HisAmM XR*
Gage, Nicholas 1939- *ConAu XR, InvJ, NewMr*
Gage-Colby, Ruth *NF*
Gagnard, Frank Lewis 1929- *WhoAm 1974*
Gagnon, Blanche 1866?-1951 *BioIn 2*
Gagnon, Henri 1883?-1958 *BioIn 5*
Gagnon, Jean-Louis 1913- *CanWW 1972,
    ConAu 23R, OxCan, OxCan Sup*
Gahagan, Marguerite Mary 1907- *BioIn 5*
Gailey, Phil *NF*
Gaillard, Edwin Samuel 1827-1885 *DcAmB 7,
    HisAmM XR*
Gaillard, M E *HisAmM XR*
Gaillardet, Theodore Frederic 1808-1882 *DcAmB 7*
Gaine, Hugh 1726?-1807 *AmAu&B, AmJnl,
    CyAL 1, REnAL*
Gaines, Robert *NF*
Gaines, William *InvJ*
Gaines, William 1700?- *NF*
Gainsborough, Richard 1896?-1969 *BioIn 8,
    BioIn 9*
Gainsway, Frederic J 1883?-1954 *BioIn 3*
Gaintan, Jorge *ForP*
Gainza Paz, Alberto 1899-1977 *BioIn 2, BioIn 3,
    BioIn 4, ConAu 73, CurBio XR, ForP,
    IntWW 1976, WhoWor 1974*
Gaither, Virgil *NF*
Galaktionov, Mikhail Romanovich 1897- *BioIn 1,
    BioIn 2*
Galanopulo, Spero *AmRP*
Galbraith, John Kenneth 1908- *AmAu&B,
    AmEA 1974, AmM&W 73S, CanWW 1972,
    CelR 1973, ConAu 21, CurBio XR, LongC,
    NewYTBE 4, REnAL, WebBD, Who 1974,
    WorAu, WrDr 1976*

Galbraith, Peter Cook 1899-1954 *BioIn 3*
Gale, George 1857-1944 *DcNAA, OxCan*
Gale, Harlow *AmJnl*
Gale, John *NF*
Gale, John Mackinnon 1925- *Au&Wr, BioIn 7*
Gale, Zona 1874-1938 *AmAu&B, AmLY,
    AnMV 1926, CnDAL, CnMD, ConAmA,
    ConAmL, DcAmB S2, DcLEL, DcNAA,
    EvLB, HisAmM XR, LongC, McGWD,
    ModWD, OxAm, Pen Am, REn, REnAL,
    TwCA, TwCA Sup, TwCW, WebBD,
    WhNAA, WisWr*
Galella, Ron 1931- *AuNews 1, BioNews 1974,
    ConAu 53, WrDr 1976*
Gales, Joseph, Elder 1761-1841 *AmAu&B, AmJnl,
    DcAmB 7, REnAL, WebBD*
Gales, Joseph, Younger 1786-1860 *AmJnl,
    BioIn 3, DcAmB 7, WebBD*
Gales, Weston Raleigh *AmJnl*
Galignani, Giovanni Antonio 1752-1821 *NewC,
    OxEng, WebBD*
Gall, Lee *NF*
Gall, Peter *NF*
Gallager, Sheldon M *NF*
Gallagher, Barclay *NF*
Gallagher, Barrett *OvPC*
Gallagher, Bill *NF*
Gallagher, Charles E 1898- *WhoAm 1974,
    WhJnl 1928*
Gallagher, Dorothy 1935- *ConAu 65*
Gallagher, Frank *BioIn 1*
Gallagher, James T *NF*
Gallagher, James Wes 1911- *WhoAm 1974*
Gallagher, James Wes see also Gallagher, Wes
Gallagher, O D *NF*
Gallagher, Robert F *OvPC*
Gallagher, Wes 1911- *BioIn 6, NewMr, OvPC,
    WhoF&I 1974*
Gallagher, Wes see also Gallagher, James Wes
Gallagher, William Davis 1808-1894 *Alli,
    Alli Sup, AmAu, AmAu&B, BbD, BiD&SB,
    BiDSA, CyAL 2, DcAmA, DcLEL,
    DcNAA, HisAmM XR, LiJA, NatCAB 9,
    OhA&B, OxAm, PoIre, REnAL*
Gallagher, William M 1923-1975 *CurBio XR*
Gallant, T Grady 1920- *ConAu 5R, WrDr 1976*
Galle, William *NF*
Gallemore, Roy Trent 1895- *WhJnl 1928*
Gallenga, Antonio Carlo Napoleone 1810-1895
    Alli Sup, BiD&SB, WebBD
Galli, Anthony P *OvPC*
Gallico, Paul William 1897-1976 *AmAu&B,
    AmNov, Au&Wr, AuNews 1, BioIn 1,
    BioIn 2, BioIn 4, BioIn 6, BioIn 9,
    ConAu 7R, ConAu 65, ConAu 69,
    ConLC 2, ConNov 1972, ConNov 1976,*

119

CurBio XR, DcLEL, EvLB, HisAmM XR,
IntWW 1974, REnAL, TwCA Sup, TwCW,
WebBD, Who 1974, WhoAm 1974,
WhJnl 1928, WhoWor 1974, WrDr 1976
Galliner, Peter 1920- *IntWW 1976*
Galling, Lorraine *OvPC*
Gallison, John 1788-1820 *Alli, HisAmM XR*
Gallo, William Victor 1922- *WhoAm 1974*
Gallob, Ben *NF*
Galloway, Clark Hewett 1898-1961 *BioIn 5,*
WhJnl 1928
Galloway, Ewing 1882?-1953 *BioIn 3*
Galloway, Joseph Lee 1941- *ConAu 73*
Galloway, Joseph W *NF*
Gallup, George Horace 1901- *AmAu&B, AmJnl,*
AmM&W 73S, BioNews 1974, CurBio XR,
EncAB, IntWW 1976, IntWW 1974, LongC,
REn, REnAL, WhoAm 1974, WhJnl 1928,
WhoWor 1974
Gallup, George Horace, III 1930- *WhoAm 1974*
Galouye, Daniel Francis 1920- *ConAu 9R*
Galphin, Bruce Maxwell 1932- *RpN,*
WhoAm 1974, WhoS&SW 1973
Galt, Herbert Randolph 1881-1926 *NF*
Galter, David J 1890-1961 *BioIn 6*
Galton, Lawrence 1913- *ConAu 57,*
HisAmM XR
Galtung, Inge *NF*
Galub, Jack *OvPC*
Galuska, Miroslav 1922- *IntWW 1976*
Galvin, Leroy Spahr 1875-1952 *BioIn 2, BioIn 3*
Galvin, W J 1884-1953 *BioIn 3*
Gamarra, Ciro *NF*
Gamble, Ed *NF*
Gamblin, Garth 1939- *NF*
Gambrell, James Bruton 1841-1921 *BiDSA,*
BioIn 3, DcNAA
Gamester, George *NF*
Gamiochippi, Fernando *NF*
Gammack, Thomas H *NF*
Gamson, Leland *NF*
Gan, Vitaly *NF*
Gander, Laurence 1915- *BioIn 7, BioIn 8*
Gander, Leonard Marsland 1902- *Au&Wr,*
BioIn 2
Gander, Rod *NF*
Gandhi, Devadas 1900-1957 *BioIn 4*
Gandhi, Feroze 1913?-1960 *BioIn 5*
Gandhi, Manilal 1892-1956 *BioIn 2, BioIn 4*
Ganju, Janki *OvPC*
Ganley, Joseph V *NF*
Gannes, Harry *AmRP*
Gannett, Frank Ernest 1876-1957 *AmAu&B,*
AmJnl, BioIn 1, BioIn 2, BioIn 4, BioIn 5,
BioIn 7, CurBio XR, HisAmM XR,
NatCAB 48, REnAL, WebBD, WhNAA,
WhJnl 1928
Gannett, Guy Patterson 1881-1954 *BioIn 3,*
BioIn 4, BioIn 6, NatCAB 44
Gannett, Lewis Stiles 1891-1966 *AmAu&B,*
CurBio XR, HisAmM XR, NewMr, REnAL,
TwCA, TwCA Sup
Gannett, Mary 1892?-1972 *BioIn 9*
Gannett, William Howard 1854-1948
HisAmM XR, NatCAB 38
Gannon, A D *NF*
Gannon, James P *NF*
Gannon, Robert 1931- *NF*
Gans, Sidney 1912?-1972 *BioIn 9, NewYTBE 3*
Ganschow, Cliff *NF*
Gansing, Gunhild *OvPC*
Gant, William 1904?-1972 *BioIn 9*
Gantz, David *NF*
Gapay, Les L *NF*

Gapen, Charles Earl 1886- *WhJnl 1928*
Garagiola, Joe 1926- *BioNews 1974, CelR 1973,*
WhoAm 1974, WhoE 1974
Garatca, Victor 1948- *NF*
Garber, D Allyn 1890?-1951 *BioIn 2*
Garber, Mary 1917- *NF*
Garber, Milton Cline 1867-1948 *BioIn 1, BioIn 3,*
NatCAB 38
Garbett, Arthur Selwyn 1883- *WhNAA,*
WhJnl 1928
Garcia, David *NF*
Garcia, Louis *OvPC*
Garcia Marquez, Gabriel Jose 1928- *CurBio XR*
Garcia Monge, Joaquin 1881-1958 *BioIn 2,*
BioIn 5, DcSpL
Garcia Moreno, Gabriel 1821-1875 *WebBD*
Garcia Pena, Roberto 1910- *BioIn 4, ForP,*
IntWW 1976
Garcia Valseca, Jose 1902?- *BioIn 2, ForP*
Gard, Alex 1899-1948 *BioIn 1*
Gard, Wayne 1899- *AmAu&B, AnMV 1926,*
BioIn 9, ConAu 2R, TexWr, WhNAA,
WhJnl 1928
Gard, William B *OvPC*
Gardella, Kay 1923- *ForWC 1970*
Gardener, Helen Hamilton 1853-1925 *Alli Sup,*
AmAu&B, AmLY, DcAmA, DcNAA,
OhA&B, WebBD
Gardette, Charles Desmarais 1830- *Alli Sup,*
BioIn 4, HisAmM XR
Gardiner, Alfred George 1865-1946 *BioIn 1,*
BioIn 5, BioIn 9, DcLEL, EvLB, LongC,
NewC, WebBD, WhoLA
Gardiner, Don d1977 *NF*
Gardiner, Harold Charles 1904-1969 *AmAu&B,*
BioIn 8, BkC 6
Gardiner, Herbert Fairbairn 1849-1924 *DcNAA*
Gardiner, J B W *HisAmM XR*
Gardiner, James B *NF*
Gardiner, John Sylvester John 1765-1830 *Alli,*
CyAL 1, DcNAA, HisAmM XR, WebBD
Gardiner, Lawrence *OvPC*
Gardiner, Sandy *NF*
Gardiner, William Howard *HisAmM XR*
Gardiner, William Howard 1934- *WhoMW 1974*
Gardner, Cassius M 1858- *WhJnl 1928*
Gardner, Charles Kitchel 1787-1869 *Alli, DcAmA,*
DcAmB 7, DcNAA, HisAmM XR
Gardner, Charles M 1872-1954 *BioIn 1*
Gardner, Dorsey 1842-1894 *Alli Sup, BiD&SB,*
DcAmA, DcNAA, HisAmM XR
Gardner, E C 1836-1915 *HisAmM XR*
Gardner, Edward Hall 1883- *WhNAA,*
WhJnl 1928
Gardner, Evelyn 1900-1956 *BioIn 4*
Gardner, Frank *NF*
Gardner, George William, Jr. 1888- *WhNAA,*
WhJnl 1928
Gardner, Gilson 1869-1935 *AmAu&B,*
DcAmB S1, DcNAA, WhNAA
Gardner, Horace J 1895-1950 *WhJnl 1928*
Gardner, Hy 1908?- *BioIn 3, WhoAm 1974*
Gardner, John Crawford 1935- *WhoAm 1974,*
WhoMW 1974
Gardner, John Edmund 1926- *Au&Wr,*
WrDr 1976
Gardner, Joseph L 1933- *ConAu 29*
Gardner, Judy *NF*
Gardner, Keith 1930- *WhoAm 1974*
Gardner, Lester D 1876-1956 *CurBio XR,*
NatCAB 44
Gardner, Marilyn 1927- *WhoAmW 1974*
Gardner, Mary Adelaide 1920- *ConAu 21R,*
DrAS 74E, WrDr 1976

Gardner, Paul *ConAu 69*
Gardner, R H 1918- *ConAu 33, WhoAm 1974, WhoE 1974*
Gardner, Ralph David 1923- *ConAu 15, OvPC, WhoAdv 1972, WhoE 1974, WhoF&I 1974, WrDr 1976*
Gardner, Richard Kent 1928- *BiDrLUS, ConAu 69, WhoAm 1974*
Gardner, Samuel Jackson 1788-1864 *Alli, Alli Sup, CyAL 1, DcAmA, DcNAA*
Gardner, Walter Hale 1917- *AmM&W 73P, BioIn 7*
Gardner, Warren S 1869- *WhJnl 1928*
Garduk, Harry *NF*
Garel, Leo 1917- *BioIn 1*
Garelick, Mary 1910- *BioIn 8*
Garfin, Alvin 1931- *WhoAm 1974*
Garfinkel, Bernard Max 1933- *WhoAm 1974*
Garfinkle, Henry *WhoAm 1974*
Gargan, Joseph *NewMr*
Garis, Howard Roger 1873-1962 *AmAu&B, BioIn 1, CarSB, ConAu 73, REnAL*
Garland, Ailsa *BioIn 9*
Garland, Charles T 1910?-1976 *ConAu 69*
Garland, James Albert 1870-1906 *DcNAA, HisAmM XR*
Garland, Phyl 1935- *ConAu 69, LivBAA*
Garland, Robert 1895-1955 *AmAu&B, REnAL*
Garner, John O 1889-1960 *NatCAB 50*
Garnett, Burt P 1887- *WhJnl 1928*
Garnett, Porter 1871-1951 *AmAu&B, HisAmM XR, WebBD*
Garno, Benjamin *HisAmM XR*
Garon, Jay *OvPC*
Garran, Andrew 1825-1901 *BioIn 2*
Garret, Wendell *NF*
Garretson, Carleton G *HisAmM XR*
Garretson, Frederick VanHon 1935?- *NF*
Garrett, B O 1897- *WhJnl 1928*
Garrett, Edward Peter 1878-1954 *HisAmM XR, WebBD*
Garrett, Edward Peter *see also* Garrett, Garet
Garrett, Emmanuel *AmRP*
Garrett, Garet 1878-1954 *AmAu&B, TwCA, TwCA Sup, WebBD*
Garrett, Garet *see also* Garrett, Edward Peter
Garrett, Gerald 1928- *ConAu 73*
Garrett, Joshua Tracy 1881- *WhJnl 1928*
Garrett, Lee 1911?-1971 *BioIn 9*
Garrett, Oliver Hart Palmer 1897-1952 *BioIn 2, BioIn 4*
Garrett, Paul 1891- *WhoAm 1974*
Garrett, W Barry *NF*
Garrett, Wilbur Eugene 1930- *WhoAm 1974, WhoS&SW 1973*
Garrigues, J C *HisAmM XR*
Garrison, Gertrude *NF*
Garrison, James H 1842-1931 *AmLY, DcAmA, DcNAA, HisAmM XR, NatCAB 18, WhNAA*
Garrison, Omar V 1913- *BioIn 3, ConAu 33, WrDr 1976*
Garrison, Theodosia *HisAmM XR*
Garrison, Troy *NF*
Garrison, W H *HisAmM XR*
Garrison, Wendell Phillips 1840-1907 *Alli Sup, AmAu&B, BiD&SB, DcAmA, DcNAA, HisAmM XR, WebBD*
Garrison, William Lloyd 1805-1879 *Alli, AmAu, AmAu&B, AmJnl, BbD, BiD&SB, BlkC, DcAmA, DcEnL, DcLEL, DcNAA, EncAB, EvLB, HisAmM XR, OxAm, REn, REnAL, WebBD*
Garrison, William Lloyd 1838-1909 *DcNAA*

Garrison, Winfred Ernest 1874-1969 *AmAu&B, AmLY, BioIn 7, BioIn 8, ConAu 1, WhNAA*
Garside, Sherwin *NF*
Garst, Robert Edward 1901?- *BioIn 1*
Gart, Murray Joseph 1924- *WhoAm 1974, WhoF&I 1974*
Garth *see* Townsend, George Alfred
Gartner, Michael Gay 1938- *WhoAm 1974*
Garver, Howard Marlyn 1910- *WhoAm 1974*
Garvey, Andrew J *HisAmM XR*
Garvey, Bruce *NF*
Garvey, Marcus Moziah 1887-1940 *EncAB, WebBD*
Garvey, Peter *NF*
Garvey, Richard Conrad 1923- *WhoAm 1974*
Garvice, Charles 1833-1920 *Alli Sup, HisAmM XR, NewC, WebBD*
Garvin, James Louis 1868-1947 *BioIn 1, BioIn 5, DcLEL, ForP, LongC, Lor&LP, NewC, WebBD*
Garvin, Ray W 1896- *WhJnl 1928*
Garvin, William S 1806-1883 *NF*
Garwood, Bill *NF*
Gary, Darnell 1952- *NF*
Gary, Gene *NF*
Gary, Jay Arthur 1891- *WhJnl 1928*
Gasch, Marie 1873?-1945 *DcNAA*
Gasch, Marie *see also* Fairfax, Beatrice
Gasch, Marie *see also* Manning, Marie
Gaskill, Gordon *NF*
Gasperini, Frank 1885?- *BioIn 1*
Gassner, John Waldhorn 1903-1967 *AmAu&B, ConAu 1, REnAL, WhNAA*
Gaston, Herbert E *NF*
Gately, Gene *OvPC*
Gately, George *NF*
Gates, Clough 1877- *WhJnl 1928*
Gates, John *AmRP, BioIn 4*
Gates, Moody Bliss 1879?-1965 *BioIn 7, HisAmM XR*
Gates, Robert Lawrence 1934- *WhoAm 1974*
Gaudiosi, Albert V *NF*
Gauer, Gitta *NF*
Gauerke, Mary *BioIn 8*
Gauerke, R G 1895- *WhJnl Sup*
Gaul, Harvey Bartlett 1881-1945 *AmSCAP 1966, WhJnl 1928, WebBD*
Gault, Henri 1929- *BioIn 8, BioIn 10*
Gaunt, Jack *NF*
Gaunt, John L, Jr. *NF*
Gaus, Gunter 1929- *IntWW 1976, WhoWor 1974*
Gauthier, Robert Edouard 1901-1966 *BioIn 7*
Gautier, Jean-Jacques 1908- *IntWW 1976, WhoWor 1974*
Gautier, Theophile 1811-1872 *AtlBL, BbD, BiD&SB, CasWL, CyWA, DcBiA, DcEuL, EuAu, EvEuW, NewC, OxEng, OxFr, Pen Eur, RComWL, REn, WebBD*
Gauvreau, Emile Henry 1891-1956 *AmJnl, BioIn 4, REnAL, WhNAA*
Gavagan, James E 1912?-1971 *BioIn 9*
Gaver, Jack 1906-1974 *AmAu&B, BiE&WWA, ConAu 53*
Gavin, Catherine *ConAu 4R*
Gavin, Edward G 1897-1956 *BioIn 4*
Gavin, John H 1883-1947 *BioIn 1, WhJnl 1928*
Gavit, John Palmer 1868-1954 *AmAu&B, BioIn 3, HisAmM XR, WhNAA*
Gavrilovich, Peter C *NF*
Gavshon, Arthur L 1916- *ConAu 7R*
Gavzer, Bernard 1921- *WhoAm 1974*
Gaw, Cooper 1877-1956 *WhJnl 1928*
Gawronski, James 1936- *NF*

Gaxotte, Pierre 1895- *IntWW 1976, OxFr, WhoWor 1974*

Gay, Edwin Francis 1867-1946 *AmJnl, DcAmB S4*

Gay, Francisque 1885-1963 *BioIn 6*

Gay, Gerald H *NF*

Gay, Robert E *WhJnl 1928*

Gay, Sydney Howard 1814-1888 *Alli Sup, AmAu, AmAu&B, AmJnl, BiD&SB, DcAmA, DcAmB 7, DcNAA, FamWC, NatCAB 2, WebBD*

Gayda, Virginio 1885-1944 *BioIn 1, CurBio XR, WebBD*

Gaylard, Doctor 1721-1736 *BioIn 2*

Gayle, Steven *NF*

Gayler, Charles 1820-1892 *Alli, Alli Sup, AmAu, AmAu&B, BiD&SB, DcAmA, DcNAA, HisAmM XR, OhA&B, REnAL*

Gayler, Charles Mills 1858-1932 *HisAmM XR, WebBD*

Gaylin, George Robert 1910- *WhoAm 1974, WhoS&SW 1973*

Gaylord, Edward King 1873-1974 *BioIn 3, BioIn 4, BioIn 8, BioIn 10, NewYTBS 5, WhoAm 1974, WhJnl 1928, WhoS&SW 1973*

Gaylord, Edward Lewis 1919- *WhoAdv 1972, WhoAm 1974, WhoF&I 1974, WhoS&SW 1973*

Gaylord, William 1945- *ConAu 69*

Gayn, Mark 1909- *WhoAm 1974*

Gaynor, Frank 1911-1961 *BioIn 5*

Gazzolo, Dorothy Haven 1911- *WhoAm 1974, WhoAmW 1974, WhoS&SW 1973*

Geake, Charles 1868?-1919 *BioIn 2*

Gealy, Edgar J 1891- *WhJnl 1928*

Geare, Mildred Mahler 1888?-1977 *ConAu 73*

Gearhart, Sam E 1887- *WhJnl 1928*

Gebler, Robert T *NF*

Gedda, George L 1941- *NF*

Geddes, Bond P 1882?-1960 *BioIn 5*

Geddes, Donald Porter 1899?-1963 *BioIn 6*

Geddie, John 1937- *ConAu 69*

Gediman, Henry James 1904- *WhoAm 1974*

Gedye, George Eric Rowe 1890-1970 *BioIn 4, TwCA, TwCA Sup*

Gee, H L 1901- *ConAu 11R*

Geer, Stephen 1930- *ConAu 69*

Geer, William, Sr. d1976 *NF*

Geeslin, Campbell *NF*

Geffen, Maxwell Myles 1896- *WhoAm 1974*

Gehman, Jesse Mercer 1901- *WhoE 1974, WhJnl Sup*

Gehman, Richard 1921-1972 *BiE&WWA, BioIn 9, NewYTBE 3*

Geiger, George Lowell 1902- *WhNAA, WhJnl 1928*

Geiger, O Frank 1864- *WhNAA, WhJnl 1928*

Geiger, Robert E *NF*

Geijer, Erik Gustaf 1783-1847 *BbD, BiD&SB, CasWL, DcEuL, EuAu, Pen Eur, WebBD*

Geike, Archibald *HisAmM XR*

Geis, Bernard 1909- *CurBio XR, WhoAm 1974, WhoF&I 1974, WhoWor 1974, WhoWorJ 1972*

Geisel, Theodor Seuss 1904- *AmAu&B, AmSCAP 1966, AuBYP, BioIn 2, BioIn 3, BioIn 4, BioIn 5, BioIn 6, BioIn 7, BioIn 8, BioIn 9, BioIn 10, ChILR 1, ConAu 13R, ConAu 15, CurBio XR, REn, REnAL, SmATA 1, TwCA, TwCA Sup, WebBD, WhoAm 1974, WhoWest 1974, WhoWor 1974*

Geisel, Theodor Seuss *see also* Seuss, Dr.

Geiselman, Arthur W, Jr. *InvJ, RpN*

Geismar, Maxwell David 1909- *AmAu&B, WhoAm 1974, WhoE 1974, WhoWor 1974, WhoWorJ 1972*

Geist, Jacob M W 1824- *NatCAB 5*

Geister, Janet M 1885?-1964 *BioIn 7*

Geladas, James 1924- *WhoF&I 1974, WhoMW 1974*

Gelatt, Roland 1920- *ConAu 13R, WhoAm 1974, WhoE 1974, WhoWor 1974*

Gelatt, Roland Bernard 1856-1917 *BioIn 5*

Gelb, Arthur 1924- *BiE&WWA, BioIn 6, ConAu 3R, InvJ, NewMr, WhoAm 1974, WhoE 1974*

Gelb, Barbara *BioIn 6*

Gelb, Leslie H *NF*

Gelders, Isidor 1869- *BioIn 1*

Gelfand, Andrew S *NF*

Geller, Uri *BioNews 1974*

Gellert, Hugo *AmRP*

Gelles, George Charles 1942- *WhoAm 1974*

Gellhorn, Martha Ellis 1908- *AmAu&B, AmNov, Au&Wr, BioIn 2, BioIn 4, ConNov 1972, ConNov 1976, DrAF 1976, IntWW 1976, OxAm, REnAL, TwCA, TwCA Sup, WebBD, WhoAm 1974, WrDr 1976*

Gellis, Ike 1908- *WhoE 1974*

Gelman, Bernard 1933- *WhoE 1974*

Gelman, David Graham 1926- *WhoAm 1974, WhoE 1974*

Gelman, Steve 1934- *BioIn 9, ConAu 25, SmATA 3, WhoE 1974*

Gelmis, Joseph Stephan 1935- *ConAu 45, WhoAm 1974*

Gelwicks, Harry R 1870?-1956 *BioIn 4*

Gemmill, Henry 1917- *WhoAm 1974, WhoE 1974, WhoS&SW 1973*

Genauer, Emily *WhoAm 1974, WhoAmA 1973, WhoGov 1972*

Gendron, George M 1949- *NF*

Genet 1892-1978 *AmAu&B, WorAu*

Genet *see also* Flanner, Janet

Genn, Lillian G 1910- *ForWC 1970, OvPC*

Genoud, Antoine Eugene 1792-1849 *WebBD*

Genoude 1792-1849 *WebBD*

Genthe, Arnold 1869-1942 *CurBio XR*

Gentile, Giovanni 1875-1944 *CasWL, CIDMEL, EvEuW, WebBD*

Gentry, Guy C 1897?-1954 *BioIn 3*

Gentry, Margaret Ann *NF*

Gentz, Will T 1882?-1952 *BioIn 2*

Geoffrey, Theodate *see* Wayman, Dorothy G

George, Collins Crusor 1909- *WhoAm 1974*

George, Henry 1839-1897 *Alli Sup, AmAu, AmAu&B, AmJnl, BbD, BiD&SB, CasWL, DcAmA, DcLEL, DcNAA, EncAB, EvLB, HisAmM XR, NewC, OxAm, OxEng, Pen Am, REn, REnAL, WebBD, WebE&AL*

George, Henry 1862-1916 *AmAu&B, BioIn 4, DcAmB 7, DcNAA, WebBD*

George, Herbert *HisAmM XR*

George, Hub *NF*

George, Manfred 1893-1965 *BioIn 5, BioIn 7, CurBio XR*

George, Marcus Benjamin 1923- *WhoAm 1974*

George, Milton *HisAmM XR*

George, Walter Lionel 1882-1926 *HisAmM XR, LongC, NewC, TwCA, WebBD*

George, Zelma W 1903- *CurBio XR*

Gepfert, Kenneth *NF*

Gephardt, Thomas Steuber 1927- *WhoAm 1974, WhoMW 1974*

Gephart, Joseph Curtin 1902-1968 *AmAu&B,*

BioIn 8, WhJnl 1928
Geppert, William L 1882- *WhNAA, WhJnl 1928*
Geraghty, James 1905- *WhoAm 1974*
Gerald, Fay *NF*
Gerald, J Edward 1906- *ConAu 5R*
Geraldine, George A *OvPC*
Gerard, Dave 1909- *ConAu 53*
Gerard, Jane 1930- *ConAu 2R*
Gerard, Jean Ignace Isidore 1803-1847 *WebBD*
Gerard, Jean Ignace Isidore *see also* Grandville
Gerasimov, Gennadi 1930- *ConAu 69*
Gerassi, John 1931- *ConAu 7R*
Geraud, Andre 1882-1974 *ConAu 53, ConAu 69, CurBio XR, NewYTBS 5, WebBD*
Gerault, Charles 1878- *WebBD*
Gerber, Thomas William 1921- *WhoAm 1974, WhoE 1974*
Gerberg, Mort *NF*
Gerbner, George 1919- *AmM&W 73S, ConAu 45, LEduc 1974, WhoAm 1974*
Gerchunoff, Alberto 1883-1950 *BioIn 1, BioIn 2, Pen Am*
Gerdener, Theo J A 1916- *IntWW 1976*
Gerdes, Louis George 1919- *WhoAm 1974, WhoF&I 1974, WhoMW 1974*
Gerdy, Robert S 1919-1965 *BioIn 7, BioIn 8*
Gerentz, Sven 1921- *IntWW 1976*
Gergen, David *NewMr*
Gerhardt, Lillian Noreen 1932- *BiDrLUS, ForWC 1970, WhoAmW 1974, WhoE 1974*
Gerin-Lajoie, Antoine 1824-1882 *BbtC, CanWr, CasWL, DcNAA, OxCan, WebBD*
Gerity, James, Jr. 1904-1973 *WhoAdv 1972, WhoAm 1974, WhoMW 1974*
Gerlach, Ernst Ludwig 1795-1877 *WebBD*
Gerlach, Hellmuth Von 1866-1935 *WebBD*
Gerlach, Wolf 1927?- *BioIn 8*
Germain, Raymond d1976 *NF*
German, William *RpN*
Germano, Eddie *NF*
Germar, William H 1911- *ConAu 23R*
Germond, Jack *NF*
Gerndon, Gene *NF*
Gernsback, Hugo 1884-1967 *AmAu&B, BioIn 7, BioIn 8, WhNAA*
Gernsback, Marcellus Harvey 1912- *WhoAm 1974, WhoWor 1974*
Gerold, Karl 1906-1973 *BioIn 9, ConAu 41, NewYTBE 4*
Gerosa, Guido 1933- *ConAu 73*
Gerould, James Thayer 1872-1951 *AmAu&B, HisAmM XR, WhJnl 1928*
Gerretsen, Charles *NF*
Gerrity, Edward J, Sr. 1897?-1978 *NF*
Gerrity, Edward Joseph, Jr. 1924- *OvPC, WhoAm 1974, WhoF&I 1974, WhoPubR 1972*
Gerrity, John *NF*
Gershanek, Sinai 1880- *WhJnl Sup*
Gershen, Martin 1924- *ConAu 33, OvPC*
Gershman, Isaac 1894-1976 *BioIn 7*
Gersoa, Guido 1933- *NF*
Gerson, Noel Bertram 1914- *AmAu&B, Au&Wr, AuBYP, BioIn 8, WhoAm 1974, WhoE 1974, WhoWor 1974, WrDr 1976*
Gerstel, Steven V *NF*
Gerstenzang, James *NF*
Gerth, Jeff *InvJ*
Gervasi, Frank Henry 1908- *AmAu&B, BioIn 2, ConAu 15, ConAu P-1, HisAmM XR*
Gesmar, Renee *NF*
Gessler, Clifford Franklin 1893- *AmAu&B, REnAL, WhNAA*
Gessner, Frank M *HisAmM XR*

Gessner, Solomon *HisAmM XR*
Gestie, Bernice Dainard 1899-1961 *BioIn 6, WhNAA*
Getlein, Frank 1921- *AmAu&B, ConAu 9R, WhoAm 1974, WhoS&SW 1973*
Getler, Michael *NF*
Getleson, James S 1894?-1956 *BioIn 4*
Getson, Philip 1884-1953 *BioIn 3*
Getter, Doyle K *NF*
Getterman, Orla *NF*
Getzloe, Lester C 1894?-1957 *BioIn 4, WhJnl 1928*
Gewecke, Clifford George, Jr. 1932- *ConAu 23R*
Gewirtz, Shelly *NF*
Geyelin, Philip Laussat 1923- *WhoAm 1974, WhoS&SW 1973*
Geyer, Georgie Anne 1935- *BioIn 7, BioIn 9, ConAu 29, ForP, ForWC 1970, OvPC, WhoAm 1974, WhoAmW 1974, WhoMW 1974, WhoWor 1974*
Ghali, Paul 1905-1970 *BioIn 2, BioIn 8*
Gheddo, Piero 1929- *ConAu 73*
Gherardi, Gherardo 1891?-1949 *BioIn 1, CnMD, McGWD*
Ghiglione, Nancy Geiger 1943- *WhoAmW 1974*
Ghilchik, David Louis *BioIn 2*
Ghiotto, Renato 1923- *ConAu 49*
Ghiselin, Michael T 1939- *ConAu 49*
Ghislanzoni, Antonio 1824-1893 *BiD&SB, WebBD*
Ghosh, Kedar *BioIn 9*
Ghosh, Tushar Kanti 1898- *IntWW 1976, WhoWor 1974*
Giaimo, Robert *NewMr*
Giandoni, William *NF*
Giannini, Alberto 1884?-1952 *BioIn 2*
Giannini, Guglielmo 1891-1960 *BioIn 1, BioIn 5*
Gibbon, Perceval 1879-1926 *CasWL, HisAmM XR, NewC, WebBD*
Gibbons, Anne Marie *NF*
Gibbons, Floyd Phillips 1887-1939 *AmAu&B, AmJnl, BioIn 1, BioIn 2, BioIn 3, BioIn 4, BioIn 9, CathA 1930, DcAmB S2, DcNAA, REnAL, TwCA, TwCA Sup, WebBD*
Gibbons, Herbert Adams 1880-1934 *AmAu&B, AmLY, BioIn 7, DcAmB S1, DcNAA, HisAmM XR, WebBD, WhNAA*
Gibbons, John 1891-1947 *BioIn 1*
Gibbons, John Harvey 1876- *WhJnl 1928*
Gibbons, John S *AmJnl*
Gibbs, Eric L 1910?-1954 *BioIn 3*
Gibbs, Sir Philip Hamilton 1877-1962 *BioIn 1, BioIn 2, BioIn 4, BioIn 6, CathA 1930, DcLEL, EvLB, FamWC, HisAmM XR, LongC, ModBL, NewC, REn, TwCA, TwCA Sup, TwCW, WebBD*
Gibbs, Wolcott 1902-1958 *AmAu&B, HisAmM XR, REnAL, WhJnl 1928*
Giberman, Marcella *NF*
Gibney, Albert J *HisAmM XR*
Gibney, Ernest Carson 1868-1951 *BioIn 2*
Gibney, Frank 1924- *BiE&WWA, BioIn 3, ConAu 69*
Giboney, Betty O'Neal 1913- *WhoAmW 1974, ForWC 1970*
Gibson, Bob *NF*
Gibson, Charles Dana 1867-1944 *AmAu&B, AmJnl, CurBio XR, DcAmA, DcAmB S3, DcNAA, HisAmM XR, OxAm, REn, REnAL, WebBD*
Gibson, Colin *NF*
Gibson, Daniel Parke 1930- *WhoAm 1974*
Gibson, James Blaine 1891- *WhJnl 1928*
Gibson, Mary *BioIn 1*
Gibson, N *NF*

Gibson, Richard 1931- *ConAu 41*
Gibson, Robert Walter 1928- *OvPC,*
    WhoAm 1974
Gibson, Thomas 1819- *BioIn 5*
Gibson, Tom *NF*
Gibson, W T *HisAmM XR*
Gibson, Walter Brown 1897- *EncMys, WhNAA,*
    WhJnl 1928
Gibson, William Hamilton 1850-1896 *Alli Sup,*
    AmAu, AmAu&B, BbD, BiD&SB, DcAmA,
    DcNAA, WebBD
Gicquel, Roger *NF*
Gidal, George 1908- *BioIn 10*
Gidal, Tim N 1909- *BioIn 9, BioIn 10,*
    ConAu 5R, SmATA 2
Giddings, Franklin Henry 1855-1931 *AmAu&B,*
    DcAmA, DcNAA, HisAmM XR, REnAL
Giddings, John *Lor&LP*
Gideon, Dave 1882?-1950 *BioIn 2*
Gieger, Henry A *NF*
Giering, Eugene Thomas 1867-1934 *WhNAA,*
    WhJnl 1928
Giese, Gilbert S 1894-1963 *NatCAB 50,*
    WhJnl 1928
Gieske, Herman Everett 1891-1954 *BioIn 3*
Giffels, Louis J 1892- *WhJnl 1928*
Gifford, Ernest *NF*
Gifford, Frank 1930- *CelR 1973, CurBio XR*
Gifford, Lester Clark 1886-1969 *WhJnl 1928*
Gifford, William 1756-1826 *Alli, AmJnl, BbD,*
    BiD&SB, BiDLA, BioIn 4, BioIn 7,
    BrAu 19, CasWL, DcEnA, DcEnL, DcEuL,
    DcLEL, EvLB, NewC, OxEng, REn,
    WebBD, WebE&AL
Giggans, Jim *BlkC*
Gigli, Ormond A *OvPC*
Gil Robles Quinones, Jose Maria 1898- *WebBD*
Gilbert, Benjamin Davis 1835-1907 *DcNAA*
Gilbert, Clinton Wallace 1871-1933 *DcNAA*
Gilbert, Dewitt 1896- *WhoAm 1974,*
    WhoGov 1972
Gilbert, Dewitt *see also* Gilbert, John DeWitt
Gilbert, Douglas *AmAu&B*
Gilbert, Douglas 1889-1948 *BioIn 1*
Gilbert, Douglas 1942- *ConAu 53*
Gilbert, Eliphalet Wheeler 1793-1853 *HisAmM XR*
Gilbert, Eugene 1926-1966 *BioIn 7*
Gilbert, Frank 1839-1899 *Alli Sup, DcNAA*
Gilbert, George 1874-1943 *CurBio XR, DcNAA*
Gilbert, J R 1888- *WhJnl 1928*
Gilbert, John DeWitt 1896- *WhJnl 1928*
Gilbert, John DeWitt *see also* Gilbert, Dewitt
Gilbert, Morris 1894?-1971 *BioIn 9, BioIn 10,*
    HisAmM XR
Gilbert, Nancy *NF*
Gilbert, Paul Thomas 1876-1953 *BioIn 3, BioIn 6,*
    NatCAB 43
Gilbert, Robert *NF*
Gilbert, Rodney 1889-1968 *BioIn 8*
Gilbert, Rose Bennett *NF*
Gilbert, Ross Kirby 1881- *WhJnl 1928*
Gilbert, Samuel *HisAmM XR*
Gilbert, Simeon *HisAmM XR*
Gilbert, Susanna *NF*
Gilbey, Quintin *BioIn 8*
Gilbreath, Frank *NF*
Gilbreth, Edward S *NF*
Gilbreth, Frank Bunker, Jr. 1911- *AmAu&B,*
    BioIn 1, BioIn 2, BioIn 9, ConAu 9R,
    CurBio XR, SmATA 2, WhoAm 1974,
    WhoS&SW 1973, WhoWor 1974
Gilchrist, Eleanor *BioIn 1*
Gilder, Jeannette Leonard 1849-1916 *Alli Sup,*
    AmAu&B, BiD&SB, DcAmA, DcAmB 7,

    DcNAA, HisAmM XR, WebBD
Gilder, Joseph Benson 1858-1936 *AmAu&B,*
    DcNAA, HisAmM XR
Gilder, Richard Watson 1844-1909 *Alli Sup,*
    AmAu, AmAu&B, BbD, BiD&SB, BioIn 6,
    BioIn 9, DcAmA, DcEnA Ap, DcLEL,
    DcNAA, EvLB, HisAmM XR, LiJA,
    OxAm, Pen Am, REn, REnAL, WebBD
Gilder, Robert Fletcher 1856-1940 *CurBio XR,*
    WebBD
Gilder, Rodman 1877-1953 *AmAu&B, BioIn 3,*
    BioIn 5, NatCAB 42
Gilder, Rosamond DeKay 1890- *AmAu&B,*
    ConAu 1R
Gilder, William Henry 1838-1900 *Alli Sup,*
    BiD&SB, DcAmA, DcAmB 7, DcNAA,
    OxCan, WebBD
Gildersleeve, Basil Lanneau 1831-1924 *Alli Sup,*
    AmAu, AmAu&B, AmJnl, BiD&SB,
    BiDSA, DcAmA, DcNAA, HisAmM XR,
    REnAL, WebBD
Gildersleeve, Mrs. C H 1834-1899 *Alli Sup,*
    DcNAA, HisAmM XR, HsB&A
Gile, Ernest S 1871-1952 *NatCAB 41*
Giles, Carl 1914?- *BioIn 2, BioIn 4*
Giles, Carl H 1935- *ConAu 29*
Giles, Robert Hartmann 1933- *WhoAm 1974*
Giles, William Elmer 1927- *WhoAm 1974,*
    WhoWor 1974
Gilgoff, Henry *NF*
Gilien, Sasha 1925?-1971 *ConAu 33*
Gilinsky, Solomon 1887?-1961 *BioIn 6*
Gilkerson, Yancey Sherard 1919- *WhoAm 1974,*
    WhoS&SW 1973
Gilkeson, Raymond H 1897- *WhJnl 1928*
Gilkin, Iwan 1858-1924 *CasWL, ClDMEL,*
    EvEuW, WebBD
Gill, Brendan 1914- *AmAu&B, ConAu 73,*
    ConNov 1972, ConNov 1976, DrAF 1976,
    Pen Am, REnAL, TwCA Sup,
    WhoAm 1974, WhoThe 1972, WrDr 1976
Gill, Derek 1919- *ConAu 49*
Gill, Frank P d1976 *NF*
Gill, George Norman 1934- *WhoAm 1974,*
    WhoS&SW 1973
Gill, Helen *BioIn 1*
Gill, John 1732-1785 *AmJnl, BioIn 2, BioIn 7,*
    DcAmB 7
Gill, Robert *NF*
Gill, William Fearing 1844-1917 *Alli Sup,*
    DcAmA, DcNAA, LiJA
Gillam, Barbara L *NF*
Gillam, Bernhard 1856-1896 *HisAmM XR*
Gillam, Burns 1870?-1954 *BioIn 3*
Gillam, F Victor *HisAmM XR*
Gillard, Francis George 1908- *IntWW 1976,*
    Who 1974, WhoWor 1974
Gillen, Albert John 1919- *WhoAm 1974*
Gillen, Daniel F *HisAmM XR*
Gillen, John Stewart 1914-1977 *IntWW 1974,*
    WhoAm 1974, WhoE 1974
Gillen, Mollie 1908- *ConAu 41*
Gillenson, Lewis William 1918- *Au&Wr,*
    ConAu 7R, WhoAm 1974
Gilles, Nicholas Chester 1924- *WhoAm 1974*
Gillespie, Charles Bowen 1872-1929 *WhJnl 1928*
Gillespie, Charles Coulston *BioIn 8*
Gillespie, Haven 1888- *AmSCAP 1966, BioIn 7*
Gillespie, John Thomas 1941- *WhoAm 1974*
Gillespie, Kingsley 1895- *WhoAm 1974*
Gillespie, Marcia Ann 1944- *AuNews 2,*
    BioIn 10, BioNews 1975, LivBAA
Gillespie, Marian Evans 1889?-1946
    AmSCAP 1966, DcNAA

Gillespie, Norvell 1913?-1973 *BioIn 9*
Gillespie, Richard H 1877-1941 *NatCAB 30*
Gillespie, Schuyler W 1884-1942 *NatCAB 30*
Gillespie, Sumter 1887-1958 *BioIn 7, WhJnl 1928*
Gillespie, William F 1888?-1952 *BioIn 2*
Gillett, Alfred S *HisAmM XR*
Gillette, Corinne Frazier *NF*
Gillette, Edward Hooker 1840-1918 *HisAmM XR*
Gillette, Robert E 1944?- *NF*
Gilliatt, Penelope 1932- *AuNews 2, ConAu 15R, ConLC 2, ConNov 1972, ConNov 1976, DrAF 1976, IntWW 1976, WrDr 1976*
Gillie, Darsie 1903-1972 *BioIn 9, BioIn 10*
Gillie, Oliver John 1937- *ConAu 65*
Gillies, Mary Davis 1900- *ConAu 25, ForWC 1970, WhoAm 1974, WhoAmW 1974*
Gilligan, Edmund 1899-1973 *AmAu&B, BioIn 4, ConAu 45, NewYTBE 4, REnAL, TwCA Sup*
Gillilan, Strickland 1869-1954 *AmAu&B, AmLY, OhA&B, REnAL, WhNAA*
Gilliom, Judy 1942?- *BioIn 10*
Gillis, James Martin 1876-1957 *AmAu&B, BioIn 1, BioIn 2, BioIn 3, BioIn 4, BioIn 5, BkC 6, CathA 1930, CurBio XR, HisAmM XR, REnAL, WhNAA*
Gillmor, Daniel S 1917?-1975 *ConAu 61*
Gillmore, Inez Haynes 1873-1970 *WebBD*
Gillmore, Inez Haynes *see also* Irwin, Inez Haynes
Gillray, James 1757-1815 *Alli, BioIn 1, BioIn 2, BioIn 7, NewC, WebBD*
Gilman, Ann 1926- *BioIn 2*
Gilman, Carl 1942?- *BioIn 8*
Gilman, Caroline Howard 1794-1888 *Alli, AmAu&B, BiD&SB, BiDSA, CyAL 1, DcAmA, DcNAA, FemPA, HisAmM XR, LiJA, LivFWS, OxAm, REnAL, WebBD*
Gilman, Charles *HisAmM XR*
Gilman, Charlotte Perkins 1860-1935 *AmAu&B, AmLY, AmRP, DcAmA, DcNAA, WebBD, WhNAA*
Gilman, Coburn 1893- *NF*
Gilman, Lawrence 1878-1939 *AmAu&B, DcAmB S2, DcNAA, HisAmM XR, REnAL, TwCA, TwCA Sup, WebBD*
Gilman, Nicholas Paine 1849-1912 *Alli Sup, AmAu&B, DcAmA, DcNAA, HisAmM XR, OhA&B*
Gilman, Peter *NF*
Gilman, Richard 1925- *ConAu 53, WhoAm 1974*
Gilman, Samuel 1791-1858 *Alli, AmAu&B, BiDSA, CyAL 1, DcAmA, DcNAA, HisAmM XR, LiJA, WebBD*
Gilman, William 1909-1978 *Au&Wr, ConAu 1R*
Gilmer, Elizabeth Meriwether 1870-1951 *AmAu&B, AmJnl, BiDSA, BioIn 1, BioIn 2, BioIn 3, CurBio XR, DcAmB S5, REnAL, WebBD, WhNAA*
Gilmer, Elizabeth Meriwether *see also* Dix, Dorothy
Gilmer, Gertrude *LiJA*
Gilmore, Albert Field 1868-1943 *BioIn 5, WhNAA*
Gilmore, Art 1912- *WhoAm 1974, WhoWest 1974*
Gilmore, Charles W 1917- *RpN, WhoAm 1974*
Gilmore, Clarence Percy 1926- *WhoAm 1974*
Gilmore, Daniel Francis 1922- *ConAu 65*
Gilmore, Douglas *NF*
Gilmore, Eddy 1907-1967 *BioIn 1, BioIn 3, BioIn 4, BioIn 8, ConAu 7R, CurBio XR*
Gilmore, Gene 1920- *ConAu 33*
Gilmore, Gordon Leonard 1908- *OvPC, WhoAm 1974, WhoF&I 1974,*

WhoPubR 1972
Gilmore, James Roberts 1823-1903 *Alli Sup, AmAu&B, BbD, BiD&SB, DcAmA, DcEnL, DcNAA, HisAmM XR, WebBD*
Gilmore, James Stanley, Jr. 1926- *WhoAm 1974, WhoAmP 1973, WhoF&I 1974, WhoMW 1974*
Gilmore, John C *NF*
Gilmore, Keith *NF*
Gilmore, Richard *HisAmM XR*
Gilmore, Thomas J *HisAmM XR*
Gilmore, William Steele 1884-1978 *WhJnl 1928*
Gilmour, Clyde *NF*
Gil Robles Quinones, Jose Maria 1898- *WebBD*
Gilroy, Edward Meyler 1905?-1967 *BioIn 8*
Gilroy, William Edgar 1876-1962 *BioIn 6, WhNAA*
Gilson, Roy Rolfe 1875-1933 *AmAu&B, DcAmA, DcNAA, WhNAA*
Gimbel, Elinor Steiner *ForWC 1970, OvPC*
Gimenez Caballero, Ernesto 1899- *BioIn 1, CasWL, CIDMEL, DcSpL, EvEuW, REn*
Gimlin, Hoyt *NF*
Gingold, Oliver J 1885-1966 *BioIn 4, BioIn 7*
Gingras, Angele DeT *OvPC*
Gingrich, Arnold 1903-1976 *AmAu&B, Au&Wr, CelR 1973, ConAu 65, ConAu 13R, ConAu 69, CurBio XR, IntWW 1976, OvPC, REnAL, WhNAA, WhoAm 1974, WhoWor 1974, WrDr 1976*
Gingrich, Curvin Henry 1880-1951 *BioIn 2, WhNAA*
Giniger, Henry 1922- *WhoS&SW 1973, WhoWor 1974*
Ginn, Opal *NewMr*
Ginna, Robert Emmett, Jr. 1925- *IntMPA 1975*
Ginnings, Daphne *NF*
Ginott, Alice *NF*
Ginsback, Pam D *NF*
Ginsberg, I *AmRP*
Ginsburg, Robert W 1900- *WhJnl Sup*
Ginsburgh, Robert *NF*
Ginter, Lewis *NF*
Ginter, Robert McNeil 1877?-1946 *BioIn 1*
Ginty, George Clay 1840-1890 *BioIn 5*
Ginzberg, Yevgeniya 1906?-1977 *ConAu 69*
Ginzburg, Alexander Ilich 1936- *BioIn 9*
Ginzburg, Evgenia Semenovna 1907?- *BioIn 8, BioIn 9*
Ginzburg, Ralph 1929- *Au&Wr, ConAu 21R, WhoAm 1974, WhoWor 1974*
Giordana, Gian Pietro 1912- *BioIn 2*
Giordana, Tullio 1878?-1950 *BioIn 2*
Giordani, Igino 1894- *BioIn 1, CathA 1930*
Giordano, Vincent 1880- *WhJnl 1928*
Giovannetti, Eugenio 1883-1951 *BioIn 2*
Giovanni, Alberto 1882-1969 *BioIn 9*
Giovannitti, Len 1920- *ConAu 13R, ConAu 15, DrAF 1976, WhoAm 1974*
Giovannoli, Harry 1866- *WhJnl 1928*
Gipson, Henry Clay *OvPC*
Giragi, Columbus 1897?- *BioIn 1*
Girard *see* Collins, Herman Leroy
Girard, Fred *NF*
Girard, Priscilla *NF*
Girardan, Ray d1971 *NF*
Girardin, Emile De 1806-1881 *BbD, BiD&SB, EvEuW, OxFr, WebBD*
Girardin, Marc *see* Saint-Marc Girardin, Francois Auguste
Giraud, Albert 1860-1929 *CasWL, CIDMEL, EvEuW, WebBD*
Giroud, Francoise 1916- *AuNews 1, BioIn 10, BioNews 1975, CurBio XR, IntWW 1976,*

NewYTBS 5, WhoWor 1974
Girson, Rochelle ConAu 23R, ForWC 1970
Gish, Pat InvJ, NewMr
Gish, Tom 1925?- BioIn 10, InvJ, NewMr
Gislason, Dorsteinn 1867-1938 BioIn 2
Gisselbrecht, Walter G 1908- WhJnl 1928
Gist, Nathan Howard 1885-1962 WhNAA,
    WhJnl 1928
Gitlow, Benjamin 1891-1965 AmRP
Gitt, Charles M 1915?- BioIn 7
Gitt, Josiah William 1884-1973 AmRP, BioIn 1,
    BioIn 3, BioIn 7, BioIn 10, NewYTBE 4,
    WhoAm 1974, WhJnl 1928
Gittings, James A OvPC
Giuliotti, Domenico 1877- BioIn 1, BioIn 3,
    CathA 1952, ClDMEL
Gius, Julius 1911- WhoAm 1974, WhoWest 1974
Givando, Joseph d1953 RpN
Given, Ivan A 1902?-1972 BioIn 9
Given, Welker 1853-1938 DcNAA, OhA&B
Givens, Alexander C 1901- WhJnl 1928
Givens, Charles Garland 1899?-1964 BioIn 7
Givens, Clarence C, Jr. 1893- WhJnl 1928
Givens, William Robert 1870?-1950 BioIn 2
Gizycka, Eleanor M see also Patterson, Eleanor
    Medill
Gizycky, G Von HisAmM XR
Gjerde, Bjartmar 1931- IntWW 1974
Gjertsen, Dorothy Fischer OvPC
Glackens, L M HisAmM XR
Glackens, William James 1870-1938 AtlBL,
    DcAmB S2, OxAm, WebBD
Gladden, Washington 1836-1918 Alli Sup,
    AmAu&B, BbD, BiD&SB, DcAmA,
    DcNAA, OhA&B, REnAL, WebBD
Gladstone, Bernard NF
Gladstone, Henry NF
Glankoff, Mort 1900- NF
Glanville, Brian 1931- BioIn 7, ConAu 7R
Glanz-Leyeles, Aaron 1889-1966 BioIn 7, BioIn 8
Glarner, Andre 1882-1953 BioIn 3
Glaser, Milton 1929- ConAu 17
Glaser, Robert Leonard 1929- WhoAdv 1972,
    WhoAm 1974
Glaser, Vera Romans ForWC 1970,
    WhoAm 1974, WhoAmW 1974
Glasgow, George 1891- BioIn 3, CathA 1952
Glasgow, Jesse Edward 1923- WhoAm 1974,
    WhoE 1974, WhoF&I 1974
Glasgow, Robert Wilbur 1916- RpN,
    WhoWest 1974
Glasgow, Robert William BioIn 3
Glasner, Isabel OvPC
Glass, Andrew James 1935- ConAu 65
Glass, Carter 1858-1946 CurBio XR, DcAmB S4,
    DcNAA, EncAB, WebBD, WhJnl 1928
Glass, Carter, Jr. 1893-1955 BioIn 4, WhJnl 1928
Glass, Charles NF
Glass, Frank P see Glass, Franklin Potts
Glass, Franklin Potts 1858-1934 BioIn 8,
    DcAmB S1, NatCAB 43, WhJnl 1928
Glass, Ian 1926- NF
Glass, Joel A NF
Glass, Powell 1887-1945 WhJnl 1928
Glass, Powell, Jr. 1917- WhoF&I 1974,
    WhoS&SW 1973
Glass, Robert Camillus 1885-1958 WhJnl 1928
Glass, Robert Henry NF
Glass, Sally NF
Glasscock, Carl Burgess 1884-1942 AmAu&B,
    WhNAA
Glasser, Selma NF
Glassman, Leo M 1897- WhJnl 1928
Glasson, William Henry 1874-1946 BiDSA,

DcAmA, HisAmM XR, WhNAA
Glatstein, Jacob 1896-1971 BioIn 9, CasWL,
    ConAu 33, NewYTBE 2, WhoWorJ 1972
Glavinovich, Rose BioIn 5
Glazier, Robert Carl 1927- WhoAm 1974
Gleasner, Diana C 1936- ConAu 65
Gleason, Arthur Huntington 1878-1923 DcNAA,
    HisAmM XR
Gleason, Eugene 1927?- BioIn 5
Gleason, Eugene Franklin 1914- ConAu 4R
Gleason, Frederick AmAu&B, HisAmM XR
Gleason, Gene NewMr
Gleason, Gene 1914- ConAu XR
Gleason, Herbert Wendell 1855- HisAmM XR
Gleason, Paul J 1902- WhJnl 1928
Gleason, Ralph Joseph 1917-1975 BioIn 10,
    ConAu 61, ConAu 65, WhoAm 1974,
    WhoWest 1974
Gleaves, Suzanne 1904- ConAu 11R
Gleeson, Fannie NF
Gleisser, Marcus David 1923- ConAu 19R,
    WhoAm 1974, WhoMW 1974
Gleissner, John M 1893-1941 WhJnl 1928
Glendinning, Malcolm 1875-1953 BioIn 2,
    BioIn 6, NatCAB 44
Glenesk, Lord 1830-1908 FamWC
Glenn, Christopher NF
Glenn, Edmund S NF
Glenn, Jacob Benjamin 1905-1974 BioIn 10,
    ConAu 9, ConAu 49, WhoWorJ 1972
Glenn, Norman NF
Glenn, W M 1888- WhNAA, WhJnl 1928
Glenn, William A OvPC
Glick, Ruth NF
Glick, Virginia Kirkus see Kirkus, Virginia
Glickman, Arthur P 1940- ConAu 61
Glimcher, Sumner OvPC
Glinn, Burt NF
Globus, Grete 1901-1970 BioIn 9
Glock, Sir William Frederick 1908- IntWW 1976
Glover, Alan S 1895?-1966 BioIn 7
Glover, Arthur James 1873-1949 BioIn 1, BioIn 2,
    WhNAA, WhJnl 1928
Glover, Lyman Beecher 1846-1915 HisAmM XR
Glover, Thaddeus HisAmM XR
Glover, William 1911- BiE&WWA,
    WhoAm 1974, WhoWor 1974
Glover, William Howard 1819-1875 WebBD
Glubok, Norman 1924- BioIn 4
Glyndon, Howard 1840-1923 Alli Sup, AmAu&B,
    DcAmA, DcEnL, DcNAA
Glyndon, Howard see also Redden, Laura Catherine
Glyndon, Howard see also Searing, Laura Catherine
    Redden
Glynn, Francis M 1884- WhJnl 1928
Glynn, Martin Henry 1871-1924 NF
Gnaegi, Charles NF
Gnam, Rene 1937- OvPC, WhoAdv 1972
Go, Puan Seng 1904- ConAu 29
Goates, Leslie 1894- WhJnl 1928
Gobetti, Piero 1901-1926 BioIn 1, ClDMEL
Goble, Emerson 1901-1969 BioIn 8, BioIn 9
Gobright, William Lawrence NF
Godard, Jean-Luc 1930- , CelR 1973, CurBio XR,
    IntWW 1976, NewYTBE 1, NewYTBE 3,
    WhoWor 1974
Godbe, William Samuel 1833-1902 HisAmM XR
Godbout, Oscar 1926-1967 BioIn 7
Goddard, Anson N HisAmM XR
Goddard, Don NF
Goddard, Mary Katherine AmJnl
Goddard, Morrill 1865-1937 AmJnl, BioIn 4,
    DcAmB S2, DcNAA, NatCAB 27
Goddard, Percival Styles 1875-1954 BioIn 3

Goddard, Peter *NF*
Goddard, Robert *NF*
Goddard, Robert d1978 *NF*
Goddard, Sarah Updike 1700?-1770? *NF*
Goddard, William 1740-1817 *Alli, AmJnl,*
BioIn 4, BioIn 6, DcAmB 7, DcNAA,
HisAmM XR
Goddard, William Giles 1794-1846 *Alli, CyAL 1*
Godey, Louis Antoine 1804-1878 *AmAu,*
AmAu&B, AmJnl, HisAmM XR, LiJA,
REn, WebBD
Godfrey, Joseph Charles, Jr. 1900- *WhJnl 1928*
Godinez, Miguel *NF*
Godkin, Edwin Lawrence 1831-1902 *Alli Sup,*
AmAu, AmAu&B, AmJnl, BbD, BiD&SB,
BioIn 2, BioIn 3, BioIn 4, BioIn 7, BioIn 8,
DcAmA, DcLEL, DcNAA, EncAB, EvLB,
FamWC, ForP, HisAmM XR, LiJA,
NewMr, OxAm, REn, REnAL, WebBD
Godsell, Geoffrey *NF*
Godwin, Charles William 1914- *WhoAm 1974*
Godwin, Earl 1881?-1956 *BioIn 4*
Godwin, Harold 1857-1931 *HisAmM XR*
Godwin, Harry E *WhJnl Sup*
Godwin, J S *HisAmM XR*
Godwin, Jay *NF*
Godwin, John 1928- *ConAu 4R*
Godwin, Parke 1816-1904 *Alli, Alli Sup, AmAu,*
AmAu&B, AmJnl, BbD, BiD&SB, BioIn 1,
BioIn 2, CyAL 2, DcAmA, DcEnL,
DcNAA, HisAmM XR, LiJA, NatCAB 35,
OxAm, REnAL, WebBD
Godwin, Tony *BioIn 10*
Goebbels, Paul Joseph 1897-1945 *ForP, OxGer,*
REn, WebBD
Goebel, Hermann J *NF*
Goebel, Julius 1857-1931 *CasWL, DcAmA,*
HisAmM XR, WebBD
Goedhart, Gerrit Jan VanHeuven 1901- *BioIn 1*
Goedsche, Hermann *NF*
Goell, Yosef *NF*
Goenka, Ramanath 1902- *IntWW 1976*
Goerch, Carl 1891- *BioIn 3, BioIn 4, BioIn 5*
Goethals, Henry Webb 1922- *WhoAm 1974,*
WhoS&SW 1973
Goette, John 1896-1974 *WhNAA, WhoAm 1974,*
WhoWor 1974
Goetz, James B 1936- *WhoAm 1974*
Goetz, Philip Becker 1870-1950 *AmAu&B,*
HisAmM XR, WhNAA
Goetzel, Ed *NF*
Goff, Earl 1906- *WhJnl 1928*
Goff, Harold 1886?-1928 *WhJnl 1928*
Going, Charles Buxton 1863- *AmAu&B, DcAmA,*
REnAL, WebBD, WhNAA
Gold, Aaron 1937- *NF*
Gold, Bill 1912- *WhoAm 1974, WhoS&SW 1973*
Gold, Bill *see also* Gold, William Emil
Gold, Don 1931- *ConAu 61*
Gold, Edward Bernard 1926- *WhoAm 1974,*
WhoF&I 1974
Gold, Gerald *NF*
Gold, Harold *WhoE 1974*
Gold, Henry Clay *NF*
Gold, Horace Leonard 1914- *AmAu&B, Au&Wr,*
BioIn 10, WorAu
Gold, Jack S 1922?-1953 *BioIn 3*
Gold, Michael 1894?-1967 *AmAu&B, AmRP,*
CnMD, ConAu XR, ModWD, OxAm,
Pen Am, REn, REnAL, TwCA, TwCA Sup,
WebE&AL
Gold, Michael *see also* Granich, Irving
Gold, Pleasant Daniel 1823-1920 *BioIn 1*
Gold, Sadie *NF*

Gold, Victor 1928- *BioIn 10, WhoPubR 1972*
Gold, William Emil 1912- *ConAu 69*
Gold, William Emil *see also* Gold, Bill
Goldbeck, Willis *NF*
Goldberg, Abraham d1942 *NF*
Goldberg, Albert Levi 1898- *WhoAm 1974,*
WhoWest 1974, WhoWorJ 1972
Goldberg, Albert N *NF*
Goldberg, Ben Zion Waife 1895?-1972 *BioIn 9,*
WhoWorJ 1972
Goldberg, Bernard *NF*
Goldberg, Bob *NF*
Goldberg, Hyman 1908?-1970 *BioIn 6, BioIn 9,*
NewYTBE 1
Goldberg, Isaac 1887-1938 *AmAu&B, DcNAA,*
HisAmM XR, REn, REnAL, TwCA,
WebBD, WhNAA
Goldberg, Jerry *NF*
Goldberg, Joshua L 1896- *OvPC, WhoWorJ 1972*
Goldberg, Lawrence Robert 1899- *WhJnl 1928*
Goldberg, Max 1911-1972 *NF*
Goldberg, Reuben Lucius 1883-1970 *AmAu&B,*
AmSCAP 1966, BioIn 1, BioIn 2, BioIn 5,
BioIn 6, BioIn 7, BioIn 8, BioIn 9,
BioIn 10, ConAu 5R, CurBio XR, WebBD,
WhNAA
Goldberg, Sidney 1931- *NF*
Goldbloom, Maurice J 1911-1977 *AmRP,*
WhoWorJ 1972
Golden, Frederic *NF*
Golden, Harold 1928- *WhoAm 1974*
Golden, Harry, Jr. *NF*
Golden, Harry Lewis 1902- *AmAu&B, BioIn 5,*
BioIn 6, BioIn 7, BioIn 8, BioIn 10,
CelR 1973, ConAu 1, ConAu 2R,
CurBio XR, Pen Am, RAdv 1, REnAL,
WhoAm 1974, WhoS&SW 1973,
WhoWor 1974, WhoWorJ 1972, WorAu
Golden, Julius 1929- *OvPC, WhoAdv 1972,*
WhoCon 1973, WhoPubR 1972,
WhoWest 1974
Golden, L L L *ConAu 23R, OvPC,*
WhoPubR 1972
Golden, Stephen *NF*
Goldenberg, Gene S 1945- *NF*
Goldenberg, Norbert 1909?-1974 *BioIn 10*
Goldenson, Leonard Harry 1905- *CurBio XR,*
IntMPA 1975, WhoAm 1974, WhoE 1974,
WhoF&I 1974, WhoGov 1972,
WhoWor 1974
Goldfine, Miriam *OvPC*
Goldfrap, John Henry 1879-1917 *DcNAA*
Goldhor, Herbert 1917- *WhoAm 1974*
Goldhurst, Richard 1927- *ConAu 57*
Golding, David 1913- *IntMPA 1975, OvPC*
Golding, Louis Thorn 1865-1961 *BioIn 6*
Goldman, Albert *AmRP*
Goldman, Albert 1927- *AmAu&B, ConAu 19R,*
DrAS 74E
Goldman, Emma 1869-1940 *AmRP, CurBio XR,*
DcNAA, OxAm, REnAL, WebBD
Goldman, Joseph 1874?-1951 *BioIn 2*
Goldman, Martin Raymond Rubin 1920- *BioIn 9,*
ConAu 69, WhoAm 1974
Goldman, Peter L 1933- *ConAu 21R, RpN*
Goldman, Ruth S *WhJnl 1928*
Goldner, Nancy 1943- *ConAu 57*
Goldring, Patrick 1921- *ConAu 29*
Goldsborough, Laird Shields 1902-1950 *BioIn 2,*
BioIn 3
Goldschlager, Seth *NF*
Goldschmidt, Meir Aaron 1819-1887 *BbD,*
BiD&SB, BioIn 7, CasWL, EuAu, EvEuW,
Pen Eur, WebBD

Goldsmith, Barbara 1931- *BioIn 10, ConAu 53, ForWC 1970, WhoAmA 1973*
Goldsmith, George F 1865-1950 *BioIn 2*
Goldsmith, J C *Alli Sup, AmJnl, HisAmM XR*
Goldsmith, John Frank 1918- *WhoAm 1974*
Goldsmith, Lucy *OvPC*
Goldsmith, Michael *NF*
Goldsmith, Robert 1882-1924 *DcNAA*
Goldstein, Alvin H, Sr. 1902-1972 *BioIn 9, ConAu 33*
Goldstein, Bernard I 1880?-1953 *BioIn 3*
Goldstein, Nathan W *OvPC*
Goldstein, Richard 1944- *BioIn 7, BioIn 10, ConAu 25*
Goldstick, Nate *NF*
Goldstien, Laurence 1937?-1972 *ConAu 33*
Goldthwaite, Stephen Grant 1868- *WhNAA, WhJnl 1928*
Goldthwaite, Thomas J 1936- *WhoAm 1974*
Goldthwaite, William M *HisAmM XR*
Goldwasser, Tom *NF*
Goldway, William *NF*
Golenbock, Peter 1946- *ConAu 57*
Golightly, Lena Mills *WhoAm 1974, WhoAmW 1974*
Golin, Milton 1921- *WhoE 1974*
Gollobin, Ronald 1941?- *NF*
Gollomb, Joseph 1881-1950 *AmAu&B, AnCL, AuBYP, BioIn 2, BioIn 4, BioIn 7, JBA 1934, JBA 1951, REnAL, TwCA, TwCA Sup*
Golobie, John d1927 *DcNAA*
Golsan, H Logan *HisAmM XR*
Golson, G Barry 1944- *ConAu 69*
Goltz, Gene 1930- *InvJ, WhoAm 1974*
Gombault, Charles Henri 1907- *IntWW 1976, WhoWor 1974*
Gomberg, Ephraim Roos 1904- *OvPC, WhoE 1974, WhoWorJ 1972*
Gomella, Guido 1905- *IntWW 1976*
Gomez, Laureano 1889-1965 *BioIn 2, BioIn 3, BioIn 7, CurBio XR, ForP*
Gomez-Wanguemert, Luis *ForP*
Gomi, Kazuo *OvPC*
Gomme, Sir George Laurence 1853-1916 *Alli Sup, WebBD*
Goncalves, A Avelino *ForP*
Gondor, Ferenc 1885?-1954 *BioIn 3*
Gonella, Guido 1905- *BioIn 1, CathA 1952, IntWW 1974, WhoWor 1974*
Gontier, A J *HisAmM XR*
Gonzales, Ambrose Elliott 1857-1926 *AmAu&B, AmJnl, BioIn 2, BioIn 9, DcNAA, REnAL*
Gonzales, Diaro *NF*
Gonzales, Donald J 1917- *RpN, WhoPubR 1972*
Gonzales, Jose *NF*
Gonzales, Laurence 1947- *NF*
Gonzales, Narciso Gener 1858-1903 *AmJnl, BioIn 2, BioIn 9, BioIn 10*
Gonzales, William Elliott 1866-1937 *BioIn 2, BioIn 9, NatCAB 28*
Gonzalez, Arturo Francis, Jr. 1928- *Au&Wr, ConAu 13, OvPC, WhoWor 1974*
Gonzalez, Eduardo L 1910- *BioIn 6*
Gonzalez, Justo 1902- *BioIn 8*
Goo, Melvin M S 1948?- *NF*
Gooch, Tom Carbry 1880-1952 *BioIn 1, BioIn 3, WhJnl 1928*
Good, Jay W 1868- *WhJnl 1928*
Good, Larry *NF*
Good, Mindy L *NF*
Good, Warren R *NF*
Goodale, George P 1843-1919 *NatCAB 18*
Goodale, James Campbell 1933- *WhoAm 1974*

Goodall, Harvey L 1836-1900 *DcAmB 7*
Goodavage, Joseph F 1925- *ConAu 25*
Goodbody, John Collett 1915- *WhoAm 1974*
Goode, Mal 1908- *BioIn 8*
Goode, Marian Elizabeth 1925- *WhoAm 1974*
Goode, Sir William Athelstane Meredith 1875-1944 *BioIn 5, DcAmA, FamWC*
Goodell, John Milton 1867-1927 *BioIn 1*
Goodell, William 1792-1878 *DcNAA, HisAmM XR*
Goodenough, Louis B 1902?-1965 *BioIn 7*
Goodenow, Donald Irving 1920- *WhoAm 1974*
Goodes, Arthur B 1874- *WhJnl 1928*
Goodfellow, Millard Preston 1892-1973 *WhoAm 1974*
Goodfriend, James *NF*
Goodhue, James Madison 1810-1852 *AmJnl, BioIn 1, BioIn 4*
Gooding, Edwin Hicks 1903- *WhJnl 1928*
Gooding, Judson 1926- *ConAu 73, WhoE 1974*
Gooding, Richard *NF*
Goodland, Walter Samuel 1863-1947 *WhJnl 1928*
Goodlett, Frank 1898- *WhJnl 1928*
Goodloe, Daniel Reaves 1814-1902 *Alli Sup, AmAu&B, BiDSA, BioIn 1, DcNAA*
Goodman, Anthony R *NF*
Goodman, Ellen Holtz 1941- *WhoAmW 1974*
Goodman, George Jerome Waldo 1930- *AmAu&B, BioIn 8, ConAu 21, WhoAm 1974*
Goodman, Henry Atlas 1924- *WhoAm 1974*
Goodman, Jack Arthur 1908-1957 *BioIn 4*
Goodman, John D *HisAmM XR*
Goodman, Joseph *HisAmM XR*
Goodman, Jules Eckert 1876-1962 *AmAu&B, HisAmM XR, McGWD, REnAL*
Goodman, Julian 1922- *CurBio XR, IntMPA 1975, IntWW 1974, OvPC, WhoAm 1974, WhoE 1974, WhoF&I 1974, WhoWor 1974*
Goodman, Lee M 1881- *WhJnl 1928*
Goodman, Martin W *RpN*
Goodman, Michael L 1881?-1953 *BioIn 3*
Goodman, Mike *InvJ*
Goodman, Mitchell 1923- *Au&Wr, BioIn 10, ConAu 1, DrAF 1976, DrAP 1975*
Goodman, Walter 1927- *ConAu 9R, WhoAm 1974, WhoE 1974*
Goodman, Warren H 1919- *OvPC, WhoPubR 1972*
Goodnow, Louis L 1885- *WhJnl 1928*
Goodnow, Marc N *WhJnl 1928*
Goodpaster, Edwin W *NF*
Goodrich, Charles T 1846-1911 *NatCAB 16*
Goodrich, Edmund d1977 *NF*
Goodrich, F E *HisAmM XR*
Goodrich, Frank Boott 1826-1894 *Alli, Alli Sup, AmAu, AmAu&B, BiD&SB, CyAL 2, DcAmA, DcAmB 7, DcEnL, DcNAA, REnAL, WebBD*
Goodrich, Frederick Elizur 1843-1925 *Alli Sup, DcNAA*
Goodrich, Kenneth Stephen 1903- *WhNAA, WhJnl 1928*
Goodrich, Samuel Griswold 1793-1860 *Alli, AmAu, AmAu&B, BbD, BbtC, BiD&SB, CarSB, CyAL 2, DcAmA, DcEnL, DcNAA, HisAmM XR, OxAm, REn, REnAL, WebBD, WhoChL*
Goodrich, Samuel Griswold *see also* Parley, Peter
Goodrich, William F *OvPC*
Goodsell, B G *HisAmM XR*
Goodsell, Daniel Ayres 1840-1909 *AmAu&B, DcAmA, DcNAA*
Goodsell, James Nelson 1929- *DrAS 74H, OvPC*

Gortatowsky, Jacob Dewey 1885-1964 *BioIn 4*, *BioIn 6*
Gorton, David A *HisAmM XR*
Goryunov, Dmitry Petrovich 1915- *IntWW 1976*, *WhoWor 1974*
Goshal, Kumar 1899-1971 *BioIn 9*, *NewYTBE 2*
Goshko, John Myron 1933- *WhoAm 1974*, *WhoWor 1974*
Goshorn, Harry R 1861?-1951 *BioIn 2*
Goshorn, Robert Charles 1890-1953 *BioIn 4*, *NatCAB 40*
Gosling, Ernest Pierce 1884- *WhJnl 1928*
Gosling, Francis George 1904- *WhJnl 1928*
Gosnell, Mariana *NF*
Gosnell, R Edward 1860-1931 *DcNAA*, *OxCan*
Goss, Chester A 1893- *WhJnl 1928*
Goss, Warren Lee 1835-1925 *Alli Sup*, *AmAu&B*, *AmLY*, *CarSB*, *DcAmA*, *DcNAA*, *WhNAA*
Gosse, Etienne 1773-1834 *WebBD*
Gosswiller, Richard *NF*
Gosztonyl, Adam 1893?-1955 *BioIn 4*
Gotblind, Theresse *NF*
Gotcher, Richard H *NF*
Goth, Trudy 1913-1974 *ForWC 1970*, *NewYTBS 5*, *OvPC*, *WhoWorJ 1972*
Goto, Motoi *NF*
Gotshall, John 1891- *WhJnl 1928*
Gott, Helen Theresa 1942- *WhoAm 1974*, *WhoAmW 1974*
Gott, Kenneth Davidson 1923- *WhoWor 1974*
Gottehrer, Barry Hugh 1935- *AmAu&B*, *ConAu 13R*
Gottfried, Manfred 1900- *AmAu&B*, *HisAmM XR*
Gottfried, Martin 1933- *BiE&WWA*, *ConAu 23R*
Gottlieb, Daniel W *NF*
Gottlieb, Edward 1903?-1961 *BioIn 6*
Gottlieb, Edward 1910- *WhoCon 1973*, *WhoPubR 1972*
Gottlieb, Herbert H *BioIn 9*
Gottlieb, Leon A 1878-1947 *BioIn 1*
Gottron, Martha V *NF*
Gottschall, Rudolf Von 1823-1909 *BiD&SB*, *EvEuW*, *OxGer*, *WebBD*
Gotwald, F G *HisAmM XR*
Goudsmit, Samuel Abraham 1902-1978 *AmM&W 73P*, *CurBio XR*, *IntWW 1974*, *WhoAm 1974*, *WhoWorJ 1972*
Gough, Marion *ForWC 1970*, *WhoAmW 1974*
Gould, Alan Jenks 1898- *BioIn 1*
Gould, Alexander S *NF*
Gould, Beatrice Blackmar 1898- *AmAu&B*, *BioIn 1*, *BioIn 2*, *BioIn 8*, *ConAu 25*, *CurBio XR*, *HisAmM XR*, *IntWW 1976*, *WhoAmW 1974*
Gould, Benjamin Apthorp 1824-1896 *Alli*, *Alli Sup*, *BiD&SB*, *DcAmA*, *DcNAA*, *HisAmM XR*, *WebBD*
Gould, Bruce 1898- *AmAu&B*, *BioIn 1*, *BioIn 2*, *BioIn 8*, *CurBio XR*, *HisAmM XR*, *WhNAA*
Gould, Mrs. Bruce *see* Gould, Beatrice Blackmar
Gould, Charles Lessington 1909- *WhoAm 1974*, *WhoF&I 1974*
Gould, Chester 1900- *BioIn 1*, *BioIn 2*, *BioIn 3*, *BioIn 4*, *BioIn 6*, *BioIn 9*, *CelR 1973*, *CurBio XR*, *EncMys*, *WhoAm 1974*, *WhoMW 1974*
Gould, Curtis *HisAmM XR*
Gould, Edward Sherman 1808?-1885 *Alli*, *Alli Sup*, *AmAu*, *AmAu&B*, *BiD&SB*, *CyAL 2*, *DcAmA*, *DcNAA*, *HisAmM XR*, *OxAm*
Gould, Edward Sherman 1837-1905 *DcNAA*

Gould, F Willis 1886- *WhJnl 1928*
Gould, Sir Francis Carruthers 1844-1925 *NewC*, *WebBD*
Gould, Jack 1914- *AmAu&B*, *NewYTBE 3*, *WhoE 1974*
Gould, Jack 1919- *WhoPubR 1972*
Gould, John Thomas 1908- *AmAu&B*, *BioIn 1*, *BioIn 4*, *ConAu 65*, *WhoAm 1974*
Gould, Kenneth Lawrence 1925- *WhoAm 1974*, *WhoF&I 1974*, *WhoS&SW 1973*
Gould, Kenneth Miller 1895-1969 *AmAu&B*, *BioIn 8*
Gould, Leslie 1902-1977 *ConAu 73*, *WhoAm 1974*
Gould, Loyal Norman 1927- *AmM&W 73S*, *OvPC*
Gould, Margaret Sarah 1900?- *BioIn 2*
Gould, Randall Chase 1898- *BioIn 2*
Gould, Stanhope *InvJ*
Gould, Sylvester Clark 1840-1909 *DcNAA*, *HisAmM XR*
Gould, Whitney M 1943?- *NF*
Goulden, Joseph *NewMr*
Goulden, Mark *Au&Wr*, *IntWW 1976*, *Who 1974*, *WhoWor 1974*
Goulding, Phil G 1921- *BioIn 7*, *BioIn 8*, *WhoAm 1974*
Gouras, Lina *ForP*
Gouraud, Powers 1881?-1954 *BioIn 3*
Gourlay, John Edgar Reginald 1854-1923 *DcNAA*
Gourley, Jay 1947- *BioIn 10*, *ConAu 73*
Gourmont, Remy De 1858-1915 *AtlBL*, *CasWL*, *ClDMEL*, *CyWA*, *EncWL*, *HisAmM XR*, *LongC*, *ModRL*, *OxFr*, *Pen Eur*, *REn*, *TwCA*, *TwCA Sup*, *WebBD*
Gover, Raymond Lewis 1927- *WhoMW 1974*
Govoni, Albert Peter 1914- *ConAu 53*, *WhoAm 1974*, *WhoWor 1974*
Gowan, Ogle Robert 1796-1876 *BbtC*, *DcNAA*
Gowdy, Curtis 1919- *WhoAm 1974*
Gowen, Emmett 1902- *AmAu&B*, *Au&Wr*, *ConAu P-1*
Gower, John Stanley 1901- *WhJnl 1928*
Goyau, Georges Pierre Louis Theophile 1869-1939 *CathA 1930*, *WebBD*
Gozder, Jodie P d1953 *BioIn 3*
Gozlan, Leon 1803-1866 *BiD&SB*, *OxFr*, *WebBD*
Gozzi, Gasparo 1713-1786 *BiD&SB*, *CasWL*, *Pen Eur*, *WebBD*
Graae, Paul *ForP*
Grabowski, Z, Anthony 1903- *ConAu 7R*
Grace, John *NF*
Grace, Teddee *NF*
Gracey, William Adolphe 1866-1944 *WhJnl 1928*
Grad, Jules *NF*
Grady, Ernest *NF*
Grady, Henry Woodfin 1850-1889 *AmAu*, *AmJnl*, *BiDSA*, *BioIn 1*, *BioIn 2*, *BioIn 3*, *BioIn 5*, *BioIn 8*, *BioIn 9*, *BioIn 10*, *DcAmB 7*, *DcLEL*, *DcNAA*, *EncAB*, *ForP*, *HisAmM XR*, *OxAm*, *REnAL*, *WebBD*
Grady, James *NF*
Grady, Sandy *NF*
Graebner, Walter 1909- *ConAu 15*, *ConAu P-1*, *CurBio XR*, *WhoAm 1974*
Graedinger, Louis B d1977 *NF*
Graefenberg, Rosie 1898- *NF*
Graemer, Bill *NF*
Graetz, F *HisAmM XR*
Graeve, Oscar *HisAmM XR*
Graffis, Herb 1893- *BioIn 2*, *WhoAm 1974*
Grafly, Dorothy 1896- *WebBD*, *WhoAm 1974*, *WhoAmA 1973*, *WhoAmW 1974*, *WhoE 1974*

Grafton, Grace *HisAmM XR*
Grafton, Samuel 1907- *AmAu&B, AmJnl,*
　CurBio XR, WhoAm 1974
Graham, Alex *NF*
Graham, Betty 1916?-1951 *BioIn 2*
Graham, Dale K *NF*
Graham, Donald 1946?- *NF*
Graham, Dillon *NF*
Graham, Edward *FamWC*
Graham, Emma d1922 *DcNAA*
Graham, Evarts Ambrose, Jr. 1921- *InvJ,*
　WhoAm 1974
Graham, Frank 1894-1965 *AmAu&B*
Graham, Frank, Jr. 1925- *AuBYP, BioIn 7,*
　BioIn 8, ConAu 9, WhoE 1974, WrDr 1976
Graham, Fred Patterson 1931- *BioIn 10,*
　ConAu 37, DrAS 74P
Graham, Gene Swann 1924- *ConAu 41,*
　DrAS 74E, RpN
Graham, George Edward 1866- *HisAmM XR*
Graham, George N 1877?- *WhJnl 1928*
Graham, George Rex 1813-1894 *AmAu,*
　AmAu&B, AmJnl, HisAmM XR, LiJA,
　REnAL, WebBD
Graham, Gordon *NF*
Graham, Harry Chrysostom 1901- *BioIn 2,*
　CurBio XR
Graham, Herbert 1895- *WhJnl 1928*
Graham, Howard Barret 1929- *WhoAm 1974*
Graham, Hugh E 1897- *WhJnl 1928*
Graham, James Francis 1915-1960 *NF*
Graham, Janet 1928- *NF*
Graham, Jarlath John 1919- *WhoAm 1974*
Graham, Joan *NF*
Graham, Joseph M 1911?-1971 *BioIn 9,*
　NewYTBE 2
Graham, Katharine 1917- *AuNews 1, BioIn 7,*
　BioIn 8, BioIn 9, BioIn 10, BioNews 1974,
　CelR 1973, CurBio XR, IntWW 1976,
　NewMr, WhoAm 1974, WhoAmW 1974,
　WhoF&I 1974, WhoS&SW 1973,
　WhoWor 1974
Graham, Lee E 1913?-1977 *ConAu 73,*
　WhoAmW 1974
Graham, Malcolm *NF*
Graham, Marcus *AmRP*
Graham, Maxtone 1924- *NF*
Graham, Philip Leslie 1915-1963 *BioIn 1, BioIn 4,*
　BioIn 5, BioIn 6, BioIn 8, CurBio XR,
　NewMr
Graham, Robert W 1902- *WhJnl 1928*
Graham, Robert Xavier 1902-1953 *BioIn 6*
Graham, Rubye *NF*
Graham, Sheilah 1908?- *AmAu&B, AuNews 1,*
　BioIn 2, BioIn 5, BioIn 6, BioIn 8, BioIn 9,
　BioNews 1974, CelR 1973, CurBio XR,
　WhoAm 1974, WhoAmW 1974, WrDr 1976
Graham, Stephen 1884-1975 *Au&Wr, DcEnL,*
　DcLEL, EvLB, HisAmM XR, LongC,
　NewC, REn, TwCA, TwCA Sup, WebBD,
　Who 1974
Graham, Stephen C *NF*
Graham, Susan 1912- *ConAu 19R*
Graham, Walter R *NF*
Graham, William Henry 1911-1951 *AmJnl,*
　BioIn 2
Grahlfs, Lincoln 1895?-1968 *BioIn 8*
Grail, Frances H d1976 *NF*
Grambling, Oliver S *NF*
Gramer, W A *NF*
Grammer, Jacob 1871-1931 *NF*
Grand-Carteret, John 1850-1927 *BiD&SB,*
　WebBD
Grandgent, Charles Hall 1862-1939 *AmAu&B,*

　AmLY, DcNAA, HisAmM XR, REnAL,
　WebBD, WhNAA
Grandin, Thomas B 1907- *WhoAm 1974,*
　WhoWest 1974
Granducci, Oeveste *OvPC*
Grandville 1803-1847 *BioIn 2, BioIn 8, OxFr,*
　WebBD
Grandy, Francis R *NF*
Grandy, Red *NF*
Granich, Irving 1894?-1967 *AmAu&B,*
　ConAu 25, Pen Am, REn, REnAL
Granier DeCassagnac, Adolphe 1808-1880 *WebBD*
Granik, Hannah Belle 1909- *WhoAm 1974,*
　WhoAmW 1974, WhoS&SW 1973
Granik, Theodore 1906-1970 *BioIn 9, CurBio XR,*
　NewYTBE 1
Granirer, Martin 1906?-1964 *BioIn 6*
Granitsas, Spyridon N *NF*
Granlund, Nils Thor 1894-1957 *BioIn 4*
Grannis, Chandler Brinkerhoff 1912-
　WhoAm 1974
Grannis, Robert M 1903-1973 *BioIn 9,*
　NewYTBE 4
Grant, Annette *NF*
Grant, B F 1857- *WhJnl 1928*
Grant, Ben Joseph 1909- *WhoAm 1974,*
　WhoF&I 1974, WhoS&SW 1973,
　WhoWor 1974
Grant, Bruce *ForP, RpN*
Grant, Bruce 1893-1977 *AuBYP, BioIn 2,*
　BioIn 7, ConAu 1R, ConAu 69, SmATA 5
Grant, Charles 1888-1965 *AmAu&B, WhNAA*
Grant, Charles *see also* Lengel, William Charles
Grant, Donald S *RpN*
Grant, E P *HisAmM XR*
Grant, Evelyn *NF*
Grant, Frances Ruth *WhoAm 1974,*
　WhoAmW 1974
Grant, George Ernest 1903-1955 *BioIn 3*
Grant, Gerald Paul 1938?- *NF*
Grant, Harry Johnston 1881-1963 *AmJnl, BioIn 2,*
　BioIn 3, BioIn 6, BioIn 9, WhNAA,
　WhJnl 1928
Grant, Howard B 1909?-1977 *NF*
Grant, Hugh Gladney 1888- *WhoAm 1974,*
　WhJnl 1928
Grant, J A 1901- *WhJnl 1928*
Grant, James 1802-1879? *Alli, Alli Sup, DcEnL,*
　FamWC
Grant, James G *NF*
Grant, Jane 1895?-1972 *BioIn 9, ConAu 25,*
　ConAu 33
Grant, Lester H *RpN*
Grant, Lou *NF*
Grant, Merrill Theodore 1932- *WhoAm 1974*
Grant, Roderick 1901-1961 *BioIn 5, WhJnl 1928*
Grant, Roderick 1941- *Au&Wr, WrDr 1976*
Grant, William *NF*
Grant, Zalin Belton 1941- *ConAu 73*
Gras, Harold W 1889- *WhJnl 1928*
Grasse, Alfredo *NF*
Grasty, Charles Henry 1863-1924 *AmAu&B,*
　AmJnl, DcNAA, HisAmM XR, NatCAB 22
Gratke, Charles 1901-1949 *BioIn 2*
Grattan, Hartley *AmRP*
Gratton, Aurele 1909-1978 *CanWW 1972*
Gratton, Georges *NF*
Gratz, Roberta B *OvPC*
Graue, Dave 1926- *NF*
Grauer, Benjamin Franklin 1908-1977 *ConAu 69,*
　CurBio XR, IntMPA 1975, NewYTBE 4,
　OvPC, WhoAm 1974, WhoWor 1974,
　WhoWorJ 1972
Grauman, Lawrence, Jr. 1935- *BioIn 10,*

ConAu 33, DrAS 74E, WhoMW 1974
Gravely, Ralph 1898- *WhNAA, WhJnl 1928*
Graves, Carl G *NF*
Graves, Charles Larcom 1856-1944 *Alli Sup, PoIre, WebBD, WhoLA*
Graves, Charles Marshall 1873?-1952 *BioIn 3*
Graves, Frank *AmRP*
Graves, George S *HisAmM XR*
Graves, H Sandham *NF*
Graves, Harold Nathan, Jr. 1915- *BioIn 2, IntWW 1976, IntWW 1974, WhoAm 1974, WhoGov 1972*
Graves, Howard *NF*
Graves, James Robinson 1820-1893 *Alli Sup, BiDSA, DcAmA, DcNAA, HisAmM XR*
Graves, John Temple 1856-1925 *BiDSA, DcAmB 7, DcNAA, HisAmM XR, WebBD*
Graves, John Temple, Jr. 1892-1961 *AmAu&B, BioIn 1, BioIn 5, WhNAA*
Graves, Louis 1883-1965 *BiDSA, BioIn 7, WhNAA*
Graves, Patricia M *NF*
Graves, Philip Perceval 1876-1953 *BioIn 2, BioIn 3*
Graves, Ralph A 1882-1932 *HisAmM XR, WhNAA*
Graves, Ralph Augustus 1924- *AmAu&B, WhoAm 1974*
Graves, Ralph Henry 1878-1939 *AmAu&B, DcNAA*
Graves, Walter A 1920- *NF*
Graves, William E *HisAmM XR*
Graves, William Whites 1871- *BioIn 1, BkC 2, CathA 1930*
Gray, Alfred Orren 1914- *ConAu 19R, DrAS 74E, WhoWest 1974, WrDr 1976*
Gray, Andy *NF*
Gray, Ann *NF*
Gray, Barry (1826-1886) see also Coffin, Robert Barry
Gray, Barry 1826-1886 *Alli Sup, AmAu&B, DcAmA, DcEnL, DcNAA*
Gray, Barry 1916- *CelR 1973, ConAu 61, NewYTBE 1*
Gray, Beverly *NF*
Gray, Claude M 1889- *WhJnl 1928*
Gray, David 1836-1888 *Alli Sup, BiD&SB, DcAmA, DcNAA*
Gray, David 1870-1968 *AmAu&B, AmLY, BioIn 2, BioIn 8, Br&AmS, DcAmA*
Gray, Denis *NF*
Gray, F T *HisAmM XR*
Gray, Francine DuPlessix 1930- *ConAu 61, WhoAmA 1973*
Gray, Francis Calley 1790-1856 *Alli, DcAmA, DcNAA, HisAmM XR*
Gray, George Hugh 1922- *ConAu 17R*
Gray, George L *HisAmM XR*
Gray, Gordon 1905- *IntMPA 1975*
Gray, Gordon 1909- *BioIn 7, CurBio XR, IntWW 1974, Who 1974, WhoAm 1974, WhoF&I 1974, WhoGov 1972, WhoS&SW 1973*
Gray, Hamilton Hunter 1827-1902 *BioIn 5*
Gray, Harold 1894-1968 *AmAu&B, AmJnl, BioIn 7, BioIn 8, BioIn 10, REnAL, WhNAA*
Gray, Harrison *NF*
Gray, Harvey L 1883- *WhJnl 1928*
Gray, J S 1890-1972 *WhoAm 1974, WhJnl 1928*
Gray, James 1899- *AmAu&B, AmNov, Au&Wr, ConAu 13R, MnnWr, REnAL, TwCA, TwCA Sup, WhNAA, WrDr 1976*
Gray, James H 1916?- *BioIn 6*

Gray, James Harry 1887?-1949 *BioIn 2*
Gray, James Richard 1859-1917 *NatCAB 12*
Gray, John Chipman *HisAmM XR*
Gray, Joseph W 1813?-1862 *DcAmB 7, NatCAB 22*
Gray, Kay 1901- *BioIn 4*
Gray, Laura *NF*
Gray, Lee Learner 1924- *ConAu 73*
Gray, Mark R 1883- *WhJnl 1928*
Gray, Reginald *NF*
Gray, Richard George 1932- *WhoAm 1974*
Gray, Stedman H 1882- *WhNAA, WhJnl 1928*
Gray, Walter S 1888?-1956 *BioIn 4*
Gray, William B *OvPC*
Gray, William Cunningham 1830-1901 *Alli Sup, DcNAA, HisAmM XR, OhA&B*
Gray, William Price 1909-1962 *BioIn 6*
Graybill, Janie *NF*
Graysmith, Robert *NF*
Grayson, A J *HisAmM XR*
Grayson, Harry 1894?-1968 *BioIn 8*
Grayson, Robert E *NF*
Grayson, William John 1788-1863 *HisAmM XR*
Grealis, Walt 1929- *NF*
Great, Maximilien *ForP*
Great Cham Of Literature see Johnson, Samuel
Greathouse, Clarence Ridgeby 1845-1899 *AmJnl, DcAmB 7*
Greaves, Arthur *NF*
Greaves, Ralph 1889- *BioIn 2*
Grebenc, Marie *NF*
Greedy, Max 1901?-1978 *NF*
Greeley, Andrew *NF*
Greeley, Bill d1977 *NF*
Greeley, Horace 1811-1872 *Alli, Alli Sup, AmAu, AmAu&B, BbD, BiD&SB, BioIn 1, BioIn 2, BioIn 3, BioIn 4, BioIn 5, BioIn 6, BioIn 7, BioIn 8, BioIn 9, BioIn 10, CasWL, CnDAL, CyAL 2, DcAmA, DcEnL, DcNAA, EncAB, EvLB, ForP, HisAmM XR, NewMr, OxAm, REn, REnAL, WebBD*
Greeley, James A 1889?-1956 *BioIn 4*
Greeley-Smith, Nixola 1880-1919 *AmJnl, BioIn 8*
Green, Abel 1900-1973 *AmSCAP 1966, BiE&WWA, BioIn 2, BioIn 3, BioIn 6, BioIn 9, CelR 1973, ConAu 41, NewYTBE 4, WhoAdv 1972, WhoAm 1974, WhoThe 1972, WhoWorJ 1972*
Green, Angela *NF*
Green, Anne Catherine Hoof *NF*
Green, Annie Douglas *HisAmM XR*
Green, Ashbel 1762-1848 *Alli, CyAL 1, DcAmA, DcNAA, HisAmM XR, WebBD*
Green, Ashbel 1928- *WhoAm 1974*
Green, Bartholomew 1666-1732 *AmJnl, DcAmB 7, OxAm, WebBD*
Green, Bert 1885-1948 *BioIn 1*
Green, Bob *NF*
Green, Charles H *NF*
Green, Charlotte 1889- *BioIn 3*
Green, Clark W *WhJnl 1928*
Green, Duff 1791?-1875 *Alli Sup, AmAu&B, AmJnl, BiDSA, BioIn 1, DcAmA, DcAmB 7, DcNAA, FamWC, WebBD*
Green, Elmer 1886-1947 *BioIn 1*
Green, George Alfred Lawrence 1868-1949 *BioIn 1, BioIn 9*
Green, George H *OvPC*
Green, Gerald 1922- *AmAu&B, BioIn 10, ConAu 15, WhoAm 1974, WhoWor 1974, WorAu*
Green, Gilbert *AmRP*
Green, Harry 1906?- *WhoAm 1974,*

Greenspun, Herman Milton *see also* Greenspun, Hank
Greenstein, Benjamin 1893-1949 *BioIn 2,*
  WhJnl 1928
Greenwald, Benjamin *OvPC*
Greenwalt, Julie *NF*
Greenway, Charles M, Jr. 1900- *WhJnl 1928*
Greenway, Charles Moore 1868-1934 *NatCAB 27*
Greenway, David S 1936?- *NF*
Greenway, Hugh D S 1935- *ConAu 73*
Greenwood, Francis William Pitt 1797-1843 *Alli,*
  CyAL 2, DcAmA, DcNAA, HisAmM XR
Greenwood, Frederick 1830-1909 *Alli Sup,*
  BioIn 2, DcEnL, NewC, WebBD
Greenwood, Grace 1823-1904 *Alli, Alli Sup,*
  AmAu, AmAu&B, BbD, BiD&SB, DcAmA,
  DcEnL, DcNAA, OxAm
Greenwood, Grace *see also* Lippincott, Sara Jane
  Clarke
Greenwood, Leonard *NF*
Greenwood, Marianne 1926- *ConAu 9*
Greenwood, Nat *NF*
Greer, Gordon G *NF*
Greer, Herbert Chester 1877-1948 *WhJnl 1928*
Greer, Hilton Ross 1879-1949 *AmAu&B, BiDSA,*
  BioIn 2, BioIn 3, DcNAA, TexWr, WhNAA
Greever, Walton Harlowe 1870-1965 *BioIn 7,*
  BioIn 9
Gregg, Frederick James *PoIre*
Gregg, Marcia *NF*
Gregg, Paul E 1876?-1949 *BioIn 2*
Gregg, Thomas 1808-1892 *Alli Sup,*
  HisAmM XR, OhA&B
Gregoire, Leon *see* Goyau, Georges Pierre Louis
  Theophile
Gregory, Alyse 1884-1967 *BioIn 1, BioIn 8,*
  BioIn 10, HisAmM XR, WhoLA
Gregory, Bettina 1946- *ConAu 69*
Gregory, Charles Edwin 1903-1961 *BioIn 6*
Gregory, Cleburne Earl 1884?- *BioIn 1*
Gregory, Clifford Verne 1883-1941 *DcAmB S3,*
  NatCAB 31, WhJnl 1928
Gregory, Elizabeth Hiatt 1872- *BioIn 1,*
  WhJnl 1928
Gregory, Gene 1923?- *BioIn 6*
Gregory, Horace Victor 1898- *HisAmM XR,*
  IntWW 1974, WebBD, WhoAm 1974,
  WhoE 1974, WhoWor 1974
Gregory, Isaac M *HisAmM XR*
Gregory, Jackson 1882-1943 *AmAu&B, AmLY,*
  DcNAA, HisAmM XR, REnAL, TwCA,
  TwCA Sup, WhNAA
Gregory, John Goadby 1856-1947 *AmAu&B,*
  BioIn 1, BioIn 5, DcNAA, DcNAA
Gregory, Lloyd Jefferson 1899- *WhoAm 1974,*
  WhJnl 1928
Gregory, Mike *NF*
Gregory, Sir Richard Arman 1864-1952 *WebBD*
Gregory, Theophilus Stephen 1897- *BioIn 1,*
  CathA 1930, Who 1974
Gregory, William H *OvPC*
Gregory, William Henry 1893-1959 *BioIn 5*
Gregson, Peter J *NF*
Gregston, Gene 1925- *WhoAm 1974,*
  WhoF&I 1974, WhoWest 1974
Grehan, Enoch 1870- *WhJnl 1928*
Grehl, Michael Tree 1928- *WhoAm 1974,*
  WhoMW 1974
Greider, William *NewMr*
Greif, Ed 1909- *OvPC, WhoPubR 1972*
Greig, D S 1885- *WhJnl 1928*
Greig, McFarlane Ian 1899- *WhJnl 1928*
Greig, Peter 1889?-1969 *BioIn 8*
Greig, S D'Alton 1885- *WhJnl 1928*

Grein, Jacob Thomas 1862-1935 *WebBD*
Greiner, Morris Esty, Jr. 1920- *WhoAdv 1972,*
  WhoAm 1974
Greneker, Claude P 1880?-1949 *BioIn 1*
Gresham, Claude Hamilton, Jr. 1922- *ConAu 7R*
Gress, Edmund G 1872- *WhJnl 1928*
Greusel, Joseph *HisAmM XR*
Grevstad, Nicolay A 1851-1940 *NatCAB 29*
Grey, Alan E *NF*
Grey, Anthony 1938- *BioIn 8, BioIn 9,*
  ConAu 29
Grey, Charles Grey 1875-1953 *BioIn 3, BioIn 8*
Grey, James C *NF*
Gribachov, Nikolai Matveyevich 1910-
  IntWW 1976
Gribayedoff, Valerian *AmJnl, HisAmM XR*
Gribbin, John F *OvPC*
Gribbroek, Eugene C *NF*
Gridley, Charles O 1897?-1966 *BioIn 7*
Gridley, Jeremy *AmJnl, HisAmM XR*
Gried, Albert O 1867- *NF*
Greig, D S 1885- *NF*
Grieg, Michael 1922- *ConAu 19R*
Grier, Albert O H 1867-1953 *WhJnl 1928*
Grier, Myrna *NF*
Grierson, Elmer Presley 1888- *WhJnl 1928*
Gries, Tom 1923?-1977 *ConAu 69*
Grieser, Norman *BioIn 1*
Griest, Elinor Preston 1921- *ForWC 1970, OvPC,*
  WhoAmW 1974
Griest, John Edmundson 1870- *WhJnl 1928*
Grieve, Mary *BioIn 7*
Grieve, Miller 1801-1878 *DcAmB 7*
Grieve, Robert 1855-1924 *DcNAA*
Griffen, Edward H 1891- *WhJnl 1928*
Griffin, A H 1911- *ConAu 21R*
Griffin, Alexander R 1903-1959 *BioIn 5*
Griffin, Benjamin F *LiJA*
Griffin, C S *NF*
Griffin, Eugene *NF*
Griffin, Frederick 1889-1946 *DcNAA*
Griffin, Gerald Edward 1907- *WhoAm 1974,*
  WhoE 1974
Griffin, Gilderoy Wells 1840-1891 *Alli Sup,*
  BiD&SB, BiDSA, DcAmA, DcNAA
Griffin, Henry Ludwig 1916- *WhoAm 1974*
Griffin, Isabel Kinnear *WhoAm 1974,*
  WhoAmW 1974
Griffin, John David 1927?-1973 *BioIn 9*
Griffin, John Howard 1920- *AmAu&B, Au&Wr,*
  AuNews 1, BioIn 3, ConAu 1, CurBio XR,
  Pen Am, WhoAm 1974, WhoTwCL,
  WhoWor 1974, WorAu, WrDr 1976
Griffin, John Toole 1923- *WhoAm 1974*
Griffin, Martin Ignatius Joseph 1842-1911
  DcAmB S1, DcNAA, HisAmM XR
Griffin, Marvin 1907- *BioIn 4, BioIn 5, BioIn 6,*
  CurBio XR
Griffin, Michael 1903?-1965 *BioIn 7*
Griffin, Oscar, Jr. *NF*
Griffin, R Allen *see* Griffin, Robert Allen
Griffin, Ramon 1903-1954 *BioIn 6, NatCAB 45*
Griffin, Richard Thomas 1932- *WhoAm 1974,*
  WhoF&I 1974
Griffin, Robert Allen 1893- *BioIn 2, CurBio XR*
Griffin, Sarah Lawrence *LiJA*
Griffin, Solomon Bulkley 1852-1925 *Alli Sup,*
  DcAmA, DcNAA, NatCAB 21
Griffin, Stuart 1917- *ConAu 7R*
Griffin, Watson 1860- *Alli Sup, BioIn 1,*
  CanNov, OxCan
Griffin, William 1897-1949 *AmJnl, BioIn 2*
Griffith, Arthur 1872-1922 *WebBD*
Griffith, Bill *NF*

Griffith, John 1876-1916 *EncAB*
Griffith, John *see also* London, Jack
Griffith, Leon Odell, Sr. 1921- *Bioln 3, ConAu 1, WrDr 1976*
Griffith, Oran Heaton 1914- *WhoAm 1974*
Griffith, R Egglesfield 1798-1850 *HisAmM XR*
Griffith, Sanford *OvPC*
Griffith, Thomas 1915- *AmAu&B, Bioln 5, ConAu 23R, IntWW 1976, RpN, WhoAm 1974, WhoF&I 1974, WrDr 1976*
Griffith, William 1876-1936 *AmAu&B, AmLY, DcNAA, HisAmM XR, WhNAA, WhJnl 1928*
Griffith, William Bebbington 1865-1952 *Bioln 2*
Griffiths, Arthur *NF*
Grifith, Bill 1944- *Bioln 10*
Grigg, J W *NF*
Grigg, John 1924- *Bioln 7, CurBio XR, Who 1974*
Grigg, Joseph W *NF*
Grigg, Joseph Williams 1910- *OvPC, WhoAm 1974*
Griggs, Ione *Bioln 3*
Griggs, Lee 1928- *ConAu 69, OvPC*
Grimes, Frank 1891-1961 *Bioln 6, TexWr, WhNAA, WhJnl 1928*
Grimes, George 1894-1964 *Bioln 8, NatCAB 51, WhNAA*
Grimes, John *NF*
Grimes, Lee 1920- *ConAu 61*
Grimes, Paul Mark *OvPC*
Grimes, William Henry 1892-1972 *Bioln 1, Bioln 9, CurBio XR, NewYTBE 3*
Grimke, Archibald Henry 1849-1930 *AmAu&B, AmLY, Bioln 4, Bioln 8, DcAmA, DcNAA, WebBD*
Grimm, Baron Friedrich Melchior Von 1723-1807 *CasWL, DcEuL, NewC, OxEng, OxFr, Pen Eur, WebBD*
Grimm, Michele *NF*
Grimm, Robert 1881-1958 *WebBD*
Grimm, Thomas M *NF*
Grimond, John J 1947?- *NF*
Grimsby, Roger *NF*
Grimsley, Roger *NF*
Grimwood, Brian *Bioln 10*
Grin, S Spencer 1928- *LEduc 1974, OvPC*
Grinnell, Charles Edward 1841-1916 *Alli Sup, DcAmA, DcNAA, HisAmM XR*
Grinnell, Frank Washburn 1873-1964 *Bioln 6, Bioln 8*
Grinnell, George Bird 1849-1938 *AmAu&B, AmLY, BbD, BiD&SB, Bioln 9, CarSB, DcAmA, DcNAA, JBA 1934, JBA 1951, OxAm, REnAL, Str&VC, WebBD, WhNAA*
Grinnell, Milon 1896- *WhNAA, WhJnl 1928*
Griscom, Bronson W d1977 *NF*
Griscom, Lloyd Carpenter 1872-1959 *Bioln 5, WebBD, WhJnl 1928*
Grisewood, Frederick Henry 1888- *Bioln 3*
Griswold, A Miner 1834-1891 *AmJnl, HisAmM XR, HsB&A, HsB&A Sup*
Griswold, Bert Joseph 1873-1927 *Bioln 2, DcNAA, IndAu 1816*
Griswold, Denny 1910- *ForWC 1970, WhoAmW 1974, WhoPubR 1972*
Griswold, Dwight P 1893-1954 *CurBio XR*
Griswold, Glenn 1886-1950 *Bioln 2*
Griswold, J *NF*
Griswold, Laurence W 1883- *WhJnl 1928*
Griswold, Rufus Wilmot 1815-1857 *Alli, AmAu, AmAu&B, BiD&SB, Bioln 1, Bioln 6, CasWL, CyAL 2, DcAmA, DcAmB 8, DcEnL, DcLEL, DcNAA, HisAmM XR,*

LiJA, OxAm, Pen Am, REnAL, WebBD
Griswold, Wesley S 1909- *ConAu 3R*
Grizzard, James Henry 1902- *WhJnl 1928*
Groat, Carl D 1887-1953 *Bioln 3*
GroenVanPrinsterer, Wilhelm 1801-1876 *WebBD*
Groer, Anne *NF*
Groger, Joseph A 1920- *USBiR 1974*
Grolund, Laurence *HisAmM XR*
Grondahl, Jens Kristian 1869-1941 *Bioln 4, NatCAB 39*
Gronert, Bernard George 1920- *WhoAm 1974*
Groom, J K 1855- *WhJnl 1928*
Gropper, William 1897-1977 *AmAu&B, AmRP, Au&Wr, CurBio XR, DcCAA, HisAmM XR, IntWW 1974, REnAL, WebBD, Who 1974, WhoAm 1974, WhoAmA 1973, WhoWor 1974, WhoWorJ 1972*
Grose, Peter Bolton 1934- *WhoAm 1974*
Groseclose, Elgin 1899- *AmAu&B, AmM&W 73S, AmNov, ConAu 21, WhoAm 1974, WhoCon 1973, WhoWor 1974, WrDr 1976*
Grosgebauer, Clare S *NF*
Gross, Alexander S *OvPC*
Gross, Bella E *WhJnl 1928*
Gross, Ben Samuel 1891- *AmAu&B, Bioln 3, Bioln 9, OvPC, WhoWorJ 1972*
Gross, Gil *NF*
Gross, Jack *NF*
Gross, Jane *NF*
Gross, Kenneth G 1938- *ConAu 25*
Gross, Leonard *Bioln 9*
Gross, Louis D 1885-1963 *Bioln 6*
Gross, Michael R *OvPC*
Gross, Milt 1895-1953 *AmAu&B, DcAmB S5, HisAmM XR, REnAL*
Gross, Milton 1912?-1973 *Bioln 6, Bioln 9, ConAu 41, NewYTBE 4*
Gross, Milton 1925?- *BioNews 1974*
Gross, Nathan Lewelyn 1907-1960 *Bioln 4, Bioln 5*
Gross, R C *NF*
Gross, Rebecca Florence 1905- *Bioln 3, ForWC 1970, RpN*
Gross, Sidney *OvPC*
Gross, Terry 1947- *NF*
Gross, William Jennings 1897-1945 *Bioln 2*
Grosse, Julius 1828-1902 *WebBD*
Grossman, Alan H *OvPC*
Grossman, Ellie *NF*
Grossman, Howard Ford 1903- *WhJnl 1928*
Grossman, Karl H 1942- *WhoAm 1974*
Grossman, Kurt R 1897-1972 *ConAu 33, WhoWorJ 1972*
Grossman, Kurt R *see also* Grossmann, Kurt R
Grossman, Lawrence Kugelmass 1931- *WhoAm 1974*
Grossman, Max R 1904- *OvPC, WhoS&SW 1973, WhoWorJ 1972*
Grossman, Vasilii Semenovich *Bioln 9*
Grossmann, Kurt R 1897-1972 *Bioln 9, Bioln 10, NewYTBE 3*
Grossmann, Kurt R *see also* Grossman, Kurt R
Grosvenor, Cyrus P *HisAmM XR*
Grosvenor, Elsie Graham Bell *HisAmM XR*
Grosvenor, Gilbert Hovey 1875-1966 *AmAu&B, Bioln 1, Bioln 2, Bioln 3, Bioln 5, CurBio XR, HisAmM XR, REnAL, WebBD, WhNAA*
Grosvenor, Gilbert Melville 1931- *Bioln 10, HisAmM XR, WhoAm 1974, WhoS&SW 1973*
Grosvenor, Melville Bell 1901- *AmAu&B,*

AmM&W 73S, BioIn 4, BioIn 5, BioIn 8, CclR 1973, ConAu 69, CurBio XR, HisAmM XR, WhoAm 1974, WhoGov 1972, WhoS&SW 1973, WhoWor 1974
Grosvenor, William Mason 1835-1900 *Alli Sup, DcAmB 8, DcNAA, NatCAB 20*
Groth, John 1908- *CurBio XR, OvPC, WhoAm 1974*
Grothmann, Carl Ellis 1922- *BioIn 7*
Grotrian, Sir Herbert *NF*
Grotz, Paul 1902- *AmArch 1970, BioIn 9*
Group, Harriet Moran *OvPC*
Groussard, Serge 1921?- *IntWW 1976, REn, WhoWor 1974*
Grout, George H 1878?-1950 *BioIn 2*
Grove, Sir George 1820-1900 *Alli Sup, BiD&SB, DcEnL, NewC, OxEng, REn, WebBD*
Grove, Kim *NF*
Grover, Preston 1900- *AmJnl, WhJnl 1928*
Groves, Charles Stuart 1867-1948 *BioIn 1*
Growald, Richard H *NF*
Growoll, Adolf 1850-1909 *AmAu&B, DcNAA, HisAmM XR*
Grozier, David F *OvPC*
Grozier, Edwin Atkins 1859-1924 *AmJnl, DcNAA, NatCAB 19*
Grozier, Richard 1887-1946 *AmJnl, BioIn 1*
Gruber, Isabelle C *NF*
Gruber, Ruth *BioIn 1, BioIn 2, ConAu 25, ForWC 1970, OvPC, WhoWorJ 1972*
Gruber, William Paul 1932- *WhoAm 1974*
Grubert, Carl 1911- *WhoAm 1974*
Gruelle, John Barton 1880?-1938 *BioIn 2, DcNAA, IndAu 1816, OhA&B, WebBD*
Gruen, John 1926- *ConAu 17R*
Gruenberg, Mark 1953- *NF*
Gruenberg, Robert 1922- *WhoAm 1974*
Gruenberg, Ruth *NF*
Gruening, Ernest 1887-1974 *AmAu&B, BioIn 4, BioIn 5, BioIn 6, BioIn 7, BioIn 10, BioNews 1974, ConAu 49, CurBio XR, HisAmM XR, IntWW 1974, NewYTBS 5, WebBD, WhoAm 1974, WhoAmP 1973*
Gruenstein, Peter *InvJ*
Gruesel, John Hubert 1866- *NF*
Gruliow, Leo 1913- *ConAu 5, ConAu 73*
Grumbach, Salomon 1884-1952 *BioIn 2, BioIn 3*
Grumhaus, Harold Francis 1903- *WhoAm 1974, WhoF&I 1974, WhoMW 1974, WhoWor 1974*
Grumich, Charles *NF*
Grund, Francis Joseph 1805?-1863 *Alli, Alli Sup, DcAmA, DcAmB S1, DcNAA, OxAm, REnAL*
Gruneisen, Charles Lewis 1806-1879 *Alli Sup, DcEnL, FamWC*
Gruner, George Frank 1925- *WhoAm 1974*
Grunewald, Hudson *NF*
Grunfeld, Frederic V 1929- *ConAu 73, OvPC, WrDr 1976*
Grunow, Julius S 1869?-1952 *BioIn 3*
Grunwald, Henry Anatole 1922- *AmAu&B, BioIn 8, BioIn 9, NewMr, WhoAm 1974*
Gruson, Sydney 1916- *BioIn 6, NewYTBE 1, WhoAm 1974, WhoWor 1974*
Grutzner, Charles *NF*
Gryzanowski, E *HisAmM XR*
Grzech, Ellen *NF*
Guado, Sergio *ConAu XR*
Guard, William J 1862-1932 *BioIn 7*
Guardia, Jorge *NF*
Guardionex, Jorge *ForP*
Guareschi, Giovanni 1908-1968 *BioIn 2, BioIn 3, BioIn 4, BioIn 7, BioIn 8, BioIn 9,*

CathA 1952, ConAu 25, EncWL, ModRL, TwCA Sup, TwCW
Guarino, Ann 1931- *ForWC 1970, WhoAmW 1974*
Gubitz, Friedrich Wilhelm 1786-1870 *WebBD*
Guccione, Robert 1931- *BioIn 8, BioIn 9, BioIn 10*
Guccione, Robert, Jr. 1956?- *AuNews 2*
Guck, Homer 1878-1949 *BioIn 2*
Gudlaughsson, Jonas 1887-1916 *BioIn 1, BioIn 2*
Gudmundsson, Guomundur 1874-1919 *BioIn 2*
Gue, Benjamin F 1828-1904 *AmAu&B, BioIn 6, DcNAA*
Gue, Benjamin T 1828-1904 *DcAmB 8*
Gueft, Olga *BioIn 6*
Guego, Firmin *WhJnl 1928*
Guehenno, Jean Marcel Jules Marie 1890-1978 *EncWL, IntWW 1974, WhoWor 1974*
Guehenno, Jean Marcel Jules Marie *see also* Guehenno, Marcel
Guehenno, Marcel 1890-1978 *CasWL*
Guehenno, Marcel *see also* Guehenno, Jean Marcel Jules Marie
Guelich, Theodor 1829-1893 *BioIn 2*
Guenther, Johann Georg *BioIn 2*
Guenther, John Lewis *ConAu 5, OvPC*
Guenther, Otto *HisAmM XR*
Guenther, Robert Wallace 1929- *WhoAm 1974*
Guenther, Robert Wallace *see also* Guenther, Wallace
Guenther, Wallace 1929- *ConAu 65*
Guenther, Wallace *see also* Guenther, Robert Wallace
Guerin, Andre Paul 1899- *IntWW 1976*
Guernsey, Alfred Hudson 1818?-1902 *Alli Sup, AmAu&B, BiD&SB, DcAmA, DcNAA, HisAmM XR*
Guernsey, Clara Florida 1839- *Alli Sup, DcAmA, DcNAA, HisAmM XR*
Guernsey, Otis Love, Jr. 1918- *AmAu&B, WhoAm 1974, WhoAm 1974*
Gueroult, Adolphe 1810-1872 *WebBD*
Guerrero, Miguel *NF*
Guerrini, John *NF*
Guesde, Jules 1845-1922 *OxFr, WebBD*
Guess, Edward Preston 1925- *ConAu 73*
Guest, Edgar Albert 1881-1959 *AmAu&B, AmJnl, CnE&AP, CurBio XR, HisAmM XR, NatCAB 44, OxAm, Pen Am, REn, REnAL, WebBD, WhNAA*
Guett, Dieter 1924- *ConAu 65*
Guggenheim, Alicia Brooks 1906-1963 *BioIn 1, BioIn 3*
Guggenheim, Alicia Brooks *see also* Patterson, Alicia
Guggenheim, Harry Frank 1890-1971 *AmJnl, BioIn 4, BioIn 5, BioIn 7, BioIn 9, CurBio XR, NewYTBE 2*
Guggenheim, Mrs. Harry Frank 1906-1963 *CurBio XR*
Guggenheim, Mrs. Harry Frank *see also* Guggenheim, Alicia Brooks
Guggenheim, Mrs. Harry Frank *see also* Patterson, Alicia
Gugliucci, Fannie 1906- *WhJnl 1928*
Guidry, Frederick H *NF*
Guidry, Vernon A, Jr. *NF*
Guild, Curtis 1827-1911 *Alli Sup, AmAu&B, BiD&SB, DcAmA, DcAmB 8, DcNAA, NatCAB 9, REnAL, WebBD*
Guild, Curtis, Jr. 1860-1915 *HisAmM XR, WebBD*
Guild, Frank S *HisAmM XR*
Guilfoyle, Ann *NF*
Guilfoyle, James H 1890-1950 *BioIn 2,*

WhJnl 1928
Guillain, Robert *ForP*
Guimaraes, Dona *WhoAmW 1974*
Guindi, M *NF*
Guinness, W Victor *WhJnl 1928*
Guinzburg, Thomas 1926- *WhoAm 1974, WhoWor 1974*
Guisewhite, Cathy *NF*
Guiterman, Arthur 1871-1943 *AmAu&B, AmLY, CnDAL, CurBio XR, DcNAA, EvLB, HisAmM XR, OxAm, REn, REnAL, Str&VC, TwCA, TwCA Sup, WebBD, WhNAA*
Guittar, Lee J *NF*
Gulbransson, Olaf 1873-1958 *BioIn 5, WebBD*
Gulek, Kasim 1910- *ForP, IntWW 1974*
Guler, Cemal Nadir 1902?- *BioIn 1*
Gulick, Luther Halsey 1828-1891 *Alli Sup, DcNAA, WebBD*
Gulick, Luther Halsey 1865-1918 *AmAu&B, DcNAA, HisAmM XR, WebBD*
Gulick, Merle A *OvPC*
Gullace, Gino 1925- *ConAu 69, OvPC*
Gulliver, Harold Strong 1935- *WhoAm 1974*
Gulliver, John P *HisAmM XR*
Gulliver, Lucile 1882-1964 *AmAu&B, AmLY, BioIn 6*
Gump, Robert Livingston 1903?- *BioIn 2*
Gumpert, Anita *NF*
Gun, Robert *HisAmM XR*
Gundell, Glenn 1904-1965 *HisAmM XR*
Gunn, Eleanor 1880?-1969 *BioIn 8*
Gunn, Herbert Smith 1904-1962 *BioIn 2, BioIn 6*
Gunn, Stanley W *AmJnl*
Gunn, Thomas Butler 1826- *Alli Sup, BioIn 4, EarABI, EarABI Sup, HisAmM XR*
Gunnison, Elisha Norman 1837-1880 *Alli Sup, DcAmA, DcNAA*
Gunnison, Herbert Foster 1858-1932 *DcNAA, WhJnl 1928*
Gunnison, Raymond M 1887-1972 *WhJnl 1928*
Gunnison, Royal Arch 1909-1946 *BioIn 1*
Gunterman, Bertha Lisette *BioIn 6*
Gunther, Jane Perry 1916- *WhoAm 1974*
Gunther, John 1901-1970 *AmAu&B, AmNov, AuBYP, BioIn 1, BioIn 2, BioIn 3, BioIn 4, BioIn 5, BioIn 6, BioIn 7, BioIn 8, BioIn 9, BioIn 10, ConAu 11R, ConAu 25, CurBio XR, EvLB, ForP, HisAmM XR, LongC, NewYTBE 1, OxAm, Pen Am, REn, REnAL, SmATA 2, TwCA, TwCA Sup, WebBD*
Gunton, George 1845-1919 *Alli Sup, DcAmA, DcNAA, HisAmM XR*
Gunts, Brent O *WhoAdv 1972, WhoAm 1974, WhoE 1974*
Gupta, Ranjan K 1944?- *NF*
Guptill, Arthur L 1891-1956 *CurBio XR, WhNAA*
Guptill, Leighton 1920- *WhoAm 1974*
Guravich, Dan *NF*
Gurly, Boyd 1888- *WhJnl 1928*
Gurney, Ephraim W 1829-1886 *HisAmM XR*
Gurney, Eric 1910- *BioIn 8*
Gurtner, Othmar 1895-1958 *BioIn 5*
Gurupadaswamy, M S 1923- *IntWW 1976*
Gusewelle, Charles Wesley 1933- *WhoAm 1974*
Gust, Dodie 1927- *NF*
Gustafson, Elton T *AuBYP, BioIn 8*
Gustafson, Grace M 1910?-1951 *BioIn 2*
Gustafson, Paul E *BioIn 2*
Gustafson, Philip H 1904?- *BioIn 1*
Gustafson, Mrs. Zadel 1841-1917 *DcNAA*
Gustaitis, Rasa 1934- *BioIn 8, ConAu 25*

Gustav, Herve 1871-1944 *NF*
Gustin, Lawrence Robert 1937- *ConAu 57*
Gustin, Wilbert H d1927 *WhJnl 1928*
Gustincic, Jurij *NF*
Gustkey, Earl 1940- *ConAu 57*
Guth, Paul 1910- *IntWW 1976*
Guthman, Edwin Otto 1919- *BioIn 2, BioIn 7, BioIn 9, ConAu 33, CurBio XR, InvJ, RpN, WhoAm 1974*
Guthrie, Alfred Bertram, Jr. 1901- *AmAu&B, AmNov, CnDAL, ConAu 57, ConNov 1972, ConNov 1976, CurBio XR, CyWA, DcLEL, DrAF 1976, IndAu 1917, RpN, ModAL, OxAm, REnAL, TwCA Sup, WhoPNW, WhoAm 1974, WhoWest 1974, WhoWor 1974, WrDr 1976*
Guthrie, Charles M *BioIn 5*
Guthrie, Thomas R *NF*
Guthrie, Wayne *NF*
Gutierrez, Oton *NF*
Gutman, John *OvPC*
Gutman, Peter *AmRP*
Gutmann, Enrique *BioIn 1*
Gutwillig, Robert Alan 1931- *AmAu&B, Au&Wr*
Gutzkow, Karl 1811-1878 *WebBD*
Guy, Harry D 1890- *WhJnl 1928*
Guys, Constantin 1802-1892 *AtlBL, BioIn 2, BioIn 4, BioIn 5, BioIn 7, OxFr, WebBD*
Guyton, David Edgar 1880-1964 *BioIn 3*
Guzman, Martin Luis 1887- *CasWL, DcSpL, DrAS 74F, ForP, IntWW 1976, LEduc 1974, Pen Am, REn*
Guzman Y Alvarez, Eliseo 1892?-1949 *BioIn 2*
Guzzo, Louis R *NF*
Gwathmey, John Hastings 1886- *AmAu&B*
Gwertzman, Bernard *NF*
Gwin, Virginia Helen 1901- *WhJnl 1928*
Gwyn, Richard 1934- *ConAu 25, OxCan Sup, WrDr 1976*
Gwynn, Denis Rolleston 1893- *Au&Wr, BioIn 1, CathA 1930, ConAu 13, ConAu P-1*
Gwynn, Edith *BioIn 1*
Gwynn, Stephen Lucius 1864-1950 *EvLB, LongC, ModBL, NewC, PoIre, TwCA, TwCA Sup, WebBD, WhoLA*
Gwynn, William *HisAmM XR*
Gwynne, Erskine 1899-1948 *DcNAA, WhoLA*
Gwynne, Howell Arthur 1865-1950 *BioIn 2, BioIn 5*
Gysi, Klaus 1912- *IntWW 1976, WhoWor 1974*
Gzowski, Peter *NF*

H

Haaf, Gunter R 1945?- *NF*
Haag, Maurice R 1911- *BioIn 1*
Haaker, Edwin L *OvPC*
Haardt, Sara Powell *HisAmM XR*
Haas, Alan D *NF*
Haas, Carl De 1817-1875 *DcNAA*
Haas, Carl De *see also* DeHaas, Carl
Haas, Charlie 1952- *ConAu 73*
Haas, Jacob Judah Aaron De 1872-1937
    DcAmB S2, WebBD
Haas, Mark Leo 1897- *WhJnl 1928*
Haas, Victor P *NF*
Habberton, John 1842-1921 *Alli Sup, AmAu,*
    AmAu&B, BbD, BiD&SB, BioIn 8, CarSB,
    DcAmA, DcBiA, DcEnL, DcNAA, EvLB,
    HisAmM XR, OxAm, REnAL, WebBD,
    WhoChL
Habe, Hans 1911-1977 *Au&Wr, BioIn 1,*
    BioIn 4, ConAu 45, ConAu 73, CurBio XR,
    IntWW 1976, OxGer, TwCA Sup,
    WhoWor 1974, WrDr 1976
Haber, Eitan *NF*
Haber, Jack 1939- *ConAu 69, NF*
Haber, Joyce 1932- *BioIn 8, BioIn 10,*
    CelR 1973, ConAu 65, IntMPA 1975
Haber, P B *WhJnl 1928*
Haberl, Franz Xavier 1840-1910 *WebBD*
Haberle, Robert *NF*
Habte, Amde M *NF*
Hach, H Theodor *HisAmM XR*
Hachel, Ali *NF*
Hacker, Helena *NF*
Hacker, Louis *AmRP*
Hackerman, Norman 1912- *BioIn 7*
Hackes, Peter Sidney 1924- *WhoAm 1974,*
    WhoS&SW 1973
Hackett, Alice Payne d1977 *HisAmM XR*
Hackett, Blanche *NF*
Hackett, Charels Megginson 1909-1970 *BioIn 9*
Hackett, Edmund Francis d1954 *BioIn 3*
Hackett, Francis 1883-1962 *AmAu&B,*
    HisAmM XR, LongC, OxAm, REnAL,
    TwCA Sup, TwCA Sup, WebBD
Hackett, John T 1900-1960 *BioIn 5,*
    HisAmM XR, WhJnl 1928
Hackett, Sir John Winthrop 1848-1916 *BioIn 2*
Hackett, Karleton Spalding 1867-1935 *WhNAA,*
    WhJnl 1928
Hackett, Paul *BioIn 3*
Hacklander, Friedrich Wilhelm Von 1816-1877
    BbD, BiD&SB, DcBiA, EvEuW, OxGer,
    WebBD
Hackleman, Pleasant Adam 1814-1862 *BioIn 7*
Haddad, William Frederick 1928- *InvJ,*
    WhoAm 1974, WhoE 1974
Hadden, Briton 1898-1929 *AmJnl, BioIn 1,*

    BioIn 2, BioIn 8, HisAmM XR,
    NatCAB 28, REnAL
Haddock, Albert 1890-1971 *NewC, WebBD*
Haddock, Albert *see also* Herbert, Sir Alan Patrick
Haddon, Frederick William 1839-1906 *BioIn 2*
Haddon, Harry Harter 1898- *WhJnl 1928*
Haddon, Sir Richard 1893-1967 *BioIn 8*
Haddon, William *HisAmM XR*
Hade, J Stover 1900- *WhJnl 1928*
Haden-Guest, Anthony *NF*
Hadfield, Edwin *NF*
Hadley, Charles Elliot 1891- *WhJnl 1928*
Hadley, Earl *NF*
Hadley, Harold 1898?-1964 *BioIn 7*
Hadley, James *HisAmM XR*
Hadley, Leila 1926- *Au&Wr, ConAu 41*
Hadley, William Waite 1866?-1960 *BioIn 5*
Hadman, Virginia 1908- *BioIn 2*
Haedens, Kleber Gustave 1913- *IntWW 1976,*
    WhoWor 1974
Haeger, Robert A *BioIn 2*
Haekal, Mohamed Hussein 1888- *BioIn 1*
Haenigsen, Harry William 1900- *AmAu&B,*
    BioIn 9, WhoAm 1974, WhJnl Sup
Haessler, Carl d1972 *NewYTBE 3*
Hafen, LeRoy R 1893- *AmAu&B, Au&Wr,*
    DrAS 74H, WhNAA, WhoAm 1974
Hafer, Fred L 1886- *WhJnl 1928*
Hafter, Rudoph P *NF*
Hagaman, C Lyle 1898- *WhJnl Sup, WhJnl 1928*
Hagaman, Harry Taylor 1869- *WhJnl 1928*
Hagedorn, Charles G *OvPC*
Hagemann, E R *LiJA*
Hagen, Richard *NF*
Hagen, Theodore *HisAmM XR*
Hager, Alice Rogers 1894- *AmAu&B, AuBYP,*
    ConAu 5R, WhoS&SW 1973
Hager, Lawrence White 1890- *WhoAm 1974,*
    WhJnl 1928, WhoS&SW 1973
Hager, Philip Dean 1937?- *NF*
Hager, Robert M 1938- *ConAu 65*
Hagerty, Christian Dane 1876- *NF*
Hagerty, James Andrew 1876-1961 *BioIn 3,*
    BioIn 6
Hagerty, James Campbell 1909- *AmJnl, BioIn 3,*
    BioIn 5, BioIn 8, CurBio XR,
    IntWW 1976, Who 1974, WhoAm 1974,
    WhoF&I 1974, WhoPubR 1972,
    WhoWor 1974
Haggard, Sewell 1879-1928 *HisAmM XR*
Haggard, William 1900?-1962 *BioIn 6*
Haggart, Stanley Mills *NF*
Haggerty, James D 1870- *WhJnl 1928*
Haggerty, James Joseph 1920- *ConAu 41,*
    SmATA 5, WhoS&SW 1973
Haggerty, Mike *NF*

138

Haggerty, Sandra *NF*
Haggerty, Thomas A 1873- *BioIn 1*
Haggett, Alice B *NF*
Hague, John 1829-1906 *DcNAA*
Hague, Robert Anderson 1904?-1953 *BioIn 3*
Hagy, Lewis Yarnall, III 1899- *WhJnl 1928*
Hagy, Ruth Geri 1911- *BioIn 4, CurBio XR*
Hahn, Changsup *NF*
Hahn, Herbert Ralph 1924- *IntMPA 1975, WhoAm 1974*
Hahn, Mannel 1895?-1954 *BioIn 3*
Hahr, Henrik A A 1911- *IntWW 1976, WhoWor 1974*
Haier, Harold R 1901- *WhJnl 1928*
Haight, Elbert E 1879- *WhJnl 1928*
Haight, Rufus James *HisAmM XR*
Haight, Theron Wilber 1840-1913 *BioIn 5*
Haight, Walter Dewey 1899?-1968 *BioIn 8*
Haight, William *NF*
Hailey, Foster 1899?-1966 *BioIn 7*
Hailmann, William Nicholas 1836-1920 *AmAu&B, DcAmA, DcNAA, HisAmM XR, OhA&B, WebBD*
Hailperin, Herman 1899-1973 *AmAu&B, Au&Wr, ConAu 5, WhoAm 1974, WhoWorJ 1972*
Haiman, Miecislaus Albin Francis Joseph 1888-1949 *BioIn 1*
Haiman, Robert S *NF*
Haines, Donald Hamilton 1886-1951 *BioIn 2, WhJnl 1928*
Haines, E M *HisAmM XR*
Haines, Harry B 1882?-1972 *WhJnl 1928*
Haines, Helen Elizabeth 1872- *HisAmM XR, REnAL*
Haines, Lynn 1876-1929 *DcNAA*
Haines, Mark P 1888- *WhJnl 1928*
Haines, Oakley P *HisAmM XR*
Hajj, E *NF*
Hajjaj, Abdul *NF*
Hake, Gordon 1899?-1962 *BioIn 6*
Halasz, Louis *NF*
Halbe, James M *OvPC*
Halberstam, David 1934- *AmAu&B, BioIn 9, CelR 1973, ConAu 69, CurBio XR, NewMr, WhoAm 1974, WhoWor 1974, WrDr 1976*
Halberstam, Michael *NF*
Halbert, Caroline A *HisAmM XR*
Halbert, N A *HisAmM XR*
Haldeman, Bruce 1862-1948 *BioIn 1, BioIn 3, NatCAB 38*
Haldeman, Walter Newman 1821-1902 *AmJnl, NatCAB 18*
Haldeman, William Birch 1846-1924 *NatCAB 18*
Haldeman-Julius, Emanuel 1889-1951 *AmRP, DcAmB S5, WebBD*
Hale, Bidwell Henry *WhJnl 1928*
Hale, Charles 1831-1882 *Alli, BioIn 3, DcAmB 8, DcNAA*
Hale, Dale *NF*
Hale, David 1791-1849 *Alli, AmJnl, DcAmB 8, NatCAB 11*
Hale, Davis *NF*
Hale, Edward *RpN*
Hale, Edward Everett 1822-1909 *Alli, Alli Sup, AmAu, AmAu&B, BbD, BiD&SB, CarSB, CnDAL, CyAL 2, CyWA, DcAmA, DcEnL, DcLEL, DcNAA, EvLB, HisAmM XR, JBA 1934, LiJA, OxAm, Pen Am, REn, REnAL, WebBD*
Hale, George Ellery 1868-1938 *DcNAA, HisAmM XR, WebBD, WhNAA*
Hale, Jeanne 1913-1969 *BioIn 8, BioIn 10*
Hale, Judson Drake 1933- *ConAu 69,*

WhoAm 1974
Hale, Leon 1921- *ConAu 19R*
Hale, Nancy 1908- *AmAu&B, Au&Wr, ConAu 5R, ConNov 1972, ConNov 1976, DrAF 1976, OxAm, REn, REnAL, TwCA Sup, WhoAm 1974, WhoAmW 1974, WhoS&SW 1973, WhoWor 1974, WrDr 1976*
Hale, Nathan 1784-1863 *Alli, AmAu&B, BioIn 1, CyAL 2, DcNAA, HisAmM XR, REnAL, WebBD*
Hale, Nathan, Jr. 1818- *Alli, HisAmM XR, LiJA*
Hale, Peter M *NF*
Hale, Philip 1854-1934 *DcAmB S1, DcNAA, WebBD, WhJnl 1928*
Hale, Ruth *HisAmM XR*
Hale, Sarah Josepha Buell 1788-1879 *Alli, Alli Sup, AmAu, AmAu&B, AmJnl, BbD, BiD&SB, BioIn 1, BioIn 3, BioIn 5, BioIn 7, CnDAL, CyAL 1, DcAmA, DcEnL, DcLEL, DcNAA, EncAB, EvLB, FemPA, HisAmM XR, LiJA, OxAm, REnAL, WebBD*
Hale, Sarah Preston Everett *HisAmM XR*
Hale, W H *HisAmM XR*
Hale, William B 1860-1938 *NatCAB 29*
Hale, William Bayard 1869-1924 *AmJnl, AmLY, BioIn 2, DcAmA, DcAmB 8, DcNAA, HisAmM XR, IndAu 1816, WebBD*
Hale, William Harlan 1910-1974 *AmAu&B, ConAu 49, HisAmM XR, NewYTBS 5, REnAL, WhoAm 1974, WhoE 1974*
Hale, William Thomas 1857-1926 *BiDSA, DcAmA, DcNAA*
Hales, Samuel Dale d1978 *NF*
Haley, Alex Palmer 1921- *BlkC, LivBAA, WhoWest 1974*
Haley, Sir William John 1901- *BioIn 1, BioIn 3, BioIn 8, BioIn 9, CurBio XR, ForP, IntWW 1974, Lor&LP, WhoAm 1974, WhoWor 1974*
Halfeld, Adolf 1898-1955 *BioIn 4*
Halik, C *NF*
Hall, A Wilford 1819-1902 *HisAmM XR*
Hall, Abraham Oakey 1826-1898 *Alli, Alli Sup, AmAu&B, DcAmA, DcAmB 8, DcNAA, HisAmM XR, WebBD*
Hall, Angus 1932- *Au&Wr, ConAu 21R, WrDr 1976*
Hall, Mrs. Bennie *WhJnl 1928*
Hall, Blakely *HisAmM XR*
Hall, Bruce *NF*
Hall, Bryant G *NF*
Hall, Clarence Wilbur 1902- *AmAu&B, WhoAm 1974, WhoWor 1974*
Hall, Claude *NF*
Hall, Clifford E *NF*
Hall, Covington *AmRP*
Hall, David 1714-1772 *AmJnl, HisAmM XR*
Hall, David 1916- *WhoAm 1974, WhoE 1974*
Hall, Edward Hagaman 1858-1936 *DcNAA*
Hall, Edward Smith 1786-1860 *BioIn 2*
Hall, Elial F *HisAmM XR*
Hall, Elizabeth 1929- *ConAu 65*
Hall, Elizabeth Wason 1912- *ConAu 4R, IndAu 1917*
Hall, Emma Gene *OvPC*
Hall, Esther Greenacre *AuBYP, BioIn 7*
Hall, Francis *AmJnl*
Hall, Frederic 1836-1918 *BioIn 6, DcNAA*
Hall, Frederick P 1859-1939 *NatCAB 31, WhJnl 1928*
Hall, Gerald Stanley 1844-1924 *HisAmM XR*

Hall, Gerry NF
Hall, Gilman HisAmM XR
Hall, Gladys 1891?-1977 ConAu 73
Hall, Gordon Langley 1929- Au&Wr, AuBYP,
    ConAu 2R
Hall, Granville Stanley 1844?-1924 Alli Sup,
    BiD&SB, DcAmA, DcNAA, HisAmM XR,
    OhA&B, OxAm, REnAL, TwCA,
    TwCA Sup, WebBD
Hall, Grover Cleveland 1888-1941 AmJnl,
    WhNAA
Hall, Grover Cleveland, Jr. 1915-1971 BioIn 9,
    NewYTBE 2
Hall, Harlan Page 1838-1907 DcNAA, OhA&B
Hall, Harold 1892-1958 BioIn 4, BioIn 5
Hall, Harrison 1785-1866 Alli, BiDSA, DcAmA,
    DcNAA, HisAmM XR
Hall, Harry NF
Hall, Helen ForWC 1970, HisAmM XR
Hall, Henri Mason 1884- BioIn 1, WhJnl 1928
Hall, Henry 1845-1920 Alli Sup, AmLY,
    DcNAA
Hall, Henry 1851-1934 Alli Sup
Hall, Henry Noble 1872-1949 BioIn 1, BioIn 2
Hall, Holworth HisAmM XR
Hall, J Basil HisAmM XR
Hall, James 1793-1868 Alli, AmAu, AmAu&B,
    AmJnl, CyAL 1, DcAmA, DcLEL, DcNAA,
    HisAmM XR, LiJA, OhA&B, OxAm,
    Pen Am, REnAL, WebBD
Hall, James Byron 1918- ConAu 1
Hall, John NF
Hall, John Elihu 1783-1829 Alli, AmAu&B,
    CyAL 1, DcAmA, DcNAA, HisAmM XR
Hall, John M HisAmM XR
Hall, John N NF
Hall, John Randolph 1892- WhNAA,
    WhJnl 1928
Hall, Josef Washington 1894-1960 AmAu&B,
    AnMV 1926, BioIn 4, BioIn 5, BioIn 6,
    CurBio XR, EvLB, TwCA, TwCA Sup,
    WebBD, WhNAA
Hall, Josef Washington see also Close, Upton
Hall, Joseph AmJnl
Hall, Joseph W, Jr. NF
Hall, Lee NF
Hall, Lemuel C 1874-1946 BioIn 1
Hall, Linda J OvPC
Hall, Marjory 1908- AuBYP, BioIn 8,
    ConAu XR, CurBio XR, WhoAmW 1974,
    WhoE 1974, WrDr 1976
Hall, Marshall Renwood 1889-1947 OhA&B,
    WhNAA, WhJnl 1928
Hall, Mary 1924?-1969 BioIn 8
Hall, Max RpN
Hall, Norman S 1896- WhJnl 1928
Hall, Oliver Leigh 1870-1946 BioIn 1
Hall, Orson Loftin 1877- WhJnl 1928
Hall, Orvan R 1900- WhJnl 1928
Hall, Payson 1915- WhoAm 1974
Hall, Ramon Lines 1890- WhJnl 1928
Hall, Richard 1925- Au&Wr, ConAu 17R,
    WrDr 1976
Hall, Robert C 1882- WhJnl 1928
Hall, Robert Dawson 1892- WhJnl 1928
Hall, Roger 1919- ConAu 29
Hall, Samuel 1740-1809 AmAu&B, REnAL
Hall, Samuel Carter 1800-1889 Alli, Alli Sup,
    BbD, BiD&SB, DcEnL, HisAmM XR,
    NewC, PoIre, WebBD
Hall, Tom HisAmM XR
Hall, Walter E 1850- WhJnl 1928
Hall, William E 1889- WhJnl 1928
Hall, William Earl 1897- BioIn 3

Hall, William Edward, Jr. 1923- DrAS 74E,
    LEduc 1974, WhoAm 1974
Hall, William Whitty 1810-1876 Alli, Alli Sup,
    BiDSA, DcAmA, DcNAA, HisAmM XR
Hall, Wilson Dudley 1922- BioIn 9, BioIn 10,
    ConAu 69, WhoAm 1974, WhoE 1974
Hall, Wilton Earle 1901- NF
Hall, Woodie NF
Halladay, Geneva 1926- NF
Halle, Katherine Murphy ConAu 41,
    WhoAm 1974
Halle, R J HisAmM XR
Hallet, Richard Matthews 1887-1967 AmAu&B,
    HisAmM XR
Hallett, Benjamin Franklin 1797-1862 BioIn 3,
    DcNAA
Hallgren, Mauritz Alfred 1899-1956 AmAu&B,
    BioIn 4, HisAmM XR, TwCA, TwCA Sup
Halliburton, Maurine HisAmM XR
Hallinan, Hazel Hunkins NF
Hallman, Eugene Sanborn 1919- CanWW 1972,
    WhoAm 1974
Hallock, Charles 1834-1917 Alli Sup, AmAu,
    AmAu&B, BiD&SB, DcAmA, DcAmB 8,
    DcNAA, HisAmM XR
Hallock, Charles 1834-1914 WebBD
Hallock, Conrad NF
Hallock, Gerard 1800-1866 AmJnl, BioIn 3,
    BioIn 9, DcAmB 8, WebBD
Hallock, Joseph Newton 1834-1913 DcAmA,
    DcNAA, HisAmM XR, NatCAB 11
Hallock, W W HisAmM XR
Hallock, Willam Allen 1794-1880 DcNAA
Halloran, Richard 1930- ConAu 29
Hallowell, Robert 1886-1939 HisAmM XR,
    WebBD
Hallowell, Sara Catherine 1833- DcNAA
Hallstrom, Bill NF
Halman, Talat Sait 1931- BioIn 9, ConAu 53,
    WhoE 1974
Halperin, Morton H 1938- AmM&W 73S,
    ConAu 9
Halpern, Alan NF
Halpin, Charles B 1864?-1955 BioIn 3
Halpine, Charles Graham 1829-1868 Alli Sup,
    AmAu, AmAu&B, BiD&SB, BioIn 9,
    CyAL 2, DcAmA, DcAmB 7, DcEnL,
    DcLEL, DcNAA, HisAmM XR, OxAm,
    PoIre, REnAL, WebBD
Halsell, Grace 1923- AuBYP, AuNews 1,
    BioIn 8, ConAu 23R, OvPC
Halsey, Abraham HisAmM XR
Halsey, Ashley BioIn 3
Halsey, Ashley, Jr. HisAmM XR,
    WhoS&SW 1973
Halsey, Francis Whiting 1851-1919 AmAu&B,
    DcAmA, DcNAA, HisAmM XR, NatCAB 9
Halstead, Albert 1867-1949 BioIn 1, BioIn 2,
    BioIn 5
Halstead, Betsy 1942?- BioIn 7
Halstead, Dirck NF
Halstead, Murat 1829-1908 AmAu, AmAu&B,
    AmJnl, BbD, BiD&SB, DcAmA, DcAmB 8,
    DcNAA, FamWC, HisAmM XR,
    NatCAB 1, OhA&B
Halton, David 1940- ConAu 73
Halton, M Giles 1867- WhJnl 1928
Halton, Matthew Henry 1904-1956 BioIn 4
Halverson, Guy NF
Ham, George Henry 1847-1926 DcNAA
Ham, James S NF
Hamada, Hidozo ForP
Hamblin, Charles Henry 1859- NF
Hamblin, Dora Jane 1920- AuBYP, ConAu 37,

For WC 1970, WhoAmW 1974
Hamblin, Francis Lebaron 1902- WhJnl 1928
Hambridge, Charles NF
Hamburg, Judith Gray NF
Hamburger, Philip Paul 1914- AmAu&B,
  ConAu 5R
Hamby, William Henry 1875-1928 DcNAA
Hamel, Ernest 1826-1898 WebBD
Hamel, John Philip 1898- WhJnl 1928
Hamer, John C NF
Hamerslag, Victor 1904-1953 BioIn 3
Hamersley, G W HisAmM XR
Hamersley, Lewis Randolph 1847-1910 DcAmA,
  DcNAA, HisAmM XR
Hamersley, Lewis Randolph, Jr. HisAmM XR
Hamersley, T H S HisAmM XR
Hamersly, G W NF
Hamerton, Philip Gilbert 1834-1894 Alli Sup,
  BbD, BiD&SB, BrAu 19, CarSB, DcBiA,
  DcEnL, EvLB, HisAmM XR, NewC,
  WebBD
Hames, Edward H HisAmM XR
Hamill, Denis NF
Hamill, Katherine NF
Hamill, Pete 1935- CelR 1973, ConAu 25,
  IntMPA 1975
Hamilton, Albert H 1925- OvPC, WhoPubR 1972
Hamilton, Alexander 1757-1804 Alli, AmAu,
  AmAu&B, AmJnl, BbD, BiD&SB, CyAL 1,
  CyWA, DcAmA, DcEnL, DcLEL, DcNAA,
  EvLB, HisAmM XR, OxAm, REn, REnAL,
  WebBD
Hamilton, Sir Charles Denis 1918- ForP,
  IntWW 1974, Lor&LP, Who 1974
Hamilton, Sir Charles Denis see also Hamilton, Sir
  Denis
Hamilton, Charles Frederick 1869-1933 DcNAA
Hamilton, Clayton Meeker 1881-1946 AmAu&B,
  AmLY, CurBio XR, DcAmB S4, DcNAA,
  HisAmM XR, REnAL, TwCA, TwCA Sup,
  WebBD, WhNAA
Hamilton, Dave 1909- ConAu 65
Hamilton, David NF
Hamilton, Sir Denis 1918- ForP, IntWW 1976,
  Who 1974, WhoWor 1974
Hamilton, Sir Denis see also Hamilton, Sir Charles
  Denis
Hamilton, Earl Jefferson 1899- AmM&W 73S,
  Au&Wr, ConAu P-1, HisAmM XR,
  WhoAm 1974, WhoWor 1974
Hamilton, Sir Frederic Howard 1865-1956 BioIn 4
Hamilton, Frederick d1885? NF
Hamilton, Gail 1833-1896 Alli Sup, AmAu,
  AmAu&B, BiD&SB, DcAmA, DcEnL,
  DcNAA, LiJA, OxAm
Hamilton, Gail see also Dodge, Mary Abigail
Hamilton, Gordon C OvPC
Hamilton, Grace Colette Durieux WhJnl 1928
Hamilton, Grant E 1862- HisAmM XR
Hamilton, Jean HisAmM XR
Hamilton, John A RpN
Hamilton, John Brown 1847-1898 DcNAA,
  HisAmM XR
Hamilton, John Durieux 1875- WhJnl 1928
Hamilton, John W NF
Hamilton, July NF
Hamilton, Lee David NF
Hamilton, Martha M NF
Hamilton, Norman Rond 1877-1964 BioIn 6,
  WhJnl 1928
Hamilton, Peter 1891- WhJnl 1928
Hamilton, Philip HisAmM XR
Hamilton, Pierce Stevens 1826-1893 BbtC,
  DcNAA, OxCan

Hamilton, R F AmJnl
Hamilton, Robert HisAmM XR
Hamilton, Roulhac NF
Hamilton, Scott B 1876?-1949 BioIn 2
Hamilton, Thomas HisAmM XR
Hamilton, Thomas Jefferson 1885-1937 WhNAA,
  WhJnl 1928
Hamilton, Tom NF
Hamilton, West Alexander 1886- WhJnl 1928
Hamilton, William 1939- ConAu 69
Hamilton, William Peter 1867-1929 DcNAA,
  WhJnl 1928
Hamilton, Williams Baskerville HisAmM XR
Hamilton, Zachary Macaulay 1872?-1950 BioIn 2
Hamlet, L Alton 1903- WhNAA, WhJnl 1928
Hamlin, Charles Eugene 1861-1921 DcNAA
Hamlin, Paul NF
Hamline, Leonidas Lent 1797?-1865 Alli Sup,
  DcAmA, DcNAA, HisAmM XR, OhA&B
Hamm, Jack 1916- BioIn 2, ConAu 5
Hamm, Margherita Arlina 1871-1907 AmAu&B,
  DcNAA, NatCAB 9
Hammann, Otto 1852-1928 WebBD
Hamment, John NF
Hammer, Richard 1928- ConAu 25, SmATA 6
Hammersmark, S AmRP
Hammerstein, Oscar 1847-1919 OxAm, WebBD
Hammerton, Sir John Alexander 1871-1949
  BioIn 1, BioIn 2, EvLB, WhoLA
Hammervik, Hans I 1947- NF
Hammesfahr, A C G HisAmM XR
Hammett, Samuel Adams 1816-1865 Alli, AmAu,
  AmAu&B, CnDAL, CyAL 2, DcAmA,
  DcNAA, OxAm, REnAL
Hammill, Grace 1895- WhJnl Sup
Hammit, Charles K HisAmM XR
Hammond, Arthur J 1871- WhJnl 1928
Hammond, Charles 1779-1840 Alli, AmJnl,
  BiDSA, DcAmB 8, OhA&B
Hammond, Charles Frederick 1879?-1951 BioIn 2
Hammond, Dorothy 1924- ConAu 69
Hammond, Harold Albert 1900- WhJnl 1928
Hammond, Harry Walter 1867-1948 BioIn 3,
  NatCAB 37
Hammond, James NF
Hammond, John Lawrence LeBreton 1872-1949
  BioIn 2, BioIn 5, WebBD
Hammond, John Winthrop 1887-1934 DcNAA
Hammond, Johnson Francis 1882-1961 BioIn 6,
  BioIn 7
Hammond, Melvin Ormond 1876-1934 DcNAA,
  OxCan
Hammond, Percy Hunter 1873-1936 AmJnl,
  DcAmB S2, DcNAA, OhA&B, REnAL,
  TwCA, TwCA Sup, WebBD
Hammond, Ray W 1880- WhJnl 1928
Hammond, Samuel H 1809-1878 Alli, Alli Sup,
  DcNAA, HsB&A
Hampson, Alfred Leete 1889?-1952 BioIn 2,
  BioIn 3
Hampson, Eugene F 1909?-1972 BioIn 9
Hampson, Fred 1902?-1955 BioIn 4
Hampson, Hillary H NF
Hampson, Stuart Hirst d1956 BioIn 4
Hampton, Benjamin Bowles 1875-1932 DcNAA,
  HisAmM XR, WhNAA
Hampton, Jesse D HisAmM XR
Hampton, Joseph Wade 1813-1855 BioIn 8
Hampton, W NF
Hamrin, Harald NF
Hamway, Ed NF
Hanan, Harry 1916- BioIn 1, WhoAmA 1973
Hanau, Stella 1890?-1972 BioIn 9
Hanauer, Joan 1931- ForWC 1970

Hance, Joseph AmJnl
Hanchett, James C OvPC
Hancock, Daniel Witt see Hancock, Dewitt
Hancock, Dewitt d1942 AmJnl
Hancock, Edward J 1874- WhJnl 1928
Hancock, Elizabeth Hazlewood 1871-1915 BiDSA,
  DcNAA
Hancock, Harrie Irving 1868-1922 DcNAA
Hancock, Malcolm 1936- ConAu 25
Hancock, Silas D HisAmM XR
Hancox, Ralph 1929- CanWW 1972
Hand, A J NF
Hand, Charles BioIn 2
Hand, Charles S NF
Hand, Ira 1879?-1949 BioIn 1
Hand, Judson 1930- NF
Handler, Meyer Srednick 1905-1978 NF
Handley, John A NF
Handley, Louis DeB 1876- WhJnl 1928
Hands, C E NF
Handy, George Charles 1886-1958 BioIn 6,
  NatCAB 43
Handy, Mary d1958 RpN
Handy, Moses P 1847-1898 AmJnl, NatCAB 16
Handy, Ray D 1879- WhJnl 1928
Handy, Robert Gillis HisAmM XR
Hanemann, H W HisAmM XR
Hanes, Frank Borden 1920- AmAu&B, BioIn 3,
  BioIn 4, ConAu 1, WhoS&SW 1973,
  WrDr 1976
Hanes, John Wesley 1892- AmJnl, WhoF&I 1974
Hanes, Leigh 1893- AmAu&B
Hanes, Thomas A 1896- WhJnl 1928
Haney, J C HisAmM XR
Haney, Jesse HisAmM XR
Haney, Lewis Henry 1882-1969 BioIn 8, WhNAA
Haney, Paul Prichard 1928- BioIn 8,
  WhoAm 1974
Hanff, Minnie Maud HisAmM XR
Hangen, Putnam Welles 1930-1970 AmAu&B,
  WhoWor 1974
Hangen, Putnam Welles see also Hangen, Welles
Hangen, Welles 1930-1970 BioIn 8, ConAu 9R
Hangen, Welles see also Hangen, Putnam Welles
Hanighen, Frank Cleary 1899-1964 BioIn 6
Hankey, Billy NF
Hankey, Clarke NF
Hanks, Marshall Bernard 1884-1948 BioIn 3,
  NatCAB 37
Hanks, Stedhan Shumway OvPC
Hanleiter, C R LiJA
Hanley, Clifford 1922- Au&Wr, BioIn 4,
  ConAu 9R, ConNov 1972, ConNov 1976,
  WrDr 1976
Hanley, Dick OvPC
Hanley, Frank BioIn 5
Hanley, James 1901- Au&Wr, CnMD Sup,
  ConDr, ConLC 3, ConLC 5, ConNov 1972,
  ConNov 1976, DcLEL, EvLB, IntWW 1974,
  LongC, ModBL, ModBL Sup, NewC,
  Pen Eng, REn, TwCA, TwCA Sup, TwCW,
  WebBD, Who 1974, WhoTwCL,
  WhoWor 1974, WrDr 1976
Hanley, James Franklin 1863-1920 NF
Hanley, Michael J NF
Hanley, Richard d1977 NF
Hanley, Richard H J 1916?-1967 BioIn 7
Hanlin, Frank 1889-1955 BioIn 3
Hanlon, Michael NF
Hanna, Charles NF
Hanna, Daniel Rhodes 1894-1962 BioIn 6
Hanna, Gordon 1920- WhoAm 1974
Hanna, Hugh Sisson 1879-1948 BioIn 1
Hanna, Lee 1930- IntMPA 1975, WhoE 1974

Hanna, Phil Townsend 1896-1957 BioIn 6,
  NatCAB 46, WhNAA
Hanna, Sam NF
Hannagan, Stephen Jerome 1899-1953 BioIn 1,
  BioIn 3, BioIn 9, CurBio XR, DcAmB S5
Hannah, Bob NF
Hannay, Arthur Burns NF
Hannay, David 1853-1934 Alli Sup, WebBD
Hannay, James 1827-1873 Alli, Alli Sup,
  BiD&SB, BioIn 4, BioIn 7, BrAu 19,
  CasWL, DcEnL, DcLEL, EvLB,
  HisAmM XR, NewC, WebBD
Hannifin, Jerry 1917- OvPC
Hanning, Hugh 1925- ConAu 25
Hannon, Evelyn OvPC
Hannum, Sara AuBYP, BioIn 8
Hanny, William P 1882?-1947 BioIn 1
Hano, Arnold 1922- AuBYP, BioIn 8, ConAu 9,
  WhoWest 1974
Hanrahan, John D 1938- NF
Hanratty, Elmarine NF
Hansbrouck, Jim NF
Hansbrough, Henry Clay 1848-1933 DcNAA
Hanschman, Nancy 1929?- BioIn 5, BioIn 6,
  CurBio XR
Hanscom, S P NF
Hansell, Jack E 1891- WhJnl 1928
Hansen, Elmer L 1890- WhJnl 1928
Hansen, Harry 1884-1977 AmAu&B, AmJnl,
  AuBYP, BioIn 1, BioIn 4, BioIn 8,
  ConAu 69, ConAu 73, CurBio XR,
  HisAmM XR, OvPC, REnAL, TwCA,
  TwCA Sup, WebBD, Who 1974,
  WhoAm 1974
Hansen, Joseph AmRP
Hansen, Leonard R 1894- WhJnl 1928
Hansen, Percy M 1890- WhJnl 1928
Hansen, Pete NF
Hansen, Robert H RpN
Hansen, Vern NF
Hansen, Walter A 1894?-1967 BioIn 8
Hansenne, Marcel 1917- BioIn 1, CurBio XR
Hanser, Richard 1909- ConAu 5R, OvPC
Hansl, Eva VomBaur 1889-1978 ForWC 1970
Hanson, Alexander Contee 1786-1819 WebBD
Hanson, Dick NF
Hanson, Elisha 1888-1962 NF
Hanson, H Rolfe 1897- WhJnl 1928
Hanson, J J OvPC
Hanson, John Wesley 1823-1901 Alli, Alli Sup,
  DcAmA, DcNAA, HisAmM XR
Hanson, Kitty AmAu&B, WhoAm 1974,
  WhoAmW 1974
Hanson, Michael Francis 1867-1950 BioIn 2,
  WhJnl 1928
Hanson, Victor Henry 1876-1945 BioIn 2
Hanson, Victor Henry, II 1930- WhoAdv 1972,
  WhoAm 1974, WhoF&I 1974,
  WhoS&SW 1973
Hanway, Patrick J HisAmM XR
Hanzsche, William Thomson 1891-1954 BioIn 3
Hapgood, Hutchins 1869-1944 AmAu&B,
  DcAmA, DcAmB S3, DcNAA,
  HisAmM XR, OxAm, REnAL, TwCA,
  TwCA Sup, WebBD, WhNAA
Hapgood, Isabel Florence 1850-1928 AmAu&B,
  BbD, DcAmA, DcAmB 8, DcNAA,
  HisAmM XR, WhNAA
Hapgood, Kate Sargent BioIn 2
Hapgood, Norman 1868-1937 AmAu&B, AmJnl,
  AmRP, BiD&SB, BioIn 4, DcAmA,
  DcAmB S2, DcNAA, HisAmM XR, OxAm,
  REnAL, TwCA, WebBD
Hapgood, Powers AmRP

Hapgood, Walter E 1873?-1949 *BioIn 1*
Happ, Wilbur R 1905- *WhJnl 1928*
Happel, Margaret E *NF*
Hara, Shiro 1908- *IntWW 1976*
Harada, Wayne *NF*
Harang, Miriam 1906?-1967 *BioIn 8*
Harbaugh, Henry 1817-1867 *Alli, Alli Sup,
AmAu, AmAu&B, CasWL, CyAL 2,
DcAmA, DcNAA, HisAmM XR, OhA&B,
PoChrch, REnAL, WebBD*
Harben, William Nathaniel 1858-1919 *AmAu&B,
AmLY, BiD&SB, BiDSA, DcAmA, DcBiA,
DcNAA, HisAmM XR, OxAm, REnAL,
WebBD*
Harbert, Elizabeth Morrisson Boynton 1845-1925
DcNAA, IndAu 1816
Harbert, Elizabeth Morrisson Boynton *see also*
Harbert, Lizzie B
Harbert, Lizzie Boynton 1845-1925 *Alli*
Harbert, Lizzie Boynton *see also* Harbert, Elizabeth
Morrisson
Harbison, Robert C 1866-1937 *WhJnl 1928*
Harbour, Jefferson Lee 1857-1931 *AmAu&B,
DcNAA, HisAmM XR*
Harbron, John Davison 1924- *Au&Wr,
CanWW 1972, ConAu 11R, OxCan Sup*
Harby, Isaac 1788-1828 *Alli, AmAu&B,
BiD&SB, BiDSA, BioIn 4, CyAL 1,
DcAmA, DcAmB 8, DcNAA*
Harchar, Harry A 1912- *AmAu&B, OvPC,
WhoAm 1974*
Harcourt-Smith, Simon *NF*
Hard, William 1878-1962 *AmLY, BioIn 2,
BioIn 6, HisAmM XR, WebBD*
Hardaway, Joseph Benson 1890?-1957 *BioIn 4*
Hardcastle, Michael 1933- *ConAu 25,
WrDr 1976*
Hardebeck, John *NF*
Harden, Edward W *AmJnl*
Harden, John William 1903- *BioIn 3, BioIn 4,
BioIn 5, WhoAdv 1972, WhoAm 1974,
WhoF&I 1974, WhoPubR 1972,
WhoS&SW 1973*
Harden, Maximilian 1861-1927 *BioIn 6, OxGer,
WebBD*
Harden, Percival L *HisAmM XR*
Hardenbergh, J E *NF*
Harder, George Albert 1899- *WhJnl 1928*
Hardie, Keir 1856-1915 *AmRP, WebBD*
Hardin, Charles T 1887- *WhJnl 1928*
Hardin, George E *BlkC*
Harding, Alfred 1892-1969 *AmAu&B, BioIn 8*
Harding, Edwin B 1887- *WhNAA, WhJnl 1928*
Harding, Gardner Ludwig 1887-1940 *DcNAA*
Harding, George Canady 1829-1881 *BioIn 2,
IndAu 1816*
Harding, Jesper 1799-1865 *AmAu&B, AmJnl,
NatCAB 22*
Harding, John William 1864-1953 *AmAu&B,
AmLY, BioIn 3, WhNAA*
Harding, Louise Graham d1964 *BioIn 7*
Harding, Mabel 1882?-1965 *BioIn 7*
Harding, Marilyn *BioIn 10*
Harding, Nelson 1879-1944 *CurBio XR*
Harding, Nelson 1924- *NF*
Harding, Richard T 1881?-1952 *BioIn 3*
Harding, Warren Gamaliel 1865-1923 *AmAu&B,
BioIn 1, BioIn 2, BioIn 3, BioIn 4, BioIn 5,
BioIn 6, BioIn 7, BioIn 8, BioIn 9,
BioIn 10, DcNAA, HisAmM XR, OhA&B,
OxAm, REn, REnAL, WebBD*
Harding, William W 1830-1889 *AmJnl,
NatCAB 22*

Hardman, Jacob Benjamin Saltsky 1882-1968
AmRP, BioIn 8
Hardt, Bob *NF*
Hardwick, Elizabeth 1916- *AmAu&B, ConAu 5,
WhoAm 1974, WhoAmW 1974, WorAu,
WrDr 1976*
Hardwick, Emery E 1885- *WhJnl 1928*
Hardy, Arnold *NF*
Hardy, Benjamin 1906?-1951 *BioIn 2*
Hardy, Don 1912-1966 *BioIn 7, BioIn 9*
Hardy, Mrs. Forman *NF*
Hardy, Guy U 1872-1947 *NatCAB 37,
WhJnl 1928*
Hardy, Oscar Jacob 1874-1950 *BioIn 3*
Hardy, Warren F 1878- *WhJnl 1928*
Hardy, William Harris 1837-1917 *BioIn 1,
DcAmB 8*
Hardy, William N 1889-1950 *BioIn 2*
Hare, James Henry 1856-1946 *DcAmB S4,
HisAmM XR, WebBD*
Harger, Charles Moreau 1862?-1955 *BioIn 3*
Hargis, James *HisAmM XR*
Hargis, Vivienne A *WhJnl 1928*
Hargroder, Charles Merlin 1926- *ConAu 73,
WhoS&SW 1973*
Hargrove, Charles R *HisAmM XR*
Hargrove, Marion 1919- *AmAu&B, CurBio XR,
REnAL, TwCA Sup*
Hargrove, Rosette *WhoAmW 1974*
Harkey, Ira, III *NF*
Harkey, Ira Brown, Jr. 1918- *BioIn 6, ConAu 57,
WhoAm 1974, WrDr 1976*
Harkness, John C *HisAmM XR*
Harkness, Peter A *NF*
Harkness, Richard Long 1907- *WhoAm 1974*
Harkrader, Charles J. 1885- *WhoAm 1974,
WhJnl 1928*
Harley, John Hunter 1865?-1947 *BioIn 1, WhoLA*
Harlin, J J *WhJnl 1928*
Harlings, Albert *NF*
Harlock, Marguerite J 1905- *WhJnl Sup*
Harlow, Harold Eugene 1925- *WhoAm 1974*
Harlow, Victor Emmanuel 1876-1958 *AmAu&B,
WhNAA*
Harm, Duane Rollo 1939- *WhoAdv 1972,
WhoAm 1974*
Harman, Fred 1902- *BioIn 1*
Harman, Jeanne Perkins 1919- *BioIn 4,
ConAu 69, ForWC 1970, OvPC,
WhoAmW 1974*
Harman, John *NF*
Harman, Moses *HisAmM XR*
Harmon, Clint *NF*
Harmon, Dudley Ann *AmJnl*
Harmon, Erskine Mortimer 1895-1965 *BioIn 7*
Harmon, Francis Stuart 1895- *WhoAm 1974,
WhJnl 1928*
Harmon, Frederick *OvPC*
Harmon, Mark K *BioIn 5*
Harmony, Henry 1873- *WhJnl 1928*
Harms, Kathleen C 1903- *WhJnl 1928*
Harmsworth, Alfred Charles William 1865-1922
FamWC, ForP, LongC, NewC, WebBD
Harmsworth, Alfred Charles William *see also*
Northcliffe, Alfred
Harmsworth, Esmond Cecil, Viscount 1898-1978
CurBio XR
Harmsworth, Geoffrey 1904- *Who 1974*
Harmsworth, Sir Harold Cecil Aubrey 1897-1952
BioIn 3
Harmsworth, Harold Sidney, Viscount 1868-1940
CurBio XR, LongC, NewC, WebBD

Harmsworth, Harold Sidney, Viscount *see also*
  Rothermere, Harold
Harmsworth, Sir Hildebrand Aubrey 1872-1929
  NewC, WebBD
Harmsworth, Vere H Esmond, Viscount 1925-
  Who 1974
Harnan, Terry 1920- *ConAu 45*
Harner, Charles Emory 1901- *WhJnl 1928,*
  WhoS&SW 1973
Harner, Herman Edwin 1898- *WhNAA,*
  WhJnl 1928
Harney, George Julian 1817-1897 *Alli Sup,*
  BioIn 7
Harney, William Wallace 1831-1912 *BiDSA,*
  BioIn 2, DcAmA, DcNAA, IndAu 1816
Harnisch, Giulio 1885?-1953 *BioIn 3*
Harper, Allanah *BioIn 1*
Harper, Burna Maude 1883- *WhJnl 1928*
Harper, Charles H 1862- *WhJnl 1928*
Harper, Dan *NF*
Harper, Fletcher 1806-1877 *AmAu&B, AmJnl,*
  HisAmM XR, LiJA, NatCAB 1, WebBD
Harper, Frances Ellen Watkins 1825-1911 *Alli Sup,*
  BlkAW, DcNAA
Harper, Henry J *LiJA*
Harper, Howard V *NF*
Harper, Howard Vincent 1904- *WhoAm 1974*
Harper, Ida Husted 1851-1931 *AmAu&B, AmLY,*
  BioIn 2, DcAmB 8, DcNAA, IndAu 1816,
  WhNAA
Harper, J C *AmJnl*
Harper, J Henry *HisAmM XR*
Harper, James 1795-1869 *AmAu&B, EncAB,*
  WebBD
Harper, James E *OvPC*
Harper, Jerry *NF*
Harper, John James 1841-1908 *BioIn 1*
Harper, Joseph S *OvPC*
Harper, Joseph Wesley 1801-1870 *HisAmM XR,*
  WebBD
Harper, Judy *NF*
Harper, Lucius Clinton 1895- *WhJnl 1928*
Harper, Patrice *NF*
Harper, Rita *NF*
Harper, Robert Story 1899-1962 *AmAu&B,*
  Au&Wr, BioIn 2, BioIn 8, OhA&B
Harper, Ru-Flo 1903- *WhJnl 1928*
Harper, Thomas Edward 1871- *WhJnl 1928*
Harper, William Hudson 1857-1946 *DcNAA*
Harper, William L *NF*
Harral, Stewart 1906-1964 *ConAu 5R*
Harrell, Arthur E *NF*
Harrell, Eugene *HisAmM XR*
Harrigan, Anthony 1925- *ConAu 21R*
Harriman, Alice 1861-1925 *DcNAA*
Harriman, John 1904-1961 *AmAu&B, AmNov,*
  BioIn 5, TwCA, TwCA Sup
Harriman, Karl Edwin 1875-1935 *AmAu&B,*
  DcAmA, DcNAA, HisAmM XR,
  NatCAB 13
Harriman, Kathleen *BioIn 1*
Harrington, Denis 1932- *ConAu 69*
Harrington, Gerald *NF*
Harrington, Guy L 1876- *WhJnl 1928*
Harrington, Harry Franklin 1882-1935 *AmJnl,*
  DcNAA, HisAmM XR, WhNAA,
  WhJnl 1928
Harrington, Joe *NF*
Harrington, John *HisAmM XR*
Harrington, John J *HisAmM XR*
Harrington, John Walker 1868-1952 *BioIn 2*
Harrington, Richard P *LiJA*
Harris, Alfred T 1911?-1971 *BioIn 9,*
  NewYTBE 2

Harris, Archie B 1880- *WhJnl 1928*
Harris, Arthur Timothy 1867-1945 *BioIn 5*
Harris, Ben Jorj *HisAmM XR*
Harris, Benjamin d1716? *AmAu, AmAu&B,*
  AmAu&B, AmJnl, NewC, OxAm, REnAL,
  WebBD
Harris, Beulah Ligon 1893-1970 *BioIn 8,*
  WhJnl 1928
Harris, C H *HisAmM XR*
Harris, Carrie Jenkins *HisAmM XR*
Harris, Carter Henry 1860-1953 *NF*
Harris, Chapin Aaron 1806-1866? *Alli, DcAmA,*
  DcNAA, HisAmM XR, WebBD
Harris, Clifford *NF*
Harris, Corra May 1869-1935 *AmAu&B, BiDSA,*
  DcNAA, HisAmM XR, WebBD, WhNAA
Harris, Dick *NF*
Harris, Don 1936?-1978 *NF*
Harris, Douglas *NF*
Harris, E *AmRP*
Harris, E H 1880- *WhJnl 1928*
Harris, Edgar Garrard 1876- *WhJnl 1928*
Harris, Edward Arnold 1910-1976 *BioIn 1,*
  ConAu 65, WhoAm 1974
Harris, Edwin V 1888-1960 *BioIn 5*
Harris, Eleanor *NF*
Harris, Eli *NF*
Harris, Emerson Pitt 1853-1937 *DcNAA,*
  WhNAA, WhJnl 1928
Harris, Emily C *NF*
Harris, Frances Kay 1917- *WhoAmW 1974*
Harris, Frank 1854?-1931 *BioIn 1, BioIn 2,*
  BioIn 4, BioIn 5, BioIn 6, BioIn 7, BioIn 9,
  BioIn 10, CnDAL, CnMD, ConAmL, EvLB,
  HisAmM XR, LongC, ModBL, NewC,
  OxAm, OxEng, Pen Eng, RAdv 1, TwCA,
  TwCA Sup, TwCW, WebBD, WhoTwCL
Harris, Garrard 1875-1927 *DcNAA, WhNAA*
Harris, Genevieve *NF*
Harris, George Washington 1814-1869 *Alli Sup,*
  AmAu, AmAu&B, BiD&SB, BiDSA,
  CnDAL, DcAmA, DcLEL, DcNAA, OxAm,
  Pen Am, REnAL, WebE&AL
Harris, Harold C 1897- *WhJnl Sup*
Harris, Harry 1918- *WhoE 1974*
Harris, Henry Wilson 1883-1955 *BioIn 3, WhoLA*
Harris, Horace Rice 1890-1956 *BioIn 4*
Harris, J W *HisAmM XR*
Harris, Jeremiah G *AmJnl*
Harris, Joel Chandler 1848-1908 *Alli Sup, AmAu,*
  AmAu&B, AmJnl, AnCL, AtlBL, AuBYP,
  BbD, BiD&SB, BiDSA, BioIn 1, BioIn 2,
  BioIn 3, BioIn 4, BioIn 5, BioIn 6, BioIn 7,
  BioIn 8, CarSB, CasWL, CnDAL, CyWA,
  DcAmA, DcAmB 8, DcBiA, DcEnA Ap,
  DcLEL, DcNAA, EncAB, EvLB,
  HisAmM XR, JBA 1934, LiJA, OxAm,
  OxEng, Pen Am, RAdv 1, REn, REnAL,
  Str&VC, WebBD, WebE&AL, WhoChL,
  YABC 1
Harris, John Carson *NF*
Harris, John D *NF*
Harris, John P 1902-1969 *BioIn 8*
Harris, Joseph 1813-1889 *BioIn 5*
Harris, Joseph 1828-1892 *Alli Sup, DcNAA,*
  HisAmM XR
Harris, Julia Collier 1875- *AmAu&B,*
  WhJnl 1928
Harris, Julian LaRose 1874-1963 *BioIn 6,*
  WhJnl 1928
Harris, Laura 1903?-1956 *BioIn 1, BioIn 4*
Harris, Lee O 1839-1909 *Alli Sup, BioIn 2,*
  DcAmA, DcNAA, IndAu 1816
Harris, Leonard 1929- *ConAu 65*

Harris, Lew NF
Harris, Louis 1921- AmM&W 73S, BioIn 7,
    CelR 1973, ConAu 13, CurBio XR,
    WhoAm 1974, WhoWor 1974
Harris, Louis Carl 1912-1978 WhoAm 1974,
    WhoS&SW 1973
Harris, Morris J NF
Harris, Nettie Magder NF
Harris, Otis 1894- WhJnl 1928
Harris, R NF
Harris, Radie ConAu 65
Harris, Ralph NF
Harris, Reginald Duckett 1920- Au&Wr, OvPC
Harris, Rex OvPC
Harris, Richard H 1920- NF
Harris, Roy Vincent 1895- BioIn 8
Harris, Samuel R HisAmM XR
Harris, Sydney Justin 1917- AmAu&B, BioIn 3,
    ConAu 61, WhoAm 1974, WhoMW 1974
Harris, T George 1924- ConAu 69,
    WhoAm 1974, WhoWest 1974,
    WhoWor 1974
Harris, Thaddeus Mason 1768-1842 Alli,
    AmAu&B, CyAL 1, DcAmA, DcNAA,
    HisAmM XR
Harris, Thomas Lake 1823-1906 Alli, Alli Sup,
    AmAu, AmAu&B, BiD&SB, DcAmA,
    DcNAA, HisAmM XR, OxAm, REnAL,
    WebBD
Harris, W B NF
Harris, Wade Hampton 1857-1935 WhJnl 1928
Harris, Walter NF
Harris, Walter C 1870- WhJnl Sup
Harris, William Charles 1830-1905 Alli Sup,
    DcAmA, DcNAA, HisAmM XR
Harris, William J OvPC
Harris, William J 1897- WhJnl 1928
Harris, William Torrey 1835-1909 Alli Sup,
    AmAu, AmAu&B, BiD&SB, BioIn 1,
    BioIn 2, BioIn 9, DcAmA, DcNAA,
    HisAmM XR, OxAm, REnAL, WebBD
Harris, Wilson NF
Harris, Winder Russell 1888-1973 NF
Harrison, Anne Blaine HisAmM XR
Harrison, Ben C 1889- WhJnl 1928
Harrison, Bernie NF
Harrison, Carter Henry 1825-1895 AmJnl,
    DcNAA
Harrison, Carter Henry 1860-1954 NF
Harrison, Dale BioIn 1
Harrison, Dale C 1895?-1978 NF
Harrison, E L T HisAmM XR
Harrison, Emma 1921?-1970 BioIn 8
Harrison, Floyd Reed 1889-1961 BioIn 6
Harrison, Gilbert Avery 1915- AmAu&B,
    BioIn 6, BioIn 10, CurBio XR,
    HisAmM XR, WhoAm 1974
Harrison, Gordon NF
Harrison, H S HisAmM XR
Harrison, Henry Sydnor 1880-1930 AmAu&B,
    BioIn 3, BioIn 8, DcAmB 8, DcNAA,
    HisAmM XR, LongC, OxAm, REnAL,
    TwCA, WebBD
Harrison, Horace H d1883 NF
Harrison, Hugh 1876- WhJnl 1928
Harrison, James 1816-1893 BioIn 2
Harrison, James 1937- ConAu 15R
Harrison, James see also Harrison, Jim
Harrison, Jay Smolens 1927-1974 ConAu 53,
    IntWW 1974, WhoAm 1974, WhoE 1974
Harrison, Jim 1937- AmAu&B, ConAu XR,
    ConLC 6, ConP 1970, ConP 1975,
    DrAF 1976, DrAP 1975, RAdv 1,
    WrDr 1976

Harrison, John Higgins 1867-1930 WhJnl 1928
Harrison, John Marshall 1914- ConAu 25,
    DrAS 74E, RpN, WhoE 1974
Harrison, John Raymond 1933- AuNews 2,
    WhoAm 1974, WhoF&I 1974,
    WhoS&SW 1973
Harrison, Joseph Graham 1912- Au&Wr,
    WhoAm 1974
Harrison, Luther 1877- WhNAA, WhJnl 1928
Harrison, Marie HisAmM XR
Harrison, Mark NF
Harrison, Mark W HisAmM XR
Harrison, Maxine OvPC
Harrison, Robert 1905?-1978 NF
Harrison, Roland R 1878-1940 NatCAB 30,
    WhJnl 1928
Harrison, Ross Granville 1870-1959 WebBD
Harrison, Russell B d1936 HisAmM XR
Harrison, Selig Seidenman 1927- HisAmM XR,
    RpN, WhoAm 1974, WhoWor 1974
Harrison, Thomas G 1883- BioIn 2, IndAu 1816
Harrison, W P HisAmM XR
Harrison, Walter Munford 1888-1961 AmJnl,
    BioIn 6, WhJnl 1928
Harrison, William 1907?-1965 BioIn 2, BioIn 7
Harrison, William Beverley HisAmM XR
Harrison, Mark 1948- WhoE 1974
Harriss, Joseph 1936- ConAu 57
Harriss, Robert Preston 1902- ConAu 73,
    WhoE 1974
Harrity, Aileen Brenon 1895?-1967 BioIn 8
Harrity, Charles NF
Harrold, Ernest William 1889-1945 BioIn 1
Harryman, A H HisAmM XR
Harsanyi, Zsolt 1887-1943 CurBio XR, Pen Eur
Harsch, Joseph Close 1905- AmAu&B, Au&Wr,
    BioIn 2, BioIn 3, CurBio XR, ForP,
    IntWW 1976, Who 1974, WhoAm 1974,
    WhoWor 1974
Harsha, Wayne V 1905- WhoAm 1974
Harshaw, Ruth NF
Hart, Bertrand K 1892- WhJnl 1928
Hart, Bob NF
Hart, Charles HisAmM XR
Hart, Charles A NF
Hart, Charles B 1850- NatCAB 13
Hart, Charles Calmer 1878-1956 BioIn 4
Hart, E Stanley HisAmM XR
Hart, Edward 1854-1931 DcNAA, HisAmM XR
Hart, H HisAmM XR
Hart, H D HisAmM XR
Hart, Harriet NF
Hart, Harry HisAmM XR
Hart, Herschell d1960 NF
Hart, Irving Warren 1899- WhNAA
Hart, J C HisAmM XR
Hart, J Wilson HisAmM XR
Hart, James NF
Hart, Jeffrey 1930- WhoAm 1974
Hart, Jerome Alfred 1854-1937 AmAu&B,
    AmLY, DcNAA, HisAmM XR, LiJA,
    NatCAB 28, WhNAA
Hart, Jim Allee 1914- AmM&W 73S,
    ConAu 13R, DrAS 74H
Hart, John 1895-1940 WhNAA
Hart, John 1948- ConAu 65
Hart, John Lewis 1931- AmAu&B, BioIn 4,
    BioIn 5, ConAu 49, WhoAm 1974
Hart, John Lewis see also Hart, Johnny
Hart, John Seely 1810-1877 Alli, Alli Sup,
    AmAu&B, CyAL 2, DcAmA, DcNAA,
    HisAmM XR, REnAL
Hart, Johnny 1931- AuNews 1, BioNews 1974
Hart, Johnny see also Hart, John Lewis

Hart, Joseph S *AmJnl*
Hart, Larry 1920- *ConAu 33*
Hart, Lester Melcher 1881- *WhJnl 1928*
Hart, R D *HisAmM XR*
Hart, William B *BioIn 1*
Hart-Davis, Duff 1936- *ConAu 29, WrDr 1976*
Harte, Bret 1836?-1902 *AmAu, AmAu&B,
   AtlBL, AuBYP, BiD&SB, CasWL, CnDAL,
   CrtT 3, CyWA, DcAmA, DcEnA, OxAm,
   Pen Am, RAdv 1, REn, REnAL,
   WebE&AL*
Harte, Bret *see also* Harte, Francis Bret
Harte, Francis Bret 1836?-1902 *Alli Sup, AmAu,
   AmJnl, BbD, CyAL 2, DcBiA, DcEnA,
   DcEnA Ap, DcEnL, DcLEL, EvLB,
   HisAmM XR, LiJA, MouLC 4, OxEng,
   WebBD*
Harte, Francis Bret *see also* Harte, Bret
Harte, Houston 1892-1972 *BioIn 9, NewYTBE 3,
   WhJnl 1928*
Harte, James D *LiJA*
Harte, Walter Blackburn 1867?-1898 *DcAmA,
   DcNAA, HisAmM XR*
Hartendorp, Abram VanHeyningen 1893- *BioIn 7,
   WhJnl 1928*
Hartford, Fernando W 1872-1938 *WhJnl 1928*
Hartford, Huntington 1911- *AmAu&B,
   BiE&WWA, CelR 1973, ConAu 17,
   CurBio XR, IntWW 1976, WhoAm 1974,
   WhoAmA 1973, WhoE 1974, WhoGov 1972*
Hartigan, William *NF*
Hartley, Robert Willard 1911-1971 *BioIn 9*
Hartley, William *NF*
Hartley, William Brown 1913- *ConAu 7R*
Hartling, Peter 1933- *CasWL, IntWW 1976,
   ModGL, OxGer, WhoWor 1974*
Hartly, Mary Mae *NF*
Hartman, Carl 1917- *OvPC, WhoWor 1974*
Hartman, Carl *see also* Hartman, Howard Carl
Hartman, Howard Carl 1917- *WhoAm 1974*
Hartman, Howard Carl *see also* Hartman, Carl
Hartman, Iris *NF*
Hartman, John Adams, Jr. 1911- *WhoAm 1974*
Hartman, John Clark 1861-1941 *DcNAA*
Hartman, L O 1876-1955 *WhJnl 1928*
Hartman, Lee Foster 1879-1941 *AmAu&B,
   BioIn 6, DcNAA, HisAmM XR,
   IndAu 1917, WhJnl 1928*
Hartman, M A *NF*
Hartman, Rachel 1920-1972 *BioIn 9, ConAu 5,
   ConAu 33, NewYTBE 3*
Hartmann, Karl Robert Eduard Von *HisAmM XR*
Hartmann, Moritz 1821-1872 *BiD&SB, CasWL,
   DcEuL, EvEuW, OxGer, WebBD*
Hartmann, William C 1869- *WhJnl 1928*
Hartnett, Robert Clinton 1904- *BioIn 2, BioIn 4,
   CurBio XR, WhoAm 1974*
Hartojo, Hari *NF*
Hartshorne, Henry 1823-1897 *Alli, Alli Sup,
   AmAu&B, BiD&SB, DcAmA, DcNAA,
   HisAmM XR*
Hartsock, Ernest 1903-1930 *AmAu&B*
Hartt, George Montgomery 1877-1954 *BioIn 3,
   WhNAA, WhJnl 1928*
Hartt, Rollin Lynde 1869-1946 *AmAu&B,
   BioIn 1, DcNAA, HisAmM XR*
Hartung, Barbara *NF*
Hartwell, Baron Michael Berry 1911-
   IntWW 1976, Who 1974, WhoWor 1974
Hartz, Jim 1940?- *AuNews 2, BioNews 1974*
Hartzell, Josiah 1833-1914 *DcNAA, OhA&B*
Hartzenbusch, Henry *OvPC*
Harvey, Alan 1919- *CanWW 1972*
Harvey, Alexander 1868-1949 *AmAu&B, AmLY,*

BioIn 2, DcNAA, HisAmM XR, WhNAA
Harvey, Charles Mitchell 1848- *BiDSA,
   HisAmM XR*
Harvey, Dorothy 1922- *NF*
Harvey, E B *HisAmM XR*
Harvey, Everett Burton 1892- *WhNAA,
   WhJnl 1928*
Harvey, George Brinton McClellan 1864-1928
   *AmAu&B, AmJnl, DcAmB 8, DcNAA,
   HisAmM XR, NatCAB 13, WebBD*
Harvey, George M *HisAmM XR*
Harvey, J H *NF*
Harvey, Jean-Charles 1891-1967 *CanWW 1972,
   CanWr, CasWL, OxCan*
Harvey, Lynwood N 1898- *WhJnl 1928*
Harvey, Paul 1918- *AmAu&B, AmJnl, BioIn 6,
   BioIn 8, BioNews 1974, CelR 1973,
   WhoAm 1974*
Harvey, Paul W 1888- *WhJnl 1928*
Harvey, R W *NF*
Harvey, Steve 1946- *NF*
Harvey, Tad *NF*
Harvey, Wells F 1879- *WhJnl 1928*
Harvey, William Hope 1851-1936 *BiDSA,
   BioIn 4, BioIn 9, DcAmA, DcNAA,
   HisAmM XR, OhA&B, OxAm, REnAL,
   WebBD, WhNAA*
Harvey-Lee, John *NF*
Harvier, Ernest *HisAmM XR*
Harway, Maxwell 1913- *OvPC, USBiR 1974,
   WhoGov 1972*
Harwood, Charles McHenry 1864-1954 *BioIn 3*
Harwood, Richard Lee 1925- *NewMr, RpN,
   WhoAm 1974*
Hasbrouck, Jacob Louis 1867- *WhJnl 1928*
Hasbrouck, John *HisAmM XR*
Hasegawa, Kazuaki *NF*
Hasegawa, Saiji 1904?-1978 *NF*
Haselden, Kyle Emerson 1913-1968 *BioIn 8,
   ConAu 5R*
Haselden, William Kerridge 1872-1953 *BioIn 3*
Haseltine, Nate 1911?-1970 *BioIn 9*
Haseltine, William Stanley *HisAmM XR*
Hasen, Irwin 1918- *NF*
Hasenack, James E 1883-1949 *BioIn 1, BioIn 2*
Haskell, Arnold Lionel 1903- *Au&Wr, ConAu 5,
   IntWW 1976, SmATA 6, Who 1974,
   WhoWor 1974*
Haskell, Burnette G *HisAmM XR*
Haskell, Henry Joseph 1874-1952 *AmJnl, BioIn 3,
   DcAmB S5, OhA&B*
Haskell, Mehitable *HisAmM XR*
Haskell, Molly *NF*
Haskell, William E 1862-1933 *NatCAB 27*
Haskell, William Edwin 1889-1953 *BioIn 3*
Haskin, Frederic Jennings 1872-1944 *AmLY,
   BioIn 1, CurBio XR, DcNAA, NatCAB 33,
   WebBD, WhNAA, WhJnl 1928*
Haslett, Arthur Woods 1906?-1969 *BioIn 8*
Hasluck, Sir Paul 1905- *CurBio XR, Who 1974*
Hass, Victor Paul 1909- *WhoAm 1974,
   WhoMW 1974*
Hassard, John Rose Greene 1836-1888 *Alli Sup,
   AmAu&B, AmJnl, BiD&SB, DcAmA,
   DcAmB 8, DcNAA, HisAmM XR,
   NatCAB 3, WebBD*
Hassaurek, Friedrich 1832?-1885 *Alli Sup,
   BiD&SB, BioIn 2, DcAmA, DcAmB 8,
   DcNAA, OhA&B*
Hassell, Sylvester 1842-1928 *BioIn 1*
Hasselquist, Tufve Nilsson 1816-1891 *BioIn 1*
Hassett, George B 1894- *WhJnl Sup*
Hastey, Stan L 1944- *NF*
Hastings, Beatrice *NF*

Hastings, Horace Lorenzo 1831-1899 *Alli Sup,*
DcAmA, DcNAA
Hastings, Hugh J 1856- *AmJnl*
Hastings, John Russel 1873-1942 *BioIn 2*
Hastings, Milo Milton 1884-1957 *BioIn 4*
Hastings, Thomas 1784-1872 *Alli, AmAu&B,*
DcNAA, HisAmM XR, OxAm, PoChrch,
REnAL
Hastrup, Aage 1919- *IntWW 1976*
Haswell, Anthony 1756-1816 *AmAu&B, AmJnl,*
DcNAA, HisAmM XR, NatCAB 8
Hatayi, John *NF*
Hatch, Alden 1898-1975 *AmAu&B, Au&Wr,*
AuBYP, ConAu 57, OvPC, WhoAm 1974
Hatch, F M 1859- *WhJnl Sup*
Hatch, George Clinton 1919- *WhoAm 1974,*
WhoF&I 1974, WhoWest 1974
Hatch, George W *HisAmM XR*
Hatch, Robert *NF*
Hatch, Ruth Streeter *ForWC 1970, OvPC*
Hatcher, Andrew Thomas 1923- *BioIn 5, BioIn 6,*
BioIn 9, WhoPubR 1972
Hatcher, Harry 1891?-1962 *BioIn 6*
Hatfield, Walter Wilbur 1882- *BioIn 4*
Hathaway, Baxter Levering 1909- *AmAu&B,*
ConAu 1, WhoAm 1974
Hathaway, Clarence *AmRP*
Hathaway, Hope *NF*
Hatlo, Jimmy 1898-1963 *BioIn 1, BioIn 2,*
BioIn 3, BioIn 6
Hatta, Mohammed 1902- *CurBio XR, ForP,*
IntWW 1974
Hatton, Frank 1846-1894 *AmJnl, DcAmB 8,*
NatCAB 4, WebBD
Hatton, Frederic 1879-1946 *AmAu&B, DcNAA*
Haugh, Irene 1906- *BioIn 3, CathA 1952*
Haught, Jim *NF*
Haughton, John Alan 1880-1951 *AmSCAP 1966,*
BioIn 2
Haugland, Vern *AmJnl*
Haugsten, Harry George 1890-1955 *BioIn 6,*
NatCAB 44
Haulenbeek, J H *HisAmM XR*
Haupt, Enid Annenberg 1906?- *BioIn 5,*
ForWC 1970, NewYTBE 1, WhoAmA 1973
Haupt, Howard C 1899?-1949 *BioIn 2*
Haureau, Jean Barthelemy 1812-1896 *WebBD*
Hause, Frank *AmJnl*
Hauser, Carl *HisAmM XR*
Hauser, Charles McCorkle 1929- *ConAu 69*
Hauser, Ernest O *HisAmM XR*
Hauser, Jacob *AmRP*
Havard, Alof H 1893- *WhJnl 1928*
Havas, Charles 1785-1858 *ForP, WebBD*
Havas, Emil 1892?-1957 *BioIn 4*
Havel, Hippolyte *AmRP*
Havell, George F *HisAmM XR*
Havemann, Ernest 1912- *BioIn 6, ConAu 4R,*
WhoE 1974
Haven, Alice Bradley Neal 1828-1863 *Alli,*
Alli Sup, AmAu, AmAu&B, CyAL 2,
DcAmA, DcNAA, HisAmM XR
Haven, Erastus Otis 1820-1881 *Alli, Alli Sup,*
CyAL 2, DcAmA, DcNAA, WebBD
Haven, Frank P 1913- *WhoAm 1974*
Haven, Gilbert 1821-1880 *Alli Sup, BiD&SB,*
DcAmA, DcNAA, WebBD
Havener, Helen *WhJnl 1928*
Havens, Shirley *NF*
Haviland, C Augustus 1832-1918 *DcNAA,*
HisAmM XR
Havlicek, Karel 1821-1856 *BiD&SB, BioIn 7,*
CasWL, EuAu, Pen Eur, WebBD
Havlicek, Karel *see also* Borovsky, Havel

Havrevold, Finn 1905- *IntWW 1976,*
WhoWor 1974
Havrilla, Alois 1891?-1952 *BioIn 3*
Hawari Ahmed, Mahmoud El- 1921- *IntWW 1976*
Hawes, Elizabeth 1903-1971 *BioIn 9, CurBio XR,*
NewYTBE 2
Hawk, Wilbur C 1881-1936 *WhJnl 1928*
Hawke, John T *NF*
Hawkes, Arthur 1871-1933 *DcNAA*
Hawkins, Desmond 1908- *ConAu 65, Who 1974*
Hawkins, Eric 1888-1969 *BioIn 1, BioIn 5,*
BioIn 6, BioIn 8, BioIn 9
Hawkins, Frank *NF*
Hawkins, Frank Nelson 1911- *WhoAm 1974*
Hawkins, Harry L 1895?-1955 *BioIn 3*
Hawkins, Jim 1944- *ConAu 73*
Hawkins, Joseph *HisAmM XR*
Hawkins, Lola A 1894- *WhJnl Sup*
Hawkins, Mary *BioIn 2*
Hawkins, Robert F *NF*
Hawkins, Thomas E *AmJnl*
Hawkins, William E 1887- *WhJnl 1928*
Hawkins, William Waller 1883-1953 *AmJnl,*
BioIn 3, BioIn 6, WhJnl 1928
Hawkins, William Waller 1912- *ConAu 4R*
Hawks, Francis Lister 1798-1866 *Alli, Alli Sup,*
AmAu, AmAu&B, BiD&SB, BiDSA,
CarSB, CyAL 2, DcAmA, DcNAA,
HisAmM XR, WebBD
Hawks, Wayne d1968 *BioIn 5, BioIn 8*
Hawley, James B 1885- *WhJnl 1928*
Hawley, Joseph Roswell 1826-1905 *AmJnl,*
BioIn 7, WebBD
Hawley, Ralph Waldo 1888-1949 *BioIn 8,*
NatCAB 50
Haworth, Peter 1889?-1948 *BioIn 1*
Hawthorne, Frank W 1852-1911 *NatCAB 6*
Hawthorne, Fred 1880-1952 *BioIn 3, WhJnl 1928*
Hawthorne, Hildegarde 1871-1952 *AmAu&B,*
AuBYP, DcAmA, HisAmM XR, JBA 1934,
JBA 1951, REnAL, WhNAA
Hawthorne, Julian 1846-1934 *Alli Sup,*
AmAu&B, AmJnl, BbD, BiD&SB, CarSB,
DcAmA, DcBiA, DcEnA, DcEnA Ap,
DcEnL, DcNAA, EncMys, HisAmM XR,
NatCAB 25, OxAm, REnAL, TwCA,
WebBD, WhNAA
Hay, Edward N 1891-1958 *NatCAB 47*
Hay, Lady Grace Marguerite Drummond
1896?-1946 *BioIn 1*
Hay, James, Jr. 1881-1936 *AmAu&B, DcNAA,*
NatCAB 28, WhNAA, WhJnl 1928
Hay, John 1915- *AmAu&B, ConAu 65,*
WhoAm 1974
Hay, John Milton 1838-1905 *Alli Sup, AmAu,*
AmAu&B, AmJnl, BbD, BiD&SB, CasWL,
DcAmA, DcAmB 8, DcBiA, DcNAA, EvLB,
HisAmM XR, IndAu 1816, LiJA, OhA&B,
OxAm, Pen Am, REn, REnAL, WebBD
Hayden, Charles Sidney 1880-1937 *NF*
Hayden, Gloria Hope *NF*
Hayden, Jay G 1884-1971 *AmJnl, BioIn 9,*
BioIn 10, NewYTBE 2, WhNAA
Hayden, John A 1884- *WhJnl 1928*
Hayden, Martin Scholl 1912- *ConAu 69,*
WhoAm 1974
Hayden, Scott 1917- *WhoE 1974*
Hayden, Victor F 1885- *WhJnl 1928*
Haydn, Hiram Collins 1907-1973 *AmAu&B,*
AmNov, Au&Wr, BioIn 1, BioIn 2,
BioIn 4, BioIn 6, BioIn 10, CnDAL,
ConAu P-1, ConNov 1972, OhA&B, OxAm,
REnAL, TwCA Sup
Haydon, John Morse, Jr. 1920- *BioIn 4,*

Hearst, George Randolph, Jr. 1927- *WhoAm 1974,
WhoWest 1974, WhoWor 1974*
Hearst, George Randolph, Sr. 1904-1972 *BioIn 2,
BioIn 5, BioIn 7, BioIn 9, NewYTBE 3*
Hearst, John Randolph 1909-1958 *BioIn 5*
Hearst, Joseph Francis 1901- *WhoAm 1974,
WhoS&SW 1973*
Hearst, Phoebe Millicent 1928?- *BioIn 1*
Hearst, Randolph Apperson 1915- *BioIn 2,
BioIn 10, IntWW 1976, NewYTBS 5,
WhoAm 1974*
Hearst, William Randolph 1863-1951 *AmAu&B,
AmJnl, BioIn 1, BioIn 2, BioIn 3, BioIn 4,
BioIn 5, BioIn 6, BioIn 7, BioIn 8, BioIn 9,
BioIn 10, DcAmB S5, EncAB, FamWC,
ForP, HisAmM XR, LongC, NatCAB 39,
OxAm, REn, REnAL, WebBD, WhJnl 1928*
Hearst, William Randolph, III *NF*
Hearst, William Randolph, Jr. 1908- *AmAu&B,
AmJnl, BioIn 2, BioIn 3, BioIn 4, BioIn 5,
CelR 1973, CurBio XR, IntWW 1976,
OvPC, Who 1974, WhoAm 1974*
Heartman, Charles F *NF*
Heath, Andrew *NF*
Heath, Daisy Winifred 1875-1954 *BioIn 3*
Heath, E Addie *HisAmM XR*
Heath, Frank H 1881- *WhJnl Sup*
Heath, Fred *AmRP*
Heath, Frederic Faries 1854-1954 *BioIn 5*
Heath, James F *NF*
Heath, Perry Sanford 1857-1927 *BioIn 2,
DcAmA, DcAmB 8, IndAu 1816, WebBD,
WhNAA*
Heath, S Burton 1898-1949 *BioIn 2, CurBio XR,
DcNAA*
Heath, Susan 1944- *NF*
Heath, William H *NF*
Heath, William Herman 1892- *WhNAA,
WhJnl 1928*
Heatherton, Harold A *WhJnl 1928*
Heatley, Leo T 1896- *WhJnl 1928*
Heaton, John Langdon 1860-1935 *AmAu&B,
AmLY, BiD&SB, DcAmA, DcAmB S1,
DcNAA, NatCAB 11, WhNAA,
WhJnl 1928*
Heatter, Gabriel 1890-1972 *BioIn 1, BioIn 5,
BioIn 6, BioIn 7, BioIn 9, CurBio XR,
NewYTBE 3*
Heavey, James J *NF*
Hebert, Felix Edward 1901- *BioIn 2, BioIn 5,
BioIn 9, CngDr 1974, CurBio XR,
NewYTBE 3, WhoAm 1974, WhoAmP 1973,
WhoGov 1972, WhoS&SW 1973*
Hebert, George J 1920- *NF*
Hebert, Jacques Rene 1755-1794 *OxFr, WebBD*
Hechinger, Fred Michael 1920- *AmAu&B,
WhoAm 1974, WhoE 1974, WhoWorJ 1972,
WrDr 1976*
Hecht, Ben 1894-1964 *AmAu&B, CnDAL,
CnMD, CnThe, ConAmA, ConAmL,
CurBio XR, DcLEL, EncMys, HisAmM XR,
LongC, McGWD, ModWD, OxAm,
Pen Am, REn, REnAL, TwCA, TwCA Sup,
WebBD*
Hecht, George Joseph 1895- *CurBio XR, OvPC,
WhNAA, WhoAm 1974, WhJnl 1928,
WhoWorJ 1972*
Heckel, Frederick C 1906?-1971 *BioIn 9,
BioIn 10*
Hecker, Isaac Thomas 1819-1888 *Alli Sup,
AmAu&B, BiD&SB, DcAmA, DcNAA,
HisAmM XR, OxAm, WebBD*
Heckman, Hugh M *OvPC*
Heckscher, August 1913- *AmAu&B, Au&Wr,*

*BiE&WWA, BioIn 5, BioIn 6, BioIn 7,
ConAu 3R, CurBio XR, IntWW 1976,
WhoAm 1974, WhoE 1974, WhoGov 1972*
Hedde, Fritz 1818-1908 *BioIn 2*
Hederman, Thomas Martin 1878-1948 *BioIn 2,
NatCAB 36*
Hederman, Thomas Martin, Jr. 1911-
WhoAm 1974, WhoS&SW 1973
Hedge, Egbert *HisAmM XR*
Hedge, Frederic Henry 1805-1890 *Alli, Alli Sup,
AmAu, AmAu&B, BbD, BiD&SB, CyAL 2,
DcAmA, DcNAA, EarABI, HisAmM XR,
LiJA, OxAm, REnAL, WebBD*
Hedges, Frank Hinckley 1895-1940 *WhNAA*
Hedley, James Alexander 1844-1916 *DcNAA*
Hedrick, Travis K 1904?-1977 *ConAu 69*
Heeren, Henry R 1908?-1963 *BioIn 6*
Heermans, Forbes 1856-1928 *AmAu&B, DcAmA,
DcNAA*
Heffernan, George P 1893?-1953 *BioIn 3*
Heffernan, Harold d1971 *NF*
Heffernan, John A 1871-1952 *BioIn 2*
Heffernan, John *ForP*
Heffernan, John William 1910- *BioIn 4, OvPC,
WhoAm 1974, WhoS&SW 1973*
Heffernan, William F 1897- *WhJnl 1928*
Heffernan, William J 1870- *WhJnl 1928*
Hefner, Hugh Marston 1926- *IntWW 1976,
WhoAm 1974, WhoF&I 1974,
WhoMW 1974, WhoWor 1974*
Heftman, Josef Haim 1888-1955 *BioIn 3*
Heg, Even Hansen 1790-1850 *BioIn 5*
Hegeler, Edward Carl *HisAmM XR*
Heiden, Konrad 1901-1966 *CurBio XR*
Heidi, Gloria *NF*
Heijermans, Herman 1864-1924 *CasWL,
CIDMEL, CnMD, CnThe, EncWL, EuAu,
McGWD, ModWD, Pen Eur, REnWD,
WebBD*
Heikal, Muhammed Hassanein 1923- *BioIn 8,
BioIn 9, BioIn 10, IntWW 1976,
NewYTBE 2, WhoWor 1974*
Heil, Jane *NF*
Heilbron, Tillie Thompson *NF*
Heilman, Joan Rattner *ConAu 57*
Heilprin, Angelo 1853-1907 *Alli Sup, AmAu,
AmAu&B, DcAmA, DcNAA, REnAL,
WebBD*
Heilprin, Michael 1823-1888 *Alli Sup, AmAu&B,
DcAmA, DcNAA, HisAmM XR, WebBD*
Heim, Allan R 1929- *WhoAm 1974*
Heimbuecher, Ruth *NF*
Heimdahl, Ralph 1909- *ConAu 69*
Heimer, Melvin Lytton 1915-1971 *BioIn 3,
ConAu 2R, ConAu 29*
Heimlich, Herbert H 1897- *WhJnl 1928*
Heine, Heinrich 1797-1856 *AtlBL, BbD,
BiD&SB, CasWL, CyWA, DcEuL, EuAu,
EvEuW, NewC, OxEng, OxFr, OxGer,
Pen Eur, RComWL, REn, WebBD*
Heine, Thomas Theodor 1867-1948 *BioIn 1*
Heinecke, Burnell *RpN*
Heineman, Henry E O 1864?-1948 *BioIn 1*
Heineman, James H *OvPC*
Heinemann, Arthur 1910- *NF*
Heinemann, George Alfred 1918- *WhoAm 1974*
Heinl, Robert D 1880-1950 *BioIn 2*
Heinl, Robert Debs, Jr. 1916- *ConAu 7R,
WhoAm 1974, WhoS&SW 1973,
WhoWor 1974*
Heins, Ethel L 1918- *BiDrLUS*
Heinssart, Paul 1923- *ConAu 29*
Heintzen, Harry *OvPC*
Heinz, W C 1915- *ConAu 5, WrDr 1976*

Heinzen, Karl Peter 1809-1880 *BioIn 2, DcAmB 8*
Heinzerling, Larry E 1945- *ConAu 73*
Heinzerling, Lynn 1906- *NF*
Heirta, Lars Johan *ForP*
Heise, Kenan 1933- *ConAu 57*
Heisey, Alan Milliken 1928- *ConAu 57*
Heishiro, Yorozuya *ForP*
Heiskell, Andrew 1915- *AmAu&B, CurBio XR, IntWW 1976, Who 1974, WhoAm 1974, WhoE 1974, WhoF&I 1974, WhoWor 1974*
Heiskell, John Netherland 1872-1972 *BioIn 1, BioIn 3, BioIn 4, BioIn 9, BioIn 10, NewYTBE 2, NewYTBE 3, WhoS&SW 1973*
Heisler, Philip Samuel 1915- *IntWW 1976, WhoAm 1974, WhoE 1974*
Heiss, John P *AmJnl*
Heissenbuttel, Helmut 1921- *CasWL, IntWW 1976, ModGL, OxGer, Pen Eur, WhoWor 1974*
Hektoen, Ludvig 1863-1951 *BioIn 1, BioIn 2, BioIn 3, CurBio XR, WebBD*
Held, Adolph 1884?-1969 *BioIn 8*
Held, John, Jr. 1889-1958 *AmAu&B, BioIn 4, BioIn 5, BioIn 6, BioIn 7, BioIn 8, BioIn 9, HisAmM XR, OxAm, REnAL, WebBD*
Heldman, Gladys *BioIn 7*
Heldt, Henning 1910?-1950 *BioIn 2, RpN*
Helgesen, Ray *BioIn 1*
Helitzer, Morris *OvPC*
Helle, Ray *NF*
Heller, Ann Williams *NF*
Heller, Deane 1924- *ConAu 9*
Heller, Jean 1942- *ConAu 73, InvJ, NewMr*
Heller, John H *WhJnl 1928*
Heller, Karen Sue *NF*
Heller, Max *NF*
Heller, Otto 1863-1941 *AmLY, DcNAA, WhNAA*
Heller, Richard H 1924- *AmAu&B, WhoAm 1974, WhoF&I 1974*
Hellinger, Mark 1903-1947 *AmAu&B, BioIn 1, BioIn 3, CurBio XR, DcNAA, REnAL*
Helliwell, Arthur *BioIn 2*
Hellman, Geoffrey Theodore 1907-1977 *AmAu&B, ConAu 69, ConAu 73, REnAL, WhoAm 1974*
Hellman, Jack 1894?-197? *NF*
Hellman, Peter *NF*
Hellyer, Paul Theodore 1923- *CanWW 1972, ConAu 69, CurBio XR, IntWW 1976, OxCan Sup, Who 1974, WhoAm 1974, WhoCan 1973, WhoMW 1974, WhoWor 1974, WrDr 1976*
Helm, William Pickett 1883-1958 *BioIn 5, WhNAA*
Helmbold, Henry K *HisAmM XR*
Helmer, Melvin Leighton 1915-1971 *BioIn 9*
Helmer, William Joseph 1936- *ConAu 73*
Helms, Jesse Alexander, Jr. 1921- *BioIn 9, BioIn 10, IntWW 1976, WhoAm 1974*
Helms, Richard McGarrah 1913- *CurBio XR, IntWW 1976, NewMr, NewYTBE 2, NewYTBE 4, USBiR 1974, WhoAm 1974, WhoS&SW 1973, WhoWor 1974*
Helmuth, Norman C 1888- *WhJnl 1928*
Heloise 1919-1977 *ConAu XR*
Heloise see also Bowles, Heloise
Heloise see also Cruse, Heloise Bowles
Helou, Charles 1911- *IntWW 1976*
Helsing, Patricia *NF*
Heltai, Andras 1931- *NF*
Hemens, Rollin DeWitt 1895-1968 *BioIn 7, BioIn 8*

Hemingway, Ernest Miller 1899-1961 *AmAu&B, AmAu&B, AmNov, AmWr, ArizL, AuNews 2, BioIn 1, BioIn 2, BioIn 3, BioIn 4, BioIn 5, BioIn 6, BioIn 7, BioIn 8, BioIn 9, BioIn 10, CasWL, CnDAL, CnMD, CnMWL, ConAmA, ConAmL, ConLC 1, ConLC 3, ConLC 6, CyWA, DcLEL, EncAB, EncWL, EvLB, ForP, HisAmM XR, LongC, ModAL, ModAL Sup, ModWD, OxAm, OxEng, Pen Am, RAdv 1, RComWL, REn, REnAL, TwCA, TwCA Sup, TwCW, WebBD, WebE&AL, WhoTwCL*
Hemingway, Leicester 1915?- *BioIn 3*
Hemingway, Mary Welsh 1908- *BioIn 7, BioIn 8, BioIn 9, BioIn 10, ConAu 73, CurBio XR, ForWC 1970, OvPC, WhoAmW 1974*
Hemment, J C *AmJnl, HisAmM XR*
Hemming, Frederick d1897 *NF*
Hemming, Roy 1928- *ConAu 61, OvPC, WhoE 1974*
Hemphill, James Calvin 1850-1927 *BiDSA, DcNAA, NatCAB 2*
Hemphill, Paul James 1936?- *AuNews 2, ConAu 49, WrDr 1976*
Hemphill, Vivia 1889-1934 *DcNAA*
Hemphill, William Arnold 1842-1902 *AmJnl*
Hempstone, Smith, Jr. 1929- *ConAu 3R, RpN, WhoAm 1974*
Hemstreet, Charles 1866- *AmAu&B, DcAmA, DcNAA, HisAmM XR*
Henault, Claude *NF*
Henault, Gilles 1920- *CanWr, OxCan, OxCan Sup*
Hence, Raymond *NF*
Hendee, Harold Cory 1887?-1952 *BioIn 2*
Hendee, Harold F 1878?-1966 *BioIn 7*
Henderickx, Herman V *NF*
Henderson, Alice Corbin 1881-1949 *AmAu&B, BioIn 2, BioIn 8, CnDAL, ConAmL, DcNAA, HisAmM XR, OxAm, REn, REnAL, WebBD*
Henderson, Daniel MacIntyre 1880-1955 *AmAu&B, AnMV 1926, BioIn 4, REnAL, WhNAA*
Henderson, Dion 1921- *BioIn 3, ConAu 9R*
Henderson, Donald *AmRP*
Henderson, Ernest McKay 1881?- *WhNAA, WhJnl 1928*
Henderson, George C 1891- *IndAu 1917, WhJnl 1928*
Henderson, Helen Weston 1874- *AmAu&B, AmLY, WhNAA*
Henderson, Sir Hubert Douglas 1890-1952 *BioIn 2, BioIn 3*
Henderson, Isaac 1850-1909 *Alli Sup, AmAu&B, BiD&SB, DcAmA, DcNAA*
Henderson, James 1883?-1949 *BioIn 2*
Henderson, James Samuel *PoIre*
Henderson, Jim R 1942?- *NF*
Henderson, Joseph Franklin 1852-1916 *HisAmM XR, HsB&A, OhA&B*
Henderson, Josephine *HisAmM XR*
Henderson, Lucie A 1872?-1953 *BioIn 3*
Henderson, Ralph Ernest 1899- *WhoAm 1974, WhJnl 1928*
Henderson, Samuel *HisAmM XR*
Henderson, W Carlton 1903- *WhJnl 1928*
Henderson, William Graham 1879-1956 *BioIn 4*
Henderson, William James 1855-1937 *AmAu&B, AmLY, BiD&SB, DcAmA, DcAmB S2, DcNAA, HisAmM XR, REnAL, TwCA, WebBD, WhNAA*
Henderson, Wilson H d1951 *BioIn 2*

Hendren, Ron 1945- *NF*
Hendrick, Burton Jesse 1870-1949 *AmAu&B,
DcAmB S4, DcLEL, HisAmM XR, LiJA,
OxAm, REnAL, TwCA, TwCA Sup,
WebBD, WhNAA*
Hendricks, J E *HisAmM XR*
Hendrickson, Dyke 1945- *NF*
Hendrix, Haile 1897?-1953 *BioIn 3*
Hendrix, Hal *NF*
Hendy, Sir Philip 1900- *IntWW 1976, Who 1974,
WhoAm 1974, WhoWor 1974*
Henehan, Mark J *OvPC*
Heney, Thomas William 1862-1928 *BioIn 2*
Hengen, William Lincoln 1914- *WhoAm 1974*
Henke, Mabel Grace 1898- *WhJnl 1928*
Henkei, Eloise *OvPC*
Henkle, Henrietta *see* Buckmaster, Henrietta
Henkle, Rae DeLancey 1883-1935 *WhNAA*
Henle, Faye d1972 *BioIn 9, ConAu 37,
NewYTBE 3*
Henle, Fritz 1909- *ConAu 73, OvPC*
Henle, Guy 1920- *WhoAm 1974, WhoE 1974*
Henley, Elizabeth C 1913?-1972 *BioIn 9*
Henley, William Ernest 1849-1903 *Alli Sup,
AtlBL, BiD&SB, BrAu 19, CasWL,
CnE&AP, DcEnA, DcEnA Ap, DcEuL,
DcLEL, EvLB, HisAmM XR, LongC,
MouLC 4, NewC, OxEng, Pen Eng, REn,
WebBD, WebE&AL*
Hennacy, Ammon 1893-1970 *AmRP, BioIn 8*
Henneman, John Bell 1864-1908 *AmAu&B,
BiDSA, DcNAA, HisAmM XR*
Hennessey, Roland Burke 1870- *HisAmM XR*
Hennessy, Duane *NF*
Hennessy, Helen *LiJA*
Hennessy, John A 1859-1951 *BioIn 2*
Hennessy, Jossleyn 1903- *Au&Wr, ConAu 9R,
WrDr 1976*
Hennessy, Michael Edmund 1866-1955 *BioIn 3*
Hennessy, Mike *NF*
Hennessy, Thomas A *NF*
Hennessy, William H, Jr. 1888- *WhJnl 1928*
Henney, Fred K 1880- *WhJnl 1928*
Hennigan, William S 1890- *WhJnl 1928*
Hennigner, Paul *NF*
Henning, Albert Frederick 1877- *WhJnl 1928*
Henning, Arthur Sears 1876-1966 *BioIn 1,
BioIn 7*
Henning, Robert A *NF*
Henninger, George Ross 1898- *BioIn 1*
Hennings, Joseph Paul 1882- *WhJnl 1928*
Hennings, Josephine Silva *ForWC 1970, OvPC,
WhoAmW 1974, WhoE 1974*
Henrichs, H F 1876- *WhJnl 1928*
Henrici, Max 1884- *WhNAA, WhJnl 1928*
Henrikson, Arthur A 1921- *NF*
Henriot, Emile 1889-1961 *EvEuW, WebBD*
Henry, Albert *HisAmM XR*
Henry, Alice 1857-1943 *DcAmB S3*
Henry, Arthur 1867-1934 *AmAu&B, DcAmA,
DcNAA*
Henry, Bill 1890-1970 *AmJnl, NewYTBE 1*
Henry, Bill *see also* Henry, William Mellors
Henry, Caleb Sprague 1804-1884 *Alli, Alli Sup,
AmAu&B, BiD&SB, CyAL 2, DcAmA,
DcNAA, HisAmM XR, REnAL*
Henry, Carl Ferdinand Howard 1913- *BioIn 8,
ConAu 13, DrAS 74P, WhoAm 1974,
WhoWor 1974*
Henry, Diane *NF*
Henry, Frank *NF*
Henry, H Taylor *AmJnl*
Henry, Harold Augustus 1895-1966 *BioIn 9*
Henry, John Case 1905- *WhoAm 1974,*

WhoS&SW 1973
Henry, Lyman H 1858- *WhJnl 1928*
Henry, O 1862-1910 *AmAu&B, AtlBL, BiDSA,
CasWL, CnDAL, CyWA, DcLEL, DcNAA,
EncMys, EncWL, EvLB, LongC, ModAL,
OxAm, OxEng, Pen Am, RAdv 1, REn,
REnAL, TwCA, TwCA Sup, TwCW,
WebBD, WebE&AL, WhoTwCL*
Henry, O *see also* Porter, William Sydney
Henry, Omer 1903- *NF*
Henry, R Norris *HisAmM XR*
Henry, Ralph L 1895- *WhNAA, WhJnl 1928*
Henry, Stokes T 1881-1957 *BioIn 4*
Henry, Thomas R *NF*
Henry, William F 1863- *WhJnl 1928*
Henry, William Mellors 1890-1970 *BioIn 4,
BioIn 7, BioIn 8, BioIn 9*
Henry, William Mellors *see also* Henry, Bill
Hensel, George Washington, Jr. 1866- *WhNAA,
WhJnl 1928*
Hensell, Hester E *ForWC 1970, OvPC*
Henshaw, Henry Wetherbee 1850-1930 *DcNAA,
HisAmM XR*
Henshaw, Julia W 1869-1937 *DcNAA, OxCan,
WhNAA*
Hensley, Stewart 1914?-1976 *ConAu 65*
Hensley, Travis Franklin 1851-1944 *BioIn 7*
Henson, Elvin G *NF*
Hentoff, Nathan Irving 1925- *AmAu&B, BioIn 7,
BioIn 8, BioIn 9, BioIn 10, ConAu 2R,
WhoAm 1974, WhoE 1974, WhoWor 1974*
Hepler, Charles D *NF*
Hepner, Arthur Wallace 1914- *RpN, WhoE 1974*
Heppe, Ralph Harold 1893- *WhJnl 1928*
Hepple, Peter 1927- *NF*
Hepworth, George Hughes 1833-1902 *Alli Sup,
AmAu&B, BbD, BiD&SB, CyAL 2,
DcAmA, DcNAA, NatCAB 4, WebBD*
Herald, George William 1911- *ConAu 73, OvPC*
Heraud, Pierre 1879-1953 *BioIn 3*
Herberg, Will 1909-1977 *AmAu&B, AmRP,
ConAu 69, DrAS 74P, WhoAm 1974*
Herbers, John N, Jr. 1923- *ConAu 33, RpN*
Herbert, Sir Alan Patrick 1890-1971 *Au&Wr,
ConAu 33, ConNov 1972, DcLEL, EvLB,
LongC, ModBL, NewC, Pen Eng, REn,
TwCA, TwCA Sup, TwCW, WebBD,
WhoThe 1972*
Herbert, Anthony *NewMr*
Herbert, B B *AmJnl, HisAmM XR*
Herbert, Bill *NF*
Herbert, Elizabeth Sweeney 1899- *CurBio XR*
Herbert, Ewing 1865?-1947 *BioIn 1*
Herbert, F Edward 1901- *WhoAm 1974*
Herbert, Gordon 1903- *WhJnl 1928*
Herbert, Harold Harvey 1888- *WhJnl Sup*
Herbert, Henry William 1807-1858 *Alli, Alli Sup,
AmAu, AmAu&B, BbD, BbtC, BiD&SB,
Br&AmS, CyAL 2, DcAmA, DcEnL,
DcLEL, DcNAA, EarABI, EarABI Sup,
HisAmM XR, HsB&A, NewC, OxAm,
REnAL*
Herbert, James C 1875- *WhJnl 1928*
Herbert, John Ruggles 1908- *OvPC,
WhoAm 1974, WhoWor 1974*
Herbert, Mary E *BbtC, DcNAA, OxCan, PoIre*
Herbert, Robert Black 1886-1954 *BioIn 3,
WhJnl 1928*
Herbert, Sarah 1824-1844 *BbtC, DcNAA,
OxCan, PoIre*
Herbert, St. Leger d1885 *FamWC*
Herblock 1909- *WhoS&SW 1973*
Herblock *see also* Block, Herbert Lawrence
Herda, D J *NF*

Herder, Ralph Barnes 1894-1955 *BioIn 3*
Herdman, Oscar *NF*
Hereford, Robert A 1902- *AuBYP, BioIn 8*
Hereford, William Richard 1871-1928 *BiDSA, DcNAA*
Heren, Louis Philip 1919- *ConAu 25, Who 1974, WhoWor 1974*
Herget, H M *HisAmM XR*
Herget, J Barlow 1942?- *NF*
Herguth, Alfons 1911- *WhoMW 1974*
Herguth, Robert J *WhoMW 1974*
Hering, Doris *BiE&WWA*
Herling, John 1907- *WhoAm 1974*
Herman, A *NF*
Herman, George Edward 1920- *ConAu 69, OvPC, WhoAm 1974, WhoWor 1974, WhoWorJ 1972*
Herman, Hal *NF*
Herman, Kenneth Neil 1954- *NF*
Herman, Leon Emerson 1887-1956 *BioIn 4*
Herman, Theodore F 1872-1948 *HisAmM XR*
Herman, W F *NF*
Hermann, George *BioIn 8*
Hermann, Karl Stephen *HisAmM XR*
Hermida, Jesus *NF*
Hern, Anthony 1916- *Au&Wr, ConAu 23R*
Hern, George Louis, Jr. 1924- *OvPC, WhoE 1974, WhoF&I 1974, WhoPubR 1972*
Herndon, Allan Charles 1890- *WhJnl 1928*
Herndon, Angelo *AmRP*
Herndon, Booten *NF*
Herndon, E Julian 1893- *WhJnl 1928*
Herndon, E W *HisAmM XR*
Herndorn, Mrs. J D *WhJnl 1928*
Hernelius, Allan 1911- *ForP, IntWW 1976, WhoWor 1974*
Hernstadt, William H 1935- *WhoAm 1974*
Herold, Don 1889-1966 *AmAu&B, BioIn 7, HisAmM XR, IndAu 1917, REnAL, WhJnl 1928*
Heron, Laurence Tunstall 1902- *ConAu 49*
Herr, Al *NF*
Herr, Michael *NF*
Herrera, Luis Alberto De d1959 *ForP*
Herrera, Philip *NF*
Herrick, Anson 1812-1868 *HisAmM XR*
Herrick, Clarence Luther 1858-1904 *Alli Sup, DcAmA, DcNAA, HisAmM XR*
Herrick, Elinore Morehouse 1895-1964 *CurBio XR*
Herrick, Jean Comstock 1902- *WhJnl 1928*
Herrick, John P 1868-1961 *NatCAB 50*
Herrick, Sophia McIlvaine Bledsoe 1837-1919 *Alli Sup, AmAu&B, BiD&SB, BiDSA, DcAmA, DcNAA, HisAmM XR, OhA&B*
Herriman, George Joseph 1880-1944 *DcAmB S3, REnAL*
Herrings, Joseph *NF*
Herrington, James L 1928- *ConAu 73*
Herrmann, Lazar 1896-1961 *AmAu&B, BioIn 6*
Herron, Ashel H *NF*
Herron, Frederick William 1906?-1967 *BioIn 8*
Herron, Lerroy W 1878- *WhJnl 1928*
Hersam, John Edward 1872-1949 *BioIn 1, BioIn 4, NatCAB 39*
Hersant, Robert *ForP*
Herschell, William 1873-1939 *BioIn 2, DcNAA, IndAu 1816*
Herschensohn, H L *NF*
Hersey, Harold Brainerd 1893-1956 *AmAu&B, AnMV 1926, BioIn 4, BioIn 6, NatCAB 45, REnAL, WhNAA*
Hersey, Heloise Edwina 1855-1933 *DcAmA, DcNAA, HisAmM XR*
Hersey, John Richard 1914- *AmAu&B, AmNov,*

BioIn 1, BioIn 2, BioIn 4, BioIn 5, BioIn 7, BioIn 8, BioIn 9, BioIn 10, CasWL, CelR 1973, CnDAL, ConAu 17R, ConLC 1, ConLC 2, ConNov 1972, ConNov 1976, CurBio XR, CyWA, DrAF 1976, DrAS 74E, HisAmM XR, IntWW 1976, LongC, ModAL, OxAm, Pen Am, RAdv 1, REn, REnAL, TwCA Sup, WebBD, Who 1974, WhoAm 1974, WhoE 1974, WhoWor 1974, WrDr 1976
Hersey, Mrs. Merle Williams *HisAmM XR*
Hersh, Seymour M 1937- *AmAu&B, AuNews 1, BioIn 8, BioIn 9, BioIn 10, ConAu 73, InvJ, NewMr, WhoAm 1974, WhoS&SW 1973*
Hershey, Burnet 1896-1971 *AmAu&B, BiE&WWA, BioIn 8, BioIn 9, BioIn 10, ConAu 25, ConAu 33, NewYTBE 2*
Hershey, Julie *NF*
Hershey, Lenore 1920- *WhoAm 1974*
Hershfield, Harry 1885-1974 *ConAu 53, NewYTBS 5*
Hershman, Arlene 1934- *WhoAm 1974*
Hershman, Oliver S 1859-1930 *NatCAB 21*
Herter, Christian Archibald 1895-1966 *CurBio XR, HisAmM XR, WebBD, WhAm 1928*
Hertle, Daniel 1824-185-? *BioIn 2*
Herts, Benjamin Russell 1888-1954 *AmAu&B, AmLY, HisAmM XR*
Herty, Charles Holmes 1867-1938 *AmJnl, DcNAA*
Hertzberg, Sidney *AmRP*
Hertzka, Theodor 1845-1924 *NF*
Herve, Aime Marie Edouard 1835-1899 *WebBD*
Herve, Gustave 1871-1944 *WebBD*
Hervey, Thomas Kibble 1799-1859 *Alli, DcEnL, NewC, WebBD*
Herzberg, Joseph Gabriel 1907-1976 *BioIn 1, ConAu 65, WhoAm 1974*
Herzberg, Max John 1886-1958 *AmAu&B, REnAL, WhNAA*
Herzberg, Oscar *HisAmM XR*
Herzl, Theodor 1860-1904 *EuAu, OxGer, WebBD*
Herzog, A W *HisAmM XR*
Heslop, J M 1923- *ConAu 37*
Hess, David *NF*
Hess, Elaine *OvPC*
Hess, Elmer 1889-1961 *CurBio XR*
Hess, Erwin *NF*
Hess, John *InvJ*
Hess, Karl, III 1923- *BioIn 7, BioIn 8, BioIn 9, NewYTBE 1*
Hess, Katie *NF*
Hess, Moses 1812-1875 *WebBD*
Hess, Sol *NF*
Hess, Thomas Baer 1920-1978 *AmAu&B, WhoAm 1974, WhoAmA 1973*
Hesse, Andreas *ForP*
Hesse, Don 1918- *WhoAm 1974, WhoAmA 1973*
Hesse, Georgia *WhoAmW 1974*
Hessey, J J Evans 1892-1956 *BioIn 4*
Hessian, Will F *WhJnl 1928*
Hessler, William Henry 1904-1965 *BioIn 7, BioIn 8, IndAu 1917, OhA&B*
Hester, William 1835-1921 *NatCAB 19*
Hester, William V 1900- *WhJnl 1928*
Hetherington, H P *NF*
Hetherington, Hector Alastair 1919- *BioIn 4, BioIn 9, ForP, IntWW 1976, Who 1974*
Hetherington, John Aikman 1907-1974 *Au&Wr, BioIn 9, ConAu 53, WhoWor 1974*
Hetherington, William Gregory 1912- *OvPC, WhoAm 1974, WhoE 1974, WhoPubR 1972*
Hettich, Arthur *NF*

Heuven Goedhart, Gerrit Jan Van 1901-1956
  BioIn 2, BioIn 3, BioIn 4, CurBio XR
Hevesi, Ludwig 1843-1910 *BiD&SB, WebBD*
Hewes, Henry 1917- *AmAu&B, BiE&WWA,*
  ConAu 13R, WhoAm 1974, WhoThe 1972,
  WhoWor 1974
Hewett, Robert *NF*
Hewit, Nathaniel Augustus 1820-1897 *Alli Sup,*
  DcAmA, DcNAA, HisAmM XR
Hewitt, Don S 1922- *WhoAm 1974, WhoE 1974*
Hewitt, Earl Smith 1892?-1959 *BioIn 5*
Hewitt, Emma Churchman 1850- *BiDSA,*
  DcAmA, HisAmM XR
Hewitt, F Vernon *NF*
Hewitt, Foster 1903- *BioIn 8*
Hewitt, John Hill 1801-1890 *AmAu, AmAu&B,*
  BiD&SB, DcAmA, DcAmB 8, DcNAA,
  HisAmM XR, LiJA, REnAL, WebBD
Hewlett, Frank West 1910- *RpN, WhoAm 1974*
Hewlett, Gregory 1907- *WhoAm 1974*
Hewlett, John Henry 1905- *BioIn 2*
Hewlett, Roger S 1911?-1977 *ConAu 73*
Hexamer, F M *HisAmM XR*
Hexter, Irving B 1897-1960 *NatCAB 47*
Hey, Robert P *NF*
Heydt, Louis Jean 1905-1960 *NF*
Heykal, Muhammed Hassanein *ForP*
Heyliger, William 1884-1955 *AmAu&B, AuBYP,*
  BioIn 3, BioIn 7, CathA 1930,
  HisAmM XR, JBA 1934, JBA 1951,
  REnAL, YABC 1
Heyman, Ken 1930- *BioIn 8, WhoAm 1974,*
  WhoE 1974
Heyman, Ruth *OvPC*
Heyman, Thomas M *OvPC*
Heyn, Edward Theodore 1867?-1950 *BioIn 2*
Heyn, Ernest V 1904- *OvPC, WhoAm 1974*
Heyward, Evelyn J *OvPC*
Heywood, Ezra H 1829-1893 *HisAmM XR*
Heywood, Lorimer D 1899-1977 *ConAu 73,*
  WhJnl 1928
Heywood, Valentine 1891-1963 *BioIn 6*
Heyworth, Peter Lawrence Frederick 1921-
  Au&Wr, ConAu 65, Who 1974,
  WhoMus 1972, WrDr 1976
Hiatt, James M *BioIn 2, IndAu 1816*
Hibbard, Addison 1887-1945 *AmAu&B*
Hibbard, Bill *NF*
Hibben, Paxton Pattison 1880-1928 *AmAu&B,*
  DcAmB 9, DcNAA, IndAu 1917, REnAL,
  WebBD
Hibbs, Ben 1901-1975 *AmAu&B, BioIn 1,*
  BioIn 5, BioIn 6, ConAu 65, CurBio XR,
  HisAmM XR, IntWW 1974, WhoAm 1974,
  WhJnl 1928
Hichborn, Franklin 1868?-1963 *BioIn 6*
Hickey, Harvey John 1904?-1959 *BioIn 5*
Hickey, James C 1876?-1952 *BioIn 2*
Hickey, Margaret 1902- *BioIn 7, ForWC 1970,*
  WhoAm 1974, WhoAmW 1974
Hickey, Neil 1931- *ConAu 1R*
Hickey, Patrick Vincent 1846-1889 *HisAmM XR,*
  NatCAB 29
Hickey, Thomas Joseph 1910?- *BioIn 4*
Hickling, Leland G *NF*
Hickman, Andrew *NF*
Hickman, Lauren C *BioIn 8*
Hickman, Michelle 1942- *NF*
Hickok, Guy C 1887?-1951 *BioIn 2*
Hickok, Lorena A 1892?-1968 *AuBYP, BioIn 8*
Hicks, Clifford Byron 1920- *AmAu&B, AuBYP,*
  BioIn 7, ConAu 5, WhoAm 1974
Hicks, Dan, Jr. 1921?- *BioIn 8, InvJ*
Hicks, Edwin P *NF*

Hicks, George 1905-1965 *AmJnl*
Hicks, Granville 1901- *AmAu&B, AmNov,*
  AmRP, CnDAL, ConAmA, ConAu 9,
  ConNov 1972, ConNov 1976, CurBio XR,
  DcLEL, OxAm, Pen Am, RAdv 1, REn,
  REnAL, TwCA, TwCA Sup, WhoAm 1974,
  WhoWor 1974, WrDr 1976
Hicks, Henry H *OvPC*
Hicks, Irl *HisAmM XR*
Hicks, Jerry D *NF*
Hicks, John 1847-1917 *AmJnl, BioIn 5, DcNAA*
Hicks, Joseph Winstead 1899-1959 *WhJnl 1928*
Hicks, Mary A 1911- *BioIn 3*
Hicks, Nancy *BlkC*
Hicks, Mrs. R B *HisAmM XR*
Hicks, Ronald Graydon 1934- *ConAu 73,*
  DrAS 74E
Hicks, Sallie *NF*
Hicks, Wilson 1897-1970 *AmAu&B, BioIn 9,*
  ConAu 29, NewYTBE 1
Hiebert, Ray Eldon 1932- *AmAu&B, ConAu 17,*
  DrAS 74E, WhoAm 1974, WhoCon 1973,
  WhoE 1974, WhoPubR 1972
Hielle, Tom *NF*
Hielscher, Theodor 1822-1907 *BioIn 2*
Hieronymus, Clara Booth Wiggins 1913-
  ConAu 73, WhoAm 1974, WhoAmW 1974,
  WhoS&SW 1973
Hiestand, Eleanor Moore *HisAmM XR*
Hifner, William A *NF*
Higbee, Elnathan Elisha *HisAmM XR*
Higdon, Harry John 1897- *BioIn 1*
Higginbotham, Alfred Leslie 1895-1967
  WhJnl 1928
Higgins, Alice 1924?-1974 *ConAu 53,*
  NewYTBS 5
Higgins, Arthur R 1900- *WhJnl 1928*
Higgins, Chester *NF*
Higgins, Chester, Jr. 1946- *ConAu 73, LivBAA*
Higgins, David William 1834-1917 *DcNAA*
Higgins, Francis Carlos 1867-1928 *BioIn 2*
Higgins, George G 1916- *NF*
Higgins, James 1916?- *BioIn 7*
Higgins, James E *NF*
Higgins, Marguerite 1920-1966 *AmAu&B, AmJnl,*
  BioIn 2, BioIn 3, BioIn 4, BioIn 5, BioIn 7,
  BioIn 8, BioIn 9, ConAu 5R, ConAu 25,
  CurBio XR
Higgins, Peggy *NF*
Higgins, Peter J J 1877- *WhJnl 1928*
Higgins, Shaun O'Leary 1948- *NF*
Higgins, Thomas d1890 *NF*
Higgins, Vera 1892-1969 *BioIn 9*
Higgs, Edward H *NF*
Higgs, James H *OvPC*
High, Gavin D *NF*
High, Stanley Hoflund 1895-1961 *AmAu&B,*
  BioIn 5, BioIn 6, HisAmM XR
Highet, Gilbert 1906-1978 *CelR 1973, ConAu 1,*
  ConAu 73, CurBio XR, IntWW 1974,
  NewYTBE 3, Who 1974, WhoAm 1974,
  WhoWor 1974
Highland, Cecil Blaine 1876?-1957 *BioIn 4*
Highland, Cecil Blaine, Jr. 1918- *WhoAm 1974*
Hight, John J 1834-1886 *BioIn 2, IndAu 1816,*
  OhA&B
Highton, Jake *NF*
Highton, Robert D *NF*
Hightower, John Marmann 1909- *BioIn 3,*
  CurBio XR, WhoAm 1974
Hilburn, Robert *NF*
Hildebrand, Hans *HisAmM XR*
Hildebrand, Jesse Richardson 1888-1951 *AmAu&B,*
  BioIn 2, HisAmM XR

Hilder, John Chapman 1892-1936 *HisAmM XR,*
WhNAA
Hilderbrand, Lon M 1893- *WhJnl 1928*
Hildreth, Charles Lotin 1856?-1896 *Alli Sup,*
AmAu&B, BiD&SB, DcAmA, DcNAA
Hildreth, James M *NF*
Hildreth, Richard 1807-1865 *Alli, AmAu,*
AmAu&B, BbD, BiD&SB, CyAL 2,
DcAmA, DcLEL, DcNAA, HisAmM XR,
OxAm, REnAL, WebBD
Hilferding, Rudolf 1877- *NF*
Hill, Adams Sherman 1833-1910 *Alli Sup,*
AmAu&B, DcAmA, DcNAA
Hill, Agnes 1842-1917 *DcNAA*
Hill, Alfred Gibson 1893- *BioIn 2, WhJnl 1928*
Hill, Ben *BioIn 1*
Hill, Charles Shattuck 1868-1948 *BioIn 1*
Hill, Daniel Harvey 1821-1889 *Alli, Alli Sup,*
AmAu&B, BiDSA, DcAmA, DcNAA,
HisAmM XR, LiJA, WebBD
Hill, E Trevor *HisAmM XR*
Hill, Ebenezer *HisAmM XR*
Hill, Edwin Conger 1884-1957 *AmAu&B,*
BioIn 4, CurBio XR, HisAmM XR,
IndAu 1917
Hill, Ernest M 1908-1958 *BioIn 4, RpN*
Hill, Evan 1919- *AmM&W 73S, ConAu 11R*
Hill, F D *NF*
Hill, Fowler 1901?-1973 *ConAu 37, WhNAA*
Hill, Frank *NF*
Hill, Frank Ernest 1888-1969 *AmAu&B, AuBYP,*
ConAu 73, REnAL, TwCA, TwCA Sup,
WebBD
Hill, Fred *NF*
Hill, Fred W 1883?-1950 *BioIn 2*
Hill, Frederic B *NF*
Hill, George *HisAmM XR*
Hill, George Canning 1825?-1898? *Alli, Alli Sup,*
BiD&SB, CarSB, DcAmA, DcNAA,
HsB&A
Hill, George Griswold 1868-1935 *NF*
Hill, Gladwin 1914- *BioIn 8, ConAu 25*
Hill, H B *NF*
Hill, H H *HisAmM XR*
Hill, Henley 1897?-1972 *BioIn 9*
Hill, Henry d1888 *NF*
Hill, Hugh *NF*
Hill, Isaac 1788-1851 *AmJnl, BioIn 6*
Hill, Issac William 1908- *ConAu 65*
Hill, J Clarence 1876- *WhJnl 1928*
Hill, Sir John 1716-1775 *Alli, BioIn 4, DcEnL*
Hill, John Alexander 1858-1916 *DcNAA,*
HisAmM XR, REnAL
Hill, John Wiley 1890-1977 *ConAu 69,*
IndAu 1917, WhoAm 1974, WhJnl 1928,
WhoPubR 1972, WhoWor 1974
Hill, L Draper 1935- *ConAu 17R, WhoAm 1974,*
WrDr 1976
Hill, Laurence *NF*
Hill, Leland Halsey 1899- *BioIn 1*
Hill, Luther Lyons 1896- *BioIn 2*
Hill, Max *NF*
Hill, Max 1904?-1949 *BioIn 2*
Hill, Milton Dean 1922?- *BioIn 1*
Hill, Norman H 1887- *WhJnl 1928*
Hill, Pamela 1938- *BioNews 1974, ForWC 1970,*
InvJ
Hill, R L 1888- *WhJnl 1928*
Hill, Ray *NF*
Hill, Russell *AmJnl*
Hill, Ruth *HisAmM XR*
Hill, Ruth K *ForWC 1970, OvPC*
Hill, Samuel *EarABI Sup, HisAmM XR*
Hill, Shandy *BioIn 8*

Hill, Thomas *HisAmM XR*
Hill, Thomas 1877- *WhJnl 1928*
Hill, Thomas Crawford 1900?-1951 *BioIn 2*
Hill, Thomas Edie 1832-1915 *Alli Sup, DcAmA,*
DcNAA, HisAmM XR
Hill, Vaughan E 1911?- *BioIn 1*
Hill, W E *HisAmM XR*
Hill, Wells L 1850- *WhJnl 1928*
Hill, William *NewMr*
Hillard, George Stillman 1808-1879 *Alli, Alli Sup,*
AmAu, AmAu&B, BbD, BiD&SB, CyAL 2,
DcAmA, DcEnL, DcNAA, HisAmM XR
Hillcourt, William 1900- *AmAu&B, AuBYP,*
WhoAm 1974
Hillebrand, Karl 1829-1884 *HisAmM XR,*
WebBD
Hillegas, Howard Clemens 1872-1918 *DcAmA,*
DcNAA
Hillenbrand, Barry R 1941- *ConAu 73*
Hillerman, Tony 1925- *ConAu 29, SmATA 6*
Hillgaertner, Georg 1824-1865 *BioIn 2*
Hilliard, John Northern 1872?-1935 *AmLY,*
DcNAA, WhNAA
Hilliard, Suzanne *OvPC, WhoAmW 1974*
Hilliard, William Arthur 1927?- *BioIn 1, BlkC*
Hillis, Marjorie 1890-1971 *BioIn 2*
Hillman, George Sidney *HisAmM XR*
Hillman, Harry *HisAmM XR*
Hillman, Henry 1912-1972 *BioIn 9, NewYTBE 3,*
WhoF&I 1974
Hillman, William 1895-1962 *BioIn 2, BioIn 6,*
HisAmM XR
Hillquit, Morris 1869-1933 *AmLY, AmRP,*
DcNAA, REnAL, WebBD
Hills, Argentina S 1906- *ForP, WhoS&SW 1973*
Hills, Denis Cecil 1913- *ConAu 65*
Hills, Laurence 1879-1941 *WhNAA*
Hills, Lee 1906- *BioIn 2, InvJ, WhoAm 1974,*
WhoMW 1974, WhoS&SW 1973,
WhoWor 1974
Hills, Wesley *InvJ*
Hills, William Henry 1859-1930 *BioIn 1,*
HisAmM XR
Hillstrom, Thomas M *NF*
Hillyard, C L 1897- *WhJnl 1928*
Hilson, Thomas *HisAmM XR*
Hiltman, John Wolfe 1862-1941 *AmAu&B,*
NatCAB 41
Hilton, Henry Hoyt 1868-1948 *AmAu&B,*
NatCAB 37
Hilton, John L 1937- *OvPC, WhoAdv 1972*
Hilton, Ned 1904?-1967 *BioIn 8*
Hilton, Ralph 1907- *ConAu 29, OvPC*
Hilts, Donna *NF*
Hilts, Phil *NF*
Himanka, Jussi W 1918- *NF*
Hinchman, Walter Swain *HisAmM XR*
Hinckle, Warren James, III 1938- *BioIn 8,*
NewMr, WhoAm 1974, WhoWest 1974,
WhoWor 1974
Hinckley, C A *HisAmM XR*
Hinckley, Theodore Ballou *NF*
Hincks, Sir Francis 1807-1885 *Alli Sup, BbtC,*
DcNAA, OxCan, WebBD
Hind, Ella Cora 1861-1942 *BioIn 5, BioIn 7*
Hinden, Stanley Jay 1927- *WhoAm 1974*
Hindle, Wilifrid Hope 1903-1967 *BioIn 7,*
ConAu 23
Hindley, Howard Lister 1870-1943 *AmAu&B,*
WhJnl 1928
Hindman, Jo *NF*
Hindmarsh, Harry Comfort 1887-1956 *BioIn 4*
Hinds, Bill *NF*
Hinds, Frank *OvPC*

DrAS 74E, WrDr 1976
Hobson, Harold 1904- *BiE&WWA, CroCD,*
　LongC, Who 1974, WhoThe 1972
Hobson, James George 1886- *WhJnl Sup*
Hobson, Laura Keane Zametkin 1900- *AmAu&B,*
　AmNov, Au&Wr, Bioln 3, Bioln 4,
　Bioln 6, ConAu 19, ConNov 1972,
　ConNov 1976, CurBio XR, REn, REnAL,
　TwCA Sup, WhoAm 1974, WhoAmW 1974,
　WrDr 1976
Hobson, Sir Oscar 1886-1961 *Bioln 5*
Hobson, Wilder 1906-1964 *AmAu&B, Bioln 6*
Hochstein, Philip 1901- *AmJnl, WhoWorJ 1972*
Hochstetter, Gustav 1873- *WebBD*
Hochstetter, Leo *OvPC*
Hocke, Gustav Rene 1908- *IntWW 1976*
Hodenfield, Chris *NF*
Hodgdon, Frederick C 1873-1946 *NatCAB 35*
Hodge, Charles 1797-1878 *Alli, Alli Sup, AmAu,*
　AmAu&B, BbD, CyAL 2, DcAmA, DcEnL,
　DcNAA, HisAmM XR, REnAL, WebBD
Hodge, Moses D *HisAmM XR*
Hodges, Ann 1928- *NF*
Hodges, Arthur Lewis 1900- *WhJnl 1928*
Hodges, Charles A 1894-1964 *Bioln 9,*
　HisAmM XR
Hodges, H P *NF*
Hodges, Leigh Mitchell 1876-1954 *AmAu&B,*
　Bioln 3, Bioln 4, NatCAB 40
Hodges, Nancy 1888-1969 *Bioln 2, Bioln 8*
Hodges, Nathaniel Dana Carlile 1852-1927
　HisAmM XR
Hodgetts, Victoria *NF*
Hodgins, Dick, Sr. *NF*
Hodgins, Eric 1899-1971 *AmAu&B, ConAu 29,*
　NewYTBE 2, REnAL, WhNAA, WorAu
Hodgins, Hawthorne H J *WhJnl 1928*
Hodgins, Joseph Louis, Jr. 1890- *WhJnl 1928*
Hodgman, Bruce E *OvPC*
Hodgson, Godfrey 1934- *ConAu 25*
Hodgson, Laurence Curran 1874-1937 *DcNAA*
Hodgson, Telfair *HisAmM XR*
Hodson, Henry Vincent 1906- *Au&Wr,*
　ConAu 7R, IntWW 1976, Who 1974,
　WhoWor 1974, WrDr 1976
Hoeber, Arthur 1854-1915 *DcNAA,*
　HisAmM XR
Hoefer, Albert, Jr. *NF*
Hoefer, Edmund 1819-1882 *BiD&SB, WebBD*
Hoefer, George 1909?-1967 *Bioln 8*
Hoefer, Hans-Juergen *NF*
Hoehling, A A 1915- *ConAu 1R*
Hoehn, Gustave *AmRP*
Hoensbroech, Count Paul Von 1852-1923 *WebBD*
Hoenshell, Don 1923- *NF*
Hoerter, Charles 1904-1974 *Bioln 4, Bioln 10,*
　NewYTBS 5
Hoest, William 1926- *Bioln 8, ConAu 69*
Hofer, Werner 1921- *Bioln 6*
Hoff, Sydney 1912- *AmAu&B, Au&Wr,*
　AuBYP, Bioln 7, Bioln 8, Bioln 9,
　ConAu 5R, ThrBJA, WhoAm 1974,
　WhoWor 1974, WhoWorJ 1972
Hoff, Virginia E 1901- *WhJnl 1928*
Hoffenstein, Samuel 1890-1947 *AmAu&B,*
　DcNAA, REnAL, TwCA, TwCA Sup,
　WebBD
Hoffer, William 1943- *ConAu 65*
Hoffman, Allan C *HisAmM XR*
Hoffman, Arthur Sullivant 1876-1966 *AmAu&B,*
　Bioln 7, HisAmM XR, REnAL, WhNAA,
　WhJnl 1928
Hoffman, Benzion 1874-1954 *Bioln 3*
Hoffman, Carl 1882-1946 *Bioln 4, NatCAB 41,*

WhJnl 1928
Hoffman, Charles Fenno 1806-1884 *Alli, AmAu,*
　AmAu&B, BiD&SB, Bioln 1, Bioln 3,
　CasWL, CnDAL, CyAL 2, DcAmA, DcBiA,
　DcEnL, DcLEL, DcNAA, EvLB,
　HisAmM XR, LiJA, OxAm, Pen Am,
　REnAL, WebBD
Hoffman, David Herbert 1933?- *NF*
Hoffman, Dean Meck 1880-1968 *Bioln 8*
Hoffman, Donald Stone 1936- *ConAu 57,*
　DrAS 74H
Hoffman, Ellen *NF*
Hoffman, Fred S *NF*
Hoffman, Harry *WhoE 1974*
Hoffman, Harry G 1911?-1977 *ConAu 69*
Hoffman, Harry H 1873?-1948 *Bioln 1*
Hoffman, Irving 1909?-1968 *Bioln 2, Bioln 5,*
　Bioln 8
Hoffman, Jeane 1920?-1966 *Bioln 2, Bioln 7*
Hoffman, Johannes 1890- *CurBio XR*
Hoffman, Linda K 1951- *NF*
Hoffman, Lisa 1919- *ConAu 29*
Hoffman, Michael Lindsay 1915- *AmEA 1974,*
　AmM&W 73S, IntWW 1976, WhoAm 1974,
　WhoGov 1972, WhoWor 1974
Hoffman, Paul 1910?-1960 *Bioln 5*
Hoffman, Paul 1934- *ConAu 45*
Hoffman, Peter *NF*
Hoffman, Robert VanAmburgh 1879-1953 *Bioln 3*
Hoffman, Sylvan 1891?-1970 *Bioln 8*
Hoffmann, C Julius *OvPC*
Hoffmann, Harry G *NF*
Hoffmann, Nehemia Dov 1860-1928 *Bioln 8*
Hoffmann, Phil 1868- *WhNAA, WhJnl 1928*
Hoffmann, Steve *NF*
Hoffnung, Gerard 1925-1959 *Bioln 5, Bioln 6,*
　Bioln 10, WhoGrA
Hofman, Peter *NF*
Hofmann, Paul 1912- *NF*
Hofmann, William F 1884?-1950 *Bioln 2*
Hofmeyr, Jan Hendrik 1845-1909 *WebBD*
Hofstetter, Elaine *NF*
Hofstra, Ann *NF*
Hogan, Barbara *NF*
Hogan, David *HisAmM XR*
Hogan, Edmund F *OvPC*
Hogan, John F *HisAmM XR*
Hogan, John Francis, Jr. 1917- *USBiR 1974,*
　WhoAm 1974, WhoGov 1972
Hogan, John Sheridan 1815?-1859 *Alli, BbtC,*
　DcNAA, PoIre
Hogan, Walter V 1892- *WhJnl 1928*
Hogan, William 1914- *WhoAm 1974*
Hogarth, Burne *NF*
Hogate, Kenneth Craven 1897-1947 *Bioln 1,*
　WhJnl 1928
Hoge, James Fulton, Jr. 1935- *Bioln 8,*
　WhoAm 1974, WhoMW 1974
Hoge, Thomas A *OvPC*
Hoge, Warren 1941- *WhoAm 1974*
Hogeboom, Amy 1891- *AuBYP, HisAmM XR*
Hogg, Tony 1925- *NF*
Hogue, John David, Jr. 1898-1958 *Bioln 6,*
　NatCAB 46, WhJnl 1928
Hohenberg, Dorothy Lannvier 1905?-1977
　ConAu 73
Hohenberg, John 1906- *AmAu&B, Bioln 2,*
　ConAu 13R, DrAS 74E, WhoAm 1974,
　WrDr 1976
Hohenlohe-Waldenburh, Stefanie Richter 1896-
　CurBio XR
Hoiles, Raymond Cyrus 1878-1970 *Bioln 6,*
　Bioln 9, NewYTBE 1
Hok, Heng *NF*

Hoke, Helen 1903- *BioIn 2, BioIn 8*
Hoke, Henry Reed 1894-1970 *BioIn 9*
Hoke, Merab *NF*
Hoke, Russell Allen 1896- *AmAu&B, WhNAA*
Hoke, Travis Henderson 1892-1947 *AmAu&B,
  HisAmM XR*
Hokinson, Helen Elna 1893-1949 *BioIn 2,
  BioIn 4, BioIn 5, DcAmB S4, NatCAB 41*
Holberg, Betty *NF*
Holberg, Joe *NF*
Holborn, Gerd *NF*
Holbrook, Alva Morris 1807?-1875 *NF*
Holbrook, James 1812-1864 *DcNAA*
Holbrook, Josiah 1788-1854 *AmAu, DcNAA,
  HisAmM XR, OhA&B, OxAm, REnAL*
Holbrook, Silas Pinckney 1796-1835 *AmAu&B,
  BiDSA, CyAL 1, DcAmA, DcNAA,
  HisAmM XR*
Holbrook, Stewart Hall 1893-1964 *AmAu&B,
  AuBYP, BioIn 7, BioIn 8, BioIn 9,
  BioIn 10, ConAu P-1, HisAmM XR, OxAm,
  REnAL, SmATA 2, ThrBJA, TwCA Sup,
  WhNAA, WhoPNW*
Holbrook, Weare *HisAmM XR*
Holbrook, Z Swift *HisAmM XR*
Holcomb, Allan Tracy 1889-1956 *BioIn 4*
Holcombe, Return Ira 1845-1916 *DcNAA,
  OhA&B*
Holden, Charles W *HisAmM XR*
Holden, Constance *NF*
Holden, David 1924-1977 *Au&Wr, ConAu 41,
  ConAu 73*
Holden, Edward Goodman 1839-1927 *DcNAA*
Holden, Inez 1906-1974 *ConAu 53*
Holden, Liberty Emery 1833-1913 *DcAmB 9*
Holden, Martha Everts 1844-1896 *AmAu&B,
  DcNAA*
Holden, Raymond Peckham 1894-1972 *AmAu&B,
  AuBYP, ConAu 7R, ConAu 37,
  NewYTBE 3, REnAL, TwCA, TwCA Sup*
Holden, Roger Cramer 1897- *WhJnl 1928*
Holden, Theodore L *NF*
Holden, W Sprague 1909-1973 *ConAu 1R,
  ConAu 45*
Holden, William Woods 1818-1892 *AmJnl,
  BioIn 5*
Holder, Charles Frederick 1851-1915 *Alli Sup,
  AmAu&B, BiD&SB, DcAmA, DcNAA,
  HisAmM XR, WebBD*
Holder, Marylynn Jeanette 1922- *WhoAmW 1974*
Holdridge, E Earl 1883- *WhJnl 1928*
Holeman, Frank 1920?- *BioIn 4*
Holiday, Mike 1950- *NF*
Holisher, Desider 1901-1972 *BioIn 9, ConAu 19,
  ConAu 37, SmATA 6, WhoWorJ 1972*
Holland, Carroll *NF*
Holland, Cecil F 1900?-1978 *WhoAmP 1973,
  WhoGov 1972*
Holland, Edward Clifford 1794-1824 *BiDSA,
  DcAmA, HisAmM XR*
Holland, Edward Clifford *see also* Holland, Edwin
  Clifford
Holland, Edwin Clifford 1794-1824 *Alli, AmAu,
  AmAu&B, CnDAL, CyAL 1, DcNAA,
  OxAm, REnAL*
Holland, Edwin Clifford *see also* Holland, Edward
  Clifford
Holland, Elmer L, Jr. *RpN*
Holland, F R *HisAmM XR*
Holland, Franklin Pierce 1852-1928 *BioIn 1,
  HisAmM XR, NatCAB 33*
Holland, George 1897?-1947 *BioIn 1*
Holland, Hal *NF*
Holland, Josiah Gilbert 1819-1881 *Alli, Alli Sup,*

*AmAu, AmAu&B, AmJnl, BbD, BiD&SB,
  BioIn 1, BioIn 2, BioIn 7, CnDAL,
  CyAL 2, DcAmA, DcBiA, DcEnL, DcLEL,
  DcNAA, EvLB, HisAmM XR, LiJA,
  OxAm, REn, REnAL, WebBD*
Holland, Lewis *HisAmM XR*
Holland, Margaret T 1871?-1948 *BioIn 1*
Holland, Ray P 1884- *AmAu&B, BioIn 9,
  WhNAA*
Holland, Robert 1940- *ConAu 33*
Hollander, Herbert S 1904?-1976 *ConAu 69*
Hollander, Jacob Harry 1871-1940 *DcAmA,
  DcNAA, HisAmM XR, WebBD*
Hollander, Richard *NF*
Hollander, Zander 1923- *ConAu 65*
Hollenbeck, Don 1905-1954 *BioIn 1, BioIn 2,
  BioIn 3, CurBio XR*
Hollenbeck, Ralph *NF*
Holles, Everett R 1904?-1978 *RpN*
Hollett, J V 1883- *WhJnl Sup*
Holley, C I *HisAmM XR*
Holley, Horace 1781-1827 *Alli, CyAL 2,
  HisAmM XR*
Holley, Horace 1887-1960 *AmAu&B, WebBD*
Holley, I B, Jr. 1919- *ConAu 37, HisAmM XR*
Holley, Lee 1933?- *BioIn 5*
Holley, Myron 1779-1841 *NF*
Holley, Orville Luther 1791-1861 *Alli, DcAmA,
  DcNAA, HisAmM XR*
Holliday, Barbara Gregg 1917- *ConAu 73,
  WhoAm 1974*
Holliday, Carl 1879-1936 *AmAu&B, AmLY,
  BiDSA, DcNAA, HisAmM XR, OhA&B,
  REnAL, WhNAA*
Holliday, John Hampden 1846-1921 *BioIn 2,
  IndAu 1816*
Holliday, Robert Cortes 1880-1946 *AmAu&B,
  BioIn 1, BioIn 4, DcNAA, HisAmM XR,
  IndAu 1917, REnAL, TwCA, TwCA Sup,
  WhNAA*
Holliday, Robert Paul 1894-1959 *WhJnl 1928*
Hollie, Pam *NF*
Hollingshead, John 1827-1904 *Alli Sup, BbD,
  BiD&SB, DcEnL, WebBD*
Hollingsworth, Robert W *NF*
Hollingworth, Clare 1914?- *BioIn 6*
Hollis, Christopher 1902-1977 *BioIn 5,
  CathA 1930, ConAu 69, ConAu 73,
  Who 1974, WrDr 1976*
Hollis, Frank E 1886- *WhJnl 1928*
Hollis, Roy Coleman 1889-1946 *BioIn 1*
Hollister, John Hamilcar 1824-1911 *HisAmM XR*
Hollister, Joseph 1877-1946 *BioIn 2, NatCAB 35*
Hollmann, Frank 1897?- *BioIn 1*
Holloway, David P 1809-1883 *NatCAB 7*
Holloway, J Starr *HisAmM XR*
Holloway, Jean *LiJA*
Holloway, William Robeson 1836-1911 *BioIn 2,
  IndAu 1816*
Hollowood, A Bernard 1910- *IntWW 1976,
  Who 1974*
Hollreiser, Len *NF*
Hollums, Ellis Clyde 1893-1949 *WhJnl 1928*
Holly, D W *HisAmM XR*
Holly, Flora Mai *LiJA*
Holly, Hazel *RpN*
Holly, Willis *NF*
Holm, Don 1918- *ConAu 33*
Holm, Ed *NF*
Holman, Ada Augusta *BioIn 1*
Holman, Alfred 1857-1930 *HisAmM XR,
  NatCAB 24*
Holman, Louis Arthur 1866-1939 *AmAu&B,
  AmLY, DcNAA*

Holmberg, Ted 1931- *WhoE 1974*
Holme, Frank 1868?-1904 *NF*
Holme, George *HisAmM XR*
Holme, John 1868-1904 *HisAmM XR*
Holmes, Allan *NF*
Holmes, Ann *NF*
Holmes, Arthur *NF*
Holmes, Barbara *BioIn 1*
Holmes, Bert *NF*
Holmes, Edison Parker 1896- *BioIn 2*
Holmes, Edward 1797-1859 *Alli*
Holmes, Ezekiel 1801-1865 *Alli, BioIn 8,*
  HisAmM XR
Holmes, Frederick Lionel 1883-1946 *AmAu&B,*
  BioIn 1, BioIn 5, WisWr
Holmes, Garrick *NF*
Holmes, George *NF*
Holmes, George Frederick 1820-1897 *BiDSA,*
  DcNAA, HisAmM XR, LiJA
Holmes, George Robert 1895-1939 *ForP*
Holmes, George Sanford 1883-1955 *BioIn 4*
Holmes, John H *AmJnl*
Holmes, John Haynes 1879-1964 *AmAu&B,*
  CurBio XR, HisAmM XR, WebBD
Holmes, Lizzie M *AmRP*
Holmes, Marilyn *NF*
Holmes, Ralph T *NF*
Holmes, Tommy 1903-1975 *ConAu 57*
Holmes, William *AmRP*
Holmesdale, Jeffery, Viscount *NF*
Holmesly, Edward Sterlin 1932- *WhoAm 1974*
Holscher, Eberhard 1890-1969 *BioIn 7, BioIn 8*
Holsendolph, Ernest *BlkC*
Holsey, Hopkins 1799-1859 *BioIn 4*
Holske, Katherine d1973 *BioIn 10*
Holsopple, Barbara 1943- *ConAu 73*
Holstrom, Ben F *RpN*
Holt, Charles *AmJnl*
Holt, Don *NF*
Holt, Edgar Crawshaw 1900-1975 *Au&Wr,*
  ConAu 3R, ConAu 61
Holt, Guy 1892-1934 *AmAu&B, DcNAA*
Holt, Hamilton 1872-1951 *AmAu&B, AmLY,*
  BioIn 2, BioIn 3, BioIn 4, BioIn 5,
  CurBio XR, DcAmB S5, HisAmM XR,
  NatCAB 40, WebBD, WhNAA
Holt, John 1721-1784 *AmAu&B, AmJnl,*
  DcAmB 9, NatCAB 23
Holt, John H *AmJnl*
Holt, Kermit *NF*
Holt, Lynne *NF*
Holt, Thad 1898- *WhoAm 1974*
Holton, Felicia Antonelli 1921- *ConAu 69*
Holton, James L 1898?-1971 *BioIn 9*
Holtzman, Jerome 1926- *ConAu 53*
Holusha, John M *NF*
Holz, Cynthia *NF*
Holzapfel, Gustav *HisAmM XR*
Holzhauer, Greg *NF*
Holzman, Arthur David 1914- *OvPC,*
  WhoGov 1972, WhoWorJ 1972
Homan, Bill *OvPC*
Homan, Helen 1893-1961 *BioIn 1, BioIn 5*
Homans, Benjamin *Alli, HisAmM XR*
Homans, Isaac Smith 1807-1879 *DcNAA,*
  HisAmM XR, NatCAB 30
Homans, Isaac Smith, Jr. 1832-1897 *Alli Sup,*
  HisAmM XR
Homsey, Sam 1933-1963 *BioIn 2, BioIn 6*
Honan, William H 1931?- *BioIn 9*
Honce, Charles Ellsworth 1895-1975 *AmAu&B,*
  ConAu 61
Honda, Chikao *ForP*
Honderich, Beland 1918- *WhoAm 1974,*

WhoE 1974
Honey, Henry R 1859- *WhNAA, WhJnl 1928*
Hong, Gary *NF*
Honig, Ana *NF*
Honig, Milton 1909?-1965 *BioIn 7*
Honig, Nat *NF*
Hood, Edwin Milton *NF*
Hood, Horace 1853-1924 *NatCAB 20*
Hood, Magnus McIntyre 1893- *WhJnl 1928*
Hood, Robert Eric 1926- *ConAu 23,*
  WhoAm 1974
Hood, Robin *NF*
Hood, Thomas 1799-1845 *Alli, AnCL, AtlBL,*
  BbD, BiD&SB, Br&AmS, BrAu 19, CarSB,
  CasWL, CnE&AP, CrtT 2, DcEnA, DcEnL,
  DcEuL, DcLEL, EvLB, MouLC 3, NewC,
  OxEng, Pen Eng, REn, Str&VC, WebBD,
  WebE&AL
Hood, Thomas 1835-1874 *Alli Sup, BiD&SB,*
  EvLB, NewC, OxEng, WebBD
Hood, Thomas *see also* Hood, Tom
Hood, Tom 1835-1874 *BrAu 19, DcEnL*
Hood, Tom *see also* Hood, Thomas
Hooey, Robert E 1897?-1949 *BioIn 2*
Hoogs, Frank L *HisAmM XR*
Hook, Theodore Edward 1788-1841 *Alli, BbD,*
  BiD&SB, BiDLA, BrAu 19, CasWL,
  DcEnA, DcEnL, DcEuL, DcLEL, EvLB,
  NewC, OxEng, WebBD
Hooke, Burford *NF*
Hooken, Horatio Clarence 1857- *NF*
Hooker, Donald Russell 1876-1946 *BioIn 1*
Hooker, George E 1861-1939 *NF*
Hooker, Richard 1878-1967 *AmAu&B, BioIn 8*
Hooker, Robert *InvJ*
Hooker, William Francis 1856-1938 *DcNAA*
Hoole, William Stanley 1903- *BioIn 2, BioIn 10,*
  LiJA, WhoAm 1974
Hooper, Edward James 1803-1882? *Alli, DcAmA,*
  DcNAA, HisAmM XR
Hooper, Franklin Henry 1862-1940 *AmAu&B,*
  CurBio XR, WhNAA
Hooper, Johnson Jones 1815-1863? *Alli, AmAu,*
  AmAu&B, BiD&SB, BiDSA, CnDAL,
  DcAmA, DcNAA, LiJA, NatCAB 11,
  OxAm, Pen Am, REn, REnAL, WebBD,
  WebE&AL
Hooper, Lucy Hamilton 1835-1893 *Alli Sup,*
  AmAu, AmAu&B, BbD, BiD&SB, CyAL 2,
  DcAmA, DcAmB 9, DcNAA, HisAmM XR
Hooper, Osman Castle 1858-1941 *AmAu&B,*
  DcNAA, OhA&B, WhJnl 1928
Hooper, Parker Morse 1877- *WhJnl 1928*
Hooper, W W *HisAmM XR*
Hooper, William DeMatoos *HisAmM XR*
Hoopes, Paul Roger 1937- *AmM&W 73S, ForP*
Hoopes, Roy 1922- *ConAu 21R*
Hooten, William Jarvis 1900- *ConAu 61,*
  WhoAm 1974, WhoS&SW 1973
Hoover, Calvin Bryce 1897-1974 *AmEA 1974,*
  AmM&W 73S, Au&Wr, ConAu 13,
  ConAu 49, ConAu P-1, HisAmM XR,
  IntWW 1974, NewYTBS 5, Who 1974,
  WhoAm 1974
Hoover, Ellison 1888-1955 *BioIn 3*
Hoover, John Page 1910- *AmM&W 73S,*
  WhoAm 1974
Hoover, Kerwin 1910- *NF*
Hoover, Robert *BioIn 1*
Hoover, Susan *NF*
Hopcraft, Arthur 1932- *ConAu 25, ConDr,*
  WrDr 1976
Hope, Chester Raines 1881-1963 *BioIn 6*
Hope, Eleanor Schorer 1891- *ForWC 1970, OvPC*

Hope, Jack NF
Hope, James Barron 1829-1887 Alli Sup, AmAu,
  AmAu&B, BiD&SB, BiDSA, DcAmA,
  DcNAA, HisAmM XR
Hope, Paul B NF
Hopf, George M 1883?-1949 BioIn 2
Hopkins, Albert A HisAmM XR
Hopkins, Alphonso Alvah 1843-1918 Alli Sup,
  AmAu&B, BiD&SB, DcAmA, DcNAA
Hopkins, Andrew Winkle 1880- WhNAA,
  WhJnl 1928
Hopkins, Bill 1928- BioIn 9, ConAu 9
Hopkins, Daniel HisAmM XR
Hopkins, Emma Curtis HisAmM XR
Hopkins, Ernest Jerome 1887- WhJnl 1928
Hopkins, Frank Louison 1885- WhJnl 1928
Hopkins, Frank S RpN
Hopkins, Garland Evans 1913- BioIn 2
Hopkins, Harry 1913- Au&Wr, ConAu 29,
  WrDr 1976
Hopkins, Henry Clayton HisAmM XR
Hopkins, Jerry 1935- ConAu 25
Hopkins, John Henry 1820-1891 Alli Sup,
  BiD&SB, BioIn 7, BioIn 9, DcAmA,
  DcNAA, HisAmM XR, PoIre
Hopkins, Livingston 1846-1927 Alli Sup, BioIn 2,
  DcNAA, HisAmM XR, OhA&B
Hopkins, Louise Macy d1963 BioIn 8
Hopkins, Mary Alden 1876-1960 AmAu&B,
  BioIn 5
Hopkins, Mary W 1931- ConAu 29
Hopkins, Pauline F HisAmM XR
Hopkins, Tom NF
Hopkinson, D H HisAmM XR
Hopkinson, Henry Thomas 1905- ConAu 19R,
  IntWW 1976, Who 1974, WhoWor 1974,
  WrDr 1976
Hopley, Mary Catherine 1856-1948 BioIn 1
Hoppe, Arthur Watterson 1925- AmAu&B,
  BioIn 6, BioIn 8, ConAu 7R, WhoAm 1974,
  WhoWest 1974, WrDr 1976
Hopper, Clarence Heller 1915- WhoAm 1974,
  WhoF&I 1974
Hopper, Hedda 1890-1966 AmAu&B, BioIn 1,
  BioIn 3, BioIn 4, BioIn 6, BioIn 7, BioIn 9,
  CurBio XR, HisAmM XR
Hopper, James Marie 1876-1956 AmAu&B,
  CurBio XR
Hopper, Mary 1923?-1975 NF
Hoppert, George NF
Hoppes, Lowell E 1913- WhoAmA 1973
Hoppin, Francis L V 1875-1946 NatCAB 34
Hoppin, William J HisAmM XR
Hopping, Kenneth E NF
Hopwood, Erie C 1877-1928 NatCAB 20,
  WhJnl 1928
Horan, Jack NF
Horan, James David 1914- AmAu&B,
  ConAu 13R, WhoAm 1974, WhoE 1974
Horbach, Michael 1924- ConAu 29
Horby, W H NF
Horgan, Charles S 1864?-1948 BioIn 1
Horgan, Denis E NF
Horgan, Stephen Henry 1854-1941 AmJnl,
  CurBio XR, DcNAA, WebBD
Horgan, Thomas P 1898?-1964 BioIn 6
Horkan, Katherine Sandford OvPC
Horn, Arthur Van OvPC
Horn, Clayton G 1906- WhoAm 1974
Horn, Edgar George 1897?-1949 BioIn 1
Horn, Edward N OvPC
Horn, Jack NF
Horn, Stanley Fitzgerald 1889- AmAu&B,
  WhoAm 1974

Horn, T N HisAmM XR
Horn, Yvonne NF
Hornaday, Mary 1906- ForWC 1970, OvPC,
  WhNAA
Hornbaker, Alice NF
Hornbeck, James Sylvanus 1908-1971
  AmArch 1970, BioIn 9, NewYTBE 2
Hornblow, Arthur, Sr. 1865-1942 Alli Sup,
  AmAu&B, CurBio XR, DcNAA,
  HisAmM XR, WebBD
Hornby, William Harry 1923- WhoAm 1974,
  WhoWest 1974
Horne, Alexander D NF
Horne, David Hamilton 1912- WhoAm 1974
Horne, George Fox BioIn 2
Horne, Josh L 1887- WhoAm 1974
Horne, Julia NF
Horne, Louther S 1887-1969 BioIn 8
Horner, Garnett Denton 1909- BioIn 9,
  WhoAm 1974, WhoS&SW 1973
Horner, Joseph, Jr. 1887- WhJnl 1928
Horner, Norman Gerald 1882-1954 BioIn 1,
  BioIn 3
Horner, Samuel AmJnl
Hornibrook, William H 1884-1946 WhJnl 1928
Hornig, Roberta NF
Horniman, Benjamin Guy 1873- BioIn 7
Hornsby, Henry H RpN
Hornung, Paul Andrew 1917- WhoAm 1974
Horowitz, Al 1907-1973 BioIn 9, ConAu XR,
  NewYTBE 4
Horowitz, David 1903- BioIn 5, ConAu 69,
  WhoWorJ 1972
Horowitz, David Charles 1937- OvPC,
  WhoAm 1974, WhoWest 1974
Horowitz, I A 1907-1973 ConAu 41
Horowitz, I A see also Horowitz, Al
Horowitz, Israel NF
Horowitz, Robert S 1924- ConAu 9R
Horrabin, James Francis 1884-1962 BioIn 6,
  BioIn 8, NewC, WebBD, WhoChL
Horrock, Nicholas M 1936- ConAu 49, InvJ,
  NewMr
Horrocks, Norman 1927- BiDrLUS, BioIn 9,
  WhoAm 1974, WhoE 1974
Horsch, Juergen F NF
Horsch, Ray L 1894- WhJnl 1928
Horsley, Terence 1904-1949 BioIn 1
Horst, Rudolph H 1878- WhJnl 1928
Horstmann, J H 1869- WhJnl 1928
Horstmeyer, Harold NF
Horton, Alan M NF
Horton, Bernard Francis 1916- WhoAm 1974,
  WhoWest 1974
Horton, Bob 1939- NF
Horton, George 1859-1942 AmAu&B, BiD&SB,
  DcAmA, DcNAA, WebBD
Horton, George M S HisAmM XR
Horton, George Reed 1895?-1972 BioIn 9
Horton, James NF
Horton, McDavid 1884-1941 WhJnl 1928
Horton, Michael OvPC
Horton, Rushmore G 1826- Alli, DcNAA
Horton, Tom NF
Horup, Viggo 1841-1902 ForP
Horvat, Janos 1944?- NF
Horvath, Imre 1940- NF
Horvitz, Samuel Aaron 1889-1956 BioIn 4,
  BioIn 6, NatCAB 43
Horwitz, Elinor Lander NF
Hoshi, Nobuo NF
Hosking, Albert J WhJnl 1928
Hosking, Robert Leroy 1931- WhoAm 1974
Hoskins, Chapin 1891- WhNAA, WhJnl 1928

Hoskins, F Lorell 1902- *WhJnl 1928*
Hoskins, Laban A 1873- *WhJnl 1928*
Hosmer, George Edwin 1867- *WhJnl 1928*
Hosmer, Margaret 1830-1897 *DcNAA*
Hosmer, William *HisAmM XR*
Hosokawa, William K 1915- *ConAu 29,*
WhoWest 1974
Hoss, Elijah Embree 1849-1919 *BiDSA, DcNAA,*
HisAmM XR
Hoss, Fred Wesley 1884- *WhJnl 1928*
Hoss, Halbert Elden 1892- *WhJnl 1928*
Hossack, Lesma *NF*
Hoste, Julius Peter 1884-1954 *BioIn 3*
Hostetter, Helen Pansy 1895- *BioIn 1,*
WhJnl 1928
Hostetter, Hugh Bingley 1880- *WhJnl 1928*
Hotaling, Edward 1937- *NF*
Hotaling, H C *AmJnl*
Hotchkiss, George S 1879- *WhJnl 1928*
Hotchkiss, George Woodward 1831-1926 *DcNAA*
Hotchkiss, Irma Helen 1880?-1951 *BioIn 2*
Hotchkiss, J Elizabeth *HisAmM XR*
Hotchkiss, Loyal Durand 1893?-1964 *BioIn 6*
Hotchkiss, Thomas Woodward 1866?-1953 *BioIn 3*
Hotchkiss, Velona Roundy *HisAmM XR*
Hotchner, Aaron Edward 1920- *AmAu&B,*
ConAu 69, OvPC, WhoAm 1974,.
WhoE 1974, WhoWor 1974
Hotson, Clarence *AmRP*
Hottelet, Richard Curt 1917- *WhoAm 1974,*
WhoWor 1974
Hotz, Robert Bergmann 1914- *WhoAm 1974,*
WhoWor 1974
Hotze, Charles Wayne 1919- *WhoAm 1974*
Hotze, Henry 1834-1887 *BioIn 6, BioIn 7*
Hougan, Jim *NF*
Hough, Elizabeth Wilson 1894?-1965 *BioIn 4,*
BioIn 7
Hough, Emerson 1857-1923 *AmAu&B, AmLY,*
BiD&SB, DcAmA, DcAmB 9, DcLEL,
DcNAA, HisAmM XR, OxAm, REn,
REnAL, TwCA, TwCA Sup, · WebBD
Hough, George A, Jr. *WhJnl 1928*
Hough, George Anthony 1868-1955 *BioIn 3,*
BioIn 4, WhNAA, WhJnl 1928
Hough, George Anthony, III 1920- *DrAS 74F*
Hough, Harold Verne 1889- *WhJnl 1928*
Hough, Henry Beetle 1896- *AmAu&B, AmNov,*
BioIn 2, BioIn 4, BioIn 5, BioIn 9,
ConAu 1R, REnAL, TwCA Sup,
WhoAm 1974
Hough, Hugh 1924- *ConAu 73, InvJ*
Hough, Patricia *OvPC*
Houghton, Albert F 1850-1937 *NatCAB 32*
Houghton, Donald *NF*
Houghton, George Frederick 1820-1870 *NF*
Houghton, George Washington Wright 1850-1891
Alli Sup, AmAu&B, BiD&SB, DcAmA,
DcNAA, HisAmM XR
Houghton, Louise Seymour 1838-1920 *Alli Sup,*
AmLY, DcAmA, DcNAA, HisAmM XR
Houghton, William Morris 1882-1960 *BioIn 5,*
HisAmM XR
Houlgate, Deke 1930- *ConAu 61*
Houlton, William *OvPC*
Houmann, Borge Kruuse 1902- *IntWW 1976,*
WhoWor 1974
Hounchell, Saul *LiJA*
Hourigan, John Aloysius 1872-1951 *BioIn 1,*
BioIn 2, BioIn 4, NatCAB 41
House, Boyce 1896-1961 *AmAu&B, BioIn 1*
House, Charles 1916- *ConAu 25*
House, Edward Howard 1836-1901 *Alli Sup,*
AmAu, AmAu&B, BiD&SB, BioIn 5,

DcAmA, DcAmB 9, DcNAA, WebBD
House, Edwin H *FamWC*
House, Jay Elmer 1870?-1936 *AmAu&B,*
DcNAA, TwCA
House, Lou *WhoAm 1974*
House, Roy Temple 1878-1963 *AmAu&B,*
WhNAA
House, Victor *NF*
Houseman, Martin P *OvPC*
Houser, Daniel M 1834-1915 *NatCAB 12*
Houser, Everett Alvin, Jr. 1900- *WhJnl 1928*
Housh, Charles Leighton 1911- *WhoAm 1974*
Housh, Esther T *HisAmM XR*
Housh, Frank E *HisAmM XR*
Housiaux, Albert 1914- *IntWW 1976*
Housley, Morris Beaufort 1903- *WhJnl 1928*
Housman, Robert L *NF*
Houssaye, Charles *NF*
Houssaye, Henri 1848-1911 *BbD, BiD&SB,*
WebBD
Housser, Frederick Broughton 1889-1936 *DcNAA*
Houston, Carmen DePinillos 1878?-1949 *BioIn 2*
Houston, George *HisAmM XR*
Houston, Herbert Sherman 1866-1956 *BioIn 1,*
BioIn 4, HisAmM XR, NatCAB 41
Houston, Noel 1909-1958 *BioIn 4, BioIn 5*
Houston, Paul Green 1942?- *NF*
Houston, William 1844-1931 *DcNAA*
Houtchens, Lawrence H *LiJA*
Hovegard, Carl *NF*
Hovey, Charles F *HisAmM XR*
Hovey, Charles Mason 1810-1887 *Alli, DcAmA,*
DcNAA, WebBD
Hovey, Graham *NF*
Hovey, Lewis R 1873- *WhJnl 1928*
Hovey, William Alfred 1841-1906 *Alli Sup,*
DcNAA
Howar, Barbara 1935?- *AuNews 1, AuNews 2,*
WrDr 1976
Howard, Alonzo H 1861?-1950 *BioIn 2*
Howard, Anthony 1933?- *BioIn 9*
Howard, August 1910- *WhoAm 1974,*
WhoE 1974, WhoWor 1974
Howard, Bailey Kneiriem 1914- *AmAu&B,*
WhoAm 1974, WhoF&I 1974
Howard, Bart B 1871-1941 *CurBio XR*
Howard, Bronson Crocker 1842-1908 *AmAu,*
AmAu&B, BbD, BiD&SB, CnDAL, CnThe,
DcAmA, DcLEL, DcNAA, EvLB, McGWD,
ModWD, OxAm, REnAL, REnWD,
WebBD, WebE&AL
Howard, Charles Danforth 1873-1944 *BioIn 2*
Howard, Charles H *HisAmM XR*
Howard, Charles P 1895- *WhJnl 1928* .
Howard, Charles Perry 1879-1938 *DcAmB S2*
Howard, Craig *NF*
Howard, Doran T *NF*
Howard, Ed 1866-1948 *BioIn 4, NatCAB 40*
Howard, Edgar 1858-1951 *BioIn 2, BioIn 3,*
DcAmB S5
Howard, Edward Percy 1869- *WhJnl 1928*
Howard, Edwin 1924- *ConAu 65*
Howard, Ernest 1860-1939 *DcNAA, WhJnl 1928*
Howard, Mrs. Frank *see* West, Lillie
Howard, George Bronson 1884-1922 *AmAu&B,*
DcNAA, EncMys, REnAL, WebBD
Howard, Hubert *FamWC*
Howard, Isabel Frances 1902- *WhJnl 1928*
Howard, Jack Rohe 1910- *AmJnl, BioIn 1,*
BioIn 3, BioIn 6, IntWW 1976,
WhoAm 1974, WhoWor 1974
Howard, James Quay 1836-1912 *Alli Sup,*
AmAu&B, DcNAA, OhA&B
Howard, Jane 1935- *BioIn 7, BioNews 1974,*

ConAu 29, OvPC
Howard, John Raymond 1837-1926 *AmAu&B,*
 DcNAA, HisAmM XR
Howard, John Tasker 1890-1964 *AmAu&B,*
 AmSCAP 1966, REnAL, TwCA Sup
Howard, Joseph, Jr. 1833-1908 *Alli Sup, AmJnl,*
 DcAmA, DcNAA, NatCAB 4
Howard, Joseph Kinsey 1906-1951 *AmAu&B,*
 BioIn 2, BioIn 4, DcAmB S5, TwCA Sup
Howard, Keble *see* Bell, John Keble
Howard, Lisa 1926-1965 *BioIn 6, BioIn 7*
Howard, Long 1896- *WhJnl 1928*
Howard, Lucy *NF*
Howard, Michael Balfe 1942- *WhoWest 1974*
Howard, N R *NF*
Howard, Nathaniel Richardson 1898-
 WhoAm 1974
Howard, Peter Dunsmore 1908-1965 *BioIn 7,*
 BioIn 8, ConAu P-1
Howard, Philip Eugene 1870-1946 *AmAu&B,*
 DcNAA, HisAmM XR
Howard, Ralph *NF*
Howard, Ray *NF*
Howard, Rhea 1892- *WhoAm 1974,*
 WhoAmP 1973, WhoS&SW 1973
Howard, Robert Staples 1924- *WhoAm 1974*
Howard, Robert West 1908- *AmAu&B, Au&Wr,*
 BioIn 10, ConAu 1, SmATA 5,
 WhoWor 1974
Howard, Roy Wilson 1883-1964 *AmAu&B,*
 AmJnl, BioIn 2, BioIn 4, BioIn 5, BioIn 6,
 BioIn 7, CurBio XR, HisAmM XR, NewMr,
 WebBD, WhNAA, WhJnl 1928
Howard, S M *HisAmM XR*
Howard, Sidney Coe 1891-1939 *AmAu&B,*
 CasWL, CnDAL, CnMD, CnThe, ConAmA,
 ConAmL, DcLEL, DcNAA, LongC,
 McGWD, ModAL, ModWD, OxAm,
 Pen Am, REn, REnAL, REnWD, TwCA,
 TwCA Sup, WebBD, WebE&AL
Howard, T C *HisAmM XR*
Howard, Thomas 1930- *ConAu 37*
Howard, Tom *NF*
Howard, William Guild *HisAmM XR*
Howay, John 1873- *NF*
Howden, Norman M 1908?- *BioIn 2*
Howe, Arthur Millidge 1867-1947 *BioIn 1*
Howe, Charles L 1932- *ConAu 19R*
Howe, Charles P 1883- *WhJnl 1928*
Howe, David Willard 1892-1969 *BioIn 1, BioIn 8,*
 WhJnl 1928
Howe, Edgar Watson 1853-1937 *Alli Sup,*
 AmAu&B, AmJnl, BiD&SB, BioIn 2,
 BioIn 3, BioIn 4, BioIn 5, BioIn 6, BioIn 8,
 CasWL, CnDAL, CyWA, DcAmA,
 DcAmB S2, DcNAA, IndAu 1816, OxAm,
 REn, REnAL, TwCA, TwCA Sup, WebBD,
 WebE&AL
Howe, Edmund Perry 1896- *WhJnl 1928*
Howe, Ernest 1875-1935 *HisAmM XR*
Howe, Gene Alexander 1886-1952 *BioIn 1,*
 BioIn 2, BioIn 4, NatCAB 41, REnAL,
 TexWr
Howe, Harold C 1886?-1970 *BioIn 8*
Howe, Harrison Estell 1881-1942 *DcNAA,*
 WebBD, WhNAA
Howe, Irving 1920- *AmAu&B, ConAu 9,*
 DrAS 74E, HisAmM XR, ModAL, RAdv 1,
 REnAL, TwCA Sup, WhoAm 1974,
 WhoWor 1974, WhoWorJ 1972
Howe, James P 1878?-1970 *BioIn 8*
Howe, John Benedict 1859-1943 *DcNAA,*
 WhJnl 1928
Howe, Joseph 1804-1873 *Alli, BbtC, BrAu 19,*

CanWr, DcLEL, OxCan, REnAL, WebBD
Howe, Julia Ward 1819-1910 *Alli, Alli Sup,*
 AmAu, AmAu&B, BbD, BiD&SB, CnDAL,
 CyAL 2, DcAmA, DcEnL, DcLEL,
 DcNAA, EvLB, FemPA, HisAmM XR,
 OxAm, OxEng, Pen Am, REn, REnAL,
 WebBD, WebE&AL
Howe, Louis McHenry 1871-1936 *NF*
Howe, Mark Antony DeWolfe 1864-1960
 AmAu&B, AmLY, BioIn 2, BioIn 4,
 BioIn 5, BioIn 6, BioIn 7, DcAmA,
 HisAmM XR, LiJA, OxAm, REn, REnAL,
 TwCA, TwCA Sup, WebBD, WhNAA
Howe, Marvine *NF*
Howe, Paul C 1900- *WhJnl 1928*
Howe, Quincy 1900-1977 *AmAu&B, BioIn 2,*
 BioIn 7, ConAu 49, ConAu 69, CurBio XR,
 DrAS 74H, ForP, IntMPA 1975,
 IntWW 1976, REnAL, WhoAm 1974
Howe, Richard J 1937- *NF*
Howe, Russell Warren 1925- *Au&Wr, ConAu 49,*
 OvPC
Howe, Samuel Gridley 1801-1876 *Alli, AmAu,*
 AmAu&B, DcAmA, DcNAA, HisAmM XR,
 OxAm, REn, REnAL, WebBD
Howe, Wallis, Jr. d1976 *NF*
Howe, Walter Nahum 1866- *WhJnl 1928*
Howe, Ward Allan d1977 *NF*
Howell, Charles Fish 1868-1943 *DcNAA,*
 NatCAB 32
Howell, Clarence Alan 1883-1955 *BioIn 3*
Howell, Clark, Jr. 1894-1966 *BioIn 4, BioIn 7*
Howell, Clark, Sr. 1863-1936 *AmJnl, BiDSA,*
 DcAmB S2, DcNAA, WebBD, WhJnl 1928
Howell, Deborah 1941- *WhoAmW 1974*
Howell, Evan Park 1839-1905 *AmJnl, NatCAB 1*
Howell, Grant W 1915- *NF*
Howell, Haney *NF*
Howell, James Bruen 1816-1880 *DcAmB 9*
Howell, Mary Catherine 1918-1973 *BioIn 10*
Howell, Norman *NF*
Howell, Richard 1869- *WhJnl 1928*
Howells, William Cooper 1807-1894 *DcAmA,*
 DcNAA, OhA&B
Howells, William Dean 1837-1920 *Alli Sup,*
 AmAu, AmAu&B, AmWr, AtlBL, BbD,
 BiD&SB, CarSB, CasWL, CnDAL, CrtT 3,
 CyAL 2, CyWA, DcAmA, DcBiA, DcEnA,
 DcEnA Ap, DcEnL, DcLEL, DcNAA,
 EncAB, EncWL, EvLB, HisAmM XR,
 LiJA, McGWD, ModAL, ModAL Sup,
 ModWD, OhA&B, OxAm, OxEng, Pen Am,
 RAdv 1, RComWL, REn, REnAL, WebBD,
 WebE&AL
Howes, Cecil 1880- *WhNAA, WhJnl 1928*
Howes, Connie B *NF*
Howes, Helen Claire *NF*
Howes, Royce B 1901-1973 *AmAu&B, BioIn 9,*
 ConAu 19, ConAu 41
Howey, Walter Crawford 1882-1954 *AmJnl,*
 BioIn 1, BioIn 3, DcAmB S5
Howkins, Elizabeth Webb 1900-1972 *BioIn 9*
Howkins, John 1945- *ConAu 65*
Howland, Edward *HisAmM XR*
Howland, Frederick Hoppin 1871-1916 *NF*
Howland, Gardiner Greene 1834-1903 *NF*
Howland, Harold Jacobs 1877-1966 *AmAu&B,*
 HisAmM XR
Howland, Hewitt Hanson 1863-1944 *AmAu&B,*
 DcNAA, HisAmM XR, IndAu 1917,
 WhJnl 1928
Howland, Howard J *HisAmM XR*
Howland, Karl V S *HisAmM XR*
Howland, Louis 1857-1934 *AmAu&B, BioIn 2,*

DcNAA, IndAu 1816
Howland, Richard S *NF*
Howland, W B *HisAmM XR*
Howland, William Bailey 1849-1917 *HisAmM XR*
Howland, William Slocum 1901- *BioIn 3,*
WhoF&I 1974
Howrilla, Bill *NF*
Hows, John William Stanhope 1797-1871 *Alli,*
Alli Sup, DcAmA, DcNAA, HisAmM XR
Howson, Elmer Thomas 1884-1944 *WhJnl 1928*
Hoxter, Curtis Joseph 1922- *OvPC,*
WhoCon 1973, WhoE 1974, WhoF&I 1974,
WhoPubR 1972
Hoy, S Frank 1892- *WhJnl 1928*
Hoy, William A d1938 *NF*
Hoy, William J 1911?-1949 *BioIn 2*
Hoye, Paul F *OvPC*
Hoyer, Robert E *OvPC*
Hoyle, Bernadette *BioIn 4, BioIn 5*
Hoyne, Thomas Temple 1875-1946 *WhJnl 1928*
Hoyt, Albert Harrison 1826- *HisAmM XR*
Hoyt, Charles Hale 1860-1900 *AmAu, AmAu&B,*
BiD&SB, CnThe, DcAmA, DcNAA,
ModWD, OxAm, REnAL, REnWD, WebBD
Hoyt, Clark Freeland 1942- *BioIn 9, ConAu 69,*
InvJ, WhoAm 1974
Hoyt, Edwin Palmer (1897) *see also* Hoyt, Palmer
Hoyt, Edwin Palmer 1897- *BioIn 1*
Hoyt, Edwin Palmer, Jr. 1923- *AuBYP,*
ConAu 3R
Hoyt, Edwin Palmer, Jr. *see also* Hoyt, Palmer, Jr.
Hoyt, Morgan H 1863?-1953 *BioIn 3*
Hoyt, Palmer (1897) *see also* Hoyt, Edwin Palmer
Hoyt, Palmer 1897- *AmJnl, BioIn 2, BioIn 3,*
BioIn 5, BioIn 8, BioIn 9, CurBio XR
Hoyt, Palmer, Jr. 1923- *BioIn 10*
Hoyt, Palmer, Jr. *see also* Hoyt, Edwin Palmer, Jr.
Hoyt, Robert E *RpN*
Hozier, Henry *FamWC*
Hrdlicka, Ales 1869-1943 *AmAu&B, AmLY,*
CurBio XR, DcNAA, HisAmM XR,
REnAL, WebBD, WhNAA
Hrebik, Jaromir 1921- *IntWW 1976,*
WhoWor 1974
Hruby, Frank M 1918- *WhoAm 1974*
Hsin, H C *NF*
Hsu, Benedict 1933- *ConAu 69*
Hubbard, Alice 1861-1915 *DcNAA*
Hubbard, Elbert 1856-1915 *AmAu&B, BbD,*
BiD&SB, BioIn 1, BioIn 2, BioIn 3,
BioIn 4, BioIn 5, BioIn 6, BioIn 9,
BioIn 10, CnDAL, DcAmA, DcLEL,
DcNAA, EvLB, HisAmM XR, OxAm, REn,
REnAL, TwCA, TwCA Sup, WebBD
Hubbard, Frank McKinney 1868-1930 *BioIn 2,*
BioIn 6, DcNAA, IndAu 1816, OhA&B,
OxAm, TwCA, TwCA Sup, WebBD,
WhNAA
Hubbard, Frank McKinney *see also* Hubbard, Kin
Hubbard, Freeman 1894- *ConAu 5R, WrDr 1976*
Hubbard, Henry Vincent 1875-1947 *DcNAA,*
WebBD, WhNAA
Hubbard, Kim *NF*
Hubbard, Kin 1868-1930 *AmAu&B, DcNAA,*
REnAL
Hubbard, Kin *see also* Hubbard, Frank McKinney
Hubbard, Leonidas, Jr. d1905 *HisAmM XR,*
OxCan
Hubbard, M F *HisAmM XR*
Hubbard, Robert L *HisAmM XR*
Hubbard, Sara Anderson 1832-1918 *DcNAA*
Hubbard, Stanley Stub 1933- *WhoAdv 1972,*
WhoAm 1974
Hubbard, Theodora K 1887-1935 *NatCAB 28*

Hubbard, Walter Whitely *WhJnl 1928*
Hubbard, Wynant Davis 1900-1961 *AmAu&B,*
BioIn 6
Hubbart, R P 1900- *WhJnl 1928*
Hubbell, Allan Hildreth 1885- *WhJnl 1928*
Hubbell, Richard Whittaker 1914- *Au&Wr,*
ConAu 13R, WhoCon 1973, WrDr 1976
Hubble, Leslie Arthur Burt 1903?- *BioIn 4*
Hubel, Gordon 1926- *WhoAm 1974*
Hubenthal, Karl Samuel 1917- *WhoAm 1974,*
WhoAmA 1973
Huber, Erwin J W 1887- *WhJnl 1928*
Huber, Gotthelf Carl 1865-1934 *DcAmB S1,*
WebBD
Huber, Ludwig Ferdinand 1764-1804 *DcEuL,*
OxGer, WebBD
Huber, Paul Speer d1946 *BioIn 1*
Huber, Paul Speer, Jr. 1921- *WhoAm 1974,*
WhoS&SW 1973
Huber, Ray Allen 1883-1958 *BioIn 4*
Huber, Theresa 1764-1829 *OxGer*
Huberman, Leo 1903-1968 *AmRP, BioIn 8,*
ConAu 1R
Hubert, Philip Gengembre 1852-1925 *DcNAA,*
OhA&B
Hubin, Allen J 1936- *ConAu 33, EncMys*
Hubler, Richard Gibson 1912- *AmAu&B,*
AmNov, BioIn 2, ConAu 3R, DrAS 74E,
WrDr 1976
Hubley, John *BioIn 6*
Hubley, Ralph I *NF*
Huck, Winifred Mason 1882-1936 *NF*
Huck, Wolfgang 1889-1967 *BioIn 7, BioIn 8*
Huckfield, Leland *HisAmM XR*
Huckle, Arthur Wycliffe 1887- *WhJnl 1928*
Huddleson, Mary 1889-1966 *BioIn 7*
Huddleston, Sisley 1883-1952 *BioIn 3, NewC,*
WebBD, WhoLA
Huddy, John *NF*
Hudelson, R Dale *NF*
Hudes, Taddeusz d1976 *NF*
Hudgins, Edwin P 1941?- *NF*
Hudnutt, Arthur C 1886- *WhJnl 1928*
Hudson, Brazillai *AmJnl*
Hudson, Charles 1795-1881 *Alli Sup, AmAu,*
AmAu&B, CyAL 2, DcAmA, DcAmB 9,
DcNAA
Hudson, Daniel Eldred 1849-1934 *DcAmB S1*
Hudson, Derek 1911- *Au&Wr, ConAu 9R,*
WrDr 1976
Hudson, Frederic 1819-1875 *Alli Sup, AmJnl,*
BiD&SB, CyAL 2, DcAmA, DcAmB S1,
DcNAA, FamWC, LiJA, NatCAB 11
Hudson, Harvey P *NF*
Hudson, Henry Norman 1814-1886 *Alli, Alli Sup,*
AmAu, AmAu&B, BbD, BiD&SB, CyAL 2,
DcAmA, DcNAA, HisAmM XR, REnAL,
WebBD
Hudson, Howard Penn *OvPC, WhoCon 1973,*
WhoPubR 1972
Hudson, J H *NF*
Hudson, James Fairchild 1846-1915 *Alli Sup,*
DcAmA, DcNAA, OhA&B
Hudson, Joseph Kennedy 1840-1907 *AmJnl,*
DcNAA, NatCAB 1
Hudson, Lionel *RpN*
Hudson, Richard 1925- *ConAu 65*
Hudson, Richard F 1884?-1965 *BioIn 4, BioIn 5,*
BioIn 6, BioIn 7
Hudson, Robert Littleton 1925- *WhoAm 1974*
Hudson, Roy *NF*
Hudson, Samuel Eddy 1870-1941 *WhJnl 1928*
Hudson, Thomas Jay 1834-1903 *DcNAA*
Hudson, William Cadwalader 1843-1915

AmAu&B, DcNAA
Hudson, William W *HisAmM XR*
Huebner, George J 1885-1956 *NatCAB 45*
Huebner, Louise *BioIn 8*
Hueffer, Francis 1845-1889 *NF*
Huergo, Maria Constanza *OvPC*
Hueston, H M *NF*
Hueffer, Francis 1845-1889 *Alli Sup, WebBD*
Huet, Coenraad Busken 1826-1886 *BioIn 1, BioIn 7*
Huet, Henri *NF*
Huff, Charles H 1888?-1959 *BioIn 5*
Huff, Darrell 1913- *ConAu 3R*
Huff, George F 1872- *WhJnl 1928*
Huff, Jacob K 1851-1910 *DcNAA*
Huff, Larry 1898- *WhJnl 1928*
Huffman, Phyllis 1937- *NF*
Hugenberg, Alfred 1865-1951 *OxGer, WebBD*
Huggett, Frank Edward 1924- *Au&Wr, ConAu 9R, WrDr 1976*
Huggins, Eddie Lou Thompson 1935- *WhoAm 1974, WhoAmW 1974*
Huggins, Edith *BlkC*
Hughes, Agnes Lockhart *AmAu&B*
Hughes, Alice d1977 *NF*
Hughes, Allen 1921- *WhoAm 1974*
Hughes, Ann H *NF*
Hughes, Blake 1914- *WhoAm 1974, WhoE 1974*
Hughes, Carolyn Bell *NF*
Hughes, Charles Frank 1891-1951 *BioIn 2, BioIn 4, NatCAB 41*
Hughes, Edward Hunter 1921- *WhoAm 1974*
Hughes, Edward P 1893-1948 *BioIn 1*
Hughes, Edward R *WhJnl 1928*
Hughes, Elinor Lambert 1906- *AmAu&B, WhoAm 1974, WhoAmW 1974*
Hughes, Emmet John 1920- *AmAu&B, BioIn 1, BioIn 3, BioIn 5, BioIn 6, BioIn 7, BioIn 8, ConAu 69, CurBio XR, Who 1974, WhoAm 1974, WhoWor 1974*
Hughes, Fred 1915- *WhoAm 1974*
Hughes, George *NF*
Hughes, George T *NF*
Hughes, Griffith R *NF*
Hughes, Hugh *WhJnl 1928*
Hughes, Hugh Price 1847-1902 *WebBD*
Hughes, James Perley 1883- *WhJnl 1928*
Hughes, Jeremiah *HisAmM XR*
Hughes, John 1930- *ConAu 1R, OvPC, RpN, Who 1974, WhoE 1974*
Hughes, John *see also* Hughes, R John
Hughes, John *see also* Hughes, Robert John
Hughes, John Stoddard 1894- *WhNAA, WhJnl 1928*
Hughes, John W *HisAmM XR*
Hughes, Justine M *NF*
Hughes, Kenneth 1899- *WhJnl Sup*
Hughes, Lawrence 1925- *WhoAm 1974*
Hughes, Lillian *NF*
Hughes, Llewellyn *HisAmM XR*
Hughes, Paul J d1955 *RpN*
Hughes, Peter F 1889- *WhJnl 1928*
Hughes, R John 1930- *WrDr 1976*
Hughes, R John *see also* Hughes, John
Hughes, R John *see also* Hughes, Robert John
Hughes, Red 1888- *WhJnl 1928*
Hughes, Richard Michael 1943- *WhoAm 1974*
Hughes, Robert John 1930- *Who 1974, WhoWor 1974*
Hughes, Robert John *see also* Hughes, John
Hughes, Robert John *see also* Hughes, R John
Hughes, Robert William 1821-1901 *Alli Sup, AmAu, BiDSA, DcAmA, DcNAA, NatCAB 7*

Hughes, Samuel Thomas 1868-1948 *BioIn 1, WhJnl 1928*
Hughes, Stephen Ormsby 1924- *ConAu 61*
Hughes, Terry A 1933- *ConAu 65*
Hughes, Thomas 1854-1934 *DcNAA*
Hughes, Waller E 1878- *WhJnl 1928*
Hughes, Walter I 1891- *WhJnl 1928*
Huglin, Henry 1915- *NF*
Hugo, Charles Victor 1826-1871 *OxFr, WebBD*
Hugo, Francois Victor 1828-1873 *WebBD*
Huhn, Heinrich 1830- *BioIn 2*
Huie, William Bradford 1910- *AmAu&B, Au&Wr, AuNews 1, BioIn 4, BioIn 6, BioIn 8, BioNews 1974, ConAu 11R, ConNov 1972, ConNov 1976, HisAmM XR, REnAL, TwCA Sup, WhoAm 1974, WhoS&SW 1973, WhoWor 1974, WrDr 1976*
Hulbert, William Davenport 1868-1913 *DcNAA, HisAmM XR*
Hulburd, David 1904-1960 *BioIn 5*
Hulen, Bertram Dyer 1889-1949 *BioIn 2*
Huling, Caroline Alden 1857-1941 *DcNAA, HisAmM XR, WhNAA*
Hull, George C 1896- *BioIn 2*
Hull, Harwood 1884?-1950 *BioIn 2*
Hull, Moses 1835- *Alli Sup, DcNAA, HisAmM XR*
Hull, O E 1866- *WhJnl 1928*
Hull, Peggy *AmJnl*
Hull, William Henry 1918- *WhoAm 1974*
Hulse, Chris *NF*
Hulse, Jerry *NF*
Hulteng, John Linne 1921- *BioIn 2, ConAu 33, DrAS 74E, RpN, WhoAm 1974*
Hultgrenn, Elmer Frederick 1876-1951 *BioIn 4, NatCAB 41*
Hulton, Edward d1904 *AmJnl, WebBD*
Hulton, Sir Edward 1870-1925 *NewC, WebBD*
Hulton, Sir Edward George Warris 1906- *Au&Wr, IntWW 1976, NewC, Who 1974, WhoWor 1974*
Hulugalle, Herbert 1899- *IntWW 1976, WhoWor 1974*
Human, Alfred E 1893-1962 *BioIn 6*
Humbaraci, D Arslan 1923- *ConAu 49*
Humber, Jack Ernest 1918- *WhoPubR 1972*
Humberg, William M *NF*
Humble, Margaret *HisAmM XR*
Hume, Brit *InvJ, NewMr*
Hume, Donald *ForP*
Hume, John E N, Jr. 1915- *WhoAm 1974*
Hume, Paul Chandler 1915- *WhoAm 1974, WhoS&SW 1973*
Hume, Rita 1917?-1953 *BioIn 3*
Hume, Robert *HisAmM XR*
Humes, Gregory T 1878-1913 *NF*
Humes, H L 1926- *AmAu&B, ConAu 7R, OxAm*
Hummel, James H *HisAmM XR*
Humpheys, Harry *NF*
Humphrey, Ada Abbott 1875?- *WhNAA, WhJnl 1928*
Humphrey, Bruce 1935- *NF*
Humphrey, Edward Porter 1809-1887 *Alli Sup, DcAmA, DcNAA, HisAmM XR*
Humphrey, F Thomas 1897?- *BioIn 2*
Humphrey, Frances A *Alli Sup, DcNAA, HisAmM XR*
Humphrey, Hal 1912?-1968 *BioIn 8*
Humphrey, Henry 1876?-1951 *BioIn 2*
Humphrey, S D *HisAmM XR*
Humphrey, Sylvia Windle *ForWC 1970, OvPC*
Humphrey, Walter R 1904- *WhJnl 1928*

Humphreys, Arthur Lee 1865-1946 *BioIn 1*
Humphreys, D *NF*
Humphreys, James 1748-1810 *AmAu&B, AmJnl*
Humphreys, Robert Thomas 1905-1965 *BioIn 7*
Humphries, Harrison B *NF*
Humphry, Derek 1930- *ConAu 41*
Humphry, James, III 1916- *WhoAm 1974*
Humphrys, Godfrey C 1894- *WhJnl 1928*
Hunebelle, Danielle 1922- *BioIn 9, BioIn 10,
  WhoWor 1974*
Huneker, James Gibbons 1860-1921 *AmAu&B,
  CnDAL, ConAmL, DcAmA, DcLEL,
  DcNAA, HisAmM XR, LongC, OxAm,
  Pen Am, RAdv 1, REn, REnAL, TwCA,
  TwCA Sup, WebBD*
Hungerford, Cyrus Cotton *BioIn 2, WhoAm 1974*
Hungerford, Herbert 1874- *WhJnl 1928*
Hunn, Max *NF*
Hunnibee, Kate *see* Lyman, Laura Elizabeth Baker
Hunnicutt, James *BioIn 8*
Hunt, Albert R *NF*
Hunt, Bruce A 1895?-1949 *BioIn 2*
Hunt, Diana 1939- *NF*
Hunt, E Howard, Jr. 1918- *AmNov, AuNews 1,
  BioNews 1974, ConAu 45, ConLC 3,
  NewYTBE 4*
Hunt, E Howard, Jr. *see also* Hunt, Everette Howard,
  Jr.
Hunt, Edward Eyre 1885-1953 *WebBD*
Hunt, Everette Howard, Jr. 1918- *AmAu&B,
  WhoAm 1974*
Hunt, Everette Howard, Jr. *see also* Hunt, E Howard,
  Jr.
Hunt, Frazier 1885-1967 *AmAu&B, AmJnl,
  BioIn 8, HisAmM XR, WebBD*
Hunt, Freeman 1804-1858 *Alli, AmAu&B,
  BiD&SB, BioIn 4, DcAmA, DcNAA,
  HisAmM XR*
Hunt, George Pinney 1918- *AuBYP, BioIn 8,
  WhoAm 1974*
Hunt, J Ray 1904- *WhoE 1974*
Hunt, John P 1915- *ConAu 33*
Hunt, L Cullen 1895- *WhJnl 1928*
Hunt, Leigh 1784-1859 *Alli, AtlBL, BiD&SB,
  BrAu 19, CnE&AP, CrtT 2, DcEuL,
  HisAmM XR, NewC, Pen Eng, RAdv 1,
  REn, WebBD, WebE&AL*
Hunt, Morton *BioIn 2*
Hunt, Percival *HisAmM XR*
Hunt, Richard 1921- *ConAu 73*
Hunt, Samuel Valentine *HisAmM XR*
Hunt, Terence *NF*
Hunt, Thomas Barry 1916?-1969 *BioIn 8*
Hunt, Todd T 1938- *ConAu 15R*
Hunt, William Dudley, Jr. 1922- *AmArch 1970,
  ConAu 33, WhoAdv 1972, WhoAm 1974,
  WrDr 1976*
Hunt, William Gibbes 1791-1833 *DcAmB 9,
  HisAmM XR, OxAm, REnAL*
Hunt, William Southworth 1879-1940 *AmAu&B,
  DcNAA, WhJnl 1928*
Hunt, William Taylor 1865- *WhJnl 1928*
Hunter, Charlayne 1942?- *BioIn 8, BioIn 9,
  BlkC*
Hunter, David *NF*
Hunter, Edward 1902-1978 *AmAu&B, AmJnl,
  Au&Wr, ConAu 7R, OvPC, WhoAm 1974,
  WhoS&SW 1973, WhoWor 1974,
  WrDr 1976*
Hunter, Edwin D *WhoS&SW 1973*
Hunter, Francis T 1894- *WhJnl 1928*
Hunter, Frank *NF*
Hunter, George M 1889- *WhJnl 1928*
Hunter, Graham *AmAu&B, WhoAmA 1973*

Hunter, James Boyd 1863-1933 *WhJnl 1928*
Hunter, James V *HisAmM XR*
Hunter, Joshua Rollin 1904-1967 *BioIn 9*
Hunter, Marjorie 1922- *ConAu 69*
Hunter, Noble 1857- *BioIn 2*
Hunter, Robert A 1921-1962 *BioIn 6*
Hunter, Stephen *NF*
Hunter, Thomas Lomax *AmAu&B*
Hunter, W F 1862- *WhJnl 1928*
Hunter, William *AmJnl, HisAmM XR*
Hunter, William Randolph 1843-1886 *DcAmA*
Hunter, William Randolph *see also* Bradford, Joseph
Huntington, Adeline Maidment 1888- *WhJnl 1928*
Huntington, Collis Potter 1821-1900 *AmJnl,
  WebBD*
Huntington, Constant 1876-1962 *NatCAB 50*
Huntington, Emily C *HisAmM XR*
Huntington, F P *HisAmM XR*
Huntington, Frederick Dan 1819-1904
  HisAmM XR, WebBD
Huntington, Richard Thomas 1889-1964 *BioIn 7*
Huntley, Chester Robert 1911-1974 *AuNews 1,
  BioIn 3, BioIn 4, BioIn 5, BioIn 6, BioIn 7,
  BioIn 8, BioIn 9, BioIn 10, ConAu 49,
  CurBio XR, ForP, WhoAm 1974,
  WhoWor 1974*
Huntley, Florence d1912 *DcNAA*
Huntly, Mary Pamela Gordon, Marchioness 1918-
  BioIn 2
Hunton, William Lee 1864-1930 *AmAu&B,
  DcNAA, WhNAA*
Huntoon, Maxwell C, Jr. *NF*
Huntress, Frank Granger 1870-1955 *BioIn 4*
Huntsman, Robert F R 1868-1945 *WhJnl 1928*
Hupe-Wallace, Philip A 1911- *NF*
Hurban, Vladimir S 1883-1949 *WebBD*
Hurban Vajansky, Svetozar 1847-1916 *CIDMEL,
  EuAu, WebBD*
Hurd, Sir Archibald 1869-1959 *NewC, WebBD*
Hurd, Carlos F 1876?-1950 *BioIn 2*
Hurd, Charles 1903-1968 *AmAu&B, BioIn 1,
  ConAu P-1*
Hurd, Charles Edwin 1833-1910 *DcNAA*
Hurd, Charles W B 1903-1968 *BioIn 8*
Hurd, G Lansing 1877- *WhJnl 1928*
Hurd, Sir Percy Angier 1864-1950 *NewC, WebBD,
  WhoLA*
Hurja, Emil *HisAmM XR*
Hurlbert, William Henry 1827-1895 *AmAu,
  AmAu&B, AmJnl, BbD, DcAmB 9,
  DcNAA, HisAmM XR, NatCAB 5*
Hurlbert, William Henry *see also* Hurlbut, William
  Henry
Hurlburt, Allen Freeman 1910- *WhoAm 1974*
Hurlbut, George C *HisAmM XR*
Hurlbut, J E *HisAmM XR*
Hurlbut, James W 1909?-1967 *BioIn 7*
Hurlbut, Jesse Lyman 1843-1930 *Alli Sup,
  DcAmA, DcNAA, HisAmM XR, TwCA*
Hurlbut, William Henry 1827-1895 *Alli, Alli Sup,
  BiDSA, DcNAA*
Hurlbut, William Henry *see also* Hurlbert, William
  Henry
Hurleigh, Robert Francis 1912- *WhoAm 1974*
Hurley, Curtis B 1896- *WhJnl 1928*
Hurley, Doran 1900-1964 *BioIn 1, BkC 2,
  CathA 1930, ConAu 5*
Hurley, Dunlea 1909?-1973 *BioIn 10*
Hurley, James Franklin 1870- *WhJnl 1928*
Hurley, James Franklin, III 1931-
  WhoS&SW 1973
Hurley, James Franklin, Jr. 1896- *WhJnl 1928*
Hurley, John R *OvPC*
Hurley, Lawrence Francis 1897-1953 *BioIn 3*

Hurly, Curtis Brown 1896- *WhJnl 1928*
Hursh, Justus Harold 1893- *WhJnl 1928*
Hurst, Hoyt *OvPC*
Hurst, Jack *NF*
Hurst, Russell E *NF*
Hurst, Vida *HisAmM XR*
Hurt, John Jeter, Jr. 1909- *WhoAm 1974*
Hurt, Walter S *HisAmM XR*
Hurwitz, Abraham 1888-1949 *BioIn 2*
Hurwitz, Henry 1886-1961 *BioIn 6*
Hurwitz, Hyman 1909?-1966 *BioIn 7*
Hurwitz, Maximilian 1887-1963 *BioIn 6*
Husar, John 1937- *NF*
Husband, Harold 1905- *CanWW 1972*
Husbands, Winifred d1960 *BioIn 5*
Huse, Charles Wells 1905- *WhoAm 1974*
Hu Shih 1891-1962 *WebBD*
Husing, Ted 1901-1962 *CurBio XR*
Husock, Howard *NewMr*
Huss, Pierre John 1906?-1966 *AmJnl, BioIn 7*
Hussain, Altaf 1900-1968 *BioIn 8*
Hussey, H Wadsworth 1926- *WhJnl 1928*
Hussey, L M *HisAmM XR*
Husslein, Joseph Casper 1873-1952 *AmAu&B,*
   BioIn 1, BioIn 3, BkC 1, CathA 1930,
   WhNAA
Hussman, Walter E 1906- *OvPC, WhoF&I 1974,*
   WhoS&SW 1973
Husted, Walter 1906- *WhoAm 1974,*
   WhoS&SW 1973
Huston, James 1820-1854 *BbtC, DcNAA, OxCan*
Huston, L D *HisAmM XR*
Huston, Luther Allison 1888- *ConAu 21,*
   WhoAm 1974, WhoS&SW 1973
Huston, Margo *NF*
Huston, McCready 1891- *AmAu&B, WhNAA,*
   WhJnl 1928
Huszar, Karoly 1882- *WebBD*
Hutchens, John Kennedy 1905- *AmAu&B,*
   ConAu 65, WhoAm 1974, WhoPNW
Hutchens, Marjorie 1924-1972 *BioIn 9*
Hutchens, Martin J *NF*
Hutcheson, James H *NF*
Hutchings, Harold Emerson 1907- *WhoAm 1974*
Hutchings, James H *HisAmM XR*
Hutchings, Richard B *HisAmM XR*
Hutchins, Stilson 1838-1912 *AmJnl, BioIn 7,*
   DcNAA
Hutchinson, Arthur Stuart Menteth 1879-1971
   Au&Wr, ConAu 29, CyWA, DcBiA,
   DcLEL, EvLB, HisAmM XR, LongC, REn,
   TwCA, TwCA Sup, TwCW, WebBD
Hutchinson, Ellen Mackay 1851- *Alli Sup, BbD,*
   BiD&SB, DcAmA, DcNAA
Hutchinson, H Lester 1904- *ConAu 17R*
Hutchinson, John *NF*
Hutchinson, Nellie *NF*
Hutchinson, Paul 1890-1956 *AmAu&B, BioIn 1,*
   BioIn 2, BioIn 4, BioIn 5, CurBio XR,
   HisAmM XR, WhNAA
Hutchinson, William K 1896-1958 *BioIn 2,*
   BioIn 4
Hutchinson, Woods 1862-1930 *DcNAA,*
   HisAmM XR, WebBD
Hutchison, Bruce 1901- *BioIn 1, BioIn 4,*
   CanWr, CasWL, CurBio XR, LongC,
   OxCan, OxCan Sup, Who 1974,
   WhoAm 1974
Hutchison, Bruce *see also* Hutchison, William Bruce
Hutchison, G Scott *NF*
Hutchison, Harold Burton 1895- *WhJnl 1928*
Hutchison, Percy Adams 1875-1952 *BioIn 2*
Hutchison, Walter D 1875- *WhJnl 1928*
Hutchison, William Bruce 1901- *CanNov,*

CanWW 1972
Hutchison, William Bruce *see also* Hutchison, Bruce
Huth, Arno *NF*
Huth, Donald Earl 1915- *WhoAm 1974*
Hutin, Marcel 1869-1950 *BioIn 2*
Hutnyan, Joseph D *NF*
Huttner, Johann Christian 1766-1847 *BioIn 2*
Huttner, Matthew 1915- *OvPC, WhoWorJ 1972*
Hutto, James Cecil 1906- *WhoAm 1974*
Hutton, Bellah 1896- *WhJnl Sup*
Hutton, J Bernard 1911- *ConAu 21R,*
   WrDr 1976
Hutton, John Alexander 1868-1947 *BioIn 2*
Hutton, Laurence 1843-1904 *Alli Sup, AmAu,*
   AmAu&B, BbD, BiD&SB, DcAmA,
   DcNAA, HisAmM XR, OxAm, REnAL,
   WebBD
Hutton, Richard Holt 1826-1897 *Alli Sup,*
   BiD&SB, BioIn 2, BioIn 6, BrAu 19,
   CasWL, DcEnL, DcLEL, EvLB, NewC,
   OxEng, WebBD
Hutton, Robert Egleston 1899- *WhJnl 1928*
Huure, Irene *ForP*
Huxley, Florence A 1882?-1955 *BioIn 3, BioIn 4*
Huxley, Leonard 1860-1933 *BioIn 2, NewC,*
   WebBD
Huxtable, Ada Louise 1921?- *CelR 1973,*
   CurBio XR, WhoAm 1974, WhoAmA 1973,
   WhoAmW 1974, WhoE 1974
Huyghe, Rene Louis 1906- *IntWW 1976,*
   WhoAm 1974, WhoWor 1974
Huyler, Jean Wiley 1935- *ConAu 69*
Huynh, Vo *NF*
Hvistendahl, Else *NF*
Hwang, Kyong-Choon *NF*
Hy, Cheng-Tse 1877?-1949 *BioIn 1*
Hyams, Edward 1910-1975 *Au&Wr, ConAu 5R,*
   ConAu 61, LongC, TwCW, Who 1974,
   WorAu, WrDr 1976
Hyams, Joe 1923- *AmAu&B, BioIn 4,*
   ConAu 17R, WhoAm 1974, WrDr 1976
Hyatt, Alpheus 1838-1902 *Alli Sup, BiD&SB,*
   DcAmA, DcNAA, WebBD
Hyatt, Jack 1894- *WhJnl 1928*
Hyatt, James C *NF*
Hyde, Douglas Arnold 1911- *BioIn 1, BioIn 2,*
   BioIn 3
Hyde, Edward Everett *HisAmM XR*
Hyde, Fillmore 1896?-1970 *BioIn 8*
Hyde, Florence Slown 1885- *WhJnl 1928*
Hyde, George Merriam 1865-1899 *HisAmM XR*
Hyde, Grant Milnor 1889-1972 *AmAu&B,*
   BioIn 5, WhNAA, WhJnl 1928
Hyde, Henry Morrow 1866-1951 *AmAu&B,*
   BioIn 2
Hyde, James Clarence *HisAmM XR*
Hyde, John *HisAmM XR*
Hyde, Mary Kendall 1858-1940 *DcNAA*
Hyde, Phoebe 1918?-1967 *BioIn 8*
Hyde, William *HisAmM XR*
Hyde, William Henry 1858-1943 *HisAmM XR*
Hyer, George 1819-1872 *BioIn 5*
Hyer, Marjorie *NF*
Hyland, Richard Francis *BioIn 1*
Hyman, Dick 1904- *ConAu 19, OvPC*
Hyman, Margaret *NF*
Hyman, Max Robinson 1859-1927 *BioIn 2,*
   IndAu 1816
Hyman, Moses *NF*
Hyman, Ralph Alan 1928- *WhoAm 1974*
Hyman, Stanley Edgar 1919-1970 *AmAu&B,*
   ConAu 25, NewYTBE 1, Pen Am, RAdv 1,
   WorAu
Hyman, Stella *BioIn 3*

Hymes, Val *NF*
Hymoff, Edward 1924- *ConAu 17R, OvPC*
Hyndman, Robert Utley 1906-1973 *BioIn 9*
Hynes, Louis *NF*
Hyon, So-Whan *NF*
Hype, Igoe *see* Igoe, Herbert A
Hyypia, Jorma 1918- *NF*

I

Iams, Jack 1910- *AmAu&B, AmNov, EncMys*
Ianuzzi, Ralph J *OvPC*
Ibsen, Sigurd 1859-1930 *WebBD*
Ichinose, Yukio *RpN*
Ickes, Harold LeClair 1874-1952 *AmAu&B,*
  CurBio XR, DcAmB S5, REnAL, WebBD
Idank, Joseph Anthony 1904- *WhNAA,*
  WhJnl 1928
Idar, Eduardo *NF*
Iddings, Lewis M 1850-1921 *NatCAB 29*
Iden, V Gilmore 1885- *WhJnl 1928*
Idol, Anna L *NF*
Ierardi, Francis B 1886-1970 *BioIn 9,*
  NewYTBE 1
Ifft, George Nicholas, II 1892- *WhJnl 1928*
Iger, Jerry *NF*
Iger, S M *NF*
Igglesden, Sir Charles 1861-1949 *BioIn 2*
Iglesias, Antonio *BioIn 3*
Iglesias, Pablo 1850-1925 *WebBD*
Ignotus, Paul 1901- *Au&Wr, ConAu 7R,*
  WrDr 1976
Igoe, Herbert A 1885-1945 *CurBio XR,*
  WhJnl 1928
Ihle, Leo J 1900-1956 *BioIn 7, NatCAB 47*
Ikenberry, Kenneth *NF*
Iker, Sam *NF*
Iliffe, Edward Mauger Iliffe, Baron 1877-1960
  BioIn 5
Illig, Joyce d1976 *NF*
Illingworth, Leslie *ForP*
Illingworth, Neil 1934- *Au&Wr, ConAu 15R*
Ilsen, Martin 1862-1946 *BioIn 1*
Ilsley, Charles Parker 1807-1887 *Alli, AmAu&B,*
  BiD&SB, DcAmA, DcNAA, HisAmM XR,
  HsB&A
Ilsley, Henry R 1873-1948 *BioIn 1*
Ilyichev, Leonid Fyodorovich 1906- *IntWW 1976,*
  WhoWor 1974
Imes, Birney 1889-1947 *WhNAA, WhJnl 1928*
Imrie, John M *NF*
Inarra, Paul 1898?-1948 *BioIn 1*
Inazawa, Kazuo *NF*
Indelman-Yinnon, Moshe 1895?-1977 *ConAu 73*
Ingalls, Claude Eugene 1877-1950 *BioIn 4,*
  NatCAB 41, WhNAA, WhJnl 1928
Ingalls, John James 1833-1900 *AmAu&B,*
  DcNAA, HisAmM XR, WebBD
Ingalls, Leonard *AuBYP, BioIn 8*
Ingersoll, Chalmers 1838-1908 *BioIn 4, BioIn 5,*
  NatCAB 39
Ingersoll, E P *HisAmM XR*
Ingersoll, Ernest 1852-1946 *Alli Sup, AmAu&B,*
  AmLY, BbD, BiD&SB, CarSB, DcAmA,
  DcNAA, HisAmM XR, REnAL, WebBD,
  WhNAA

Ingersoll, Jared 1722-1781 *Alli, CyAL 1, WebBD*
Ingersoll, John H 1925- *ConAu 73*
Ingersoll, John N 1817-1881 *BioIn 1*
Ingersoll, Ralph McAllister 1900- *AmAu&B,*
  AmJnl, Au&Wr, BioIn 1, BioIn 4, BioIn 5,
  BioIn 6, ConAu 13, ConAu P-1,
  CurBio XR, IntWW 1976, REnAL,
  TwCA Sup, WhNAA, Who 1974,
  WhoAm 1974, WhoE 1974
Ingersoll, Robert 1933- *NF*
Ingersoll, Vera Nelson d1953 *BioIn 3*
Ingerson, Carl I *HisAmM XR*
Ingham, Curtis *NF*
Ingham, Harvey 1858-1949 *AmJnl, BioIn 2*
Ingham, Irena 1900- *BioIn 1*
Ingle, Bob *NF*
Ingle, Edward 1861-1924 *Alli Sup, BiDSA,*
  DcAmA, DcNAA, LiJA
Ingling, Dorothy Radcliffe *OvPC*
Inglis, Brian 1916- *ConAu 19R, Who 1974*
Inglis, William d1902 *NF*
Inglis, William 1872-1949 *BioIn 2, DcNAA,*
  HisAmM XR
Inglis, William O 1862?-1949 *NF*
Ingraham, Herbert R 1906?-1968 *BioIn 8*
Ingram, Sir Bruce Stirling 1877-1963 *BioIn 2,*
  BioIn 4, BioIn 5, BioIn 6
Ingram, Derek 1925- *ConAu 9R*
Ingram, Herbert *FamWC, ForP*
Ingram, Jim *NF*
Ingrim, Ward D 1910- *WhoAm 1974*
Inkeles, Alex 1920- *AmM&W 73S, ConAu 1,*
  ForP, LEduc 1974, WhoAm 1974,
  WhoWor 1974
Inlander, Maxine *NF*
Inman, Harry A 1896- *WhJnl 1928*
Inman, Henry 1837-1899 *AmAu, AmAu&B,*
  CnDAL, DcAmA, DcNAA, HisAmM XR,
  OxAm, REnAL
Inman, John 1805-1850 *CyAL 2, DcAmB 9,*
  HisAmM XR, NatCAB 9
Inman, Julia *NF*
Inman, Thomas *NF*
Innerst, Preston *NF*
Innes, Guy *NF*
Innes, James 1833- *NF*
Inouye, Ken 1929?-1950 *AmJnl, BioIn 2*
Inskip, Leonard *NF*
Insolia, Anthony Edward 1926- *WhoE 1974*
Interlandi, Frank *NF*
Interlandi, Phil *NF*
Inukai, Ki Tsuyoshi 1855-1932 *WebBD*
Inzuna, Jorge *ForP*
Ipekci, Abdi 1929- *IntWW 1976*
Ireland, Alexander 1810-1894 *Alli Sup*
Ireland, Alleyne 1871-1951 *AmLY, BiD&SB,*

BioIn 2, DcAmA
Ireland, George Thomas 1866?-1963 *BioIn 6*
Ireland, William 1880-1935 *BioIn 2, BioIn 3*
Iremonger, Frederic Athelwold 1878-1952 *BioIn 3*
Irish, John Powell 1843-1923 *NatCAB 12*
Irish, W E 1890- *WhJnl 1928*
Ironson, Jack *NF*
Irvin, Bede d1944 *AmJnl*
Irvin, George Bede *see* Irvin, Bede
Irvin, Rea 1881-1972 *BioIn 9, NewYTBE 3,
WhoAmA 1973*
Irvin, Robert W *BioIn 9*
Irvine, Benjamin Franklin d1940 *WhNAA,
WhJnl 1928*
Irvine, E Eastman 1883?-1948 *BioIn 1*
Irvine, F Eugene *HisAmM XR*
Irvine, Reed J 1922- *NewMr*
Irvine, Ward 1895- *WhJnl 1928*
Irving, Arthur P 1893- *WhJnl 1928*
Irving, Helen *FemPA, HisAmM XR*
Irving, Howard *HisAmM XR*
Irving, Jay 1900?-1970 *BioIn 8*
Irving, Mary *HisAmM XR*
Irving, Washington 1783-1859 *Alli, AmAu,
AmAu&B, AmWr, AtlBL, BbD, BiD&SB,
CarSB, CasWL, CnDAL, CrtT 3, CyAL 1,
CyWA, DcAmA, DcBiA, DcEnA, DcEnL,
DcLEL, DcNAA, DcSpL, EncAB, EvLB,
HisAmM XR, LiJA, MouLC 3, OxAm,
OxCan, OxEng, Pen Am, RAdv 1, REn,
REnAL, WebBD, WebE&AL, WhoChL,
WisWr*
Irving, Wilbur *BioIn 3*
Irving, William 1766-1821 *Alli, AmAu, BiD&SB,
CyAL 1, DcAmA, HisAmM XR, OxAm,
REnAL, WebBD*
Irwin, Don *NF*
Irwin, Frank Newton, Jr. 1902- *WhJnl 1928*
Irwin, Inez Haynes 1873-1970 *AmAu&B, CarSB,
REnAL, TwCA, TwCA Sup, WhNAA*
Irwin, James P *HisAmM XR*
Irwin, James Wesley 1902- *WhoAm 1974,
WhJnl Sup, WhoPubR 1972*
Irwin, Richard B *HisAmM XR*
Irwin, Theodore 1907- *AmAu&B, ConAu 65,
WhoAm 1974*
Irwin, W Arthur 1898- *WhoAm 1974*
Irwin, Wallace Admah 1875-1959 *AmAu&B,
CnDAL, ConAmL, DcAmA, HisAmM XR,
OxAm, REn, REnAL, Str&VC, TwCA,
TwCA Sup, WebBD*
Irwin, Will 1873-1948 *AmAu&B, AmJnl,
EncMys, OxAm, REnAL, WebBD, WhNAA*
Irwin, Will *see also* Irwin, William Henry
Irwin, William Arthur 1898- *CanWW 1972,
IntWW 1976*
Irwin, William Henry 1873-1948 *AmAu&B,
BioIn 1, BioIn 2, BioIn 4, DcAmB S4,
DcNAA, HisAmM XR, NatCAB 35, TwCA,
TwCA Sup*
Irwin, William Henry *see also* Irwin, Will
Isaacs, Abram Samuel 1851-1920 *Alli Sup,
AmLY, DcAmA, HisAmM XR, WebBD*
Isaacs, Arnold R *NF*
Isaacs, Asher 1902-1963 *AmAu&B*
Isaacs, Benno *NF*
Isaacs, Edith Juliet Rich 1878-1956 *AmAu&B,
BioIn 4, REnAL, WhNAA*
Isaacs, Harold Robert 1910- *AmAu&B,
AmM&W 73S, AmRP, ConAu 3R,
WhoAm 1974, WhoWor 1974,
WhoWorJ 1972*
Isaacs, Norman Ellis 1908- *WhoAm 1974*
Isaacs, Samuel Myer 1804-1878 *DcAmB 9,*

HisAmM XR, WebBD
Isaacs, Stephen D 1937- *NF*
Isaacson, Charles David 1891-1936 *DcNAA,
WhNAA*
Isakovsky, Mikhail Vasilyevich 1900-1973 *CasWL,
ConAu 41, NewYTBE 4*
Isbell, Florence B *NF*
Isbell, Tom *NF*
Iselin, John Jay 1933- *WhoAm 1974*
Isham, Frederic Stewart 1866-1922 *Alli Sup,
AmAu&B, DcAmA, DcNAA*
Ishibashi, Tanzan 1884-1973 *CurBio XR,
NewYTBE 4*
Ishihara, Hiroshi *RpN*
Ishikawa, Sam *OvPC*
Ishimaru, Kazuto *NF*
Israel, David *NF*
Israel, Elaine 1945- *ConAu 53*
Israel, Larry Herbert 1919- *WhoAm 1974,
WhoF&I 1974, WhoS&SW 1973*
Israel, Leon 1887-1955 *BioIn 3*
Israels, Josef 1906-1954 *BioIn 3*
Iswolsky, Helene 1896-1975 *ConAu 7R*
Itevesi, Ludwig 1843-1910 *NF*
Ittleson, Al *NF*
Ivers, James D 1909?-1964 *BioIn 6*
Iversen, Olaf 1902-1959 *BioIn 5*
Iverson, Caroline *BioIn 1*
Iverson, Genie 1942- *ConAu 65*
Ives, Charles Pomeroy, II 1903- *WhoAm 1974,
WhoE 1974*
Ives, Frederick Eugene 1856-1937 *AmJnl,
HisAmM XR, WebBD*
Ives, Vernon *BioIn 1*
Ivey, Alfred G *RpN*
Ivey, James Burnett 1925- *WhoAm 1974,
WhoAmA 1973, WhoWor 1974*
Ivin, Daniel *ForP*
Ivins, Haddon 1886- *WhJnl 1928*
Ivins, Molly *NewMr*
Ivry, Isaac *NF*
Iwama, Frank *NF*
Iwamoto, Hiroshi *NF*
Iwanaga, Yakichi *NF*
Iwaszkiewicz, Jaroslaw 1894- *CasWL, CIDMEL,
CnMD, EncWL, IntWW 1976, ModSL 2,
ModWD, Pen Eur, WhoWor 1974*
Izard, Ralph *NF*
Izban, Samuel 1905- *ConAu 49*
Izurieta Obando, Gustavo 1914?-1978 *NF*
Izzard, Wesley Sherman 1900- *WhoAm 1974,
WhoS&SW 1973*

J

J A *see* Alden, John
J P M *see* Wheeler, Andrew Carpenter
Jabavu, Noni 1919?- *BioIn 6*
Jablonski, Wanda Mary *WhoAm 1974, WhoAmW 1974*
Jabotinsky, Vladimir 1880-1940 *WebBD*
Jabri, Marwan *OvPC*
Jaccaci, Auguste *HisAmM XR*
Jackman, Arthur E *NF*
Jackman, Florence *NF*
Jackman, Francis P *NF*
Jacks, Allan *NF*
Jackson, A L *WhJnl 1928*
Jackson, Alan R *HisAmM XR*
Jackson, Albert 1904- *WhJnl 1928*
Jackson, Alfred Graham 1892?-1965 *BioIn 7*
Jackson, Allan 1905?-1976 *ConAu 65*
Jackson, Brooks *InvJ, NewMr*
Jackson, C D 1902-1964 *BiE&WWA, CurBio XR*
Jackson, C D *see also* Jackson, Charles D
Jackson, Carol 1911- *BioIn 3, CathA 1952*
Jackson, Charles D 1902-1964 *NatCAB 51*
Jackson, Charles D *see also* Jackson, C D
Jackson, Charles Samuel 1860-1924 *BioIn 1, NatCAB 33*
Jackson, Charles Tenney 1874- *AmAu&B, AmLY, HisAmM XR, WhNAA, WisWr*
Jackson, D Brooks *NF*
Jackson, David K *LiJA*
Jackson, David L 1941?- *BlkC*
Jackson, Donald Dale 1935- *ConAu 49*
Jackson, Dorothy St. John *NF*
Jackson, Eddie *NF*
Jackson, Edward 1856-1942 *DcNAA, HisAmM XR*
Jackson, Elmer Martin, Jr. 1906- *WhNAA, WhoAm 1974, WhoE 1974, WhoF&I 1974, WhJnl 1928*
Jackson, Francis 1789-1861 *Alli Sup, HisAmM XR*
Jackson, Gardner 1897-1965 *BioIn 7*
Jackson, George R *HisAmM XR*
Jackson, Gerald V 1926?- *BlkC*
Jackson, Harold Charles LeBaron 1894-1954 *BioIn 3*
Jackson, Herbert G, Jr. 1928- *ConAu 37, WrDr 1976*
Jackson, Herbert M 1878- *WhJnl 1928*
Jackson, Holbrook 1874-1948 *DcLEL, EvLB, LongC, NewC, REn, TwCA, TwCA Sup, WebBD*
Jackson, James O 1940?- *NF*
Jackson, John Day 1868-1961 *BioIn 5, BioIn 7, WhJnl 1928*
Jackson, John P *FamWC*
Jackson, Joseph 1867-1946 *AmAu&B, DcNAA, WhNAA*
Jackson, Joseph D *NF*
Jackson, Joseph Henry 1894-1955 *AmAu&B, BioIn 1, BioIn 3, BioIn 4, DcAmB S5, HisAmM XR, REnAL, TwCA, TwCA Sup, WhNAA*
Jackson, Katherine Gauss 1904-1975 *ConAu 57, ForWC 1970, WhoAm 1974, WhoAmW 1974, WhoE 1974*
Jackson, Lionel Stewart 1915- *WhoAm 1974*
Jackson, Maria Foster 1862-1956 *BioIn 4*
Jackson, Methro *HisAmM XR*
Jackson, Michael *NF*
Jackson, Philip Ludwell 1893-1953 *BioIn 5, NatCAB 42, WhJnl 1928*
Jackson, Richard Seymour 1910- *WhoAm 1974, WhoE 1974, WhoF&I 1974*
Jackson, Robert 1911- *Au&Wr, ConAu 9R*
Jackson, Robert Hill 1934- *WhoAm 1974*
Jackson, Robert L 1935- *ConAu 73, InvJ*
Jackson, Samuel 1910- *BioIn 9*
Jackson, Sheldon 1834-1909 *Alli Sup, BiD&SB, DcAmA, DcNAA, HisAmM XR*
Jackson, Solomon Henry 1787-1837 *BioIn 8*
Jackson, Stuart 1943?- *BioIn 2, BioIn 3*
Jackson, William Spencer 1934- *OvPC, WhoE 1974*
Jackson, Wilma 1931- *ConAu 73*
Jacob, Alaric 1909- *Au&Wr, BioIn 2, ConAu 7R*
Jacob, Edward Frederick Fulford 1882-1928 *DcNAA*
Jacob, Edward Frederick Fulford *see also* Jacob, Edwin F Fulford
Jacob, Edward Frederick Fulford *see also* Jacob, Fred
Jacob, Edwin Frederick Fulford 1882-1928 *CanNov*
Jacob, Edwin Frederick Fulford *see also* Jacob, Edward F Fulford
Jacob, Edwin Frederick Fulford *see also* Jacob, Fred
Jacob, Fred 1882-1928 *OxCan*
Jacob, Fred *see also* Jacob, Edward Frederick Fulford
Jacob, Fred *see also* Jacob, Edwin Frederick Fulford
Jacobs, Arthur 1922- *ConAu 7R, WhoMus 1972*
Jacobs, Barbara *NF*
Jacobs, Beth *AuBYP, BioIn 8*
Jacobs, Bradford McElderry 1920- *WhoAm 1974, WhoE 1974*
Jacobs, David *BioIn 6*
Jacobs, Flora Gill 1918- *AuBYP, BioIn 8, BioIn 10, ConAu 1R, ForWC 1970, SmATA 5*
Jacobs, Frederic B 1880-1942 *NatCAB 31, WhJnl 1928*
Jacobs, Harold D 1890-1959 *WhJnl 1928*

Jacobs, Harvey 1915- *ConAu 21R, IndAu 1917*
Jacobs, Herbert A 1903- *ConAu 15R*
Jacobs, Howard 1908- *ConAu 65,*
  WhoS&SW 1973
Jacobs, Jane 1916- *AmAu&B, ConAu 21R,*
  WhoAm 1974, WhoAmW 1974,
  WhoWor 1974
Jacobs, Jesse *NF*
Jacobs, Julian S 1887-1972 *BioIn 9*
Jacobs, Lawrence L 1906- *WhJnl 1928*
Jacobs, Mary *OvPC*
Jacobs, Michel 1877-1958 *WhNAA, WhJnl 1928*
Jacobs, Milton D 1881- *WhJnl 1928*
Jacobs, Montague 1913?-1967 *BioIn 7*
Jacobs, Paul 1918-1978 *AmAu&B, BioIn 7,*
  BioIn 9, BioNews 1974, ConAu 13R,
  ConAu 73, NewYTBS 5, WhoAm 1974,
  WhoWest 1974, WhoWor 1974
Jacobs, Samuel 1821-1891 *BioIn 2, IndAu 1816*
Jacobs, William Plummer 1893-1948 *HisAmM XR*
Jacobsen, Berne Selvig 1906- *WhoAm 1974,*
  WhoWest 1974
Jacobsen, Charles 1899- *WhJnl Sup*
Jacobsen, Sybil Victoria *BioIn 7*
Jacobson, Bernard 1936- *WhoAm 1974*
Jacobson, Fred Felix Arnold 1924- *OvPC,*
  WhoE 1974, WhoF&I 1974, WhoPubR 1972
Jacobson, Gershon *NF*
Jacobson, Howard Boone 1925- *ConAu 2R*
Jacobson, Julius 1922- *ConAu 45*
Jacobson, Mark *NF*
Jacobson, Philip *NF*
Jacobson, Robert *NF*
Jacobson, Sydney 1908- *IntWW 1976,*
  Who 1974, WhoWor 1974
Jacobson, Walter *NF*
Jacobus, Melancthon Williams 1816-1876 *Alli,*
  Alli Sup, DcAmA, DcNAA, HisAmM XR
Jacoby, Annalee *NF*
Jacoby, Jim *NF*
Jacoby, Melville 1916-1942 *AmJnl*
Jacoby, Paul E 1897?-1954 *BioIn 3*
Jacoby, Susan *NF*
Jacomo, Antonio 1900-1951 *BioIn 2*
Jacot DeBoinod, Bernard Louis 1898-1977
  ConAu 9
Jacowitz, Jacob *NF*
Jacquemard, Simonne 1924- *IntWW 1976*
Jacquet, Lloyd 1898- *WhJnl 1928*
Jacquin, Edwin N 1899- *WhJnl 1928*
Jacquot, Charles Jean Baptiste *see* Mirecourt,
  Eugene De
Jaeger, Peter *NF*
Jaekel, Frederic Blair 1882-1943 *AmAu&B*
Jaffe, Andrew *NF*
Jaffe, Eddie 1913?- *BioIn 4, BioIn 8*
Jaffe, Jacob H *OvPC*
Jaffe, Louis Isaac 1888-1950 *BioIn 2, BioIn 3*
Jaffe, Phillip J *AmRP*
Jaffe, Sam *NF*
Jaffee, Allan *OvPC*
Jaffray, William Gladstone 1870-1949 *BioIn 2*
Jaffrey, Liz Weissblatt *OvPC*
Jagendorf, Morita *OvPC*
Jaggard, Geoffrey 1902-1970 *ConAu 21*
Jagger, Claude A *NF*
Jahn, Ernst Adalbert 1929- *ConAu 69*
Jahn, Joseph Michael 1943- *ConAu 49*
Jain, Girilal 1922- *Au&Wr, ConAu 11R*
Jain, Shanti Prasad 1912-1977 *IntWW 1974,*
  WhoWor 1974
Jaklitsch, Joseph John, Jr. 1919- *BioIn 8,*
  WhoAm 1974, WhoE 1974, WhoF&I 1974
Jakobson, Max 1923- *IntWW 1976,*

WhoGov 1972, WhoWor 1974
James, Alfred *NF*
James, B *NF*
James, Bernice C *NF*
James, Betty *NF*
James, David Henry 1881- *Au&Wr*
James, Ed *HisAmM XR*
James, Edmund Janes 1855-1925 *Alli Sup,*
  DcAmA, DcNAA, HisAmM XR, WebBD
James, Edwin Hugh 1917- *WhoAdv 1972*
James, Edwin Leland 1890-1951 *AmJnl, BioIn 2,*
  BioIn 3, DcAmB S5
James, Francis 1918- *BioIn 4, BioIn 5, BioIn 9*
James, Frank Lowher 1841-1907 *HisAmM XR*
James, Geoffrey *NF*
James, George Hobson 1886- *WhJnl 1928*
James, George Wharton 1858-1923 *AmAu&B,*
  AmLY, DcAmA, DcNAA, HisAmM XR,
  LiJA, WebBD
James, Gloria *NF*
James, Henry Moore 1885- *WhJnl 1928*
James, Howard *NF*
James, Joe *BioIn 7*
James, Leamon Dewey, Jr. 1932?- *NF*
James, Lee *NF*
James, Lionel 1871-1955 *BioIn 3, FamWC,*
  WhoLA
James, Marquis 1891-1955 *AmAu&B,*
  DcAmB S5, OxAm, REnAL, TwCA,
  TwCA Sup, WebBD, WhNAA
James, Rembert Faulkner 1905- *OvPC,*
  WhoAm 1974
James, Rick *NF*
James, Roy Harrison 1889- *WhJnl 1928*
James, Sidney Lorraine 1906- *WhoAm 1974,*
  WhoS&SW 1973
James, Stanley Bloomfield 1869-1951 *BioIn 1,*
  BioIn 2, CathA 1930
James, Timothy M *NF*
James, U P *HisAmM XR*
James, W H *NF*
James, Walter 1912- *Au&Wr, ConAu 7R,*
  Who 1974
James, Weldon Bernard 1912- *ConAu 1R, RpN*
James, William Grant *HisAmM XR*
James, William H *NF*
James, Winfield Henry 1918- *NewYTBE 3,*
  WhoAdv 1972, WhoAm 1974, WhoE 1974
James, Winifred Lewellin 1876-1941 *BioIn 2*
Jameson, Henry B *NF*
Jameson, John Franklin 1859-1937 *Alli Sup,*
  AmAu&B, DcAmA, DcNAA, HisAmM XR,
  OxAm, REnAL, WebBD
Jameson, Sam *NF*
Jamieson, Bob *NF*
Jamieson, Edward Leo 1929- *WhoAm 1974*
Jamieson, Francis Anthony 1904-1960 *BioIn 5,*
  BioIn 6, NatCAB 43
Jamieson, John 1909- *BioIn 3*
Jamieson, Nina d1932 *DcNAA*
Jamieson, William Darius 1873-1949 *BioIn 2*
Jampel, David M *OvPC*
Jamsa, Matti 1928?- *BioIn 4*
Janensch, Paul *NF*
Janes, Edward C 1908- *AuBYP, BioIn 8*
Janet, Pierre Marie Felix 1859-1947 *WebBD*
Janeway, Eliot 1913- *AmAu&B, CurBio XR,*
  IntWW 1974, WhoAm 1974, WhoWor 1974,
  WrDr 1976
Janeway, Michael Charles 1940- *WhoAm 1974*
Janicki, Edward *NF*
Janin, Jules Gabriel 1804-1874 *BiD&SB, EvEuW,*
  OxFr, WebBD
Janka, Katherine *NF*

Janos, Leo *NF*
Jans, H P *NF*
Janson, Donald D 1921- *ConAu 5R, RpN*
Janson, Joseph Bror, II 1928- *WhoAm 1974*
Janssen, Peter *BioIn 9*
Janssen, Richard *NF*
Januszewski, Frank 1886?-1953 *BioIn 3*
Janvier, Meredith 1872-1936 *AmAu&B, DcNAA*
Janvier, Thomas Allibone 1849-1913 *Alli Sup, AmAu, AmAu&B, BbD, BiD&SB, DcAmA, DcAmB 9, DcEnA Ap, DcLEL, DcNAA, HisAmM XR, OxAm, REnAL, WebBD*
Jaques, Milton G *NF*
Jara, Anibal 1892- *BioIn 3*
Jaramillo, Emilio d1949 *BioIn 2*
Jares, Joe 1937- *ConAu 33, WrDr 1976*
Jarnagin, Roy A 1886- *WhJnl 1928*
Jarnagin, W C 1879- *WhJnl 1928*
Jaroff, Leon *NF*
Jaros, Natalie F *OvPC*
Jarrar, Farouk *ForP*
Jarreau, Rollo Carnal 1869- *BioIn 2*
Jarrell, Sanford 1896?-1962 *BioIn 6*
Jarrett, Vernon D 1921- *BlkC*
Jarrett, Will *NF*
Jarriel, Tom *NF*
Jarrold, Ernest 1850-1912 *DcAmA, DcNAA*
Jarves, James Jackson 1818-1888 *Alli, Alli Sup, AmAu, AmAu&B, BiD&SB, CyAL 2, DcAmA, DcNAA, OxAm, REnAL, WebBD*
Jarvis, Charles E *WhJnl Sup*
Jarvis, J *NF*
Jarvis, Jack 1914?- *BioIn 2*
Jarvis, Lucy Howard 1919- *CurBio XR, OvPC, WhoAm 1974, WhoAmW 1974, WhoE 1974, WhoWor 1974*
Jarvis, Russel 1791-1853 *NF*
Jarvis, Russell *AmJnl*
Jarvis, William Henry Pope 1876-1944 *DcNAA, OxCan*
Jautard, Valantin *NF*
Jaures, Jean Leon 1859-1914 *OxFr, REn, WebBD*
Javers, Ronald A 1946?- *NF*
Javits, Marion Ann Borris 1924?- *BioIn 6, WhoAmW 1974, WhoE 1974*
Jay, Douglas Patrick Thomas 1907- *Au&Wr, ConAu 65, IntWW 1976, IntWW 1974, Who 1974, WhoWor 1974*
Jay, Frank *OvPC*
Jay, Griff 1880?-1951 *BioIn 2*
Jay, Peter 1937- *IntWW 1976, Who 1974*
Jay, Peter A 1940- *NF*
Jay Bee *see* Bradford, Joseph
Jayne, David d1977 *NF*
Jaynes, Oliver Brown 1895- *WhNAA, WhJnl 1928*
Jean, Andre *BioIn 1*
Jean, Emile 1896- *WhJnl 1928*
Jeancard, Pierre 1921?- *BioIn 7*
Jeannerat, Pierre Gabriel 1902- *Au&Wr, ConAu 7R*
Jeans, Allen E *NF*
Jedlicka, Albert 1914- *WhoMW 1974*
Jefferds, Warren C 1878- *WhJnl 1928*
Jefferson, Ted B *BioIn 7*
Jefferys, Upton S 1864?-1950 *BioIn 2*
Jeffress, Edwin Bedford 1887- *WhJnl 1928*
Jeffrey, Adi-Kent Thomas 1916- *ConAu 37, OvPC, WrDr 1976*
Jeffrey, Lord Francis 1773-1850 *Alli, BbD, BiD&SB, BrAu 19, CasWL, CrtT 2, DcEnA, DcEnL, DcEuL, DcLEL, EvLB, MouLC 3, NewC, OxEng, Pen Eng, WebBD, WebE&AL*

Jeffries, Brian *NF*
Jeffries, Georgia 1948- *NF*
Jehu, Ivor Stewart 1908-1960 *BioIn 5*
Jelliffe, Smith Ely 1866-1945 *CurBio XR, DcNAA, HisAmM XR, WhNAA*
Jellinek, George *NF*
Jellinghaus, Carl Frederic 1917- *WhoAm 1974*
Jemail, Jimmy 1893?-1978 *NF*
Jencks, Hugh *OvPC*
Jencks, Richard William 1921- *WhoAm 1974, WhoF&I 1974*
Jenison, E M 1866- *WhJnl 1928*
Jenkins, Arthur 1851-1903 *NatCAB 25*
Jenkins, Burris, Jr. 1896-1966 *BioIn 4, WhJnl 1928*
Jenkins, Burris Atkins 1869-1945 *AmAu&B, BiDSA, DcNAA, WhNAA*
Jenkins, C Ray *RpN*
Jenkins, Carol *BlkC*
Jenkins, Charles Christopher 1882-1943 *BioIn 1, CanNov, DcNAA*
Jenkins, Charles Francis 1865-1951 *AmAu&B, HisAmM XR, NatCAB 43, WhNAA*
Jenkins, Charles W *HisAmM XR*
Jenkins, Dan 1916- *BioIn 9, IntMPA 1975*
Jenkins, David *NF*
Jenkins, Geoffrey 1920- *Au&Wr, ConAu 7R*
Jenkins, George T 1889- *WhJnl 1928*
Jenkins, Herschel V 1871-1960 *NatCAB 47*
Jenkins, Howard Malcolm 1842-1902 *Alli Sup, AmAu&B, DcAmA, DcNAA, NatCAB 25*
Jenkins, James Francis 1884- *WhJnl 1928*
Jenkins, John 1813-1898 *Alli Sup, BbtC, DcNAA, HisAmM XR*
Jenkins, John Stilwell 1818-1852 *Alli, AmAu, AmAu&B, BiD&SB, DcAmA, DcNAA*
Jenkins, Lillian *BioIn 3*
Jenkins, Loren *NF*
Jenkins, MacGregor 1869-1940 *AmAu&B, CurBio XR, DcNAA, HisAmM XR, WhNAA, WhJnl 1928*
Jenkins, Paul 1898- *WhJnl 1928*
Jenkins, Roy Harris 1920- *Au&Wr, BioIn 7, BioIn 8, BioIn 9, BioIn 10, ConAu 9, CurBio XR, IntWW 1974, Who 1974, WhoWor 1974, WorAu, WrDr 1976*
Jenkins, Ruth A *NF*
Jenkins, Simon 1943- *NF*
Jenkinson, Isaac 1825-1911 *BioIn 2, IndAu 1816, OhA&B*
Jenks, Alan *NF*
Jenks, Edward North 1910?-1962 *BioIn 6*
Jenks, Francis *HisAmM XR*
Jenks, George Charles 1850-1929 *AmAu&B, DcAmB 10, DcNAA, HsB&A, REnAL, WebBD*
Jenks, George Charles *see also* Lawson, W B
Jenks, Homer 1914- *WhoAm 1974, WhoE 1974*
Jenks, Howard *NF*
Jenks, Tudor 1857-1922 *AmAu&B, AmLY, BiD&SB, CarSB, DcAmA, DcNAA,; HisAmM XR, REnAL*
Jenks, W O *WhJnl 1928*
Jenness, Lucian 1900- *WhJnl 1928*
Jennett, Richard P *BioIn 6*
Jennings, Charles S d1961 *RpN*
Jennings, Claude A C *NF*
Jennings, Dean Southern 1905-1969 *AmAu&B, BioIn 8*
Jennings, George A 1850-1936 *NatCAB 27*
Jennings, James 1888-1957 *BioIn 4*
Jennings, Janet A *NF*
Jennings, John Joseph 1853-1909 *BiDSA, DcNAA*
Jennings, Louis John 1836?-1893 *Alli Sup, AmJnl*

Jennings, M R NF
Jennings, Paul Francis 1918- Au&Wr,
  ConAu 9R, NewC
Jennings, Peter Charles 1938- WhoAm 1974,
  WhoE 1974
Jennings, Robert Maurice 1924- WhoAm 1974
Jensen, C Gregory NF
Jensen, Cecil Leon 1902- BioIn 1, WhoAm 1974
Jensen, Holger NF
Jensen, Margaret E NF
Jensen, Maxine Dowd 1919- ConAu 65
Jensen, Oliver Ormerod 1914- ConAu 25,
  CurBio XR, DrAS 74H, WhoAm 1974,
  WhoE 1974, WhoWor 1974
Jensen, Wilhelm 1837-1911 BiD&SB, CasWL,
  EvEuW, OxGer, WebBD
Jensen, William E NF
Jenson, Lee NF
Jernegan, W L NF
Jerome, Ed NF
Jerome, Fred NF
Jerome, Jerome Klapka 1859-1927 Alli Sup, BbD,
  BiD&SB, CasWL, CyWA, DcBiA,
  DcEnA Ap, DcLEL, LongC, EvLB,
  McGWD, ModBL, ModWD, NewC, OxEng,
  Pen Eng, REn, TwCA, TwCW, WebBD
Jerome, Leonard NF
Jerome, Victor J 1897?-1965 AmRP, BioIn 7
Jerrold, Douglas William 1803-1857 Alli, BbD,
  BiD&SB, BrAu 19, DcEnA, DcEnL,
  DcEuL, DcLEL, EvLB, HisAmM XR,
  McGWD, NewC, OxEng, Pen Eng, WebBD
Jersom, Herman AmRP
Jerus, James B 1897- WhJnl 1928
Jessee, Ernest NF
Jessen, Ernest Forrest 1890-1971 BioIn 2,
  BioIn 9, NewYTBE 2
Jessup, Elon Huntington 1885-1958 BioIn 4
Jessup, John Knox 1907- WhoAm 1974
Jessup, Tom NF
Jessye, Eva Alberta 1897- AmSCAP 1966,
  BlkAW, WhJnl Sup
Jester, Lewis T 1893- WhNAA, WhJnl 1928
Jeter, Frank Hamilton 1891-1955 WhJnl 1928
Jett, Monroe D 1898- WhJnl 1928
Jett, Tish NF
Jewell, Derek 1927- ConAu 33, WrDr 1976
Jewell, Edmund F d1978 NF
Jewell, Edward Alden 1888-1947 AmAu&B,
  DcNAA, TwCA, TwCA Sup
Jewell, Harry Sanford 1867-1945 BioIn 3,
  NatCAB 37
Jewell, Marshall H 1857- NatCAB 11
Jewell, Richard Leland 1914?-1967 BioIn 7
Jewett, Eleanor 1892- WhNAA, WhJnl 1928
Jewett, John Howard 1843-1925 AmAu&B,
  DcAmA, DcNAA
Jhabvala, Sarica D NF
Jiler, George H OvPC
Jiler, Harry OvPC
Jimenez, Antonio E NF
Jimenez, Carlos A 1914-1969 BioIn 8
Jinks, Robert Larry 1929- WhoAm 1974,
  WhoF&I 1974, WhoS&SW 1973
Joachim, Jerome 1898-1956 NatCAB 47
Joachim, Marie 1906- NF
Jobes, William P NF
Jobim, Danton ForP
Joesten, Joachim 1905- CurBio XR
Johannson, Bertram H NF
Johansson, Axel ForP
John, DeWitt 1915- IntWW 1976, Who 1974,
  WhoAm 1974, WhoE 1974, WhoWor 1974
Johns, B T NF

Johns, George Sibley 1857-1941 AmJnl,
  WhJnl 1928
Johns, June 1925- ConAu 57
Johns, Richard P 1939- NF
Johns, William Earl 1893-1968 ConAu 73,
  WhoChL
Johnsen, Grace 1911- WhoAm 1974,
  WhoAmW 1974
Johnson, Albert NF
Johnson, Albert 1869-1957 BioIn 4
Johnson, Alden Porter 1914-1972 BioIn 9
Johnson, Alfonso 1890- WhJnl 1928
Johnson, Alfred Sidney 1860-1925 HisAmM XR
Johnson, Alvin Saunders 1874-1971 AmAu&B,
  BioIn 1, BioIn 2, BioIn 3, HisAmM XR,
  REnAL, TwCA Sup, WebBD
Johnson, Andrew 1853-1879 BioIn 1
Johnson, Arthur Charles, Sr. 1874-1950 BioIn 2,
  WhJnl 1928
Johnson, Bea d1976 ConAu 65
Johnson, Benjamin F, Of Boone see Riley, James
  Whitcomb
Johnson, Bernard Lyman 1883-1947 BioIn 1,
  BioIn 3, NatCAB 37
Johnson, Bob NF
Johnson, Burges 1877-1963 AmAu&B, AmLY,
  HisAmM XR, NatCAB XR, REnAL,
  WebBD, WhNAA, WhJnl 1928
Johnson, C Stuart HisAmM XR
Johnson, C W NF
Johnson, Carl H 1904- WhJnl 1928
Johnson, Carlton Myles 1925- RpN,
  WhoAm 1974
Johnson, Carrie NF
Johnson, Cecil Haven 1887- WhJnl 1928
Johnson, Charles 1948- BioIn 8
Johnson, Charles D 1888- WhJnl 1928
Johnson, Charles Edgar 1902- WhJnl 1928
Johnson, Charles Raymond 1925- ConAu 65,
  WhoMW 1974
Johnson, Charles W 1843-1905 DcNAA
Johnson, Christohper 1931- ConAu 13R
Johnson, Connie S 1951- NF
Johnson, Crockett 1906-1975 AmJnl, Au&Wr,
  AuBYP, BioIn 1, BioIn 5, BioIn 8, BioIn 9,
  ConAu XR, CurBio XR, SmATA 1,
  ThrBJA, WhoAmA 1973
Johnson, Curtis Boyd 1875-1950 BioIn 2, BioIn 4,
  NatCAB 41
Johnson, Curtis Lee 1928- WhoAm 1974,
  WhoMW 1974
Johnson, Diantha NF
Johnson, Doctor see Johnson, Samuel
Johnson, Don NF
Johnson, Dorothy Marie 1905- Au&Wr,
  ConAu 5R, ForWC 1970, SmATA 6,
  WhoPNW
Johnson, Mrs. E NF
Johnson, E D BioIn 1
Johnson, Earl NF
Johnson, Edgar WhJnl 1928
Johnson, Edith WhJnl 1928
Johnson, Edward Gilpin NF
Johnson, Edward Marion 1893- WhJnl 1928
Johnson, Emory Richard 1864-1950 DcAmA,
  HisAmM XR, WebBD
Johnson, Erskine 1910?- BioIn 2
Johnson, F Hilliard HisAmM XR
Johnson, Ferd 1905- ConAu 69
Johnson, Francis 1837-1908 BioIn 2, HsB&A,
  HsB&A Sup, IndAu 1816
Johnson, Frank NF
Johnson, Frank S OvPC
Johnson, Frederick C 1853- NatCAB 11

Johnson, Frederick Green 1890-1941 *WhNAA,*
 WhJnl 1928
Johnson, Gail Borden *NF*
Johnson, Gerald White 1890- *AmAu&B, AnCL,*
 AuBYP, BioIn 2, BioIn 3, BioIn 4, BioIn 7,
 BioIn 9, BioIn 10, CnDAL, HisAmM XR,
 OxAm, REnAL, ThrBJA, TwCA Sup,
 WebBD, WhNAA, WhoAm 1974,
 WhJnl 1928, WhoWor 1974
Johnson, Grace *NF*
Johnson, Guion Griffis 1900- *TexWr, WhNAA,*
 WhoAmW 1974, WhJnl 1928
Johnson, Harold Bowtell 1880-1949 *BioIn 1,*
 BioIn 2, WhJnl 1928
Johnson, Harriett *ForWC 1970, WhoAm 1974,*
 WhoAmW 1974, WhoE 1974
Johnson, Haynes Bonner 1931- *AmAu&B,*
 ConAu 7R, NewMr, WhoAm 1974,
 WhoS&SW 1973
Johnson, Helen Kendrick 1844-1917 *AmAu&B,*
 HisAmM XR
Johnson, Henry Lewis *HisAmM XR*
Johnson, Herbert 1878-1946 *AmAu&B*
Johnson, Herbert Henry 1875-1957 *BioIn 1,*
 BioIn 4
Johnson, Hillary J 1950- *NF*
Johnson, Horace 1893-1964 *AmSCAP 1966,*
 BioIn 1, WhoMus 1972
Johnson, Hugh Samuel 1882-1942 *AmAu&B,*
 AmJnl, CurBio XR, DcNAA, HisAmM XR,
 WebBD
Johnson, Humphrey Wynne 1925-1976 *ConAu 61*
Johnson, J Percy H 1873?-1952 *BioIn 1, BioIn 2*
Johnson, Jalmar Edwin 1905- *ConAu 7R,*
 WhoAm 1974
Johnson, James J *HisAmM XR*
Johnson, Jeanette Ninas *BioIn 4, BioIn 5*
Johnson, John, Jr. *BlkC*
Johnson, John A 1861-1909 *NF*
Johnson, John Harold 1918- *BioNews 1974, BlkC,*
 CelR 1973, CurBio XR, EncAB,
 IntWW 1976, WhoAm 1974, WhoMW 1974
Johnson, Joseph French 1853-1925 *AmAu&B,*
 AmJnl, AmLY, DcAmA, DcNAA
Johnson, Julian 1886?-1965 *BioIn 7*
Johnson, Kathryn 1929- *ConAu 33*
Johnson, Keen 1895-1970 *NewYTBE 1,*
 WhJnl 1928
Johnson, Kenneth P *NF*
Johnson, Larry A *NF*
Johnson, Lionel Pigot 1867-1902 *AtlBL, BrAu 19,*
 CasWL, CnE&AP, DcEnA Ap, DcEuL,
 DcLEL, EvLB, HisAmM XR, LongC,
 NewC, OxEng, Pen Eng, PoIre, REn,
 WebBD, WebE&AL
Johnson, Malcolm Blaine 1913- *WhoAm 1974,*
 WhoS&SW 1973
Johnson, Malcolm L 1937- *ConAu 69*
Johnson, Malcolm Malone 1904-1976 *BioIn 1,*
 BioIn 2, BioIn 6, ConAu 65, ConAu 69,
 CurBio XR
Johnson, Martyn *HisAmM XR*
Johnson, Mary Louise Holton *OvPC*
Johnson, Michael Lillard 1943- *ConAu 53,*
 DrAS 74E
Johnson, Mike *NF*
Johnson, Morgan H d1888 *NF*
Johnson, Nunnally 1897-1977 *AmAu&B,*
 ConAu 69, CurBio XR, IntMPA 1975,
 REnAL, WhoAm 1974, WhoWor 1974
Johnson, Oliver 1809-1889 *Alli Sup, AmAu&B,*
 BiD&SB, DcAmA, DcNAA, HisAmM XR,
 OxAm
Johnson, Oliver S *NF*

Johnson, Paul Bede 1928- *Au&Wr, BioIn 7,*
 ConAu 17R, ForP, Who 1974,
 WhoWor 1974, WrDr 1976
Johnson, Paul Cornelius 1904- *WhoAm 1974*
Johnson, Philander Chase 1866-1939 *AmAu&B,*
 DcAmA, DcNAA, REnAL
Johnson, Philip A *OvPC*
Johnson, Philip J *RpN*
Johnson, Pussyfoot *see* Johnson, William Eugene
Johnson, Ray Bird 1891?-1950 *BioIn 2*
Johnson, Raymond Edward 1904- *WhoAm 1974,*
 WhJnl 1928, WhoS&SW 1973,
 WhoWor 1974
Johnson, Richard 1927- *NF*
Johnson, Richard N 1900?-1971 *AmJnl,*
 NewYTBE 2
Johnson, Robert Cummings 1864- *NF*
Johnson, Robert Edward 1922- *WhoAm 1974,*
 WhoMW 1974
Johnson, Robert Harold 1890?-1948 *BioIn 1*
Johnson, Robert Livingston 1894-1966 *BioIn 3,*
 BioIn 7, CurBio XR, HisAmM XR
Johnson, Robert Underwood 1853-1937 *AmAu&B,*
 AmLY, BbD, BiD&SB, BioIn 2, BioIn 4,
 BioIn 6, DcAmA, DcAmB S2, DcNAA,
 HisAmM XR, IndAu 1816, LiJA,
 NatCAB 46, OxAm, REn, REnAL, TwCA,
 TwCA Sup, WebBD, WhNAA
Johnson, Robert Wayne 1947- *NF*
Johnson, Robert Wilson 1888-1963 *WhJnl 1928*
Johnson, Roy Ruggles 1883?-1973 *BioIn 9*
Johnson, Samuel 1709-1784 *Alli, AtlBL, BbD,*
 BiD&SB, BrAu, CasWL, CnE&AP, CrtT 2,
 CyWA, DcBiA, DcEnA, DcEnA Ap,
 DcEnL, DcEuL, DcLEL, EvLB, MouLC 2,
 NewC, OxAm, OxEng, Pen Eng, RComWL,
 REn, WebBD, WebE&AL
Johnson, Sol C 1868- *WhNAA, WhJnl 1928*
Johnson, Stanley J F 1921?-1978 *NF*
Johnson, Stanley Phillips 1892-1946 *HisAmM XR*
Johnson, Stephen *NF*
Johnson, Suzanne *OvPC*
Johnson, Thomas A 1928- *BlkC*
Johnson, Thomas Moore 1851-1919 *HisAmM XR*
Johnson, Tom *NF*
Johnson, Vance *RpN*
Johnson, Verdenal Hoag 1924- *WhoAm 1974,*
 WhoAmW 1974, WhoE 1974
Johnson, W F *LiJA*
Johnson, Walter A 1874- *WhJnl 1928*
Johnson, Walter Alexander *HisAmM XR*
Johnson, Walter Christopher 1878-1966 *BioIn 1,*
 BioIn 7
Johnson, Wayne Eaton 1930- *WhoAm 1974*
Johnson, William Eugene 1862-1945 *AmLY,*
 NatCAB XR, OhA&B, WebBD, WhNAA
Johnson, William Martin 1862- *HisAmM* XR
Johnson, William Weber 1909- *AmAu&B,*
 AuBYP, BioIn 8, ConAu 17R,
 WhoAm 1974, WhoWest 1974, WrDr 1976
Johnson, Willis Fletcher 1857-1931 *AmAu&B,*
 DcNAA, HisAmM XR
Johnson, Wingate Memory 1885-1963 *BioIn 2*
Johnson, Wyatt Thomas, Jr. 1941- *WhoAm 1974,*
 WhoGov 1972
Johnston, Albert H 1914- *ConAu 69*
Johnston, Albert Wheeler 1871?-1952 *BioIn 3*
Johnston, Alexander Carter 1879-1952 *BioIn 3,*
 WhJnl 1928
Johnston, Alva 1888-1950 *BioIn 3, REnAL*
Johnston, Bertha 1864-1953 *BioIn 3*
Johnston, Dave *NF*
Johnston, Emery K 1897- *WhJnl 1928*
Johnston, Ernest, Jr. 1940?- *BlkC*

Johnston, Frances B NF
Johnston, Frederick Mair 1903- Who 1974
Johnston, George Herbert 1896- WhJnl 1928
Johnston, George Palmer, Jr. 1918- WhoAm 1974
Johnston, Harold S NF
Johnston, Harry d1967 BioIn 7
Johnston, Henry B NF
Johnston, Herbert 1858- WhJnl 1928
Johnston, James AmJnl
Johnston, Josiah Stoddard 1833-1913 DcAmA,
    DcNAA
Johnston, Laurie AuBYP, BioIn 8
Johnston, Louisa Mae 1925- AuBYP, BioIn 8
Johnston, Mary Elizabeth WhoAm 1974,
    WhoAmW 1974
Johnston, Myrna HisAmM XR
Johnston, Oswald L NF
Johnston, P P HisAmM XR
Johnston, Ralph E 1902- AuBYP, BioIn 8
Johnston, Remington Allen 1875-1946 BioIn 2,
    IndAu 1816
Johnston, Richard James Humphreys 1910-
    AmAu&B, OvPC, WhoAm 1974
Johnston, Richard Wyckoff 1915- WhoAm 1974
Johnston, Robert Malcus 1895- WhJnl 1928
Johnston, Stanley 1900-1962 BioIn 6
Johnston, T R 1893- WhNAA, WhJnl 1928
Johnston, W J HisAmM XR
Johnston, William Andrew 1871-1929 AmAu&B,
    DcAmB 10, DcNAA, WebBD, WhJnl Sup
Johnstone, Archibald R 1896?- BioIn 1
Johnstone, Hubert McBean 1879?-1919 NF
Johnstone, Lammy 1946- NF
Johson, Thomas NF
Jolas, Eugene 1894-1952 OxAm, REn, REnAL
Jolas, Maria BioIn 8
Jolidon, Larry NF
Joliffe, H R 1904- ConAu 4R
Jolley, Thomas Glenn 1944?- BioIn 9,
    NewYTBE 2
Jonas, Charles 1840-1896 BioIn 5
Jonas, Gerald 1935- ConAu 65, DrAP 1975
Jonas, Gilbert 1930- OvPC, WhoPubR 1972
Jonas, S A BiDSA
Jones, Alexander 1802-1863 Alli, AmJnl, BiDSA,
    DcAmA, DcAmB 10, DcNAA, HisAmM XR
Jones, Alexander Francis 1891-1966 BioIn 2,
    BioIn 7, BioIn 9
Jones, Alfred 1888?-1943 WhJnl 1928
Jones, Brendan NF
Jones, Carl A OvPC
Jones, Carl Allen 1879-1950 BioIn 2, BioIn 4
Jones, Carl Waring 1887-1957 BioIn 4
Jones, Carter Brooke NF
Jones, Catherine Parker d1977 NF
Jones, Charles A TexWr
Jones, Charles A 1815?-1851 Alli, DcNAA,
    HisAmM XR, OhA&B
Jones, Charles Henry 1848-1913 AmJnl,
    HisAmM XR, NatCAB 1
Jones, Clarence H, Jr. InvJ, RpN
Jones, Claudia AmRP
Jones, Clayton 1951- NF
Jones, Clement 1915- Who 1974
Jones, Coleman Bond 1895-1959 BioIn 5
Jones, Cranston Edward 1918- ConAu 2R,
    WhoAm 1974, WhoE 1974
Jones, David NF
Jones, David E 1866?-1948 BioIn 1
Jones, Dewey Roscoe 1899- WhJnl 1928
Jones, DuPre NF
Jones, Dwight Bangs 1900-1958 NF
Jones, E Penrose HisAmM XR
Jones, Earl J 1893-1958 BioIn 4

Jones, Edward D NF
Jones, Ellis O 1874?-1967 AmRP, BioIn 8
Jones, Everett L 1892?-1954 BioIn 3
Jones, George NF
Jones, George 1811-1891 AmJnl, BioIn 7,
    BioIn 10, NatCAB 1, WebBD
Jones, George Clifford 1884- WhJnl 1928
Jones, George J WhJnl 1928
Jones, Georgia H Lloyd 1875- WhJnl 1928
Jones, Gerald NF
Jones, Gerre Lyle 1926- OvPC, WhoE 1974,
    WhoF&I 1974, WhoPubR 1972
Jones, Gifford NF
Jones, Gilbert S 1879?-1954 BioIn 3
Jones, Griffith 1722-1786 Alli, DcEnL
Jones, H Lee 1898- WhJnl 1928
Jones, Harry C HisAmM XR
Jones, Haydon 1870?-1954 BioIn 3
Jones, Helen Louise 1903-1973 BioIn 4, BioIn 9
Jones, Herschel Vespasian 1861-1928 AmAu&B,
    DcAmB 10
Jones, Howard Mumford 1892- AmAu&B,
    Au&Wr, CnDAL, DrAS 74E, HisAmM XR,
    IntWW 1974, OxAm, RAdv 1, REnAL,
    TwCA Sup, WebBD, WhNAA,
    WhoAm 1974, WhoE 1974, WhoWor 1974
Jones, Howard Palfrey 1899-1973 CurBio XR,
    NewYTBE 4, WhoAm 1974, WhJnl 1928
Jones, Idwal 1890?-1964 AmAu&B, AmNov,
    CurBio XR, HisAmM XR, REnAL
Jones, Mrs. Inis 1878-1938 DcNAA
Jones, Iris Sanderson 1932- ConAu 73
Jones, J Hannum HisAmM XR
Jones, James HisAmM XR
Jones, James Alfred 1902- BioIn 1
Jones, James Athearn 1790?-1854 AmAu&B,
    DcNAA
Jones, James Clinton 1922- ConAu 69
Jones, James Henry 1907?-1977 ConAu 73
Jones, Jefferson 1891-1965 BioIn 7, WhNAA
Jones, Jenkin Lloyd 1843-1918 Alli Sup,
    AmAu&B, AmLY, DcAmA, DcNAA,
    HisAmM XR, WisWr
Jones, Jenkin Lloyd 1911- BioIn 3, BioIn 4,
    BioIn 5, BioIn 8, ConAu 9R,
    WhoF&I 1974, WhoS&SW 1973
Jones, Jesse H HisAmM XR
Jones, Jesse Holman 1874-1956 CurBio XR,
    EncAB, WebBD
Jones, John A HisAmM XR
Jones, John Beauchamp 1810-1866 Alli, Alli Sup,
    AmAu, AmAu&B, BiD&SB, BiDSA,
    BioIn 4, BioIn 8, DcAmA, DcAmB 10,
    DcLEL, DcNAA, OxAm, REnAL
Jones, John Clement 1915- Who 1974,
    WhoWor 1974
Jones, John Price 1877-1964 BioIn 7, BioIn 8,
    WhNAA
Jones, John Tilford, Jr. 1917- WhoAm 1974,
    WhoF&I 1974, WhoS&SW 1973
Jones, John W HisAmM XR
Jones, John William HisAmM XR
Jones, Johnny NF
Jones, Joseph J 1907- BioIn 2, Br&AmS
Jones, Joseph L 1897- WhoAm 1974,
    WhoE 1974
Jones, Ken NF
Jones, Kenley 1935- ConAu 69
Jones, Kiler K HisAmM XR
Jones, Lamoyne Arthur 1911- OvPC,
    WhoE 1974, WhoF&I 1974
Jones, Leonard Augustus 1832-1909 Alli Sup,
    DcAmA, DcNAA, HisAmM XR
Jones, Llewellyn 1884-1961 AmAu&B,

HisAmM XR, WhJnl 1928
Jones, Lombard C *HisAmM XR*
Jones, Lucien Arthur 1895- *WhJnl Sup*
Jones, Lucy 1912?-1966 *BioIn 7*
Jones, Lynn *NF*
Jones, Mabel 1860-1920 *DcNAA*
Jones, Major *see* Thompson, William Tappan
Jones, Mark Perrin 1902-1959 *BioIn 7,
    NatCAB 48*
Jones, Mark Perrin, III 1932- *WhoAmP 1973*
Jones, Mary MacCracken d1950 *BioIn 2*
Jones, Matte *WhJnl 1928*
Jones, Maurice *RpN*
Jones, Meriwether *AmJnl*
Jones, Merle Silas 1905- *WhoAm 1974,
    WhoWor 1974*
Jones, Mervyn 1922- *Au&Wr, ConAu 45,
    ConNov 1972, ConNov 1976, Who 1974,
    WrDr 1976*
Jones, Milton Wakefield 1930- *NF,
    WhoAdv 1972, WhoWest 1974*
Jones, Nard 1904-1972 *AmAu&B, AmNov,
    REnAL, WhNAA, WhoPNW*
Jones, Patrick L d1915 *AmJnl*
Jones, Paul *NF*
Jones, Paul A 1882- *WhJnl 1928*
Jones, Paul John 1897-1974 *BioIn 2, ConAu 53*
Jones, Paul L 1896- *WhJnl 1928*
Jones, Phil *NF*
Jones, Ralston 1926- *NF*
Jones, Regina *NF*
Jones, Richard 1926- *Au&Wr, ConAu 49,
    WrDr 1976*
Jones, Richard Lloyd 1873-1963 *HisAmM XR,
    WhNAA, WhJnl 1928*
Jones, Richard Lloyd, Jr. 1909- *BioIn 2, BioIn 4,
    WhoS&SW 1973*
Jones, Richard Montgomery 1907- *WhoAm 1974*
Jones, Richard Seelye *AmJnl*
Jones, Richard W *NF*
Jones, Robert F 1934- *ConAu 49*
Jones, Robert Letts 1913- *OvPC, WhoAm 1974,
    WhoF&I 1974, WhoWest 1974*
Jones, Robert Marion 1919- *WhoAm 1974*
Jones, Robert Russell 1927- *ConAu 69*
Jones, Robert S *NF*
Jones, Robert Webster 1874?-1947 *BioIn 1*
Jones, Robert William 1884- *WhNAA,
    WhJnl 1928*
Jones, Rochelle *NF*
Jones, Sir Roderick 1877-1962 *BioIn 2, BioIn 6*
Jones, Roger M *HisAmM XR*
Jones, Ruby Aileen Hiday 1908- *ConAu P-1,
    ForWC 1970, IndAu 1917, WhoAmW 1974,
    WhoMW 1974*
Jones, Rufus Matthew 1863-1948 *AmAu&B,
    AmLY, CurBio XR, DcNAA, HisAmM XR,
    LongC, REnAL, TwCA Sup, WhNAA*
Jones, Russell 1918- *AmJnl, BioIn 4,
    CurBio XR, WhoWor 1974*
Jones, Thomas, Jr. *HisAmM XR*
Jones, Thomas L *OvPC*
Jones, Thomas P 1774-1848 *HisAmM XR*
Jones, Thomas Samuel, Jr. 1882-1932 *AmAu&B,
    AnMV 1926, DcNAA, REnAL, WhNAA*
Jones, Thomas W 1875?-1954 *BioIn 3*
Jones, Tony *NF*
Jones, Victor Owen 1905-1970 *BioIn 8, BioIn 10,
    RpN*
Jones, Vincent Starbuck 1906- *WhoAm 1974,
    WhoE 1974, WhoWor 1974*
Jones, W S *HisAmM XR*
Jones, Weimar *BioIn 5*
Jones, Wesley Thompson 1901- *WhJnl 1928*

Jones, Will Owen 1862-1928 *WhJnl 1928*
Jones, William 1936- *NF*
Jones, William Hugh 1939- *InvJ, WhoAm 1974*
Jones, William N 1883- *WhJnl 1928*
Jones, William Russell 1889- *WhNAA,
    WhJnl 1928*
Jones, William S 1863-1939 *NatCAB 30*
Jones, William V 1865- *WhJnl 1928*
Jones, Yardley *NF*
Jonsson, Einar 1880- *BioIn 2*
Jordan, Clyde C 1930- *WhoAm 1974*
Jordan, Don Franklin *OvPC*
Jordan, Dulcina 1833-1895 *BioIn 2*
Jordan, Eileen *BioIn 4*
Jordan, Elizabeth Garver 1867-1947 *AmAu&B,
    BioIn 1, BioIn 4, BkC 2, CarSB,
    CathA 1930, DcAmA, DcNAA,
    HisAmM XR, REnAL, WebBD, WhNAA,
    WisWr*
Jordan, Fred 1925- *WhoAm 1974*
Jordan, George F 1891- *WhJnl 1928*
Jordan, James J 1856- *NatCAB 4*
Jordan, John A 1843-1917 *DcNAA*
Jordan, Laurence Dormer 1903- *WhJnl 1928*
Jordan, Lewis 1912- *WhoAm 1974, WhoE 1974*
Jordan, Max 1895-1977 *BioIn 1, CathA 1930*
Jordan, Mildred A 1901- *AmAu&B, AmNov,
    SmATA 5, TwCA Sup*
Jordan, Monica *see* Caruba, Alan
Jordan, Philip Furneaux 1902-1951 *BioIn 2*
Jordan, Robert Paul 1921- *ConAu 29*
Jordan, Thomas 1819-1895 *Alli Sup, BiDSA,
    BioIn 5, DcAmA, DcAmB 10, WebBD*
Jordan, Virgil 1892-1965 *CurBio XR*
Jordan, W Alec 1914- *BioIn 2, WhoE 1974,
    WhoF&I 1974, WhoPubR 1972*
Jordan, Wilhelm 1819-1904 *BbD, BiD&SB,
    EvEuW, OxGer, WebBD*
Jordan, Will F 1871- *WhJnl 1928*
Jordan, William George 1864-1928 *AmAu&B,
    DcAmA, DcNAA, HisAmM XR*
Jordan, Winfield B *WhJnl 1928*
Jordon, Edward 1800-1869 *BioIn 3*
Jorgensen, Axel Emil 1877- *WhJnl 1928*
Jorgensen, Johannes 1866-1956 *CathA 1930,
    EncWL, Pen Eur, WebBD*
Jorgenson, Bruce *NF*
Josaphat, Israel Beer 1816-1899 *WebBD*
Josaphat, Israel Beer *see also* Reuter, Baron Paul
    Julius Von
Joseloff, G *NF*
Joseloff, Stanley 1907- *AmSCAP 1966, OvPC*
Joseph, Alexander Henry 1911- *WhoAm 1974,
    WhoE 1974, WhoF&I 1974*
Joseph, Arthur *HisAmM XR*
Joseph, Clay Evans 1894- *WhJnl 1928*
Joseph, David Henry 1886-1966 *BioIn 7,
    WhJnl 1928*
Joseph, Gabe 1907- *WhoAm 1974*
Joseph, J Arthur *NF*
Joseph, Richard 1910-1976 *AmAu&B,
    CelR 1973, ConAu 3R, ConAu 69,
    WhoAm 1974, WhoE 1974, WhoWor 1974*
Joseph, Thomas *NF*
Josephs, Ray 1912- *ConAu 9R, WhoAm 1974,
    WhoF&I 1974, WhoPubR 1972,
    WhoWorJ 1972, WrDr 1976*
Josephson, Matthew 1899-1978 *AmAu&B,
    ConAmA, NewYTBE 3, OxAm, Pen Am,
    REn, REnAL, TwCA, TwCA Sup, WebBD,
    WhoAm 1974, WhoWor 1974,
    WhoWorJ 1972*
Josephy, Alvin M, Jr. 1915- *ConAu 19R,
    OxCan Sup, WhoAm 1974, WhoE 1974,*

WrDr 1976
Josey, Jairus Anthony *WhJnl 1928*
Josie, Edith 1921?- *BioIn 7*
Joslin, Theodore Goldsmith 1890-1944 *DcNAA,
HisAmM XR, WhJnl 1928*
Joslyn, Jay *NF*
Jost, Joseph A *NF*
Josten, Josef *BioIn 2*
Jourdain, Paul 1877-1954 *BioIn 3*
Journeyman *see* Nock, Albert Jay
Jouve, Geraud Henri 1901- *IntWW 1976,
WhoWor 1974*
Jouvenel, Henry De 1876-1935 *BioIn 2, BioIn 5,
WebBD*
Jovanovic, Jovan 1833-1904 *BbD, BiD&SB,
WebBD*
Jovanovic, Jovan *see also* Zmaj, Jovan Jovanovic
Jovine, Francesco 1902-1950 *BioIn 2, CasWL,
EncWL, EvEuW, Pen Eur*
Joy, George 1783-1847 *BioIn 6*
Joy, James Richard 1863-1957 *AmAu&B,
BioIn 4, DcAmA, WhNAA*
Joy, Sally *NF*
Joy, Verne E 1876-1964 *BioIn 8, WhJnl 1928*
Joya, Mock *NF*
Joyant, Maurice 1864-1930 *BioIn 6*
Joyce, Christopher R *NF*
Joyce, James Avery 1902- *Au&Wr, BioIn 5,
ConAu 65, CurBio XR, WhoAm 1974,
WhoWor 1974*
Joyce, Philip Halton 1928- *WhoAm 1974*
Joyce, Thomas H *RpN*
Joye, Judy *NF*
Joyner, Andrew 1856?-1951 *BioIn 2*
Juan, Jose Vega *NF*
Juckett, Eunice Telfer *NF*
Judd, David Wright 1838-1888 *Alli Sup, DcAmA,
DcNAA, HisAmM XR*
Judd, Edwin E 1890- *WhJnl 1928*
Judd, Maurice *NF*
Judd, O B *HisAmM XR*
Judd, Orange 1822-1892 *HisAmM XR,
NatCAB 8, WebBD*
Judge, Diane 1931- *NF*
Judge, Frank *NF*
Judge, William Quan 1851-1896 *AmAu,
AmAu&B, DcNAA, HisAmM XR, WebBD*
Judges, Frederick B 1897- *WhJnl 1928*
Judson, Clara Ingram 1879-1960 *AmAu&B,
AuBYP, CarSB, CurBio XR, IndAu 1816,
JBA 1951, OxCan, WhNAA, WhJnl 1928*
Judson, Edward Zane Carroll 1823-1886 *Alli Sup,
AmAu, AmAu&B, DcAmA, DcNAA,
HisAmM XR, HsB&A, OhA&B, OxAm,
REn, REnAL, WebBD*
Judy, Bernard *NF*
Judy, Stephen N *NF*
Judy, Will 1891- *ConAu 7R, WhNAA*
Juergens, Hubert F 1892?-1962 *BioIn 6*
Julian, Carl B 1885- *WhJnl 1928*
Julian, Constance 1863- *BioIn 3, CathA 1952*
Julian, Forbes 1902- *WhJnl 1928*
Julian, Isaac Hoover 1823-1911? *BiDSA, BioIn 2,
DcAmA, DcNAA, IndAu 1816*
Julian, John A L 1867- *WhJnl 1928*
Julien, Louis Antoine *HisAmM XR*
Juling, Ray Greene *HisAmM XR*
Julius, Hoffman C *OvPC*
June, Jennie 1829-1901 *Alli Sup, AmAu,
AmAu&B, BiD&SB, DcAmA, DcEnL,
DcNAA, WebBD*
June, Jennie *see also* Croly, Jane Cunningham
Jungk, Robert 1913- *BioIn 3, WhoWor 1974*
Junius Americus *see* Endicott, Charles Moses

Junor, John Donald Brown 1919- *IntWW 1976,
WhoWor 1974*
Jupo, Frank J 1904- *AuBYP, BioIn 5, BioIn 8,
ConAu 7R, SmATA 7, WrDr 1976*
Jurgen-Fischer, Klaus 1930- *BioIn 7*
Jurney, Dorothy Misener 1909- *BioIn 9, BioIn 10,
ForWC 1970, WhoAm 1974, WhoAmW 1974*
Jury, John G *HisAmM XR*
Just, Ward Swift 1935- *ConAu 25, WhoAm 1974*
Juster, Harry *NF*
Justice, Blair 1927- *ConAu 45*
Justus, Roy Braxton 1901- *WhoAm 1974,
WhoAmA 1973*

K

Kabaker, Harvey M NF
Kabel, Jerry NF
Kadis, Philip M NF
Kael, Pauline 1919- AmAu&B, Au&Wr,
    CelR 1973, ConAu 45, CurBio XR,
    ForWC 1970, IntMPA 1975, WhoAm 1974,
    WhoAmW 1974, WrDr 1976
Kaempffert, Waldemar Bernhard 1877-1956
    BiDPara, BioIn 4, CurBio XR,
    HisAmM XR, WebBD
Kaese, Harold 1909?-1975 ConAu 57
Kaestner, Erich 1899-1974 ConAu 49, ConAu 73,
    NewYTBS 5
Kaestner, Erich see also Kastner, Erich
Kaff, Albert E OvPC
Kahana, Yoram 1939- NF
Kahl, Norman A NF
Kahler, Charlotte NF
Kahler, Hugh MacNair 1883-1969 AmAu&B,
    BioIn 8, HisAmM XR, REnAL, WhNAA
Kahles, Charles W 1878- AmJnl, WhJnl 1928
Kahn, Alexander 1881-1962 BioIn 6
Kahn, David 1930- ConAu 25, WrDr 1976
Kahn, Ely Jacques, Jr. 1916- AmAu&B, Au&Wr,
    BioIn 4, ConAu 65, NewYTBE 3,
    TwCA Sup, WhoAm 1974, WhoE 1974,
    WhoWorJ 1972
Kahn, Gustave 1859-1936 CasWL, CIDMEL,
    EvEuW, OxFr, Pen Eur, REn, WebBD
Kahn, Howard 1886-1951 BioIn 2, WhJnl 1928
Kahn, J Kesner NF
Kahn, Jack M 1952- NF
Kahn, James M 1903?-1978 NF
Kahn, Joan 1914?- BioIn 3, BioIn 8
Kahn, Joseph Gabriel 1913- WhoAm 1974
Kahn, Roger 1927- AuBYP, BioIn 4, BioIn 8,
    BioIn 9, ConAu 25
Kahn-Ackermann, Georg 1918- IntWW 1976
Kaikini, P R 1912- ConAu 61
Kain, F E 1886- WhJnl 1928
Kaine, Elinor 1936?- BioIn 8, BioIn 9
Kaisari, Uri 1899?-1979 NF
Kaiser, Bill 1937- ConAu XR
Kaiser, Dave 1943- NF
Kaiser, Lloyd Eugene 1927- WhoAm 1974,
    WhoE 1974
Kaiser, Robert Blair 1930- ConAu 9R
Kaiser, Robert Greeley 1943- ConAu 65, NewMr
Kaiser, Robert S NF
Kalb, Barry NF
Kalb, Bernard NF
Kalb, Marvin Leonard 1930- AmAu&B,
    ConAu 5R, WhoAm 1974, WhoS&SW 1973,
    WhoWor 1974
Kalber, Floyd NF
Kalenick, Sandy 1945- NF

Kaler, James Otis 1848-1912 Alli Sup, AmAu&B,
    BiD&SB, CarSB, DcAmA, DcNAA,
    JBA 1934, JBA 1951, NatCAB 13, OxAm
Kaliff, Joe NF
Kalisch, Bertram 1902- IntMPA 1975, OvPC
Kalisch, David 1820-1872 BbD, BiD&SB, OxGer,
    WebBD
Kalischer, Peter AmJnl, HisAmM XR
Kalish, Karen NF
Kalker, Phil NF
Kallai, Gyula 1910- IntWW 1976, WhoWor 1974
Kallgren, Everett 1900?-1969 BioIn 8
Kalmar, Vicki 1946- NF
Kalmbach, Albert Carpenter 1910- WhoAm 1974
Kalmus, Allan Henry 1917- OvPC, WhoE 1974,
    WhoF&I 1974, WhoPubR 1972
Kaltenborn, Hans Von 1878-1965 AmAu&B,
    AmJnl, BioIn 1, BioIn 2, BioIn 4, BioIn 5,
    BioIn 7, BioIn 8, CurBio XR, REnAL,
    WebBD, WhNAA, WhJnl 1928
Kalusky, Rebecca AuBYP, BioIn 8
Kamalick, Joseph NF
Kamath, Madhav Vithal 1921- ConAu 69
Kamei, Asahi NF
Kamerman, Sylvia E 1916- ConAu XR
Kamerman, Sylvia E see also Burack, Sylvia
    Kamerman
Kaminski, Szymon 1891?-1950 BioIn 2
Kamm, Henry 1925- NewMr
Kamm, Herbert 1917- WhoAm 1974
Kamphausen, Hugo 1863- WhNAA, WhJnl 1928
Kanabayashi, Masayoshi NF
Kanaga, Consuelo 1894?-1978 NF
Kandahl, Torolv 1899- IntWW 1976
Kandel, Myron OvPC
Kandell, Jonathan NF
Kane, Charles Edward 1893- WhJnl 1928
Kane, Frank R 1925- NF
Kane, Harnett Thomas 1910- AmAu&B, AmNov,
    CathA 1952, REn, REnAL, TwCA Sup,
    WhoS&SW 1973
Kane, Herbert J E d1953 RpN
Kane, Larry NF
Kane, Lawrence L NF
Kane, Maurice R 1906?-1965 BioIn 7
Kane, Maury NF
Kane, Riki 1943- NF
Kane, Robert S 1925- ConAu 9R, OvPC
Kane, William J 1889?-1951 BioIn 2
Kane, William R 1885- HisAmM XR,
    WhJnl 1928
Kaneko, Kentaro HisAmM XR
Kaneko, Kiichi AmRP
Kanfer, Stefan NF
Kann, Peter Robert 1942- WhoAm 1974
Kannawin, John NF

Kantar, Eddie NF
Kanter, Penny NF
Kantor, MacKinlay 1904-1977 AmAu&B,
   AmNov, AuBYP, CnDAL, ConAmA,
   ConAu 61, ConAu 73, ConNov 1972,
   ConNov 1976, DcLEL, EncMys, ModAL,
   OxAm, Pen Am, REn, REnAL, TwCA,
   TwCA Sup, TwCW, WebBD, WhoAm 1974,
   WrDr 1976
Kantor, Seth 1926- NF
Kantorowicz, Alfred 1899- IntWW 1976
Kantotowich, Haim AmRP
Kany, A S 1884- WhJnl 1928
Kany, Howard L OvPC
Kapel, Saul NF
Kaplan, Bernard NF
Kaplan, Don 1879?-1952 BioIn 3
Kaplan, H Eliot HisAmM XR
Kaplan, Milton Lewis 1920- BioIn 8
Kaplan, Morris OvPC
Kaplan, Nat AmRP
Kaplan, Richard 1929- ConAu 73, WhoAm 1974
Kaplow, Herb NF
Kapp, Friedrich 1824-1884 Alli Sup, BiD&SB,
   HisAmM XR, WebBD
Kappel, Ted NF
Kappelman, Murray NF
Kappen, Charles Vaughan 1910- ConAu 11R,
   DrAS 74E
Kaps, Carola NF
Kapstein, Jonathan OvPC
Kapuscinski, Ryszard 1932- IntWW 1976
Karafin, Harry J 1915?- BioIn 7
Karakushansky, Shabtai 1901-1977 NF
Karasik, Ellen NF
Karch, R Randolph 1902- NF
Kareda, Urjo NF
Karen, Lauri E 1927- NF
Karen, Ruth 1922- AuBYP, BioIn 8,
   ConAu 19R, OvPC, SmATA 9,
   WhoAmW 1974, WrDr 1976
Karger, Gus J 1866-1924 AmJnl
Karig, Walter 1898-1956 AmAu&B, AmNov,
   REnAL, TwCA Sup
Kariotis, Theodore NF
Karmen, Roman 1906-1978 IntWW 1974,
   WhoWor 1974
Karmin, Mayanne S NF
Karmin, Monroe William 1929- InvJ,
   WhoAm 1974, WhoS&SW 1973
Karnes, Grace T 1892- WhJnl 1928
Karnow, Stanley A 1925- ConAu 57, RpN,
   WhoAm 1974, WhoWor 1974
Karp, Richard NF
Karp, Walter NF
Karpeles, Gustav 1848-1909 WebBD
Karpf, Jerome J 1897?-1964 BioIn 7
Karpf, Jerome J, Jr. OvPC
Karpin, Fred L 1913- ConAu 15
Karpowicz, Ray Anthony 1925- WhoAdv 1972,
   WhoAm 1974
Karr, Albert R NF
Karr, Alphonse 1808-1890 BbD, BiD&SB, OxFr,
   WebBD
Karsell, Thomas G RpN
Karsner, David 1889-1941 AmAu&B, CurBio XR,
   DcNAA
Karstaedt, Clinton F 1888- WhJnl 1928
Kase, Max 1898-1974 BioIn 10, NewYTBS 5
Kashiwahara, Ken NF
Kasmire, Robert Diaz 1926- WhoAm 1974
Kassell, Hilda OvPC
Kasson, Frank H 1852- HisAmM XR
Kastle, Martin HisAmM XR

Kastner, Erich 1899-1974 AuBYP, CasWL,
   CIDMEL, CnMD, CurBio XR, EncWL,
   EvEuW, IntWW 1974, ModGL, ModWD,
   OxGer, Pen Eur, ThrBJA, Who 1974,
   WhoChL, WhoWor 1974, WorAu
Kastner, Erich see also Kaestner, Erich
Kasturi Ranga Iyengar, S d1923 BioIn 8
Kataev, Evgeni Petrovich see Petrov, Evgeni
   Petrovich
Kataev, Valentin Petrovich 1897- CasWL,
   CIDMEL, CnMD, DcRusL, EncWL,
   EvEuW, McGWD, ModSL 1, Pen Eur,
   REn, TwCW, WhoWor 1974
Katayama, Sen AmRP
Katcher, David A BioIn 1
Katel, Jacques 1916-1965 BioIn 7
Kates, Charles 1912?- BioIn 1
Katibah, Habib Ibrahim 1891?-1951 BioIn 2
Katkov, Mikhail Nikiforovich 1818-1887 BioIn 3,
   BioIn 7, BioIn 8, CasWL, DcEuL, DcRusL,
   EvEuW, WebBD
Katkov, Norman 1918- AmAu&B, AmNov,
   BioIn 1, BioIn 2, ConAu 15
Kato, Masuo NF
Kato, Tsugio 1929- NF
Kato, Yoshiro BioIn 5
Katz, Dolores Jean 1945- WhoAmW 1974
Katz, Gertrude 1915- NF
Katz, Harvey NewMr
Katz, Jerome F OvPC
Katz, Kaufman Ray OvPC
Katz, Leonard 1926- ConAu 21R
Katz, Ralph NF
Katz, Wallace Rice 1890- WhJnl 1928
Katzander, Shirley Saltzman 1921- ForWC 1970,
   WhoPubR 1972
Katzen, Bobby NF
Katzenelson-Shazar, Rachel NF
Katzman, Allen 1937- BioIn 10, ConAu 29,
   DrAP 1975, WrDr 1976
Katzman, Larry NF
Kaub, Redfield NF
Kauffman, Erle 1900- BioIn 2
Kauffman, Reginald Wright 1877-1959 AmAu&B,
   BioIn 7, HisAmM XR, REnAL, WebBD,
   WhNAA
Kauffman, Ruth Wright 1883-1952 AmAu&B,
   WebBD
Kauffman, Victor 1868- NF
Kauffmann, John Hoy 1925- WhoAm 1974,
   WhoS&SW 1973, WhoWor 1974
Kauffmann, Philip Christopher 1895-1954 BioIn 3
Kauffmann, Rudolph Max 1882-1958 BioIn 4
Kauffmann, Samuel Hay 1898-1971 AmJnl,
   BioIn 1, BioIn 5, BioIn 9, NewYTBE 2
Kauffmann, Stanley 1916- AmAu&B, Au&Wr,
   ConAu 7R, LongC, Pen Am, WorAu,
   WrDr 1976
Kaufman, Abe AmRP
Kaufman, Al NF
Kaufman, Anton 1882- WhNAA, WhJnl 1928
Kaufman, Gerald 1930- ConAu 23R
Kaufman, George Simon 1889-1961 AmAu&B,
   CasWL, CnDAL, CnMD, CnThe, ConAmA,
   ConAmL, CurBio XR, DcLEL, EvLB,
   LongC, McGWD, ModWD, NewYTBE 3,
   OxAm, Pen Am, REn, REnAL, REnWD,
   TwCA, TwCA Sup, TwCW, WebBD,
   WebE&AL
Kaufman, Hal NF
Kaufman, Herbert 1878-1947 AmAu&B, AmLY,
   BioIn 1, DcNAA, HisAmM XR
Kaufman, Isidore 1892-1978 NF
Kaufman, Julian Mortimer 1918- WhoAdv 1972,

WhoAm 1974, WhoWest 1974
Kaufman, Kenneth Carlyle 1887-1945 AmAu&B
Kaufman, Mervyn NF
Kaufman, Michael NF
Kaufman, S Jay 1886-1957 BioIn 4, WhJnl 1928
Kaufman, Sue 1926-1977 ConAu XR, ConLC 3,
    DrAF 1976, WhoAm 1974, WrDr 1976
Kaufman, Wolfe 1905?-1970 ConAu 29
Kaufmann, Myron S 1921- BioIn 4, ConAu 25
Kaufmann, Paula C NF
Kaufmann, Sigismund 1825-1889 BioIn 2
Kaul, Donald 1934- ConAu 65
Kautsky, Karl Johann 1854-1938 AmRP, WebBD
Kautz, John Arthur 1860-1938 WhJnl 1928
Kavaler, Arthur R OvPC
Kavanagh-Camp, Fletcher NF
Kavanaugh, Julie NF
Kavanaugh, Ted OvPC
Kaveny, Edward T 1896- WhJnl 1928
Kawada, Kikuji 1933?- BioIn 10
Kawakami, Kiyoshi Kari 1875-1949 BioIn 2,
    WebBD
Kawanago, Makoto 1931- NF
Kay, Gerta NF
Kay, Jane Holtz NF
Kay, Keith NF
Kay, Margaret 1944?- BioIn 8
Kay, Princess NF
Kay, T H 1884- WhJnl 1928
Kay, Virginia 1927?-1969 BioIn 8, ForWC 1970
Kaye, C Frank 1863- WhJnl 1928
Kaye, Sidney D 1895- WhJnl 1928
Kayenbergh, Marie Emile Albert see Giraud, Albert
Kaylor, Robert NF
Kaynor, Joseph Clifford 1887- WhJnl 1928
Kazickas, Jurate NF
Kazin, Alfred 1915- AmAu&B, Au&Wr,
    CasWL, CelR 1973, ConAu 4R, CurBio XR,
    DrAS 74E, HisAmM XR, IntWW 1974,
    OxAm, Pen Am, RAdv 1, REn, REnAL,
    TwCA Sup, WhoAm 1974, WhoWor 1974,
    WhoWorJ 1972
Kazmayer, Robert Henderson 1908- WhoAm 1974
Keane, Albert W 1888?- WhJnl 1928
Keane, Bil 1922- BioIn 9, ConAu 33,
    SmATA 4, WhoAmA 1973
Keane, Charles Peter 1886-1950 BioIn 2
Keane, Clifton Joseph BioIn 7
Keane, Jim NF
Keane, K NF
Kearney, Donald Leo 1918- OvPC, WhoAdv 1972
Kearney, George Fairchild 1895-1960 WhNAA,
    WhJnl 1928
Kearney, Martin J HisAmM XR
Kearney, Vincent S 1913- BioIn 4
Kearns, Frank NF
Kearns, Robert M NF
Keasler, John 1921?- BioIn 2, BioIn 5
Keast, Laurie NF
Keat, James Sussman 1929- WhoAm 1974
Keate, James Stuart 1913- CanWW 1972,
    WhoCan 1973, WhoWor 1974
Keate, Jeff NF
Keating, Bern 1915- ConAu XR, SmATA XR,
    WrDr 1976
Keating, Brian NewMr
Keating, Catherine J NF
Keating, Edward 1875-1965 BioIn 8, NatCAB 51
Keating, Edward M 1925- ConAu 15R
Keating, Franke NF
Keating, H H F 1926- ConAu 33
Keating, John G 1917?-1968 BioIn 8
Keating, John McLeod 1830-1906 AmAu,
    AmAu&B, DcAmB 10, DcNAA

Keating, John W HisAmM XR
Keating, Joseph F NF
Keating, Joseph Ignatius Patrick 1865-1939
    BioIn 1, CathA 1930, WhoLA
Keating, Leo Bernard 1915- ConAu 29,
    SmATA 10
Keating, Leo Bernard see also Keating, Bern
Keating, Michael 1932- ConAu 49
Keating, William John 1927- WhoAm 1974,
    WhoAmP 1973, WhoGov 1972,
    WhoMW 1974
Keatley, Robert Leland 1935- WhoAm 1974
Keats, Liloth NF
Keats, M NF
Keats, William NF
Keavy, Hubbard 1902- BioIn 9, WhoAm 1974,
    WhoWest 1974
Keble, Howard see Bell, John Keble
Keck, Harry 1897-1965 NF
Keddell, Georgina 1913- ConAu 25
Keefe, Frederick Henry 1881-1943 BioIn 2,
    NatCAB 34
Keefe, William McG 1894- WhJnl 1928
Keegan, Anne NF
Keegan, Charlie NF
Keegan, William J 1895?-1954 BioIn 3
Keel, Pinckney NF
Keeler, Bronson C d1909 Alli Sup, DcNAA
Keeler, Harry Stephen 1894?-1967 AmAu&B,
    EncMys, HisAmM XR, WhNAA
Keeler, James Edward NF
Keeler, James Edward 1857-1900 HisAmM XR
Keeler, O B 1882-1950 BioIn 2, WhNAA
Keeler, Ralph Olmstead 1840-1873 Alli Sup,
    AmAu&B, BioIn 6, DcAmA, DcAmB 10,
    DcNAA, OhA&B, OxAm
Keeley, James 1867-1934 AmAu&B, AmJnl,
    BioIn 3
Keeley, Joseph Charles 1907- AmAu&B,
    ConAu 25, WhoAm 1974
Keeley, Richard NF
Keemle, Louis F 1898?-1952 BioIn 3
Keenan, Edward A 1893- WhJnl 1928
Keenan, Henry Francis 1850?-1928 Alli Sup,
    AmAu&B, AmLY, BiD&SB, DcAmA,
    DcBiA, DcNAA, HisAmM XR, OxAm,
    REnAL
Keenan, Thomas J 1859-1927 NatCAB 5
Keenan, William D WhJnl 1928
Keene, Charles Samuel 1823-1891 WebBD
Keene, Tom H 1888- WhJnl 1928
Keenen, Thomas J AmJnl
Keener, Sidney Clarence 1888- WhJnl 1928
Keepers, W Floyd 1896- WhNAA, WhJnl 1928
Keer, Charles H HisAmM XR
Kees, Beverly NF
Keese, George Pomeroy HisAmM XR
Keet, Alfred Ernest HisAmM XR
Keeton, Kathy AuNews 2, BioNews 1974
Keever, Jack 1938- ConAu 53
Keffir, Frank M 1875- WhJnl 1928
Kehoe, Lawrence HisAmM XR
Keif, Aubrey 1898- WhNAA, WhJnl 1928
Keifer, Louis Frederick 1894- WhoAm 1974,
    WhoF&I 1974
Keilholz, F J 1898- WhJnl 1928
Keilmann, Earl David 1886- WhJnl 1928
Keim, Charles Joseph 1922- ConAu 33,
    DrAS 74E, WhoAm 1974
Keimer, Samuel 1688-1739 Alli, AmAu,
    AmAu&B, AmJnl, CyAL 1, DcAmA,
    EarAbl, HisAmM XR, OxAm, REnAL
Keiper, Charles A 1881- WhJnl 1928
Keiser, George Camp 1900-1956 BioIn 4

Keith, Adelphus Bartlett 1877?- *NatCAB 12,*
   WhJnl 1928
Keith, Carl W 1927- *NF*
Keith, Edgar Talbert 1890- *WhJnl 1928*
Keith, Robert *NF*
Kelen, Emery 1896- *ConAu 9R*
Kelen, Emery *see also* Kelen, Imre
Kelen, Imre 1896- *BioIn 1, BioIn 2, BioIn 6*
Kelen, Imre *see also* Kelen, Emery
Kelheur, Charles Leonard 1871-1964 *WhJnl 1928*
Kelland, Clarence Budington 1881-1964 *AmAu&B,*
   AmNov, HisAmM XR, OxAm, REn,
   REnAL, TwCA, TwCA Sup, WebBD,
   WhNAA
Kelleher, Agnes Anne 1900- *WhoAmW 1974,*
   WhJnl 1928
Kellen, William V *Alli Sup, HisAmM XR*
Keller, A R *HisAmM XR*
Keller, Albert Calloway 1874-1956 *HisAmM XR*
Keller, Allan 1904- *ConAu 29*
Keller, Beverly *NF*
Keller, Charles Walter, Jr. 1898- *WhNAA,*
   WhJnl 1928
Keller, Frederick Gottlob *AmJnl*
Keller, Heinz *BioIn 8*
Keller, Jack 1911- *WhoAm 1974*
Keller, James T 1870?-1957 *BioIn 4*
Keller, John W *NF*
Keller, Leroy 1905- *WhoAm 1974, WhoE 1974*
Keller, Oliver J 1898-1968 *WhJnl 1928*
Keller, Ralph Olmstead 1840-1873 *HisAmM XR*
Keller, Reamer *NF*
Keller, Victor *NF*
Keller, William G *NF*
Kellerman, Don 1927?- *BioIn 3*
Kelley, Cecil B *NF*
Kelley, Charles Darrell 1888- *WhJnl 1928*
Kelley, George W 1879- *WhNAA, WhJnl 1928*
Kelley, Gertrude 1882?-1955 *BioIn 3*
Kelley, Hubert Williams 1898?-1959 *BioIn 5*
Kelley, James *HisAmM XR*
Kelley, James Herbert 1875-1948 *BioIn 1*
Kelley, John Tyrone 1882- *WhJnl 1928*
Kelley, Joseph L *NF*
Kelley, Wayne P *RpN*
Kelley, William Melvin 1894- *WhJnl 1928*
Kelley, William Valentine 1843-1927 *DcNAA,*
   HisAmM XR
Kellgren, Johan Henrik 1751-1795 *BbD, BiD&SB,*
   CasWL, DcEuL, EuAu, EvEuW, WebBD
Kellner, Gottlieb Theodor 1819-1898 *BioIn 2*
Kellner, Mark Allen 1957- *NF*
Kellock, Harold *HisAmM XR*
Kellog, William Scripps 1897- *WhJnl 1928*
Kellogg, Alice Maud 1862-1911 *DcNAA,*
   HisAmM XR
Kellogg, Ansel Nash 1832-1866 *AmJnl, BioIn 5,*
   HisAmM XR
Kellogg, Arthur Piper 1878-1934 *HisAmM XR*
Kellogg, Clara *HisAmM XR*
Kellogg, Daniel Fiske 1865-1920 *BioIn 2,*
   NatCAB 34
Kellogg, E M *HisAmM XR*
Kellogg, Edward Leland *HisAmM XR*
Kellogg, F Beulah *HisAmM XR*
Kellogg, Frederick W 1866-1940 *NatCAB 31*
Kellogg, G D *NF*
Kellogg, Gertrude *HisAmM XR*
Kellogg, Mark d1876 *BioIn 2*
Kellogg, Paul Underwood 1879-1958 *AmAu&B,*
   BioIn 5, BioIn 9, EncAB, HisAmM XR,
   WhNAA
Kellogg, Ross William 1888- *WhJnl 1928*
Kellogg, Warren Franklin 1860- *Alli Sup.*

   DcAmA, HisAmM XR
Kelly, A O J 1870-1911 *HisAmM XR*
Kelly, Blanche Mary 1881- *BioIn 1, BkC 4,*
   CathA 1930
Kelly, Bradley 1894-1969 *BioIn 8*
Kelly, Chris *NF*
Kelly, Eric Philbrook 1884-1960 *AmAu&B, AnCL,*
   AuBYP, JBA 1934, JBA 1951, REnAL,
   WebBD, WhNAA, YABC 1
Kelly, Eugene 1877-1948 *HisAmM XR*
Kelly, Florence Finch 1858-1939 *AmAu&B,*
   CurBio XR, DcAmA, DcNAA, WhNAA
Kelly, Frank K 1914- *BioIn 3, ConAu 1R, RpN*
Kelly, Fred Charters 1882-1959 *AmAu&B,*
   BioIn 5, OhA&B, WhNAA
Kelly, Gilbert W 1878?-1948 *BioIn 1*
Kelly, H V *NF*
Kelly, Harold Edward 1864- *AmAu&B*
Kelly, Harry *InvJ*
Kelly, Harry *AmRP*
Kelly, Harry J *NF*
Kelly, Jack W 1913?-1966 *BioIn 7*
Kelly, James J *NF*
Kelly, Jerome G 1932?- *NF*
Kelly, John 1822-1886 *WebBD*
Kelly, John C 1852-1920 *HisAmM XR*
Kelly, John F 1900?-1970 *BioIn 8*
Kelly, John Grant 1872-1962 *WhJnl 1928*
Kelly, John H 1885-1933 *NatCAB 26*
Kelly, John M 1919?-1968 *BioIn 8*
Kelly, John Patrick 1927- *RpN, WhoAm 1974,*
   WhoS&SW 1973
Kelly, John Paul 1915- *OvPC, WhoPubR 1972,*
   WhoS&SW 1973
Kelly, John William 1875- *NF*
Kelly, Jonathan Falconbridge 1817?-1855? *Alli,*
   AmAu, AmAu&B, BiD&SB, DcNAA,
   OxAm, REnAL
Kelly, Kevin 1934- *BiE&WWA, WhoAm 1974,*
   WhoE 1974
Kelly, Loudon *NF*
Kelly, Marguerite Lelong 1932- *ConAu 65*
Kelly, Milton 1927- *WhoAm 1974*
Kelly, Orr *NF*
Kelly, Pat Brown *NF*
Kelly, Raymond J 1898-1967 *BioIn 7*
Kelly, Robert M 1836-1913 *NatCAB 11*
Kelly, Sandra *NF*
Kelly, Stephen E 1920?-1978 *NF*
Kelly, Thomas Howard 1895-1967 *AmAu&B,*
   Au&Wr, BioIn 8, HisAmM XR
Kelly, Virginia W *NF*
Kelly, Walt 1913-1973 *AmAu&B, AmJnl,*
   AmSCAP 1966, BioIn 1, BioIn 2, BioIn 3,
   BioIn 4, BioIn 6, BioIn 10, CelR 1973,
   ConAu 45, ConAu 73, CurBio XR,
   NewYTBE 4, REnAL, WhoAm 1974
Kelsey, Charles Edward 1862-1931 *HisAmM XR*
Kelsey, Ray T 1897- *WhJnl 1928*
Kelso, Clarence A *OvPC*
Kelso, Harry O 1872- *BioIn 3*
Kelson, Allen H 1940- *NF*
Kelton, Steve 1889- *WhJnl 1928*
Kemble, Edward Cleveland 1827?-1886 *DcNAA*
Kemble, Edward Windsor 1861-1933 *DcNAA,*
   HisAmM XR, OxAm, REnAL, WebBD
Kemble, William Penn 1876-1957 *BioIn 6,*
   NatCAB 43
Kemeny, George 1875?-1952 *BioIn 2*
Kemezis, Paul *NF*
Kemler, Edgar *BioIn 4*
Kempe, Richard J *OvPC*
Kempner, Mary Jean 1913-1969 *ConAu 29,*
   HisAmM XR, SmATA 10

Kempski, Hans Ulrich 1922?- *BioIn 5*
Kempson, Grover Cleveland 1894-1949 *BioIn 1, WhJnl 1928*
Kempster, Norman 1936- *NF*
Kempton, James Murray (1918) *see also* Kempton, Murray
Kempton, James Murray 1918- *AmAu&B, WhoAm 1974*
Kempton, James Murray, Jr. 1945?-1971 *ConAu 33, NewYTBE 2*
Kempton, Murray 1918- *AmAu&B, BioIn 6, BioIn 9, BioIn 10, CelR 1973, CurBio XR, WorAu*
Kempton, Murray *see also* Kempton, James Murray
Kempton, Willett Main 1900- *WhJnl 1928*
Kemsley, James Gomer Berry, Viscount 1883-1968 *BioIn 2, BioIn 3, BioIn 8, CurBio XR, Lor&LP*
Kemsley, Lionel Barry, Viscount 1909- *Who 1974*
Kendall, Ada Louise 1865?-1950 *BioIn 2*
Kendall, Amos 1789-1869 *Alli, Alli Sup, AmAu&B, AmJnl, BiD&SB, BiDSA, BioIn 2, BioIn 7, DcAmA, DcAmB 10, DcNAA, EncAB, WebBD*
Kendall, Clarence M 1887- *WhJnl 1928*
Kendall, Cricket 1906?-1972 *BioIn 9*
Kendall, David W d1976 *NF*
Kendall, Donald M *RpN*
Kendall, Frederick C 1889-1965 *BioIn 7, WhJnl Sup*
Kendall, Frederick W 1863- *WhJnl 1928*
Kendall, George Wilkins 1809-1867 *Alli, AmAu, AmAu&B, AmJnl, BiD&SB, BiDSA, BioIn 3, DcAmA, DcAmB 10, DcNAA, FamWC, OxAm, REnAL, WebBD*
Kendall, James *AmRP*
Kendall, John Smith 1874- *AmAu&B, AmLY, BiDSA, WhNAA*
Kendall, Linda D *NF*
Kendall, Otis H *HisAmM XR*
Kendig, Frank 1941?- *BioIn 9*
Kendrick, Alexander *RpN*
Kendrick, Charles *HisAmM XR*
Kendrick, Thomas R *NF*
Kenealy, Ahmed John 1854- *DcAmA, HisAmM XR*
Kenealy, Alexander 1864- *AmJnl, Lor&LP*
Kenen, Isaiah L 1905- *NF, WhoWorJ 1972*
Kenmare, Valentine Edward Charles Browne 1891-1943 *BioIn 4*
Kenn, Warren W *OvPC*
Kennan, George 1845-1924 *Alli Sup, AmAu&B, BbD, BiD&SB, BioIn 1, BioIn 6, BioIn 9, DcAmA, DcAmB 10, DcNAA, HisAmM XR, OhA&B, OxAm, REn, REnAL, WebBD*
Kennan, Ralph H *OvPC*
Kennedy, Berenice Connor *ForWC 1970, OvPC, WhoAmW 1974*
Kennedy, Bill *NF*
Kennedy, Bruce M 1929- *ConAu 57*
Kennedy, Crammond 1842-1918? *Alli Sup, AmAu&B, BiD&SB, DcAmA, DcNAA, HisAmM XR*
Kennedy, D Raymond 1892- *WhJnl 1928*
Kennedy, Davis Lee 1938- *WhoAm 1974*
Kennedy, Delos J 1885- *WhJnl 1928*
Kennedy, Edward 1905?-1963 *BioIn 1, BioIn 6*
Kennedy, Frederick Washington 1875-1952 *BioIn 1, BioIn 3, NatCAB 45*
Kennedy, George 1899?-1977 *ConAu 73*
Kennedy, Howard Angus 1861-1938 *CanNov, DcNAA, OxCan, WhNAA*
Kennedy, Jacob M 1864- *NatCAB 14*

Kennedy, James Harrison *HisAmM XR*
Kennedy, James Henry 1849-1934 *DcNAA, OhA&B*
Kennedy, John Bright 1894-1961 *BioIn 6, CurBio XR, HisAmM XR*
Kennedy, John Pendleton 1795-1870 *Alli, Alli Sup, AmAu, AmAu&B, BbD, BiD&SB, BiDSA, CasWL, CnDAL, CyAL 1, CyWA, DcAmA, DcBiA, DcLEL, DcNAA, EvLB, HisAmM XR, LiJA, OxAm, OxEng, Pen Am, REnAL, WebBD, WebE&AL*
Kennedy, John Russell *NF*
Kennedy, Lois J *OvPC*
Kennedy, Nancy *NF*
Kennedy, Olin Wood 1874- *WhJnl 1928*
Kennedy, Paul P 1904?-1967 *BioIn 7*
Kennedy, Robert Emmet 1910- *WhoAm 1974*
Kennedy, Roland A *WhJnl 1928*
Kennedy, Stetson 1916- *BioIn 4, ConAu 5*
Kennedy, Thomas J d1953 *BioIn 3*
Kennedy, Walker 1857-1909 *BiDSA, DcAmA, DcNAA*
Kennedy, Walter Scott 1874- *WhJnl 1928*
Kennedy, William 1924- *BioIn 8, WhoAm 1974*
Kennedy, William Sloane 1850-1929 *Alli Sup, AmAu&B, BbD, BiD&SB, DcAmA, DcNAA, OhA&B, WebBD*
Kennedy, X J 1929- *AmAu&B, ConAu XR, ConP 1970, ConP 1975, DrAP 1975, Pen Am, WhoAm 1974, WhoWor 1974, WorAu, WrDr 1976*
Kenner, Zvi Moshe 1915- *WhoWorJ 1972*
Kennerley, Mitchell 1878- *AmAu&B, HisAmM XR*
Kennerly, David Hume 1947- *AuNews 2, WhoAm 1974*
Kenney, George 1896?-1955 *BioIn 3*
Kenney, Herbert P, Jr. *NF*
Kenney, Jack *NF*
Kenney, James Pritchard 1893- *WhJnl 1928*
Kennicott, Donald 1881-1965 *AmAu&B*
Kenny, Charles A *BioIn 1*
Kenny, Herbert Andrew 1912- *ConAu 41, WhoAm 1974, WhoE 1974*
Kenny, Michael 1863-1946 *BioIn 1, BkC 2, CathA 1930, DcNAA*
Kenny, Nicholas Napoleon 1895-1975 *AmAu&B, AmSCAP 1966, BioIn 3, BioIn 4, BioIn 10, WhoAm 1974, WhoS&SW 1973*
Kent, Arthur *OvPC*
Kent, Francis B *OvPC*
Kent, Frank L *NF*
Kent, Frank Richardson 1877-1958 *AmAu&B, AmJnl, BioIn 4, BioIn 5, ForP, HisAmM XR, REnAL, WebBD, WhNAA, WhJnl 1928*
Kent, George *NF*
Kent, Ira Rich 1876-1945 *AmAu&B, HisAmM XR*
Kent, Jack 1920- *AmAu&B, WhoAm 1974*
Kent, Kurt 1940- *NF*
Kent, Mabel *HisAmM XR*
Kent, Norman 1903-1972 *BioIn 9, WhoE 1974*
Kent, Peter *NF*
Kent, Thomas *NF*
Kent, Thomas J R *OvPC*
Kent, Tom *NF*
Kent, W H *NF*
Kentera, Chris William 1925- *WhoAm 1974*
Kentera, George Richard 1922- *WhoAm 1974*
Kenvyn, Ronald 1884- *WhJnl 1928*
Kenworthy, Carroll H 1904- *WhoAm 1974, WhoS&SW 1973*
Kenworthy, E W *NF*

Kenyon, Bernice Lesbia 1897- AmAu&B,
  WhNAA
Kenyon, Charles Moir 1916- WhoAm 1974
Kenyon, Elmer 1886?-1949 BioIn 1
Kenyon, Nellie WhJnl 1928
Kenyon, Paul BioIn 1
Kenyon, Robert Edwin, Jr. 1908- WhoAdv 1972,
  WhoAm 1974, WhoPubR 1972
Keogh, James 1916- BioIn 8, BioIn 9,
  ConAu 45, HisAmM XR, IntWW 1976,
  IntWW 1974, USBiR 1974, WhoAm 1974,
  WhoE 1974, WhoGov 1972
Keppler, Herbert 1925- WhoAm 1974,
  WhoF&I 1974
Keppler, Joseph 1838-1894 AmAu&B, AmJnl,
  REnAL, WebBD
Keppler, Joseph, Jr. 1872- HisAmM XR
Ker, Frederick Innes 1885- CanWW 1972,
  Who 1974, WhoCan 1973, WhJnl 1928
Keratry, Comte Emile De 1832-1905 WebBD
Kerby, Frederick M 1886- WhJnl 1928
Kerby, Philip NF
Kerby, Philip C 1893?-1969 BioIn 8
Kerby, William Frederick 1908- IntWW 1974,
  WhoAm 1974, WhoE 1974, WhoF&I 1974
Kerensky, Oleg 1930- ConAu 29, WhoMus 1972,
  WrDr 1976
Kerfoot, John Barrett 1865-1927 DcNAA,
  HisAmM XR
Kerg, Charles Scott 1904- WhJnl 1928
Kerhouel, Gaeton see Vigne, Paul
Kerillis, Henri De 1889-1958 BioIn 4
Kerkhoff, Jack BioIn 3
Kerman, Keith NF
Kern, Alfred E 1895- WhJnl 1928
Kern, Edward 1925?- BioIn 6
Kern, Frederick John 1864-1931 WhJnl 1928
Kern, Harold G 1899-1976 BioIn 1
Kern, Harry Frederick 1911- WhoAm 1974
Kern, Janet 1924- ConAu 7R
Kern, Richard Arminius 1891- HisAmM XR,
  WhoAm 1974
Kerner, Edmund NF
Kerner, Fred 1921- AmAu&B, CanWW 1972,
  ConAu 9R, OvPC, WhoAm 1974,
  WhoE 1974, WhoF&I 1974, WhoWor 1974,
  WhoWorJ 1972, WrDr 1976
Kerney, James 1873-1934 DcAmB S1, DcNAA
Kerney, James, Jr. 1910- BioIn 9, WhoAm 1974,
  WhoE 1974
Kernighan, Robert Kirkland 1857-1926 DcNAA,
  Polre
Keropian, Haig NF
Kerr, Adelaide ForWC 1970, OvPC
Kerr, Alvah Milton 1858-1924 AmAu&B,
  DcNAA, HisAmM XR, OhA&B
Kerr, Charles S AmRP
Kerr, George F 1869?-1953 BioIn 3
Kerr, Ian OvPC
Kerr, Joe HisAmM XR
Kerr, Joseph M 1894- WhJnl 1928
Kerr, Orpheus C 1836-1901 Alli Sup, AmAu,
  AmAu&B, BbD, BiD&SB, CnDAL,
  DcAmA, DcEnL, DcLEL, DcNAA, OxAm,
  REn, WebBD
Kerr, Orpheus C see also Newell, Robert Henry
Kerr, Philip Henry 1882-1940 WebBD
Kerr, Robert Kenneth 1898-1953 BioIn 6,
  NatCAB 43
Kerr, Sophie 1880-1965 AmAu&B, AmNov,
  TwCA, TwCA Sup, WebBD, WhNAA
Kerr, Victor NF
Kerr, Walter Francis 1913- AmAu&B,
  AmSCAP 1966, Au&Wr, BioIn 1,

ConAu 7R, CurBio XR, IntWW 1976,
  OxAm, REnAL, WhoAm 1974, WhoE 1974,
  WhoWor 1974, WorAu, WrDr 1976
Kerrigan, Edwin S 1901- WhJnl 1928
Kerry, Tom AmRP
Kershner, Howard Eldred 1891- AmAu&B,
  ConAu 23, ConAu 73, WhoAm 1974
Kerwin, James L NF
Keshen, Albert Sidney 1905- OvPC
Keshet, Sylvie 1930- BioIn 9
Keshishian, Levon 1917- NF
Kesler, Carl Reed 1898- WhJnl 1928
Kessel, Joseph 1898- BioIn 1, BioIn 5, BioIn 7,
  CasWL, CIDMEL, EncWL, IntWW 1976,
  REn, WhoWor 1974, WorAu
Kessie, Jack Joel 1927- WhoAm 1974
Kessinger, Augustus C 1842- WhJnl 1928
Kessler, Abel E OvPC
Kessler, Felix NF
Kessler, Gene 1898- WhJnl 1928
Kessler, Ronald 1943- ConAu 69, InvJ, NewMr
Kesten, Yehuda 1926- BioIn 8
Kester, Reuben P 1869- WhJnl 1928
Kester, Vaughan 1869-1911 AmAu&B, BiDSA,
  DcAmA, DcAmB 10, DcNAA, OhA&B,
  TwCA, WebBD
Kesterton, Wilfred 1914- ConAu 41
Kesting, Theodore 1918- WhoAm 1974,
  WhoF&I 1974
Ketalaer, Nicholas ForP
Ketcham, Hank 1920- BioIn 3, BioIn 4,
  CurBio XR
Ketcham, Hank see also Ketcham, Henry King
Ketcham, Henry King 1920- AmAu&B,
  WhoAm 1974, WhoAmA 1973,
  WhoWest 1974, WhoWor 1974
Ketcham, Henry King see also Ketcham, Hank
Ketcham, Carleton J 1897- WhNAA
Ketchum, John Buckhout 1837-1914 DcAmA,
  DcNAA
Ketchum, Thomas Carleton Lee 1862?-1927
  DcNAA
Ketele, S NF
Kettell, Samuel 1800-1855 Alli, AmAu&B,
  BiD&SB, CyAL 2, DcAmA, DcNAA,
  HisAmM XR, OxAm, REnAL
Kettell, Thomas Prentice HisAmM XR
Kettner, Mangus G 1882?-1951 BioIn 2
Kevess, Arthur 1916?-1973 BioIn 9
Kewes, Karol 1924- ConAu 9R
Key, Pierre VanRensselaer 1872-1945 AmAu&B,
  DcNAA, WebBD, WhNAA
Key, Theodore 1912- AmAu&B, BioIn 3,
  BioIn 9, ConAu 13R, HisAmM XR,
  WhoAm 1974, WhoAmA 1973,
  WhoWorJ 1972
Key, Thomas J HisAmM XR
Key, Wilson Bryan 1925- ConAu 49
Keyes, Frances Parkinson 1885-1970 AmAu&B,
  AmNov, BkCL, CathA 1930, ConAu 5R,
  ConAu 25, EvLB, LongC, Pen Am, REn,
  TwCA, TwCA Sup, TwCW, WebBD,
  WhNAA
Keyes, George T HisAmM XR
Keyes, Helen 1874-1951 BioIn 2
Keyes, Homer Eaton 1875-1938 NatCAB 28,
  WhNAA
Keyes, Paul William 1924- WhoAm 1974
Keylor, Arthur W WhoF&I 1974
Keynes, Baron John Maynard 1883-1946 DcLEL,
  EvLB, HisAmM XR, LongC, NewC,
  OxEng, REn, TwCA, TwCA Sup, WebBD,
  WebE&AL
Keys, Clement Melville 1876-1952 DcAmB S5,

HisAmM XR
Keys, Henry *NF*
Keyser, Earl Edward 1903-1955 *BioIn 3*
Keyser, Harriette A 1841- *Alli Sup,*
HisAmM XR
Keyser, W Fenwick 1912?-1968 *BioIn 8*
Keyserlingk, Robert Wendelin Henry 1905-
BioIn 1, BioIn 3, CanWW 1972,
CathA 1952
Khalatbari, Adel-Sultan 1901?-1977 *ConAu 69*
Khalil, Abou *NF*
Khan, Mohammed Akram 1869?-1968 *BioIn 8*
Khan, Sadruddin Aga *NF*
Kidd, Paul *RpN*
Kidney, James A *NF*
Kieckhefer, Erwin D *RpN*
Kielty, Bernardine *AuBYP, BioIn 8, REnAL*
Kiely, Benedict 1919- *Au&Wr, BioIn 9,*
CathA 1952, ConAu 1, ConNov 1972,
ConNov 1976, WorAu, WrDr 1976
Kieran, Evelyn *NF*
Kieran, James Michael 1901?-1952 *BioIn 2*
Kieran, John Francis 1892- *AmAu&B, BioIn 1,*
BioIn 2, BioIn 3, BioIn 4, BioIn 5, BioIn 7,
BioIn 8, BioIn 9, CathA 1930, REn,
REnAL, WebBD, WhoAm 1974, WhoE 1974
Kiernan, Leo 1899-1952 *AmJnl, BioIn 2*
Kiernan, Mike *NewMr*
Kiernan, Walter 1902-1978 *BioIn 2, ConAu 73,*
WhoAm 1974
Kieser, Ellwood E 1929- *WhoAm 1974*
Kiest, Edwin John 1861-1941 *BioIn 5,*
NatCAB 42, WhJnl 1928
Kifner, John W 1942?- *NF*
Kift, Jane Leslie *WhNAA, WhJnl 1928*
Kiker, Douglas 1930- *Au&Wr, ConAu 65*
Kilbon, Roland 1891?-1952 *BioIn 3*
Kilbourn, Jonathan 1916?-1976 *ConAu 65*
Kilbracken, Lord John Raymond Godley 1920-
Au&Wr, BioIn 4, BioIn 6, ConAu 7R,
Who 1974, WrDr 1976
Kilburger, Wilbur Francis 1914- *WhoAm 1974*
Kilby, Cyrus Hamlin 1828- *DcNAA*
Kildal, Arne *HisAmM XR*
Kildare, Owen Frawley 1864-1911 *AmAu&B,*
DcNAA
Kiley, Aloysius Bernard 1900?-1949 *BioIn 1*
Kilgallen, Dorothy 1913-1965 *BioIn 1, BioIn 2,*
BioIn 3, BioIn 4, BioIn 5, BioIn 6, BioIn 7,
BioIn 8, CurBio XR
Kilgallen, James Lawrence 1888- *BioIn 1,*
BioIn 2, BioIn 4, BioIn 8, ForP, OvPC
Kilgore, Bernard 1908-1967 *BioIn 2, BioIn 5,*
BioIn 8
Kilian, Michael *NF*
Kilker, Frank *BioIn 2*
Killam, Charles Avery 1900- *WhJnl 1928*
Killam, Izaak Walton 1885-1955 *BioIn 4*
Killam, Walter H 1882- *WhJnl 1928*
Killanin, Baron Michael Morris 1914- *BioIn 9,*
CurBio XR, IntWW 1974, Who 1974
Killeen, Charles d1891 *NF*
Killenberg, George Andrew 1917- *WhoAm 1974,*
WhoF&I 1974
Killilea, Thomas Rutledge 1892?-1947 *BioIn 1*
Killion, George 1901- *CurBio XR*
Killion, John Joseph *HisAmM XR*
Kilmer, Forrest Junior 1921- *WhoAm 1974*
Kilmer, Joyce 1886-1918 *AmAu&B, AmLY,*
AmSCAP 1966, CnDAL, ConAmL, DcLEL,
DcNAA, HisAmM XR, LiJA, LongC,
OxAm, REn, REnAL, Str&VC, TwCA,
WebBD
Kilner, Frederic Richard 1892-1963 *NatCAB 50*

Kilpatrick, Carroll 1913- *ConAu 69, RpN,*
WhoAm 1974, WhoS&SW 1973
Kilpatrick, Charles Otis 1922- *WhoAm 1974,*
WhoS&SW 1973
Kilpatrick, George 1888- *WhJnl 1928*
Kilpatrick, James Jackson, Jr. 1920- *AmAu&B,*
AuNews 1, AuNews 2, BioIn 2, BioIn 5,
BioIn 6, BioIn 9, BioNews 1974, ConAu 1R,
NewMr, WhoAm 1974, WhoS&SW 1973
Kilvert, Cory 1879-1946 *BioIn 1*
Kim, H Edward *NF*
Kim, Hyung Sup *NF*
Kim, James *NF*
Kim, Sung Soo 1890?-1955 *BioIn 3*
Kim, Tae-Ung *NF*
Kim, Tae-Won *NF*
Kim, Yong-Koo *RpN*
Kim, Yong-Tae 1936?- *NF*
Kim, Young Il *NF*
Kim, Young Kyoon *NF*
Kimball, Alice Mary *NF*
Kimball, Arthur Reed 1855-1933 *BioIn 7,*
DcNAA, HisAmM XR, NatCAB 47
Kimball, B Palmer 1894- *WhJnl 1928*
Kimball, C D 1879- *WhJnl 1928*
Kimball, Fred M *HisAmM XR*
Kimball, Grace Atkinson *HisAmM XR*
Kimball, Ingalls 1874-1933 *AmJnl, HisAmM XR,*
NatCAB 30
Kimball, Mrs. Lou H *HisAmM XR*
Kimball, Vera F 1903- *WhoAm 1974,*
WhoAmW 1974, WhoS&SW 1973
Kimball, Ward 1910?- *BioIn 10*
Kimble, Leslie D 1893- *WhJnl 1928*
Kimbrell, Woody *NF*
Kimbrough, Emily 1899- *AmAu&B, Au&Wr,*
ConAu 17R, IndAu 1917, OxAm, REnAL,
SmATA 2, WhoWor 1974, WorAu,
WrDr 1976
Kimbrough, Jess *AmRP, BlkAW*
Kimche, Jon 1909- *WhoWor 1974*
Kimel, David M 1897- *WhJnl 1928*
Kimmel, Oscar H 1877- *WhJnl 1928*
Kincaid, Dorothy *NF*
Kincaid, Harrison R 1836- *NatCAB 7*
Kincaid, Jamaica *NF*
Kincaid, Jim *NF*
Kincaid, Mary *BioIn 6*
Kincaid, Randall Rich 1903-1971 *BioIn 9*
Kincey, Robert W 1895- *WhJnl 1928*
Kinch, Sam E, Jr. 1940- *ConAu 45*
King, A E *NF*
King, A Rowden *WhJnl 1928*
King, Alfred William Vernon 1897-1957 *BioIn 4*
King, Brian B 1947- *NF*
King, Caroline Blanche 1871-1947 *DcNAA,*
WhJnl Sup
King, Carroll E 1893- *WhNAA, WhJnl 1928*
King, Cecil Harmsworth 1901- *BioIn 2, BioIn 4,*
BioIn 5, BioIn 6, BioIn 7, BioIn 8, BioIn 9,
ForP, IntWW 1976, Lor&LP, Who 1974,
WhoWor 1974, WrDr 1976
King, Charles 1789-1867 *WebBD*
King, Clyde Lyndon *HisAmM XR*
King, Cy *NF*
King, Cyril Bernard 1905- *WhoAm 1974*
King, Earl *OvPC*
King, Edward Smith 1848-1896 *AmAu, AmAu&B,*
DcAmB 10, DcNAA, HisAmM XR
King, Eileen *NF*
King, Eleanor Anthony 1901-1949 *BioIn 2*
King, Fay *WhJnl 1928*
King, Francis Scott *HisAmM XR*
King, Frank H *NF*

King, Frank O 1883-1969 *AmAu&B*, *AmJnl*,
  BioIn 1, *BioIn 2*, *BioIn 3*, *BioIn 8*
King, Geraldine B *NF*
King, Mrs. H C *HisAmM XR*
King, Henry 1842-1915 *AmAu&B*, *DcAmB 10*,
  NatCAB 24
King, Henry D *NF*
King, Herbert Booth *HisAmM XR*
King, Homer D 1896- *BioIn 3*, *BioIn 4*
King, Horatio Collins 1837-1918 *Alli Sup*,
  DcAmA, *DcNAA*, *HisAmM XR*
King, James 1822-1856 *AmJnl*, *BioIn 1*, *BioIn 2*,
  BioIn 4, *BioIn 7*, *BioIn 8*
King, James Bruce 1922- *WhoWest 1974*
King, Jerry *NF*
King, John *HisAmM XR*
King, John Lewis 1879?-1949 *AmJnl*, *BioIn 2*
King, Joseph *HisAmM XR*
King, Larry L 1929- *BioIn 8*, *BioIn 9*,
  ConAu 15R, *NewMr*
King, Loretta *OvPC*
King, Lyman M *WhJnl 1928*
King, Mary *WhJnl 1928*
King, Murray *AmRP*
King, O H P 1902- *AmJnl*, *ConAu 2R*
King, Oswin Kerryn 1889- *WhNAA*, *WhJnl 1928*
King, Padraic 1886- *WhJnl Sup*
King, Ralph *NF*
King, Ralph 1928- *Au&Wr*
King, Robert Cotton 1931- *WhoAm 1974*,
  WhoF&I 1974, *WhoMW 1974*
King, Rufus 1755-1827 *AmAu&B*, *WebBD*
King, Rufus 1814-1876 *BioIn 5*, *BioIn 7*,
  HisAmM XR, *WebBD*
King, Rufus 1817-1891 *Alli Sup*, *DcNAA*,
  OhA&B
King, Seth S *AuBYP*, *BioIn 8*, *WhoE 1974*
King, Stoddard 1889-1933 *AmAu&B*,
  AmSCAP 1966, *DcNAA*, *REnAL*, *WebBD*
King, Terry Johnson 1929-1978 *ConAu 17R*
King, Warren Thomas 1916-1978 *WhoAm 1974*,
  WhoAmA 1973, *WhoE 1974*, *WhoWor 1974*
King, William Gaut 1907-1949 *BioIn 2*
King, William L *Alli Sup*
King, William Lyon Mackenzie 1874-1950
  CurBio XR, *OxCan*, *WebBD*, *WhNAA*
King, William Peter 1871-1953 *HisAmM XR*,
  WhNAA
King, Wyncie 1883?-1961 *BioIn 5*
Kingdon, Frank 1894-1972 *BioIn 9*, *ConAu 33*,
  CurBio XR, *NewYTBE 3*, *REnAL*
Kingman, Elias *AmJnl*
Kingsbury, Albert B 1860- *WhJnl 1928*
Kingsbury, Edward Martin 1854-1946 *BioIn 1*,
  BioIn 2, *NatCAB 36*
Kingsbury, Harry D 1874?-1949 *BioIn 1*
Kingsbury, Theodore Bryant 1828- *BiDSA*, *LiJA*
Kingsbury-Smith, Joseph 1908- *CelR 1973*,
  IntWW 1976, *WhoAm 1974*, *WhoWor 1974*
Kingsbury-Smith, Joseph *see also* Smith, Kingsbury
Kingsley, Henry 1830-1876 *Alli Sup*, *BbD*,
  BiD&SB, *BrAu 19*, *CarSB*, *CyWA*,
  DcBiA, *DcEnA*, *DcEnL*, *DcEuL*, *DcLEL*,
  EvLB, *HsB&A*, *NewC*, *OxEng*, *Pen Eng*,
  REn, *WebBD*, *WebE&AL*
Kingsley, Nathan 1926- *OvPC*, *USBiR 1974*
Kingsley, Robert E *OvPC*
Kingsley, Walter Ingalls 1923- *WhoAm 1974*
Kingston, William Beatty 1837- *Alli Sup*,
  BiD&SB, *FamWC*
Kinkaid, Mary Holland 1861-1948 *BioIn 1*,
  WhNAA
Kinkead, Eugene 1906- *ConAu 1R*
Kinkead, Robin *NF*

Kinley, Daniel Dalton 1917- *WhoAm 1974*
Kinmonth, Jesse Lyle 1870- *WhJnl 1928*
Kinnaird, Clark 1901- *AmAu&B*, *Au&Wr*,
  ConAu 45, *WhoAm 1974*, *WhJnl 1928*
Kinnaman, J O *HisAmM XR*
Kinne, Birge 1894- *WhJnl 1928*
Kinne, Fred B *NF*
Kinney, Coates 1826-1904 *Alli Sup*, *AmAu&B*,
  BiD&SB, *DcAmA*, *DcNAA*, *OhA&B*
Kinney, Dallas *NF*
Kinney, Ed *NF*
Kinney, Harrison 1921- *ConAu 1R*
Kinney, Henry Walsworth 1879- *AmAu&B*,
  AmLY, *WhNAA*
Kinney, Jay 1950- *BioIn 10*
Kinney, Thomas T 1821-1900 *NatCAB 6*
Kinney, William Burnet 1799-1880 *DcAmB 10*,
  NatCAB 13
Kinnison, Charles Shadrach 1889- *OhA&B*,
  WhNAA
Kinnosuke, Adachi *HisAmM XR*
Kinovsky, Benn 1899- *WhJnl 1928*
Kinross, Baron John P D Balfour 1904-1976
  Who 1974
Kinross, Baron John P D Balfour *see also* Kinross,
  Lord Patrick
Kinross, Lord Patrick 1904-1976 *Au&Wr*,
  ConAu 9R, *ConAu 65*
Kinross, Lord Patrick *see also* Kinross, Baron John P
  D Balfour
Kinsella, Frank J 1891- *WhJnl 1928*
Kinsella, Thomas 1832-1884 *AmJnl*, *NatCAB 9*
Kinser, Betty W *NF*
Kinsolving, Lester 1927?- *BioIn 9*
Kinsolving, William Grady 1890- *WhJnl 1928*
Kinter, W L *NF*
Kintner, Robert Edmonds 1909- *AmJnl*, *BioIn 2*,
  BioIn 5, *BioIn 6*, *BioIn 7*, *BioIn 9*,
  CurBio XR
Kiplinger, Austin Huntington 1918- *AmAu&B*,
  BioIn 3, *ConAu 57*, *WhoAm 1974*,
  WhoS&SW 1973, *WhoWor 1974*
Kiplinger, Willard Monroe 1891-1967 *AmAu&B*,
  BioIn 1, *BioIn 7*, *BioIn 8*, *CurBio XR*,
  HisAmM XR, *OhA&B*
Kirby, Blaik 1928- *NF*
Kirby, J P *NF*
Kirby, Jack *NF*
Kirby, Louis Paul 1870- *BioIn 2*
Kirby, Rollin 1875-1952 *AmAu&B*, *AmJnl*,
  BioIn 2, *BioIn 3*, *BioIn 7*, *CurBio XR*,
  DcAmB S5, *HisAmM XR*, *NatCAB 47*,
  WebBD, *WhJnl 1928*
Kirby, S R *HisAmM XR*
Kirby, William 1817-1906 *Alli Sup*, *BbtC*,
  BiD&SB, *CanWr*, *CasWL*, *DcLEL*,
  DcNAA, *OxAm*, *OxCan*, *OxCan Sup*, *REn*,
  REnAL
Kirchhofer, Alfred Henry 1892- *BioIn 5*,
  WhoAm 1974, *WhJnl 1928*
Kirchner, Raphael *HisAmM XR*
Kirchoff, Glenn *NF*
Kirchwey, Freda 1893-1976 *AmAu&B*, *BioIn 1*,
  ConAu 61, *CurBio XR*, *HisAmM XR*,
  IntWW 1974, *NewMr*, *WhoAm 1974*,
  WhoAmW 1974
Kirk, Betty *OvPC*
Kirk, Donald 1938- *ConAu 37*, *OvPC*,
  WrDr 1976
Kirk, Edward Cameron 1856-1933 *HisAmM XR*,
  WhNAA
Kirk, John Foster 1824-1904 *Alli Sup*, *AmAu*,
  AmAu&B, *BbtC*, *BiD&SB*, *CyAL 2*,
  DcAmA, *DcNAA*, *HisAmM XR*, *WebBD*

Kirk, L J *NF*
Kirk, Lucile Dvorak 1898- *ForWC 1970,*
 WhoAm 1974, WhoAmW 1974
Kirk, Norman A 1937- *NF*
Kirk, Robert 1929- *NF*
Kirk, Russell Amos 1918- *AmAu&B, Au&Wr,*
 AuNews 1, ConAu 1, WhoAm 1974,
 WhoMW 1974, WhoWor 1974, WorAu,
 WrDr 1976
Kirk, Thomas *HisAmM XR*
Kirk, William Frederick 1877-1927 *DcNAA,*
 WisWr
Kirk, Wilmeth 1920?- *BioIn 3*
Kirke, Edmund *see* Gilmore, James Roberts
Kirkham, James M 1872- *WhJnl 1928*
Kirkhorn, Michael J 1938?- *NF*
Kirkland, Bruce 1949- *NF*
Kirkland, Caroline Matilda Stansbury 1801-1864
 Alli, Alli Sup, AmAu, AmAu&B, BbD,
 BiD&SB, CyAL 2, DcAmA, DcNAA,
 OxAm, REn, REnAL, WebBD
Kirkland, Elithe Hamilton 1907- *BioIn 2*
Kirkland, John Thornton 1770-1840 *AmAu&B,*
 BiD&SB, DcAmA, HisAmM XR
Kirkland, Joseph 1830-1894 *Alli Sup, AmAu,*
 AmAu&B, BbD, BiD&SB, CasWL,
 DcAmA, DcLEL, DcNAA, EvLB,
 HisAmM XR, OxAm, REn, REnAL,
 WebBD
Kirkley, John L 1935?- *BioIn 10*
Kirkman, Donald Christian 1929- *WhoAm 1974*
Kirkpatrick, Clayton 1915- *BioIn 10,*
 WhoAm 1974, WhoF&I 1974,
 WhoMW 1974, WhoWor 1974
Kirkpatrick, Curry 1943?- *BioIn 9*
Kirkpatrick, E E 1913?- *BioIn 9*
Kirkpatrick, Helen 1909- *AmJnl, CurBio XR*
Kirkpatrick, J D *HisAmM XR*
Kirkpatrick, M Glen 1889- *WhNAA, WhJnl 1928*
Kirkpatrick, Russell 1897- *WhJnl 1928*
Kirkpatrick, Sidney Dale 1894-1973 *BioIn 2,*
 BioIn 5, BioIn 8, BioIn 9, BioIn 10,
 NewYTBE 4
Kirkpatrick, T J *HisAmM XR*
Kirkus, Virginia 1893- *AmAu&B, ConAu XR,*
 CurBio XR
Kirkwood, Irwin R 1878-1927 *AmJnl, NatCAB 22*
Kirkwood, Marie *WhNAA, WhJnl 1928*
Kirkwood, William Paul 1867- *WhNAA,*
 WhJnl 1928
Kirolos, W *NF*
Kirsch, Robert 1922- *AmAu&B, ConAu 33,*
 WhoAm 1974
Kirschbaum, Richard Warren 1894-1948 *BioIn 1,*
 DcNAA
Kirschenbaum, Jacob 1885?-1946 *BioIn 1*
Kirschten, Ernest 1902-1974 *ConAu 49,*
 ConAu P-1
Kirshner, James M 1886?-1952 *BioIn 3*
Kirstein, George Garland 1909- *AmAu&B,*
 WhoAm 1974
Kirstein, Jane 1916-1968 *BioIn 8*
Kirstein, Lincoln 1907- *AmAu&B, CurBio XR,*
 IntWW 1974, WhoAm 1974,
 WhoAmA 1973, WhoWor 1974
Kirsten, Sidney W *OvPC*
Kirtland, Helen Johns *OvPC*
Kirtland, Jared Potter *HisAmM XR*
Kisch, Egon Erwin 1885-1948 *BioIn 1, Pen Eur*
Kiser, Bill 1927?- *BioIn 10*
Kiser, Samuel Ellsworth 1862-1942 *AmAu&B,*
 AmJnl, DcAmA, DcNAA, HisAmM XR,
 OhA&B, WhNAA, WhJnl 1928
Kisfaludy, Karoly 1788-1830 *BbD, BiD&SB,*

 CasWL, EuAu, McGWD, Pen Eur, WebBD
Kisfaludy, Sandor 1772-1844 *BbD, BiD&SB,*
 CasWL, EuAu, Pen Eur, WebBD
Kish, Frances *ForWC 1970, OvPC*
Kish, Henrietta *OvPC*
Kishiki, Kazuyoshi *NF*
Kishon, Ephraim 1924- *Au&Wr, ConAu 49,*
 ForP, REnWD
Kisly, Lorraine *NF*
Kisonak, Richard 1929?-1973 *BioIn 10*
Kisor, Henry 1940- *ConAu 73*
Kissane, Cyril E *WhJnl 1928*
Kissling, Dorothy Hight 1904- *BioIn 2*
Kitay, William *NF*
Kitchen, Denis 1946- *BioIn 10*
Kitchen, Herminie 1901-1973 *BioIn 10*
Kitchen, Karl Kingsley 1885-1935 *AmAu&B,*
 DcNAA, OhA&B, WhJnl 1928
Kitchin, Lee Coleman 1934- *WhoAm 1974,*
 WhoF&I 1974
Kitman, Marvin 1929- *AmAu&B, BioIn 7,*
 BioIn 8, WhoAm 1974
Kitson, Harry Dexter 1886-1959 *BioIn 1, BioIn 2,*
 BioIn 5, BioIn 9, CurBio XR, IndAu 1816,
 WhNAA
Kittell, Albert George 1881-1943 *WhJnl 1928*
Kittell, Clyde Stillwell 1900?-1955 *BioIn 3*
Kittredge, William Albion 1890- *WhJnl 1928*
Kitts, William *NF*
Kivity, Nissim 1926- *NF*
Kivlighan, Thomas, Jr. *WhJnl 1928*
Klaczko, Julian 1828-1908 *BiD&SB*
Kladstrup, Don 1943- *NF*
Klaich, Dolores 1936- *ConAu 49*
Klaischer, Peter *HisAmM XR*
Klapp, Eugene *HisAmM XR*
Klar, Zoltan 1893?-1966 *BioIn 7*
Klass, Sholom 1916- *ConAu 23R*
Klass, Sholom *see also* Klass, Sidney
Klass, Sidney 1916- *WhoAm 1974*
Klass, Sidney *see also* Klass, Sholom
Klatzkin, Jakob 1882-1948 *BioIn 1, BioIn 2*
Klauber, Edward 1887-1954 *BioIn 3*
Klauber, M L *HisAmM XR*
Klausler, Alfred Paul 1910- *ConAu 23,*
 WhoAm 1974
Klavan, Eugene *BioIn 7*
Klaver, Martin Arnold 1900- *AmAu&B*
Klaw, Barbara *NF*
Klaw, Spencer 1920- *ConAu 25*
Klee, Victor L 1894- *WhJnl 1928*
Kleene, Tom 1915- *NF*
Klees, Stan *NF*
Kleiman, Robert 1918- *ConAu 15, OvPC*
Klein, Alfred 1887- *WhoWorJ 1972*
Klein, Alfred M 1901-1963 *BioIn 6*
Klein, Dennis *NF*
Klein, Edward 1936- *ConAu 69*
Klein, Herbert George 1918- *BioIn 5, BioIn 7,*
 BioIn 8, BioIn 9, BioIn 10, CurBio XR,
 IntWW 1976, WhoAm 1974, WhoAmP 1973,
 WhoGov 1972, WhoS&SW 1973
Klein, Herman 1856- *WhoLA*
Klein, J Edward 1920- *OvPC, WhoPubR 1972*
Klein, Joe *NF*
Klein, Julius 1901- *BioIn 1, BioIn 3, BioIn 7,*
 CurBio XR, OvPC, WhoAm 1974,
 WhoPubR 1972, WhoWorJ 1972
Klein, Norman 1897-1948 *DcNAA, WhNAA*
Klein, Roger H 1937-1968 *BioIn 8, BioIn 9*
Klein, Samuel *NF*
Klein, William Livingston 1851-1931 *DcNAA*
Klein, Willie 1913- *WhoAm 1974*
Klein, Woody 1929- *BioIn 9, ConAu 15R*

Kleinberg, Howard *NF*
Kleine, Glen 1936- *ConAu 73*
Kleiner, Dick *NF*
Kleiner, Rheinhart 1892?-1949 *BioIn 1, BioIn 2*
Kleinman, Robert 1918- *ConAu 15R*
Kleinschmidt, Edward E 1875-1977 *NF*
Kleist, Heinrich Von 1777-1811 *AtlBL, BiD&SB,
  CasWL, CnThe, CyWA, DcEuL, EuAu,
  EvEuW, McGWD, OxGer, Pen Eur,
  RComWL, REn, REnWD, WebBD*
Klem, John *OvPC*
Klemens, Theodore, Jr. *OvPC*
Klemesrud, Judy *NF*
Klerr, Edward 1899-1961 *BioIn 2, BioIn 6*
Kleu, S J *RpN*
Klien, H Arthur *BioIn 8*
Kline, Ben G 1894- *WhJnl 1928*
Kline, Burton 1877- *AmAu&B, AmLY, WhNAA*
Kline, Charles H, Jr. 1910-1967 *BioIn 7,
  WhJnl 1928*
Kline, Charles Talcott 1911- *OvPC, WhoAm 1974*
Kline, F Gerald *NF*
Kline, Fred W *NF*
Kline, Gardiner 1878- *WhJnl 1928*
Kline, George 1757?-1820 *AmAu&B*
Kline, Henry Blue *HisAmM XR*
Kline, John H 1874- *WhJnl 1928*
Kline, John K 1875- *WhJnl 1928*
Kline, Johnny J 1888- *WhJnl 1928*
Kline, Joseph *NF*
Kline, Sidney *OvPC*
Kline, William Jay 1848-1930 *WhNAA,
  WhJnl 1928*
Kling, Ken 1895-1970 *BioIn 1, BioIn 8,
  NewYTBE 1, WhJnl 1928*
Klinger, David 1909- *WhoAm 1974*
Klinger, Kurt 1914- *ConAu 19R*
Klingman, Lawrence *OvPC*
Klinkner, Anthony Ferdinand 1880- *CathA 1930,
  WhNAA, WhJnl 1928*
Klobuchar, James John 1928- *ConAu 73,
  WhoMW 1974*
Klock, John N 1865-1938 *NatCAB 32*
Kloess, Robert W 1900- *WhJnl 1928*
Klopsch, Louis 1852-1910 *HisAmM XR*
Klose, Kevin 1940- *ConAu 53*
Kloss, Gerald *NF*
Klouda, J P 1893- *WhJnl 1928*
Kluckhohn, Frank Louis 1907-1970 *BioIn 9,
  ConAu 7R, ConAu 29, NewYTBE 1*
Kluge, John Werner 1914- *WhoAm 1974*
Kluge, Paul Frederick 1942- *ConAu 73*
Kluger, Richard 1934- *ConAu 9R, WhoAm 1974,
  WhoE 1974*
Kluttz, Jerry 1907- *WhoAm 1974,
  WhoS&SW 1973*
Knap, Ted *NF*
Knapp, Adeline 1860-1909 *DcAmA, DcNAA*
Knapp, Arnold 1869-1956 *HisAmM XR*
Knapp, Charles W 1848-1916 *NatCAB 18*
Knapp, Chauncey Langdon 1809-1898 *NF*
Knapp, Cleon T *NF*
Knapp, Frank Bradley 1878- *WhJnl 1928*
Knapp, George 1814-1883 *DcAmB 10,
  NatCAB 19*
Knapp, George Leonard 1872- *AmAu&B*
Knapp, George R *HisAmM XR*
Knapp, Herman *HisAmM XR*
Knapp, Isaac *HisAmM XR*
Knapp, John 1816-1888 *NatCAB 12*
Knapp, Joseph Palmer 1864-1951 *DcAmB S5,
  HisAmM XR, NatCAB 39*
Knapp, O H *HisAmM XR*
Knapp, Richard *NF*

Knapp, Samuel Lorenzo 1783-1838 *Alli, AmAu,
  AmAu&B, BiD&SB, CyAL 1, DcAmA,
  DcNAA, HisAmM XR, OxAm, REnAL*
Knapp, William *OvPC*
Knaufft, Ernest 1864- *HisAmM XR*
Knauth, Percy 1914- *ConAu 57*
Knauth, Victor W 1895?-1977 *ConAu 73*
Knebel, Fletcher 1911- *AmAu&B, Au&Wr,
  AuNews 1, BioIn 7, BioNews 1975,
  ConAu 1R, ConNov 1972, ConNov 1976,
  NewYTBS 5, WhoAm 1974, WhoE 1974,
  WhoWor 1974, WrDr 1976*
Knecht, Karl Kae 1883- *WhNAA,
  WhoAmA 1973, WhJnl 1928*
Kneeland, Abner 1774-1844 *Alli, AmJnl,
  DcAmA, DcNAA, HisAmM XR, OxAm*
Kneeland, Frank H 1879- *WhJnl 1928*
Kneeland, Samuel 1697-1769 *AmAu&B, AmJnl*
Kneer, H H *AmJnl*
Kneisly, Nathaniel Mckay 1892- *WhoAm 1974*
Knelman, Martin 1943- *ConAu 73*
Knerr, Harold Hering 1882-1949 *BioIn 2, BioIn 4,
  BioIn 7, NatCAB 40*
Knickerbocker, Cholly *see* Cassini, Igor Loiewski
Knickerbocker, Cholly *see* Paul, Maury Henry Biddle
Knickerbocker, Hubert Renfro 1898-1949
  *AmAu&B, AmJnl, BioIn 2, CurBio XR,
  DcNAA, ForP, REnAL*
Knickerbocker, Paine 1912- *BiE&WWA,
  IntMPA 1975, WhoAm 1974, WhoWest 1974*
Knickerbocker, Suzy *see* Mehle, Aileen
Knickerbocker, William Skinkle 1892-1972
  AmAu&B, HisAmM XR, WhNAA
Knight, Albion Williamson *HisAmM XR*
Knight, Arthur 1916- *ConAu 41, IntMPA 1975,
  WhoAm 1974*
Knight, Charles 1791-1873 *Alli, Alli Sup, BbD,
  BiD&SB, BrAu 19, CasWL, DcEnA,
  DcEnL, DcLEL, EvLB, NewC, OxEng,
  WebBD*
Knight, Charles Landon 1867-1933 *AuNews 2,
  BioIn 1, BioIn 2, OhA&B, WhJnl 1928*
Knight, Charlotte *BioIn 3*
Knight, Clifford 1886- *AmAu&B, BioIn 2,
  BioIn 4, WhNAA*
Knight, Edward Frederick 1853- *Alli Sup,
  FamWC*
Knight, Frank A 1907-1956 *BioIn 4*
Knight, Frank Hyneman 1885-1972 *ConAu 33,
  HisAmM XR, NewYTBE 2*
Knight, Franklin *HisAmM XR*
Knight, H Ralph 1895- *ConAu 25, HisAmM XR*
Knight, Harold Audas 1890-1954 *BioIn 3,
  WhJnl 1928*
Knight, Hugh McCown 1905- *ConAu 5R*
Knight, Jacqueline *NF*
Knight, James Landon 1909- *BioIn 5,
  WhoAm 1974, WhoS&SW 1973*
Knight, Jim *NF*
Knight, John James 1863-1927 *BioIn 2*
Knight, John Shively 1894- *AmJnl, AuNews 2,
  BioIn 1, BioIn 3, BioIn 4, BioIn 5, BioIn 8,
  CurBio XR, HisAmM XR, IntWW 1976,
  InvJ, WhoAm 1974, WhoF&I 1974,
  WhJnl 1928, WhoMW 1974,
  WhoS&SW 1973, WhoWor 1974*
Knight, John Shively, III 1945-1975 *AuNews 2,
  BioIn 10*
Knight, Kit 1952- *NF*
Knight, Lucian Lamar 1868-1933 *AmAu&B,
  BiDSA, DcNAA, WhNAA*
Knight, Marion Ada d1957 *BioIn 4*
Knight, Mark H 1897- *WhJnl 1928*
Knight, Mary *NF*

Knight, Norman 1924- *WhoAm 1974,*
 WhoE 1974, WhoF&I 1974
Knight, Oliver 1919- *ConAu 21R*
Knight, Peter *AuBYP*
Knight, R I E *NF*
Knight, Robin 1943- *ConAu 73*
Knight, Walker Leigh 1924- *ConAu 37,*
 WhoAm 1974
Knight, Wallace Edward 1926- *ConAu 65,*
 DrAF 1976
Knight, William Wesley 1909- *WhoAm 1974*
Knight, Young David 1899- *WhJnl 1928*
Knightley, Philip 1929- *ConAu 25*
Knights, Peter Roger 1938- *ConAu 37,*
 DrAS 74H
Knipe, Humphry 1941- *ConAu 37*
Kniskern, Maynard 1912- *WhoAm 1974*
Knister, Raymond 1900-1932 *CanNov, CanWr,*
 DcLEL, DcNAA, HisAmM XR, OxCan
Knoblaugh, H Edward 1904- *CathA 1930*
Knobler, Peter *NF*
Knogsley, Nathan *OvPC*
Knoll, Erwin *NF*
Knoll, Richard, Jr. *OvPC*
Knop, Werner 1912?-1970 *BioIn 1, BioIn 9,*
 ConAu 29
Knopf, Samuel *HisAmM XR*
Knorpp, Walter Wesley 1891- *WhoAm 1974*
Knorr, Hermann *ForP*
Knott, Jean 1883- *WhNAA, WhJnl 1928*
Knott, John Francis 1878-1963 *BioIn 4*
Knott, Richard Wilson 1849-1917 *HisAmM XR*
Know, Frances *NF*
Knowland, J F *NF*
Knowland, Joseph Russell 1873-1966 *BioIn 2,*
 BioIn 5, BioIn 7, WhJnl 1928
Knowland, Joseph William 1930- *WhoAm 1974,*
 WhoF&I 1974
Knowland, William Fife 1908-1974 *BioIn 5,*
 BioIn 7, BioIn 10, CurBio XR,
 NewYTBS 5, Who 1974, WhoAmP 1973,
 WhoWest 1974, WhoWor 1974
Knowles, Charles Oswald 1875-1956 *BioIn 4*
Knowles, Clayton 1908-1978 *ConAu 73*
Knowles, Eric 1899- *WhJnl 1928*
Knowles, James Davis 1798-1838 *Alli, DcAmA,*
 DcNAA, HisAmM XR
Knowles, Sir James Thomas 1831-1908 *BioIn 1,*
 DcEuL, NewC, WebBD
Knowles, John 1926- *AmAu&B, Au&Wr,*
 CasWL, ConAu 17R, ConLC 1, ConLC 4,
 ConNov 1972, ConNov 1976, DrAF 1976,
 RAdv 1, SmATA 8, WhoAm 1974,
 WhoWor 1974, WorAu, WrDr 1976
Knowles, Ron *NF*
Knowles, Ruth S *OvPC*
Knowles, Vernon 1890?-1951 *BioIn 2*
Knowlton, Will P *BioIn 4*
Knox, Collie T 1897?-1977 *BioIn 1, ConAu 73*
Knox, Edmund George Valpy 1881-1971 *Au&Wr,*
 BioIn 4, BioIn 9, ConAu 29, DcLEL, EvLB,
 LongC, NewC, NewYTBE 2, TwCA,
 TwCA Sup, WebBD
Knox, Sir Errol Galbraith 1889-1949 *BioIn 2,*
 BioIn 5
Knox, Frances M *NF*
Knox, Franklin 1874-1944 *AmAu&B, AmJnl,*
 BioIn 1, BioIn 3, BioIn 5, CurBio XR,
 DcAmB S3, WebBD
Knox, Franklin *see also* Knox, William Franklin
Knox, John Armoy 1850-1906 *Alli Sup, AmJnl,*
 DcNAA, HisAmM XR
Knox, Thomas Wallace 1835-1896 *Alli Sup,*
 AmAu, AmAu&B, BbD, BiD&SB, CarSB,

DcAmA, DcAmB 10, DcNAA, FamWC,
 HisAmM XR, REnAL
Knox, Walter 1863-1892 *BioIn 2, IndAu 1816*
Knox, William 1928- *ConAu 2R, WrDr 1976*
Knox, William David *BioIn 9*
Knox, William Franklin 1874-1944 *EncAB*
Knox, William Franklin *see also* Knox, Franklin
Knudsen, Don *NF*
Knudsen, Jim *NF*
Knudson, Gale *NF*
Knuemann, Carl 1922- *NF*
Knutson, Harold 1880-1953 *BioIn 1, BioIn 3,*
 CurBio XR, DcAmB S5
Knutson, Lawrence L *NF*
Knyvett, William *NF*
Kobak, Edgar 1895-1962 *CurBio XR,*
 WhJnl 1928
Kobbe, Gustav 1857-1918 *Alli Sup, AmAu&B,*
 AmLY, BiD&SB, DcAmA, DcNAA,
 HisAmM XR, WebBD
Kober, Arthur 1900-1975 *AmAu&B, Au&Wr,*
 BiE&WWA, ConAu 13, ConAu P-1,
 IntMPA 1975, ModWD, OxAm, REn,
 REnAL, TwCA, TwCA Sup, WhoAm 1974,
 WhoWorJ 1972
Kober, Barbara *NF*
Kobler, Christopher *NF*
Kobre, Sidney 1907- *ConAu 65*
Koch, Carl *OvPC*
Koch, Marion 1904- *WhJnl 1928*
Koch, Thilo 1920- *ConAu 25*
Kocher, A Lawrence 1885-1969 *BioIn 8*
Kochetov, Vsevolod Anisimovich 1912-1973
 BioIn 10, ConAu 45, NewYTBE 4,
 WhoWor 1974
Kocivar, Ben 1916- *WhoAm 1974*
Koeberlein, Leo *NF*
Koehl, Edgar 1887- *WhJnl 1928*
Koehler, George Applegate 1921- *IntMPA 1975,*
 WhoAm 1974
Koehler, Joseph M 1900-1977 *WhJnl 1928*
Koehler, Margaret Hudson *NF*
Koehler, Robert Earl 1924- *WhoAm 1974,*
 WhoS&SW 1973
Koehler, Sylvester Rosa 1837-1900 *Alli Sup,*
 AmAu&B, BiD&SB, DcAmA, DcNAA,
 HisAmM XR
Koenig, Frederick *AmJnl*
Koenig, Gea *NF*
Koenig, George C 1896?-1950 *BioIn 2*
Koenig, Helmut *NF*
Koenig, Lester d1976 *AmRP*
Koenig, Rhoda *NF*
Koenigsberg, Moses 1878-1945 *AmAu&B, AmJnl,*
 BiDSA, DcAmB S3, DcNAA, NatCAB XR,
 REnAL, WhNAA, WhJnl 1928
Koeppen, George 1833-1897 *BioIn 5*
Koestler, Arthur 1905- *Au&Wr, BioIn 1,*
 BioIn 2, BioIn 3, BioIn 4, BioIn 5, BioIn 6,
 BioIn 7, BioIn 8, BioIn 9, CasWL,
 CnMWL, ConAu 1, ConLC 1, ConLC 3,
 ConLC 6, ConNov 1972, ConNov 1976,
 CurBio XR, CyWA, EncWL, ForP,
 HisAmM XR, IntWW 1976, LongC,
 ModBL, NewC, NewYTBE 1, OxEng,
 Pen Eng, REn, TwCA Sup, TwCW,
 WebBD, WebE&AL, Who 1974, WhoTwCL,
 WhoWor 1974, WhoWorJ 1972, WrDr 1976
Koeves, Tibor 1903- *BioIn 3*
Koff, Richard Myram 1926- *WhoAm 1974*
Kofoed, Jack *see* Kofoed, John Christian
Kofoed, John Christian 1894- *BioIn 1, BioIn 8,*
 ConAu 5R
Kofoed, William H *WhJnl 1928*

Kogan, Herman 1914- *ConAu 9R, WhoAm 1974, WhoMW 1974*
Kohl, Helga R *OvPC*
Kohl, John Y *WhJnl 1928*
Kohlberg, Alfred *NF*
Kohler, Charlotte 1908- *DrAS 74E, WhoAm 1974, WhoAmW 1974, WhoS&SW 1973*
Kohler, Herbert C 1891-1953 *WhJnl 1928*
Kohler, Ruth 1906-1953 *BioIn 3, BioIn 5*
Kohler, Saul 1928- *ConAu 69*
Kohlmeier, Louis Martin, Jr. 1926- *ConAu 49, NewMr, WhoAm 1974, WhoS&SW 1973*
Kohlsaat, Herman Henry 1853-1924 *AmAu&B, AmJnl, DcNAA, HisAmM XR, NatCAB 19*
Kohn, August 1868-1930 *AmLY, DcNAA, WhNAA*
Kohn, Diana *NF*
Kohn, Howard 1948?- *BioIn 9, InvJ*
Kohn, Sherwood Davidson 1927- *NF*
Kohout, Pavel 1928- *ConAu 45*
Kois, John *NewMr*
Koitzsch, Martin J 1895- *WhJnl 1928*
Kolatch, Myron 1926- *WhoAm 1974*
Kolcsey, Ferencz 1790-1838 *BbD, BiD&SB, WebBD*
Kole, John William 1934- *RpN, WhoS&SW 1973*
Kolenberg, Bernard *NF*
Koller, Lawrence Robert 1912-1967 *BioIn 8, ConAu 1*
Kollmar, Richard Tompkins 1910-1971 *BioIn 1, BioIn 2, BioIn 3, BioIn 9, CurBio XR, HisAmM XR*
Kollock, Shepard 1750-1839 *AmAu&B, DcAmB 10, HisAmM XR, NatCAB 10*
Kolodin, Irving 1908- *AmAu&B, CurBio XR, REnAL, WhoAm 1974, WhoMus 1972, WhoWor 1974*
Kolsby, Edwin B *OvPC*
Koltun, Frances Lang 1922- *BioIn 5, ConAu 23R, ConAu 69, ForWC 1970, WhoAmW 1974*
Komroff, Manuel 1890-1974 *AmAu&B, AmNov, AuBYP, CnDAL, ConAu 4R, ConAu XR, HisAmM XR, NewYTBS 5, OxAm, REnAL, SmATA 2, TwCA, TwCA Sup, WebBD, WhoAm 1974, WhoWor 1974, WrDr 1976*
Konadu, S A 1932- *ConAu 23R*
Kondo, Ken *NF*
Kondracke, Morton M 1939?- *NF*
Kondrashov, Stanislav N 1928- *ConAu 69*
Konig, Irene *NF*
Koning, Johan 1887?-1946 *BioIn 1*
Koo, Samuel 1941- *NF*
Koop, Theodore Frederick 1907- *WhoAm 1974*
Kopelin, Louis *AmRP, HisAmM XR*
Kopetzky, Samuel Joseph 1876-1950 *BioIn 2*
Kopinski, T *NF*
Kopkind, Andrew David 1935- *AmAu&B, ConAu 29, HisAmM XR, InvJ, NewMr, WhoAm 1974, WhoS&SW 1973, WhoWor 1974, WrDr 1976*
Koppel, Ted *NF*
Kopper, Philip *NF*
Koppett, Leonard 1923- *ConAu 25, WhoE 1974, WhoWorJ 1972*
Korab, Henri De 1891?-1954 *BioIn 3*
Kordel, Lelord *NF*
Korengold, Robert J 1929- *RpN, USBiR 1974*
Kormendi, Ferenc 1900-1972 *AmAu&B, AmNov, ConAu 37, NewYTBE 3, WorAu*
Korn, Gerald Edward 1921- *WhoAm 1974*
Kornberg, Warren Stanley 1927- *WhoAm 1974*
Kornfeder, Joseph Zack 1897-1963 *BioIn 6*
Korngold, Julius 1860-1945 *CurBio XR*

Kornheiser, Tony *NF*
Kornitzer, Bela 1910-1964 *BioIn 2, BioIn 7*
Korody, Tony 1951- *NF*
Korper, Fordham 1940- *NF*
Korrudi, Eduard 1885-1955 *NF*
Korry, Edward Malcolm 1922- *BioIn 9, BioIn 10, IntWW 1976, WhoAm 1974, WhoAmP 1973*
Korsch, Karl *AmRP*
Korsen, Stephen Eugene 1913- *OvPC, WhoPubR 1972*
Koshetz, Herbert 1907?-1977 *ConAu 73*
Kosmak, George W 1873-1954 *NatCAB 44*
Kosman, William *NF*
Kosner, Edward A 1937- *WhoAm 1974*
Kosolapov, Valery Alexeevich 1910- *IntWW 1976, WhoWor 1974*
Kossuth, Lajos 1802-1894 *ForP, OxGer, Pen Eur, WebBD*
Kossuth, Lajos *see also* Kossuth, Louis
Kossuth, Louis 1802-1894 *AmJnl, HisAmM XR*
Kossuth, Louis *see also* Kossuth, Lajos
Kostash, Myrna 1944- *ConAu 65*
Koster, John 1945- *ConAu 53*
Koterba, Ed 1918?- *BioIn 5*
Kotlowitz, Robert 1924- *ConAu 33, ConLC 4, DrAF 1976, WhoAm 1974, WhoF&I 1974*
Kotulak, Ronald 1935- *WhoAm 1974, WhoMW 1974*
Kotz, Nathan Kallison 1932- *WhoAm 1974, WhoS&SW 1973*
Kotz, Nathan Kallison *see also* Kotz, Nick
Kotz, Nick 1932- *ConAu 29*
Kotz, Nick *see also* Kotz, Nathan Kallison
Kotzebue, August Friedrich Ferdinand Von 1761-1819 *AtlBL, BbD, BiD&SB, CasWL, CnThe, DcEuL, EuAu, EvEuW, HisAmM XR, McGWD, NewC, OxEng, OxFr, OxGer, Pen Eur, REn, REnWD, WebBD*
Kotzky, Alex Sylvester 1923- *WhoAm 1974*
Kountz, Carol *NF*
Kouwenhoven, John Atlee 1909- *AmAu&B, ConAu 1R, DrAS 74E, LiJA, WhoAm 1974, WhoAmA 1973, WrDr 1976*
Kovach, Bill 1932- *ConAu 69*
Kovacs, Alexander 1930?-1977 *ConAu 73*
Kovacs, Istvan 1927- *NF*
Koval, Patricia O'Brien 1936?- *NF*
Koven, Joseph *AmRP*
Koven, Ronald *NF*
Koves, Helen *HisAmM XR*
Kowal, John Paul 1942- *NF*
Kozloff, Max 1933- *AmAu&B, WhoAm 1974, WhoAmA 1973*
Kracht, A Clemens 1887- *WhJnl 1928*
Kraemer, Henry 1868-1924 *DcNAA, HisAmM XR*
Kraemer, Joseph Louis 1872- *WhJnl 1928*
Krafsur, Samuel S *NF*
Kraft, Hy 1899-1975 *BiE&WWA, ConAu 41, ConAu 57*
Kraft, Joseph 1924- *AmAu&B, BioIn 7, ConAu 9R, WhoAm 1974, WhoS&SW 1973, WrDr 1976*
Kraft, Ole Bjorn 1893- *BioIn 2, BioIn 3, CurBio XR*
Kraft, Virginia 1932- *ConAu 21R, ForWC 1970, WhoAmW 1974, WhoE 1974*
Kraglund, John 1922- *WhoAm 1974*
Krahmer, Arthur 1901-1971 *BioIn 9*
Kram, Debbie *InvJ*
Kramer, Chris *BioIn 9*
Kramer, Dale 1911-1966 *AmAu&B, BioIn 7*
Kramer, Gene 1927- *ConAu 69*

Kramer, Hilton 1928- *WhoAmA 1973*
Kramer, Jack *OvPC*
Kramer, Kenneth 1904- *WhoAm 1974*
Kramer, Mark W *OvPC*
Kramer, Peter G *NF*
Kramer, Sidney B *OvPC*
Kramp, Louis J 1912?-1965 *BioIn 7*
Kraner, Thomas J *OvPC*
Kranidiotis, Nicos 1911- *IntWW 1976*,
  WhoWor 1974
Kranish, Arthur 1928- *NF*
Kranz, Philip *NF*
Kraslow, David J 1926- *ConAu 29*, *InvJ*, *RpN*,
  WhoAm 1974
Krasna, Norman 1909- *AmAu&B*, *BiE&WWA*,
  CurBio XR, *IntMPA 1975*, *McGWD*,
  WhoAm 1974, *WhoThe 1972*
Krassner, Paul 1932- *AmAu&B*, *BioIn 7*,
  BioIn 8, *BioIn 10*, *ConAu 21R*,
  WhoAm 1974
Kratsch, E C 1893- *WhJnl 1928*
Kraus, Adolf 1850-1928 *NF*
Kraus, Albert L 1920- *ConAu 41*, *RpN*
Kraus, Joseph H 1898-1967 *BioIn 8*
Kraus, Karl 1874-1936 *CasWL*, *ClDMEL*,
  CnMD, *CnMWL*, *EncWL*, *McGWD*,
  ModGL, *ModWD*, *OxGer*, *Pen Eur*,
  WebBD, *WhoTwCL*, *WorAu*
Kraus, Rene Raoul 1902-1947 *BioIn 1*,
  CurBio XR, *DcNAA*
Kraus, Robert 1925- *AmAu&B*, *AuBYP*,
  BioIn 8, *BioIn 9*, *ConAu 33*, *SmATA 4*,
  ThrBJA, *WhoAm 1974*, *WhoE 1974*
Krause, Alex *NF*
Krause, George Carey 1885- *WhJnl 1928*
Krauss, Mitchell *NF*
Krauss, Robert G 1924- *ConAu 1R*
Kravencho *FamWC*
Kravitz, Nathaniel 1902?- *ConAu 49*,
  WhoWorJ 1972
Kravsow, Irving *NF*
Krebs, Alvin *NF*
Krebs, Betty Dietz *ForWC 1970*
Krebs, Walter Winston 1894-1974 *WhoAm 1974*
Krecker, Preston B *NF*
Kredenser, Gail 1936- *ConAu 21R*
Kreger, William Castles 1924- *WhoAm 1974*
Kreh, Bernard 1925- *ConAu 57*
Krehbiel, Henry Edward 1854-1923 *AmAu&B*,
  BiD&SB, *DcAmA*, *HisAmM XR*, *OhA&B*,
  WebBD
Kreiling, Ernie *NF*
Krementz, Jill 1940- *AuNews 1*, *AuNews 2*,
  BioNews 1975, *ConAu 41*, *WhoAm 1974*,
  WhoAmW 1974
Kremp, Herbert 1928- *IntWW 1976*
Krents, Milton Ellis 1911- *WhoAm 1974*,
  WhoWorJ 1972
Kretchmar, Ella M *HisAmM XR*
Kretchmer, Arthur 1940- *WhoAm 1974*
Kretzmer, Herbert 1925- *Who 1974*,
  WhoThe 1972
Kreuger, Miles *BioIn 10*
Kreuttner, Caroline 1878?-1958 *BioIn 4*, *BioIn 5*
Krieghbaum, Hillier 1902- *ConAu 5R*, *DrAS 74E*
Krieghoff, William George d1930 *NF*
Kriegsman, Alan Mortimer 1928- *WhoAm 1974*
Krimsky, George A *NF*
Krisher, Bernard 1931- *WhoAm 1974*
Krishnan, Harihar *NF*
Krishnaswami, P N *RpN*
Kriska, Jerome S *OvPC*
Kriss, Ronald P 1934- *BioIn 9*, *ConAu 69*
Kristensen, Sven Moller 1909- *IntWW 1976*,

WhoWor 1974
Kristol, Irving 1920- *BioIn 10*, *ConAu 25*,
  CurBio XR, *NewMr*
Krivickas, Grazina E *NF*
Krivitskii, Aleksandr Iurevich 1910- *BioIn 10*
Kriwanek, G *NF*
Krock, Arthur 1886-1974 *AmAu&B*, *AmJnl*,
  AuNews 1, *BioIn 1*, *BioIn 2*, *BioIn 3*,
  BioIn 5, *BioIn 6*, *BioIn 7*, *BioIn 8*, *BioIn 9*,
  CelR 1973, *ConAu 33*, *ConAu 49*,
  CurBio XR, *EncAB*, *NewMr*, *NewYTBS 5*,
  WebBD, *WhNAA*, *WhoAm 1974*,
  WhoS&SW 1973, *WhoWor 1974*
Kroeger, Adolph Ernst 1837-1882 *Alli Sup*,
  BiD&SB, *BiDSA*, *DcAmA*, *DcAmB 10*,
  DcNAA, *HisAmM XR*
Kroger, William Meers 1913- *WhoAm 1974*
Kroker, Bruno *OvPC*
Kroll, Jack *NF*
Kromayer, Hernrich E 1900- *NF*
Kromm, Franklin Herbert, Jr. 1910- *WhoAm 1974*
Kron, Joan *NF*
Kronenberger, Louis 1904- *AmAu&B*, *Au&Wr*,
  BiE&WWA, *ConAu 4R*, *CurBio XR*,
  DrAS 74E, *HisAmM XR*, *OhA&B*, *OxAm*,
  REnAL, *TwCA Sup*, *WhoAm 1974*,
  WhoThe 1972, *WhoWor 1974*,
  WhoWorJ 1972, *WrDr 1976*
Kroner, Jack *AmRP*
Kropotkin, Igor Nicholas 1918- *WhoAm 1974*
Krosney, Herbert *NF*
Krouser, James Caryl 1903- *WhJnl 1928*
Krouser, James Joseph 1876- *WhJnl 1928*
Krouser, Wenley Baily 1902- *WhJnl 1928*
Krout, John Allen 1896- *AmAu&B*, *DrAS 74H*,
  HisAmM XR, *OhA&B*, *WhoAm 1974*
Krout, Mary Hannah 1857-1927 *BioIn 3*, *DcAmA*,
  DcNAA, *IndAu 1816*
Krows, Arthur Edwin 1892-1958 *BioIn 4*
Kruckman, Arnold 1880?-1959 *BioIn 5*
Krueger, Howard Hamel 1886- *WhJnl 1928*
Krueger, Jack Burke 1908- *WhoAm 1974*,
  WhoS&SW 1973
Kruidenier, David 1921- *WhoAdv 1972*,
  WhoAm 1974, *WhoF&I 1974*
Krukowski, Nancy Harrow 1930- *WhoAm 1974*
Krulak, Victor Harold 1913- *WhoAm 1974*
Krum, Tyrrell DeYoe 1900- *WhJnl 1928*
Krumbhaar, E B *HisAmM XR*
Krumme, Richard *NF*
Krusenstiern, Alfred Von *OvPC*
Kruszka, Michael 1860-1918 *BioIn 5*
Krutch, Joseph Wood 1893-1970 *AmAu&B*,
  Au&Wr, *BiE&WWA*, *CnDAL*, *ConAmA*,
  ConAmL, *ConAu 2R*, *ConAu 25*,
  CurBio XR, *DcLEL*, *EvLB*, *HisAmM XR*,
  NewYTBE 1, *OxAm*, *Pen Am*, *REn*,
  REnAL, *TwCA*, *TwCA Sup*, *WebBD*,
  WhNAA, *WhJnl 1928*
Kryszak, Mary 1876-1945 *BioIn 5*
Kryter, Charles C 1873-1944 *NatCAB 33*
Kubes, Victor *NF*
Kubic, Milan *NF*
Kubilius, Walter 1918- *WhoF&I 1974*
Kubly, Herbert 1915- *ConAu 7R*, *CurBio XR*,
  WhoAm 1974
Kucharsky, David E 1931- *ConAu 65*
Kudlaty, Ed *NF*
Kudo, Yoroski *OvPC*
Kuehn, James Marshall 1926- *WhoAm 1974*
Kuehner, Norman 1895-1943 *BioIn 2*
Kuekes, Edward Daniel 1901- *BioIn 3*,
  CurBio XR, *WhoAm 1974*, *WhoAmA 1973*
Kuenzel, William Albert 1884-1964 *WhJnl 1928*

Kugel, Frederick A 1915?-1960 *BioIn 5*
Kugelmass, Joseph Alvin 1910-1972 *AmAu&B,*
 AuBYP, BioIn 8, BioIn 9, BioIn 10,
 ConAu 7R, ConAu 33, WhNAA,
 WhoAm 1974
Kugimiya, Tokio 1872- *BioIn 1*
Kugler, Norman *NF*
Kuh, Frederick Robert 1895-1978 *BioIn 1,*
 WhoS&SW 1973
Kuh, Katharine 1904- *AmAu&B, ConAu 13R,*
 ForWC 1970, WhoAm 1974, WhoAmA 1973,
 WhoAmW 1974, WhoWor 1974
Kuhn, Adalbert 1812-1881 *WebBD*
Kuhn, Ernst 1846-1920 *WebBD*
Kuhn, Ferdinand 1905-1978 *AmAu&B,*
 ConAu 5R, HisAmM XR, IntWW 1976,
 WhoAm 1974
Kuhn, Irene Corbally 1900- *BioIn 1, BioIn 8,*
 ConAu P-1, CurBio XR, ForWC 1970,
 OvPC, WhoAmW 1974, WhoE 1974
Kuhn, Mary Ann *NF*
Kuhn, Oliver Owen 1886-1937 *NF*
Kuhn, Ruth E *NF*
Kuhne, Ferdinand Gustav 1806-1888 *OxGer,*
 WebBD
Kuhnelt-Leddihn, Erik Maria 1909- *BioIn 1,*
 BioIn 3
Kuhns, William R 1897?-1972 *BioIn 9*
Kukic, Tom *NF*
Kuleshov, Arkady A 1915?-1978 *NF*
Kulick, Harold *AmJnl*
Kulick, Vera *OvPC*
Kullen, Sol 1913- *WhoAm 1974*
Kumpa, Peter John 1926- *RpN, WhoAm 1974,*
 WhoWor 1974
Kun, Bela 1885-1937 *WebBD*
Kung, Teh-Pai *BioIn 1*
Kunhardt, Philip Bradish, Jr. 1928- *BioIn 9*
Kunitz, Stanley Jasspon 1905- *AmAu&B,*
 CnE&AP, ConAu 41, ConLC 6, ConP 1970,
 ConP 1975, DrAP 1975, HisAmM XR,
 IntWW 1974, ModAL, ModAL Sup, OxAm,
 Pen Am, RAdv 1, REn, REnAL,
 WebE&AL, WhoAm 1974, WhoTwCL,
 WhoWor 1974, WhoWorJ 1972, WorAu,
 WrDr 1976
Kunke, Laverne J *OvPC*
Kunkel, N Murray 1904- *WhJnl 1928*
Kunkin, Art *NewMr*
Kuntz, John H J 1904- *WhJnl 1928*
Kuntze, C Donald *OvPC*
Kunz, Marji *NF*
Kunz, Virginia B 1921- *ConAu 21R*
Kupcinet, Irving 1912- *BioIn 1, BioIn 5,*
 BioIn 6, BioIn 10, CelR 1973,
 WhoAm 1974, WhoMW 1974
Kupferberg, Herbert 1918- *ConAu 29, OvPC,*
 WhoWorJ 1972, WrDr 1976
Kuprin, Alexander *HisAmM XR*
Kuralt, Charles Bishop 1934- *WhoAm 1974*
Kuramitsu, Masashi *NF*
Kurata, Susumu *NF*
Kurdyumov, Nikolai *NF*
Kurilenkov, Vasilii 1904?-1952 *BioIn 2*
Kurkjian, Stephen *InvJ*
Kurnakov-Kozelskil, Sergei Nikolaevich d1949
 BioIn 2
Kuroda, Kazuo *RpN*
Kuroha, Yoshisa *NF*
Kuroki, Ben 1918- *BioIn 2, WhoWest 1974*
Kursh, Harry 1919- *ConAu 9, OvPC*
Kurtacic, Efraim *NF*
Kurtz, Charles M 1855-1909 *HisAmM XR*
Kurtz, Henry L 1889?-1951 *BioIn 2*

Kurtz, W *HisAmM XR*
Kurtzman, Harvey *AmAu&B*
Kurzer, Siegmund F 1907?-1973 *BioIn 9*
Kurzman, Dan 1927?- *AmAu&B, ConAu 69*
Kusheloff, David *NF*
Kushner, Rose 1929- *ConAu 61*
Kustermeir, Rudolf 1893?-1977 *ConAu 73*
Kutschera, Peter C *OvPC*
Kuttnor, Robert L *NF*
Kuusinen, Hertta 1904-1974 *CurBio XR*
Kuypers, Harold M 1897- *WhJnl 1928*
Kuypers, John Anton 1869-1940 *BioIn 5,*
 WhJnl 1928
Kwapil, Joseph F 1882- *WhJnl 1928*
Kwitny, Jonathan 1941- *ConAu 49, InvJ*
Kwon, Yung Su *NF*
Kyle, Duncan 1930- *ConAu XR, WrDr 1976*
Kyle, Fleming Clason 1929- *WhoS&SW 1973*
Kyle, John Hamilton 1925- *WhoAm 1974*
Kyle, Melvin Grove 1858-1933 *DcNAA,*
 HisAmM XR, OhA&B, WhNAA
Kyncl, Karel *NF*
Kyner, Leonore 1903?- *BioIn 1*
Kyu-Hwan, Kim *ForP*

L

Laas, William 1910?-1975 *ConAu 61, OvPC*
Labadie, Jo *AmRP*
LaBarre, Harriet *NF*
Labarthe, Andre 1902-1967 *BioIn 8*
Labat, Gaston P 1843-1908 *DcNAA*
Labaut, Lucien A *AmJnl*
Labin, Suzanne 1913- *ConAu 29*
Labouchere, Henry DuPre 1831-1912 *Alli Sup,
    BbD, BiD&SB, BioIn 4, BioIn 6, BioIn 9,
    FamWC, HisAmM XR, NewC, WebBD*
Labouisse, Eve Denise 1904- *IntWW 1976*
Labouisse, Eve Denise *see also* Curie, Eve
Laboulaye, Edouard Rene Lefebvre De 1811-1883
    *BbD, BiD&SB, CarSB, DcBiA, JBA 1934,
    JBA 1951, WebBD*
LaBree, Benjamin *HisAmM XR*
Labree, Lawrence *HisAmM XR*
Labrie, Jacques 1784-1831 *BbtC, BioIn 2,
    DcNAA, OxCan*
Labrot, William H 1900-1949 *BioIn 1*
Labunski, Angus *OvPC*
Labunski, Stephen Bronislaw 1924- *WhoAdv 1972,
    WhoAm 1974, WhoE 1974, WhoF&I 1974*
Lacagnina, Arnaldo *OvPC*
LaCamera, Anthony *WhoE 1974*
Lacerda, Carlos 1914-1977 *BioIn 3, BioIn 6,
    BioIn 7, BioIn 9, ConAu 69, ForP,
    IntWW 1976, WhoWor 1974*
Lacey, Robert 1944- *Au&Wr, ConAu 33,
    WrDr 1976*
Lachenmeyer, O H 1893- *WhJnl 1928*
Lackaye, Wilton *HisAmM XR*
Lackey, Herndon 1893- *WhJnl 1928*
Lacombe, Gabriel 1905?-1973 *ConAu 37*
LaCoss, Louis 1889?-1966 *BioIn 7*
LaCossitt, Henry 1901-1962 *BioIn 2, BioIn 6,
    HisAmM XR*
Lacretelle, Jacques Amaury Gaston De 1888-
    IntWW 1976, WhoWor 1974, WebBD
Lacretelle, Jean Charles Dominique De 1766-1855
    BiD&SB, OxFr, WebBD
Lacretelle, Pierre Louis De 1751-1824 *BiD&SB,
    OxFr, WebBD*
LaCroix, Robert De *BioIn 8*
Lacy, W Gibbons 1897- *WhJnl 1928*
LaDany, L *ForP*
Ladd, Frederic Pierpont 1870-1947 *DcNAA*
LaFarge, John 1880-1963 *AmAu&B, BioIn 1,
    BioIn 2, BioIn 3, BioIn 4, BioIn 5, BioIn 6,
    BioIn 7, BioIn 8, CurBio XR, HisAmM XR,
    WebBD*
Laffan, William Mackay 1848-1909 *AmAu&B,
    AmJnl, DcAmB 10, DcNAA, NatCAB 30,
    WebBD*
Laffler, William D *NF*
Laffont, Robert 1916- *BioIn 8*

Lafleur, Benoit *NF*
LaFollete, Gerry G 1933?- *NF*
LaFollette, Robert Marion 1855-1925 *DcNAA,
    HisAmM XR, NewMr, REn, REnAL,
    WebBD*
LaFollette, Suzanne *HisAmM XR*
LaFond, Edward M 1875- *WhJnl 1928*
Lafortune, Nap 1886- *WhJnl 1928*
Lagarde, Ernest *HisAmM XR*
Lagate, Henry R *HisAmM XR*
Lagemann, John Kord 1910?-1969 *BioIn 8*
Lagercrantz, Olof 1911- *IntWW 1976,
    WhoWor 1974*
LaGorce, John Oliver 1879-1959 *AmAu&B,
    BioIn 3, BioIn 4, BioIn 5, CurBio XR,
    HisAmM XR*
Lagore, Joseph O 1900- *WhJnl 1928*
LaGuardia, Fiorello Henry 1882-1947 *BioIn 1,
    BioIn 2, CurBio XR, EncAB, HisAmM XR,
    REn, WebBD*
Lague, Louise E *NF*
Laguerre, Andre 1915?- *BioIn 10*
LaHatte, Patricia *BioIn 8*
Lahey, Edwin Aloysius 1902-1969 *BioIn 1,
    BioIn 4, BioIn 6, BioIn 8, InvJ, RpN*
LaHines, Elizabeth 1882?-1951 *BioIn 2*
Lahr, John 1941- *AmAu&B, ConAu 25,
    DrAF 1976, WrDr 1976*
Lahr, Raymond Merrill 1914-1973 *BioIn 9,
    ConAu 41, WhoS&SW 1973*
Laidler, Harry Wellington 1884-1970 *AmRP,
    ConAu 5, ConAu 29, CurBio XR,
    NewYTBE 1, WebBD, WhNAA*
Laing, Neff 1876- *WhJnl 1928*
Laing, Peter *NF*
Laird, Charlton G 1901- *ConAu 13, WhJnl 1928*
Laird, Landon *BioIn 4*
Laird, Melvin Robert 1922- *ConAu 65,
    CurBio XR, IntWW 1976, NewYTBE 2,
    NewYTBE 4, WebBD, Who 1974,
    WhoAm 1974, WhoAmP 1973,
    WhoGov 1972, WhoS&SW 1973,
    WhoWor 1974*
Laird, Stephen 1915- *WhoAm 1974,
    WhoWor 1974*
Laird, William J 1918- *WhoAm 1974,
    WhoF&I 1974, WhoMW 1974*
Lait, George 1906-1958 *BioIn 4*
Lait, Jack 1883-1954 *AmAu&B, AmLY XR,
    BioIn 2*
Lait, Jack *see also* Lait, Jacquin Leonard
Lait, Jacquin Leonard 1883-1954 *BioIn 1,
    BioIn 2, BioIn 3, DcAmB S5, WhJnl 1928*
Lait, Jacquin Leonard *see also* Lait, Jack
Laitin, Joseph 1914- *BioIn 7, WhoGov 1972*
LaJoie, Raymond A 1920- *WhoPubR 1972*

Landon, Herman 1882-1960 *AmAu&B*
Landon, Melville DeLancey 1839-1910 *Alli Sup,
AmAu, AmAu&B, AmJnl, BiD&SB,
DcAmA, DcLEL, DcNAA, OxAm, REnAL*
Landon, Percival 1869-1927 *NF*
Landorf, Joyce *AuNews 1, BioIn 9*
Landquist, John 1881- *IntWW 1976*
Landregan, Steve *NF*
Landrey, Wilbur G *OvPC*
Landrum, Lynn W 1891- *BioIn 2, TexWr*
Landry, Robert *NF*
Landry, Robert John 1903-1977 *AmAu&B,
WhoAm 1974, WhoWor 1974*
Landsberg, Morrie *NF*
Landstone, Charles 1891-1978 *WhoThe 1972*
Landy, James Richard 1867- *WhNAA,
WhJnl 1928*
Lane, Bill *NF*
Lane, Charles d1870 *BioIn 5, BioIn 6*
Lane, Charles C *NF*
Lane, Charles Howard 1908- *WhoAdv 1972,
WhoAm 1974*
Lane, Clement Quirk 1897-1958 *BioIn 5*
Lane, Gertrude Battles 1874-1941 *CurBio XR,
DcAmB S3, HisAmM XR, WhJnl 1928*
Lane, J Charles *NF*
Lane, Joan F *OvPC*
Lane, John *NF*
Lane, John Veasey 1861- *WhJnl 1928*
Lane, Laura 1913- *ForWC 1970*
Lane, Laurence William 1890-1967 *HisAmM XR*
Lane, Laurence William, Jr. 1919- *WhoF&I 1974*
Lane, Lydia *NF*
Lane, Margaret 1907- *Au&Wr, ConAu 25,
LongC, NewC, WebBD, Who 1974,
WhoAmW 1974, WhoWor 1974, WorAu*
Lane, Melvin Bell 1922- *WhoAm 1974*
Lane, Nancy 1938- *ForWC 1970, WhoAm 1974*
Lane, Ralph Norman Angell 1872-1967 *LongC,
NewC, WebBD*
Lane, Ralph Norman Angell *see also* Angell, Sir
Norman
Lane, Samuel W *HisAmM XR*
Lane, Thomas Alphonsus 1906-1975 *ConAu 15R,
WhoS&SW 1973*
Lane, Thomas H *LiJA*
Lane, William Preston, Jr. 1892-1967 *BioIn 2,
BioIn 3, BioIn 8, CurBio XR*
Lane, Winthrop D *HisAmM XR*
Laney, Al *BioIn 5*
Laney, James E 1882- *WhJnl 1928*
Lang, Andre 1893- *IntWW 1976, McGWD*
Lang, Andrew 1844-1912 *Alli Sup, AnCL,
AuBYP, BbD, BiD&SB, BiDPara, BrAu 19,
CarSB, CasWL, DcBiA, DcEnA,
DcEnA Ap, DcEuL, DcLEL, EvLB,
HisAmM XR, JBA 1934, LongC, ModBL,
NewC, OxEng, Pen Eng, REn, Str&VC,
WebBD, WebE&AL, WhoChL*
Lang, Andy *NF*
Lang, Daniel 1915- *AmAu&B, ConAu 7R,
WhoAm 1974*
Lang, Harry *NF*
Lang, Jack 1921- *ConAu 5R*
Lang, John S *NF*
Lang, Ossian H *HisAmM XR*
Lang, Paul Henry 1901- *AmAu&B,
IntWW 1974, REnAL, WhoMus 1972*
Lang, Ronald A 1936- *OvPC, WhoPubR 1972*
Lang, Thompson Hughes 1946- *WhoAm 1974,
WhoWest 1974*
Lang, Will 1914?-1968 *BioIn 8*
Langdon, Charles C 1805-1889 *NatCAB 18*
Langdon, Palmer Hall 1868- *WhNAA,*

WhJnl 1928
Langdon, Thomas Calvin 1900- *WhJnl Sup*
Langdon-Davies, John 1897- *NewC, TwCA,
TwCA Sup, WebBD*
Lange, Helene 1848-1930 *OxGer, WebBD*
Lange, Kelly *NF*
Lange, Louie A 1914- *WhoMW 1974*
Lange, Louie Angustus 1854-1917 *BioIn 5*
Lange, Sven 1868-1930 *WebBD*
Langeland, Knud 1813-1888 *BioIn 5*
Langell, Jerome Edwin 1910- *WhoAm 1974*
Langer, Adolph A 1872?-1948 *BioIn 1*
Langer, Ralph Ernest 1937- *WhoAm 1974*
Langguth, A J 1933- *ConAu 61*
Langguth, Theodore E *WhJnl 1928*
Langley, Donald C *NF*
Langley, James McLellan 1894-1968 *BioIn 8*
Langley, John Newport 1852-1925 *BioIn 3,
BioIn 9, WebBD*
Langley, Milford C 1896- *WhJnl 1928*
Langley, Roger 1930- *ConAu 73*
Langley, Wright 1935- *ConAu 57*
Langlois, Joseph Godefroy 1866-1928 *DcNAA*
Langlow, Leonard S 1891- *WhJnl 1928*
Langone, John 1929- *ConAu 49*
Langton, William W *HisAmM XR*
Langtree, Samuel Daly *HisAmM XR*
Langworth, Richard Michael 1941- *ConAu 73*
Langworthy, I P *HisAmM XR*
Lanham, Edwin Moultrie 1904- *OvPC,
WhoAm 1974*
Lanier, Albert Gallatin *HisAmM XR*
Lanier, Charles Day 1868-1945 *Br&AmS,
HisAmM XR*
Lanier, Henry Wysham 1873-1958 *AmAu&B,
BiDSA, BioIn 4, HisAmM XR, REnAL,
WhNAA*
Lanier, Lyle *HisAmM XR*
Lanigan, George Thomas 1845-1886 *Alli Sup,
AmAu&B, BbD, BbtC, BiD&SB, CanWr,
DcAmA, DcAmB 10, DcLEL, DcNAA,
HisAmM XR, NatCAB 8, OxAm, OxCan,
PoIre, REn, REnAL, WebBD*
Lanigan, Harold Webster 1875- *WhJnl 1928*
Lanker, Brian Timothy 1947- *WhoAm 1974*
Lanman, Charles 1819-1895 *Alli, Alli Sup,
AmAu, AmAu&B, BbtC, BiD&SB,
CyAL 1, DcAmA, DcNAA, EarABI,
HisAmM XR, OhA&B, OxCan, REnAL*
Lanni, Clement G 1888-1963 *WhNAA*
Lano, Joan F *OvPC*
Lanocita, Arturo 1904- *IntWW 1976*
Lans, Asher B W *OvPC*
Lansdell, Sarah Wilkerson 1920- *WhoAm 1974,
WhoAmW 1974, WhoS&SW 1973*
Lansden, Ollie P *BioIn 1*
Lansdon, Floyd *NF*
Lansinger, John M 1892- *WhJnl 1928*
Lansky, Bernie *NF*
Lansner, Kermit Irvin 1922- *BioIn 9,
WhoAm 1974, WhoE 1974*
Lanston, Tolbert *AmJnl*
Lanter, Ralph *NF*
Lants, Gerry *NF*
Lanz Duret, Miguel *ForP*
Lapham, G Moore *OvPC*
Lapham, Lewis Henry 1935- *WhoAm 1974*
Lapham, William Berry 1828-1894 *Alli Sup,
DcAmA, DcAmB 10, DcNAA, HisAmM XR*
Lapides, George *NF*
Lapierre, Dominique 1931- *CelR 1973,
ConAu 69, WhoWor 1974*
Lapin, Sergei Georgievich 1912- *IntWW 1974,
WhoWor 1974*

Lapolla, Paul Mccormick 1919- *WhoAm 1974*
Lapping, Brian 1937- *ConAu 25, WrDr 1976*
Lapping, Edward Carl 1899- *WhoAm 1974, WhoE 1974*
Laprade, William Thomas 1883-1975 *AmAu&B, HisAmM XR, WhNAA, WhoAm 1974, WhoS&SW 1973, WhoWor 1974*
Larbaud, Valery 1881-1957 *CasWL, CIDMEL, EncWL, EvEuW, NewC, OxFr, Pen Eur, REn, TwCA, TwCA Sup, TwCW, WebBD*
Larcom, Lucy 1824-1893 *Alli, Alli Sup, AmAu, AmAu&B, BiD&SB, DcAmA, DcLEL, DcNAA, HisAmM XR, OxAm, REnAL, WebBD*
Lardner, David *AmJnl*
Lardner, George Edmund, Jr. 1934- *ConAu 73, WhoS&SW 1973*
Lardner, John Abbott 1912-1960 *AmAu&B, BioIn 1, BioIn 3, BioIn 5, BioIn 6, HisAmM XR*
Lardner, Rex 1881-1941 *AmAu&B, REnAL*
Lardner, Ring 1885-1933 *AmSCAP 1966, AmWr, AtlBL, CasWL, CnDAL, CnMWL, ConAmA, ConAmL, CyWA, DcLEL, EncWL, HisAmM XR, LongC, ModAL, ModAL Sup, OxAm, Pen Am, RAdv 1, REn, REnAL, TwCA, TwCA Sup, TwCW, WebBD, WebE&AL, WhNAA, WhoTwCL*
Lardner, Ring *see also* Lardner, Ringgold Wilmer
Lardner, Ringgold Wilmer 1885-1933 *AmAu&B, DcAmB S1, DcNAA, EvLB*
Lardner, Ringgold Wilmer *see also* Lardner, Ring
Lareau, Edmond 1848-1890 *DcNAA, OxCan*
Large, Arlen J 1931- *NF*
Lariar, Lawrence 1908- *AmAu&B, Au&Wr, BioIn 2, BioIn 6, ConAu P-1, WhoAm 1974, WhoAmA 1973*
Larison, Cornelius Wilson 1837-1910 *Alli Sup, BioIn 3, DcNAA*
Larkin, Aimee *HisAmM XR*
Larkin, Alfred S, Jr. 1947?- *NF*
Larkin, H James 1888- *WhJnl 1928*
Larkin, William Joseph 1867- *WhJnl 1928*
Larned, Augusta 1835-1924 *Alli Sup, AmAu&B, DcAmA, DcNAA, HisAmM XR*
Larned, Deborah *NF*
Larned, Josephus Nelson 1836-1913 *Alli Sup, AmAu&B, DcAmA, DcNAA, WebBD*
Larned, William Augustus *HisAmM XR*
Larned, William Edmund, Jr. 1919- *WhoAm 1974*
Larned, William Trowbridge d1928 *DcNAA*
Laro, Arthur Emmett 1912- *BioIn 5, WhoAm 1974, WhoWor 1974*
Larrabee, Carroll Burton 1896- *WhoAm 1974*
Larrabee, Charles B *HisAmM XR*
Larrabee, Donald Richard 1923- *WhoAm 1974*
Larrabee, Eric 1922- *AmAu&B, ConAu 1R, DrAS 74H, WhoAm 1974, WhoE 1974, WhoWor 1974*
Larrabee, William Clark 1802-1859 *Alli Sup, DcAmA, DcNAA, HisAmM XR, IndAu 1816, OhA&B*
Larrabee, William Henry 1829-1913 *BioIn 2, DcNAA, IndAu 1816*
Larratt, Pamela *NF*
Larric, Jack 1888-1941 *DcNAA*
Larrimore, Don Martin *OvPC*
Larrimore, George Shockly 1890?- *WhNAA, WhJnl 1928*
Larsen, Carl W *RpN*
Larsen, Egon 1904- *Au&Wr, ConAu 9R, WrDr 1976*
Larsen, Erling 1909- *BioIn 6, ConAu 13, MnnWr*

Larsen, Hanna Astrup 1873-1945 *AmAu&B, BioIn 1, DcNAA, REnAL, WebBD, WhNAA*
Larsen, Jonathan Z *InvJ*
Larsen, Leonard E *NF*
Larsen, Lisa *NF*
Larsen, Roy Edward 1899- *CurBio XR, HisAmM XR, IntWW 1976, Who 1974, WhoAm 1974, WhoF&I 1974, WhoGov 1972, WhoWor 1974*
Larson, Anna McManus 1917- *NF*
Larson, Arnold Byron 1900- *WhJnl Sup*
Larson, George Charles 1942- *ConAu 65*
Larson, Kay 1946- *NF*
Larson, Ralph Kermit Thomas 1901- *BioIn 8*
Larson, Reed *NF*
Larson, Roy 1929- *WhoAm 1974*
Lartz, C B 1889- *WhJnl 1928*
Lasch, Robert 1907- *RpN, WhoAm 1974*
Laschever, Barnett D 1924- *AuBYP, BioIn 8, ConAu 4R*
Lasdon, Oscar 1909-1971 *BioIn 9, NewYTBE 2*
Lash, Joseph P 1909- *AmRP, ConAu 17R, CurBio XR, HisAmM XR, WhoAm 1974, WhoE 1974*
Lasher, Albert Charles 1928- *ConAu 25, WhoF&I 1974*
Lasher, George Starr 1885-1964 *BioIn 6, WhJnl 1928*
Lasher, Philip 1894- *WhJnl 1928*
Lask, Thomas *NF*
Lasker, Bruno *NF*
Lasker, Edward 1829-1884 *BioIn 7*
Lasker, Myles Frank 1893- *WhJnl 1928*
Lasky, Melvin Jonah 1920- *Au&Wr, ConAu 53, Who 1974*
Lasky, Victor 1918- *AmAu&B, AuNews 1, BioIn 8, BioNews 1975, CelR 1973, ConAu 5R, WhoAm 1974, WhoE 1974, WhoWorJ 1972, WrDr 1976*
Lasley, Ross A 1899?-1973 *BioIn 9, NewYTBE 4*
Lass, Abraham Harold 1907- *BioIn 2, ConAu 9, NewYTBE 2*
Lassen, Kurt *NF*
Lassen, Vilhelm 1861-1908 *ForP*
Lasseter, Robert C, Jr. *RpN*
Lassetter, William Casper 1887- *WhNAA, WhJnl 1928*
Lasswell, Frederick 1916- *BioIn 6*
Lastelic, Joseph Anthony *NF*
Lasteyrie DuSaillant, Philibert De 1759-1849 *WebBD*
Latchaw, David Austin 1861-1948 *BioIn 1*
Latchem, E W *NF*
Latham, Aaron 1943- *ConAu 33*
Latham, Frank B 1910- *ConAu 49, SmATA 6*
Latham, James 1891- *WhJnl Sup*
Latham, Joseph Claude 1875- *WhJnl 1928*
Latham, Joyce 1943- *NF*
Latham, William I *NF*
Lathan, Robert *NF*
Lathrop, George Parsons 1851-1898 *Alli Sup, AmAu, AmAu&B, BbD, BiD&SB, DcAmA, DcLEL, DcNAA, HisAmM XR, LiJA, OxAm, REn, REnAL, WebBD*
Lathrop, John, Jr. 1772-1820 *Alli, AmAu, AmAu&B, CyAL 1, DcNAA, HisAmM XR*
Latimer, Frederick P 1875-1940 *NatCAB 30*
Latimer, George *NewMr*
Latimer, James Carter 1894- *WhJnl 1928*
Latorre, Marion J *NF*
Latta, Thomas Albert 1872-1931 *DcNAA, WhNAA, WhJnl 1928*
Lattimore, Owen 1900- *AmAu&B,*

*AmM&W 73S, CurBio XR, HisAmM XR,
IntWW 1974, OxAm, REnAL, TwCA Sup,
WebBD, Who 1974, WhoAm 1974,
WhoWor 1974*
Lattin, Frank H *HisAmM XR*
Laube, Clifford James 1891-1974 *BioIn 1,
CathA 1930, ConAu 53, NewYTBS 5,
WhJnl 1928*
Laube, Heinrich 1806-1884 *BbD, BiD&SB,
CasWL, DcEuL, EuAu, EvEuW, OxGer,
Pen Eur, REn, WebBD*
Laubengayer, Robert J 1884-1958 *WhJnl 1928*
Lauder, Valarie 1926?- *BioIn 1*
Lauer-Leonardi, Boris 1905?-1971 *BioIn 9,
NewYTBE 2*
Lauferty, Lilian 1887-1958 *AmAu&B, AmNov,
BioIn 4*
Laugel, Auguste *HisAmM XR*
Laughlin, George A 1862-1936 *NatCAB 27,
WhNAA, WhJnl 1928*
Laughlin, James Laurence 1850-1933 *Alli Sup,
BiD&SB, DcAmA, HisAmM XR, OhA&B,
WebBD*
Lauinger, Philip Charles 1900- *WhoAm 1974*
Laurance, Erwin 1912- *WhoAm 1974,
WhoF&I 1974*
Laurence, Florence Davidow *OvPC*
Laurence, John 1939- *ConAu 69, WhoAm 1974*
Laurence, Michael M 1940- *ConAu 33*
Laurence, William Leonard 1888-1977 *AmAu&B,
BioIn 4, BioIn 6, CurBio XR, OvPC,
REnAL, WhoAm 1974, WhoWor 1974,
WhoWorJ 1972*
Laurent, Jacques 1919- *IntWW 1976,
NewYTBE 2, REn*
Laurent, Lawrence Bell 1925- *ConAu 69,
WhoAm 1974, WhoS&SW 1973*
Laurent, Michel *NF*
Laurentie, Pierre Sebastien 1793-1876 *BbD,
BiD&SB, WebBD*
Laurie, Annie 1869-1936 *WhNAA*
Laurie, Annie see also Black, Winifred
Laurie, James 1947- *ConAu 69*
Laurie, Joe 1893-1954 *BioIn 3*
Laurie, Patrick Gammie 1833-1902 *BioIn 5*
Laut, Agnes Christina 1871-1936 *AmAu&B,
CanNov, CanWr, DcAmA, DcNAA,
HisAmM XR, JBA 1934, JBA 1951,
OxCan, REnAL, WebBD, WhNAA*
Lautens, Gary *NF*
Lauterbach, Richard Edward 1914-1950 *BioIn 2,
RpN*
Lautier, Louis R 1896-1962 *BioIn 3, BioIn 6*
Lavan, George *AmRP*
LaVarre, William Johanne, Jr. 1898- *AmAu&B,
HisAmM XR, WhNAA, WhoAm 1974*
LaVelle, Mike 1933- *BioIn 9, ConAu 65*
Lavender, Janice Marie B De *OvPC*
Laventhol, David Abram 1933- *WhoAm 1974*
Laver, Tina *NF*
Lavery, Emmet Godfrey 1902- *CurBio XR,
WhoAm 1974, WhoWor 1974*
Lavine, Harold 1915- *AmAu&B, ConAu 41,
WhoAm 1974, WhoE 1974, WhoWor 1974,
WrDr 1976*
Lavine, Mel *NF*
Lavine, Sigmund Arnold 1908- *AuBYP,
ConAu 3R, SmATA 3, WrDr 1976*
Lavino, William *NF*
Law, Andrew 1749-1821 *DcNAA, HisAmM XR*
Law, Robert Adger 1879-1961 *AmAu&B, TexWr*
Lawler, Gordon Joseph 1911- *WhoAm 1974*
Lawler, Thomas Bonaventure 1864-1945 *AmAu&B,
DcAmA, NatCAB 35*

Lawley, Francis Charles 1825-1901 *BioIn 2,
Br&AmS*
Lawlor, Daniel Joseph 1875-1950 *BioIn 3,
NatCAB 38*
Lawlor, Florine 1925- *ConAu 65*
Lawlor, Patrick Anthony 1893- *Au&Wr, BioIn 1,
ConAu P-1, DcLEL, WrDr 1976*
Lawlor, William B *WhJnl Sup*
Lawrence, Alberta 1875- *AmAu&B, OhA&B,
WhNAA*
Lawrence, Anthony *BioIn 9*
Lawrence, Benjamin Franklin 1877-1965 *WhNAA,
WhJnl Sup*
Lawrence, Charles Edward 1870-1940 *CurBio XR,
NewC, WebBD, WhoLA*
Lawrence, David 1888-1973 *AmAu&B, AmJnl,
BioIn 2, BioIn 3, BioIn 6, BioIn 9,
BioIn 10, ConAu 41, CurBio XR, ForP,
HisAmM XR, NewMr, NewYTBE 4,
REnAL, WebBD, WhJnl 1928,
WhoS&SW 1973*
Lawrence, David, Jr. 1942- *ConAu 73,
WhoAm 1974*
Lawrence, Dick 1916- *WhoAm 1974*
Lawrence, Edgar Harcourt St. Leger d1977 *NF*
Lawrence, George A W 1911- *OvPC,
WhoPubR 1972*
Lawrence, George Andrew 1914- *WhoF&I 1974*
Lawrence, Isaac *HisAmM XR*
Lawrence, J J *HisAmM XR*
Lawrence, James Ernest 1889-1957 *BioIn 4,
WhJnl 1928*
Lawrence, Jim *BioIn 8*
Lawrence, John Frederick 1934- *WhoAm 1974*
Lawrence, Joseph Stagg 1896-1950 *HisAmM XR*
Lawrence, Josephine 1890?-1978 *AmAu&B,
AmNov, OxAm, REn, REnAL, TwCA,
TwCA Sup, WebBD, WhNAA,
WhoAm 1974, WhoAmW 1974, WhoE 1974*
Lawrence, Linda *NF*
Lawrence, Margery 1880?-1969 *WebBD*
Lawrence, R B 1882?-1951 *BioIn 2*
Lawrence, R D 1921- *ConAu 65*
Lawrence, Richard A *NF*
Lawrence, Roy K 1886- *WhJnl 1928*
Lawrence, Scott M *NF*
Lawrence, Seymour 1926- *WhoAm 1974,
WhoE 1974*
Lawrence, Sharon 1945- *ConAu 65*
Lawrence, William Howard 1916-1972 *BioIn 9,
ConAu 33, ForP, NewYTBE 3,
WhoS&SW 1973*
Laws, Raymond C *OvPC*
Lawson, David *RpN*
Lawson, Donna Roberta 1937- *ConAu 41*
Lawson, Evelyn 1917- *ConAu 57*
Lawson, H L 1900- *ConAu 5R, WhNAA,
WhJnl 1928*
Lawson, H L W *NF*
Lawson, J Murray 1848-1925 *DcNAA*
Lawson, James 1799-1880 *Alli, AmAu,
AmAu&B, BioIn 9, CyAL 2, DcAmA,
DcNAA, OxAm, REnAL*
Lawson, Jessie Kerr 1839?-1917 *DcNAA*
Lawson, John Davison 1852-1921 *Alli Sup,
AmLY, DcAmA, DcNAA, HisAmM XR*
Lawson, Mike *NF*
Lawson, Nigel 1932- *ForP, Who 1974,
WhoWor 1974*
Lawson, T Arthur 1891- *WhJnl 1928*
Lawson, Theodore W *HisAmM XR*
Lawson, Thomas William 1857-1925 *Alli Sup,
AmAu&B, AmJnl, DcAmA, DcNAA,
HisAmM XR, OxAm, WebBD*

Lawson, Victor Fremont 1850-1925 *AmAu&B,
AmJnl, BioIn 1, BioIn 2, BioIn 8,
DcAmB 11, WebBD*
Lawson, W B 1850-1929 *HisAmM XR, REnAL,
WebBD*
Lawson, W B *see also* Jenks, George Charles
Lawton, Harry Wilson 1927- *ConAu 33*
Lawton, J *NF*
Laybourne, Lawrence Eugene 1913-1976
ConAu 65, WhoAm 1974
Laycock, George 1921- *ConAu 5, SmATA 5*
Layton, Lord Walter Thomas Layton 1884-1966
BioIn 7, WebBD
Lazard, Sidney *NF*
Lazare, Bernard 1865-1903 *BioIn 1, BioIn 7*
Lazareff, Helene Gordon 1907?- *BioIn 6, BioIn 7*
Lazareff, Pierre 1907-1972 *BioIn 1, BioIn 4,
BioIn 9, ConAu 33, CurBio XR,
NewYTBE 3*
Lazarus, George 1932- *WhoMW 1974*
Lazarus, Herman 1905?-1966 *BioIn 7*
Lazarus, Margaret Connelly 1869?-1966 *BioIn 7*
Lazarus, Marx E *HisAmM XR*
Lazarus, Mell 1927- *ConAu 19R, WhoAm 1974*
Lazell, Fred, Jr. 1901- *WhJnl 1928*
Lazell, Fred J 1870-1940 *DcNAA, WhJnl 1928*
Lazurick, Robert 1895-1968 *BioIn 8*
Lea, Luke 1879-1945 *BioIn 1, CurBio XR,
DcAmB S3, WhJnl 1928*
Lea, Tom 1907- *AmAu&B, OxAm, REnAL,
TwCA Sup, WhoAm 1974, WhoAmA 1973,
WhoS&SW 1973, WhoWor 1974*
Leacacos, John Peter 1908- *ConAu 25,
WhoAm 1974*
Leach, Anna *HisAmM XR*
Leach, C J *NF*
Leach, DeWitt C 1822-1909 *NatCAB 17*
Leach, George A d1892 *NF*
Leach, Harper *NF*
Leach, Henry Goddard 1880-1970 *AmAu&B,
AmLY, HisAmM XR, NatCAB XR,
REnAL, WhNAA*
Leach, Jesse S 1878- *WhJnl 1928*
Leach, Paul Roscoe 1890-1977 *BioIn 2, BioIn 4,
ConAu 73, IndAu 1917*
Leach, Robin *NF*
Leach, Ruby *WhJnl 1928*
Leadabrand, Russ *NF*
Leader, Henry J 1909?-1972 *BioIn 9*
Leadlay, Edward 1890?-1951 *BioIn 2*
Leadley, A Thomas 1890- *WhJnl 1928*
Leahy, J Gordon *OvPC*
Leahy, Thomas Richard 1921- *WhoAm 1974*
Leahy, William Augustus 1867-1941 *AmAu&B,
DcAmA, DcNAA, PoIre*
Leake, Paul R 1891- *WhJnl 1928*
Leamer, Laurence Allen 1941- *ConAu 65*
Leamy, Edmund Stanislaus 1889-1962 *BioIn 6,
Str&VC*
Lean, E Tangye 1911-1974 *ConAu 53*
Lear, John 1909- *AmAu&B, ConAu 37,
WhoAm 1974, WhoMW 1974, WrDr 1976*
Lear, Martha Weinman 1930- *ConAu 9R*
Leard, John Earnshaw 1916- *ConAu 73,
WhoAm 1974, WhoS&SW 1973*
Learmond, Douglas *NF*
Learoyd, Harold J 1867-1957 *BioIn 4*
Leary, Bill *NF*
Leary, Francis T 1914?-1968 *BioIn 8*
Leary, John J *WhoE 1974*
Leary, John Joseph, Jr. 1874-1944 *CurBio XR,
DcNAA, WhNAA, WhJnl 1928*
Leary, Mary Ellen *RpN*
Leary, Warren *NF*

Lease, Mary Elizabeth 1853-1933 *DcAmA,
DcNAA, HisAmM XR*
Leasor, James 1923- *Au&Wr, ConAu 4R,
Who 1974*
Leath, William Ferguson 1872- *WhJnl 1928*
Leatherbee, Mary 1911?-1972 *BiE&WWA,
BioIn 9*
Leatherock, Wesley Kenneth 1897-1949 *BioIn 6,
NatCAB 43*
Leavell, David Cox 1904- *WhoAm 1974,
WhoS&SW 1973*
Leavey, Laurence Andrew 1910-1964 *BioIn 1,
BioIn 7*
Leavitt, Dudley 1772-1851 *AmAu&B*
Leavitt, John McDowell 1824-1909 *Alli Sup,
DcAmA, DcNAA, HisAmM XR, OhA&B*
Leavitt, Joshua 1794-1873 *Alli, DcNAA,
HisAmM XR*
Leavitt, Thaddeus W H 1844?-1909 *DcNAA,
OxCan*
Leavy, Jim 1928- *WhoAm 1974*
Lebedeff, Vladimir Ivanovich 1882?-1956 *BioIn 4*
LeBerthon, Ted 1892?-1960 *BioIn 5*
Lebkicher, John V R *NF*
LeBlanc, Rena Dictor *NF*
Leblanc, Romeo A 1927- *IntWW 1976*
Leboulaye, Edouard Rene Lefebure De 1811-1883
NF
Lebovitz, Harold Paul 1916- *WhoAm 1974*
Lebow, Sylvan 1912- *WhoAm 1974,
WhoWorJ 1972*
LeBreton, Edmond *NF*
LeBuffe, Francis Peter 1885-1954 *BioIn 1,
BioIn 3, BkC 2, CathA 1930*
Lechenperg, Harald 1904- *BioIn 10*
Lechlitner, Ruth *HisAmM XR*
Leckie, Robert 1920- *AuBYP, BioIn 8,
ConAu 13R*
Lecler, Paula *OvPC*
Ledbetter, Frank *WhJnl 1928*
Lederer, Charles 1856-1925 *AmJnl, HisAmM XR*
Lederer, Edith *NF*
Lederer, Esther Pauline 1918- *BioIn 4, BioIn 7,
BioIn 10*
Lederer, Esther Pauline *see also* Landers, Ann
Lederer, Joseph 1927- *ConAu 73, OvPC*
Lederer, Muriel 1929- *NF*
LeDoux, Harold *NF*
Leduc, Harry *NF*
LeDuchat, Jacob 1658-1735 *BioIn 9*
Lee, Adrian *NF*
Lee, Albert 1868-1946 *AmAu&B, AmLY,
BiDSA, BioIn 2, DcAmA, DcNAA,
HisAmM XR, NatCAB 36*
Lee, Alfred McClung 1906- *AmM&W 73S,
ConAu 1R, WhoAm 1974, WhoWor 1974,
WrDr 1976*
Lee, Alfred W *AmJnl*
Lee, Algernon 1873-1954 *HisAmM XR*
Lee, Alwyn 1912?-1970 *BioIn 9*
Lee, Anne *WhJnl 1928*
Lee, Bee Virginia 1902- *HisAmM XR*
Lee, Bill *NF*
Lee, Bob *NF*
Lee, Charles 1913- *AmAu&B, ConAu 33,
DrAS 74E, WhoAm 1974, WhoE 1974*
Lee, Clark Gould 1907-1953 *AmJnl, BioIn 3,
CurBio XR*
Lee, David C *NF*
Lee, Dick 1887?-1967 *BioIn 8*
Lee, Eleanor *NF*
Lee, Everett S 1891- *BioIn 2*
Lee, Francis W S 1870- *WhJnl 1928*
Lee, Frank L 1886- *WhJnl 1928*

Lee, Franklyn Warner 1864-1898 *DcNAA*
Lee, Glenn Clifford 1910?- *BioIn 2*
Lee, Hal Fitzhugh 1901?-1959 *BioIn 2, BioIn 5*
Lee, Harrell 1907- *WhJnl 1928*
Lee, Harry W 1870- *WhJnl 1928*
Lee, Henry 1782-1867 *BioIn 3*
Lee, Henry 1911- *ConAu 5R*
Lee, Hubert Floyd 1900- *WhoAm 1974*
Lee, Hugh Johnson 1871-1944 *WhJnl 1928*
Lee, Ivy Ledbetter 1877-1934 *AmJnl, BiDSA, DcNAA, WebBD*
Lee, Ivy Ledbetter, Jr. 1909- *WhoAm 1974, WhoF&I 1974*
Lee, James F 1905?-1975 *ConAu 61*
Lee, James Melvin 1878-1929 *AmAu&B, DcNAA, HisAmM XR, NatCAB 23, WhJnl 1928*
Lee, Jeff *NF*
Lee, John 1931- *ConAu 25*
Lee, Lawrence 1903- *AmAu&B, ConAu 25, DrAS 74E, WhoAm 1974, WhoE 1974, WrDr 1976*
Lee, Mary Ann 1939- *WhoAmW 1974, WhoS&SW 1973*
Lee, Mike *NF*
Lee, Morris Matthews 1877?-1956 *BioIn 4*
Lee, Olive B *HisAmM XR*
Lee, Paul Kern *NF*
Lee, Ray E 1904- *WhJnl 1928*
Lee, Richard *NewMr*
Lee, Richard *HisAmM XR*
Lee, Robert E *RpN*
Lee, Robert P *WhJnl Sup*
Lee, Robert Wright 1916- *WhoS&SW 1973*
Lee, Rohama *OvPC*
Lee, Sarah Tomerlin *HisAmM XR, WhoAm 1974, WhoAmW 1974*
Lee, Soo Keun 1923?- *BioIn 8*
Lee, Stan 1922?- *BioIn 9*
Lee, William F *HisAmM XR*
Lee, Wong Hee *NF*
Lee, Yan Phou *Alli Sup, WhJnl 1928*
Leech, Alfred B 1918?-1974 *ConAu 49*
Leech, Edward Towner 1892-1949 *BioIn 2, WhJnl 1928*
Leech, Harper 1885-1951 *BioIn 2*
Leech, John 1817-1864 *Alli, BioIn 2, BioIn 3, BioIn 8, Br&AmS, DcEnL, NewC, WebBD*
Leech, Lewis Harper 1885-1951 *WhJnl 1928*
Leech, Russell B 1882- *WhJnl 1928*
Leeds, Stanton B 1886?-1964 *BioIn 7*
Leek, Stephen B *NF*
Leekley, Richard N 1912-1976 *ConAu 69*
Leeney, Robert Joseph 1916- *WhoAm 1974*
Leepson, Marc 1945- *NF*
Leept, Gerardus *ForP*
Lees, Dan 1927- *ConAu 33*
Lees, Gene 1928- *ConAu 23R*
Lees, W Thomson 1889- *WhNAA, WhJnl 1928*
Leeser, Isaac 1806-1868 *Alli, BioIn 4, BioIn 5, BioIn 7, DcAmA, DcNAA, WebBD*
Leet, Frank R 1881?-1949 *BioIn 2*
Leet, Glen 1908- *HisAmM XR, WhoAm 1974, WhoE 1974, WhoWor 1974*
Lefaivre, Georgiana 1873?-1951 *BioIn 2*
LeFan, Mike 1946- *NF*
LeFanu, Joseph Sheridan 1814-1873 *Alli Sup, AtlBL, BbD, BiD&SB, BioIn 1, BioIn 5, BioIn 9, BrAu 19, CasWL, CyWA, DcEnA, DcEnL, DcEuL, DcLEL, EncMys, EvLB, HsB&A, NewC, OxEng, Pen Eng, PoIre, REn, WebBD*
Lefevre, Edwin 1871-1943 *AmAu&B, AmLY, DcAmA, DcNAA, HisAmM XR, REnAL*
Leff, Phil *NF*

Leffel, James *HisAmM XR*
Leffelaar, Hendrik Louis 1929- *ConAu 5*
Leffingwell, Charles Wesley 1840-1928 *DcNAA, HisAmM XR*
Leftwich, James Adolf 1902- *ConAu 41, WhoAm 1974*
Legantsov, Vladislav *NF*
Legare, Hugh Swinton 1797-1843 *Alli, AmAu&B, BiDSA, CyAL 2, DcAmA, DcNAA, HisAmM XR, LiJA, OxAm, REnAL, WebBD*
Legare, J D *HisAmM XR*
Legare, James W *HisAmM XR*
Legate, David M DeC 1905- *Au&Wr, BioIn 8*
Legett, T B *HisAmM XR*
Legg, Leopold George Wickham 1877-1963 *BioIn 6*
Leggert, Glenn H 1890- *WhJnl 1928*
Leggett, Craig *NF*
Leggett, William 1801?-1839 *Alli, AmAu, AmAu&B, AmJnl, BiD&SB, BioIn 1, BioIn 2, CyAL 2, DcAmA, DcAmB 11, DcLEL, DcNAA, HisAmM XR, OxAm, REnAL*
Legrand, Duard Madison, Jr. 1915-1978 *WhoAm 1974, WhoS&SW 1973*
Legum, Colin 1919- *Au&Wr, ConAu 1R, SmATA 10, WrDr 1976*
Lehane, Daniel J 1914?-1966 *BioIn 7*
Lehman, John F, Jr. 1942- *ConAu 15R*
Lehman, Milton 1917-1966 *BioIn 7, ConAu 13, ConAu P-1*
Lehman, Stan *NF*
Lehmann, John Frederick 1907- *Au&Wr, CasWL, ConAu 9, ConP 1970, ConP 1975, DcLEL, EvLB, IntWW 1976, LongC, ModBL, NewC, OxEng, Pen Eng, REn, TwCA, TwCA Sup, TwCW, WebE&AL, Who 1974, WhoWor 1974, WrDr 1976*
Lehmann, Rudolph Chambers 1856-1929 *TwCA, TwCA Sup, WebBD*
Lehmann-Haupt, Christopher *NF*
Lehmer, Larry *NF*
Lehrbas, Lloyd Allan 1898-1964 *BioIn 2, BioIn 7, CurBio XR*
Lehrer, James *BioIn 7*
Lehrman, Hal 1911- *OvPC, WhoWorJ 1972*
Lehrman, Nat *NF*
Leiber, Fritz 1910- *AmAu&B, ConAu 45, ConNov 1976, DrAF 1976, WrDr 1976*
Leiberman, Irv 1922- *NF*
Leibing, Peter *NF*
Leibovitz, Annie *NF*
Leibowitz, Irving 1922- *ConAu 11R, WhoAm 1974*
Leichter, Otto 1898?-1973 *BioIn 9, ConAu 41*
Leifer, Anita E *NF*
Leigh, Randolph 1891-1953 *BioIn 3*
Leigh, Ruth 1895- *WhNAA, WhJnl 1928*
Leighton, George Ross 1902-1966 *BioIn 7*
Leighton, Isabel *OvPC*
Leiper, George Armstrong *OvPC*
Leiper, Henry Smith 1891-1975 *AmAu&B, ConAu 53, CurBio XR*
Leipheimer, Edwin George 1880- *WhJnl 1928*
Leisenring, Peter W 1884- *WhJnl 1928*
Leiser, Ernest Stern 1921- *WhoAm 1974*
Leishman, Allan *NF*
Leishman, David *NF*
Leisk, David Johnson 1906-1975 *AuBYP, ConAu 9R, ConAu 57, CurBio XR, SmATA 1, ThrBJA*
Leisk, David Johnson *see also* Johnson, Crockett
Leissler, Kurt *NF*
Leitch, David *BioIn 9*

Leiter, Clayton A 1872- *WhNAA, WhJnl 1928*
Leiter, Otho Clarke 1878- *WhNAA, WhJnl 1928*
Leiterman, Douglas *RpN*
Leitner, Gottlieb Wilhelm 1840-1899 *Alli Sup,*
  BiD&SB, WebBD
Leitner, Karl 1878?-1954 *BioIn 3*
Lekus, Max *OvPC*
Leland, Austin Porter 1907- *WhoAm 1974*
Leland, Charles Godfrey 1824-1903 *Alli, Alli Sup,*
  AmAu, AmAu&B, BbD, BiD&SB, BioIn 5,
  BioIn 6, BioIn 8, BioIn 9, CasWL,
  CyAL 2, DcAmA, DcEnA, DcEnA Ap,
  DcEnL, DcNAA, EvLB, HisAmM XR,
  OxAm, OxEng, Pen Am, REn, WebBD
Leland, Timothy 1937- *InvJ, WhoAm 1974*
Lelyveld, Joseph Salem 1937- *WhoAm 1974,*
  WhoWor 1974
Lema, Celso Collazo *NF*
Lemaitre, Jules 1853-1914 *BbD, CIDMEL,*
  DcEuL, McGWD, ModWD, OxFr, REn,
  TwCA, TwCA Sup, WebBD
Leman, Albert N 1897?-1972 *BioIn 9,*
  NewYTBE 3
Lemay, Gaston *FamWC*
Lemay, Georges 1857-1902 *DcNAA*
Lemelin, Roger 1919- *BioIn 3, BioIn 10,*
  CanWW 1972, CanWr, CasWL,
  IntWW 1976, OxCan, OxCan Sup, REnAL,
  TwCW
Lemert, James Bolton 1935- *ConAu 73,*
  WhoWest 1974
Lemkowitz, Florence *NF*
Lemley, Walter H *HisAmM XR*
Lemmer, George James 1895-1950 *BioIn 2*
Lemmon, George *NF*
Lemmon, Jack *NF*
Lemmon, Kenneth 1911- *ConAu 65*
Lemmon, Robert Stell 1885-1964 *AmAu&B,*
  AuBYP
Lemoinne, John Marguerite Emile 1815-1892
  WebBD
Lemon, Mark 1809-1870 *Alli, Alli Sup, BbD,*
  BiD&SB, BioIn 7, BioIn 9, BrAu 19,
  CasWL, DcEnA, DcEnL, DcEuL, DcLEL,
  EvLB, NewC, OxEng, REn, WebBD
Lemond, Alan Roy 1938- *WhoAm 1974*
Lemont, George 1927- *ConAu 65*
Lemov, Penelope *NF*
Lenahan, Edward Patrick 1925- *WhoAm 1974*
Leng, Rock Jo-Shui *NF*
Lengel, John B *NF*
Lengel, William Charles 1888-1965 *AmAu&B,*
  BioIn 5, BioIn 7, HisAmM XR, WhNAA
Lengyel, Emil 1895- *AmAu&B, AmM&W 73S,*
  BioIn 4, BioIn 9, ConAu 9, CurBio XR,
  DrAS 74H, REnAL, SmATA 3, TwCA,
  TwCA Sup, WebBD, WhNAA,
  WhoAm 1974, WhoWor 1974
Lenhoff, Alan 1951- *ConAu 73*
Lenin, Nikolai 1870-1924 *ForP, REn, WebBD*
Lenin, Nikolai *see also* Lenin, Vladimir Ilyich
Lenin, Vladimir Ilyich 1870-1924 *CasWL,*
  DcRusL, OxEng
Lenin, Vladimir Ilyich *see also* Lenin, Nikolai
Lennon, Florence Becker 1895- *ConAu 15,*
  DrAP 1975, OvPC
Lennox, Patrick Joseph 1862-1943 *AmAu&B*
Lennox, Lord William Pitt 1799-1881 *Alli Sup,*
  BiD&SB, BrAu 19, DcEnL, NewC, WebBD
Lens, Sidney 1912- *AmRP, AuBYP, ConAu 1,*
  WhoAm 1974, WhoWor 1974
Lenson, Robert H *HisAmM XR*
Lent, John A 1936- *ConAu 29, WrDr 1976*
Lent, R E 1891- *WhJnl 1928*

Lentz, Ellen *NF*
Lentz, Rex V 1902- *WhJnl 1928*
Lenz, Frank G *HisAmM XR*
Lenz, Sidney S 1873- *HisAmM XR, WhNAA,*
  WhJnl 1928
Leokum, A *NF*
Leonard, Albert 1857-1931 *HisAmM XR*
Leonard, Baird 1889-1941 *AmAu&B, DcNAA,*
  HisAmM XR
Leonard, Bill 1916- *CurBio XR*
Leonard, Bill *see also* Leonard, William Augustus, II
Leonard, Daniel 1740-1829 *AmAu, AmAu&B,*
  AmJnl, DcAmA, DcNAA, OxAm, REnAL
Leonard, Ella S *HisAmM XR*
Leonard, Frank E 1896?-1970 *BioIn 9,*
  NewYTBE 1
Leonard, George B 1923- *ConAu 9R*
Leonard, George K, Jr. 1915- *ConAu 17R*
Leonard, Harry *HisAmM XR*
Leonard, John 1939- *AmAu&B, BioIn 9,*
  BioIn 10, ConAu 13R, DrAF 1976,
  WhoE 1974
Leonard, Jonathan Norton 1903-1975 *ConAu 61,*
  WhoAm 1974
Leonard, P A *HisAmM XR*
Leonard, Paul Alfred 1911- *WhoAm 1974*
Leonard, Richard 1921- *WhoAm 1974*
Leonard, Sherrill Ellsworth 1904- *WhJnl 1928*
Leonard, William Augustus, II 1916- *BioIn 5,*
  WhoAm 1974
Leonard, William Augustus, II *see also* Leonard, Bill
Leonard, William Daniel 1912- *WhoAm 1974*
Leone, Vivien *OvPC*
Leonhardt, Rudolf Walter 1921- *ConAu 9R,*
  IntWW 1976, WhoWor 1974
Leonhart, James Chancellor *WhJnl 1928*
LePelley, Guernsey 1910- *WhoAm 1974,*
  WhoE 1974
Lepman, Jella 1891?-1970 *BioIn 9*
Lerman, Leo 1914- *ConAu 45, WhoAmA 1973,*
  WhoWorJ 1972
Lerner, Harry *NF*
Lerner, James 1911- *WhoAm 1974*
Lerner, Leo Alfred 1907-1965 *AmAu&B, BioIn 7*
Lerner, Max 1902- *AmAu&B, AmM&W 73S,*
  AmRP, Au&Wr, AuNews 1, BioIn 4,
  BioIn 5, BioIn 7, BioNews 1974, CelR 1973,
  ConAu 13R, CurBio XR, HisAmM XR,
  IntWW 1976, OxAm, Pen Am, REnAL,
  TwCA, TwCA Sup, WebBD, Who 1974,
  WhoAm 1974, WhoE 1974, WhoWor 1974,
  WhoWorJ 1972, WrDr 1976
Lerner, Richard Edward 1941- *ConAu 73*
Lernoux, Penny 1940- *OvPC*
Leroux, Gaston 1868-1927 *CasWL, EncMys,*
  LongC, OxFr, TwCA, WebBD
LeRoux, Henri 1860-1925 *WebBD*
Leroux, Pierre 1797-1871 *BiD&SB, BioIn 3,*
  OxFr, WebBD
LeRoy, L David 1920- *WhoAm 1974,*
  WhoAmP 1973, WhoS&SW 1973
LeRoy, Virginia Barlow 1867- *WhJnl 1928*
Lerude, Warren L *NF*
Lerwill, Leonard Leston 1900- *WhNAA,*
  WhJnl 1928
LeSage, John M *FamWC*
Lescarboura, Austin C 1891-1962 *HisAmM XR,*
  WhNAA
Lescaze, Lee *NF*
Lesher, Dean Stanley 1902- *WhoAm 1974*
Lesins, Knuts 1909- *ConAu 73, Pen Eur*
Leslie, Miss *see* Leslie, Eliza
Leslie, Amy 1860-1939 *AmAu&B, DcNAA,*
  WhNAA

Leslie, Annie Louise 1870-1948 *WhNAA*
Leslie, Annie Louise *see also* Leslie, Mrs. J E
Leslie, Cecilie 1914?- *ConAu 17R,*
WhoAmW 1974
Leslie, Eliza 1787-1858 *Alli, AmAu, AmAu&B,*
BiD&SB, CyAL 1, DcAmA, DcNAA,
EarABI, HisAmM XR, OxAm, Polre,
REnAL
Leslie, Frank 1821-1880 *AmAu&B, AmJnl,*
EncAB, HisAmM XR, OxAm, REnAL,
WebBD
Leslie, Mrs. Frank 1836-1914 *BiDSA, WebBD,*
HisAmM XR
Leslie, Mrs. Frank *see also* Leslie, Miriam F F S
Leslie, Mrs. J E 1870-1948 *WhNAA, WhJnl 1928*
Leslie, Jacque *NF*
Leslie, Sir John Randolph Shane 1885-1971 *EvLB,*
WebBD
Leslie, Sir John Randolph Shane *see also* Leslie, Sir
Shane
Leslie, Miriam Florence Folline Squier 1836-1914
Alli Sup, AmAu, AmAu&B, DcNAA,
REnAL
Leslie, Miriam Florence Folline Squier *see also*
Leslie, Mrs. F
Leslie, Sir Shane 1885-1971 *CathA 1930,*
ConAu 33, DcLEL, HisAmM XR, LongC,
ModBL, NewC, Polre, TwCA, TwCA Sup,
WhoLA
Leslie, Sir Shane *see also* Leslie, Sir John Randolph
Shane
Leslie, Warren *Bioln 2, Bioln 6*
Leslie, Warren, III 1927- *ConAu 9*
Lesner, Samuel Joel 1909- *WhoAm 1974,*
WhoMW 1974
Lesperance, Jean Talon 1838-1891 *DcNAA*
Less, Gunther L *OvPC*
Lesser, Isaac *HisAmM XR*
Lessing, Bruno 1870-1940 *AmAu&B, AmLY XR,*
CurBio XR, DcNAA, HisAmM XR
Lessing, Bruno *see also* Block, Rudolph
Lessing, Gotthold Ephraim 1729-1781 *AtlBL,*
BbD, BiD&SB, CasWL, CnThe, CyWA,
DcEuL, EuAu, EvEuW, McGWD, NewC,
OxEng, OxGer, Pen Eur, RComWL, REn,
REnWD, WebBD
Lessing, Lawrence Peter 1908- *Bioln 6,*
WhoAm 1974
LesStrang, Jacques 1926- *ConAu 65*
Lester, Barnett Benjamin 1912- *USBiR 1974,*
WhoAm 1974, WhoS&SW 1973
Lester, John *NF*
Lester, Julius B 1939- *AmAu&B, AuBYP,*
BlkAW, ChlLR 2, ConAu 17, LivBAA,
WhoAm 1974
L'Estrange, Sir Roger 1616-1704 *Alli, AmJnl,*
Bioln 1, Bioln 3, Bioln 9, BrAu, CasWL,
DcEnA, DcEnL, DcEuL, DcLEL, EvLB,
NewC, OxEng, Pen Eng, REn, WebBD,
WebE&AL
Lesueur, Larry 1909- *CurBio XR*
Lesure, Thomas B *NF*
Letellier DeSaint Just, Eustache 1894-1952 *Bioln 3*
Letofsky, Irv *NF*
Letourneau, Joseph H *OvPC*
Lett, Mark *NF*
Lett, William Pittman 1819?-1892 *BbtC, DcNAA,*
Polre
Letzler, Walter A *WhJnl 1928*
Leubsdorf, Carl P 1938- *ConAu 73*
Leupp, Francis Ellington 1849-1918 *AmAu&B,*
AmJnl, AmLY, DcAmB 11, DcNAA,
HisAmM XR, NatCAB 15
Levasseur, Nazaire 1848-1927 *DcNAA*

Leventhal, Albert Rice 1907-1976 *ConAu 61,*
ConAu 65, WhoAm 1974
Leveque, Joseph Mark 1868-1911 *BiDSA,*
HisAmM XR
Levere, Jane *NF*
Levering, Albert 1869-1929 *HisAmM XR*
Leverton, Garrett Hasty 1896-1949 *Bioln 2,*
DcNAA
Levesque, Rene 1922- *Bioln 8, Bioln 9,*
CanWW 1972, CurBio XR, NewYTBE 1,
OxCan Sup, WhoAm 1974, WhoE 1974,
WhoWor 1974
Levett, Bruce *NF*
Levett, Michael *NewMr*
Levey, Robert F *NF*
Levey, Robert Lewis 1939?- *NF*
Levey, Stanley 1914-1971 *Bioln 9, NewYTBE 2*
Levi, Arrigo *NF*
Levi, Carlo 1902-1975 *Bioln 3, Bioln 4, CasWL,*
CnMWL, ConAu 53, ConAu 65,
CurBio XR, EncWL, EvEuW, IntWW 1974,
ModRL, Pen Eur, REn, TwCA Sup,
TwCW, WhoWor 1974
Levi, Emmanuel *NF*
Levi, Isaac A *OvPC*
Levick, Louis E 1899?-1968 *Bioln 8*
LeVien, John Douglas 1918- *OvPC,*
WhoAm 1974, WhoWor 1974
Levien, Sonya *HisAmM XR*
Leviero, Anthony Harry 1905-1956 *Bioln 3,*
Bioln 4, CurBio XR
Levin, Alan M 1926- *WhoAm 1974*
Levin, Ann 1953- *NF*
Levin, Arnie *NF*
Levin, Arthur *NF*
Levin, Bernard *BiE&WWA, WrDr 1976*
Levin, Felice Michaels 1928- *ForWC 1970, OvPC*
Levin, Harry C *OvPC*
Levin, Marj Jackson *NF*
Levin, Marlin 1921- *ConAu 65, OvPC*
Levin, Martin *NF*
Levin, Meyer 1905- *AmAu&B, AmNov, AmRP,*
Au&Wr, AuNews 1, BiE&WWA,
BioNews 1974, CelR 1973, CnMD,
ConAu 11R, ConNov 1972, ConNov 1976,
CurBio XR, DcLEL, ModAL, OxAm,
Pen Am, REn, REnAL, TwCA, TwCA Sup,
WhoAm 1974, WhoWorJ 1972, WrDr 1976
Levin, Ruben 1902- *WhoAm 1974,*
WhoF&I 1974, WhoS&SW 1973
Levine, David 1926- *Bioln 8, Bioln 9, Bioln 10,*
CurBio XR
Levine, Ghita *NF*
Levine, Irving Raskin 1922- *AmAu&B, Bioln 5,*
ConAu 15R, CurBio XR, ForP,
WhoAm 1974, WhoWor 1974,
WhoWorJ 1972
Levine, Isaac Don 1892- *AmAu&B, Bioln 9,*
ConAu 13R, OvPC, REnAL, WhNAA,
WhoAm 1974, WhoWorJ 1972
Levine, Morris Benjamin 1912- *WhoAm 1974*
Levine, Paul *NF*
Levine, Richard *Bioln 9*
Levine, Samuel P *NF*
Levine, Suzanne *NF*
Levine, Theodore 1918?-1972 *Bioln 9,*
NewYTBE 3
Levins, Peter 1896?-1950 *Bioln 2*
Levinson, Edward 1901- *WhJnl 1928*
Levinson, Will *NF*
Levison, Hal *InvJ*
Levison, M A *HisAmM XR*
Levison, Teddi *Bioln 8*
Levison, W H *HisAmM XR*

Levitan, Stuart Dean NF
Levitas, Mitchell R RpN
Levitas, Samuel Moisewitch 1894-1961 BioIn 5
Leviton, Ralph OvPC
Levitt, Robert Daniels 1910-1958 BioIn 4
Levy, Alan 1932- BioIn 7, BioIn 9, ConAu 9,
    OvPC, WrDr 1976
Levy, Alton 1915-1965 BioIn 7
Levy, Arthur Jay 1892?-1955 BioIn 3
Levy, Carol 1931- WhoAm 1974
Levy, Claudia NF
Levy, Henry W 1908- WhNAA, WhJnl 1928,
    WhoWorJ 1972
Levy, Joseph M 1900?-1965 BioIn 7
Levy, Leo Samuel 1886-1961 BioIn 5,
    WhJnl 1928
Levy, Leon 1895-1978 WhoAm 1974, WhoE 1974
Levy, Leonce 1866- WhNAA, WhJnl 1928
Levy, Louis 1887?-1950 BioIn 2
Levy, Louis 1895-1952 BioIn 2
Levy, Maury Z NF
Levy, Michael R NF
Levy, Phyllis NF
Levy, Robert 1926- WhoAm 1974
Lew, Timothy Tinfang 1891-1947 BioIn 1
Lewellen, Charles NewMr
Lewes, George Henry 1817-1878 Alli, Alli Sup,
    BiD&SB, BrAu 19, CasWL, DcEnA,
    DcEnL, DcEuL, DcLEL, EvLB, NewC,
    OxEng, Pen Eng, REn, WebBD
Lewi, Isidor 1850-1939 NF
Lewin, Charles J 1902-1965 BioIn 7
Lewin, Milton 1904?-1967 BioIn 7
Lewin, Murray 1899?-1943 CurBio XR
Lewin, Robert M 1904- WhoAm 1974
Lewine, Frances L NF
Lewinsohn, Richard 1894- NF
Lewinson, Minna NF
Lewis, Alfred 1912-1968 BioIn 8
Lewis, Alfred E NF
Lewis, Alfred Henry 1858?-1914 AmAu&B,
    AmJnl, AtlBL, AuBYP, BiD&SB, CnDAL,
    DcAmA, DcAmB 11, DcLEL, DcNAA,
    EncMys, HisAmM XR, OhA&B, OxAm,
    REnAL, WebBD
Lewis, Anthony 1927- AmAu&B, BioIn 3,
    BioIn 4, BioIn 7, ConAu 11R, CurBio XR,
    RpN, Who 1974, WhoAm 1974
Lewis, Arthur H 1906- ConAu 1
Lewis, Barbara NF
Lewis, Beth NF
Lewis, Boyd DeWolf 1905- BioIn 2,
    WhoAm 1974
Lewis, Byron J d1950 BioIn 2
Lewis, Carl Benjamin 1917- OvPC,
    WhoF&I 1974, WhoPubR 1972
Lewis, Carolyn NewMr
Lewis, Charles Bertrand 1842-1924 Alli Sup,
    AmAu, AmAu&B, AmJnl, BbD, BiD&SB,
    DcAmA, DcNAA, HisAmM XR, HsB&A,
    NatCAB 6, OhA&B, OxAm, REnAL,
    WebBD
Lewis, Charles Fletcher 1890-1971 BioIn 9,
    NewYTBE 2
Lewis, Charles J 1940- NF
Lewis, Charlotte HisAmM XR
Lewis, Charlton Thomas 1834-1904 Alli Sup,
    AmAu, AmJnl, BiD&SB, DcAmA, DcNAA,
    HisAmM XR, NatCAB 38, WebBD
Lewis, Chester Milton 1914- BiDrLUS,
    CurBio XR, WhoAm 1974
Lewis, Clark Q 1919?- BioIn 2
Lewis, Claude A 1934- BlkC
Lewis, Constance d1940 DcNAA

Lewis, Dan NF
Lewis, David 1942- ConAu 69
Lewis, David Lanier 1927- ConAu 69,
    DrAS 74H, WhoAm 1974, WhoPubR 1972
Lewis, Diocesian 1823-1886 Alli Sup, BbD,
    BlkAW, DcAmA, DcNAA
Lewis, Dominic Bevan Wyndham 1891-1969
    BioIn 8, BioIn 9, CathA 1930, ConAu 25,
    DcLEL, EvLB, LongC, ModBL, NewC,
    Pen Eng, REn, TwCA, TwCA Sup, WebBD
Lewis, Edward NF
Lewis, Edward J NF
Lewis, Edward Williams 1899- WhoAm 1974
Lewis, Enoch 1776-1856 Alli, DcAmA, DcNAA,
    HisAmM XR
Lewis, Ernest I 1873-1947 NatCAB 43
Lewis, Finlay NF
Lewis, Flora 1920?- BioIn 6, BioIn 9,
    ForWC 1970, WhoAmW 1974
Lewis, Fulton, III 1936- WhoAm 1974
Lewis, Fulton, Jr. 1903-1966 AmJnl, BioIn 1,
    BioIn 2, BioIn 3, BioIn 4, BioIn 7,
    CurBio XR
Lewis, George 1943- NF
Lewis, George Alexander 1846- WhJnl 1928
Lewis, Sir George Cornewall 1806-1863 Alli,
    Alli Sup, BbD, BiD&SB, BrAu 19, DcEnL,
    EvLB, NewC, OxEng, WebBD
Lewis, H N F HisAmM XR
Lewis, Hal NF
Lewis, Harry Sinclair 1885-1951 CasWL,
    DcAmB S5, EvLB
Lewis, Harry Sinclair see also Lewis, Sinclair
Lewis, Henry Alfred HisAmM XR
Lewis, Henry Harrison 1863-1923 DcNAA,
    HisAmM XR, IndAu 1816
Lewis, Henry Steele 1900-1954 BioIn 3
Lewis, Herbert Clyde 1909?-1950 BioIn 2
Lewis, Hobart Durbin 1909- IntWW 1976,
    WhoAm 1974
Lewis, Hugh A 1894-1964 BioIn 7
Lewis, Ida BioIn 9, LivBAA
Lewis, Irwin A OvPC
Lewis, Jack 1916- NF
Lewis, Janice NF
Lewis, Jim NF
Lewis, John 1858-1935 DcNAA
Lewis, John Philip 1903-1961 BioIn 6
Lewis, John W, Jr. NF
Lewis, Mrs. Juan HisAmM XR
Lewis, Judd Mortimer 1867-1945 AmAu&B,
    BiDSA, BioIn 4, BioIn 7, DcNAA, TexWr,
    WhNAA
Lewis, Larry 1928- NF
Lewis, LaVern 1884- WhJnl 1928
Lewis, Lloyd Downs 1891-1949 AmAu&B,
    BioIn 1, BioIn 2, DcAmB S4, DcNAA,
    IndAu 1917, REnAL
Lewis, Lucia BioIn 5
Lewis, M Botts 1870- WhJnl 1928
Lewis, Matthew NF
Lewis, Morris 1875- WhJnl 1928
Lewis, Murray 1912-1967 BioIn 8
Lewis, Paul M NF
Lewis, Ralph Ferguson 1918- ConAu 29,
    WhoAm 1974, WrDr 1976
Lewis, Richard Stanley 1916- ConAu 57,
    WhoAm 1974
Lewis, Robert NF
Lewis, Robert C 1920?-1971 BioIn 9,
    NewYTBE 2
Lewis, Robert D NF
Lewis, Robert E 1890- WhNAA, WhJnl 1928
Lewis, Robert Emerson 1901- WhJnl 1928

Lewis, Ross Aubrey 1902-1977 *BioIn 3*
Lewis, Roy 1913- *ConAu 7R, WrDr 1976*
Lewis, Samuel H *HisAmM XR*
Lewis, Sinclair 1885-1951 *AmAu&B, AmNov, AmRP, AmWr, AtlBL, CnDAL, CnMD, CnMWL, ConAmA, ConAmL, CyWA, DcLEL, EncWL, LongC, ModAL, ModAL Sup, ModWD, OxAm, OxEng, Pen Am, RAdv 1, RComWL, REn, REnAL, TwCA, TwCA Sup, TwCW, WebBD, WebE&AL, WhNAA, WhoTwCL*
Lewis, Sinclair *see also* Lewis, Harry Sinclair
Lewis, Spearman 1879-1954 *NF*
Lewis, Taylor *HisAmM XR*
Lewis, Ted 1901?- *BioIn 7*
Lewis, Theophilus 1891- *BioIn 4, BlkAW*
Lewis, Todd *NF*
Lewis, Tracy Hammond 1890-1951 *BioIn 2, BioIn 4, OhA&B*
Lewis, William *AmJnl*
Lewis, William Eugene d1924 *NF*
Lewis, Sir Willmott Harsant 1877-1950 *BioIn 1, BioIn 2, BioIn 4, BioIn 5, CurBio XR*
Lewis, Zachariah 1773-1840 *NatCAB 11*
Lewisohn, Ludwig 1883-1955 *AmAu&B, AmLY, AmNov, BiDSA, CnDAL, ConAmA, ConAmL, DcLEL, HisAmM XR, ModAL, OhA&B, OxAm, Pen Am, REn, REnAL, TwCA, TwCA Sup, WebBD, WhNAA*
Lewthwaite, Gilbert A *NF*
Lexow, Friedrich 1827-1872 *BioIn 2*
Leyendecker, Joseph Christian 1874-1951 *DcAmB S5*
Leypoldt, Augusta Harriet 1849-1919 *BioIn 1*
Leypoldt, Frederick 1835-1884 *Alli Sup, DcNAA, HisAmM XR, REnAL, WebBD*
Leys, Sir Cecil 1877-1950 *BioIn 2*
Leysmith, Walter F 1886?-1954 *BioIn 3*
Lherbas, Lloyd *NF*
Li, Chiang-Kwang 1915- *ConAu 73*
Li, Ling-Ai *OvPC*
Liang, Ch'i-Ch'ao 1873-1929 *BioIn 2, BioIn 3, BioIn 9, CasWL, DcOrL 1, WebBD*
Lias, Godfrey *ConAu 7R*
Libbey, John M *HisAmM XR*
Libby, Paul *WhJnl Sup*
Liberman, Alexander 1912- *DcCAA, WhoAmA 1973, WhoE 1974*
Lichtenberg, James *NF*
Lichtenberg, Margaret Klee *NF*
Lichtenstein, Grace 1941- *ConAu 49*
Lichty, George Maurice 1905- *BioIn 2, WhoAm 1974*
Lickey, Annabelle 1905- *WhJnl 1928*
Lico, Claudia E *NF*
Liddell, Marlane *NF*
Liddell Hart, Sir Basil Henry 1895-1970 *CurBio XR, DcLEL, EvLB, LongC, NewC, TwCA, TwCA Sup, WebBD*
Liddle, Theron *NF*
Lidgett, John Scott 1854-1953 *BioIn 3, BioIn 4*
Lidman, David Louis 1905- *ConAu 69, WhNAA, WhJnl 1928*
Lieb, Frederick George 1888- *AuBYP, BioIn 7, ConAu 69, WhNAA, WhJnl 1928*
Lieb, Jack *OvPC*
Lieb, William 1870?-1951 *BioIn 2*
Lieberman, Henry Richard 1916- *WhoAm 1974, WhoWorJ 1972*
Lieberman, Herman 1889-1963 *BioIn 6*
Liebknecht, Wilhelm 1826-1900 *BbD, BiD&SB, OxGer, REn, WebBD*
Liebling, Abbot Joseph 1904-1963 *AmAu&B, BioIn 1, BioIn 2, BioIn 4, BioIn 5, BioIn 6,*

BioIn 8
Liecty, Austin N 1866- *WhJnl 1928*
Liederman, Al 1911- *WhoAm 1974*
Liefde, Jacob De *FamWC*
Lienert, Robert M *NF*
Liepa, Alex *OvPC*
Liepmann, Heinz 1905-1966 *BioIn 7, TwCA, TwCA Sup*
Liermark, Dorothy *NF*
Liessin, Abraham 1872-1938 *NF*
Lietzmann, Sabina *NF*
Liggett, Robert B 1885- *WhJnl 1928*
Liggett, Thomas 1918- *ConAu 5, WrDr 1976*
Liggett, Walter William 1886-1935 *AmAu&B, DcAmB S1, DcNAA*
Light, George Washington 1809-1868 *CyAL 2, DcAmA, DcNAA*
Light, Herbert Cary d1946 *BioIn 1*
Light, Murray B *NF*
Lightbrown, Mary Jane *BioIn 6*
Lighter, Edwin H 1898- *WhJnl 1928*
Lignac, Xavier De 1912?- *BioIn 7*
Lilienthal, Alfred Morton 1913- *ConAu 37, WhoAm 1974, WhoWor 1974*
Lilienthal, Meta 1876-1948 *BioIn 1*
Lilienthal, Samuel 1815-1891 *Alli Sup, DcNAA, HisAmM XR*
Lillard, Benjamin 1847- *Alli Sup, HisAmM XR*
Lillie, Helen 1915- *ConAu 65*
Lillie, John S *AmJnl, HisAmM XR*
Lillitos, Nick *NF*
Lilly, Doris 1926- *BioIn 5, CelR 1973, ConAu 29*
Lilly, Joseph 1900?-1965 *BioIn 7*
Limpert, John A 1934- *NF*
Limprecht, Hollis *NF*
Limpus, Lowell M 1897-1957 *BioIn 4, RpN*
Lin, Sam Chu *NF*
Linck, Tony *OvPC*
Lincoln, Charles H 1870- *WhJnl 1928*
Lincoln, Charles Monroe 1866-1950 *BioIn 2*
Lincoln, Joseph Freeman 1900-1962 *AmAu&B, BioIn 6*
Lind, Karl G 1894- *WhNAA, WhJnl 1928*
Lindau, Paul 1839-1919 *BbD, BiD&SB, EvEuW, OxGer, WebBD*
Lindau, Rudolf 1829-1910 *BiD&SB, WebBD*
Linde, Carl *NF*
Linde, Otto Zur 1873-1938 *CIDMEL, EncWL, OxGer, WebBD*
Lindeman, Bard *NF*
Lindeman, Charles B 1891?-1969 *BioIn 8*
Lindeman, Eduard Christian 1885-1953 *HisAmM XR, WhNAA*
Linden, Einar T 1886- *WhJnl 1928*
Lindenberger, Edwin F 1887- *WhJnl 1928*
Linderman, Frank Bird 1869-1938 *AmAu&B, DcNAA, JBA 1934, JBA 1951, OhA&B, OxAm, REnAL, WhNAA*
Lindgren, H A 1875?- *WhJnl 1928*
Lindheim, Leon 1912- *NF*
Lindley, Denver 1904- *WhoAm 1974*
Lindley, Ernest Kidder 1899- *AmAu&B, AmJnl, CurBio XR, DrAS 74H, HisAmM XR, IndAu 1917, WhoAm 1974, WhJnl 1928*
Lindner, Clarence Richard 1890-1952 *BioIn 2, BioIn 4, NatCAB 40*
Lindquist, Jennie Dorothea 1899-1977 *AuBYP, BioIn 2, BioIn 4, BioIn 6, BioIn 7, ConAu 69, MorJA*
Lindsay, Arthur Oliver 1878-1956 *BioIn 4, BioIn 7, NatCAB 47*
Lindsay, Edward Emerson 1899- *WhoAm 1974*
Lindsay, G W *NF*

Lindsay, George Andrew 1867- WhJnl 1928
Lindsay, George Clayton 1912- WhoAm 1974
Lindsay, George David 1862-1946 BioIn 3,
   NatCAB 38, WhJnl 1928
Lindsay, Mrs. H C HisAmM XR
Lindsay, Sir Harry Alexander Fanshawe 1881-
   BioIn 3
Lindsay, James Gordon 1892-1965 BioIn 9
Lindsay, James Hubert 1862-1933 DcNAA,
   WhJnl 1928
Lindsay, John J RpN
Lindsay, John Vliet 1921- AmSCAP 1966,
   CelR 1973, CurBio XR, IntWW 1974,
   NewYTBE 2, NewYTBE 3, NewYTBE 4,
   NewYTBS 5, Who 1974, WhoAm 1974,
   WhoAmP 1973, WhoE 1974, WhoGov 1972,
   WhoWor 1974
Lindsay, Leon NF
Lindsay, Sir Lionel Arthur 1874-1961 BioIn 5,
   BioIn 8
Lindsay, Luella WhJnl 1928
Lindsay, Norman Alfred William 1879-1969
   BioIn 4, BioIn 6, BioIn 8, BioIn 9,
   BioIn 10, DcLEL, LongC, Pen Eng, REn,
   TwCA, TwCA Sup, TwCW, WebBD,
   WhoChL
Lindsay, Patricia d1974 BioIn 10
Lindsay, Philip 1906-1958 LongC, NewC,
   WebBD
Lindsay, Powell S NF
Lindsay, Robert 1924- AmM&W 73S
Lindsay, Thomas Fanshawe 1910- Au&Wr,
   BioIn 3, CathA 1952, ConAu 23
Lindsey, Benjamin Barr 1869-1943 AmAu&B,
   BiDSA, BioIn 8, BioIn 9, DcNAA,
   HisAmM XR, LongC, REnAL. WebBD
Lindsey, Bill NF
Lindsey, Charles 1820-1908 Alli Sup, BbtC,
   DcNAA, OxCan
Lindsley, J Berrien 1822-1897 HisAmM XR
Lindsley, Lorna 1889-1956 BioIn 4
Lindstrom, Carl E 1896-1969 BioIn 5, BioIn 8,
   ConAu 3R
Lindstrom, Pia 1938- CelR 1973
Lindstrom, Ulla 1909- BioIn 1, IntWW 1974
Line, Les 1935- NF
Linebarger, R G 1879- WhJnl 1928
Linedecker, Clifford L 1931- ConAu 73
Linen, James Alexander, III 1912- HisAmM XR,
   IntWW 1976, OvPC, WhoAm 1974,
   WhoF&I 1974, WhoWor 1974
Linen, James Alexander, IV 1938- WhoMW 1974
Liney, John NF
Linford, Ernest H 1907- DrAS 74E, RpN
Ling, Wilfred NF
Lingan, J M AmJnl
Lingle, Caroline Gray HisAmM XR
Lingle, Jake d1930 AmJnl
Lingle, Roy Petran 1885- WhJnl 1928
Lingo, Karen 1947- NF
Linguet, Simon Nicolas Henri 1736-1794 BiD&SB,
   OxFr, WebBD
Link, Mary NF
Link, Ruth 1923- ConAu 29
Link, Stanley 1894?-1957 BioIn 1, BioIn 4
Link, Theodore C 1905?-1974 BioIn 1, BioIn 10,
   NewYTBS 5
Linkert, Lo NF
Linkletter, John Austin 1923- ConAu 69
Linkroum, Richard BioIn 8
Links, Marty BioIn 1
Linn, Bandel BioIn 1
Linn, Thomas Calvin 1894?-1972 BioIn 9,

NewYTBE 3
Linn, William Alexander 1846-1917 DcAmA,
   DcNAA, NatCAB 26
Lins, Marcelo NF
Linscott, Robert Newton 1886-1964 BioIn 7
Linscott, Roger Bourne 1920- WhoAm 1974
Linsley, D S HisAmM XR
Linthicum, Jesse Allison 1891-1959 BioIn 5
Linthicum, Richard 1859-1934 AmAu&B,
   DcAmA, DcNAA
Linton, Eliza Lynn 1822-1898 Alli Sup, BiD&SB,
   BrAu 19, CasWL, DcEnL, DcEuL, DcLEL,
   EvLB, HsB&A Sup, NewC, WebBD
Linton, James M 1873- WhJnl 1928
Linton, Margaret Reynolds WhoAm 1974,
   WhoAmW 1974, WhoWor 1974
Linton, William James 1812-1897 Alli Sup,
   AmAu&B, BbD, BiD&SB, BrAu 19,
   DcAmA, DcEnL, EarABI, EarABI Sup,
   NewC, REnAL
Lintott, Kate E J 1872?-1968 BioIn 8
Lipman, David 1931- ConAu 23R, WhoAm 1974,
   WhoMW 1974, WrDr 1976
Lippa, Si NF
Lippard, George 1822-1854 Alli, AmAu,
   AmAu&B, BiD&SB, DcAmA, DcLEL,
   DcNAA, HisAmM XR, OhA&B, OxAm,
   REnAL
Lippert, Jack Kissane 1902- WhoAm 1974
Lipphard, William Benjamin 1886-1971 AmAu&B,
   BioIn 6, BioIn 9, ConAu 29, IndAu 1917,
   NewYTBE 2, WhNAA
Lippincott, Joshua Ballinger 1813-1886 AmAu&B,
   WebBD
Lippincott, Leander K Alli Sup, HisAmM XR
Lippincott, Sara Jane Clarke 1823-1904 Alli,
   AmAu, AmAu&B, BbD, BioIn 1, CarSB,
   CyAL 2, DcAmA, DcEnL, DcNAA,
   FemPA, HisAmM XR, OxAm
Lippincott, Sara Jane Clarke see also Greenwood,
   Grace
Lippman, Theo, Jr. 1929- ConAu 33
Lippmann, Walter 1889-1974 AmAu&B, AmJnl,
   AmRP, AuNews 1, BioIn 1, BioIn 2,
   BioIn 4, BioIn 5, BioIn 6, BioIn 7, BioIn 8,
   BioIn 9, BioIn 10, BioNews 1975,
   CelR 1973, ConAmA, ConAu 9R,
   ConAu 53, CurBio XR, DcLEL, DrAS 74E,
   EncAB, ForP, HisAmM XR, IntWW 1974,
   LongC, NewYTBS 5, OxAm, Pen Am,
   REn, REnAL, TwCA, TwCA Sup, WebBD,
   WhNAA, Who 1974, WhoAm 1974,
   WhJnl 1928, WhoWor 1974
Lipschitz, Chaim Ure 1912- Au&Wr, BioIn 7,
   CurBio XR, WhoAm 1974, WhoWor 1974,
   WhoWorJ 1972
Lipscomb, Andrew Adgate 1816-1890 Alli Sup,
   BiDSA, DcAmA, DcNAA, HisAmM XR
Lipscombe, Edward Hart 1858- BioIn 8
Lipsett, Robert NF
Lipsky, Louis 1876-1963 WebBD
Lipsyte, Robert 1938- ConAu 19R, SmATA 5
Lipton, Dean 1919- ConAu 29, WrDr 1976
Lisagor, Peter Irvin 1915-1976 BioIn 9,
   ConAu 69, ForP, RpN, WhoAm 1974,
   WhoS&SW 1973
Lish, Gordon Jay 1934- WhoAm 1974,
   WhoE 1974
Lisker, Jerry NF
Lissner, Will 1908- AmEA 1974, OvPC,
   WhoE 1974
Lissueris, Meyer HisAmM XR
List, Georg Friedrich 1789-1846 DcAmB 11
Lista Y Aragon, Alberto 1775-1848 BiD&SB,

CasWL, DcEuL, DcSpL, EuAu, Pen Eur, WebBD
Lister, Charles Baynard 1898-1951 *BioIn 2*
Lister, Harold 1922- *ConAu 73*
Lister, Walter Bartlett 1899?-1967 *BioIn 1, BioIn 7*
Liston, Carol Foley 1938- *WhoE 1974*
Liston, Harold V *RpN*
Liston, Jim *NF*
Liston, Robert A 1927- *AuBYP, BioIn 8, ConAu 19, SmATA 5*
Litchfield, A *HisAmM XR*
Litchfield, Paul *HisAmM XR*
Litchfield, Robert Orbin d1977 *ConAu 73*
Litchman, Charles Henry 1849-1902 *AmRP*
Liter, Calvin Pollard 1900- *WhJnl 1928*
Litfin, Richard Albert 1918- *WhoAm 1974*
Littauer, Kenneth *HisAmM XR*
Littell, Eliakim 1797-1870 *Alli, AmAu&B, DcLEL, HisAmM XR, LiJA, NatCAB 24, OxAm, REnAL, WebBD*
Littell, Philip 1868-1943 *AmAu&B, CurBio XR, DcNAA, HisAmM XR*
Littell, Robert 1896-1963 *AmAu&B, BioIn 6, BioIn 8, NatCAB 50, WhNAA, WhJnl 1928*
Littell, Robert S d1896 *HisAmM XR*
Litten, Frederic Nelson 1885-1951 *AmAu&B, AuBYP, BioIn 2, BioIn 8, WhNAA*
Littick, Orville Beck 1890-1953 *BioIn 3, WhJnl 1928*
Littick, William Oliver 1867-1941 *BioIn 3, NatCAB 38*
Little, Arthur W, Jr. 1900- *WhJnl 1928*
Little, Carl Victor 1894-1959 *BioIn 3, BioIn 5*
Little, Emma Holmer 1887-1972 *BioIn 9, NewYTBE 3*
Little, James Henry 1903- *WhJnl 1928*
Little, John Dutton 1894- *ConAu 65*
Little, John T *OvPC*
Little, O W 1867- *WhJnl 1928*
Little, Richard Henry 1869-1946 *AmAu&B, BioIn 1, REnAL*
Little, Ruby A Black *see* Black, Ruby Aurora
Little, Samuel George 1903-1974 *BioIn 2, BioIn 9, ConAu 49, WhoAm 1974*
Little, Stuart W 1921- *BiE&WWA, ConAu 45, WrDr 1976*
Little, Thomas Russell 1911- *Au&Wr, ConAu 13R*
Little, Tom 1898?-1972 *BioIn 9, NewYTBE 3*
Little, William D, Jr. 1921- *WhoF&I 1974, WhoS&SW 1973*
Little, William Dee 1888- *WhJnl 1928*
Littledale, Clara Savage 1891-1956 *BioIn 1, BioIn 2, BioIn 4, CurBio XR*
Littledale, Freyda *BioIn 9*
Littledale, Harold Aylmer 1885-1957 *BioIn 4*
Littlefield, George Emery 1844-1915 *AmAu&B, DcNAA*
Littlefield, Walter 1867-1948 *AmAu&B, BioIn 1, BioIn 3, DcNAA, NatCAB 37, REnAL*
Littleford, William Donaldson 1914- *WhoAdv 1972, WhoAm 1974, WhoF&I 1974*
Littlejohn, A F 1892- *WhJnl 1928*
Littlejohn, David 1937- *ConAu 41, DrAS 74E*
Littlejohns, G Michael *NF*
Littlewood, Thomas B 1928- *ConAu 29*
Litz, David *NF*
Litz, Roger *NF*
Liu, David S C *OvPC*
Liu, Sydney *NF*
Liuhala, Allan *ForP*
Lively, Kenneth E *NF*
Livengood, William Winfred 1881-1962 *BioIn 6*

Livermore, D P *HisAmM XR*
Livermore, Mary Ashton Rice 1820-1905 *Alli Sup, AmAu, AmAu&B, BbD, BiD&SB, DcAmA, DcNAA, HisAmM XR, WebBD*
Livermore, Mercer Pilcher *BioIn 5, OvPC*
Livernash, Edward James 1866- *HisAmM XR*
Livesay, Dorothy 1909- *AuNews 2, CanWW 1972, CanWr, CasWL, ConAu 25, ConLC 4, ConP 1970, ConP 1975, DcLEL, OxCan, OxCan Sup, REnAL, WrDr 1976*
Livesay, Florence Hamilton Randal 1874-1953 *AmLY, CanNov, OxCan, WhNAA*
Livesay, John Frederick Bligh 1875-1944 *BioIn 1, DcNAA, OxCan*
Livingood, Jay 1932- *NF*
Livingston, Bob *NF*
Livingston, J A 1905- *AmEA 1974, ConAu 1R, WhoAm 1974, WhoE 1974*
Livingston, J A *see also* Livingston, Joseph Arnold
Livingston, James Arthur 1877- *WhJnl 1928*
Livingston, Joseph Arnold 1905- *AmM&W 73S, WhoF&I 1974*
Livingston, Joseph Arnold *see also* Livingston, J A
Livingstone, William *NF*
Livingstone, William, Jr. 1844- *NF*
Livingstone, William Pringle 1865?-1950 *BioIn 2*
Lizelius, Antti *ForP*
Llang, Ch'i-Ch'ao 1873-1929 *BioIn 8*
Llano, Rodrigo De 1890- *BioIn 4*
Lleras Camargo, Alberto 1906- *CurBio XR, ForP, IntWW 1976*
Llergo, Regino Hernandez *NF*
Llewellyn, Emma C *OvPC*
Llorens, David 1939-1973 *BlkAW, NewYTBE 4, WhoAm 1974*
Lloyd, Allan M *OvPC*
Lloyd, Charles Mostyn 1878-1946 *BioIn 1*
Lloyd, D R *HisAmM XR*
Lloyd, Demarest 1883-1937 *NatCAB 28*
Lloyd, Everett 1881- *AmAu&B, TexWr, WhNAA, WhJnl 1928*
Lloyd, Henry Demarest 1847-1903 *AmAu, AmAu&B, BiD&SB, BioIn 2, BioIn 4, BioIn 6, BioIn 10, DcAmA, DcAmB 11, DcNAA, HisAmM XR, NatCAB 28, OxAm, Pen Am, REnAL, WebBD*
Lloyd, John A 1901- *WhNAA, WhoAm 1974, WhoF&I 1974, WhJnl 1928*
Lloyd, Mary *WhJnl 1928*
Lloyd, Nelson McAllister 1873?-1933 *AmAu&B, DcNAA, DcAmA*
Lloyd, Norman *NF*
Lloyd, O B 1914?- *BioIn 5*
Lloyd, Robin *NF*
Lloyd, Sam *HisAmM XR*
Lloyd, Walter Hamilton 1896-1956 *BioIn 4, WhJnl 1928*
Lloyd-Smith, Parker *NF*
Lo, Betty *NF*
Loayza, Tomas Alejandro 1901?- *BioIn 2*
Lobb, Charlotte 1935- *ConAu 65*
LoBello, Nino 1921- *ConAu 29, OvPC*
Lobrano, Gustave Stubbs 1902-1956 *BioIn 4*
Lobsenz, Norman Mitchell 1919- *AmAu&B, ConAu 9R, OvPC, SmATA 6*
Lochbiler, Don 1908- *ConAu 49*
Locher, Fred 1886- *WhJnl 1928*
Lochner, John C 1871- *WhJnl 1928*
Lochner, Louis Paul 1887-1975 *AmJnl, BioIn 4, ConAu 53, ConAu 65, CurBio XR, IntWW 1976, OvPC, WhoAm 1974, WhoE 1974*
Lochridge, Benjamin Sturges 1917- *WhoAm 1974*
Locke, Charles O 1896?-1977 *ConAu 69*

Locke, David Ross 1833-1888 *Alli Sup, AmAu,*
AmAu&B, AmJnl, BbD, BiD&SB, CasWL,
CnDAL, CyAL 2, DcAmA, DcAmB 11,
DcLEL, DcNAA, EvLB, HisAmM XR,
NatCAB 6, OhA&B, OxAm, Pen Am, REn,
REnAL, WebBD
Locke, David Ross *see also* Nasby, Petroleum
Vesuvius
Locke, Edith Raymond 1921- *WhoAm 1974,*
WhoAmW 1974, WhoE 1974
Locke, Francis P *RpN*
Locke, James 1869-1928 *DcNAA*
Locke, Justin *HisAmM XR*
Locke, L G *NF*
Locke, Michael 1943- *ConAu 73*
Locke, Raymond Friday *NF*
Locke, Richard Adams 1800-1871 *Alli, AmAu,*
AmAu&B, AmJnl, DcAmA, DcAmB 11,
DcNAA, NatCAB 13, OxAm, WebBD
Locke, Robinson 1856-1920 *AmAu&B, REnAL*
Locke, Walter 1875-1957 *AmAu&B, BioIn 4,*
OhA&B
Locker-Lampson, Oliver Stillingfleet 1881-1954
WebBD
Lockerby, Frank McCarthy 1899-1969 *BioIn 10,*
WhJnl 1928
Lockerman, Doris *BioIn 1*
Lockett, Edward B 1905- *NF*
Lockett, John W 1881- *WhJnl 1928*
Lockhart, Jack Herbert 1909- *WhoAm 1974*
Lockhart, John Gibson 1794-1854 *Alli, AtlBL,*
BbD, BiD&SB, BioIn 1, BioIn 3, BioIn 9,
BioIn 10, BrAu 19, CasWL, DcEnA,
DcEnL, DcEuL, DcLEL, EvLB, MouLC 3,
NewC, OxEng, Pen Eng, RAdv 1, REn,
WebBD, WebE&AL
Lockhart, Sir Robert Hamilton Bruce 1887-1970
BioIn 4, DcLEL, EvLB, TwCA, TwCA Sup,
WebBD
Lockhart, Sir Robert Hamilton Bruce *see also* Bruce
Lockhart, R H
Lockheimer, F Roy *OvPC*
Lockley, Fred 1871-1958 *AmAu&B, WhNAA*
Locklin, Bruce *InvJ*
Lockridge, Patricia *HisAmM XR*
Lockridge, Richard 1898- *AmAu&B, CurBio XR,*
EncMys, REnAL, TwCA, TwCA Sup,
WhoAm 1974
Lockwood, August Graham *WhoAm 1974*
Lockwood, Donald A *WhJnl 1928*
Lockwood, Douglas 1918- *ConAu 21R*
Lockwood, George Browning 1872-1932 *BioIn 2,*
DcNAA, IndAu 1816, WhJnl 1928
Lockwood, Howard *HisAmM XR*
Lockwood, Ingersoll 1841-1918 *Alli Sup,*
AmAu&B, DcAmA, DcNAA, HisAmM XR
Lockwood, Kenneth F 1881?-1948 *BioIn 1*
Lockwood, Lee Jonathan 1932- *BioIn 7,*
ConAu 37, WhoAm 1974
Lockwood, Louise Field 1923- *WhoAm 1974*
Lockwood, Sara L *WhJnl Sup*
Lodge, Edwin A *HisAmM XR*
Lodge, Henry Cabot 1850-1924 *Alli Sup, AmAu,*
AmAu&B, BbD, BiD&SB, Br&AmS,
DcAmA, DcNAA, HisAmM XR, LiJA,
OxAm, REnAL, WebBD
Lodge, Henry Cabot 1902- *CelR 1973,*
ConAu 53, CurBio XR, IntWW 1976,
WebBD, WhNAA, Who 1974,
WhoAm 1974, WhoAmP 1973, WhJnl 1928,
WhoWor 1974
Lodge, John Christian 1862-1950 *BioIn 2, BioIn 3*
Lodge, Joseph Norman 1899-1964 *BioIn 2,*
BioIn 7

Lodge, Paul *HisAmM XR*
Lodovichetti, Arthur Victor 1909- *WhoAm 1974,*
WhoS&SW 1973
Loeb, Edward *NF*
Loeb, Hanau Wolf 1865-1927 *HisAmM XR,*
WhNAA
Loeb, James, Jr. 1908- *CurBio XR*
Loeb, Madeleine H 1905?-1974 *ConAu 45,*
NewYTBS 5
Loeb, Marshall Robert 1929- *ConAu 23R,*
WhoE 1974
Loeb, Richard *AmJnl*
Loeb, Sophie Irene Simon 1876-1929 *DcAmB 11,*
DcNAA, WebBD
Loeb, William 1905- *BioIn 4, BioIn 6, BioIn 8,*
BioIn 9, BioIn 10, CurBio XR,
NewYTBE 2, WhoAm 1974, WhoE 1974
Loebl, Suzanne *ConAu 69*
Loeser, John C *OvPC*
Loeser, John Charles 1905- *WhJnl 1928*
Loewenthal, Henry *NF*
Loewenthal, Johann Jakob 1810-1876 *WebBD*
Loftis, Anne 1922- *ConAu 45*
Lofton, John 1941?- *BioIn 9, BioIn 10*
Lofton, John D, Jr. *NF*
Lofton, John Marion 1919- *ConAu 11R,*
WhoAm 1974, WrDr 1976
Loftus, Joseph Anthony 1907- *RpN,*
WhoAm 1974, WhoAmP 1973,
WhoF&I 1974, WhoGov 1972
Loftus, William, Jr. 1901- *WhJnl 1928*
Logan, George B *NF*
Logan, Harlan DeBaun 1904- *BioIn 1,*
HisAmM XR
Logan, Hugh J, Jr. 1874- *WhJnl 1928*
Logan, John Daniel 1869-1929 *DcLEL, DcNAA,*
OxCan
Logan, John Gordon 1871?-1950 *BioIn 2*
Logan, Joseph C 1905- *WhJnl 1928*
Logan, Olive 1839-1909 *Alli Sup, AmAu,*
AmAu&B, BiD&SB, DcAmA, DcAmB 10,
DcNAA, HisAmM XR, HsB&A, OhA&B,
REnAL
Logan, W C *HisAmM XR*
Loggins, William K 1948- *NF*
Loh, Jules 1931- *BlkC, ConAu 33*
Lohrke, Eugene William 1897-1953 *AmAu&B,*
BioIn 3, BioIn 4, TwCA, TwCA Sup
Loir, Theo *NF*
Loizeaux, Marie Duvernoy 1905- *BiDrLUS,*
BioIn 5, ForWC 1970, WhoAmW 1974
Lokey, Eugene M 1892?-1956 *BioIn 4*
Lollar, Coleman Aubrey 1946- *ConAu 49*
Lomax, Almena *BlkC*
Lomax, Jane T *HisAmM XR*
Lomax, Joseph 1809- *NatCAB 14*
Lomax, Louis Emanuel 1922-1970 *AmAu&B,*
BioIn 5, BioIn 7, BioIn 8, BioIn 9,
ConAu 25, NewYTBE 1
Lombard, Helen 1905- *CurBio XR*
Lombardi, John Robert 1942- *WhoAm 1974*
Lomoe, Orville E 1914- *NF*
London, Charmian *AmAu&B, WhNAA*
London, Jack 1876-1916 *AmAu&B, AmRP,*
AmWr, AtlBL, AuBYP, AuNews 2,
BiD&SB, CarSB, CasWL, CnDAL,
ConAmL, CyWA, DcAmA, DcBiA, DcLEL,
DcNAA, EncAB, EncMys, EncWL,
HisAmM XR, JBA 1934, LiJA, LongC,
ModAL, ModAL Sup, OxAm, OxCan,
OxEng, Pen Am, RAdv 1, RComWL, REn,
REnAL, Str&VC, TwCA, TwCA Sup,
TwCW, WebBD, WebE&AL, WhoTwCL
Lonergan, Michael d1953 *BioIn 3*

Long, Adam F 1898?-1972 *BioIn 9*, *NewYTBE 3*
Long, Charles 1938- *ConAu 65*
Long, Charles Ramsay 1872-1946 *WhNAA*,
    WhJnl 1928
Long, Clyde C 1905- *WhJnl 1928*
Long, Donald Hooper 1896- *WhJnl 1928*
Long, E John 1900- *WhJnl 1928*
Long, Edward Ernest 1880-1956 *BioIn 4*, *WhoLA*
Long, Ferdinand George 1870?-1948 *BioIn 1*
Long, Forrest Edwin 1895- *WhoAm 1974*
Long, George T 1871?-1948 *BioIn 1*
Long, George Washington 1913-1958 *BioIn 5*
Long, Gerald 1923- *IntWW 1976*, *Who 1974*,
    WhoAm 1974, *WhoWor 1974*
Long, Howard Rusk 1909- *ConAu 7R*,
    DrAS 74E, *WhoAm 1974*, *WrDr 1976*
Long, Hubert M 1873- *WhJnl 1928*
Long, Jess E 1874- *WhJnl 1928*
Long, John Budd 1894-1962 *BioIn 2*, *BioIn 6*,
    BioIn 7, *NatCAB 49*
Long, John C *NF*
Long, John Cuthbert 1892- *AmAu&B*,
    ConAu P-1, *WhoAm 1974*
Long, Joseph Harvey 1863-1958 *BioIn 5*, *BioIn 9*,
    WhJnl 1928
Long, Luman Harrison 1907-1971 *BioIn 9*,
    NewYTBE 2
Long, Paul Walker 1896-1961 *BioIn 5*,
    WhJnl 1928
Long, Percy Waldron 1876-1952 *AmAu&B*,
    HisAmM XR, *NatCAB 41*, *WhNAA*
Long, Ralph *NF*
Long, Ray 1878-1935 *AmAu&B*, *DcNAA*,
    HisAmM XR, *IndAu 1917*, *WhNAA*
Long, S W H *NF*
Long, Scott 1917- *WhoAm 1974*
Long, Sidney David 1873- *WhJnl 1928*
Long, Tania 1913- *BioIn 1*, *CurBio XR*
Long, Tudor Seymour *HisAmM XR*
Long, W *NF*
Long, Walker 1896-1961 *NatCAB 46*
Long, Wellington 1924?- *BioIn 3*
Long, William *NF*
Longacre, Charles Smull 1871-1958 *BioIn 5*,
    WhNAA
Longacre, James Barton 1794-1869 *HisAmM XR*
Longan, B George 1879-1942 *WhJnl 1928*
Longan, George Baker *see* Longan, B George
Longcope, T Ridgway 1891- *WhJnl 1928*
Longfellow, William Pitt Preble 1836-1913 *DcAmA*,
    DcNAA, *HisAmM XR*
Longgood, William Frank 1917- *ConAu 2R*
Longhurst, Henry Carpenter 1909-1978 *Au&Wr*,
    BioIn 9, *BioIn 10*, *Who 1974*
Longley, Alcander 1832-1918 *DcNAA*,
    HisAmM XR, *OhA&B*
Longman, Irwin 1841-1918 *AmAu&B*, *DcNAA*
Longman, Irwin *see also* Lockwood, Ingersoll
Longstreet, Augustus Baldwin 1790-1870 *Alli*,
    AmAu, *AmAu&B*, *BbD*, *BiD&SB*, *BiDSA*,
    CasWL, *CnDAL*, *CyAL 2*, *CyWA*, *DcAmA*,
    DcLEL, *DcNAA*, *HisAmM XR*, *OxAm*,
    Pen Am, *REn*, *REnAL*, *WebBD*,
    WebE&AL
Longstreet, Helen Dortch d1962 *AmAu&B*,
    BiDSA
Longuet, Marcel 1877?-1949 *BioIn 2*
Longwell, Daniel 1899-1968 *BioIn 8*
Longwell, William H 1839-1921 *NatCAB 19*
Longworth, Richard Cole 1936?- *NF*
Longworth, Robert L *WhJnl 1928*
Lonnrot, Elias 1802-1884 *BiD&SB*, *CyWA*,
    DcEuL, *EuAu*, *ForP*, *Pen Eur*, *WebBD*
Lons, Hermann 1866-1914 *CasWL*, *CIDMEL*,

EvEuW, *OxGer*, *WebBD*
Loofbourrow, John G 1902?-1964 *BioIn 6*
Looker, Earle 1895-1976 *AmAu&B*, *ConAu 29*,
    ConAu 65, *WhNAA*
Loomis, Alfred Fullerton 1890-1968 *AmAu&B*,
    BioIn 8, *BioIn 10*, *REnAL*, *WhNAA*
Loomis, Frederic Morris 1877-1949 *DcNAA*
Loomis, Henry 1919- *IntWW 1974*,
    WhoAm 1974, *WhoAmP 1973*,
    WhoGov 1972, *WhoWor 1974*
Loomis, Ken *NF*
Loomis, Lee P 1884-1964 *BioIn 2*, *BioIn 6*
Loomis, Pascal *HisAmM XR*
Loomis, William Warner 1876-1947 *BioIn 1*
Loomis, Zela Hadley 1891- *WhJnl 1928*
Looms, George 1886-1926 *DcNAA*
Loory, Stuart Hugh 1932- *ConAu 25*, *InvJ*,
    WhoAm 1974
Loose, Heinrich 1810-1872 *BioIn 2*
Lopenzina, Gary A *NF*
Loper, James Leaders 1931- *WhoAm 1974*
Lopes, Norberto *ForP*
Lopez, Andrew 1910- *WhoAm 1974*
Lopez, Eddie 1940?-1971 *BioIn 9*, *NewYTBE 2*
Lopez, Luisita *NF*
Lopez, Rafael Anglada *NF*
Lopez, Salvador P 1911- *IntWW 1976*,
    WhoWor 1974
Lopez Cisnero, Alberto *BioIn 7*
Lopez Moctezuma, Juan 1931?- *BioIn 8*
Lopez Y Fuentes, Gregorio 1892?-1966 *BioIn 7*
Lorance, John 1864?-1953 *BioIn 3*
Lorant, Stefan 1901- *AmAu&B*, *Au&Wr*,
    AuNews 1, *BioIn 1*, *BioIn 8*, *ConAu 5R*,
    DrAS 74H, *IntWW 1976*, *Who 1974*,
    WhoAm 1974, *WrDr 1976*
Lord, Chester Sanders 1850-1933 *AmJnl*,
    DcAmB S1, *DcNAA*, *NatCAB 25*
Lord, Christine *NF*
Lord, Daniel Aloysius 1888-1955 *AmAu&B*,
    BioIn 1, *BioIn 3*, *BkC 1*, *CathA 1930*,
    WhNAA
Lord, David Nevins 1792-1880 *Alli*, *Alli Sup*,
    DcAmA, *DcNAA*, *HisAmM XR*
Lord, Graham 1943- *ConAu 53*
Lord, Henry G 1865-1961 *NatCAB 46*
Lord, Kenneth *NF*
Lord, Merrill M 1891?-1954 *BioIn 3*
Lord, Mrs. R I H 1880- *WhJnl 1928*
Lord, Russell 1895- *AmAu&B*, *BioIn 1*,
    WhJnl 1928
Lord, Shirley 1934- *ConAu XR*
Lorenz, Alfred Lawrence, Jr. 1937- *ConAu 45*,
    DrAS 74E
Lorenz, Edmund Simon 1854-1942 *Alli Sup*,
    AmSCAP 1966, *DcNAA*, *HisAmM XR*,
    NatCAB 32, *OhA&B*
Lorenz, Lee Sharp 1932- *WhoAm 1974*
Lorenz, Selma G *NF*
Lorenzo, Christopher M *NF*
Lorimer, George Horace 1868-1937 *AmAu&B*,
    BbD, *BiD&SB*, *BiDSA*, *BioIn 1*, *BioIn 2*,
    BioIn 3, *BioIn 4*, *DcAmA*, *DcAmB S2*,
    DcNAA, *HisAmM XR*, *NatCAB 27*, *OxAm*,
    REn, *REnAL*, *WebBD*, *WhJnl 1928*
Lorimer, Graeme 1903- *AmAu&B*,
    HisAmM XR, *WhoAm 1974*, *WhoE 1974*
Loring, Ellis Gray 1803-1858 *HisAmM XR*
Loring, Frederick Wadsworth 1848-1871 *Alli Sup*,
    AmAu, *AmAu&B*, *DcAmA*, *DcAmB 11*,
    DcNAA
Loring, James *HisAmM XR*
Loring, Paule Stetson 1899- *BioIn 5*
Lorsung, Thomas N 1938- *NF*

Lorton, Eugene 1869-1949 *BioIn 1, BioIn 2, BioIn 4, NatCAB 40*
Losee, Charles D *NF*
Loshak, David 1933- *ConAu 41*
Lossing, Benson John 1813-1891 *Alli, Alli Sup, AmAu, AmAu&B, BbD, BiD&SB, BioIn 2, BioIn 8, CyAL 2, DcAmA, DcNAA, EarABI, EarABI Sup, WebBD*
Lostutter, Melvin Simmons 1895-1958 *IndAu 1917, WhJnl 1928*
Loth, David Goldsmith 1899- *AmAu&B, Au&Wr, BioIn 3, ConAu 3R, OvPC, WhoAm 1974, WhJnl Sup, WrDr 1976*
Loth, Paul V *HisAmM XR*
Lothar, Ernst 1890- *AmAu&B, AmNov, CurBio XR, TwCA Sup*
Lothrop, Daniel 1831-1892 *AmAu&B, DcNAA, HisAmM XR, WebBD*
Lotito, Rocco *NF*
Lotspeich, Roy Nichols 1882-1951 *BioIn 2, BioIn 6, NatCAB 44*
Lott, Monroe *see* Howard, Edwin
Lottell, Philip 1868-1943 *NatCAB 32*
Loubet, Nat *NF*
Loucheim, Katie 1903- *BioIn 7, BioIn 8, BioIn 9*
Louchheim, Donald Harry 1937- *WhoAm 1974*
Loud, Grover Cleveland 1890-1968 *BioIn 8, BioIn 9*
Loudon, John Claudius 1783-1843 *Alli, BiDLA, BrAu 19, DcEnL, WebBD*
Loudon, Samuel 1727-1813 *AmAu&B, AmJnl, OxAm, REnAL, WebBD*
Loughborough, Jim *NF*
Loughborough, Mary Ann Webster 1836-1887 *AmAu&B, BiDSA, DcAmA, DcNAA, LivFWS*
Loughbridge, J *HisAmM XR*
Loughran, G *NF*
Loughran, Robert T *BioIn 4*
Louis, Victor E 1929?- *BioIn 8, BioIn 9, NewYTBE 2*
Lounsbury, George Fenner 1872-1958 *WhNAA, WhJnl 1928*
Lounsbury, Thomas Raynesford 1838-1915 *Alli Sup, AmAu, AmAu&B, BiD&SB, DcAmA, DcNAA, HisAmM XR, OxAm, REn, WebBD*
Louviere, Vernon Ray 1920- *WhoAm 1974*
Love, Alfred Henry 1830-1913 *HisAmM XR, OxAm*
Love, Judy *NF*
Love, Kennett 1924- *OvPC*
Love, Philip Hampton 1905-1977 *ConAu 73, WhoAm 1974, WhoS&SW 1973*
Love, Robertus Donnell 1867-1930 *AmAu&B, DcAmB 11, DcNAA, HisAmM XR, WhNAA, WhJnl 1928*
Lovejoy, Bahija *OvPC*
Lovejoy, Clarence Earle 1894-1974 *AmAu&B, Au&Wr, BioIn 6, BioIn 10, ConAu 5R, ConAu 45, NewYTBS 5, WhNAA, WhJnl 1978*
Lovejoy, Elijah Parish 1802-1837 *AmAu, EncAB, HisAmX XR, OxAm, REnAL, WebBD*
Lovejoy, Mary Evelyn 1847-1928 *DcNAA*
Lovejoy, Owen 1811-1864 *DcNAA, HisAmM XR, OxAm, WebBD*
Lovejoy, Sharron *NF*
Lovelace, Delos Wheeler 1894-1967 *AmAu&B, AuBYP, ConAu 7R, ConAu 25, MnnWr, SmATA 7, TwCA, TwCA Sup, WhNAA*
Lovelace, Douglas Cooper 1916- *WhoAm 1974*
Lovelady, Steve *NewMr*

Lovell, Bernard M *OvPC*
Lovell, Graham *NF*
Lovell, Ronald P 1937- *ConAu 73*
Loveman, Amy 1881-1955 *AmAu&B, BioIn 1, BioIn 2, BioIn 4, BioIn 5, BioIn 6, CurBio XR, DcAmB S5, NatCAB 44, REnAL*
Loveman, Samuel 1885?-1976 *ConAu 65*
Loveridge, George Y 1904- *BioIn 2*
Lovestone, Joe *AmRP*
Lovett, J T *HisAmM XR*
Lovewell, Paul A 1876- *WhNAA, WhJnl 1928*
Loving, Edward Pierre 1894?-1950 *BioIn 2*
Low, Alfred Maurice 1860-1929 *DcAmA, HisAmM XR*
Low, Alfred Maurice *see also* Low, Maurice
Low, Bob *NF*
Low, Sir David Alexander Cecil 1891-1963 *BioIn 1, BioIn 2, BioIn 4, BioIn 5, BioIn 6, CurBio XR, ForP, HisAmM XR, WebBD*
Low, Donald Anthony 1927- *ConAu 73, WhoWor 1974*
Low, Frederick Rollins 1860-1936 *DcNAA, WhNAA, WhJnl 1928*
Low, George Prescott 1913- *OvPC, WhoAm 1974*
Low, Maurice 1860-1929 *NewC, WebBD*
Low, Maurice *see also* Low, Alfred Maurice
Low, Russell Cutler 1882?-1957 *BioIn 4*
Low, Sir Sidney James Mark 1857-1932 *BioIn 2, WebBD*
Low Cloud, Charles Round 1872-1949 *BioIn 2, BioIn 5, BioIn 9*
Lowe, Arthur H 1894- *WhJnl 1928*
Lowe, Caroline *AmRP*
Lowe, Charles 1828-1874 *HisAmM XR*
Lowe, Charles 1848- *Alli Sup*
Lowe, Corinne Martin 1882-1952 *BioIn 2*
Lowe, Frank 1921?-1977 *NF*
Lowe, Herman Albert 1905-1961 *BioIn 5*
Lowe, Janet *NF*
Lowe, Margaret Hurst *NF*
Lowe, Vivian *OvPC*
Lowell, Charles 1782-1861 *Alli, DcAmA, DcNAA, HisAmM XR*
Lowell, Francis Cabot *HisAmM XR*
Lowell, James Russell 1819-1891 *Alli, Alli Sup, AmAu, AmAu&B, AmJnl, AtlBL, BbD, BiD&SB, BioIn 2, BioIn 3, BioIn 4, BioIn 5, BioIn 6, BioIn 8, BioIn 9, CasWL, CnDAL, CnE&AP, CrtT 3, CyAL 2, CyWA, DcAmA, DcEnA, DcEnA Ap, DcEnL, DcLEL, DcNAA, DcSpL, EvLB, HisAmM XR, LiJA, MouLC 4, OxAm, OxEng, Pen Am, RAdv 1, REn, REnAL, Str&VC, WebBD, WebE&AL*
Lowell, John *Alli*
Lowell, Juliet 1901- *AmAu&B, ConAu 1, ForWC 1970, OvPC, WhNAA, WhoAm 1974, WhoAmW 1974*
Lowell, Orson 1871-1956 *BioIn 4, HisAmM XR*
Lowenfels, Walter 1897-1976 *AmAu&B, ConAu 9R, ConP 1970, ConP 1975, DrAP 1975, Pen Am, RAdv 1, WrDr 1976*
Lowengard, Leon 1886- *WhJnl 1928*
Lowens, Irving 1916- *BiDrLUS, ConAu 17R, DrAS 74H, LiJA, WhoAm 1974, WhoS&SW 1973, WrDr 1976*
Lowenstein, Douglas *NF*
Lowenstein, Gabriel Abraham 1889-1965 *BioIn 9*
Lowenstein, Ludwig 1898?-1968 *BioIn 8*
Lowenstein, Ralph Lynn 1930- *BioIn 7, ConAu 17R, ForP, WhoAm 1974*
Lowenthal, Marvin 1890-1969 *AmAu&B, BioIn 4, BioIn 8, BioIn 9, TwCA, TwCA Sup*

Lower, Elmer Wilson 1913- *BioIn 8,*
IntMPA 1975, OvPC, WhoAm 1974
Lowery, Raymond 1918- *WhoS&SW 1973*
Lowery, Samuel R 1830?- *BioIn 8*
Lowie, Robert Harry 1883-1957 *AmAu&B,*
OxCan, REnAL, WebBD, WhNAA
Lowman, Josephine *NF*
Lowman, Lester Alvin *WhJnl 1928*
Lowndes, Arthur 1858-1917 *HisAmM XR*
Lowrey, Burling *NF*
Lowrey, Ed C 1888- *WhJnl 1928*
Lowrey, Frederick C *HisAmM XR*
Lowrie, Henry *NF*
Lowrie, Richard 1876- *WhJnl 1928*
Lowry, Edward George 1876-1943 *CurBio XR,*
DcNAA, NatCAB 32
Lowry, Helen B *NF*
Lowther, William A *NF*
Loy, Damon *NF*
Loy, Kathy *NF*
Loy, Matthias 1828-1915 *Alli Sup, AmAu&B,*
DcAmA, DcNAA, OhA&B
Loyd, Gene *NF*
Lozano, Dolores Lanz Duret *ForP*
Lozano, Ignacio E 1886-1953 *BioIn 3*
Lozano, Ignacio Eugenio, Jr. 1927- *WhoF&I 1974,*
WhoWest 1974
Lozoya, Francisco *NF*
Lu, David 1906?- *BioIn 2*
Lubar, Robert 1920- *ConAu 73, WhoAm 1974*
Lubben, John Frederick 1866- *WhJnl 1928*
Lubeck, Robert E *NF*
Lubell, Samuel 1911- *AmAu&B, Au&Wr,*
BioIn 3, BioIn 4, ConAu 15R, CurBio XR,
WhoAm 1974, WhoS&SW 1973,
WhoWor 1974, WhoWorJ 1972
Lubinski, Kurt 1900?-1955 *BioIn 4*
Lubis, Mochtar 1922- *BioIn 9, CasWL,*
ConAu 29, IntWW 1976, WhoWor 1974
Lubkin, Gloria Becker 1933- *AmM&W 73P*
Luby, James Patrick Kenyon 1856-1925 *DcNAA*
Luby, Thomas Clarke 1822-1901 *Alli Sup,*
DcAmA, DcNAA
Lucas, Christopher *ForP*
Lucas, Clarence Bickford 1930- *WhoAm 1974*
Lucas, Clarence L 1898- *WhJnl 1928*
Lucas, Edward Verrall 1868-1938 *CarSB, DcLEL,*
EvLB, LongC, ModBL, NewC, OxEng,
Pen Eng, REn, Str&VC, TwCA,
TwCA Sup, TwCW, WebBD, WhoChL,
WhoLA
Lucas, Jacob 1825- *BioIn 2*
Lucas, Jim Griffing 1914-1970 *AmJnl, BioIn 9,*
ForP, NewYTBE 1, WhoS&SW 1973
Lucas, Lawrence Edward 1933- *BioIn 9,*
ConAu 65, LivBAA
Lucas, Peter *NewMr*
Lucas, Robert L *NF*
Lucas, Robert Warren 1912- *WhoAm 1974*
Lucas, Samuel 1818-1868? *Alli, Alli Sup, DcEnL*
Lucca, Pauline *HisAmM XR*
Luccock, Halford Edward 1885-1960 *AmAu&B,*
CurBio XR, REnAL
Luccock, Naphtali 1853-1916 *DcAmA, DcNAA,*
HisAmM XR, OhA&B
Luce, Claire Boothe 1903- *NewYTBE 4,*
WhoThe 1972, WrDr 1976
Luce, Claire Boothe *see also* Boothe, Clare
Luce, Claire Boothe *see also* Luce, Clare Boothe
Luce, Clare Boothe 1903- *AmAu&B, Au&Wr,*
CathA 1930, CelR 1973, ConAu 45,
IntWW 1976, McGWD, OvPC, OxAm,
REn, REnAL, TwCA Sup, WhoAm 1974,
WhoAmP 1973, WhoWor 1974

Luce, Clare Boothe *see also* Boothe, Clare
Luce, Clare Boothe *see also* Luce, Claire Boothe
Luce, Henry, III 1925- *CelR 1973, IntWW 1976,*
OvPC, WhoAm 1974, WhoE 1974,
WhoF&I 1974, WhoWor 1974
Luce, Henry Robinson 1898-1967 *AmAu&B,*
AmJnl, BioIn 1, BioIn 2, BioIn 3, BioIn 5,
BioIn 6, BioIn 7, BioIn 8, BioIn 9,
CurBio XR, EncAB, ForP, HisAmM XR,
REn, REnAL, WebBD
Luce, Mrs. Henry Robinson 1903- *Who 1974*
Luce, Mrs. Henry Robinson *see also* Boothe, Clare
Luce, Mrs. Henry Robinson *see also* Luce, Claire
Boothe
Luce, Mrs. Henry Robinson *see also* Luce, Clare
Boothe
Luce, Robert Bonner 1921- *HisAmM XR,*
WhoAm 1974
Lucentini, Mauro 1924- *ConAu 69*
Lucey, Charles Timothy 1905- *WhoAm 1974*
Lucey, Thomas C *OvPC*
Lucey, William L *LiJA*
Luchaire, Jean 1900?-1946 *BioIn 1, BioIn 2*
Luchsinger, Fred W 1921- *IntWW 1976,*
WhoWor 1974
Lucker, J M *ForP*
Lucker, Joop 1915?- *BioIn 3*
Luckett, Hubert Pearson 1916- *OvPC,*
WhoAm 1974
Luckett, James Douglas 1891- *BioIn 2*
Luckey, Samuel 1791-1869 *DcNAA,*
HisAmM XR
Lucky, Fred *NF*
Lucy, Sir Henry 1845-1924 *Alli Sup, NewC,*
WebBD
Ludcke, G L *NF*
Ludington, Nicholas *NF*
Ludlow, Donald *ForP*
Ludlow, Fitz-Hugh 1836-1870 *AmAu&B,*
DcNAA, HisAmM XR
Ludlow, Henry S 1870-1938 *NatCAB 28*
Ludlow, John Malcolm Forbes 1821-1911 *Alli Sup,*
WebBD
Ludlow, Louis Leon 1873-1950 *BioIn 2,*
IndAu 1917
Ludlow, Lynn 1933- *NF*
Ludlow, Park *see* Brown, Theron
Ludvigsen, Karl 1934- *ConAu 73*
Ludwig, Richard A *WhJnl 1928*
Ludwigson, John Ormont 1938- *WhoAm 1974*
Luedtke, Kurt *NF*
Luehrs, Kirk A *NF*
Luft, Friedrich 1911- *IntWW 1976*
Luft, Herbert G *IntMPA 1975*
Lugard, Lady Flora Louise 1852-1929 *BioIn 1*
Luger, Johan *NF*
Lugrin, Charles Henry 1846-1917 *DcNAA*
Lujan, Nestor *ForP*
Lukas, J Anthony 1933- *AmAu&B, ConAu 49,*
WhoAm 1974
Luke, Hugh *NF*
Lukens, Henry Clay 1838-1900? *Alli Sup, AmAu,*
AmAu&B, BiD&SB, DcAmA, DcNAA,
NatCAB 13, OxAm
Lukin, Nikolai Mikhailovich 1885-1940 *BioIn 10*
Lukochevichus, Jonas *NF*
Lukomski, Jess *NF*
Lukovets, Aleksei I 1921?-1977 *NF*
Luks, Fred 1917- *NF*
Luks, George Benjamin 1867-1933 *AmJnl,*
DcAmB S1, HisAmM XR, WebBD
Lull, Richard Swann 1867-1957 *HisAmM XR,*
WhNAA
Lum, Arlene *NF*

Lum, Dyer Daniel *Alli Sup, AmRP, DcNAA, HisAmM XR*
Lumley, Arthur 1837-1912 *EarABI, EarABI Sup, HisAmM XR*
Lummis, Charles Fletcher 1859-1928 *AmAu&B, AmLY, BiD&SB, DcAmA, DcNAA, HisAmM XR, OhA&B, OxAm, WebBD, WhNAA*
Lumsden, Francis A d1860 *AmJnl, FamWC, NatCAB 13*
Lumsden, Marshall *NF*
Lunacharskii, Anatolii Vasilevich 1875-1933 *BioIn 9*
Lund, Eric *NF*
Lund, Robert *NF*
Lund, Svend Aage 1900- *IntWW 1976, WhoWor 1974*
Lundberg, Wayne 1935- *NF*
Lundeen, Earnest Warren 1894- *WhNAA, WhJnl 1928*
Lundorg, Florence *HisAmM XR*
Lundquist, Carl 1913- *OvPC*
Lundy, Benjamin 1789-1839 *Alli, AmJnl, BiD&SB, HisAmM XR, OhA&B, OxAm, REnAL, WebBD*
Lundy, Walker *InvJ*
Lunt, George 1803-1885 *Alli, Alli Sup, AmAu, AmAu&B, BiD&SB, CyAL 2, DcAmA, DcAmB 11, DcNAA, HisAmM XR*
Lunzer, Jean H *NF*
Lupo, Alan 1938- *ConAu 41*
Lupton, Frank L *HisAmM XR*
Lupton, Mrs. Henry M 1874- *WhJnl 1928*
Lurie, Jesse Z 1913- *WhoWorJ 1972*
Lurie, Meyer *OvPC*
Lurie, Ranan R 1932- *BioIn 9, ConAu 57, OvPC*
Lurie, Richard G 1919- *ConAu 23, OvPC*
Lurie, Ted R 1909-1974 *BioIn 10, NewYTBS 5, WhoWor 1974*
Lurton, Douglas Ellsworth 1897-1956 *BioIn 4*
Lush, Charles Keeler 1861- *BiD&SB, DcAmA, DcNAA, WhNAA*
Lusinchi, Victor *NF*
Lusk, Addison K 1885- *WhJnl 1928*
Lusk, Edward Franklyn 1900- *WhJnl 1928*
Lusk, Robert Davies 1902-1962 *BioIn 9, WhJnl 1928*
Luskin, John 1908- *ConAu 45*
Luter, John 1919- *DrAS 74E, OvPC, WhoAm 1974, WhoE 1974, WhoWor 1974*
Lutes, Della Thompson d1942 *AmAu&B, AmLY, CurBio XR, DcNAA, HisAmM XR, WhNAA*
Lutfi Al-Sayyid, Ahmad 1871?-1963 *BioIn 6*
Luther, James Wallace 1940- *ConAu 69*
Luther, Mark Lee 1872- *AmAu&B, DcAmA, HisAmM XR, WhNAA*
Luther, Mary Lou *NF*
Luthi, Adrian *NF*
Lutjen, George Prentis *OvPC*
Lutrell, Estelle *LiJA*
Lutwach, Leonard I *LiJA*
Lutz, Antonio F *OvPC*
Lutz, C Arthur *HisAmM XR*
Lutz, Francis Earle 1890?-1958 *BioIn 5*
Lutz, William W 1919- *ConAu 49*
Lux, John Francis 1896- *BioIn 2*
Luz, Myriam *OvPC*
Ly-Qui, Chung 1940- *ConAu 29*
Lyall, Mrs. Gavin Tudor 1928- *Who 1974*
Lyall, Mrs. Gavin Tudor *see also* Lyall, Katharine Elizabeth
Lyall, Mrs. Gavin Tudor *see also* Whitehorn, Katharine Elizabeth

Lyall, Gavin Tudor 1932- *Au&Wr, ConAu 9R, EncMys, Who 1974, WrDr 1976*
Lyall, Katharine Elizabeth 1928- *ConAu 7R*
Lyall, Katharine Elizabeth *see also* Whitehorn, Katharine E
Lydon, Christopher *NF*
Lyford, Harry Burgh 1899- *WhJnl 1928*
Lyght, Charles Everard 1901- *WhoAm 1974*
Lyle, Eugene P, Jr. 1873- *AmAu&B, AmLY, BiDSA, HisAmM XR, WhNAA*
Lyman *FamWC*
Lyman, Ambrose W *NF*
Lyman, Harold William 1893- *WhJnl 1928*
Lyman, Joseph Bardwell 1829-1872 *Alli Sup, BiD&SB, BioIn 7, DcAmA, DcNAA, HisAmM XR*
Lyman, Laura Elizabeth Baker 1831- *BiD&SB*
Lyman, Lauren Dwight 1891-1972 *BioIn 9, NewYTBE 3*
Lyman, Robert Hunt 1864-1937 *NatCAB 28, WhNAA, WhJnl 1928*
Lyman-Green, D *NF*
Lynahan, Gertrude 1900- *WhJnl 1928*
Lynch, Charles Burchill 1919- *CanWW 1972, OvPC*
Lynch, Charles Ivers *BioIn 2*
Lynch, Denis Tilden 1884?-1966 *BioIn 7*
Lynch, Francis Michael 1899- *BioIn 1*
Lynch, Frederick 1867-1934 *HisAmM XR*
Lynch, George Edward *WhJnl 1928*
Lynch, Jay Patrick 1945- *BioIn 10*
Lynch, Jim 1931- *NF*
Lynch, John Francis 1917- *WhoAm 1974, WhoS&SW 1973, WhoWor 1974*
Lynch, John W 1904- *BioIn 1, CathA 1930*
Lynch, Mitchell *NF*
Lynch, Patrick Neeson 1817-1882 *BiDSA, HisAmM XR*
Lynd, Robert 1879-1949 *BioIn 1, BioIn 2, BioIn 4, BioIn 5, BioIn 6, DcLEL, EvLB, LongC, ModBL, NewC, REn, TwCA, TwCA Sup, WebBD*
Lynd, Robert Staughton 1892-1970 *AmAu&B, ConAu 29, DcLEL, IndAu 1917, LongC, NewYTBE 1, OxAm, Pen Am, REnAL, TwCA, TwCA Sup, WebBD*
Lynde, Hunter 1900- *WhJnl Sup*
Lynde, Myron Stanford 1931- *BioIn 4*
Lynde, Myron Stanford *see also* Lynde, Stan
Lynde, Stan 1931- *ConAu 65, WhoAm 1974*
Lynde, Stan *see also* Lynde, Myron Stanford
Lynden, Patricia 1937- *ConAu 73*
Lyne, John Alexander 1857- *WhJnl 1928*
Lyneis, Dick 1935- *NF*
Lynes, Joseph Russell, Jr. 1910- *WhoAm 1974*
Lynes, Joseph Russell, Jr. *see also* Lynes, Russell
Lynes, Russell 1910- *AmAu&B, Au&Wr, BioIn 3, BioIn 4, BioIn 5, BioIn 8, BioIn 9, CelR 1973, ConAu 2R, CurBio XR, OxAm, REnAL, WhoAmA 1973, WhoWor 1974*
Lynes, Russell *see also* Lynes, Joseph Russell, Jr.
Lynett, Edward James 1906?-1966 *BioIn 7*
Lynett, Elizabeth Ruddy 1902-1959 *BioIn 5*
Lynn, Emerson E 1898- *WhJnl 1928*
Lynn, Gordon Wauhope 1903- *WhJnl 1928*
Lynn, John Arnold, Jr. 1891- *WhJnl 1928*
Lynn, Joyce *NF*
Lynn, Melda *NF*
Lyon, Allie *NF*
Lyon, George H 1890-1971 *BioIn 9, NewYTBE 2*
Lyon, Gideon Allen 1867-1951 *BioIn 2*
Lyon, Harris Merton 1883-1916 *AmAu&B, DcNAA, HisAmM XR, REnAL*
Lyon, Herb 1919?-1968 *BioIn 8*

Lyon, James *NF*
Lyon, Jean 1902?-1960 *BioIn 5*
Lyon, John *HisAmM XR*
Lyon, Matthew 1750-1833 *AmJnl*
Lyon, Richard Hill 1846-1907 *BioIn 2,*
   IndAu 1816
Lyon, Robert d1858 *NF*
Lyon, Stewart *NF*
Lyon, Thomas Stewart 1866-1946 *BioIn 1*
Lyon, W *NF*
Lyons, Barrow 1889?-1959 *BioIn 5*
Lyons, Daniel *HisAmM XR*
Lyons, Daniel 1920- *BioIn 9, ConAu 41,*
   WhoAm 1974, WhoE 1974, WhoWor 1974
Lyons, Enid Muriel 1897- *BioIn 7, BioIn 10,*
   IntWW 1974, Who 1974, WhoWor 1974
Lyons, Eugene 1898- *AmAu&B, BioIn 2,*
   BioIn 4, BioIn 8, ConAu 9R, CurBio XR,
   HisAmM XR, OvPC, OxAm, REn, REnAL,
   TwCA, TwCA Sup, WhoAm 1974,
   WhoWor 1974, WhoWorJ 1972
Lyons, Harriet *NF*
Lyons, Herbert *RpN*
Lyons, James Edward 1902- *WhoAdv 1972,*
   WhJnl 1928
Lyons, James Henry 1925-1973 *BioIn 10,*
   WhoAm 1974, WhoE 1974
Lyons, Joel Curtis 1897- *WhNAA, WhJnl 1928*
Lyons, Joseph *NF*
Lyons, Josephine *ForWC 1970, OvPC*
Lyons, Leonard 1906-1976 *AmJnl, BioIn 2,*
   BioIn 3, BioIn 5, BioIn 8, BioIn 10,
   CelR 1973, ConAu 69, NewYTBS 5,
   WhoAm 1974, WhoE 1974, WhoWorJ 1972
Lyons, Louis M *RpN*
Lyons, Norbert 1883?-1971 *BioIn 9*
Lyons, Richard D 1928- *OvPC*
Lyons, Richard I *NF*
Lyons, Ronald J *NF*
Lyst, John Henry 1933- *WhoAm 1974*
Lytle, Andrew Nelson 1902- *AmAu&B, AmNov,*
   ConAu 9, ConNov 1972, ConNov 1976,
   CyWA, DrAF 1976, HisAmM XR, OxAm,
   Pen Am, RAdv 1, REnAL, WhoAm 1974,
   WorAu, WrDr 1976
Lytle, Stewart *NF*
Lyttelton, Humphrey Richard Adeane 1921-
   IntWW 1976, WhoMus 1972
Lytton, Baron Edward G E Lytton Bulwer-
   1803-1873 *Alli, Alli Sup, BiDLA, BrAu 19,*
   CasWL, DcEnA, DcEuL, DcLEL, EvLB,
   HsB&A, NewC, OxEng, Pen Eng, REn,
   WebBD
Lytton, Baron Edward George E L B *see also*
   Bulwer-Lytton, Edward

M

M Quad *see* Lewis, Charles Bertrand
Maas, Peter 1929- *AmAu&B, BioNews 1974, InvJ, NewMr, WhoAm 1974, WrDr 1976*
Maas, Willard 1911-1971 *AmAu&B, ConAu 13, ConAu 29, ConAu P-1*
Maas, William H 1889- *WhNAA, WhJnl 1928*
Maass, William George 1925- *WhoAm 1974*
Mabie, Hamilton Wright 1845?-1916 *Alli Sup, AmAu&B, AnCL, BbD, BiD&SB, CarSB, DcAmA, DcNAA, HisAmM XR, OxAm, REnAL, TwCA, TwCA Sup, WebBD*
Mabie, Janet 1893?-1961 *BioIn 2, BioIn 6*
Mabley, Jack 1915- *WhoAm 1974, WhoMW 1974*
Mabon, Prescott Cliffton 1905- *WhoAm 1974*
Macadam, John *BioIn 4*
MacAfee, Helen 1884-1956 *BioIn 4, BioIn 6, HisAmM XR*
MacAlarney, Robert Emmet 1873-1945 *BioIn 1, CurBio XR, DcNAA, WhJnl 1928*
MacAlister, Merle *HisAmM XR*
MacArthur, C L *HisAmM XR*
MacArthur, Charles 1895-1956 *AmAu&B, CnDAL, McGWD, ModWD, OxAm, REn, REnAL, WebBD*
MacArthur, D Wilson 1903- *ConAu 11R*
MacArthur, James 1866-1909 *AmAu&B*
MacArthur, Peter 1866-1924 *HisAmM XR*
MacArthur, Robert Stuart 1841-1923 *BiD&SB, DcAmA, DcNAA, HisAmM XR*
Macaskie, Francis Gilbert 1912?-1952 *BioIn 2*
Macaulay, D *HisAmM XR*
Macaulay, S Armour 1897- *WhJnl 1928*
Macaulay, Lord Thomas Babington Macaulay 1800-1859 *Alli, AtlBL, BbD, BiD&SB, BrAu 19, CasWL, CrtT 3, CyWA, DcEnA, DcEuL, DcLEL, EvLB, MouLC 3, NewC, OxEng, Pen Eng, RAdv 1, REn, WebBD, WebE&AL*
Macaulay, Zachary 1768-1838 *Alli, WebBD*
Macauley, Charles *NF*
Macauley, Doris *OvPC*
Macauley, Doris Johnston *OvPC*
Macauley, Robie Mayhew 1919- *AmAu&B, BioIn 10, ConAu 1, ConNov 1972, ConNov 1976, DrAF 1976, DrAS 74E, OxAm, WhoAm 1974, WorAu, WrDr 1976*
Macausland, Earle Rutherford 1893- *WhoAm 1974*
MacBeath, Innis 1928- *WrDr 1976*
MacCallum, H C *NF*
MacCann, Richard Dyer 1920- *ConAu 9R, DrAS 74E*
MacCardle, Ross C 1901-1964 *BioIn 6, BioIn 9*
MacCarthy, James Philip 1869-1920 *DcNAA*
Macciocchi, Maria Antoinetta 1922- *ConAu 73*

MacColl, Rene 1905-1971 *BioIn 4, BioIn 9, ForP*
MacCormac, John 1890-1958 *BioIn 4*
MacDermot, Hugh Ernest 1888- *BioIn 4, CanWW 1972*
MacDermot, Thomas Henry 1870-1933 *BioIn 3, BioIn 9*
MacDonagh, Michael 1860- *BioIn 1, CathA 1930, WhoLA*
MacDonald, Alexander 1908- *BioIn 1, BioIn 2*
MacDonald, Alexander Black 1861-1942 *NF*
MacDonald, Bert *NF*
MacDonald, Carlyle *NF*
MacDonald, Craig 1949- *ConAu 57*
Macdonald, David *NF*
Macdonald, David Ian 1914?-1953 *BioIn 3*
Macdonald, Donald 1857-1932 *BioIn 2*
MacDonald, Duncan *OvPC, WhoAmW 1974, WhoE 1974*
Macdonald, Dwight 1906- *AmAu&B, AmRP, BioIn 1, BioIn 4, BioIn 8, CelR 1973, ConAu 29, CurBio XR, ModAL, OxAm, Pen Am, RAdv 1, WhoAm 1974, WhoTwCL, WorAu, WrDr 1976*
MacDonald, Edward 1900- *CathA 1930*
Macdonald, Edward C *WhJnl 1928*
MacDonald, Edward J 1900- *BioIn 1*
MacDonald, Elizabeth P *BioIn 1*
MacDonald, George Everett Hussey 1857-1944 *DcNAA*
Macdonald, George S 1866-1945 *NatCAB 34*
Macdonald, Gerald E 1901- *WhJnl 1928*
Macdonald, Glenn 1901- *WhJnl 1928*
MacDonald, Gregory 1903- *BioIn 1, CathA 1930*
MacDonald, Harrison C 1889- *WhJnl 1928*
Macdonald, James Aloysius 1874-1964 *BioIn 3, BioIn 6, BioIn 7*
MacDonald, John *NF*
Macdonald, Kenneth 1905- *ConAu 73, WhoAm 1974*
MacDonald, Neil *NF*
Macdonald, Peter Mcintyre 1916- *WhoAm 1974*
Macdonald, Potts 1877- *WhJnl 1928*
Macdonald, Robert Taylor 1930- *WhoAm 1974, WhoWor 1974*
Macdonald, Ronald Gordon 1899- *AmM&W 73P, BioIn 3, BioIn 6, BioIn 7, WhoAm 1974*
MacDonald, Walter *NF*
MacDonald, William 1863-1938 *AmAu&B, DcNAA, HisAmM XR, WebBD, WhNAA*
Macdonald, William Arthur 1890-1951 *BioIn 2*
MacDonell, Archibald Gordon 1895-1941 *EvLB, LongC, TwCA, TwCA Sup, TwCW, WebBD*
MacDonnell, Sir John *NF*
Macdonnell, Norman 1916- *WhoAm 1974*
MacDougall, A Kent 1931- *ConAu 45*
Macdougall, Allan Ross 1893-1956 *BioIn 4*

MacDougall, Curtis Daniel 1903- *AmM&W 73S,*
Au&Wr, ConAu 53, WhoAm 1974
Macdougall, David *HisAmM XR*
MacDougall, Sally 1875?-1973 *BioIn 9,*
NewYTBE 4
MacDougall, Sarah *WhJnl Sup, WhJnl 1928*
MacDougall, William *NF*
MacDowell, Rachel *NF*
Mace, Harry Fred 1922?-1963 *BioIn 6*
Mace, Jean 1815-1894 *BiD&SB, CarSB, WebBD*
MacEoin, Gary 1909- *ConAu 1, OvPC,*
WrDr 1976
Macfadden, Bernarr 1868-1955 *AmAu&B, AmJnl,*
ForP, HisAmM XR, NatCAB 45, REnAL,
WhNAA, WhJnl 1928
Macfarlane, Andrew Walker 1928- *WhoAm 1974*
Macfarlane, Clark 1871-1918 *HisAmM XR*
Macfarlane, John *NF*
MacFarquhar, Roderick 1930- *ConAu 21R*
MacGahan, Januarius Aloysius 1844-1878 *Alli Sup,*
AmAu, AmAu&B, AmJnl, BbD, BiD&SB,
BioIn 9, DcAmA, DcNAA, FamWC,
OhA&B, WebBD
MacGeorge, Robert Jackson 1811?-1884 *BbtC,*
BioIn 1, DcNAA, OxCan
MacGibbond, John *HisAmM XR*
MacGillivray, Charles J 1887- *WhJnl 1928*
MacGowan, Gault 1894- *AmJnl, CurBio XR*
MacGowan, Grace *HisAmM XR*
Macgowan, John Encil 1831-1903 *NatCAB 1*
Macgowan, Kenneth 1888-1963 *AmAu&B,*
REnAL, WhNAA
MacGregor, Alasdair Alpin 1899-1970 *ConAu 29,*
ConAu P-1, WhoLA
Macgregor, Greg *OvPC*
MacGregor, James 1925- *ConAu 13*
MacGregor, Theodore Douglas 1878?-1969 *BioIn 8*
MacGregor-Hastie, Roy 1929- *AuBYP, BioIn 9,*
ConAu 1, SmATA 3, WrDr 1976
MacGuineas, Carol *NF*
Machacek, John W 1940- *WhoAm 1974*
Machado, China *BioIn 8*
Machamer, Jefferson 1900?-1960 *BioIn 5,*
HisAmM XR
MacHarg, William Briggs 1872-1951 *AmAu&B,*
EncMys, HisAmM XR, WhNAA
Machen, Arthur 1863-1947 *Alli Sup, CasWL,*
CyWA, DcLEL, EncMys, EvLB, LongC,
ModBL, NewC, OxEng, Pen Eng, REn,
TwCA, TwCA Sup, TwCW, WebBD
Machlin, Milton Robert 1924- *AmAu&B,*
Au&Wr, ConAu 4R, WhoAm 1974
MacInnes, Colin 1914-1976 *ConAu 65,*
ConAu 69, Who 1974, WhoWor 1974
Mack, E B *AmJnl*
Mack, Gene 1890?-1953 *BioIn 3*
Mack, Isaac Foster 1837-1912 *BioIn 9*
Mack, John Talman 1846-1914 *BioIn 6,*
NatCAB 43
Mack, Lath *NF*
Mack, Norman E 1858-1932 *NatCAB 26*
Mack, Raymond Francis 1912- *WhoAdv 1972,*
WhoAm 1974
Mack, William 1865-1941 *BioIn 2, DcNAA,*
NatCAB 35, WhNAA
Mackall, Leonard Leopold 1879-1937 *AmAu&B*
Mackay, Barbara E 1944- *NF*
Mackay, Charles 1814-1889 *Alli, Alli Sup, BbtC,*
BiD&SB, BrAu 19, DcEnL, EvLB, NewC,
WebBD
Mackay, Don *NF*
Mackay, Donald *WhJnl Sup*
Mackay, Donald 1925- *CanWW 1972*
MacKay, Douglas 1900-1938 *DcNAA, OxCan*

Mackay, Edward B *WhJnl 1928*
Mackay, Ian 1898-1952 *BioIn 1, BioIn 3*
MacKay, John Fields 1868-1954 *BioIn 3*
Mackay, John W 1831-1902 *AmJnl*
Mackay, Robert *HisAmM XR*
MacKay, Ruth *BioIn 2*
MacKay, Shane 1926- *CanWW 1972, RpN*
Mackaye, William Ross 1934- *WhoAm 1974*
Mackeever, Samuel A *HisAmM XR*
MacKenzie, Andrew 1911- *ConAu 49*
Mackenzie, Cameron 1882-1921 *DcNAA,*
HisAmM XR
Mackenzie, Catherine 1894-1949 *BioIn 2,*
DcNAA
Mackenzie, Sir Compton 1883-1972 *Au&Wr,*
CasWL, CathA 1930, ConAu 21, ConAu 37,
ConNov 1972, DcLEL, EncWL, EvLB,
HisAmM XR, LongC, ModBL, NewC,
NewYTBE 3, OxEng, Pen Eng, REn,
TwCA, TwCA Sup, TwCW, WebBD,
WebE&AL, WhoChL, WhoLA, WhoTwCL
Mackenzie, DeWitt 1885-1962 *AmAu&B, BioIn 6*
MacKenzie, F A *NF*
MacKenzie, Fred 1905- *ConAu 25*
Mackenzie, George C 1883- *WhJnl 1928*
Mackenzie, Hector *HisAmM XR*
MacKenzie, John Pettibone 1930- *ConAu 65*
Mackenzie, Louis Burton 1880- *BioIn 7*
Mackenzie, Robert Shelton 1809-1881 *Alli,*
Alli Sup, AmAu, AmAu&B, BbD, BiD&SB,
CyAL 2, DcAmA, DcAmB 12, DcNAA,
HisAmM XR, NewC, PoIre
Mackenzie, William Lyon 1795-1861 *Alli, BbtC,*
BioIn 4, BioIn 6, BioIn 7, BioIn 8, BioIn 9,
DcLEL, DcNAA, OxCan, WebBD
Mackey, Albert Gallatin 1807-1881 *Alli, Alli Sup,*
BiD&SB, BiDSA, DcAmA, DcNAA,
HisAmM XR
Mackey, David Ray 1917- *WhoAm 1974*
Mackey, Garland L 1892- *WhJnl 1928*
Mackey, Joseph *BioIn 1*
Mackie, V J *NF*
Mackin, Cassie 1939- *BioIn 9*
Mackin, Cassie *see also* Mackin, Catherine Patricia
Mackin, Catherine Patricia 1939- *ForWC 1970,*
WhoS&SW 1973
Mackin, Catherine Patricia *see also* Mackin, Cassie
Mackinnon, Cyrus Leland 1916- *WhoAm 1974,*
WhoF&I 1974
MacKinnon, Eugene 1898-1951 *BioIn 2*
Mackintosh, Sir Alexander 1858-1948 *BioIn 5*
Macklin, E H *NF*
Macklin, J *NF*
Macklin, William *NF*
MacLane, Mary 1881-1929 *AmAu&B, DcAmA,*
DcNAA
MacLaurin, Barbara *NF*
Maclean, Frances *NF*
Maclean, Frank E 1872- *WhJnl 1928*
Maclean, John *NF*
MacLean, John Bayne *NF*
Maclean, W A *NF*
MacLeish, Archibald 1892- *AmAu&B,*
AmSCAP 1966, AmWr, BiE&WWA,
CasWL, CelR 1973, CnDAL, CnE&AP,
CnMD, CnMWL, CnThe, ConAmA,
ConAmL, ConAu 9, ConDr, ConLC 3,
ConP 1970, ConP 1975, CroCD, CurBio XR,
CyWA, DcLEL, DrAP 1975, EncWL,
EvLB, HisAmM XR, IntWW 1974, LongC,
McGWD, ModAL, ModAL Sup, ModWD,
OxAm, OxEng, Pen Am, RAdv 1, REn,
REnAL, SixAP, TwCA, TwCA Sup,
TwCW, WebBD, WebE&AL, WhNAA,

Who 1974, WhoAm 1974, WhoThe 1972,
WhoWor 1974, WrDr 1976
Macleish, Kenneth 1917-1977 ConAu 73,
WhoAm 1974
MacLeish, Roderick 1926- ConAu 41,
WhoAm 1974, WhoS&SW 1973
MacLennan, Frank Pitts 1855-1933 NatCAB 11,
WhNAA, WhJnl 1928
Macleod, Harry NF
Macleod, Henry Williams 1911- WhoAm 1974
MacLeod, Margaret d1946 BioIn 1
MacLeod, Robert F 1917- NF
Macleod, William 1850-1929 BioIn 2
Maclure, Stuart 1926- ConAu 61
MacMahan, Anna 1846-1919 DcNAA
MacMahon, Tom 1892- WhJnl 1928
MacManus, Clive d1953 NF
MacMaster, Frank 1891?-1972 BioIn 9,
NewYTBE 3
Macmillan, Alexander 1815-1896 WebBD
MacMillen, Frank H 1906?-1948 BioIn 1
MacMurray, George J BioIn 2
Macnab, Brenton A NF
Macnamee, W Bruce 1890?-1958 BioIn 4
MacNaughton, Ernest Boyd 1880-1960 BioIn 2,
BioIn 3, BioIn 5, BioIn 7
MacNeil, Neil 1891-1969 AmAu&B, BioIn 3,
BioIn 5, BioIn 8, CathA 1952, ConAu 19,
ConAu 29, ConAu P-1, CurBio XR, OxCan,
WrDr 1976
MacNeill, Ben Dixon 1888?-1960 AmAu&B,
BioIn 5
MacNelly, Jeffrey Kenneth 1947- WhoAm 1974,
WhoAmA 1973
Macnow, Yoko Hamada OvPC
Macomber, Ben 1876- WhJnl 1928
Macomber, Frank NF
Macon, John Alfred 1851-1891 Alli Sup, BiDSA,
DcAmA, DcNAA
MaCoy, Ramelle C BioIn 2
MacPeek, Walter G 1902-1973 BioIn 9,
ConAu 29, ConAu 41, SmATA 4, WhNAA
Macphail, William Curtis 1921- WhoAm 1974
MacPherson, Charles J 1856- WhJnl 1928
Macpherson, Duncan 1924?- BioIn 7
Macpherson, Kenneth 1902?-1971 BioIn 9,
ConAu 29, NewYTBE 2
MacPherson, Malcolm NF
MacPherson, Margaret L AuBYP, BioIn 7
MacPherson, Stuart BioIn 1
MacPherson, Thomas George 1915- AuBYP,
BioIn 8, ConAu 1
MacQuarrie, Gordon 1900-1956 BioIn 5
Macqueen, Thomas 1803-1861 BioIn 1
Macqueen-Pope, Walter James 1888-1960 BioIn 5
Macquire, J R HisAmM XR
MacRae, D B NF
Macrae, Norman Alastair Duncan 1923- BioIn 2
Macready, John A HisAmM XR
MacReynolds, George 1861-1950 BioIn 2
MacRorie, Janet 1891-1950 BioIn 2
MacShimming, Roy NF
MacTavish, Wilfrid Lawrence 1891-1951 BioIn 2,
WhJnl 1928
Macune, C W HisAmM XR
MacVane, John Franklin 1912- ConAu 65,
WhoWor 1974
Macy, John Albert 1877-1932 AmAu&B,
ConAmL, DcNAA, HisAmM XR, OxAm,
REnAL, TwCA, WebBD, WhNAA
Macy, Josiah Noel 1900- BioIn 9, WhoAm 1974
Madden, Daniel Michael 1916- ConAu 65
Madden, E S 1919- ConAu 11R
Madden, Eva Anne 1863- AmAu&B, AmLY,

BiDSA
Madden, George A 1850- NatCAB 5
Madden, Richard L NF
Maddock, Kenneth d1971 BioIn 9
Maddocks, Melvin NF
Maddox, John 1925?- BioIn 7
Maddox, William Johnston 1887- WhNAA,
WhJnl 1928
Mader, B William NF
Mader, Joseph H, Jr. WhJnl 1928
Madisen, Erik L 1893-1960 NatCAB 48
Madlee, Dorothy 1917- ConAu 19R,
ForWC 1970
Madsen, I E 1912?-1965 BioIn 7
Maduro, Carlota OvPC
Maeda, Hisashi RpN
Maenpaa, Risto NF
Maerker-Branden, A Paul 1888- WhJnl 1928
Maeroff, Gene Irving 1939- ConAu 61,
WhoAm 1974
Maes, Charles C 1883- WhJnl 1928
Maevsky, Viktor Vasiliyevich 1921- IntWW 1976
Magdoff, Harry NF
Magee, Carleton Cole 1873-1946 BioIn 1, BioIn 3
Magee, J L HisAmM XR
Magee, James V NF
Magee, Knox 1877-1934 DcNAA
Magee, Ray Alvin 1888- WhJnl 1928
Magee, Rex B 1888- WhJnl 1928
Magee, Thomas HisAmM XR
Mager, Charles Augustus 1878-1956 BioIn 4
Mages, George T 1860- WhJnl 1928
Magidoff, Robert 1905-1970 AmAu&B, BioIn 1,
ConAu 19, ConAu P-1
Magila, Louis NF
Maginn, William 1793-1842 Alli, BbD, BiD&SB,
BioIn 4, BrAu 19, CasWL, DcEnL, DcLEL,
EvLB, NewC, OxEng, PoIre, REn, WebBD
Magnet, Alejandro 1919- IntWW 1976,
WhoWor 1974
Magnuson, Don 1911?- BioIn 1
Magon, Enrique Flores NF
Magon, Ricardo Flores NF
Magoun, George Frederic 1821-1896 DcNAA,
HisAmM XR
Magowan, Vivien NF
Maguire, Frederick W RpN
Mahar, Edward A 1900?-1973 BioIn 9,
NewYTBE 4
Maher, Arthur J NF
Maher, John J NF
Mahin, Helen Ogden 1880- IndAu 1917,
WhNAA, WhJnl 1928
Mahmoud, Samy NF
Mahon, Derek 1941- BioIn 10, ConP 1970,
ConP 1975, WrDr 1976
Mahoney, Daniel Joseph 1880-1963 BioIn 6
Mahoney, Daniel Joseph, Jr. 1927- WhoAm 1974,
WhoMW 1974
Mahoney, John NF
Mahoney, John Thomas 1905- AmAu&B,
ConAu 11, ConAu P-1
Mahoney, John Thomas see also Mahoney, Tom
Mahoney, Tom 1905- OvPC, TexWr,
WhoAm 1974
Mahoney, Tom see also Mahoney, John Thomas
Mahoney, Vincent 1902?-1949 BioIn 2
Mahoney, William G OvPC
Mahony, Bertha E BioIn 2
Mahony, Francis Sylvester 1804-1866 Alli, BbD,
BrAu 19, CasWL, DcEnL, DcLEL, EvLB,
NewC, OxEng, PoIre, REn, WebBD
Mahony, Walter Butler 1877-1954 HisAmM XR,
NatCAB 39

Mahony, Walter Butler, Jr. 1914- *WhoAm 1974*
Mahtab, Harekrushna 1899- *IntWW 1976*
Mahuran, Stuart Ansala 1892-1953 *BioIn 3*
Maidenberg, Hyman Jonah 1928- *WhoAm 1974*
Maidenburg, Ben 1910- *WhoAm 1974,*
WhoMW 1974, WhoWorJ 1972
Maidment, Carrie 1868?-1949 *BioIn 2*
Maidment, Frederick H 1869-1952 *BioIn 2,*
WhJnl 1928
Maier, Harold R 1901- *NF*
Maier, Irwin 1899- *WhoAm 1974,*
WhoMW 1974, WhoWor 1974
Mailer, Norman Kingsley 1923- *AmAu&B,*
ConAu 11, IntWW 1976, WhoAm 1974
Mailey, Arthur Alfred 1888- *BioIn 2*
Mailly, William 1871-1912 *AmRP, DcAmB 12*
Maines, George H *NF*
Mainwaring, Bernard 1897-1957 *BioIn 7,*
NatCAB 48
Mainwaring, William Lewis 1935- *WhoAm 1974*
Mais, Stuart Petre Brodie 1885-1975 *Au&Wr,*
ConAu 57, ConAu 69, DcLEL, EvLB,
LongC, NewC, TwCA, TwCA Sup, WebBD,
Who 1974, WhoLA
Maisch, John Michael 1831-1893 *Alli Sup,*
DcNAA, HisAmM XR
Maitland, Derek 1943- *ConAu 29, WrDr 1976*
Maitland, James A 1835?- *Alli, Alli Sup,*
AmAu&B, DcNAA
Maitlin, Robert W 1942- *NF*
Majerski, Thomas J *NF*
Major, Gerri *NF*
Major, Herve *CanWW 1972*
Major, Jack *NF*
Major, Ralph H, Jr. 1920- *OvPC, WhoPubR 1972*
Makela, Benjamin R 1922- *WhoAm 1974*
Makepeace, Gordon *NF*
Makow, Henry 1949- *ConAu 7R*
Makower, S V *NF*
Malabari, Behramji Maharbanji 1854-1912
Alli Sup, BiD&SB, NewC, WebBD
Malabre, Alfred Leopold, Jr. 1931- *ConAu 65*
Malamud, Phyllis *NF*
Malamuth, Charles 1900?-1965 *BioIn 7*
Malaparte, Curzio 1898-1957 *BioIn 4, CasWL,*
ClDMEL, CnMD, EncWL, EvEuW,
ModRL, Pen Eur, REn, TwCA Sup, TwCW
Malarkey, Martin Francis, Jr. 1918-
WhoAm 1974, WhoS&SW 1973
Malatesta, Enrico 1850-1932 *WebBD*
Malbin, Michael Jacob 1943- *ConAu 73*
Malcolm, Andrew 1943- *ConAu 53*
Malcolm, Mollan *WhJnl 1928*
Malcuzynski, Karol 1922- *IntWW 1976*
Maldonado, Alexander *RpN*
Maldonado, Hernan *NF*
Malek, Leona Alford *NF*
Maler, Angel Lerma 1919- *WhoAm 1974*
Malik, Adam 1917- *CurBio XR, IntWW 1976,*
NewYTBE 1, NewYTBE 2, WhoWor 1974
Malik, Michael Abdul *ForP*
Malin, Don 1896- *AmSCAP 1966, BioIn 7*
Malin, Jay 1927- *ConAu 19R*
Malino, Emily *NF*
Malinowski, John A *NewMr*
Maliwanag, Vicente *NF*
Malkani, K R *RpN*
Malkenson, Arthur Lyon 1881-1956 *BioIn 4*
Malkin, Lawrence *NF*
Malkum Khan, Mirza 1834?-1908 *BioIn 9,*
CasWL
Mallakh, Kamal El 1918- *IntWW 1976,*
WhoWor 1974
Mallea, Eduardo 1903- *CasWL, CyWA,*

DcCLAA, EncWL, IntWW 1976, Pen Am,
TwCW, WhoWor 1974, WorAu
Mallet, Elizabeth *NF*
Mallet DuPan, Jacques 1749-1800 *BioIn 3,*
DcEuL, OxFr, WebBD
Mallett, Elizabeth *NF*
Mallette, Malcolm Francis 1923- *BioIn 4*
Malley, Thomas A 1900?-1964 *BioIn 7*
Malliet, A M Wendell 1896- *WhJnl 1928*
Mallison, Sam T *WhJnl Sup*
Malloch, Douglas 1877-1938 *AmAu&B, DcNAA,*
NatCAB 28, Str&VC, WhNAA,
WhJnl 1928
Mallon, George Barry *NF*
Mallon, Isabel Allderdice 1857-1898 *DcNAA,*
HisAmM XR
Mallon, Paul 1901-1950 *AmJnl*
Mallon, Winifred 1879-1954 *BioIn 3*
Mallory, Bolton *HisAmM XR*
Mallory, George S *HisAmM XR*
Mallory, M H *HisAmM XR*
Mallovy, Naomi 1923- *NF*
Mallowe, Mike *NF*
Malloy, Charles *HisAmM XR*
Malloy, Louise d1947 *BioIn 1*
Malmin, Rasmus 1865- *WhJnl 1928*
Malone, Albert Wise 1880- *WhJnl 1928*
Malone, Edwin Scott, III 1938- *WhoAm 1974*
Malone, Kemp 1889-1971 *AmAu&B,*
HisAmM XR, NewYTBE 2, REnAL
Malone, Richard Sankey 1909- *CanWW 1972,*
ForP, WhoAm 1974, WhoCan 1973,
WhoMW 1974, WhoWor 1974
Malone, Robert James 1892?-1966 *BioIn 7*
Malone, Ted *see* Russell, Frank Alden
Maloney, Cornelius F 1900- *WhJnl 1928*
Maloney, Earl H 1894- *WhJnl 1928*
Maloney, Joseph A 1902?- *BioIn 7*
Maloney, Kathleen *NF*
Maloney, Leonard James 1892- *WhJnl 1928*
Maloney, Russell 1910-1948 *REnAL*
Maloney, Thomas James 1906- *OvPC,*
WhoAm 1974
Malot, Hector Henri 1830-1907 *AuBYP, BbD,*
BiD&SB, BioIn 7, DcBiA, EvEuW, OxFr,
WebBD
Maloy, Richard Joseph 1924- *WhoAm 1974,*
WhoS&SW 1973
Mama, Soya *BioIn 9*
Mammen, E H 1896- *WhJnl 1928*
Manahan, Patrice *NF*
Manassah, Ed *NF*
Manchester, Harland 1898-1977 *ConAu 4R,*
ConAu 73
Manchester, William 1922- *BioIn 7, CelR 1973,*
ConAu 1R, CurBio XR, HisAmM XR,
IntWW 1976, Who 1974, WhoAm 1974,
WhoE 1974, WhoWor 1974
Mancini, Anthony 1939- *ConAu 73*
Mancur, J H *HisAmM XR*
Mandel, Kim H *OvPC*
Mandelbaum, Michael *NF*
Mandell, George S 1867-1934 *NatCAB 25*
Mandell, Samuel P 1833-1920 *NatCAB 28*
Mandigo, John H *HisAmM XR*
Maney, Richard 1892-1968 *BioIn 1, BioIn 2,*
BioIn 4, BioIn 6, BioIn 7, BioIn 8, BioIn 9,
CurBio XR, REnAL
Manford, Erasmus *HisAmM XR*
Mangan, Sherry *NF*
Mangold, Tom 1934- *ConAu 69*
Manheim, Michael Philip *NF*
Maniere, Alfred *HisAmM XR*
Manigault, Peter 1927- *WhoAm 1974,*

WhoS&SW 1973, WhoWor 1974
Manion, Marilyn *NF*
Mankiewicz, Frank Fabian 1924- *BioIn 8,
BioIn 9, BioIn 10, WhoAm 1974*
Mankiewicz, Herman Jacob 1897-1953 *DcAmB S5*
Manley, James R *HisAmM XR*
Manley, Joseph Homan 1842-1905 *DcAmB 12*
Manley, Robert H *NF*
Manly, Chesly 1905- *AmAu&B*
Mann, Arthur Henry *Lor&LP*
Mann, Arthur William 1901-1963 *AmJnl*
Mann, Donald Nathaniel 1920- *WhoAm 1974,
WhoF&I 1974, WhoMW 1974*
Mann, E D *HisAmM XR*
Mann, Henry 1848-1915 *DcAmA, DcNAA,
HisAmM XR*
Mann, Jack 1925?- *BioIn 5*
Mann, Jim *WhoAdv 1972*
Mann, Karl Mowry 1888- *WhJnl 1928*
Mann, Louis R 1896- *WhJnl 1928*
Mann, Martin 1920- *OvPC, WhoAm 1974*
Mann, Milton B 1937- *ConAu 45*
Mann, Prestonia *AmRP, HisAmM XR*
Mann, Robert S 1891- *WhJnl 1928*
Mann, Roderick *NF*
Mann, Steve *NF*
Mann, William D'Alton 1839-1920 *BioIn 5,
BioIn 7, DcNAA, HisAmM XR, OhA&B*
Mann, William W *HisAmM XR*
Manners, Dorothy *BioIn 10, CelR 1973,
WhoAm 1974, WhoAmW 1974*
Manners, Mary *HisAmM XR*
Mannes, Marya 1904- *AmAu&B, BioIn 5,
BioIn 6, BioIn 7, BioIn 9, CelR 1973,
ConAu 2R, CurBio XR, DrAF 1976,
ForWC 1970, NewYTBE 2, WhoAmW 1974,
WorAu, WrDr 1976*
Mannin, Ethel 1900- *Au&Wr, ConAu 53,
ConNov 1976, DcLEL, EvLB, IntWW 1976,
LongC, NewC, Pen Eng, REn, TwCA,
TwCA Sup, WebBD, Who 1974, WrDr 1976*
Manning, Alice *HisAmM XR*
Manning, Arthur Brewster 1913- *WhoAm 1974,
WhoF&I 1974, WhoS&SW 1973*
Manning, Arthur L 1898- *WhJnl 1928*
Manning, Daniel 1831-1887 *NatCAB 2, WebBD*
Manning, Elizabeth Macdonald 1919-
*WhoAm 1974, WhoAmW 1974, WhoE 1974,
WhoF&I 1974*
Manning, Farley 1909- *OvPC, WhoE 1974,
WhoF&I 1974, WhoPubR 1972*
Manning, Gordon 1917- *WhoAm 1974*
Manning, Herbert A 1875-1959 *NatCAB 47*
Manning, James Henry 1854-1925 *NatCAB 1*
Manning, John C d1967 *NF*
Manning, John H 1820?- *EarABI, EarABI Sup,
HisAmM XR*
Manning, Margaret *NF*
Manning, Marie 1873?-1945 *AmAu&B, AmJnl,
AmLY, BioIn 1, CurBio XR, DcAmB S3,
DcNAA, REnAL*
Manning, Marie *see also* Fairfax, Beatrice
Manning, Reginald West 1905- *BioIn 2,
CurBio XR, WhoAm 1974*
Manning, Robert Joseph 1919- *BioIn 7, BioIn 9,
ConAu 69, IntWW 1976, RpN,
WhoAm 1974, WhoE 1974*
Manning, Steven *OvPC*
Manning, Walter Webster 1875-1931 *HisAmM XR*
Manning, William Raymond 1920- *WhoAm 1974,
WhoS&SW 1973*
Manocchia, Benito 1934- *ConAu 69*
Manolis, Paul George 1928- *WhoAm 1974*
Manos, Charles 1923- *ConAu 29*

Manry, Robert 1918-1971 *ConAu 21, ConAu 29*
Mansbridge, Frederick Ronald 1905-
WhoAm 1974, WhoWor 1974
Mansell, Thomas Norman 1904- *WhoAm 1974*
Mansfield, Edward Deering 1801-1880 *Alli,
Alli Sup, AmAu, AmAu&B, BbD, BiD&SB,
BioIn 9, DcAmA, DcNAA, HisAmM XR,
OhA&B*
Mansfield, James Carroll 1896- *WhJnl 1928*
Mansfield, Peter 1928- *ConAu 65*
Mansfield, Richard H 1888?- *BioIn 2*
Mansfield, William Douglass 1878-1952 *BioIn 4,
NatCAB 41*
Manship, Charles Phelps 1881-1947 *WhJnl 1928*
Manship, Charles Phelps, Jr. 1908- *WhoAdv 1972,
WhoAm 1974, WhoF&I 1974,
WhoS&SW 1973*
Manship, Douglas L 1918- *WhoAdv 1972,
WhoAm 1974, WhoS&SW 1973*
Manship, Douglas L, Jr. *NF*
Manson, Frederic E 1860- *WhJnl 1928*
Manson, Harold P 1918- *OvPC, WhoWorJ 1972*
Manson, Richard 1901-1954 *BioIn 3*
Mansour, Atallah 1934?- *BioIn 6*
Mant, Ken *NF*
Mant, Russell *NF*
Mantel, S G *AuBYP, BioIn 8*
Mantell, Suzanne *NF*
Manthey, Marlene *NF*
Manthey, Wilhelm M *NF*
Manthorne, Mary Elizabeth Arnold 1909-
BiDrLUS, WhoAm 1974, WhoAmW 1974
Mantle, Burns 1873-1948 *AmAu&B, DcNAA,
HisAmM XR, REnAL, TwCA, TwCA Sup,
WhNAA*
Mantle, Burns *see also* Mantle, Robert Burns
Mantle, Robert Burns 1873-1948 *CurBio XR,
DcAmB S4, WebBD, WhJnl 1928*
Mantle, Robert Burns *see also* Mantle, Burns
Mantler, Heinrich *NF*
Manuel, Bruce *NF*
Manz, Henry W 1896- *WhJnl 1928*
Manzi, Riccardo 1913- *BioIn 3, WhoGrA*
Manzini, Raimundo *ForP*
Mapes, James Jay 1806-1866 *Alli, HisAmM XR*
Mapes, Victor 1870-1943 *AmAu&B, AmLY,
CurBio XR, DcNAA, WhNAA*
Mapp, Alt J, Jr. 1925- *ConAu 4R*
Mara, Margaret McHugh 1880-1966 *BioIn 7*
Maranixx, Elliott *NF*
Marbaker, Edward Ellsworth 1888-1954 *BioIn 1,
BioIn 3*
Marberry, M M 1905-1968 *ConAu 21*
Marble, Earl *HisAmM XR*
Marble, Manton Malone 1835-1917 *AmAu&B,
AmJnl, BioIn 5, BioIn 9*
Marbrook, Djelloul 1934- *ConAu 73*
Marbut, F B 1905- *ConAu 33*
Marcello, Amedeo Alfred 1904- *WhoAm 1974,
WhoF&I 1974*
March, Alden 1869-1942 *DcAmA, DcNAA*
March, Charles Wainwright 1815-1864 *Alli,
AmAu&B, DcAmA, DcNAA*
March, Joseph Moncure 1899-1977 *AmAu&B,
ConAu 69, OxAm, REn, REnAL*
Marchand, Felix Gabriel 1832-1900 *BbD, BbtC,
BiD&SB, DcNAA, OxCan*
Marchi, Giacomo *see* Bassani, Giorgio
Marcil, Tancrede 1880?-1955 *BioIn 3*
Marcil, William Christ 1936- *WhoAm 1974*
Marcin, Max 1879-1948 *AmAu&B, DcNAA,
EncMys, REnAL, WebBD*
Marcosson, Isaac Frederick 1877-1961 *AmAu&B,
BioIn 5, BioIn 9, HisAmM XR, REnAL,*

WebBD
Marcotte, Anna M HisAmM XR
Marcousis, Louis HisAmM XR
Marcum, Walter F 1889- WhJnl 1928
Marcus, Edwin 1885?-1961 BioIn 4, BioIn 6
Marcus, Frank 1928- Au&Wr, CnThe,
    ConAu 45, ConDr, CroCD, McGWD,
    WhoThe 1972, WrDr 1976
Marcus, Greil NF
Marcus, Jerry NF
Marcus, Joe 1933- ConAu 65
Marcus, Joseph Anthony 1894-1960 BioIn 5,
    BioIn 7
Marcus, Leonard Marshall 1930- WhoAm 1974,
    WhoE 1974
Marcus, Ruth NF
Marcus, Steven 1928- AmAu&B, ConAu 41,
    DrAS 74E
Marcy, Leslie AmRP
Marcy, Mary AmRP
Marden, George A 1839-1906 NatCAB 6
Marden, Luis 1913- WhoAm 1974,
    WhoS&SW 1973
Marden, Orison Swett 1850-1924 AmAu&B,
    BiD&SB, BioIn 5, DcAmA, DcAmB 12,
    DcNAA, HisAmM XR, REnAL, WebBD
Marden, Philip Sanford 1874-1963 AmAu&B,
    BioIn 6, WhJnl 1928
Marden, William 1947- ConAu 61
Marder, Irving BioIn 8
Marder, Murrey RpN
Marella, Philip Daniel 1929- WhoAm 1974
Mares, Richard Allan 1928- WhoAm 1974
Mares, William J BioIn 9
Margalit, Dan NF
Margo, Bruno 1901?- BioIn 7
Margold, Stella OvPC
Margolies, Marjorie Sue 1942- BioIn 10,
    ConAu 65
Margolis, Irwin NF
Margolis, Jon NF
Margolis, Tru NF
Margolius, Sidney 1911- ConAu 21R,
    WhoE 1974
Margoshes, Joseph 1866-1955 BioIn 3
Margoshes, Samuel NF
Marguerittes, Julie De 1814-1866 BiD&SB,
    DcNAA
Margulies, Leo 1900-1975 ConAu 61, OvPC
Marhoefer, Barbara 1936- ConAu 61
Mariano, Frank 1931?-1976 ConAu 69
Marieton, Paul 1862-1911 WebBD
Marimov, William K 1948?- NF
Marin, Amador NF
Marin, Jean 1909- IntWW 1976, WhoWor 1974
Marin Sola, Ramon 1832-1902 BioIn 8
Marine, Gene 1926- ConAu 65, WhoAm 1974
Marinescu, Teodor 1922- IntWW 1976,
    WhoWor 1974
Marinetti, Emilio Filippo Tommaso 1876-1944
    WebBD
Marinoni, Hippolyte 1823-1904 WebBD
Mario, Giuseppe HisAmM XR
Mario, Jessie Meriton 1832-1906 BioIn 7, BioIn 9
Mario, Jessie White HisAmM XR
Marion, Frances 1890?-1973 AmAu&B, AmNov,
    ConAu 41, NewYTBE 4
Maris, Albert Branson 1893- HisAmM XR,
    WhoAm 1974
Mark, Mary Ellen 1940- NF
Mark, Norman NF
Mark, Ross ForP
Mark, Weinbaum 1890- WhJnl 1928
Markbreit, Leopold 1842- NatCAB 12

Markel, Helen 1925- ForWC 1970
Markel, Lester 1894-1977 BioIn 1, BioIn 3,
    BioIn 5, ConAu 37, ConAu 73, CurBio XR,
    ForP, IntWW 1976, NewYTBE 3,
    WhoAm 1974, WhoWorJ 1972, WrDr 1976
Marken, William NF
Markens, Isaac 1846-1928 DcNAA
Markey, Gene 1895- AmAu&B, ConAu P-1,
    WhoAm 1974
Markey, Lawrence Morris 1899-1950 AmAu&B,
    BioIn 2
Markham, Clarence Matthew, Jr. 1911- ConAu 69,
    WhoF&I 1974
Markham, Edgar Cary 1870?-1959 BioIn 5
Markham, James M NF
Markham, James Walter 1910-1972
    AmM&W 73S, ConAu 21
Markham, Reuben Henry 1887-1949 BioIn 2,
    BioIn 4, DcNAA
Markham, William Colfax 1868-1961 BioIn 1,
    BioIn 6, BioIn 8, OhA&B
Markle, Robert NF
Marko, Milos 1922- IntWW 1976,
    WhoWor 1974
Markowitz, Arnold M 1937?- NF
Marks, Arnold 1912- IntMPA 1975,
    WhoAm 1974
Marks, Avery C, Jr. 1887-1935 NF
Marks, Bessie B 1900- WhJnl Sup
Marks, Dorothy NF
Marks, Edward Bennett 1911- USBiR 1974,
    WhoGov 1972
Marks, Frederick M NF
Marks, John D NewMr
Marks, John Ryan 1895- WhJnl 1928
Marks, Leonard Harold 1916- CurBio XR,
    IntWW 1974, WhoAm 1974, WhoAmP 1973,
    WhoS&SW 1973
Marks, Montague HisAmM XR
Marks, Richard Lee 1923?- BioIn 2
Marks, Stan 1929- ConAu 29, WrDr 1976
Markus, Robert NF
Marlatt, Walter Thomas 1874-1925 BioIn 5
Marlens, Al 1927- WhoAm 1974
Marlette, Douglas NF
Marley, Faye BioIn 4
Marley, Frank Elsworth WhJnl Sup
Marley, Harold P HisAmM XR
Marling, John Leake 1825-1856 DcAmB 12,
    NatCAB 13
Marlow, George Stanley Withers 1889-1948
    BioIn 1
Marlow, James 1903-1968 BioIn 8
Marlowe, Thomas 1868-1935 BioIn 2
Marmon, William NF
Marmon, William F, Jr. 1942- NF
Marmor, Helen OvPC
Marnell, William H 1907- ConAu 23R,
    DrAS 74E
Marnes, John NF
Marochetti, George Charles Marie 1894-1952
    BioIn 3
Marot, Helen 1865-1940 DcNAA, HisAmM XR,
    WhNAA
Marotta, Giuseppe 1902-1963 BioIn 2, BioIn 6,
    CasWL, EncWL, EvEuW
Marple, Allen Clark 1901-1968 BioIn 8,
    HisAmM XR
Marple, F T HisAmM XR
Marquand, Allan 1853-1924 AmAu&B, DcNAA,
    WebBD
Marquand, John Phillips 1893-1960 AmAu&B,
    AmNov, AmWr, CasWL, CnDAL,
    ConLC 2, CyWA, DcLEL, DrAF 1976,

EncMys, EncWL, EvLB, LongC, ModAL,
OxAm, Pen Am, RAdv 1, REn, REnAL,
TwCA, TwCA Sup, TwCW, WebBD,
WebE&AL
Marquardt, Frederic Sylvester 1905- WhoAm 1974
Marques, Luis ForP
Marques, Pedro Correia ForP
Marquez, Guillermo Martinez OvPC
Marquis, C C 1860- WhJnl 1928
Marquis, Don Robert Perry 1878-1937 AmAu&B,
AmJnl, AmLY, BiDPara, CnDAL,
CnE&AP, ConAmA, ConAmL, DcAmB S2,
DcLEL, DcNAA, EvLB, HisAmM XR,
ModAL, OhA&B, Pen Am, RAdv 1, REn,
REnAL, Str&VC, TwCA, TwCA Sup,
TwCW, WebBD, WhNAA
Marquis, J Clyde HisAmM XR
Marquis, Vivienne 1922?-1966 BioIn 7
Marquiss, Walter Otis 1892?-1957 BioIn 4
Marranca, Bonnie 1947- ConAu 65
Marraro, Howard R LiJA, NewYTBE 3
Marriner, Harry Lee 1872-1914 DcNAA
Marriner, William M HisAmM XR
Marrion, James HisAmM XR
Marriott, Charles 1869-1957 LongC, ModBL,
TwCA, TwCA Sup, WebBD
Marriott, Crittenden 1867-1932 AmAu&B,
AmLY, DcNAA, WhNAA
Marriott, Edward Evarts 1865-1927 WhJnl Sup,
WhJnl 1928
Marriott, Frederick Alfred HisAmM XR
Marriott, Raymond Bowler 1913- Au&Wr
Marro, Anthony InvJ
Marroquin Rojas, Clemente 1897?-1978 NF
Marryshow, Theophilus Albert 1887-1958 BioIn 5
Marseilles, Charles 1846- NatCAB 11
Marsh, Blair Rose WhJnl 1928
Marsh, Charles Edward 1887?-1964 BioIn 7
Marsh, Dave 1945?- BioIn 10
Marsh, Don NF
Marsh, F H V 1897- WhJnl 1928
Marsh, Fred T 1895?-1963 BioIn 6
Marsh, George HisAmM XR
Marsh, Harmon W 1861- WhJnl 1928
Marsh, Harry W HisAmM XR, NewYTBE 4
Marsh, Henry EarABI, HisAmM XR
Marsh, J T B HisAmM XR
Marsh, Lou NF
Marsh, R W BioIn 9
Marsh, Reginald 1898-1954 CurBio XR, DcCAA,
WebBD
Marsh, Robert Charles 1924- ConAu 15R,
WhoAm 1974, WhoMW 1974,
WhoWor 1974
Marsh, W Ward d1971 NF
Marshall, Alfred 1884-1965 ConAu 5
Marshall, Alfred, Jr. 1921- WhJnl 1928
Marshall, Benny 1920?-1969 BioIn 8
Marshall, Charles Clinton HisAmM XR
Marshall, Chester Allen NF
Marshall, Clarence G 1884- WhJnl 1928
Marshall, Edna 1898-1926 WhJnl Sup,
WhJnl 1928
Marshall, Edward 1869-1933 AmJnl, DcAmA,
DcNAA, FamWC, HisAmM XR,
WhJnl 1928
Marshall, Edward Chauncey 1824-1898 Alli,
Alli Sup, DcAmA, DcNAA
Marshall, Frank Arthur 1865- WhJnl 1928
Marshall, Fred F 1894- WhJnl 1928
Marshall, H E LiJA
Marshall, Henry W, Jr. 1892-1952 NatCAB 45
Marshall, Henry Wright 1865-1951 BioIn 2,
BioIn 6, NatCAB 45

Marshall, Isaac May 1865- WhJnl 1928
Marshall, James A 1895- WhJnl 1928
Marshall, James B HisAmM XR
Marshall, James Leslie 1891?-1957 BioIn 4
Marshall, James Wilson HisAmM XR
Marshall, Jan NF
Marshall, John BioIn 9
Marshall, John L RpN
Marshall, John Norman 1905- Au&Wr
Marshall, Lawrence NF
Marshall, Margaret 1900?-1974 BioIn 10,
HisAmM XR
Marshall, Marguerite Mooers 1887-1964
AmAu&B, WhNAA, WhJnl 1928
Marshall, Mary Duffee 1886- WhJnl 1928
Marshall, Ray Gifford 1881-1946 BioIn 1
Marshall, Robert A NF
Marshall, Roger V OvPC
Marshall, Samuel Lyman Atwood 1900-1977
AmAu&B, AuBYP, BioIn 3, BioIn 5,
BioIn 8, ConAu 73, CurBio XR,
WhoAm 1974, WorAu
Marshall, Scott NF
Marshall, Ty NF
Marshall, Verne 1889-1965 BioIn 7, CurBio XR
Marshall, W H 1826?- Alli Sup
Marson, Philip 1892- ConAu 11R
Marsters, Ann 1916- AmSCAP 1966,
WhoAmW 1974
Marston, Edward Walton 1884-1950 BioIn 2
Martell, Edward Drewett 1909- Au&Wr, BioIn 7,
CurBio XR, Who 1974
Martens, Georg Friedrich Von 1756-1821 WebBD
Marth, Del 1925- ConAu 61
Marthen, Joseph NF
Marti-Ibanez, Felix 1912?-1972 BioIn 9,
ConAu 33, NewYTBE 3
Martignoni, Margaret E 1907?-1974 BioIn 10
Martin, Alexander HisAmM XR
Martin, Allen B OvPC
Martin, Ann Ray NF
Martin, Arnold Engle 1914?-1956 BioIn 4
Martin, Artemas HisAmM XR
Martin, Arthur Patchett 1851-1902 Alli Sup,
BiD&SB, BioIn 2
Martin, Ben Ellis HisAmM XR
Martin, Boyce WhJnl 1928
Martin, Charles E 1910?- OvPC, WhoAm 1974,
WhoAmA 1973, WhoE 1974
Martin, Charles Francis 1866-1955 BioIn 3
Martin, Charles Morris 1891- AuBYP, BioIn 7
Martin, Chet NF
Martin, David C 1943- NF
Martin, Douglas DeVeny 1889-1963 BioIn 6
Martin, Douglas Vass, Jr. 1894- WhJnl 1928
Martin, Dudley B OvPC
Martin, Dwight 1921-1978 WhoAm 1974,
WhoWor 1974
Martin, E P 1874- WhJnl Sup
Martin, Edgar Everett 1898?-1960 BioIn 5
Martin, Edward Sandford 1856-1939 Alli Sup,
AmAu&B, AmLY, BiD&SB, DcAmA,
DcAmB S2, DcNAA, HisAmM XR,
REnAL, TwCA, WebBD, WhNAA
Martin, Everett G NF
Martin, Fletcher 1904- BioIn 3, CurBio XR,
DcCAA, WhoAm 1974, WhoAmA 1973
Martin, Fletcher P RpN
Martin, Fowler NF
Martin, Frank Lee 1881-1941 AmAu&B,
CurBio XR, DcNAA, WhNAA
Martin, Frank Lee 1912?- BioIn 4
Martin, Franklin Henry 1857-1935 DcNAA,
WebBD, WhNAA

Martin, Fred W *WhJnl 1928*
Martin, Frederick Roy 1871-1952 *AmAu&B,*
 AmJnl, NatCAB 41
Martin, G A 1878- *WhJnl 1928*
Martin, George 1889- *WhNAA, WhJnl 1928*
Martin, George Ernest 1894-1968 *BioIn 10*
Martin, George Justis *BioIn 2*
Martin, George Wilbur 1930- *WhoAm 1974*
Martin, Gould B 1902- *WhJnl 1928*
Martin, Harold *HisAmM XR*
Martin, Harold Eugene 1923- *WhoAm 1974,*
 WhoS&SW 1973
Martin, Harold Harber 1910- *BioIn 1, ConAu 61,*
 WhoAm 1974, WhoS&SW 1973
Martin, Harold Percy 1869?-1950 *BioIn 2*
Martin, Harry Brownlow 1873-1959 *BioIn 5,*
 WhJnl 1928
Martin, Harry Leland 1908-1958 *BioIn 1,*
 BioIn 5, CurBio XR
Martin, Irving 1865- *WhJnl 1928*
Martin, Irving, Jr. 1893- *WhJnl 1928*
Martin, Irving Lewthwaite 1918-1967 *BioIn 1,*
 BioIn 9
Martin, Jack E *NF*
Martin, John *OvPC*
Martin, John Alexander 1839-1889 *DcAmB 12,*
 DcNAA
Martin, John B Taylor 1896- *WhJnl 1928*
Martin, John Bartlow 1915- *AmAu&B, Au&Wr,*
 BioIn 3, BioIn 4, BioIn 7, ConAu 15R,
 CurBio XR, IntWW 1974, OhA&B
Martin, John C 1882- *AmJnl, WhJnl 1928*
Martin, John H *OvPC*
Martin, John Joseph 1893- *AmAu&B,*
 WhoAm 1974
Martin, John Stuart 1900-1977 *ConAu 9R,*
 ConAu 69, HisAmM XR
Martin, John W 1901- *WhJnl 1928*
Martin, Joseph *NF*
Martin, Joseph H 1875- *WhJnl 1928*
Martin, Joseph William, Jr. 1884-1968 *CurBio XR,*
 WebBD
Martin, Jurek 1942- *NF*
Martin, Kingsley 1897-1969 *BioIn 2, BioIn 5,*
 BioIn 7, BioIn 8, BioIn 9, BioIn 10,
 ConAu 5R, ConAu 25, DcLEL, LongC,
 NewC
Martin, L John 1921- *ConAu 57*
Martin, Lannie Hayes *HisAmM XR*
Martin, Lawrence 1895- *ConAu P-1, WhNAA*
Martin, Linda Grant *NF*
Martin, Louis Emanuel 1912- *WhoAmP 1973*
Martin, Lowry 1885- *WhJnl 1928*
Martin, M W *NF*
Martin, Marian *NF*
Martin, Marion Charles 1904- *WhJnl 1928*
Martin, Martha d1925 *BioIn 2, DcNAA*
Martin, Melvin F *WhJnl 1928*
Martin, Mildred Crowl 1912- *NF*
Martin, Myron W 1901- *WhJnl 1928*
Martin, Neil A 1939- *NF*
Martin, Paul Logan 1912-1978 *WhoAm 1974,*
 WhoS&SW 1973
Martin, Pete 1901- *BiE&WWA*
Martin, Pete *see also* Martin, Thorton
Martin, Pete *see also* Martin, W Thorton
Martin, Peter Bird *NF*
Martin, Quinn 1891- *WhJnl 1928*
Martin, Ralph Guy 1920- *AmAu&B, AuBYP,*
 ConAu 5R, OvPC, WhoAm 1974,
 WhoE 1974, WrDr 1976
Martin, Robert *NF*
Martin, Robert H 1892- *WhJnl 1928*
Martin, Robert Hugh 1858- *WhJnl 1928*

Martin, Robert P *RpN*
Martin, Ron *NF*
Martin, Ronald D *NF*
Martin, Santford 1886-1957 *BioIn 4*
Martin, Sir Theodore 1816-1909 *Alli, Alli Sup,*
 BbD, BiD&SB, BrAu 19, DcEnA,
 DcEnA Ap, DcEnL, DcEuL, EvLB, NewC,
 OxEng, WebBD
Martin, Thomas Commerford 1856-1924 *Alli Sup,*
 DcNAA, HisAmM XR, WebBD
Martin, Thornton 1901- *BioIn 6*
Martin, Thorton *see also* Martin, Pete
Martin, Thorton *see also* Martin W Thorton
Martin, Victor 1889- *WhJnl 1928*
Martin, W Thornton 1901- *HisAmM XR*
Martin, W Thorton *see also* Martin, Pete
Martin, W Thorton *see also* Martin, Thorton
Martin, Wilbur Forrest 1924- *WhoAm 1974*
Martin-Dillon, Paul Revere Francis 1884- *BioIn 1*
Martindale, James Vaughan 1894- *WhoAm 1974*
Martineau, Jean Colbert *OvPC*
Martineau, Pierre D 1905?-1965 *BioIn 7*
Martinek, Frank Victor 1895- *AmAu&B*
Martinez, Al 1929- *ConAu 57*
Martinez, Mexico Pavlino *NF*
Martinez, Raymond J 1889- *ConAu 61*
Martinez Aparicio, Carlos 1891-1959 *BioIn 5*
Martinez-Marquez, Guillermo 1900- *NF*
Martingale, Hawser *see* Sleeper, John Sherburne
Martire, Vincent David *OvPC*
Marty, Martin Emil 1928- *ConAu 5, CurBio XR,*
 DrAS 74H, WhoAm 1974, WhoWor 1974,
 WrDr 1976
Martyn, Henry *HisAmM XR*
Martyn, Sarah Towne Smith 1805-1879 *Alli Sup,*
 AmAu, AmAu&B, BiD&SB, DcAmA,
 DcNAA, HisAmM XR
Martyn, Stan *NF*
Martyn, Thomas J C *NF*
Martyr, J Leighton 1898- *WhJnl 1928*
Martz, Laurence J 1933- *ConAu 69*
Marus, John 1903?-1952 *BioIn 3*
Marvel, Tom 1902?-1970 *BioIn 8*
Marvin, C N 1857- *WhJnl Sup, WhJnl 1928*
Marvin, Dwight 1880-1972 *BioIn 3, BioIn 9,*
 NewYTBE 3, WhNAA
Marvin, E P *HisAmM XR*
Marvin, Fred Richard 1868-1939 *DcNAA*
Marvin, George *HisAmM XR*
Marvin, Joseph B *HisAmM XR*
Marvin, Winthrop Lippitt 1863-1926 *DcAmA,*
 DcNAA
Marx, Frank 1910- *WhoAm 1974*
Marx, Karl 1818-1883 *BiD&SB, CasWL,*
 CyWA, EuAu, LongC, OxEng, OxFr,
 OxGer, RComWL, REn, WebBD
Marx, Karl 1876-1966 *BioIn 7, BioIn 8,*
 BioIn 10, ForP
Marx, Kenneth Samuel 1939- *ConAu 69*
Marxhausen, August *NF*
Maryles, Daisy *NF*
Marzo, Eduardo 1852-1929 *BioIn 1*
Mashruwala, Kishorilal G 1891?-1952 *BioIn 3*
Maskery, Mary Ann *NF*
Maskin, George *NF*
Masley, Peter A *NF*
Masliansky, Z H *NF*
Maslowski, Karl H *NF*
Mason, Bernard Sterling 1896-1953 *AmAu&B,*
 OhA&B
Mason, Daniel Gregory 1873-1953 *AmAu&B,*
 AmSCAP 1966, HisAmM XR, OxAm,
 REnAL, WhNAA
Mason, Dave *NF*

Mason, David Hastings 1829-1903 *Alli Sup,*
  DcAmA, DcNAA, NatCAB 10
Mason, Edward F 1888- *WhJnl 1928*
Mason, Frank Earl 1893- *WhoAm 1974,*
  WhJnl 1928
Mason, Gregory 1889-1968 *AmAu&B, BioIn 3,*
  BioIn 8, HisAmM XR
Mason, H P *NF*
Mason, Harriet 1866- *WhJnl 1928*
Mason, James M *HisAmM XR*
Mason, Jay E 1891- *WhJnl 1928*
Mason, Jerry *HisAmM XR*
Mason, Joseph B *OvPC*
Mason, Joseph Warren Teets 1879-1941 *AmAu&B,*
  CurBio XR, DcNAA, WhNAA
Mason, Julian Starkweather 1876-1954 *BioIn 3,*
  BioIn 7, NatCAB 48, WhJnl 1928
Mason, Louise Emily d1946 *DcNAA*
Mason, Margaret *BioIn 2*
Mason, Martha Sprague 1864-1949 *BioIn 2*
Mason, Paul *OvPC*
Mason, R B *HisAmM XR*
Mason, Renee Fortunee *OvPC*
Mason, Robert 1912- *BioIn 2, WhoAm 1974,*
  WhoS&SW 1973
Mason, Robert T 1900- *WhJnl 1928*
Mason, Roberto *NF*
Mason, Samuel 1878?-1950 *BioIn 2*
Mason, Thomas *HisAmM XR*
Mason, Walt 1862-1939 *AmAu&B, AmJnl,*
  DcAmB S2, DcNAA, EvLB, HisAmM XR,
  LongC, NatCAB 30, TwCA, WebBD
Mason, William Edward 1905- *WhJnl 1928*
Mason, William Powell *HisAmM XR*
Masraff, Yussef *NF*
Massa, Richard Wayne 1932- *AmM&W 73S,*
  ConAu 57, DrAS 74E
Massachusettensis *see* Leonard, Daniel
Massai, Elisa *NF*
Massaquoi, Hans Jurgen 1926- *BlkC, ConAu 69,*
  WhoAm 1974
Massaro, John J *NF*
Masse, Andre *OvPC*
Masseck, Clinton Joseph *NF*
Massee, May 1881-1966 *BioIn 1, BioIn 2,*
  BioIn 4, BioIn 5, BioIn 7, BioIn 8
Massengill, Frederick I *WhJnl 1928*
Massey, Gerald 1828-1907 *Alli, Alli Sup, BbD,*
  BiD&SB, BrAu 19, DcEnA, DcEnL,
  DcEuL, DcLEL, EvLB, HisAmM XR,
  NewC, REn, WebBD, WebE&AL
Massey, Sarah Lee *NF*
Massi, Frank 1909- *WhoAm 1974*
Massie, Robert K 1929- *BioIn 8*
Massimino, Sal *OvPC*
Massingham, Harold John 1888-1952 *DcLEL,*
  EvLB, LongC, NewC, TwCA, TwCA Sup,
  WebBD, WhoLA
Massingham, Henry William 1860-1924 *LongC,*
  NewC, WebBD
Massip, Roger 1904- *IntWW 1976,*
  WhoWor 1974
Massock, Richard G *OvPC*
Massock, Richard Gilbert 1900- *WhJnl Sup*
Masson, David 1822-1907 *Alli, Alli Sup,*
  BiD&SB, BrAu 19, DcEnA, DcEnL,
  DcEuL, DcLEL, EvLB, LongC, NewC,
  OxEng, Pen Eng, WebBD
Masson, Joseph Gaudiose Irenee 1896-1955 *BioIn 4*
Masson, Thomas Lansing 1866-1934 *AmAu&B,*
  DcAmB S1, DcNAA, HisAmM XR, WebBD
Masson, Walter *NF*
Massot, Henri Victor Joseph 1903- *IntWW 1976,*
  WhoWor 1974

Massow, Rosalind *ForWC 1970, OvPC,*
  WhoAm 1974, WhoAmW 1974
Mast, Casper Leo, Jr. 1909- *WhoAm 1974*
Mast, Phineas Price *HisAmM XR*
Masters, Ann V *ForWC 1970, OvPC*
Masters, Dexter 1908- *BioIn 3*
Masters, E Woodworth *HisAmM XR*
Masters, George E 1899- *WhJnl Sup*
Masters, Ira Harwood 1877-1956 *BioIn 4*
Masterson, Bat 1853-1921 *WebBD*
Masterson, Bat *see also* Masterson, William Barclay
Masterson, Thomas A d1901 *NF*
Masterson, Tom 1912-1972 *BioIn 9, NewYTBE 3*
Masterson, William Barclay 1853-1921 *BioIn 4,*
  BioIn 5, BioIn 6, BioIn 8, BioIn 9, WebBD
Mastro, Garrett *NF*
Mastro, Susan Duff 1945- *ConAu 69*
Mastroianni, Tony *NF*
Mather, Frank Jewett, Jr. 1868-1953 *AmAu&B,*
  HisAmM XR, REnAL, TwCA, TwCA Sup,
  WebBD, WhNAA
Mather, Frederic Gregory 1844-1925 *DcNAA,*
  OhA&B
Mather, Maurice Whittemore 1866?-1950 *BioIn 2*
Mather, Stephen Tyng 1867-1930 *WebBD*
Matheson, Roderick O 1876- *WhJnl 1928*
Mathew, David J *ForP*
Mathews, Carol *NF*
Mathews, Cornelius 1817-1889 *Alli, Alli Sup,*
  AmAu, AmAu&B, BbD, BiD&SB, CasWL,
  CyAL 2, DcAmA, DcNAA, HisAmM XR,
  OxAm, REnAL
Mathews, Garrett 1949- *NF*
Mathews, Glenn D 1896- *WhJnl 1928*
Mathews, Jason *HisAmM XR*
Mathews, John F *NF*
Mathews, John L *HisAmM XR*
Mathews, Linda M *NF*
Mathews, Shailer 1863-1941 *AmAu&B,*
  CurBio XR, DcNAA, HisAmM XR,
  WhNAA
Mathews, Tom *NF*
Mathews, William 1818-1909 *Alli Sup, AmAu,*
  AmAu&B, BiD&SB, DcAmA, DcAmB 12,
  DcNAA, HisAmM XR
Mathews, William Rankin 1893-1969 *BioIn 8,*
  WhNAA, WhJnl 1928
Mathews, William Smythe Babcock 1837-1912
  Alli Sup, AmAu&B, DcAmA, DcNAA,
  HisAmM XR
Mathias, Benjamin *HisAmM XR*
Mathiason, Carolyn S *NF*
Mathieu, Beatrice 1904-1976 *ConAu 65,*
  WhoAm 1974
Mathieu, Charles L 1891?-1950 *BioIn 2*
Mathieu, Richard C *OvPC*
Mathiews, Franklin K 1873?-1950 *BioIn 2*
Mathis, James V *RpN*
Mathison, Richard Randolph 1919- *ConAu 3R*
Matis, David *NF*
Matlick, Dayton Harris 1934- *WhoAm 1974*
Matney, William C, Jr. 1924- *BlkC, ConAu 69*
Matos, Huber *ForP*
Matos Segueira, Gustavo De 1880-1962 *BioIn 6*
Matsell, George Washington 1811-1877 *Alli Sup,*
  DcNAA, HisAmM XR
Matson, Carlton Kingsbury 1890-1948 *BioIn 1*
Matsuo, Yoshiharu *NF*
Matsuyama, Yukio *OvPC*
Matteos, Elizabeth R *NF*
Matteson, W T *HisAmM XR*
Matthewman, Lisle DeVaux 1867-1904 *DcAmA,*
  DcNAA
Matthews, Albert *LiJA*

Matthews, Anne Murray McIllhenney
 ForWC 1970, WhoAmW 1974, WhoE 1974
Matthews, Brander 1852-1929 *AmAu, AmAu&B,*
 BiD&SB, BiDSA, CnDAL, ConAmL,
 DcAmA, DcNAA, OxAm, Pen Am, REn,
 REnAL, WebBD
Matthews, Brander *see also* Matthews, James
 Brander
Matthews, Burrows 1893-1954 *BioIn 3,*
 WhJnl 1928
Matthews, Mrs. Burrows *see* Matthews, Anne M
 McIllhenney
Matthews, Cornelius *HisAmM XR*
Matthews, Curt 1934- *ConAu 73*
Matthews, Franklin 1858-1917 *DcAmB 12,*
 DcNAA
Matthews, G C *HisAmM XR*
Matthews, George E 1855- *NatCAB 12*
Matthews, Herbert Lionel 1900-1977 *AmAu&B,*
 Au&Wr, AuBYP, BioIn 1, BioIn 4,
 BioIn 8, BioIn 9, BioIn 10, ConAu 1R,
 ConAu 73, CurBio XR, IntWW 1976,
 REnAL, WhoAm 1974, WhoWor 1974
Matthews, James *HisAmM XR*
Matthews, James Brander 1852-1929 *Alli Sup,*
 AmAu, BbD, DcLEL, DcNAA
Matthews, James Brander *see also* Matthews,
 Brander
Matthews, James Newson 1828-1888 *Alli Sup,*
 DcNAA
Matthews, John L 1869- *WhJnl 1928*
Matthews, Les 1933?- *BioIn 9, BlkC*
Matthews, Marcia C J *HisAmM XR*
Matthews, Norman W *NF*
Matthews, Ralph D 1904- *WhJnl 1928*
Matthews, Ronald 1903-1967 *BioIn 7*
Matthews, Thomas Stanley 1901- *AmAu&B,*
 Au&Wr, BioIn 2, BioIn 3, BioIn 5,
 ConAu P-1, CurBio XR, HisAmM XR,
 OhA&B, REnAL, Who 1974, WhoAm 1974,
 WrDr 1976
Matthews, Victor *NF*
Matthiessen, Peter 1927- *AmAu&B, Au&Wr,*
 ConAu 9, ConLC 5, ConNov 1972,
 ConNov 1976, DrAF 1976, WhoAm 1974,
 WhoWor 1974, WorAu, WrDr 1976
Mattick, Paul *AmRP*
Mattioli, Francesco *OvPC*
Mattison, Anna C *HisAmM XR*
Mattson, George *NF*
Mattson, Hans 1832-1893 *AmAu&B, DcNAA*
Mattson, Marie *NF*
Matusovskii, Mikhail L'vovich 1915- *BioIn 2*
Matyash, Vladimir N *NF*
Maudoodi, Syed Abul'Ala 1903- *BioIn 8*
Maue, John Adam 1877- *WhJnl 1928*
Mauldin, Bill 1921- *CelR 1973, CurBio XR,*
 OxAm, REnAL, WhoAmA 1973
Mauldin, Bill *see also* Mauldin, William Henry
Mauldin, William Henry 1921- *AmAu&B, AmJnl,*
 BioIn 1, BioIn 2, BioIn 3, BioIn 4, BioIn 5,
 BioIn 6, BioIn 7, BioIn 9, CurBio XR,
 TwCA Sup, WhoAm 1974, WhoMW 1974,
 WhoWor 1974
Mauldin, William Henry *see also* Mauldin, Bill
Maule, Frances 1879-1966 *BioIn 4, BioIn 7*
Maule, Hamilton Bee 1915- *AuBYP, BioIn 7,*
 BioIn 9, BioIn 10, ConAu 1R, WhoAm 1974
Maule, Harry E 1886-1971 *HisAmM XR,*
 NewYTBE 1, WhNAA
Maule, Henry *NF*
Maulnier, Thierry 1909- *IntWW 1976, McGWD,*
 WhoWor 1974
Maulsby, William Shipman 1890- *WhJnl 1928*

Maund, Alfred 1923- *ConAu 4R*
Maupin, Will M 1863- *WhJnl 1928*
Maurer, Gilbert Charles 1928- *WhoAm 1974,*
 WhoE 1974, WhoF&I 1974
Maurer, James *AmRP*
Maurer, Wesley Henry 1897- *AmM&W 73S,*
 WhoAm 1974, WhJnl 1928
Maurer, Yolanda *NF*
Mauriac, Francois 1885-1970 *AtlBL, CasWL,*
 CathA 1930, CIDMEL, CnMD, CnMWL,
 ConAu 25, ConLC 4, CyWA, EncWL,
 EvEuW, LongC, McGWD, ModRL,
 ModWD, NewYTBE 1, OxEng, OxFr,
 Pen Eur, RComWL, REn, REnWD, TwCA,
 TwCA Sup, TwCW, WebBD, WhoTwCL
Maurice, Arthur Bartlett 1873-1946 *AmAu&B,*
 BioIn 1, DcAmA, DcNAA, HisAmM XR,
 LiJA, REnAL, WhNAA
Maurice, Sir Frederick 1871-1951 *BioIn 2,*
 BioIn 9, Lor&LP, WebBD
Maurice, John D *NF*
Maurin, Peter 1877-1949 *AmRP, CathA 1952*
Maurras, Charles 1868-1952 *BioIn 1, BioIn 2,*
 BioIn 3, CasWL, CIDMEL, EncWL,
 EvEuW, NewC, OxFr, Pen Eur, REn,
 WebBD, WorAu
Maury, Donald P 1939?- *BioIn 10*
Maury, Magruder Gordon 1878-1948 *BioIn 1,*
 BioIn 2, DcNAA, NatCAB 36, WhNAA,
 WhJnl 1928
Maury, Matthew Fontaine 1806-1873 *Alli,*
 Alli Sup, AmAu&B, BbD, BiD&SB,
 BiDSA, CyAL 2, DcAmA, DcNAA,
 HisAmM XR, REnAL, WebBD
Maury, Reuben 1899- *BioIn 1, BioIn 9,*
 WhoAm 1974
Maus, Mike *NF*
Maver, Aian *NF*
Mavity, Nancy Barr 1890- *AmAu&B, WhNAA*
Mawhinney, George M *NF*
Mawson, Christopher Orlando Sylvester 1870-1938
 AmAu&B, NatCAB 29, REnAL, TwCA
Max, Alfred *NF*
Maxa, Kathleen 1949- *NF*
Maxa, Rudolph Joseph, Jr. 1949- *ConAu 65*
Maxey, David R 1936- *ConAu 73*
Maxfield, David M *NF*
Maxse, Leopold James 1864-1932 *BioIn 1,*
 BioIn 2
Maxson, Edgar Potter *WhJnl 1928*
Maxted, Stanley 1897-1963 *BioIn 6*
Maxwell, Allen 1915- *WhoS&SW 1973*
Maxwell, Clair *HisAmM XR*
Maxwell, Elsa 1883-1963 *AmSCAP 1966,*
 CurBio XR
Maxwell, Floyd 1897- *WhJnl 1928*
Maxwell, J William 1919- *AmM&W 73S*
Maxwell, Lee Wilder *HisAmM XR*
Maxwell, Otis Allen 1915- *WhoAm 1974*
Maxwell, Perriton 1868-1947 *AmAu&B, DcAmA,*
 HisAmM XR
Maxwell, Phyllis *NF*
Maxwell, Rod *NF*
Maxwell, W Kee 1879- *WhJnl 1928*
Maxwell, William 1755?-1809 *AmJnl, OhA&B*
Maxwell, William 1784-1857 *BiDSA, DcNAA,*
 HisAmM XR
Maxwell, William 1908- *AmAu&B, AmNov,*
 AuBYP, ConNov 1972, ConNov 1976,
 CurBio XR, OxAm, REn, TwCA Sup,
 WhoAm 1974, WhoWor 1974, WrDr 1976
Maxwell, William Donald 1900- *BioIn 2*
May, A Wilfred 1900-1969 *BioIn 8*
May, Antoinette *NF*

May, Arthur Franklin 1922- *WhoAm 1974*
May, Donald H *NF*
May, E Lawson 1897-1976 *WhJnl 1928*
May, Edgar 1929- *ConAu 9, WhoAm 1974, WhoAmP 1973, WhoWor 1974*
May, Emily H *HisAmM XR*
May, James Boyer 1904- *AmAu&B, ConAu P-1*
May, James Garfield 1881- *WhJnl 1928*
May, Philip William 1864-1903 *BioIn 1, BioIn 2, BioIn 6, WebBD*
May, Robert S *OvPC*
May, Robert Stephen 1929- *ConAu 29, WrDr 1976*
May, Tom d1927 *NF*
May, Walter W R 1888-1978 *NatCAB XR*
May, William *NF*
Mayborn, Ward Carlton 1879-1958 *BioIn 4, BioIn 7, NatCAB 47, WhJnl 1928*
Mayborn, William A 1888- *WhJnl 1928*
Mayer, Albert P 1902- *WhJnl 1928*
Mayer, Allan J *NF*
Mayer, Barb *NF*
Mayer, Francis VonRossdell 1874-1946 *BioIn 2*
Mayer, Henry 1868-1954 *DcAmA, HisAmM XR*
Mayer, Henry *see also* Mayer, Hy
Mayer, Hy 1868-1954 *AmAu&B, BioIn 3*
Mayer, Hy *see also* Mayer, Henry
Mayer, Jean 1920- *AmM&W 73P, CurBio XR, WhoAm 1974, WhoAmP 1973, WhoE 1974, WhoWor 1974*
Mayer, Margaret *NF*
Mayer, Martin Prager 1928- *AmAu&B, Au&Wr, BioIn 3, BioIn 6, BioIn 8, ConAu 5, WhoAm 1974, WorAu*
Mayer, Milton 1908- *ConAu 37, DrAS 74E, WhoAm 1974, WhoE 1974, WhoWor 1974*
Mayes, Herbert Raymond 1900- *AmAu&B, BioIn 1, BioIn 5, BioIn 6, BioIn 10, HisAmM XR*
Mayfield, Julian 1928- *AmAu&B, BlkAW, ConAu 13, ConNov 1972, ConNov 1976, LivBAA, WhoAm 1974, WrDr 1976*
Mayfield, Molly *BioIn 1*
Mayfield, Sara 1905- *ConAu 25*
Mayhall, William Franklin 1854-1917 *NatCAB 18*
Mayhem, Sir Basil *NF*
Mayhew, Henry 1812-1887 *Alli, Alli Sup, BiD&SB, BrAu 19, CarSB, DcEnA, DcEnL, DcLEL, OxEng, Pen Eng, WebBD, WebE&AL*
Maynard, Jacob Beckwith 1819-1902 *BioIn 2, IndAu 1816*
Maynard, Robert C 1937?- *NF*
Mayne, Calvin W *RpN*
Mayne, John 1759-1836 *Alli, BiD&SB, BiDLA, BrAu 19, DcEnL, EvLB*
Mayne, Richard 1926- *Au&Wr, ConAu 13R, WrDr 1976*
Mayo, Anna *NF*
Mayo, Caswell O *HisAmM XR*
Mayo, Earl Williams 1873-1957 *AmAu&B, AmLY, BioIn 4, DcAmA, HisAmM XR*
Mayo, Lawrence Shaw 1888- *AmAu&B, LiJA*
Mayo, Sarah Carter Edgarton 1819-1848 *Alli, AmAu, AmAu&B, DcAmA, FemPA*
Mayol, Frank 1885- *WhJnl 1928*
Mayor, Alfred Hyatt 1934- *ConAu 65*
Mayorga-Rivas, Rodolfa 1905- *NF*
Mayrand, Oswald 1876-1969 *BioIn 8, WhJnl 1928*
Mays, Livingston T 1873?-1952 *BioIn 3*
Mays, VanZandt 1902- *WhJnl 1928*
Mazade, Louis Charles Jean Robert De 1821-1893 *WebBD*

Mazeline, Guy 1900- *WebBD*
Mazie, David M *RpN*
Mazo, Earl 1919- *AmAu&B, ConAu 37, OvPC, WhoAm 1974, WhoS&SW 1973, WhoWorJ 1972*
Mazzola, Anthony T 1923- *CelR 1973*
Mbita, Hashim Iddi 1933- *IntWW 1976*
McAdam, Charles Vincent 1892- *WhoAm 1974*
McAdam, Edward Lippincott 1905-1969 *BioIn 8*
McAdams, Clark 1874-1935 *DcAmB S1, WhNAA, WhJnl 1928*
McAdoo, Richard Budd 1920- *WhoAm 1974*
McAdory, J R, Jr. *NF*
McAfee, Helen 1884-1956 *NatCAB 43*
McAleer, John Joseph 1923- *ConAu 21R, DrAS 74E, WhoE 1974*
McAlister, Durwood 1927- *WhoS&SW 1973*
McAlister, Durwood *see also* McAlister, Luther Durwood
McAlister, Luther Durwood 1927- *WhoAm 1974, WhoS&SW 1973*
McAlister, Luther Durwood *see also* McAlister, Durwood
McAllister, Addams Stratton 1875-1946 *WebBD*
McAllister, Gilbert 1906-1964 *BioIn 6*
McAllister, John T *NF*
McAllister, Ward 1827-1895 *AmAu&B, DcNAA, REn, WebBD*
McAlpin, Harry S 1906- *BioIn 3*
McAlpin, Robert *NF*
McAlpin, Tod *NF*
McAlpine, Eadmonn *AmRP*
McAnally, David Rice 1810-1895 *AmAu&B, BiD&SB, BiDSA, DcAmA, DcAmB 11, DcNAA*
McAndrew, William 1863-1937 *HisAmM XR, WhNAA*
McAndrew, William Robert 1914-1968 *BioIn 6, BioIn 8*
McAneny, George 1869-1953 *HisAmM XR, WebBD*
McAnney, Burnett Olcott 1891-1962 *BioIn 6*
McArdle, Willis Kenneth 1911- *HisAmM XR, WhoAm 1974*
McAree, John Verner 1876-1958 *BioIn 4*
McArthur, George *NF*
McArthur, Jack *NF*
McArthur, Peter 1866-1924 *AmLY, CanWr, DcLEL, DcNAA, OxCan*
M'Carthy, Justin 1830-1912 *NewC, WebBD*
M'Carthy, Justin *see also* McCarthy, Justin
McAtamney, Hugh Entwistle 1860-1929 *DcNAA*
McAtee, Waldo Lee 1883-1962 *BioIn 9, IndAu 1917, WhNAA*
McBeath, Faye *AmJnl*
McBee, Susanna *NF*
McBreen, T J 1888- *WhJnl 1928*
McBride, Clyde Edward 1882- *WhJnl 1928*
McBride, Henry 1867-1962 *AmAu&B*
McBride, Isaac d1941 *AmRP, DcNAA*
McBride, Marion *NF*
McBride, Mary Margaret 1899-1976 *AmAu&B, BioIn 1, BioIn 3, BioIn 4, BioIn 5, BioIn 9, ConAu 65, ConAu 69, CurBio XR, WhoAm 1974, WhoAmW 1974*
McBride, William M 1894- *WhJnl 1928*
McBryde, John McLauren, Jr. 1870- *BiDSA, HisAmM XR*
McBurney, John *HisAmM XR*
McCabe, Carol L *NF*
McCabe, Charles Bernard 1899-1970 *BioIn 8, NewYTBE 1*
McCabe, Charles R *BioIn 5*
McCabe, Edward Preston *NF*

McCabe, Frank, Jr. 1899- *WhJnl 1928*
McCabe, Frederick Augustus 1911- *WhoAm 1974*
McCabe, Gibson 1911- *AmAu&B, CurBio XR,
  NewYTBE 2, WhoAm 1974, WhoF&I 1974*
McCabe, James Dabney, Jr. 1842-1883 *AmAu&B,
  BiDSA, DcAmA, DcNAA, HisAmM XR,
  PoIre*
McCabe, James Dabney, Sr. 1808-1875 *BiDSA*
McCabe, Lida Rose 1865-1938 *AmAu&B,
  DcNAA, OhA&B*
McCabe, Michael 1864- *WhJnl 1928*
McCabe, Peter *NF*
McCabe, Ray *NF*
McCabe, Robert Copland 1869?-1958 *BioIn 4*
McCabe, St. Clair Landerkin 1915- *CanWW 1972,
  WhoAm 1974, WhoF&I 1974*
McCabe, Thomas Joseph *WhJnl 1928*
McCabe, William Raphael 1884?- *BioIn 1*
McCadden, George E *OvPC*
McCafferty, James *NF*
McCaffrey, James P 1899?-1974 *BioIn 10,
  NewYTBS 5*
McCaffrey, Joseph Francis 1920- *WhoAm 1974,
  WhoGov 1972, WhoS&SW 1973*
McCahill, Charles Francis 1886-1969 *BioIn 2,
  BioIn 8*
McCain, George Nox 1856-1934 *DcNAA*
McCain, Thomas Hart Benton 1839-1898 *BioIn 2,
  IndAu 1816*
McCall, Anne Bryan *HisAmM XR*
McCall, Francis *NF*
McCall, James *HisAmM XR*
McCall, Thomas Lawson 1913- *NewYTBE 2,
  WhoAm 1974, WhoAmP 1973,
  WhoGov 1972*
McCall, Thomas Lawson *see also* McCall, Tom
McCall, Tom 1913- *BioNews 1974, CurBio XR,
  IntWW 1976*
McCall, Tom *see also* McCall, Thomas Lawson
McCall, William Harry 1910- *OvPC,
  WhoAm 1974, WhoWor 1974*
McCalla, Gary Edward 1931- *WhoAm 1974*
McCallum, Andrew *HisAmM XR*
McCallum, Earl 1899- *WhJnl 1928*
McCallum, George P, Jr. 1902-1969 *BioIn 10,
  WhJnl 1928*
McCallum, William L 1865- *WhJnl 1928*
McCalmont, David B 1876-1947 *NatCAB 37*
McCambridge, William J 1889-1964 *NatCAB 51*
McCandlish, Edward Gerstell 1887-1946 *BioIn 1,
  DcNAA, OhA&B, WhJnl 1928*
McCaniel, C C 1886- *WhJnl 1928*
McCann, Alfred Watterson 1879-1931 *DcAmB 11,
  DcNAA, WebBD*
McCann, Charles Mallette 1893-1959 *BioIn 5*
McCann, David Anthony 1929- *WhoAm 1974*
McCann, Hank *NF*
McCann, John A *HisAmM XR*
McCardell, Roy L 1870- *AmAu&B, BiDSA*
McCardle, Carl Wesley 1904-1972 *BioIn 3,
  BioIn 9, ConAu 37, NewYTBE 3*
McCardle, Dorothy Bartlett 1904-1978 *BioIn 9,
  WhoAm 1974*
McCarrens, John S 1869-1943 *CurBio XR,
  NatCAB 32*
McCarroll, James 1814-1892 *AmAu, AmAu&B,
  BbtC, DcAmB 11, DcNAA, OxCan, PoIre*
McCarroll, Marion Clyde 1893?-1977 *ConAu 73*
McCarter, William J, Jr. 1929- *WhoAm 1974*
McCarthey, Fred *NF*
McCarthy, Charles F 1903- *WhJnl 1928*
McCarthy, Clem 1882-1962 *CurBio XR*
McCarthy, Colman *NF*
McCarthy, Cornelius Stephen 1916- *WhoAm 1974*

McCarthy, Dan B *NF*
McCarthy, Denis Aloysius 1870-1931 *AmLY,
  DcNAA, PoIre, WhNAA*
McCarthy, Edward James 1914- *WhoAm 1974*
McCarthy, Glenn Herbert 1907- *BioIn 1, BioIn 2,
  BioIn 4, BioIn 5, BioIn 8*
McCarthy, James R 1900- *WhJnl Sup*
McCarthy, Joe 1915- *ConAu 2R*
McCarthy, Julia *OvPC*
McCarthy, Justin (1830-1912) *see also* M'Carthy,
  Justin
McCarthy, Justin 1830-1912 *BbD, BiD&SB,
  BrAu 19, DcEnA, DcEnA Ap, DcEnL,
  EvLB, HisAmM XR, LongC, OxEng,
  Pen Eng, PoIre, TwCA*
McCarthy, Justin 1908?- *BioIn 5*
McCarthy, Justin Gerald 1915-1978 *RpN,
  WhoS&SW 1973*
McCarthy, Lawrence 1893- *WhJnl 1928*
McCarthy, Lee *NF*
McCarthy, Leon J 1894- *WhJnl 1928*
McCarthy, Marvin 1902- *BioIn 2*
McCarthy, Max *see* McCarthy, Richard Dean
McCarthy, Patrick J 1951- *NF*
McCarthy, Richard Dean 1927- *ConAu 41,
  WhoAm 1974, WhoAmP 1973*
McCarthy, Robert J 1892- *WhJnl 1928*
McCarthy, Ruth *NF*
McCarthy, William T 1908-1973 *BioIn 10,
  NewYTBE 4, WhoE 1974*
McCartney, James H 1925- *ConAu 73, RpN*
McCartney, Roy *NF*
McCarty, Charles Walter 1891- *BioIn 1,
  WhJnl 1928*
McCarty, John Lawton 1901- *TexWr,
  WhJnl 1928*
McCarty, P *NF*
McCary, Robert L d1960 *RpN*
McCauley, Bruce Gordon *WhoAm 1974,
  WhoF&I 1974, WhoWor 1974*
McCausland, Elizabeth 1899-1965 *NF*
McCaw, Raymond Henry 1886-1959 *BioIn 5*
McClain, John D *NF*
McClanahan, William J 1907- *WhoAm 1974,
  WhoS&SW 1973*
McClaran, William B 1898- *WhJnl 1928*
McClary, Eula 1886?-1946 *BioIn 1*
McClary, Jacquelyn B *NF*
McClary, Jane McIlvaine *OvPC*
McClary, Jane Stevenson 1919- *ConAu 2R,
  ForWC 1970*
McClatchy, C K *NF*
McClatchy, Carlos K 1891- *WhJnl 1928*
McClatchy, Charles Kenny 1858-1936 *BioIn 4,
  DcAmB S2, WhNAA, WhJnl 1928*
McClatchy, Eleanor 1900?- *BioIn 2,
  WhoAmW 1974*
McClatchy, James *NF*
McClean, Robert Bowles 1877- *WhJnl 1928*
McCleery, William 1911- *ConAu 1R*
McClellan, Diana B *NF*
McClellan, George Brinton 1865-1940 *AmAu&B,
  AmLY, DcAmA, DcAmB S2, DcNAA,
  WebBD*
McClelland, David Clarence 1917- *AmAu&B,
  AmM&W 73S, ConAu 25, WhoAm 1974*
McClelland, Douglas Wayne 1934- *ConAu 41,
  WhoAm 1974*
McClenahan, Howard *HisAmM XR*
McClendon, Sarah 1910?- *BioIn 4, BioIn 6,
  CelR 1973*
McClintock, James Harvey 1864-1934 *DcAmB S1,
  DcNAA, WhNAA*
McClintock, John 1814-1870 *BbD, BiD&SB,*

DcAmA, DcNAA, HisAmM XR, WebBD
McClintock, John Norris 1846-1914 *DcNAA,*
HisAmM XR
McClintock, Marshall 1906-1967 *AuBYP,*
BioIn 7, BioIn 9, ConAu P-1, SmATA 3
McClintock, Wayne E *NF*
McCloskey, John C *LiJA*
McCloskey, Marie *NF*
McCloud, Norman C *HisAmM XR*
McCloy, Helen 1866?-1950 *BioIn 2*
McCloy, William C *NF*
McCluggage, Denise *BioIn 4*
McClung, Alexander d1855 *AmAu&B*
McClung, Alfred C 1881- *WhJnl 1928*
McClung, Mary J *BioIn 1*
McClure, Alexander Kelly 1828-1909 *AmAu&B,*
AmJnl, DcAmA, DcNAA, HisAmM XR,
NatCAB 1, REnAL
McClure, Alexander Wilson 1808-1865 *AmAu&B,*
DcAmA, DcNAA
McClure, Arthur H 1904?-1963 *BioIn 6*
McClure, Darrell *NF*
McClure, H H *HisAmM XR*
McClure, Hal *OvPC*
McClure, James Warren 1919- *WhoAm 1974*
McClure, John *HisAmM XR*
McClure, John Peebles 1893-1956 *AmAu&B*
McClure, Robert Emerson 1896- *AmAu&B,*
OhA&B
McClure, Samuel Grant 1863-1948 *BioIn 1,*
WhJnl 1928
McClure, Samuel Sidney 1857-1949 *AmAu&B,*
AmJnl, BioIn 1, BioIn 2, BioIn 5, BioIn 6,
BioIn 7, DcAmB S4, DcNAA, EncAB,
HisAmM XR, LiJA, REn, REnAL, WebBD,
WhNAA
McClure, William K 1922- *IntMPA 1975, OvPC*
McClurg, Alexander Caldwell 1832-1901
HisAmM XR, WebBD
McCluskey, William *HisAmM XR*
McColl, Patricia *NF*
McCollough, A E *WhJnl 1928*
McCollough, Albert W 1917- *NF*
McCollough, Clair R 1903- *WhoAm 1974,*
WhoF&I 1974
McCollum, Earl 1889-1947 *BioIn 1*
McCollum, Fay James 1883- *WhJnl 1928*
McCombe, Leonard 1923- *WhoAm 1974*
McCombs, G B 1909- *WhoAm 1974*
McCombs, Julia C *NF*
McCombs, Maxwell Elbert 1938- *AmM&W 73S,*
ConAu 73
McCombs, Philip A 1944- *ConAu 49*
McConachie, Bob *NF*
McConagha, Alan C 1932- *WhoAm 1974*
McConaughy, James Lukens 1915?-1958 *BioIn 4*
McConaughy, John 1884-1933 *DcNAA*
McConnachie, Brian John 1942- *WhoAm 1974*
McConnell, Frank H 1895?-1966 *BioIn 7*
McConnell, John Griffith 1911- *BioIn 4,*
CanWW 1972, WhoAm 1974
McConnell, John Wilson 1877-1963 *BioIn 6*
McConnell, Mary Lamar Knight *OvPC*
McConnell, Mickey *BioIn 4*
McConnell, Oviatt 1898?-1953 *BioIn 3*
McConnell, Raymond Arnott, Jr. 1915-
WhoAm 1974
McConville, George *NF*
McCoo, Wayman *NF*
McCord, D J *HisAmM XR*
McCord, David Thompson Watson 1897-
ConAu 73, WhoAm 1974, WhoWor 1974
McCord, Fred *NF*
McCord, Myron Hawley 1840-1908 *BioIn 5*

McCord, Robert *NF*
McCormack, Donald P *OvPC*
McCormack, Michael *NF*
McCormack, Pat S *OvPC*
McCormack, Thomas Joseph 1932- *WhoAm 1974*
McCormally, John Patrick 1922- *RpN,*
WhoMW 1974
McCormick, Alexander Agnew 1863- *NF*
McCormick, Anne Elizabeth O'Hare 1881-1954
AmAu&B, BioIn 1, BioIn 2, BioIn 3,
BioIn 4, BioIn 5, CurBio XR, DcAmB S5,
WebBD
McCormick, Bernard *BioIn 10*
McCormick, Cyrus Hall 1809-1884 *AmJnl,*
HisAmM XR, WebBD
McCormick, Donald King 1911- *ConAu 11R,*
ConAu 73, WrDr 1976
McCormick, Edith *NF*
McCormick, Eliot *HisAmM XR*
McCormick, Elsie 1894-1962 *BioIn 6*
McCormick, Frederick d1951 *NF*
McCormick, George Brinton 1865- *WhJnl 1928*
McCormick, George Chalmers 1872- *WhJnl 1928*
McCormick, James 1920- *ConAu 25*
McCormick, Joe *WhJnl 1928*
McCormick, Joseph Medill 1877-1925 *AmAu&B,*
AmJnl, DcAmB 11, NatCAB 19, WebBD
McCormick, Kenneth Dale 1906- *BioIn 9,*
WhoAm 1974
McCormick, Kenneth F *RpN*
McCormick, Richard Cunningham 1832-1901
DcAmA, DcAmB 11, DcNAA
McCormick, Robert *NF*
McCormick, Robert Rutherford 1880-1955
AmAu&B, AmJnl, BioIn 1, BioIn 2,
BioIn 3, BioIn 4, BioIn 7, CurBio XR,
DcAmB S5, NatCAB 41, REnAL, WebBD,
WhJnl 1928
McCormick, Tom *NF*
McCormick, Vance Criswell 1872-1946 *BioIn 1,*
BioIn 2, NatCAB 35, WebBD
McCormick, Virginia Taylor 1873- *AmAu&B,*
AnMV 1926, WhNAA
McCormick, William 1866-1923 *AmLY, DcNAA*
McCormick, William B 1868- *HisAmM XR*
McCorquidale, Malcolm S 1900- *WhJnl 1928*
McCoy, Alvin Scott *NF*
McCoy, Bruce R 1896- *WhJnl 1928*
McCoy, George W d1962 *NF*
McCoy, Horace 1897-1955 *AmAu&B, AmNov,*
OxAm, REnAL, TexWr, WhNAA,
WhJnl 1928, WorAu
McCoy, Jackson 1890- *WhJnl 1928*
McCoy, Ralph Edward 1915- *BiDrLUS,*
ConAu 37, DrAS 74H, WhoAm 1974
McCoy, Samuel Duff 1882-1964 *AmAu&B,*
BioIn 6, WebBD, WhJnl 1928
McCracken, George Herbert 1899- *WhoAm 1974,*
WhJnl 1928
McCraken, Robert Stanton 1924- *WhoAm 1974*
McCraken, Tracy Stephenson 1894-1960 *BioIn 3,*
BioIn 5
McCrary, Ernest S *OvPC*
McCrary, Jinx 1919- *BioIn 1, BioIn 2, BioIn 3,*
CurBio XR
McCrary, John Reagan 1910- *BioIn 1, BioIn 2,*
BioIn 3
McCrary, John Reagan *see also* McCrary, Tex
McCrary, Tex 1910- *CurBio XR, IntMPA 1975*
McCrary, Tex *see also* McCrary, John Reagan
McCraw, Jim *NF*
McCray, E Ward 1917- *NF*
McCray, Floyd E *WhJnl 1928*
McCready, Albert Lee 1918- *WhoAm 1974*

McCready, Ben W 1901- *WhJnl 1928*
McCready, Ernest W 1869?-1950 *BioIn 2*
McCready, John E Blakeny 1839- *NF*
McCready, Robert H 1872- *WhJnl 1928*
McCready, Robert N *NF*
McCreary, Elmer White *WhJnl 1928*
McCrindle, Joseph F 1923- *ConAu 29*
McCrohon, Maxwell *NF*
McCue, George Robert 1910- *WhoAm 1974*
McCuish, John Berridge 1906-1962 *BioIn 8,*
  NatCAB 50
McCulla, James 1913- *BioIn 9*
McCullagh, Cecil Richard 1897- *WhJnl 1928*
McCullagh, Clement George 1905-1952 *BioIn 1,*
  BioIn 3, BioIn 7
McCullagh, Francis 1874-1956 *AmJnl, BioIn 1,*
  BioIn 4, BkC 2, CathA 1930
McCullagh, George *NF*
McCullagh, James B *NF*
McCullagh, Joseph Burbridge 1842-1896
  AmAu&B, AmJnl, BioIn 8, DcAmB 12,
  FamWC
McCullin, Donald 1935- *IntWW 1976*
McCulloch, Frank Walter 1920- *BioIn 3,*
  WhoAm 1974
McCulloch, George F 1855-1915 *NF*
McCulloch, John Herries *BioIn 3, CanNov,*
  OxCan
McCulloch, Thomas 1776?-1843 *BbtC, CanWr,*
  DcNAA, OxCan
McCulloh, James H 1781-1869 *BioIn 4*
McCullough, Collin 1929- *BioIn 9*
McCullough, Ernest 1867-1931 *DcNAA,*
  WhJnl 1928
McCullough, Esther Morgan d1957 *BioIn 4*
McCullough, J B *NF*
McCullough, John E *HisAmM XR*
McCullough, John Gerard 1917- *WhoAm 1974,*
  WhoE 1974
McCullough, John M *NF*
McCullough, William J 1902?-1954 *BioIn 3*
McCullum, Dorothy *OvPC*
McCully, Helen 1902?-1977 *ConAu 73*
McCune, Thomas C *HisAmM XR*
McCurdy, Fleming Blanchard 1875-1952 *BioIn 3*
McCurdy, Jack 1933- *ConAu 69*
McCurdy, Patrick Pierre 1928- *BioIn 10, OvPC,*
  WhoF&I 1974, WhoS&SW 1973
McCurdy, Wesley 1881- *WhJnl 1928*
McCurry, Myron 1895- *WhJnl 1928*
McCutcheon, Ben Frederick 1875-1934 *AmAu&B,*
  BioIn 2, DcNAA, IndAu 1816
McCutcheon, George Barr 1866-1928 *AmAu&B,*
  BiD&SB, CnDAL, DcAmA, DcBiA, DcLEL,
  DcNAA, EncMys, EvLB, IndAu 1816,
  LongC, OxAm, REn, REnAL, TwCA,
  TwCA Sup, WebBD, WhNAA
McCutcheon, John Tinney 1870-1949 *AmAu&B,*
  AmJnl, BioIn 1, BioIn 2, HisAmM XR,
  IndAu 1816, REnAL, WebBD
McCutcheon, John Tinney, Jr. 1917- *ConAu 69,*
  WhoAm 1974, WhoMW 1974
McDaniel, George W, Jr. 1894- *WhJnl 1928*
McDaniel, Raymond Lamar 1925- *WhoAm 1974*
McDaniel, Ted *NF*
McDaniels, Jim *NF*
McDermott, Edwin Francis 1896- *WhJnl Sup*
McDermott, Hugh Farrar 1833-1890 *DcAmA,*
  DcNAA, PoIre
McDermott, Jack Chipman 1905-1966 *BioIn 7*
McDermott, John Ralph 1921-1977 *ConAu 69*
McDermott, Michael J 1894-1955 *CurBio XR*
McDevitt, Hugh Vincent 1905- *WhJnl 1928*
McDonagh, Martin J B 1888- *WhJnl 1928*

McDonald, Daniel 1833-1916 *BioIn 2, DcNAA,*
  IndAu 1816
McDonald, Dick *NF*
McDonald, E H *HisAmM XR*
McDonald, E M *HisAmM XR*
McDonald, Erwin Lawrence 1907- *ConAu 23,*
  ConAu 73, WhoF&I 1974, WhoS&SW 1973
McDonald, Frances *WhJnl 1928*
McDonald, Frank 1941?- *BioIn 9*
McDonald, Iverach 1908- *Lor&LP, Who 1974*
McDonald, James 1896-1962 *BioIn 6*
McDonald, John Clark 1916- *USBiR 1974,*
  WhoAm 1974, WhoGov 1972, WhoWor 1974
McDonald, John W *NF*
McDonald, Lee R 1887- *WhJnl 1928*
McDonald, Lucile Saunders 1898- *AuBYP,*
  ConAu 3R, ForWC 1970, SmATA 10,
  WhoAmW 1974, WhoPNW
McDonald, Paula 1939?- *AuNews 1*
McDonald, Roy 1901- *WhoAm 1974,*
  WhoS&SW 1973
McDonald, W N *HisAmM XR*
McDonnall, J P *HisAmM XR*
McDonnell, John M 1866- *WhJnl 1928*
McDonough, Frank Wheatley 1905-1950 *BioIn 2,*
  HisAmM XR
McDougal, Edward F *OvPC*
McDougal, Herbert F 1876- *WhJnl 1928*
McDougal, Violet 1897- *WhJnl 1928*
McDougall, Walter *AmJnl*
McDougall, William Henry, Jr. 1909- *BioIn 2,*
  BioIn 3, CathA 1952, RpN
McDowall, John R *HisAmM XR*
McDowell, Albert *HisAmM XR*
McDowell, Anne Elizabeth 1826-1901
  HisAmM XR
McDowell, Bart 1923- *ConAu 25*
McDowell, Charles, Jr. 1926- *ConAu 2R*
McDowell, Edwin Stewart 1935- *ConAu 11R,*
  WhoAm 1974, WrDr 1976
McDowell, Franklin Davey 1888-1965 *CanNov,*
  CanWr, DcLEL, OxCan
McDowell, Jack Sherman 1914- *WhoAm 1974*
McDowell, John Ralph 1902-1957 *BioIn 4*
McDowell, Margaret Meyers 1895-1955 *BioIn 4*
McDowell, Rachel Kollock 1880-1949 *BioIn 1,*
  BioIn 2
McDowell, Samuel W 1882- *WhJnl 1928*
McDowell, Ted Gaylor 1902- *WhJnl 1928*
McEachin, Hec A *HisAmM XR*
McElhattan, Dean *NF*
McElheny, Victor K *RpN*
McElhone, James F *WhJnl 1928*
McElrath, Thomas 1807-1888 *AmJnl, DcNAA,*
  HisAmM XR, NatCAB 3
McElroy, George H 1902- *WhJnl 1928*
McElroy, John 1846-1929 *AmAu&B, DcNAA,*
  HisAmM XR, OhA&B
McElroy, William Henry 1838-1918 *DcAmA,*
  DcNAA
McElwain, Alan *NF*
McEnerny, Harry 1860-1941 *NatCAB 31*
McEvoy, Arthur E 1886?- *BioIn 4*
McEvoy, Bernard 1842-1932 *DcNAA, WhNAA*
McEvoy, Dennis 1918- *ConAu 73, OvPC*
McEvoy, George E *HisAmM XR*
McEvoy, Joseph Patrick 1895-1958 *AmAu&B,*
  HisAmM XR, REnAL, WebBD
McEwen, Arthur *AmJnl, HisAmM XR*
McFadden, James Patrick 1930- *WhoAm 1974*
McFarland, Hays 1890- *WhJnl 1928*
McFarland, Hood *NF*
McFarland, John Horace *HisAmM XR*
McFarland, John Thomas 1851-1913 *DcNAA,*

HisAmM XR, IndAu 1917
McFarland, Kermit 1905-1972 *BioIn 9,*
WhJnl 1928
McFarland, Wilma *AuBYP, BioIn 8*
McFeatters, Ann Carey *NF*
McFeatters, Dale *NF*
McFeely, Otto *BioIn 1*
McGaan, Dianne *NF*
McGaffin, William 1910- *ConAu 25,*
WhoAm 1974, WhoS&SW 1973
McGann, George T *OvPC*
McGannon, Donald Henry 1920- *CurBio XR,*
IntMPA 1975, IntWW 1976, WhoAm 1974,
WhoE 1974, WhoF&I 1974
McGarry, Joseph Martin 1917- *OvPC,*
WhoAm 1974, WhoPubR 1972
McGarry, William R 1872-1942 *NatCAB 39*
McGarvy, Carol *NF*
McGaughey, William Howard Taft 1912-
IndAu 1917, OvPC, WhoAm 1974,
WhoPubR 1972
McGaw, Bill 1914?- *BioIn 7*
McGeachy, J Burns 1899-1966 *BioIn 7,*
WhJnl 1928
McGeary, William *NF*
McGee, Frank 1921-1974 *BioIn 6, BioIn 7,*
BioIn 10, CelR 1973, CurBio XR, ForP,
NewYTBS 5, WhoAm 1974
McGee, Thomas D'Arcy 1825-1868 *BbtC,*
BrAu 19, CanWr, DcNAA, HisAmM XR,
NewC, OxCan, PoIre, REn, REnAL,
WebBD
McGeehan, William O'Connell 1879-1933 *AmJnl,*
DcAmB S1
McGettigan, E J *WhJnl 1928*
McGhee, Zach 1881- *BiDSA*
McGibbeny, Daniel J *NF*
McGiffert, Robert C 1922- *ConAu 49*
McGiffin, Don 1889- *WhJnl 1928*
McGiffin, William Junkin 1893- *BioIn 2*
McGill, Angus *WrDr 1976*
McGill, Anna Blanche 1874- *BiDSA*
McGill, Harold A 1876?-1952 *BioIn 3, BioIn 5*
McGill, Ralph Emerson 1898-1969 *AmJnl,*
BioIn 1, BioIn 2, BioIn 5, BioIn 8, BioIn 9,
BioIn 10, ConAu 7R, ConAu 25,
CurBio XR
McGilligan, Patrick Michael 1951- *ConAu 65*
McGillivray, Don *NF*
McGilvray, Robert D *NF*
McGinley, Conde J 1890?-1963 *BioIn 6*
McGinley, Phyllis 1905-1978 *AmAu&B, Au&Wr,*
AuBYP, CelR 1973, CnE&AP, CnMWL,
ConAu 9, ConP 1970, ConP 1975,
CurBio XR, EvLB, IntWW 1974, JBA 1951,
LongC, ModAL, OxAm, Pen Am, RAdv 1,
REn, REnAL, SmATA 2, TwCA Sup,
TwCW, WhoAm 1974, WhoAmW 1974,
WhoTwCL, WhoWor 1974, WrDr 1976
McGinnis, Arthur Joseph 1911- *WhoAdv 1972,*
WhoAm 1974
McGinnis, John Hathaway 1883- *AmAu&B,*
TexWr, WhNAA
McGinnis, Sonia *NF*
McGinnis, Thomas Charles 1925- *ConAu 65,*
WhoAm 1974, WhoE 1974
McGinniss, Joe 1942- *AmAu&B, AuNews 2,*
ConAu 25, WrDr 1976
McGinty, Brian *NF*
McGinty, J Roy 1887?- *BioIn 1*
McGivern, Maureen Daly 1921- *ConAu 11R*
McGivern, Maureen Daly *see also* Daly, Maureen
McGlachlin, Edward 1840-1931 *BioIn 5*
McGlynn, Edward *HisAmM XR*

McGlynn, P S 1850- *WhJnl 1928*
McGoff, John *NF*
McGovern, Bob *NF*
McGovern, Chauncey Montgomery *HisAmM XR*
McGovern, James Lawrence 1869-1952 *BioIn 2*
McGovern, John 1850-1917 *AmAu&B, BioIn 2,*
DcAmA, DcAmB 12, DcNAA,
HisAmM XR, IndAu 1816, PoIre
McGovern, Joseph James 1925- *WhoAm 1974*
McGovern, Mary *NF*
McGovern, Michael R 1940?- *NF*
McGovern, William P d1977 *NF*
McGowan, John P *HisAmM XR*
McGowen, Roscoe Emmett 1879?-1966 *BioIn 7*
McGrady, Mike 1933- *ConAu 49, SmATA 6*
McGrady, Patrick M, Jr. 1932- *ConAu 29*
McGrane, Bert *NF*
McGrath, Alice *BioIn 7*
McGrath, C A 1892- *WhJnl 1928*
McGrath, John J *NF*
McGrath, Mary *NF*
McGrath, William C *NF*
McGraw, James H 1860-1948 *NF*
McGraw, James H, Jr. 1893- *WhJnl 1928*
McGreevey, William *NF*
McGregor, Craig 1933- *Au&Wr, ConAu 23R,*
SmATA 8
McGregor, Donald Anderson 1879- *WhJnl 1928*
McGregor, Hugh *HisAmM XR*
McGrory, Mary 1918- *AuNews 2, BioIn 5,*
BioIn 8, ForP, NewMr, WhoAmW 1974
McGuffin, J B *NF*
McGuinnes, James Kevin 1894-1950 *BioIn 2*
McGuinness, James Pearse 1919?- *BioIn 3*
McGuire, Frances *AuBYP, BioIn 7*
McGuire, Frank G *NF*
McGuire, J A *HisAmM XR*
McGuire, James P 1903?-1955 *BioIn 3*
McGuire, James Richard 1917- *WhoAm 1974*
McGuire, Mark *NF*
McGuire, Paul R 1893- *WhJnl 1928*
McGuire, R G 1903- *WhJnl 1928*
McGuire, Walter P 1881?-1951 *BioIn 2*
McGurn, Barrett 1914- *BioIn 1, BioIn 7,*
ConAu 4R, CurBio XR, OvPC,
WhoAm 1974, WhoE 1974,
WhoS&SW 1973, WrDr 1976
McHale, William Francis 1920-1962 *BioIn 6*
McHam, David 1933- *ConAu 73*
McHarry, Charles 1914?-1976 *BioIn 5*
McHenry, James 1785-1845 *AmAu, AmAu&B,*
BbD, BiD&SB, DcAmA, DcLEL, DcNAA,
NewC, OxAm, PoIre, REnAL
McHolland, Joseph D 1898- *WhJnl 1928*
McHose, Harry William 1904- *WhJnl 1928*
McHugh, Eugene J 1893-1962 *BioIn 6,*
WhJnl 1928
McHugh, Raymond Joseph 1924- *OvPC,*
WhoS&SW 1973
McHugh, Robert Paul 1917- *WhoAm 1974*
McIlhany, Sterling Fisher 1930- *BioIn 8,*
WhoAm 1974, WhoE 1974, WhoF&I 1974,
WhoWor 1974
McIlquham, John 1947- *NF*
McIlrath, W F *NF*
McIlvaine, Jane 1919- *AuBYP, BioIn 7,*
ConAu XR
McIlwain, William Franklin, Jr. 1925- *ConAu 1R,*
WhoAm 1974
McIlwain, William H *RpN*
McInerney, John E 1896?-1951 *BioIn 2*
McInerny, Timothy Anthony 1902-1965 *BioIn 7*
McInnes, Neil 1924- *NF*
McIntosh, Alexander Angus 1874-1950 *BioIn 2*

McIntosh, Charles Jarvis 1871- *WhJnl 1928*
McIntosh, J I 1858- *WhJnl 1928*
McIntosh, John *HisAmM XR*
McIntosh, John 1930- *ConAu 21*
McIntosh, Ned *NF*
McIntyre, Bruce Herbert 1930- *WhoAm 1974*
McIntyre, Dave *NF*
McIntyre, E R 1888- *WhJnl 1928*
McIntyre, Marvin Hunter 1878-1943 *BioIn 1,*
CurBio XR
McIntyre, Oscar Odd 1884-1938 *AmAu&B,*
AmJnl, BioIn 2, BioIn 4, DcAmB S2,
DcNAA, NatCAB 36, OhA&B, REnAL,
TwCA, WebBD, WhNAA
McIntyre, Robert B *NF*
McIntyre, William 1916- *ConAu 37*
McKalip, Paul *NF*
McKay, Alexander 1886-1953 *NatCAB 42*
McKay, Charlotte E *HisAmM XR*
McKay, Claude 1890-1948 *AmAu&B, BlkAW,*
CasWL, CathA 1930, ConAmA, DcLEL,
DcNAA, OxAm, REn, REnAL, TwCA,
TwCA Sup, WebBD, WebE&AL
McKay, Claude Eric Fergusson 1878- *BioIn 6*
McKay, David 1860-1918 *NatCAB 42*
McKay, Dorothy 1903?-1974 *BioIn 10*
McKay, Floyd John 1936?- *NF*
McKay, James *HisAmM XR*
McKay, James T *HisAmM XR*
McKay, Jim 1921- *CurBio XR, WhoAm 1974*
McKay, John Angus 1865- *HisAmM XR,*
WhJnl 1928
McKay, Robert *HisAmM XR*
McKay, William *NF*
McKay, Winsor 1869-1934 *AmJnl*
McKeag, Ernest Lionel 1896- *Au&Wr,*
ConAu P-1
McKean, Douglas Franklin 1911- *WhoAm 1974*
McKean, William V 1820-1903 *AmJnl,*
NatCAB 8
McKee, Alexander E *WhJnl 1928*
McKee, Mary Carolyn 1900- *WhJnl Sup*
McKee, Richard A *NF*
McKee, Thomas H *HisAmM XR*
McKeel, Sam Stewart 1926- *WhoAm 1974*
McKeen, Joseph 1914- *WhoAm 1974*
McKeever, John Herbert *WhJnl 1928*
McKeithan, Daniel M *LiJA*
McKelvey, John Jay 1863-1947 *AmLY, BioIn 1,*
DcNAA, WhNAA
McKelvie, Bruce Alistair 1889-1960 *OxCan,*
WhNAA
McKelvie, Samuel Roy 1881-1956 *BioIn 3,*
BioIn 4, BioIn 9, WhJnl 1928
McKelway, Benjamin Mosby 1895-1976 *BioIn 1,*
BioIn 2, BioIn 4, BioIn 5, ConAu 69,
CurBio XR, IntWW 1976, WhoAm 1974,
WhoGov 1972
McKelway, John M *NF*
McKelway, St. Clair 1845-1915 *AmJnl,*
NatCAB 17, WebBD
McKelway, St. Clair 1905- *AmAu&B, ConAu 5,*
WhoAm 1974, WhoWor 1974
McKenna, Edward Lawrence 1893?-1953 *BioIn 3*
McKenna, Francis Eugene 1921- *BiDrLUS,*
CurBio XR
McKenna, Robert E 1915- *WhoAm 1974*
McKenney, Robert Lee 1865-1947 *NF*
McKenney, Ruth 1911-1972 *AmAu&B,*
ConAu 37, CurBio XR, LongC,
NewYTBE 3, OhA&B, OxAm, REn,
REnAL, TwCA, TwCA Sup, WebBD
McKenzie 1871- *NF*
McKenzie, Andrew D 1882?-1953 *BioIn 3*

McKenzie, D A 1871- *WhJnl 1928*
McKenzie, Edward Warren 1898- *WhJnl 1928*
McKenzie, Vernon 1887-1963 *WhNAA*
McKeogh, Arthur 1890-1937 *HisAmM XR*
McKeon, Almira Guild *HisAmM XR*
McKeon, John Edgar 1892- *WhJnl 1928*
McKeough, Richard Blair 1927- *WhoAm 1974,*
WhoE 1974, WhoF&I 1974
McKeown, Lorraine L *NF*
McKeown, William Taylor 1921- *OvPC,*
WhoAm 1974
McKernan, Maureen 1894- *WhJnl 1928*
McKerrow, Ronald Brunlees 1872-1940 *DcLEL,*
LongC, NewC, OxEng, REn, WebBD
McKibbin, Brian G *OvPC*
McKie, Ronald 1909- *ConAu 11R*
McKiernan, John F 1897?-1954 *BioIn 3*
McKiernan, Thomas P 1894- *WhJnl 1928*
McKillop, David Holmes 1916- *WhoAm 1974,*
WhoGov 1972
McKim, James Miller 1810-1874 *HisAmM XR*
McKinley, Carlyle 1847-1904 *AmAu, AmAu&B,*
BiDSA, DcAmB 12, DcNAA
McKinley, Douglas Webster 1917- *WhoAm 1974*
McKinney, Donald Lee 1923- *ConAu 73,*
WhoAm 1974
McKinney, Emma 1872?- *BioIn 3*
McKinney, Howard 1890- *BioIn 1*
McKinney, J P 1847- *WhJnl 1928*
McKinney, James H *NF*
McKinney, Joan *NF*
McKinney, Robert Moody 1910- *BioIn 4, BioIn 5,*
CurBio XR, IntWW 1974, WhoAm 1974
McKinney, Thomas L *AmJnl*
McKinnon, Clinton Dotson 1906- *BioIn 1,*
WhoAm 1974, WhoAmP 1973
McKinnon, Hector Brown 1890- *CanWW 1972,*
Who 1974
McKinsey, Folger 1866-1950 *BiDSA, BioIn 4*
McKinstry, Edwin L 1877- *WhJnl 1928*
McKinven, Mary Jane *NF*
McKissick, James Rion 1884-1944 *BioIn 1,*
WhJnl 1928
McKnight, Charles 1826-1881 *AmAu&B,*
DcAmA, DcNAA, HisAmM XR,
NatCAB 22
McKnight, Colbert Augustus 1916- *BlkC,*
WhoAm 1974, WhoF&I 1974,
WhoS&SW 1973
McKnight, Felix R *NF*
McKnight, Gerald 1919- *ConAu 15R*
McKnight, Pete *see* McKnight, Colbert Augustus
McKnight, Sheldon *NF*
McKone, John J 1890- *WhJnl 1928*
McLachlan, Donald *Lor&LP*
McLain, John Scudder 1853-1931 *DcNAA,*
OhA&B
McLaren, Fred *BioIn 10*
McLaughlin, Bill *NF*
McLaughlin, Edward F *NF*
McLaughlin, John J 1889?-1956 *BioIn 4*
McLaughlin, Kathleen *OvPC, WhoAm 1974,*
WhoAmW 1974
McLaughlin, Marguerite 1882- *WhJnl 1928*
McLaughlin, Marya *BioIn 7*
McLaughlin, Mignon *ConAu 11R*
McLaughlin, Robert 1908-1973 *AmAu&B,*
AmNov, ConAu 3R, ConAu 45
McLaughlin, Russell J 1894-1975 *WhJnl 1928*
McLaughlin, William G *HisAmM XR*
McLaughlin, William J d1970 *BioIn 9*
McLean, Andrew 1848- *NatCAB 13*
McLean, Charles 1892?-1948 *BioIn 1*
McLean, David J 1879?-1950 *BioIn 2*

McLean, Edward Beale 1886-1941 *AmJnl,*
  DcAmB S3
McLean, Emily Pratt *HisAmM XR*
McLean, Frank *LiJA*
McLean, George Agnew *HisAmM XR*
McLean, Jack *NF*
McLean, John Emery 1865- *HisAmM XR,*
  WhNAA
McLean, John R 1849-1916 *AmJnl, NatCAB 1*
McLean, Robert 1891- *AmJnl, BioIn 2, BioIn 5,*
  BioIn 9, CurBio XR, IntWW 1974, WebBD,
  WhoE 1974, WhoWor 1974
McLean, S B Wiley *AmJnl*
McLean, Washington *AmJnl*
McLean, William L, III *NF*
McLean, William L, Jr. 1895-1954 *AmJnl,*
  BioIn 1, BioIn 3
McLean, William Lippard 1852-1931 *AmJnl,*
  WebBD
McLellan, Archibald *NF*
McLellan, Diana *NF*
McLemore, Henry 1907?-1968 *BioIn 2, BioIn 3,*
  BioIn 8
McLendon, Gordon Barton 1921- *WhoAm 1974,*
  WhoE 1974, WhoS&SW 1973
McLendon, Sarah 1910?- *ConAu 73*
McLendon, Will Loving 1925- *ConAu 9,*
  DrAS 74F
McLendon, Winzola *NF*
McLennan, John S 1863- *WhJnl 1928*
McLeod, Donald E *NF*
McLeod, John Freeland 1917- *ConAu 69*
McLeod, Robert Emmett *NF*
McLinn, George 1884?-1953 *BioIn 3*
McLintock, Peter 1916- *WhoAm 1974*
McLoughlin, Ellen Veronica *WhoAm 1974,*
  WhoAmW 1974
McLucas, Carl Daniel 1898- *WhJnl 1928*
McLuhan, Herbert Marshall 1911- *CasWL,*
  DrAS 74E, IntWW 1974, Pen Am,
  WhoAm 1974, WhoWor 1974
McLuhan, Herbert Marshall *see also* McLuhan,
  Marshall
McLuhan, Marshall 1911- *AmAu&B,*
  CanWW 1972, CanWr, CelR 1973,
  ConAu 9, CurBio XR, NewC, OxCan,
  OxCan Sup, WebBD, Who 1974, WhoTwCL,
  WorAu, WrDr 1976
McLuhan, Marshall *see also* McLuhan, Herbert
  Marshall
McLuitock, F S *HisAmM XR*
McMahon, Bryan T 1950- *ConAu 45,*
  DrAP 1975
McMahon, Francis Elmer 1906- *WhoAm 1974*
McMahon, Helen *LiJA*
McMahon, Louis F 1894- *WhJnl Sup*
McMahon, Robert A 1900- *WhJnl 1928*
McMann, Renville Hupfel, Jr. 1927- *WhoAm 1974*
McManus, George 1884-1954 *AmJnl, BioIn 2,*
  BioIn 3, BioIn 6, DcAmB S5, NatCAB 45,
  REnAL, WebBD
McManus, Irene *NF*
McManus, James T *AmRP*
McManus, Jason *NF*
McManus, Jim *NF*
McManus, John T 1904-1961 *BioIn 6*
McManus, Marjorie 1950- *ConAu 73*
McManus, R C *NF*
McMaster, Frank d1972 *NF*
McMaster, James Alphonsus 1820-1886 *AmJnl,*
  BioIn 2, DcAmB 12, HisAmM XR
McMaster, Robert H 1877- *WhJnl 1928*
McMasters, William H 1873?-1968 *BioIn 8*
McMichael, Clayton 1844-1906 *NatCAB 2*

McMichael, Morton 1807-1879 *AmAu&B, AmJnl,*
  HisAmM XR, NatCAB 2, REnAL
McMichael, Ross D 1902- *WhJnl 1928*
McMillan, Emilie *HisAmM XR*
McMillan, George Scholefield 1895?-1968 *BioIn 8*
McMillan, H C *HisAmM XR*
McMillen, Robert D 1916- *BioIn 3*
McMillen, Wheeler 1893- *AmAu&B, AuBYP,*
  BioIn 2, BioIn 7, ConAu 33, HisAmM XR,
  OhA&B, WhNAA, WhoAm 1974,
  WhoS&SW 1973
McMillin, Miles James 1913- *WhoAm 1974*
McMillion, Bonner 1921- *BioIn 3, ConAu 15R*
McMorrow, Fred 1925- *ConAu 57*
McMullan, John *InvJ*
McMullen, Larry *NF*
McMullen, Roy 1911- *ConAu 25*
McMullin, Georges *WhJnl 1928*
McMunn, Earl William 1910- *WhoAm 1974*
McMurchy, Wilton G 1872-1923 *NatCAB 6*
McMurray, J Donald 1911-1969 *BioIn 8*
McMurray, J M 1860- *WhJnl 1928*
McMurray, Wayne Dennett 1897-1974 *BioIn 10,*
  WhoE 1974
McMurtrie, Francis Edwin 1884-1949 *BioIn 1*
McMurtry, Lewis S *HisAmM XR*
McNair, Sylvia 1924- *NF*
McNair, W J *NF*
McNally, Augustin 1875- *WhJnl 1928*
McNally, Joel *NF*
McNamara, Bob *NF*
McNamara, John S 1908?-1977 *ConAu 69*
McNamee, Graham 1888-1942 *BioIn 7,*
  CurBio XR
McNamee, M William 1887- *WhJnl 1928*
McNamee, Theodore *HisAmM XR*
McNaughton, F F 1890- *WhJnl 1928*
McNaughton, Frank 1906?- *BioIn 2*
McNeal, Thomas Allen 1853-1942 *AmAu&B,*
  DcNAA, OhA&B, WhJnl 1928
McNear, Bette Hitchcock 1924?- *ForWC 1970,*
  WhoAmW 1974
McNeary, William F B 1891- *WhJnl 1928*
McNeely, David M 1940?- *NF*
McNeil, Hector 1910-1955 *CurBio XR*
McNeil, J A *NF*
McNeil, Marshall 1904- *WhoAm 1974,*
  WhoS&SW 1973
McNeil, Neil Venable 1927- *RpN, WhoAm 1974*
McNeil, Robert S *NF*
McNeill, Charles James 1912- *WhoAm 1974,*
  WhoE 1974
McNeill, Donald J 1945?-1968 *BioIn 8*
McNeill, John Charles 1874-1907 *BiDSA, BioIn 1,*
  BioIn 3, BioIn 5, CnDAL, DcNAA
McNeill, Mary E 1926?-1967 *BioIn 8*
McNeill, Warren *NF*
McNeish, James 1931- *ConAu 69, WrDr 1976*
McNell, John Charles 1874-1907 *BioIn 4*
McNellis, Maggi 1917- *BioIn 1, BioIn 3,*
  BioIn 4, CurBio XR, IntMPA 1975
McNellis, Margaret *see* McNellis, Maggi
McNickle, R George 1922?-1972 *BioIn 9,*
  NewYTBE 3
McNierney, Michael *NF*
McNish, Charles Otis 1918- *WhoAm 1974*
McNitt, Virgil Venice 1881-1964 *BioIn 6,*
  WhJnl 1928
McNulty, Faith 1918- *ConAu 49, WrDr 1976*
McNulty, Henry Piper 1913- *OvPC,*
  WhoPubR 1972
McNulty, John 1895-1956 *BioIn 1, BioIn 2,*
  BioIn 4, OhA&B, REnAL
McNutt, John T *OvPC*

McNutt, William Slavens *HisAmM XR*
McPeak, Ival *HisAmM XR*
McPhail, James A, Jr. 1903- *WhJnl Sup*
McPhaul, John James 1904- *ConAu 9R*,
  WhoMW 1974
McPhee, John Charman 1903- *WhJnl 1928*
McPhee, Rodolph P 1868- *WhJnl 1928*
McPherson, Donald R *NF*
McPherson, Myra *NF*
McPherson, William Alexander 1933- *ConAu 69*,
  WhoAm 1974, WhoWor 1974
McPherson, William Lenhart 1865-1930 *DcNAA*,
  WhNAA
McQuade, DeRosset 1934?-1978 *NF*
McQuary, Joan Susan 1922- *WhoAm 1974*
McQueen, Silke *NF*
McQueen, Thomas 1803-1861 *BbtC*
McQuigg, Clancey *NF*
McQuilkin, Albert H *HisAmM XR*
McQuillan, Brice *NF*
McQuillan, Laurence J *NF*
McRae, Dee *NF*
McRae, Hamish 1943- *ConAu 57*
McRae, Milton Alexander 1858-1930 *AmAu&B*,
  AmJnl, DcNAA, NatCAB 16, OhA&B,
  WebBD, WhJnl 1928
McRee, James F 1911?-1969 *BioIn 8*
McReynolds, Martin *NF, OvPC*
McRosky, Mrs. Racine 1873-1915 *DcNAA*
McSheehy, Henry James 1852-1911 *BioIn 2*,
  IndAu 1816
McSherry, Elizabeth A *NF*
McSherry, William *NF*
McSkimming, Roy *NF*
McSpadden, Joseph Walker 1874-1960 *AmAu&B*,
  BioIn 5, REnAL
McSurely, Alexander d1953 *BioIn 3*
McSwigan, Marie 1907-1962 *AuBYP, BkC 6*,
  ConAu 73, CurBio XR, MorJA, WhNAA
McTaggart, Fred 1939- *ConAu 65*
McTavish, Newton McFaul 1877-1941 *DcNAA*
McThomas, Robert G, Jr. *NF*
McTigue, John D *OvPC*
McVay, Rosanne 1916- *OvPC*
McVeigh, Anthony P *NF*
McVeigh, Linda 1946?- *BioIn 7*
McVeigh, Thomas M 1868-1935 *NatCAB 26*
McVickar, Harry W *HisAmM XR*
McVicker, James Hubert *HisAmM XR*
McWain, Andrew Jackson 1860-1949 *BioIn 1*,
  BioIn 2, WhJnl 1928
McWain, Donald Merton 1899- *WhJnl 1928*
McWhirter, A Ross 1925-1975 *ConAu 19R*
McWhirter, Bill *NF*
McWhirter, Glenna *NF*
McWhirter, William *NF*
McWhirter, William Allan 1888?-1955 *BioIn 3*
McWilliams, Al *NF*
McWilliams, Carey 1905- *AmAu&B, AmRP*,
  BioIn 3, BioIn 8, CelR 1973, ConAu 45,
  CurBio XR, LiJA, NewMr, OxAm, REnAL,
  TwCA Sup, WhoAm 1974, WhoWor 1974
McWilliams, La-Nora 1943- *BioIn 8*
McWilliams, Marie Joan 1925- *WhoAm 1974*
Meacham, William Shands 1900- *WhoAm 1974*
Mead, Darius *HisAmM XR*
Mead, Edwin Doak 1849-1937 *Alli Sup*,
  AmAu&B, BiD&SB, BioIn 4, DcAmA,
  DcAmB S2, DcNAA, HisAmM XR, LiJA,
  WhNAA
Mead, Everett K 1894- *WhJnl 1928*
Mead, Frederic Malcolm 1915- *WhoAm 1974*
Mead, Garth L *RpN*
Mead, William B *NF*

Meade, Walter *NF*
Meador, Elihu Newton 1878-1959 *BioIn 6*,
  NatCAB 44
Meador, J E D *NF*
Meagher, Ed *InvJ*
Meagher, Philip 1898?-1971 *BioIn 9*
Mealey, Michael *NF*
Meaney, Donald *NF*
Means, John N *NF*
Means, Marianne Hansen 1934- *BioIn 6*,
  ConAu 11R, WhoAm 1974, WhoAmW 1974,
  WhoS&SW 1973
Meany, Edmond Stephen 1862-1935 *DcAmB S1*,
  DcNAA
Meany, Thomas William 1903-1964 *BioIn 7*
Mears, F C *NF*
Mears, Walter R 1935- *NF*
Mears, William Hodgson 1900- *WhJnl 1928*
Mearson, Lyon 1888-1966 *AmAu&B, WhNAA*,
  WhJnl 1928
Mebane, Daniel *HisAmM XR*
Mebane, John Harrison 1909- *Au&Wr*,
  ConAu 15R, WhoAm 1974, WrDr 1976
Mechanicus, Philip 1889-1944 *BioIn 8*
Mechem, Charles Stanley, Jr. 1930- *WhoAm 1974*,
  WhoF&I 1974
Mechlin, Leila 1874-1949 *WhNAA*
Mechlin, Sheldon M *OvPC*
Meckel, Frank A 1894- *WhJnl 1928*
Mecker, Louis 1894- *WhJnl 1928*
Mecklin, John M 1918-1971 *BioIn 9, ConAu 33*,
  NewYTBE 2
Mecom, Benjamin 1732-1777? *AmAu&B, AmJnl*,
  HisAmM XR
Meda, Luigi *BioIn 1*
Medary, Samuel 1801-1864 *AmJnl*
Medbery, James Knowles 1838-1873 *Alli Sup*,
  DcNAA
Medbury, John P 1894- *WhJnl 1928*
Medes, W J *HisAmM XR*
Medill, Joseph 1823-1899 *AmAu&B, AmJnl*,
  BioIn 1, BioIn 2, DcAmB 12, ForP, OxAm,
  WebBD
Medley, Kenneth W *NF*
Medley, Mary Louise 1907- *BioIn 8*
Medwick, Lucille 1922?-1971 *BioIn 9*,
  NewYTBE 2
Mee, Arthur Henry 1875-1943 *BioIn 1, BioIn 5*,
  BioIn 8, DcLEL, EvLB, LongC, WebBD,
  WhoChL
Mee, Fiona *NF*
Meegan, John J 1891?-1953 *BioIn 3*
Meehan, Patrick J *HisAmM XR*
Meehan, Thomas 1826-1901 *Alli Sup, AmAu*,
  DcAmA, DcNAA, HisAmM XR
Meehan, Thomas Francis 1854-1942 *BioIn 5*,
  CurBio XR, DcNAA
Meek, Alexander Beaufort 1814-1865 *Alli, AmAu*,
  AmAu&B, BiD&SB, BiDSA, DcAmA,
  DcNAA, HisAmM XR, OxAm, REnAL
Meek, Loyal George 1918- *ConAu 73*
Meek, Phillip Joseph 1937- *WhoAm 1974*
Meek, Samuel Williams 1895- *WhoAm 1974*
Meek, Walter William 1935?- *NF*
Meek, William *NF*
Meeker, Claude 1861-1929 *NF*
Meeker, Nathan Cook 1817-1879 *Alli Sup*,
  AmAu&B, BioIn 4, DcAmA, DcAmB 12,
  DcNAA, OhA&B, OxAm, REnAL
Meeker, Ralph 1845-1921 *NatCAB 19*
Meeker, Robert J 1899- *WhJnl 1928*
Meekins, Lynn Roby 1862-1933 *BiDSA, DcAmA*,
  DcNAA
Meeks, James L 1877-1941 *NatCAB 31*

Meell, Edward Joseph 1936- WhoAm 1974
Meeman, Edward John 1889-1966 BioIn 7,
  BioIn 9, WhJnl 1928
Megali, S NF
Megargee, Louis N HisAmM XR
Megged, Aharon 1920- CasWL, ConAu 49,
  WhoWorJ 1972, WorAu, WrDr 1976
Meggy, Percy AmJnl
Meginnis, John Franklin 1827-1899 DcNAA,
  NatCAB 10
Mehan, Joseph A OvPC
Mehl, Ernest BioIn 4
Mehle, Aileen 1919- BioIn 6, BioIn 7, BioIn 8,
  BioIn 9, BioIn 10, CelR 1973
Mehnert, Klaus 1906- ConAu 1, IntWW 1976,
  WhoWor 1974, WrDr 1976
Mehrtens, Ruth BioIn 3
Mehta, Ved Parkash 1934- Au&Wr, ConAu 1R,
  CurBio XR, Who 1974, WhoWor 1974,
  WorAu, WrDr 1976
Meibert, Virgil Elmer 1934- WhoAm 1974
Meier, Gerhard J 1927- WhoAm 1974
Meier, Larry AmJnl
Meigs, Josiah 1757-1822 AmAu&B, CyAL 1
Meigs, Merrill C 1883-1968 BioIn 8
Meily, Clarence AmRP
Mein, John AmAu&B, AmJnl, REnAL
Meinholtz, Fred E NF
Meisels, Andrew 1933- OvPC, WhoWorJ 1972
Meiser, Edward A 1865-1951 BioIn 4,
  NatCAB 40
Meisler, Stanley 1931- ConAu 73, WhoAm 1974
Mejanel, M FamWC
Mekas, Jonas 1922- BioIn 7, BioIn 9, BioIn 10
Mekeel, Charles Haviland HisAmM XR
Melady, John F 1903?-1965 BioIn 7
Melancon, Claude BioIn 4, OxCan Sup
Melas, Evi 1930- ConAu 65
Melcher, Frederic Gershom 1879-1963 AmAu&B,
  CurBio XR, HisAmM XR, WhJnl 1928
Melhorn, Nathan Raymond 1871-1952 BioIn 2,
  OhA&B, WhNAA
Melhuish, Martin NF
Meline, James Florant 1811-1873 Alli Sup,
  AmAu&B, BiD&SB, DcAmA, DcNAA,
  HisAmM XR, OhA&B
Melk, Vivien Bernard 1895- BioIn 1
Mellen, George Alfred 1874- WhJnl 1928
Mellett, Donald Ring 1891-1926 AmJnl, BioIn 1
Mellett, Lowell 1884-1960 BioIn 5, CurBio XR,
  HisAmM XR
Mellinkoff, Abe NF
Melliss, David M HisAmM XR
Mellon, Mary d1946 BioIn 1
Mellor, William Bancroft 1906- ConAu 61
Mellors, John Parkin 1920- ConAu 65
Mellow, James Robert 1926- WhoAm 1974,
  WhoAmA 1973
Mellquist, Proctor 1915- HisAmM XR,
  WhoAm 1974
Melone, Harry R 1893- WhJnl 1928
Meloney, Marie Mattingly d1943 AmAu&B,
  HisAmM XR, WebBD
Meloney, Marie Mattingly see also Meloney, Mrs.
  William Brown
Meloney, Mrs. William Brown d1943 CurBio XR
Meloney, William Brown 1878-1925 AmAu&B,
  DcNAA, WebBD
Melton, Oliver Quimby, Jr. 1922-1977 WhJnl 1928,
  WhoS&SW 1973
Melton, Ona AmJnl
Melton, Rollan Doyle 1931- WhoAm 1974
Melton, Wightman Fletcher 1867-1944 AmAu&B,
  BiDSA, DcNAA, WhNAA, WhJnl 1928

Meltzer, Charles Henry 1853-1936 HisAmM XR
Meltzer, R 1945- BioIn 10
Meltzer, Robert d1941 AmRP
Menakhem, Boraisho 1888-1949 NF
Menamin, R S HisAmM XR
Mencher, Melvin 1927- ConAu 73, DrAS 74E,
  RpN
Mencke, Johann Burkhard 1674-1732 OxGer,
  WebBD
Mencke, Otto 1644-1707 WebBD
Mencken, Henry Louis 1880-1956 AmAu&B,
  AmLY, AmWr, AtlBL, BioIn 1, BioIn 2,
  BioIn 3, BioIn 4, BioIn 5, BioIn 6, BioIn 7,
  BioIn 8, BioIn 9, BioIn 10, CasWL,
  CnDAL, CnMWL, ConAmA, ConAmL,
  CyWA, DcLEL, EncAB, EncWL, EvLB,
  HisAmM XR, LiJA, LongC, ModAL,
  ModAL Sup, OxAm, OxEng, Pen Am,
  RAdv 1, REn, REnAL, TwCA, TwCA Sup,
  TwCW, WebBD, WebE&AL, WhNAA,
  WhJnl 1928, WhoTwCL
Mendell, Seth HisAmM XR
Mendelsohn, Robert NF
Mendelsohn, Rona NF
Mendelson, Mary Adelaide Jones 1917-
  BioNews 1974, InvJ, NewMr,
  WhoAmW 1974
Mendelssohn, Moses 1729-1786 BiD&SB, CasWL,
  DcEuL, EuAu, EvEuW, OxGer, REn,
  WebBD
Mendenhall, James William 1844-1892 DcAmA,
  DcNAA, HisAmM XR, OhA&B
Mendes, Catulle 1841?-1909 BbD, BiD&SB,
  CasWL, CIDMEL, EuAu, EvEuW, LongC,
  OxFr, Pen Eur, REn, WebBD
Mendes, Frederic DeSola 1850-1927 WebBD
Mendum, Josiah P HisAmM XR
Menees, Tim NF
Menendez Pidal, Ramon 1869-1968 CasWL,
  CIDMEL, DcSpL, EvEuW, REn, WebBD
Meneses, Enrique 1929- ConAu 25, OvPC
Meng, Lois Perry NF
Meng, Warren Douglas WhJnl 1928
Mengenhauser, Jane NF
Menke, Frank Grant 1885-1954 BioIn 1, BioIn 3,
  OhA&B
Menken, Jules 1900-1957 BioIn 4
Menkin, Peter NF
Menn, Thorpe 1912- WhoAm 1974
Menninger, Walt NF
Menon, Vatakke Kurupath Narayana 1911-
  IntWW 1976, WhoWor 1974
Menoni, Hector NF
Menpes, Mortimer 1859-1938 WebBD
Menzel, Wolfgang 1798-1873 BiD&SB, DcEuL,
  OxGer, WebBD
Menzies, George 1796?-1847 BbtC, BioIn 1
Menzies, Ian Stuart 1920- RpN, WhoAm 1974
Mera, Steven M NF
Merahn, Lawrence Wilburn 1909- WhoAm 1974
Meras, Phyllis 1931- ConAu 41
Mercelis, Lester 1891- WhJnl 1928
Mercer, Charles 1917- ConAu 1R,
  WhoAm 1974, WhoE 1974
Mercer, Hamilton d191-? BioIn 2, IndAu 1816
Mercer, James Sidney 1880-1945 BioIn 2,
  NatCAB 34
Mercer, Willis HisAmM XR
Mercier, A F NF
Mercier, Desire Joseph 1851-1926 WebBD
Mercur, William 1898?-1972 BioIn 9
Meredith, Edwin Thomas 1876-1928 DcAmB 12,
  HisAmM XR, WebBD

Meredith, Edwin Thomas, Jr.1906-1966 *HisAmM XR*
Meredith, George 1828-1909 *Alli, Alli Sup,*
  AtlBL, BbD, BiD&SB, BrAu 19, CasWL,
  CnE&AP, CrtT 3, CyWA, DcBiA, DcEnA,
  DcEnA Ap, DcEnL, DcEuL, DcLEL, EvLB,
  HisAmM XR, LongC, MouLC 4, NewC,
  OxEng, Pen Eng, RAdv 1, REn, WebBD,
  WebE&AL
Meredith, Gertrude *HisAmM XR*
Meredith, Hugh *AmJnl*
Meredith, Thomas 1795-1850 *BioIn 1,*
  HisAmM XR
Mergen, M F 1894- *WhJnl 1928*
Mergenthaler, Ottmar 1854-1899 *AmJnl, OxAm,*
  WebBD
Merguson, Walter *BlkC*
Merick, Wendell S *NF*
Merino, Adolfo G *NF*
Meritt, Benjamin Dean 1899- *DrAS 74H,*
  HisAmM XR, IntWW 1974, Who 1974,
  WhoAm 1974
Meriwether, Bowman S 1906- *WhJnl 1928*
Meriwether, Mrs. Hunter M *WhJnl 1928*
Meriwether, Walter Scott 1861?-1950 *BioIn 2*
Merkel, Andrew Doane 1884-1954 *BioIn 3*
Merkling, Frank 1924- *BioIn 10, WhoAm 1974,*
  WhoE 1974, WhoF&I 1974
Merlis, George 1940- *BioIn 9, ConAu 33*
Merrell, Jesse H 1938- *NF*
Merrell, Sarah Lawrence Perry 1883?-1966 *BioIn 7*
Merriam, Dan 1771-1823 *WebBD*
Merriam, Ebenezer 1777-1858 *WebBD*
Merriam, Edmund Franklin 1847-1930 *AmLY,*
  DcNAA, HisAmM XR, WhNAA
Merriam, Franklin A 1857- *NF*
Merriam, George 1773-1802 *WebBD*
Merriam, George Spring 1843-1914 *Alli Sup,*
  BiD&SB, DcAmA, DcNAA, HisAmM XR
Merrick, Frank B *NF*
Merrick, L H 1882- *WhJnl 1928*
Merrick, Lula *WhJnl 1928*
Merrifield, Richard F 1905?-1977 *NF*
Merrill, Albert J *HisAmM XR*
Merrill, Arch 1895?-1974 *BioIn 6, ConAu 49*
Merrill, Bradford *NF*
Merrill, Cedric V 1895- *WhJnl 1928*
Merrill, Charles Addison 1889?-1951 *BioIn 2*
Merrill, Daniel Roy 1889- *BioIn 2*
Merrill, Estelle M H *HisAmM XR*
Merrill, Jean Fairbanks 1923- *AuBYP, BioIn 3,*
  BioIn 4, BioIn 5, BioIn 7, BioIn 8, BioIn 9,
  BioIn 10, ConAu 1, ForWC 1970,
  SmATA 1, ThrBJA, WhoAmW 1974,
  WhoE 1974, WrDr 1976
Merrill, John C 1888?-1954 *BioIn 3*
Merrill, John Calhoun 1924- *ConAu 73,*
  DrAS 74E, ForP, WhoAm 1974
Merrill, John Douglas 1865-1940 *CurBio XR*
Merrill, Louis Taylor 1896-1960 *BioIn 5*
Merrill, Philip *WhoAm 1974*
Merrill, Richard *NF*
Merrill, Samuel 1855-1932 *Alli Sup, DcNAA*
Merrill, William Bradford 1861-1928 *DcNAA,*
  NatCAB 1
Merrill, William Henry d1907 *AmJnl*
Merriman, Ann L 1934- *NF*
Merriman, Franklin A 1857- *WhJnl 1928*
Merriman, Truman A *NF*
Merritt, Abraham 1884-1943 *AmAu&B, BioIn 7,*
  DcNAA, NatCAB 32, REnAL, WorAu
Merritt, Allan J *NF*
Merritt, Carroll B 1881- *WhJnl 1928*
Merritt, Jesse F 1889- *WhJnl 1928*

Merritt, Mabel Witte 1887- *WhJnl 1928*
Merritt, W Davis *NF*
Merry, Robert Ellsworth 1920- *WhoAm 1974*
Merryman, Plew Mildred 1892- *WhJnl 1928*
Merson, Ben *OvPC*
Merwin, David 1900- *AmJnl, WhJnl 1928*
Merwin, Frederic Eaton 1907- *WhoAm 1974*
Merwin, Henry Bannister *HisAmM XR*
Merwin, James Burtis *HisAmM XR*
Merwin, Samuel 1874-1936 *AmAu&B, AmLY,*
  DcAmA, DcNAA, EncMys, HisAmM XR,
  LongC, OxAm, REnAL, TwCA, WebBD,
  WhNAA
Merz, Charles 1893-1977 *AmAu&B, AmJnl,*
  ConAu 73, CurBio XR, HisAmM XR,
  IntWW 1976, OhA&B, TwCA, TwCA Sup,
  WhNAA, Who 1974, WhJnl 1928
Mesinger, Maxine *NF*
Meskil, Paul *NF*
Meskill, Robert 1918?-1970 *BioIn 8*
Mesonero Y Romanos, Ramon De 1803-1882
  BiD&SB, EuAu, WebBD
Mesplet, Fleury 1735-1794 *OxCan*
Mesquita, Julio, Sr. d1927 *ForP*
Mesquita Filho, Julio d1969 *ForP*
Messenger, Lillian 1843-1921 *DcNAA*
Messick, Dale 1906- *BioIn 5, BioIn 6,*
  CurBio XR, WhoAm 1974
Messick, Hank 1922- *ConAu XR, InvJ, NewMr*
Messick, Henry H 1922- *ConAu 45*
Messick, Henry H see also Messick, Hank
Messina, Marc Anthony *OvPC*
Metcalf, Clyde Webster 1895- *WhJnl 1928*
Metcalf, Elizabeth 1904- *BioIn 1*
Metcalf, Frederick Thomas 1921- *WhoAm 1974*
Metcalf, George Pierce 1890?-1957 *BioIn 4*
Metcalf, George R 1914- *ConAu 25*
Metcalf, Henry Harrison 1841-1932 *DcNAA,*
  HisAmM XR, NatCAB 22, WhNAA
Metcalf, James *HisAmM XR*
Metcalf, James H 1894- *WhJnl 1928*
Metcalf, Lorettus Sutton 1837- *HisAmM XR,*
  NatCAB 1
Metcalf, Nelson Case 1872- *WhJnl 1928*
Metcalf, Ralph 1861-1939 *NF*
Metcalf, Richard Lee 1861-1954 *NF*
Metcalf, Stephen Olney 1857-1950 *AmJnl,*
  BioIn 2, BioIn 4, NatCAB 41
Metcalfe, James J 1906- *CathA 1952*
Metcalfe, James Stetson 1858-1927 *AmAu&B,*
  DcNAA, HisAmM XR
Metcalfe, Kristina *NF*
Methvin, Eugene H 1934- *ConAu 29*
Metz, Clinton Edgar 1905?- *WhJnl 1928*
Metz, Robert H 1929- *ConAu 61*
Metz, Robert Roy 1929- *WhoAm 1974,*
  WhoE 1974
Metz, Robert T *OvPC*
Metz, Tim *NF*
Metzdorf, Robert Frederic 1912-1975 *BiDrLUS,*
  ConAu 57, WhoAm 1974
Metzelthin, Pearl Violette 1894-1948 *CurBio XR,*
  DcNAA
Metzer, Joseph F 1901?-1954 *BioIn 3*
Metzger, George 1939- *BioIn 10*
Metzger, Howell Peter 1931- *AmM&W 73P,*
  WhoWest 1974
Metzger, Ted *NF*
Metzger, Thomas Warren 1887-1949 *BioIn 3,*
  NatCAB 37
Metzke, Gretchen 1906- *WhJnl 1928*
Metzker, Isaac 1901- *ConAu 45, WhoWorJ 1972*
Metzler, Ken 1929- *ConAu 53*
Metzner, Monika M *NF*

Mewhinney, Hubert 1905?- *BioIn 2*
Meyer, A C *HisAmM XR*
Meyer, Agnes Elizabeth 1887-1970 *BioIn 1,
BioIn 2, BioIn 3, BioIn 9, ConAu 29,
CurBio XR, NewYTBE 1*
Meyer, Albert 1870- *WebBD*
Meyer, Alfred 1936?- *BioIn 9*
Meyer, Arthur 1844-1924 *WebBD*
Meyer, Arthur B 1916- *BioIn 3, WhoAm 1974*
Meyer, Ben Franklin 1903- *WhoAm 1974,
WhoS&SW 1973*
Meyer, Bernard *OvPC*
Meyer, Cord, Jr. 1920- *BioIn 1, BioIn 9,
CurBio XR, NewYTBE 4*
Meyer, Edith 1895- *BioIn 1, BioIn 10*
Meyer, Eric E 1892- *WhJnl 1928*
Meyer, Ernest Louis 1892-1952 *BioIn 2, BioIn 9,
WhNAA*
Meyer, Eugene 1875-1959 *AmJnl, BioIn 1,
BioIn 3, BioIn 5, CurBio XR*
Meyer, Eugene L *NewMr*
Meyer, Frank Straus 1909-1972 *AmAu&B,
ConAu 33, ConAu P-1, NewYTBE 3*
Meyer, Frederick A *NF*
Meyer, George Homer 1858-1926 *DcNAA*
Meyer, Gerald Justin 1940- *WhoMW 1974*
Meyer, Hans B 1901- *NF*
Meyer, Helen 1907- *WhoAm 1974,
WhoAmW 1974, WhoGov 1972*
Meyer, Henry Coddington 1844-1935 *DcNAA,
HisAmM XR*
Meyer, Henry Coddington, Jr. 1870- *WhNAA*
Meyer, Herbert Alton 1886-1950 *BioIn 2*
Meyer, John *NF*
Meyer, John Louis 1881- *WhJnl 1928*
Meyer, Karl Ernest 1928- *AmAu&B, ConAu 3R,
NewMr, WhoWor 1974*
Meyer, Larry L *NF*
Meyer, Lawrence R 1941- *ConAu 73*
Meyer, Leonard E 1887- *WhJnl 1928*
Meyer, Paul 1874- *WhJnl 1928*
Meyer, Philip Edward 1930- *AmM&W 73S,
ConAu 65, InvJ, WhoS&SW 1973*
Meyer, Pieter Johannes 1909- *IntWW 1976*
Meyer, Richard E *NF*
Meyer, Rose D *NF*
Meyer, Susan E 1940- *ConAu 45, WhoAm 1974*
Meyer, Sylvan Hugh 1921- *RpN, WhoAm 1974,
WhoS&SW 1973, WhoWor 1974*
Meyerhoff, A E 1895- *WhJnl 1928*
Meyers, Arthur J *NF*
Meyers, Augustus A *HisAmM XR*
Meyers, Edith 1895- *BioIn 8*
Meyers, Edward *NF*
Meyers, Georg Nelson 1915- *BioIn 1,
WhoAm 1974*
Meyers, Robert T *OvPC*
Meyerson, Ron *NF*
Meynell, Alice 1847-1922 *Alli Sup, BbD,
BiD&SB, CnE&AP, DcEnA, DcEnA Ap,
DcEuL, DcLEL, EvLB, HisAmM XR,
LongC, ModBL, NewC, Pen Eng, REn,
TwCA, TwCA Sup, WebBD*
Meynell, Wilfrid 1852-1948 *Alli Sup, BioIn 1,
BioIn 3, CathA 1930, DcLEL, EvLB,
LongC, NewC, WebBD*
Mezerik, A G *NF*
Miall, Edward 1809-1881 *Alli, Alli Sup, DcEnL,
WebBD*
Mich, Daniel Danforth 1905-1965 *BioIn 2,
BioIn 7, HisAmM XR*
Mich, Isabella Taves *OvPC*
Michael, Cassius K *WhJnl 1928*
Michael, Charles R 1876-1954 *BioIn 3*

Michaelis, Alfred *OvPC*
Michaelis, Aline 1885- *TexWr, WhNAA,
WhJnl 1928*
Michaelis, Anthony *BioIn 4*
Michaelis, Richard C 1839-1909 *DcNAA*
Michaelis, Sulamith S 1887?-1958 *BioIn 5*
Michaels, Audrey *OvPC*
Michaels, James Walker 1921- *WhoAm 1974*
Michaels, Ken *NF*
Michaels, Ruth Gruber *ConAu XR, OvPC*
Michaels, Ruth Gruber *see also* Gruber, Ruth
Michaels, Willard Arthur 1917- *WhoAm 1974,
WhoS&SW 1973*
Michaelson, Mike *NF*
Michaud, Joseph Francois 1767-1839 *BiD&SB,
OxFr, WebBD*
Michaud, Louis Gabriel 1773-1858 *WebBD*
Michel, George *AmRP*
Michel, John Leopold 1894- *WhJnl 1928*
Michelfelder, William 1912- *BioIn 3*
Micheli, Bruno 1894?-1954 *BioIn 3*
Michels, John *HisAmM XR*
Michels, Marcia *NF*
Michelson, Charles 1869?-1948 *BioIn 1, BioIn 2,
BioIn 3, CurBio XR, DcAmB S4, REnAL,
WhJnl 1928*
Michelson, Edward J 1915- *WhoAm 1974,
WhoS&SW 1973, WhoWorJ 1972*
Michelson, Gustav *HisAmM XR*
Michener, Charles *NF*
Michie, Allan Andrew 1915-1973 *AuBYP,
BioIn 8, BioIn 10, ConAu 45, CurBio XR,
NewYTBE 4*
Mickel, Ernest Preston 1910- *WhoAm 1974*
Mickel, Louis Blanchard 1888-1972 *BioIn 4,
BioIn 9, WhJnl 1928*
Mickelson, Paul R 1899-1958 *BioIn 5,
WhJnl 1928*
Mickelson, Walter K 1897- *WhJnl 1928*
Middlesworth, Mike *NF*
Middleton, Drew 1913- *AmAu&B, Au&Wr,
BioIn 1, CurBio XR, IntWW 1976, REnAL,
Who 1974, WhoAm 1974, WhoWor 1974*
Middleton, Edgar C *NF*
Middleton, Jesse Edgar 1872- *CanNov, OxCan,
WhNAA*
Middleton, Lamar 1901?-1969 *BioIn 8*
Middleton, Scudder 1888-1959 *BioIn 5*
Middleton, Thomas H 1926- *NF*
Midgley, John *ForP*
Midgley, Leslie 1915- *BioIn 8, WhoAm 1974*
Midgley, Wilson 1887- *BioIn 1*
Midr, Ludovic *ForP*
Midura, Edmund *NF*
Miernik, M B *NF*
Mifflin, J Houston *HisAmM XR*
Mighels, Henry Rust 1830-1879 *AmAu&B*
Migne, Jacques Paul 1800-1875 *CasWL, OxFr,
WebBD*
Mignet, Francois Auguste Marie 1796-1884
BiD&SB, OxFr, WebBD
Mihaesco, Eugene *NF*
Mihajlov, Mihajlo *ForP*
Mikita, Joseph Karl 1918- *WhoAm 1974,
WhoE 1974, WhoF&I 1974*
Mikkelsen, Henning Dahl 1915?- *BioIn 1*
Mikkelsen, Michael A 1865-1941 *NatCAB 30*
Mikos, Nick G *OvPC*
Mikutowicz, Sharon *NF*
Milam, Marin Scott *NF*
Milans, Henry Fetter 1861-1946 *BioIn 1, DcNAA*
Milbauer, Richard S *OvPC*
Miles, Carlton Wright 1884-1954 *AmAu&B,
BioIn 3, WhNAA*

Miles, Josephine 1902- *WhJnl 1928*
Miles, Lovick Pierce 1871-1953 *NF*
Miley, Norma E *OvPC*
Milford, Morton Marshall 1883- *WhJnl 1928*
Milholland, Inez *HisAmM XR*
Milian, Emilio *NF*
Milius, Peter L *NF*
Milks, Harold Keith 1908- *WhoAm 1974*
Mill, James 1773-1836 *Alli, BbD, BiD&SB,*
   BiDLA, BrAu 19, CasWL, DcEnA, DcEnL,
   DcEuL, DcLEL, EvLB, NewC, OxEng,
   Pen Eng, WebBD
Millar, George Reid 1910- *ConAu 73*
Millar, J Halket 1899- *ConAu 11R*
Millar, Jeffery Lynn 1942- *ConAu 69*
Millar, Robert Cameron 1900- *BioIn 5*
Millar, Ronald 1891?-1946 *BioIn 1*
Millard, Bailey 1859-1941 *AmAu&B, CurBio XR,*
   DcNAA, HisAmM XR, REnAL, WhNAA
Millard, Frank Bailey *see* Millard, Bailey
Millard, H *HisAmM XR*
Millard, Thomas Franklin Fairfax 1868-1942
   DcNAA
Millas Correa, Orlando 1918- *IntWW 1976*
Millau, Christian *BioIn 8*
Milldyke, William 1937- *NF*
Mille, Herve 1909- *IntWW 1976*
Mille, Pierre 1864-1941 *BioIn 1, CIDMEL, REn,*
   WebBD
Miller, A T 1895- *WhJnl 1928*
Miller, Alan Robert 1929- *ConAu 73*
Miller, Alexander Quintella 1874- *BioIn 4*
Miller, Alfred E d1920 *NF*
Miller, Allister Mitchell 1865-1951 *BioIn 2*
Miller, Andrew *HisAmM XR*
Miller, Ben *AmJnl*
Miller, Bertha E 1882-1969 *BioIn 3, BioIn 5,*
   BioIn 7, BioIn 8, BioIn 10
Miller, Boyd L *NF*
Miller, Carl Patterson, Sr. 1897- *WhoAm 1974,*
   WhoWor 1974
Miller, Catherine Lanham *NF*
Miller, Charles Grant 1866-1928 *DcNAA,*
   OhA&B
Miller, Charles Ransom 1849-1922 *AmJnl,*
   NatCAB 1, WebBD
Miller, Charles Roger Donohue 1899-1964 *BioIn 6*
Miller, Charles William Emil 1863-1934
   HisAmM XR, WhNAA
Miller, Christopher Blackburn 1885-1956 *BioIn 4*
Miller, Cincinnatus Heine 1841?-1913 *Alli Sup,*
   AmAu, AmAu&B, BbD, BiD&SB, CyAL 2,
   DcAmA, DcNAA, EvLB, HisAmM XR,
   IndAu 1816, MouLC 4, REnAL, WebBD
Miller, Cincinnatus Heine *see also* Miller, Joaquin
Miller, Claude Harris 1875-1950 *BioIn 2*
Miller, Daniel Clarence 1876- *WhJnl 1928*
Miller, David 1932?- *NF*
Miller, David A 1869-1958 *NatCAB 47*
Miller, David Aaron 1896?-1965 *BioIn 2, BioIn 4,*
   BioIn 7
Miller, David J *BioIn 8*
Miller, Donald D *BioIn 8*
Miller, Donald Peter 1906- *WhoAm 1974,*
   WhoE 1974
Miller, Douglass Wood 1895- *WhJnl 1928*
Miller, E E 1879- *WhJnl 1928*
Miller, Edgar H *OvPC*
Miller, Edgar H, Jr. *OvPC*
Miller, Edward 1760-1812 *Alli, CyAL 1,*
   HisAmM XR, WebBD
Miller, Edward Marion 1903- *RpN,*
   WhoAm 1974
Miller, Edwin *NF*

Miller, Elizabeth Duer *HisAmM XR*
Miller, Emily Clark Huntington 1833-1913
   Alli Sup, AmAu, AmAu&B, BbD, BiD&SB,
   DcAmA, DcNAA, HisAmM XR
Miller, Eugene 1925- *WhoAm 1974,*
   WhoF&I 1974, WhoMW 1974,
   WhoPubR 1972
Miller, Floyd 1892- *WhJnl 1928*
Miller, Floyd J 1886-1954 *BioIn 3, WhJnl 1928*
Miller, Francis Trevelyan 1877-1959 *AmAu&B,*
   AmLY, HisAmM XR
Miller, Frank *NF*
Miller, Frank A 1904- *WhJnl 1928*
Miller, Frank Harvey 1867-1945 *BioIn 2,*
   NatCAB 35, WhJnl 1928
Miller, Fred *NF*
Miller, Frederick 1904- *ConAu 25*
Miller, Frederick Alfred 1868-1954 *BioIn 3,*
   BioIn 6, NatCAB 44, WhJnl 1928
Miller, Gene Edward 1928- *InvJ, NewMr,*
   WhoAm 1974, WhoS&SW 1973
Miller, Geoff *NF*
Miller, George E 1863-1934 *WhJnl Sup,*
   WhJnl 1928
Miller, George LaF 1829-1920 *NatCAB 19*
Miller, George W 1873?-1950 *BioIn 2*
Miller, Gerald *WhJnl 1928*
Miller, Gerald 1927?-1970 *BioIn 8*
Miller, Harlan *HisAmM XR*
Miller, Harold Blaine 1903- *OvPC,*
   WhoAm 1974, WhoPubR 1972
Miller, Harriet Parks 1852- *WhJnl 1928*
Miller, Heinrich *AmJnl*
Miller, Helen Hill 1899- *Au&Wr, ConAu 11R,*
   ForWC 1970, WhoAm 1974,
   WhoAmW 1974, WhoS&SW 1973,
   WhoWor 1974, WrDr 1976
Miller, Hope Ridings 1909- *ConAu 25,*
   ForWC 1970, WhNAA, WhoAm 1974
Miller, Horace B *HisAmM XR*
Miller, Horatio H, Jr. 1896- *WhJnl 1928*
Miller, Howard *WhoAm 1974*
Miller, Hoyt 1883-1957 *BioIn 4*
Miller, Irma Ganz 1916- *NF*
Miller, J Bruen *HisAmM XR*
Miller, J J *HisAmM XR*
Miller, Jack C 1900- *WhJnl 1928*
Miller, James Elwood 1918- *WhoAm 1974*
Miller, James L 1897-1964 *BioIn 4, BioIn 7*
Miller, James Martin 1859-1939 *DcNAA*
Miller, Jay d1977 *NF*
Miller, Jeanne Irene 1915-1961 *BioIn 6*
Miller, Joaquin 1841?-1913 *Alli Sup, AmAu,*
   AmAu&B, BiD&SB, CasWL, CnDAL,
   CrtT 3, CyAL 2, DcAmA, DcEnA Ap,
   DcEnL, DcLEL, DcNAA, EvLB, LongC,
   OxAm, OxEng, Pen Am, REn, REnAL,
   Str&VC, WebBD
Miller, Joaquin *see also* Miller, Cincinnatus Heine
Miller, John 1781-1846 *NF*
Miller, John Anderson 1895-1964 *AmAu&B,*
   BioIn 6
Miller, John Duncan 1902-1977 *Who 1974*
Miller, John E *HisAmM XR*
Miller, John G *OhA&B*
Miller, John Godfrey 1870- *WhJnl 1928*
Miller, John Henry 1702-1782 *AmAu&B, CasWL,*
   NatCAB 24, REnAL
Miller, John Joseph James 1936?- *BioIn 4*
Miller, John Stephen 1942- *WhoAm 1974*
Miller, John W *HisAmM XR*
Miller, Joseph Dana 1864-1939 *AmAu&B,*
   DcNAA, HisAmM XR, WhNAA
Miller, Josiah 1828-1870 *NF*

Miller, Judith *NF*
Miller, Karl 1932?- *BioIn 8*
Miller, Katherine E *BioIn 8*
Miller, Kelton Bedell 1860-1941 *BioIn 1,*
   NatCAB 33
Miller, Kenneth *OvPC*
Miller, Kirk *NF*
Miller, Laura Haralson 1874- *WhJnl 1928*
Miller, Laurel *WhJnl 1928*
Miller, Lawrence K 1907- *BioIn 9*
Miller, Lee Graham 1902-1961 *IndAu 1917,*
   WhJnl 1928
Miller, Lewis *HisAmM XR*
Miller, Lischen M *HisAmM XR*
Miller, Lois Mattox *WhoAm 1974,*
   WhoAmW 1974
Miller, Lou 1915?- *BioIn 5*
Miller, Louis E *NF*
Miller, Louis Gerard 1913- *WhoAm 1974*
Miller, Loye Wheat, Jr. 1930- *WhoAm 1974,*
   WhoS&SW 1973
Miller, Lynn S 1891- *WhJnl 1928*
Miller, Mark *AuBYP, BioIn 7, HisAmM XR*
Miller, Mary Sue *NF*
Miller, Max 1899?-1967 *AmAu&B, Au&Wr,*
   BioIn 1, BioIn 2, BioIn 4, BioIn 8,
   ConAu 3R, ConAu 25, CurBio XR, REnAL,
   TwCA, TwCA Sup, WhNAA
Miller, Maxwell Peter 1919?- *BioIn 2*
Miller, Merle 1919- *AmAu&B, AmNov,*
   Au&Wr, AuNews 1, CelR 1973, ConAu 9R,
   CurBio XR, REn, REnAL, WhoWor 1974,
   WorAu, WrDr 1976
Miller, Merrill *NF*
Miller, Mike *NF*
Miller, Milton R 1886- *WhJnl 1928*
Miller, Nathan 1927- *ConAu 53, WhoAm 1974,*
   WhoS&SW 1973
Miller, Neville D 1881- *WhJnl 1928*
Miller, Norman Charles, Jr. 1934- *ConAu 37,*
   WhoAm 1974
Miller, Paul 1906- *AmJnl, BioIn 1, BioIn 4,*
   WhoAm 1974, WhoE 1974, WhoF&I 1974,
   WhJnl 1928, WhoWor 1974
Miller, Robert Branson 1906- *WhoAm 1974,*
   WhoF&I 1974
Miller, Robert Branson, Jr. 1935- *WhoAm 1974*
Miller, Robert C *RpN*
Miller, Robert L 1908- *BioIn 9*
Miller, Roland E 1912-1957 *NatCAB 50*
Miller, Ross C 1886- *WhJnl 1928*
Miller, Roswell *HisAmM XR*
Miller, Ruth Elizabeth 1921- *BioIn 2*
Miller, S A *HisAmM XR*
Miller, Samuel Kyle 1880- *WhJnl 1928*
Miller, Saul 1918- *WhoAm 1974,*
   WhoS&SW 1973, WhoWorJ 1972
Miller, Sherman R 1910-1968 *BioIn 8*
Miller, Spencer 1891-1968 *BioIn 3, BioIn 8*
Miller, Thomas 1876- *WhJnl 1928*
Miller, Tom *NF*
Miller, Truman W *HisAmM XR*
Miller, W B *AmJnl*
Miller, Walter 1864-1949 *AmAu&B, BiDSA,*
   DcNAA, WhNAA
Miller, Wanda *NF*
Miller, Warren Hastings 1876-1966 *AmAu&B,*
   WhNAA
Miller, Wayne W 1898- *WhJnl 1928*
Miller, Webb 1892-1940 *AmAu&B, AmJnl,*
   BioIn 4, CurBio XR, DcAmB S2, DcNAA
Miller, William 1912- *AmEA 1974, DrAS 74H*
Miller, William Burke 1905- *BioIn 6*
Miller, William Johnson *BioIn 4, RpN,*

WhoAm 1974
Millerand, Alexandre 1859-1943 *CurBio XR,*
   WebBD, WhoLA
Millet, Francis Davis 1846-1912 *Alli Sup, AmAu,*
   AmAu&B, BiD&SB, DcAmA, DcNAA,
   FamWC, WebBD
Millet, Josiah B 1853-1938 *HisAmM XR,*
   NatCAB 28
Millett, Ralph Linwood 1878-1954 *BioIn 3*
Millett, Ralph Linwood, Jr. 1919- *WhoAm 1974,*
   WhoF&I 1974, WhoS&SW 1973
Millican, Jim *NF*
Millier, Henry *NF*
Milligan, Carl Glover 1885- *WhJnl 1928*
Milliken, D L *HisAmM XR*
Milliken, Stanley Torrey 1889?-1954 *BioIn 3*
Millikin, Jill *NF*
Millis, Walter 1899-1968 *AmAu&B, BioIn 4,*
   BioIn 8, ConAu 9, ConAu 37, ConAu P-1,
   HisAmM XR, OxAm, REn, REnAL,
   TwCA, TwCA Sup, WebBD
Millner, Simon L 1882?-1952 *BioIn 2*
Millones, Peter *NF*
Millott, Daniel J *OvPC*
Mills, Betty *NF*
Mills, Bill *AmRP*
Mills, Cynthia J *NF*
Mills, David 1831-1903 *NF*
Mills, Gordon T 1922- *WhoAm 1974,*
   WhoE 1974
Mills, J Warner *HisAmM XR*
Mills, James 1932- *BioIn 9*
Mills, Jeffrey *NF*
Mills, John G 1857-1943 *NatCAB 32*
Mills, Kay *NF*
Mills, Nathaniel *AmJnl*
Mills, Ralph *NF*
Mills, Rilla Dean 1942- *WhoAm 1974*
Mills, Russell 1944- *NF*
Millstein, Rose Silverman 1903?-1975 *ConAu 61*
Millward, Russel Hastings 1877- *WhJnl 1928*
Milmine, Georgine *HisAmM XR*
Milmoe, Eugene *NF*
Milne, Alan Alexander 1882-1956 *AnCL, AuBYP,*
   BkCL, CarSB, CasWL, ChlLR 1, CnMD,
   DcLEL, EncMys, EvLB, HisAmM XR,
   JBA 1934, JBA 1951, LongC, McGWD,
   ModBL, ModWD, NewC, OxEng, Pen Eng,
   RAdv 1, REn, Str&VC, TwCA, TwCA Sup,
   TwCW, WebBD, WhoChL, WhoLA,
   YABC 1
Milne, Donald George 1927- *WhoAm 1974*
Milne, John K *NF*
Milne, Robert Scott *NF*
Milner, Alfred 1854-1925 *DcEuL, LongC,*
   WebBD
Milner, Art 1923- *NF*
Milner, Jay 1926- *ConAu 1R*
Milner, Violet Georgina Cecil 1872-1958 *BioIn 5*
Miloff, Harold *OvPC*
Milton, Arthur Gregory 1911- *OvPC,*
   WhoAm 1974
Milton, George Fort 1869-1924 *BiDSA, BioIn 4,*
   BioIn 5
Milton, George Fort 1894-1955 *AmAu&B,*
   DcAmB S5, REnAL, WhNAA, WhJnl 1928
Milton, John 1608-1674 *Alli, AtlBL, BbD,*
   BiD&SB, BrAu, CasWL, CnE&AP, CnThe,
   CrtT 2, CyWA, DcEnA, DcEnA Ap,
   DcEnL, DcEuL, DcLEL, EvLB, ForP,
   HisAmM XR, HsB&A, MouLC 1, NewC,
   OxEng, Pen Eng, PoChrch, RAdv 1,
   RComWL, REn, REnWD, WebBD,
   WebE&AL

Milton, Patricia A *OvPC*
Mims, Joseph Starke 1883-1955 *BioIn 2, BioIn 7,*
NatCAB 47
Mims, Latham *NF*
Minahan, John 1933- *ConAu 45*
Minahan, Victor Ivan 1881-1954 *BioIn 5*
Minahan, Victor Ivan 1921- *WhoAm 1974*
Mine, Hiromichi *NF*
Miner, Charles 1780-1865 *Alli, AmAu&B,*
DcAmA, DcNAA, NatCAB 5
Miner, Charles Sydney 1906- *ConAu 19,*
ConAu P-1, OvPC
Miner, E N *HisAmM XR*
Miner, Edward Herbert *HisAmM XR*
Miner, Floyd B 1872- *WhJnl 1928*
Miner, George Roberts *HisAmM XR*
Miner, Paul Virgil 1911- *WhoAm 1974,*
WhoMW 1974
Miner, William Harvey 1877-1934 *AmAu&B,*
DcNAA
Mines, John Flavel 1835-1891 *Alli Sup, BiD&SB,*
DcAmA, DcNAA
Mingos, Howard L 1891-1955 *BioIn 4,*
WhJnl 1928
Minh, Ngo Cong 1921- *WhoAm 1974*
Miniberger, Vaclav J 1883- *WhJnl 1928*
Minick, Michael 1945- *ConAu 65*
Minifie, James MacDonald 1900-1974
CanWW 1972, ConAu 49, NewYTBS 5,
OxCan, OxCan Sup
Mink, Randy 1949- *NF*
Minkoff, N B 1893-1958 *NF*
Minnery, Thomas *NF*
Minney, Rubeigh James 1895- *Au&Wr,*
ConAu 7R, Who 1974, WhoLA
Minnigerode, Fitzhugh Lee 1878-1948 *BioIn 1*
Minnocci, Bob 1954- *NF*
Minor, Benjamin Blake 1818-1904? *Alli,*
AmAu&B, BiDSA, HisAmM XR, LiJA
Minor, D Kimball *HisAmM XR*
Minor, Robert 1884-1952 *AmRP, BioIn 1,*
BioIn 3, BioIn 4, CurBio XR, DcAmB S5
Minor, Virginia Otey *HisAmM XR*
Minor, Wilson 1922?- *BioIn 8*
Minot, George Richards 1758-1802 *Alli, AmAu,*
CyAL 1, DcNAA, HisAmM XR, OxAm
Minot, John Clair 1872-1941 *AmAu&B, AmLY,*
HisAmM XR, WhNAA, WhJnl 1928
Minotos, Spiros *NF*
Minow, Newton Norman 1926- *ConAu 15R,*
CurBio 1962, IntWW 1974, WhoAm 1974,
WhoAmP 1973, WhoF&I 1974,
WhoMW 1974, WhoWor 1974,
WhoWorJ 1972, WrDr 1976
Minteer, Edwin Dillin 1891- *WhoAm 1974*
Minter, James Gideon, Jr. 1930- *WhoAm 1974*
Minton, Bruce *AmRP*
Minton, Lynn *NF*
Minton, Maurice M *HisAmM XR*
Mintz, Anita *NF*
Mintz, Michael *NF*
Mintz, Morton Abner 1922- *ConAu 15, InvJ,*
NewMr, RpN, WhoAm 1974,
WhoS&SW 1973
Mintz, Moses *NF*
Mirabella, Grace 1930- *BioIn 9, CelR 1973,*
WhoAm 1974, WhoAmW 1974
Miracle, Phillip *NF*
Miranda, Fernando *HisAmM XR*
Miranda, M Pacheco De *ForP*
Mirbeau, Octave 1850-1917 *BioIn 1, BioIn 2,*
BioIn 6, BioIn 7, CasWL, CIDMEL,
CnMD, EncWL, EuAu, EvEuW, McGWD,
ModWD, OxFr, WebBD

Mirecourt, Eugene De 1812-1880 *BiD&SB,*
WebBD
Mirel, Elizabeth Post *NF*
Miriam 1861-1944 *CasWL, WebBD*
Miro'Quesada, Aurelio 1907-1950 *BioIn 2*
Misch, Robert Jay 1905- *ConAu 23, OvPC,*
WhoE 1974
Misener, Herbert R 1877- *WhJnl 1928*
Mishkin, Leo *OvPC*
Mishra, Vishwa Mohan 1937- *ConAu 61,*
DrAS 74E
Misselwitz, Henry Francis 1900- *WhNAA*
Missiroli, Mario 1886-1974 *ConAu 53,*
IntWW 1974
Mitchel, Frederick Augustus 1839-1918 *Alli Sup,*
AmAu&B, BiD&SB, DcAmA, DcNAA,
OhA&B
Mitchel, John 1815-1875 *Alli Sup, BioIn 1,*
BioIn 2, BioIn 3, BrAu 19, CasWL,
DcAmB 13, DcNAA, NewC, OxEng,
WebBD
Mitchell, Adrian 1932- *Au&Wr, BioIn 8,*
ConAu 33, ConNov 1972, ConNov 1976,
ConP 1970, ConP 1975, WrDr 1976
Mitchell, Arthur Harris 1916- *WhoAm 1974*
Mitchell, Arthur J *HisAmM XR*
Mitchell, Charles H J 1880- *WhJnl 1928*
Mitchell, D D *HisAmM XR*
Mitchell, David Inscho *HisAmM XR*
Mitchell, Donald Grant 1822-1908 *Alli, Alli Sup,*
AmAu, AmAu&B, BbD, BiD&SB, CarSB,
CnDAL, CyAL 2, DcAmA, DcBiA, DcEnL,
DcLEL, DcNAA, EvLB, HisAmM XR,
OxAm, REn, REnAL, WebBD
Mitchell, E V *NF*
Mitchell, Edmund 1861-1917 *Alli Sup, AmAu&B,*
DcNAA
Mitchell, Edward Page 1852-1927 *AmAu&B,*
AmJnl, DcNAA, HisAmM XR, NatCAB 4,
REnAL
Mitchell, Elizabeth Pryse *NF*
Mitchell, Elliot Cobbs 1891- *WhJnl 1928*
Mitchell, Frederick Cleveland 1933- *WhoAm 1974*
Mitchell, George Dean 1866-1950 *HisAmM XR,*
NatCAB 38
Mitchell, Greg 1947- *ConAu 73*
Mitchell, Hal E 1869- *WhJnl 1928*
Mitchell, Harley B *HisAmM XR*
Mitchell, Harry B d1955 *NF*
Mitchell, Helen *BioIn 2*
Mitchell, Henry Z 1884-1965 *NatCAB 51*
Mitchell, Isaac 1759-1812 *AmAu, AmAu&B,*
DcNAA, OxAm, REnAL
Mitchell, James Vincent 1903- *WhJnl 1928*
Mitchell, Jerry 1905?-1972 *BioIn 9, ConAu 33*
Mitchell, Jim 1950- *BioIn 10*
Mitchell, John 1863- *BioIn 8*
Mitchell, John Ames 1845-1918 *AmAu,*
AmAu&B, BiD&SB, DcAmA, DcNAA,
HisAmM XR, OxAm, REnAL, WebBD
Mitchell, John J *HisAmM XR*
Mitchell, John P, Jr. 1863-1929 *BioIn 8*
Mitchell, Joseph Quincy 1908- *BioIn 3,*
WhoAm 1974
Mitchell, Kate L *AmRP*
Mitchell, Lester Edwin 1888- *WhJnl 1928*
Mitchell, Margaret Munnerlyn 1900-1949 *NF*
Mitchell, Patrick *OvPC*
Mitchell, Phyllis *NF*
Mitchell, Robert E *LiJA*
Mitchell, Robert Watson 1910- *WhoAm 1974,*
WhoE 1974
Mitchell, S D *HisAmM XR*
Mitchell, Stanley 1884- *WhJnl 1928*

Mitchell, Stewart 1892-1957 *BioIn 4*,
HisAmM XR, OhA&B
Mitchell, William J *NF*
Mitchill, Samuel Latham 1764-1831 *Alli, AmAu,*
CyAL 1, DcAmA, DcNAA, HisAmM XR
Mitelberg, Louis *see* Tim
Mitford, Jessica 1917- *AmAu&B, ConAu 1,*
CurBio XR, IntWW 1974, InvJ, NewC,
WhoAmW 1974, WhoWor 1974, WorAu,
WrDr 1976
Mitford, John 1781-1859 *Alli, BiDLA, BrAu 19,*
DcEnL, NewC, WebBD
Mitford, John 1782-1831 *Alli, BrAu 19, DcEnL*
Mitgang, Herbert 1920- *AmAu&B, ConAu 11R,*
WhoAm 1974, WhoE 1974, WhoWor 1974,
WhoWorJ 1972, WrDr 1976
Mitov, Entcho *NF*
Mitre, Bartolome 1821-1906 *CasWL, DcSpL,*
ForP, Pen Am, WebBD
Mitre, Jorge *NF*
Mitre, Luis 1869-1950 *BioIn 2*
Mix, J Rowland *HisAmM XR*
Mix, Sheldon A 1927- *NF*
Mixter, Paul 1900- *WhJnl 1928*
Mizelle, Virginia P *OvPC*
Mizuno, Shigeo *ForP*
Mnacko, Ladislav 1919- *CasWL, ConAu 29,*
EncWL, ModSL 2, Pen Eur, TwCW
Moats, Alice-Leone 1911?- *BioIn 2, ConAu 15,*
ConAu P-1, CurBio XR
Moberley, Leeds 1905?-1970 *BioIn 8*
Mobley, Dozier *NF*
Mobley, Jack *NF*
Mobley, Radford E 1905?-1969 *BioIn 8*
Moc, Miroslav 1928- *IntWW 1976*
Mock, John C 1900- *WhJnl 1928*
Mockel, Albert Henri Louis 1866-1945 *WebBD*
Mockridge, Norton 1915- *BioIn 8, WhoE 1974*
Modder, Montagu Frank 1891-1958 *BioIn 4,*
BioIn 5
Modean, Erik W *OvPC*
Modell, Frank *NF*
Moderwell, Hiram Kelly *NF*
Modisane, Bloke 1923- *BioIn 6, ConP 1970,*
Pen Cl, TwCW
Modisett, Harry Edwin 1896- *WhJnl Sup*
Moe, Barbara 1937- *ConAu 69*
Moehlman, Henry J 1896- *WhJnl 1928*
Moers, Ellen 1928- *AmAu&B, Au&Wr,*
ConAu 9, DrAS 74E, ForWC 1970,
WhoAm 1974, WhoAmW 1974
Moffa, Ettore 1885?-1954 *BioIn 3*
Moffat, Charles Bethune 1859-1935 *BioIn 2*
Moffat, Frances Rowan Ayres *WhoAm 1974,*
WhoAmW 1974
Moffat, Samuel *NF*
Moffat, William David 1866-1946 *AmAu&B,*
BioIn 1, DcAmA, DcNAA, WhJnl 1928
Moffatt, Lester E 1888?-1948 *BioIn 1*
Moffet, Hugh R 1863- *BioIn 6, WhJnl 1928*
Moffet, Victor L 1895- *WhJnl 1928*
Moffett, Alfred Robert 1934- *WhoAm 1974*
Moffett, Cleveland Langston 1863-1926 *AmAu&B,*
DcAmB 13, DcNAA, EncMys,
HisAmM XR, NatCAB 14, WebBD
Moffett, Fred Dudley 1873- *WhJnl 1928*
Moffett, Hugh 1910- *ConAu 73, OvPC*
Moffett, Samuel Erasmus 1860-1908 *DcAmA,*
DcNAA, HisAmM XR
Moffett, Samuel J *NF*
Moffitt, Jack 1901?- *BioIn 2*
Moffitt, Mabel *HisAmM XR*
Mogel, Leonard Henry 1922- *WhoAm 1974*
Mohassess, Ardeshir 1938- *BioIn 9*

Mohbat, Joseph Emile 1938?- *NF*
Mohr, Charles 1929- *WhoWor 1974*
Mohs, Mayo *NF*
Mojsov, Lazar 1920- *IntWW 1976,*
WhoAm 1974, WhoE 1974, WhoGov 1972,
WhoWor 1974
Mok, Michel 1888?-1961 *BioIn 5*
Mokarzel, S A 1881?-1952 *BioIn 2*
Molden, Ernst 1886-1953 *BioIn 3*
Molden, Herbert George 1912- *WhoAm 1974*
Molden, Otto Richard 1918- *BioIn 6*
Mole, John W *BioIn 7*
Moleon, Ary *NF*
Moley, Raymond 1886-1975 *AmAu&B, BioIn 1,*
BioIn 8, ConAu 61, CurBio XR,
HisAmM XR, OhA&B, REn, REnAL,
WebBD, WhNAA, WhoAm 1974
Molica, James *NF*
Molinari, Gustave De 1819-1912 *WebBD*
Molino, Emily *NF*
Mollenhauer, Robert D *OvPC*
Mollenhoff, Clark Raymond 1921- *AmAu&B,*
BioIn 3, BioIn 5, BioIn 7, BioIn 8,
ConAu 19R, CurBio XR, InvJ, NewMr,
NewYTBE 1, RpN, WhoAm 1974,
WhoWor 1974
Moller, Lars 1842-1926 *BioIn 6*
Mollison, Andrew, Jr. *NF*
Mollman, John Peter 1931- *WhoAm 1974*
Mollo, Victor 1909- *Au&Wr, ConAu 11R,*
Who 1974, WrDr 1976
Molloy, John T *NF*
Molloy, Paul George 1920- *BioIn 6, BioIn 10,*
ConAu 2R, WhoAm 1974, WhoMW 1974
Molloy, Robert William 1906-1977 *AmAu&B,*
AmNov, ConAu 29, ConAu 69, CurBio XR,
REnAL, TwCA Sup, WhoAm 1974,
WhoE 1974
Molnar, Ferenc 1878-1952 *AtlBL, CasWL,*
ClDMEL, CnMD, CnThe, CyWA, EncWL,
EvEuW, LongC, McGWD, ModWD,
Pen Eur, REn, REnWD, TwCA,
TwCA Sup, WebBD
Molner, Joseph 1907?-1968 *BioIn 8*
Moloney, Stephen J 1896?-1951 *BioIn 2*
Molony, Charles 1911- *RpN, WhoGov 1972*
Molyneaux, Peter 1882-1953 *BioIn 3, TexWr*
Molyneux, Robert E 1917?-1968 *BioIn 8*
Mommaert, Jean *ForP*
Monaghan, Charles Andrew 1932- *WhoAm 1974*
Monaghan, John J d1977 *NF*
Monahan, James Gideon 1855-1923 *BioIn 1,*
BioIn 5
Monahan, Margaret *AmRP*
Monahan, Michael 1865-1933 *AmAu&B, BioIn 6,*
DcNAA, HisAmM XR, REnAL, WhNAA
Monberg, Helene C 1918- *NF*
Mondadori, Alberto 1914-1976 *ConAu 65,*
IntWW 1976, WhoWor 1974
Mondadori, Giorgio 1917- *ForP, WhoWor 1974*
Monelli, Paolo 1894- *IntWW 1976,*
WhoWor 1974
Moneta, Ernesto Teodoro 1833-1918 *BioIn 9,*
WebBD
Monette, J W *HisAmM XR*
Monfort, Francis Cassatte 1844-1928 *Alli Sup,*
AmLY, BioIn 2, DcAmA, DcNAA,
IndAu 1816, OhA&B
Monfort, Joseph Glass 1810-1906 *OhA&B*
Monks, Noel 1907- *BioIn 4*
Monnier, Claude Michel 1938- *IntWW 1976*
Monnier, Henri Bonaventure 1799-1877 *BioIn 2,*
BioIn 7, CasWL, EuAu, EvEuW, OxFr,
Pen Eur, WebBD

Monro, Harold Edward 1879-1932 *AnCL,*
 BioIn 2, BioIn 7, DcLEL, EvLB, LongC,
 ModBL, NewC, OxEng, Pen Eng, REn,
 TwCA, TwCA Sup, WebBD, WebE&AL,
 WhoLA, WhoTwCL
Monroe, A F 1913- *OvPC, WhoPubR 1972*
Monroe, Bill *NF*
Monroe, Charles O 1881- *WhJnl 1928*
Monroe, Harriet 1860-1936 *AmAu&B, AmLY,*
 BiD&SB, BioIn 1, BioIn 4, BioIn 5,
 BioIn 6, BioIn 8, BioIn 10, CasWL,
 CnDAL, ConAmL, DcAmA, DcAmB S2,
 DcNAA, EvLB, HisAmM XR, LongC,
 NatCAB 28, OxAm, Pen Am, REn,
 REnAL, TwCA, TwCA Sup, WebBD,
 WhNAA
Monroe, J R *HisAmM XR*
Monroe, Lilla Day *WhNAA, WhJnl 1928*
Monroe, Lucy *HisAmM XR*
Monroe, Meade 1907- *WhoAm 1974*
Monroe, Ross *NF*
Monroe, Valerie 1950- *NF*
Monroe, William Blanc 1920- *BioIn 10*
Monroney, Aimer Stillwell Mike 1902- *CurBio XR,*
 WhoAm 1974
Monsarrat, Ann Whitelaw 1937- *ConAu 73,*
 WrDr 1976
Monsen, Per 1913- *ForP, IntWW 1976,*
 WhoWor 1974
Monsey, Derek 1921- *ConAu 4R*
Monsky, Leo 1907?-1966 *BioIn 7*
Monsky, Mark 1941- *ConAu 65*
Monson, Karen Ann 1945- *WhoAm 1974*
Montagu, Ivor 1904- *Au&Wr, BioIn 9,*
 ConAu 15, IntWW 1974, Who 1974,
 WhoWor 1974, WrDr 1976
Montague, Charles Edward 1867-1928 *BioIn 2,*
 DcLEL, EvLB, LongC, OxEng, Pen Eng,
 REn, TwCA, TwCW, WebBD
Montague, Charles Howard 1858-1889 *Alli Sup,*
 AmAu&B, BiD&SB, DcAmA, DcNAA
Montague, Evelyn Aubrey 1900?-1948 *BioIn 1*
Montague, James *NF*
Montague, James Jackson 1873-1941 *CurBio XR,*
 DcNAA
Montague, John 1929- *ConAu 11R*
Montague, Katherine *NF*
Montalban, Leonardo 1887-1946 *BioIn 1*
Montalbano, William D 1940- *NF*
Montale, Eugenio 1896- *CasWL, CIDMEL,*
 CnMWL, ConAu 19, EncWL, EvEuW,
 IntWW 1976, ModRL, Pen Eur, REn,
 TwCW, WhoTwCL, WhoWor 1974, WorAu
Montalembert, Charles Forbes 1810-1870 *BioIn 2,*
 BioIn 3, BioIn 4, BioIn 5, BioIn 8, WebBD
Montana, Bob 1920-1975 *BioIn 10,*
 WhoAm 1974, WhoAmA 1973, WhoE 1974,
 WhoWor 1974
Montanelli, Indro 1909- *IntWW 1976,*
 WhoWor 1974
Montaner, Carlos Alberto 1943- *DrAS 74F*
Montant, Jane *WhoAmW 1974*
Montefiore, Joshua 1762-1843 *Alli, BiDLA,*
 DcAmA, DcNAA
Montegut, Jean Baptiste Joseph Emile 1826?-1895
 DcEuL, WebBD
Monteiro, Edmundo *ForP*
Montenegro, Adolfo 1878?-1951 *BioIn 2*
Montenegro, Roberto Martinez 1942?-1978 *NF*
Monterosso, Carlo 1921- *ConAu 29*
Montes, Antonio Llano 1924- *ConAu 69*
Montgomery, A J *NF*
Montgomery, Alexander *HisAmM XR*
Montgomery, Charles A *HisAmM XR*

Montgomery, Charlotte *NF*
Montgomery, David 1937- *IntWW 1976*
Montgomery, Ed 1918- *NF*
Montgomery, Edward S *NF*
Montgomery, George *NF*
Montgomery, George Edgar 1855-1898
 HisAmM XR
Montgomery, H F *HisAmM XR*
Montgomery, Harry 1902- *WhoAm 1974*
Montgomery, Harry E 1876- *WhJnl 1928*
Montgomery, Harry Thomas 1909- *RpN,*
 WhoAm 1974
Montgomery, Henry A 1887-1957 *NF*
Montgomery, James *HisAmM XR*
Montgomery, James 1771-1854 *Alli, BbD,*
 BiD&SB, BiDLA, BrAu 19, DcEnA,
 DcEnL, DcEuL, DcLEL, EvLB, NewC,
 Pen Eng, PoChrch, PoIre, WebBD,
 WebE&AL
Montgomery, James Calder 1885- *WhJnl 1928*
Montgomery, James E 1884-1960 *NatCAB 48*
Montgomery, James F 1933?- *NF*
Montgomery, Jim 1927- *WhoAm 1974,*
 WhoS&SW 1973
Montgomery, John 1847- *WhJnl 1928*
Montgomery, John Alexander 1908- *WhoAm 1974,*
 WhoS&SW 1973
Montgomery, John D *OvPC*
Montgomery, John Osborn 1921- *WhoMW 1974,*
 WhoPubR 1972
Montgomery, Paul *NF*
Montgomery, Ruth Shick 1912- *AuNews 1,*
 BioIn 1, BioIn 4, BioIn 9, ConAu 4R,
 CurBio XR, ForWC 1970, WhoAm 1974,
 WhoAmW 1974, WhoWor 1974, WrDr 1976
Montgomery, Vaida Stewart 1888-1959 *AmAu&B,*
 REnAL, TexWr, WhNAA
Montgomery, Whitney Maxwell 1877-1966
 AmAu&B, AnMV 1926, REnAL, TexWr,
 WhNAA
Montgomery-Massingberd, Hugh 1946?- *BioIn 9*
Montigny, Henri Gaston Testard De 1870-1914
 DcNAA
Montlosier, F D DeReynaud, Comte De 1755-1838
 WebBD
Montor, Henry *NF*
Montpetit, Andre Napoleon 1840-1898 *DcNAA*
Montrose, Sherman 1905?-1956 *BioIn 4*
Monypenny, William Flavelle 1866-1912 *TwCA,*
 WebBD
Moodle, Thomas H 1877?-1948 *BioIn 1*
Moody, Blair 1902-1954 *BioIn 2, BioIn 3,*
 BioIn 7, CurBio XR, DcAmB S5,
 NatCAB 47
Moody, Charles Amadon *HisAmM XR*
Moody, Clarence L 1895- *WhJnl 1928*
Moody, Clarence W 1892- *WhJnl 1928*
Moody, Dwight Lyman 1900-1972 *BioIn 9,*
 NewYTBE 3, WhJnl 1928
Moody, John 1868-1958 *AmAu&B, BkC 2,*
 CathA 1930, HisAmM XR, REnAL,
 WebBD
Moody, Winfield Scott 1856- *AmAu&B*
Moon, Ben L *NF*
Moon, Eric Edward 1923- *BioIn 7, BioIn 8*
Moon, John C *NF*
Moon, Julie M J *NF*
Moon, Owen 1872-1947 *BioIn 1, BioIn 2,*
 NatCAB 35
Moon, Parker Thomas 1892-1936 *CathA 1930,*
 DcNAA, HisAmM XR, WhNAA
Moon, Robert 1925- *ConAu 73*
Moon, Toh Sang *OvPC*
Mooney, Booth 1912-1977 *ConAu 49, ConAu 69*

Mooney, Charles Patrick Joseph 1865-1926
  AmAu&B, BioIn 1, DcNAA
Mooney, Chase Curran 1913-1973 BioIn 10,
  ConAu 19
Mooney, Elizabeth C 1918- ConAu 61
Mooney, Herbert R HisAmM XR
Mooney, John 1899?-1952 BioIn 3
Mooney, Martin BioIn 1
Mooney, Michael Macdonald 1930- ConAu 65
Mooney, Richard E RpN
Moora, Robert L 1912?-1971 BioIn 9,
  NewYTBE 2
Moorad, George 1908-1949 BioIn 2, DcNAA,
  IndAu 1917
Moore, A HisAmM XR
Moore, Acel 1940- ConAu 69
Moore, Alexander Pollock 1867-1930 AmJnl,
  WebBD
Moore, Anne Carroll 1871-1961 AmAu&B,
  AuBYP, ConAu 73, JBA 1934, JBA 1951,
  REnAL, WhNAA
Moore, Arthur 1906?-1977 ConAu 69
Moore, Arthur James, Jr. 1922- OvPC,
  WhoAm 1974
Moore, Arthur S HisAmM XR
Moore, Augustus Martin d1910 PoIre
Moore, Barbara 1934- ConAu 53, WrDr 1976
Moore, Bernard 1904- ConAu 69
Moore, Bob 1910-1950 NF
Moore, Bobbie Conlan BioIn 10
Moore, Brian 1921- Au&Wr, CanWr, CasWL,
  ConAu 1R, ConLC 1, ConLC 3, ConLC 5,
  ConNov 1972, ConNov 1976, DrAF 1976,
  ModBL Sup, NewC, OxCan, OxCan Sup,
  Pen Eng, RAdv 1, REn, REnAL, TwCW,
  WebE&AL, WorAu, WrDr 1976
Moore, Buel Willard 1906- WhJnl 1928
Moore, Burton L 1905- WhJnl 1928
Moore, C W 1903- WhJnl 1928
Moore, Charles 1855-1942 AmAu&B, DcAmA,
  DcAmB S3, DcNAA
Moore, Charles C HisAmM XR
Moore, Charles Leonard HisAmM XR
Moore, Charles W HisAmM XR
Moore, Clarence W OvPC
Moore, Cornelius 1806- Alli, Alli Sup, DcNAA,
  HisAmM XR
Moore, Cullen Lanius BioIn 8
Moore, D D T HisAmM XR
Moore, Don HisAmM XR
Moore, E Clifton 1892-1949 BioIn 2
Moore, Edward 1712-1757 Alli, BiD&SB, BrAu,
  CasWL, DcEnL, DcEuL, EvLB, NewC,
  OxEng, PoIre
Moore, Edward Colman 1877-1935 DcNAA,
  WhJnl 1928
Moore, Edward E 1866-1940 BioIn 2,
  IndAu 1816, OhA&B
Moore, Eldon 1901-1954 BioIn 3
Moore, Elizabeth 1881?-1953 BioIn 3
Moore, Ellis Oglesby 1924- WhoAm 1974
Moore, Evan InvJ
Moore, Frances AmRP
Moore, Frank Frankfort 1855-1931 Alli Sup, BbD,
  BiD&SB, LongC, TwCA, WebBD
Moore, Fred NF
Moore, Frederick Ferdinand 1877- AmAu&B,
  WhNAA
Moore, Frederick Randolph 1857-1943 DcAmB S3
Moore, Gilbert 1935- BioIn 9
Moore, Guy W WhJnl 1928
Moore, Mrs. H G HisAmM XR
Moore, Hannah 1857-1927 DcNAA
Moore, Harold Alexander 1897-1947 BioIn 2,

NatCAB 36
Moore, Harold Arthur 1903- WhJnl 1928
Moore, Harold E NF
Moore, Henry Napier 1893-1963 BioIn 6,
  WhJnl 1928
Moore, Henry Philip 1858- WhJnl 1928
Moore, Henry Wallace 1898- WhJnl 1928
Moore, Herbert S AmJnl
Moore, Horatio Booth 1900- WhJnl 1928
Moore, Idora McClellan 1843-1929 AmAu&B,
  DcNAA
Moore, Idora McClellan see also Moore, Idora
  Plowman
Moore, Idora Plowman 1843-1929 BiDSA
Moore, Idora Plowman see also Moore, Idora
  McClellan
Moore, J Quitman HisAmM XR
Moore, Jack Hoyt 1888- WhJnl 1928
Moore, Jackson T 1865-1944 NatCAB 36
Moore, Jacob Bailey 1797-1853 Alli, AmAu&B,
  DcAmA, DcAmB 13, DcNAA, WebBD
Moore, James H 1857- WhJnl 1928
Moore, John Foot HisAmM XR
Moore, John L NF
Moore, John Trotwood 1858-1929 AmAu&B,
  AmLY, BiD&SB, BiDSA, DcAmA,
  DcAmB 13, DcNAA, OxAm, REnAL
Moore, John Weeks 1807-1889 Alli, Alli Sup,
  AmAu&B, CyAL 2, DcAmA, DcNAA
Moore, Joseph Hampton 1864- NF
Moore, Joseph West Alli Sup, DcAmA, DcNAA
Moore, Lilian 1917- BioIn 7, ConAu 1
Moore, Lloyd NF
Moore, Lyford 1910?- BioIn 2
Moore, Marcus W, Jr. NF
Moore, Marianne Craig 1887-1972 AmAu&B,
  AmWr, AnCL, AnMV 1926, CasWL,
  CnDAL, CnE&AP, CnMWL, ConAmA,
  ConAmL, ConAu 1, ConAu 33, ConLC 1,
  ConLC 2, ConLC 4, ConP 1970, DcLEL,
  EncWL, EvLB, ForWC 1970, HisAmM XR,
  LongC, ModAL, ModAL Sup, OxAm,
  OxEng, Pen Am, RAdv 1, REn, REnAL,
  SixAP, TwCA, TwCA Sup, TwCW,
  WebBD, WebE&AL, WhoTwCL
Moore, Matthew Coleman 1874-1952 BioIn 4,
  NatCAB 41
Moore, Myrna Drake HisAmM XR
Moore, Pamela NF
Moore, Rebecca Deming 1877-1935 DcNAA
Moore, Robert F 1898?-1964 BioIn 6
Moore, Robert Roy 1899- WhJnl 1928
Moore, Robert Tilden 1882- WhJnl 1928
Moore, Rosalind OvPC
Moore, Roy Donald 1887-1954 AmJnl, BioIn 2,
  BioIn 3, BioIn 4
Moore, Ruth Ellen 1908- AmAu&B, ConAu 4R,
  ForWC 1970, WhoAm 1974
Moore, S H HisAmM XR
Moore, Mrs. S V HisAmM XR
Moore, Samuel Taylor 1893-1974 AmAu&B,
  ConAu 53, WhNAA
Moore, T HisAmM XR
Moore, Thomas Emmett 1861-1950 BioIn 2,
  OhA&B
Moore, Thomas H 1876- WhJnl 1928
Moore, Thomas Hendrick 1898- BioIn 3,
  CathA 1952
Moore, Thomas J InvJ
Moore, Thomas P 1928- WhoAm 1974
Moore, Thomas Waldrop 1918- CurBio XR,
  IntMPA 1975, WhoAm 1974, WhoF&I 1974,
  WhoGov 1972, WhoWor 1974
Moore, Thornton C 1914?-1948 BioIn 1

Moore, Virginia 1903- *AmAu&B, AnMV 1926, WhJnl Sup*
Moore, W Robert *HisAmM XR*
Moore, Waldo Wightman 1895- *WhJnl 1928*
Moore, Warner Richard 1903- *WhoAm 1974, WhoE 1974*
Moore, Wickliffe Beckham 1900- *BioIn 9*
Moore, William Emmet 1878-1941 *DcNAA, WhJnl 1928*
Moore, William Paul 1900- *WhJnl 1928*
Moore, William Russell 1910?-1950 *BioIn 2*
Moore, William Taylor 1901- *WhoAm 1974, WhoS&SW 1973*
Moore, William Thomas 1832-1926 *BiDSA, DcAmA, DcNAA, HisAmM XR, OhA&B*
Moore-Smith, Jeannette 1897-1946 *BioIn 1*
Moorehead, Alan McCrae 1910- *Au&Wr, BioIn 4, BioIn 6, BioIn 9, ConAu 7R, IntWW 1976, LongC, NewC, REn, TwCA Sup, WhoWor 1974, WrDr 1976*
Moores, Richard 1909- *ConAu 69*
Moorhead, Ethel *BioIn 7*
Moorhead, Frank Graham 1876- *NF*
Moorhead, Ralph W 1897- *WhJnl 1928*
Moorhead, Raynolds G 1884?-1947 *BioIn 1*
Moorhouse, Geoffrey 1931- *ConAu 25, WrDr 1976*
Moorhouse, Hopkins J 1882- *WhNAA*
Moorsom, Sasha 1931- *ConAu 69*
Moosa, Spencer *NewMr*
Mootz, William *NF*
Moque, Alice Lee 1865-1919 *DcNAA*
Mora, Ferenc 1879-1934 *BioIn 4, CasWL, EvEuW, Pen Eur*
Morabito, Rocco 1920- *WhoAm 1974, WhoS&SW 1973*
Moraes, Frank Robert 1907-1974 *BioIn 4, BioIn 10, ConAu 13, ConAu 49, ConAu P-1, CurBio XR, WhoWor 1974*
Moraes Neto, Prudente De 1904?-1977 *NF*
Moraitinis, Timos 1874?-1952 *BioIn 3*
Morales, Jose Pablo 1828-1882 *PueRA*
Moran, Frank T 1872?-1949 *BioIn 2*
Moran, James Sterling 1909?- *BioIn 1, BioIn 2, BioIn 3, ConAu 9R*
Moran, John d1890 *NF*
Moran, John W *NF*
Moran, Joseph M *OvPC*
Moran, Thomas E *NF*
Moran, Thomas L 1899-1963 *NatCAB 50*
Moravia, Alberto 1907- *Au&Wr, CasWL, CIDMEL, CnMD, CnMWL, ConAu XR, ConLC 2, CurBio XR, CyWA, EncWL, EvEuW, IntWW 1976, LongC, ModRL, OxEng, Pen Eur, REn, TwCA Sup, TwCW, WebBD, Who 1974, WhoTwCL, WhoWor 1974*
Morden, Harold M 1900?-1947 *BioIn 1*
More, Alberto *NF*
More, Paul Elmer 1864-1937 *AmAu&B, AmLY, BiD&SB, BiDSA, CasWL, CnDAL, ConAmA, ConAmL, DcAmA, DcAmB S2, DcLEL, DcNAA, EvLB, HisAmM XR, LongC, ModAL, OxAm, Pen Am, REn, REnAL, TwCA, TwCA Sup, WebBD, WhNAA*
Moreau, Daniel Howard 1898-1963 *BioIn 9, WhJnl 1928*
Moreau, John Adam 1938- *ConAu 37*
Moreau, Ron *NF*
Morehead, Albert Hodges 1909-1966 *AmAu&B, AmSCAP 1966, ConAu 13, ConAu P-1, CurBio XR*
Morehouse, Clifford Phelps 1904- *AmAu&B,*

ConAu 9, WhoAm 1974
Morehouse, Edward 1915?-1978 *NF*
Morehouse, Frederic Cook 1868-1932 *AmAu&B, BioIn 5, DcNAA*
Morehouse, Leslie C 1892- *WhJnl 1928*
Morehouse, Linden Husted *HisAmM XR*
Morehouse, Rebecca *NF*
Morehouse, Ward 1901-1966 *AmAu&B, BioIn 7, BioIn 8, ConAu 25, CurBio XR, REnAL, WebBD, WhJnl 1928*
Morel, Edmund Dene 1873-1924 *BioIn 8*
Morel, Eugene d1952 *BioIn 3*
Moreland, John Richard 1880-1947 *AmAu&B, AnMV 1926, WhNAA*
Morelli, Lorenzo 1878?-1950 *BioIn 2*
Morello, Ted *NF*
Moremen, Grace E *ConAu 45*
Moreno, N Z *OvPC*
Moreno, Pedro R 1947- *ConAu 69*
Moreno-Verdin, Luis *NF*
Morford, Henry 1823-1881 *Alli Sup, AmAu, AmAu&B, BiD&SB, DcAmA, DcAmB 13, DcNAA, OxAm, WebBD*
Morford, William J 1896- *WhJnl 1928*
Morgan, Appleton 1845-1928 *AmAu&B, AmLY, DcAmA, DcNAA, HisAmM XR*
Morgan, Bob *NF*
Morgan, Charles Langbridge 1894-1958 *CasWL, CnMD, CnThe, CroCD, DcLEL, EvLB, LongC, ModBL, ModWD, NewC, OxEng, Pen Eng, REn, TwCA, TwCA Sup, TwCW, WebBD, WebE&AL, WhoLA*
Morgan, Charles Mann 1886- *WhJnl 1928*
Morgan, Dan *NewMr*
Morgan, Donald *OvPC*
Morgan, Edward Paddock 1910- *AmAu&B, BioIn 3, BioIn 4, BioIn 6, BioIn 7, BioIn 8, ConAu 19, ConAu P-1, CurBio XR, ForP, WhoAm 1974, WhoS&SW 1973, WhoWor 1974*
Morgan, Ethel L Skooglund 1898- *WhJnl 1928*
Morgan, Frank *NF*
Morgan, Fred Royal 1885?-1947 *BioIn 1*
Morgan, Frederick 1922- *ConAu 19, ConP 1975, DrAP 1975, WhoF&I 1974, WrDr 1976*
Morgan, George 1854-1936 *AmAu&B, AmLY, DcNAA, WhNAA, WhJnl 1928*
Morgan, George B 1900- *WhJnl 1928*
Morgan, Gwen *ForWC 1970*
Morgan, H Richards 1895- *WhJnl 1928*
Morgan, Harry W *OvPC*
Morgan, Helen Laufman 1896- *WhJnl 1928*
Morgan, Horace H *Alli Sup, HisAmM XR*
Morgan, Howe V 1892- *WhJnl 1928*
Morgan, J Elizabeth *NF*
Morgan, James 1861-1955 *AmAu&B, BioIn 3, BioIn 4, WhNAA*
Morgan, Jefferson 1940- *ConAu 73*
Morgan, Joe Warner 1912- *Au&Wr, ConAu 9R, IndAu 1917, WhoAm 1974*
Morgan, Joy Elmer 1889- *AmAu&B, CurBio XR, WhoAm 1974*
Morgan, Lael 1936- *ConAu 53, WrDr 1976*
Morgan, Lloyd Brooks 1935- *WhoAm 1974*
Morgan, Louise *ConAu 9R, ForWC 1970*
Morgan, Lucy Ware *BioIn 10*
Morgan, Maria *NF*
Morgan, Marshall *NF*
Morgan, Mary *NF*
Morgan, Matt *HisAmM XR*
Morgan, Middie *AmJnl*
Morgan, Mike *NF*
Morgan, Neil 1924- *AmAu&B, ConAu 5R, WhoAm 1974, WrDr 1976*

Morgan, Paul J 1892- *WhJnl 1928*
Morgan, Perry Eugene 1927- *RpN, WhoAm 1974*
Morgan, Robert E *HisAmM XR*
Morgan, Roy Edward 1908- *WhoAm 1974*
Morgan, Thomas Bruce 1926- *BioIn 7, BioIn 9,
ConAu 13R, WhoE 1974*
Morgan, Thomas Brynmor 1886-1972 *BioIn 9,
ConAu 37, NewYTBE 3, OhA&B*
Morgan, Truman S 1868-1940 *NatCAB 37*
Morgan, Victor H 1879-1946 *BioIn 1,
WhJnl 1928*
Morgan, Wiley L 1874- *WhJnl 1928*
Morgan, William James *NF*
Morgan, William Yoast 1866-1932 *DcNAA,
NatCAB 23, OhA&B, WhNAA,
WhJnl 1928*
Morgan-Powell, Samuel 1867-1962 *BioIn 6,
WhNAA*
Morgello, Clem *NF*
Morgenstern, Dan *NF*
Morgenstern, George Edward 1906- *WhoAm 1974*
Morgenstern, Soma 1891?-1976 *ConAu 65*
Morgenthau, Henry, Jr. 1891-1967 *BioIn 1,
CurBio XR, WebBD, WhJnl 1928*
Mori, Shozo 1900?-1953 *BioIn 3*
Moriarty, Eugene J 1907?-1970 *BioIn 8*
Moriarty, Florence Jarman *WhoAm 1974,
WhoAmW 1974, WhoE 1974*
Moriarty, Tim 1923- *ConAu 61*
Morin, Pat *NF*
Morin, Relman George 1907-1973 *AmJnl,
BioIn 5, ConAu 3R, ConAu 41, CurBio XR*
Morinaga, Kyoichi *RpN*
Morisey, A Alexander 1913- *BlkC,
WhoPubR 1972*
Morison, George H 1888-1962 *BioIn 6*
Morison, John *NF*
Morison, John Hopkins 1808-1896 *Alli, Alli Sup,
DcAmA, DcNAA, HisAmM XR*
Morison, Robert F *NF*
Morisseau, James J *OvPC*
Moritz, Frederick A *NF*
Morley, Charles B 1944- *NF*
Morley, Christopher Darlington 1890-1957
*AmAu&B, AmJnl, AmNov, CarSB, CasWL,
CnDAL, ConAmA, ConAmL, DcLEL,
EvLB, LongC, ModAL, OxAm, OxEng,
Pen Am, REn, REnAL, Str&VC, TwCA,
TwCA Sup, WebBD, WhNAA*
Morley, Felix Muskett 1894- *AmAu&B,
AmM&W 73S, WebBD, WhoAm 1974*
Morley, Frank 1860-1937 *DcNAA, HisAmM XR*
Morley, Frederic A 1916?-1952 *BioIn 2*
Morley, Henry 1822-1894 *Alli, Alli Sup, BbD,
BiD&SB, BrAu 19, DcEnA, DcEnL,
DcEuL, DcLEL, EvLB, NewC, Pen Eng,
REn, WebBD*
Morley, John, Viscount 1838-1923 *Alli, BbD,
BiD&SB, BrAu 19, CasWL, DcEnA,
DcEnL, DcEuL, DcLEL, HisAmM XR,
LongC, NewC, OxEng, Pen Eng, WebBD*
Morley, John, Viscount *see also* Morley Of
Blackburn, J, Viscount
Morley Of Blackburn, John, Viscount 1838-1923
EvLB
Morley Of Blackburn, John, Viscount *see also*
Morley, J, Viscount
Moroso, John Antonio 1874-1957 *BioIn 2, BioIn 4*
Morphy, Edward R *HisAmM XR*
Morphy, Paul Charles 1837-1884 *WebBD*
Morrah, Dave 1914- *BioIn 4, ConAu XR,
SmATA XR*
Morrah, Dermot 1896-1974 *ConAu 29,
ConAu 53, NewYTBS 5*

Morrell, J B *NF*
Morrell, Kenneth E *NF*
Morrill, Dewitt G *OvPC*
Morrill, Joseph S *HisAmM XR*
Morrill, Miron Anderson 1898- *WhJnl 1928*
Morrill, S P *NF*
Morris, Alton Chester 1903- *ConAu 15,
DrAS 74E, WhoCon 1973*
Morris, Bailey U *NF*
Morris, Ben Rankin 1922- *WhoAm 1974*
Morris, Charles Dexter 1883-1954 *BioIn 3,
BioIn 6, NatCAB 45*
Morris, Charles D'Urban 1827-1886 *Alli Sup,
DcAmA, HisAmM XR*
Morris, Charles Eugene 1884- *OhA&B,
WhJnl 1928*
Morris, Christopher 1938- *ConAu 21R*
Morris, Claud *BioIn 7*
Morris, Dan 1912- *ConAu 21R*
Morris, Donald R 1924- *Au&Wr, ConAu 19R*
Morris, Edmund 1804-1874 *Alli Sup, DcAmA,
DcNAA*
Morris, Everett B 1889-1967 *BioIn 7, ConAu P-1*
Morris, Frank Daniel *HisAmM XR*
Morris, George 1866-1944 *NF*
Morris, George 1887- *WhNAA*
Morris, George D *NF*
Morris, George L K 1905- *AmRP, DcCAA,
WhoAm 1974, WhoAmA 1973,
WhoWor 1974*
Morris, George Perry 1864-1921 *AmLY,
HisAmM XR*
Morris, George Pope 1802-1864 *Alli, AmAu,
AmAu&B, AmJnl, BiD&SB, BioIn 1,
CyAL 2, DcAmA, DcAmB 13, DcLEL,
DcNAA, EvLB, HisAmM XR, LiJA,
OxAm, REnAL, WebBD*
Morris, Geraldine *OvPC*
Morris, Harrison Smith 1856-1948 *AmAu&B,
BbD, BiD&SB, DcAmA, DcNAA,
HisAmM XR, WhNAA*
Morris, Helen Swift *HisAmM XR*
Morris, Hugh *RpN*
Morris, Hugh L *NF*
Morris, Inez *NF*
Morris, James 1926- *BioIn 6, BioIn 7,
ConAu 3R, CurBio XR, IntWW 1974,
NewYTBS 5, Who 1974*
Morris, James *see also* Morris, Jan
Morris, James B 1890- *WhJnl 1928*
Morris, Jan 1926- *ConAu 53, IntWW 1976,
NewYTBS 5, Who 1974, WrDr 1976*
Morris, Jan *see also* Morris, James
Morris, Jeannie 1935?- *BioIn 9*
Morris, Joe Alex 1904- *ConAu 65, HisAmM XR*
Morris, Joe Alex, Jr. 1927- *ConAu 73,
WhoAm 1974*
Morris, John 1907?- *BioIn 2*
Morris, John G *OvPC*
Morris, John Milton 1906- *WhoAm 1974*
Morris, Judith 1947- *NF*
Morris, Julie *NF*
Morris, M D *OvPC*
Morris, Malcolm 1849- *Alli Sup, HisAmM XR*
Morris, Mary 1913- *ConAu 53*
Morris, Mel 1930- *ConAu 69*
Morris, Mowbray *BioIn 2*
Morris, Norman S 1931- *ConAu 33*
Morris, Phyllis 1894- *WhoThe 1972*
Morris, Robert *Alli, HisAmM XR*
Morris, Robert 1818-1882 *Alli, Alli Sup, BiDLA,
DcNAA, HisAmM XR*
Morris, Roger R *NF*
Morris, William 1834-1896 *Alli, Alli Sup,*

AtlBL, BbD, BiD&SB, BrAu 19, CasWL,
CnE&AP, CrtT 3, DcBiA, DcEnA,
DcEnA Ap, DcEnL, DcEuL, EvLB,
HisAmM XR, MouLC 4, NewC, OxEng,
Pen Eng, RAdv 1, RComWL, REn,
Str&VC, WebBD, WebE&AL
Morris, William 1913- *AmAu&B, ConAu 19,*
OvPC, WhoAm 1974
Morris, William Grayson 1899- *WhJnl 1928*
Morris, William Shivers 1903-1967 *Bioln 7*
Morris, William Shivers, III 1934- *WhoAm 1974,*
WhoF&I 1974, WhoS&SW 1973
Morris, Willie 1934- *AuNews 2, Bioln 8,*
Bioln 9, CelR 1973, ConAu 19R,
DrAF 1976, IntWW 1976, NewMr,
WhoAm 1974, WhoE 1974, WhoWor 1974
Morris, Willis *LiJA*
Morrisey, James J 1901- *WhJnl 1928*
Morrison, Arthur 1863-1945 *BbD, BiD&SB,*
DcEnA Ap, DcLEL, EncMys, EvLB,
HisAmM XR, LongC, NewC, TwCA,
TwCA Sup, WebBD, WhoLA
Morrison, Charles Clayton 1874-1966 *Bioln 1,*
Bioln 2, Bioln 7, Bioln 9, OhA&B,
WhNAA
Morrison, Charles Munro 1881-1950 *Bioln 2,*
WhNAA, WhJnl 1928
Morrison, Chester *NF*
Morrison, Chester L 1899?-1966 *Bioln 7*
Morrison, Donal MacLachlan 1922- *WhoAm 1974*
Morrison, George Ernest 1862-1920 *Bioln 2,*
Bioln 7, Bioln 8, Bioln 9, NewC, WebBD
Morrison, Harold 1919- *WhoAm 1974,*
WhoWor 1974
Morrison, Herb 1905?- *Bioln 7*
Morrison, Hobe 1904- *BiE&WWA,*
WhoThe 1972
Morrison, Ian 1910?-1950 *Bioln 2*
Morrison, J P *HisAmM XR*
Morrison, Jesse A 1871- *WhJnl 1928*
Morrison, Joseph Lederman 1918- *AmAu&B,*
ConAu 5R
Morrison, Leo 1898?-1974 *Bioln 10*
Morrison, Philip *NF*
Morrison, Theodore 1901- *AmAu&B, ConAu 1,*
DrAS 74E, HisAmM XR, OxAm, REnAL,
TwCA Sup, WhoAm 1974, WrDr 1976
Morrison, William J 1876- *WhJnl 1928*
Morrison-Fuller, J *HisAmM XR*
Morriss, Frank 1923- *ConAu 5, WrDr 1976*
Morriss, Mack 1920?-1976 *ConAu 65*
Morriss, Ruth Moore 1898?-1961 *Bioln 5*
Morrissey, David A 1880?-1947 *Bioln 1*
Morrissey, Donald R 1903- *WhJnl 1928*
Morrissey, George 1909-1972 *Bioln 9*
Morrow, Edward Andrew 1915?-1969 *Bioln 8*
Morrow, Elise 1922- *Bioln 1*
Morrow, Felix *AmRP*
Morrow, George 1869?-1955 *Bioln 3*
Morrow, Honore Willsie 1880-1940 *AmAu&B,*
CurBio XR, DcNAA, HisAmM XR, OxAm,
REnAL, TwCA, WebBD, WisWr
Morrow, Hugh *HisAmM XR*
Morrow, L C 1888- *WhJnl 1928*
Morrow, L W W 1888- *WhJnl 1928*
Morrow, Marco 1869-1959 *HisAmM XR,*
OhA&B, WhNAA, WhJnl 1928
Morrow, Michael *NewMr*
Morrow, Stephen 1939- *ConAu 73*
Morrow, Tom 1903?- *Bioln 5*
Morrow, Walter Alexander 1894-1949 *Bioln 1,*
Bioln 2
Morrow, William 1873-1931 *AmAu&B*
Morrow, Winston Vaughan 1887- *WhJnl 1928*

Morsch, Dale *NF*
Morsch, Karl 1926- *IntWW 1976*
Morse, Edwin Wilson 1855-1924 *DcNAA,*
NatCAB 30
Morse, Hiram Boardman 1865?-1952 *Bioln 3*
Morse, Jane *NF*
Morse, Jedediah 1761-1826 *Alli, AmAu,*
AmAu&B, BiDLA, CyAL 1, DcAmA,
DcNAA, HisAmM XR, OxAm, REnAL,
WebBD
Morse, John Torrey, Jr. 1840-1937 *Alli Sup,*
AmAu&B, BiD&SB, DcAmA, DcAmB S2,
DcNAA, WebBD
Morse, Joseph Laffan 1902-1969 *Bioln 3, Bioln 8*
Morse, Josiah Mitchell 1912- *ConAu 65,*
DrAS 74E, WhoE 1974
Morse, L L *NF*
Morse, Richard Cary 1795-1868 *HisAmM XR,*
WebBD
Morse, Robert *OvPC*
Morse, Samuel 1888-1946 *Bioln 1, DcNAA*
Morse, Samuel H *HisAmM XR*
Morse, Sherman W *NF*
Morse, Sidney E 1835- *NatCAB 13*
Morse, Sidney Edwards 1794-1871 *Alli, AmAu,*
AmAu&B, DcAmA, DcNAA, HisAmM XR,
REnAL, WebBD
Morse, Sidney H *HisAmM XR*
Morse, Mrs. T Vernette *HisAmM XR*
Morse, Wilbur 1903?-1955 *Bioln 3*
Morss, Samuel E 1852-1903 *AmJnl, NatCAB 1*
Mortensen, Arthur Marion *NF*
Mortensson-Egnund, Ivar 1857-1934 *WebBD*
Mortier, Alfred 1865-1937 *WebBD*
Mortimer, C *HisAmM XR*
Mortimer, F C *NF*
Mortimer, John Lynn 1908- *ConAu 69*
Mortimer, Lee 1904-1963 *AmAu&B, Bioln 2,*
Bioln 6, HisAmM XR
Mortimer, Penelope 1918- *ConAu 57, Who 1974*
Mortimer, Raymond 1895- *IntWW 1976, LongC*
Mortison, Carl L 1889?-1963 *Bioln 6*
Mortland, Samuel Gayley 1879- *WhJnl 1928*
Morton, Bruce *NF*
Morton, Carlos 1947- *ConAu 73, DrAF 1976,*
DrAP 1975
Morton, Charles W 1899-1967 *AmAu&B,*
Bioln 2, Bioln 7, Bioln 8, REnAL
Morton, David 1886-1957 *AmAu&B,*
AnMV 1926, HisAmM XR, REn, REnAL,
Str&VC, WebBD, WhNAA
Morton, Edward 1858-1922 *NF*
Morton, Esther *Bioln 3*
Morton, Frank 1869-1923 *Bioln 2*
Morton, Frederick William 1859- *DcAmA,*
HisAmM XR
Morton, Guy Eugene 1884-1948 *Bioln 1, CanNov,*
DcNAA
Morton, Henry 1836-1902 *Alli Sup, DcAmA,*
DcNAA, HisAmM XR, WebBD
Morton, Henry Vollam 1892- *Au&Wr, DcLEL,*
EvLB, IntWW 1976, LongC, TwCA,
TwCA Sup, WebBD, Who 1974,
WhoWor 1974
Morton, Howard E 1878-1938 *AmAu&B*
Morton, John Bingham 1893- *Bioln 1, Bioln 5,*
CathA 1930, LongC, WebBD, WorAu
Morton, John Bingham *see also* Morton, John C A B
M
Morton, John Cameron Andrieu Bingham M 1893-
IntWW 1976, Who 1974
Morton, John Cameron Andrieu Bingham M *see also*
Morton, John B
Morton, Joseph, Jr. 1914?-1945 *AmJnl,*

ConAu XR
Morton, Julius Sterling 1832-1902 *HisAmM XR,*
    WebBD
Morton, Marmaduke B 1859- *WhJnl 1928*
Morton, Oliver S *NF*
Morton, Oliver Throck 1860-1898 *BioIn 2,*
    DcAmA, DcNAA, IndAu 1816
Morton, Oren Frederic 1857-1926 *DcNAA,*
    WhNAA
Morton, William *AmAu&B, AmJnl*
Morus *see* Lewinsohn, Richard
Morwitz, Edward 1815-1893 *BioIn 2*
Mosby, A *NF*
Mosby, Thomas Speed 1874-1954 *BioIn 6,*
    NatCAB 45
Mosby, Wade Hamilton 1917- *WhoAm 1974*
Moscow, Alvin 1925- *AmAu&B, AuBYP,*
    ConAu 2R, SmATA 3
Moscow, Henry I 1905?- *BioIn 1*
Moscow, Warren 1908- *BioIn 1, ConAu 23R,*
    WhoE 1974, WhoWorJ 1972
Mosebach, Fred 1871- *WhJnl 1928*
Moseley, Douglas W *OvPC*
Moseley, Ray Neal 1932- *WhoAm 1974*
Moseley, Sydney Alexander 1888-1961 *BioIn 5,*
    BioIn 6
Moser, Frank H 1886-1964 *BioIn 7, BioIn 9*
Moser, Hanns 1921?-1953 *BioIn 3*
Moser, Nathan *AmRP*
Moses, Barr 1874- *WhJnl 1928*
Moses, Sir Charles Joseph Alfred 1900-
    IntWW 1976, WhoWor 1974
Moses, Frank Rae 1883-1944 *BioIn 2,*
    NatCAB 34
Moses, George Higgins 1869-1944 *CurBio XR,*
    DcAmB S3, HisAmM XR, NatCAB XR,
    WebBD
Moses, Herbert 1884-1972 *BioIn 6, BioIn 9,*
    NewYTBE 3
Moses, Montrose Jonas 1878-1934 *AmAu&B,*
    DcAmB S1, DcNAA, HisAmM XR, OxAm
Mosessohn, David Nehemiah 1883-1930 *WebBD,*
    WhJnl 1928
Mosessohn, Moses Dayyan 1884-1940 *WebBD*
Mosessohn, Nehemiah 1853-1926 *WebBD*
Mosettig, Michael David 1942- *WhoAm 1974*
Mosher, Ann 1906?-1968 *BioIn 8*
Mosher, Paul R *OvPC*
Mosher, Thomas Bird 1852-1923 *AmAu&B,*
    DcNAA, HisAmM XR, LongC, OxAm,
    WebBD
Moskin, John Robert 1923- *AmAu&B,*
    ConAu 19R, DrAS 74H, OvPC,
    WhoAm 1974, WhoE 1974, WhoWor 1974,
    WhoWorJ 1972
Moskowitz, Belle Lindner 1877-1933 *WebBD*
Moskowitz, Gene *NF*
Moskowitz, Milton *NF*
Mosler, Henry 1841-1920 *WebBD*
Mosley, Leonard 1913- *Au&Wr, WrDr 1976*
Mosley, Zack Terrell 1906- *WhoAm 1974,*
    WhoAmA 1973
Moss, Edward Bayard 1874?-1948 *BioIn 1*
Moss, G E *WhJnl 1928*
Moss, Geoffrey *NF*
Moss, Howard 1922- *AmAu&B, Au&Wr,*
    ConAu 1, ConP 1970, ConP 1975,
    DrAP 1975, Pen Am, RAdv 1,
    WhoAm 1974, WhoWor 1974, WorAu,
    WrDr 1976
Moss, Jeanette K *NF*
Moss, Joseph F 1903- *WhJnl 1928*
Moss, Norman 1928- *ConAu 49*
Moss, William *AmJnl*

Moss, William Watkins, Jr. 1893- *WhJnl 1928*
Mossberg, Walter S *NF*
Mossman, William Templeton *HisAmM XR*
Most, Johann Joseph 1846-1906 *AmJnl, AmRP,*
    DcNAA
Moszkowski, Alexander 1851-1934 *WebBD*
Motherwell, Hiram 1888-1945 *BioIn 1, BioIn 2,*
    CurBio XR, DcNAA, IndAu 1917
Motherwell, William 1797-1835 *Alli, BiD&SB,*
    BrAu 19, DcEnA, DcEnL, DcLEL, EvLB,
    NewC, OxEng, REn, WebBD
Mothner, Ira Sanders 1932- *ConAu 21R,*
    WhoE 1974
Motley, Arthur Harrison 1900- *AuNews 2,*
    BioNews 1974, CurBio XR, WhoAdv 1972,
    WhoAm 1974, WhoE 1974
Mott, Ed *HisAmM XR*
Mott, Edward Harold 1845-1920 *DcNAA,*
    NatCAB 18
Mott, Frank Luther 1886-1964 *AmAu&B,*
    BioIn 2, BioIn 4, BioIn 6, BioIn 7, BioIn 8,
    BioIn 9, ConAu 4R, CurBio XR, LiJA,
    OxAm, REn, REnAL, TwCA Sup, WebBD,
    WhNAA
Mott, H S *HisAmM XR*
Motteux, Peter Anthony 1660?-1718 *Alli, BrAu,*
    CasWL, DcEnL, DcLEL, OxEng, WebBD
Mottola, Michele 1904-1971 *BioIn 9*
Motz, John Edward 1909- *CanWW 1972,*
    WhoMW 1974
Motz, W J 1870- *WhJnl 1928*
Mouat, Lucia 1936- *NF*
Mould, George 1894- *ConAu 57*
Moulier, Fernand 1913- *NF*
Moult, Thomas 1895-1974 *Au&Wr, LongC,*
    NewC, WebBD, Who 1974
Moulton, Charles Wells 1859-1913 *Alli Sup,*
    AmAu&B, DcNAA, HisAmM XR
Moulton, Charlotte G *NF*
Moulton, Forest Ray 1872-1952 *WebBD, WhNAA*
Moulton, Roy K 1880- *WhJnl 1928*
Mount, Ferdinand 1939- *ConAu 21R*
Mount, Mrs. P W *HisAmM XR*
Mountsier, Robert 1888?-1972 *BioIn 9,*
    ConAu 37
Moursi, Rajaa *NF*
Movitz, Milton *OvPC*
Mowbray, Charles W *AmRP*
Mowbray, J P *see* Wheeler, Andrew Carpenter
Mowery, Edward Joseph 1906-1970 *BioIn 3,*
    BioIn 9, CurBio XR, NewYTBE 1
Mowrer, Edgar Ansel 1892-1977 *AmAu&B,*
    AmJnl, Au&Wr, BioIn 2, BioIn 4, BioIn 6,
    BioIn 8, ConAu 15, ConAu 69, ConAu P-1,
    CurBio XR, DrAS 74P, IntWW 1976,
    OvPC, REnAL, TwCA, TwCA Sup,
    WhNAA, Who 1974, WhoAm 1974,
    WhoE 1974
Mowrer, Lilian Thomson *ConAu 65, CurBio XR,*
    WhNAA, WrDr 1976
Mowrer, Paul Scott 1887-1971 *AmAu&B, AmJnl,*
    BioIn 1, BioIn 3, ConAu 5R, ConAu 29,
    NewYTBE 2, REnAL, WebBD, WhNAA
Mowrer, Richard *AmJnl*
Moxley, Warden N *NF*
Moy, Ernest K 1895- *WhJnl 1928*
Moya, Alejandro *NF*
Moyed, Ralph *NF*
Moyer, Alan Dean 1928- *WhoAm 1974*
Moyer, Harry B 1882?-1950 *BioIn 2*
Moyer, Paul Edward 1888- *BioIn 2*
Moyers, Bill 1934- *AuNews 1, ConAu 61,*
    CurBio XR, IntWW 1976, NewMr,
    Who 1974, WhoAm 1974, WhoAmP 1973,

Mungo, Ray *NewMr*
Munhall, Horace E 1887?-1952 *BioIn 2*
Munk, Erika 1937?- *BioIn 10, ConAu 19*
Munkacsi, Martin 1896-1963 *BioIn 10*
Munkittrick, Richard Kendall 1853-1911
    AmAu&B, BiD&SB, DcAmA, DcNAA,
    HisAmM XR, PoIre
Munn, Bruce Watson 1911- *BioIn 6,*
    WhoAm 1974, WhoE 1974, WhoWor 1974
Munn, Charles Allen d1924 *HisAmM XR*
Munn, Charles Clark 1848-1917 *AmAu&B,*
    BiD&SB, CarSB, DcAmA, DcNAA,
    HisAmM XR
Munn, James C d1976 *NF*
Munn, Orson Desaix 1824-1907 *HisAmM XR*
Munoz, Luis *NF*
Munoz Meany, Enrique 1908-1951 *BioIn 2*
Munro, Dana Carleton 1866-1933 *AmAu&B,*
    DcAmA, DcNAA, HisAmM XR, WebBD
Munro, David A d1910 *HisAmM XR*
Munro, Eleanor C 1928- *AuBYP, BioIn 7,*
    ConAu 4R
Munro, George 1825-1896 *HisAmM XR*
Munro, John Richard 1931- *WhoAm 1974,*
    WhoE 1974, WhoF&I 1974
Munro, Leslie Knox 1901-1974 *ConAu 49,*
    CurBio XR, NewYTBS 5, WhoWor 1974
Munro, Neil 1864-1930 *BbD, BiD&SB, CasWL,*
    DcLEL, EvLB, LongC, Pen Eng, TwCA,
    WebBD
Munro, Norman L *HisAmM XR*
Munro, Robert Ross 1913- *CanWW 1972,*
    WhoCan 1973
Munro, Robert Ross *see also* Munro, Ross
Munro, Ross 1913- *OxCan, WhoAm 1974,*
    WhoWor 1974
Munro, Ross *see also* Munro, Robert Ross
Munro, Wallace 1863?-1948 *BioIn 1*
Munro, William Bennett 1875-1957 *AmAu&B,*
    AmLY, OxCan, WebBD, WhNAA
Munroe, Frederick Mitchell *HisAmM XR*
Munroe, Kirk 1850-1930 *Alli Sup, AmAu&B,*
    BbD, BiD&SB, BiDSA, CarSB, DcAmA,
    DcNAA, HisAmM XR, JBA 1934, OxAm,
    TwCA
Munroe, Mary Norris *NF*
Munroe, Pat 1916- *WhoAm 1974*
Munsell, Joel 1808-1880 *Alli, Alli Sup,*
    AmAu&B, CyAL 2, DcAmA, DcNAA,
    REnAL
Munsey, Frank Andrew 1854-1925 *Alli Sup,*
    AmAu&B, AmJnl, BioIn 3, BioIn 9, CarSB,
    DcAmA, DcNAA, HisAmM XR,
    REnAL, WebBD, WhJnl Sup
Munsey, Pierce 1877- *WhJnl 1928*
Munson, Don 1908- *ConAu 73*
Munson, Gorham Bert 1896-1969 *AmAu&B,*
    AuBYP, CnDAL, ConAu P-1, HisAmM XR,
    OxAm, Pen Am, REnAL, TwCA,
    TwCA Sup, WebBD
Munson, Halsey J 1908?-1960 *BioIn 5*
Munson, Oliver Goldsmith 1856-1933 *BioIn 5*
Munves, James 1922- *ConAu 5R*
Muramaya, Nagataka 1894-1977 *IntWW 1976,*
    WhoWor 1974
Murayama, Choken *ForP*
Murayama, Ofuji *BioIn 7*
Murayama, Ryohei 1850-1933 *NF*
Murchie, R Deane 1889- *WhJnl 1928*
Murdoch, Henry T 1902- *WhJnl 1928*
Murdoch, Sir Keith Arthur 1886-1952 *BioIn 3*
Murdoch, Keith Rupert 1931- *Who 1974,*
    WhoWor 1974
Murdoch, Keith Rupert *see also* Murdoch, Rupert

Murdoch, Louis R 1876- *WhJnl 1928*
Murdoch, Rupert 1931- *ForP, IntWW 1976,*
    Who 1974
Murdoch, Rupert *see also* Murdoch, Keith Rupert
Murdock, Fridge *HisAmM XR*
Murdock, Gertrude M *HisAmM XR*
Murdock, John Nelson *HisAmM XR*
Murdock, Kenneth Ballard 1895-1975 *AmAu&B,*
    ConAu 61, IntWW 1974, Who 1974,
    WhoAm 1974
Murdock, Marcellus Marion 1883-1970 *BioIn 4,*
    WhJnl 1928
Murdock, Victor 1871-1945 *BioIn 2, CurBio XR,*
    DcAmB S3, HisAmM XR, NatCAB 35,
    WhNAA, WhJnl 1928
Muret, Jules Henri Maurice 1870-1954 *WebBD*
Murill, Hugh Ambrose, Jr. 1894- *WhJnl 1928*
Murillo Toro, Manuel 1815-1880 *WebBD*
Murkland, Harry Banta 1902?-1966 *BioIn 7*
Murn, Thomas X *NF*
Murphey, Frances B *BioIn 9*
Murphy, Arthur Richard, Jr. 1915- *WhoAm 1974*
Murphy, Bernard 1847-1918 *NatCAB 18*
Murphy, Lady Blanche *HisAmM XR*
Murphy, Carl 1889-1967 *WhJnl 1928*
Murphy, Charles *NF*
Murphy, Charles J V *NF*
Murphy, Daniel *HisAmM XR*
Murphy, Donald P 1895- *WhJnl 1928*
Murphy, Donald Ridgway 1895- *BioIn 4*
Murphy, Edgar Gardner 1869-1913 *BioIn 8,*
    DcAmA
Murphy, Edward T 1896?-1965 *BioIn 7*
Murphy, Edwin Greenslade 1867-1939 *BioIn 2*
Murphy, Francis P 1896- *WhoAm 1974*
Murphy, Frank G *NF*
Murphy, Frederick E 1872-1940 *BioIn 4, BioIn 7,*
    CurBio XR, DcAmB S2, NatCAB 47
Murphy, Henry Cruse 1810-1882 *Alli, Alli Sup,*
    AmAu, AmAu&B, AmJnl, BiD&SB,
    CyAL 2, DcAmA, DcNAA, PoIre, REnAL
Murphy, J Edwin *BioIn 1*
Murphy, J Elmer 1914- *CanWW 1972,*
    WhoAdv 1972
Murphy, J Reginald 1934- *BioIn 10*
Murphy, J Reginald *see also* Murphy, John Reginald
Murphy, J Reginald *see also* Murphy, Reg
Murphy, Jack Raymond, Jr. 1923- *WhoAm 1974*
Murphy, James E *AmJnl*
Murphy, Jim *NF*
Murphy, Jimmy 1891-1970 *BioIn 7, BioIn 9*
Murphy, John Cullen *NF*
Murphy, John H, Sr. 1840-1922 *NF*
Murphy, John Reginald 1934- *NewYTBS 5, RpN*
Murphy, John Reginald *see also* Murphy, J Reginald
Murphy, John Reginald *see also* Murphy, Reg
Murphy, John T 1860-1932 *BioIn 5, WhJnl 1928*
Murphy, Joseph M 1894?-1968 *BioIn 8*
Murphy, Lawrence C *OvPC*
Murphy, Lawrence R *LiJA*
Murphy, Lawrence William 1895-1969 *WhNAA*
Murphy, Mark 1912?-1952 *BioIn 3*
Murphy, Michael Edward 1930- *LiJA,*
    WhoMW 1974
Murphy, Paul I *OvPC*
Murphy, Paul V 1888?-1954 *BioIn 3*
Murphy, Reg 1934- *ConAu 33, WhoAm 1974,*
    WhoS&SW 1973
Murphy, Reg *see also* Murphy, J Reginald
Murphy, Reg *see also* Murphy, John Reginald
Murphy, Richard J 1861- *NatCAB 3*
Murphy, Robert William 1902-1971 *AuBYP,*
    BioIn 8, BioIn 9, ConAu 29, ConAu P-1,
    SmATA 10

Murphy, Sam *NF*
Murphy, Thomas S 1925- *WhoAm 1974,*
  WhoE 1974, WhoS&SW 1973
Murphy, William Charles 1898-1949 *BioIn 2*
Murphy, William J 1859-1918 *NatCAB 20*
Murray, Albert A 1889-1964 *BioIn 6*
Murray, Anthony *NF*
Murray, Bill *NF*
Murray, Bredett C 1837-1924 *NatCAB 6*
Murray, Carolyn S *NF*
Murray, Charles Theodore 1843-1924 *Alli Sup,*
  AmAu&B, AmLY, BiDSA, BioIn 2,
  DcNAA, IndAu 1816
Murray, David 1925- *WhoAm 1974*
Murray, David Christie 1847-1907 *Alli Sup, BbD,*
  BiD&SB, BrAu 19, DcBiA, DcEnA,
  DcEnA Ap, EncMys, EvLB, NewC, WebBD
Murray, Donald M 1924- *AmAu&B, AuBYP,*
  BioIn 8, ConAu 4R, WhoAm 1974
Murray, Dorothy 1918- *NF*
Murray, Frank E 1903?-1957 *BioIn 4*
Murray, Geoffrey 1907?-1970 *BioIn 8*
Murray, George 1889-1961 *BioIn 6, BioIn 8*
Murray, George 1909- *ConAu 19R*
Murray, George Francis 1929- *WhoAm 1974*
Murray, George McIntosh 1900-1970 *Au&Wr,*
  ConAu P-1, Lor&LP
Murray, Grace Peckham *HisAmM XR*
Murray, Grenville 1824-1881 *BiD&SB, NewC,*
  WebBD
Murray, J D 1825- *BbtC*
Murray, J Edward 1915- *BioIn 1, WhoAm 1974*
Murray, J Harley 1910?-1977 *ConAu 73*
Murray, James 1946- *ConAu 49*
Murray, James T 1881- *WhJnl 1928*
Murray, Jim 1919- *ConAu 65*
Murray, Joan 1941- *LivBAA*
Murray, Joe *NF*
Murray, John 1778-1843 *Alli, BrAu 19, DcEnA,*
  DcEnL, DcEuL, NewC, WebBD
Murray, Joseph W 1879-1959 *WhJnl 1928*
Murray, Lieutenant *see* Ballou, Maturin Murray
Murray, Luanne *NF*
Murray, Margaret Teresa 1888- *BioIn 8*
Murray, Marian *ConAu 41, SmATA 5*
Murray, Max *BioIn 1*
Murray, Michele 1933-1974 *BioIn 10, ConAu 49,*
  NewYTBS 5, SmATA 7
Murray, Riley *NF*
Murray, Robert Null 1903- *WhoAm 1974*
Murray, William 1926- *Au&Wr, BioIn 3*
Murray-Aaron, Eugene 1852- *DcNAA,*
  HisAmM XR
Murrin, James Albert 1894- *WhJnl 1928*
Murrow, Edward Roscoe 1908-1965 *AmJnl,*
  BioIn 1, BioIn 2, BioIn 3, BioIn 4, BioIn 5,
  BioIn 6, BioIn 7, BioIn 8, BioIn 9,
  BioIn 10, CurBio XR, EncAB,
  HisAmM XR, InvJ, REnAL, WebBD
Murry, John Middleton 1889-1957 *BioIn 1,*
  BioIn 2, BioIn 4, BioIn 5, BioIn 6, BioIn 7,
  BioIn 8, CasWL, DcLEL, EvLB, LongC,
  ModBL, NewC, OxEng, Pen Eng, REn,
  TwCA, TwCA Sup, TwCW, WebBD,
  WebE&AL, WhoLA, WhoTwCL
Murry, Philip H 1842- *BioIn 8*
Murtagh, W J *AmJnl*
Murtaugh, T Edward 1877?-1950 *BioIn 2*
Murtland, Blanche Nevins 1878- *AnMV 1926,*
  WhJnl 1928
Musa, Salamah 1887-1959 *BioIn 7*
Muschel, Herbert *AmJnl*
Muse, William Foster 1860-1931 *WhJnl 1928*
Musel, R S *NF*

Musgrave, Arthur Benson 1910- *AmM&W 73S,*
  RpN
Musgrave, Noel Henry 1903-1971 *BioIn 9*
Musial, Joe 1905?-1977 *ConAu 69*
Musick, Charles *NF*
Musick, John Roy 1849?-1901 *Alli Sup,*
  AmAu&B, BiD&SB, BiDSA, DcAmA,
  DcNAA
Musil, Robert 1880-1942 *AtlBL, BioIn 10,*
  CasWL, CIDMEL, CnMD, CnMWL,
  EncWL, EvEuW, McGWD, ModGL, OxGer,
  Pen Eur, REn, TwCA Sup, TwCW,
  WhoTwCL
Musselwhite, Harry Webster 1868-1955 *BioIn 4,*
  WhJnl 1928
Musser, Benjamin Francis 1889-1951 *AmAu&B,*
  AnMV 1926, BkC 3, CathA 1930, REnAL,
  WhNAA
Musser, John Herr, Jr. 1883-1947 *DcNAA,*
  HisAmM XR, WhNAA
Mussey, Henry Raymond 1875-1940 *DcNAA,*
  HisAmM XR
Mussey, Mabel H B *HisAmM XR*
Mussolini, Benito 1883-1945 *CasWL, CurBio XR,*
  EvEuW, ForP, REn, WebBD, WhoLA
Mustafa Kamel 1874-1908 *WebBD*
Mustard, Wilfred Pirt 1864-1932 *DcNAA,*
  HisAmM XR, WhNAA
Muste, Abraham Johannes *AmRP, CurBio XR*
Mutch, David *NF*
Muth, John Francis 1918- *WhoAm 1974*
Muthig, John *NF*
Muto, Al *AmJnl*
Mutschlechner, Joseph 1855?-1950 *BioIn 2*
My, Huynh Thanh *NF*
Mydans, Carl 1907- *AmJnl, WhoAm 1974,*
  WhoE 1974
Mydans, Shelley Smith 1915- *CurBio XR*
Myers, Arthur 1920?- *ConAu 19R,*
  WhoAm 1974
Myers, Charles Samuel 1873-1946 *WebBD*
Myers, Clarence Arnold 1885- *WhJnl 1928*
Myers, Dan *NF*
Myers, Debs 1911?-1971 *BioIn 9, NewYTBE 2*
Myers, Edward Spencer 1894- *WhJnl 1928*
Myers, Fran *BioIn 5*
Myers, Frank A 1848-1930 *DcNAA, IndAu 1917*
Myers, Fred G *OvPC*
Myers, Geoffrey *NF*
Myers, Gustavus 1872-1942 *AmAu&B, BioIn 4,*
  CurBio XR, DcAmB S3, DcLEL, DcNAA,
  HisAmM XR, OxAm, OxCan, TwCA,
  TwCA Sup, WhNAA
Myers, Hortense 1913- *ConAu 1R, ForWC 1970*
Myers, Irving B 1888- *WhJnl 1928*
Myers, J F *NF*
Myers, Joseph Simmons 1867-1953 *BioIn 3,*
  OhA&B, WhJnl 1928
Myers, Lanning 1882- *WhJnl 1928*
Myers, M *NF*
Myers, O R 1860- *WhJnl 1928*
Myers, Robert John 1924- *WhoAm 1974*
Myers, Rollo Hugh 1892- *AmAu&B, Au&Wr,*
  ConAu 19R, WhoMus 1972
Myers, Russ *NF*
Myers, Vernon C 1911- *WhoAm 1974,*
  WhoF&I 1974
Myers, William J G 1868?-1953 *BioIn 3*
Mygatt, Gerald 1887-1955 *BioIn 3*
Mylander, Charles H 1891?-1949 *BioIn 2*
Mylander, Maureen 1937- *ConAu 53*
Mylander, William Herman 1903- *BioIn 2*
Myler, Joseph L 1905?-1973 *ConAu 41*
Mynders, Alfred D 1888-1969 *BioIn 8*

Myrick, Frank Beckwith 1908-1969 *BioIn 8,*
  BioIn 10
Myrick, Harry Pierce 1857-1916 *BioIn 5*
Myrick, Herbert 1860-1927 *AmAu&B, DcNAA,*
  HisAmM XR, NatCAB 25
Myrus, Donald 1927- *BioIn 8, ConAu 1*
Myshuha, Luke 1887?-1955 *BioIn 3*

N

Naar, Joseph L 1843-1905 *NatCAB 13*
Nabeshima, Keizo *NF*
Nabl, Franz 1883-1974 *BioIn 10, OxGer*
Naccache, Ursula *NF*
Nachman, Gerald Weil 1938- *ConAu 65,*
  WhoAm 1974
Nachman, M Milton 1887- *WhJnl 1928*
Nadal, Ehrman Syme 1843-1922 *Alli Sup, AmAu,*
  AmAu&B, BiD&SB, BiDSA, DcAmA,
  DcNAA, HisAmM XR
Nadar 1820-1910 *BioIn 4, BioIn 5, BioIn 7,*
  WebBD
Nadar *see also* Tournachon, Felix
Nadel, Gerald 1945?-1977 *ConAu 73*
Nadel, Norman 1915- *BiE&WWA,*
  WhoThe 1972
Nader, Ralph 1934- *AmAu&B, CelR 1973,*
  CurBio XR, EncAB, IntWW 1974, NewMr,
  Who 1974, WhoWor 1974
Nadir, Isaac Moishe 1885-1943 *DcNAA*
Naemeka, Tony Ike *NF*
Naft, Stephen 1878?-1956 *BioIn 4*
Nagao, Yasushi *NF*
Nagel, Claire *NF*
Nagler, Barney 1912- *ConAu 19R*
Nagorski, Andrew *NF*
Nagorski, Zygmunt, Jr. 1912- *ConAu 73*
Nagourney, Herbert 1926- *WhoAm 1974*
Nagurny, Nick *NF*
Nagy, John D *NF*
Nahl, Charles 1818-1878 *HisAmM XR*
Nahum, Penny L De *NF*
Naidu, Padmaja *HisAmM XR*
Naismith, Grace 1904- *ConAu 65, ForWC 1970,*
  OvPC
Naismith, Helen 1929- *ConAu 69*
Naive, Allen Thomas 1893- *WhJnl 1928*
Najarian, Ross *NF*
Naka, Akira *NF*
Nakamaru, Kaoru 1937?- *BioIn 10*
Nakamura, Hiroaki *OvPC*
Nakamura, Teru 1938?- *NF*
Nakanishi, Hiroshi *NF*
Nakasa, Nathaniel *RpN*
Nakatsuka, Lawrence Kaoru 1920- *RpN,*
  WhoAmP 1973
Nakayama, Tsunehiko *NF*
Naleche, Etienne, Comte De 1865-1947 *WebBD*
Nance, John *NF*
Naning, Jean *NF*
Nankivell, Frank Arthur 1869-1959 *BioIn 5,*
  HisAmM XR, WebBD
Nannen, Henri 1913- *IntWW 1976,*
  WhoWor 1974
Nannes, Caspar Harold 1906- *ConAu 9*
Napier, David *AmJnl*

Napolitano, Gian Gaspare 1907-1966 *BioIn 7*
Narashimhan, Gopalan d1977 *NF*
Narcross, C P *HisAmM XR*
Nares, Robert 1753-1829 *Alli, BiDLA, NewC,*
  WebBD
Narkeliunaite, Salomeja 1920- *NF*
Narodny, Ivan 1870?-1953 *BioIn 3*
Nasby, Petroleum Vesuvius 1833-1888 *Alli Sup,*
  AmAu, AmAu&B, BiD&SB, CnDAL,
  DcAmA, DcEnL, DcLEL, DcNAA, EvLB,
  OhA&B, OxAm, Pen Am, REn, REnAL,
  WebBD
Nasby, Petroleum Vesuvius *see also* Locke, David
  Ross
Nash, Bruce *NF*
Nash, Eno *see* Stevens, Austin
Nash, Harry Douglas 1900?-1954 *BioIn 3*
Nash, Helen W *OvPC*
Nash, Jay Robert 1934- *ConAu 21R, IndAu 1917*
Nash, Jessie Madeline 1943- *ConAu 69*
Nash, Mary F 1900- *WhJnl 1928*
Nash, Max *NF*
Nash, Michael *NF*
Nash, Ruth Cowan *ForWC 1970, OvPC*
Nash, Samuel W 1893?-1949 *BioIn 2*
Nash, Willard Glover 1833-1893 *Alli Sup,*
  BioIn 2, IndAu 1816
Nash, William Francis 1847-1916 *BioIn 5*
Nashashibi, Nasser Eddin 1924- *IntWW 1976*
Nasmyth, Charles *FamWC*
Nason, Elias 1811-1887 *Alli, Alli Sup,*
  AmAu&B, BiD&SB, CyAL 2, DcAmA,
  DcNAA, HisAmM XR
Nason, Harry B, Jr. 1895- *WhJnl 1928*
Nast, Conde Montrose 1873?-1942 *AmAu&B,*
  DcAmB S3, HisAmM XR
Nast, Thomas 1840-1902 *AmJnl, BioIn 3,*
  BioIn 7, BioIn 8, BioIn 9, EarABI,
  EarABI Sup, EncAB, OxAm, REn, REnAL,
  WebBD
Nastvogel, Kurt Uwe 1948- *BioIn 8*
Natanson, George 1928- *ConAu 73, OvPC*
Natesan, G A *BioIn 8*
Nathan, Adele Gutman *ForWC 1970, OvPC,*
  WhoAm 1974, WhoAmW 1974
Nathan, Bernard E *OvPC*
Nathan, David 1926- *ConAu 29, WrDr 1976*
Nathan, Emily *OvPC*
Nathan, George Jean 1882-1958 *AmAu&B,*
  CnDAL, ConAmA, ConAmL, CurBio XR,
  DcLEL, HisAmM XR, IndAu 1816, LongC,
  ModAL, NatCAB XR, OxAm, OxEng,
  Pen Am, REn, REnAL, TwCA, TwCA Sup,
  WebBD
Nathan, Henry C *HisAmM XR*
Nathan, Paul S 1913- *WhoAm 1974*

Nathanson, Yale S 1895- *WhJnl 1928*
Naudeau, Ludovic 1872-1949 *BioIn 2*
Naughton, James M *NF*
Naumann, Oscar Edward 1912- *WhoAm 1974*
Navas, Jesus Anez *NF*
Navasky, Victor Saul 1932- *ConAu 21,*
  WhoE 1974
Nax, Charles W 1881- *WhJnl 1928*
Naylor, Aubrey W *HisAmM XR*
Naylor, John H *WhJnl 1928*
Naylor, John L 1898- *WhJnl 1928*
Naylor, Margot Lodge 1907- *ConAu 11R*
Neal, Austin E 1869-1941 *DcNAA*
Neal, Fred Warner 1915- *AmM&W 73S,*
  ConAu 5, RpN, WhoAm 1974,
  WhoAmP 1973, WrDr 1976
Neal, Harold L, Jr. 1924- *WhoAm 1974,*
  WhoE 1974, WhoF&I 1974
Neal, James Madison 1925- *ConAu 73*
Neal, John 1793-1876 *Alli, Alli Sup, AmAu,*
  AmAu&B, BbD, BbtC, BiD&SB, CasWL,
  CnDAL, CyAL 1, DcAmA, DcEnL, DcLEL,
  DcNAA, EvLB, HisAmM XR, HsB&A,
  LiJA, OxAm, Pen Am, REnAL, WebBD
Neal, Joseph Clay 1807-1847 *Alli, AmAu,*
  AmAu&B, BiD&SB, CyAL 2, DcAmA,
  DcAmB 13, DcLEL, DcNAA, HisAmM XR,
  OxAm, REnAL
Neal, Lloyd Gilbert 1901- *WhJnl 1928*
Neal, Robert Miller 1901-1950 *BioIn 2*
Neal, Robert Wilson 1871-1939 *DcNAA*
Neal, Roy *NF*
Neale, Walter 1873-1933 *AmAu&B, BiDSA,*
  DcNAA, HisAmM XR
Neall, Adelaide W 1884- *WhJnl Sup*
Nease, Jack *NF*
Neblett, Mrs. Boyd S 1878- *WhJnl 1928*
Neeb, Harry A 1850-1934 *NatCAB 27*
Needham, Henry Beach 1871-1915 *AmJnl,*
  DcNAA
Needham, James P 1891- *WhJnl 1928*
Needham, John R 1873- *WhJnl 1928*
Needham, R J *NF*
Needham, Wilbur *AmRP*
Needham, William P 1853-1899 *BioIn 2,*
  IndAu 1816
Neef, Walter *AmJnl*
Neergaard, Niels 1854-1936 *WebBD*
Neesham, Robin *OvPC*
Neff, Donald *NF*
Neff, Ward Andrew 1891-1959 *BioIn 5, BioIn 7,*
  NatCAB 49, WhJnl 1928
Nefftzer, Auguste 1820-1876 *WebBD*
Negre, Maurice 1901- *IntWW 1976*
Negronida, Peter Richard 1938- *WhoAm 1974*
Neher, Fred 1903- *WhoAmA 1973*
Neideg, William Jonathan d1955 *AmAu&B*
Neigoff, Michael 1920- *ConAu 5R,*
  WhoAm 1974
Neihardt, John Gneisenau 1881-1973 *AmAu&B,*
  AmLY, AnMV 1926, CnDAL, ConAmA,
  ConAmL, ConAu 13, ConAu P-1,
  IntWW 1974, OxAm, REn, REnAL, TwCA,
  TwCA Sup, WebBD, WhoMW 1974
Neikirk, William *NF*
Neil, Edward J d1936 *NF*
Neil, George Mahon 1907-1957 *BioIn 4*
Neil, Helen 1906?-1964 *BioIn 7*
Neilan, Edward *OvPC*
Neill, Paul 1892-1940 *NF*
Neill, Rolfe 1932- *WhoAm 1974, WhoE 1974*
Neilson, John 1776-1848 *Alli, BbtC, OxCan,*
  WebBD
Neilson, Rutgers 1892- *WhJnl 1928*

Neily, Harry 1881- *WhJnl 1928*
Neimore, J J *BlkC*
Nelan, Bruce W *NF*
Nell, William Cooper 1816-1874 *Alli, AmAu,*
  AmAu&B, BioIn 9, DcNAA, REnAL,
  WebBD
Nellor, William *NF*
Nelsen, Wallie *NF*
Nelson, Alice-Dunbar *WhJnl 1928*
Nelson, Allen H 1879-1944 *NatCAB 33*
Nelson, Ames *NF*
Nelson, Arla Reed 1912- *WhoAm 1974,*
  WhoF&I 1974
Nelson, Arthur Magnus 1876- *WhJnl 1928*
Nelson, Benjamin H *OvPC*
Nelson, Bentley 1888- *WhJnl 1928*
Nelson, C Hjalmar 1905- *WhoAm 1974*
Nelson, Charles Edgar 1889- *WhJnl 1928*
Nelson, Cordner 1918- *ConAu 29, WrDr 1976*
Nelson, Edna *BioIn 6*
Nelson, Frank L 1873-1947 *BioIn 1, WhJnl 1928*
Nelson, Frederic Cooke 1893- *BioIn 1*
Nelson, Godfrey Nicholas 1878-1954 *BioIn 3*
Nelson, Harry 1923- *WhoAm 1974,*
  WhoWest 1974
Nelson, Henry Loomis 1846-1908 *Alli Sup,*
  AmAu, AmAu&B, BbD, BiD&SB, DcAmA,
  DcNAA, LiJA
Nelson, Jack 1929- *BioIn 9, ConAu XR, InvJ,*
  NewMr
Nelson, Jack *see also* Nelson, John Howard
Nelson, James Anthony 1920- *BioIn 8,*
  WhoAdv 1972
Nelson, John 1873-1936 *DcNAA*
Nelson, John Howard 1929- *BioIn 9, ConAu 29,*
  RpN, WhoAm 1974, WhoS&SW 1973
Nelson, John Howard *see also* Nelson, Jack
Nelson, Josephine 1898- *WhJnl 1928*
Nelson, Lars-Erik *NF*
Nelson, Nels Robert 1923- *WhoAm 1974*
Nelson, Raymond 1892- *WhJnl 1928*
Nelson, Robert C 1931?- *NF*
Nelson, Robert Duane 1920- *WhoAdv 1972,*
  WhoAm 1974, WhoF&I 1974
Nelson, Robert J 1877- *WhJnl 1928*
Nelson, Robin *NF*
Nelson, Roy Paul 1923- *ConAu 19R, DrAS 74E,*
  WhoWest 1974, WrDr 1976
Nelson, W Dale 1927- *NF*
Nelson, Walter Henry 1928- *AmAu&B,*
  ConAu 15, OvPC, WhoAm 1974
Nelson, Warren L *NF*
Nelson, William C 1871?-1954 *BioIn 3*
Nelson, William Rockhill 1841-1915 *AmJnl,*
  BioIn 1, BioIn 2, BioIn 3, DcAmB 12,
  ForP, WebBD
Nemer, Jack *Lor&LP*
Nenni, Pietro 1891- *CurBio XR, ForP,*
  IntWW 1976
Nenning, Charles N 1886- *WhJnl 1928*
Neotz, C H 1869- *WhJnl 1928*
Nerman, Einar 1888- *IntWW 1976,*
  WhoWor 1974
Nerman, Ture 1886- *BioIn 1, CIDMEL*
Neruda, Jan 1834-1891 *BbD, BiD&SB, CasWL,*
  CIDMEL, DcEuL, EuAu, EvEuW, Pen Eur,
  WebBD
Nesbit, Wilbur Dick 1871-1927 *AmAu&B, AmJnl,*
  BioIn 2, DcNAA, IndAu 1816, OhA&B
Nesoff, Bob 1938- *NF*
Nessel, Jack *NF*
Nessen, Ronald H 1934- *BioNews 1974,*
  NewYTBS 5
Nesterowicz, Melania 1876?-1951 *BioIn 2*

Neth, Cecil Berle 1924- *WhoAm 1974*
Nettleton, Alvred Bayard 1838-1911 *DcAmB 13,*
　DcNAA, OhA&B
Nettleton, Ida *NF*
Nettleton, Mary 1906-1965 *BioIn 7*
Neu, George 1878-1927 *WhJnl Sup, WhJnl 1928*
Neubacher, Jim *NF*
Neubauer, Chuck *InvJ*
Neubauer, Kurt *OvPC*
Neuberger, Richard Lewis 1912-1960 *AmAu&B,*
　BioIn 2, BioIn 3, BioIn 4, BioIn 5, BioIn 7,
　CurBio XR
Neuerbourg, Hanns *NF*
Neuharth, Allen Harold 1924- *WhoAm 1974,*
　WhoF&I 1974
Neuman, Ladd A 1942?- *NF*
Neumann, Jonathan 1950?- *NF*
Neumann, Louis d1892 *NF*
Neuschotz, Charles *AmRP*
Nevard, Jacques 1925-1977 *NF*
Nevill, John Tobin 1901- *WhJnl 1928*
Neville, Glenn 1906-1965 *BioIn 7*
Neville, John *WhoS&SW 1973*
Neville, Paul Edwin 1919-1969 *BioIn 8*
Neville, Robert 1905-1970 *BioIn 2, BioIn 8,*
　NewYTBE 1
Nevin, David *NF*
Nevin, Hugh Williamson 1902- *WhJnl 1928*
Nevin, James Banks 1873-1931 *WhJnl 1928*
Nevin, John Edwin *NF*
Nevin, Louis *NF*
Nevin, Robert Peebles 1820-1908 *Alli Sup,*
　AmAu&B, DcAmA, DcAmB 13, DcNAA,
　OhA&B
Nevin, Theodore Williamson 1854-1918 *DcNAA*
Nevin, William Channing 1844-1920 *Alli Sup,*
　AmAu&B, AmLY, BiD&SB, DcAmA,
　OhA&B　　　　　　　　　　.
Nevin, William Wilberforce 1836-1899 *Alli Sup,*
　DcAmA, DcNAA
Nevins, Albert J 1915- *AuBYP, BioIn 3,*
　BioIn 7, BkC 6, CathA 1952, ConAu 5,
　OvPC, WhoAm 1974
Nevins, Allan 1890-1971 *AmAu&B, BioIn 8,*
　BioIn 9, BioIn 10, ConAu 5R, ConAu 29,
　CurBio XR, EncAB, LongC, NewYTBE 2,
　OxAm, Pen Am, REn, REnAL, TwCA,
　TwCA Sup, WebBD
Nevins, James F d1892 *NF*
Nevins, Winfield Scott 1850-1921 *DcAmA,*
　DcNAA, NatCAB 19
Nevinson, Henry Woodd 1856-1941 *BioIn 5,*
　EvLB, LongC, NewC, TwCA, TwCA Sup,
　WebBD
New, Clarence Herbert 1862-1933 *DcAmA,*
　DcNAA
New, Harry Stewart 1858-1937 *DcAmB S2,*
　WebBD
Newberry, Perry 1870-1938 *AmAu&B, AmLY,*
　DcNAA
Newbery, John 1713-1767 *Alli, BrAu, DcLEL,*
　NewC, REn, REnAL, WebBD, WhoChL
Newbold, Fleming 1873-1949 *AmJnl, BioIn 1,*
　WhJnl 1928
Newbolt, Sir Henry John 1862-1938 *CarSB,*
　DcEnA Ap, DcLEL, EvLB, LongC, ModBL,
　NewC, OxEng, Pen Eng, REn, TwCA,
　TwCA Sup, WebBD
Newborn, Roy I *OvPC*
Newbranch, Harvey Ellsworth 1875-1959 *BioIn 1,*
　BioIn 5, BioIn 6, NatCAB 44
Newby, Eric 1919- *Au&Wr, BioIn 9,*
　ConAu 7R, Who 1974, WrDr 1976
Newcomb, Richard Fairchild 1913- *AmAu&B,*

ConAu 1R, *WhoAm 1974*
Newcombe, Jack *AuBYP, BioIn 8*
Newcombe, Leo Raymond 1921- *WhoAm 1974*
Newcomer, Lee M 1880- *WhJnl 1928*
Newell, Frank S *WhJnl 1928*
Newell, Peter 1862-1924 *AmAu&B, CarSB,*
　DcAmA, DcNAA, OxAm, WebBD
Newell, Robert Henry 1836-1901 *Alli, AmAu,*
　AmAu&B, AmJnl, BiD&SB, CnDAL,
　DcAmA, DcAmB 13, DcEnL, DcLEL,
　DcNAA, EvLB, NatCAB 11, OxAm, REn,
　REnAL, WebBD
Newell, Robert Henry *see also* Kerr, Orpheus C
Newell, William *AmJnl*
Newell, William F 1918?-1977 *NF*
Newett, George A *BioIn 7*
Newfield, Jack 1939- *AmAu&B, BioIn 8,*
　BioIn 10, ConAu 21R, InvJ, WhoAm 1974
Newfield, Maurice 1893-1949 *BioIn 2*
Newgate, J Baxter 1947- *NF*
Newhall, Scott 1914- *BioIn 8, BioIn 9,*
　WhoAm 1974, WhoWest 1974
Newhouse, Nancy *NF*
Newhouse, Norman Nathan 1906- *WhoAm 1974*
Newhouse, Samuel Irving 1896- *AmJnl, BioIn 2,*
　BioIn 3, BioIn 5, BioIn 6, BioIn 7,
　CurBio XR, IntWW 1976, WhoAm 1974,
　WhoE 1974
Newhouse, Wynter Reed 1915- *WhoAm 1974*
Newkirk, Newton 1870-1938 *AmAu&B, DcNAA*
Newland, Lynn C *NF*
Newlin, Stewart *NF*
Newlinski, Philipp Michael De 1841-1899 *BioIn 5*
Newman, Abram 1882- *WhJnl Sup, WhJnl 1928*
Newman, Amy *NF*
Newman, Andrew Joseph, Jr. 1917- *WhoAm 1974*
Newman, Cecil Earl 1903- *BioIn 8,*
　WhoAm 1974,ˑ WhoF&I 1974
Newman, Claude d1976 *NF*
Newman, David 1937- *BioIn 8, IntMPA 1975,*
　WhoAm 1974
Newman, Earl F 1901- *WhJnl 1928*
Newman, Edwin Harold 1919- *BioIn 6, BioIn 7,*
　BioIn 8, BioNews 1974, CelR 1973,
　ConAu 69, CurBio XR, WhoAm 1974,
　WhoE 1974
Newman, Elias 1903- *OvPC, WhoAm 1974,*
　WhoAmA 1973, WhoWorJ 1972
Newman, Eugene William 1845- *BiDSA, DcNAA*
Newman, Frances *WhJnl 1928*
Newman, H W Richard *NF*
Newman, Harold *OvPC*
Newman, Harry *AmJnl*
Newman, Henry Hardin 1894?- *BioIn 1*
Newman, James Roy 1907-1966 *AmAu&B,*
　BioIn 7, BioIn 9
Newman, Cardinal John Henry 1801-1890 *Alli,*
　Alli Sup, AtlBL, BbD, BiD&SB, BrAu 19,
　CasWL, CrtT 3, CyWA, DcEnA, DcEnL,
　DcEuL, DcLEL, EvLB, MouLC 4, NewC,
　OxEng, Pen Eng, PoChrch, REn, WebBD,
　WebE&AL
Newman, John Jeffrey 1907-1953 *BioIn 3*
Newman, Joseph *OvPC*
Newman, Joseph Simon 1891-1960 *AmAu&B,*
　OhA&B
Newman, Larry G *OvPC*
Newman, M W 1917- *WhoAm 1974*
Newman, Neil 1886?-1951 *BioIn 2*
Newman, Peter Charles 1929- *CanWW 1972,*
　ConAu 11R, OxCan, OxCan Sup,
　WhoE 1974, WhoWorJ 1972
Newman, Stanley 1935- *WhoAm 1974*
Newman, Yale 1923- *OvPC, USBiR 1974,*

Nilsson, Hjalmar 1860-1936 *DcNAA*
Nilsson, Victor 1867-1942 *AmAu&B, AmLY*
Nimmer, David *NF*
Nimnicht, Nona 1930- *ConAu 73*
Nims, John Frederick 1913- *AmAu&B,*
CathA 1952, ConAu 15, ConP 1970,
ConP 1975, DrAP 1975, DrAS 74E, OxAm,
REn, REnAL, TwCA Sup, WhoAm 1974,
WhoWor 1974, WrDr 1976
Ninomiya, Joanne Miyako 1940- *WhoAm 1974,*
WhoAmW 1974
Nipson, Herbert 1916- *BioIn 10, WhoAm 1974*
Nirdlinger, C F *HisAmM XR*
Nirdlinger, Charles J *HisAmM XR*
Nirdlinger, Samuel F *HisAmM XR*
Nisard, Desire 1806-1888 *DcEuL, OxFr, REn,*
WebBD
Nisberg, Jack L *OvPC*
Nisbett, William Charles 1877-1955 *BioIn 4*
Nissen, Carl B 1884- *WhJnl 1928*
Nissenson, Aaron 1897-1964 *BioIn 6*
Niswiski, Norbert *NF*
Niven, L A 1883- *WhJnl 1928*
Niven, Paul 1924?-1970 *BioIn 8, NewYTBE 1*
Nixon, Edward L 1910?-1949 *BioIn 1*
Nixon, Floyd S 1890-1972 *NF*
Nixon, Glenn C *RpN*
Nixon, Oliver Woodson 1825-1905? *DcAmA,*
DcNAA, OhA&B
Nixon, Raymond Blalock 1903- *AmM&W 73S,*
ForP, WhoAm 1974
Nixon, William Penn 1833-1912 *AmJnl,*
DcAmB 13, NatCAB 9
Nkosi, Lewis P 1936- *ConAu 65, RpN*
Noah, Jacob J *NF*
Noah, Mordecai Manuel 1785-1851 *Alli, AmAu,*
AmAu&B, AmJnl, BbD, BiD&SB, BioIn 1,
BioIn 2, BioIn 4, BioIn 8, BioIn 9,
CyAL 1, DcAmA, DcAmB 13, DcLEL,
DcNAA, HisAmM XR, OxAm, REnAL,
WebBD
Nobel, David W *HisAmM XR*
Nobile, Philip 1941- *WhoE 1974*
Noble, Alden Charles *HisAmM XR*
Noble, Daniel Earl 1901- *WhoAm 1974*
Noble, Edmund 1853-1937 *Alli Sup, BiD&SB,*
DcAmA, DcNAA, HisAmM XR
Noble, Frederic Perry 1863-1945 *BioIn 2,*
NatCAB 35
Noble, Frederick Alphonso *HisAmM XR*
Noble, Gil *BlkC*
Noble, Howard A 1898- *WhJnl 1928*
Noble, Roberto J 1904?-1969 *BioIn 8*
Nobs, Ernst 1886-1957 *CurBio XR*
Nocella, Sam *NF*
Nocera, Joseph *InvJ*
Nock, Albert Jay 1873?-1945 *AmAu&B,*
CurBio XR, DcAmB S3, DcNAA,
HisAmM XR, OxAm, REnAL, TwCA,
TwCA Sup
Nocton, Edward J 1868?-1947 *BioIn 1*
Noe, James A, Jr. *WhoS&SW 1973*
Noe, James Albert 1893-1976 *WhoAm 1974,*
WhoAmP 1973
Noeggerath, Emil 1827-1895 *HisAmM XR*
Noel, Eugenio 1885-1936 *BioIn 1, CIDMEL*
Noel, Frank d1966 *NF*
Noel, Lucie 1899?-1972 *BioIn 9, NewYTBE 3*
Noel, Pappy d1966 *NF*
Noel, Sterling 1903- *Au&Wr, WhoF&I 1974*
Nofziger, Ed *NF*
Noggle, Mears B 1902- *WhJnl 1928*
Nohe, Camille H 1891- *WhJnl 1928*
Nokes, John Richard 1915- *WhoAm 1974*

Nokes, R Gregory 1938?- *NF*
Nolan, Brian 1911-1966 *BioIn 2, BioIn 7,*
BioIn 8, ConAu XR
Nolan, Martin F *NF*
Nolan, Mary *HisAmM XR*
Noland, Stephen Croan 1887-1962 *BioIn 3,*
IndAu 1917
Nolasco, Teddy De *BioIn 6*
Nolen, Barbara 1902- *WhoAmW 1974,*
WhoE 1974
Nolen, William A *NF*
Noll, Henry 1877- *WhJnl 1928*
Nolte, Carl 1933- *NF*
Nomad, Max 1880?-1973 *AmAu&B, BioIn 8,*
BioIn 9, ConAu 41
Noonan, Josiah A 1813-1882 *BioIn 5*
Noonan, Ollie *NF*
Noonan, Ray John 1914- *WhoMW 1974*
Noone, Anna A 1900-1965 *BioIn 7*
Noor, Bob *NF*
Norcross, Theodore White 1883-1965 *BioIn 7*
Norcross, W F *HisAmM XR*
Nordau, Max Simon 1849-1923 *BbD, BiD&SB,*
DcEuL, EvEuW, LongC, TwCA Sup,
WebBD
Nordell, Hans Roderick 1925- *WhoAm 1974,*
WhoE 1974
Norden, Albert 1904- *IntWW 1974*
Norden, Robert B 1924- *WhoAm 1974,*
WhoE 1974
Nordhoff, Charles 1830-1901 *Alli, Alli Sup,*
AmAu, AmAu&B, AmJnl, BbD, BiD&SB,
CarSB, CnDAL, CyAL 2, DcAmA,
DcAmB 13, DcNAA, HisAmM XR,
OhA&B, OxAm, REnAL, WebBD
Nordin, Gustaf Adolph 1911- *WhoAm 1974,*
WhoWest 1974
Nordlinger, Stephen Edward 1930- *WhoAm 1974*
Norgaard, Noland *NF*
Norman, Albert E *OvPC*
Norman, Amandus 1865-1931 *BioIn 3*
Norman, Dan *NF*
Norman, Dorothy 1905- *ConAu 25,*
WhoAmA 1973
Norman, Geoffrey *NF*
Norman, Sir Henry 1858-1939 *Alli Sup, BbD,*
BiD&SB, DcAmA, NewC, WebBD
Norman, John T *NF*
Norman, Joyce Ann 1937- *ConAu 65*
Norman, Philip *BioIn 5*
Normark, Don *NF*
Norrell, Byron 1875- *WhJnl 1928*
Norris, Benjamin Franklin 1870-1902 *DcAmB 13,*
DcNAA, EncAB, WebBD
Norris, Benjamin Franklin *see also* Norris, Frank
Norris, Charles Gilman 1881-1945 *AmAu&B,*
CnDAL, ConAmL, CurBio XR, DcAmB S3,
DcNAA, HisAmM XR, LongC, OxAm,
REnAL, TwCA, TwCA Sup, WebBD
Norris, David Windsor 1876-1949 *BioIn 2,*
WhJnl 1928
Norris, Edward James *HisAmM XR*
Norris, Frank 1870-1902 *AmAu&B, AmJnl,*
AmWr, AtlBL, BbD, BiD&SB, CasWL,
CnDAL, CrtT 3, CyWA, DcAmA, DcBiA,
DcLEL, DcNAA, EvLB, FamWC,
HisAmM XR, LongC, ModAL, OxAm,
OxEng, Pen Am, RAdv 1, REn, REnAL,
TwCA, TwCA Sup, TwCW, WebE&AL
Norris, Frank *see also* Norris, Benjamin Franklin
Norris, Hoke 1913-1977 *ConAu 11R, ConAu 73,*
ConNov 1972, ConNov 1976, RpN,
WhoAm 1974, WrDr 1976
Norris, J A 1929- *ConAu 25*

Norris, J Parker *HisAmM XR*
Norris, Jane E *NF*
Norris, John *NF*
Norris, Leonard M 1913?- *BioIn 2, BioIn 3*
Norris, Paul *NF*
Norris, True L 1848-1920 *NatCAB 20*
Norsen, Nathaniel 1915?-1974 *BioIn 10*
North, Christopher 1785-1854 *BbD, BiD&SB,
   BrAu 19, CasWL, DcEnA, DcEnL, DcEuL,
   DcLEL, EvLB, NewC, Pen Eng, REn,
   WebBD, WebE&AL*
North, Christopher *see also* Wilson, John
North, Don *NF*
North, Ernest Dressel 1858- *AmAu&B*
North, H Lee 1884- *WhJnl 1928*
North, James Mortimer 1886-1956 *BioIn 4,
   WhJnl 1928*
North, Jessica Nelson 1894- *AmAu&B,
   HisAmM XR, TwCA, TwCA Sup*
North, Joseph 1904-1976 *BioIn 5, ConAu 2R,
   ConAu 69*
North, Simon Newton Dexter 1848-1924 *BioIn 6,
   DcNAA, LiJA*
North, Sterling 1906-1974 *AmAu&B, AmNov,
   Au&Wr, AuBYP, BioIn 2, ConAu 5R,
   ConAu 53, CurBio XR, NewYTBS 5,
   REnAL, SmATA 1, ThrBJA, TwCA,
   TwCA Sup, WhoAm 1974, WhoE 1974*
North, William *HisAmM XR*
Northart, Leo Joseph 1929- *ConAu 69*
Northcliffe, Alfred Harmsworth, Viscount
   1865-1922 *BioIn 1, BioIn 2, BioIn 3,
   BioIn 4, BioIn 5, BioIn 7, BioIn 9, DcLEL,
   Lor&LP, OxEng*
Northcliffe, Alfred Harmsworth, Viscount *see also*
   Harmsworth, A
Northcott, Kaye *NewMr*
Northcross, Grace *NF*
Northington, James Montgomery 1885-1964
   BioIn 8, NatCAB 50
Northrop, Benjamin d1900 *NF*
Northrop, Guy Santee, Jr. 1923- *WhoAm 1974*
Northrop, N B *NF*
Northrup, Bowen *NF*
Northshield, Robert J *NF*
Northup, Stephen D *NF*
Norton, Adelaide I d1950 *NF*
Norton, Andrews 1786-1853 *Alli, AmAu,
   AmAu&B, CyAL 1, DcAmA, DcEnL,
   DcNAA, HisAmM XR, OxAm*
Norton, B Hammatt *AmJnl*
Norton, Catharine *NF*
Norton, Charles Benjamin 1825-1891 *Alli,
   Alli Sup, DcAmA, DcNAA, HisAmM XR*
Norton, Charles E 1905- *WhJnl 1928*
Norton, Charles Eliot 1827-1908 *Alli, Alli Sup,
   AmAu, AmAu&B, BbD, BiD&SB, CarSB,
   CyAL 2, DcAmA, DcNAA, EncAB, EvLB,
   HisAmM XR, LiJA, LongC, OxAm,
   Pen Am, REn, WebBD*
Norton, Charles Ledyard 1837-1909 *Alli Sup,
   BbD, BiD&SB, DcAmA, DcNAA,
   HisAmM XR*
Norton, Conrad *NF*
Norton, Edward C 1937?- *NF*
Norton, Elliot 1903- *BiE&WWA, CelR 1973,
   WhoAm 1974, WhoThe 1972*
Norton, Frank Henry 1836-1921 *Alli Sup,
   DcAmA, DcNAA*
Norton, Frank R B 1909- *ConAu 61, SmATA 10*
Norton, George Lowell 1837-1923 *HisAmM XR*
Norton, Harold F 1837-1923 *WhJnl Sup*
Norton, Harry J d1879 *BioIn 7*
Norton, Howard Melvin 1911- *BioIn 1,*

ConAu 4R, CurBio XR, WhoAm 1974
Norton, Jacob *HisAmM XR*
Norton, Jerry W 1946- *NF*
Norton, John H 1858-1916 *BioIn 7*
Norton, Robert L 1886?-1948 *BioIn 1*
Norton, Roy 1869-1942 *AmAu&B, DcNAA*
Norton, S *NF*
Norton-Taylor, Duncan 1904- *BioIn 2,
   WhoAm 1974*
Nossiter, Bernard Daniel 1926- *ConAu 41,
   NewMr, RpN, WhoAm 1974, WhoWor 1974*
Notson, Robert C 1902- *WhoAm 1974,
   WhoWest 1974*
Nourissier, Francois 1927- *IntWW 1976,
   WhoWor 1974*
Nourse, Dale *NF*
Novack, George 1905- *AmRP, ConAu 49,
   WhoAm 1974, WhoWor 1974*
Novak, Michael *NF*
Novak, Ralph *NF*
Novak, Robert David Sanders 1931- *BioIn 7,
   ConAu 13R, WhoAm 1974*
Novaseda, Tina *NF*
Nover, Barnet 1899-1973 *BioIn 1, BioIn 9,
   ConAu 41, NewYTBE 4, WhoWor 1974*
Nover, Naomi *NF*
Novikov, Nikolai Ivanovich 1744-1818 *BioIn 1,
   BioIn 7, BioIn 9, BioIn 10, WebBD*
Novikov, Olga Kireev 1840-1925 *BioIn 2, WebBD*
Novitz, Charles R 1934- *ConAu 69*
Novomesky, Ladislav 1904-1976 *ConAu 69,
   IntWW 1976, ModSL 2, WhoWor 1974*
Novotney, John A *NF*
Nowak, Tadeusz 1930- *IntWW 1976*
Nowogrodsky, Emanuel 1891?-1967 *BioIn 8*
Noyes, Alexander Dana 1862-1945 *AmLY,
   DcAmA, DcAmB S3, DcNAA,
   HisAmM XR, WhJnl 1928*
Noyes, Crosby Stuart 1825-1908 *AmJnl,
   DcAmB 13, NatCAB 5, NatCAB 28,
   WebBD*
Noyes, Crosby Stuart 1921- *WhoAm 1974,
   WhoS&SW 1973*
Noyes, Frank Brett 1863-1948 *AmJnl, BioIn 1,
   BioIn 2, DcAmB S4, WebBD, WhJnl 1928*
Noyes, Frank Eugene 1856-1941 *WhJnl 1928*
Noyes, George W *HisAmM XR*
Noyes, James Oscar 1829-1872 *Alli, BiDSA,
   DcAmA, DcNAA, HisAmM XR*
Noyes, Linwood Irving 1894-1964 *BioIn 2,
   BioIn 6, BioIn 8, NatCAB 51, WhJnl 1928*
Noyes, Newbold 1892-1942 *AmJnl, DcNAA*
Noyes, Newbold 1918- *BioIn 1, BioIn 6,
   WhoAm 1974, WhoS&SW 1973*
Noyes, Theodore Williams 1858-1946 *AmJnl,
   BioIn 1, BioIn 6, DcAmA, DcNAA,
   WebBD*
Noyes, William Albert 1857-1941 *AmLY,
   DcAmA, HisAmM XR*
Nuckols, William P 1905- *CurBio XR*
Nugent, Allyne Velome *BioIn 1*
Nugent, Art *NF*
Nugent, John *AmJnl*
Nugent, John Peer 1930?- *ConAu 15R,
   WhoAm 1974*
Nugent, Tom 1943- *ConAu 49*
Nuhn, Clifford J 1903?-1969 *BioIn 8*
Nunan, Thomas 1868?-1957 *BioIn 4*
Nunberg, Ralph M 1903?-1949 *BioIn 1*
Nunez De Arce, Gaspar 1834-1903 *BbD, BiD&SB,
   CasWL, CIDMEL, DcSpL, EuAu, McGWD,
   Pen Eur, WebBD*
Nunn, Gary *NF*
Nunn, Robert Alexander 1904- *WhJnl 1928*

Nunn, W R 1926- *NF*
Nurenberg, Thelma 1903- *AuBYP, BioIn 8,*
   ConAu 69
Nursey, Walter R 1847-1927 *DcNAA*
Nuschke, Otto 1883-1957 *BioIn 4*
Nussbaum, Lowell B 1901- *WhJnl 1928*
Nussbaum, Martin *NF*
Nussbaum, Max Ehrlich 1907- *WhoAm 1974,*
   WhoS&SW 1973
Nutt, Alfred Trubner 1856-1910 *Alli Sup, WebBD*
Nutter, Joseph W 1900?-1948 *BioIn 1*
Nutter, William Herbert 1874-1941 *DcNAA*
Nxumalo, Henry 1917-1957 *AfA 1, BioIn 4*
Nyblom, Lennart 1915?- *BioIn 3*
Nycop, Carl Adam 1909- *BioIn 5, ForP*
Nydick, David 1929- *WhoE 1974*
Nye, Bill 1850-1896 *AmAu, AmAu&B, CnDAL,*
   DcAmA, DcLEL, DcNAA, HisAmM XR,
   REnAL, WebBD
Nye, Bill *see also* Nye, Edgar Wilson
Nye, Edgar Wilson 1850-1896 *Alli Sup, AmAu,*
   AmJnl, BbD, BiD&SB, BioIn 2, BioIn 5,
   BioIn 9, DcAmA, DcAmB 13, DcLEL,
   DcNAA, HisAmM XR, OxAm, WebBD,
   WisWr
Nye, Edgar Wilson *see also* Nye, Bill
Nye, Gerald P 1892-1971 *CurBio XR,*
   NatCAB XR, NewYTBE 2, WebBD
Nye, Phila 1871- *BioIn 1*
Nyhan, David *NF*
Nylund, Felix Alexander 1907- *BioIn 2*
Nyren, Karl 1921- *NF*

O

O Henry *see* Porter, William Sydney
O K *see* Novikov, Olga Kireev
Oak, Liston M 1895-1970 *BioIn 8, NewYTBE 1*
Oakes, George Washington 1861-1931 *AmAu&B, OhA&B, WebBD*
Oakes, George Washington *see also* Ochs, George Washington
Oakes, George Washington *see also* Ochs-Oakes, George Washington
Oakes, George Washington 1909-1965 *BioIn 9*
Oakes, John Bertram 1913- *BioIn 5, BioIn 8, ConAu 15R, IntWW 1976, WhoAm 1974, WhoE 1974, WhoWorJ 1972*
Oakes, Ken *NF*
Oakey, Charles Cochran 1845-1908 *BioIn 2, DcNAA, IndAu 1816*
Oakley, Don 1927- *ConAu 29, SmATA 8*
Oakley, Ray M 1876- *WhJnl 1928*
Oaksmith, Alvin *HisAmM XR*
Oaksmith, Appleton *HisAmM XR*
Oaksmith, Edward *HisAmM XR*
Oaksmith, Sidney *HisAmM XR*
Oancia, David 1929- *BioIn 7, CanWW 1972*
Oat, William H 1867?-1947 *BioIn 1*
Oatis, William Nathan 1914- *BioIn 2, BioIn 3, BioIn 8, WhoAm 1974, WhoWor 1974*
Ober, Josephine Robb *WhJnl 1928*
Oberbeck, Stephen K *NF*
Oberdorfer, Don *NF*
Oberg, Erik 1881-1951 *BioIn 1, BioIn 2*
Oberholtzer, Ellis Paxson 1868-1936 *AmAu&B, DcAmA, DcAmB S2, DcNAA, HisAmM XR, LiJA, WhNAA*
Oberlin, Lindley B 1870- *WhJnl 1928*
Obermaier, Hannes *BioIn 5*
Oberman, Mike *NF*
Oberman, Ron *NF*
Obermayer, Herman Joseph 1924- *ConAu 65, WhoF&I 1974, WhoS&SW 1973*
Oberndorf, Ludwig 1887?-1966 *BioIn 7, WhNAA*
Obert, John *RpN*
Obis, Paul 1951- *NF*
O'Boyle, Doug *NF*
O'Brady, Frederic *BioIn 6*
O'Brian, Jack 1914- *IntMPA 1975*
O'Brien, Alfred S 1889?-1951 *BioIn 2*
O'Brien, Andrew William 1910- *ConAu 25*
O'Brien, Conor Cruise 1917- *CurBio XR, IntWW 1974, Who 1974, WhoWor 1974, WorAu, WrDr 1976*
O'Brien, Dillon 1817-1882 *Alli Sup, DcNAA, PoIre*
O'Brien, Edward Joseph Harrington 1890-1941 *AmAu&B, BioIn 1, CathA 1930, CnDAL, CurBio XR, DcNAA, HisAmM XR, LongC, OxAm, REnAL, TwCA, TwCA Sup,*
WebBD, WhNAA
O'Brien, Edward William 1916- *WhoAm 1974, WhoS&SW 1973*
O'Brien, Fitz-James 1828?-1862 *Alli Sup, AmAu, AmAu&B, BbD, BiD&SB, BioIn 7, CnDAL, DcAmA, DcAmB 13, DcNAA, HisAmM XR, OxAm, Pen Am, PoIre, REn, REnAL*
Obrien, Florence J 1865- *WhJnl 1928*
O'Brien, Frank George 1843-1920 *DcNAA*
O'Brien, Frank Michael 1875-1943 *AmAu&B, AmJnl, DcNAA, HisAmM XR, NatCAB 32, REnAL, WhJnl 1928*
O'Brien, Frank P 1844- *NatCAB 1*
O'Brien, Frederick 1869-1932 *AmAu&B, ConAmL, DcAmB 13, DcNAA, HisAmM XR, OhA&B, OxAm, REnAL, TwCA, WebBD, WhNAA*
O'Brien, Harry Russell 1889- *HisAmM XR, WhJnl 1928*
O'Brien, Howard Vincent 1888-1947 *AmAu&B, BioIn 1, DcNAA, REnAL*
O'Brien, James Bronterre 1805-1864 *PoIre, WebBD*
O'Brien, John Cornelius 1894-1964 *BioIn 1, BioIn 1, BioIn 7*
O'Brien, John Gerald *WhJnl 1928*
O'Brien, John Harrington 1908- *WhoAm 1974*
O'Brien, John J 1887?-1965 *BioIn 7*
O'Brien, John Martin 1909?-1964 *BioIn 7*
O'Brien, John T 1860?-1950 *BioIn 2*
O'Brien, Leo W 1900- *CurBio XR*
O'Brien, Merrill *OvPC*
O'Brien, Patricia *NF*
O'Brien, Patrick Joseph 1892-1938 *AmAu&B, DcNAA*
O'Brien, Robert C 1918-1973 *BioIn 9, ChlLR 2, ConAu XR, SixAP*
O'Brien, Robert Lincoln 1865-1955 *AmJnl, BioIn 4, DcAmB S5, HisAmM XR, WhNAA, WhJnl 1928*
O'Brien, Robert R 1889- *WhJnl 1928*
O'Brien, Thomas A *OvPC*
O'Brien, Thomas Harry 1892- *WhJnl 1928*
O'Brien, William 1852-1928 *PoIre, WebBD*
O'Brien, William D 1895?-1951 *BioIn 2*
O'Brien, William Edward 1891- *WhJnl 1928*
O'Brien, William F 1900- *WhJnl 1928*
O'Brien, William J 1882- *WhJnl 1928*
O'Brine, Jack 1906?-1970 *BioIn 9*
O'Bryan, Maud 1914- *WhoS&SW 1973*
Obst, David *InvJ, NewMr*
O'Callaghan, Edmund Bailey 1797-1880 *Alli, Alli Sup, AmAu, AmAu&B, BbtC, CyAL 2, DcAmA, DcNAA, OxCan*
Ocampo, Victoria 1891-1979 *DcCLAA,*

IntWW 1976, WhoWor 1974
Ochiltree, Thomas H 1912- *NF*
Ochs, Adolph Shelby 1895-1974 *BioIn 10,
NewYTBS 5, WhJnl 1928*
Ochs, Adolph Simon 1858-1935 *AmAu&B,
AmAu&B, AmJnl, BioIn 1, BioIn 2,
BioIn 3, BioIn 4, BioIn 5, BioIn 6, BioIn 7,
BioIn 8, BioIn 9, EncAB, ForP,
HisAmM XR, NatCAB XR, OxAm, REn,
REnAL, WebBD, WhJnl 1928*
Ochs, George Washington 1861-1931 *AmJnl*
Ochs, George Washington *see also* Oakes, George
Washington
Ochs, George Washington *see also* Ochs-Oakes,
George Washington
Ochs, Milton Barlow 1864-1955 *BioIn 1, BioIn 3,
WebBD*
Ochs-Oakes, George Washington 1861-1931
HisAmM XR, WhJnl 1928
Ochs-Oakes, George Washington *see also* Oakes,
George Washington
Ochs-Oakes, George Washington *see also* Ochs,
George Washington
Ockene, Robert M 1934?-1969 *BioIn 8*
O'Connell, Daniel *NF*
O'Connell, Denis *NF*
O'Connell, Herb *NF*
O'Connell, James Henry 1878- *WhJnl 1928*
O'Connell, John James, III 1921- *HisAmM XR,
WhoAm 1974*
O'Connell, Lillian G *OvPC*
O'Connell, Margaret F 1935-1977 *ConAu 73*
O'Connell, Theodore William, Jr. 1928-
WhoAm 1974
O'Conner, James *HisAmM XR*
O'Conner, William Douglas 1832-1889 *DcAmB 13,
HisAmM XR*
O'Conner, William Douglas *see also* O'Connor,
William Douglas
O'Connor, Daniel P *OvPC*
O'Connor, Feargus Edward 1794-1855 *WebBD*
O'Connor, Harvey 1897- *AmAu&B, AmRP,
ConAu 7R, WhoAm 1974*
O'Connor, Hugh 1894-1967 *BioIn 8, WhJnl 1928*
O'Connor, James Matthew, Jr. 1895- *WhJnl 1928*
O'Connor, Jerome William 1923- *WhoAm 1974,
WhoMW 1974*
O'Connor, John *NF*
O'Connor, John Carroll 1869-1946 *BioIn 1,
WhJnl 1928*
O'Connor, John James 1895- *WhJnl 1928*
O'Connor, John Woolf 1902-1978 *AmAu&B,
ConAu 7R, WhoAm 1974, WhoPNW*
O'Connor, Joseph 1841-1908 *DcAmA, DcNAA,
NatCAB 13, PoIre*
O'Connor, Maurice J d1899 *NF*
O'Connor, Patricia Ann *NF*
O'Connor, Patrick 1899- *BioIn 3, BkC 3*
O'Connor, Patrick 1915- *AuBYP, ConAu XR,
EncMys, SmATA 2*
O'Connor, Patrick *see also* O'Connor Wibberley,
Leonard Patrick
O'Connor, Patrick *see also* Wibberley, Leonard
O'Connor, Richard 1915-1975 *AmAu&B,
ConAu 57, ConAu 61, IndAu 1917, LiJA,
WhoAm 1974, WhoE 1974*
O'Connor, Thomas Burton 1914-1952 *BioIn 3*
O'Connor, Thomas F 1886- *WhJnl 1928*
O'Connor, Thomas Power 1848-1929 *Alli Sup,
BioIn 2, DcLEL, HisAmM XR, LongC,
NewC, OxEng, WebBD*
O'Connor, William Douglas 1832-1889 *Alli Sup,
AmAu, AmAu&B, BbD, BiD&SB, BioIn 1,
BioIn 2, BioIn 3, CnDAL, DcAmA,*

DcNAA, OxAm, PoIre, REnAL, WebBD
O'Connor, William Douglas *see also* O'Conner,
William Douglas
O'Connor Wibberley, Leonard Patrick 1915-
Au&Wr
O'Connor Wibberley, Leonard Patrick *see also*
Wibberley, Leonard
O'Conor, Joseph *NF*
Oddo, Sandra Schmidt 1937- *ConAu 65*
O'Dell, DeForest 1898-1958 *BioIn 4, BioIn 7*
O'Dell, Edith *HisAmM XR, WhJnl 1928*
Odell, Emery Alvin 1871-1953 *BioIn 5*
Odell, Frank Iglehart 1886- *BioIn 2, IndAu 1816*
Odell, Jay C, Jr. *RpN*
Odell, Joseph Henry 1871-1929 *DcNAA,
HisAmM XR*
Odell, Rice 1928- *NF*
Odell, Wallace 1876?- *WhJnl 1928*
Oden, Henry *NF*
Oden, Marjorie Ann *OvPC*
Odervain, James M d1884 *NF*
Odion, Henry W *NF*
O'Donnell, Daniel Kane 1838-1871 *Alli Sup,
AmAu&B, DcAmA, DcNAA, PoIre*
O'Donnell, Francis X *NF*
O'Donnell, Hugh Arnott *WhJnl 1928*
O'Donnell, Jack *HisAmM XR*
O'Donnell, James *BioIn 1*
O'Donnell, John 1870-1954 *BioIn 4, NatCAB 40,
WhJnl 1928*
O'Donnell, John Eugene 1902- *WhJnl 1928*
O'Donnell, John Francis 1837-1874 *BrAu 19,
PoIre*
O'Donnell, John Parsons 1896-1961 *BioIn 6*
O'Donnell, Larry *NF*
O'Donnell, Peadar 1893- *BioIn 1, TwCA,
TwCA Sup*
O'Donnell, Peter *EncMys*
O'Donnell, Red *NF*
O'Donnell, Thomas Clay 1881-1962 *BioIn 6*
O'Donnell, Tim *NF*
O'Donnell, William F 1878- *WhJnl 1928*
O'Donoghue, John 1813-1893 *Alli Sup, PoIre*
O'Donoghue, John J W *HisAmM XR*
O'Donovan, Edmond 1838-1883 *Alli Sup, FamWC*
O'Donovan, Jeremiah 1831- *PoIre*
O'Donovan, Patrick 1918- *BioIn 3, ForP*
O'Dwyer, John R *OvPC*
O'Dwyer, William *HisAmM XR*
Oechsner, Frederick C 1902- *AmJnl, CurBio XR*
Oehler, Alfred G *WhJnl 1928*
Oehm, Gustav M 1894- *WhJnl 1928*
Oelbaum, Jerome *NF*
Oelsner, Lesley *BioIn 9*
Oeri, Albert 1875-1950 *BioIn 2*
Oestreicher, John Cahill 1905-1951 *BioIn 2*
Oestreicher, Walter M 1873- *WhJnl 1928*
Oexle, Joseph *NF*
O'Farrill, Romulo, Jr. 1917- *ForP, WhoWor 1974*
O'Farrill, Romulo, Sr. *ForP*
Offit, Sidney 1928- *ConAu 1, DrAF 1976,
SmATA 10, WhoAm 1974, WhoE 1974,
WrDr 1976*
O'Flaherty, Hal 1890-1972 *BioIn 2, BioIn 9*
O'Flaherty, James O, Jr. d1939 *NF*
O'Flaherty, Terrence 1917- *ConAu 73,
WhoWest 1974*
O'Furey, Joseph P 1876- *WhJnl 1928*
Ofusa, Junnosuke *NF*
O'Gara, James Vincent, Jr. 1918-1979 *BioIn 7,
WhoAdv 1972, WhoAm 1974, WhoE 1974*
Ogata, Taketora 1888-1956 *BioIn 4*
Ogawa, Masaru 1915- *IntWW 1976,
WhoWor 1974*

Ogawa, Satoshi NF
Ogawa, Sei NF
Ogburn, William Fielding 1886-1959 AmAu&B,
    CurBio XR, HisAmM XR, TwCA Sup,
    WhNAA
Ogden, Alfred Warner WhJnl 1928
Ogden, Christopher NF
Ogden, Herbert Gouverneur HisAmM XR
Ogden, Herschel Coombs 1869-1943 AmJnl,
    NatCAB 32
Ogden, Michael Joseph 1911- BioIn 2,
    WhoAm 1974
Ogden, Robert Curtis 1836-1913 DcNAA,
    HisAmM XR
Ogden, Rollo 1856-1937 AmAu&B, AmJnl,
    BioIn 4, DcAmA, DcAmB S2, DcNAA,
    HisAmM XR, OhA&B, WebBD,
    WhJnl 1928
Ogden, Theodore Roosevelt NF
Ogg, Frederick Austin 1878-1951 HisAmM XR
Ogilvie, Cecil Claude 1900- WhJnl 1928
Ogilvie, Edward L 1873- WhJnl 1928
Ogilvie, Thomas Fleisher 1892-1955 BioIn 3
Ogilvie, William Henry 1869-1964 Br&AmS,
    WebBD
Ogina, Naoki NF
Ogle, Claude M 1891- WhJnl 1928
Ogle, Ed NF
Ogle, Robert Carroll 1890?-1968 BioIn 8
Oglesby, Carl WhoAm 1974
Oglesby, John NF
Ognibene, Peter J 1941- NF
O'Grady, Donald NF
O'Guin, W W 1886- WhJnl 1928
O'Hagan, Anne 1869- DcAmA, HisAmM XR
O'Hagan, Thomas 1855-1939 Alli Sup,
    CathA 1930, DcLEL, DcNAA, OxCan,
    PoIre, WhNAA
O'Hanlon, Thomas J 1933- ConAu 61
O'Hara, Barratt 1881-1969 NF
O'Hara, Bernard S 1887?-1965 BioIn 7
O'Hara, Edward A 1887?-1972 BioIn 9
O'Hara, John 1905-1970 AmAu&B, AmNov,
    AmWr, BiE&WWA, CasWL, CnDAL,
    CnMD, ConAmA, ConAu 5R, ConAu 25,
    ConLC 1, ConLC 2, ConLC 3, ConLC 6,
    CurBio XR, CyWA, DcLEL, EncWL,
    EvLB, LongC, ModAL, ModAL Sup,
    NewYTBE 1, OxAm, OxEng, Pen Am,
    RAdv 1, REn, REnAL, TwCA, TwCA Sup,
    TwCW, WebBD, WebE&AL, WhoTwCL
O'Hara, Neal Russell 1893-1962 AmAu&B
O'Hara, Peg NF
O'Hara, Theodore 1820-1867 AmAu, AmAu&B,
    BbD, BiDSA, BioIn 3, CnDAL, DcAmA,
    DcAmB 14, OxAm, PoIre, REnAL, WebBD
O'Hara, Thomas Patrick 1913-1974 BioIn 10,
    NewYTBS 5
O'Hare, James H NF
O'Hare, Kate Richards AmRP
Ohe, Marianna NF
O'Hearn, Walter D 1910?-1969 BioIn 8
O'Higgins, Don 1922- NF
O'Higgins, Harvey Jerrold 1876-1929 AmAu&B,
    AmJnl, AmLY, CanNov, ConAmL,
    DcAmB 14, DcLEL, DcNAA, EncMys,
    HisAmM XR, OxAm, TwCA, WebBD,
    WhNAA
O'Higgins, Patrick BioIn 9
Ohley, William D 1900- WhJnl 1928
Ohliger, Dorothy L NF
Ohrt, Frederick Schemetzer 1891- WhJnl 1928
Ohser, Erich 1906?-1944 BioIn 2
Oishi, Gene NF

Ojetti, Ugo 1871-1946 BioIn 1, CasWL,
    CIDMEL, WebBD
Ojike, Mbonu 1914?- CurBio XR
Oka, Takashi NF
Oka, Tom NF
Okabe, Masaaki NF
Okamura, Akihiko NF
O'Kane, Don H WhJnl 1928
O'Keef, Herbert Edward, Jr. 1908- WhoAm 1974,
    WhoS&SW 1973
O'Kelly, Sean Thomas 1882?-1966 CurBio XR,
    WebBD, WhoLA
Okin, Robert RpN
Okker, Willa 1907- WhJnl 1928
Oko, Adolph Sigmund 1883-1944 BioIn 1
Okpaku, Joseph 1943- ConAu 29, NewYTBE 1
Okuley, Bert W NF
Okullu, Henry 1929- BioIn 10, ForP
Olafsson, Jon 1850-1916 BioIn 2
O'Laughlin, John Callan 1873-1949 AmAu&B,
    HisAmM XR
Olcheski, Bill 1925- ConAu 61
Olcott, Frances Jenkins AmAu&B, JBA 1934,
    JBA 1951, REnAL
Olcott, John W 1936- NF
Olcott, Ralph T 1861-1932 NatCAB 25
Olcott, William OvPC
Old Bachelor, An see Curtis, George William
Old Block, The see Delano, Alonzo
Older, Fremont 1856-1935 AmJnl, BioIn 2,
    BioIn 5, BioIn 7, BioIn 9, DcAmB S1,
    DcNAA, WhNAA, WhJnl 1928
Olderman, Murray 1922- ConAu 45
Oldfield, A Barney OvPC
Oldham, Evelyn NF
Oldisworth, William 1680-1734 Alli, BioIn 1,
    DcEnL
Oldmeadow, Ernest James 1867-1949 BioIn 1,
    BioIn 2, CathA 1930, LongC
Olds, Elizabeth Fagg OvPC
Olds, Greg NewMr
Oldschool, Oliver see Dennie, Joseph
Oldschool, Oliver see Sargent, Nathan
O'Leary, Dillon d1978 NF
O'Leary, Dostaler 1908-1965 BioIn 7, OxCan
O'Leary, James F 1905?-1970 BioIn 9
O'Leary, Jeremiah A, Jr. NF
O'Leary, M Grattan NF
O'Leary, Ralph Semmes 1911-1963 BioIn 6
O'Leary, Richard A WhoAm 1974, WhoE 1974
O'Leary, Thomas Vincent 1910?- ConAu 5R,
    WhoPubR 1972
Oler, Wesley Marion 1856- HisAmM XR
Oleson, N Lee NF
Olgin, Moissaye J AmRP
Oliphant, Laurence 1829-1888 Alli, Alli Sup,
    BbD, BiD&SB, BioIn 4, BrAu 19, CasWL,
    DcBiA, DcEnA, DcEnL, DcEuL, DcLEL,
    EvLB, HisAmM XR, NewC, OxEng,
    Pen Eng, REn, WebBD
Oliphant, Patrick Bruce 1935- BioIn 7, BioIn 8,
    BioIn 9, WhoAm 1974
Olive, Ralph NF
Olive, Theodore R 1901- BioIn 8
Oliveira, Barradas De ForP
Oliveira Lima, Manoel De 1865-1928 BioIn 9
Oliver, Betty 1911?- BioIn 1
Oliver, Daniel NF
Oliver, Don NF
Oliver, Edith 1913- BiE&WWA, WhoAm 1974,
    WhoAmW 1974, WhoThe 1972
Oliver, Edwin Austin 1855-1924 DcNAA
Oliver, Frederick Scott 1864-1934 BioIn 2
Oliver, George Sturges 1878-1963 BioIn 9

Oliver, Jacob Lewis 1886- *WhJnl 1928*
Oliver, John Madison 1905- *WhJnl 1928*
Oliver, Martha 1845-1916 *DcAmA, DcNAA*
Oliver, Owen *NF*
Oliver, Pat *NF*
Oliver, Robert Tarbell 1909- *ConAu 5,*
DrAS 74E, ForP, WhoAm 1974, WrDr 1976
Oliver, Warner *HisAmM XR*
Olivera, Lucho *NF*
Olivia *DcNAA*
Olivier, Stuart 1880- *AmJnl*
Olivier-Lecamp, Max Jules Alexis Marcel 1914-
IntWW 1976
Ollemans, Dominicus Hugo 1909-1963 *BioIn 6*
Olmos, Harold *NF*
Olmstead, Agnes *BioIn 2*
Olmstead, John Wesley *HisAmM XR*
Olmsted, Frederick Law 1822-1903 *Alli, Alli Sup,*
AmAu, AmAu&B, AtlBL, BbD, BiD&SB,
CyAL 2, DcAmA, DcNAA, HisAmM XR,
LiJA, OxAm, REnAL, WebBD
Olney, George Washington 1835-1916 *DcNAA*
Olney, Roy 1891-1949 *BioIn 2*
Olofson, Darwin R *NF*
O'Loughlin, Daniel *HisAmM XR*
O'Loughlin, Edward T 1877?-1950 *BioIn 2*
O'Loughlin, Peter *NF*
O'Loughlin, Robert S *HisAmM XR*
Olsen, Arthur Joseph 1920- *BioIn 9,*
USBiR 1974, WhoAm 1974, WhoGov 1972
Olsen, Jack 1925- *ConAu XR, WhoAm 1974*
Olsen, Jack *see also* Olsen, John Howard
Olsen, John Edward 1925- *ConAu 19R,*
IndAu 1917
Olsen, John Howard *see also* Olsen, Jack
Olsen, Lucille P *BioIn 10*
Olsen, Poul Rovsing 1922- *IntWW 1976,*
WhoWor 1974
Olshaker, Mark *NF*
Olshan, Mort *NF*
Olshausen, Theodor 1802-1869 *BioIn 2, WebBD*
Olson, Alan *OvPC*
Olson, Alma Louise 1883?-1964 *BioIn 6*
Olson, Cal 1924- *WhoAm 1974*
Olson, Clarence E *NF*
Olson, Gene 1922- *AuBYP, BioIn 7*
Olson, Jane Virginia 1916- *ForWC 1970,*
WhoAmW 1974
Olson, John *NF*
Olson, Lynne *NF*
Olson, Oscar K *BioIn 1*
Olson, Sidney 1908- *ConAu P-1*
Olson, Ted 1899- *AmAu&B, AnMV 1926,*
ConAu 49, WhNAA
Olson, Theodore B *see* Olson, Ted
Olson, W G *NF*
Oltmans, Willem L 1925- *ConAu 57*
Olwell, Lee U *NF*
O'Malley, Anthony J 1880-1947 *BioIn 1,*
WhJnl 1928
O'Malley, Dominick *NF*
O'Malley, Ernie 1897?-1957 *BioIn 4*
O'Malley, Frank Ward 1875-1932 *AmAu&B,*
DcNAA, REnAL, WebBD, WhNAA
Omang, Joanne *NF*
Omansky, Dorothy Linder 1905?-1977 *ConAu 73,*
OvPC
O'Mara, Richard P *NF*
Omarr, Sydney *NF*
Omberg, Arthur Chalmers 1909- *WhoAm 1974*
O'Mealia, Leo Edward 1884-1960 *BioIn 5*
O'Meara, Edward Francis 1915- *WhoAm 1974*
Omeara, Stephen 1854-1918 *BioIn 5*
Omohundro, Charlotte *NF*

Onderdonk, Benjamin Tredwell 1791-1861 *Alli,*
HisAmM XR
Onderdonk, William H *HisAmM XR*
One Of The Barclays *see* Otis, Mrs. Harrison Gray
O'Neal, George *NF*
O'Neal, James 1875- *AmLY, HisAmM XR,*
IndAu 1816, WhNAA, WhJnl 1928
O'Neil, Gerard *InvJ*
O'Neil, Harriet I 1903- *WhJnl 1928*
O'Neil, James Francis 1898- *CurBio XR,*
WhoAm 1974, WhoF&I 1974
O'Neil, Terry 1949- *ConAu ,61*
O'Neil, William M 1898- *WhJnl 1928*
O'Neill, Edward *NF*
O'Neill, Eugene M 1850- *NatCAB 5*
O'Neill, Gerard Michael 1942- *ConAu 69,*
WhoAm 1974
O'Neill, Harold Edgar 1888-1942 *DcNAA*
O'Neill, Hugh Daniel 1942?- *BioIn 6*
O'Neill, James *NF*
O'Neill, James, Jr. 1920- *BiE&WWA*
O'Neill, Martin 1909?- *BioIn 8*
O'Neill, Michael James 1922- *WhoAm 1974,*
WhoE 1974
O'Neill, Raymond Bernard 1907-1972 *BioIn 9,*
NewYTBE 3
O'Neill, Rose Cecil 1874-1944 *AmAu&B,*
DcAmB S3, DcNAA, TwCA, TwCA Sup,
WebBD
O'Neill, Sarge *NF*
O'Neill, Stephen *NF*
Onetti, Juan Carlos 1909- *CasWL, DcCLAA,*
IntWW 1976, Pen Am, WhoTwCL,
WhoWor 1974
Ongaro, Alberto 1925- *ConAu 25*
Onis, Juan De *NF*
Onkel Tom *see* Hevesi, Ludwig
Onruang, Chirabha *RpN*
Opie, Evarts Walton 1893- *WhJnl 1928*
Opie, Hierome Lindsay 1880-1943 *BioIn 1,*
NatCAB 33, WhJnl 1928
Opie, Thomas Fletcher 1883-1957 *BioIn 4*
Opoku, Bright Michael *NF*
Opotowsky, Maurice Leon 1931- *WhoAm 1974*
Opotowsky, Stan 1923- *ConAu 1R,*
IntMPA 1975
Oppedahl, John *NF*
Oppegard, M M *NF*
Oppenheimer, Evelyn 1907- *ConAu 3R,*
ForWC 1970
Oppenheimer, Franz 1864-1943 *CurBio XR,*
HisAmM XR
Oppenheimer, George 1900-1977 *AmAu&B,*
BiE&WWA, ConAu 15R, ConAu 73,
IntMPA 1975, WhoAm 1974
Opper, Frederick Burr 1857-1937 *AmAu&B,*
AmJnl, AuNews 1, BioIn 2, BioIn 4,
BioIn 6, DcAmB S2, DcNAA,
HisAmM XR, NatCAB 44, OhA&B, OvPC,
REnAL, WebBD, WhNAA, WhJnl 1928
Optic, Oliver 1822-1897 *AmAu, AmAu&B,*
BiD&SB, CnDAL, DcAmA, DcEnL,
DcNAA, OxAm, REnAL
Optic, Oliver *see also* Adams, William Taylor
Orage, Alfred Richard 1873-1934 *BioIn 2,*
BioIn 7, LongC, Pen Eng, REn, TwCA,
TwCA Sup
Oravets, John D *NF*
Orazem, A Ed 1903- *WhJnl 1928*
Orben, Robert *NF*
Orchard, Harry *HisAmM XR*
Orchard, Thomas *OvPC*
Orcutt, C R *HisAmM XR*
Orcutt, Edward *HisAmM XR*

Ordovensky, Patrick J *NF*
O'Rear, Frankie *NF*
Orear, J Davis *HisAmM XR*
O'Rear, John *NF*
Orear, Leslie Fray 1911- *WhoAm 1974*
O'Regan, Richard Arthur 1919- *ConAu 73,
WhoAm 1974, WhoWor 1974*
Orehek, Don *NF*
O'Reilly, Don 1913- *WhoS&SW 1973*
O'Reilly, Edward Synnott 1880-1946 *DcNAA*
O'Reilly, Jane 1936- *ConAu 73*
O'Reilly, John Boyle 1844-1890 *Alli Sup, AmAu,
AmAu&B, BbD, BiD&SB, BioIn 1, BioIn 2,
BioIn 4, BioIn 7, BrAu 19, CnDAL,
DcAmA, DcLEL, DcNAA, EncAB, EvLB,
HisAmM XR, OxAm, PoIre, REn, REnAL,
WebBD*
O'Reilly, Mary Boyle 1873-1937 *DcNAA*
O'Reilly, Miles 1829-1868 *AmAu, BiD&SB,
DcAmA, DcEnL, DcNAA, OxAm, PoIre,
WebBD*
O'Reilly, Miles *see also* Halpine, Charles Graham
O'Reilly, Moe *OvPC*
O'Reilly, Thomas Costigan 1905-1962 *BioIn 5,
BioIn 6*
O'Reilly, Tom *NF*
Oren, Uri 1931- *ConAu 65*
Orff, Frank *HisAmM XR*
Orff, Samuel *HisAmM XR*
O'Rielly, Henry 1806-1886 *DcNAA*
O'Riley, John *NF*
Orkin, Ruth *WhoAmA 1973*
Orlando, Guido 1906- *BioIn 3, BioIn 7, BioIn 9*
Orlando, Ruggero 1907- *OvPC, WhoAm 1974,
WhoWor 1974*
Orlin, Gerald I *NF*
Orloff, Ed Sam 1923- *ConAu 69*
Ormesson, Jean D', Comte 1925- *IntWW 1976*
Ormond, John 1923- *ConAu 65, ConP 1970,
ConP 1975, WrDr 1976*
Ormond, John Raper *HisAmM XR*
Ormsbee, Thomas Hamilton 1890-1969 *AmAu&B,
BioIn 8*
Ormsby, George V 1884?-1950 *BioIn 2*
Ormsby, John S 1869- *AnMV 1926, PoIre,
WhJnl 1928*
Ornes, German Emilio 1919- *OvPC,
WhoWor 1974*
O'Rourke, Clem D 1887- *WhJnl 1928*
O'Rourke, Lawrence Michael 1938- *ConAu 69*
O'Rourke, P J 1947- *NF*
Orr, Carey 1890-1967 *BioIn 7*
Orr, Cecil 1909?- *BioIn 1*
Orr, Charles *AmRP*
Orr, Clifford 1899-1951 *BioIn 2*
Orr, John Charles 1858- *WhoLA*
Orr, John William 1815-1887 *Alli, EarABI Sup,
HisAmM XR*
Orr, Lois *AmRP*
Orr, Lyndon *HisAmM XR*
Orr, Nathaniel *HisAmM XR*
Orr, Ralph *NF*
Orr, T E *HisAmM XR*
Orr, Thomas, Jr. *OvPC*
Orr, William Anderson 1883-1950 *BioIn 2*
Orris, John *HisAmM XR*
Orsini, Betty *InvJ*
Ortega, Felix A *NF*
Ortega, Frank Garcia 1889?-1967 *BioIn 8*
Orth, Maureen *NF*
Orton, Alvin *NF*
Orton, Vrest Teachout 1897- *AmAu&B,
ConAu 33, WhNAA, WhoAm 1974,
WrDr 1976*

Orvis, John *HisAmM XR*
Osbahr, Bernard F *BioIn 2*
Osbon, Bradley Sillick 1828-1912 *Alli Sup,
AmAu&B, AmJnl, DcNAA, FamWC*
Osborn, Charles 1775-1850 *HisAmM XR,
IndAu 1816, OhA&B*
Osborn, Chase Salmon 1860-1949 *BioIn 1,
BioIn 2, BioIn 3, BioIn 5, BioIn 6,
DcAmB S4, DcNAA, IndAu 1816, REnAL,
WhNAA*
Osborn, Chase Salmon, Jr. *NF*
Osborn, Clifton Carlisle *HisAmM XR*
Osborn, E B *NF*
Osborn, Erastus William 1860-1930 *WhJnl 1928*
Osborn, George Augustus 1884-1972 *WhJnl 1928*
Osborn, Helen *WhJnl 1928*
Osborn, John W 1794-1866 *NatCAB 18*
Osborn, Norris Galpin 1858-1932 *AmAu&B,
DcNAA, NatCAB 25*
Osborn, Selleck 1782?-1826 *Alli, AmAu,
AmAu&B, CyAL 1, DcAmA, DcAmB 14,
DcNAA*
Osborne, Burl *NF*
Osborne, Charles D 1888- *WhJnl 1928*
Osborne, Charles Devens 1895-1961 *BioIn 5*
Osborne, Charles Francis 1855-1914 *DcNAA,
HisAmM XR*
Osborne, Edwin A 1901?-1947 *BioIn 1*
Osborne, James 1943- *BioIn 10*
Osborne, John 1907- *BioIn 8, BioIn 9,
ConAu 61, NewMr, WhoAm 1974*
Osborne, Joseph Alexander 1860-1948 *BioIn 3,
NatCAB 38*
Osborne, Mary Frances 1897- *WhJnl 1928*
Osborne, Scott *NF*
Oschay, Henry H 1895- *WhJnl 1928*
Osgood, Charles *BioIn 10*
Osgood, James R 1836- *AmAu&B*
Osgood, Nancy *NF*
Osgood, Samuel 1812-1880 *Alli, Alli Sup,
AmAu&B, BbD, BiD&SB, CyAL 2,
DcAmA, DcNAA, HisAmM XR*
O'Shaughnessy, Arthur *HisAmM XR*
O'Shaughnessy, James 1863?-1950 *BioIn 2*
O'Shea, Arthur 1897?-1950 *BioIn 2*
O'Shea, John Augustus 1840- *Alli Sup, FamWC*
Osherowitch, Mendel 1889-1965 *BioIn 7*
Oshima, Ichiro *ForP*
Osius, Larry Clark 1930- *WhoAm 1974,
WhoS&SW 1973*
Oskison, John Milton 1874-1947 *AmAu&B,
DcNAA, HisAmM XR*
Osmanczyk, Edmund Jan 1913- *IntWW 1976,
WhoWor 1974*
Osmer, Margaret *NF*
Osnos, Peter *NewMr*
Osoba, Olusegun 1941?- *NF*
Osol, Bernice Bede 1934- *NF*
Osolin, Charles A *NF*
Ossietzky, Carl Von 1889-1938 *OxGer, Pen Eur,
WebBD*
Ossoli, Margaret Fuller 1810-1850 *CyAL 2*
Ossoli, Margaret Fuller *see also* Fuller, Margaret
Ossoli, Margaret Fuller *see also* Fuller, Sarah
Margaret
Osteen, Hubert Graham 1870- *WhJnl 1928*
Osten, Jerry *NF*
Osterhout, Robert S 1869- *WhJnl 1928*
Osterling, Anders Johan 1884- *CasWL, CIDMEL,
IntWW 1976, Pen Eur, WhoWor 1974*
Ostling, Richard N 1940- *ConAu 53*
Ostroff, Ron *NF*
Ostrom, Merle Campbell 1889- *WhJnl 1928*
Ostrow, Marty *NF*

Ostrow, Ronald J *InvJ, NF, RpN*
Ostrum, James E *NF*
O'Sullivan, Daniel E 1858?-1946 *Bioln 1, PoIre*
O'Sullivan, J Reilly *OvPC*
O'Sullivan, Jeremiah Leo 1894- *Bioln 5, WhJnl 1928*
O'Sullivan, Joan *ForWC 1970*
O'Sullivan, John Louis 1813-1895 *AmAu&B, DcAmB 14, EncAB, HisAmM XR*
O'Sullivan, Kevin Patrick 1928- *WhoAm 1974*
O'Sullivan, P Michael *NF*
O'Sullivan, Seumas 1879-1958 *CasWL, DcLEL, EncWL, EvLB, LongC, NewC, PoIre, TwCA, TwCA Sup, WebBD*
Oswald, Eleazar *AmJnl*
Oswald, Felix *HisAmM XR*
Oswald, John Clyde 1872-1938 *AmAu&B, DcNAA, HisAmM XR, OhA&B, WhNAA*
Otani, Satoshi *RpN*
Otero, Lisandro *ForP*
Otero Vizcarrondo, Henrique 1882?-1952 *Bioln 3*
Oteru, Seiichi *NF*
Otey, Carter, Jr. 1898- *WhJnl 1928*
Othen, John 1872- *WhJnl 1928*
Othman, Frederick Campbell 1905-1958 *Bioln 1, Bioln 2, Bioln 5*
Otis, Bass 1784-1861 *HisAmM XR*
Otis, Charles 1872- *WhJnl 1928*
Otis, Charles Augustus 1868-1953 *Bioln 3*
Otis, Denise *NF*
Otis, Elita Proctor *HisAmM XR*
Otis, Eliza A W 1833-1904 *NatCAB 14*
Otis, Mrs. Harrison Gray 1796-1873 *Alli, AmAu&B, DcNAA*
Otis, Harrison Gray 1837-1917 *AmJnl, Bioln 2, DcNAA, WebBD*
Otis, James 1725-1783 *Alli*
Otis, James 1848-1912 *Alli Sup, BiD&SB, DcAmA, DcNAA, JBA 1934, JBA 1951, OxAm*
Otis, James *see also* Kaler, James Otis
Otis, Marian 1879-1960 *Bioln 6*
Otis, Oscar *Bioln 9*
O'Toole, Thomas *NF*
Ott, Carol J *NF*
Ottaway, David B *NF*
Ottaway, E J 1871- *WhJnl 1928*
Ottaway, James H 1911- *WhoAm 1974*
Ottaway, James H, Jr. *NF*
Ottaway, Mark *NF*
Otten, Alan L *NF*
Ottenad, Thomas W *NF*
Ottenberg, Miriam 1914- *ConAu 7R, ForWC 1970, InvJ, NewMr, WhoAmW 1974, WhoWorJ 1972*
Ottendorfer, Anna Sartorius Uhl 1815-1884 *NF*
Ottendorfer, Oswald 1826-1900 *AmJnl, Bioln 2, CasWL*
Ottenfeld, Helen H 1902- *WhJnl 1928*
Ottesen, Keith *NF*
Ottley, James Henry 1851-1922 *HisAmM XR, NatCAB 24*
Ottley, Roi 1906-1960 *AmAu&B, Bioln 5, CurBio XR, REnAL*
Otto, Virginia *NF*
Ottolengui, Rodrigues 1861-1937 *DcNAA, HisAmM XR*
Ottone, Piero 1924- *IntWW 1976*
Otwell, Ralph Maurice 1926- *RpN, WhoAm 1974*
Ouellet, Jo *NF*
Ouimet, Adolphe 1840-1910 *DcNAA*
Ouimet, Marcel 1915- *CanWW 1972*
Oulahan, Richard 1918- *ConAu 33*
Oulahan, Richard V 1867-1931 *AmJnl,*

NatCAB 27
Oursler, Charles Fulton 1893-1952 *WebBD*
Oursler, Charles Fulton *see also* Ousler, Fulton
Oursler, Fulton 1893-1952 *AmAu&B, AuBYP, Bioln 1, Bioln 2, Bioln 3, Bioln 4, Bioln 6, Bioln 7, Bioln 8, CathA 1930, CurBio XR, DcSpL, LiJA, REn, REnAL, TwCA Sup, WhNAA*
Oursler, Fulton *see also* Oursler, Charles Fulton
Oursler, Grace 1900-1955 *Bioln 4*
Oursler, William Charles 1913- *ConAu 7R, OvPC, WhoAm 1974, WhoWor 1974*
Oursler, William F *OvPC*
Ousley, Clarence 1863-1948 *Bioln 1*
Outcault, Richard Felton 1863-1928 *AmAu&B, AmJnl, Bioln 3, DcNAA, HisAmM XR, OhA&B, REnAL, WebBD*
Outland, Ethel R 1909- *WhJnl 1928*
Outler, Jesse *NF*
Outze, Berge 1912- *IntWW 1976*
Ovalle Castillo, Dario 1884?-1949 *Bioln 2*
Overall, John Wilford 1823?-1899 *BiDSA, DcAmA, DcNAA, HisAmM XR*
Overby, Charles L *NF*
Overgard, William *NF*
Overton, Grant Martin 1887-1930 *AmAu&B, DcNAA, HisAmM XR, TwCA, WebBD*
Oviatt, Edwin 1874-1955 *Bioln 3, HisAmM XR*
Oviatt, Ray *NF*
Ovington, Ray *AuBYP, Bioln 8*
Owen, Cecil 1903?-1954 *Bioln 3*
Owen, Chandler *BlkC*
Owen, Ernest L 1886- *WhJnl 1928*
Owen, F A *HisAmM XR*
Owen, Frank 1905- *Bioln 1, Who 1974*
Owen, Fred K 1865- *WhJnl 1928*
Owen, Helen Mildred d1946 *Bioln 1*
Owen, Sir James *NF*
Owen, John 1929- *WhoAm 1974*
Owen, June 1915?-1964 *Bioln 6*
Owen, Kenneth F *NF*
Owen, Mary Eugenia d1965 *Bioln 1, Bioln 2, Bioln 7*
Owen, Robert Dale 1801-1877 *Alli, Alli Sup, AmAu, AmAu&B, BbD, BiD&SB, CyAL 2, DcAmA, DcEnL, DcNAA, HisAmM XR, IndAu 1816, REnAL, WebBD*
Owen, Russell 1889-1952 *AmAu&B, AuBYP, Bioln 2, Bioln 3, Bioln 7, REnAL, WebBD*
Owen, Samuel *Alli, HisAmM XR*
Owen, Sidney M 1838- *HisAmM XR, NatCAB 14*
Owen, Stewart D 1898?-1970 *Bioln 9*
Owen, Tom The Bee Hunter *see* Thorpe, Thomas Bangs
Owen, William 1802-1842 *Bioln 10, HisAmM XR*
Owens, Bill 1938- *ConAu 73*
Owens, Bob *NewMr*
Owens, Dewey M 1901- *WhJnl 1928*
Owens, Ford G 1892-1977 *WhJnl 1928*
Owens, Hamilton 1888-1967 *Bioln 4, Bioln 7*
Owens, John W 1884?-1968 *Bioln 8, HisAmM XR*
Owens, Leo Edward 1889- *WhoAm 1974*
Owens, Millwee 1892- *WhJnl 1928*
Owens, Patrick J 1929- *ConAu 73, RpN*
Owens, R B *HisAmM XR*
Owens, Russell D *NF*
Ownby, Jim *OvPC*
Owne, Sidney M *HisAmM XR*
Oxenford, John 1812-1877 *Alli, BrAu 19, DcEnL, WebBD*
Oyen, Henry 1883-1921 *DcNAA, HisAmM XR*

Ozeki, Tetsuya   *NF*

P

OhA&B, OxAm
Pansy see also Alden, Isabella Macdonald
Panter-Downes, Molle 1906- BioIn 1, BioIn 4
Paoli, Pia 1930- ConAu 25
Papaconstantinou, Theophylactos 1905-
IntWW 1976
Papanek, Jan 1896- WhoWor 1974
Pape, Esther Cleveland 1895- WhJnl 1928
Pape, Mona Jeanne 1898- WhJnl 1928
Pape, William Jamieson 1873-1961 BioIn 5,
BioIn 6, CurBio XR, WhJnl 1928
Papillaud, Henri 1867?-1950 BioIn 2
Papini, Giovanni 1881-1956 CasWL, CathA 1930,
ClDMEL, CnMWL, EncWL, EvEuW,
LongC, Pen Eur, REn, TwCA, TwCA Sup,
TwCW, WebBD, WhoLA
Pappas, Ike NF
Paprocki, Thomas P 1901?-1973 BioIn 9
Paquette, Georgiana S 1905- BioIn 2
Paquin, Jo NF
Paquin, S S NF
Paradowski, Pamela NF
Paramore, Edward E 1895?-1956 BioIn 4
Parasuram, Tattamangalam V I RpN
Parca, Gabriella 1930?- BioIn 7
Pardo Bazan, Emilia, Condesa De 1852?-1921
BiD&SB, CasWL, ClDMEL, DcSpL,
EncWL, EuAu, EvEuW, ModRL, Pen Eur,
REn, WebBD
Pardridge, William DeWeese 1916- BioIn 1,
WhoS&SW 1973
Pare, Jean NF
Parenteau, Shirley NF
Parer, Damien AmJnl
Parham, James Avery 1881- WhJnl 1928
Parham, Joseph Byars 1919- ConAu 65
Paris, Jeanne WhoAm 1974, WhoAmW 1974,
WhoE 1974
Parish, Elijah 1762-1825 Alli, AmAu&B,
DcAmA, DcNAA, HisAmM XR, OxAm
Parish, Howard Wells 1890- WhJnl 1928
Parisi, Paul A BioIn 6
Park, David B 1894- WhJnl 1928
Park, Edward NF
Park, Edwards Amasa 1808-1900 Alli, Alli Sup,
AmAu, DcAmA, DcNAA, HisAmM XR
Park, Frances 1895-1950 AmAu&B
Park, Hamilton Grey 1888?-1965 BioIn 3,
BioIn 7
Park, John HisAmM XR
Park, John Alsey 1885-1956 BioIn 4, WhJnl 1928
Park, Kwon-Sang RpN
Park, Roy Hampton 1910- Au&Wr,
WhoAdv 1972, WhoAm 1974, WhoE 1974,
WhoF&I 1974
Park, Ruth Au&Wr, BioIn 3, BioIn 6,
CathA 1952, TwCW
Parke, Robert B NF
Parker, Addison B 1869- WhJnl 1928
Parker, Alexander McKay 1884- WhJnl 1928
Parker, Andrew McClean 1890- WhJnl 1928
Parker, Angela Claire 1949?- BlkC
Parker, Arthur Caswell 1881-1955 AmAu&B,
REnAL, WebBD
Parker, Austin 1893-1938 DcNAA
Parker, Brant NF
Parker, Cedric 1907?-1978 BioIn 2
Parker, Charles S 1839- WhJnl 1928
Parker, Daniel Francis 1893-1967 BioIn 2,
BioIn 4, BioIn 6, BioIn 7
Parker, Dorothy Rothschild 1893-1967 AmAu&B,
AmSCAP 1966, BioIn 1, BioIn 4, BioIn 6,
BioIn 7, BioIn 8, BioIn 9, BioIn 10,
CasWL, CnDAL, CnE&AP, ConAmA,

ConAu 19, ConAu 21, ConAu 25, DcLEL,
EvLB, HisAmM XR, LongC, ModAL,
OxAm, Pen Am, RAdv 1, REn, REnAL,
TwCA, TwCA Sup, TwCW, WebBD
Parker, Eddi NF
Parker, Eliza R HisAmM XR
Parker, Frank HisAmM XR
Parker, George Bertram 1886-1949 BioIn 2,
BioIn 4, NatCAB 39, WhJnl 1928
Parker, George Frederick 1847-1928 AmJnl,
AmLY, BioIn 2, DcNAA, HisAmM XR,
IndAu 1816, WhNAA
Parker, Sir Gilbert 1862-1932 BbD, BiD&SB,
CanWr, DcAmA, DcBiA, DcEnA Ap,
DcNAA, HisAmM XR, LongC, NewC,
OxAm, OxCan, REn, REnAL, TwCA,
TwCA Sup, WebBD
Parker, Gladys 1909?-1966 BioIn 1, BioIn 7
Parker, Harold HisAmM XR
Parker, Henry G HisAmM XR
Parker, Henry Taylor 1867-1934 AmAu&B,
DcAmB S1, DcNAA, WebBD
Parker, J Roy 1895- WhJnl 1928
Parker, James 1714-1770 AmAu&B, AmJnl,
HisAmM XR, OxAm
Parker, James Reid 1909- AmAu&B,
WhoAm 1974
Parker, Joel 1799-1873 Alli, DcAmA, DcNAA,
HisAmM XR
Parker, John HisAmM XR
Parker, John 1926?- BioIn 3, BioIn 9
Parker, Knowlton 1897- WhJnl 1928
Parker, Maynard NF
Parker, Ralph 1907?-1964 BioIn 6, BioIn 7
Parker, Robert 1920- NF
Parker, Robert B 1906-1955 BioIn 3
Parker, Theodore 1810-1860 Alli, AmAu,
AmAu&B, BbD, BiD&SB, CasWL,
CyAL 2, DcAmA, DcEnL, DcLEL,
DcNAA, EvLB, HisAmM XR, LiJA,
OxAm, REn, REnAL, WebBD
Parker, Thomas F HisAmM XR
Parker, Wally NF
Parker, Walter J 1888- WhJnl 1928
Parker, William 1891?-1967 BioIn 7
Parker, William Belmont 1871-1934 AmAu&B,
AmLY, DcNAA, HisAmM XR
Parkerson, John 1885-1978 NF
Parkes, Sir Henry 1815-1896 Alli Sup, DcLEL,
WebBD
Parkes, Roger 1933- ConAu 53
Parkhill, Forbes 1892- ConAu 4R, WhNAA
Parkhurst, Charles 1845-1921 BioIn 3
Parkhurst, E R NF
Parkhurst, Michael InvJ
Parkin, Elmer William 1911- WhoAm 1974
Parkin, George R NF
Parkinson, James W HisAmM XR
Parkinson, Margaret Barton 1927-
WhoAmW 1974, WhoE 1974
Parkinson, R F 1885- WhJnl 1928
Parkman-Ray, Margaret Anne Moore 1939-
AmM&W 73S, WhoAm 1974
Parks, Albert E 1897?-1977 NF
Parks, Edmund 1911- ConAu 69
Parks, Gordon Alexander Buchanan 1912-
ConAu 41, CurBio XR, LivBAA,
WhoAm 1974, WhoE 1974, WhoWor 1974
Parks, John Shields 1870- NF
Parks, Michael NF
Parks, William 1698?-1750 AmAu&B, AmJnl,
NatCAB 20
Parks, Winfield 1932?-1977 NF
Parkyn, Herbert A HisAmM XR

Parley, Peter 1793-1860 *Alli, AmAu, AmAu&B,*
BiD&SB, BrAu 19, DcAmA, DcEnL,
DcNAA, OxAm, REn, REnAL, WebBD,
WhoChL
Parley, Peter *see also* Goodrich, Samuel Griswold
Parloa, Maria 1843-1909 *Alli Sup, DcAmA,*
DcNAA, HisAmM XR
Parmele, George H 1867?-1951 *BioIn 2*
Parmelee, Edmund F 1861- *WhJnl 1928*
Parmelee, Howard Coon 1874-1959 *BioIn 5,*
BioIn 6, WhJnl 1928
Parmenter, Ross 1912- *ConAu 17R*
Paro, Tom Edward 1923- *WhoAm 1974*
Parodi, Anton Gaetano 1923- *IntWW 1976,*
WhoWor 1974
Parr, Elizabeth *NF*
Parr, Grant *NF*
Parr, John *HisAmM XR*
Parr, Raymond E *OvPC*
Parra, Jorge E *NF*
Parrett, William J 1874- *WhJnl 1928*
Parri, Ferruccio 1890?- *CurBio XR*
Parrini, Primo 1898-1961 *BioIn 6*
Parris, John *OvPC*
Parris, John A 1914- *BioIn 3*
Parrish, Philip Hammon 1896-1956 *AmAu&B,*
BioIn 4
Parrish, Randall 1858-1923 *AmAu&B, AmLY,*
DcAmA, DcNAA
Parrish, Wayne William 1907- *BioIn 4, BioIn 5,*
CurBio XR, WhoAm 1974, WhoS&SW 1973
Parrott, Reg 1916-1948 *NF*
Parry, Albert 1901- *AmAu&B, BioIn 5,*
BioIn 6, ConAu 1, CurBio XR, DrAS 74H,
WhoAm 1974, WhoWor 1974, WrDr 1976
Parry, Duke N 1893- *WhJnl 1928*
Parry, Will H 1864-1917 *NatCAB 18*
Parsons, Albert Richard 1848-1887 *AmJnl,*
AmRP, DcNAA, HisAmM XR
Parsons, Arch *RpN*
Parsons, Charles West *HisAmM XR*
Parsons, Floyd William 1880-1941 *DcNAA,*
HisAmM XR, NatCAB 30, WhNAA,
WhJnl 1928
Parsons, Geneve Shaffer *BioIn 8*
Parsons, Geoffrey 1879-1956 *AmAu&B, BioIn 2,*
BioIn 4, BioIn 6, NatCAB 46, TwCA,
TwCA Sup
Parsons, Geoffrey, Jr. 1908- *WhoAm 1974,*
WhoF&I 1974, WhoWor 1974
Parsons, George Frederic 1840-1893 *AmAu&B,*
BiD&SB, DcAmA, DcNAA, HisAmM XR
Parsons, Harriet *CurBio XR, IntMPA 1975,*
WhoAm 1974, WhoAmW 1974,
WhoWest 1974
Parsons, Louella O 1881-1972 *AmAu&B, BioIn 1,*
BioIn 2, BioIn 3, BioIn 6, BioIn 7, BioIn 9,
BioIn 10, ConAu 37, CurBio XR,
HisAmM XR, REnAL, WhoAmW 1974,
WhJnl 1928
Parsons, Lucy B *AmRP*
Parsons, O F *HisAmM XR*
Parsons, Percy Allen 1879-1963 *BioIn 6*
Parsons, Thomas *NF*
Parsons, W D *BioIn 2*
Parsons, W Drake *AmJnl*
Parsons, W H *WhJnl 1928*
Parsons, Wilfrid 1887-1958 *AmAu&B, BioIn 1,*
BioIn 4, BioIn 5, BioIn 6, BkC 4,
CathA 1930, NatCAB 44, TwCA,
TwCA Sup
Partch, Virgil Franklin, II 1916- *Au&Wr,*
BioIn 1, CurBio XR, WhoAm 1974,
WhoAmA 1973

Parton, Ethel 1862-1944 *AmAu&B, DcNAA,*
JBA 1934, JBA 1951, REnAL
Parton, James 1912- *AmAu&B, DrAS 74H,*
WhoAm 1974
Parton, Lemuel Frederick d1943 *AmAu&B*
Parton, Margaret *BioIn 5, OvPC*
Parton, Sara Payson Willis 1811-1872 *Alli, AmAu,*
AmAu&B, AmJnl, BbD, BiD&SB, DcNAA,
EncAB, HisAmM XR, REnAL, WebBD
Parton, Sara Payson Willis *see also* Fern, Fanny
Parton, Sara Willia Eldridge *HisAmM XR*
Partridge, Sir Bernard 1861-1945 *BioIn 5,*
CurBio XR, LongC, WebBD
Partridge, Charles *Alli, HisAmM XR*
Partridge, Frederick 1867-1952 *BioIn 3*
Partridge, Marianne *NF*
Parturier, Francoise 1919?- *BioIn 9,*
NewYTBE 2
Parvin, Thomas *AmJnl*
Pascal, David 1918- *ConAu 9, WhoAm 1974,*
WhoAmA 1973, WhoE 1974
Pascal, Nicole *NF*
Pascalis, Felix 1750?-1833 *HisAmM XR*
Paschal, George Washington 1812-1878 *Alli,*
Alli Sup, DcAmB 14, DcNAA
Paschall, Edwin 1799-1869 *BiDSA, DcNAA*
Paschall, Harry Barton 1897- *NF*
Paschall, John 1879-1953 *BioIn 3*
Paschen, Bernice *NF*
Pascin, Jules *HisAmM XR*
Pascoe, C E *HisAmM XR*
Pascoe, Elizabeth Jean *ConAu 69*
Pasley, Fred D 1888?-1951 *BioIn 2*
Pasmanik, Wolf *DrAP 1975*
Pasquin, Anthony 1761-1818 *Alli, AmAu,*
CnDAL, DcNAA, OxAm, OxEng
Pasquin, Anthony *see also* Williams, John
Passano, Edward B 1872-1946 *NatCAB 36*
Passano, William Moore 1902- *WhoAm 1974*
Passera, Carlos A *NF*
Passfield, Baron *see* Webb, Sidney James
Passy, Paul Edouard 1859-1940 *WebBD*
Pastore, Arthur Ralph, Jr. 1922- *ConAu 19R,*
WhoS&SW 1973
Pastore, Evelyn 1918?-1965 *BioIn 7*
Pastoret, Phil *NF*
Pataky, Ron *NF*
Patcevitch, Iva 1900- *WhoAm 1974*
Patch, Buel W 1899- *WhJnl 1928*
Patchell, Roy 1886- *WhJnl 1928*
Patchin, Frank Glines 1861-1925 *AmAu&B,*
DcNAA
Patchin, Robert H 1881-1955 *NatCAB 45*
Pate, Herbert J 1903- *WhJnl 1928*
Patenotre, Eleanor Elverson 1870- *AmJnl*
Patenotre, Raymond 1900-1951 *BioIn 2*
Paterson, Andrew Barton 1864-1941 *BioIn 2,*
BioIn 4, BioIn 7, BioIn 8, BioIn 9, CasWL,
DcLEL, LongC, Pen Eng, WebBD,
WebE&AL
Paterson, Isabel Bowler 1886?-1961 *AmAu&B,*
WebBD
Paterson, Lawrence Patrick *BioIn 9*
Paterson, Thomas *NF*
Pates, Gordon 1916- *WhoAm 1974,*
WhoWest 1974
Patmore, Derek Coventry 1908- *ConAu 7R*
Patricelli, Leonard Joseph 1907- *WhoAm 1974,*
WhoE 1974
Patrick, Charles *NF*
Patrick, Douglas Arthur 1905- *ConAu 17R,*
WhoE 1974
Patrick, John Corbin 1905- *WhoAm 1974*
Patrick, Sam *NF*

Patrick, Ted 1901-1964 *AmAu&B, BioIn 6*
Patt, G H *NF*
Patten, David 1888- *BioIn 2*
Patten, Roland Taylor 1864- *WhJnl Sup*
Patten, William H 1865-1936 *NatCAB 27*
Patterson, A D *HisAmM XR*
Patterson, Ada *AmAu&B, AmJnl, WhNAA*
Patterson, Alicia 1906-1963 *AmAu&B, BioIn 4, BioIn 5, BioIn 6, CurBio XR*
Patterson, Alicia *see also* Guggenheim, Alicia Brooks
Patterson, Anne Virginia Sharpe 1841-1913 *BioIn 2, HsB&A Sup, IndAu 1816, OhA&B*
Patterson, Blaine S 1893- *WhJnl 1928*
Patterson, Burd Shippen 1859-1924 *DcNAA*
Patterson, Carolyn Bennett *NF*
Patterson, Catherine M *HisAmM XR*
Patterson, Charles Brodie 1854-1917 *DcAmA, DcNAA, HisAmM XR*
Patterson, Charles S *HisAmM XR*
Patterson, Eleanor Medill 1881-1948 *AmAu&B, AmJnl, BioIn 1, BioIn 7, CurBio XR, DcAmB S4, WebBD*
Patterson, Elmore C *HisAmM XR*
Patterson, Eugene Corbett 1923- *InvJ, WhoAm 1974, WhoS&SW 1973, WhoWor 1974*
Patterson, Francis Ford, Jr. 1867-1935 *NatCAB 29*
Patterson, Graham 1881-1969 *CurBio XR, HisAmM XR*
Patterson, Grove 1881-1956 *BioIn 3, BioIn 4, WhJnl 1928*
Patterson, H W 1884- *WhJnl 1928*
Patterson, Helen M *WhJnl 1928*
Patterson, Hugh Baskin, Jr. 1915- *BioIn 5, OvPC, WhoAm 1974, WhoS&SW 1973*
Patterson, James *OvPC*
Patterson, Jerome Calvin 1911- *WhoMW 1974*
Patterson, Joseph Medill 1879-1946 *AmAu&B, AmJnl, BioIn 1, BioIn 2, CurBio XR, DcAmB S4, ForP, HisAmM XR, NatCAB 36, WebBD, WhJnl 1928*
Patterson, Lawrence Patrick *BlkC*
Patterson, Louis *NF*
Patterson, Paul Chenery 1878-1952 *BioIn 2, BioIn 3, WhJnl 1928*
Patterson, Rachelle A *NF*
Patterson, Raymond Albert 1856-1909 *DcNAA, NatCAB 25*
Patterson, Robert J *NF*
Patterson, Robert Mayne 1832-1911 *Alli Sup, AmAu&B, DcAmA, DcNAA*
Patterson, Robert P 1891-1952 *CurBio XR*
Patterson, Robert W 1850-1910 *AmJnl, NatCAB 12*
Patterson, Samuel D *Alli, HisAmM XR*
Patterson, Thomas M 1840- *AmJnl, NatCAB 12*
Patterson, Tom 1920- *WhoThe 1972*
Patterson, Virginia 1841-1913 *DcNAA*
Patterson, W MacLean 1912?-1976 *NF*
Patterson, William Dudley 1910- *WhoAm 1974, WhoWor 1974*
Patterson, Wright A 1870-1954 *BioIn 3, HisAmM XR*
Patti, Ercole 1904-1976 *BioIn 7, ConAu 69*
Pattie, J Delton *NF*
Pattington, Meader G 1905- *NF*
Pattison, James William 1844-1915 *DcNAA, HisAmM XR*
Patton, Alfred Spencer 1824?-1888 *Alli, DcAmA, HisAmM XR*
Patton, B A *AmRP*
Patton, Francis Landey 1843-1932 *Alli Sup, AmAu&B, DcAmA, DcNAA, HisAmM XR, WebBD*

Patton, Harvey W, Jr. 1916?-1978 *NF*
Patton, Harvey W, Sr. *NF*
Patton, Will A 1890- *WhJnl 1928*
Patton, William Weston 1821-1889 *Alli, Alli Sup, DcAmA, DcNAA, HisAmM XR*
Pattullo, George 1879-1967 *AmAu&B, HisAmM XR*
Patty, Stanton H *NF*
Paturis, Cleo *NF*
Pauker, Loretta *NF*
Paul, Arthur 1925- *WhoAm 1974, WhoF&I 1974*
Paul, George Howard 1826-1890 *BioIn 5*
Paul, Jan S 1929- *NF*
Paul, Jeanne *NF*
Paul, John 1834-1905 *Alli Sup, AmAu, AmAu&B, BbD, BiD&SB, DcAmA, DcNAA, REnAL, WebBD*
Paul, John *see also* Webb, Charles Henry
Paul, John Gilman D'Arcy 1886?-1972 *BioIn 9, HisAmM XR, NewYTBE 3*
Paul, Leslie Allen 1905- *Au&Wr, BioIn 2, BioIn 8, ConAu 1, LongC, WrDr 1976*
Paul, Maury Henry Biddle 1890-1942 *AmAu&B, BioIn 1, REnAL*
Paul, Robert Galloway *HisAmM XR*
Paul, Steve 1941?- *BioIn 7*
Paulding, Gouverneur 1897?-1965 *BioIn 7*
Paulding, James Kirke 1778-1860 *Alli, AmAu, AmAu&B, BbD, BiD&SB, CasWL, CnDAL, CyAL 2, DcAmA, DcEnL, DcLEL, DcNAA, EvLB, HisAmM XR, LiJA, OxAm, Pen Am, REn, REnAL, WebBD*
Pauley, Gay *ForWC 1970, WhoAm 1974, WhoAmW 1974, WhoE 1974*
Pauley, Jane *NF*
Pauli, William E *NF*
Paulin, L R E *NF*
Paulson, Holgar D 1887- *BioIn 5*
Paulson, John Doran 1915- *WhoAm 1974*
Paulu, Burton 1910- *AmM&W 73S, ConAu 15, DrAS 74E, ForP, WrDr 1976*
Paulus, John Douglas 1917- *ConAu 69, WhoE 1974, WhoF&I 1974*
Paulus, Mildred H *NF*
Pauly, David *NF*
Pauson, Charles Shipman *HisAmM XR*
Paustovsky, Konstantin 1892-1968 *ConAu 25*
Pavlik, Linda *InvJ*
Pawle, Gerald 1913- *Au&Wr, ConAu 5R*
Paxson, Richard, Jr. *NF*
Paxton, Edwin John 1877-1961 *BioIn 1, BioIn 8, NatCAB 50, RpN, WhJnl 1928*
Paxton, Edwin John 1912- *BioIn 1*
Paxton, Harry T 1915?- *BioIn 2, HisAmM XR*
Paxton, John R *HisAmM XR*
Paxton, W N *NF*
Payette, Virginia *NF*
Payette, William Colin 1913- *OvPC, WhoAm 1974, WhoE 1974*
Paylidis, Manos *NF*
Payn, James 1830-1898 *Alli, Alli Sup, BbD, BiD&SB, BrAu 19, DcBiA, DcEnA, DcEnA Ap, DcEnL, DcLEL, EncMys, EvLB, HisAmM XR, HsB&A, NewC, OxEng, REn, WebBD*
Payne, Barrie 1897- *WhJnl 1928*
Payne, Charles *WhJnl 1928*
Payne, Christopher Harrison 1848-1925 *BioIn 8*
Payne, David L *AmJnl*
Payne, Dee 1918- *NF*
Payne, Edward F 1870?-1955 *BioIn 3*
Payne, Eugene Gray *NF*
Payne, F F *NF*

Payne, Franklin S *BioIn 4*
Payne, G Logan 1876- *WhJnl 1928*
Payne, George Henry 1876-1945 *AmAu&B,*
　AmLY, BioIn 2, DcNAA, HisAmM XR,
　WhNAA
Payne, Henry M d1883 *NF*
Payne, J Lambert *NF*
Payne, John Howard 1791?-1852 *Alli, AmAu,*
　AmAu&B, BbD, BiD&SB, BioIn 1, BioIn 2,
　BioIn 3, BioIn 4, BioIn 8, BioIn 9, CasWL,
　CnDAL, CyAL 1, DcAmA, DcEnL, DcLEL,
　DcNAA, LiJA, OxAm, OxEng, Pen Am,
　REn, REnAL, WebBD
Payne, Kenneth Wilcox 1890-1962 *AmAu&B,*
　BioIn 6, HisAmM XR
Payne, Les *InvJ*
Payne, Melvin Monroe 1911- *WhoAm 1974,*
　WhoS&SW 1973, WhoWor 1974
Payne, Philip 1867- *AmAu&B, OhA&B*
Payne, Philip A 1893-1927 *AmJnl, WhJnl Sup*
Payne, Sanford C, Jr. *NF*
Payne, Sid d1976 *NF*
Payne, Will 1865-1954 *AmAu&B, BioIn 3,*
　DcAmA, HisAmM XR, WhNAA
Payne, William Archibald 1909- *WhoAm 1974,*
　WhoS&SW 1973
Payne, William Morton 1858-1919 *Alli Sup,*
　AmAu&B, BiD&SB, DcAmA, DcNAA,
　HisAmM XR, LiJA
Payne, William W 1837-1928 *HisAmM XR*
Payne, Winona 1865?-1949 *BioIn 1*
Paynter, Henry M d1960 *NF*
Payton, B L *NF*
Payton, J *NF*
Paz, Ezequiel Pedro 1871-1953 *BioIn 3, ForP*
Paz, Jose Camilo 1842-1912 *BioIn 2*
Paz, Jose Clemente *ForP*
Peabody, Andrew Preston 1811-1893 *Alli,*
　Alli Sup, AmAu, AmAu&B, BbD, CyAL 1,
　CyAL 2, DcAmA, DcNAA, HisAmM XR,
　LiJA, OxAm, WebBD
Peabody, Elizabeth Palmer 1804-1894 *Alli,*
　Alli Sup, AmAu, AmAu&B, BiD&SB,
　CnDAL, DcAmA, DcNAA, HisAmM XR,
　LiJA, OxAm, REnAL, WebBD
Peabody, Ephraim 1807-1856 *Alli, DcAmA,*
　HisAmM XR
Peabody, George Foster 1852-1938 *BioIn 2,*
　BioIn 4
Peabody, Oliver William Bourne 1799-1848 *Alli,*
　AmAu&B, CyAL 2, DcAmA, DcNAA,
　HisAmM XR
Peabody, Velton 1936- *ConAu 53*
Peace, Bony Hampton 1873- *WhJnl 1928*
Peace, Bony Hampton, Jr. 1906- *WhoS&SW 1973*
Peace, Roger Craft 1899-1968 *BioIn 1, WhNAA*
Peacock, E E *NF*
Peacock, G Raymond 1908- *WhJnl 1928*
Peacock, Gibson *AmJnl*
Peacock, Mary Willa 1942- *ConAu 69,*
　ForWC 1970
Peacock, William T 1905?-1967 *BioIn 8*
Peacocke, Emilie H *NF*
Peak, Bob *BioIn 9*
Pearce, George W *NF*
Pearce, John Ed *RpN*
Pearce, Richard Elmo 1909- *ConAu 1R,*
　WhoAm 1974, WhoWest 1974
Pearl, Hal 1914?-1975 *ConAu 61*
Pearl, Ralph 1910- *ConAu 73*
Pearlman, Sy *NF*
Pearlmutter, Morris *OvPC*
Pearlstine, Norman *NF*
Pearne, Thomas H *HisAmM XR*

Pearsall, J H *NF*
Pearsall, Robert *NF*
Pearse, H H S *FamWC*
Pearson, Sir Arthur 1866-1921 *BioIn 2, LongC*
Pearson, Sir Arthur *see also* Pearson, Sir Cyril
　Arthur
Pearson, Arthur Clemens *HisAmM XR*
Pearson, Charles D *NF*
Pearson, Charles H 1895?-1972 *BioIn 9*
Pearson, Sir Cyril Arthur 1866-1921 *WebBD*
Pearson, Sir Cyril Arthur *see also* Pearson, Sir
　Arthur
Pearson, Drew 1897-1969 *AmAu&B, AmJnl,*
　BioIn 1, BioIn 2, BioIn 4, BioIn 6, BioIn 7,
　BioIn 8, BioIn 9, BioIn 10, ConAu 5R,
　ConAu 25, CurBio XR, ForP, InvJ, NewMr,
　REnAL, TwCA Sup
Pearson, Edmund Lester 1880-1937 *AmAu&B,*
　CarSB, DcAmB S2, DcNAA, LongC,
　OxAm, REnAL, TwCA, WebBD, WhNAA
Pearson, G Fred *NF*
Pearson, George R *HisAmM XR*
Pearson, Haydn Sanborn 1901-1967 *BioIn 7*
Pearson, Henry Clemens 1858-1936 *Alli Sup,*
　DcNAA, NatCAB 27
Pearson, James Larkin 1879- *AmAu&B,*
　AnMV 1926, BiDSA, WhJnl 1928
Pearson, John E 1906- *WhJnl 1928*
Pearson, Leon Morris 1899-1963 *BioIn 2, BioIn 6*
Pearson, Lois R 1923- *NF*
Pearson, Paul Martin 1871- *AmLY,*
　HisAmM XR
Pearson, Richard M 1899-1957 *NatCAB 46*
Pearson, Ruth *NF*
Pease, Albert S 1828-1914 *NatCAB 16*
Pease, Andrew Jackson 1900- *WhJnl 1928*
Pease, Joseph Ives 1809-1883 *HisAmM XR*
Pease, Lucius Curtis 1869-1963 *BioIn 1, BioIn 2,*
　BioIn 6, CurBio XR, REnAL, WhJnl 1928
Pease, Lute *see* Pease, Lucius Curtis
Pease, Theodore Calvin 1887-1948 *BioIn 1,*
　DcNAA, WhNAA
Pease, Zephaniah Walter 1861-1933 *DcNAA*
Peaslee, Charlotte *OvPC*
Peattie, Elia Wilkinson 1862-1935 *AmAu&B,*
　BiD&SB, DcAmA, DcNAA
Peavey, Hubert Haskell 1881-1937 *BioIn 5*
Pechin, William *HisAmM XR*
Peck, Abraham 1945- *ConAu 73, WhoAm 1974*
Peck, Clair Beach 1884-1959 *BioIn 5*
Peck, Ellen *NF*
Peck, F Hamilton 1899?-1971 *BioIn 9*
Peck, George 1797-1876 *Alli, AmAu&B,*
　DcAmA, DcNAA, HisAmM XR, REnAL
Peck, George Washington 1817-1859 *Alli,*
　Alli Sup, AmAu, AmAu&B, CyAL 2,
　DcAmA, DcAmB 14, DcNAA,
　HisAmM XR, OhA&B
Peck, George Wilbur 1840-1916 *AmAu,*
　AmAu&B, AmJnl, BbD, BiD&SB, CarSB,
　CnDAL, DcAmA, DcAmB 14, DcNAA,
　HisAmM XR, OxAm, Pen Am, REn,
　REnAL, WebBD, WhoChL, WisWr
Peck, Harry Thurston 1856-1914 *AmAu,*
　AmAu&B, BiD&SB, DcAmA, DcNAA,
　HisAmM XR, OxAm, REn, REnAL
Peck, John B 1918?-1973 *BioIn 10*
Peck, John Mason 1789-1858 *Alli, AmAu,*
　AmAu&B, BiDSA, DcAmA, DcNAA,
　HisAmM XR, OxAm
Peck, Leroy Eugene 1922- *WhoAm 1974,*
　WhoWest 1974
Peck, Priscilla *WhoAm 1974, WhoAmW 1974*
Peck, Robert B 1885-1972 *BioIn 3, BioIn 9,*

New YTBE 3
Peck, Ruth Boyer *NF*
Peck, Templeton 1908- *WhoAm 1974,*
   WhoWest 1974
Peck, William Farley 1840-1908 *DcAmA, DcNAA*
Peck, William J *WhJnl 1928*
Peck, William Jay 1853-1920 *BioIn 3, BioIn 4*
Peckham, Content *BioIn 2*
Peckham, Stanton 1906- *BioIn 10,*
   WhoAm 1974, WhoWest 1974
Pederson, Kern *NF*
Peebles, Dick 1918- *WhoAm 1974,*
   WhoS&SW 1973
Peebles, William Buchanan 1899?-1957 *BioIn 4*
Peek, M L 1897- *WhJnl 1928*
Peel, Harris 1923- *OvPC, WhoGov 1972*
Peeler, Ernie 1913?-1950 *AmJnl, BioIn 2*
Peer, Elizabeth *NF*
Peerman, Dean Gordon 1931- *ConAu 13R,*
   WhoAm 1974
Peery, Richard *NF*
Peet, Creighton B 1899-1977 *AuBYP, BioIn 7,*
   ConAu 69
Peet, Herbert Marlin 1892- *WhJnl 1928*
Peet, Hubert William 1886-1950 *BioIn 3*
Peet, John 1915?- *BioIn 2*
Peet, Louis Harman 1863-1905 *DcNAA*
Peet, Stephen Denison 1831?-1914 *Alli Sup,*
   AmAu&B, BiD&SB, DcAmA, DcNAA,
   HisAmM XR, OhA&B, REnAL
Peet, William 1879- *WhJnl 1928*
Peffer, Lillian d1951 *BioIn 2*
Peffer, William Alfred 1831-1912 *AmAu,*
   AmAu&B, DcAmA, DcAmB 14, DcNAA,
   HisAmM XR
Pegler, Arthur James 1864?-1961 *BioIn 5*
Pegler, Westbrook 1894-1969 *AmAu&B, AmJnl,*
   BioIn 1, BioIn 3, BioIn 4, BioIn 6, BioIn 7,
   BioIn 8, BioIn 9, BioIn 10, CurBio XR,
   OxAm, WebBD
Peipert, James *NF*
Peirce, Bradford Kinney 1819-1889 *Alli, Alli Sup,*
   AmAu&B, DcAmA, DcNAA
Peirce, Neal R 1932- *ConAu 25,*
   WhoS&SW 1973, WrDr 1976
Peithman, Stephen *NF*
Peixotto, Benjamin Franklin 1834-1890
   DcAmB 14, HisAmM XR
Peixotto, Daniel Levy Maduro *HisAmM XR*
Peker, Charles G 1878- *WhJnl 1928*
Pekkanen, John R 1939?- *NF*
Pelham, Robert A 1859-1943 *BioIn 8, DcAmB S3*
Pelham, William *HisAmM XR*
Pell, Gene *NF*
Pell, John H G *HisAmM XR*
Pelletan, Pierre Clement Eugene 1813-1884
   BiD&SB, WebBD
Pelletier, George E 1900- *WhJnl Sup*
Pelletier, Georges 1882-1947 *CanWr*
Pelletier, Gerard 1919- *CanWW 1972,*
   IntWW 1976, OxCan Sup, WhoAm 1974,
   WhoCan 1973, WhoE 1974, WhoWor 1974
Pelletier, J Arthur 1874?-1954 *BioIn 3*
Pellew, George 1859-1892 *BiD&SB, DcAmA,*
   DcNAA, HisAmM XR
Peloubet, Francis Nathan 1831-1920 *DcNAA,*
   HisAmM XR
Pelt, A 1892- *CurBio XR*
Pelton, E R *HisAmM XR*
Pelton, O *HisAmM XR*
Peltz, Hamilton *NF*
Peltz, Mary Ellis 1896- *AmAu&B, CurBio XR,*
   WhoAm 1974, WhoAmW 1974
Pelz, Eduard 1800-1876 *BioIn 2*

Pemberton, Brock 1885-1950 *CurBio XR,*
   DcAmB S4
Pemberton, Sir Max 1863-1950 *BbD, BiD&SB,*
   BioIn 2, BioIn 8, DcBiA, DcEnA Ap,
   EncMys, EvLB, HisAmM XR, LongC,
   NewC, WebBD, WhoChL, WhoLA
Pence, Harry 1874- *WhJnl 1928*
Pendell, Thomas G 1867?-1947 *BioIn 1*
Pendleton, Hugh *HisAmM XR*
Pendleton, James Madison 1811-1891 *Alli,*
   Alli Sup, BiDSA, DcAmA, DcNAA,
   HisAmM XR, OhA&B
Pendleton, Louis Beauregard 1861-1939 *DcNAA*
Pendleton, Philip C *HisAmM XR*
Pendleton, Roger *NF*
Pendleton, S C *HisAmM XR*
Pendleton, W K *HisAmM XR*
Pendray, Leatrice May 1905-1971 *BioIn 9,*
   New YTBE 2
Pendred, Loughnan St. Lawrence 1870-1953
   BioIn 1, BioIn 3, WhoLA
Pendrell, Ernest *NF*
Penfield, Edward 1866-1925 *AmAu&B, DcNAA,*
   HisAmM XR, WebBD
Penfield, Edward 1872- *WhJnl 1928*
Penfield, Frederic Courtland 1855-1922 *DcAmA,*
   DcAmB 14, DcNAA
Penfield, Roderick Campbell 1864-1921
   HisAmM XR
Penfield, Wilder, III *NF*
Penfold, John Spies 1904?-1948 *BioIn 1*
Penn, I Garland *NF*
Penn, Stanley William 1928- *InvJ, NewMr,*
   WhoAm 1974, WhoE 1974
Pennekamp, John David 1897-1978 *AmJnl,*
   BioIn 1, WhoS&SW 1973
Pennell, Joseph 1857-1926 *HisAmM XR, LiJA,*
   WebBD
Penney, Pat *NF*
Penney, William N *NF*
Pennington, Wayne *OvPC*
Pennington, Weldon Jerry 1919- *WhoAm 1974,*
   WhoF&I 1974
Pennoyer, Clarence 1896?-1950 *BioIn 2*
Penny, Arthur Guy 1886- *WhJnl 1928*
Penny, Prudence *see* Goldberg, Hyman
Pennypacker, Anna Maria Whitaker 1876-1952
   BioIn 2
Pennypacker, Isaac Rusling 1852-1935 *AmAu&B,*
   DcAmA, DcNAA, NatCAB 13
Penrose, Lady d1977 *NF*
Pense, Edward J Barker 1848- *NF*
Pense, Michael Lorenzo *NF*
Pentcheff, Nicolas *OvPC*
Pentecost, George Frederick 1843?-1921 *Alli Sup,*
   BbD, BiD&SB, DcAmA, DcNAA,
   HisAmM XR
Penton, Brian Con 1904-1951 *BioIn 2, DcLEL,*
   TwCW
Pentz, Sara *NF*
Pepe, Phil 1935- *ConAu 25*
Pepis, Betty 1916?-1968 *BioIn 8*
Pepler, Hilary Douglas Clark 1878-1951 *BioIn 1,*
   BioIn 3, CathA 1930
Pepper, Charles Melville 1859-1930 *DcAmA,*
   DcNAA, NatCAB 22, OhA&B
Pepper, Choral C *NF*
Pepper, Curtis Bill 1920- *ConAu XR, OvPC*
Pepper, Curtis G 1920- *ConAu 23R*
Pepper, Curtis G *see also* Pepper, Curtis Bill
Pepper, E I D *HisAmM XR*
Pepper, Warren S *NF*
Pepper, William Mullin, Jr. 1903-1975 *ConAu 57,*
   WhoAm 1974, WhJnl 1928

Pepperday, Thomas M 1887- *WhJnl 1928*
Pepperpod, Pip *see* Stoddard, Charles Warren
Peralva, Osvaldo *ForP*
Percival, Harold Waldwin 1868- *HisAmM XR,*
   WhNAA
Percival, James Gates 1795-1856 *Alli, AmAu,*
   AmAu&B, BbD, BiD&SB, CyAL 1,
   DcAmA, DcEnL, DcLEL, DcNAA, EvLB,
   HisAmM XR, OxAm, REnAL, WebBD,
   WisWr
Percy, Harry L *AmJnl*
Peregrine *see* Deutscher, Isaac
Pereira, Ary Alves *NF*
Pereira, Harold Bertram 1890- *Au&Wr,*
   ConAu 9R
Perelman, Sidney Joseph 1904- *AmAu&B,*
   Au&Wr, AuNews 1, AuNews 2, CnDAL,
   ConAu 73, ConDr, ConLC 3, ConLC 5,
   DcLEL, LongC, McGWD, OxAm, Pen Am,
   RAdv 1, REn, REnAL, TwCA, TwCA Sup,
   TwCW, WebBD, WebE&AL, WrDr 1976
Peretz, Don 1922- *AmM&W 73S, OvPC,*
   WhoWorJ 1972
Peretz, Martin *WhoAm 1974*
Perew, Thomos 1946- *NF*
Perez, Alvaro 1917- *BioIn 2, USBiR 1974*
Perez, H Hugo 1923- *NF*
Perez DeArce, Guillermo 1873-1958 *BioIn 4*
Perez Palacio, Matilde *ForP*
Perfall, Arthur *OvPC*
Perham, John Cargil 1918- *WhoAm 1974*
Peri, John J 1895- *WhJnl 1928*
Perine, George E *HisAmM XR*
Perkerson, Angus 1888- *BioIn 4, WhJnl 1928*
Perkerson, Medora Field *NF*
Perkes, Dan 1931- *ConAu 69*
Perkin, Robert Lyman 1914-1978 *WhoPubR 1972,*
   WhoWest 1974
Perkins, Bertram J 1885?-1964 *BioIn 7*
Perkins, C L 1885- *WhJnl 1928*
Perkins, Eli *see* Landon, Melville DeLancey
Perkins, Erasmus *see* Cannon, George
Perkins, F N *NF*
Perkins, Frederick Beecher 1828-1899 *AmAu&B,*
   HisAmM XR, REnAL
Perkins, Harold Everett 1900-1952 *BioIn 2,*
   BioIn 3
Perkins, Henry Drewry 1865?-1955 *BioIn 3*
Perkins, J MacLary *NF*
Perkins, Jack *NF*
Perkins, Jacob Randolph 1878-1959 *BioIn 5*
Perkins, James Handasyd 1810-1849 *Alli,*
   AmAu&B, CyAL 2, DcAmA, DcNAA,
   HisAmM XR, OhA&B
Perkins, Jay L *NF*
Perkins, Maxwell Evarts 1884-1947 *AmAu&B,*
   BioIn 1, BioIn 2, BioIn 3, BioIn 6, BioIn 9,
   NatCAB 37, REnAL
Perkins, Newton Stephens 1925- *ConAu 49*
Perkins, Robert *NF*
Perkins, Sidney Albert 1865-1955 *BioIn 3,*
   BioIn 4, BioIn 6, NatCAB 46
Perkins, Terry William 1936- *WhoAm 1974*
Perkinson, William J 1921?-1969 *BioIn 8*
Perl, Susan 1922- *BioIn 8, ConAu 17R,*
   WhoE 1974
Perley 1820-1887 *AmAu, AmAu&B, OxAm,*
   REnAL
Perley *see also* Poore, Benjamin Perley
Perley, Frank E 1871?-1947 *BioIn 1*
Perley, Sidney 1858-1928 *AmAu&B, DcAmA,*
   DcNAA, HisAmM XR, WhNAA
Perlman, J Samuel 1900- *CanWW 1972,*
   WhoAm 1974

Perlmutter, Alvin *NF*
Perls, Eugenia Soderberg 1904?-1973 *ConAu 37*
Permar, Robert 1896- *WhJnl 1928*
Perna, Rita A *OvPC*
Peroutka, Ferdinand 1895?-1978 *NF*
Perrault, Giles 1931- *BioIn 7*
Perrazzelli, Antonio *OvPC*
Perreault, John 1937- *AmAu&B, ConAu 45,*
   ConP 1970, DrAP 1975
Perrin, Dwight Stanley 1888-1952 *BioIn 1,*
   BioIn 3
Perrin, William Henry 1834-1891 *Alli Sup,*
   DcNAA
Perrine, William *HisAmM XR*
Perris, E A *Lor&LP*
Perrone, Pio 1876-1952 *BioIn 2*
Perry, Bliss 1860-1954 *AmAu&B, BbD,*
   BiD&SB, BioIn 1, BioIn 2, BioIn 3,
   BioIn 4, BioIn 5, BioIn 6, CnDAL,
   ConAmL, DcAmA, HisAmM XR, LiJA,
   LongC, OxAm, REn, REnAL, TwCA,
   TwCA Sup, WebBD
Perry, Charlotte *NF*
Perry, Christopher J, Sr. d1921 *NF*
Perry, Enoch Wood *HisAmM XR*
Perry, Erma *NF*
Perry, Eugene Ashton 1864-1948 *HisAmM XR,*
   NatCAB 34
Perry, Fred C 1888- *BioIn 2*
Perry, George d1890 *HisAmM XR*
Perry, George Dorn 1887-1940 *WhJnl 1928*
Perry, James 1756-1821 *Alli, BiDLA, DcEnL,*
   ForP
Perry, Jean *BlkC*
Perry, John H *AmJnl*
Perry, John Holliday 1881-1952 *BioIn 1, BioIn 3*
Perry, John Holliday, Jr. 1917- *WhoAm 1974,*
   WhoS&SW ·1973, WhoWor 1974
Perry, Katherine *HisAmM XR*
Perry, Lawrence 1875-1954 *AmAu&B, BioIn 3,*
   WhJnl 1928
Perry, Lincoln *NF*
Perry, Margaret *NF*
Perry, Merton Dale 1929-1970 *BioIn 9,*
   NewYTBE 1
Perry, Nelson R 1894?-1964 *BioIn 7*
Perry, Nora 1831-1896 *Alli Sup, AmAu,*
   AmAu&B, BbD, BiD&SB, CarSB, DcAmA,
   DcAmB 14, DcNAA, HisAmM XR, REnAL
Perry, O H *HisAmM XR*
Perry, Rufus Lewis 1834-1895 *BioIn 8, DcAmA,*
   DcAmB 14, DcNAA
Perry, Stuart Hoffman 1874-1957 *BioIn 1,*
   BioIn 4, WhNAA, WhJnl 1928
Perry, Thomas Sergeant 1845-1928 *Alli Sup,*
   AmAu, AmAu&B, BiD&SB, DcAmA,
   DcNAA, HisAmM XR, OxAm, REnAL
Perry, Wallace 1883-1956 *BioIn 6, NatCAB 45,*
   WhJnl 1928
Perry, Will 1933- *ConAu 65*
Perry, William Arthur 1886- *WhJnl 1928*
Persimmon *see* Robinson, William Erigena
Persky, Mordecai 1931- *WhoAm 1974,*
   WhoE 1974
Person, Bernard *NF*
Personne 1834-1896 *Alli*
Personne *see also* DeFontaine, Felix Gregory
Persons, William Frank 1876-1955 *HisAmM XR*
Pertinax 1878- *WebBD*
Pertinax 1882-1974 *ConAu XR, WebBD,*
   Who 1974
Pertinax *see also* Geraud, Andre 1882-1974
Peshkov, Aleksei Maksimovich 1868-1936 *DcRusL,*
   McGWD, REn, REnWD

Peshkov, Aleksei Maksimovich *see also* Gorky, Maxim
Pesmen, Sandra 1931- *WhoAm 1974*
Pestelli, Gino 1894?-1965 *BioIn 7*
Petacque, Arthur M *InvJ*
Petajaniemi, Eero 1907- *IntWW 1976*
Petal, Marvin *NF*
Peterman, Cy *NF*
Peterman, Ivan *OvPC*
Peters, Abraham *HisAmM XR*
Peters, Absalom 1793-1869 *Alli, DcNAA, HisAmM XR*
Peters, Art 1928?-1973 *BioIn 9*
Peters, Bernard 1827- *NatCAB 1*
Peters, Charles *NewMr*
Peters, Charles Hamilton 1907- *CanWW 1972, WhoWor 1974*
Peters, Curtis Arnoux 1904-1968 *LongC, WebBD*
Peters, Curtis Arnoux *see also* Arno, Peter
Peters, Doris Revere *OvPC*
Peters, Frank Lewis, Jr. 1930- *WhoAm 1974, WhoMW 1974*
Peters, Frederick Romer 1874-1935 *BioIn 2, NatCAB 35, WhJnl 1928*
Peters, Howard H 1877-1963 *NatCAB 51*
Peters, Jim *NF*
Peters, Joseph C *OvPC*
Peters, Lulu Hunt 1873-1930 *DcNAA, HisAmM XR, WhNAA*
Peters, Madison Clinton 1859-1918 *Alli Sup, AmAu&B, DcAmA, DcNAA, HisAmM XR*
Peters, Margedant *HisAmM XR*
Peters, Mike *NF*
Peters, Pearl 1877- *WhJnl 1928*
Peters, Philip Williams 1878- *WhJnl 1928*
Peters, Richard F 1897?-1965 *BioIn 7*
Peters, Russell Holt 1899- *WhJnl 1928*
Peters, William 1921- *AmAu&B, ConAu 11R, WhoAm 1974, WhoE 1974*
Petersen, Agnes Joy *WhJnl 1928*
Petersen, Clarence G 1933- *NF*
Petersen, Harald 1893- *BioIn 2, IntWW 1974*
Petersen, Hjalmer 1890-1968 *NF*
Petersen, Mark Edward 1900- *BioIn 2, WhoF&I 1974*
Petersen, Raymond Joseph 1919- *WhoAdv 1972, WhoAm 1974*
Peterson, Albert E *OvPC*
Peterson, Arthur 1851-1932 *Alli Sup, DcAmA, DcNAA*
Peterson, Bettelou *WhoAmW 1974*
Peterson, Mrs. Charles Jacobs *HisAmM XR*
Peterson, Charles Jacobs 1819-1887 *Alli, AmAu, AmAu&B, AmJnl, BbD, BbtC, BiD&SB, DcAmA, DcNAA, HisAmM XR, HsB&A Sup, NatCAB 28, OxAm, REnAL*
Peterson, Clyde *NF*
Peterson, Eldridge 1905-1977 *BioIn 4, ConAu 73, WhoAm 1974*
Peterson, Elmer *NF*
Peterson, Elmer P 1884?-1969 *BioIn 8*
Peterson, Elmer Theodore 1884- *HisAmM XR, WhJnl 1928*
Peterson, Elmer W *NF*
Peterson, Florence Klauer 1913?-1964 *BioIn 7*
Peterson, Franklynn 1938- *NF*
Peterson, George Lester 1902- *WhoAm 1974*
Peterson, George W 1877- *WhJnl 1928*
Peterson, Harold 1939- *ConAu 29*
Peterson, Henry 1818-1891 *Alli, Alli Sup, AmAu, AmAu&B, BbD, BiD&SB, DcAmA, DcNAA, HisAmM XR, REnAL, WebBD*
Peterson, Herbert 1870- *WhJnl 1928*
Peterson, Jackie *NF*

Peterson, James Walden 1906- *WhJnl 1928*
Peterson, John E *NF*
Peterson, Jon *NF*
Peterson, Karl Lee 1919- *WhoAm 1974*
Peterson, Knut *ForP*
Peterson, L V 1875- *WhJnl 1928*
Peterson, Martin Severin 1897- *AmM&W 73P, ConAu 1, WhNAA, WhoAm 1974, WrDr 1976*
Peterson, R V *NF*
Peterson, Robert W 1925- *ConAu 33*
Peterson, Theodore Bernard 1918- *AmM&W 73S, DrAS 74E, ForP, LEduc 1974, WhoAm 1974*
Peterson, Victor Herbert 1916- *OvPC, WhoAm 1974*
Peterson, Virgilia 1904-1966 *AmAu&B, BioIn 3, BioIn 6, BioIn 7, BioIn 8, ConAu 25, CurBio XR, WorAu*
Peterson, Wilbur C 1898- *WhJnl 1928*
Petree, James Foster 1893-1970 *BioIn 9*
Petrie, Sir Charles 1895-1977 *BioIn 2, BioIn 4, ConAu 19, IntWW 1976, Who 1974, WhoWor 1974*
Petrie, Charles Barker 1900-1956 *BioIn 4*
Petrie, John W *HisAmM XR*
Petrie, Yvonne Elaine 1927-1978 *ForWC 1970, WhoAmW 1974*
Petroff, Eugene 1902-1942 *CurBio XR*
Petrou, David Michael 1949- *NF*
Petrov, Evgeni Petrovich 1903-1942 *CasWL, CIDMEL, CnMWL, DcRusL, EvEuW, ModSL 1, Pen Eur, TwCA, TwCW, WebBD*
Petrov, Ivan 1842- *BioIn 7*
Petrovic', Mihajlo 1868-1949 *BioIn 2*
Petry, Martin 1868- *WhJnl 1928*
Pett, Laurence J *OvPC*
Pett, Saul *NF*
Petta, Joseph Louis 1905- *WhJnl 1928*
Pettey, Tom S 1894- *WhJnl 1928*
Petti, Michael A 1915- *NF*
Pettigrew, John *HisAmM XR*
Pettingill, Lillian *HisAmM XR*
Pettit, Tom *see* Pettit, William Thomas
Pettit, William Thomas 1931- *WhoAm 1974*
Pettitt, Edward G 1916?-1967 *BioIn 8*
Pettus, Allen *NF*
Petty, Mary 1899-1976 *ConAu 65*
Peuzner, Antoine *HisAmM XR*
Peverelly, Charles A *Alli*
Pew, Marlen Edwin 1878-1936 *BioIn 6, HisAmM XR*
Peyser, Ethel Rose 1887-1961 *AmAu&B, BioIn 6, WhNAA*
Peyton, Bernard 1928?- *BioIn 2*
Peyton, Wesley Grant, Jr. 1925- *WhoAm 1974, WhoWest 1974*
Peyton-Griffin, R T 1890?-1950 *BioIn 2*
Pfaeffle, Walter 1938- *NF*
Pfeifer, Ellen Claire 1947- *WhoAm 1974*
Pfeifer, Luanne 1932- *NF*
Pfeiffer, C Boyd 1937- *ConAu 57*
Pfeiffer, Ewald W 1902- *WhJnl 1928*
Pfeiffer, George, II *NF*
Pfeiffer, Mary 1904- *BioIn 4*
Pfirshing, C *HisAmM XR*
Pfister, Charles Frederick 1859-1927 *BioIn 5*
Pfister, Walter John 1900- *Au&Wr, WhJnl 1928*
Pfund, Edward H 1870- *WhJnl 1928*
Phelan, Charlotte *NF*
Phelan, David Samuel 1841-1915 *DcAmB 14, DcNAA*
Phelan, Harold E 1916?-1971 *BioIn 9,*

New YTBE 2
Phelan, James InvJ
Phelan, James 1856-1891 Alli Sup, AmAu&B,
　BiDSA, DcAmA, DcNAA
Phelan, Michael 1816-1871 Alli, DcNAA,
　HisAmM XR
Phelan, Thomas F 1878?-1954 BioIn 3
Phelon, William Arlie 1871-1925 DcNAA
Phelps, Ashton 1913- WhoAm 1974,
　WhoS&SW 1973
Phelps, Charles H HisAmM XR
Phelps, Don G 1930?- BlkC
Phelps, E H HisAmM XR
Phelps, Edith May 1881- BioIn 5
Phelps, Edward Bunnell 1863-1915 DcAmA,
　DcNAA, HisAmM XR
Phelps, Henry Pitt 1844- DcNAA
Phelps, Hubbard OvPC
Phelps, Mary Hutchins 1900- WhJnl 1928
Phelps, Miriam E NF
Phelps, Moses Stuart HisAmM XR
Phelps, Phelps 1897- OvPC, WhoAm 1974,
　WhoWor 1974
Phelps, Sheffield 1864- NatCAB 11
Phelps, William Lyon 1865-1943 AmAu&B,
　CnDAL, ConAmL, CurBio XR, DcAmA,
　DcAmB S3, DcNAA, EvLB, HisAmM XR,
　LiJA, LongC, OxAm, REnAL, TwCA,
　TwCA Sup, WebBD
Phifer, Charles Lincoln 1860-1931 DcNAA
Philbin, Tom NF
Philbrick, John Dudley 1818-1886 Alli, DcAmA,
　DcNAA, HisAmM XR
Philbrick, Samuel HisAmM XR
Philcox, Fred NF
Philes, George Philip 1828-1913 AmAu&B,
　HisAmM XR
Philip, Percy J 1886-1956 AmJnl, BioIn 4
Philips, Albert Freeman 1850- WhJnl 1928
Philips, Melville Alli Sup, DcNAA
Philleo, Calvin Wheeler HisAmM XR
Phillimore Of Shiplake, Baron Godfrey W 1879-1947
　BioIn 1
Phillip, Lee June WhoAm 1974
Phillippi, Hank NF
Phillippi, Wendell Crane 1918- WhoAm 1974
Phillips, Alene M 1896- WhJnl 1928
Phillips, Bessie I 1880?-1954 BioIn 2, BioIn 3
Phillips, Cabell 1905?-1975 ConAu 61
Phillips, Coles 1912-1959 HisAmM XR
Phillips, David Atlee 1922- ConAu 69,
　WhoAm 1974, WhoGov 1972
Phillips, David Graham 1867-1911 AmAu&B,
　AmJnl, CnDAL, DcAmA, DcAmB 14,
　DcLEL, DcNAA, HisAmM XR,
　IndAu 1816, LongC, NewMr, OhA&B,
　OxAm, REn, REnAL, TwCA, TwCA Sup,
　WebBD, WebE&AL
Phillips, David Julius 1924- OvPC,
　WhoAmP 1973, WhoF&I 1974,
　WhoPubR 1972
Phillips, Donald S NF
Phillips, Eleazer d1732? AmJnl
Phillips, Elizabeth M BlkC
Phillips, Ellen NF
Phillips, George A OvPC
Phillips, George Searle 1818?-1889 Alli, BiD&SB,
　DcAmA, DcEnL, DcNAA, HisAmM XR
Phillips, Gifford 1918- BioIn 2, WhoAm 1974,
　WhoAmA 1973
Phillips, Grace Eustis 1899?-1966 BioIn 7
Phillips, Harmon 1903- WhoAm 1974,
　WhoS&SW 1973
Phillips, Harry Irving 1887-1965 AmJnl, BioIn 7,

CurBio XR
Phillips, Harry Irving see also Phillips, Henry Irving
Phillips, Henry Albert 1880-1951 AmAu&B,
　BioIn 2, BioIn 3, WhNAA
Phillips, Henry Irving 1887-1965 AmAu&B
Phillips, Henry Irving see also Phillips, Harry Irving
Phillips, Herb NF
Phillips, Hubert 1891-1964 BioIn 5, BioIn 6,
　LongC
Phillips, Irving W 1908- ConAu 65,
　WhoAmA 1973
Phillips, James H NF
Phillips, Jean Brown ForWC 1970, OvPC,
　WhoAmW 1974
Phillips, Jeffrey R NF
Phillips, John 1914- BioIn 1, BioIn 3, BioIn 5
Phillips, John Arthur 1842-1907 DcNAA
Phillips, John David 1920- WhoAm 1974,
　WhoE 1974
Phillips, John Sanburn 1861-1949 AmAu&B,
　DcAmB S4, HisAmM XR, NatCAB 38,
　Pen Am, REnAL
Phillips, Kevin Price 1940- BioIn 10, ConAu 65,
　WhoAm 1974, WhoAmP 1973
Phillips, Laughlin 1924- WhoAm 1974
Phillips, Lena Madesin 1881-1955 CurBio XR
Phillips, Leslie Gordon OvPC
Phillips, Loyal 1905- WhoAm 1974,
　WhoS&SW 1973
Phillips, Mary 1881- BioIn 1, BioIn 7
Phillips, McCandlish NF
Phillips, Morris 1834-1904 DcAmA, DcNAA,
　HisAmM XR, NatCAB 9
Phillips, Moses Dresser HisAmM XR
Phillips, Naphtali 1773-1870 BioIn 4
Phillips, Norman 1916?-1965 BioIn 7
Phillips, Osmond NF
Phillips, Pauline Esther Friedman 1918- AmAu&B,
　BioIn 4, BioIn 5, BioIn 8, ConAu 1R,
　CurBio XR
Phillips, Pauline Friedman see also VanBuren,
　Abigail
Phillips, Percival NF
Phillips, Ralph E HisAmM XR
Phillips, Ruby Hart 1900?- BioIn 5, ForWC 1970
Phillips, Ruth Alexandria 1902?-1970 BioIn 9
Phillips, Sherman NF
Phillips, Theodore O OvPC
Phillips, Virginia Vincent OvPC
Phillips, Walter Polk 1846-1920 Alli Sup,
　AmAu&B, DcAmB 14, DcNAA,
　NatCAB 19
Phillips, Warren Henry 1926- BioIn 10,
　IntWW 1976, OvPC, WhoAm 1974,
　WhoE 1974, WhoF&I 1974
Phillips, Wayne 1925?- BioIn 5
Phillips, Willard 1784-1873 Alli, AmAu&B,
　DcAmA, DcNAA, HisAmM XR
Phillips, William 1907- AmRP, ConAu 29,
　DrAS 74E, WhoAm 1974
Phillips, William Hamilton 1830-1916 DcNAA
Philp, Kenward d1886 NF
Philp, Richard Nelson 1943- ConAu 69
Philpott, Anthony J 1861?-1952 BioIn 2
Phinizy, Bowdre 1871- WhJnl 1928
Phipps, Hubert Beaumont 1906?-1969 BioIn 8
Phipps, John H 1904- WhoAm 1974
Phithayakorn, Sumalee NF
Phleger, Marjorie BioIn 9
Phoebus, George HisAmM XR
Phoebus, J W NF
Phoebus, William HisAmM XR
Phoenix, John 1823-1861 Alli, AmAu, AmAu&B,
　BiD&SB, CnDAL, DcAmA, DcEnL,

DcNAA, OxAm
Phoenix, John *see also* Derby, George Horatio
Phraner, Stanley L 1894- *WhJnl 1928*
Piatt, Donn 1819-1891 *Alli Sup, AmAu&B, BiD&SB, DcAmA, DcAmB 14, DcNAA, HisAmM XR, NatCAB 13, OhA&B, WebBD*
Piatt, John James 1835-1917 *Alli, Alli Sup, AmAu, AmAu&B, BbD, BiD&SB, BioIn 2, CnDAL, CyAL 2, DcAmA, DcAmB 14, DcLEL, DcNAA, HisAmM XR, IndAu 1816, OhA&B, OxAm, REnAL, WebBD*
Picabia, Francis 1879-1953 *AtlBL, HisAmM XR*
Picard, Laurent Augustine 1927- *CanWW 1972, IntWW 1976, WhoCan 1973, WhoWor 1974*
Picchia, Menotti Del 1892- *IntWW 1976*
Pichel, Isaac 1866?-1954 *BioIn 3*
Pichon, Stephen Jean Marie 1857-1933 *BioIn 9, WebBD*
Pick, Frederick Walter 1912-1949 *BioIn 2*
Pickard, Glenn H 1879- *WhJnl 1928*
Pickard, Samuel Thomas 1828-1915 *AmAu&B, DcAmA, DcNAA, HisAmM XR*
Pickens, Robert S 1900?-1978 *NF*
Pickens, Thomas M 1930- *NF*
Pickens, William *NF*
Pickerell, Albert George 1912- *ConAu 25, DrAS 74E, WhoAm 1974, WhoWest 1974, WhoWor 1974*
Pickerell, James Howard 1936- *WhoAm 1974, WhoE 1974*
Pickering, Edward Davies 1912- *IntWW 1976, Who 1974, WhoWor 1974*
Pickering, Henry Bowditch 1840-1911 *NF*
Pickering, Jack *NF*
Pickering, Loring 1812-1892 *NatCAB 25*
Pickering, Loring 1888-1959 *BioIn 5, BioIn 7, NatCAB 48*
Pickering, Ruth *NF*
Pickett, Albert 1771-1850 *Alli, HisAmM XR*
Pickett, Charles W 1857- *WhJnl 1928*
Pickett, Mrs. George Edward *HisAmM XR*
Pickett, H H *NF*
Pickett, John Erasmus 1885-1952 *HisAmM XR*
Pickett, John W *HisAmM XR*
Pickett, Marvin Harold 1899- *WhJnl 1928*
Pickle, Peregrine 1834-1919 *WebBD*
Pickle, Peregrine *see also* Upton, George Putman
Pickoff, Dave *NF*
Pickrel, Paul 1917- *ConAu 9, DrAS 74E, HisAmM XR, WhoAm 1974*
Pickrell, Homer P 1885- *WhJnl 1928*
Picou, Thomas *NF*
Picton, John *NF*
Picton, Thomas 1822-1891 *AmAu, AmAu&B, DcAmB 14, DcNAA, NatCAB 13*
Pidgeon, Edward E *NF*
Piel, Gerard 1915- *ConAu 57, CurBio XR, WhoAm 1974*
Pier, Arthur Stanwood 1874-1966 *AmAu&B, AmLY, BiD&SB, BioIn 9, CarSB, DcAmA, HisAmM XR, JBA 1934, JBA 1951, REnAL, WhNAA*
Pieraccini, Giovanni 1918- *IntWW 1976, WhoWor 1974*
Pierard, Louis 1886-1951 *BioIn 2*
Pierce, Arthur Dudley 1897- *ConAu 1R*
Pierce, David H 1898?-1949 *BioIn 2*
Pierce, Frank G *HisAmM XR*
Pierce, George Foster 1811-1884 *BiDSA, DcNAA, HisAmM XR*
Pierce, Gilbert Ashville 1839-1901 *Alli Sup, AmAu, AmAu&B, BioIn 2, DcNAA,*

IndAu 1816, WebBD
Pierce, Grace Adele d1923 *DcNAA*
Pierce, Harian A *HisAmM XR*
Pierce, Harriet Ristine 1881- *WhJnl 1928*
Pierce, Harry Solon 1877-1945 *BioIn 5*
Pierce, Herbert Allen 1881-1958 *BioIn 4*
Pierce, James Melville *HisAmM XR*
Pierce, Jesse W 1878-1925 *WhJnl Sup*
Pierce, Julian Irving 1864?-1947 *BioIn 1*
Pierce, Marvin 1893-1969 *HisAmM XR*
Pierce, Phil E 1912- *NF*
Pierce, Ponchitta Anne 1942- *WhoAm 1974, WhoAmW 1974, WhoE 1974, WhoF&I 1974*
Pierce, Ruby Edna 1888- *WhNAA, WhJnl 1928*
Pierce, Shelly 1898-1956 *BioIn 4*
Pierce, Solon Wesley 1831-1903 *BioIn 5*
Piercy, Joseph William 1866- *WhJnl 1928*
Pierotti, John 1911- *BioIn 4, WhoAm 1974, WhoAmA 1973*
Pierpoint, Robert *NF*
Pierrot *see* Arnold, George
Pierrot, George Francis 1898- *AmAu&B, AuNews 2, ConAu 7R, IntWW 1976, WhNAA, WhoAm 1974, WhJnl 1928*
Piersel, James Vincent 1901?-1962 *BioIn 6*
Piersol, George Morris 1880-1966 *HisAmM XR*
Pierson, Arthur Tappan 1837-1911 *Alli Sup, DcAmA, DcNAA, HisAmM XR*
Pierson, Charles E 1905?-1967 *BioIn 7*
Pierson, Delavan Leonard 1867-1952 *BioIn 3, DcNAA, WhNAA*
Pierson, John *NF*
Pierson, Lillian R *OvPC*
Pierson, Romaine 1868- *HisAmM XR*
Pierson, Walter G *HisAmM XR*
Pietri, Nilsa *NF*
Pietschmann, Richard John, III 1940- *ConAu 69*
Pigeon, Charles D *HisAmM XR*
Piggot, Robert *HisAmM XR*
Piggott, J S *NF*
Pignatelli, Conchita 1888?-1972 *BioIn 9*
Pigney, Joseph Page 1908- *ConAu 3R*
Pigott, Richard 1828?-1889 *Alli Sup, LongC, WebBD*
Pigue, W W 1884- *WhJnl 1928*
Pike, Albert 1809-1891 *Alli, AmAu, AmAu&B, BbD, BiD&SB, BiDSA, CnDAL, CyAL 2, DcCAA, DcLEL, DcNAA, EvLB, OxAm, REnAL*
Pike, Charles *NF*
Pike, David F *NF*
Pike, James Shepherd 1811-1882 *Alli Sup, AmAu, AmAu&B, AmJnl, BioIn 1, BioIn 4, DcAmA, DcAmB 14, DcNAA*
Pike, Manley H *HisAmM XR*
Pike, William P *NF*
Pilarski, Laura 1926- *ConAu 29, OvPC*
Pilat, Oliver Ramsay 1903- *AmAu&B, ConAu 7R*
Pilcher, Lewis Stephen 1845-1934 *Alli Sup, BioIn 1, DcNAA, HisAmM XR, WhNAA*
Pileggi, Nicholas *InvJ*
Pilkington, Betty *ConAu 69*
Pill, Howard E 1900- *WhJnl 1928*
Pillai, Maraveedy Gopal G 1939?- *NF*
Pillai, Shankar *BioIn 10*
Pillsbury, Arthur Judson 1854-1937 *DcNAA, HisAmM XR*
Pillsbury, Fred *RpN*
Pillsbury, John Elliott *HisAmM XR*
Pillsbury, Parker 1809-1898 *Alli Sup, AmAu&B, DcAmA, DcNAA, HisAmM XR, OxAm, WebBD*
Pilsbury, Caroline T *HisAmM XR*

Pilsworth, Graham NF
Pim, William Paul 1885-1950 BioIn 2
Pinard, Guy Andre 1938- WhoAm 1974
Pinchot, Amos HisAmM XR
Pinckney, Henry Laurens 1794-1863 AmAu&B,
    BiDSA
Pincus, Joseph William 1876-1951 BioIn 2
Pincus, Robert B 1944- WhoAm 1974
Pincus, Walter Haskell 1932- WhoAm 1974
Pindell, Henry M 1860- NatCAB 18
Pine, Art NF
Pines, Burton NF
Pines, Robert A 1897?-1949 BioIn 2
Pinkard, Maceo 1897-1962 AmSCAP 1966,
    NatCAB 48
Pinkerman, John NF
Pinkerton, Roy David 1885- WhoAm 1974
Pinkerton, Stewart NF
Pinkerton, William M RpN
Pinkham, Edwin George 1876-1948 BioIn 1,
    DcNAA
Pinkley, Virgil 1907?- BioIn 1
Pinkney, Edward Coote 1802-1828 Alli, AmAu,
    AmAu&B, BiD&SB, BiDSA, BioIn 3,
    BioIn 8, CyAL 2, DcAmA, DcLEL,
    DcNAA, EvLB, OxAm, REnAL, WebBD
Pinkson, Leon J 1878- WhJnl 1928
Pinkstaff, Marsha 1943?- BioIn 9
Pinkus, Matthew NF
Pinner, Felix 1880- NF
Pinney, Gregor W 1936?- NF
Pinney, Roy 1911- ConAu 7R
Pino, Angel NF
Pinover, Irving NF
Pinter, Walter NF
Pinto, Edmund NF
Pintong, Nilawan 1916- BioIn 9
Pioneer see Yates, Raymond Francis
Piovene, Count Guido 1907-1974 CasWL,
    ConAu 53, EncWL, IntWW 1974,
    NewYTBE 1, Pen Eur, REn, WhoWor 1974,
    WorAu
Pipal, George Henry 1916- WhoAm 1974,
    WhoWor 1974
Piper, Edgar Bramwell 1865-1928 IndAu 1917,
    WhJnl 1928
Piper, Edwin Ford 1871-1939 AmAu&B, DcNAA,
    HisAmM XR, REnAL, WhNAA
Piper, Harold NF
Pipkin, Charles Wooten 1899-1941 DcNAA,
    WhNAA
Pipp, Edwin G, Jr. NF
Pipp, Edwin G, Sr. 1864-1935 NF
Pippen, Rodger Hamill 1888-1959 BioIn 5
Pippert, Wesley Gerald 1934- ConAu 53
Pippett, Roger NF
Pires, Joe ConAu XR
Pirtle, Caleb Jackson, III 1941- ConAu 69
Piscione, Pamela NF
Pitkin, Helen 1877- BiDSA, DcAmA
Pitkin, Robert Bolter 1910- WhoAm 1974
Pitkin, Walter Boughton 1878-1953 AmAu&B,
    BioIn 3, BioIn 4, CurBio XR, DcAmB S5,
    HisAmM XR, OxAm, REnAL, TwCA,
    TwCA Sup, WebBD
Pitman, Jack NF
Pitrof, George A BioIn 8
Pitt, Lee 1926- OvPC, WhoF&I 1974,
    WhoWest 1974
Pitt, Robert Healy 1853-1937 HisAmM XR
Pitt, Theodore L HisAmM XR
Pittock, Henry L 1835- NatCAB 16
Pitts, Denis 1930- ConAu 65
Pitts, Frederic G 1896?-1973 BioIn 10

Pitzele, Merlyn Stuart 1911- BioIn 3,
    WhoAm 1974
Pixley, Frank 1867-1919 LiJA, OhA&B
Place, Eric NF
Place, G M BioIn 2
Place, Harold Curtis 1895- WhNAA,
    WhJnl 1928
Plaisted, Frederick William 1865-1943 CurBio XR
Plaisted, Harris Merrill 1828-1898 NF
Plant, Albert F NF
Plante, Bill NF
Plante, James F OvPC
Plants, James F OvPC
Plaschke, Paul Albert 1880-1954 BioIn 3
Plasterer, Lowell 1889- WhJnl 1928
Plater, Ronald RpN
Platero, Dillon 1926- BioIn 9
Platero, John NF
Platt, Charles D NF
Platt, David AmRP
Platt, Edmund 1865-1939 AmLY, DcNAA,
    WhNAA
Platt, F L 1872- WhJnl 1928
Platt, Frank L 1888-1959 BioIn 5
Platt, Kin 1911- BioIn 8, ConAu 19R,
    WhoAm 1974
Platt, S H HisAmM XR
Platter, J NF
Plawin, Paul NF
Player, Cyril d1952 NF
Player, William Oscar 1906-1951 BioIn 2
Playfair, Wilfrid Ernest 1882-1953 BioIn 3
Pleasant, Richard d1961 BioIn 6
Pleasants, Henry 1910- AmAu&B, WrDr 1976
Pleasants, John Hampden 1797-1846 AmJnl,
    DcAmB 15, NatCAB 7
Plenn, Jaime 1905?-1978 OvPC
Pletcher, Eldon 1922- WhoAm 1974
Pletz, Mary Ellis 1896- BioIn 3
Plimpton, Florus Beardsley 1830-1886 Alli Sup,
    DcNAA, NatCAB 5, OhA&B
Plimpton, George 1927- AuNews 1, BioIn 7,
    BioIn 8, BioIn 9, BioIn 10, CelR 1973,
    ConAu 21R, CurBio XR, NewYTBE 1,
    SmATA 10, WhoAm 1974, WhoWor 1974
Plimpton, George Arthur 1855-1936 AmAu&B,
    DcNAA, NatCAB 27, REnAL
Plopper, Julie Jynelle 1916- ConAu 69
Plotkin, David George 1899-1968 BioIn 8
Plotnik, Arthur 1937- BiDrLUS, BioIn 8,
    ConAu 69
Plough, Kenneth A 1891-1947 NatCAB 49
Plowden, Gene 1906- ConAu 21R
Plum, David Banks 1869-1948 BioIn 1,
    WhJnl 1928
Plumb, Charlie 1942- ConAu 49
Plumb, Preston B 1837-1891 DcAmB 15
Plumb, Robert RpN
Plummer, Charles Arnold 1898-1961 BioIn 6
Plummer, Evans E 1899- WhJnl 1928
Plummer, Herbert C 1903?-1955 BioIn 3
Plummer, Walter Percy 1883-1933 NF
Plunkett, Count George Noble 1851-1948
    CathA 1952, PoIre, WebBD
Plunkett, Henry Grattan HisAmM XR
Plunkett, John James 1927- WhoAm 1974
Pluntze, Jack NF
Pobers, Michel BioIn 1
Poblete, Omar NF
Podell, Jack Jerry 1927- WhoAm 1974
Podhoretz, Midge BioIn 9
Podhoretz, Norman 1930- AmAu&B, Au&Wr,
    BioIn 6, BioIn 8, BioIn 9, CelR 1973,
    ConAu 9R, CurBio XR, NewYTBE 3,

Pen Am, WhoAm 1974, WhoWor 1974,
WorAu
Poe, Clarence Hamilton 1881-1964 *AmLY,*
BiDSA, BioIn 3, BioIn 5, BioIn 7, BioIn 9,
HisAmM XR
Poe, David *HisAmM XR*
Poe, Edgar Allan 1809-1849 *Alli, AmAu,*
AmAu&B, AmWr, AnCL, AtlBL, BbD,
BiD&SB, BiDSA, CasWL, CnDAL,
CnE&AP, CrtT 3, CyAL 2, CyWA,
DcAmA, DcBiA, DcEnA, DcEnL, DcLEL,
DcNAA, EncAB, EncMys, EvLB,
HisAmM XR, LiJA, MouLC 3, OxAm,
OxEng, Pen Am, RAdv 1, RComWL, REn,
REnAL, Str&VC, WebBD, WebE&AL
Poe, Edgar Allen 1906- *WhoAm 1974*
Poelsma, Dominic *NF*
Poffenbarger, Livia Simpson 1862-1937 *AmAu&B*
Pohl, Frederick 1919- *AmAu&B, ConAu 61*
Poinier, Arthur Best 1911- *WhoAm 1974*
Poinsett, Alex Caesar 1926- *ConAu 29, LivBAA*
Poirier, Richard 1925- *AmAu&B, AmRP,*
ConAu 1, DrAS 74E, WhoAm 1974,
WhoE 1974
Pokress, Jack *NF*
Pokriefka, F A 1887- *WhJnl 1928*
Pol, Heinz 1901-1972 *BioIn 9*
Polachek, Victor H 1876-1940 *AmAu&B*
Polack, William Gustave 1890-1950 *BioIn 2,*
WhNAA
Polakoff, Joseph *NF*
Polevoi, Boris Nikolaevich 1908- *IntWW 1976,*
WhoWor 1974
Poliakoff, Vladimir 1881?-1956 *BioIn 4*
Poliakov, Alexander 1908-1942 *CurBio XR*
Policano, Joseph D *OvPC*
Polier, Rex *NF*
Poling, Daniel Alfred 1884-1968 *AmAu&B,*
BioIn 7, BioIn 8, BioIn 10, CurBio XR,
OhA&B
Poling, James *NF*
Polinow, Samuel *AmRP*
Politella, Dario 1921- *ConAu 13R, DrAS 74E,*
WhoE 1974, WrDr 1976
Polk, George W 1913?-1948 *BioIn 1*
Polk, Irwin J 1925- *NF*
Polk, James R 1937- *BioNews 1974, ConAu 69,*
InvJ
Polk, Leonidas Lafayette 1837-1892 *BioIn 1,*
BioIn 2, HisAmM XR
Polk, Milton D *WhJnl 1928*
Polk, Peggy *NF*
Polk, William Tannahill 1896-1955 *BioIn 3,*
BioIn 4
Polk, Willis *HisAmM XR*
Pollack, Harvey 1913- *ConAu 7R*
Pollack, Jack Harrison 1914- *AmAu&B, BioIn 4,*
CurBio XR, OvPC
Pollack, Merrill S 1924- *BioIn 3, ConAu 7R*
Pollak, Eugen 1890- *NF*
Pollak, Gustav 1849-1919 *AmAu&B, DcNAA*
Pollak, Oskar 1893-1963 *BioIn 6*
Pollak, Richard *NF*
Pollan, Clay *NF*
Pollard, Alfred William *HisAmM XR*
Pollard, Charles Louis *HisAmM XR*
Pollard, Edward A 1831?-1872 *Alli, Alli Sup,*
AmAu, AmAu&B, AmJnl, BiD&SB,
BiDSA, DcAmA, DcAmB 15, DcNAA,
HisAmM XR, REnAL, WebBD
Pollard, Harold Stanley 1878-1953 *AmAu&B,*
BioIn 3
Pollard, Hugh Bertie Campbell 1888- *BioIn 2,*
Br&AmS

Pollard, Jack 1926- *ConAu 29*
Pollard, James Edward 1894- *ConAu 15,*
ConAu P-1, DrAS 74H, OhA&B,
WhoAm 1974
Pollard, Joseph Percival 1869-1911 *AmAu&B,*
DcNAA, HisAmM XR
Pollard, Mary Orenda 1873?- *BioIn 2*
Pollock, Channing 1880-1946 *AmAu&B, AmLY,*
AmSCAP 1966, CnDAL, CurBio XR,
DcNAA, HisAmM XR, ModWD, OxAm,
REn, REnAL, TwCA, TwCA Sup, WebBD,
WhNAA
Pollock, Edward A *HisAmM XR*
Pollock, Francis *NF*
Pollock, Horatio Milo 1868-1950 *AmLY, BioIn 2,*
WhNAA
Pollock, Sir John 1878-1963 *BioIn 2, LongC,*
WhoLA
Pollock, Richard P *NF*
Pollock, Walter Herries 1850-1926 *Alli Sup,*
BiD&SB, TwCA, WebBD
Polonskii, Iakov Petrovich 1820-1898 *BioIn 1,*
BioIn 2, BioIn 9
Polson, Izil I 1894- *WhJnl 1928*
Polttoon, Milford *NF*
Polyakov, Vasily Ivanovich 1913- *IntWW 1976,*
WhoWor 1974
Polyzoides, Adamanitos Th 1885-1969 *BioIn 8,*
WhJnl 1928
Pomeroy, A Nevin 1859- *WhJnl 1928*
Pomeroy, Brick *see* Pomeroy, Marcus Mills
Pomeroy, Brick *see* Pomeroy, Mark
Pomeroy, Cashel *HisAmM XR*
Pomeroy, Marcus Mills 1833-1896 *Alli Sup,*
AmAu, AmAu&B, BiD&SB, BioIn 5,
BioIn 9, DcAmA, DcNAA, HisAmM XR,
WisWr
Pomeroy, Marcus Mills *see also* Pomeroy, Mark
Pomeroy, Mark 1833-1896 *Alli, AmJnl*
Pomeroy, Mark *see also* Pomeroy, Marcus Mills
Pomfret, John *RpN*
Pompadur, I Martin 1935- *WhoAm 1974,*
WhoF&I 1974
Pompey, Joseph H *NF*
Pond, Elizabeth *NF*
Pond, Frederick Eugene 1856-1925 *Alli Sup,*
AmAu&B, BiD&SB, DcAmA, DcNAA,
NatCAB 10, OhA&B, REnAL
Pond, George Edward 1837-1899 *Alli Sup,*
AmAu&B, DcAmA, DcAmB 15, DcNAA,
HisAmM XR, NatCAB 10
Pond, Philip Ray 1900- *WhJnl 1928*
Pond, Seymour G 1898- *WhJnl 1928*
Ponsot, Marie *HisAmM XR*
Ponte, Lowell Alton 1946- *WhoAm 1974,*
WhoWest 1974
Ponting, Herbert 1882- *BioIn 2, WhJnl 1928*
Pool, Mary Jane *WhoAm 1974, WhoAmW 1974*
Pool, Stephen D *LiJA*
Pool, William Frederick *HisAmM XR*
Poole, Ernest Cook 1880-1950 *DcAmB S4,*
HisAmM XR, WebBD
Poole, Fitch 1803-1873 *AmAu&B, DcAmB 15*
Poole, Gary Thomas 1931- *WhoAm 1974,*
WhoF&I 1974
Poole, Gray *BioIn 7*
Poole, John Bayard 1912- *WhoAm 1974,*
WhoE 1974, WhoF&I 1974, WhoMW 1974
Poole, Robert *NF*
Poole, William Morris 1908- *BioIn 1*
Pooler, James S 1905-1967 *NF*
Poor, Chlipke *AmRP*
Poor, Henry Varnum 1812-1905 *Alli, Alli Sup,*
AmAu&B, DcAmB 15, DcNAA, EncAB,

HisAmM XR, *REnAL*, *WebBD*
Poor, Henry William 1844-1915 *AmAu&B*,
  NatCAB 16
Poor, John Barton 1915- *WhoAm 1974*,
  WhoE 1974
Poore, Benjamin Perley 1820-1887 *Alli*, *Alli Sup*,
  AmAu, *AmAu&B*, *BiD&SB*, *BioIn 9*,
  DcAmA, *DcAmB 15*, *DcNAA*,
  HisAmM XR, *OxAm*, *REnAL*, *WebBD*
Poore, Charles Graydon 1902-1971 *AmAu&B*,
  HisAmM XR, *NewYTBE 2*
Poorman, Paul Arthur 1930- *WhoAm 1974*
Pooton, James *NF*
Pope, Albert Augustus 1843-1909 *HisAmM XR*
Pope, Alvin E 1873- *WhJnl 1928*
Pope, Edwin 1928- *ConAu 73*, *WhoS&SW 1973*
Pope, Ernest Russel 1910- *OvPC*, *USBiR 1974*
Pope, F L *HisAmM XR*
Pope, Generoso 1927?- *BioIn 8*, *BioIn 9*
Pope, Gerald S *HisAmM XR*
Pope, John Edwin, III 1928- *WhoAm 1974*
Pope, O C *HisAmM XR*
Pope, Quentin 1900?-1961 *BioIn 5*
Pope, Vernon 1905- *WhoAm 1974*,
  WhoPubR 1972
Pope, Virginia 1886?-1978 *BioIn 4*
Pope, Wilson 1866-1953 *BioIn 3*
Popescu, Dumitru 1928- *IntWW 1976*
Popham, John Nicholas 1910?- *BioIn 4*
Popkin, Zelda 1898- *AmAu&B*, *AmNov*,
  ConAu 25, *CurBio XR*, *WhoWorJ 1972*,
  WrDr 1976
Popov, Dimitrii Mikhailovich d1952 *BioIn 2*
Poppele, J R 1898- *IntMPA 1975*, *WhoAm 1974*
Poppy, John 1942?- *BioIn 9*
Por, Ödon *AmRP*
Porche, Wladimir 1910- *IntWW 1976*,
  WhoWor 1974
Porcupine, Peter 1762?-1835 *Alli*, *BrAu 19*,
  DcEnL, *DcLEL*, *EvLB*, *NewC*, *OxAm*,
  WebBD
Porcupine, Peter *see also* Cobbett, William
Pore, Harry Ross 1872?-1949 *BioIn 2*
Porges, Frederick 1890?-1978 *NF*
Poritt, Edward *HisAmM XR*
Porritt, Arthur 1872- *BioIn 1*, *WhoLA*
Porta, Agustin Della *NF*
Porte, Andrew *NF*
Porte-Crayon 1816-1888 *DcEnL*, *WebBD*
Porte-Crayon *see also* Strother, David Hunter
Portell, Jose Maria *NF*
Porteous, Clark *RpN*
Porter, Amy 1906?-1971 *BioIn 1*, *BioIn 9*
Porter, Andrew 1928- *ConAu 53*, *WhoMus 1972*,
  WrDr 1976
Porter, Bruce *HisAmM XR*, *LiJA*
Porter, Charles Bell 1896?-1948 *BioIn 1*
Porter, Charlotte *HisAmM XR*
Porter, Darwin Fred 1937- *ConAu 69*
Porter, Ellis *NF*
Porter, Henry H *HisAmM XR*
Porter, Janet *NF*
Porter, John Addison 1856-1900 *Alli Sup*,
  BiD&SB, *DcAmA*, *DcNAA*, *NatCAB 9*,
  NatCAB 28
Porter, Joseph Whitcomb 1824-1901 *Alli Sup*,
  DcNAA, *HisAmM XR*
Porter, Lee *NF*
Porter, Maurice S 1873- *WhJnl 1928*
Porter, McKenzie 1911- *OxCan*
Porter, Philip Wiley 1900- *ConAu 69*
Porter, Robert Percival 1852-1917 *Alli Sup*,
  AmAu&B, *AmJnl*, *DcAmA*, *DcAmB 15*,
  DcNAA, *WebBD*

Porter, Roy P 1907-1947 *BioIn 1*, *DcNAA*
Porter, Rufus 1792-1884 *AmAu&B*, *DcNAA*,
  HisAmM XR
Porter, Russell *NF*
Porter, Steve *NF*
Porter, Sylvia Field 1913- *AmAu&B*, *BioIn 1*,
  BioIn 3, *BioIn 5*, *BioIn 6*, *BioIn 9*,
  CurBio XR, *ForWC 1970*, *WhoAm 1974*,
  WhoE 1974
Porter, T D *HisAmM XR*
Porter, T O *HisAmM XR*
Porter, William E 1918- *ConAu 69*
Porter, William Earl *BioIn 3*
Porter, William Lee 1931- *WhoAm 1974*
Porter, William Sydney 1862-1910 *AmAu&B*,
  AmJnl, *AtlBL*, *CasWL*, *CnDAL*, *DcLEL*,
  DcNAA, *EncMys*, *EvLB*, *HisAmM XR*,
  LiJA, *LongC*, *OhA&B*, *OxAm*, *OxEng*,
  Pen Am, *REn*, *REnAL*, *TwCA*, *TwCA Sup*,
  WebBD, *WebE&AL*
Porter, William Sydney *see also* Henry, O
Porter, William Trotter 1809-1858 *Alli*,
  AmAu&B, *AmJnl*, *BioIn 4*, *BioIn 9*,
  DcAmB 15, *DcNAA*, *HisAmM XR*, *LiJA*,
  OxAm, *REnAL*
Porterfield, Allen Wilson 1877-1952 *AmAu&B*,
  HisAmM XR, *WhNAA*
Porterfield, William H 1872-1927 *NatCAB 21*
Portis, Charles 1933- *AmAu&B*, *ConAu 45*
Portisch, Hugo 1927- *ConAu 21R*,
  WhoWor 1974
Portman, Victor R *NF*
Poschinger, Heinrich Von 1845-1911 *WebBD*
Posener, Salomon 1876?-1946 *BioIn 1*
Posey, Alexander Lawrence 1873-1908 *AmAu&B*,
  DcAmB 15, *DcNAA*, *REnAL*
Posey, Ron *NF*
Posner, Ben 1914- *USBiR 1974*, *WhoAm 1974*,
  WhoGov 1972, *WhoS&SW 1973*,
  WhoWor 1974
Posner, Jack *NF*
Posner, Michael Louis 1932- *WhoAm 1974*,
  WhoS&SW 1973
Post, A L *NF*
Post, Alice 1853-1947 *BioIn 1*
Post, Bert F 1890- *WhJnl 1928*
Post, Charles Cyrel 1846- *DcAmA*, *DcNAA*
Post, Charles Johnson 1873-1956 *BioIn 4*,
  WhNAA
Post, David *NF*
Post, Elizabeth *NF*
Post, Emily Price 1873-1960 *AmAu&B*, *BioIn 1*,
  CurBio XR, *WebBD*
Post, Frank A *BioIn 2*, *BioIn 3*
Post, George W *HisAmM XR*
Post, Homer A 1888- *ConAu 25*
Post, Howard *NF*
Post, Israel *HisAmM XR*
Post, Louis Freeland 1849-1928 *DcNAA*,
  HisAmM XR, *OhA&B*, *WhNAA*
Post, Lyman D *HisAmM XR*
Post, Maveric 1870-1943 *AmAu&B*, *WhNAA*
Post, Maveric *see also* Mapes, Victor
Post, Richard W *NF*
Post, Robert P 1911-1943 *AmJnl*, *CurBio XR*
Postal, Bernard 1905- *ConAu 5R*, *WhoE 1974*,
  WhoWorJ 1972
Postgate, John William 1851- *AmJnl*, *DcNAA*
Postgate, Raymond William 1896-1971 *Au&Wr*,
  BioIn 4, *BioIn 9*, *ConAu 5*, *DcLEL*,
  EncMys, *EvLB*, *LongC*, *Pen Eng*, *TwCA*,
  TwCA Sup, *TwCW*, *WhoLA*
Poston, Ted 1906-1974 *BioIn 1*, *BioIn 9*,
  BlkAW, *BlkC*, *NewYTBS 5*

Prasad, Sharada *RpN*
Pratt, Charles E *Alli Sup, HisAmM XR*
Pratt, Charles Stuart 1854-1921 *AmAu&B, DcAmA, DcNAA, HisAmM XR, WhNAA*
Pratt, Cornelia Atwood d1929 *AmAu&B, DcAmA, DcNAA, HisAmM XR, OhA&B*
Pratt, D Anson *HisAmM XR*
Pratt, Donald L 1896?-1965 *BioIn 7*
Pratt, Edwin John 1883-1964 *CanWr, CasWL, DcLEL, EvLB, LongC, NewC, OxCan, OxCan Sup, OxEng, Pen Eng, REn, REnAL, TwCA Sup, WebBD, WebE&AL, WhNAA*
Pratt, Eliza Anna Farman 1843?-1907 *AmAu&B, WebBD*
Pratt, Eliza Anna Farman *see also* Farman, Ella
Pratt, Eliza Anna Farman *see also* Pratt, Ella Ann Farman
Pratt, Ella Ann Farman 1843?-1907 *Alli Sup, BbD, BiD&SB, DcAmA, DcNAA*
Pratt, Ella Ann Farman *see also* Farman, Ella
Pratt, Ella Ann Farman *see also* Pratt, Eliza Anna Farman
Pratt, Elmer C 1874- *WhJnl 1928*
Pratt, Fletcher 1897-1956 *AmAu&B, AuBYP, CurBio XR, REnAL, TwCA Sup, WhNAA*
Pratt, Frances N *HisAmM XR*
Pratt, Harold J 1895?-1965 *BioIn 7*
Pratt, Harry Noyes 1879-1944 *AmAu&B, HisAmM XR, WhNAA*
Pratt, John 1831-1900 *DcAmB 15*
Pratt, Leonard *NF*
Pratt, Orson 1811-1881 *Alli, BiD&SB, DcAmA, DcNAA, HisAmM XR*
Pratt, Richard Henry 1891-1973 *BioIn 10*
Pratt, Sarah 1853-1942 *BioIn 2*
Pratt, Sereno Stansbury 1858-1915 *DcAmB 15, DcNAA*
Pratt, Thomas H 1893- *WhJnl 1928*
Pratt, William Bates 1895- *WhJnl 1928*
Pratt, William V 1869-1957 *CurBio XR*
Pratte, Alf 1938- *NF*
Prattis, Percival L 1895- *BioIn 8, WhJnl 1928*
Pray, Isaac Clark 1813-1869 *Alli, AmAu&B, DcAmA, DcAmB 15, DcNAA, HisAmM XR, WebBD*
Prebble, John Edward Curtis 1915- *Au&Wr, ConAu 7R, Who 1974, WrDr 1976*
Prebeck, Florence *HisAmM XR*
Preetorius, Edward L 1866-1915 *NatCAB 16*
Preetorius, Emil 1827-1905 *BioIn 2, DcAmB 15*
Preger, Paul D, Jr. 1926- *ConAu 49*
Prehodka, Henry *OvPC*
Preiser, Theodore H *OvPC*
Preiss, David Lee 1935- *ConAu 69, WhoAm 1974*
Prendergast, Charles J, Jr. *WhoAm 1974*
Prendergast, Curtis *NF*
Prenner, Manuel 1901-1972 *BioIn 9*
Prenosil, Stanley W 1893?-1967 *BioIn 7*
Prentice, George Dennison 1802-1870 *Alli, AmAu, AmJnl, BbD, BiD&SB, BiDSA, CyAL 2, DcAmA, DcAmB 15, DcNAA, HisAmM XR, NatCAB 3, OxAm, REnAL*
Prentice, Marion Alcott *HisAmM XR*
Prentice, Pierrepont Isham *HisAmM XR*
Prentiss, Charles 1774-1820 *Alli, CyAL 1, DcAmA, DcNAA*
Prentiss, John William 1898-1953 *BioIn 5, NatCAB 42*
Prentiss, Mark O d1948 *BioIn 1*
Presbrey, Frank *HisAmM XR*
Presbrey, Paul 1910?- *BioIn 2*
Prescott, Eustis *HisAmM XR*

Prescott, John Sherwin, Jr. 1927- *WhoAdv 1972, WhoAm 1974, WhoE 1974, WhoF&I 1974*
Prescott, Orville 1906- *AmAu&B, AuBYP, ConAu 41, CurBio XR, REnAL, WhoAm 1974*
Prescott, Peter S 1935- *BioIn 9, BioIn 10, ConAu 37*
Prescott, W W *HisAmM XR*
Present, Ruth Helene 1903- *WhJnl 1928*
Press, Harry *RpN*
Press, Otto 1880- *WhJnl 1928*
Pressense, Edmond Dehaut De 1824-1891 *BbD, BiD&SB, WebBD*
Presser, Theodore 1848-1925 *DcNAA, HisAmM XR, WebBD*
Pressman, Gabriel 1923?- *BioIn 4, BioIn 6*
Prestbo, John A 1941- *ConAu 49*
Prestgard, Kristian 1866-1946 *BioIn 2*
Preston, Charles *NF*
Preston, Dickson J 1914- *ConAu 61*
Preston, Edward *ConAu XR*
Preston, H E 1857-1926 *BioIn 2, Br&AmS*
Preston, Henry Raymond 1874-1944 *BioIn 2, NatCAB 34*
Preston, John *AmRP, HisAmM XR*
Preston, Keith 1884-1927 *AmJnl, DcNAA, REnAL, WhNAA*
Preston, Malcom H 1920- *NF*
Preston, Paul 1822-1891 *AmAu, DcNAA*
Preston, Paul *see also* Picton, Thomas
Preston, Raymond Abner 1892?-1956 *BioIn 4*
Preston, Ruth 1906- *ForWC 1970*
Preston, T H *NF*
Preston, W B *NF*
Preuss, Arthur 1871-1934 *BioIn 1, CathA 1930, DcNAA*
Previte-Orton, Charles William 1877-1947 *BioIn 1, BioIn 2, BioIn 5*
Prevost, Alain 1930?-1971 *ConAu 33*
Prevost-Paradol, Lucien Anatole 1829-1870 *BbD, BiD&SB, OxFr, WebBD*
Prew, Robert J *NF*
Prewett, Virginia *OvPC*
Prezzolini, Giuseppe 1882- *BioIn 1, CasWL, CIDMEL, WebBD*
Priaulx, Allan *OvPC*
Pribichevich, Stoyan 1905?-1976 *ConAu 65, CurBio XR*
Price, Arthur L 1879- *WhJnl 1928*
Price, Burr 1888-1952 *BioIn 2*
Price, Byron 1891- *AmJnl, BioIn 1, BioIn 6, CurBio XR, IntWW 1976, WebBD, Who 1974*
Price, Charles W 1857- *HisAmM XR*
Price, Don 1921-1974 *BioIn 9, BioIn 10*
Price, Eleanor *NF*
Price, Emerson d1977 *NF*
Price, Emmet Russel 1874- *WhJnl 1928*
Price, Mrs. Frances N *WhJnl 1928*
Price, Frank J 1860-1939 *AmAu&B, AmLY*
Price, G Jefferson, III *NF*
Price, Garrett 1896- *BioIn 8*
Price, George Ward 1886-1961 *BioIn 1, BioIn 4, BioIn 6*
Price, Granville 1906- *DrAS 74E, WhoAm 1974*
Price, James G *NF*
Price, Lucien 1883-1964 *AmAu&B, BioIn 3, BioIn 7*
Price, Marion Woodrow 1914- *WhoAm 1974*
Price, Max 1927- *WhoAm 1974*
Price, Raymond Kissam, Jr. 1930- *BioIn 8, OvPC, WhoAm 1974, WhoGov 1972, WhoS&SW 1973*
Price, Roger Taylor *WhoAm 1974*

Price, Samuel Norton 1896- *WhJnl 1928*
Price, Stanley 1931- *Au&Wr, ConAu 13R, WrDr 1976*
Price, Tom *NF*
Price, Vincent Barrett 1940- *ConAu 69*
Price, Warren Elbridge 1864- *HisAmM XR*
Price, Warwick James 1870-1934 *AmAu&B, AmLY, DcNAA, OhA&B, WhNAA*
Price, Wesley *HisAmM XR*
Price, Willard DeMille 1887- *AmAu&B, Au&Wr, AuBYP, ConAu 4R, IntWW 1976, WhNAA, WhoAm 1974, WrDr 1976*
Price, William *HisAmM XR*
Price, William Thompson 1846-1920 *AmAu, AmAu&B, DcNAA, WebBD*
Price, William W *AmJnl*
Price, Woodrow 1914- *WhoS&SW 1973*
Prickitt, Charles N 1898- *WhJnl 1928*
Prickitt, Helen C 1903- *WhJnl 1928*
Pride, Armistead Scott 1906- *DrAS 74E, WhoAm 1974*
Priest, J Percy 1900-1956 *CurBio XR, NatCAB 46*
Priestly, Lee 1904- *BioIn 8*
Prieth, Benedict *HisAmM XR*
Prill, Luis Merton 1882- *WhJnl 1928*
Prime, Edward Dorr Griffin 1814-1891 *Alli, Alli Sup, DcAmA, DcNAA, WebBD*
Prime, Samuel Irenaeus 1812-1885 *Alli, Alli Sup, AmAu&B, BbD, BiD&SB, CyAL 2, DcAmA, DcNAA, HisAmM XR, WebBD*
Prime, Thomas Norton 1906- *WhJnl 1928*
Prime, William Cowper 1825-1905 *Alli, Alli Sup, AmAu&B, BbD, BiD&SB, CyAL 2, DcAmA, DcAmB 15, DcNAA, HisAmM XR, NatCAB 13, WebBD*
Primm, Alexander Timon, III 1914- *WhoAm 1974, WhoF&I 1974, WhoWor 1974*
Primo, Albert T 1935- *ConAu 73*
Prina, L Edgar *NF*
Prina, Lee Lorick *NF*
Prince, Alan *NF*
Prince, Albert I 1893?-1956 *BioIn 4*
Prince, Lemuel B 1892-1961 *NatCAB 50*
Prince, Richard 1947- *NF*
Prince, Thomas 1721?-1748 *Alli, AmJnl, BioIn 5*
Princigalli, Ada 1931?- *BioIn 9*
Pringle, Henry Fowles 1897-1958 *AmAu&B, BioIn 4, BioIn 5, BioIn 6, HisAmM XR, OxAm, OxCan, REnAL, TwCA, TwCA Sup, WebBD*
Pringle, James Donald *NF*
Pringle, James Matthew Joseph 1919?-1970 *BioIn 5, BioIn 8*
Pringle, John Martin Douglas 1912- *Au&Wr, BioIn 10, ConAu 13R, IntWW 1976, Who 1974, WhoWor 1974, WrDr 1976*
Pringle, Laurence 1935- *BioIn 9, SmATA 4*
Pringle, Peter 1940- *ConAu 69*
Pringle, Thomas 1789-1834 *Alli, BrAu 19, CasWL, DcEnL, DcLEL, EvLB, NewC, OxEng, Pen Eng, WebBD, WebE&AL*
Prinkey, John *NF*
Prinkhall, Jim *InvJ, NewMr*
Prinsky, Bob *NF*
Printz, Peggy 1945- *ConAu 73*
Prioleau, John Randolph Hamilton 1882-1954 *BioIn 3*
Prior, Charles Henry 1900- *WhJnl 1928*
Prior, Melton *FamWC*
Priscilla, Louis 1906-1956 *BioIn 4*
Prisk, Charles H 1875-1940 *NatCAB 32, WhJnl 1928*
Prist, Frank d1944 *AmJnl*

Pritchard, Allen *NF*
Pritchard, John Wagner 1851-1924 *DcNAA, WhNAA*
Pritchett, Florence 1920-1965 *BioIn 1, BioIn 7*
Pritchett, Sir Victor Sawdon 1900- *Au&Wr, CasWL, ConAu 61, ConLC 5, ConNov 1972, ConNov 1976, DcLEL, EncWL, IntWW 1976, LongC, ModBL, ModBL Sup, NewC, OxEng, Pen Eng, RAdv 1, REn, TwCA Sup, TwCW, WebBD, Who 1974, WhoTwCL, WhoWor 1974, WrDr 1976*
Prittie, T Cornelius Farmer 1913- *ConAu 2R*
Pritzker, J N *OvPC*
Prizant, M *AmRP*
Probert, Lionel Charles 1883- *WhJnl 1928*
Probst, Leonard 1921- *ConAu 65*
Prochnau, William W 1937- *ConAu 33*
Procter, Harry *BioIn 1, BioIn 5*
Proctor, Albert Abram 1902- *WhJnl 1928*
Proctor, Harry George 1882-1946 *DcNAA*
Proctor, J Harris *HisAmM XR*
Proctor, John C *NF*
Proctor, John James 1833?-1909 *BbtC, DcNAA, OxCan*
Proctor, Priscilla 1945- *ConAu 65*
Proctor, Richard Anthony 1837-1888 *Alli, Alli Sup, BbD, BiD&SB, DcEnL, HisAmM XR, WebBD*
Proctor, William 1941- *ConAu 37*
Proctor, William, Jr. *HisAmM XR*
Proffitt, Nick *NF*
Prothero, Sir George Walter 1848-1922 *Alli Sup, NewC, TwCA, WebBD*
Prothero, Rowland Edmund 1852?-1937 *Alli Sup, NewC, TwCA, TwCA Sup, WebBD, WhoLA*
Proudfoot, Andrea 1866?-1949 *BioIn 2*
Proudfoot, Jim *NF*
Proudhon, Pierre Joseph 1809-1865 *AtlBL, BbD, BiD&SB, BioIn 1, BioIn 2, BioIn 4, BioIn 7, BioIn 8, CasWL, DcEuL, EuAu, OxFr, REn, WebBD*
Proujan, Carl 1929- *WhoAm 1974, WhoE 1974*
Prout, Father 1804-1866 *WebBD*
Prout, Father *see also* Mahony, Francis Sylvester
Prout, H E *HisAmM XR*
Prouvost, Jean 1885-1978 *BioIn 1, BioIn 3, BioIn 5, BioIn 8, ForP, IntWW 1976, WhoWor 1974*
Provencher, Joseph Alfred Norbert 1843-1887 *BioIn 4*
Provost, Wally 1922- *WhoAm 1974*
Pruette, Lorine Livingston 1896- *AmAu&B, WebBD*
Pruitt, Walter C 1886- *WhJnl 1928*
Pry, Polly *AmAu&B*
Pry, Polly *see also* Campbell, Leonel
Pryce-Jones, Alan Payan 1908- *AmAu&B, DcLEL, IntWW 1976, NewC, Who 1974, WhoAm 1974, WhoWor 1974*
Pryor, Hubert 1916- *WhoAm 1974, WhoF&I 1974*
Pryor, Roger Atkinson 1828-1919 *BiDSA, DcNAA, WebBD*
Przesmycki, Zenon 1861-1944 *CasWL, WebBD*
Pucci, Enrico 1879-1952 *BioIn 3*
Puckette, Charles McDonald 1887-1957 *BioIn 4*
Puddepha, Derek 1930- *ConAu 61*
Puenkoesti, Elisabeth De d1948 *BioIn 1*
Puffer, Charles C 1841-1915 *NatCAB 17*
Pugh, Edgar 1888- *WhJnl 1928*
Pugh, Edwin *HisAmM XR*
Pugh, Leonard E 1875-1931 *NatCAB 22,*

WhJnl 1928
Pugh, Thomas *RpN*
Pugner, Mark *NF*
Pujo, Maurice 1872?-1955 *BioIn 4, WebBD*
Pulaski, Jack *NF*
Pulay, George 1923- *ConAu 45*
Puleo, Vincent 1942- *NF*
Pulham, Charles d1887 *NF*
Pulitzer, Albert 1851-1909 *AmJnl*
Pulitzer, Herbert 1895-1957 *AmJnl, BioIn 4*
Pulitzer, Joseph 1847-1911 *AmAu&B, AmJnl,*
  BioIn 1, BioIn 2, BioIn 3, BioIn 3, BioIn 4,
  BioIn 5, BioIn 6, BioIn 7, BioIn 8, BioIn 9,
  BioIn 10, CasWL, DcAmB 15, DcLEL,
  EncAB, EvLB, FamWC, ForP,
  HisAmM XR, Lor&LP, OxAm, REn,
  REnAL, WebBD
Pulitzer, Joseph, II 1885-1955 *AmAu&B, AmJnl,*
  BioIn 3, BioIn 4, CurBio XR, WebBD
Pulitzer, Joseph, Jr. 1913- *CelR 1973,*
  IntWW 1976, InvJ, WhoAm 1974,
  WhoAmA 1973, WhoMW 1974,
  WhoWor 1974
Pulitzer, Michael Edgar 1930- *WhoAm 1974*
Pulitzer, Ralph 1879-1939 *AmAu&B, AmJnl,*
  BioIn 3, BioIn 4, BioIn 7, DcAmB S2,
  DcNAA, NatCAB 37, WebBD, WhNAA,
  WhJnl 1928
Pullan, Patricia *NF*
Pullen, Emma *NF*
Pullen, Weston Carpenter, Jr. 1916- *WhoAm 1974,*
  WhoE 1974
Pulliam, Eugene Collins 1889-1975 *AuNews 2,*
  BioIn 2, BioIn 7, BioIn 9, IndAu 1917,
  IntWW 1976, WhoAm 1974, WhJnl 1928,
  WhoMW 1974, WhoWest 1974,
  WhoWor 1974
Pulliam, Eugene Smith 1914- *WhoAm 1974*
Pulliam, Myrta 1947- *InvJ, NewMr*
Pullman, Marian M *HisAmM XR*
Pulsifer, Harold Trowbridge 1886-1948 *AmAu&B,*
  BioIn 1, BioIn 2, HisAmM XR,
  NatCAB 36, REnAL, WhNAA
Pun, Chiu-Yin *RpN*
Puner, Helen W 1915- *ConAu 7R*
Purcell, Carl 1902?-1964 *BioIn 7*
Purcell, Harold 1888?-1952 *BioIn 3, BioIn 3*
Purcell, John Wallace *AuBYP, BioIn 8*
Purcell, William 1830- *NatCAB 1*
Purdom, Charles Benjamin 1883-1965 *BioIn 2,*
  BioIn 7, ConAu P-1, LongC, WhoLA
Purdue, Marc *OvPC*
Purdy, Kenneth William 1913-1972 *Au&Wr,*
  BioIn 1, BioIn 2, BioIn 9, ConAu 37,
  HisAmM XR, NewYTBE 3, WhoAm 1974
Purington, Julia M *HisAmM XR*
Purkiser, Westlake Taylor 1910- *DrAS 74P,*
  WhoAm 1974
Purnell, Fillimore R 1868- *WhJnl 1928*
Purser, John R 1935- *WhoPubR 1972*
Puscas, George 1927- *WhoAm 1974*
Pusey, Elbert N 1876- *WhJnl 1928*
Pusey, Merlo John 1902- *AmAu&B,*
  AmM&W 73S, Au&Wr, BioIn 2, BioIn 3,
  BioIn 9, ConAu 11R, CurBio XR,
  DrAS 74H, OxAm, REnAL, TwCA Sup,
  WhoAm 1974, WhoE 1974, WhJnl 1928,
  WrDr 1976
Putman, John J *NF*
Putnam, Allen *HisAmM XR*
Putnam, Arthur James 1893?-1966 *BioIn 7*
Putnam, George *Alli, Alli Sup, HisAmM XR*
Putnam, George 1872-1961 *NF*
Putnam, George 1914?- *BioIn 4, BioIn 6,*

BioIn 8
Putnam, George Haven 1844-1930 *Alli Sup,*
  AmAu&B, BbD, BiD&SB, DcAmA,
  DcNAA, REnAL, WebBD, WhNAA
Putnam, George Israel 1860-1937 *AmAu&B,*
  DcAmA, DcNAA
Putnam, George Palmer 1814-1872 *Alli,*
  AmAu&B, BbD, BiD&SB, DcAmA,
  DcNAA, HisAmM XR, LiJA, REn,
  REnAL, WebBD
Putnam, George Palmer 1887-1950 *EvLB, WebBD*
Putnam, Harry C 1907- *WhJnl 1928*
Putnam, J Bishop 1848-1915 *HisAmM XR*
Putnam, John J 1903- *WhJnl 1928*
Putnam, Mary Lowell *HisAmM XR*
Putnam, Samuel 1892-1950 *AmAu&B, BioIn 1,*
  REnAL, TwCA Sup
Putnam, Sumner 1909?-1967 *BioIn 7*
Putney, Mabel F *WhJnl 1928*
Putrament, Jerzy 1910- *IntWW 1976*
Putzel, Michael 1942- *ConAu 73*
Puzo, Virginia *NF*
Pye, Mort 1918- *WhoAm 1974, WhoE 1974*
Pyke, Geoffrey Nathaniel 1893?-1948 *BioIn 1,*
  BioIn 5
Pyle, Dolores *NF*
Pyle, Ernest Taylor 1900-1945 *AmAu&B, AmJnl,*
  BioIn 1, BioIn 2, BioIn 3, BioIn 4, BioIn 5,
  BioIn 6, BioIn 7, BioIn 8, BioIn 9,
  DcAmB S3, DcNAA, IndAu 1917,
  TwCA Sup
Pyle, Ernest Taylor *see also* Pyle, Ernie
Pyle, Ernie 1900-1945 *AmAu&B, CurBio XR,*
  NatCAB 33, OxAm, REn, REnAL
Pyle, Ernie *see also* Pyle, Ernest Taylor
Pyle, Harold Gibson 1902- *WhoAm 1974,*
  WhoS&SW 1973
Pyle, Richard H *NF*
Pyles, Floyd W d1977 *NF*
Pyles, Joseph Gilpin *HisAmM XR*
Pyne, Joe 1925-1970 *NewYTBE 1*
Pyne, John *HisAmM XR*

Q

Q *see* Quiller-Couch, Sir Arthur Thomas
Qoboza, Percy P 1940?- *NF*
Quaal, Ward Louis 1919- *WhoAm 1974,*
　WhoF&I 1974, WhoMW 1974
Quackenbos, G P *HisAmM XR*
Quad, John K 1904- *WhJnl 1928*
Quad, M 1842-1924 *AmAu, AmAu&B, DcAmA,*
　DcNAA, HsB&A, OhA&B, REnAL,
　WebBD
Quad, M *see also* Lewis, Charles Bertrand
Qualey, Jacob S 1905?-1970 *BioIn 9, RpN*
Quarberg, Lincoln 1898- *WhJnl 1928*
Quarles, Benjamin 1904- *ConAu 1, DrAS 74H*
Quarles, Norma *NF*
Quart, Julie *NF*
Quartermain, Leslie Bowden 1896-1973 *BioIn 10*
Quarton, William Barlow 1903- *WhoAm 1974,*
　WhoF&I 1974
Queen, Alan *NF*
Queen, Bella *NF*
Queen, Frank *HisAmM XR*
Queen, Robert Isaac 1919- *IntMPA 1975, OvPC,*
　WhoCon 1973, WhoE 1974, WhoF&I 1974,
　WhoPubR 1972
Quellet, Jo *NF*
Quennell, Peter 1905- *IntWW 1976, Who 1974*
Quequelle, Frederick *HisAmM XR*
Quesada, Aurelio Miro *NF*
Quesenberry, Preston Banks 1934?-1964 *BioIn 7*
Quezada, Abel 1921- *BioIn 6, ConAu 5*
Quick, Arnold *BioIn 8*
Quick, Herbert 1861-1925 *AmAu&B, CnDAL,*
　ConAmL, DcBiA, HisAmM XR, OxAm,
　REnAL, TwCA, WebBD
Quickel, Stephen 1936- *ConAu 73*
Quidde, Ludwig 1858-1941 *CurBio XR, WebBD,*
　WhoLA
Quigg, Horace Dasher 1911- *AmAu&B, OvPC,*
　WhoAm 1974
Quigg, J Travis *HisAmM XR*
Quigg, Lemuel Ely 1863-1919 *DcAmB 15,*
　DcNAA
Quigg, Murray T 1891-1956 *NatCAB 43*
Quigg, Philip W 1920- *ConAu 11R*
Quigley, James *NF*
Quigley, John 1927- *Au&Wr, ConAu 19R,*
　WrDr 1976
Quigley, Martin Schofield 1917- *WhoAm 1974*
Quigley, Walter R 1896- *WhJnl 1928*
Quijano, Manuel DeJesus 1884-1950 *BioIn 1,*
　BioIn 2
Quillard, Pierre 1864-1912 *WebBD*
Quillen, Robert 1887-1948 *AmAu&B, REnAL,*
　WhNAA
Quiller-Couch, Sir Arthur Thomas 1863-1944 *BbD,*
　BiD&SB, CasWL, CurBio XR, DcBiA,

DcEnA, DcEnA Ap, DcLEL, EvLB,
　HisAmM XR, JBA 1934, LongC, ModBL,
　NewC, OxEng, Pen Eng, RAdv 1, REn,
　TwCA, TwCA Sup, TwCW, WebBD
Quimby, Harriet 1884-1912 *NF*
Quin, Dan *AmAu&B, CnDAL, DcAmA,*
　DcNAA, OhA&B, OxAm, REnAL
Quin, Dan *see also* Lewis, Alfred Henry
Quinby, D F *HisAmM XR*
Quinby, William Emory 1835-1908 *BioIn 1,*
　NatCAB 1
Quince, Peter 1774-1803 *Alli, AmAu, DcNAA,*
　OxAm
Quince, Peter *see also* Story, Isaac
Quincy, Edmund 1808-1877 *Alli, AmAu,*
　AmAu&B, BiD&SB, CnDAL, DcAmA,
　DcNAA, HisAmM XR, WebBD
Quiner, Edwin Bentlee 1816-1868 *BioIn 5,*
　DcNAA
Quinlan, Mary Kay *NF*
Quinlan, Sterling Carroll 1916- *ConAu 5,*
　WhoAm 1974, WhoMW 1974
Quinn, Charles *NF*
Quinn, Frank *HisAmM XR*
Quinn, J Alvan *NF*
Quinn, James Leland 1875-1960 *BioIn 5*
Quinn, Jane Bryant 1939- *WhoAmW 1974*
Quinn, John Collins 1925- *BioIn 10*
Quinn, Joseph Martin 1912-1979 *OvPC,*
　WhoWest 1974
Quinn, Ralph Hughes 1893- *WhJnl 1928*
Quinn, Sally 1941- *AuNews 2, ConAu 65,*
　WhoAm 1974
Quinn, Thomas C 1864- *HisAmM XR*
Quinn, W *NF*
Quint, Alonzo Hall 1828-1896 *Alli, Alli Sup,*
　CyAL 2, DcAmA, DcNAA, HisAmM XR
Quint, Bert 1930- *ConAu 69*
Quint, Wilder Dwight 1863-1936 *AmAu&B,*
　DcNAA
Quirk, James Robert 1884-1932 *HisAmM XR,*
　WhJnl 1928
Quirk, Leslie W 1882- *AmAu&B, CarSB,*
　WhNAA, WisWr
Quirk, William H *OvPC*
Quisenberry, Anderson Chenault 1850-1921
　AmAu&B, AmLY, DcNAA

R

Raab, Selwyn 1934- *BioIn 9, ConAu 73, InvJ, NewMr*
Raaz, Lois *WhJnl Sup*
Rabe, Wilmer Taylor 1921- *WhoMW 1974*
Rabel, Ed *NF*
Raben, Joseph 1924- *ConAu 69, DrAS 74E, WhoE 1974*
Rabi, Yitzhak *NF*
Rabinovich, Abraham 1933- *ConAu 61*
Rabinovich, Joseph *NF*
Rabinowitch, Eugene 1901-1973 *AmAu&B, AmM&W 73P, BioIn 6, ConAu 41, NewYTBE 4, WhoWorJ 1972*
Rabinowitz, Ezekiel 1892- *ConAu 25, WhoE 1974, WhoWorJ 1972*
Raboy, Mac 1914?-1967 *BioIn 8*
Rabwin, Marcella 1908- *NF*
Rachel, Elisa *HisAmM XR*
Rachlis, Eugene 1920- *ConAu 5R*
Rackowe, Alec 1897- *ConAu 25*
Racusin, Maurice Jay 1892-1962 *BioIn 6*
Radcliffe, Ann Ward 1764-1823 *BbD, BiD&SB, BrAu, BrAu 19, CasWL, CrtT 2, CyWA, DcBiA, DcEnA, DcEuL, DcLEL, EncMys, EvLB, MouLC 2, NewC, OxEng, Pen Eng, RAdv 1, REn, WebBD, WebE&AL*
Radcliffe, John Anderson 1881-1944 *BioIn 2, NatCAB 34*
Radcliffe, Redonia *NF*
Raddatz, Leslie *NF*
Radder, Norman John 1894- *WhJnl 1928*
Raddock, Charles 1916-1972 *BioIn 9, WhoWorJ 1972*
Radek, Karl Bernardovich 1885- *AmRP, WebBD*
Rademaekers, William *NF*
Raden, Don *NF*
Rader, Dotson 1942- *CelR 1973, ConAu 61*
Radin, Jacqueline 1939?-1973 *BioIn 10, NewYTBE 4*
Radl, Shirley Louise 1935- *ConAu 69*
Radloff, William Hamilton 1914- *WhoAm 1974*
Rado, Martha 1881- *WhJnl 1928*
Radulescu, Ioan Heliade 1802-1872 *WebBD*
Raduta, Henry *NF*
Rae, Arne Gundersen 1896?-1953 *BioIn 3*
Rae, Bruce 1892-1962 *BioIn 6, BioIn 7, NatCAB 47*
Rae, George Bronson *FamWC*
Rae, William Elder 1908- *WhoAm 1974*
Rae, William Fraser 1835- *Alli Sup, OxCan*
Raeke, Carolyn S *NF*
Raemaekers, Louis 1869-1956 *BioIn 4, HisAmM XR, WebBD*
Raff, Joseph A *OvPC*
Raffaelli, Jean *BioIn 7*
Rafferty, B V 1896- *WhJnl Sup*

Rafferty, Kathleen *OvPC*
Rafinesque, Constantine Smalz 1784?-1842 *Alli, AmAu&B, CyAL 1, DcAmA, DcNAA, HisAmM XR, OxAm, REnAL*
Rafshoon, Gerald *BioIn 10*
Ragan, David 1925- *ConAu 65*
Ragan, Samuel Talmadge 1915- *AmAu&B, ConAu 15R, WhoAm 1974, WhoWor 1974*
Ragghianti, Carlo Ludovico 1910- *IntWW 1976*
Ragland, Sam *HisAmM XR*
Ragner, Bernhard 1891?-1947 *BioIn 1*
Rago, Henry Anthony 1915-1969 *AmAu&B, ConAu 25, HisAmM XR, WorAu*
Ragon, Sylvia 1901- *WhJnl 1928*
Ragsdale, Silas Baggett 1896- *TexWr, WhJnl 1928, WhoS&SW 1973*
Ragsdale, Warner B 1898- *ConAu 73*
Ragsdale, Wilmott 1915- *DrAS 74E, OvPC*
Raguet, Condy 1784-1842 *Alli, DcAmA, DcNAA, HisAmM XR, WebBD*
Rahbek, Knud Lyne 1760-1830 *CasWL, WebBD*
Rahn, Pete *NF*
Rahv, Philip 1908-1973 *AmAu&B, AmRP, ConAu 45, ModAL, ModAL Sup, NewYTBE 4, NewYTBS 5, Pen Am, REnAL, TwCA Sup*
Rai, Raghu *NF*
Raidy, William Anthony 1923- *NF*
Raihall, Richard Lee 1936- *WhoAm 1974*
Raine, William MacLeod 1871-1954 *AmAu&B, AmLY, EvLB, REnAL, TwCA, TwCA Sup, WebBD, WhNAA*
Raines, Howell 1943- *ConAu 73*
Rainey, John M 1880?-1947 *BioIn 1*
Raju, Gopal *OvPC*
Rakoczi, Prince Ferenc *ForP*
Rakosi, Jeno 1842-1929 *WebBD*
Rakowski, Mieczyslaw Franciszek 1926- *IntWW 1976*
Rakstis, Ted J *NF*
Ralbovsky, Martin Paul 1942- *ConAu 49*
Ralph, Julian 1853-1903 *AmAu&B, AmJnl, BiD&SB, DcAmA, DcAmB 15, DcNAA, FamWC, HisAmM XR, NatCAB 1, OxCan, REnAL, WebBD*
Ralston, John Craig 1879?- *BioIn 1*
Rama, Carlos Manuel 1921- *IntWW 1976, WhoWor 1974*
Rama, Rao K 1896- *BioIn 7*
Ramage, Adam *AmJnl*
Ramage, Burr James 1858- *Alli Sup, BiDSA, HisAmM XR*
Rambo, Ralph 1895?- *BioIn 9*
Ramirez Y Ramirez, Enrique *ForP*
Ramm, Fredrik d1943 *CurBio XR*
Ramming, Heinrich *BioIn 2*

Ramos, Angel 1902?-1960 *BioIn 5*
Ramos-Shahani, Leticia V *BioIn 6*
Ramsay, Marion F *NF*
Ramsaye, Terry 1885-1954 *AmAu&B, BioIn 3, REnAL, WhNAA*
Ramsdell, Irving 1901?-1965 *BioIn 7*
Ramsden, T *HisAmM XR*
Ramsey, Glenn d1977 *NF*
Ramsey, Judith 1939- *NF*
Ramsey, Paul W 1905-1976 *ConAu 69, WhoGov 1972*
Ramsey, Roy S 1920?-1976 *ConAu 65*
Ramsey, Stewart *NF*
Ramsey, Ted L 1898- *WhJnl 1928*
Ranc, Arthur 1831-1908 *WebBD*
Ranck, Than Vanneman 1874-1947 *BioIn 1*
Rand, Abby *ForWC 1970*
Rand, Addison 1896- *AuBYP, BioIn 7*
Rand, Asa 1783-1871 *Alli, DcAmA, DcNAA, HisAmM XR*
Rand, Avery L 1851-1918 *NatCAB 39*
Rand, Ayn 1905- *AmAu&B, AmNov, CasWL, CelR 1973, ConAu 15, ConLC 3, ConNov 1972, ConNov 1976, ForWC 1970, OxAm, Pen Am, REn, REnAL, TwCA Sup, WebBD, WebE&AL, WhoAm 1974, WhoAmW 1974, WhoTwCL, WrDr 1976*
Rand, Christopher Temple Emmet 1912-1968 *AmAu&B, BioIn 8, RpN*
Rand, Clayton Thomas 1891-1971 *BioIn 9, ConAu 5R, ConAu 29*
Rand, Harry 1913- *OvPC, WhoPubR 1972*
Rand, John C 1842-1911 *NatCAB 28*
Rand, Lester *NF*
Randal, Jonathan C *NF*
Randal, Judith Ellen 1929- *WhoAm 1974, WhoAmW 1974*
Randall, Charles Edgar, Jr. 1897- *ConAu 41, WhNAA*
Randall, George Maxwell 1810-1873 *Alli, DcNAA, HisAmM XR*
Randall, J Parke 1927- *AmArch 1970*
Randall, James Ryder 1839-1908 *AmAu, AmAu&B, BiD&SB, BiDSA, BioIn 3, DcAmA, DcAmB 15, DcNAA, EvLB, OxAm, REn, REnAL, WebBD*
Randall, Michael Bennett 1919- *BioIn 7, IntWW 1976, Who 1974, WhoWor 1974*
Randall, Samuel 1778-1864 *AmAu&B, DcAmB 15*
Randall, Samuel Sidwell 1809-1881 *Alli, Alli Sup, DcAmA, DcNAA, HisAmM XR*
Randall, Theodore A *HisAmM XR*
Randall, Wayne L 1883?-1967 *BioIn 7*
Randall, Willard Sterne 1942- *ConAu 69*
Randall-Diehl, Anna *HisAmM XR*
Randau, Clem J 1895-1954 *BioIn 3*
Randerson, J Howard 1890- *WhJnl 1928*
Randles, Anthony Victor, Jr. 1942- *ConAu 65*
Randles, Slim 1942- *ConAu XR*
Randolph, A Philip 1889- *BlkC, CelR 1973, CurBio XR*
Randolph, Mrs. Frankie *NewMr*
Randolph, Innes 1837-1887 *BiDSA, BioIn 3*
Randolph, Jennings 1902- *CurBio XR, CngDr 1974, IntWW 1974, WhoAm 1974, WhoAmP 1973, WhoE 1974, WhoGov 1972, WhJnl 1928*
Randolph, John W 1903?-1961 *BioIn 5*
Randon, Don *NF*
Rands, How *NF*
Raney, Bates O 1899-1968 *BioIn 8, WhJnl 1928*
Raney, William 1916?-1964 *BioIn 7*
Rangan, Kasturi *NF*

Range, Peter Ross *OvPC*
Rangel, Carlos *ForP*
Rankin, James 1923- *WhoAm 1974, WhoS&SW 1973*
Rankin, Jeremiah Eames 1828-1904 *Alli, Alli Sup, AmAu, AmAu&B, BbD, BiD&SB, DcAmA, DcNAA, HisAmM XR, OhA&B, REnAL*
Rankin, John 1793-1886 *BiDSA, DcAmA, DcNAA, HisAmM XR, OhA&B, WhNAA*
Rankin, Louise 1897?-1951 *BioIn 2*
Rankin, Robert A 1949- *NF*
Rankin, Robert James 1896- *CanWW 1972*
Ransom, Beverly C *HisAmM XR*
Ransom, John Crowe 1888-1974 *AmAu&B, AmWr, CasWL, CelR 1973, CnDAL, CnE&AP, CnMWL, ConAmA, ConAu 5, ConAu 49, ConLC 2, ConLC 4, ConLC 5, ConP 1970, ConP 1975, CurBio XR, CyWA, DcLEL, EvLB, HisAmM XR, LongC, ModAL, ModAL Sup, NewYTBE 3, NewYTBS 5, OhA&B, OxAm, Pen Am, RAdv 1, REn, REnAL, SixAP, TwCA, TwCA Sup, TwCW, WebBD, WebE&AL, WhoAm 1974, WhoTwCL, WhoWor 1974*
Ransome, Arthur Michell 1884-1967 *Alli Sup, AuBYP, CarSB, CasWL, ConAu 73, DcLEL, EvLB, JBA 1934, JBA 1951, LongC, NewC, Pen Eng, REn, TwCA, TwCA Sup, WebBD, WhoChL, WhoLA*
Rao, R P 1924- *ConAu 13R*
Raper, Dewey D 1898?-1977 *NF*
Raper, James Arthur 1887-1948 *BioIn 2, NatCAB 36, WhJnl 1928*
Raper, John Wolfe 1870-1950 *BioIn 2, OhA&B*
Rapoport, Daniel 1933- *WhoAm 1974*
Rapoport, Roger 1946- *ConAu 33, InvJ*
Rapp, Joel *AuNews 1*
Rapp, Paul C *OvPC*
Rapp, Wilhelm 1828-1907 *BioIn 2, DcAmA, DcAmB 15, OhA&B*
Rapp, William Jourdan 1895-1942 *AmAu&B, CurBio XR, DcNAA*
Rappoport, Ken 1935- *ConAu 53*
Rardin, Claude S 1879- *WhJnl 1928*
Rardin, John B 1909- *WhJnl 1928*
Rasanen, George P *NF*
Rascoe, Burton 1892-1957 *AmAu&B, BioIn 1, BioIn 4, BioIn 9, HisAmM XR, OxAm, REnAL, TwCA, TwCA Sup, WebBD*
Rash, Bryson Brennan 1913- *BioIn 10, WhoAm 1974*
Rashke, Richard *InvJ*
Raskin, Abraham Henry 1911- *BioIn 4, WhoAm 1974*
Raskin, Barbara *NF*
Rasmussen, Geraldine *BioIn 5*
Rasmussen, Harry Elwood 1893-1968 *BioIn 10*
Rasmussen, Nils C *OvPC*
Rasmusson, Halvor 1900-1961 *BioIn 6*
Raspberry, William J 1935?- *BioIn 9, BlkC*
Raster, Hermann 1827-1891 *BioIn 1, BioIn 2*
Ratchford, B U *AmEA 1974, HisAmM XR*
Ratcliff, John Drury 1903- *AmAu&B, BioIn 5, NewYTBE 4, WhNAA, WhoAm 1974*
Ratcliffe, Samuel Kerkham 1868-1958 *BioIn 5*
Rathbone, Henry Bailey 1871-1945 *AmAu&B*
Rathbun, Stephen *NF*
Rather, Dan 1931- *AuNews 1, BioIn 10, BioNews 1974, ConAu 53, CurBio XR, InvJ, OvPC*
Rathom, John Revelstoke 1868-1923 *DcAmA, HisAmM XR, NatCAB 20*
Ratiani, Georgi M 1918?-1978 *NF*
Ratisbonne, Louis Fortune Gustave 1827-1900

OxFr, *WebBD*
Ratliff, Richard Charles 1922- *ConAu 65*
Ratner, Joe E *HisAmM XR*
Ratner, Rochelle 1948- *ConAu 33, DrAP 1975, WrDr 1976*
Ratner, Vic *NF*
Rattee, Stanley George 1893-1953 *BioIn 3*
Rattenbury, Arnold 1921- *ConAu 29*
Rattiner, Dan 1940?- *BioIn 10*
Rattray, Jeanette 1893?-1974 *BioIn 10*
Rattray, William Jordan 1835-1883 *Alli Sup, DcNAA, OxCan*
Rau, Chalapathi M *IntWW 1976*
Rau, Herb *NF*
Rauch, Hans Georg 1939- *BioIn 8*
Rauch, Rudolph S *NF*
Raum, Thomas *NF*
Raumer, Karl Von *HisAmM XR*
Ravage, John M *NF*
Rave, Herman Charles Frederick 1849?-1929 *BioIn 2, IndAu 1816*
Ravegnani, Giuseppe 1895- *IntWW 1976*
Raven, Anton A *HisAmM XR*
Raven-Hill, Leonard 1867-1942 *BioIn 5, WebBD*
Ravis, Howard S *NF*
Rawitch, Robert *InvJ*
Rawles, Wallace X 1900- *WhJnl 1928*
Rawling, Charles A *HisAmM XR*
Rawling, Sylvester J C *NF*
Rawlings, Augustus *HisAmM XR*
Rawls, Wendell L, Jr. 1941- *ConAu 73*
Rawson, Eleanor Stierhem *BioIn 8, ForWC 1970, OvPC, WhoAmW 1974*
Rawson, Kenneth L *BioIn 8, OvPC*
Ray, Al *NF*
Ray, Charles Bennett 1807-1886 *DcAmB 15*
Ray, Charles Henry 1821-1870 *AmJnl, BioIn 4, BioIn 10, NatCAB 29*
Ray, Cyril 1908- *Au&Wr, ConAu 7R, Who 1974, WrDr 1976*
Ray, E Lansing 1884-1955 *BioIn 1, BioIn 4, WhJnl 1928*
Ray, Edgar Wayne 1911- *WhoAm 1974, WhoS&SW 1973*
Ray, Grace Ernestine *WhJnl 1928*
Ray, Jacques Jean d1976 *NF*
Ray, Marie Beynon 1890?-1969 *BioIn 8*
Ray, Michele 1938?- *BioIn 7, BioIn 8*
Ray, William Isaac, Jr. 1914- *WhoAm 1974, WhoS&SW 1973*
Raymond, Alexander Gillespie 1909-1956 *BioIn 1, BioIn 2, BioIn 4*
Raymond, Allen 1892-1957 *BioIn 4*
Raymond, Arthur *BioIn 9, WhoAmP 1973*
Raymond, Henry Jarvis 1820-1869 *Alli, AmAu, AmAu&B, AmJnl, BbD, BiD&SB, BioIn 2, BioIn 9, BioIn 10, CyAL 2, DcAmA, DcNAA, ForP, HisAmM XR, OxAm, REnAL, WebBD*
Raymond, Henry Warren 1847-1925 *AmLY, DcNAA*
Raymond, Jack 1918- *OvPC, WhoAm 1974*
Raymond, James H *HisAmM XR*
Raymond, Jim *NF*
Raymond, John *NF*
Raymond, John Francis 1925- *AuBYP, BioIn 8, WhoS&SW 1973*
Raymond, Robert L *HisAmM XR*
Raymond, Rossiter Worthington 1840-1918 *Alli, Alli Sup, AmAu&B, CarSB, DcAmA, DcNAA, HisAmM XR, OhA&B, WebBD*
Raymond, Steve 1940- *ConAu 49*
Raymont, Henry 1926?- *BioIn 5, RpN*
Rayne, Alan *see* Tobin, James Edward

Rayne, Martha *HisAmM XR*
Rayner, Emma d1926 *AmAu&B, DcAmA, DcNAA*
Raynolds, W W *NF*
Rea, Gardner 1892-1966 *AmAu&B, BioIn 1, BioIn 7, BioIn 8, CurBio XR*
Rea, John J *NF*
Rea, Richard A 1880- *WhJnl 1928*
Rea, Wayne 1883- *WhJnl 1928*
Read, Alexander Louis 1914- *WhoAm 1974*
Read, Ben H 1888- *WhJnl 1928*
Read, E C K *OvPC*
Read, Glory 1927- *ForWC 1970, WhoCon 1973, WhoPubR 1972*
Read, Harry Cyril 1892- *WhJnl 1928*
Read, Helen Appleton 1887-1974 *ConAu 53, WhoAm 1974, WhoAmA 1973*
Read, Lessie S 1891- *WhJnl 1928*
Read, Lizzie Bunnell 1834-1909 *BioIn 8*
Read, M C *HisAmM XR*
Read, Opie Pope 1852-1939 *Alli Sup, AmAu&B, AmJnl, BbD, BiD&SB, BioIn 4, BioIn 7, CnDAL, DcAmA, DcAmB S2, DcLEL, DcNAA, EvLB, HisAmM XR, LiJA, OhA&B, OxAm, REn, REnAL, TwCA, WebBD*
Read, Peggy *NF*
Reade, Frank *HisAmM XR*
Reade, John 1837-1919 *Alli Sup, BbtC, BiD&SB, DcNAA, OxCan, PoIre*
Reade, William A *AmJnl*
Readel, John D *HisAmM XR*
Reader, Francis Smith 1842-1928 *DcNAA*
Reading, Paul *NF*
Reagan, Cindy *OvPC*
Reagan, Ronald 1911- *BioNews 1974, CelR 1973, CurBio XR, IntMPA 1975, IntWW 1974, NewYTBE 1, NewYTBS 5, WhoAm 1974, WhoGov 1972, WhoWest 1974, WhoWor 1974*
Reakes, George Leonard 1889- *BioIn 4*
Realf, Richard 1834-1878 *Alli, AmAu, AmAu&B, BbD, BiD&SB, CnDAL, DcAmA, DcNAA, HisAmM XR, OxAm, REnAL*
Ream, Laura 1828-1913 *BioIn 2, IndAu 1816, OhA&B*
Reamer, Lawrence *NF*
Rearden, Jim 1925- *ConAu 65*
Reardon, Maureen *NF*
Reasoner, Harry 1923- *AmAu&B, AuNews 1, BioIn 7, BioIn 8, BioNews 1975, CelR 1973, CurBio XR, ForP, IntMPA 1975, WhoAm 1974, WhoE 1974*
Reasons, George *InvJ*
Reavis, Ed *NF*
Reavis, Holland S *HisAmM XR*
Reavis, Logan Uriah 1831-1889 *Alli, Alli Sup, BiDSA, DcAmA, DcNAA, HisAmM XR*
Reavis, Smith Freeman 1893-1940 *CurBio XR*
Rebatet, Lucien 1903-1972 *ConAu 37*
Reber, Ben J 1900- *WhJnl 1928*
Reber, Norman Franklin 1909- *WhoAm 1974*
Rechnitzer, Ferdinand Edsted 1894- *AuBYP, BioIn 7*
Reck, W Emerson 1903- *ConAu 61, WhoMW 1974, WhoPubR 1972*
Record, James Robert 1885-1973 *BioIn 2*
Record, Phil 1929- *NF*
Recouly, Raymond 1876-1950 *BioIn 2, HisAmM XR, WebBD*
Reddell, William Jennings 1915- *WhoAm 1974, WhoS&SW 1973*
Redden, Laura Catherine 1840-1923 *Alli, DcEnL*

Redden, Laura Catherine *see also* Searing, Laura
   Catherine
Reddick, DeWitt Carter 1904- *ConAu 7R,*
   DrAS 74E, WhoAm 1974
Reddin, Thomas J 1916?- *BioIn 8, BioIn 9*
Redding, Cyrus 1785-1870 *Alli, BiDLA, DcEnL*
Redding, Josephine *HisAmM XR*
Reddy, G K *RpN*
Reddy, John F X 1912?-1975 *ConAu 53*
Redeker, Bill *NF*
Redfern, Caleb H *NF*
Redfield, Charles M *WhJnl 1928*
Redfield, Justus Starr 1810-1888 *AmAu&B*
Redfield, W D *HisAmM XR*
Redman, Ben Ray 1896-1961 *AmAu&B,*
   AnMV 1926, Au&Wr, REnAL, WebBD
Redman, Peggy Dowat *HisAmM XR*
Redmond, Daniel George 1896-1955 *BioIn 3,*
   HisAmM XR
Redmond, Daniel George, Jr. *HisAmM XR*
Redmont, Bernard Sidney 1918- *ConAu 73,*
   OvPC, WhoAm 1974, WhoWor 1974
Redmont, Dennis F 1942- *OvPC*
Redpath, James 1833-1891 *Alli, Alli Sup, AmAu,*
   AmAu&B, BbD, BiD&SB, BioIn 3, BioIn 4,
   DcAmA, DcAmB 15, DcNAA,
   HisAmM XR, OxAm, REnAL, WebBD
Redwood, Hugh 1883- *BioIn 1, BioIn 4, BioIn 7*
Reed, Alma M d1966 *BioIn 7*
Reed, C McF *HisAmM XR*
Reed, Caleb 1797-1854 *Alli, DcNAA*
Reed, Clyde Martin 1871-1949 *WhJnl 1928*
Reed, David 1790-1870 *BioIn 3*
Reed, Dean *NF*
Reed, Douglas 1895-1976 *Au&Wr, BioIn 3,*
   BioIn 4, CathA 1952, NewC, TwCA,
   TwCA Sup, WebBD, Who 1974
Reed, Ed 1907- *WhoAm 1974*
Reed, Edward Bliss 1872-1940 *AmAu&B,*
   CurBio XR, DcNAA, HisAmM XR
Reed, Edward Tennyson 1860-1933 *BioIn 2,*
   BioIn 4
Reed, Gideon F T *HisAmM XR*
Reed, H V *HisAmM XR*
Reed, Harrison 1813-1899 *BioIn 5, BioIn 8*
Reed, Henry Carlyle 1915- *WhoAm 1974*
Reed, Isaac 1742-1807 *Alli, BioIn 1, CasWL,*
   DcEnL, WebBD
Reed, Isaac George, Jr. 1836-1903 *Alli, Alli Sup,*
   DcNAA, HisAmM XR
Reed, Jim 1915- *WhoAm 1974, WhoPubR 1972*
Reed, John 1757-1845 *DcAmB 15*
Reed, John 1887-1920 *AmAu&B, AmLY,*
   AmRP, BioIn 1, BioIn 3, BioIn 4, BioIn 5,
   BioIn 6, BioIn 7, BioIn 8, DcNAA, LongC,
   ModAL, OxAm, Pen Am, REn, REnAL,
   TwCA, TwCA Sup, WebBD
Reed, Jon Michael 1946- *NF*
Reed, Joseph P *HisAmM XR*
Reed, Larry *NF*
Reed, Martha Hemphill *NF*
Reed, Mortimer P 1872- *WhJnl 1928*
Reed, Myra G *HisAmM XR*
Reed, Perley Isaac 1887- *WhJnl 1928*
Reed, Rex 1938?- *AuNews 1, BioIn 8, BioIn 9,*
   CelR 1973, ConAu 53, CurBio XR,
   NewYTBE 3, WhoE 1974, WrDr 1976
Reed, Richard Everett 1931- *WhoAm 1974*
Reed, Robert Willard 1891?-1949 *BioIn 2*
Reed, Roy E *RpN*
Reed, Russ 1923?- *BioIn 9*
Reed, Sue *NF*
Reed, T Murray *BioIn 2*
Reed, T Smith *HisAmM XR*

Reed, Travis Dean 1930- *WhoAm 1974,*
   WhoS&SW 1973
Reed, Wallace Putnam 1849-1903 *BiDSA,*
   DcNAA
Reed, William A 1870- *WhJnl 1928*
Reed, William Hale 1874-1950 *BioIn 4,*
   NatCAB 40, WhJnl 1928
Reeder, Pearl Ann 1900- *WhoAm 1974,*
   WhoAmW 1974
Reedy, George Edward, Jr. 1917- *BioIn 5,*
   BioIn 6, BioIn 7, BioIn 8, ConAu 29,
   IntWW 1974, WhoAm 1974
Reedy, Jerry 1937- *NF*
Reedy, William B *HisAmM XR*
Reedy, William Marion 1862-1920 *AmAu&B,*
   BioIn 5, BioIn 6, DcAmB 15, DcNAA,
   HisAmM XR, LiJA, OxAm, REnAL,
   TwCA, WebBD
Reedy, William Thomas 1896- *WhJnl 1928*
Reef, Arthur 1917- *OvPC, WhoF&I 1974,*
   WhoPubR 1972
Reef, Betty *OvPC*
Rees, Albert 1921- *AmM&W 73S, ConAu 29,*
   HisAmM XR
Rees, David 1928- *Au&Wr, ConAu 11R*
Rees, Edwin Henry 1922-1974 *WhoWest 1974*
Rees, James 1802-1885 *Alli, Alli Sup, DcAmA,*
   DcNAA
Rees-Mogg, William 1928- *Au&Wr, BioIn 8,*
   BioIn 9, IntWW 1976, Lor&LP, Who 1974,
   WhoWor 1974
Reese, Benjamin Harrison 1888-1974 *BioIn 2,*
   BioIn 10, InvJ, WhoAm 1974, WhJnl 1928
Reese, Cara *NF*
Reese, Charles Lee, Jr. 1903- *BioIn 9,*
   WhoAm 1974, WhoE 1974
Reese, David J 1871- *WhJnl 1928*
Reese, Heloise 1919-1977 *ConAu 11R, ConAu 73*
Reese, Heloise *see also* Bowles, Heloise
Reese, Heloise *see also* Cruse, Heloise Bowles
Reese, Samuel *BioIn 6*
Reeve, Arthur Benjamin 1880-1936 *AmAu&B,*
   AmLY, CathA 1930, DcNAA, EncMys,
   HisAmM XR, REnAL, TwCA, TwCA Sup,
   WhNAA
Reeve, Henry 1813-1895 *Alli, Alli Sup, BioIn 1,*
   BrAu 19, CasWL, DcEnL, DcEuL, EvLB,
   NewC, WebBD
Reeve, James Knapp 1856-1933 *DcAmA, DcNAA,*
   HisAmM XR, OhA&B
Reeves, D LeRoy 1872?-1949 *BioIn 2*
Reeves, E C *WhJnl 1928*
Reeves, Earl C 1889?-1962 *BioIn 6, IndAu 1917*
Reeves, Lee 1921?-1973 *BioIn 9*
Reeves, Richard 1936- *NF*
Reeves, Robert R 1901?-1950 *BioIn 2*
Reeves, William Pember 1857-1932 *CasWL,*
   DcLEL, TwCW, WebBD, WebE&AL
Reeves, William Peters 1865-1945 *IndAu 1917*
Regan, Dick *NF*
Regan, John *NF*
Reger, Erik 1893-1954 *BioIn 1, BioIn 3, OxGer*
Rehak, Peter 1936- *OvPC*
Rehberg, Chuck *NF*
Rehns, Charles *NF*
Reibetantz, Carl Julius 1827-1894 *BioIn 2*
Reibsamen, Gary G *OvPC*
Reice, Sylvie Schuman *AmAu&B, ForWC 1970,*
   WhoAm 1974, WhoAmW 1974
Reich, Kenneth 1938- *ConAu 69*
Reichart, Ronald J 1935- *NF*
Reichler, Oxie 1898- *BioIn 4*
Reichley, Anthony James 1929- *BioIn 4*
Reick, William Charles 1864-1924 *DcAmB 15*

Reid, Ace *BioNews 1974*
Reid, Alastair 1926- *AuBYP, ConAu 7R, ConP 1970, ConP 1975, WorAu, WrDr 1976*
Reid, Albert Turner 1873-1955 *BioIn 4*
Reid, Alexander James 1846-1910 *BioIn 5*
Reid, Clementine *NF*
Reid, Ed *InvJ*
Reid, Edge Robeson 1904- *WhoAm 1974*
Reid, Helen Rogers 1882-1970 *AmJnl, BioIn 1, BioIn 2, BioIn 3, BioIn 7, BioIn 9, CurBio XR, ForWC 1970, NewYTBE 1*
Reid, Hiram Alvin 1834-1906 *DcNAA, OhA&B*
Reid, John C *NF*
Reid, John Morrison 1820-1896 *Alli Sup, DcAmA, DcNAA, HisAmM XR*
Reid, Kenneth 1893-1960 *NatCAB 50*
Reid, Louis Raymond 1889?-1965 *BioIn 7*
Reid, Malcolm 1941- *ConAu 53, OxCan Sup*
Reid, Ogden Mills 1882-1947 *AmAu&B, AmJnl, BioIn 1, DcAmB S4, NatCAB 33, WebBD, WhJnl 1928*
Reid, Ogden Rogers 1925- *BioIn 4, BioIn 5, CngDr 1974, CurBio XR, IntWW 1976, WhoAm 1974, WhoAmP 1973, WhoE 1974, WhoGov 1972*
Reid, Ormond Roy *WhJnl 1928*
Reid, Philip Joseph 1865- *WhJnl 1928*
Reid, Richard 1896-1961 *BioIn 5*
Reid, Richard C 1930- *NF*
Reid, Sydney Robert Charles Forneri 1857-1936 *DcAmA, DcNAA*
Reid, Thomas Boyd 1843-1925 *BioIn 5*
Reid, Thomas R, III *NF*
Reid, Sir Thomas Wemyss 1842-1905 *Alli Sup, BbD, BiD&SB, BrAu 19, CasWL, DcLEL, EvLB, WebBD*
Reid, Victor Stafford 1913- *BioIn 9, ConAu 65, ConNov 1972, ConNov 1976, LongC, Pen Eng, WebE&AL, WhoWor 1974, WrDr 1976*
Reid, Whitelaw 1837-1912 *Alli, AmAu, AmAu&B, AmJnl, BbD, BiD&SB, BioIn 1, BioIn 2, BioIn 3, BioIn 5, CyAL 2, DcAmA, DcAmB 15, DcNAA, EncAB, FamWC, HisAmM XR, OhA&B, OxAm, REnAL, WebBD*
Reid, Whitelaw 1913- *CurBio XR, OvPC, Who 1974, WhoAm 1974, WhoF&I 1974, WhoWor 1974*
Reiersen, Johann Reinert 1810-1864 *BioIn 6*
Reif, Rita 1929- *ConAu 41*
Reifenberg, Jan *NF*
Reifsnider, Mrs. Calvin Kryder *HisAmM XR*
Reifsnider, Donna *NF*
Reil, Frank T 1908?-1951 *BioIn 2*
Reiley, Henry Baker 1875-1962 *BioIn 7, NatCAB 48, WhJnl 1928*
Reiley, Henry Baker, Jr. 1908- *WhoF&I 1974*
Reiley, Kenneth C *NF*
Reilly, Charles A 1887- *WhJnl 1928*
Reilly, Charles Francis, Jr. 1910- *WhoAm 1974, WhoF&I 1974, WhoS&SW 1973*
Reilly, Charles Phillips *NF*
Reilly, Donald *NF*
Reilly, Henry Joseph 1881-1963 *HisAmM XR*
Reilly, Louis W 1853- *HisAmM XR, PoIre*
Reilly, Maurice T 1900-1962 *NatCAB 47*
Reilly, Trish *NF*
Reilly, Walter Benedict 1888-1961 *BioIn 7, NatCAB 49*
Reiman, F Albert 1901- *WhJnl 1928*
Reimann, Guenter 1904- *AmEA 1974, AmM&W 73S, OvPC, WhoF&I 1974*
Reimann, Hans 1889- *BioIn 3*

Reimert, William Daniel 1902-1969 *BioIn 10*
Reinach, Joseph 1856-1921 *BioIn 8, OxFr, WebBD*
Reincke, Helmut *NF*
Reinecke, William O 1886- *WhJnl 1928*
Reingold, Edwin M *NF*
Reinhardt, Ad 1913-1967 *DcCAA*
Reinhart, Edgar 1883?-1954 *BioIn 3*
Reinhart, Robert *OvPC*
Reinhold, Frieder *NF*
Reinhold, Robert *NF*
Reiniger, Scott Hale *OvPC*
Reinitz, Bertram 1897- *WhJnl 1928*
Reinsch, James Leonard 1908- *WhoAm 1974, WhoF&I 1974, WhoS&SW 1973*
Reinsch, Paul Samuel 1869-1923 *AmAu&B, AmLY, DcAmA, DcNAA, HisAmM XR, WebBD, WisWr*
Reisler, Susan *NF*
Reisz, David *AmRP*
Reiter, J Clarence 1893- *WhJnl 1928*
Relf, Samuel 1776-1823 *Alli, BiDSA, DcNAA*
Rembao, Alberto 1895?-1962 *BioIn 6*
Rembold, Chris H *WhJnl 1928*
Remington, A G *HisAmM XR*
Remington, Dale *NF*
Remington, Frederic 1861-1909 *AmAu, AmAu&B, AtlBL, CnDAL, DcAmA, DcLEL, DcNAA, HisAmM XR, OxAm, REn, REnAL, WebBD*
Remington, George David 1925- *WhoAm 1974*
Remington, Harold George 1881?-1946 *BioIn 1*
Remington, Joseph D *OvPC*
Remmel, Arthur K 1886-1941 *NatCAB 32, WhJnl 1928*
Remsberg, Bonnie Kohn 1937- *ConAu 69, Who Am 1974, WhoAmW 1974*
Remsberg, Charles Andruss 1936- *ConAu 57, WhoAm 1974*
Remsen, Ira 1846-1927 *Alli Sup, AmAu&B, BiDSA, DcAmA, DcNAA, HisAmM XR, WebBD, WhNAA*
Remy, Henri 1811?-1867 *BiDSA, DcNAA*
Renard, Jacques C *NF*
Renard, Jules 1864-1910 *CasWL, ClDMEL, CnMD, EncWL, EuAu, EvEuW, McGWD, ModWD, OxFr, Pen Eur, WebBD*
Renaud, Ralph Edward 1881-1948 *BioIn 1*
Renaudot, Theophraste 1586-1653 *OxFr, WebBD*
Renberg, Werner *AmEA 1974, OvPC*
Rendel, John 1905-1978 *NF*
Renegar, Horace Calvin 1901?- *WhoAm 1974, WhJnl Sup, WhoS&SW 1973*
Renfrew, Glen M *OvPC*
Renfrow, Perry Wade *WhJnl 1928*
Renier, Leon 1857?-1950 *BioIn 2*
Renner, Thomas C 1928- *ConAu 73, InvJ*
Rennert, Leo *NF*
Rennie, Rutherford 1897?-1956 *BioIn 4*
Reno, June Mellies *OvPC*
Renold, Evelyn *NF*
Rensberger, Boyce *NF*
Rense, Paige *NF*
Renshaw, Anderson N 1891- *WhJnl 1928*
Renshaw, Charles Clark, Jr. 1920- *WhoAm 1974*
Rentz, J Fred 1924- *WhoAm 1974*
Renwick, George *NF*
Repington, Charles A'Court 1858-1925 *LongC, REn, WebBD*
Repp, William 1936- *NF*
Reppert, Barton C *NF*
Rerick, John H 1830- *BioIn 2, IndAu 1816*
Resch, F A *NF*

Resnick, David *OvPC*
Resnick, Louis 1891-1941 *CurBio XR,*
  WhJnl 1928
Resnickoff, Philomeme *NF*
Ress, Paul *NF*
Ressner, Phil *BioIn 8*
Reston, James B, Jr. 1941- *ConAu 37*
Reston, James Barrett 1909- *AmAu&B, AmJnl,*
  AuNews 1, AuNews 2, BioIn 1, BioIn 2,
  BioIn 3, BioIn 4, BioIn 5, BioIn 6, BioIn 7,
  BioIn 8, BioIn 9, BioIn 10, CelR 1973,
  ConAu 65, CurBio XR, ForP, IntWW 1976,
  InvJ, NewMr, OhA&B, REnAL, WebBD,
  WhoAm 1974, WhoS&SW 1973,
  WhoWor 1974, WrDr 1976
Reston, Scotty *see* Reston, James Barrett
Restrepo, Fabio 1887?-1949 *BioIn 2*
Reswick, William 1889?-1954 *BioIn 3*
Retlaw, S P 1878- *WhNAA*
Retlaw, S P *see also* Steinhaeuser, Walter Philip
Reuter, Madalynne *NF*
Reuter, Baron Paul Julius Von 1816-1899 *ForP,*
  REn, WebBD
Reuterdahl, Henry 1871-1925 *HisAmM XR,*
  WebBD
Reutlinger, Harry Frank 1896?-1962 *BioIn 1,*
  BioIn 5, BioIn 6
Reutzel, Emil William, Jr. 1923- *WhoAm 1974*
Revel, Jean-Francois 1924- *CurBio XR,*
  IntWW 1974, NewYTBE 2, WhoWor 1974
Revell, Aldric R *RpN*
Revell, Nellie 1872?-1958 *BioIn 3, BioIn 5*
Reventlow, Count Ernst Zu 1869-1943 *CurBio XR,*
  WebBD
Revere, Richard Halworth 1915- *NF*
Reves, Emery 1904- *BioIn 1, CurBio XR*
Revusky, Abraham 1889-1946 *DcNAA*
Rewey, E M *NF*
Rexdale, Robert 1859-1929 *Alli Sup, DcAmA,*
  DcNAA
Rexroth, Kenneth 1905- *AmAu&B, CelR 1973,*
  CnE&AP, ConAu 5, ConDr, ConLC 1,
  ConLC 2, ConLC 6, ConP 1970,
  ConP 1975, DrAP 1975, EncWL,
  IndAu 1917, IntWW 1976, ModAL,
  ModAL Sup, OxAm, Pen Am, RAdv 1,
  REn, REnAL, TwCA Sup, WebE&AL,
  WhoAm 1974, WhoTwCL, WhoWest 1974,
  WhoWor 1974, WrDr 1976
Rey, Larry *NF*
Reybaud, Louis 1799-1879 *WebBD*
Reyburn, Wallace 1913- *ConAu 49*
Reyes, Narciso G 1914- *IntWW 1976,*
  Who 1974, WhoAm 1974, WhoGov 1972,
  WhoWor 1974
Reyes Mozo, Alberto *ForP*
Reymert, James DeNoon 1821-1896 *BioIn 5*
Reynolds, Ann *NF*
Reynolds, Barbara 1942- *ConAu 73*
Reynolds, Donald Worthington 1906- *BioIn 1,*
  OvPC, WhoAm 1974, WhoS&SW 1973,
  WhoWest 1974
Reynolds, Frank 1923- *BioIn 8, WhoAm 1974,*
  WhoWor 1974
Reynolds, George William MacArthur 1814-1879
  Alli, BioIn 2, BrAu 19, DcLEL
Reynolds, Gilbert Elmer 1884- *WhJnl 1928*
Reynolds, J D 1907?-1968 *BioIn 8*
Reynolds, J Lacey *NF*
Reynolds, Jack *NF*
Reynolds, John *HisAmM XR*
Reynolds, John Parker 1820-1912 *HisAmM XR*
Reynolds, Quentin James 1902-1965 *AmAu&B,*
  AmJnl, AuBYP, BioIn 2, BioIn 4, BioIn 6,

  BioIn 7, BioIn 8, ConAu 73, CurBio XR,
  HisAmM XR, LiJA, LongC, REnAL,
  TwCA Sup
Reynolds, Ruth 1904?-1971 *BioIn 9, NewYTBE 2*
Reynolds, Stanley M 1885- *WhJnl 1928*
Reynolds, Thomas C *HisAmM XR*
Reynolds, Thomas F *NF*
Reynolds, Wendell Sanford 1898- *WhJnl 1928*
Reynolds, William Kilby 1848-1902 *DcNAA*
Reynolds, William Morton 1812-1876 *Alli,*
  Alli Sup, DcAmA, DcNAA, HisAmM XR
Rhawn, Heister Gule 1892- *WhoAm 1974,*
  WhJnl 1928
Rhett, Robert Barnwell, Jr. 1800-1876 *AmJnl,*
  BiDSA
Rhetts, JoAnn *NF*
Rhinewine, Abraham 1887-1932 *DcNAA,*
  WhNAA
Rhoades, Judith G *NF*
Rhoads, Geraldine Emeline 1914- *ForWC 1970,*
  WhoAm 1974, WhoAmW 1974
Rhoads, H G 1894- *WhJnl 1928*
Rhoads, James E 1828-1895 *HisAmM XR*
Rhoads, Margaret W *HisAmM XR*
Rhoads, Samuel 1862- *HisAmM XR*
Rhode, Eric 1934- *ConAu 21R*
Rhode, Robert Bartlett 1916- *ConAu 19R,*
  DrAS 74E
Rhodes, Anne *HisAmM XR*
Rhodes, Bradford 1845-1924 *HisAmM XR*
Rhodes, Clifford Oswald 1911- *Au&Wr,*
  ConAu 65, Who 1974, WrDr 1976
Rhodes, Frank *FamWC*
Rhodes, Harrison Garfield 1871-1929 *AmAu&B,*
  DcNAA, HisAmM XR, OhA&B, WebBD
Rhodes, James Rutherford 1882- *WhJnl 1928*
Rhodes, Kent *NF*
Rhodes, Lynwood Mark 1931- *NF*
Rhodes, Richard 1937- *ConAu 45*
Rhodes, Rufus W *NF*
Rhodes, William *NF*
Rhodin, Eric Nolan 1916- *ConAu 3R*
Rhondda, Margaret Haig, Viscountess 1883-1958
  BioIn 1, BioIn 5
Rhone, Kenneth Dean 1907- *WhoAm 1974,*
  WhoE 1974
Rhude, Forbes *NF*
Rhydwen, David 1918- *BiDrLUS*
Rhys, Dynevor *HisAmM XR*
Ribalow, Harold U 1919- *ConAu 5R,*
  WhoWorJ 1972, WrDr 1976
Ribbens, Dennis *NF*
Riblet, Carl, Jr. *NF*
Riboud, Marc *BioIn 9*
Ricalton, James *FamWC*
Ricci, Rolandi *HisAmM XR*
Rice, Albert 1907-1976 *ConAu XR*
Rice, Albert *see also* Leventhal, Albert Rice
Rice, Allen Thorndike 1851-1889 *Alli Sup, AmJnl,*
  DcNAA, HisAmM XR, LiJA, NatCAB 3
Rice, Allen Thorndike *see also* Rice, Charles Allen
  Thorndike
Rice, Arthur L 1870-1946 *HisAmM XR*
Rice, Charles Allen Thorndike 1851-1889
  AmAu&B, BioIn 2, BioIn 3, DcAmB 15,
  DcNAA
Rice, Charles Allen Thorndike *see also* Rice, Allen
  Thorndike
Rice, Charles Duane 1910-1971 *AuBYP, BioIn 7,*
  BioIn 9, NewYTBE 2
Rice, Cy 1905-1971 *ConAu 33, ConAu P-1*
Rice, Edwin Wilbur, Sr. 1831-1929 *Alli Sup,*
  AmAu&B, AmLY, DcAmA, DcNAA,
  NatCAB 3, WhNAA

Rice, George *HisAmM XR*
Rice, Grantland 1880-1954 *AmAu&B, AmJnl,*
  BioIn 1, BioIn 3, BioIn 4, BioIn 7,
  CurBio XR, HisAmM XR, REnAL,
  WhJnl 1928
Rice, Harvey 1800-1891 *Alli, Alli Sup,*
  AmAu&B, BbD, BiD&SB, DcAmA,
  DcNAA, OhA&B
Rice, Isaac Leopold 1850-1915 *Alli Sup, DcAmA,*
  DcNAA, HisAmM XR
Rice, Joseph Mayer 1857-1934 *AmLY, DcAmA,*
  DcNAA, HisAmM XR, NatCAB 12
Rice, Philip Blair *HisAmM XR*
Rice, Robert *NF*
Rice, Roger Douglas 1921- *WhoAm 1974,*
  WhoF&I 1974, WhoWest 1974
Rice, Wallace DeGroot Cecil 1859-1939 *AmAu&B,*
  DcAmA, DcNAA, HisAmM XR, WhNAA
Rice, William A *OvPC*
Rice, William Gorham, Jr. 1892- *WhJnl 1928*
Rice, William Herbert 1877?-1948 *BioIn 1*
Rich, Alan 1924- *AmAu&B, ConAu 11R,*
  WhoAm 1974, WhoE 1974
Rich, Corinne *WhJnl 1928*
Rich, Elizabeth H *OvPC*
Rich, Frank 1949- *ConAu 73*
Rich, H S *HisAmM XR*
Rich, H Thompson 1893- *AnMV 1926,*
  HisAmM XR
Rich, Helen *OvPC*
Rich, Jacob 1832-1913 *NatCAB 15*
Rich, John *NF*
Rich, John H, Jr. *OvPC*
Rich, Spencer A *NF*
Rich, Stanley 1923- *OvPC, USBiR 1974*
Richan, Avard 1897- *WhJnl 1928*
Richard, Calvin Aird 1930- *WhoAm 1974*
Richard, Clarence E 1896- *WhJnl 1928*
Richard, Gabriel 1767-1832 *NF*
Richard, James Robert 1900-1977 *ConAu XR*
Richard, Joseph W *HisAmM XR*
Richard, Mary Ellen *HisAmM XR*
Richard, Randall *InvJ*
Richards, Carol *NF*
Richards, Clay F *NF*
Richards, Daniel H *AmJnl*
Richards, Dave *AmRP*
Richards, David Dudley 1889- *WhJnl 1928*
Richards, Donovan M *NF*
Richards, Douglas D *NF*
Richards, Earle Blake 1915- *CanWW 1972,*
  WhoAm 1974, WhoF&I 1974, WhoWor 1974
Richards, Emmet 1889- *WhJnl 1928*
Richards, Florence Smith *OvPC*
Richards, Francis John 1901-1965 *BioIn 7*
Richards, Frederick Thompson *HisAmM XR*
Richards, George Livingston *HisAmM XR*
Richards, George Warren 1869-1955 *AmLY,*
  HisAmM XR, WhNAA
Richards, Guy 1905-1979 *ConAu 61*
Richards, Harry Sanger 1868-1929 *DcNAA,*
  WhJnl 1928
Richards, J W *HisAmM XR*
Richards, James Maude 1907- *Au&Wr, BioIn 9,*
  ConAu 5
Richards, Joseph H *HisAmM XR*
Richards, Louis L *NF*
Richards, Ray 1894?-1950 *AmJnl, BioIn 2*
Richards, Robert W 1904- *WhJnl 1928*
Richards, Walker *HisAmM XR*
Richards, Willard *HisAmM XR*
Richards, William C 1888-1956 *BioIn 4*
Richardson, Albert Deane 1833-1869 *Alli,*
  Alli Sup, AmAu, AmAu&B, AmJnl, BbD,

BiD&SB, BioIn 3, DcAmA, DcAmB 15,
  DcNAA, FamWC, HisAmM XR, HsB&A,
  OhA&B
Richardson, Allen H *HisAmM XR*
Richardson, Amadeo *NF*
Richardson, Anna Steese Sausser 1865-1949
  BioIn 1, BioIn 2, DcNAA, OhA&B
Richardson, Beale H 1843- *Alli*
Richardson, Burton Taylor 1906- *CanWW 1972,*
  IntWW 1976, WhoWor 1974
Richardson, C B *HisAmM XR*
Richardson, Charles B *HisAmM XR*
Richardson, Charles Francis 1851-1913 *Alli Sup,*
  AmAu, AmAu&B, DcAmA, DcNAA,
  HisAmM XR, OxAm, REnAL
Richardson, Clifton F 1891- *WhJnl 1928*
Richardson, David B *OvPC*
Richardson, David Nelson 1832-1898 *Alli Sup,*
  DcNAA
Richardson, Donovan 1895?-1967 *BioIn 8*
Richardson, Dorothy 1875-1955 *AmAu&B,*
  HisAmM XR
Richardson, Francis A 1838-1926 *AmJnl*
Richardson, Francis H 1855- *NatCAB 13*
Richardson, Fred 1862-1937 *HisAmM XR*
Richardson, George Tilton 1863-1938 *AmAu&B,*
  DcNAA
Richardson, Harold Ward 1900-1954 *BioIn 3*
Richardson, J J *AmJnl*
Richardson, James Hugh 1894-1963 *BioIn 3,*
  BioIn 4, BioIn 6, WhJnl 1928
Richardson, James Patrick 1921- *BioIn 6, MnnWr*
Richardson, John *NF*
Richardson, Leander Pease 1856-1918 *Alli Sup,*
  AmAu&B, DcAmA, DcNAA, HisAmM XR,
  OhA&B
Richardson, Lou *HisAmM XR*
Richardson, Midge Turk 1930- *ConAu 65*
Richardson, Nathaniel Smith 1810-1883 *Alli,*
  DcAmA, DcNAA, HisAmM XR
Richardson, Paula 1933- *BioIn 2*
Richardson, Robert 1826- *Alli*
Richardson, Robert Lorne 1860-1921 *DcNAA*
Richardson, Solon *HisAmM XR*
Richardson, Stanley *NF*
Richardson, Stephen J *NF*
Richardson, Wayne A *OvPC*
Richardson, Willard 1802-1875 *DcAmB 15*
Richardson, William Alan 1907- *WhoAm 1974*
Richardson, William Arthur 1919?-1968 *BioIn 8*
Richardson, William Duncan 1885-1947 *BioIn 1*
Richardson, William H *HisAmM XR*
Richardson, William W 1866-1912 *NatCAB 18*
Richelieu *see* Robinson, William Erigena
Richert, Earl Harvey 1914- *BioIn 8,*
  WhoAm 1974, WhoS&SW 1973
Richey, Dorothy *NF*
Richman, Milton 1922- *ConAu 69*
Richman, Phyllis C *NF*
Richmond, Al 1913- *ConAu 41, WhoWest 1974*
Richmond, Sir Bruce Lyttelton 1871-1964 *WebBD*
Richmond, Carl W 1900- *WhJnl 1928*
Richmond, Cora Linn Victoria 1840-1923 *Alli Sup,*
  DcNAA, HisAmM XR
Richmond, Dick 1933- *ConAu 61*
Richmond, Forrest 1879- *WhJnl 1928*
Richmond, Leonard *BioIn 2, BioIn 5*
Richmond, William Ebenezer *NF*
Richter, Anne 1905- *BioIn 4, BioIn 8*
Richter, Francis C *HisAmM XR*
Richter, Frederick 1890?-1963 *BioIn 6*
Richter, Henry *HisAmM XR*
Richter, Mischa 1910- *BioIn 1*
Rick, Frank *NF*

Rickard, Thomas Arthur 1864-1953 *AmLY,*
BioIn 1, OxCan, WebBD
Rickards, Colin 1937- *ConAu 25*
Rickatson-Hatt, Bernard 1898?-1966 *BioIn 7*
Ricke, Nancy *NF*
Ricke, Tom *NF*
Ricker, Dorothy *NF*
Rickerby, Arthur B 1921?-1972 *BioIn 9,*
NewYTBE 3
Ricketts, Albert Davis 1928?- *BioIn 5*
Rickey, Harry N 1871?-1948 *BioIn 1*
Ricklefs, Roger Ulrich 1940- *WhoAm 1974,*
WhoE 1974
Rickner, Jean Michel 1951- *NF*
Riddel, Samuel Hopkins *HisAmM XR*
Riddell, Charlotte Eliza Lawson 1832-1906
Alli Sup, BbD, BiD&SB, DcEnL, NewC,
WebBD
Riddell, Charlotte Eliza Lawson *see also* Riddell,
Mrs. J H
Riddell, Baron George Allardice 1865-1934 *BioIn 2,*
WebBD
Riddell, Mrs. J H 1832-1906 *Alli, DcLEL*
Riddell, Mrs. J H *see also* Riddell, Charlotte Eliza
Lawson
Riddell, James Gilmour 1912- *WhoAm 1974*
Riddell, William *BioIn 10*
Ridder, Bernard Herman 1883-1975 *BioIn 10*
Ridder, Bernard J 1913- *WhoAm 1974,*
WhoF&I 1974, WhoWest 1974
Ridder, E Joseph 1886- *WhJnl 1928*
Ridder, E Joseph *see also* Ridder, Joseph Edward
Ridder, Eric 1918- *WhoAm 1974, WhoE 1974,*
WhoF&I 1974
Ridder, Herman 1851-1915 *AmJnl, HisAmM XR,*
WebBD
Ridder, Herman Henry 1908-1969 *BioIn 8*
Ridder, Joseph Bernard 1920- *WhoAm 1974*
Ridder, Joseph Edward 1886- *BioIn 7, BioIn 8*
Ridder, Joseph Edward *see also* Ridder, E Joseph
Ridder, Marie 1925- *ConAu 73*
Ridder, Robert Blair 1919- *WhoAm 1974*
Ridder, Ruth 1887-1969 *BioIn 8*
Ridder, Victor Frank 1886-1963 *BioIn 6*
Ridder, Walter Thompson 1917- *BioIn 5,*
WhoAm 1974
Riddle, Maxwell 1907- *ConAu 7R,*
WhoMW 1974
Riddle, Ned *NF*
Rideing, William Henry 1853-1918 *Alli Sup,*
AmAu, AmAu&B, AmLY, BiD&SB,
CarSB, DcAmA, DcNAA, HisAmM XR
Ridenour, C Frank 1884- *WhJnl 1928*
Ridenour, Millard W 1884- *WhJnl 1928*
Ridenour, Ron 1939- *ConAu 69, NewMr*
Rideout, E G *HisAmM XR*
Rider, Fremont 1885-1962 *AmAu&B,*
HisAmM XR, NatCAB 50, REnAL, WebBD
Rider, Fremont 1917- *OvPC*
Rider, Gene *OvPC*
Rider, John Russell 1923- *ConAu 25, DrAS 74E,*
WhoMW 1974
Rider, Sidney *HisAmM XR*
Rider-Taylor, Henry *HisAmM XR*
Ridge, Edney 1886- *WhJnl 1928*
Ridge, John Rollin 1827-1867 *AmAu&B, DcNAA,*
OxAm, REnAL
Ridgeway, Frank *NF*
Ridgeway, James Fowler 1936- *AmAu&B,*
BioIn 7, HisAmM XR, InvJ, WhoAm 1974
Ridgway, Erman Jesse 1867-1943 *AmAu&B,*
HisAmM XR
Riding, Laura 1901- *AmAu&B, CnDAL,*
CnE&AP, ConAmA, ConAu XR, ConLC 3,

ConP 1970, ConP 1975, DcLEL, EvLB,
HisAmM XR, IntWW 1974, LongC, OxAm,
Pen Am, RAdv 1, REnAL, SixAP, TwCA,
TwCA Sup, WebBD, WhNAA, Who 1974,
WhoTwCL, WrDr 1976
Ridings, J Willard 1894?-1948 *BioIn 1*
Ridley, C W *NF*
Ridley, J Kent 1890- *WhJnl 1928*
Ridsdale, Sir William 1890-1957 *BioIn 4*
Riedberger, Christine 1938?- *BioIn 7*
Riedinger, Robert Joseph 1925- *WhoAm 1974,*
WhoE 1974, WhoF&I 1974
Riegel, Oscar Wetherhold 1902- *AmM&W 73S,*
OvPC, WhoAm 1974, WhJnl 1928
Riegle, Meredith *NF*
Rieke, Foster Frederick 1905-1970 *BioIn 9*
Riel, Eric A *OvPC*
Rienits, Rex 1909-1971 *Au&Wr, ConAu 29,*
ConAu P-1
Ries, Henry *OvPC*
Riesel, Victor 1917- *BioIn 1, BioIn 2, BioIn 4,*
BioIn 5, OvPC, WhoAm 1974,
WhoGov 1972, WhoWor 1974
Rifbjerg, Klaus 1931- *CasWL, CroCD, EncWL,*
IntWW 1976, Pen Eur, WhoWor 1974
Rifkin, Sandra *NF*
Rigby, Cora *NF*
Riger, Rebecca *OvPC*
Riger, Robert 1924- *WhoAm 1974*
Riggenbach, Jan *NF*
Riggs, Arthur Stanley 1879-1952 *AmAu&B,*
HisAmM XR
Riggs, Edward Gridley 1856-1924 *NF*
Riggs, James A *HisAmM XR*
Riggs, John R *NF*
Riggs, Robert *Alli, ForP*
Right Cross *see* Armstrong, Paul
Righter, Carroll 1900- *CelR 1973, CurBio XR*
Righter, James Haslam 1916- *WhoAm 1974,*
WhoF&I 1974
Rightor, Henry 1870-1922 *BiDSA, DcNAA*
Rigos, John Nestor *OvPC*
Riis, Jacob August 1849-1914 *AmAu&B, AmJnl,*
BbD, BiD&SB, BioIn 1, BioIn 3, BioIn 6,
BioIn 7, BioIn 8, BioIn 9, BioIn 10,
DcAmA, DcAmB 15, DcNAA, EncAB,
HisAmM XR, NatCAB 13, OxAm, REn,
REnAL, WebBD
Riis, John 1882-1946 *BioIn 1*
Riis, Roger William 1894-1953 *BioIn 2, BioIn 3*
Riker, Daniel C *NF*
Riley, Elihu Samuel 1845- *DcNAA*
Riley, Franklin Studebaker, Jr. 1924- *OvPC,*
WhoPubR 1972, WhoWest 1974
Riley, James 1848-1930 *AmAu&B, AmLY,*
DcAmA, DcNAA, PoIre
Riley, James Whitcomb 1849-1916 *Alli Sup,*
AmAu, AmAu&B, AmSCAP 1966, BbD,
BiD&SB, BlkAW, CarSB, CasWL, CnDAL;
DcAmA, DcEnA Ap, DcLEL, DcNAA,
EvLB, HisAmM XR, IndAu 1816,
JBA 1934, LongC, OxAm, Pen Am,
RAdv 1, REn, REnAL, Str&VC, WebBD
Riley, Lawrence 1897?-1975 *ConAu 61*
Riley, Patrick Gavan Duffy 1927- *OvPC,*
WhoAm 1974, WhoWor 1974
Riley, Phil Madison 1882-1926 *DcNAA, WhNAA*
Riley, R David *NF*
Riley, Roy, Jr. 1943?-1977 *ConAu 73*
Riley, Thomas 1943- *NF*
Riley, Thomas Harry 1902-1960 *BioIn 5*
Riley, Thomas Joseph 1900-1977 *ConAu 73,*
WhoE 1974
Riley, Woodbridge 1869-1933 *AmAu&B,*

DcNAA, HisAmM XR, OxAm, REnAL
Rimington, Critchell 1907-1976 AmAu&B,
ConAu 61, WhoAm 1974
Rind, Clementina AmJnl
Rindal, S Bertram 1897- WhJnl 1928
Rindl, Robert 1892-1961 BioIn 5
Rines, George Edwin 1860-1951 BioIn 2, BioIn 3
Rinfret, Fernand 1883-1939 DcNAA
Ring, Robert C 1905?-1957 BioIn 4
Ringle, William H NF
Ringwald, George NF
Rinkle, Will Davis 1890- WhJnl 1928
Rintels, David 1939- ConAu 73
Rintoul, Robert Stephen 1787-1858 BioIn 4,
DcEnL
Riordan, Eileen Lardner OvPC
Riordan, James 1949- NF
Rios, Jose Gregorio 1931- NF
Riotto, Guy Michael 1943- ConAu 73
Ripka, Hubert 1895-1958 BioIn 4
Ripley, George 1802-1880 Alli, AmAu,
AmAu&B, AmJnl, BiD&SB, CasWL,
CnDAL, CyAL 2, DcAmA, DcEnL, DcLEL,
DcNAA, EncAB, HisAmM XR, LiJA,
NatCAB 3, OxAm, Pen Am, REn, REnAL,
WebBD
Ripley, Josephine NF
Ripley, Robert LeRoy 1893-1949 AmAu&B,
BioIn 1, BioIn 4, BioIn 5, BioIn 6, BioIn 9,
BioIn 10, CurBio XR, DcAmB S4,
NatCAB 41, OxAm, REnAL, WhJnl Sup
Ripley, Warren 1921- ConAu 33
Rippin, Jane 1882-1953 BioIn 3
Ripskis, Al Louis InvJ
Risaliti, John Michael 1946- NF
Riseling, John J W 1888?-1977 ConAu 73
Risher, Eugene 1934?- NF
Risk, T F HisAmM XR
Risko, Jan 1930- IntWW 1976, WhoWor 1974
Risser, James InvJ
Risso, Mario NF
Ritchey, Michael 1943?- NF
Ritchie, Robert Welles 1879-1942 AmAu&B,
DcNAA, NatCAB 32
Ritchie, Thomas 1778-1854 Alli, AmJnl,
DcAmB 15, NatCAB 7, WebBD
Ritchie, Thomas, Jr. AmJnl
Ritchie-Calder, Baron Peter 1906- IntWW 1974,
Who 1974, WhoWor 1974
Ritchie-Calder, Baron Peter see also Calder, Ritchie
Ritis, Beniamino De 1889-1956 BioIn 4
Ritner, Peter V 1927?-1976 ConAu 69
Rittenberg, Louis 1892-1962 BioIn 6
Rittenhouse, Jessie Belle 1869-1948 AmAu&B,
AmLY, AnMV 1926, DcAmB S4, REn,
REnAL, TwCA, TwCA Sup, WhNAA
Ritter, Ed 1917- ConAu 19R
Ritter, Frederick W 1881?-1948 BioIn 1
Ritter, John 1942- NF
Ritter, Leo J 1919?-1968 BioIn 8
Ritter, Marcelino ForP
Rittig, Johann 1829?-1885 BioIn 2
Ritz, Dorothy d1977 NF
Ritz, Joseph P 1929- ConAu 21R
Ritzau, E N ForP
Riutor, Raul H NF
Rivaroli, Antoine 1753-1801 BioIn 3, BioIn 7,
WebBD
Rivas, Victor Manuel 1909?-1965 BioIn 7
Rivera, Geraldo 1943- BioIn 9, BioIn 10,
BioNews 1974, CelR 1973, CurBio XR,
NewMr, NewYTBE 2
Rivera Otero, Rafael 1903-1958 BioIn 4
Rivero, Jose Ignacio 1895-1944 CurBio XR

Rivers, Caryl 1937- ConAu 49, NewYTBE 2
Rivers, J D 1898- WhJnl 1928
Rivers, Lucille NF
Rivers, Pearl 1849-1896 Alli Sup, AmAu,
AmAu&B, BiDSA, DcAmA, DcNAA
Rivers, Pearl see also Nicholson, Eliza Jane Poitevent
Rivers, William Lawrence 1925- ConAu 19R,
WhoWest 1974
Rivers-Coffey, Rachel 1943- ConAu 73
Rives, John Cook 1795-1864 Alli, AmAu&B,
AmJnl, DcAmB 15, NatCAB 3
Rives, William T 1912?- BioIn 1
Rivett, Rohan Deakin 1917- Au&Wr, ConAu 25,
IntWW 1976, WhoWor 1974, WrDr 1976
Riviere, Jacques 1886-1925 CasWL, CIDMEL,
EncWL, OxFr, Pen Eur, REn, WebBD,
WorAu
Rivington, Charles 1688-1742 WebBD
Rivington, Charles 1754-1831 WebBD
Rivington, Francis 1745-1822 WebBD
Rivington, Francis 1805-1885 WebBD
Rivington, James 1724-1802 Alli, AmJnl, BioIn 5,
CyAL 1, DcAmB 15, HisAmM XR, WebBD
Rivington, John 1779-1841 WebBD
Rivington, John 1812-1886 WebBD
Rivington, Septimus 1846-1926 WebBD
Rizzuto, Francisco, Jr. ForP
Roach, Celia May 1897- WhJnl 1928
Roach, Gwendolyn BioIn 2
Roach, James 1907- WhoAm 1974, WhoE 1974
Roach, James P d1978 NF
Roads, David J OvPC
Roales, Judith M NF
Roalman, A R NF
Roane, Spencer 1762-1822 Alli, BiDSA
Roark, Eldon 1897- BioIn 1, WhoAm 1974
Robards, Sherman M 1939- ConAu 61
Robards, Terry ConAu XR
Robb, Arthur Thomas 1893?-1962 BioIn 6,
HisAmM XR
Robb, Charles J 1856- WhJnl 1928
Robb, Don B 1870- WhJnl 1928
Robb, Eugene Spivey 1910-1969 BioIn 8
Robb, Gene NF
Robb, Inez AmJnl, BioIn 1, BioIn 3, BioIn 5,
BioIn 6, CurBio XR, ForP
Robb, James AmRP
Robb, Walter NF
Robbins, Al NF
Robbins, Alan Pitt NF
Robbins, Charles H D OvPC
Robbins, Frank Egleston 1884- BioIn 3
Robbins, J J HisAmM XR
Robbins, James 1879-1962 BioIn 6, WhJnl 1928
Robbins, Janice OvPC
Robbins, Jhan OvPC
Robbins, Leon H 1886- WhJnl 1928
Robbins, Leonard Harman 1877-1947 BioIn 1,
DcNAA, REnAL
Robbins, Mary Caroline 1841-1912 Alli Sup,
AmAu&B, DcAmA, DcNAA
Robbins, Merton C 1875-1937 NatCAB 37
Robbins, Mildred Brown ConAu 33,
ForWC 1970, WhoWest 1974
Robbins, William A NF
Robbins, William H NF
Rober-Reynaud, Henri 1875-1951 BioIn 2
Roberge, Frank BioIn 4
Robert, Dent H 1863-1917 NatCAB 17
Robert, Evelyn 1909?-1972 BioIn 9
Roberton, Thomas Beattie 1879-1936 DcNAA
Roberts, Anthony K NF
Roberts, Avis C BioIn 2
Roberts, Bill 1924- NF

Roberts, Bill 1914?-1978 *NF*
Roberts, C Wesley 1903-1975 *CurBio XR*
Roberts, Cecil Edric Mornington 1892-1976
  *Au&Wr, ConAu 69, DcLEL, LongC, NewC,
  TwCA, TwCA Sup, WebBD, WhNAA,
  Who 1974, WrDr 1976*
Roberts, Chalmers McGeagh 1910- *AmAu&B,
  ConAu 41, ForP, IntWW 1974,
  WhoAm 1974, WhoS&SW 1973*
Roberts, Charles *BioIn 2, BioIn 7*
Roberts, Charles A 1900- *WhJnl 1928*
Roberts, Charles Wesley 1916- *ConAu 19R,
  WhoS&SW 1973*
Roberts, Clete 1910?- *BioIn 2*
Roberts, Daniel *AmRP*
Roberts, David H 1902- *WhJnl 1928*
Roberts, Doug *NF*
Roberts, Edward P *HisAmM XR*
Roberts, Edwin Albert, Jr. 1932- *ConAu 23,
  WhoE 1974*
Roberts, Ellis Henry 1827-1918 *Alli Sup, DcAmA,
  DcNAA*
Roberts, Elmer 1863-1937 *AmLY, BioIn 2,
  DcNAA, IndAu 1816, WhNAA*
Roberts, Elzey 1892-1962 *BioIn 6, WhJnl 1928*
Roberts, Eugene Leslie, Jr. 1932- *InvJ,
  WhoAm 1974, WhoE 1974*
Roberts, Eugene Leslie, Jr. *see also* Roberts, Gene L
Roberts, Gene L 1932- *NewMr, RpN,
  WhoE 1974*
Roberts, Gene L *see also* Roberts, Eugene Leslie, Jr.
Roberts, George *AmJnl, HisAmM XR*
Roberts, George D *WhJnl 1928*
Roberts, George Simon 1860-1940 *DcNAA*
Roberts, Harold *AmRP*
Roberts, Harold C *HisAmM XR*
Roberts, Harris W 1888- *WhJnl 1928*
Roberts, Harry E 1883-1925 *WhJnl Sup,
  WhJnl 1928*
Roberts, Henry Buchtel 1903?-1960 *BioIn 5*
Roberts, J M *NF*
Roberts, John 1890?-1968 *BioIn 4, BioIn 8*
Roberts, Kenneth Lewis 1885-1957 *AmAu&B,
  AmNov, CasWL, CnDAL, ConAmA,
  DcLEL, EvLB, HisAmM XR, LongC,
  ModAL, OxAm, OxCan, Pen Am, REn,
  REnAL, TwCA, TwCA Sup, TwCW,
  WebBD, WhNAA*
Roberts, Leslie 1896- *BioIn 1, CanWW 1972,
  OxCan, OxCan Sup, WhNAA*
Roberts, Mary 1871-1956 *BioIn 4*
Roberts, Michael 1945- *ConAu 69*
Roberts, Sir Percy *NF*
Roberts, Rick *NF*
Roberts, Roy Allison 1887-1967 *AmJnl, BioIn 1,
  BioIn 6, BioIn 7*
Roberts, Ruby Altizer 1907- *ForWC 1970*
Roberts, Samuel J 1858-1913 *NatCAB 17*
Roberts, Sandy *NF*
Roberts, Stanley 1933- *WhoAm 1974*
Roberts, Steven V 1943- *ConAu 61*
Roberts, Susan *OvPC*
Roberts, Tom *NF*
Roberts, Walker 1941- *NF*
Roberts, Walter Adolphe 1886-1962 *AmAu&B,
  AmNov, BioIn 6, BioIn 9, WhNAA*
Roberts, Willa *HisAmM XR*
Roberts, William R 1896- *WhJnl 1928*
Robertson, Alexander *AmJnl, BbtC*
Robertson, Archibald Thomas 1911?-1965 *BioIn 1,
  BioIn 7*
Robertson, Arlynn *NF*
Robertson, Ben, Jr. 1903-1943 *AmJnl,
  CurBio XR, DcNAA, NatCAB 32*

Robertson, Cameron A 1898- *WhJnl 1928*
Robertson, Cary 1902- *RpN, WhoS&SW 1973*
Robertson, Don 1929- *ConAu 9R, SmATA 8*
Robertson, E J *Lor&LP*
Robertson, Earl Edward 1886-1950 *BioIn 6,
  NatCAB 45*
Robertson, Frank *NF*
Robertson, G S *NF*
Robertson, Harrison 1856-1939 *AmAu&B,
  AmLY, BiDSA, DcAmA, DcNAA,
  NatCAB 29, WhNAA*
Robertson, Hugh Winfield 1888- *NewYTBE 3,
  WhJnl 1928*
Robertson, Irving E *NF*
Robertson, Jack W *NF*
Robertson, James 1740- *AmAu&B, AmJnl,
  DcAmB 16*
Robertson, John *NF*
Robertson, John Henry 1909-1965 *BioIn 7*
Robertson, John Mackinnon 1856-1933 *EvLB,
  LongC, NewC, Pen Eng, WebBD, WhoLA*
Robertson, John Ross 1841-1918 *Alli Sup,
  BioIn 9, DcNAA, OxCan*
Robertson, Lloyd *NF*
Robertson, Morgan 1861-1915 *HisAmM XR*
Robertson, Nan *NF*
Robertson, Nathan W d1951 *RpN*
Robertson, Nugent *HisAmM XR*
Robertson, Sparrow 1855-1941 *BioIn 1*
Robertson, Stewart *WhJnl 1928*
Robertson, Thomas Aaron 1883?-1950 *BioIn 2*
Robertson, Thomas B *NF*
Robertson, Wilbur W 1868- *WhJnl 1928*
Robertson, William Cornelius 1882- *WhJnl 1928*
Robertson, William Franklin 1917- *WhoAm 1974*
Robertson, William Joseph 1888- *WhJnl 1928*
Robertson-Scott, John William 1866-1962 *BioIn 2,
  BioIn 4, BioIn 6, BioIn 7*
Robey, John *HisAmM XR*
Robey, Ralph West 1899-1972 *BioIn 9,
  ConAu 37, CurBio XR, NewYTBE 3*
Robicheaux, Virginia *NF*
Robidoux, Louis Philippe 1897-1957 *BioIn 4*
Robie, Virginia 1878- *AmLY, HisAmM XR,
  WhNAA*
Robinette, Kathryn *NF*
Robins, Denise Naomi 1897- *ConAu 65*
Robins, Edward 1862-1943 *AmAu&B, AmLY,
  BiD&SB, CurBio XR, DcAmA, DcNAA*
Robins, Eric *NF*
Robinson, Albert Gardner 1855-1932 *DcAmA,
  DcNAA*
Robinson, Alice Gram *ForWC 1970,
  WhoAm 1974, WhoAmW 1974*
Robinson, Alice Wade d1952 *BioIn 2*
Robinson, Bill 1918- *ConAu XR*
Robinson, Boardman 1876-1952 *AmAu&B,
  BioIn 3, CurBio XR, DcAmB S5, DcCAA,
  HisAmM XR, WebBD*
Robinson, Carl *NF*
Robinson, Charles 1912?-1965 *BioIn 5, BioIn 7*
Robinson, Charles Mulford 1869-1917 *AmAu&B,
  DcAmA, DcAmB 16, DcNAA,
  HisAmM XR, WebBD*
Robinson, Charles S 1892- *WhJnl 1928*
Robinson, Cliff d1977 *NF*
Robinson, Crabb *scc* Robinson, Henry Crabb
Robinson, David Moore 1880-1958 *AmAu&B,
  AmLY, HisAmM XR, WebBD, WhNAA*
Robinson, Doane 1856-1946 *AmAu&B, AmLY,
  DcAmA, HisAmM XR, WhNAA*
Robinson, Donald 1913- *BioIn 2, ConAu 25*
Robinson, Douglas *NF*
Robinson, E H *HisAmM XR*

Robinson, Edward 1794-1863 *Alli, AmAu,
    AmAu&B, CyAL 1, DcAmA, DcEnL,
    DcNAA, HisAmM XR, WebBD*
Robinson, Edwin Meade 1878-1946 *AmAu&B,
    BioIn 1, BioIn 2, DcNAA, IndAu 1816,
    OhA&B, REnAL, WhNAA*
Robinson, Edwin Meade *see also* Robinson, Ted
Robinson, Eldred J 1894- *WhJnl 1928*
Robinson, Elsie 1883-1956 *BioIn 3, BioIn 4*
Robinson, Ezekiel Gilman 1815-1894 *Alli,
    Alli Sup, DcAmA, DcNAA, HisAmM XR,
    WebBD*
Robinson, Frank M 1926- *ConAu 49*
Robinson, Frank Torrey 1845-1898 *DcAmA,
    DcNAA*
Robinson, Frederic Hugo 1890-1923 *BioIn 2,
    NatCAB 35*
Robinson, Geoffrey 1874?-1918 *WebBD*
Robinson, Gerold Tanquary 1892-1971
    HisAmM XR
Robinson, Grace *OvPC*
Robinson, H D *Alli, HisAmM XR*
Robinson, Harriet Jane Hanson 1825-1911
    *Alli Sup, AmAu&B, DcAmA, DcNAA,
    HisAmM XR, OxAm, REnAL*
Robinson, Harry A 1942- *BioIn 9*
Robinson, Harry Perry 1859-1930 *DcAmA,
    HisAmM XR*
Robinson, Helen 1878-1923 *DcNAA*
Robinson, Henry Crabb 1775-1867 *Alli, BiD&SB,
    BioIn 3, BioIn 5, BioIn 7, BioIn 9,
    BrAu 19, CasWL, DcEnL, DcEuL, DcLEL,
    EvLB, FamWC, NewC, OxEng, Pen Eng,
    WebBD*
Robinson, Henry Morton 1898-1961 *AmAu&B,
    AmNov, CathA 1952, CurBio XR, REnAL,
    TwCA Sup, WhNAA*
Robinson, Howard Perley 1874?-1950 *BioIn 2*
Robinson, Hubbell 1905-1974 *ConAu 53,
    NewYTBS 5, WhoAm 1974*
Robinson, Irwin *NF*
Robinson, James Algernon 1854- *WhJnl 1928*
Robinson, James G *OvPC*
Robinson, Jerry *OvPC*
Robinson, Sir John *FamWC*
Robinson, John *NF*
Robinson, John Hovey 1825- *Alli, HisAmM XR*
Robinson, Jonah L 1856- *NatCAB 13*
Robinson, Judith *OxCan*
Robinson, Katherine Prentis Woodroofe 1939-
    LEduc 1974, WhoAm 1974, WhoAmW 1974
Robinson, Leonard Wallace 1912- *ConAu 69,
    DrAF 1976*
Robinson, Lisa *NF*
Robinson, Louie *LivBAA*
Robinson, Marilyn *NF*
Robinson, Maurice 1884?-1953 *BioIn 3*
Robinson, Maurice Richard 1895- *CurBio XR,
    WhoAm 1974, WhJnl 1928*
Robinson, Nugent 1840?-1906? *Alli Sup,
    HisAmM XR, PoIre*
Robinson, Pat 1890?-1964 *BioIn 7*
Robinson, Paul D 1898?-1974 *BioIn 10*
Robinson, Philip Stewart 1849-1902 *Alli Sup,
    BiD&SB*
Robinson, Prescott W *OvPC*
Robinson, Ralph D *HisAmM XR*
Robinson, Raymond Kenneth 1920- *BioIn 7,
    WhoAm 1974, WhoE 1974*
Robinson, Richard 1945- *BioIn 10, ConAu 57*
Robinson, Robert 1927- *Au&Wr, ConAu 11R,
    WrDr 1976*
Robinson, Selma 1899?-1977 *ConAu 73*
Robinson, Solon 1803-1880 *Alli, AmAu,*

    *AmAu&B, BiDSA, DcAmA, DcNAA,
    HisAmM XR, IndAu 1816, NatCAB 3,
    OxAm, REnAL*
Robinson, Spencer W 1903- *WhJnl 1928*
Robinson, Ted 1878-1946 *AmJnl, REnAL*
Robinson, Ted *see also* Robinson, Edwin Meade
Robinson, Thomas Lambard 1907- *BioIn 4*
Robinson, Virginia *NF*
Robinson, Walter C *HisAmM XR*
Robinson, Walter Irving 1884- *WhJnl 1928*
Robinson, Wayne 1916- *BiE&WWA, ConAu 2R,
    WhoAm 1974*
Robinson, Wilfriedt 1871- *BioIn 3*
Robinson, William Edward 1900-1969 *CurBio XR*
Robinson, William Erigena 1814-1892 *Alli, AmJnl,
    DcAmB 16, DcNAA, PoIre*
Robinson, William Heath 1872-1944 *BioIn 5,
    BioIn 8, BioIn 10, CurBio XR, WebBD,
    WhoChL*
Robinson, William Josephus 1867-1936 *AmLY,
    AmRP, BioIn 2, DcNAA*
Robinson, William Stevens 1818-1876 *Alli Sup,
    AmAu&B, DcAmA, DcAmB 16, DcNAA*
Robinson, William Wheeler 1918- *ConAu 7R*
Robison, David *NF*
Robison, Helen J *OvPC*
Robles, Sebastian Tomas 1902?-1959 *BioIn 5*
Roblin, Sir Redmond *OxCan*
Robling, Mrs. John S *RpN*
Robling, John Stevens 1922- *OvPC,
    WhoMW 1974, WhoPubR 1972*
Robson, Jean *WhJnl 1928*
Robson, Jeremy 1939- *BioIn 10, ConAu 5*
Robson, John 1824-1892 *BioIn 8*
Robson, William Alexander 1895- *Au&Wr,
    IntWW 1976, Who 1974*
Rocha Martins, Francisco Jose Da 1879-1952
    BioIn 2, BioIn 3
Rochacker, J H *HisAmM XR*
Roche, Arthur Somers 1883-1935 *AmAu&B,
    DcAmB S1, DcNAA, TwCA, WebBD*
Roche, G W 1870- *WhJnl 1928*
Roche, James Jeffrey 1847-1908 *Alli Sup, AmAu,
    AmAu&B, BbD, BiD&SB, BioIn 5,
    DcAmA, DcAmB 16, DcNAA,
    HisAmM XR, LiJA, PoIre, REnAL,
    WebBD*
Roche, Jeremiah J *NF*
Roche, John P 1923- *AmAu&B, AmM&W 73S,
    ConAu 69, DrAS 74H, IntWW 1974,
    WhoAm 1974, WhoE 1974, WhoGov 1972*
Roche, Mary McDermott d1977 *ForWC 1970*
Roche, R A *NF*
Rochefort, Henri 1830-1913 *BioIn 7, WebBD*
Rochette, Edward C *NF*
Rochon, Edwin Waterbury 1918- *WhoAm 1974*
Rock, Howard 1911- *BioIn 9*
Rockafellow, Ralph *HisAmM XR*
Rockne, Dick 1939- *ConAu 61*
Rockwell, F F 1884- *ConAu 49*
Rockwell, Jane 1929- *ConAu 65*
Rockwell, Sidney J 1888- *WhJnl 1928*
Rockwood, Nathan C 1884- *WhJnl 1928*
Rod, Edouard 1857-1910 *BbD, BiD&SB,
    CasWL, EuAu, EvEuW, HisAmM XR,
    OxFr, WebBD*
Roda Roda, Alexander Friedrich Ladislaus
    1872-1945 *WebBD*
Rodale, Jerome Irving 1898-1971 *AmAu&B,
    BioIn 7, BioIn 8, BioIn 9, BioIn 10,
    ConAu 29*
Rodale, Robert 1930- *ConAu 53*
Rodden, Mike 1891-1978 *NF*
Rode, Charles R 1825-1865 *Alli, HisAmM XR*

Rode, Edith 1879-1956 *BioIn 1, CasWL*
Rodemeyer, John *WhJnl 1928*
Rodenberg, Julius 1831-1914 *BbD, BiD&SB, BioIn 3, DcEuL, OxGer, WebBD*
Rodenwold, Zelta 1895- *BioIn 1*
Roder, James W 1908-1958 *BioIn 5*
Roderick, Dorrance Douglas 1900- *WhoAm 1974, WhJnl 1928, WhoS&SW 1973*
Roderick, John P *NF*
Roderick, Lee *NF*
Roderick, S V *HisAmM XR*
Roderick, Virginia *HisAmM XR*
Rodewalt, Vance *NF*
Rodger, Esca G *WhNAA, WhJnl 1928*
Rodgers, Cleveland 1885-1956 *BioIn 4*
Rodgers, Cleveland *see also* Rogers, Cleveland
Rodgers, Wilfrid C *RpN*
Rodgers, William H 1918- *ConAu 19R*
Rodino DiMiglione, Marcello 1906- *IntWW 1976, WhoWor 1974*
Rodker, John 1894- *HisAmM XR*
Rodman, Selden 1909- *AmAu&B, AmRP, ConAu 5, OxAm, REn, REnAL, SmATA 9, TwCA Sup, WhoAm 1974, WhoAmA 1973, WhoWor 1974*
Rodney, Lester *AmRP*
Rodolf, Charles Clark *HisAmM XR*
Rodrigo, Robert 1928- *ConAu 13R*
Rodriguez, Carlos Rafael 1913- *BioIn 6, IntWW 1976*
Rodriguez, Dennis *NF*
Rodriguez, Eugenio *NF*
Rodriguez Cerna, Jose 1894?-1952 *BioIn 3*
Rodriguez Larreta, Eduardo 1888- *BioIn 2*
Rodriguez-Morejon, Gerardo 1893?-1966 *BioIn 7*
Rodriquez, Juan *NF*
Roe, Frederic Gordon 1894- *Au&Wr, BioIn 10, Br&AmS, ConAu 9, Who 1974, WhoLA, WrDr 1976*
Roe, George Mortimer 1848-1916 *NatCAB 12, OhA&B*
Roe, Herman 1886- *AmJnl, WhJnl 1928*
Roe, Rolla E 1864?-1942 *BioIn 1*
Roe, Wellington 1898-1952 *BioIn 2, WhNAA*
Roeder, Bill *NF*
Roeder, Gus C *NF*
Roesch, Roberta *NF*
Roesch, W Eugene 1898-1952 *BioIn 3*
Roeser, Carl d1897 *BioIn 2*
Roesler, Gustav Adolf 1818-1855 *BioIn 2*
Roesler, Robert Harry 1927- *WhoAm 1974, WhoS&SW 1973*
Roessner, Elmer 1900-1972 *BioIn 9, NewYTBE 3*
Roethe, Henry Edgar 1866-1939 *BioIn 5*
Roetter, Charles Frederick 1919- *ConAu 61*
Roevekamp, Fred *RpN*
Roewe, Janet Mae *NF*
Rogaly, Joseph *ForP*
Rogan, Helen *NF*
Roger, Charles 1819-1878 *Alli, BbtC, DcNAA, OxCan*
Rogers, Alexander Hamilton 1868-1942 *BioIn 3, NatCAB 37*
Rogers, Boody *BioIn 2*
Rogers, Cameron 1900- *AmAu&B, Au&Wr, HisAmM XR, WhNAA*
Rogers, Cedric *AuBYP, BioIn 7*
Rogers, Charles Elkins 1892- *AmM&W 73S, WhNAA, WhJnl 1928*
Rogers, Charles O *AmJnl*
Rogers, Cleveland 1885-1956 *AmAu&B*
Rogers, Cleveland *see also* Rodgers, Cleveland
Rogers, Cornish *BioIn 8*
Rogers, David Barss 1899-1967 *BioIn 8*

Rogers, Dick *NF*
Rogers, Donald Irwin 1918- *BioIn 6, ConAu 57, WhoAm 1974*
Rogers, E L 1877- *WhJnl 1928*
Rogers, Edward H *HisAmM XR*
Rogers, Edwin A *NF*
Rogers, Ernest 1897-1964 *BioIn 4, BioIn 8*
Rogers, George McIntosh 1879-1949 *BioIn 2, WhJnl 1928*
Rogers, H R 1892- *WhJnl 1928*
Rogers, Helen Jean *ForWC 1970*
Rogers, Hopewell Lindenberger 1876-1948 *BioIn 1*
Rogers, Irving Emerson 1902- *WhoAm 1974*
Rogers, J A *NF*
Rogers, James Tracy 1921- *ConAu 45, WhoAmP 1973*
Rogers, Jason 1868-1932 *DcNAA, WhJnl 1928*
Rogers, John G *NF*
Rogers, John Rankin 1838-1901 *AmAu&B, DcAmA, DcNAA*
Rogers, John T 1881- *BioIn 1, WhJnl 1928*
Rogers, Joseph *WhJnl 1928*
Rogers, Joseph Morgan 1861-1922 *BiDSA, DcNAA, OhA&B*
Rogers, Lela Emogen 1890-1977 *AmSCAP 1966*
Rogers, Loula Kendall *BiDSA, LivFWS*
Rogers, Margaret B 1938- *NF*
Rogers, Michael 1950- *ConAu 49, DrAF 1976*
Rogers, Nathaniel Peabody 1794-1846 *Alli, BioIn 1, BioIn 2, DcNAA, HisAmM XR*
Rogers, Paul Brinkley *NF*
Rogers, Robert *NF*
Rogers, Robert Cameron 1862-1912 *AmAu&B, BiD&SB, DcAmA, DcNAA, REnAL*
Rogers, Stephen 1912- *OvPC, WhoAm 1974*
Rogers, Steve *InvJ, NewMr*
Rogers, W G 1896- *ConAu 11R*
Rogers, Walter Stowell 1877-1965 *BioIn 7*
Rogers, Warren Joseph, Jr. 1922- *AmAu&B, ForP, WhoAm 1974, WhoWor 1974*
Rogers, Will 1879-1935 *AmAu&B, AmJnl, CnDAL, DcAmB S1, DcNAA, HisAmM XR, LongC, NatCAB 33, OxAm, Pen Am, REn, REnAL, TwCA, TwCA Sup, WebBD, WhJnl 1928*
Rogers, William Allen 1854-1931 *AmAu&B, AmJnl, BioIn 3, BioIn 8, DcNAA, HisAmM XR, OhA&B*
Rogers, William F 1870- *WhJnl 1928*
Rogers, William Garland 1896-1978 *AmAu&B, AuBYP, ConAu 9, WrDr 1976*
Rogers, William J 1891- *WhJnl 1928*
Rogers, William Penn Adair 1879-1935 *DcNAA, EncAB, EvLB*
Rogerson, Cliff *NF*
Roget, Samuel Romilly 1875-1952 *BioIn 3*
Rogin, Gilbert Leslie 1929- *ConAu 65, WhoAm 1974*
Rogoff, Harry 1882-1971 *BioIn 9, ConAu 33, NewYTBE 2, WhNAA, WhoWorJ 1972*
Rohde, Helmut 1925- *IntWW 1976*
Rohde, William Lloyd 1901- *WhJnl 1928*
Rohe, Alice 1875?-1957 *BioIn 4*
Rohe, Robert L 1894- *WhJnl 1928*
Rohr, William Henry 1888- *WhJnl 1928*
Rohrbach, Paul 1869- *WebBD*
Rohrer, Fred 1867-1936 *BioIn 2, IndAu 1816*
Rojas, Alberto *NF*
Rojas, Gloria *NF*
Rojas-Vela, Enrique *OvPC*
Roland, Albert 1925- *ConAu 61, USBiR 1974*
Roland, Charles 1831-1918 *OhA&B*
Rolens, Fred M 1880- *WhJnl 1928*
Rolfe, John F 1880- *WhJnl 1928*

Rolfe, William James 1827-1910 *Alli, Alli Sup,
  AmAu, AmAu&B, BbD, BiD&SB, DcAmA,
  DcNAA, REnAL, WebBD*
Rolleston, Thomas William Hazen 1857-1920
  Alli Sup, BioIn 2, CasWL, PoIre, WebBD
Rollin, Betty *ConAu 13R, ForWC 1970*
Rollins, Bryant 1937- *BlkAW, ConAu 49,
  LivBAA*
Rollins, Byron *NF*
Rollins, Carole *NF*
Rollins, Mabel *HisAmM XR*
Rolt-Wheeler, Francis William 1876-1960
  *AmAu&B, AmLY, JBA 1934, JBA 1951,
  WhNAA, WhoLA*
Roman, Alexander J *NF*
Roman, Anton *HisAmM XR, LiJA*
Roman, Cris A *NF*
Romano, Armando 1883?-1963 *BioIn 6*
Romanoff, Harry 1892?-1970 *BioIn 7, BioIn 8,
  BioIn 9*
Romanones, Aline 1921- *BioIn 8*
Romanov, Aleksey Vladimirovich 1908-
  IntWW 1976
Romanov, Pavel Konstantinovich 1913-
  IntWW 1976
Romantsov, Yuri V *NF*
Romeike, Henry *NF*
Romer, John Irving 1869-1933 *BioIn 2,
  HisAmM XR*
Romero, Pepe 1911- *BioIn 3, BioIn 4*
Romine, Joanne *NF*
Romulo, Carlos Pena 1899- *AmAu&B, BioIn 1,
  BioIn 2, BioIn 3, BioIn 4, BioIn 5, BioIn 6,
  BioIn 8, CathA 1930, ConAu 15R,
  CurBio XR, IntWW 1976, WhNAA,
  WhoWor 1974*
Ron, Moshe *NF*
Ronald, Sir Robert *NF*
Ronald, Stephen *NF*
Ronald, W R 1879-1951 *BioIn 2*
Rondon, Hector *NF*
Rongen, Bjoern 1906- *ConAu 29, SmATA 10*
Ronnen, Yorham 1933- *NF*
Ronning, Nils Nilsen 1870-1962 *BioIn 6*
Ronstrom, Maud *BioIn 1*
Rood, Henry Edward 1867-1954 *AmAu&B,
  BiD&SB, BioIn 3, DcAmA*
Roode, Albert De *HisAmM XR*
Roodenburg, Nancy McKee 1909?-1972 *BioIn 9*
Rook, Charles Alexander 1861-1946 *BioIn 1*
Rooney, Edmund J, Jr. *RpN*
Rooney, John *NF*
Roos, B Mathieu *OvPC*
Roos, Delmar Barney *NF*
Roosenburg, Henriette 1916?-1972 *Au&Wr,
  BioIn 4, BioIn 9, BioIn 10, ConAu 37,
  NewYTBE 3*
Roosevelt, Edith Kermit 1927?- *BioIn 5,
  ConAu 69, ForWC 1970, WhoS&SW 1973*
Roosevelt, Eleanor 1884-1962 *AmAu&B, BioIn 1,
  BioIn 2, BioIn 3, BioIn 4, BioIn 5, BioIn 6,
  BioIn 7, BioIn 8, BioIn 9, BioIn 10,
  BioNews 1974, CurBio XR, HisAmM XR,
  LongC, OxAm, REn, REnAL, WebBD*
Roosevelt, Nicholas 1893- *AmAu&B, BioIn 3,
  WebBD, WhoAm 1974, WhJnl 1928,
  WhoWest 1974*
Roosevelt, Robert Barnwell 1829-1906 *Alli,
  Alli Sup, AmAu&B, BiD&SB, CyAL 2,
  DcAmA, DcNAA, WebBD*
Root, Ernest Rob 1862-1953 *BioIn 1, OhA&B,
  WhNAA*
Root, Frank Albert 1837-1926 *AmAu&B, DcNAA*
Root, Helen Isabel 1873-1945 *BioIn 1*

Root, Lin *ConAu 69, OvPC*
Root, Louis Carroll 1868-1939 *HisAmM XR*
Root, O T *HisAmM XR*
Root, Walstein *NF*
Root, Waverley Lewis 1903- *AmAu&B,
  ConAu 25, CurBio XR, WhoAm 1974,
  WrDr 1976*
Root, Wells 1900- *IntMPA 1975, WhJnl 1928*
Ropelewski, Robert *NF*
Roper, Burns Worthington 1925- *WhoCon 1973,
  WhoE 1974*
Roper, Charles A 1887-1954 *BioIn 3*
Roper, Elmo Burns, Jr. 1900- *AmAu&B,
  CurBio XR, NewYTBE 2*
Roper, James E *NF*
Roques, Valeska Von *NF*
Rorer, Sarah Tyson 1849-1937 *Alli Sup, DcAmA,
  DcNAA, HisAmM XR*
Rorty, James 1890-1973 *AmAu&B, BioIn 9,
  ConAu 41, NewYTBE 4, WhNAA*
Rosapepe, Joseph S 1913- *OvPC, WhoPubR 1972*
Rosbaud, Paul 1896-1963 *BioIn 6*
Roscoe, George Boggs 1907- *ConAu 65,
  WhoS&SW 1973*
Roscoe, Theodore *HisAmM XR*
Rose, Ada Campbell 1902?-1976 *AmAu&B,
  ConAu 65*
Rose, Alfred W 1902- *WhJnl 1928*
Rose, Billy 1899-1966 *AmSCAP 1966,
  BiE&WWA, BioIn 1, BioIn 2, BioIn 3,
  BioIn 4, BioIn 5, BioIn 6, BioIn 7, BioIn 8,
  CurBio XR*
Rose, Camille Davied 1893- *ConAu 21, OvPC*
Rose, Camille Davied *see also* Davied, Camille
Rose, Carl 1903-1971 *BioIn 9, ConAu 29,
  NewYTBE 2*
Rose, Donald Frank 1890-1964 *AmAu&B,
  BioIn 1*
Rose, Edward 1849-1904 *BioIn 6*
Rose, Eliot Joseph Benn 1909- *IntWW 1976,
  Who 1974, WhoWor 1974, WrDr 1976*
Rose, Elizabeth 1915- *ConAu 73*
Rose, Janet B *NF*
Rose, Jerry A 1933-1965 *BioIn 7*
Rose, John Lawrence 1908- *WhoAm 1974*
Rose, Louis *InvJ*
Rose, Louis H 1880- *BioIn 2*
Rose, Marcus A 1888-1964 *BioIn 6*
Rose, Norman Sherwin *WhJnl 1928*
Rose, Oscar *OvPC*
Rose, Philip Sheridan *HisAmM XR*
Rose, Richard C *NF*
Rose, Robert Leonard 1924- *WhoAm 1974,
  WhoWest 1974*
Rose, Stuart 1899?-1975 *BioIn 7, ConAu 61,
  HisAmM XR*
Rose, Thornton Turner 1910- *WhoAm 1974*
Rose, William Ganson 1878-1957 *OhA&B*
Rose, William Palen 1889- *ConAu 57,
  HisAmM XR, WhNAA, WhoAm 1974,
  WhJnl 1928*
Rosebault, Charles Jerome 1864-1944 *AmAu&B*
Rosebault, W M *NF*
Roseberry, Cecil R 1902- *ConAu 21R*
Roseboro, Viola 1857-1945 *AmAu&B, BiDSA,
  DcAmA, DcNAA, HisAmM XR*
Rosecrans, Charles D, Jr. d1950? *AmJnl*
Rosecrans, E J *HisAmM XR*
Rosefsky, Robert S *NF*
Rosen, Dan 1935- *NF*
Rosen, Fred *OvPC*
Rosen, Gerald R *NF*
Rosen, Jane K *NF*
Rosen, Jay *NF*

Rosen, Lew *DcNAA, HisAmM XR*
Rosen, Baron Roman Romanovich 1847-1921
  WebBD
Rosen, Saul David 1906- *WhoAm 1974,*
  WhoE 1974
Rosenbaum, Arthur *NF*
Rosenbaum, David *NF*
Rosenbaum, Edward Philip 1916-1963 *BioIn 6*
Rosenbaum, Helen *NF*
Rosenbaum, Jack *NF*
Rosenbaum, Maurice 1907- *ConAu 17R,*
  SmATA 6
Rosenbaum, Richard D *OvPC*
Rosenbaum, Ron *InvJ*
Rosenberg, Adolphus *HisAmM XR*
Rosenberg, Alfred 1893-1946 *CurBio XR, LongC,*
  REn, WebBD
Rosenberg, Felix *HisAmM XR*
Rosenberg, Harold 1906-1978 *AmAu&B,*
  ConAu 21, Pen Am, WhoAm 1974,
  WhoAmA 1973, WhoWorJ 1972, WorAu
Rosenberg, Harold H 1882- *WhJnl 1928*
Rosenberg, James L 1898- *WhJnl 1928*
Rosenberg, Morris *NF*
Rosenberg, Shirley Sirota 1925- *ConAu 21R,*
  WhoAmW 1974
Rosenberger, William J 1889- *WhJnl 1928*
Rosenblatt, Fred 1914- *ConAu 41*
Rosenblatt, Joe 1933- *ConP 1970, ConP 1975,*
  OxCan Sup, WrDr 1976
Rosenblatt, Roger 1940- *NF*
Rosenblum, Mort 1943- *ConAu 73, OvPC*
Rosenblum, Robert *NF*
Rosenburg, John M 1918- *AuBYP, BioIn 7,*
  ConAu 23, OvPC, SmATA 6
Rosendale, Donald P *OvPC*
Rosenfeld, Albert Hyman 1920- *ConAu 65*
Rosenfeld, Alvin 1919- *ConAu 73, OvPC*
Rosenfeld, Arnold Solomon 1933- *ConAu 65,*
  WhoAm 1974
Rosenfeld, Harriet E *NF*
Rosenfeld, Harry Morris 1929- *ConAu 69,*
  NewMr
Rosenfeld, Paul Leopold 1890-1946 *AmAu&B,*
  CnDAL, CurBio XR, DcAmB S4, DcNAA,
  OxAm, REnAL, TwCA, TwCA Sup,
  WebBD, WhJnl 1928
Rosenfeld, Stephen S *NF*
Rosenfeld, Sydney 1855-1931 *BiDSA, DcNAA,*
  HisAmM XR
Rosenfield, Genie H *HisAmM XR*
Rosenfield, James A 1943- *ConAu 49*
Rosengarten, Isaac 1886-1961 *BioIn 5*
Rosenheim, Andrew *NF*
Rosenhouse, Harvey *BioIn 3*
Rosenkrantz, Linda 1934- *BioIn 8, ConAu 25*
Rosenkranz, Karl *HisAmM XR*
Rosenman, Daniel *OvPC*
Rosenmuller, Karel Frantisek *ForP*
Rosenthal, Abraham Michael 1922- *AmAu&B,*
  BioIn 5, BioIn 6, BioIn 7, ConAu 21R,
  CurBio XR, HisAmM XR, IntWW 1976,
  NewMr, WhoAm 1974, WhoE 1974,
  WhoF&I 1974
Rosenthal, Alan *NF*
Rosenthal, Edwin S 1914- *OvPC*
Rosenthal, Eric 1905- *Au&Wr, ConAu 9R*
Rosenthal, Harold 1914- *BioIn 2, WhoWorJ 1972*
Rosenthal, Harry Frederick 1927- *ConAu 65*
Rosenthal, Irving *NF*
Rosenthal, Jacob 1935- *WhoAm 1974,*
  WhoS&SW 1973
Rosenthal, Jaime *ForP*
Rosenthal, Jakob *NF*

Rosenthal, Joseph 1911- *AmJnl, ConAu 69,*
  CurBio XR, OvPC
Rosenthal, Julian 1879?-1948 *BioIn 1*
Rosenthal, Richard *OvPC*
Rosenthal, Ricky *NF*
Rosenthal, Roy G 1896- *WhJnl 1928,*
  WhoWorJ 1972
Rosenthal, Samuel M 1886- *WhJnl 1928*
Rosenzweig, David *InvJ*
Rosenzweig, Mark *NF*
Rosenzweig, Richard S *NF*
Rosewater, Charles Colman 1874?-1946 *BioIn 1*
Rosewater, Edward 1841-1906 *BioIn 10,*
  DcAmB 16
Rosewater, Victor 1871-1940 *AmAu&B, BioIn 4,*
  DcAmA, DcAmB S2, DcNAA, WhNAA
Rosin, Axel G 1907- *WhoAm 1974*
Rosinski, Herbert 1903-1962 *BioIn 6*
Roskolenko, Harry 1907- *BioIn 9, ConAu 13R,*
  WrDr 1976
Rosley, Henry W 1886- *WhJnl 1928*
Ross, Alan 1922- *Au&Wr, ConAu 11R,*
  ConP 1970, ConP 1975, LongC, ModBL,
  NewC, TwCA Sup, Who 1974, WrDr 1976
Ross, Albion 1906- *BioIn 4, DrAS 74E*
Ross, Alexander *NF*
Ross, Allan K 1898- *WhJnl 1928*
Ross, Betty *ConAu 69, ForWC 1970,*
  WhJnl 1928
Ross, Billy Irvan 1925- *AmM&W 73S,*
  ConAu 57, WhoAdv 1972, WhoAm 1974,
  WhoCon 1973, WhoS&SW 1973
Ross, Carl *AmRP*
Ross, Charles Griffith 1885-1950 *AmAu&B,*
  AmJnl, CurBio XR, DcAmB S4,
  NatCAB 42, WebBD
Ross, Colin 1885-1945 *BioIn 5*
Ross, Donald T *NF*
Ross, Edmund Gibson 1826-1907 *BioIn 2,*
  BioIn 4, BioIn 5, BioIn 7, DcAmB 16,
  DcNAA, OhA&B
Ross, Edward Alsworth 1866-1951 *AmAu&B,*
  AmLY, DcAmA, HisAmM XR, REnAL,
  WebBD, WhNAA, WisWr
Ross, Erle Franklin 1894- *WhJnl 1928*
Ross, Fred E 1913- *BioIn 3, BioIn 4*
Ross, George M 1822-1879 *NF*
Ross, Harold Wallace 1892-1951 *AmAu&B,*
  AmJnl, BioIn 1, BioIn 2, BioIn 3, BioIn 4,
  BioIn 5, BioIn 7, BioIn 8, CurBio XR,
  DcAmB S5, LongC, REn, REnAL
Ross, Hugh Munro 1870-1954 *BioIn 3*
Ross, Irwin *NF*
Ross, Ishbel 1897-1975 *AmAu&B, AmNov,*
  BioIn 1, ConAu 61, ForWC 1970
Ross, James Davidson 1924- *ConAu 49*
Ross, James M 1882- *WhJnl 1928*
Ross, Janet Anne Duff-Gordon 1842-1927 *Alli Sup,*
  WebBD
Ross, Ken *NF*
Ross, Lillian 1926- *AmAu&B, BioIn 6, BioIn 8,*
  BioIn 9, ConAu 11R, RAdv 1,
  WhoAm 1974, WorAu
Ross, Madeline Dane 1901?-1972 *BioIn 9,*
  ForWC 1970, NewYTBE 3
Ross, Morris M 1850-1915 *BioIn 2, IndAu 1816*
Ross, Nancy *see* DeRoin, Nancy
Ross, Philip 1939- *ConAu 69*
Ross, Philip Dansken 1858-1949 *BioIn 2, DcNAA,*
  WhJnl 1928
Ross, Robert B *NF*
Ross, Ruth N *BioIn 9, BlkC, ForWC 1970*
Ross, Stanley 1914- *OvPC, WhoAdv 1972,*

WhoAm 1974, WhoWor 1974
Ross, Thomas Bernard 1929- *ConAu 29, NewMr, RpN, WhoAm 1974, WhoS&SW 1973, WhoWor 1974*
Ross, Victor Harold 1878-1934 *DcNAA*
Ross-Duggan, John K 1890-1967 *BioIn 7*
Ross Williamson, Hugh 1901- *Au&Wr, ConAu 17R, IntWW 1976, LongC, Who 1974*
Rossa *see* O'Donovan, Jeremiah
Rosse, Joseph 1892?-1951 *BioIn 2*
Rossel, Marie-Therese Anne 1910- *IntWW 1976, WhoWor 1974*
Rosset, Barnet Lee, Jr. 1922- *CurBio XR, WhoAm 1974, WhoWor 1974*
Rossetti, Lucy *WebBD*
Rossi, Columbia *OvPC*
Rossi, Mario 1916- *ConAu 5R*
Rossi, Richard A *NF*
Rossie, M W *NF*
Rossiter, Al *NF*
Rossiter, Al, Jr. *NF*
Rossiter, E M 1890- *WhJnl 1928*
Rosskam, Charles A 1901- *WhJnl 1928*
Rosskam, Edwin *NF*
Rosso, Henry D *NF*
Rossoll, Harry *BioIn 9*
Rosten, Leo Calvin 1908- *AmAu&B, Au&Wr, ConAu 7R, ConNov 1972, ConNov 1976, CurBio XR, OxAm, Pen Am, REn, REnAL, TwCA, TwCA Sup, WhNAA, Who 1974, WhoAm 1974, WhoWor 1974, WhoWorJ 1972, WrDr 1976*
Rostock, Frank Witte 1882-1960 *BioIn 7, NatCAB 48, WhJnl 1928*
Roswell, Harold H *HisAmM XR*
Rotandaro, Fred *NF*
Roth, Andrew 1919- *Au&Wr, ConAu 53, WrDr 1976*
Roth, Arnold 1929- *ConAu 21R, WhoE 1974*
Roth, Ben 1909-1960 *BioIn 5*
Roth, Earl Ralph 1894- *WhJnl 1928*
Roth, Herb 1887?-1953 *BioIn 3*
Roth, Richard 1949- *NF*
Rotha, Paul 1907- *Au&Wr, ConAu 9, CurBio XR, IntMPA 1975, IntWW 1976, Who 1974, WhoWor 1974, WrDr 1976*
Rothacker, Wilheim 1828-1859 *BioIn 2*
Rothberg, Abraham 1922- *AmAu&B, ConAu 33, WhoAm 1974*
Rothberg, Donald M *NF*
Rothe, Emil 1826-1895 *BioIn 2*
Rothermere, Esmond C H, Viscount 1898-1978 *BioIn 1, CurBio XR, IntWW 1976, Who 1974*
Rothermere, Harold S H, Viscount 1868-1940 *BioIn 2, CurBio XR, LongC, Lor&LP, NewC*
Rothermere, Harold S H, Viscount *see also* Harmsworth, Harold S
Rothery, Agnes 1888-1952 *CurBio XR*
Rothkirch, Edward V *NF*
Rothman, Abraham Don 1896-1968 *BioIn 8*
Rothman, Benjamin 1897?-1973 *BioIn 10, NewYTBE 4*
Rothman, David *InvJ*
Rothschild, Alfred 1894?-1972 *ConAu 37*
Rothschild, Alonzo 1862-1915 *DcNAA*
Rothstein, Arthur 1915- *ConAu 57*
Rothstein, Ralph *NF*
Rothweiler, Paul Roger 1931- *ConAu 65*
Rothwell, Richard Pennefather 1836-1901 *DcAmA, DcNAA, HisAmM XR*
Rotkin, Charles E 1916- *ConAu 5, OvPC*

Rotteck, Carl *BioIn 2*
Rotter, Helen *BioIn 2*
Roudybush, Alexandra Brown 1911- *ConAu 65*
Roueche, Berton 1911- *AmAu&B, Au&Wr, BioIn 5, ConAu 2R, CurBio XR, DrAF 1976, REnAL, WhoAm 1974, WhoWor 1974*
Rougier, Michael *NF*
Rouiller, C A *HisAmM XR*
Roulston, Marjorie 1890-1971 *BioIn 9*
Roulstone, George *AmJnl*
Roumanille, Joseph 1818-1891 *BiD&SB, CasWL, CIDMEL, EuAu, OxFr, Pen Eur, REn, WebBD*
Round, William Marshall Fitts 1845-1906 *Alli Sup, AmAu&B, DcAmA, DcAmB 16, DcNAA*
Rounsavell, Nathaniel *AmJnl*
Rounseville, William R *HisAmM XR*
Rountree, Martha 1916- *CurBio XR*
Rountree, Maude McIver 1875- *AmAu&B, WhNAA*
Rourke, Remy 1885-1966 *BioIn 7*
Rourke, Violet B 1924- *NF*
Rous, John Henry 1912- *WhoAm 1974, WhoS&SW 1973*
Rouse, E S S 1795-1883 *Alli, HisAmM XR, OhA&B*
Rouson, John 1908?- *BioIn 2, BioIn 8*
Roussel, Claude 1919- *IntWW 1976*
Rousset, David 1912- *BioIn 4, BioIn 8, TwCA Sup*
Routh, Eugene Coke 1874- *BioIn 2*
Routh, James Edward 1879- *AmAu&B, HisAmM XR, WhNAA, WhJnl 1928*
Routh, Jonathan *BioIn 3, WrDr 1976*
Rovere, Richard Halworth 1915- *AmAu&B, AmRP, BioIn 2, BioIn 4, BioIn 8, ConAu 49, ForP, NewMr, OxAm, REnAL, WhoAm 1974, WhoWor 1974*
Rowan, Carl Thomas 1925- *AmAu&B, BioIn 2, BioIn 4, BioIn 5, BioIn 6, BioIn 7, BioIn 8, BioIn 9, BioIn 10, BlkC, CurBio XR, LivBAA, Who 1974, WhoAm 1974, WhoAmP 1973, WhoS&SW 1973, WhoWor 1974*
Rowan, Charles T *NF*
Rowan, Ford 1943- *ConAu 69, InvJ*
Rowan, Helen 1926?-1972 *BioIn 9, ConAu 37, NewYTBE 3*
Rowan, James *AmRP*
Rowan, Roy *NF*
Rowe, Clifford G *NF*
Rowe, George H *NF*
Rowe, Gilbert Theodore 1875-1965 *HisAmM XR, WhNAA*
Rowe, H E C 1902- *WhJnl 1928*
Rowe, Henry Theodore 1906-1974 *BioIn 10*
Rowe, James Lester, Jr. 1948- *ConAu 69*
Rowe, Josiah P, Jr. *WhJnl 1928*
Rowe, Percy *NF*
Rowe, Viola Carson *AuBYP, BioIn 7, ConAu 1*
Rowell, Chester Harvey 1867-1948 *BioIn 1, CurBio XR, DcAmB S4, HisAmM XR*
Rowell, George Presbury 1838-1908 *AmAu&B, AmJnl, DcNAA, HisAmM XR*
Rowell, Henry Thompson 1904-1974 *BioIn 9, ConAu 13, ConAu P-1, WhoWor 1974*
Rowen, Hobart 1918- *ConAu 11R, OvPC, WhoAm 1974, WhoF&I 1974, WhoS&SW 1973*
Rowland, Hardy 1908?- *BioIn 1*
Rowland, Helen 1875-1950 *AmAu&B, REnAL, WhJnl 1928*
Rowland, Henry Cottrell 1874-1933 *AmAu&B,*

DcNAA, HisAmM XR
Rowland, Stanley J, Jr. 1928- *BioIn 5,
ConAu 13R*
Rowlands, Marvin Lloyd, Jr. 1926- *WhoAm 1974*
Rowley, Anthony 1939- *ConAu 61*
Rowley, Claude Arthur 1882-1945 *BioIn 2,
NatCAB 34*
Rowley, Frank E 1869-1913 *NatCAB 16*
Rowley, Louis Napoleon, Jr. 1909- *BioIn 7,
WhoAm 1974*
Rowley, Peter 1934- *ConAu 65*
Rowse, Arthur E 1926- *OvPC*
Rowson, Richard Cavanagh 1926- *AmEA 1974,
AmM&W 73S, OvPC*
Rowson, Susanna 1762-1824 *HisAmM XR,
WebBD*
Roxon, Lillian 1933?-1973 *BioIn 8, BioIn 10,
NewYTBE 1, NewYTBE 4*
Roy, Basanta Koomar d1949 *BioIn 1, BioIn 2*
Roy, M N *AmRP*
Roy, Malcolm Miller 1888-1960 *BioIn 5*
Roy, Michael 1913-1976 *ConAu 65*
Roy, Michel *NF*
Roy, S G *NF*
Royal, Anne 1769-1854 *AmJnl, HisAmM XR*
Royal, Anne *see also* Royall, Anne Newport
Royal, John F D 1887?-1978 *NF*
Royal, Joseph 1837-1902 *BbtC, DcNAA, OxCan*
Royall, Anne Newport 1769-1854 *Alli, AmAu,
AmAu&B, BiDSA, BioIn 3, BioIn 4,
BioIn 5, BioIn 7, BioIn 8, BioIn 9,
BioIn 10, DcAmA, DcLEL, DcNAA,
EncAB, HisAmM XR, OxAm, REnAL*
Royall, Anne Newport *see also* Royal, Anne
Royall, John Mabry 1873- *WhJnl 1928*
Royce, Knut *InvJ*
Royer, Charles *NF*
Royer, John S *HisAmM XR*
Royko, Mike 1932- *BioIn 7, WhoAm 1974,
WhoMW 1974*
Royle, John C 1878- *WhJnl 1928*
Roys-Gavit, E M *HisAmM XR*
Royse, Pat *NF*
Royster, Vermont Connecticut 1914- *AmAu&B,
BioIn 1, BioIn 3, BioIn 7, BioIn 8, BioIn 9,
ConAu 21R, CurBio XR, IntWW 1974,
WhoAm 1974, WhoS&SW 1973, WrDr 1976*
Rozanov, Igor *NF*
Ruark, Robert Chester 1915-1965 *AmAu&B,
BioIn 1, BioIn 2, BioIn 3, BioIn 4, BioIn 5,
BioIn 6, BioIn 7*
Rubattel, Rodolphe 1896-1961 *CurBio XR*
Rubens, Doris *BioIn 1*
Rubicam, Harry Cogswell, Jr. 1902- *AuBYP,
BioIn 7, ConAu 17*
Rubicam, Marian *NF*
Rubin, Jacob A 1910-1972 *ConAu 37,
ConAu P-1, NewYTBE 3*
Rubin, James H 1947?- *NF*
Rubin, Jerry 1938- *AmAu&B, ConAu 69*
Rubin, Louis Decimus, Jr. 1923- *ConAu 1,
DrAS 74E, HisAmM XR, WhoAm 1974*
Rubin, Morris Harold 1911- *WhoAm 1974*
Rubinstein, Martin *NF*
Ruble, Paul E 1926?- *NF*
Rublee, Horace 1829-1896 *Alli, BioIn 5*
Rubner, Alex *NF*
Ruby, Harold Austin 1899- *WhJnl 1928*
Ruby, Michael A 1943?- *NF*
Rucher, L V B 1882- *WhJnl 1928*
Rucker, Bryce Wilson 1921- *ConAu 11R,
DrAS 74E*
Rucker, Frank Warren 1886- *ConAu 4R,
WhJnl 1928*

Rudd, Arthur S *WhJnl 1928*
Rudd, Augustin Goelet 1890?-1968 *BioIn 8*
Rudd, Basil Gordon 1890- *WhJnl Sup*
Rudd, Hughes Day 1921- *AmAu&B, BioIn 7,
BioIn 10, BioNews 1974, ConAu 73,
WhoAm 1974*
Rudder, Virginia L 1941- *ConAu 65*
Ruddy, Howard Shaw 1856-1922 *DcNAA*
Ruder, Melvin Harvey 1915- *BioIn 9,
WhoAm 1974, WhoWest 1974*
Rudin, Ellen *BioIn 6*
Rudin, John 1876-1954 *NatCAB 43*
Rudis, Al *NF*
Rudman, Kal *BioIn 9*
Rudnitsky, Howard *NF*
Rudolf, Anthony 1942- *Au&Wr, ConAu 61,
WrDr 1976*
Rudy, Ann *NF*
Rudy, William H *NF*
Rudyard, Charlotte *AmAu&B, HisAmM XR*
Rue, Lars 1893?-1965 *BioIn 7*
Ruecker, A 1884- *WhJnl 1928*
Rufa, Robert H *NF*
Ruff, Eric *NF*
Ruff, G Elson 1904- *AmAu&B*
Ruff, John Dougherty 1859- *WhJnl 1928*
Ruffin, Edmund 1794-1865 *Alli, AmAu&B,
BiDSA, DcNAA, HisAmM XR, WebBD*
Ruffner, Josa Morgan *OvPC*
Ruffner, Mary *NF*
Rugaber, Walter *NF*
Ruge, Arnold 1803-1880 *BiD&SB, WebBD*
Ruggles, David *BlkC*
Rugile, Paul *OvPC*
Ruhe, Percy B 1881- *WhJnl 1928*
Ruhen, Olaf 1911- *Au&Wr, ConAu 1R,
WrDr 1976*
Ruhl, Arthur Brown 1876-1935 *AmAu&B, AmLY,
DcAmB S1, DcNAA, HisAmM XR*
Ruhl, Robert Waldo 1880-1967 *BioIn 8*
Ruhle, Otto *AmRP*
Ruiz DeElvira, Maria D *NF*
Rukeyser, Louis 1933- *ConAu 65*
Rukeyser, Merryle Stanley 1897-1974 *ConAu 23,
WhoAm 1974, WhJnl 1928, WhoWorJ 1972*
Rukeyser, Merryle Stanley, Jr. 1931-
WhoAm 1974
Rukeyser, William Simon 1939- *ConAu 69,
WhoAm 1974, WhoWor 1974*
Rule, Elton H 1917- *WhoAm 1974,
WhoF&I 1974*
Rule, William 1839- *WhJnl 1928*
Rumiantsev, Aleksey Matveyevich 1905-
IntWW 1976
Rumley, Larry *NF*
Rummell, Leo Leavitt 1893- *WhJnl Sup*
Runde, Fred J 1887-1965 *BioIn 7, WhJnl 1928*
Rundell, Oliver S 1881- *WhJnl 1928*
Rundle, Walter G 1906?- *BioIn 1, RpN*
Rundt, Arthur 1881- *NF*
Runes, Dagobert David 1902- *AmAu&B,
ConAu 25, WhoAm 1974, WhoWorJ 1972*
Runge, David August 1912- *WhoAm 1974*
Runnells, David Leslie 1893- *WhJnl 1928*
Runnion, Ray 1898- *WhJnl 1928*
Runyon, Alfred Damon *see* Runyon, Damon
Runyon, Alfred Milton 1905- *WhoAm 1974*
Runyon, Damon 1884?-1946 *AmAu&B, AmJnl,
BioIn 1, BioIn 2, BioIn 3, BioIn 4, BioIn 5,
BioIn 7, BioIn 8, CasWL, CnDAL,
CnMAL, CurBio XR, DcAmB S4, DcLEL,
DcNAA, EncMys, EvLB, HisAmM XR,
LongC, ModAL, ModWD, NatCAB 39,
OxAm, Pen Am, REn, REnAL, TwCA,*

TwCA Sup, TwCW, WebBD, WebE&AL
Runyon, John William 1887-1967 *BioIn 7*
Rupe, William S 1886-1959 *NatCAB 46*
Rupley, David Besore 1895- *WhJnl 1928*
Rupp, Carla Marie *NF*
Rupp, Werner Andrew 1880-1963 *BioIn 9*
Rupp, William 1839-1904 *HisAmM XR*
Ruppel, Louis 1903-1958 *BioIn 1, BioIn 4, HisAmM XR*
Ruppius, Otto 1819-1864 *BioIn 2, CasWL, OxGer*
Rusch, Dave 1936?- *BioIn 5*
Ruse, Harold Jesse 1897- *WhJnl 1928*
Rusher, William Allen 1923- *WhoAm 1974, WhoE 1974, WrDr 1976*
Rushmore, Howard 1912-1958 *BioIn 4, BioIn 5*
Rusk, Ralph Leslie 1888-1962 *AmAu&B, ConAu 5, LiJA, REnAL*
Ruskin, Elinor *NF*
Russ, Lavinia 1904- *BioIn 9, ConAu 25*
Russel, Alexander 1814-1876 *Alli, DcEnL*
Russel, J S *NF*
Russell, Addison Peale 1826-1912 *Alli Sup, AmAu&B, BiD&SB, DcAmA, DcNAA, NatCAB 6, OhA&B*
Russell, Andrew J *NF*
Russell, Arthur Joseph 1861- *AmAu&B, WhJnl 1928*
Russell, Benjamin 1761-1845 *Alli, AmAu&B, AmJnl, DcAmB 16*
Russell, Bruce Alexander 1903?-1963 *BioIn 6*
Russell, Cecilia Marie 1907?-1950 *BioIn 2*
Russell, Charles Edward 1860-1941 *AmAu&B, AmJnl, AmLY, AmRP, CurBio XR, DcAmA, DcAmB S3, DcNAA, HisAmM XR, NatCAB XR, OxAm, REnAL, TwCA, TwCA Sup, WebBD, WhNAA*
Russell, Charles Taze 1852-1916 *AmAu&B, DcNAA, HisAmM XR, WebBD*
Russell, Don 1899- *ConAu 2R*
Russell, E F *HisAmM XR*
Russell, Edwin F 1914- *WhoAm 1974*
Russell, Elijah *HisAmM XR*
Russell, Ernest *HisAmM XR*
Russell, Eugene Howard 1893- *WhJnl 1928*
Russell, Ezekiel *HisAmM XR*
Russell, Foster Meharry *BioIn 7*
Russell, Frank Alden 1908- *BioIn 1*
Russell, Frank J 1880- *WhJnl 1928*
Russell, Fred 1906- *BioIn 2, BioIn 4*
Russell, George H 1871- *WhJnl 1928*
Russell, George William 1867-1935 *AtlBL, CasWL, DcLEL, EncWL, EvLB, HisAmM XR, LongC, McGWD, ModBL, ModWD, NewC, OxEng, PoIre, REn, TwCA, TwCA Sup, WebBD, WebE&AL*
Russell, Henry Benajah 1859-1945 *AmAu&B, DcAmA, DcNAA, WhNAA, WhJnl 1928*
Russell, J Stuart 1892-1960 *NF*
Russell, J T *HisAmM XR*
Russell, Jacob *HisAmM XR*
Russell, James Webster, Jr. 1921- *WhoAm 1974*
Russell, John *HisAmM XR, LiJA*
Russell, John 1885-1956 *AmAu&B, EncMys, REnAL, TwCA*
Russell, John 1919- *Au&Wr, ConAu 13R*
Russell, John Andrew 1865-1936 *DcNAA*
Russell, John B *HisAmM XR*
Russell, Lucius T 1870?-1948 *BioIn 1*
Russell, Mark *NF*
Russell, Martin 1934- *Au&Wr, ConAu 73, WrDr 1976*
Russell, Martin J 1845- *NatCAB 10*

Russell, Mary A *NF*
Russell, Mary S *NF*
Russell, Morris Craw 1840-1913 *DcNAA*
Russell, Peggy *NF*
Russell, Phillips 1884- *AmAu&B, BioIn 3, BioIn 4, WhNAA*
Russell, Ray 1924- *ConAu 3R, WhoWest 1974, WrDr 1976*
Russell, W A *NF*
Russell, Walter 1871-1963 *AmAu&B, AmLY, HisAmM XR, WhNAA*
Russell, William 1798-1873 *Alli, DcAmA, DcNAA, HisAmM XR*
Russell, William Clark 1844-1911 *Alli Sup, BbD, BiD&SB, BrAu 19, CyWA, DcBiA, DcEnA, DcEnA Ap, DcLEL, EncMys, EvLB, HisAmM XR, NewC, OxEng, REn, WhoChL*
Russell, Sir William Howard 1820-1907 *Alli, Alli Sup, BbD, BbtC, BiD&SB, BioIn 2, BioIn 3, BioIn 6, BioIn 9, BrAu 19, DcEnA, DcEnA Ap, DcEnL, EvLB, FamWC, ForP, NewC, OxEng, REn, REnAL, WebBD*
Russwurm, John Brown 1799-1851 *AmJnl, BioIn 7, BioIn 8, BioIn 9, BlkC, ForP*
Rust, George W *HisAmM XR*
Rust, Samuel *AmJnl*
Rust, William 1903-1949 *BioIn 1*
Rustin, Bayard 1910- *AmRP, ConAu 53, CurBio XR, LivBAA, WebBD, WhoAm 1974, WhoWor 1974*
Ruston, Perry Lounsbery 1906- *WhoAm 1974*
Rutberg, Sidney 1924- *ConAu 69*
Ruth, Charles H 1889- *WhJnl 1928*
Ruth, Philippa *NF*
Ruthenberg, Charles E *AmRP*
Rutherford, Rutledge *HisAmM XR*
Ruthnaswamy, Mariadas 1885- *BioIn 3, CathA 1952*
Rutland, Robert Allen 1922- *ConAu 45, DrAS 74H, WhoAm 1974*
Rutledge, Gordon 1886- *WhJnl 1928*
Rutledge, Joseph Lister 1883-1957 *BioIn 4, WhNAA*
Rutledge, Peter *NF*
Rutman, Laurence 1906- *WhoAm 1974*
Rutt, Christian Ludwig 1859-1937 *DcNAA*
Rutter, Frank *NF*
Rutter, Owen 1889-1944 *NewC, WebBD, WhoLA*
Ruttkay, Georg 1890-1955 *BioIn 4*
Ruyerson, James Paul 1931- *ConAu XR*
Ruzic, Neil Pierce 1930- *ConAu 17R, WhoAdv 1972, WhoAm 1974, WhoF&I 1974, WhoWor 1974*
Ryall, George Francis Trafford 1888- *WhJnl 1928*
Ryan, Barbara Haddad *NF*
Ryan, Bill *NF*
Ryan, Bob 1946- *ConAu 49*
Ryan, Calvin T 1888- *WhJnl 1928*
Ryan, Claude 1925- *CanWW 1972, OxCan Sup, WhoE 1974, WhoWor 1974*
Ryan, Clendenin J *HisAmM XR*
Ryan, Cornelius John 1920-1974 *BioIn 2, BioIn 7, ConAu 53, ConAu 69, OvPC, Who 1974, WhoAm 1974, WhoE 1974, WhoWor 1974*
Ryan, Frank H 1889?-1954 *BioIn 3*
Ryan, George Benedict 1879-1951 *BioIn 2, WhJnl 1928*
Ryan, Guy *NF*
Ryan, Jennifer Q 1952- *NF*
Ryan, John Barry 1900?-1966 *BioIn 7*
Ryan, Joseph J 1910?-1976 *ConAu 69*

Ryan, Leo A 1889- *WhJnl 1928*
Ryan, Marsha *NF*
Ryan, Paddy *HisAmM XR*
Ryan, Richard A *NF*
Ryan, Samuel 1824-1907 *BioIn 5*
Ryan, Steve *NF*
Ryan, Ted *NF*
Ryan, Thomas Kenneth 1905- *WhoAm 1974*
Ryan, Thomas Stewart *NF*
Ryan, William Lawrence 1911- *WhoAm 1974,*
   WhoWor 1974
Ryang, Chol Yong *NF*
Ryckman, Charles Silcott 1898- *BioIn 5,*
   WhJnl 1928
Ryckman, J H *AmRP*
Ryckman, John W *HisAmM XR*
Rydell, Wendy 1927- *BioIn 9, ConAu 33,*
   SmATA 4, WrDr 1976
Ryder, George Conklin 1920- *WhoAm 1974*
Ryder, John Maxim 1899- *WhJnl 1928*
Ryder, Robert Oliver 1875-1936 *BioIn 2, DcNAA,*
   OhA&B, WhJnl 1928
Ryder, William Hering *HisAmM XR*
Ryerson, Adolphus Egerton 1803-1882 *BbtC,*
   DcNAA, WebBD
Ryffle, Robert *InvJ*
Rygg, Andrew Nilsen 1868-1951 *BioIn 1, BioIn 2*
Ryland, Cally Thomas *AmAu&B*
Ryle, Gilbert 1900-1976 *Au&Wr, ConAu 73,*
   IntWW 1974, LongC, OxEng, Who 1974,
   WhoWor 1974, WorAu, WrDr 1976
Ryskind, Morrie 1895- *AmAu&B, BiE&WWA,*
   ConDr, IntMPA 1975, ModWD, WebBD,
   WhNAA, WhoWorJ 1972
Ryu, Shintaro 1901?-1967 *BioIn 8*

S

Saab, Edouard 1929-1976 *ConAu 65*
Saal, Hubert *NF*
Saarinen, Aline Bernstein Louchheim 1914-1972
  *AmAu&B, BioIn 7, BioIn 9, BioIn 10,
  ConAu 37, CurBio XR, NewYTBE 3,
  WhoGov 1972*
Sabban, Roberta *NF*
Saben, Mowry 1870-1950 *BioIn 2*
Sabharwal, Pran *NF*
Sabin, Francene *ConAu 69*
Sabin, Joseph 1821-1881 *Alli, Alli Sup, AmAu,
  AmAu&B, BbD, BiD&SB, DcAmA,
  DcNAA, HisAmM XR, REnAL, WebBD*
Sabin, Louis 1930- *ConAu 69*
Sabine, Gordon *NF*
Sabol, Blair 1947- *NF*
Sabry, Zak *NF*
Sacher, Harry *NF*
Sachs, Moshe Y *NF*
Sachs, Sylvia *WhoAmW 1974*
Sack, A J *HisAmM XR*
Sack, John 1930- *BioIn 7, ConAu 21R,
  WhoE 1974*
Sack, Leo R 1889-1956 *NF*
Sackett, Leland Russell, Jr. 1923- *WhoAm 1974*
Sackett, Russell *NewMr*
Sackett, Sheldon Fred 1902-1968 *BioIn 1, BioIn 8*
Sackett, William Edgar 1848-1926 *DcNAA*
Sacks, Jack *NF*
Saco, Ken *BioIn 8*
Sadak, Necmeddin 1890-1953 *BioIn 1, BioIn 2,
  BioIn 3, CurBio XR*
Sadanand, Swaminathan 1900-1953 *BioIn 3*
Sadd, H S *HisAmM XR*
Saddler, Owen Leslie 1911- *WhoAm 1974*
Sadovy, John *NF*
Saen, H *NF*
Saenger, Gustav 1865-1935 *AmSCAP 1966,
  BioIn 1*
Saerchinger, Cesar Victor Charles 1884-1971
  AmAu&B, WebBD
Saez, Juan V *RpN*
Safer, Morley 1931- *AuNews 2, BioIn 8,
  BioIn 10, InvJ, WhoAm 1974*
Saffer, Rex 1900- *WhJnl 1928*
Saffir, Leonard *OvPC*
Safford, Harold Arthur 1897- *WhJnl 1928*
Safire, William L 1929- *BioIn 9, BioIn 10,
  ConAu 19R, CurBio XR, NewYTBE 4,
  WhoAm 1974*
Safran, Claire 1930- *ForWC 1970,
  WhoAm 1974, WhoAmW 1974*
Safran, Don *NF*
Sagan, Bruce 1928?- *BioIn 4*
Sagar, Easwar *NF*
Sage, Bob *NF*

Sage, Bruce Hornbrook 1909- *BioIn 7*
Sage, James A *WhJnl 1928*
Sagendorf, Bud *NF*
Sagendorph, Robb Hansell 1900-1970 *AmAu&B,
  ConAu 7R, ConAu 29, CurBio XR*
Sager, Lois *RpN*
Saginer, Jean O 1907- *NF*
Sagnier, Thierry 1946- *ConAu 53*
Sahanek, Tatana *BioIn 10*
Said, Ahmed *BioIn 5*
Saikowski, Charlotte *WhoAmW 1974*
Sainer, Arthur 1924- *ConAu 49, ConDr,
  WrDr 1976*
Sainsbury, Frances *NF*
St. Clair, Victor 1851-1930 *Alli Sup, DcNAA*
St. Clair, Victor *see also* Browne, George Waldo
St. Denis, Walter 1877-1947 *BioIn 1*
St. George, Andrew *NF*
St. John, Jeffrey *NF*
St. John, John Pierce *HisAmM XR*
St. John, Robert 1902- *AmAu&B, Au&Wr,
  BioIn 1, BioIn 3, BioIn 4, BioIn 5,
  ConAu 2R, CurBio XR, WhoAm 1974,
  WhoWor 1974, WrDr 1976*
St. John, Samuel 1813-1876 *Alli, DcNAA,
  HisAmM XR*
St. John, Tracy *NF*
St. John, Wylly Folk 1908- *ConAu 21R,
  ForWC 1970, SmATA 10, WhoAmW 1974,
  WrDr 1976*
St. Johns, Adela Rogers 1894- *AmAu&B,
  AuNews 1, BioIn 8, CelR 1973,
  ForWC 1970, WhoAm 1974,
  WhoAmW 1974, WrDr 1976*
Saint-Marc Girardin, Francois Auguste 1801-1873
  BbD, BiD&SB, OxFr, WebBD
St. Michel, Jean-Paul *NF*
St. Pierre, Telesphore 1869-1912 *DcNAA*
Sainte-Beuve, Charles Augustin 1804-1869 *AtlBL,
  BbD, BiD&SB, CasWL, CyWA, DcEnL,
  DcEuL, EuAu, EvEuW, LiJA, NewC,
  OxEng, OxFr, Pen Eur, RComWL, REn,
  WebBD*
Saintsbury, George Edward Bateman 1845-1933
  *Alli Sup, AtlBL, BbD, BiD&SB, DcEnA,
  DcEnA Ap, DcLEL, EvLB, HisAmM XR,
  LongC, ModBL, NewC, OxEng, Pen Eng,
  RAdv 1, TwCA, TwCA Sup, WebBD*
Saito, Eiichi 1910- *IntWW 1976*
Saito, Hiroyuki 1917- *ConAu 61*
Saito, Torao d1971 *BioIn 9*
Sajous, Charles Euchariste DeMedicis 1852-1929
  *Alli Sup, DcAmA, DcNAA, HisAmM XR,
  WebBD, WhNAA*
Sakai, Toshio *NF*
Sakdalan, Frank *NF*

Sakler, Ernesto *NF*
Saksena, Mary Madge *NF*
Sala, George Augustus Henry 1828-1895 *Alli,*
Alli Sup, BbD, BiD&SB, BrAu 19, CasWL,
DcEnA, DcEnA Ap, DcEnL, DcEuL,
DcLEL, EvLB, FamWC, HisAmM XR,
NewC, OxEng, REn, REnAL, WebBD
Sala, John 1879?-1954 *BioIn 3*
Salamoun, Jiri 1935- *BioIn 10*
Salant, Richard S 1914- *CurBio XR,*
IntMPA 1975, WhoAm 1974
Salas, Jack *NF*
Salazar, Fanny Zampini *NF*
Salazar, Ralph *OvPC*
Salazar, Ruben 1928-1970 *BioIn 8, BioIn 9,*
WhoS&SW 1973
Salcedo, Jose Joaquin *ForP*
Salditch, Martin *NF*
Sale, Kirkpatrick 1937- *ConAu 13R*
Salinger, Herman 1905- *AmAu&B, ConAu 13,*
ConAu P-1, DrAS 74F, HisAmM XR,
WhoAm 1974, WhoWor 1974, WrDr 1976
Salinger, Pierre Emil George 1925- *BioIn 5,*
BioIn 6, BioIn 7, BioIn 8, ConAu 19R,
CurBio XR, IntWW 1976, WhoAm 1974,
WhoAmP 1973, WhoS&SW 1973,
WhoWor 1974
Salisbury, Dorothy 1891?-1976 *ConAu 69*
Salisbury, Harrison Evans 1908- *AmAu&B,*
Au&Wr, BioIn 3, BioIn 4, BioIn 5,
BioIn 6, BioIn 7, CelR 1973, ConAu 2R,
CurBio XR, IntWW 1976, MnnWr, NewMr,
REnAL, Who 1974, WhoAm 1974,
WhoE 1974, WhoWor 1974, WorAu,
WrDr 1976
Salisbury, Morse 1898- *WhJnl 1928*
Salisbury, Philip 1892?-1967 *BioIn 8*
Sallans, George Herbert *BioIn 1, CanNov,*
OxCan, WhJnl 1928
Salley, D Bruce *NF*
Sallows, Ben J 1888?-1950 *BioIn 2*
Salmans, Sandra *NF*
Salmon, Clarke 1889- *WhJnl 1928*
Salmon, Lucy Maynard 1853-1927 *AmAu&B,*
DcAmA, DcNAA
Salmon, Robert 1918- *IntWW 1976,*
WhoWor 1974
Salmona, Stelio 1928?-1973 *BioIn 10*
Saloman, M I *NF*
Salomon, Erich 1886-1944 *BioIn 10*
Salpeter, Harry *NF*
Salsberg, Arthur P 1929- *NF*
Salsinger, H G 1887-1958 *NF*
Salto, Ivan *NF*
Saltonstall, Richard, Jr. 1937- *ConAu 33*
Saltus, Francis Saltus *HisAmM XR*
Saltus, Freeman M 1866-1950 *BioIn 2*
Saltz, Donald *NF*
Saltzberg, Geraldine 1892?-1972 *BioIn 9,*
NewYTBE 3
Saluson, Harold Whiting *HisAmM XR*
Salutsky, J B *AmRP*
Salzano, Carlo J *NF*
Salzberg, Louis 1929?- *BioIn 8*
Salzman, Alexander E *OvPC*
Salzman, Ed 1931- *NF*
Samalman, Alexander 1904-1956 *WhJnl 1928*
Samayoa Chinchilla, Carlos 1898- *IntWW 1974*
Sambourne, Edward Linley 1844-1910 *WebBD*
Sammis, Fred Rutledge 1912- *WhoAm 1974*
Sammons, Robert *NF*
Sammons, Wheeler 1889- *WhJnl 1928*
Samonisky, Harris 1895- *WhJnl 1928*
Samovitz, Fannie 1900- *WhJnl 1928*

Sample, James *NF*
Sample, Joseph Scanlon 1923- *WhoAm 1974,*
WhoWest 1974
Sampson, Anthony 1926- *ConAu 1R,*
IntWW 1976, Who 1974, WhoWor 1974
Sampson, Lewis D *HisAmM XR*
Samra, Cal 1931- *ConAu 37*
Samson, Henry T 1897- *WhJnl 1928*
Samson, Jack *NF*
Samson, John G *RpN*
Samuels, Arthur H 1888-1938 *HisAmM XR*
Samuels, Charles 1902- *ConAu 4R*
Samuels, Gertrude *AuBYP, BioIn 7,*
ConAu 11R, ForWC 1970, WhoWorJ 1972
Sanborn, Alvan Francis 1866-1966 *AmAu&B,*
AmLY, DcAmA
Sanborn, Cyrus Ashton Rollins 1882-1970 *BioIn 10*
Sanborn, Edward H *HisAmM XR*
Sanborn, Franklin Benjamin 1831-1917 *Alli Sup,*
AmAu, AmAu&B, BioIn 8, DcAmA,
DcAmB 16, DcNAA, HisAmM XR, OxAm,
REnAL, WebBD
Sanborn, John Bell 1876- *WhJnl 1928*
Sanborn, Pitts 1879?-1941 *AmAu&B,*
CurBio XR, DcNAA, TwCA
Sanborn, Walter Lyman 1879- *WhJnl 1928*
Sanburn, Richard Louis 1912- *WhoAm 1974,*
WhoWest 1974
Sanche, DeReneau 1884- *WhJnl 1928*
Sanchez, Blas *NF*
Sanchez, Florencio 1875-1910 *CasWL, CnThe,*
CyWA, DcSpL, McGWD, ModWD,
Pen Am
Sanchez, Robert C *BioIn 2*
Sanchez-Silva, Jose Maria 1911- *ConAu 73,*
ThrBJA
Sancton, John William 1919?- *BioIn 1*
Sancton, Thomas *HisAmM XR, RpN*
Sand, Edward Austin 1911- *WhoAm 1974*
Sandburg, Carl 1878-1967 *AmAu&B,*
AmSCAP 1966, AmWr, AnCL, AtlBL,
AuBYP, CasWL, CnDAL, CnE&AP,
CnMWL, ConAmA, ConAmL, ConAu 7R,
ConAu 25, ConLC 1, ConLC 4, CurBio XR,
CyWA, DcLEL, EncAB, EncWL, EvLB,
HisAmM XR, LongC, ModAL, ModAL Sup,
OxAm, OxEng, Pen Am, RAdv 1, REn,
REnAL, SixAP, SmATA 8, Str&VC,
TwCA, TwCA Sup, TwCW, WebBD,
WebE&AL, WhoTwCL, WisWr
Sandel, Ardis 1921- *OvPC, WhoAm 1974*
Sander, Ellen 1944- *ConAu 41, WhoAmW 1974*
Sanders, Allison 1902- *WhoS&SW 1973*
Sanders, Alvin Howard 1860- *HisAmM XR,*
WhJnl 1928
Sanders, Charles L *NF*
Sanders, Cora Francis *HisAmM XR*
Sanders, Daniel 1819-1897 *WebBD* ‧
Sanders, Donald *NF*
Sanders, George N 1812-1873 *HisAmM XR*
Sanders, Jacquin 1922- *ConAu 3R*
Sanders, James Harvey 1832-1899 *DcNAA,*
HisAmM XR, OhA&B
Sanders, Lawrence *BioIn 8*
Sanders, Leonard Marion, Jr. 1929- *ConAu 11R,*
WhoAm 1974
Sanders, Marion K 1905-1977 *ConAu 33,*
ConAu 73, ForWC 1970
Sanders, Marlene 1931- *ConAu 65, ForWC 1970*
Sanders, Ronald 1932- *ConAu 23, WhoAm 1974,*
WrDr 1976
Sanders, Sol 1926- *ConAu 49*
Sanders, William Willard 1930- *BioIn 9,*
WhoAm 1974

Sanderson, Albert *HisAmM XR*
Sanderson, George Alfred 1906-1959 *BioIn 5*
Sanderson, Harvey D 1901- *WhJnl 1928*
Sanderson, John 1783-1844 *Alli, AmAu,
    AmAu&B, CyAL 1, DcAmA, DcNAA,
    HisAmM XR, OxAm, REnAL*
Sanderson, Uluth Mitchell, Jr. 1900- *WhJnl 1928*
Sandes, John 1863-1938 *BioIn 2, PoIre*
Sandeson, William Seymour 1913- *WhoAm 1974*
Sandgren, John *AmRP*
Sandison, George *NF*
Sandler, Irving 1925- *ConAu 29*
Sandoval, Richard C *NF*
Sandrof, Ivan 1912?-1979 *BioIn 10*
Sands, Frank E 1863-1951 *BioIn 2, WhJnl 1928*
Sands, Robert Charles 1799-1832 *Alli, AmAu,
    AmAu&B, BioIn 1, CyAL 2, DcAmA,
    DcAmB 16, DcLEL, DcNAA, EvLB,
    HisAmM XR, OxAm, REnAL, WebBD*
Sands, Samuel *HisAmM XR*
Sands, William *HisAmM XR*
Sands, William B *HisAmM XR*
Sandwell, Bernard Keble 1876-1954 *BioIn 2,
    BioIn 3, BioIn 4, CanWr, DcLEL, OxCan*
Sandy, Dick *NF*
Sandys, Edwyn William 1860-1909 *DcNAA,
    HisAmM XR*
Sanford, Arthur B *HisAmM XR*
Sanford, David Boyer 1943- *HisAmM XR,
    WhoAm 1974*
Sanford, Graham 1876- *WhJnl 1928*
Sanford, Harold Williams 1890-1950 *BioIn 2*
Sanford, John *AmRP*
Sanford, Leda 1934- *ConAu 65*
Sanford, Steadman Vincent 1871- *AmLY,
    WhNAA, WhJnl 1928*
Sanford, Thomas K, Jr. 1921-1977 *ConAu 73*
Sanford, Vernon Todd 1905- *WhJnl 1928*
Sang, Paul 1914- *ConAu 13R*
Sanger, Arthur E *AmRP*
Sanger, Fritz Paul 1901- *IntWW 1976,
    WhoWor 1974*
Sanger, George Partridge 1819-1890 *Alli, BioIn 3*
Sanger, Joseph P 1840-1926 *HisAmM XR*
Sanger, Margaret 1883-1966 *AmAu&B,
    CurBio XR, EncAB, HisAmM XR, LongC,
    OxAm*
Sanger, Richard Paulett 1930- *BioIn 9,
    WhoAm 1974, WhoE 1974*
Sangster, Charles 1822-1893 *Alli, BbtC,
    BiD&SB, BrAu 19, CanWr, DcLEL,
    DcNAA, OxCan, REn, REnAL, WebE&AL*
Sangster, Margaret Elizabeth 1894?- *AmAu&B,
    WebBD*
Sangster, Margaret Elizabeth Munson 1838-1912
    *Alli Sup, AmAu, AmAu&B, BbD, BiD&SB,
    DcAmA, DcNAA, HisAmM XR, REnAL,
    WebBD*
Sanial, Lucien 1836-1927 *DcNAA, HisAmM XR*
Sankaran Nair, Sir Chettur 1857-1934 *WebBD*
Sann, Paul 1914- *AmAu&B, Au&Wr,
    ConAu 13, WhoAm 1974, WhoE 1974*
Sansom, Art *NF*
Sanson, Kenneth Dudley, Jr. 1932- *WhoAm 1974*
Sansone, Sam *NF*
Sansoucy, Arthur Eugene 1880-1950 *BioIn 4,
    NatCAB 40*
Sansweet, Stephen Jay 1945- *ConAu 61*
Santelices, Sergio *OvPC*
Santiago Castillo, Jose' 1888- *BioIn 2*
Santora, I J 1930- *NF*
Santora, Phillip Joseph 1911- *WhoAm 1974*
Santoro, Al 1899?-1978 *NF*
Santos, Eduardo 1888-1974 *BioIn 10, ForP,*

New YTBS 5, WebBD
Santos, Enrique 1886?-1971 *BioIn 9*
Saperstein, Jacob *NF*
Saperstein, M J *NF*
Saphier, William *HisAmM XR*
Saphir, Moritz Gottlieb 1795-1858 *BiD&SB,
    OxGer, WebBD*
Saporiti, Piero *BioIn 2*
Saporta, Marc 1923- *ConAu 21R, IntWW 1976,
    WhoWor 1974*
Sapp, Frederick Arthur 1877-1955 *BioIn 6,
    NatCAB 45*
Sarasohn, Judy *NF*
Sarasohn, Kasriel Z 1835- *NF*
Sarbin, Hershel Benjamin 1924- *WhoAm 1974*
Sarcey, Francisque 1827?-1899 *BbD, BiD&SB,
    CIDMEL, DcEuL, HisAmM XR, OxFr,
    WebBD*
Sarcey, Yvonne 1869-1950 *BioIn 2*
Sarchet, Corbin Marquand 1871- *WhJnl 1928*
Sarda, Shankar *RpN*
Sardinha, Antonio 1887?-1925 *BioIn 1, CIDMEL*
Sarett, Lew 1888-1954 *AmAu&B, AnMV 1926,
    CnDAL, ConAmA, ConAmL, HisAmM XR,
    OxAm, REn, REnAL, TwCA, TwCA Sup,
    WebBD, WhNAA*
Sarfatti, Margherita Grassini 1886-1961 *WebBD*
Sargeant, Howland H 1911- *CurBio XR,
    WhoAm 1974, WhoWor 1974*
Sargeant, Winthrop 1903- *ConAu 29,
    WhoAm 1974, WhoWor 1974, WrDr 1976*
Sargent, Charles Sprague 1841-1927 *Alli Sup,
    BiD&SB, DcAmA, DcNAA, WebBD*
Sargent, David R *NF*
Sargent, Dwight Emerson 1917- *AmAu&B,
    OvPC, RpN, WhoAm 1974*
Sargent, Epes 1813-1880 *Alli, Alli Sup, AmAu,
    AmAu&B, BbD, BiD&SB, BioIn 6,
    CnDAL, CyAL 2, DcAmA, DcAmB 16,
    DcLEL, DcNAA, HisAmM XR, OxAm,
    REnAL, WebBD*
Sargent, George Henry 1867-1931 *AmAu&B,
    DcAmB 16, DcNAA, WhNAA*
Sargent, John Osborne 1811-1891 *Alli, Alli Sup,
    CyAL 2, DcAmA, DcAmB 16, DcNAA,
    HisAmM XR, WebBD*
Sargent, Nathan 1794-1875 *Alli, Alli Sup,
    AmAu, AmAu&B, BiD&SB, DcAmA,
    DcAmB 16, DcNAA, HisAmM XR,
    NatCAB 13*
Sargent, Tony *NF*
Sargint, Herman John Jeffers 1882?-1951 *BioIn 2*
Sarjent, Abel *HisAmM XR*
Sarka, Charles *NF*
Sarkar, Chanchal *RpN*
Sarkar, Vinanti R 1944- *NF*
Sarker, Chanchal *ForP*
Sarlat, Noah 1918- *WhoAm 1974*
Sarnoff, David 1891-1971 *AmJnl, CurBio XR,
    EncAB, New YTBE 1, New YTBE 2,
    WebBD, WhoWorJ 1972*
Sarnoff, Robert W 1918- *AmJnl, CurBio XR,
    IntMPA 1975, IntWW 1974, Who 1974,
    WhoAm 1974, WhoAmA 1973, WhoE 1974,
    WhoF&I 1974, WhoGov 1972,
    WhoWor 1974*
Sarnoff, Thomas Warren 1927- *WhoAm 1974,
    WhoF&I 1974, WhoWest 1974,
    WhoWor 1974*
Sarolea, Charles 1870-1953 *BioIn 3, BioIn 4,
    WebBD, WhoLA*
Saroni, Herman S *HisAmM XR*
Saroyan, Arshalyus 1923-1974 *ConAu 53*
Sarris, Andrew 1928- *AmAu&B, BioIn 9,*

ConAu 21R
Sarro, Ronald A *NF*
Sarruf, Fuad 1900- *IntWW 1976, WhoWor 1974*
Sartain, Geraldine *ForWC 1970, OvPC*
Sartain, John 1808-1897 *Alli, AmAu&B, DcAmA, DcNAA, HisAmM XR, WebBD*
Sartre, Jean-Paul 1905- *Au&Wr, BiE&WWA, CasWL, CelR 1973, ClDMEL, CnMD, CnMWL, CnThe, ConAu 9, ConLC 1, ConLC 4, CroCD, CurBio XR, CyWA, EncWL, EvEuW, ForP, IntWW 1976, LongC, McGWD, ModRL, ModWD, NewYTBE 2, OxEng, OxFr, Pen Eur, RComWL, REn, REnWD, TwCA Sup, TwCW, WebBD, Who 1974, WhoThe 1972, WhoTwCL, WhoWor 1974*
Sasscer, Harrison 1924?-1969 *BioIn 8*
Sassen, David E *NF*
Sasso, Joey *NF*
Satakopan, Rangaswamy d1976 *NF*
Satchell, Michael *NF*
Sato, Nobuyaki *NF*
Satpathy, Nandini 1931- *IntWW 1976*
Satterfield, Archie 1933- *ConAu 57*
Satterlee, Marie M *OvPC*
Satterwhite, Henry Allen 1902- *WhoAm 1974, WhoF&I 1974*
Sattler, Otto 1872-1950 *BioIn 2, CasWL*
Sattler, Warren 1934- *ConAu 65*
Satyukov, Pavel Alexeevich 1911- *IntWW 1976, WhoWor 1974*
Sauckel, Fritz 1894-1946 *CurBio XR, WebBD*
Sauer, Abram E *NF*
Sauer, Mack 1896-1960 *BioIn 7, NatCAB 47*
Sauerbrei, Harold 1916- *WhoAm 1974*
Sauers, Allen 1901- *WhJnl 1928*
Sauerwein, Jules 1880- *WebBD*
Saumenig, Frederick Boyd 1843- *WhJnl 1928*
Saunders, Allen 1899- *ConAu 69*
Saunders, Carl Maxon 1890-1974 *BioIn 2, CurBio XR, NewYTBS 5*
Saunders, Dero Ames 1913- *AmAu&B, WhoAm 1974*
Saunders, Dudley *NF*
Saunders, Fritchie *NF*
Saunders, George L 1866- *WhJnl 1928*
Saunders, John Monk 1897-1940 *AmAu&B, CurBio XR, DcNAA*
Saunders, Keith 1910- *ConAu 57*
Saunders, Ripley Dunlap 1856-1915 *DcAmA, DcNAA*
Saunders, William 1823- *Alli Sup, Lor&LP*
Saunders, William Laurence 1835-1891 *AmAu, AmAu&B, BiDSA, BioIn 3, DcNAA*
Saunders, William Laurence 1856-1931 *WhNAA*
Saunders, William Oscar 1884-1940 *BioIn 6*
Sauter, Van Gordon 1935- *ConAu 73, WhoAm 1974*
Sauvage, Leo *NF*
Sauve, Jeanne 1922- *CanWW 1972, IntWW 1976, WhoCan 1973*
Sauveur, Albert 1863-1939 *DcNAA, HisAmM XR, WhNAA*
Savage, Alvin Mackenzie 1921- *WhoAm 1974*
Savage, G S F *Alli, HisAmM XR*
Savage, Harry 1936- *OvPC, WhoPubR 1972*
Savage, Hugh 1883- *WhJnl 1928*
Savage, James 1767- *Alli, BiDLA*
Savage, James 1784-1873 *Alli, AmAu&B, CyAL 2, DcAmA, DcNAA, HisAmM XR, WebBD*
Savage, James F 1939- *ConAu 73, InvJ, NewMr*
Savage, John 1828-1888 *Alli, AmAu, AmAu&B, BbD, BiD&SB, CyAL 2, DcAmA,*

DcAmB 16, DcNAA, NatCAB 11, PoIre, WebBD
Savage, Noel *NF*
Savage, Pauline Elizabeth 1904- *WhJnl 1928*
Savary, Charles 1845-1889 *DcNAA*
Savell, Morton *HisAmM XR*
Savery, Ranald 1903?-1974 *BioIn 1*
Savik, Stein *NF*
Savitch, Jessica Beth 1947- *ForWC 1970*
Savory, Philip Maxwell Hugh 1889-1965 *BioIn 7*
Savoy, Hubert 1869?-1951 *BioIn 2*
Sawada, Kyoichi d1970 *BioIn 9*
Sawatsky, John *NF*
Sawislak, Arnold B *NF*
Sawyer, Caroline Mehitabel 1812-1894 *Alli, AmAu&B, CyAL 2, DcAmA, DcNAA, FemPA*
Sawyer, Robert William 1917- *BioIn 5*
Sawyer, Walter Leon 1862-1915 *DcAmA, DcNAA, HisAmM XR*
Saxe, John Godfrey 1816-1887 *Alli, Alli Sup, AmAu, AmAu&B, AnCL, AuBYP, BbD, BiD&SB, CnDAL, CyAL 2, DcAmA, DcEnL, DcLEL, DcNAA, HisAmM XR, OxAm, REnAL, WebBD*
Saxe, Kathleen *NF*
Saxon, C M *HisAmM XR*
Saxon, Charles David 1920- *AmAu&B, WhoAm 1974, WhoAmA 1973, WhoE 1974*
Saxon, John A 1886-1947 *BioIn 1, DcNAA*
Saxon, Lyle 1891-1946 *AmAu&B, CurBio XR, DcNAA, HisAmM XR, REnAL, TwCA, TwCA Sup, WebBD, WhNAA*
Saxton, Andrew B 1856- *WhJnl 1928*
Saxton, Brian E *NF*
Saxton, Eugene Francis 1884-1943 *BioIn 6, DcAmB S3, HisAmM XR*
Sayegh, Fayez Abdullah 1922- *BioIn 4, ConAu 9, CurBio XR*
Sayer, Lydia *HisAmM XR*
Sayer, Robert W 1880- *WhJnl 1928*
Sayers, Elliseva *ForWC 1970, OvPC*
Sayers, John Edward *Lor&LP*
Sayler, Oliver Martin 1887-1958 *BioIn 5, IndAu 1917, WhNAA*
Sayles, E Roy 1875- *WhJnl 1928*
Saylor, Harry T 1893- *WhJnl 1928*
Saylor, Henry Hodgman 1880-1967 *AmAu&B, AmLY, BioIn 3, BioIn 4, BioIn 7, BioIn 8, BioIn 9, WhNAA*
Saylor, Oliver Martin 1887- *AmAu&B*
Sayre, Harrison Monell 1894-1974 *BioIn 10, WhoAm 1974, WhoWor 1974*
Sayre, Joel 1900- *AmAu&B, AmNov*
Sayre, Nora *NewMr*
Sayres, Ross *RpN*
Sayrs, Henry John 1904- *ConAu 7R*
Saywer, K Maurees 1905- *WhJnl 1928*
Scaduto, Al *NF*
Scaglia, Giovanni Battista 1910- *IntWW 1976, WhoWor 1974*
Scala, Mary Louise 1949- *NF*
Scalera, Paul S 1920?-1953 *BioIn 3*
Scali, John Alfred 1918- *BioIn 7, BioIn 9, BioIn 10, ConAu 65, CurBio XR, IntWW 1976, NewYTBE 2, NewYTBE 3, WhoAm 1974, WhoS&SW 1973, WhoWor 1974*
Scally, William F *NF*
Scamardella, Rose Ann *NF*
Scamehorn, R John 1905- *WhJnl 1928*
Scammon, J Young 1812-1890 *Alli, AmJnl*
Scandur, Leonard *NF*
Scanlon, Cornelius Thomas 1906-1959 *BioIn 8,*

NatCAB 51
Scarborough, Cayce C BioIn 7
Scarborough, Harold Ellicott 1897-1935 DcNAA
Scarborough, John Barret 1891- WhoAm 1974
Scarf, Margaret 1932?- NF
Scarfe, Gerald A 1936- BioIn 7, BioIn 8,
 IntWW 1976
Scarfoglio, Eduardo 1860-1917 BioIn 1, WebBD
Scarpelli, Henry NF
Scates, Shelby Tamms 1931- RpN,
 WhoWest 1974
Scavullo, Francesco NF
Scelba, Mario 1901- CurBio XR, IntWW 1976,
 WhoWor 1974
Schaaf, Miv NF
Schaal, Albert A HisAmM XR
Schaap, Richard Jay 1934- AmAu&B,
 ConAu 11R, NewMr, WhoE 1974
Schabelitz, R F HisAmM XR
Schaber, Will OvPC
Schacher, Gerhard 1896-1953 BioIn 3
Schacht, Beulah BioIn 1
Schade, Louis 1829-1903 BioIn 2, HisAmM XR
Schade, Walter Bradford WhJnl 1928
Schaefer, A 1878- WhJnl 1928
Schaefer, H NF
Schaefer, Jack Warner 1907- AmAu&B, Au&Wr,
 AuBYP, ConAu 19R, ConAu P-1, OhA&B,
 SmATA 3, ThrBJA, WhoAm 1974,
 WhoWest 1974
Schaeffer, George C HisAmM XR
Schaefle, William J 1875- WhJnl Sup
Schaertel, Terry Davidson NF
Schafer, Horst NF
Schafer, Ilse NF
Schafer, Wilhelm 1868-1952 CasWL, CIDMEL,
 ModGL, OxGer, WebBD
Schaffer, Boguslaw 1929- IntWW 1976
Schaffer, Jan NF
Schaffer, Louis 1889?-1953 BioIn 3
Schakne, Robert 1926- ConAu 65
Schaleben, Arville Orman 1907- ConAu 3R
Schallert, Edwin NF
Schanberg, Sidney Hillel 1934- ConAu 69
Schanche, Don A 1926- ConAu 5R
Schanen, William F 1913?-1971 BioIn 8, BioIn 8,
 BioIn 9, NewYTBE 2
Schanz, John J 1891- WhJnl 1928
Schapiro, Sid OvPC
Schapper, Henry OvPC, WhoPubR 1972
Schara, Ron 1942- NF
Scharf, John Thomas 1843-1898 Alli Sup, AmAu,
 AmAu&B, BiDSA, DcAmA, DcNAA,
 WebBD
Schau, Virginia NF
Schaub, Howard Churchill 1863-1947 BioIn 1
Schauffler, Harry K 1900- WhJnl 1928
Schechner, Richard 1934- BiE&WWA,
 ConAu 45, DrAS 74E, WhoThe 1972
Schechter, Abel Alan CurBio XR, OvPC,
 WhoF&I 1974
Schechter, Ben OvPC
Schechter, Solomon 1847?-1915 DcNAA, REnAL,
 WebBD
Schecter, Jerrold L 1932- ConAu 23R, RpN
Scheele, William Earl 1920- AuBYP, ThrBJA,
 WhoAm 1974
Scheer, Elliott Brown 1898- WhJnl 1928
Scheer, Julian Weisel 1926- AmAu&B, AuBYP,
 BioIn 8, ConAu 49, SmATA 8,
 WhoAm 1974, WhoGov 1972
Scheer, Robert 1936- AmAu&B, BioIn 8
Scheetz, James William 1941- NF
Scheibel, Kenneth Maynard 1920- WhoAm 1974,

WhoWor 1974
Scheibla, Shirley Hobbs 1919- ConAu 41,
 ForWC 1970, WhoAm 1974
Scheidemann, Philipp 1865-1939 REn, WebBD
Scheleen, Joseph Carl 1904- WhoS&SW 1973
Schell, F Cresson 1857-1942 HisAmM XR
Schell, Jonathan 1943- ConAu 73
Schell, Tom NF
Schellhardt, Timothy D NF
Schellhase, Louise M WhJnl Sup
Schem, Alexander Jacob 1826-1881 Alli,
 AmAu&B, DcAmA, DcNAA, WebBD
Schemm, J C HisAmM XR
Schemmel, William NF
Schenberg, Roy M OvPC
Schenck, Leopold 1843-1886 HisAmM XR,
 NatCAB 4
Schendorf, Hilliard Arthur 1918- OvPC,
 WhoF&I 1974, WhoPubR 1972
Scher, Jacob 1908-1961 BioIn 6
Scherbatof, Mara 1908-1956 BioIn 4
Scherck, G 1894- WhJnl 1928
Scherer, D J NF
Scherer, Edmond 1815-1889 BbD, BiD&SB,
 CIDMEL, DcEuL, OxFr, WebBD
Scherer, Raymond Lewis 1919- WhoAm 1974,
 WhoWor 1974
Scherman, Bernadine Kielty 1890?-1973 BioIn 10,
 ConAu 45
Scherman, Harry 1887-1969 AmAu&B,
 CurBio XR, WebBD, WhoWorJ 1972
Scherman, William Harris 1913- WhoAdv 1972,
 WhoAm 1974
Schermerhorn, Jack NF
Schermerhorn, James 1865-1941 AmAu&B,
 NatCAB XR
Schermerhorn, Jane NF
Scherr, Elliott Brown 1898- NF
Scherr, Max 1916?- BioIn 8, NewMr
Scherwitz, George Harold 1900- WhJnl 1928
Scheuer, Jim OvPC
Scheuer, Steven H NF
Schevitsch, Serge HisAmM XR
Schickel, Richard 1933- AuNews 1,
 BioNews 1974, ConAu 3R, WhoAm 1974,
 WhoE 1974, WrDr 1976
Schickele, Rene 1885-1940 CasWL, CIDMEL,
 CnMD, EncWL, EvEuW, ModGL, OxGer,
 Pen Eur, REn, TwCA, TwCA Sup, WebBD
Schieffer, Bob 1937- NF
Schier, Ernest 1918- WhoE 1974
Schiff, Bennet NF
Schiff, Dorothy 1903- AmAu&B, BioIn 4,
 BioIn 5, BioIn 7, BioIn 8, CelR 1973,
 CurBio XR, ForWC 1970, IntWW 1976,
 WhoAm 1974, WhoAmW 1974, WhoE 1974,
 WhoWor 1974, WhoWorJ 1972
Schiffer, Robert L OvPC
Schifferes, Justus Julius 1907- BioIn 1, ConAu 5
Schifman, Ben Bylah 1913- WhoAm 1974,
 WhoWorJ 1972
Schiller, Johann Christoph Friedrich Von 1759-1805
 BbD, BiD&SB, CasWL, DcEuL, EuAu,
 EvEuW, HisAmM XR, NewC, OxEng,
 OxFr, OxGer, WebBD
Schiller, Marlene NF
Schilplin, Fred 1868?-1949 BioIn 1, BioIn 2
Schimberg, Albert Paul 1885-1949 BioIn 1,
 BioIn 2, BkC 4, CathA 1930
Schimmel, Hendrik Jan 1823-1906 Alli Sup,
 CasWL, EuAu, EvEuW, WebBD
Schindelmyer, F J 1886- WhJnl 1928
Schindler, Aaron NF
Schinto, Jeanne NF

Schiottz-Christensen, Alf Krabbe 1909- IntWW 1976
Schipley, Joseph P 1893- NF
Schiren, Charles Adolph HisAmM XR
Schirmer, Joseph E NF
Schissler, Paul 1892?-1968 BioIn 8
Schjeldahl, Peter 1942- DrAP 1975, Pen Am
Schlacht, Harry H 1893-1961 BioIn 5, BioIn 7, NatCAB 47
Schlaeger, Eduard BioIn 2
Schlafly, Hubert Joseph, Jr. 1919- WhoAm 1974, WhoF&I 1974
Schlamm, William S 1904-1978 AmAu&B, Au&Wr
Schlegel, August Wilhelm Von 1767-1845 AtlBL, BbD, BiD&SB, CasWL, DcEnL, DcEuL, DcSpL, EuAu, EvEuW, HisAmM XR, NewC, OxEng, OxFr, OxGer, Pen Eur, REn, REnWD, WebBD
Schlegel, Carl Wilhelm Friedrich Von 1772-1829 EvEuW
Schlegel, Carl Wilhelm Friedrich Von see also Schlegel, F
Schlegel, Carl Wilhelm Friedrich Von see also Schlegel, Karl W F
Schlegel, Friedrich Von 1772-1829 AtlBL, BiD&SB, CasWL, DcEuL, EuAu, NewC, OxEng, OxGer, REn, REnWD
Schlegel, Friedrich Von see also Schlegel, Carl Wilhelm F
Schlegel, Friedrich Von see also Schlegel, Karl Wilhelm F
Schlegel, Karl Wilhelm Friedrich Von 1772-1829 BbD, Pen Eur
Schlegel, Karl Wilhelm Friedrich Von see also Schlegel, Carl W F
Schlegel, Karl Wilhelm Friedrich Von see also Schlegel, F
Schleicher, John A HisAmM XR
Schlemihl, Peter see Thoma, Ludwig
Schleppey, Blanche 1861-1927 BioIn 2
Schlesinger, Arthur Meier 1888-1965 AmAu&B, ConAu 5, ConAu 25, DcLEL, OhA&B, OxAm, REn, REnAL, TwCA, TwCA Sup, WebBD, WhNAA
Schlesinger, Arthur Meier, Jr. 1917- AmAu&B, Au&Wr, AuNews 1, ConAu 1, CurBio XR, HisAmM XR, OhA&B, OxAm, Pen Am, REn, REnAL, TwCA Sup, WebBD, WhoAm 1974, WrDr 1976
Schlesinger, Rudolf 1901-1969 BioIn 9
Schlesinger, Stephen C 1942- ConAu 57
Schlich, Paul J HisAmM XR
Schline, Sandy NF
Schloss, Murray S HisAmM XR
Schlosser, Alexander Leo 1888-1943 CurBio XR, DcNAA, WhJnl 1928
Schlosser, Herbert Samuel 1926- IntMPA 1975, WhoAm 1974
Schlumpf, Viktor NF
Schmalzried, Darlene NF
Schmeck, Harold M, Jr. 1923- ConAu 17, RpN
Schmemann, Serge 1945- NF
Schmick, William F, III NF
Schmick, William Frederick 1883-1963 BioIn 2, BioIn 6
Schmick, William Frederick, Jr. 1913- WhoE 1974, WhoWor 1974
Schmid, John M 1876-1947 BioIn 1, WhJnl 1928
Schmid, Randolph E NF
Schmidt, Ann Downing NF
Schmidt, Carl Gottlieb 1845-1922 BioIn 5
Schmidt, Carl Henry 1835-1888 BioIn 5
Schmidt, Dana Adams 1915- AmAu&B, BioIn 2,

ConAu 11R, OvPC, RpN, WhoWor 1974
Schmidt, Felix 1885- WhJnl 1928
Schmidt, Frederick d1951 BioIn 2
Schmidt, George NF
Schmidt, Julian 1818-1886 OxGer, WebBD
Schmidt, Karl HisAmM XR
Schmidt, Leopold 1860-1927 NF
Schmidt, Margaret Fox 1925- ConAu 65
Schmidt, Sandra 1937- ConAu XR
Schmidt, Stanley Albert 1944- ConAu 61
Schmidt, Stephen NF
Schmidt, William E 1947- ConAu 73
Schmitt, Bernadotte Everly 1886-1969 AmAu&B, ConAu 1R, OhA&B, OxAm, TwCA, TwCA Sup, WebBD
Schmitt, Gladys 1909-1972 AmAu&B, AmNov, Au&Wr, ConAu 1, ConAu 37, CurBio XR, NewYTBE 3, OxAm, REnAL, TwCA Sup, WhoAmW 1974
Schmitt, Henry Joseph 1909- WhoAm 1974
Schmitt, Nikolaus d1870 BioIn 2
Schmitt, Peter NF
Schmolze, Karl Heinrich 1823-1859 BioIn 2
Schnapper, Morris AmRP
Schnauffer, Carl Heinrich 1823-1854 BioIn 2
Schneider, Ad NF
Schneider, Alfred Reuben 1926- WhoAm 1974, WhoWorJ 1972
Schneider, Charles Harold 1912- BioIn 6, WhoAm 1974, WhoS&SW 1973
Schneider, Charles Ivan 1923- WhoAm 1974, WhoWest 1974
Schneider, Franz, Jr. NF
Schneider, George 1823-1905 BioIn 2, DcAmB 16
Schneider, Howie AuNews 2
Schneider, John Arnold 1926- IntMPA 1975, WhoAm 1974, WhoF&I 1974
Schneider, Lou NF
Schneider, Otto J HisAmM XR
Schneider, Paul A 1891- WhJnl 1928
Schneider, Roger L NF
Schneider, Walter E 1904- WhJnl 1928
Schneiderman, Harry 1885-1975 ConAu 61, WhoWorJ 1972
Schnell, Harry J HisAmM XR
Schnitzler, John L 1866- WhJnl 1928
Schoeffler, Moritz 1813-1875 BioIn 5
Schoelcher, Victor 1804-1893 Alli, WebBD
Schoelkopf, Dean Harold 1932- WhoAm 1974
Schoenberner, Franz 1892-1970 BioIn 1, BioIn 3, BioIn 4, BioIn 8
Schoenbrun, David Franz 1915- AmAu&B, BioIn 5, BioIn 6, ConAu 49, CurBio XR, WhoAm 1974, WhoWor 1974
Schoenfeld, Clarence Albert 1918- AmM&W 73S, ConAu 1R
Schoenfeld, Eugene 1935- BioIn 8, BioIn 10
Schoening, Roger Warren 1928- WhoAm 1974
Schoenleb, Edwin A NF
Schoenstein, Paul 1902-1974 BioIn 8, BioIn 10, NewYTBS 5, WhoAm 1974
Schoenstein, Ralph 1933- BioIn 5, ConAu 13R
Schoff, Stephen Alonzo 1818-1904 HisAmM XR
Schoffelmayer, Victor H BioIn 2, TexWr
Schofield, Charles Edwin 1894-1951 BioIn 2
Schofield, Graham L 1886- WhJnl 1928
Schofield, James E 1888- WhJnl 1928
Schofield, William Greenough 1909- BioIn 3, CathA 1952, ConAu 7R, WhoE 1974, WhoF&I 1974
Scholer, Jacob 1807-1885 BioIn 2
Scholes, Frank NF
Scholes, Percy Alfred 1877-1958 LongC, TwCA Sup, WebBD, WhoLA

Scholl, Aurelien 1833-1902 BioIn 2, BioIn 6,
  OxFr
Scholl, John 1922- ConAu 11R
Scholnick, Joseph B 1921- OvPC, WhoCon 1973,
  WhoPubR 1972, WhoWest 1974
Schomer, Howard 1915- AmAu&B, DrAS 74P,
  WhoAm 1974, WhoWor 1974
Schonberg, Harold C 1915- AmAu&B,
  IntWW 1976, WhoAm 1974, WhoE 1974,
  WhoWor 1974
Schonbrunn, S M OvPC
Schonfaber, J F HisAmM XR
Schonfeld, Moses 1910- WhoWorJ 1972
Schoningh, Franz Josef 1902-1960 BioIn 5
Schooley, Raymond H 1884- WhJnl 1928
Schopp, Ludwig 1895-1949 BioIn 2
Schorer, Brint, Jr. NF
Schorr, Burton L NF
Schorr, Daniel Louis 1916- AuNews 2, BioIn 5,
  BioIn 9, ConAu 65, CurBio XR, InvJ,
  NewMr, WhNAA, WhoAm 1974,
  WhoWor 1974
Schorr, Jose IntMPA 1975
Schorr, Norman A 1920- OvPC, WhoPubR 1972,
  WhoWorJ 1972
Schott, Webster 1927- BioIn 10, ConAu 49
Schottelkotte, James Edward 1930- WhoAm 1974,
  WhoMW 1974
Schouler, William 1814-1872 Alli, AmAu&B,
  DcAmA, DcNAA, OhA&B, WebBD
Schrader, Frederick Franklin 1857-1943 AmAu&B,
  AmLY, WhNAA
Schrader, Martin Harry 1925- WhoAm 1974
Schrag, Peter 1931- ConAu 15R, WhoAm 1974,
  WrDr 1976
Schram, Jolly 1934- NF
Schram, Martin Jay 1942- NF
Schramm, R VonHorrum HisAmM XR
Schramm, Wilbur Lang 1907- ForP,
  HisAmM XR, IntWW 1976, OhA&B,
  REnAL, WhoAm 1974
Schrantz, Ward L 1890- WhJnl 1928
Schreiber, Charles Jaques 1929- OvPC,
  WhoE 1974
Schreiber, Le Anne NF
Schreider, Frank 1924- ConAu 7R, USBiR 1974
Schreiner, George Abel NF
Schreiner, Samuel Agnew, Jr. 1921- ConAu 65
Schricker, Henry F 1883-1966 CurBio XR
Schriftgiesser, Karl 1903- AmAu&B, BioIn 4,
  ConAu P-1, OvPC, REnAL, TwCA Sup,
  WhJnl 1928
Schroder, Armund A Schulze 1925- ConAu 13R
Schroder, Daniel Richard 1899- WhJnl 1928
Schroeder, Eric G 1896- WhJnl 1928
Schroeder, Francis DeNeufville 1901-1952 BioIn 3
Schroeder, Mary 1903- ConAu 17, ConAu 73,
  WhoAmW 1974
Schroeder, Peter C NF
Schroeder, Raymond C 1889- WhJnl 1928
Schroeder, Rilla HisAmM XR
Schroeder, Theodore HisAmM XR
Schroeder, Willard 1913- WhoAm 1974
Schroers, John 1858- NatCAB 12
Schroeter, Bob NF
Schroeter, Eduard 1811- BioIn 2
Schropp, A B WhJnl 1928
Schropp, John K R 1880- WhJnl 1928
Schroth, Frank D 1884-1974 AmAu&B, BioIn 10,
  NewYTBS 5
Schroth, Raymond A d1977 NF
Schroth, Thomas Nolan 1920- WhoAm 1974
Schruth, Peter Elliott 1917- WhoAdv 1972,
  WhoAm 1974

Schubert, Paul 1899- BioIn 1
Schuchat, David G NF
Schucking, Levin 1814-1883 OxGer, WebBD
Schudt, William Arthur, Jr. 1906- WhoAm 1974
Schue, Harold Franklin 1899- WhJnl 1928
Schuenemann-Pott, Friedrich 1826?-1881 BioIn 2
Schuette, Oswald Francis 1882-1953 BioIn 3
Schulberg, B P 1892-1957 NF
Schulberg, Stuart NF
Schulenburg, Detlev Friedrich Achaz 1910?-
  BioIn 2
Schuler, Gottlieb Frederick Henry 1854-1926
  BioIn 2
Schuler, Loring Ashley 1886-1968 AmAu&B,
  BioIn 8, HisAmM XR, WhNAA
Schulkers, Robert Franc 1890- OhA&B,
  WhJnl 1928
Schuller, Robert NF
Schulman, Bob NF
Schulman, Grace ConAu 65, DrAP 1975,
  DrAS 74E
Schulman, Jack 1914- WhoAm 1974
Schulman, Milton 1913- NF
Schulman, Sammy NF
Schulman, Victor 1876?-1951 BioIn 2
Schulte, Henry Frank 1924- AmM&W 73S,
  ConAu 25, DrAS 74E, LEduc 1974, OvPC,
  WrDr 1976
Schultz, Gladys Denny 1895- HisAmM XR
Schultz, Gladys Denny see also Shultz, Gladys Denny
Schultz, Ignac 1894-1954 BioIn 3
Schultz, John H HisAmM XR
Schultz, Lester C 1900- WhJnl 1928
Schultz, Morton J NF
Schultz, Sigrid Lillian AmJnl, BioIn 1,
  CurBio XR, OvPC, WhoAm 1974
Schultz, Terri 1946- ConAu 65
Schultz, Whitt N 1920- NF
Schultze, Bunny 1866-1939 REnAL
Schultze, Bunny see also Schultze, Carl Emil
Schultze, Carl Emil 1866-1939 AmAu&B, AmJnl,
  DcNAA, WebBD
Schultze, Carl Emil see also Schultze, Bunny
Schulz, Charles Monroe 1922- AmAu&B, AmJnl,
  AuBYP, BioIn 4, BioIn 5, BioIn 6, BioIn 7,
  BioIn 8, BioIn 9, ConAu 9R, CurBio XR,
  MnnWr, SmATA 10, ThrBJA,
  WhoAm 1974, WhoAmA 1973, WrDr 1976
Schulz, Dietrich W NF
Schulz, Ralph R OvPC
Schumacher, Ann M NF
Schuman, Frederick Lewis 1904- AmAu&B,
  AmM&W 73S, AmRP, Au&Wr, BioIn 1,
  BioIn 3, BioIn 4, ConAu 45, IntWW 1974,
  TwCA, TwCA Sup, WhNAA, WhoAm 1974,
  WhoWor 1974, WrDr 1976
Schuman, Frederick Lewis see also Shuman,
  Frederick Lewis
Schumann, Maurice 1911- CurBio XR,
  IntWW 1974, Who 1974, WhoWor 1974
Schumeister, James NF
Schuon, Karl BioIn 7
Schur, Sylvia OvPC
Schurmacher, Emile Carlos 1903-1976 BioIn 2,
  ConAu 69
Schurz, Carl 1829-1906 Alli, Alli Sup, AmAu,
  AmAu&B, BbD, BiDSA, BioIn 1, BioIn 2,
  BioIn 3, BioIn 5, BioIn 6, BioIn 7, BioIn 8,
  BioIn 9, DcAmA, DcNAA, EncAB,
  HisAmM XR, OxAm, REnAL, WebBD,
  WisWr
Schurz, Franklin Dunn 1898- WhoAm 1974,
  WhoF&I 1974, WhJnl 1928
Schuster, Ad B 1884- WhJnl 1928

Schuster, Gary F NF
Schuster, Max Lincoln 1897-1970 AmAu&B,
    BioIn 9, ConAu 29, CurBio XR,
    NewYTBE 1, REnAL, WebBD,
    WhoWorJ 1972
Schutz, Bob NF
Schutzer, Paul George 1930-1967 NF
Schuyler, Elmer L 1863- WhJnl 1928
Schuyler, George Samuel 1895-1977 AmAu&B,
    AmRP, BioIn 7, BlkAW, ConAu 73,
    HisAmM XR, WhoAm 1974, WhJnl 1928
Schuyler, Montgomery 1843-1914 AmAu&B,
    BioIn 3, BioIn 4, DcAmA, DcAmB 16,
    DcNAA, HisAmM XR
Schuyler, Robert Livingston 1883-1966 AmAu&B,
    ConAu P-1, HisAmM XR
Schuyler, William M 1877?-1950 BioIn 2
Schwab, Fred HisAmM XR
Schwab, John Christopher 1865-1916 AmAu&B,
    DcAmA, DcNAA, HisAmM XR
Schwab, Samuel S 1886?-1949 BioIn 2
Schwalberg, Carol 1930- ConAu 69
Schwartz, Berl NF
Schwartz, Bolton OvPC
Schwartz, David NF
Schwartz, Delmore 1913-1966 AmAu&B, AtlBL,
    CasWL, CnDAL, CnE&AP, CnMWL,
    ConAu 17, ConAu 25, ConLC 2, ConLC 4,
    ConP 1975, CurBio XR, EncWL,
    HisAmM XR, ModAL, ModAL Sup, OxAm,
    Pen Am, RAdv 1, REn, REnAL, SixAP,
    TwCA, TwCA Sup, TwCW, WebE&AL,
    WhoTwCL
Schwartz, George Leopold 1891- BioIn 2,
    Who 1974
Schwartz, Harry 1919- AmM&W 73S,
    WhoWorJ 1972
Schwartz, Jack 1939?- NF
Schwartz, Leland InvJ
Schwartz, Lew 1907-1971 BioIn 9, NewYTBE 2
Schwartz, Lloyd NF
Schwartz, Loretta NF
Schwartz, Marvin David 1926- WhoAm 1974,
    WhoAmA 1973
Schwartz, Michael InvJ
Schwartz, Pamela NF
Schwartz, Tony NF
Schwartzkopff, Gerhard NF
Schwarz, Daniel 1908- WhoAm 1974,
    WhoE 1974
Schwarz, Leo Walder 1906-1967 BioIn 8,
    ConAu 5
Schwarz, Ted ConAu XR
Schwarz, Theodore R, Jr. 1945- ConAu 65
Schwarz, Walter 1930- Au&Wr, ConAu 13R
Schwarzmann, A HisAmM XR
Schwarzschild, Leopold 1891-1950 BioIn 2
Schwarzwalder, John Carl 1917- WhoAm 1974,
    WhoMW 1974
Schwedhelm, Karl 1915- IntWW 1976
Schweid, Barry NF
Schweiker, Jim NF
Schweitzer, Avarm 1923- WhoWorJ 1972
Schwimmer, Rosika NF
Schwinn, Walter Kelly 1901- WhJnl 1928
Schwitters, Kurt 1887-1948 OxGer, Pen Eur,
    WebBD
Scism, Don 1893- WhNAA, WhJnl 1928
Sclove, Louise H OvPC
Scobie, Hugh 1811-1853 BbtC, BioIn 1
Scofield, James Steve 1928- BiDrLUS,
    WhoAm 1974
Scofield, John 1914- WhoAm 1974,
    WhoS&SW 1973

Scoggin, Margaret Clara 1905-1968 BioIn 8,
    CurBio XR
Scoggins, C Verne 1902- WhJnl 1928
Scoggins, Charles Elbert 1888-1955 HisAmM XR
Scoles, Isaac HisAmM XR
Scott, Alice NF
Scott, Angelo Cyrus 1857-1949 IndAu 1917,
    NatCAB 37
Scott, Austin D 1939?- BlkC
Scott, C A NF
Scott, C P 1846-1932 ForP, LongC
Scott, C P see also Scott, Charles Prestwich
Scott, Charles Frederick 1860- WhJnl 1928
Scott, Charles Prestwich 1846-1932 BioIn 1,
    BioIn 2, BioIn 5, BioIn 9, Lor&LP, WebBD
Scott, Charles Prestwich see also Scott, C P
Scott, Edith 1885- WhJnl 1928
Scott, Edwin A WhJnl 1928
Scott, Emmet Jay 1873-1957 AmAu&B, WhNAA
Scott, Frances NF
Scott, Frank Hall 1848-1912 HisAmM XR
Scott, Frank Harrelson 1896- WhJnl 1928
Scott, Franklin William 1877-1950 AmAu&B,
    AmJnl, AmLY, BioIn 2, LiJA
Scott, Fred Newton 1860-1931 AmAu&B,
    DcNAA, IndAu 1816, REnAL, WebBD
Scott, Gavin 1936- NF
Scott, George Edwin 1925- Au&Wr, BioIn 4,
    ConAu '29, Who 1974, WrDr 1976
Scott, Greg NF
Scott, Harvey Whitefield 1838-1910 AmAu&B,
    AmJnl, DcNAA, NatCAB 16, REnAL
Scott, Henry E HisAmM XR
Scott, Herward Sydney 1865- WhJnl 1928
Scott, Howard AmRP
Scott, Hugh 1908- BioIn 3
Scott, Isaiah Benjamin 1854-1931 BioIn 1
Scott, J Thomas 1872-1948 BioIn 1
Scott, Jack 1942- BioIn 2, BioIn 5
Scott, James A 1924- OvPC, WhoPubR 1972
Scott, James Brown AmAu&B, DcNAA,
    WebBD, WhNAA
Scott, James White 1926- WhoAm 1974
Scott, James Wilmot 1849-1895 AmAu&B,
    AmJnl, DcAmB 16, NatCAB 2
Scott, Joe NF
Scott, John NF
Scott, John 1783-1821 Alli, BioIn 4
Scott, John 1912-1976 AmAu&B, Au&Wr,
    ConAu 7R, OvPC, WhoAm 1974
Scott, John L OvPC
Scott, John Russell 1879-1949 BioIn 2
Scott, John W HisAmM XR
Scott, John Wilson 1915- AmM&W 73P,
    CanWW 1972
Scott, Julian 1846-1901 HisAmM XR
Scott, Leonard HisAmM XR
Scott, M K NF
Scott, Milton Robinson 1841-1921 DcNAA,
    OhA&B
Scott, Nadine NF
Scott, Niki 1943- NF
Scott, Oliver NF
Scott, Otto J OvPC
Scott, Owen 1898- WhJnl 1928
Scott, Patrick NF
Scott, Philip H NF
Scott, Rachel NewMr
Scott, Richard ForP
Scott, Robert 1860- NF
Scott, Sidney D 1890- BioIn 1
Scott, Stanley Southall 1933- BioIn 10,
    WhoAm 1974, WhoAmP 1973
Scott, Thomas A AmJnl

Scott, Vernon *NF*

Scott, W J *HisAmM XR*

Scott, Sir Walter 1771-1832 *Alli, AnCL, AtlBL, BbD, BiD&SB, BiDLA, BiDLA Sup, BrAu 19, CarSB, CasWL, CnE&AP, CrtT 2, CyWA, DcBiA, DcEnA, DcEnA Ap, DcEnL, DcEuL, DcLEL, EvLB, HisAmM XR, HsB&A, MouLC 3, NewC, OxEng, Pen Eng, PoChrch, RAdv 1, RComWL, REn, Str&VC, WebBD, WebE&AL, WhoChL*

Scott, Walter 1867-1938 *WebBD*

Scott, Walter 1906- *WhNAA*

Scott, William Walter 1853-1931 *DcNAA*

Scott, Winfield Townley 1910-1968 *AmAu&B, ConAu 7R, ConAu 25, ModAL, ModAL Sup, OxAm, Pen Am, REn, REnAL, TwCA Sup*

Scott-James, Rolfe Arnold 1878- *BioIn 7*

Scott-Watson, Keith *NF*

Scouton, William O *NF*

Scovel, Henry Sylvester 1869-1905 *AmJnl, DcAmB 16, FamWC*

Scoville, F C 1886- *WhJnl 1928*

Scoville, Joseph Alfred 1815-1864 *Alli, AmAu, AmAu&B, DcAmA, DcAmB 16, DcEnL, DcNAA, HisAmM XR*

Scoville, Samuel, Jr. 1872-1950 *AmAu&B, BioIn 2, HisAmM XR, JBA 1934, JBA 1951, REnAL, WhNAA*

Scriba, Jay 1926- *NF*

Scribner, Arthur Hawley 1859-1932 *AmAu&B, NatCAB 36, WebBD*

Scribner, Charles 1821-1871 *AmAu&B, WebBD*

Scribner, Charles 1854-1930 *AmAu&B, WebBD*

Scribner, Charles 1890-1952 *AmAu&B, HisAmM XR, NatCAB 45, WebBD*

Scribner, David Gordon 1926- *WhoAm 1974*

Scribner, John Blair 1850-1879 *WebBD*

Scripp, Charles *HisAmM XR*

Scripps, Charles Edward 1920- *AmAu&B, AmJnl, BioIn 3, IntWW 1974, WhoAm 1974, WhoF&I 1974, WhoMW 1974*

Scripps, Edward Wyllis 1854-1926 *AmAu&B, AmJnl, BioIn 2, BioIn 3, BioIn 5, BioIn 7, BioIn 9, BioIn 10, EncAB, ForP, NatCAB 28, REnAL, WebBD*

Scripps, Edward Wyllis 1909- *AmAu&B, WhoAm 1974*

Scripps, Edward Wyllis, II 1929- *WhoE 1974, WhoF&I 1974*

Scripps, Ellen Browning 1836-1932 *AmAu&B, AmJnl, BioIn 6, BioIn 9, DcAmB 16, NatCAB 28, WebBD*

Scripps, George H *AmJnl*

Scripps, James Edmund 1835-1906 *AmAu, AmAu&B, AmJnl, BioIn 1, DcAmA, DcNAA, NatCAB 28, WebBD*

Scripps, James G 1886-1921 *AmJnl, NatCAB 22*

Scripps, John *AmJnl*

Scripps, John L 1818-1866 *AmJnl, NatCAB 7*

Scripps, John P 1912- *AmAu&B, AmJnl, WhoAm 1974*

Scripps, Robert Paine 1895-1938 *AmAu&B, AmJnl, BioIn 4, DcAmB S2, WebBD*

Scripps, William A 1838-1914 *NatCAB 36*

Scripps, William Edmund 1882-1952 *AmAu&B, BioIn 2, BioIn 3, DcAmB S5, WhJnl 1928*

Scrivner, Guy 1894- *WhJnl 1928*

Scroggie, George E *WhJnl 1928*

Scroggs, William Oscar 1879- *HisAmM XR, WhNAA*

Scruggs, William Lindsay 1836-1912 *BiDSA, DcAmA, DcNAA, NatCAB 2*

Scudder, Edward Wallace 1882-1953 *BioIn 3*

Scudder, Edward Wallace, Jr. 1911- *WhoE 1974*

Scudder, Horace Elisha 1838-1902 *Alli, Alli Sup, AmAu, AmAu&B, BbD, BiD&SB, BioIn 1, BioIn 3, CarSB, DcAmA, DcNAA, HisAmM XR, JBA 1934, LiJA, OxAm, REn, REnAL*

Scudder, M L *HisAmM XR*

Scudder, Preston *HisAmM XR*

Scudder, Richard B 1913- *BioIn 9, WhoAm 1974*

Scudder, Samuel Hubbard 1837-1911 *Alli Sup, BbtC, DcAmA, DcNAA, HisAmM XR, OxCan, WebBD*

Scudder, Wallace McIlvane 1853-1931 *AmAu&B*

Scull, Guy Hamilton 1876-1920 *DcNAA*

Scull, John 1765-1828 *AmAu&B, AmJnl*

Scully, Frank 1892-1964 *AmAu&B, AmRP, BioIn 4, BioIn 6, BioIn 7, BkC 5, ConAu 5, WhNAA*

Scully, John C *OvPC*

Scully, Julia *NF*

Scully, Michael 1898?-1958 *BioIn 5*

Scully, William A 1881-1936 *NatCAB 27*

Seabrook, William Buehler 1886-1945 *AmAu&B, CurBio XR, DcNAA, REnAL, TwCA, TwCA Sup, WhNAA*

Seacrest, Fred 1894- *WhJnl 1928*

Seacrest, Joseph Claggett 1864-1942 *BioIn 3, NatCAB 37*

Seacrest, Joseph Rushton 1920- *WhoAm 1974, WhoMW 1974*

Seacrest, Joseph Winger 1895-1978 *WhoAm 1974*

Seagle, Don *RpN*

Seal, Robert Donald 1902- *WhJnl 1928*

Seale, Ellis C 1878-1960 *NatCAB 49*

Seals, John H d1906 *HisAmM XR, NatCAB 2*

Seaman, Barbara 1935- *ConAu 29*

Seaman, Barrett 1945- *ConAu 73*

Seaman, Elizabeth Cochrane 1867-1922 *AmAu, AmAu&B, BioIn 3, BioIn 4, BioIn 5, BioIn 7, BioIn 8, BioIn 9, BioIn 10, CnDAL, DcAmB 16, DcNAA, OxAm, REn, REnAL, WebBD*

Seaman, Elizabeth Cochrane *see also* Cochrane, Elizabeth

Seaman, Sir Owen 1861-1936 *Alli Sup, EvLB, LongC, NewC, TwCA, TwCA Sup, WebBD*

Seaman, William Casper 1925- *WhoAm 1974*

Seamon, Mayo C 1901- *WhJnl 1928*

Seamon, Richard Morris 1919- *BioIn 5, WhoAm 1974*

Searing, Laura Catherine Redden 1840-1923 *Alli Sup, AmAu&B, BiD&SB, BiDSA, DcAmA, DcAmB 16, DcNAA, HisAmM XR*

Searing, Laura Catherine Redden *see also* Redden, Laura Catherine

Searle, Ronald 1920- *Au&Wr, BioIn 1, BioIn 2, BioIn 4, BioIn 5, BioIn 6, ConAu 9, IntWW 1976, NewC, WhoAm 1974, WhoGrA, WhoWor 1974, WrDr 1976*

Sears, Barnas 1802-1880 *Alli, CyAL 1, DcAmA, DcNAA, HisAmM XR, WebBD*

Sears, E G *HisAmM XR*

Sears, Edmund Hamilton 1810-1876 *Alli, Alli Sup, AmAu, AmAu&B, DcAmA, DcNAA, HisAmM XR, OhA&B, PoChrch, REnAL, WebBD, WebE&AL*

Sears, Edward Isidore 1819?-1876 *Alli, AmAu&B, DcNAA, HisAmM XR, PoIre*

Sears, Henry *HisAmM XR*

Sears, John VanDerZee 1835- *DcNAA*

Sears, Joseph Hamblen 1865-1946 *AmAu&B, DcNAA, HisAmM XR, NatCAB 13*

Sears, Robert 1810-1892 *Alli, AmAu&B,*

DcNAA, HisAmM XR
Sears, U I 1870- *WhJnl 1928*
Sears, Val 1927- *ConAu 73*
Seaton, Fay N 1882?-1952 *BioIn 3*
Seaton, Frederick Andrew 1909-1974 *BioIn 4,*
 BioIn 5, BioIn 10, WhoAmP 1973,
 WhoGov 1972
Seaton, Siebert Frederick 1901- *WhJnl 1928*
Seaton, William Winston 1785-1866 *Alli,*
 AmAu&B, AmJnl, BiDSA, BioIn 3,
 BioIn 9, DcAmB 16, WebBD
Seaver, Horace Holley 1810-1889 *DcNAA,*
 HisAmM XR
Seaver, William A *HisAmM XR*
Seavers, Fanny P *HisAmM XR*
Seawell, Donald Ray 1912- *WhoAm 1974,*
 WhoE 1974, WhoF&I 1974, WhoThe 1972
Seawell, Molly Elliot 1860-1916 *AmAu&B,*
 BiD&SB, BiDSA, CarSB, DcAmA, DcBiA,
 DcNAA, HisAmM XR, TwCA
Sebaei, Youssef 1918?-1978 *NF*
Sebestyen, Gyorgy 1930- *Au&Wr, ConAu 9R*
Secondari, John Hermes 1919-1975 *AmAu&B,*
 Au&Wr, ConAu 57, ConAu 61, CurBio XR,
 WhoAm 1974, WhoE 1974, WhoF&I 1974
Secondsight, Solomon 1785-1845 *AmAu,*
 AmAu&B, DcNAA, NewC
Secondsight, Solomon *see also* McHenry, James
Secrest, Andrew M *RpN*
Seddon, T *HisAmM XR*
Sedell, Avery 1914- *NF*
Sedgwick, Arthur George 1844-1915 *Alli Sup,*
 AmAu&B, AmJnl, DcAmA, DcAmB 16,
 DcNAA, HisAmM XR, NatCAB 27,
 NewMr, WebBD
Sedgwick, Ellery 1872-1960 *AmAu&B, BioIn 1,*
 BioIn 5, DcAmA, HisAmM XR, LiJA,
 REnAL, WebBD
Sedgwick, Hubert M 1867?-1950 *BioIn 2*
Sedgwick, Theodore 1811-1859 *Alli, AmAu&B,*
 CyAL 2, DcAmA, DcNAA, WebBD
Sedley, Henry 1831?-1899 *Alli, AmAu&B,*
 BiD&SB, DcAmA, DcNAA, HisAmM XR
See, Richard H *HisAmM XR*
Seeger, Murray A *RpN*
Seelmeyer, Richard W *NF*
Seely, Herman Gastrell 1891- *WhJnl 1928*
Seely, Howard *HisAmM XR*
Seely, Walter Hoff 1873-1936 *HisAmM XR*
Seeman, Bernard 1911- *Au&Wr, ConAu 23R,*
 WhoE 1974, WhoF&I 1974
Seep, Thomas W *NF*
Seese, George 1882?-1955 *BioIn 3*
Sefrit, Charles G 1860-1925 *WhJnl Sup*
Sefrit, Frank I 1867- *WhJnl 1928*
Segal, Albert E 1903- *WhJnl 1928*
Segal, Alfred 1883- *BioIn 2, BioIn 3*
Segal, Harvey Hirst 1922- *AmEA 1974,*
 AmM&W 73S, ConAu 4R
Segal, J I 1896-1954 *NF*
Segal, Robert *NF*
Segal, William Charles 1909- *WhoAm 1974*
Segar, Elzie Crisler 1894-1938 *AmJnl, DcNAA,*
 WebBD
Seger, Gerhart H 1896?-1967 *BioIn 7*
Segerstedt, Torgny S d1945 *BioIn 3, ForP*
Segev, Shmuel *NF*
Seghers, Anna 1900- *CasWL, CIDMEL,*
 CurBio XR, EncWL, EvEuW, ForP,
 IntWW 1976, ModGL, OxGer, Pen Eur,
 REn, TwCA, TwCA Sup, WebBD,
 WhoWor 1974
Seghers, Pierre 1906- *IntWW 1976,*
 WhoWor 1974

Segrave, Edmond 1904-1971 *BioIn 9, ConAu 29*
Sehlstedt, Albert, Jr. *NF*
Seib, Charles Bach 1919- *InvJ, WhoAm 1974*
Seibel, Fred O 1887?-1969 *BioIn 8*
Seibel, George 1872-1958 *AmAu&B, WhNAA*
Seiberling, Dorothy *NF*
Seibold, Louis 1866?-1945 *AmJnl, CurBio XR,*
 DcAmB S3, DcNAA, NatCAB XR
Seidel, Phyllis *BioIn 9*
Seiden, Matthew J *NF*
Seidenbaum, Art 1930- *ConAu 29*
Seidenfaden, Erik 1910- *IntWW 1976,*
 WhoWor 1974
Seidl, Johann Gabriel 1804-1875 *OxGer, WebBD*
Seifert, E W 1898- *WhJnl Sup*
Seifert, Jaroslav 1901- *CasWL, EvEuW,*
 IntWW 1976, ModSL 2, Pen Eur,
 WhoWor 1974
Seifrit, Edwin Jacob 1894- *WhJnl 1928*
Seigel, Kalman 1917- *ConAu 25*
Seigenthaler, John Lawrence 1927- *RpN,*
 WhoAm 1974, WhoS&SW 1973
Seigenthaler, Walter A 1894- *WhJnl 1928*
Seil, William Jonathan 1866- *WhJnl 1928*
Seiler, R E 1893- *WhJnl 1928*
Seitel, Fraser Paul 1946- *NF*
Seitlin, Charlotte *OvPC*
Seitz, Don Carlos 1862-1935 *AmAu&B, AmLY,*
 DcAmB S1, DcNAA, LiJA, OhA&B,
 OxCan, REnAL, TwCA
Seitz, Nicholas Joseph 1939- *NF*
Sekey, Suzanne *BioIn 3*
Selby, Earl 1917?- *BioIn 2*
Selby, John 1897- *BioIn 2, ConAu 1R*
Selden, Charles Albert 1870-1949 *BioIn 1*
Selden, Harry L *OvPC*
Seldes, George 1890- *AmAu&B, AmRP,*
 Au&Wr, BioIn 3, BioIn 4, ConAu 7R,
 CurBio XR, HisAmM XR, NewMr, OxAm,
 REnAL, TwCA, TwCA Sup, WebBD,
 WhNAA, WhoAm 1974, WhJnl 1928,
 WrDr 1976
Seldes, Gilbert Vivian 1893-1970 *AmAu&B,*
 Au&Wr, CnDAL, ConAu 7R, ConAu 29,
 HisAmM XR, OxAm, Pen Am, REnAL,
 TwCA, TwCA Sup, WebBD
Seldin, Alexander 1882?-1949 *BioIn 2*
Seldis, Henry James 1925-1978 *WhoAm 1974,*
 WhoAmA 1973, WhoWest 1974
Self, Edwin Forbes 1920- *ConAu 69,*
 WhoWest 1974
Self, Gloria *NF*
Selig, Harris Leon 1880-1960 *BioIn 5*
Seligman, Daniel 1924- *WhoAm 1974,*
 WhoF&I 1974
Seligman, DeWitt *HisAmM XR*
Seligmann, Jean *NF*
Selikovitsch, Goetzel 1863-1926 *DcAmB 16*
Selim *see* Woodworth, Samuel
Selinko, Annemarie 1914- *Au&Wr, CurBio XR*
Sell, Henry Blackman 1889-1974 *AmAu&B,*
 BioIn 1, BioIn 2, BioIn 9, HisAmM XR,
 NewYTBS 5, WhoAm 1974
Sell, Ted 1928- *ConAu 69*
Sellar, Robert 1841-1919 *Alli Sup, DcNAA,*
 OxCan
Sellars, James *NF*
Sellers, Isaiah 1802?-1864 *AmAu&B, OxAm,*
 REnAL, WebBD
Sellers, Matthew Bacon 1869-1932 *WebBD*
Sellers, Paul *NF*
Sellers, Thomas 1920?-1972 *BioIn 9*
Sellers, William *AmJnl*
Sellew, Edwin P *HisAmM XR*

Sellin, Thorstein HisAmM XR
Selover, Marshall 1897- WhJnl 1928
Selsam, Howard 1903-1970 BioIn 9, ConAu 29,
  NewYTBE 1
Seltsam, William Henry 1897-1968 BioIn 8
Seltzer, George Schofield 1883?-1950 BioIn 2
Seltzer, Louis Benson 1897- AmAu&B, BioIn 1,
  BioIn 2, BioIn 3, BioIn 4, BioIn 5, BioIn 7,
  CurBio XR
Seltzer, Ruth 1916- WhoAm 1974,
  WhoAmW 1974, WhoE 1974
Selwyn, Amy NF
Selz, Lucile NF
Selzer, Richard 1928- ConAu 65
Sematones, Frank 1925- NF
Semple, Robert NF
Sender, Toni 1888- CurBio XR
Sendler, David A 1938- ConAu 65
Seney, Edgar F, Jr. RpN
Seng, Tay Bock NF
Sengstacke, Frederick D NF
Sengstacke, John Herman Henry 1912- BioIn 2,
  BioIn 8, BlkC, CurBio XR, WhoAm 1974
Sengstacke, Whittier A 1916- WhoAm 1974,
  WhoWor 1974
Senner, Joseph Henry 1846-1908 NF
Sensenderfer, Robert E P 1883?-1957 BioIn 4
Senter, Erasmus Gilbert 1865-1942 BioIn 2
Sentner, P David 1898-1975 ConAu 57,
  WhoAm 1974
Sepdiveda, Orlando ForP
Seppy, Thomas P NF
Serafin, Barry NF
Serao, Matilda 1856-1927 BbD, BiD&SB,
  CasWL, CIDMEL, DcBiA, EvEuW,
  Pen Eur, REn, WebBD
Sereno, El WebBD
Serge, Victor 1890-1947 AmRP, TwCA Sup
Sergel, Charles Hubbard 1861-1926 DcNAA
Sergel, Johan Tobias 1740-1814 BioIn 4
Sergel, Roger L HisAmM XR
Sergio, Lisa 1905- ConAu 61, CurBio XR
Serling, Robert Jerome 1918- ConAu 45,
  WhoE 1974
Serrati, Menotti NF
Serrill, Theodore Andrew 1911- WhoPubR 1972
Serrin, William NF
SerVaas, Beurt Richard 1919- BioIn 9,
  WhoAm 1974, WhoF&I 1974
SerVaas, Cory Synhorst 1924- WhoAm 1974
SerVaas, Sandra Jean 1947- WhoAm 1974
Servadio, Gaia 1938- Au&Wr, ConAu 25,
  WrDr 1976
Servan-Schreiber, Emile 1888?-1967 BioIn 8
Servan-Schreiber, Jean-Claude 1918- BioIn 7,
  IntWW 1976, WhoWor 1974
Servan-Schreiber, Jean-Jacques 1924- BioIn 3,
  BioIn 4, BioIn 8, BioIn 9, BioIn 10,
  CurBio XR, ForP, IntWW 1976, Who 1974,
  WhoWor 1974
Servan-Schreiber, Jean Louis 1937- BioIn 9
Serviss, Garrett Putnam 1851-1929 Alli Sup,
  AmLY, BioIn 1, DcAmA, DcNAA, REnAL,
  WebBD, WhNAA
Sesser, Stan InvJ
Sessions, Charles H 1868- WhJnl 1928
Sessions, Wesley O 1896- WhJnl 1928
Sestero, Nat Aldo 1914- WhoAm 1974
Set, Alan HisAmM XR
Seth, James 1860- DcAmA, HisAmM XR
Sethe, Paul 1901-1967 BioIn 7
Sether, J Wenpell OvPC
Seton, Al OvPC
Sette Camara, Jose 1920- IntWW 1976,

WhoWor 1974
Settel, Arthur 1911- WhoGov 1972,
  WhoPubR 1972, WhoWorJ 1972
Seuss, Dr. 1904- AmAu&B, AuBYP, MorJA,
  REn, REnAL, SmATA 1, Str&VC, TwCA,
  TwCA Sup, WhoChL, WrDr 1976
Seuss, Dr. see also Geisel, Theodor Seuss
Sevareid, Eric 1912- AmAu&B, AmJnl,
  AuNews 1, BioIn 1, BioIn 4, BioIn 5,
  BioIn 7, BioIn 8, BioNews 1974, CelR 1973,
  ConAu 69, CurBio XR, ForP, IntMPA 1975,
  IntWW 1974, NewMr, WhoAm 1974,
  WhoWor 1974
Severance, Frank Hayward 1856-1931 AmAu&B,
  AmLY, DcAmA, DcNAA, OxCan, WhNAA
Severance, Luther 1797-1855 NatCAB 13
Severance, Mary Harriman HisAmM XR
Severo, Richard 1932- ConAu 73
Severson, John 1932?- BioIn 7
Sevier, O'Neil 1874?-1950 BioIn 2
Sewall, Samuel E HisAmM XR
Sewall, William J 1866- WhJnl 1928
Seward, Frederick William 1830-1915 Alli Sup,
  BioIn 7, DcAmB 16, DcNAA
Sewell, Alfred L HisAmM XR
Sewell, Elizabeth HisAmM XR
Sewell, William George Grant 1829-1862 Alli,
  BbtC, DcNAA
Seybold, G E 1868- WhJnl 1928
Seybold, Geneva B 1900- WhJnl 1928
Seydel, Mildred ConAu 37
Seymore, James W NF
Seymour, Alan 1927- ConAu 53, ConDr,
  TwCW, WrDr 1976
Seymour, Arthur Hallock 1928- WhoAm 1974
Seymour, Charles C B 1829-1869 Alli, DcNAA
Seymour, Edward Loomis Davenport 1888-1956
  BioIn 1, BioIn 4, WhNAA
Seymour, Forrest W 1905- BioIn 1,
  WhoAm 1974
Seymour, Gideon Deming 1901-1954 BioIn 3,
  BioIn 6, InvJ, NatCAB 43, WhJnl 1928
Seymour, H S 1876- WhJnl 1928
Seymour, Henry James HisAmM XR
Seymour, Horatio Winslow 1854-1920 AmJnl,
  DcAmA, DcNAA, NatCAB 10, NatCAB 27
Seymour, Mary F HisAmM XR
Seymour, Ralph Fletcher 1876-1966 HisAmM XR
Shabad, Theodore 1922- ConAu 25, WhoE 1974
Shabecoff, Phillip NF
Shachtman, Max AmRP
Shackelford, Ruby P 1889- WhJnl 1928
Shackell, Aubrey Earle 1902- WhJnl 1928
Shackell, Robert George 1868- WhJnl 1928
Shackelton, Walter D NF
Shackford, Roland Herbert 1908- ConAu 3R,
  WhoAm 1974, WhoS&SW 1973,
  WhoWor 1974
Shackleton, Robert 1860-1923 AmAu&B,
  DcNAA, OhA&B
Shafer, Boyd Carlisle 1907- AmAu&B,
  ConAu 17, DrAS 74H, OhA&B,
  WhoAm 1974
Shafer, Burr 1899-1965 BioIn 7, BioIn 8
Shafer, Chet 1887?- BioIn 1
Shafer, Paul W 1893-1954 CurBio XR
Shafer, Ronald G 1939- ConAu 65
Shaffer, Carroll 1884- WhJnl 1928
Shaffer, Helen B NF
Shaffer, Jesse R, Jr. 1928- WhoAm 1974
Shaffer, John Charles 1853-1943 AmJnl, WhNAA
Shaffer, Samuel NF
Shafik, Doria 1919- CurBio XR, IntWW 1974
Shah, Diane Kiver 1945- ConAu 73

Shah, Raymond 1928- NF
Shain, Percy NF
Shainmark, Eliezer L 1900- WhoAm 1974,
  WhoWorJ 1972
Shakespeare, Frank J, Jr. 1925- IntWW 1976,
  WhoGov 1972
Shale, James B HisAmM XR
Shales, Thomas W NF
Shalett, Sidney 1911?-1965 BioIn 7
Shalit, Gene 1931?- BioIn 10
Shallman, Aron NF
Shallman, Lazaro 1905?-1978 NF
Shallus, Francis HisAmM XR
Shanahan, Eileen NF
Shanahan, Michael J NF
Shanahan, William D OvPC
Shanard, Marjorie Burns OvPC
Shand, Bob 1884- WhJnl 1928
Shand, Robert Gordon 1896-1966 BioIn 7
Shandler, Philip NF
Shandy, Hill 1901- WhJnl 1928
Shane, Paul NF
Shaner, Earl L 1890- WhJnl 1928
Shaner, Howard Seymour 1895- WhJnl 1928
Shaner, Joseph E BioIn 1
Shank, Joseph E 1892- ConAu 25
Shankar 1902- BioIn 2, IntWW 1976
Shanke, Edwin A NF
Shanks, Bruce McKinley 1908- WhoAm 1974,
  WhoAmA 1973
Shanks, Edward Richard Buxton 1892-1953
  BioIn 3, BioIn 7, WebBD
Shanks, Maria Gore 1876?-1950 BioIn 2
Shanks, Michael James 1927- ConAu 5R,
  Who 1974, WrDr 1976
Shanks, Sanders 1891-1949 BioIn 2
Shanks, William Franklin Gore 1837-1905
  AmAu&B, BiD&SB, BiDSA, DcAmA,
  DcNAA, NatCAB 3
Shanly, Charles Dawson 1811-1875 Alli,
  AmAu&B, DcAmA, HisAmM XR, PoIre
Shannon, Anthony NF
Shannon, Charles Barry 1891?-1946 BioIn 1
Shannon, Donald Hawkins 1923- OvPC,
  WhoAm 1974, WhoE 1974
Shannon, E Ralph 1888- WhJnl 1928
Shannon, Herb 1917- WhoWest 1974
Shannon, James NF
Shannon, Lewis William 1859- NF
Shannon, Margaret Rutledge 1917- WhoAm 1974,
  WhoAmW 1974, WhoS&SW 1973
Shannon, Thomas Vincent 1874- WhJnl 1928
Shannon, W P HisAmM XR
Shannon, William Vincent 1927- AmAu&B,
  ConAu 11R, WhoAm 1974
Shanor, Donald Read 1927- ConAu 61
Shantz, Stanley S 1902- WhJnl Sup
Shapiro, Fred C 1931- ConAu 19R
Shapiro, Harvey 1924- AmAu&B, ConAu 41,
  ConP 1970, ConP 1975, DrAP 1975,
  WhoAm 1974, WrDr 1976
Shapiro, Henry 1906- RpN, WhoAm 1974,
  WhoWor 1974, WhoWorJ 1972
Shapiro, Karl Jay 1913- AmAu&B, AnCL,
  CasWL, CnDAL, CnE&AP, ConAu 1,
  ConLC 4, ConP 1970, ConP 1975, DcLEL,
  DrAF 1976, DrAP 1975, DrAS 74E,
  EncWL, EvLB, HisAmM XR, IntWW 1974,
  ModAL, ModAL Sup, OxAm, Pen Am,
  RAdv 1, REn, REnAL, SixAP, TwCA Sup,
  TwCW, WebBD, WebE&AL, WhoAm 1974,
  WhoTwCL, WhoWorJ 1972, WrDr 1976
Shapiro, Lionel 1908-1958 OxCan
Shapiro, Melvin 1938- WhoAm 1974

Shapiro, Rebecca AuBYP, BioIn 8
Shaplen, Joseph 1893-1946 BioIn 1
Shaplen, Robert Modell 1917- AmAu&B,
  ConAu 9R, RpN, WhoAm 1974,
  WhoWor 1974, WrDr 1976
Sharfman, Bern NF
Sharkey, Donald C 1912-, BioIn 3, BkC 3,
  CathA 1952, OhA&B
Sharkey, Joseph Edward 1877-1958 BioIn 4,
  WhNAA
Sharman, Chuck BioIn 8
Sharp, B Marion 1896- WhJnl 1928
Sharp, Eliot Hall 1903- OvPC, WhoAm 1974,
  WhoF&I 1974
Sharp, Eugene W NF
Sharp, Hal NF
Sharp, Lee J 1893- WhJnl 1928
Sharp, Roger 1935- ConAu 73
Sharp, Sidney 1870-1943 AmAu&B, WhNAA
Sharp, Sidney see also Mapes, Victor
Sharp, T E 1892- WhJnl 1928
Sharpe, Bill 1903- BioIn 3, BioIn 4, BioIn 5
Sharpe, Constance NF
Sharpe, Ernest Alonzo 1916- AmM&W 73S
Sharpe, John Allen 1873- WhJnl 1928
Sharpe, Paul M 1914?- BioIn 8
Shatley, James NF
Shattuc, W B HisAmM XR
Shattuck, Frances BioIn 4
Shattuck, George Brune 1844-1923 BioIn 3,
  HisAmM XR, WebBD
Shattuck, Jim NF
Shaub, Earl L 1886- BioIn 6
Shaver, Bud NF
Shavin, Norman 1926- NF
Shaw, Adele Marie 1865?-1941 AmAu&B,
  AmLY, DcNAA, HisAmM XR, WhNAA
Shaw, Albert 1857-1947 Alli Sup, AmAu&B,
  BbD, BiD&SB, BioIn 1, BioIn 2, DcAmA,
  DcAmB S4, DcNAA, HisAmM XR,
  NatCAB 34, OhA&B, OxAm, REnAL,
  WebBD, WhNAA
Shaw, Albert, Jr. HisAmM XR
Shaw, Alexander Preston 1879- BioIn 1
Shaw, Arch Wilkinson 1876- HisAmM XR,
  WhJnl 1928
Shaw, Archer H 1876- OhA&B, WhJnl 1928
Shaw, Bernard NF
Shaw, Bernard 1856-1950 CurBio XR, CyWA,
  LongC, REnWD
Shaw, Bernard see also Shaw, George Bernard
Shaw, Bruno 1905- BioIn 1, OvPC,
  WhoAm 1974
Shaw, Bunny BioIn 3
Shaw, Bynum 1923- ConAu 3R
Shaw, Charles Emory HisAmM XR
Shaw, Chet 1898- BioIn 2
Shaw, David 1943- ConAu 49
Shaw, Dean Brian 1933- NF
Shaw, Donald Lewis 1936- ConAu 61, DrAS 74H
Shaw, Edgar Dwight 1871-1931 AmAu&B
Shaw, Edward NF
Shaw, Edward R 1870- WhJnl 1928
Shaw, Elton Raymond 1886-1955 NatCAB 48,
  WhNAA
Shaw, Fred d1972 BioIn 9
Shaw, Gaylord 1942- NF
Shaw, George Bernard 1856-1950 Alli Sup,
  AtlBL, BiD&SB, CasWL, CnMD, CnMWL,
  CnThe, DcBiA, DcEnA Ap, DcLEL,
  EncWL, EvLB, McGWD, ModBL,
  ModBL Sup, ModWD, NewC, OxEng,
  Pen Eng, RComWL, REn, REnWD, TwCA,
  TwCA Sup, TwCW, WebBD, WebE&AL,

WhoTwCL
Shaw, George Bernard *see also* Shaw, Bernard
Shaw, Grace Goodfriend 1920- *ForWC 1970,*
OvPC, WhoAmW 1974
Shaw, Harry *WhJnl 1928*
Shaw, Harry C 1873- *WhJnl 1928*
Shaw, Harry Lee, Jr. 1905- *WhoAm 1974*
Shaw, Henry Wheeler 1818-1885 *Alli, Alli Sup,*
AmAu, AmAu&B, BbD, BiD&SB, CasWL,
CnDAL, DcAmA, DcEnL, DcLEL, DcNAA,
EvLB, HisAmM XR, OhA&B, OxAm,
OxEng, Pen Am, REn, REnAL, WebBD
Shaw, Howard *HisAmM XR*
Shaw, James Gerard 1909- *BioIn 3, BioIn 4,*
BkC 5
Shaw, John *NF*
Shaw, Lawrence Hugh 1940- *AmEA 1974,*
AmM&W 73S, ConAu 69
Shaw, Len G *NF*
Shaw, Leon 1872- *WhJnl 1928*
Shaw, Mildred Lee 1899- *WhJnl 1928*
Shaw, Peter J *NF*
Shaw, Ray *ConAu 33, ForWC 1970, OvPC,*
SmATA 7, WhoAmW 1974, WrDr 1976
Shaw, Reeves 1886-1952 *BioIn 2*
Shaw, Roger 1903-1959 *BioIn 5, BioIn 7,*
HisAmM XR
Shaw, Samuel Craig 1874- *WhJnl 1928*
Shaw, Shullen *NF*
Shaw, W B *NF*
Shaw, Wilfred Byron 1881- *AmAu&B, BioIn 1,*
HisAmM XR
Shaw, William Smith 1778-1826 *Alli, AmAu&B,*
HisAmM XR
Shawhan, Ralph 1903?- *BioIn 1*
Shawn, William 1907- *AmAu&B, BioIn 2,*
BioIn 9, CelR 1973, IntWW 1976, NewMr,
WhoAm 1974, WhoWor 1974
Shay, Arthur 1922- *ConAu 33, SmATA 4,*
WhoAm 1974, WhoMW 1974
Shay, Felix *HisAmM XR*
Shea, Catherine L *NF*
Shea, Frank R 1908-1978 *NF*
Shea, Hamilton 1914- *WhoAm 1974*
Shea, John Augustus 1802-1845 *Alli, AmAu&B,*
DcAmA, DcNAA, PoIre
Shea, John Dawson Gilmary 1824-1892 *Alli,*
Alli Sup, AmAu, AmAu&B, BbD, BbtC,
BiD&SB, CyAL 2, DcAmA, DcNAA,
HisAmM XR, OxAm, OxCan, WebBD
Sheaffer, Louis 1912- *Au&Wr, ConAu XR,*
WrDr 1976
Sheahan, James Washington 1824-1883 *Alli,*
AmJnl, DcNAA
Sheahan, John *NF*
Shean, J Fred 1891- *WhJnl 1928*
Shearer, Ted *NF*
Shearon, Lowe 1868?-1948 *BioIn 1*
Shearon, William H 1914-1963 *BioIn 1, BioIn 3,*
BioIn 6
Shecter, Leonard 1926-1974 *BioIn 10, ConAu 45,*
NewYTBS 5
Shedd, Fred Fuller 1871-1937 *BioIn 4,*
DcAmB S2
Sheean, Vincent 1899-1975 *AmAu&B, AmNov,*
BioIn 1, BioIn 2, BioIn 3, BioIn 4, BioIn 5,
CnDAL, ConAmA, ConAu 61, CurBio XR,
HisAmM XR, NewYTBS 5, OxAm, REn,
REnAL, TwCA, TwCA Sup, WebBD
Sheed, Wilfrid John Joseph 1930- *AmAu&B,*
ConLC 2, ConLC 4, ConNov 1972,
ConNov 1976, DrAF 1976, ModAL Sup,
NewC, WhoAm 1974, WorAu, WrDr 1976
Sheehan, Bill *NF*

Sheehan, Ed *NF*
Sheehan, John William, Jr. 1884- *WhJnl 1928*
Sheehan, Joseph Matthew 1914-1970 *BioIn 9,*
NewYTBE 1
Sheehan, Marion Turner 1914?-1968 *BioIn 8*
Sheehan, Neil 1936- *ConAu 29, NewMr,*
NewYTBE 2, WhoAm 1974
Sheehan, Paul Vincent 1904- *ConAu 33,*
DrAS 74E, WhoAm 1974, WhoWest 1974,
WrDr 1976
Sheehan, Perley Poore 1875-1943 *AmAu&B,*
DcNAA, OhA&B, WhNAA
Sheehan, Richard G 1922-1966 *BioIn 7*
Sheehan, Robert Wade 1903-1971 *BioIn 9,*
NewYTBE 2
Sheehan, Susan 1937- *Au&Wr, ConAu 21R,*
WhoAmW 1974, WrDr 1976
Sheehan, William *OvPC*
Sheehan, William A 1883-1956 *BioIn 4*
Sheehan, Winfield R 1883-1945 *CurBio XR*
Sheehy, Gail 1937?- *BioIn 9, ConAu 49,*
NewMr
Sheekman, Arthur 1901-1978 *IntMPA 1975*
Sheen, Marion J 1902?-1955 *BioIn 3*
Sheerin, Chris H 1903- *WhJnl 1928*
Sheets, Millard Owen 1907- *DcCAA,*
WhoAm 1974
Sheffer, Eugene *NF*
Shefrin, David Z *OvPC*
Shehan, Henry *HisAmM XR*
Shehan, Thomas F *OvPC*
Sheils, Merrill *NF*
Sheinman, Mort *NF*
Sheinwold, Alfred 1912- *ConAu 61,*
WhoAm 1974, WhoWor 1974
Shelby, Gertrude Mathews 1881-1936 *AmAu&B,*
DcNAA
Sheldon, Alexander E *HisAmM XR*
Sheldon, Arthur Frederick 1868-1935 *AmLY,*
DcNAA, HisAmM XR
Sheldon, Charles Monroe 1857-1946 *AmAu&B,*
AmJnl, BiD&SB, BioIn 1, BioIn 2,
CurBio XR, DcAmA, DcLEL, DcNAA,
EvLB, HisAmM XR, LongC, OxAm, REn,
REnAL, TwCA, TwCA Sup, WebBD
Sheldon, Courtney Roswell 1920- *USBiR 1974,*
WhoAm 1974, WhoE 1974, WhoWor 1974
Sheldon, Electra *HisAmM XR*
Sheldon, George *NF*
Sheldon, Grace Carew 1855- *DcNAA*
Sheldon, Isabella 1871?-1951 *BioIn 2*
Sheldon, James H *OvPC*
Sheldon, John P 1792-1871 *AmJnl, BioIn 5*
Sheldon, Preston King 1892?-1972 *BioIn 9*
Sheldon, W Raymond 1893- *WhJnl 1928*
Shellman, Henry J d1894 *NF*
Shelton, Gilbert *NF*
Shelton, Herbert M 1895- *WhJnl 1928*
Shelton, Isabelle *NF*
Shelton, Lynn 1912?- *BioIn 3*
Shelton, O M *NF*
Shelton, Robert *NF*
Shelton, Sam J *NF*
Shelton, William Ellington 1905-1970 *BioIn 9*
Shelton, William Hazen 1901-1955 *BioIn 5,*
NatCAB 42
Shelton, William Henry 1840-1932 *AmAu&B,*
AmLY, DcNAA, HisAmM XR
Shelton, William Roy 1919- *AuNews 1,*
ConAu 5R, SmATA 5
Shemanski, Frances 1925- *ForWC 1970*
Shen, Linda *NF*
Shen, Shan *RpN*
Shenfeld, Gary *OvPC*

Shenkel, William T d1944 *AmJnl, BioIn 3*
Shenker, Israel 1925- *WrDr 1976*
Sheodon, Frederick *HisAmM XR*
Shepard, Elaine 1923- *BioIn 6, ConAu 21R,*
OvPC
Shepard, Elizabeth G d1899 *DcNAA*
Shepard, Gary *NF*
Shepard, H D *AmJnl*
Shepard, Isaac Fitzgerald 1816-1889 *Alli,*
AmAu&B, DcAmA, DcNAA
Shepard, Nathaniel *NF*
Shepard, P W *HisAmM XR*
Shepard, Richard *NF*
Shepard, Thomas Rockwell, Jr. 1918-
WhoAdv 1972, WhoAm 1974, WhoE 1974,
WhoF&I 1974
Shepard, Thomas W *HisAmM XR*
Shepherd, Emalene *NF*
Shepherd, Forrest *HisAmM XR*
Shepherd, Grace 1897- *WhJnl 1928*
Shepherd, Jack 1937- *ConAu 57*
Shepherd, James *NF*
Shepherd, Jean *AmAu&B, AuNews 2, OvPC*
Shepherd, Jean 1923- *CelR 1973*
Shepherd, Richard *NF*
Shepherd, William Gunn 1878-1933 *AmJnl,*
DcNAA, HisAmM XR, OhA&B
Shepherdson, Francis W *HisAmM XR*
Shepilov, Dmitri Trofimovitch 1905?- *BioIn 4,*
CurBio XR, IntWW 1976, WhoWor 1974
Shepler, Fred B 1891- *WhJnl 1928*
Shepler, Ned 1896- *WhJnl 1928*
Shepley, James Robinson 1917- *IntWW 1976,*
WhoAm 1974, WhoF&I 1974
Shepp, Daniel B 1863-1940 *NatCAB 31*
Sheppard, Barry 1937- *AmRP, ConAu 61*
Sheppard, Don 1926?- *BioIn 1*
Sheppard, Edmund Ernest 1855-1924 *DcNAA,*
OxCan
Sheppard, Eugenia Benbow 1910- *BioIn 5,*
BioIn 6, BioIn 9
Sheppard, George 1819-1912 *BbtC, BioIn 2,*
DcNAA
Sheppard, Harper Donelson 1868-1951 *BioIn 2,*
BioIn 4
Sheppard, Nathan 1834-1888 *Alli Sup, AmAu&B,*
BiDSA, DcAmA, DcNAA
Sheppard, R Z *NF*
Sheppard, Sally 1917- *ConAu 69*
Sheppe, Edwin S, Sr. *WhJnl 1928*
Sheps, Elias 1892-1963 *BioIn 6*
Sher, Zelig 1888-1971 *BioIn 9*
Sherard, Robert Harborough 1861-1943
CurBio XR, HisAmM XR
Sheraton, Mimi *NF*
Shercliff, Jose *NF*
Shere, Dennis 1940- *WhoAm 1974*
Shere, Sam *NF*
Sheridan, Bart 1912- *OvPC, WhoAm 1974,*
WhoWest 1974
Sheridan, Dave 1943- *BioIn 10*
Sheridan, Martin 1914- *OvPC, WhNAA,*
WhoAm 1974, WhoF&I 1974,
WhoPubR 1972
Sheridan, Mary *NF*
Sheridan, Robert E *OvPC*
Sheridan, Sarah Ann *NF*
Sheridan, Thomas 1684?-1738 *Alli, DcAmA,*
ForP, PoIre, WebBD
Sheridan, Walter 1916?- *BioIn 8*
Sherin, George A *HisAmM XR*
Sherk, Mrs. J M *WhJnl 1928*
Sherley, Connie *NF*
Sherlock, Chesla Clella 1895-1938 *DcNAA,*

HisAmM XR, WhNAA, WhJnl 1928
Sherman, Albion F 1893- *WhJnl 1928*
Sherman, Arnold 1932- *ConAu 33, WrDr 1976*
Sherman, Benjamin Franklin 1836-1915 *BioIn 5*
Sherman, Charles Sumner 1871- *WhJnl 1928*
Sherman, Clifton Lucien 1866-1946 *AmAu&B*
Sherman, Edgar Leslie 1873-1946 *BioIn 3*
Sherman, Frederic Fairchild 1874-1940
CurBio XR, DcNAA
Sherman, George *NF*
Sherman, Jerry 1930- *OvPC, WhoPubR 1972*
Sherman, John D *NF*
Sherman, John Dickinson 1859-1926 *NF*
Sherman, Loren A 1844-1914 *NatCAB 16*
Sherman, Maurice Sinclair 1873-1947 *BioIn 1,*
WhJnl 1928
Sherman, Patrick 1928- *WhoAm 1974*
Sherman, Ray Wesley 1884-1971 *BioIn 9,*
ConAu 33
Sherman, Sharon F *NF*
Sherman, Stuart Pratt 1881-1926 *AmAu&B,*
ConAmA, ConAmL, DcLEL, DcNAA,
EvLB, HisAmM XR, OxAm, Pen Am,
REnAL, TwCA
Sherman, William S 1946- *InvJ*
Shero, Jeffrey *NF*
Sherr, Linda *NF*
Sherrill, John Bascom 1864- *WhJnl 1928*
Sherrill, Robert Glenn 1925- *ConAu 21R,*
NewMr, WhoS&SW 1973
Sherrod, Blackie 1920- *AuNews 2*
Sherrod, Blackie see also Sherrod, William Forrest
Sherrod, Robert Lee 1909- *AmAu&B, BioIn 3,*
BioIn 6, CurBio XR, HisAmM XR,
IntWW 1976, OvPC, WhoAm 1974,
WhoS&SW 1973
Sherrod, William Forrest 1920- *WhoAm 1974,*
WhoS&SW 1973
Sherrod, William Forrest see also Sherrod, Blackie
Sherry, Mrs. Arthur H *RpN*
Sherwin, Lewis *HisAmM XR*
Sherwin, Louis 1883?-1978 *NF*
Sherwin, Mark 1919?-1962 *BioIn 6*
Sherwood, Elizabeth Julia 1883-1963 *BioIn 6*
Sherwood, Emily Lee 1843- *DcAmA*
Sherwood, Hugh C 1928- *ConAu 29, WrDr 1976*
Sherwood, Isaac Ruth 1835-1925 *AmAu&B,*
DcNAA, OhA&B
Sherwood, James Manning 1814-1890 *Alli,*
Alli Sup, DcAmA, DcNAA, HisAmM XR
Sherwood, John R *NF*
Sherwood, Kate Brownlee 1841-1914 *Alli Sup,*
AmAu&B
Sherwood, Kate Brownlee see also Sherwood,
Katharine M Brownlee
Sherwood, Katharine Margaret Brownlee 1841-1914
DcAmA, DcNAA, NatCAB 2, OhA&B
Sherwood, Katharine Margaret Brownlee see also
Sherwood, Kate B
Sherwood, Robert Emmet 1896-1955 *AmAu&B,*
CasWL, CnDAL, CnMD, CnThe, ConAmA,
CurBio XR, CyWA, DcAmB S5, DcLEL,
EncWL, EvLB, HisAmM XR, LongC,
McGWD, ModAL, ModWD, OxAm,
Pen Am, REn, REnAL, REnWD, TwCA,
TwCA Sup, TwCW, WebBD, WebE&AL
Sherwood, Virginia *NF*
Shevelson, Harris 1916?- *BioIn 1*
Shevey, Sandra *NF*
Shew, Edward Spencer 1908-1977 *Au&Wr,*
ConAu 1R, ConAu 69
Shideler, H W 1873- *WhJnl 1928*
Shidle, Norman Glass 1895- *AmAu&B,*
ConAu 17, WhJnl 1928

Shiel, Matthew Phipps 1865-1947 *BbD, DcLEL, EncMys, LongC, NewC, TwCA, TwCA Sup, WebBD, WhoLA*
Shields, Edward Gustavus 1870- *WhJnl 1928*
Shields, Edward J *NF*
Shields, George Oliver 1846-1925 *Alli Sup, AmAu, AmAu&B, AmLY, DcAmA, DcNAA, HisAmM XR, OhA&B*
Shields, Jerry *BioIn 10*
Shields, Lacey Herbert 1878- *WhJnl 1928*
Shields, Mark 1889?-1953 *BioIn 3*
Shields, Mrs. S A *HisAmM XR*
Shier, Carlton S 1875- *WhJnl 1928*
Shifrin, Carole A *NF*
Shiga, Yoshio 1901- *IntWW 1976, WhoWor 1974*
Shih, Comet K M *NF*
Shillaber, Benjamin Penhallow 1814-1890 *Alli, Alli Sup, AmAu, AmAu&B, BbD, BiD&SB, CarSB, CnDAL, DcAmA, DcAmB 17, DcEnL, DcLEL, DcNAA, HisAmM XR, OxAm, REnAL, WebBD*
Shillaber, William *NF*
Shimansky, O K 1872- *WhJnl 1928*
Shimizu, Teiji *NF*
Shimkin, Arthur 1922- *WhoAm 1974*
Shindler, Merrill *NF*
Shine, Neal James 1930- *WhoAm 1974*
Shinkman, Paul Alfred 1897- *WhoAm 1974*
Shinn, Bill *AmJnl*
Shinn, Charles Howard 1852-1924 *Alli Sup, AmLY, BbD, BiD&SB, DcAmA, DcNAA, HisAmM XR*
Shinn, Earl 1837-1886 *Alli Sup, DcAmA, DcNAA, HisAmM XR*
Shinn, Earl *see also* Strahan, Edward
Shinn, Everett 1876-1953 *CurBio XR, DcAmB S5, DcCAA, WebBD*
Shinn, Milicent Washburn 1858-1940 *AmLY, BiD&SB, CurBio XR, DcAmA, DcNAA, HisAmM XR, LiJA, WhNAA*
Shinnar, Beno 1913?-1970 *BioIn 9*
Shinnick, William C 1895?-1957 *BioIn 4*
Shipard, W A 1867- *WhJnl 1928*
Shipler, David *NF*
Shipley, Joseph T 1893- *AmAu&B, AnMV 1926, BioIn 2, ConAu 15R, REnAL, WhNAA, WhoAm 1974, WhJnl 1928, WhoThe 1972, WrDr 1976*
Shipman, Elydia Foss 1881- *WhJnl 1928*
Shipman, Evan 1903?-1957 *BioIn 4*
Shipman, George Elias 1820-1893 *Alli Sup, DcNAA, HisAmM XR*
Shipman, Louis Evan 1869-1933 *AmAu&B, BiD&SB, DcAmA, DcNAA, HisAmM XR*
Shipp, Bill *NF*
Shipp, Cameron 1903-1961 *AmAu&B, BioIn 6*
Shipp, Nelson 1892- *ConAu 57*
Shippey, Lee 1884-1969 *AmAu&B, BioIn 5, BioIn 8, HisAmM XR, WhNAA*
Shippy, Richard 1927- *NF*
Shipton, Audus Walton 1893-1964 *BioIn 8, NatCAB 51*
Shirakawa, Michinobu *RpN*
Shire, Al *NF*
Shirer, William Lawrence 1904- *AmAu&B, AmJnl, Au&Wr, AuBYP, BioIn 1, BioIn 2, BioIn 3, BioIn 4, BioIn 6, BioIn 7, BioIn 8, ConAu 9R, CurBio XR, IntWW 1976, OxAm, REn, REnAL, TwCA Sup, WebBD, Who 1974, WhoAm 1974, WhoWor 1974, WrDr 1976*
Shires, Thomas Donald 1909- *WhoAm 1974*
Shirey, Dave *InvJ*

Shirlaw, Walter 1838-1909 *HisAmM XR*
Shirley, Anne 1919- *BioIn 1*
Shirley, Dana *HisAmM XR*
Shirley, Hardy Lomax 1900- *AmM&W 73P, BioIn 1, BioIn 2, BioIn 3, BioIn 7, ConAu 37, IndAu 1917, WhoAm 1974*
Shirley, William *NF*
Shivanandan, Mary *NF*
Shively, Carlton A 1891?-1952 *BioIn 2*
Shively, John W *RpN*
Shklovsky, Isaac Vladimirovich 1865- *NF*
Shlonsky, Abraham 1900?-1973 *ConAu 41, WhoWor 1974*
Shloss, Leon W d1976 *NF*
Shmidt, Otto Iulevich 1891- *BioIn 1*
Shnayerson, Robert Beahan 1925- *BioIn 9, WhoAm 1974, WhoE 1974*
Shneiderman, Samuel I *NF*
Shober, Charles Ernest *HisAmM XR*
Shoemaker, Donald Cleavenger 1912- *AmAu&B*
Shoemaker, Francis Henry 1889-1958 *NF*
Shoemaker, Henry Wharton 1882-1958 *AmAu&B, AmLY, BioIn 5*
Shoemaker, Vaughn 1902- *AmAu&B, BioIn 1, BioIn 3, WhoAm 1974, WhoAmA 1973, WhoWor 1974*
Shoemaker, Vivien Keatley 1909?-1972 *BioIn 9*
Shoemaker, W C *NF*
Shoenfield, Allen 1896?-1979 *NF*
Shoffner, Charles P 1868?- *WhJnl 1928*
Shofield, John *ForP*
Shogan, Robert *NF*
Sholes, Charles Clark 1816-1867 *BioIn 5*
Sholes, Christopher Latham 1819-1890 *AmJnl, BioIn 3, BioIn 5, BioIn 7, BioIn 8, DcAmB 17, WebBD*
Sholis, Victor Adam 1910- *WhoAm 1974, WhoS&SW 1973*
Shollenberger, Lewis Winnbert 1916- *WhoAdv 1972, WhoAm 1974*
Shonting, Howard Leroy 1909- *WhoF&I 1974*
Shonts, Theodore Perry *HisAmM XR*
Shontz, Patricia Jane 1933- *AmEA 1974, WhoAm 1974*
Shoop, Clarence Fred 1883- *WhJnl 1928*
Shoop, Duke 1905-1957 *BioIn 4*
Shope, T S 1874- *WhJnl 1928*
Shoquist, Joseph William 1925- *WhoAm 1974, WhoF&I 1974, WhoWor 1974*
Shor, Franc Marion Luther 1914- *WhoAm 1974*
Shor, George Gershon 1884-1967 *BioIn 7, WhJnl 1928*
Shore, Benjamin *NF*
Shore, Rufus A 1876- *WhJnl 1928*
Shore, Sidney *OvPC*
Shore, Viola Brothers 1895- *WhJnl 1928*
Shorey, John L *HisAmM XR*
Shorey, Paul 1857-1934 *AmAu&B, BiD&SB, DcNAA, HisAmM XR, WhNAA*
Shoriki, Matsutaro 1885-1969 *BioIn 3, BioIn 4, BioIn 5, BioIn 6, BioIn 8, CurBio XR, ForP*
Shorris, Earl 1936- *ConAu 65*
Short, Carlton Bryce 1888-1946 *BioIn 1, BioIn 2, NatCAB 35*
Short, Charles Wilkins *Alli, HisAmM XR*
Short, Donald H 1904-1969 *BioIn 8*
Short, Harvey M 1866- *WhJnl 1928*
Short, Howard Elmo 1907- *ConAu 61, DrAS 74P, WhoAm 1974, WhoWor 1974*
Short, Joseph Hudson, Jr. 1904-1952 *AmJnl, BioIn 2, BioIn 3, BioIn 8, CurBio XR, WhNAA, WhJnl 1928*
Shorter, Clement King 1857-1926 *BiD&SB,*

DcEnA Ap, DcLEL, EvLB, HisAmM XR,
  LongC, NewC, TwCA, WebBD
Shoshano, Rose 1895?-1968 *BioIn 8*
Shoskes, Henry 1891-1964 *BioIn 6*
Shosteck, Patti *NF*
Shott, Hugh Ike 1868-1953 *BioIn 3, BioIn 6,*
  NatCAB 46
Shott, James Howard 1895-1957 *BioIn 6,*
  NatCAB 46
Shotwell, Thomas Cooper 1867?-1957 *BioIn 4*
Showalter, W D *HisAmM XR*
Showalter, William Joseph 1878-1935
  HisAmM XR
Showers, Paul C 1910- *ConAu 1R*
Showker, Kay *NF*
Shrader, Frederick F *HisAmM XR*
Shrady, George Frederick 1837-1907 *DcAmB 17,*
  DcNAA, HisAmM XR, WebBD
Shreve, Thomas Hopkins 1808-1853 *Alli,*
  AmAu&B, BiDSA, DcAmA, DcNAA,
  HisAmM XR, OhA&B
Shridharani, Krishanalal Jethalal 1911-1960
  BioIn 5, CurBio XR
Shriner, Charles Anthony 1853-1945 *DcNAA,*
  OhA&B, WhNAA
Shriner, Ralph Lloyd 1899- *AmM&W 73P,*
  BioIn 2, WhNAA, WhoAm 1974
Shriver, John Shultz 1857-1915 *Alli Sup, BiDSA,*
  DcAmA, DcNAA
Shropshire, John H *NF*
Shroyer, Frederick Benjamin 1916- *AmAu&B,*
  ConAu 13R, DrAS 74E, IndAu 1917,
  WhoAm 1974, WhoWest 1974
Shryock, James N 1895- *WhJnl 1928*
Shub, Anatole 1928- *WhoAm 1974*
Shub, Boris 1912-1965 *BioIn 7*
Shub, David 1887-1973 *BioIn 9, BioIn 10,*
  ConAu 41, NewYTBE 4
Shuford, Cecil Eugene 1907- *AuNews 1,*
  ConAu 13R, DrAS 74E, WhoAm 1974
Shuker, Gregory Brown 1932- *WhoAm 1974*
Shuler, Marjorie *WhNAA*
Shull, George Harrison 1874-1954 *WebBD,*
  WhNAA
Shull, Leo 1913- *BiE&WWA, WhoAdv 1972,*
  WhoAm 1974, WhoThe 1972
Shull, Richard K *NF*
Shulman, Arthur 1927- *OvPC, WhoAm 1974*
Shulman, Milton 1913- *Au&Wr, Who 1974,*
  WhoThe 1972, WrDr 1976
Shulsky, Sam *NF*
Shultes, Mildred *WhJnl 1928*
Shults, A B *HisAmM XR*
Shultz, Gladys Denny 1895- *ConAu 49*
Shultz, Gladys Denny *see also* Schultz, Gladys Denny
Shumaker, James H *NF*
Shuman, A L 1872- *WhJnl 1928*
Shuman, Edwin Llewellyn 1863-1941 *AmAu&B,*
  AmJnl, AmLY, DcAmA, DcNAA,
  NatCAB 15, WhNAA
Shuman, Frederick Lewis 1904- *HisAmM XR*
Shuman, Frederick Lewis *see also* Schuman,
  Frederick Lewis
Shuman, Ik 1893?-1965 *BioIn 1, BioIn 7*
Shuman, James B 1932- *ConAu 61*
Shuman, Joseph 1903- *WhoAm 1974*
Shuman, Nicholas Roman 1921- *WhoAm 1974,*
  WhoWor 1974
Shunick, Maurice E 1890- *WhJnl 1928*
Shupak, Rose *NF*
Shupeck, Ian D *NF*
Shupert, George Thomas 1904- *IntMPA 1975,*
  WhoAm 1974, WhoF&I 1974,
  WhoS&SW 1973

Shurick, Edward Palmes 1912- *WhoAm 1974,*
  WhoE 1974, WhoF&I 1974
Shurkin, Joel N 1938- *ConAu 69*
Shuster, Alvin 1930?- *NF*
Shuster, George Nauman 1894-1977 *AmAu&B,*
  BkC 4, CathA 1930, ConAu 69,
  CurBio XR, DrAS 74E, IntWW 1974,
  REnAL, TwCA, TwCA Sup, WebBD,
  WhoAm 1974, WhoWor 1974
Shuster, William Morgan 1877-1960 *HisAmM XR,*
  NatCAB 47, WebBD
Shuttee, Mary Margaret *WhJnl Sup*
Shuttlesworth, Dorothy 1907- *BioIn 9, SmATA 3*
Shuttleworth, Jack *HisAmM XR*
Shuttleworth, Jane *AuNews 1*
Shuttleworth, John 1937- *AuNews 1*
Shutts, Frank B 1870-1947 *WhJnl 1928*
Shwartz, Pinchas 1902?-1963 *BioIn 6*
Siatos, Thomas John 1923- *WhoAm 1974*
Sibley, Frank Palmer 1872?-1949 *BioIn 2*
Sibley, Hiram Ellis 1891- *WhJnl 1928*
Sibley, John LaBarre 1928-1974 *BioIn 10,*
  NewYTBS 5
Sibley, William Giddings 1860-1935 *AmLY,*
  DcNAA, OhA&B, WhNAA, WhJnl 1928
Siddall, John MacAlpine 1874-1923 *DcNAA,*
  HisAmM XR, NatCAB 19, OhA&B
Siddiqui, Manzur *RpN*
Siddon, Arthur J *NF*
Sidebotham, Herbert 1872-1940 *BioIn 2, BioIn 5*
Sider, Don 1933- *NF*
Sidey, Hugh Swanson 1927- *WhoAm 1974,*
  WhoWor 1974
Sidlo, Thomas L 1888- *WhJnl 1928*
Sidore, Saul O 1907-1964 *BioIn 9*
Siebert, Frederick Seaton 1902- *ForP,*
  WhoAm 1974, WhJnl Sup
Siebert, Horst A *NF*
Siegal, Allan *NF*
Siegart, Alice *NF*
Siegel, Barry *NF*
Siegel, Eli 1902-1978 *AmAu&B, ConAu 19,*
  ConP 1970, ConP 1975, REnAL,
  WhoAm 1974, WhoE 1974, WhoWorJ 1972,
  WrDr 1976
Siegel, Eric *NF*
Siegel, Marcia B 1932- *ConAu 69*
Siegel, Marvin *NF*
Siegel, Morris *NF*
Siegel, Seymour Nathaniel 1908- *NewYTBE 2,*
  OvPC, WhoAm 1974, WhoE 1974,
  WhoWorJ 1972
Siegenthaler, Robert *NF*
Siegrist, Mary d1953 *AmAu&B*
Sieniawski, Michael *OvPC*
Siepmann, Eric Otto *BioIn 4*
Sierra, Justo 1814-1861 *BioIn 2*
Sifford, Charles Darrell 1931- *WhoAm 1974,*
  WhoS&SW 1973
Sifton, Sir Clifford 1861-1929 *OxCan, WebBD*
Sifton, Clifford 1893-1976 *CanWW 1972,*
  WhoAm 1974, WhoCan 1973, WhoWor 1974
Sifton, John W *WhJnl 1928*
Sifton, Michael Clifford 1931- *CanWW 1972,*
  WhoAm 1974, WhoCan 1973, WhoE 1974
Sifton, Paul F 1897-1972 *CnMD, ConAu 33,*
  ModWD, NewYTBE 3, WhJnl 1928
Sifton, Victor 1897-1961 *BioIn 5, BioIn 6*
Sigal, Clancy 1926- *AmAu&B, ConAu 1,*
  ConNov 1972, ConNov 1976, DrAF 1976,
  Pen Am, WhoAm 1974, WorAu, WrDr 1976
Sigale, Merwin K *OvPC*

Sigel, Albert 1827-1884 *BioIn 2*
Sigel, Franz 1824-1902 *BioIn 1, BioIn 2,*
 BioIn 3, BioIn 7, HisAmM XR, WebBD
Signer, Robert A *NF*
Sigourney, Lydia Howard Huntley 1791-1865 *Alli,*
 AmAu, AmAu&B, BbD, BiD&SB, CarSB,
 CasWL, CnDAL, CyAL 1, DcAmA, DcEnL,
 DcLEL, DcNAA, EvLB, FemPA,
 HisAmM XR, OxAm, PoChrch, REnAL,
 WebBD
Sikes, Allen Belknap 1900- *WhJnl 1928*
Sikes, William Wirt 1836-1883 *Alli, Alli Sup,*
 AmAu&B, DcAmA, DcAmB 17, DcNAA,
 HsB&A
Silberkleit, Louis Horace 1905- *WhoAm 1974*
Silberman, Arlene *NF*
Silberman, Charles Eliot 1925- *AmAu&B,*
 ConAu 9R, WhoAm 1974, WhoE 1974,
 WhoWorJ 1972, WrDr 1976
Silberman, James Henry 1927- *AmAu&B,*
 WhoAm 1974, WhoE 1974
Silberman, Peter H *NF*
Silberstein, Michael E 1876?-1950 *BioIn 2*
Silbey, Stanley Peter *OvPC*
Silha, Otto Adelbert 1919- *WhoAm 1974*
Silin, Bert *NF*
Silk, Leonard Solomon 1918- *AmM&W 73S,*
 ConAu 1R, NewYTBE 1, WhoAm 1974,
 WrDr 1976
Sillen, Samuel 1910-1973 *BioIn 9, ConAu 41,*
 NewYTBE 4
Silliman, Benjamin 1779-1864 *Alli, AmAu, BbD,*
 BbtC, CyAL 1, DcAmA, DcNAA,
 HisAmM XR, OxCan, REnAL, WebBD
Silliman, Benjamin, Jr. 1816-1885 *Alli, CyAL 1,*
 DcAmA, DcNAA, HisAmM XR, WebBD
Silliman, Harry Inness 1876-1950 *BioIn 2,*
 WhJnl 1928
Sillince, W A 1906- *BioIn 1*
Silone, Ignazio 1900-1978 *CasWL, CIDMEL,*
 CnMD, CnMWL, ConAu 25, ConLC 4,
 CyWA, EncWL, EvEuW, IntWW 1976,
 LongC, ModRL, NewYTBE 3, Pen Eur,
 REn, TwCA, TwCA Sup, TwCW, WebBD,
 Who 1974, WhoTwCL, WhoWor 1974
Silsbee, William *HisAmM XR*
Silva Espejo, Rene *ForP*
Silveira Sampaio, Jose De 1913?-1964 *BioIn 7*
Silver, Dick *NF*
Silver, Helen Paltis *NF*
Silver, John *HisAmM XR*
Silver, Roy *NF*
Silverman, Al 1926- *AuBYP, BioIn 7, BioIn 10,*
 ConAu 11R, WhoAm 1974
Silverman, Alvin Michaels 1912- *ConAu 11R,*
 WhoAm 1974, WhoWorJ 1972
Silverman, J Herbert *OvPC*
Silverman, Robert Jay 1940- *LEduc 1974*
Silverman, Sime 1872-1933 *AmAu&B,*
 HisAmM XR, NatCAB 24
Silverman, Sime *see also* Silverman, Simon J
Silverman, Simon J 1872-1933 *BioIn 1*
Silverman, Simon J *see also* Silverman, Sime
Silverman, Syd 1932- *BiE&WWA, IntMPA 1975,*
 WhoAm 1974
Silverman, William *NF*
Silvers, Robert B 1929- *AmAu&B, OvPC,*
 WhoAm 1974, WhoE 1974
Silversmith, Julius *Alli, HisAmM XR*
Silverstein, Mickie *BioIn 8*
Silverstein, Shelby 1932- *BioIn 6, WhoAm 1974*
Silvestre, Paul Armand 1837-1901 *OxFr, WebBD*
Sim, John Cameron 1911- *ConAu 25,*
 WhoAm 1974, WrDr 1976

Sima, Andor Andre *OvPC*
Simak, Clifford Donald 1904- *BioIn 6, BioIn 7,*
 ConAu 4R, ConLC 1, MnnWr, WorAu
Simar, Bill H *NF*
Simavi, Sedat 1895?-1953 *BioIn 3*
Simeral, Charles Delmar 1875-1947 *BioIn 3,*
 NatCAB 37
Simmons, Azariah *AmJnl*
Simmons, Bonnie 1923?- *BioIn 2*
Simmons, Boyd Tetherly 1912- *RpN,*
 WhoAm 1974
Simmons, Charles 1924- *WhoAm 1974,*
 WhoE 1974
Simmons, Edward Alfred 1875-1931 *HisAmM XR*
Simmons, Eleanor Booth 1869?-1950 *BioIn 2*
Simmons, George E 1898- *WhJnl Sup*
Simmons, George Henry 1852-1937 *BioIn 1,*
 BioIn 4, DcAmB S2, HisAmM XR
Simmons, James Wright 1800?-1867? *Alli, BiDSA,*
 CyAL 2, DcNAA, HisAmM XR
Simmons, John O 1892- *WhJnl 1928*
Simmons, Mabel Clarke 1899- *WhoAm 1974,*
 WhoAmW 1974, WhoS&SW 1973
Simmons, Matty 1926- *ConAu 29, WhoAm 1974,*
 WhoF&I 1974
Simmons, Roscoe Conkling 1878-1951 *BioIn 2,*
 BioIn 7, DcAmB S5
Simmons, Thomas Jefferson 1914- *WhoAm 1974,*
 WhoS&SW 1973
Simmons, Walter 1908- *AmJnl, WhoAm 1974*
Simms, Jacob E *BlkC*
Simms, Kenneth Lee 1916- *WhoAm 1974*
Simms, Leroy Alanson 1905- *WhoAm 1974,*
 WhoS&SW 1973, WhoWor 1974
Simms, Peter 1925- *ConAu 21R*
Simms, William Gilmore 1806-1870 *Alli, AmAu,*
 AmAu&B, BbD, BiD&SB, BiDSA, CasWL,
 CnDAL, CyAL 2, CyWA, DcAmA, DcBiA,
 DcEnL, DcLEL, DcNAA, EvLB,
 HisAmM XR, HsB&A, HsB&A Sup, LiJA,
 OxAm, OxEng, Pen Am, REn, REnAL,
 WebBD, WebE&AL
Simms, William Philip 1881-1957 *AmJnl, BioIn 4,*
 BioIn 7, NatCAB 47
Simon, Andre Louis 1877-1970 *Au&Wr,*
 ConAu 29, LongC, WebBD
Simon, Anthony Tony 1921- *AmAu&B,*
 WhoAm 1974, WhoE 1974
Simon, Bob *NF*
Simon, David Jenkins *NF*
Simon, Eliav *OvPC*
Simon, George 1893-1963 *BioIn 6*
Simon, George Thomas 1912- *ConAu 25,*
 WhoAm 1974
Simon, Henry William 1901-1970 *AmAu&B,*
 BioIn 9, ConAu 5, ConAu 29, NewYTBE 1
Simon, Herman *HisAmM XR*
Simon, Howard *InvJ*
Simon, Joan *NF*
Simon, John 1925- *BiE&WWA, ConAu 21R,*
 WhoThe 1972, WorAu
Simon, Max *NF*
Simon, Paul 1928- *BioIn 2, WhoAm 1974,*
 WhoAmP 1973, WhoGov 1972,
 WhoMW 1974
Simon, Todd 1913- *WhoAm 1974*
Simon, Tony 1921- *AmAu&B, ConAu 5R*
Simonds, Frank Herbert 1878-1936 *AmAu&B,*
 AmJnl, BioIn 4, DcAmB S2, DcNAA,
 HisAmM XR, TwCA, WebBD
Simonds, John E *NF*
Simonds, William 1822-1859 *Alli, AmAu&B,*
 BiD&SB, DcAmA, DcNAA
Simonds, William Adams 1887-1963 *AmAu&B,*

ConAu P-1

Simonov, Konstantin Mikhailovich 1915- BioIn 4,
 BioIn 6, CasWL, CnMD, CroCD, DcRusL,
 EncWL, EvEuW, IntWW 1976, McGWD,
 ModSL 1, ModWD, Pen Eur, REn,
 TwCA Sup, TwCW, WhoWor 1974
Simons, Algie Martin 1870-1950 AmRP,
 DcAmB S4, HisAmM XR, WhNAA
Simons, Dolph Collins 1904- WhoF&I 1974,
 WhJnl 1928
Simons, Dolph Collins, Jr. 1930- WhoAm 1974
Simons, Gerard J M 1876?-1948 BioIn 1
Simons, Howard 1929- ConAu 65, NewMr,
 RpN, WhoAm 1974, WhoS&SW 1973
Simons, Lewis M NF
Simons, Michael Laird 1843-1880 Alli Sup,
 DcNAA
Simons, W C 1871- WhJnl 1928
Simonton, James William 1823-1882 AmJnl,
 DcAmB 17
Simonton, Thomas C G OvPC
Simpich, Frederick, Jr. 1878-1950 BioIn 2,
 HisAmM XR, WhJnl 1928
Simpson, Andrew J 1883- WhJnl 1928
Simpson, B O WhJnl 1928
Simpson, Carole NF
Simpson, Dave NF
Simpson, Kirke Larue 1880-1972 BioIn 6,
 BioIn 9, ConAu 37, NewYTBE 3
Simpson, Len L NF
Simpson, Lewis Pearson 1916- ConAu 19,
 DrAS 74E, WhoAm 1974, WhoS&SW 1973,
 WrDr 1976
Simpson, Peggy A NF
Simpson, Richard W BioIn 1
Simpson, Robert 1886-1934 AmAu&B, DcNAA
Simpson, Robert 1895-1972 BioIn 9
Simpson, Samuel L 1845-1899 DcNAA
Simpson, Stephen 1789-1854 Alli, AmAu,
 AmAu&B, DcNAA, HisAmM XR, LiJA,
 NatCAB 5
Simpson, Victor NF
Simpson, William 1864-1956 BioIn 4
Sims, Al NF
Sims, Burt 1918- WhoWest 1974
Sims, Carl W 1941?- NF
Sims, Edward Howell 1923- AmAu&B, Au&Wr,
 ConAu 1R, WhoAm 1974, WhoWor 1974
Sims, George Robert 1847-1922 Alli Sup, BbD,
 BiD&SB, BioIn 1, BrAu 19, EncMys,
 EvLB, LongC, NewC, WebBD
Sims, Hugo S 1893- WhNAA
Sims, Hugo S, Jr. 1921- CurBio XR
Sims, J NF
Sims, Lydel AuBYP, BioIn 8
Sims, Patsy 1938- WhoAmW 1974
Sims, Philip Hal 1886-1949 DcNAA,
 HisAmM XR
Sims, Watson S RpN
Sinasi, Ibrahim 1826-1871 CasWL, DcOrL 3,
 ForP, REnWD
Sinclair, Angus 1841-1919 DcNAA, HisAmM XR
Sinclair, Bruce NF
Sinclair, Ernest Keith 1914- IntWW 1976,
 Who 1974, WhoWor 1974
Sinclair, Frank 1895- WhJnl 1928
Sinclair, Gordon 1900- AuNews 1, BioIn 10,
 BioNews 1974, CanWW 1972
Sinclair, Joseph Samuels 1922- WhoAm 1974,
 WhoF&I 1974
Sinclair, Upton Beall 1878-1968 AmAu&B,
 AmAu&B, AmNov, AmRP, AuBYP,
 BiDPara, CasWL, CnDAL, ConAmA,
 ConAmL, ConAu 5, ConAu 25, ConLC 1,

CurBio XR, CyWA, DcAmA, DcLEL,
 EncWL, EvLB, HisAmM XR, LongC,
 ModAL, OxAm, OxEng, Pen Am, RAdv 1,
 REn, REnAL, SmATA 9, TwCA,
 TwCA Sup, TwCW, WebBD, WebE&AL,
 WhNAA, WhoTwCL
Sinclair, Ward NF
Sindermann, Horst 1915- IntWW 1976,
 WhoWor 1974
Sindlinger, Albert NF
Sine, Maurice 1928- BioIn 6, WhoGrA
Siner, Robert NF
Sines, John H WhJnl 1928
Singer, Harry 1917?-1967 BioIn 7
Singer, Henry OvPC
Singer, Isaac Bashevis 1904- AmAu&B, AmWr,
 AnCL, Au&Wr, AuBYP, AuNews 1,
 AuNews 2, BioIn 8, BioIn 9, BioIn 10,
 CasWL, CelR 1973, ChlLR 1, ConAu 1R,
 ConLC 1, ConLC 3, ConLC 6,
 ConNov 1972, ConNov 1976, CurBio XR,
 DrAF 1976, EncWL, IntWW 1976,
 ModAL Sup, NewYTBE 1, NewYTBE 3,
 Pen Am, SmATA 3, ThrBJA, TwCW,
 WebE&AL, WhoAm 1974, WhoE 1974,
 WhoTwCL, WhoWor 1974, WorAu,
 WrDr 1976
Singer, Isidore 1859-1939 AmAu&B, DcNAA,
 WebBD
Singer, Jack AmJnl
Singer, Joseph Howard 1922- OvPC,
 WhoPubR 1972
Singer, Kurt Deutsch 1911- AmAu&B, Au&Wr,
 ConAu 49, CurBio XR, WhoAm 1974,
 WhoWest 1974, WhoWor 1974
Singer, Martin Melvin 1928- WhoAm 1974
Singer, Samuel Loewenberg 1911- ConAu 65,
 WhoAm 1974
Singerly, Benjamin HisAmM XR
Singerly, William Miskey 1832-1898 AmAu&B,
 AmJnl, NatCAB 1
Singh, Khushwant 1915- CasWL, ConAu 9,
 ConNov 1972, ConNov 1976, IntWW 1976,
 Pen Eng, REn, WebE&AL, WhoWor 1974,
 WrDr 1976
Singh, Ratan NF
Singleton, Donald Edward 1936- WhoAm 1974
Singmaster, John Alden 1852-1926 DcNAA,
 HisAmM XR
Sinnott, Arthur Joseph 1886-1944 BioIn 2,
 NatCAB 34
Sinnott, James P 1890?-1955 BioIn 4
Sinor, John 1930- ConAu 69
Sinsabaugh, Chris NF
Sionil, Jose F 1924- ConAu 23R
Sions, Harry 1905?-1974 BioIn 10, NewYTBS 5
Sip, Emil ForP
Sippel, John 1920- NF
Sirius 1902- WhoWor 1974
Sirius see also Beuve-Mery, Hubert
Sirkin, Abraham M 1914- OvPC, WhoAm 1974,
 WhoGov 1972
Sisk, Hanson R 1892- WhJnl 1928
Sisk, Richard NF
Sissman, Louis Edward 1928-1976 ConAu 65,
 WhoAdv 1972, WhoAm 1974, WhoE 1974
Sisson, Edgar Grant 1875-1948 AmJnl, BioIn 1,
 DcNAA, HisAmM XR
Sisson, Frederick Reynolds 1908?-1957 BioIn 4
Sitomer, Curtis J NF
Sitterley, James E 1877-1945 NatCAB 34
Sitton, Claude Fox 1925- WhoAm 1974,
 WhoS&SW 1973
Sitton, Harold Thomas Jack 1915- WhoAm 1974

Siu, Stephen *NF*
Sivaram, M *ForP*
Siviter, William Henry 1858-1939 *HisAmM XR*
Sixta, George *BioIn 1*
Sizemore, Richard Clayborne 1924- *WhoAm 1974*
Sjostrom, George William 1924- *WhoAm 1974*
Skacel, Milan B *OvPC*
Skaith, Dorothea Henrietta 1911?- *BioIn 1*
Skala, Martin 1935- *WhoAm 1974*
Skartvedt, Dan 1945- *NF*
Skavlan, Einar 1882-1954 *BioIn 3*
Skelly, John T *NF*
Skelly, Robert *HisAmM XR*
Skene, Don 1897-1938 *DcNAA*
Skewes, James H 1888- *WhJnl 1928*
Skiddy, Lawrence J 1892?-1951 *BioIn 2*
Skidmore, Howard Franklyn 1917- *OvPC,
   WhoAm 1974, WhoF&I 1974,
   WhoPubR 1972*
Skidmore, Ian 1929- *BioIn 10, ConAu 61*
Skien, Michael T *NF*
Skillin, Edward Simeon 1904- *BioIn 1, BioIn 2,
   BioIn 7, CurBio XR, WhoAm 1974*
Skilman, Thomas T *HisAmM XR*
Skingley, Peter *NF*
Skinner, Charles Montgomery 1852-1907
   AmAu&B, DcAmA, DcNAA
Skinner, Constance Lindsay 1882?-1939 *AmAu&B,
   CanNov, DcLEL, DcNAA, JBA 1934,
   MorJA, OxAm, OxCan, Str&VC, TwCA,
   TwCA Sup, WebBD, WhNAA, YABC 1*
Skinner, Frederick Gustavus *HisAmM XR*
Skinner, Hilary *FamWC*
Skinner, John Herbert 1864-1958 *BioIn 7,
   NatCAB 47*
Skinner, John Stuart 1788-1851 *Alli, AmAu&B,
   BiDSA, BioIn 2, DcNAA, HisAmM XR,
   NatCAB 2*
Skinner, Liam C 1908- *BioIn 3, CathA 1952*
Skinner, Olivia 1919- *WhoAm 1974,
   WhoAmW 1974*
Skinner, Richard Dana 1893-1941 *CathA 1930,
   DcNAA, HisAmM XR*
Skinner, Sam *NF*
Skinner, Thomas *NF*
Sklarewitz, Norman 1924- *ConAu 69*
Skoglund, Goesta 1904- *ConAu 65*
Skole, Robert *NF*
Skolnich, Sherman *NF*
Skolnik, Alfred M 1920?-1977 *ConAu 69*
Skolsky, Sidney 1905- *BioIn 2, BioIn 3,
   CelR 1973, IntMPA 1975, WhoAm 1974,
   WhoWorJ 1972*
Skou-Hansen, Tage 1925- *Au&Wr, ConAu 13R*
Skow, John *NF*
Skrotzki, Bernhardt G A 1907-1963 *BioIn 6*
Skuce, Lou d1951 *BioIn 2*
Slack, E F *NF*
Slack, Munsey 1879- *WhJnl 1928*
Slaight, John W *NF*
Slane, Henry Pindell 1920- *WhoAm 1974*
Slappey, Sterling Greene 1917- *ConAu 65,
   WhoAm 1974*
Slate, Ted *NF*
Slater, Charlotte Wolpers 1944- *ConAu 65*
Slater, George d1889 *NF*
Slater, Hughes DeCourcy 1874- *HisAmM XR,
   WhJnl 1928*
Slater, Layton Ernest Alfred 1916- *IntWW 1976*
Slater, Leonard 1920- *ConAu 15R, OvPC,
   WhoWest 1974*
Slater, Robert *NF*
Slattery, William J *NF*
Slaughter, Adolph James 1928- *WhoAm 1974,*

WhoGov 1972
Slaughter, Louis 1941?- *BioIn 10*
Slavitt, David Rytman 1935- *Au&Wr,
   ConAu 21R, ConLC 5, ConNov 1972,
   ConNov 1976, ConP 1970, ConP 1975,
   DrAF 1976, DrAP 1975, WrDr 1976*
Slayter, Bill *NF*
Sleed, Joel *NF*
Sleeper, John Sherburne 1794-1878 *Alli,
   AmAu&B, AmJnl, DcAmA, DcNAA,
   NatCAB 13*
Sleet, Moneta, Jr. 1926- *WhoE 1974*
Sleicher, John A 1848- *NatCAB 13*
Sleight, Alfred Collins *WhJnl 1928*
Slep, Daniel Neff 1872-1953 *BioIn 6, NatCAB 45*
Slep, Harry 1836-1922 *BioIn 4, NatCAB 39*
Slessor, Kenneth 1901-1971 *BioIn 4, BioIn 6,
   BioIn 7, BioIn 8, BioIn 9, CasWL,
   ConP 1970, DcLEL, LongC, Pen Eng, REn,
   TwCW, WebE&AL, WorAu*
Slevin, Joseph Raymond 1918- *AmM&W 73S,
   WhoS&SW 1973*
Sloan, Albert Lewis 1886-1947 *BioIn 1*
Sloan, Carl *NF*
Sloan, John 1871-1951 *AmRP, AtlBL,
   DcAmB S5, HisAmM XR, OxAm, REn,
   REnAL, WebBD*
Sloan, John N W 1898- *NF*
Sloan, Laurence Henry 1889-1949 *BioIn 1,
   DcNAA, IndAu 1917*
Sloan, Lester 1942?- *NF*
Sloan, Lloyd Lawrence 1922- *WhoAm 1974*
Sloan, Oscar B *HisAmM XR*
Sloan, Robert Chalmers 1864- *WhJnl 1928*
Sloan, Robin Adams *NF*
Sloan, Tom *NF*
Sloanaker, William *HisAmM XR*
Sloane, Arthur John 1875- *WhJnl 1928*
Sloane, Bob 1927- *NF*
Sloane, Leonard 1932- *ConAu 21R, WhoE 1974*
Sloane, Thomas O'Conor 1851-1940 *Alli Sup,
   DcAmA, DcNAA, WebBD*
Sloane, William Milligan 1850-1928 *Alli Sup,
   AmAu&B, BiD&SB, DcAmA, DcNAA,
   HisAmM XR, OhA&B, WebBD*
Slocombe, Charles S d1946 *BioIn 1*
Slocombe, George Edward 1894-1963 *LongC,
   NewC, WebBD*
Slocum, George M 1889- *WhJnl 1928*
Slocum, Richard William 1901-1957 *BioIn 3,
   BioIn 4*
Slocum, William Joseph Michael, Jr. 1912?-1974
   BioIn 5, ConAu 53
Sloggatt, Arthur Hastings 1917?-1975 *BioIn 10,
   ConAu 61*
Slomovitz, Philip 1896- *OvPC, WhJnl 1928*
Slonim, Marc 1894-1976 *AmAu&B, ConAu 65,
   REnAL, WorAu*
Slonim, Yoel 1884-1944 *NF*
Slonimski, Antoni 1895-1976 *CasWL, CIDMEL,
   ConAu 65, IntWW 1974, ModSL 2,
   Pen Eur, WhoWor 1974*
Sloper, Leslie Akers 1883-1949 *BioIn 2*
Slosser, Bob Gene 1929- *ConAu 65*
Slosson, Edwin Emery 1865-1929 *AmAu&B,
   AmLY, DcNAA, HisAmM XR, WebBD,
   WhNAA, WhJnl 1928*
Slosson, Preston William 1892- *AmAu&B,
   Au&Wr, ConAu 61, WhNAA,
   WhoAm 1974*
Slote, Bernice *NF*
Slott, Mollie 1896?-1967 *BioIn 1, BioIn 7*
Slottman, George V 1903-1958 *NatCAB 44*
Slough, Robert E 1890- *WhJnl 1928*

Slover, Samuel LeRoy 1873-1959 *BioIn 5, BioIn 7*
Sloyan, Patrick J *NF*
Small, Albion Woodbury 1854-1926 *Alli Sup, AmAu&B, AmLY, DcNAA, HisAmM XR, WebBD*
Small, Alex 1894?-1965 *BioIn 7*
Small, Elden 1876-1934 *AmAu&B, DcNAA*
Small, F O *HisAmM XR*
Small, Len 1862-1936 *NF*
Small, Leslie Charles 1886-1957 *BioIn 6, NatCAB 44*
Small, Sam 1851-1931 *DcNAA*
Small, Wesley Parker 1900- *WhJnl 1928*
Small, William *NF*
Smalley, Alton D *NF*
Smalley, Eugene Virgil 1841-1899 *Alli Sup, AmAu&B, DcAmA, DcAmB 17, DcNAA, HisAmM XR, OhA&B*
Smalley, George Washburn 1833-1916 *AmAu&B, AmJnl, BbD, BiD&SB, BioIn 9, DcAmA, DcAmB 17, DcNAA, FamWC, HisAmM XR, OxAm, REnAL, WebBD*
Smalley, P J *HisAmM XR*
Smalley, V H *NF*
Smallwood, Clement 1902?-1963 *BioIn 6*
Smallwood, Joseph Roberts 1900- *BioIn 2, BioIn 3, BioIn 5, BioIn 9, BioIn 10, CanWW 1972, CurBio XR, IntWW 1976, OxCan, WhoCan 1973, WhoE 1974*
Smallzreid, Katherine Ann *NF*
Smart, David Archibald 1892-1952 *CurBio XR, DcAmB S5, NatCAB 43*
Smart, Graydon F *NF*
Smart, John Kenneth 1932- *WhoAm 1974*
Smart, William Buckwalter 1922- *WhoAm 1974, WhoWest 1974*
Smedley, Agnes 1894-1950 *AmAu&B, AmRP, BioIn 2, BioIn 4, CurBio XR, DcAmB S4, TwCA, TwCA Sup*
Smedley, David *NF*
Smeltzer, William H 1899- *WhJnl 1928*
Smiley, Charles Wesley 1846-1926 *HisAmM XR*
Smiley, David Elmer 1879- *WhJnl 1928*
Smiley, Nixon *NF*
Smillie, James 1807-1885 *HisAmM XR*
Smith, A Earl 1884- *BioIn 4*
Smith, A Merriman 1913-1970 *BioIn 3, BioIn 7*
Smith, A Merriman *see also* Smith, Merriman
Smith, A Morton 1903- *WhJnl 1928*
Smith, A Philbrook 1898- *WhJnl 1928*
Smith, A R 1884- *WhJnl 1928*
Smith, A Robert 1925- *ConAu 73, WhoAm 1974*
Smith, Adam *see* Goodman, George Jerome Waldo
Smith, Al *NF*
Smith, Alaric M 1859-1943 *BioIn 2, NatCAB 35*
Smith, Albert H 1902- *BioIn 5, WhoAm 1974, WhJnl Sup*
Smith, Albert Richard 1816-1860 *Alli, BiD&SB, BrAu 19, DcEnL, EvLB, NewC, WebBD*
Smith, Alexander R 1861- *HisAmM XR*
Smith, Alfred Emanuel 1873-1944 *AmAu&B, AmJnl, CurBio XR, DcAmB S3, DcNAA, HisAmM XR, OxAm, REn, REnAL, WebBD*
Smith, Alison *NF*
Smith, Anthony John Francis 1926- *Au&Wr, ConAu 11R, WrDr 1976*
Smith, Arthur Croxton 1865-1952 *BioIn 2, BioIn 3, Br&AmS*
Smith, Arthur Douglas Howden 1887-1945 *AmAu&B, DcNAA*
Smith, Arthur L J 1860-1946 *BioIn 1*
Smith, Arthur Maxson 1873-1962 *BioIn 8*
Smith, Arthur R d1977 *NF*

Smith, Austin Edward 1912- *AmM&W 73P, BioIn 2, CurBio XR, HisAmM XR, WhoAm 1974*
Smith, Ballard *NF*
Smith, Benjamin Bosworth 1794- *Alli, HisAmM XR*
Smith, Beverly Waugh, Jr. 1898-1972 *BioIn 1, BioIn 2, BioIn 4, BioIn 9, HisAmM XR, NewYTBE 3*
Smith, Bradley 1910- *ConAu 5*
Smith, Brainard G 1846-1930 *NatCAB 22*
Smith, Buckner Jett 1886- *WhJnl 1928*
Smith, C R F 1898- *WhJnl 1928*
Smith, C Ruggles 1903- *WhJnl 1928*
Smith, Cabell *NF*
Smith, Camerson *NF*
Smith, Carl 1878?-1950 *BioIn 2*
Smith, Caroline L *Alli Sup, DcNAA*
Smith, Cecil Howard, III 1917- *ConAu 69, WhoAm 1974, WhoWest 1974*
Smith, Charles 1768-1808 *Alli, BiDLA, DcNAA, HisAmM XR*
Smith, Charles Emory 1842-1908 *AmAu&B, AmJnl, DcAmB 17, NatCAB 11*
Smith, Charles Henry 1826-1903 *Alli Sup, AmAu, AmAu&B, AmJnl, BiD&SB, BiDSA, CnDAL, DcAmA, DcAmB 17, DcLEL, DcNAA, HisAmM XR, OxAm, REnAL, WebBD*
Smith, Charles J *NF*
Smith, Charles R *NF*
Smith, Charles Stephenson 1877-1964 *NF*
Smith, Charles W 1874- *WhJnl 1928*
Smith, Charles William 1840-1914 *BioIn 1*
Smith, Charlotte *HisAmM XR*
Smith, Chester L d1973 *BioIn 9*
Smith, Clarence J 1874- *WhJnl 1928*
Smith, Clay S 1895- *WhJnl Sup*
Smith, Clifford *NF*
Smith, Conrad Frederick 1904- *WhJnl 1928*
Smith, Dan *NF*
Smith, Daniel B 1792-1883 *Alli, DcNAA, HisAmM XR*
Smith, Darr *BioIn 3*
Smith, David 1872?-1957 *BioIn 4*
Smith, David C 1931- *ConAu 69*
Smith, Dean E 1923- *ConAu 9R*
Smith, Delavan 1861-1922 *AmJnl, NatCAB 19*
Smith, Delos Owen 1905-1973 *ConAu 41, WhoAm 1974, WhoWor 1974*
Smith, Denys H H 1899?-1962 *BioIn 6*
Smith, Dick 1889- *WhJnl 1928*
Smith, Donald Lloyd 1935- *WhoAm 1974, WhoE 1974*
Smith, Donald R *NF*
Smith, Donna *NF*
Smith, Dorman Henry 1892-1956 *BioIn 4*
Smith, Douglas 1918- *ConAu 73, WhoAm 1974*
Smith, Duncan MacMillan 1863?-1956 *BioIn 4*
Smith, E Norman 1871-1957 *BioIn 4, WhNAA, WhJnl 1928*
Smith, Edgar Pichard 1920- *WhoAm 1974*
Smith, Edgar Valentine 1873?-1953 *BioIn 3*
Smith, Edith C *NF*
Smith, Edward H 1881?- *WhJnl 1928*
Smith, Edwin E 1862- *WhJnl 1928*
Smith, Elias 1769-1846 *DcAmA, DcNAA, HisAmM XR*
Smith, Elihu Hubbard 1771-1798 *Alli, AmAu, AmAu&B, CyAL 1, DcAmA, DcNAA, HisAmM XR, OxAm, Pen Am, REnAL*
Smith, Elizabeth T 1897- *WhJnl 1928*
Smith, Ellison W *OvPC*
Smith, Elmo 1909-1968 *BioIn 5, BioIn 8*

Smith, Erle Hazlett 1890- *WhJnl 1928*
Smith, Ernest *NF*
Smith, Ernest Gray 1873-1945 *BioIn 1,
   NatCAB 33*
Smith, Eugenia Clair *BioIn 1*
Smith, Floyd Leon 1887- *WhJnl 1928*
Smith, Francis Shubael 1819-1887 *Alli, AmAu&B,
   DcNAA, HisAmM XR*
Smith, Frank Clifford 1865-1937 *DcNAA*
Smith, Frank Hovey 1881?-1957 *BioIn 4*
Smith, Frank L 1885?-1953 *BioIn 3*
Smith, Frank P *HisAmM XR*
Smith, Franklin G *NF*
Smith, Fraser *NF*
Smith, Fred 1898?-1976 *ConAu 69*
Smith, Fred Colfax 1882- *BioIn 1*
Smith, Fred E 1862- *WhJnl 1928*
Smith, Frederick *OvPC*
Smith, Frederick George 1880- *BioIn 2,
   IndAu 1816, WhNAA*
Smith, Frederick Rutledge 1925- *WhoAm 1974,
   WhoE 1974*
Smith, Gean *HisAmM XR*
Smith, Geoffrey *NF*
Smith, George *HisAmM XR*
Smith, Mrs. George *NF*
Smith, George 1789-1846 *WebBD*
Smith, George 1824-1901 *DcEuL, NewC, REn,
   WebBD*
Smith, George 1833- *Alli Sup*
Smith, George Campbell d1933 *NF*
Smith, George Henry 1873-1931 *AmAu&B,
   DcAmB 17, DcNAA*
Smith, George M *NF*
Smith, George VanRiper 1937- *WhoAm 1974*
Smith, George W E 1896- *WhJnl 1928*
Smith, Gerald B 1909- *ConAu 25*
Smith, Gerald Hewitt 1912-1955 *NatCAB 45*
Smith, Gerald L K 1898?-1976 *CurBio XR*
Smith, Gideon B *HisAmM XR*
Smith, Godfrey 1926- *Au&Wr, ConAu 9R*
Smith, Goldwin 1823-1910 *Alli, Alli Sup, BbD,
   BiD&SB, BioIn 1, BioIn 2, BioIn 4,
   BrAu 19, CanWr, DcEnA, DcEnA Ap,
   DcEnL, DcEuL, DcLEL, DcNAA, EvLB,
   HisAmM XR, LongC, NewC, OxCan,
   OxEng, REn, REnAL, WebBD*
Smith, Goldwin 1912- *ConAu 41*
Smith, Gretchen L d1972 *BioIn 9*
Smith, Guy Lincoln, IV 1949- *WhoGov 1972*
Smith, H Allen 1907-1976 *AuNews 2, CelR 1973,
   ConAu 5R, ConAu 65, CurBio XR,
   HisAmM XR, LongC, REn, REnAL,
   WhoAm 1974, WhoE 1974, WrDr 1976*
Smith, H C 1863- *BioIn 8*
Smith, Mrs. H M F *HisAmM XR*
Smith, Hal Harrison 1876-1953 *BioIn 3,
   WhJnl 1928*
Smith, Harold D 1900- *WhJnl 1928*
Smith, Harris 1921- *ConAu 49*
Smith, Harrison 1888-1971 *AmAu&B, BioIn 3,
   BioIn 9, ConAu 29, CurBio XR,
   HisAmM XR, NewYTBE 2*
Smith, Harry B 1876- *WhJnl 1928*
Smith, Harry Bache 1860-1936 *AmAu&B,
   AmSCAP 1966, BiD&SB, DcAmA,
   DcAmB S2, DcNAA, REnAL, WebBD*
Smith, Harry E *WhJnl 1928*
Smith, Harry James 1880-1918 *AmAu&B,
   DcNAA, HisAmM XR*
Smith, Harry King, Jr. 1896- *WhJnl Sup*
Smith, Harry T 1876-1954 *BioIn 3*
Smith, Hazel Freeman Brannon 1914?- *BioIn 7,
   BioIn 10, CurBio XR*

Smith, Hedrick Laurence 1933- *ConAu 65,
   WhoS&SW 1973*
Smith, Helen Huntington *HisAmM XR*
Smith, Henry Boynton 1815-1877 *Alli, AmAu&B,
   DcAmA, DcNAA, HisAmM XR, WebBD*
Smith, Henry Justin 1875-1936 *AmAu&B,
   BioIn 4, BioIn 9, DcAmB S2, DcNAA,
   HisAmM XR, REnAL, WhNAA,
   WhJnl 1928*
Smith, Henry M *Alli, HisAmM XR*
Smith, Henry Worthington *HisAmM XR*
Smith, Herbert Atwood 1878-1959 *WhJnl 1928*
Smith, Herbert Leary, Jr. 1923- *AmArch 1970*
Smith, Hoke 1855-1931 *AmJnl, BiDSA,
   HisAmM XR, WebBD*
Smith, Horace Wemyss 1825-1891 *Alli, DcAmA,
   DcNAA*
Smith, Howard 1937- *BioIn 10*
Smith, Howard Kingsbury 1914- *AmAu&B,
   BioIn 6, BioIn 8, BioNews 1974, CelR 1973,
   ConAu 45, CurBio XR, ForP, IntMPA 1975,
   IntWW 1976, WhoAm 1974,
   WhoS&SW 1973, WhoWor 1974,
   WrDr 1976*
Smith, Howard Leslie 1861- *WhNAA,
   WhJnl 1928*
Smith, Howard Strachan 1902- *WhJnl 1928*
Smith, Howard Van 1910- *ConAu 5R*
Smith, Hugh *NF*
Smith, Huntington 1857-1926 *Alli Sup,
   AmAu&B, HisAmM XR*
Smith, J H *NF*
Smith, J H, Jr. *OvPC*
Smith, Jack Clifford 1916- *BioIn 5, ConAu 69,
   WhoWest 1974*
Smith, Jacob 1914- *NF*
Smith, James *NF*
Smith, James 1802?-1857 *Alli*
Smith, James 1820?-1888 *Alli, DcNAA*
Smith, James 1820-1910 *BioIn 2*
Smith, James M 1901- *WhJnl 1928*
Smith, James Walter 1868-1948 *HisAmM XR*
Smith, Jane Maxwell d1965 *BioIn 7*
Smith, Jay *InvJ*
Smith, Jeannette H 1876- *WhJnl Sup*
Smith, Jerome Howard 1861-1941 *BioIn 3,
   BioIn 8*
Smith, Jerome VanCrowninshield 1800-1879 *Alli,
   Alli Sup, AmAu&B, DcAmA, DcNAA,
   HisAmM XR*
Smith, Jessica 1895- *ConAu 49, ForWC 1970,
   WhoAm 1974, WhoAmW 1974*
Smith, John 1924- *Au&Wr, ConP 1970,
   ConP 1975, WrDr 1976*
Smith, John Chabot 1915- *ConAu 69*
Smith, John Jay 1798-1881 *Alli, AmAu&B,
   CyAL 1, DcAmA, DcNAA, HisAmM XR*
Smith, John Laurence 1861- *PoIre*
Smith, John Lawrence 1860- *BioIn 2,
   IndAu 1816*
Smith, John Merlin Powis 1866-1932 *AmAu&B,
   DcNAA, WebBD, WhNAA*
Smith, John Talbot 1855-1923 *Alli Sup, DcAmA,
   DcNAA, HisAmM XR*
Smith, John Vincent *NF*
Smith, John Wilfred 1891?- *BioIn 3*
Smith, Joseph E 1873-1962 *BioIn 9*
Smith, Joseph Edward Adams 1822-1896 *Alli Sup,
   DcAmA, DcNAA*
Smith, Joseph T *HisAmM XR*
Smith, Joseph Y *NF*
Smith, Judson 1837-1906 *Alli Sup, DcAmA,
   DcNAA, HisAmM XR, OhA&B, WebBD*
Smith, Julia Holmes *NF*

Smith, Ken 1902- *ConAu 45*
Smith, Kingsbury 1908- *ForP, HisAmM XR*
Smith, Kingsbury *see also* Kingsbury-Smith, Joseph
Smith, Lamont 1893- *WhJnl 1928*
Smith, Langdon 1858-1908 *BiDSA, DcAmA, DcNAA*
Smith, Larry L *NF*
Smith, Laura Alexandrine d1935 *Alli Sup, BioIn 2, IndAu 1816*
Smith, Lee 1937- *ConAu 73*
Smith, Leo A 1892- *WhJnl 1928*
Smith, Leonard *OvPC*
Smith, Leslie Slawson 1928- *WhoAm 1974*
Smith, Lillian 1897-1966 *ConAu 17, ConAu 25, CurBio XR*
Smith, Liz 1923- *ConAu 65, ForWC 1970*
Smith, Lloyd Pearsall 1822-1886 *Alli, Alli Sup, AmAu&B, CyAL 1, DcNAA, WebBD*
Smith, Louis Graham 1878?-1952 *BioIn 2*
Smith, Louise *NF*
Smith, Lucius Edwin 1822-1900 *Alli, DcNAA*
Smith, M H *NF*
Smith, Margaret F *NF*
Smith, Marjorie Aileen Matthews 1918- *WhoAm 1974, WhoAmW 1974*
Smith, Mary Alice 1896-1970 *BioIn 9, ForWC 1970*
Smith, Mary Elizabeth *see* Smith, Liz
Smith, Mason Rossiter *OvPC*
Smith, Matthew John Wilfred 1891-1960 *AmAu&B, BioIn 1, BioIn 5, BkC 4*
Smith, Max 1874- *NF*
Smith, Merriman 1913-1970 *AmAu&B, BioIn 8, BioIn 9, ConAu 1R, ConAu 29, CurBio XR*
Smith, Merriman *see also* Smith, A Merriman
Smith, Michael Townsend 1935- *AmAu&B, BioIn 10, ConAu 21R, WhoAm 1974*
Smith, Mildred Catharine 1891-1973 *BioIn 10, ConAu 45, ForWC 1970, HisAmM XR, NewYTBE 4*
Smith, Neil Homer 1909?-1972 *ConAu 37*
Smith, Nicholas 1836-1911 *AmAu&B, BioIn 4, DcNAA, OxCan*
Smith, Orlando Jay 1842-1908 *BioIn 2, DcAmA, DcNAA, IndAu 1816*
Smith, Ormond Gerald 1860-1933 *AmAu&B, DcAmB S1, HisAmM XR*
Smith, Palmer 1891-1955 *BioIn 3, WhJnl 1928*
Smith, Pattie Sherwood 1909?-1974 *ConAu 53*
Smith, Paul Clifford 1908-1976 *BioIn 1, BioIn 2, BioIn 3, BioIn 4, BioIn 7, ConAu 65, CurBio XR, HisAmM XR*
Smith, Paul Jordan 1885-1971 *AmRP, REnAL, WhNAA*
Smith, Paul Linwood 1897- *WhJnl 1928*
Smith, Philip W *NF*
Smith, Raymond E 1897- *WhJnl 1928*
Smith, Rebecca *HisAmM XR*
Smith, Red 1905- *CelR 1973, CurBio XR, REnAL*
Smith, Red *see also* Smith, Walter Wellesley
Smith, Rex 1898-1959 *BioIn 5, BioIn 7, CurBio XR, NatCAB 48*
Smith, Richard Austin 1911- *AmAu&B, ConAu 19R, WhoAm 1974*
Smith, Richard M 1946- *ConAu 73*
Smith, Richard Penn 1799-1854 *Alli, AmAu, AmAu&B, BiD&SB, CnDAL, CyAL 2, DcAmA, DcNAA, HisAmM XR, REnAL, WebBD*
Smith, Robert *Alli, HisAmM XR*
Smith, Robert A *NF*
Smith, Robert Arthur 1944- *ConAu 69*
Smith, Robert Aura 1899-1959 *AmAu&B,*

BioIn 1, BioIn 5
Smith, Robert B 1901- *WhJnl 1928*
Smith, Robert Burns 1929- *WhoAm 1974*
Smith, Robert C *RpN*
Smith, Robert Gray 1942- *WhoAm 1974*
Smith, Robert James 1925- *WhoAm 1974*
Smith, Robert L 1893- *WhJnl 1928*
Smith, Robert M *NewMr, OvPC*
Smith, Robert Pearsall *HisAmM XR*
Smith, Robert Sidney (1877-1935) *see also* Smith, Sidney
Smith, Robert Sidney 1877-1935 *DcAmB S1*
Smith, Robert Sidney 1904-1969 *HisAmM XR*
Smith, Robert William 1916- *WhoAm 1974*
Smith, Roger Haskell 1932- *ConAu 69, WhoAm 1974*
Smith, Roswell 1829-1892 *AmAu&B, HisAmM XR, LiJA, WebBD*
Smith, Roysce *NF*
Smith, Ruel Perley 1869-1937 *AmAu&B, DcNAA, WhJnl 1928*
Smith, Sally W *NF*
Smith, Samuel D 1891- *WhJnl 1928*
Smith, Samuel Francis 1808-1895 *Alli, Alli Sup, AmAu, AmAu&B, BiD&SB, CyAL 2, DcAmA, DcLEL, DcNAA, EvLB, HisAmM XR, OxAm, PoChrch, REn, WebBD, WebE&AL*
Smith, Samuel Harrison 1772-1845 *Alli, AmJnl, DcAmB 17, DcNAA, HisAmM XR, NatCAB 20*
Smith, Samuel Stephenson 1897-1961 *AmAu&B, BioIn 6, BioIn 8*
Smith, Sandy *InvJ, NewMr*
Smith, Saqui 1860-1924 *Alli Sup, DcNAA*
Smith, Sarah Towne *HisAmM XR*
Smith, Seba 1792-1868 *Alli, AmAu, AmAu&B, AmJnl, BbD, BiD&SB, CnDAL, CyAL 2, DcAmA, DcEnL, DcLEL, DcNAA, HisAmM XR, OxAm, REn, REnAL, WebBD*
Smith, Selden C 1874-1939 *NatCAB 29*
Smith, Seymour Wemyss 1896-1932 *DcNAA, WhNAA*
Smith, Sherwin D *OvPC*
Smith, Sidney 1877-1935 *AmAu&B, AmJnl, DcNAA, WebBD*
Smith, Sidney *see also* Smith, Robert Sidney
Smith, Stanford 1919- *OvPC, WhoAm 1974, WhoF&I 1974*
Smith, Stanley Roger 1947?- *BioIn 9*
Smith, Stephe R 1851?- *DcNAA*
Smith, Susy 1911- *BiDPara, ConAu 5R, ForWC 1970, WhoAmW 1974*
Smith, Mrs. Sydney *HisAmM XR*
Smith, Sydney 1771-1845 *Alli, AtlBL, BbD, BiD&SB, BrAu 19, CasWL, DcEnA, DcEnL, DcEuL, DcLEL, EvLB, NewC, OxAm, OxEng, Pen Eng, WebBD, WebE&AL*
Smith, Sydney Goodsir 1915-1975? *Au&Wr, CasWL, ConAu 57, ConP 1970, ConP 1975, EncWL, EvLB, HisAmM XR, ModBL, Pen Eng, WorAu*
Smith, Talbot T 1888- *WhJnl 1928*
Smith, Terence 1938- *ConAu 73*
Smith, Thomas *HisAmM XR*
Smith, Mrs. Thomas K *HisAmM XR*
Smith, Thomas Robert 1880-1942 *AmAu&B, CurBio XR, DcNAA, HisAmM XR*
Smith, Toby *NF*
Smith, Tom Wash *HisAmM XR*
Smith, Vern E *NF*
Smith, Vieva Dawley 1888?-1971 *BioIn 9*

Smith, Virginia Otto *WhJnl 1928*
Smith, Vivus W 1804-1881 *NatCAB 5*
Smith, W Courtright 1883- *WhJnl 1928*
Smith, W Eugene d1978 *NewYTBS 5*
Smith, W Hazelton *HisAmM XR*
Smith, W Ray 1897- *WhJnl 1928*
Smith, Walker C *AmRP*
Smith, Walter Wellesley 1905- *BioIn 1, BioIn 2, BioIn 3, BioIn 4, BioIn 5, BioIn 6, CurBio XR, REnAL*
Smith, Walter Wellesley *see also* Smith, Red
Smith, Wayne C 1888?-1966 *BioIn 7*
Smith, Wendell 1914-1972 *BioIn 9, BioNews 1974, NewYTBE 3*
Smith, Weston 1901- *WhoAm 1974, WhoE 1974, WhoF&I 1974, WhoWor 1974*
Smith, Wilbur R C 1872-1941 *NatCAB 30*
Smith, Wilfred d1977 *NF*
Smith, William 1727-1803 *Alli, AmAu, AmAu&B, CyAL 1, DcAmA, DcNAA, HisAmM XR, LiJA, OxAm, Pen Am, REn, REnAL, WebBD*
Smith, Sir William 1813-1893 *Alli, BbD, BiD&SB, BioIn 6, BrAu 19, DcEnL, DcEuL, EvLB, NewC, OxEng, WebBD*
Smith, William 1873?-1948 *BioIn 1*
Smith, William A J *HisAmM XR*
Smith, William Andrew 1802-1870 *BiDSA, DcAmA, DcNAA*
Smith, William B *HisAmM XR*
Smith, William B S 1909-1951 *BioIn 2*
Smith, William E *NF*
Smith, William Gardner 1926-1974 *BioIn 9, BlkAW, ConAu 53, ConAu 65, LivBAA, NewYTBS 5, Pen Am*
Smith, William Henry 1825-1891 *WebBD*
Smith, William Henry 1833-1896 *Alli Sup, AmAu&B, DcAmA, DcAmB 17, DcNAA, HisAmM XR, NatCAB 19, OhA&B*
Smith, William Henry 1839-1935 *BioIn 2, DcNAA, IndAu 1816*
Smith, William J 1877- *WhJnl 1928*
Smith, William Richmond 1868-1934 *DcNAA*
Smith, William Waugh 1845-1912 *DcNAA*
Smith, William Wolfe *NF*
Smith, William Wye 1827-1917 *Alli Sup, BbtC, DcNAA, OxCan*
Smithee, James N 1842- *NatCAB 7*
Smithwick, John G *HisAmM XR*
Smitley, Robert Lincoln 1881?-1964 *BioIn 7*
Smits, Lee J d1974 *NF*
Smitt-Ingebretsen, Herman 1891-1961 *BioIn 6*
Smolar, Boris 1897- *ConAu 41, WhoAm 1974, WhoWorJ 1972*
Smothers, Frank *NF*
Smyllie, Robert Maire d194-? *BioIn 5*
Smyser, Adam Albert 1920- *WhoAm 1974, WhoWest 1974*
Smyth, Albert Henry 1863-1907 *AmAu, AmAu&B, DcAmA, DcNAA, HisAmM XR, LiJA*
Smyth, Bernard John 1915- *BioIn 2, BioIn 6, WhoAm 1974*
Smyth, Clifford 1866-1943 *DcNAA, WhNAA*
Smyth, Dan *NF*
Smyth, David 1929- *ConAu 61*
Smyth, Egbert Coffin 1829-1904 *Alli, Alli Sup, DcAmA, DcNAA, HisAmM XR, WebBD*
Smyth, Ethel Mary 1858-1944 *CurBio XR*
Smyth, Jeannette *NF*
Smyth, Joel Douglas 1941- *WhoAm 1974*
Smyth, Joseph Hilton 1901- *AmAu&B, AmJnl,*

HisAmM XR
Smythe, Albert Ernest Stafford 1861-1947 *DcNAA, PoIre*
Smythe, Andrew E *HisAmM XR*
Smythe, Reggis *NF*
Smythe, Reginald 1918?- *AuNews 1, BioIn 10*
Smythe, William Ellsworth 1861-1922 *DcAmA, DcNAA, HisAmM XR, NatCAB 17, WhNAA*
Snaddon, Andrew William 1921- *CanWW 1972, WhoAm 1974*
Snagge, John Derrick Mordaunt 1904- *BioIn 7, Who 1974*
Snead-Cox, John George 1855-1939 *BioIn 1, CathA 1930*
Snedden, Charles Willis 1913- *BioIn 4, WhoAm 1974*
Snedden, William J 1903- *WhJnl 1928*
Sneed, A C *HisAmM XR*
Sneh, Moshe 1909-1972 *BioIn 9, NewYTBE 3*
Snell, Dave 1936- *NF*
Snell, David 1921- *WhoAm 1974, WhoF&I 1974, WhoS&SW 1973, WhoWor 1974*
Snell, George 1909- *AmAu&B, AmNov*
Snell, John *WhJnl 1928*
Snell, Leroy Waite 1886- *WhJnl 1928*
Snelling, William Joseph 1804-1848 *Alli, AmAu, AmAu&B, AmJnl, DcAmA, DcAmB 17, DcLEL, DcNAA, HisAmM XR, OxAm, REnAL, WebBD*
Snellman, J V *ForP*
Snelson, P B 1878- *WhJnl 1928*
Snevily, Henry Mansfield 1886-1954 *BioIn 3*
Sneyd, Doug *NF*
Snider, Arthur J *WhoAm 1974*
Snider, Gerald A 1896- *WhJnl 1928*
Snider, William Davis 1920- *WhoAm 1974, WhoF&I 1974, WhoS&SW 1973*
Sniffen, Michael J *NF*
Snitowsky, Mike *NF*
Snively, John H *Alli Sup, HisAmM XR*
Snoddy, Abbie *BioIn 2*
Snodgrass, J E *HisAmM XR*
Snodgrass, Rhey T 1880- *HisAmM XR, WhJnl 1928*
Snook, Albert M 1869- *WhJnl 1928*
Snow, Carmel 1890-1961 *BioIn 5, BioIn 6, HisAmM XR*
Snow, Edgar Parks 1905-1972 *AmAu&B, Au&Wr, BioIn 3, BioIn 4, BioIn 5, BioIn 9, BioIn 10, ConAu 33, CurBio XR, HisAmM XR, REn, REnAL, TwCA, TwCA Sup, WebBD*
Snow, Edgar Rowe 1902- *ConAu 9R*
Snow, Francis Haffkine 1876?-1949 *BioIn 1*
Snow, Francis Lawrence 1882- *WhJnl 1928*
Snow, Francis Woolson 1877-1949 *DcNAA*
Snow, George K *HisAmM XR*
Snow, Helen Foster 1907- *ConAu 57, ForWC 1970, WrDr 1976*
Snow, John B *NF*
Snow, R A *HisAmM XR*
Snow, Richard F *NF*
Snow, Samuel Sheffield 1828?- *DcNAA*
Snow, Sydney I 1888- *WhJnl Sup*
Snow, W G M 1904- *WhJnl 1928*
Snow, Walter 1905-1973 *BioIn 9*
Snowden, Dorothy Parr *NF*
Snowden, Isaac Clarkson *HisAmM XR*
Snowden, William W *HisAmM XR*
Snowdon, Lord 1930- *NewYTBE 1*
Snowdon, Lord *see also* Armstrong-Jones, Antony

Snowdon, Lord *see also* Snowdon, Anthony Armstrong-Jones, Earl
Snowdon, Antony Armstrong-Jones, Earl 1930- *IntWW 1974, Who 1974*
Snowdon, Anthony Amstrong-Jones, Earl *see also* Armstrong- Jones, A
Snowdon, Antony Armstrong-Jones, Earl *see also* Snowdon, Lord
Snyder, Brodie *NF*
Snyder, Burwell C 1883- *WhJnl 1928*
Snyder, Charles McCoy 1859- *AmAu&B, DcAmA, HisAmM XR*
Snyder, Clarence, Jr. 1881- *WhJnl Sup*
Snyder, Donald Bertram 1897- *AmAu&B*
Snyder, Gerald S 1933- *ConAu 61*
Snyder, Henry Burgess 1884- *WhJnl 1928*
Snyder, J R 1885- *WhJnl 1928*
Snyder, Jimmy *NF*
Snyder, Louis Irving, Jr. 1912- *WhoAm 1974*
Snyder, Murray 1911-1969 *BioIn 4, BioIn 5, BioIn 8*
Snyder, Tom 1936?- *BioIn 10*
Snyder, W P *HisAmM XR*
Soanes, Wood 1894- *WhJnl Sup*
Sobel, Bernard 1887-1964 *AmAu&B, BiE&WWA, BioIn 3, BioIn 6, ConAu 5R, IndAu 1917, REnAL, WhNAA*
Sobel, Lester Albert 1919- *AmAu&B, ConAu '21, WhoAm 1974, WhoE 1974*
Sobol, Donald J 1924- *AuBYP, BioIn 8, BioIn 9, BioIn 10, ConAu 1, SmATA 1*
Sobol, Louis 1896- *AmAu&B, BioIn 1, BioIn 8, ConAu 29, IntMPA 1975*
Sobolev, Leonid 1898-1971 *ConAu 29*
Sobolewski, E *HisAmM XR*
Sobrino, Jose *NF*
Soby, James Thrall 1906- *AmAu&B, REnAL, TwCA Sup, WhoAm 1974, WhoAmA 1973*
Sochurek, Howard J *RpN*
Socolow, Sanford 1928- *WhoE 1974*
Soderlind, Sterling Eugene 1926- *WhoAm 1974*
Soderstrom, E A 1897- *WhJnl 1928*
Soglow, Otto 1900-1975 *AmAu&B, BioIn 3, ConAu 57, CurBio XR, REnAL, WhoAm 1974, WhoAmA 1973*
Sogno, Edgardo 1915?- *BioIn 3*
Sohn, Joseph 1867-1935 *AmAu&B*
Sokol, Edward 1913?- *BioIn 2*
Sokolov, Alexander V 1943- *ConAu 73*
Sokolov, Raymond A 1941?- *BioIn 9, BioIn 10*
Sokolov, Sasha *ConAu XR*
Sokolow, Nahum 1861-1936 *CasWL, WebBD*
Sokolsky, George Ephraim 1893-1962 *AmAu&B, AmJnl, BioIn 3, BioIn 6, BioIn 7, CurBio XR, ForP, NatCAB 49*
Sokorski, Wlodzimierz 1908- *IntWW 1976, WhoWor 1974*
Solano, Armando 1897?-1953 *BioIn 3*
Solano, Solita 1888-1975 *ConAu 61*
Solberg, Carl 1915- *ConAu 73*
Solender, Robert Lawrence 1923- *WhoAdv 1972, WhoAm 1974*
Soler, Jose Antonio Martinez 1947?- *NF*
Soler, Jose M 1890- *WhJnl 1928*
Sollmann, William Frederick 1881-1951 *BioIn 2, BioIn 3*
Solman, Paul 1945?- *NF*
Solomon, George 1940- *ConAu 45*
Solomon, Goody Love 1929- *ConAu 57, WhoAmW 1974*
Solomon, Neil 1937- *ConAu 65*
Solomon, Philip Samuel *NF*
Solomon, Stephen David 1950- *ConAu 69*
Solotaroff, Theodore 1928- *BioIn 8, ConAu 11R,*

DrAF 1976
Soloviev, Mikhail 1908- *BioIn 3*
Solow, Herbert 1903-1964 *AmAu&B, AmRP, BioIn 7*
Soloyanis, Constantine *OvPC*
Soltis, Andrew Eden, Jr. 1947- *ConAu 49, WhoAm 1974*
Somerby, Charles P *HisAmM XR*
Somerby, Frederic Thomas 1814-1871 *DcNAA*
Somers, Florence *NF*
Somers, Frederic M 1850-1894 *HisAmM XR, NatCAB 22*
Somerset, Isabella Caroline 1851-1921 *WebBD*
Somerset, Isabella Caroline *see also* Somerset, Lady Henry
Somerset, Lady Henry 1851-1921 *Alli Sup*
Somerset, Lady Henry *see also* Somerset, Isabella Caroline
Somerset, Joseph Bernard 1928- *WhoAm 1974*
Somerville, Alexander 1811-1885 *BbtC, BioIn 8, DcNAA, OxCan*
Somerville, Charley *NF*
Somerville, Henry 1889-1953 *BioIn 1, BioIn 3, CathA 1930*
Somerville, Hugh 1922- *ConAu 9R*
Sommer, Theo 1930- *IntWW 1976*
Sommers, Martin 1900-1963 *BioIn 6, HisAmM XR*
Sommers, Naomi Swett 1889- *WhJnl 1928*
Sondern, Frederic 1911?-1966 *BioIn 7*
Sonneborn, Harry Lee 1919- *WhoAm 1974*
Sonneck, Oscar George Theodore 1873-1928 *AmAu&B, BioIn 1, DcNAA, REnAL, WebBD*
Sonnichsen, Albert 1878-1931 *AmAu&B, DcAmB 17, DcNAA, REnAL*
Sonnichsen, Charles Leland 1901- *DrAS 74E, WhoAm 1974*
Sons, Raymond William 1920- *NF*
Sonstein, Bill *NF*
Sontag, Frederick Hermann 1924- *OvPC, WhoAm 1974, WhoAmP 1973, WhoCon 1973, WhoE 1974, WhoPubR 1972*
Sontag, Henriette *HisAmM XR*
Sontag, Susan 1933- *AmAu&B, CelR 1973, ConAu 19, ConLC 1, ConLC 2, ConNov 1972, ConNov 1976, CurBio XR, DrAF 1976, ModAL, Pen Am, RAdv 1, WhoAm 1974, WhoAmW 1974, WhoE 1974, WhoTwCL, WhoWor 1974, WorAu, WrDr 1976*
Sontheimer, Morton *WhoPubR 1972*
Soong, Norman 1910?-1969 *BioIn 8*
Soper, John H 1846-1944 *NatCAB 48*
Sopris, William St. Vrain 1898- *WhJnl 1928*
Sorel, Edward 1929- *BioIn 8, ConAu 9, WhoAm 1974, WhoE 1974, WhoWor 1974*
Sorel, Georges 1847-1922 *CasWL, CIDMEL, LongC, OxFr, REn, WebBD, WorAu*
Sorensen, Grace *HisAmM XR*
Sorensen, Holger R 1909- *IntWW 1976*
Sorensen, Robert *NF*
Sorensen, Thomas Chaikin 1926- *BioIn 5, ConAu 23, WhoAm 1974, WhoF&I 1974, WrDr 1976*
Sorenson, Robert *NF*
Sorge, Reinhard M *NF*
Sorge, Richard 1895-1944 *BioIn 2, BioIn 3, BioIn 4, BioIn 7, BioIn 8*
Soria, Dorle *BioIn 1*
Sorin, Edward Frederick 1814-1893 *AmAu&B*
Sorley Walker, Kathrine *Au&Wr, ConAu 7R, WrDr 1976*

Sorokin, Pitirim Alexandrovic 1889-1968
  AmAu&B, BiDPara, ConAu 5, ConAu 25,
  CurBio XR, HisAmM XR, REnAL,
  TwCA Sup, WebBD, WhNAA
Sorrells, John Harvey 1896-1948 *AmAu&B,*
  BioIn 1
Sorrels, William Wright 1924- *WhoAm 1974,*
  WhoS&SW 1973
Sosa, Enrique *NF*
Sosey, Frank H 1864- *WhJnl 1928*
Sosin, Gene *OvPC*
Sosin, Mark J *NF*
Soskin, William H 1899-1952 *AmAu&B,*
  WhJnl Sup
Soth, Lauren Kephart 1910- *BioIn 4, BioIn 10,*
  CurBio XR, WhoAm 1974
Sotheran, Alice Hyneman Rhine 1840- *NF*
Sotheran, Charles 1847-1902 *Alli Sup, DcAmA,*
  DcNAA
Souchon, Paul 1879-1951 *BioIn 2*
Soudder, Edward Wallace, Jr. 1911- *WhoAm 1974*
Souki, Samir *BioIn 3*
Soule, Franklin 1810-1882 *DcNAA*
Soule, Gardner 1913- *ConAu 5R*
Soule, George Henry, Jr. 1887-1970 *AmAu&B,*
  BioIn 8, ConAu 21, ConAu 29, CurBio XR,
  HisAmM XR, NewYTBE 1, REnAL,
  TwCA, TwCA Sup, WebBD, WhNAA
Soule, J H *HisAmM XR*
Soule, Joshua 1781-1867 *Alli, HisAmM XR*
Souney, William T *OvPC*
Sousa, John Philip, III 1913- *WhoAm 1974*
Sousley, James Clarence 1867- *WhJnl 1928*
Souter, David Henry 1862-1935 *BioIn 2*
Souter, Gerry 1940- *NF*
Southall, H Langtry 1896- *WhJnl 1928*
Southall, James Cocke 1828-1897 *Alli Sup,*
  AmAu&B, DcAmB 17, DcNAA
Southam, Harry Stevenson 1875-1954 *BioIn 3*
Southam, John David 1909-1954 *BioIn 3*
Southam, Robert Wilson 1914- *CanWW 1972,*
  WhoAm 1974
Southam, William 1843-1932 *NF*
Southam, William James 1877?-1957 *BioIn 4*
Southard, Shelby Edward 1914- *WhoAm 1974*
Southerland, Daniel *NF*
Southern, William Neil, Jr. 1864-1956 *AmAu&B,*
  BioIn 4, WhJnl Sup
Southwick, John Leonard 1858-1932 *NatCAB 31,*
  WhJnl 1928
Southwick, Solomon 1773-1839 *Alli, AmAu&B,*
  AmJnl, DcAmB 17, DcNAA, NatCAB 4,
  REnAL
Southwick, Thomas P *NF*
Southwood, Lord Julius Salter Elias *Lor&LP*
Southworth, Edward F 1872-1946 *NatCAB 34*
Southworth, George W 1851- *WhJnl 1928*
Souvaine, Mabel Hill *AmAu&B*
Sovola, Ed 1919?- *BioIn 2*
Sower, Christopher 1693-1758 *AmAu&B, AmJnl,*
  CasWL, EarABI, OxAm
Sower, Christopher, III 1754-1799 *AmAu&B,*
  AmJnl, WebBD
Spade, Fred *BioIn 1*
Spadolini, Giovanni 1925- *IntWW 1976,*
  WhoWor 1974
Spadone, F G *NF*
Spaeth, Sigmund Gottfried 1885-1965 *AmAu&B,*
  AmSCAP 1966, ConAu 5R, CurBio XR,
  HisAmM XR, REnAL, TwCA, TwCA Sup,
  WebBD, WhNAA
Spahn, Philip *OvPC*
Spahr, Charles Barzillai 1860-1904 *DcAmA,*

DcNAA, HisAmM XR, OhA&B
Spake, Amanda *InvJ*
Spalding, Jack Johnson 1913- *ConAu 69,*
  WhoAm 1974, WhoS&SW 1973
Spalding, James Reed 1821-1872 *Alli, AmAu,*
  NatCAB 5
Spalding, Martin John 1810-1872 *Alli, AmAu&B,*
  BiD&SB, BiDSA, DcAmA, DcNAA,
  HisAmM XR, WebBD
Spalding, William Andrew 1852-1941 *AmLY,*
  BioIn 6, DcAmA, DcNAA
Spalla, Bery *NF*
Spangler, Andrew M 1818-1897 *DcNAA*
Spann, Eleanor *HisAmM XR*
Spargo, John 1876-1966 *AmAu&B, AmLY,*
  AmRP, HisAmM XR, REnAL, WebBD,
  WhNAA
Spargo, Mary *NF*
Sparhawk, Edward V *HisAmM XR*
Sparkes, Boyden 1890-1954 *AmAu&B, BioIn 3,*
  HisAmM XR, OhA&B
Sparks, Allister *RpN*
Sparks, Frank Melville 1877-1950 *BioIn 2*
Sparks, Fred 1915- *BioIn 3, BioIn 4, OvPC*
Sparks, George McIntosh 1888-1958 *BioIn 5,*
  BioIn 9, WhNAA, WhJnl 1928
Sparks, Jared 1789-1866 *Alli, AmAu, AmAu&B,*
  AmJnl, BiD&SB, BioIn 3, BioIn 6, BioIn 9,
  CyAL 1, DcAmA, DcNAA, EncAB,
  HisAmM XR, LiJA, OxAm, REn, REnAL,
  WebBD
Sparks, John S, Jr. *OvPC*
Sparling, Earl 1897-1951 *BioIn 2*
Sparn, Edwin F *OvPC*
Spaulding, Charles D *HisAmM XR*
Spaulding, Eugene W *HisAmM XR*
Spaulding, John Pearson 1923- *NewYTBS 5,*
  WhoAm 1974
Spaulding, Martha *NF*
Speaks, Charles *OvPC*
Spear, Elmer E 1887- *WhJnl 1928*
Spear, Ivan I 1894- *WhJnl 1928*
Spear, Joe *NewMr*
Spear, John William 1856-1943 *BioIn 4,*
  NatCAB 40
Spear, Joseph C *NF*
Spear, Samuel Thayer 1812-1891 *Alli, Alli Sup,*
  DcAmA, DcNAA, HisAmM XR
Spear, William R *NF*
Speare, Charles F 1875?-1961 *BioIn 5*
Spearman, Walter 1908- *BioIn 3, BioIn 4,*
  ConAu 29
Spears, Jackie *NF*
Spears, John Randolph 1850-1936 *AmAu&B,*
  BiD&SB, DcAmA, DcNAA, HisAmM XR,
  NatCAB 9, OhA&B, WebBD
Spears, Lee *NF*
Spears, Monroe Kirk 1916- *ConAu 5, DrAS 74F,*
  HisAmM XR, WhoAm 1974
Spector, Maurice *AmRP*
Spectorsky, Auguste Comte 1910-1972 *AmAu&B,*
  BioIn 6, BioIn 9, BioIn 10, ConAu 17,
  ConAu 33, CurBio XR, REnAL
Spedon, Andrew Learmont 1831-1884 *BbtC,*
  DcNAA
Speed, John Gilmer 1853-1909 *AmAu&B,*
  BiD&SB, BiDSA, DcAmA, DcNAA,
  HisAmM XR, NatCAB 10
Speed, Keats 1879-1952 *AmJnl, BioIn 2,*
  BioIn 3, WhNAA
Speer, Clifford d1945 *NF*
Speer, John 1817- *NatCAB 7*
Speer, Talbot Taylor 1895- *WhoAm 1974,*
  WhoE 1974, WhoF&I 1974

Speer, Victor *NF*
Speer, William McMurtrie 1865-1923 *NF*
Speers, Archer *NF*
Speers, Leland C 1876-1946 *BioIn 1*
Speidel, Glenn *NF*
Speidel, Merritt Charles 1879-1960 *AmJnl,
    BioIn 1, BioIn 2, BioIn 5*
Speiser, Jean *ConAu 69*
Spence, Francis Stephens 1850-1917 *NF*
Spence, Hartzell 1908- *AmAu&B, AmNov,
    ConAu 5, CurBio XR, REnAL,
    WhoAm 1974*
Spence, William G 1885- *WhJnl 1928*
Spencer, Anna Garlin 1851-1931 *DcAmB 17,
    DcNAA, WhNAA*
Spencer, Anna W *HisAmM XR*
Spencer, Arthur *HisAmM XR*
Spencer, Bella Zilfa 1840-1867 *Alli, DcAmA,
    DcNAA, HisAmM XR*
Spencer, Bernard 1909-1963 *BioIn 8, ModBL,
    TwCW, WorAu*
Spencer, Charles H 1870- *WhJnl 1928*
Spencer, Dale R 1925- *ConAu 57*
Spencer, Duncan C *NF*
Spencer, F Gilman *NF*
Spencer, Frank *NF*
Spencer, Frederick *AmRP*
Spencer, Herbert 1820-1903 *Alli, Alli Sup, BbD,
    BiD&SB, BrAu 19, CasWL, DcEnA,
    DcEnA Ap, DcEnL, DcLEL, EvLB,
    HisAmM XR, NewC, OxEng, Pen Eng,
    REn, WebBD, WebE&AL*
Spencer, Hiram Ladd 1829-1915 *Alli, DcNAA*
Spencer, John 1885-1957 *BioIn 4, WhJnl 1928*
Spencer, Lorillard 1860-1912 *HisAmM XR*
Spencer, Mary Hoffman *WhJnl Sup*
Spencer, Mary V *HisAmM XR*
Spencer, Matthew Lyle 1881-1969 *AmJnl, AmLY,
    BioIn 8, WhNAA, WhJnl 1928*
Spencer, Murlin *NF*
Spencer, O L *NF*
Spencer, Robert B 1872- *WhJnl 1928*
Spencer, Steven M 1905- *ConAu 13, ConAu P-1,
    HisAmM XR, RpN*
Spencer, Stewart *NF*
Spencer, W Vaughan 1899-1940 *NatCAB 46*
Spencer, Warren 1888-1965 *AmAu&B, WhNAA*
Spencer, Warren *see also* Lengel, William Charles
Spender, Edward Harold 1864-1926 *WebBD*
Spender, John Alfred 1862-1942 *BioIn 1, BioIn 5,
    ForP, LongC, Lor&LP, NewC, WebBD,
    WhoLA*
Spender, Lilian Headland 1838-1895 *Alli Sup,
    WebBD*
Spender, Stephen 1909- *Au&Wr, CasWL,
    CnE&AP, CnMD, CnMWL, ConAu 9,
    ConLC 1, ConLC 2, ConLC 5, ConP 1970,
    ConP 1975, CurBio XR, CyWA, DcLEL,
    EncWL, EvLB, HisAmM XR, IntWW 1976,
    LongC, ModBL, ModBL Sup, ModWD,
    NewC, OxEng, Pen Eng, RAdv 1, REn,
    TwCA, TwCA Sup, TwCW, WebBD,
    WebE&AL, Who 1974, WhoTwCL,
    WhoWor 1974, WrDr 1976*
Speranza, Gino 1872-1927 *HisAmM XR*
Spergel, Howard K 1938?- *NF*
Sperling, Godfrey, Jr. 1915- *BioIn 9, BioIn 10,
    WhoAm 1974, WhoS&SW 1973*
Sperry, Watson R 1842- *NatCAB 1*
Spewack, Bella Cohen 1899- *AmAu&B, Au&Wr,
    ConDr, McGWD, ModWD, REn, REnAL,
    TwCA, TwCA Sup, WebBD, WhoAm 1974*
Spewack, Samuel 1899-1971 *AmAu&B, Au&Wr,
    BiE&WWA, CnMD, ConAu 33, McGWD,*

*ModWD, NewYTBE 2, REn, REnAL,
    TwCA, TwCA Sup, WebBD, WhJnl 1928*
Speyer, Edward 1884- *WhJnl 1928*
Spiegel, Robert H 1922- *NF*
Spiegelman, Judy 1942- *NF*
Spielmann, Marion Harry 1858-1948 *LongC,
    WhoLA*
Spiers, Paul H, Jr. *OvPC*
Spiker, Laurence J 1898?-1950 *BioIn 2*
Spikol, Art *NF*
Spiller, Robert Ernest 1896- *AmAu&B, ConAu 5,
    DrAS 74E, HisAmM XR, LiJA, REnAL,
    WhNAA, WhoAm 1974*
Spilman, Charles H *NF*
Spina, Tony 1914- *ConAu 69*
Spingarn, Joel Elias 1875-1939 *AmAu&B, AmLY,
    AnMV 1926, CnDAL, DcAmA, DcLEL,
    DcNAA, HisAmM XR, OxAm, REn,
    REnAL, TwCA, WebBD, WhNAA*
Spink, Albert H *HisAmM XR*
Spink, Charles Claude Johnson 1916-
    WhoAdv 1972, WhoAm 1974, WhoMW 1974
Spink, John George Taylor 1888-1962 *BioIn 1,
    BioIn 5, BioIn 6*
Spiro, Amster 1893?-1956 *BioIn 4*
Spitzer, Maurice 1900- *BioIn 8*
Spitzer, Silas 1896?-1973 *BioIn 9*
Spitzler, Robert Theodore 1931- *WhoAm 1974*
Spivack, Robert Gerald 1915-1970 *BioIn 8,
    NewYTBE 1*
Spivak, John Louis 1897- *AmAu&B, BioIn 8,
    WhoAm 1974*
Spivak, Jonathan M *NF*
Spivak, Lawrence Edmund 1900- *BioIn 2,
    BioIn 4, BioIn 6, BioIn 9, CurBio XR,
    HisAmM XR, IntMPA 1975, WhoAm 1974,
    WhoS&SW 1973, WhoWorJ 1972*
Spizman, Leib 1903-1963 *BioIn 6*
Splint, Fred C *HisAmM XR*
Splint, Sarah Field d1959 *HisAmM XR*
Spofford, William Benjamin 1892-1972 *BioIn 9,
    NewYTBE 3*
Spooner, Alden Jeremiah 1810-1881 *Alli,
    AmAu&B, DcNAA*
Spooner, Chesler M d1976 *NF*
Spooner, Judah 1748-1807 *NatCAB 19*
Spotswood, William *HisAmM XR*
Spraggett, Allen 1932- *ConAu 25*
Spragg, Andrew 1921?- *BioIn 1*
Sprague, Charles Arthur 1887-1969 *BioIn 1,
    BioIn 2, BioIn 5, BioIn 8, HisAmM XR,
    WhJnl 1928*
Sprague, George E 1895- *WhJnl 1928*
Sprague, Hugh Almeron 1866- *WhJnl 1928*
Sprague, Marshall 1909- *ConAu 4R, DrAS 74H,
    OhA&B*
Sprague, Timothy Dwight 1819?-1849 *Alli,
    HisAmM XR*
Sprague, William Cyrus 1860-1922 *DcAmA,
    DcNAA, HisAmM XR, OhA&B*
Spremo, Boris *NF*
Sprigg, D A *HisAmM XR*
Sprigge, Sir Squire 1860-1937 *BioIn 2, BioIn 3,
    WhoLA*
Sprigle, Ray 1886-1957 *BioIn 1, BioIn 2,
    BioIn 4, OhA&B*
Spring, Bob *NF*
Spring, Howard 1889-1965 *ConAu P-1,
    CurBio XR, DcLEL, EvLB, LongC, NewC,
    Pen Eng, REn, TwCA, TwCA Sup, TwCW,
    WebBD, WhoChL*
Spring, Johann Arnold 1845-1924 *BioIn 7*
Spring, Norma 1917- *ConAu 61*
Spring, Samuel 1746-1819 *Alli, DcNAA,*

HisAmM XR, WebBD
Springer, Axel Casar 1912- *BioIn 4, BioIn 6, BioIn 7, BioIn 8, CurBio XR, ForP, IntWW 1976*
Springer, Gertrude 1879- *BioIn 2, HisAmM XR*
Springer, John 1916- *ConAu 53, HisAmM XR, IntMPA 1975, WhoCon 1973*
Springer, John L 1915- *ConAu 2R*
Springer, Louis A *NF*
Springer, Marguerite Warren *HisAmM XR*
Spritzler, Marvin D *NF*
Spurgeon, John J *NF*
Spy *see* Ward, Sir Leslie
Squibob, John P *see* Derby, George Horatio
Squibob, John P *see* Phoenix, John
Squier, Ephraim George 1821-1888 *Alli, Alli Sup, AmAu, AmAu&B, BbD, CyAL 2, DcAmA, DcAmB 17, DcEnL, DcNAA, EarABI Sup, HisAmM XR, OhA&B, OxAm, REnAL, WebBD*
Squier, Miriam Florence *AmAu, HisAmM XR*
Squier, S L 1900- *WhJnl 1928*
Squire, C B *OvPC*
Squire, George Hardie 1871-1950 *BioIn 2*
Squire, Sir John Collings 1884-1958 *BioIn 2, DcLEL, EvLB, LongC, ModBL, ModWD, NewC, Pen Eng, REn, TwCA, TwCA Sup, TwCW, WebBD, WebE&AL, WhNAA*
Squires, Grant *AmJnl*
Squires, James D 1943?- *NF*
Squires, James E *NF*
Squires, Jim *InvJ*
Squirru, Rafael 1925- *WhoS&SW 1973*
Srere, Benson M 1928- *WhoAm 1974*
Srinath, M G *NF*
Srinivasan, C R 1889-1962 *BioIn 6*
Srinivasan, Kasturi 1887-1959 *BioIn 9*
Sroda, Dirk *BioIn 8*
Srodes, James *NF*
Stabile, Toni *ForWC 1970, OvPC*
Stabler, C Norman 1901- *WhJnl 1928*
Stace, Arthur W 1875-1950 *BioIn 2, WhJnl 1928*
Stacey, Joseph *NF*
Stacey, Thomas Charles Gerrard 1930- *Au&Wr, BioIn 5, ConAu 9R*
Stackelberg, Baroness Garnett *NF*
Stacker, Margaret 1875- *WhJnl 1928*
Stackpole, Edward James, Jr. 1894-1967 *AmAu&B, ConAu 1, WhJnl 1928*
Stackpole, Edward James, Sr. 1861-1936 *AmAu&B, DcNAA, NatCAB 27, WhNAA, WhJnl 1928*
Stackpole, Peter *NF*
Stacpoole, Henry DeVere 1863-1951 *EvLB, HisAmM XR, PolRe, TwCW, WebBD*
Stadtfeld, Curtis Karl 1935- *ConAu 49, WhoMW 1974, WhoPubR 1972*
Staffin, Anne *NF*
Stafford, Charles L *NF*
Stafford, Dale 1908-1973 *NF*
Stafford, James V 1914?-1971 *BioIn 9*
Stagg, George T *OvPC*
Stahl, John Meloy 1860-1944 *AmAu&B, DcNAA, WhNAA*
Stahl, Lesley *AuNews 2*
Stahl, Nancy *WhoAmW 1974*
Stahlman, Edward Bushrod 1843-1930 *BioIn 5*
Stahlman, Frank Carl 1872?-1949 *BioIn 1*
Stahlman, James Geddes 1893-1976 *BioIn 2, IntWW 1974, WhoAm 1974, WhoF&I 1974, WhJnl 1928, WhoS&SW 1973*
Stahr, John S *HisAmM XR*
Staihar, Janet *NF*
Stainbrook, Richard D *OvPC*

Stair, Edward Douglas 1859-1951 *BioIn 2, BioIn 4, NatCAB 39*
Stall, Robert *NF*
Stallard, John 1935- *ConAu 49*
Stallings, Laurence 1894-1968 *AmAu&B, CnDAL, ConAmA, ConAmL, HisAmM XR, McGWD, ModWD, OxAm, Pen Am, REn, REnAL, TwCA, TwCA Sup, WebBD*
Stallins, Henry Arnold 1888- *WhJnl 1928*
Stamaty, Stanley 1916- *WhoAmA 1973*
Stambler, Irwin 1924- *AuBYP, BioIn 8, BioIn 10, ConAu 5, SmATA 5, WrDr 1976*
Stampa, George Loraine 1875-1951 *BioIn 2*
Stampfer, Friedrich 1874-1957 *BioIn 4*
Stamprech, Franz 1906- *IntWW 1976, WhoWor 1974*
Stanard, William Glover 1858-1933 *AmAu&B, BiDSA, DcNAA*
Standard, James N 1940?- *NF*
Standish, Milton R 1891- *WhJnl 1928*
Standish, Myles 1907- *IntMPA 1975, WhoAm 1974*
Standish, Myles E 1893?-1971 *BioIn 9*
Stanek, Adam *NF*
Stanford, Alfred Boller 1900- *AmAu&B, ConAu P-1, WebBD, WhNAA, WhoAm 1974*
Stanford, Donald Elwin 1913- *ConAu 13, DrAS 74E, WhoS&SW 1973, WrDr 1976*
Stanger, Ila Ann 1940- *ConAu 65, WhoAm 1974*
Stankevich, Boris 1928- *BioIn 9, ConAu 23, SmATA 2*
Stanley, Allison F 1897- *WhJnl 1928*
Stanley, Amy Leslie Marie *see* West, Lillie
Stanley, Cassius Miller 1878- *WhNAA, WhJnl 1928*
Stanley, Donald 1925- *WhoAm 1974, WhoWest 1974*
Stanley, Edward *BioIn 1*
Stanley, Fred 1890?-1949 *BioIn 1*
Stanley, Harry 1894- *WhJnl 1928*
Stanley, Sir Henry Morton 1841-1904 *Alli Sup, AmAu&B, AmJnl, BbD, BiD&SB, BioIn 1, BioIn 2, BioIn 3, BioIn 4, BioIn 5, BioIn 6, BioIn 7, BioIn 8, BioIn 9, BrAu 19, CarSB, DcAmA, DcEnA, DcEnA Ap, EvLB, FamWC, HisAmM XR, OxAm, OxEng, REn, REnAL, WebBD*
Stanley, Hiram Alonzo 1859- *AmAu&B, DcAmA, DcNAA, NatCAB 13*
Stanley, Hiram M *HisAmM XR*
Stanley, James Berney 1844- *WhJnl 1928*
Stanley, John 1940- *ConAu 21R*
Stanley, Marie 1860-1939 *DcNAA*
Stanley, Marie *see also* West, Lillie
Stanley, Terri *NF*
Stanoyevich, Milivoy Stoyan 1882- *AmAu&B, WhNAA*
Stansbury, Charles Frederick 1854-1922 *DcNAA, HisAmM XR*
Stansbury, Henry H *NF*
Stansbury, Herb, Jr. *NF*
Stansfield, Elaine 1926- *NF*
Stanton, Charles Spelman 1868-1947 *BioIn 1*
Stanton, Eleanor *NF*
Stanton, Elizabeth Cady 1815-1902 *Alli Sup, AmAu, AmAu&B, BbD, BiD&SB, DcAmA, DcNAA, EncAB, HisAmM XR, OxAm, REn, REnAL, WebBD*
Stanton, Frank Lebby 1857-1927 *AmAu&B, AmJnl, AmSCAP 1966, BbD, BiDSA, DcAmA, DcAmB 17, DcNAA, HisAmM XR, OxAm, REn, REnAL, WebBD*

Stanton, Gerrit Smith 1845-1927 *DcNAA*
Stanton, Hazel 1896?-1966 *BioIn 7*
Stanton, Henry Brewster 1805-1887 *Alli, Alli Sup, BiD&SB, DcAmA, DcAmB 17, DcNAA, NatCAB 2, WebBD*
Stanton, Pam *BioIn 10, BioNews 1975*
Stanton, Robert Livingston 1810-1885 *Alli, DcAmA, DcNAA, HisAmM XR, OhA&B*
Stanton, Roger 1928- *BioIn 10, BioNews 1975, WhoF&I 1974, WhoMW 1974*
Stanton, Theodore 1851-1925 *Alli Sup, AmLY, BiD&SB, DcAmA, DcNAA, HisAmM XR*
Stanwood, Edward 1841-1923 *Alli Sup, AmAu&B, DcAmA, DcNAA, HisAmM XR, NatCAB 9*
Stapel, John C 1893- *WhJnl 1928*
Stapler, Harry 1919- *ConAu 61*
Staples, Arthur Gray 1861-1940 *DcNAA, WhJnl 1928*
Staples, Owen 1866-1949 *BioIn 2*
Staples, Paul William 1907- *InvJ, WhoWest 1974*
Stapleton, Constance *NF*
Stapleton, Jack 1899- *WhJnl 1928*
Stapleton, Jean 1942- *ConAu 69*
Stapley, Ray *NF*
Star, Cima *NF*
Star, Jack 1920- *ConAu 73*
Starbuck, Alexander 1841-1925 *DcNAA*
Starbuck, C C *HisAmM XR*
Starbuck, Calvin W *AmJnl*
Starbuck, Frank Raymond 1876-1951 *BioIn 5*
Starbuck, Frank Washburn 1845-1929 *BioIn 5*
Starey, A B *HisAmM XR*
Starger, Martin 1932- *WhoAm 1974, WhoE 1974*
Stark, Al *NF*
Stark, C J 1882- *WhJnl 1928*
Stark, C Nick *NF*
Stark, Eliot M *OvPC*
Stark, George Washington 1884-1966 *WhJnl 1928*
Stark, J Clifford *OvPC*
Stark, Leonard *NF*
Stark, Louis 1888-1954 *BioIn 2, BioIn 3, CurBio XR, DcAmB S5*
Stark, Morton S *OvPC*
Stark, Norm *NF*
Stark, Raymond 1919- *ConAu 73*
Stark, Richard S *OvPC*
Stark, Susan Rothenberg 1940- *WhoAm 1974, WhoAmW 1974*
Starke, H F Gerhard 1916- *IntWW 1976*
Starken, Louis Edward 1904- *WhJnl 1928*
Starkey, James Sullivan 1879-1958 *CasWL, DcLEL, EvLB, LongC, NewC, PoIre, TwCA, TwCA Sup, WebBD*
Starkey, James Sullivan *see also* O'Sullivan, Seumas
Starkman, Moshe 1906-1975 *BioIn 10, ConAu 57, WhoWorJ 1972*
Starnes, Richard 1922- *BioIn 5, WhoAm 1974, WhoS&SW 1973*
Starobin, Joseph R 1913-1976 *AmRP, ConAu 45, ConAu 69*
Starr, Alfred *HisAmM XR*
Starr, Cecile 1921- *ConAu 65, CurBio XR*
Starr, D L *NF*
Starr, David 1922- *WhoAm 1974, WhoE 1974*
Starr, Elisha 1806-1893 *BioIn 5*
Starr, Ella *HisAmM XR*
Starr, Frank 1938- *ConAu 69*
Starr, Jimmy *NF*
Starr, Joshua 1907-1949 *BioIn 2, BioIn 3*
Starr, Kevin *NF*
Starr, Leonard *NF*
Starr, Louis Morris 1917- *ConAu 53, DrAS 74H*

Starr, Marjorie 1921- *WhoAm 1974, WhoAmW 1974*
Starr, Martin 1902-1967 *BioIn 7*
Starr, Steve Dawson 1944- *WhoAm 1974, WhoS&SW 1973*
Starr-Hunt, Jack 1893?-1951 *BioIn 2*
Starrett, Charles 1884- *IntMPA 1975, WhJnl 1928*
Starrett, Charles Vincent Emerson 1886-1974 *AuBYP, DcLEL, EncMys, REn, REnAL, TwCA, TwCA Sup, WhNAA*
Starrett, Charles Vincent Emerson *see also* Starrett, Vincent
Starrett, Helen Ekin 1840-1920 *Alli Sup, DcAmA, DcNAA, HisAmM XR*
Starrett, Vincent 1886-1974 *AmAu&B, ConAu 45, ConAu 73, HisAmM XR, LiJA, NewYTBS 5, WebBD*
Starrett, Vincent *see also* Starrett, Charles Vincent Emerson
Starrett, W Kamp 1890?-1952 *BioIn 2*
Starrett, William A *HisAmM XR*
Starzel, Frank Joseph 1904?- *AmJnl, BioIn 1*
Stasio, Marilyn Louise 1940?- *ConAu 33, ForWC 1970*
Statham, Richard W *NF*
Stauderman, Albert Philip 1910- *WhoAm 1974, WhoE 1974*
Stauffer, Charles Albert 1880- *BioIn 1, WhJnl 1928*
Stauffer, David McNeely 1845-1913 *AmAu&B, DcNAA, WebBD*
Stauffer, John Keim *NF*
Stauffer, Oscar Stanley 1886- *AmJnl, WhoAm 1974, WhJnl 1928*
Stauffer, Peter W *NF*
Stauffer, Stanley Howard 1920- *WhoAm 1974*
Staunton, Helen M 1913- *ForWC 1970*
Stayskal, Wayne *NF*
Stead, Robert James Campbell 1880-1959 *CanNov, CanWr, DcLEL, OxCan, WhNAA, WhJnl 1928*
Stead, Ronald Maillard *NF*
Stead, William Thomas 1849-1912 *Alli Sup, BiD&SB, BioIn 1, BioIn 4, BioIn 5, BioIn 6, BioIn 9, BioIn 10, BrAu 19, DcLEL, HisAmM XR, LongC, Lor&LP, NewC, OxEng, WebBD*
Steadman, Ralph 1936- *BioIn 8, BioIn 10, WhoChL*
Steadwell, B Samuel 1871- *WhNAA*
Stealey, Orlando Oscar 1842-1928 *BioIn 2, IndAu 1816*
Stearns, George Luther 1809-1867 *HisAmM XR*
Stearns, Harold Edmund 1891-1943 *AmAu&B, BioIn 4, CurBio XR, DcAmB S3, DcLEL, DcNAA, HisAmM XR, OxAm, TwCA, TwCA Sup*
Stearns, Jessie *OvPC*
Stearns, John Newton 1829-1895 *Alli, AmAu&B, CarSB, DcNAA, HisAmM XR*
Stearns, L Earl 1898- *WhJnl 1928*
Stearns, William A *NF*
Stearus, Leslie B 1886- *WhJnl 1928*
Steckman, Lillian L *BioIn 1*
Stedman, Edmund Clarence 1833-1908 *Alli, Alli Sup, AmAu, AmAu&B, BiD&SB, CnDAL, CyAL 2, DcAmA, DcEnA Ap, DcEnL, DcLEL, DcNAA, EvLB, FamWC, HisAmM XR, LiJA, OxAm, OxCan, REn, REnAL, WebBD*
Steed, Henry Wickham 1871-1956 *BioIn 4, DcLEL, EvLB, ForP, NewC, TwCA, TwCA Sup, WebBD*

Steedman, Marguerite Couturier 1908- *ConAu 4R*
Steeg, Jules 1836-1898 *WebBD*
Steeger, Henry 1903- *AmAu&B, ConAu 41,*
   HisAmM XR, WhoAm 1974
Steel, Johannes 1906- *BioIn 1, CurBio XR,*
   OvPC
Steel, Ronald 1931- *ConAu 9*
Steele, Archibald Trojan 1903- *BioIn 1,*
   WhoWest 1974
Steele, Earle 1883- *WhJnl 1928*
Steele, Fred Elton, III *OvPC*
Steele, Jack 1914- *WhoS&SW 1973*
Steele, James Bruce, Jr. 1943- *InvJ, NewMr,*
   WhoAm 1974
Steele, James King 1875-1937 *AmAu&B, BioIn 1,*
   DcNAA, NatCAB 33, WhNAA
Steele, John *NF*
Steele, John Lawrence 1917- *AmAu&B, ForP,*
   RpN, WhoAm 1974
Steele, Jonathan *NF*
Steele, Raymond Graydon 1886- *WhJnl 1928*
Steele, Sir Richard 1672-1729 *Alli, AtlBL, BbD,*
   BiD&SB, BrAu, CasWL, CnThe, CrtT 2,
   CyWA, DcEnA, DcEnL, DcEuL, DcLEL,
   EvLB, ForP, McGWD, MouLC 2, NewC,
   OxEng, Pen Eng, PoIre, RAdv 1, REn,
   REnWD, WebBD, WebE&AL
Steele, Richard Charles 1917- *WhoAm 1974*
Steele, Robert 1860-1944 *BioIn 1*
Steele, Robert Edward, III 1920- *OvPC,*
   WhoPubR 1972
Steele, Robert Michael 1942- *WhoAm 1974*
Steele, Rufus Mills 1877-1935 *AmAu&B, DcNAA*
Steele, Sally *NF*
Steele, Virginia M 1929?-1971 *BioIn 9*
Steele, Walter Simeon 1890-1960 *BioIn 5*
Steell, Willis 1859?-1941 *AmAu&B, CurBio XR,*
   DcNAA
Steen, Sid *NF*
Steep, George Wail *HisAmM XR*
Steer, George *NF*
Stees, John Grove 1909?- *BioIn 4*
Steevens, George Warrington 1869-1900 *DcEuL,*
   DcLEL, EvLB, FamWC, LongC, WebBD
Stefan, Paul 1879-1943 *CurBio XR*
Stefanile, Selma *NF*
Steffek, Edwin F *NF*
Steffen, Don Carl *OvPC*
Steffens, Joseph Lincoln 1866-1936 *DcAmA,*
   DcLEL, DcNAA, EncAB
Steffens, Joseph Lincoln *see also* Steffens, Lincoln
Steffens, Lincoln 1866-1936 *AmAu&B, AmJnl,*
   BioIn 1, BioIn 2, BioIn 3, BioIn 4, BioIn 5,
   BioIn 6, BioIn 8, BioIn 9, BioIn 10,
   DcAmB S2, HisAmM XR, LongC, ModAL,
   NewMr, OxAm, Pen Am, REn, REnAL,
   TwCA, TwCA Sup, WebBD, WebE&AL
Steffens, Lincoln *see also* Steffens, Joseph Lincoln
Stefferud, Alfred 1903- *BioIn 8, ConAu 15,*
   WhoAm 1974, WhoE 1974
Steibel, Gerald L *OvPC*
Steif, William *RpN*
Steig, William 1907- *AmAu&B, BioIn 8,*
   BioIn 9, CelR 1973, CurBio XR,
   WhoAm 1974, WhoAmA 1973, WhoE 1974,
   WhoWor 1974
Steiger, Andrew Jacob 1900-1970 *BioIn 9,*
   ConAu 5R
Steiger, Paul *NF*
Steigleman, Walter 1907- *BioIn 4*
Steimer, Al *NF*
Steimer, Fred *NF*
Stein, Aaron Marc 1906- *ConAu 9R, EncMys*
Stein, Albert Louis 1902- *WhJnl Sup*

Stein, Benjamin *NF*
Stein, Edwin Carroll 1909?-1970 *BioIn 8*
Stein, Fred W 1905-1970 *BioIn 8, NewYTBE 1*
Stein, Harry *NF*
Stein, Herb 1928- *ConAu 65*
Stein, J Morris 1889- *WhJnl 1928*
Stein, John *NF*
Stein, Leon 1912- *ConAu 17R, WhoAm 1974,*
   WhoE 1974, WhoF&I 1974, WhoWorJ 1972
Stein, Ludwig 1859-1930 *NF*
Stein, Meyer Lewis 1920- *AmM&W 73S,*
   AuBYP, BioIn 8, ConAu 17R, DrAS 74E,
   SmATA 6, WhoE 1974
Stein, Mike *NF*
Stein, Robert 1924- *AmAu&B, ConAu 49,*
   WhoAdv 1972, WhoAm 1974, WhoF&I 1974
Steinbeck, John 1902-1968 *AmAu&B, AmNov,*
   AmWr, BiE&WWA, CasWL, CnDAL,
   CnMD, CnMWL, CnThe, ConAmA,
   ConAu 1, ConAu 25, ConLC 1, ConLC 5,
   CurBio XR, CyWA, DcLEL, EncWL,
   EvLB, LongC, McGWD, ModAL, ModWD,
   OxAm, OxEng, Pen Am, RAdv 1,
   RComWL, REn, REnAL, SmATA 9,
   TwCA, TwCA Sup, TwCW, WebBD,
   WebE&AL, WhoTwCL
Steinberg, Harris Bernard 1912-1969 *BioIn 2,*
   BioIn 8
Steinberg, Isaac *NF*
Steinberg, Michael 1928- *WhoAm 1974,*
   WhoE 1974
Steinberg, Rafael Mark 1927- *ConAu 61,*
   WhoAm 1974, WhoE 1974
Steinberg, Saul 1914- *AmAu&B, BioIn 1,*
   BioIn 2, BioIn 3, BioIn 4, BioIn 5, BioIn 7,
   BioIn 8, BioIn 9, CelR 1973, CurBio XR,
   DcCAA, IntWW 1976, OxAm, REn,
   WhoAm 1974, WhoGrA, WhoWor 1974
Steinberg, Selig Philip 1899- *WhJnl 1928*
Steinberg, Sigfrid Henry 1899-1969 *BioIn 9*
Steinborn, Edward 1873- *WhJnl 1928*
Steinche, Karl Kristan 1880- *BioIn 2*
Steincrohn, Peter Joseph 1899- *AmAu&B,*
   Au&Wr, CurBio XR, WhoAm 1974,
   WhoWorJ 1972
Steinebach, Frank G 1896- *WhJnl 1928*
Steinem, Gloria 1936?- *AmAu&B, BioIn 7,*
   BioIn 8, BioIn 9, BioIn 10, BioNews 1974,
   CelR 1973, ConAu 53, CurBio XR,
   WhoAm 1974, WhoAmW 1974
Steiner, Arthur *OvPC*
Steiner, Edward Alfred 1866-1956 *HisAmM XR,*
   OhA&B, WebBD
Steiner, George 1929- *ConAu 73, IntWW 1974,*
   Who 1974, WhoAm 1974, WhoWor 1974
Steiner, Jean Francois *BioIn 7*
Steiner, Paul 1921- *ConAu 9R*
Steiner, Shari 1941- *ConAu 73*
Steinfeld, Thomas Albert 1917- *WhoAdv 1972,*
   WhoAm 1974
Steinfirst, James U *OvPC*
Steinhaeuser, Walter Philip 1878- *AmAu&B,*
   WhNAA
Steinitz, William 1836-1900 *DcNAA,*
   HisAmM XR
Steinke, William 1885-1958 *BioIn 4*
Steinle, Paul Michael *OvPC*
Steinman, James Hale 1886-1962 *BioIn 6*
Steinman, John Frederick 1884- *WhoAm 1974*
Steinmann, Marion 1929- *NF*
Steinmann, Ted 1900- *WhJnl 1928*
Steirman, Hy 1921- *ConAu 29, WhoAm 1974*
Stella, Charles Guy, Jr. 1931- *WhoAm 1974*
Stelly, Matthias 1916- *AmM&W 73P,*

Stevens, Morris H 1843-1923 *NatCAB 19*
Stevens, Mortimer I *HisAmM XR*
Stevens, Oscar Lundgren 1871-1958 *BioIn 4,*
  WhJnl 1928
Stevens, Otheman *HisAmM XR*
Stevens, Sharon 1949- *NF*
Stevens, Thomas 1855- *Alli Sup, AmAu&B,*
  DcAmA, DcNAA, FamWC, HisAmM XR
Stevens, Thomas Wood 1880-1942 *AmAu&B,*
  AmLY, DcNAA, HisAmM XR
Stevens, Walter Barlow 1848-1939 *AmAu&B,*
  BiDSA, DcAmA, DcNAA, NatCAB 12
Stevens, Warder W 1845-1927 *BioIn 2,*
  IndAu 1816
Stevens, William James 1915?- *BioIn 3*
Stevenson, Adlai Ewing 1900-1965 *AmAu&B,*
  ConAu 15, ConAu P-1, CurBio XR,
  HisAmM XR, OxAm, REn, REnAL,
  WebBD, WhJnl Sup
Stevenson, Alec Brock 1895- *AmAu&B,*
  HisAmM XR
Stevenson, Burton Egbert 1872-1962 *AmAu&B,*
  BiD&SB, DcAmA, EvLB, OhA&B, REn,
  REnAL, TwCA, TwCA Sup, WebBD,
  WhNAA, WhJnl 1928
Stevenson, Charles John 1889?-1965 *BioIn 7*
Stevenson, E Robert 1882- *AmAu&B,*
  CurBio XR, WhJnl 1928
Stevenson, Edward Irenaeus Prime 1868-1942
  Alli Sup, AmAu&B, AmLY, BiD&SB,
  DcAmA, DcNAA, WhNAA
Stevenson, Emma Reh 1897- *WhJnl 1928*
Stevenson, Fay 1895- *WhJnl 1928*
Stevenson, Frederick Boyd 1869- *WhJnl 1928*
Stevenson, George 1799-1856 *BioIn 2*
Stevenson, James 1930?- *BioIn 8*
Stevenson, L L 1879-1953 *NF*
Stevenson, R W 1904- *WhJnl 1928*
Stevenson, William 1749?-1821 *Alli, BiDLA*
Stevenson, William 1925- *BioIn 4, ConAu 13R*
Steward, Hal David 1922- *ConAu 69*
Steward, Thomas Edward 1889- *WhJnl 1928*
Stewart, B Anthony *HisAmM XR*
Stewart, Bill *NF*
Stewart, Charles I *NF*
Stewart, Charles P *NF*
Stewart, Charles Samuel 1795-1870 *Alli, DcAmA,*
  DcNAA, HisAmM XR
Stewart, Donald Ogden 1894- *AmAu&B, AmRP,*
  BiE&WWA, CarSB, CurBio XR, DcLEL,
  HisAmM XR, OhA&B, Pen Am,
  REnAL, TwCA, TwCA Sup, WebBD,
  WhNAA, WhoAm 1974, WhJnl 1928
Stewart, Douglas Alexander 1913- *BioIn 10,*
  CasWL, ConDr, ConP 1970, ConP 1975,
  DcLEL, Pen Eng, TwCW, WebE&AL,
  WhoWor 1974, WorAu, WrDr 1976
Stewart, Edward Joseph 1894-1951 *BioIn 2*
Stewart, Elizabeth 1907- *BioIn 2, BioIn 8*
Stewart, Evelyn Seeley 1901-1978 *ForWC 1970*
Stewart, Ford 1909?-1970 *BioIn 9, NewYTBE 2*
Stewart, Frank 1893?- *BioIn 1, WhoS&SW 1973*
Stewart, George 1848-1906 *Alli Sup, DcLEL,*
  DcNAA, OxCan
Stewart, George A *HisAmM XR*
Stewart, Gilbert W, Jr. *RpN*
Stewart, Henry *Alli Sup, DcNAA,*
  HisAmM XR
Stewart, Ian *NF*
Stewart, James *NF*
Stewart, John Leighton 1876-1940 *BioIn 2,*
  NatCAB 34, WhJnl 1928
Stewart, Kenneth Norman 1901-1978 *AmAu&B,*
  CurBio XR, DrAS 74H, RpN

Stewart, Margaret 1912- *ConAu 25*
Stewart, Maxwell Slutz 1900- *WhoAm 1974*
Stewart, Oliver 1895- *Au&Wr, ConAu 7R,*
  Who 1974
Stewart, Orville H *NF*
Stewart, Paul A *OvPC*
Stewart, Rhea Talley 1915- *ConAu 41*
Stewart, Richard Henry 1931?- *NF*
Stewart, Robert T 1920?-1977 *ConAu 73*
Stewart, Rowe 1876- *WhJnl 1928*
Stewart, Russ 1909- *BioIn 5, WhoAm 1974,*
  WhoF&I 1974
Stewart, Sam *NF*
Stewart, T A *HisAmM XR*
Stewart, Thomas *NF*
Stewart, W R 1869- *WhJnl 1928*
Stewart, Walter 1931- *OxCan Sup*
Stewart, William *NF*
Stewart, William Henry 1870?- *WhJnl 1928*
Steyer, Robert *NF*
Steyn, Robert C *RpN*
Stick, David 1919- *BioIn 3, BioIn 4, BioIn 5*
Stickley, Gustave 1858- *HisAmM XR*
Stickney, Joseph L 1848-1907 *AmJnl, FamWC*
Stieglitz, Alfred 1864-1946 *AmAu&B, AtlBL,*
  CurBio XR, EncAB, HisAmM XR, OxAm,
  REn, REnAL, WebBD, WhNAA
Stieglitz, Ronald M *OvPC*
Stieri, Emanuele 1891-1959 *BioIn 5*
Stiff, Robert Martin 1931- *WhoAm 1974,*
  WhoS&SW 1973
Stiles, Chester F *NF*
Stiles, Chuck *NF*
Stiles, Henry Reed 1832-1909 *Alli, Alli Sup,*
  AmAu&B, DcAmA, DcNAA, HisAmM XR,
  OhA&B, WebBD
Stiles, Hinson 1893-1969 *AmAu&B, BioIn 8*
Stiles, James Esmond 1889-1960 *BioIn 5,*
  WhJnl 1928
Stiles, Kent Brooklyn 1886?-1961 *BioIn 5*
Stiles, Martin 1927- *AmM&W 73P, BioIn 8,*
  WhoAm 1974
Stiles, Meredith Newcomb 1880-1937 *DcNAA*
Stiles, Paul W 1895- *WhJnl 1928*
Still, Andrew Taylor 1828-1917 *DcNAA, WebBD*
Still, C Henry 1920- *ConAu 11R, WhoWest 1974*
Still, Charles Edwin 1872-1949 *BioIn 2, DcNAA*
Still, Colin 1888- *BioIn 8*
Still, Louise Morgan *AmAu&B*
Still, Stephen Allen 1919- *WhoAm 1974,*
  WhoWest 1974
Stille, Ugo *NF*
Stilley, Francis 1918- *OvPC*
Stilley, Francis *see also* Stilley, Frank
Stilley, Frank 1918- *ConAu 61*
Stillman, Don 1945?- *BioIn 2*
Stillman, James *HisAmM XR*
Stillman, Mildred 1890-1950 *BioIn 2*
Stillman, William James 1828-1901 *Alli Sup,*
  AmAu, AmAu&B, BbD, BiD&SB, BioIn 4,
  DcAmA, DcAmB 18, DcNAA,
  HisAmM XR, WebBD
Stillson, Jerome B *AmJnl*
Stimmel, Thomas Stribling 1925- *WhoAm 1974,*
  WhoS&SW 1973
Stimpson, George William 1896-1952 *BioIn 1,*
  BioIn 3, REnAL, WhNAA, WhJnl 1928
Stimpson, Mary Stoyell 1857-1939 *DcNAA, LiJA*
Stimson, A R 1905- *WhJnl 1928*
Stimson, George *HisAmM XR*
Stimson, N R *AmJnl, HisAmM XR*
Stindt, Gary *NF*
Stindt, Gerhard S *OvPC*
Stiner, William H *NF*

Stines, Fred, Jr. 1925- *WhoAm 1974*
Stinnett, Caskie 1911- *ConAu 5, WhoAm 1974*
Stinson, George *HisAmM XR*
Stirling, Edmund 1861- *WhJnl 1928*
Stirrup *see* Brent, Henry Johnson
Stitser, Rollin C 1899- *WhJnl 1928*
Stitt, Donald L 1891- *WhJnl 1928*
Stitt, Teddy *NF*
Stock, William 1902- *WhJnl 1928*
Stockbridge, Frank Parker 1870-1940 *AmAu&B,
   CurBio XR, DcNAA, HisAmM XR,
   WhNAA*
Stockdale, John M 1822-1897 *NatCAB 17*
Stockham, Alice Bunker 1833-1912 *DcAmA,
   DcNAA, HisAmM XR, OhA&B*
Stockholm, Arne *NF*
Stocking, Milan H *WhJnl 1928*
Stocking, William 1840-1930 *DcNAA*
Stocklin, William Albert 1910- *WhoAm 1974*
Stockly, Walter D 1905-1955 *BioIn 3*
Stocks, Carl Winslow 1884- *BioIn 2, WhJnl 1928*
Stocks, R K *WhJnl 1928*
Stockton, Frank Richard 1834-1902 *Alli, AmAu,
   AmAu&B, AuBYP, BbD, BiD&SB, CarSB,
   CnDAL, CyAL 2, DcLEL, EncMys, EvLB,
   HisAmM XR, JBA 1934, LiJA, OxAm,
   OxEng, RAdv 1, REn, WebBD*
Stockton, J Roy 1893?-1972 *ConAu 37*
Stockton, John d1876 *NF*
Stockton, Thomas T 1853- *NatCAB 5*
Stockton, William 1943?- *NF*
Stockwell, Richard E 1917- *AmEA 1974, RpN,
   WhoAm 1974, WhoF&I 1974*
Stockwell, Stephen N *AmJnl*
Stoddard, Burdett C *NF*
Stoddard, Charles Augustus 1833-1920 *AmAu&B,
   AmLY, DcAmA, DcNAA, HisAmM XR*
Stoddard, Charles Coleman 1876?-1961 *BioIn 6*
Stoddard, Charles Warren 1843-1909 *Alli,
   Alli Sup, AmAu, AmAu&B, AmJnl,
   BiD&SB, BkC 4, CnDAL, DcAmA, DcLEL,
   DcNAA, HisAmM XR, OxAm, REnAL,
   WebBD*
Stoddard, Henry Luther 1861-1947 *BioIn 3,
   BioIn 7, BioIn 9, DcNAA, HisAmM XR,
   NatCAB 38, REnAL*
Stoddard, Hope 1900- *AuBYP, BioIn 8,
   ConAu 49, SmATA 6*
Stoddard, Joseph, Jr. *HisAmM XR*
Stoddard, Richard Henry 1825-1903 *Alli,
   Alli Sup, AmAu, AmAu&B, BbD, BiD&SB,
   CnDAL, CyAL 2, DcAmA, DcEnA Ap,
   DcEnL, DcLEL, DcNAA, EvLB,
   HisAmM XR, LiJA, OxAm, REn, REnAL,
   WebBD*
Stoddard, William Osborn 1835-1925 *Alli Sup,
   AmAu, AmAu&B, BiD&SB, CarSB,
   DcAmA, DcNAA, OxAm, REnAL, WebBD*
Stoddart, Henry *HisAmM XR*
Stoddart, Joseph Marshall 1845-1921 *AmAu&B,
   HisAmM XR*
Stoeppelwerth, Melicey d1977 *NF*
Stoever, Martin Luther 1820-1870 *Alli, DcAmA,
   DcNAA, HisAmM XR*
Stoffel, Albert Law 1909- *ConAu 65*
Stoianoff, Ellen Ardery 1937- *ForWC 1970*
Stoiber, Rudolf 1925- *NF*
Stoil, Ted 1920?-1967 *BioIn 8*
Stojadinovic, Milan 1888-1961 *BioIn 6*
Stokes, Carl Burton 1927- *BioIn 9, BioIn 10,
   ConAu 69, CurBio XR, InvJ, WhoAm 1974,
   WhoAmP 1973, WhoWor 1974*
Stokes, Charles Edwin 1901- *WhJnl 1928*
Stokes, Frederick Abbot 1857-1939 *Alli Sup,*

AmAu&B, DcAmB S2, DcNAA, REnAL
Stokes, Geoffrey 1940- *ConAu 69*
Stokes, Harold Phelps 1887-1970 *BioIn 8,
   NewYTBE 1, WebBD*
Stokes, Horace Wilson 1886-1950 *NF*
Stokes, James Graham Phelps 1872-1960 *BioIn 8,
   WebBD*
Stokes, Richard Leroy 1882-1957 *BioIn 3,
   BioIn 4, CathA 1952, IndAu 1917*
Stokes, Robert S *NF*
Stokes, Rose Harriet Pastor Wieslander 1879-1933
   DcNAA, WebBD
Stokes, Thomas Lunsford 1898-1958 *AmJnl,
   BioIn 1, BioIn 4, BioIn 5, CurBio XR*
Stokley, James 1900- *AmAu&B, WhoAm 1974,
   WhJnl 1928*
Stolberg, Benjamin 1891-1951 *AmRP,
   DcAmB S5, HisAmM XR, WhNAA*
Stole, Bert *NF*
Stoler, Peter *NF*
Stoliar, Matias 1885?-1951 *BioIn 2*
Stoll, Albert, Jr. 1884- *WhJnl 1928*
Stoll, John G 1879?-1959 *BioIn 5*
Stolley, Richard Brockway 1928- *OvPC,
   WhoAm 1974, WhoE 1974*
Stone, A J *HisAmM XR*
Stone, Arthur Fairbanks 1863-1944 *DcNAA*
Stone, Arthur L 1865- *WhJnl 1928*
Stone, Benjamin C 1891?-1953 *BioIn 3*
Stone, Candace *NF*
Stone, Chuck 1924- *BlkAW, LivBAA*
Stone, Claude Ulysses 1879-1957 *BioIn 4,
   BioIn 6, NatCAB 44*
Stone, David 1929- *ConAu 5R*
Stone, David Marvin 1817-1895 *Alli, AmAu&B,
   DcAmA, DcNAA, NatCAB 1*
Stone, Desmond 1921- *RpN, WhoAm 1974*
Stone, Douglas *NF*
Stone, Earl Lewis 1915- *BioIn 9*
Stone, Emerson *NF*
Stone, Everett R *OvPC*
Stone, Herbert Lawrence 1872-1955 *BioIn 4*
Stone, Herbert Stuart 1871-1915 *DcNAA, LiJA*
Stone, I F 1907- *AmRP, CelR 1973, ConAu 61,
   CurBio XR, InvJ, NewMr, WhoAm 1974,
   WhoWor 1974*
Stone, I F *see also* Stone, Isidor Feinstein
Stone, Isidor Feinstein 1907- *AmAu&B, BioIn 8,
   BioIn 9, BioIn 10, WrDr 1976*
Stone, Isidor Feinstein *see also* Stone, I F
Stone, James H 1847-1914 *NF*
Stone, John L, Jr. *OvPC*
Stone, John Nelson 1835-1919 *BioIn 5*
Stone, Louis T *AmJnl*
Stone, Lucinda Hinsdale 1814-1900 *NF*
Stone, Lucy 1818-1893 *AmAu&B, BiD&SB,
   HisAmM XR, OxAm, REn, WebBD*
Stone, Marilla *WhJnl 1928*
Stone, Martin 1915- *WhoAm 1974*
Stone, Marvin Lawrence 1924- *ConAu 69,
   WhoAm 1974, WhoWorJ 1972*
Stone, Melville Elijah 1848-1929 *AmAu&B,
   AmJnl, BioIn 7, BioIn 9, DcAmB 18,
   DcNAA, EncAB, HisAmM XR, REnAL,
   WebBD, WhJnl 1928*
Stone, Nelly *NF*
Stone, Ormond 1847-1933 *HisAmM XR*
Stone, Percy *NF*
Stone, Phillip M *NF*
Stone, Robert Granville 1907- *AmM&W 73P,
   WhoAm 1974*
Stone, Scott Clinton Stuart 1932- *ConAu 25,
   WhoAm 1974*
Stone, Thomas Jefferson 1916- *WhoAm 1974,*

WhoWor 1974
Stone, Vernon Alfred 1929- *ConAu 65,
DrAS 74E*
Stone, Walker 1904-1973 *BioIn 9, BioIn 10,
NewYTBE 4, WhoS&SW 1973*
Stone, Warren Sanford 1860-1925 *WebBD*
Stone, Wilbur Fisk 1833-1920 *DcNAA*
Stone, William Leete 1792-1844 *Alli, AmAu,
AmAu&B, AmJnl, BbtC, CyAL 1, DcAmA,
DcAmB 18, DcNAA, HisAmM XR, LiJA,
NatCAB 7, OxAm, REnAL, WebBD*
Stone, William Leete, Jr. 1835-1908 *Alli, Alli Sup,
AmAu&B, DcAmA, DcNAA, WebBD*
Stone, Witmer 1866-1939 *AmAu&B, AmLY,
DcAmA, DcNAA, WebBD, WhNAA*
Stoneback, C E 1890- *WhJnl 1928*
Stonebraker, Jesse Nelson 1886- *WhJnl 1928*
Stoneham, Gordon *NF*
Stoneman, Frank B 1857-1941 *WhJnl 1928*
Stong, Philip Duffield 1899-1957 *AmAu&B,
AmNov, CnDAL, ConAmA, CyWA, MorJA,
OxAm, REnAL, Str&VC, TwCA,
TwCA Sup, WebBD*
Stoop, Norma McLain *ConAu 65*
Stoppard, Tom 1937- *Au&Wr, CnThe, ConDr,
ConLC 1, ConLC 3, ConLC 4, ConLC 5,
CroCD, CurBio XR, EncWL, IntWW 1974,
McGWD, ModBL Sup, ModWD,
NewYTBE 3, NewYTBS 5, WebE&AL,
Who 1974, WhoThe 1972, WhoTwCL,
WrDr 1976*
Storer, George Butler 1899-1975 *IntMPA 1975,
WhoAm 1974, WhoF&I 1974,
WhoS&SW 1973*
Storey, S *NF*
Storey, Wilbur Fisk 1819-1884 *AmJnl, BioIn 8*
Storin, Edward Michael 1929- *WhoAm 1974*
Storke, Charles Albert 1847-1936 *DcNAA*
Storke, Thomas More 1876-1971 *BioIn 5,
BioIn 6, BioIn 9, CurBio XR, NewYTBE 2*
Storke, William Frederick Joseph 1922-
WhoAm 1974
Storm, George *NF*
Storm, Marian 1892?-1975 *BioIn 10, ConAu 61*
Stormont, Gilbert R 1843-1930 *BioIn 2,
IndAu 1816*
Storrow, James J, Jr. 1917- *WhoAm 1974*
Storrow, Linda Eder *NF*
Storrs, Caryl B 1870-1920 *DcNAA*
Storrs, Leslie Simons 1901- *WhJnl 1928*
Storrs, Richard Salter 1787-1873 *Alli, Alli Sup,
AmAu&B, DcNAA, HisAmM XR, WebBD*
Storrs, Richard Salter 1821-1900 *Alli, AmAu&B,
BiD&SB, DcAmA, DcNAA, WebBD*
Story, Francis *AmJnl*
Story, H L 1879- *WhJnl 1928*
Story, Isaac 1774-1803 *Alli, AmJnl, AmAu, AmAu&B,
CyAL 1, DcAmA, DcNAA, OxAm, REnAL,
WebBD*
Stouffer, Lloyd 1909- *OvPC*
Stouffer, W C 1892?- *WhJnl 1928*
Stout, Charles Holt 1903- *WhoAm 1974,
WhoWest 1974*
Stout, Chauncey Field 1878?-1972 *BioIn 9*
Stout, E H *HisAmM XR*
Stout, Elihu *AmJnl*
Stout, Oliver B *NF*
Stout, Robert Joe 1936- *ConAu 65, DrAF 1976*
Stout, Wesley Winans 1889-1972 *BioIn 9,
CurBio XR, HisAmM XR, NewYTBE 2,
WhJnl 1928*
Stout, William Bushnell 1880-1956 *WebBD*
Stovall, Pleasant Alexander 1857-1935 *BiDSA,
DcAmB S1, DcNAA*

Stovall, Wallace Fisher 1869-1950 *BioIn 2*
Stowe, Leland 1899- *AmAu&B, AmJnl, BioIn 1,
BioIn 3, BioIn 4, CurBio XR, IntWW 1976,
REnAL, TwCA Sup, WebBD, WhoAm 1974,
WhoWor 1974*
Stowell, Charles Henry 1850-1932 *Alli Sup,
DcAmA, DcNAA, HisAmM XR*
Stowell, Henry 1834-1918 *NatCAB 17*
Stowell, John *NF*
Stowell, Kenneth Kingsley 1894-1969 *BioIn 8,
HisAmM XR*
Stowell, Louisa Reed 1850- *HisAmM XR*
Stowitts, Earl O 1882?-1953 *BioIn 3*
Strachan, Al *NF*
Strachey, John St. Loe 1860-1927 *BioIn 5,
BioIn 6, DcLEL, WebBD*
Strafford, Peter *NF*
Strahan, Alexander *HisAmM XR*
Strahan, Edward 1837-1866 *Alli Sup, DcAmA,
DcNAA, HisAmM XR*
Strahan, Edward *see also* Shinn, Earl
Straight, Dorothy Whitney *HisAmM XR*
Straight, Michael Whitney 1916- *AmAu&B,
BioIn 1, ConAu 5R, ConNov 1972,
ConNov 1976, CurBio XR, HisAmM XR,
WhoGov 1972, WrDr 1976*
Straight, Willard Dickerman 1880-1918 *AmAu&B,
HisAmM XR, WebBD*
Straker, Robert Lincoln 1899-1959 *BioIn 5,
BioIn 7*
Strakhov, Nikolai Nikolaevich 1828-1896 *BioIn 9*
Straley, Wilson 1877-1952 *BioIn 2*
Strandberg, Carl Vilhelm August 1818-1877
CasWL, WebBD
Strandvold, Georg 1883-1960 *BioIn 5*
Strang, Lewis Clinton 1869-1935 *AmAu&B,
BiD&SB, DcAmA, DcNAA*
Strange, E Z *NF*
Strange, Susan 1923- *ConAu 49*
Strange, William 1902- *BioIn 1, CanNov*
Strasburg, Mary Elizabeth 1923?-1968 *BioIn 8*
Strasburg, William E *OvPC*
Strassburger, Ralph Beaver 1883-1959 *BioIn 5*
Strasser, Otto 1897-1974 *ConAu 53, CurBio XR,
IntWW 1974, NewYTBS 5, REn, WebBD*
Strassmeyer, Mary 1929- *ForWC 1970,
WhoAm 1974, WhoAmW 1974*
Stratton, Lloyd 1895-1961 *BioIn 5*
Straub, Leonard *ForP*
Straub, W L 1867- *WhJnl Sup*
Straus, Michael W 1897- *CurBio XR*
Straus, Nathan, Jr. 1889-1961 *AmAu&B,
CurBio XR, HisAmM XR, WebBD*
Straus, R Peter 1923- *WhoAm 1974,
WhoS&SW 1973*
Straus, Ralph 1882- *NF*
Straus, Roger W, Jr. 1917- *CelR 1973,
HisAmM XR, OvPC, WhoAm 1974*
Strause, Isaac Rice 1859-1934 *BioIn 2,
IndAu 1816*
Strauss, Anna Lord 1899- *CurBio XR,
HisAmM XR, WhoAm 1974,
WhoAmW 1974*
Strauss, Arthur J 1898- *WhJnl 1928*
Strauss, Eduard *HisAmM XR*
Strauss, Jack *NF*
Strauss, Juliet Virginia 1863-1918 *BioIn 2,
IndAu 1816*
Strauss, Moses 1872-1938 *OhA&B, WhJnl 1928*
Strauss, Samuel 1869?-1953 *BioIn 3*
Strauss, Theodore *HisAmM XR*
Strausz-Hupe, Robert 1903- *AmAu&B,
AmM&W 73S, ConAu 9, HisAmM XR,
IntWW 1976, USBiR 1974, WhoAm 1974,*

WhoAmP 1973, WhoGov 1972,
WhoWor 1974
Strawser, Neil *NF*
Strayer, Louis W 1869-1922 *NF*
Straznicky, Edwin R *HisAmM XR*
Streano, Vince 1945- *ConAu 53*
Streator, George Walter 1902?-1955 *BioIn 4*
Strebig, James J 1907?-1951 *BioIn 2*
Street, Alfred Billings 1811-1881 *Alli, AmAu,*
AmAu&B, BbtC, BiD&SB, CyAL 2,
DcAmA, DcNAA, HisAmM XR, HsB&A,
OxAm, WebBD
Street, Arthur George 1892-1966 *BioIn 7,*
BioIn 8, ConAu 13, ConAu P-1, DcLEL,
LongC, TwCW
Street, Francis d1883 *HisAmM XR*
Street, James 1903-1954 *AmAu&B, AmNov,*
CnDAL, CurBio XR, REnAL, TwCA Sup
Street, Joseph M 1782-1840 *AmJnl*
Street, Julian 1879-1947 *AmAu&B, DcNAA,*
HisAmM XR, REnAL, TwCA, TwCA Sup,
WebBD, WhNAA
Streeter, Carroll Perry 1898-1975 *AmAu&B,*
BioIn 10, WhJnl 1928
Streeter, Dan *NF*
Streicher, Julius 1885-1946 *CurBio XR, REn,*
WebBD
Streit, Clarence Kirshman 1896- *AmAu&B,*
BioIn 1, BioIn 2, BioIn 3, BioIn 4,
ConAu 2R, CurBio XR, IntWW 1976,
OxAm, REnAL, TwCA, TwCA Sup,
WebBD, Who 1974, WhoAm 1974
Streithorst, Tom *NF*
Strell, George W *HisAmM XR*
Strelsin, Alfred A 1898- *OvPC, WhoAm 1974*
Stressburger, Ralph B 1883- *WhJnl 1928*
Stretch, George E *OvPC*
Stretch, Harold A 1890?-1951 *BioIn 2*
Stretch, Jane A *BioIn 6*
Strickland, Edwin 1917- *BioIn 4*
Strickland, Joseph 1929?- *NF*
Strickland, Mabel Edeline 1899- *IntWW 1976,*
Who 1974, WhoWor 1974
Strickland, W P *HisAmM XR*
Strickler, George Arnold 1904- *WhoAm 1974*
Strickler, Homer Edison 1914?-1955 *BioIn 4*
Stridsberg, Gustaf 1877?-1943 *CurBio XR*
Strindberg, August 1849-1912 *AtlBL, BiD&SB,*
CnMD, CnThe, CyWA, DcEuL, EuAu,
HisAmM XR, LongC, McGWD, ModWD,
NewC, OxEng, OxGer, Pen Eur, RComWL,
REn, REnWD, TwCA, TwCA Sup, WebBD,
WhoTwCL
Stringer, William Henry 1908-1976 *ConAu 65,*
USBiR 1974, WhoAm 1974
Stringfellow, J H *HisAmM XR*
Strobel, Marion 1895- *AmAu&B, HisAmM XR*
Strode, William Hall, III 1937- *WhoAm 1974,*
WhoS&SW 1973
Stroh, Nicholas 1938?-1971 *BioIn 9, BioIn 10*
Strohm, John Louis 1912- *AmAu&B, Au&Wr,*
BioIn 1, OvPC, WhoAm 1974
Strohmeyer, John 1924- *RpN, WhoAm 1974*
Strom, Russell Rex 1890- *WhJnl 1928*
Stromme, Peer Olsen 1856-1921 *DcAmB 18,*
DcNAA
Strong, Anna Louise 1885-1970 *AmAu&B,*
AmRP, BioIn 1, BioIn 2, BioIn 3, BioIn 4,
BioIn 8, BioIn 9, ConAu 29, CurBio XR,
HisAmM XR, NewYTBE 1, OhA&B,
TwCA, TwCA Sup, WebBD, WhNAA
Strong, Barbara *NF*
Strong, Charles H 1853-1936 *NatCAB 27*
Strong, Edwin J 1894-1954 *BioIn 3*

Strong, George Gordon 1913- *CanWW 1972,*
WhoAdv 1972, WhoAm 1974
Strong, Jacob H 1885-1960 *NatCAB 47*
Strong, Jonathan *HisAmM XR*
Strong, Kent *NF*
Strong, Lydia 1906?-1966 *BioIn 7*
Strong, Oliver Smith 1864-1951 *BioIn 2*
Strong, Robert Emery 1902- *WhJnl 1928*
Strong, T W *HisAmM XR*
Strong, Walter Ansel 1883-1931 *AmAu&B,*
AmJnl, BioIn 2, DcAmB 18
Strong, William Duncan *HisAmM XR*
Strongin, Theodore 1918- *WhoAm 1974*
Stross, R Marshall *OvPC*
Strother, David Hunter 1816-1888 *AmAu&B,*
BbD, BiD&SB, BiDSA, DcAmA, DcEnL,
DcNAA, EarABI, EarABI Sup, WebBD
Strother, French 1883-1933 *DcNAA,*
HisAmM XR, WhNAA
Strother, Robert S *BioIn 2*
Strother, Susie *BioIn 5*
Stroud, Joe H *NF*
Stroud, M F *NF*
Strout, Richard Lee 1898- *AmAu&B, BioIn 8,*
BioIn 10, ConAu 69, WhoAm 1974
Struby, Cynthia J *NF*
Strunk, Harry Decosta 1892-1960 *BioIn 7,*
NatCAB 49
Strunsky, Simeon 1879-1948 *AmAu&B, BioIn 1,*
BioIn 3, BioIn 4, ConAmL, DcAmB S4,
DcNAA, NatCAB 37, REnAL, TwCA,
TwCA Sup, WebBD
Strusberg, Peter *NF*
Struve, Gustav 1805-1870 *BioIn 5, DcNAA,*
WebBD
Stryker, James 1792-1864 *Alli, HisAmM XR*
Stryker, Perrin 1908- *AmAu&B, ConAu 7R,*
WhoAm 1974, WrDr 1976
Stuart, Sir Campbell 1885- *BioIn 2, WhNAA,*
WhoLA
Stuart, Carl K 1890-1963 *WhJnl Sup*
Stuart, Carlos *HisAmM XR*
Stuart, Charles T 1883-1958 *HisAmM XR*
Stuart, Daniel 1766-1846 *Alli, BiDLA, DcLEL,*
OxEng
Stuart, George Donnell 1896- *WhJnl 1928*
Stuart, Henry Longan 1875?-1928 *DcNAA,*
TwCA
Stuart, James 1764-1840? *Alli, PoIre*
Stuart, James A 1880-1975 *WhJnl 1928*
Stuart, John McHugh 1885-1957 *BioIn 4,*
WhJnl 1928
Stuart, Kenneth 1891-1945 *CurBio XR*
Stuart, Kenneth James 1905- *HisAmM XR,*
WhoAm 1974, WhoAmA 1973
Stuart, Mary Louise 1923?-1969 *BioIn 8*
Stuart, Peter C *NF*
Stuart, William d1886 *NF*
Stuart, William Hervey 1874-1962 *BioIn 6*
Stuart, William Plato 1879-1960 *WhNAA*
Stuck, Franz Von 1863-1928 *BioIn 9*
Stuckenschmidt, H H 1901- *ConAu 25*
Stuckey, William *NF*
Stucky, William McDowell 1916-1961 *BioIn 5,*
RpN
Studebaker, Herbert Earl 1891- *WhJnl 1928*
Studebaker, John W *NF*
Studer, Augustus C 1854-1922 *NatCAB 31*
Studley, George W *HisAmM XR*
Stuebing, Douglas 1913- *ConAu 25, OxCan Sup*
Stuhlmann, Gunther 1927- *ConAu 25,*
WhoE 1974
Stumm, Francis A 1898- *WhJnl 1928*
Stuntz, Albert Edward 1902-1976 *ConAu 65*

Stuntz, Laurance F 1908- *ConAu 61*
Sturdevant, Fred E 1875?-1954 *BioIn 3*
Sturdevant, Lafayette Monroe 1856-1923 *BioIn 5*
Sturdevant, William L 1915?- *BioIn 2, BioIn 5*
Sturges, Dwight C 1874-1940 *NF*
Sturgis, Russell 1836-1909 *AmAu&B, DcAmA, DcNAA, HisAmM XR, WebBD*
Sturrup, Ron 1926?- *BioIn 7*
Stursberg, Peter 1913- *BioIn 8, CanWW 1972, OxCan Sup*
Sturtevant, Catherine d1970 *BioIn 8*
Sturtevant, John Loomis 1865- *WhJnl 1928*
Sturtevant, Peter Mann, Jr. 1943- *ConAu 69*
Stutler, Boyd Blynn 1899?-1970 *AmAu&B, ConAu 23*
Stuttaford, Genevieve *NF*
Stutz, Harry George 1885-1954 *BioIn 3*
Stutz, Sara D 1932- *NF*
Stutzman, James S *OvPC*
Styles, Cary W *NF*
Styles, William Brewster 1923- *WhoAm 1974, WhoMW 1974*
Stylites, Simeon *see* Luccock, Halford Edward
Suard, J B A *NF*
Sudomier, William V *NF*
Sufian, Vicki *NF*
Sugar, Andrew *NF*
Sugartail 1814-1869 *AmAu&B*
Sugartail *see also* Harris, George Washington
Sugiura, Masaki *NF*
Sugrue, Thomas 1907-1953 *CurBio XR, REnAL, TwCA Sup*
Suits, Robert A *NF*
Sulek, Miroslav 1918- *IntWW 1976*
Sulgrove, Berry Robinson 1828-1890 *BioIn 2, IndAu 1816*
Sulkin, Sidney 1918- *ConAu 5R*
Sullens, Frederick 1877-1957 *BioIn 1, BioIn 4*
Sulley, Phillip Francis 1884-1953 *BioIn 3*
Sullivan, A M 1896- *AnCL, BkC 3, ConAu 29, CurBio XR, REnAL*
Sullivan, Alexander Martin 1830-1884 *Alli Sup, PoIre*
Sullivan, Alexander Martin 1871-1959 *BioIn 3, BioIn 5*
Sullivan, Daniel Joseph 1935- *WhoAm 1974*
Sullivan, Donal 1910-1971 *AmJnl*
Sullivan, Ed 1902-1974 *BioIn 2, BioIn 3, BioIn 4, BioIn 5, BioIn 6, BioIn 7, BioIn 8, BioIn 10, BioNews 1974, CelR 1973, CurBio XR, IntMPA 1975, NewYTBS 5, WhoWor 1974*
Sullivan, Ed *see also* Sullivan, Edward Vincent
Sullivan, Edward Dean 1888-1938 *AmAu&B, DcNAA*
Sullivan, Edward Vincent 1902-1974 *AmJnl, IntWW 1974, WhoAm 1974*
Sullivan, Edward Vincent *see also* Sullivan, Ed
Sullivan, Ellen L *OvPC*
Sullivan, Francis John 1892-1976 *ConAu 65, ConAu P-1*
Sullivan, Francis John *see also* Sullivan, Frank
Sullivan, Frank (1892-1976) *see also* Sullivan, Francis John
Sullivan, Frank 1892-1976 *AmAu&B, BioIn 9, ConAu 25, HisAmM XR, LongC, REn, REnAL, TwCA, TwCA Sup, WebBD, WhoAm 1974*
Sullivan, Frank 1912-1975 *ConAu 61*
Sullivan, George D 1899- *WhJnl 1928*
Sullivan, George Edward 1927- *AuBYP, BioIn 8, BioIn 9, ConAu 13, SmATA 4, WrDr 1976*
Sullivan, J Wesley *RpN*
Sullivan, Jack *HisAmM XR*

Sullivan, James William 1848-1938 *BiD&SB, DcAmA, DcAmB S2, DcNAA*
Sullivan, John R *WhJnl 1928*
Sullivan, Lawrence 1898-1968 *AmAu&B, BioIn 8*
Sullivan, Margaret Frances 1847-1903 *Alli Sup, BbD, DcAmA, DcNAA, PoIre*
Sullivan, Marguerite Hoxie *NF*
Sullivan, Mark 1874-1952 *AmAu&B, AmJnl, BioIn 3, BioIn 4, BioIn 5, BioIn 9, CathA 1952, DcAmB S5, ForP, HisAmM XR, NatCAB 42, OxAm, REn, REnAL, TwCA, TwCA Sup, WebBD, WhNAA*
Sullivan, Martin 1934- *ConAu 29, OxCan Sup*
Sullivan, Matthew G 1888?-1952 *BioIn 3*
Sullivan, Michael B 1938- *OvPC*
Sullivan, Mike *NF*
Sullivan, Richard C C *OvPC*
Sullivan, Robert E *NF*
Sullivan, Robert Francis 1913- *WhoAm 1974*
Sullivan, Ruth *NF*
Sullivan, Scott *NF*
Sullivan, T S *HisAmM XR*
Sullivan, Walter B 1885-1921 *NatCAB 19*
Sullivan, Walter Seagar 1918- *AmAu&B, AmM&W 73P, BioIn 6, ConAu 3R, IntWW 1976, WhoAm 1974, WhoWor 1974, WrDr 1976*
Sully, Francois 1927-1971 *BioIn 9, ConAu 25, ConAu 29*
Sulzberger, Arthur Hays 1891-1968 *AmAu&B, AmJnl, BioIn 1, BioIn 2, BioIn 3, BioIn 7, BioIn 8, CurBio XR, REnAL, WebBD*
Sulzberger, Arthur Ochs 1926- *BioIn 8, CelR 1973, CurBio XR, IntWW 1976, OvPC, Who 1974, WhoAm 1974, WhoE 1974, WhoF&I 1974, WhoWor 1974*
Sulzberger, Cyrus Leo 1912- *Au&Wr, BioIn 3, BioIn 4, BioIn 7, BioIn 8, BioIn 9, CelR 1973, ConAu 53, CurBio XR, ForP, IntWW 1976, REnAL, WhoAm 1974, WhoWor 1974*
Sulzberger, Iphigene 1892?- *BioIn 9, BioIn 10*
Summerfield, Charles 1810-1867 *Alli, Alli Sup, AmAu, AmAu&B, DcNAA, OxAm*
Summerfield, Charles *see also* Arrington, Alfred W
Summerfield, Jack D 1927- *ConAu 23*
Summerill, Thomas C 1901- *WhJnl 1928*
Summerill, William A 1862- *WhJnl 1928*
Summerlin, Sam 1928- *ConAu 45, WhoAm 1974, WhoE 1974*
Summers, Alden Bernard, Jr. 1939- *WhoAm 1974*
Summers, Anthony Bruce 1942- *ConAu 69*
Summers, Elmer Lee 1898?- *BioIn 1*
Summers, Iverson B 1864-1926 *NatCAB 20*
Summers, James C *NF*
Summers, Thomas Osmond 1812-1882 *Alli, Alli Sup, BiDSA, DcAmA, DcNAA, HisAmM XR*
Summers, William *NF*
Summers, William Henry 1897-1951 *BioIn 3*
Summy, Clayton F *HisAmM XR*
Sumner, Allene Myra 1895- *WhNAA, WhJnl 1928*
Sumner, Charles Allen 1835-1903 *Alli Sup, DcAmA, DcNAA*
Sumner, David 1937- *ConAu 57*
Sumner, William Allison 1892- *WhJnl 1928*
Sumner, William Graham 1921- *WhoAm 1974*
Sundberg, Clifford Stanley 1918- *WhoAm 1974*
Sunde, Tenold R 1900-1959 *BioIn 5*
Sunderland, J Y *HisAmM XR*
Sundine, August 1882- *WhJnl 1928*
Sundy, Robert M *OvPC*

HisAmM XR, WhNAA
Sweetser, Charles Humphreys 1841-1871 *Alli,*
AmJnl, DcAmA, DcNAA, HisAmM XR
Sweetser, Delight 1873-1903 *BioIn 2, DcNAA,*
IndAu 1816
Sweetser, Henry Edward *AmJnl, HisAmM XR*
Sweezy, Paul Marlor 1910- *AmAu&B,*
AmEA 1974, AmM&W 73S, AmRP,
ConAu 1
Sweinhart, Henry Lee 1878-1949 *BioIn 1,*
BioIn 3, NatCAB 38
Swem, Earl Gregg 1870-1965 *AmAu&B*
Swennes, Harvey E 1899- *WhJnl 1928*
Swenson, Allan A 1933- *OvPC*
Swenson, Gilbert O 1896- *WhJnl 1928*
Swenson, Peggye 1933- *ConAu 73*
Swensson, Paul S *NF*
Swetland, H L *HisAmM XR*
Swetland, Horace M *HisAmM XR*
Swett, Sophie 1858-1912 *AmAu&B,*
HisAmM XR
Swietochowski, Aleksander 1849-1938 *BioIn 1,*
CasWL, CIDMEL
Swift, Jonathan 1667-1745 *Alli, AtlBL, BbD,*
BiD&SB, BrAu, CarSB, CasWL, CnE&AP,
CrtT 2, CyWA, DcBiA, DcEnA,
DcEnA Ap, DcEnL, DcEuL, DcLEL, EvLB,
HsB&A, MouLC 2, NewC, OxEng,
Pen Eng, PoIre, RAdv 1, RComWL, REn,
WebBD, WebE&AL, WhoChL
Swift, Josiah Otis 1871-1948 *AmAu&B, BioIn 1,*
WhJnl 1928
Swift, Otis Peabody 1896-1971 *BioIn 9,*
NewYTBE 2, WhJnl 1928
Swift, Robert *NF*
Swiger, Wilbur Moore 1892- *WhJnl 1928*
Swiggett, Glen Levin 1867-1961 *BiDSA, BioIn 7,*
IndAu 1917, WhNAA
Swindell, Larry 1929- *ConAu 25*
Swineford, Alfred P 1836-1909 *DcNAA, OhA&B*
Swing, David 1830-1894 *Alli Sup, DcAmA,*
DcNAA, HisAmM XR, OhA&B
Swing, Raymond Gram 1887-1968 *AmAu&B,*
AmJnl, BioIn 1, BioIn 3, BioIn 4, BioIn 6,
BioIn 8, CurBio XR, HisAmM XR, LongC,
OhA&B, TwCA Sup, WebBD
Swingle, Frank B 1876- *WhJnl 1928*
Swingler, Randall *NF*
Swinnerton, Frank Arthur 1884- *ConNov 1972,*
ConNov 1976, CyWA, DcLEL, EvLB,
IntWW 1974, LongC, ModBL, NewC,
Pen Eng, RAdv 1, REn, TwCA,
TwCA Sup, TwCW, WebBD, Who 1974,
WhoLA, WhoWor 1974, WrDr 1976
Swinnerton, James Guilford 1875-1974 *BioIn 10,*
NewYTBS 5
Swinney, Fred Harold 1890- *WhJnl 1928*
Swinton, John 1829-1901 *Alli Sup, AmAu&B,*
BbD, BiD&SB, BioIn 1, BioIn 8, DcAmA,
DcAmB 18, DcNAA
Swinton, Stanley Mitchell 1919- *BioIn 5, OvPC,*
WhoAm 1974
Swinton, William 1833-1892 *Alli, Alli Sup,*
AmAu, AmAu&B, BiD&SB, BioIn 5,
CyAL 2, DcAmA, DcAmB 18, DcNAA,
HisAmM XR, OxAm, REnAL, WebBD
Swire, Joseph *NF*
Swisshelm, Emmett 1898- *WhJnl 1928*
Swisshelm, Jane Grey Cannon 1815-1884 *Alli,*
Alli Sup, AmAu&B, AmJnl, BbD, BiD&SB,
BioIn 1, BioIn 3, BioIn 4, BioIn 6, BioIn 8,
DcAmA, DcNAA, HisAmM XR
Switzler, William Franklin 1819-1906 *Alli Sup,*
AmAu, AmAu&B, BiDSA, DcAmB 18,

DcNAA
Swofford, Hugh Gile *OvPC*
Swope, Herbert Bayard 1882-1958 *AmJnl,*
BioIn 1, BioIn 4, BioIn 5, BioIn 6, BioIn 7,
CurBio XR, REn, REnAL, WebBD
Swope, John H 1904- *WhJnl 1928*
Swope, Tom 1888?-1969 *BioIn 8*
Swords, James *NF*
Swords, Thomas *HisAmM XR*
Sybel, Heinrich Von 1817-1895 *BbD, BiD&SB,*
DcEuL, WebBD
Sychrava, Lev 1887?-1958 *BioIn 4*
Sydnor, Charles Sackett 1898-1954 *AmAu&B,*
HisAmM XR, WhNAA
Syer, William Alan *NF*
Sykes, Charles Henry 1882-1942 *AmAu&B,*
CurBio XR, HisAmM XR
Sykes, Jay G 1922- *ConAu 45*
Sylvester, Arthur 1901- *BioIn 6, BioIn 7,*
NewMr
Sylvester, E H *HisAmM XR*
Sylvester, James Joseph 1814-1897 *Alli Sup,*
HisAmM XR, WebBD
Sylvester, Richard H 1830- *NatCAB 3*
Sylvester, Robert 1907-1975 *AmAu&B, BioIn 10,*
ConAu 57, ConAu 61, WhoAm 1974,
WhoE 1974
Syme, David 1827-1908 *BioIn 2, BioIn 7*
Symonds, Edward *OvPC*
Symonds, Gene 1926?-1955 *BioIn 3, BioIn 4*
Symonds. Maurice 1891 *WhJnl 1928*
Symons, Arthur 1865-1945 *Alli Sup, AtlBL,*
BiD&SB, CasWL, CnE&AP, DcEnA A∤
DcLEL, EvLB, LongC, ModBL, NewC,
OxEng, Pen Eng, REn, TwCA, TwCA Sup.
TwCW, WebBD, WebE&AL
Symons, George Edgar 1903- *AmM&W 73P,*
BioIn 4, WhoAm 1974
Symontowne, Russ 1897?-1950 *BioIn 2*
Synon, John James 1909?-1972 *BioIn 9*
Syse, Glenna Marie Lowes *WhoAm 1974,*
WhoAmW 1974
Syverson, Henry *BioIn 5*
Syvertsen, Edythe 1921- *ConAu 73*
Syvertsen, George 1932?-1970 *BioIn 8,*
NewYTBE 1
Szabo, Thomas 1921?-1969 *BioIn 8*
Szamuely, Tibor 1925-1972 *BioIn 9*
Szaniawski, Jerzy 1886-1970 *CasWL, CnMD,*
ConAu 29, CroCD, ModWD, Pen Eur
Szapiro, Jerzy 1895-1962 *BioIn 6*
Szasz, Bela 1910- *BioIn 9, BioIn 10*
Szebenyei, Joseph 1879?-1953 *BioIn 2, BioIn 3*
Szekely, Izso 1878?-1966 *BioIn 7*
Szenes, Sigmond 1894?-1951 *BioIn 2*
Szep, Paul *NF*
Szeps, Moritz *NF*
Szinnyey, Stephen Ivor 1863-1919 *DcNAA*
Szulc, Tad 1926- *AmAu&B, ConAu 9,*
ConAu 11R, ForP, InvJ, NewMr, OvPC,
WhoAm 1974, WhoWor 1974, WrDr 1976
Szyk, Arthur 1894-1951 *BioIn 1, BioIn 2,*
BioIn 3, BioIn 5, CurBio XR, DcAmB S5
Szymborska, Wislawa 1923- *CasWL,*
IntWW 1976

T

T R B *see* Strout, Richard Lee
Taafe, William *NF*
Tabarly, Pierre Ph Noel 1930- *NF*
Taber, George McCaffrey 1942- *ConAu 65*
Taber, Gladys 1899- *AmAu&B, BioIn 1, BioIn 2, BioIn 3, BioIn 5, ConAu 5, CurBio XR, HisAmM XR, WhoAm 1974, WhoAmW 1974*
Taber, Harry Persons 1865- *HisAmM XR*
Taber, William R *HisAmM XR*
Tabor, Frank 1919- *NF*
Tabor, Grace *HisAmM XR, WhNAA*
Tabor, Peder 1891- *IntWW 1976, WhoWor 1974*
Tabori, Paul 1908-1974 *Au&Wr, ConAu 5R, ConAu 53, IntMPA 1975, NewYTBS 5, WrDr 1976*
Tabouis, Genevieve R 1892- *BioIn 1, BioIn 9, CurBio XR, WebBD*
Tache, Joseph Charles 1821?-1894 *CanWr, DcNAA, OxCan*
Tad 1877-1929 *AmAu&B, WebBD*
Tad *see also* Dorgan, Thomas Aloysius
Tadad, Francisco 1939- *IntWW 1976*
Tafel, Gustav 1830-1908 *BioIn 2, OhA&B*
Taff, Paul Kenneth 1920- *WhoAm 1974, WhoE 1974*
Taft, Charles Phelps 1843-1929 *NatCAB 23, WebBD, WhJnl 1928*
Taft, Edward A *HisAmM XR*
Taft, Hulbert 1877-1959 *AmJnl, BioIn 2, BioIn 5, BioIn 6, NatCAB 43, WhJnl 1928*
Taft, William Howard 1915- *ConAu 15R, DrAS 74E, WhoAm 1974*
Tager, Sally *NF*
Taggart, John H 1821-1892 *NatCAB 5*
Taggiasco, Ronald J *OvPC*
Tai, Tseng-Yi *NF*
Taillandier, Rene Gaspard Ernest 1817-1879 *BiD&SB, WebBD*
Taine, Hippolyte Adolphe 1828-1893 *AtlBL, BbD, BiD&SB, CasWL, CIDMEL, CyWA, DcEnL, DcEuL, EuAu, EvEuW, NewC, OxEng, OxFr, Pen Eur, REn, WebBD*
Taines, Beatrice 1923- *ConAu 73*
Taishoff, Lawrence Bruce 1933- *WhoAm 1974, WhoF&I 1974*
Taishoff, Sol Joseph 1904- *ConAu 73, WhoAm 1974, WhoF&I 1974, WhoS&SW 1973, WhoWor 1974, WhoWorJ 1972*
Tait, Dorothy 1902?-1972 *ConAu 33*
Tait, Gordon *OvPC*
Takahama, Tato *NF*
Takaishi, Shingoro 1878-1967 *BioIn 7*
Takeuchi, Richard *NF*
Takoda, Miskrit *NF*

Talbert, Ansel Edward McLaurine 1912- *AuBYP, BioIn 5, BioIn 8, OvPC, WhoAm 1974, WhoS&SW 1973*
Talbert, Robert *NF*
Talbot, Dean Marion *HisAmM XR*
Talbot, E H *HisAmM XR*
Talbot, Edward Allen 1801-1839 *Alli, BbtC, DcNAA, OxCan*
Talbot, Francis Xavier 1889-1953 *AmAu&B, BioIn 3, BkC 2, CathA 1930*
Talbot, Gayle 1901?-1956 *BioIn 4*
Talbot, J J *HisAmM XR*
Talbot, James E *NF*
Talbott, Earl G 1906?-1967 *BioIn 8*
Talbott, Greenville Pace 1868- *WhJnl 1928*
Talburt, Harold M 1895-1966 *BioIn 7*
Talese, Gay 1932- *AmAu&B, AuNews 1, BioNews 1974, ConAu 4R, CurBio XR, WhoAm 1974, WhoE 1974, WhoWor 1974, WrDr 1976*
Taliaferro, Alfred 1905?-1969 *BioIn 8*
Talis Qualis 1818-1877 *WebBD*
Talis Qualis *see also* Strandberg, Carl Vilhelm August
Talley, Rick *NF*
Talley, Victor W 1894-1973 *BioIn 9, NewYTBE 4*
Tallyai, Daniel *ForP*
Talmage, Thomas DeWitt 1832-1902 *Alli Sup, AmAu, AmAu&B, BbD, BiD&SB, DcAmA, DcNAA, HisAmM XR, HsB&A, REnAL, WebBD*
Talney, Allen 1902?- *BioIn 9*
Talyarkhan, Frene *BioIn 1*
Tamarkin, Robert *NF*
Tames, George *NF*
Tammen, Harry Heye 1856-1924 *AmJnl, BioIn 2, BioIn 4, DcAmB Sx, HisAmM XR*
Tan, Mark *NF*
Tan, Ronnie *NF*
Tanakadate, H *NF*
Tanenbaum, Mary 1915- *OvPC*
Tankard, James William, Jr. 1941- *ConAu 73*
Tanksley, Ruth Loring *NF*
Tannehill, Wilkins 1787-1858 *Alli, BiDSA, BioIn 3, DcAmA, DcNAA, REnAL*
Tanner, Benjamin Tucker 1835-1923 *Alli, Alli Sup, BiD&SB, DcAmA, DcNAA, HisAmM XR*
Tanner, Edward Everett, III 1921-1976 *AmAu&B, ConAu 69, CurBio XR, WhoAm 1974, WorAu, WrDr 1976*
Tanner, Henry 1918- *ConAu 73, RpN, WhoAm 1974*
Tanner, John *HisAmM XR*
Tanner, Murray G 1900?-1953 *BioIn 3*

Tanner, Thomas B 1893?-1965 *BioIn 7*
Tanzer, Lester 1929- *ConAu 19R,*
　WhoS&SW 1973
Tapley, D J *Alli Sup, HisAmM XR*
Tappan, Arthur 1786-1865 *AmAu&B, AmJnl,*
　HisAmM XR, WebBD
Tappan, Eli Todd 1824-1888 *Alli, AmAu&B,*
　DcAmA, DcNAA, WebBD
Tappan, Lewis 1788-1873 *Alli, Alli Sup,*
　AmAu&B, DcAmA, DcNAA, HisAmM XR,
　WebBD
Tapper, Thomas 1864-1958 *DcAmA,*
　HisAmM XR
Tapping, A J *NF*
Tapping, Theodore Hawley 1889- *WhJnl 1928*
Tapply, Horace Gardner 1910- *ConAu 15R,*
　WhoAm 1974, WhoE 1974
Tara, Janet *NF*
Tarasov, Leo P 1913- *BioIn 8*
Tarasov, Vasilii Vasil'evich 1927?- *BioIn 6*
Tarbell, Arthur W 1872-1946 *DcNAA,*
　HisAmM XR
Tarbell, Ida Minerva 1857-1944 *AmAu&B,*
　AmJnl, BiD&SB, CnDAL, CurBio XR,
　DcAmA, DcAmB S3, DcLEL, DcNAA,
　EncAB, HisAmM XR, LiJA, NewMr,
　OxAm, REn, REnAL, TwCA, TwCA Sup,
　WebBD, WhNAA
Tarbox, Increase Niles 1815-1888 *Alli, Alli Sup,*
　AmAu&B, DcAmA, DcNAA, HisAmM XR
Tarchiani, Alberto 1885-1964 *BioIn 2, BioIn 7,*
　CurBio XR
Tardieu, Andre Pierre Gabriel Amedee 1876-1945
　CurBio XR, HisAmM XR, WebBD
Tardivel, Jules-Paul 1851-1905 *CanWr, DcNAA,*
　OxCan
Tardy, W T *NF*
Tarleton, Fiswoode 1890-1931 *AmAu&B, DcNAA*
Tarman, Fred E 1889- *WhJnl 1928,*
　WhoS&SW 1973
Tarr, Edgar Jordan 1881-1950 *BioIn 2*
Tarran, Geoffrey d1978 *NF*
Tarte, Joseph Israel 1848-1907 *DcNAA, OxCan*
Tarud, Raul *ForP*
Tarver, Jackson Williams 1917- *BioIn 4,*
　WhoAdv 1972, WhoAm 1974,
　WhoS&SW 1973
Tarver, Micajah *HisAmM XR*
Tarvin, Pryor G 1876?-1950 *BioIn 2*
Tarzi, Mahmud 1868-1935 *BioIn 8, DcOrL 3*
Tarzian, Mary *WhoAm 1974, WhoAmW 1974,*
　WhoWor 1974
Tarzian, Sarkes 1900- *WhoAm 1974*
Tasaki, Hanama 1913- *BioIn 2*
Taschereau, Jules Antoine 1801-1874 *WebBD*
Tashiro, Kikuo 1917- *IntWW 1976*
Tashrak 1872-1926 *WebBD*
Tasistro, Louis Fitzgerald 1808?-1868? *Alli,*
　DcNAA, HisAmM XR
Tasker, John Dana 1904- *BioIn 2, BioIn 3,*
　HisAmM XR
Tassin, Ray 1926- *ConAu 53*
Tassler, Bernard W *WhJnl 1928*
Tassos, Alex *OvPC*
Tastrum, Edward P *NF*
Tatanis, Peter P 1884?-1959 *BioIn 5*
Tatay, Sandor 1910- *IntWW 1976,*
　WhoWor 1974
Tate, Allen 1899- *AmAu&B, AmWr, Au&Wr,*
　CasWL, CathA 1952, CnDAL, CnE&AP,
　ConAmA, ConAu 5, ConLC 2, ConLC 4,
　ConLC 6, ConNov 1972, ConNov 1976,
　ConP 1970, ConP 1975, CurBio XR,
　DrAF 1976, DrAP 1975, DrAS 74E,

EncWL, HisAmM XR, IntWW 1974,
　LongC, ModAL, ModAL Sup, OxAm,
　Pen Am, RAdv 1, REn, REnAL, SixAP,
　TwCA, TwCA Sup, TwCW, WebBD,
　WebE&AL, WhoAm 1974, WhoS&SW 1973,
　WhoTwCL, WhoWor 1974, WrDr 1976
Tate, Allen *see also* Tate, John Orley Allen
Tate, Cassandra 1945?- *NF*
Tate, Donald *NF*
Tate, Frederick L 1889- *CanWW 1972,*
　WhJnl 1928
Tate, John Orley Allen 1899- *EvLB,*
　HisAmM XR
Tate, John Orley Allen *see also* Tate, Allen
Tate, Shirley M *OvPC*
Tatman, George S 1903- *WhJnl 1928*
Tattersail, Richard *NF*
Tatu, Michel 1933- *ConAu 25, WhoWor 1974*
Tatum, Josiah *HisAmM XR*
Taub, Harald J *OvPC*
Taubeneck, George *NF*
Taubkin, Irvin Stearns 1906- *OvPC,*
　WhoS&SW 1973
Taubman, Howard 1907- *AmAu&B, BiE&WWA,*
　CurBio XR, IntWW 1976, WhoThe 1972
Taubman, Howard *see also* Taubman, Hyman
　Howard
Taubman, Hyman Howard 1907- *WhoAm 1974*
Taubman, Hyman Howard *see also* Taubman,
　Howard
Taul, Anthony M *NF*
Taussig, Frank William 1859-1940 *Alli Sup,*
　AmAu&B, AmLY, CurBio XR, DcAmA,
　DcNAA, HisAmM XR, REnAL, WebBD,
　WhNAA
Taussig, Harriet Burket 1908- *ConAu 37*
Taussig, Lucy *HisAmM XR*
Tavares De Sa, Hernane 1911- *BioIn 5*
Taves, Brydon 1914-1943 *AmJnl*
Taves, Isabella 1915- *ConAu 23, OvPC,*
　WhoAmW 1974
Tawney, James A 1900- *NF*
Tawney, Richard Henry 1880-1962 *BioIn 2,*
　CasWL, DcLEL, LongC, NewC, Pen Eng,
　REn, TwCA, TwCA Sup
Tax, Sol 1907- *AmAu&B, AmM&W 73S,*
　ConAu 5, IntWW 1974, WhoAm 1974,
　WhoGov 1972, WhoWor 1974,
　WhoWorJ 1972
Tay Pay *see* O'Connor, Thomas Power
Tayleure, Clifton W 1832-1891 *AmAu&B*
Taylor, Adrian *NF*
Taylor, Allan K *BioIn 2*
Taylor, Arthur M 1875?-1951 *BioIn 2*
Taylor, Arthur Robert 1935- *IntWW 1974,*
　NewYTBE 3, WhoAm 1974, WhoF&I 1974
Taylor, Bayard 1825-1878 *Alli, Alli Sup, AmAu,*
　AmAu&B, AmJnl, BbD, BiD&SB, CasWL,
　CnDAL, CyAL 2, DcAmA, DcBiA,
　DcEnA Ap, DcEnL, DcLEL, DcNAA,
　EvLB, HisAmM XR, LiJA, OxAm, OxEng,
　Pen Am, REn, REnAL, WebBD
Taylor, Ben L 1897- *WhJnl 1928*
Taylor, Benjamin Franklin 1819-1887 *Alli,*
　Alli Sup, AmAu, AmAu&B, BbD, BiD&SB,
　DcAmA, DcAmB 18, DcNAA,
　HisAmM XR, OhA&B
Taylor, Bert Leston 1866-1921 *AmAu&B, AmJnl,*
　BioIn 8, DcAmB 18, DcNAA,
　HisAmM XR, REnAL, TwCA, TwCA Sup,
　WebBD
Taylor, Bob Byron 1932- *WhoAm 1974,*
　WhoS&SW 1973
Taylor, Charles Fayette 1827-1899 *Alli, Alli Sup,*

DcAmA, DcNAA, HisAmM XR, WebBD
Taylor, Charles Henry 1846-1921 AmJnl, DcAmB 18, NatCAB 35
Taylor, Charles Henry 1867-1941 BioIn 2, BioIn 5
Taylor, David S 1868- WhJnl 1928
Taylor, Deems 1885-1966 AmSCAP 1966, CurBio XR, OxAm, REnAL, TwCA, TwCA Sup, WebBD
Taylor, Deems see also Taylor, Joseph Deems
Taylor, Demetria 1903?-1977 NF
Taylor, E E 1861- WhJnl 1928
Taylor, Earl Howard 1891- HisAmM XR, WhNAA, WhJnl 1928
Taylor, Edmond OvPC
Taylor, Edmond Lapierre 1908- BioIn 1
Taylor, Eli HisAmM XR
Taylor, Ella C 1867- WhJnl 1928
Taylor, Elliott 1898-1953 BioIn 3
Taylor, Floyd 1902-1951 BioIn 2, BioIn 4, NatCAB 40
Taylor, Frank J 1894-1972 AmAu&B, Au&Wr, ConAu 37, ConAu P-1, HisAmM XR, WhNAA
Taylor, Frank L 1900-1962 BioIn 6
Taylor, Frank W 1887-1961 BioIn 5
Taylor, Garner W 1887-1965 BioIn 7, WhJnl 1928
Taylor, George Boardman 1832-1907 Alli, Alli Sup, BiDSA, CarSB, DcAmA, DcNAA, HisAmM XR
Taylor, George Frederick 1928- WhoAm 1974
Taylor, George Rogers 1895- AmAu&B, AmEA 1974, AmM&W 73S
Taylor, Graham 1851-1938 AmLY, DcNAA, HisAmM XR, OxAm
Taylor, Graham Romeyn 1880-1942 AmLY, HisAmM XR, NatCAB 31, WhNAA
Taylor, H R HisAmM XR
Taylor, Harmon Robert 1896- WhJnl 1928
Taylor, Harry E 1893- WhJnl 1928
Taylor, Sir Henry 1800-1886 Alli, Alli Sup, BbD, BiD&SB, BrAu 19, CasWL, DcEnA, DcEnL, DcEuL, DcLEL, EvLB, NewC, OxEng, WebBD
Taylor, Henry Archibald Au&Wr, Lor&LP, Who 1974
Taylor, Henry Junior 1902- AmAu&B, BioIn 1, CelR 1973, ConAu 23, IntWW 1976, WhoAm 1974
Taylor, Henry Noble 1929?-1960 AmJnl, BioIn 5
Taylor, Herbert W NF
Taylor, Horace Adolphus 1837-1910 BioIn 5
Taylor, Howard Blaine 1909-1977 ForP, WhoWest 1974
Taylor, Irene S OvPC
Taylor, Mrs. J D 1877- WhJnl 1928
Taylor, J Orville Alli, HisAmM XR
Taylor, Jack InvJ
Taylor, James Alfred 1878-1956 BioIn 4
Taylor, James Bayard 1825-1878 Alli, DcAmA
Taylor, James Bayard see also Taylor, Bayard
Taylor, James Earl 1845-1901 HisAmM XR
Taylor, James Wickes 1819-1893 Alli, DcAmA, DcAmB 18, DcNAA, OhA&B
Taylor, Jean Sharley NF
Taylor, Joan Chatfield NF
Taylor, John d1832 Alli
Taylor, John 1781-1864 Alli
Taylor, John 1921- ConAu 23R
Taylor, John Edward 1791-1844 DcEuL, NewC, WebBD
Taylor, John Ingalls 1911- WhoAm 1974, WhoE 1974

Taylor, John L BlkC
Taylor, John Percy 1883?-1954 BioIn 3
Taylor, John Phelps 1841-1915 HisAmM XR
Taylor, John Russell 1935- Au&Wr, ConAu 5R, Who 1974, WhoThe 1972, WrDr 1976
Taylor, Joseph 1878- WhJnl 1928
Taylor, Joseph A OvPC
Taylor, Joseph B 1887?- WhJnl 1928
Taylor, Joseph Deems 1885-1966 AmAu&B, WhJnl 1928
Taylor, Joseph Deems see also Taylor, Deems
Taylor, Lawrence E NF
Taylor, Leon NF
Taylor, Lillian NF
Taylor, Margerie Venables 1881?-1963 BioIn 7
Taylor, Marian 1909-1973 BioIn 2, BioIn 10
Taylor, Marshall William 1846-1887 Alli Sup, BiDSA, BioIn 8, DcAmA, DcNAA, OhA&B
Taylor, Melvin N 1903- WhJnl 1928
Taylor, Merlin Moore 1886- WhJnl 1928
Taylor, Moseley 1894?-1952 BioIn 2
Taylor, Nora NF
Taylor, Oscar Newland 1896- WhJnl 1928
Taylor, Pat NF
Taylor, Peter NF
Taylor, Ray Jefferson 1918-1977 ConAu 69, WhoS&SW 1973
Taylor, Richard 1902-1970 BioIn 1, BioIn 2, BioIn 8, BioIn 9, CurBio XR, NewYTBE 1
Taylor, Robert 1902- WhoAm 1974
Taylor, Robert J NF
Taylor, Robert Lewis 1912- AmAu&B, Au&Wr, ConAu 3R, ConNov 1972, ConNov 1976, CurBio XR, OxAm, REnAL, SmATA 10, WhoAm 1974, WhoE 1974, WhoWor 1974, WorAu, WrDr 1976
Taylor, Robert Love 1850-1912 AmAu&B, BiDSA, DcNAA, WebBD
Taylor, Robert W 1898- WhJnl 1928
Taylor, Ruth Gash NF
Taylor, Samuel Harvey 1807-1871 Alli, DcAmA, DcNAA, HisAmM XR
Taylor, Sherril Wightman 1924- WhoAm 1974
Taylor, Stuart S NF
Taylor, Tim 1920-1974 ConAu 45, ConAu 53, NewYTBS 5
Taylor, Tom 1817-1880 Alli, Alli Sup, BbD, BiD&SB, BrAu 19, DcEnA, DcEnL, DcEuL, DcLEL, EncMys, EvLB, McGWD, NewC, OxEng, REn, WebBD
Taylor, Toni OvPC
Taylor, V V HisAmM XR
Taylor, W B HisAmM XR
Taylor, W J NF
Taylor, W L 1881- WhJnl 1928
Taylor, Walter A NF
Taylor, Willene 1898- WhJnl Sup
Taylor, William Alexander 1837-1912 Alli Sup, DcAmA, DcNAA, OhA&B
Taylor, William Davis 1908- WhoAm 1974, WhoE 1974, WhoWor 1974
Taylor, William Howland 1901-1966 Au&Wr, BioIn 7
Taylor, William Osgood 1871-1955 AmJnl, BioIn 4
Taylor, Zack 1927- ConAu 65
Tchelietchev, Pavel HisAmM XR
Tchernowitz, Chaim 1871-1949 BioIn 1, BioIn 2
Tchernychev, Viatcheslav NF
Teague, James OvPC
Teague, Robert 1929- BioIn 8
Teahen, John K NF
Teall, Dorothy Judd 1898?-1946 BioIn 1
Teall, Edna A West 1881-1968 BioIn 8, WhNAA

Teall, Edward Nelson 1880-1947 *AmAu&B*,
  DcNAA, *HisAmM XR*, *WhJnl 1928*
Teall, Gardner Callahan 1878-1956 *BioIn 4*,
  HisAmM XR
Teatsorth, Ralph C 1908?-1966 *BioIn 7*
Tebbel, John 1912- *AmAu&B*, *CurBio XR*,
  ForP, *HisAmM XR*, *LiJA*, *WhoAm 1974*
Tebeau, Joe *NF*
Teeters, Bert A 1895- *WhJnl 1928*
Tefft, Benjamin Franklin 1813-1885 *Alli*, *Alli Sup*,
  DcAmA, *DcNAA*, *HisAmM XR*
Tegetmeier, William Bernhard 1816-1912 *Alli*,
  Alli Sup, *WebBD*
Teichner, Miriam *NF*
Teixeira DeMattos, Alexander Louis 1865-1921
  LongC, *WebBD*
Telford, Thomas *HisAmM XR*
Telthorst, Ann 1952- *NF*
Teltsch, Kathleen *NF*
Tempest, Rone, III *NF*
Temple, Sir Richard Carnac 1850-1931 *Alli Sup*,
  WebBD, *WhoLA*
Templeton, Ben *NF*
Templeton, Charles B 1916?- *BioIn 5*,
  CanWW 1972
Templeton, Herminie *HisAmM XR*
Templeton, Joe *NF*
Templeton, Lee *NF*
Templin, Hugh C 1896- *WhJnl 1928*
TenBerge, Jacobus *OvPC*
Tenenbaum, Frances 1919- *ConAu 73*
Tenenbaum, Samuel *WhJnl 1928*
Tennant, Emma 1937- *ConAu 65*, *WhoTwCL*
Tennant, John *NF*
Tennant, William Brydon 1870-1940 *BioIn 2*,
  NatCAB 34
Tenney, Horace Addison 1820-1906 *BioIn 5*,
  DcNAA
Tenney, William Jewett 1811-1883 *Alli*, *DcAmA*,
  DcNAA
Tenniel, Sir John 1820-1914 *Alli*, *BioIn 1*,
  BioIn 2, *BioIn 4*, *BioIn 8*, *BioIn 9*,
  JBA 1934, *JBA 1951*, *LongC*, *NewC*, *REn*,
  Str&VC, *WebBD*, *WhoChL*
Tennyson, G B 1930- *BioIn 10*, *ConAu 21*,
  WrDr 1976
Teodoro, Jorge 1912?-1952 *BioIn 3*
Ter Horst, Jerald Franklin 1922- *AuNews 1*,
  BioIn 10, *BioNews 1974*, *CurBio XR*,
  NewYTBS 5, *WhoAm 1974*
Teresi, Dick *NF*
Terhune, Albert Payson 1872-1942 *AmAu&B*,
  AmLY, *AuBYP*, *BiD&SB*, *CnDAL*,
  CurBio XR, *DcAmA*, *DcNAA*, *EvLB*,
  HisAmM XR, *JBA 1934*, *OxAm*, *REnAL*,
  TwCA, *TwCA Sup*, *WebBD*, *WhNAA*
Terhune, Everit B 1876- *WhJnl 1928*
Terkel, Studs Louis 1912- *AmAu&B*, *CurBio XR*,
  WhoAm 1974, *WhoMW 1974*
Terkelsen, Terkel Madsen 1904- *IntWW 1976*,
  WhoWor 1974
Ternes, Alan *NF*
Terracini, Umberto Elia 1895- *IntWW 1976*,
  WhoWor 1974
Terrazas, Silvestre 1873-1944 *BioIn 9*
Terrell, Frank G *HisAmM XR*
Terrell, John V *NF*
Terrell, Roy Alfred, Jr. 1923- *WhoAm 1974*
Terrenoire, Louis 1908- *IntWW 1976*,
  WhoWor 1974
Terrett, Courtenay 1901-1950 *BioIn 2*,
  WhJnl 1928
Terrill, Rogers 1900- *BioIn 1*
Terry, Clifford Lewis 1937- *WhoAm 1974*,

Teall, Edward Nelson *WhoMW 1974*
Terry, G C 1895- *WhJnl 1928*
Terry, Henry C *NF*
Terry, J Harold 1906- *NF*
Terry, J William 1895-1966 *BioIn 7*
Terry, John B d1944 *AmJnl*, *RpN*
Terry, Joseph Guilford 1890- *NF*
Terry, Paul H 1887?-1971 *BioIn 7*, *BioIn 9*,
  NewYTBE 2
Terry, Wallace H, II 1938?- *NF*
Terry, Walter 1913- *AmAu&B*, *AuBYP*,
  BioIn 8, *ConAu 23R*, *ForP*, *WhoAm 1974*
Tervo, Penna 1901-1956 *BioIn 4*
Testut, Charles 1818-1892 *AmAu&B*, *BiDSA*,
  DcAmB 18, *DcNAA*, *REnAL*
Tetirick, Teddy Linn 1893- *WhJnl 1928*
Tetlow, Edwin 1905- *ConAu 17R*, *WhoAm 1974*
Tetrick, Willis Guy 1883-1956 *BioIn 6*,
  NatCAB 45, *WhJnl 1928*
Tetu, Horace 1842-1915 *DcNAA*
Teubner, Charles William 1899- *WhJnl 1928*
Teubner, Ferdinand Cary 1921- *WhoAdv 1972*
Tevis, Robert Starley 1899- *WhJnl 1928*
Tewson, William Orton 1877-1947 *BioIn 1*,
  WhJnl 1928
Thacher, W F G 1879- *WhNAA*, *WhJnl Sup*,
  WhJnl 1928
Thacker, Edward N 1858- *WhJnl 1928*
Thackeray, Anne *HisAmM XR*
Thackeray, William Makepeace 1811-1863 *Alli*,
  AtlBL, *BbD*, *BiD&SB*, *BrAu 19*, *CarSB*,
  CasWL, *CrtT 3*, *CyWA*, *DcBiA*, *DcEnA*,
  DcEnA Ap, *DcEnL*, *DcEuL*, *DcLEL*, *EvLB*,
  HisAmM XR, *HsB&A*, *MouLC 3*, *NewC*,
  OxAm, *OxEng*, *Pen Eng*, *RAdv 1*,
  RComWL, *REn*, *WebBD*, *WebE&AL*,
  WhoChL
Thackrey, Dorothy S 1903- *BioIn 1*, *BioIn 2*,
  CurBio XR
Thackrey, Eugene P 1902- *WhJnl 1928*
Thackrey, Russell I 1904- *ConAu 37*,
  WhoAm 1974
Thackrey, Theodore Olin 1901- *AmJnl*, *BioIn 1*,
  BioIn 2, *OvPC*
Thai, Nguyen *RpN*
Thaler, Karol C *NF*
Thalhever, August *NF*
Thalken, Margaret Mary 1926- *WhoAm 1974*,
  WhoAmW 1974
Thallheimer, Joseph *NF*
Thatcher, J S *AmJnl*
Thatcher, Oxbridge *AmJnl*
Thatcher, Peter O *HisAmM XR*
Thatcher, Samuel Cooper *HisAmM XR*
Thaves, Bob *NF*
Thaxter, Adam Wallace 1832-1864 *Alli*, *DcAmA*,
  DcNAA, *HisAmM XR*
Thayer, Alexander Wheelock 1817-1897 *Alli*,
  Alli Sup, *BiD&SB*, *DcAmA*, *DcNAA*,
  HisAmM XR, *OxAm*, *REnAL*, *WebBD*
Thayer, Ernest Lawrence 1863-1940 *AuBYP*,
  BioIn 6, *BioIn 8*, *CurBio XR*, *EvLB*,
  WebBD
Thayer, Eugene Butler 1853-1931 *BioIn 5*
Thayer, Frank 1890-1965 *BioIn 9*, *OhA&B*
Thayer, Gideon F 1793-1864 *HisAmM XR*
Thayer, John Adams 1861-1936 *AmAu&B*,
  DcNAA, *HisAmM XR*, *REnAL*
Thayer, Marjorie *BioIn 4*
Thayer, Oliver F 1895- *WhJnl 1928*
Thayer, Scofield *NF*
Thayer, Thomas Baldwin 1812-1886 *Alli*, *BioIn 3*,
  DcAmA, *DcNAA*, *HisAmM XR*
Thayer, Walter Nelson 1910- *WhoAm 1974*

Thayer, William Adams 1865?-1952 *BioIn 2*
Thayer, William Makepeace 1820-1898 *Alli,*
Alli Sup, AmAu&B, BbD, BiD&SB, CarSB,
DcAmA, DcNAA, HisAmM XR
Thayer, William Roscoe 1859-1923 *Alli Sup,*
AmAu&B, DcAmA, DcNAA, HisAmM XR,
OxAm, REnAL, TwCA, WebBD
Theil, Leon S *OvPC, WhoPubR 1972*
Theis, Grover 1896?-1950 *BioIn 2*
Theis, John William 1911- *WhoAm 1974*
Theiss, Lewis Edwin 1878-1963 *AmAu&B,*
AuBYP, BioIn 6, BioIn 8, WhNAA,
WhJnl 1928
Thelen, Gil 1938- *ConAu 73*
Thibault, David 1892- *WhJnl 1928*
Thickens, Richard E 1889-1954 *NatCAB 40*
Thieblin, Nicholas Leon 1834-1888 *DcNAA*
Thiem, George 1897- *WhJnl Sup*
Thieme, August 1822-1879 *BioIn 2*
Thieriot, Charles DeYoung 1915- *BioIn 4,*
WhoWor 1974
Thimmesch, Nicholas Palen 1927- *ConAu 15R,*
WhoAm 1974
Thirer, Irene 1904-1964 *BioIn 6, WhJnl 1928*
Thisleton, George *HisAmM XR*
Thisted, Amos d1977 *NF*
Thistlethwaite, Mark 1879-1947 *BioIn 1*
Thivierge, Joseph Narcisse 1887- *WhJnl 1928*
Thoams, Gardener J *WhJnl 1928*
Tholens, Henry 1866-1942 *NatCAB 32*
Thom, Adam 1802-1890 *Alli, Alli Sup, BbtC,*
DcNAA, EvLB
Thoma, Ludwig 1867-1921 *CasWL, CIDMEL,*
CnMD, EncWL, EuAu, EvEuW, McGWD,
ModWD, OxGer, WebBD
Thomas, A A *HisAmM XR*
Thomas, A Russell 1894- *WhJnl 1928*
Thomas, Abel 1807-1880 *NF*
Thomas, Albert Ellsworth 1872-1947 *AmAu&B,*
AmLY, DcNAA, REnAL, WebBD
Thomas, Aubrey *NF*
Thomas, Barbara 1945- *NF*
Thomas, Beth Wood 1916- *NF*
Thomas, Bill 1934- *ConAu 61*
Thomas, Bob *NF*
Thomas, Burt R 1881-1964 *WhJnl 1928*
Thomas, Cecil *Lor&LP*
Thomas, Chandler B *BioIn 2*
Thomas, Charles 1882- *WhJnl 1928*
Thomas, Charles Swain 1868-1943 *AmAu&B,*
DcNAA, IndAu 1917, REnAL, WhJnl 1928
Thomas, Chauncey 1872- *AmAu&B, WhNAA*
Thomas, Cynthia *NF*
Thomas, Ebenezer Smith 1780-1844 *AmAu,*
AmAu&B, BiDSA, BioIn 9, DcAmA,
DcNAA, OhA&B
Thomas, Frank 1898- *WhJnl 1928*
Thomas, Frank Morehead 1868-1921 *DcNAA,*
HisAmM XR
Thomas, Frederick William 1806-1866 *Alli,*
AmAu, AmAu&B, BiD&SB, BiDSA,
CyAL 2, DcAmA, DcAmB 18, DcLEL,
DcNAA, HisAmM XR, OhA&B, OxAm,
REnAL
Thomas, Gardner J *NF*
Thomas, Gordon 1933- *ConAu 9R*
Thomas, Helen A 1920- *BioIn 7, WhoAm 1974,*
WhoAmW 1974, WhoWor 1974
Thomas, Horace E 1882- *WhJnl 1928*
Thomas, Howard H 1897- *WhJnl 1928*
Thomas, Ifor *HisAmM XR*
Thomas, Isaiah 1749-1831 *Alli, AmAu,*
AmAu&B, AmJnl, BiD&SB, CyAL 1,
DcAmA, DcNAA, EarABI, EarABI Sup,

HisAmM XR, LiJA, NatCAB 6, OxAm,
REnAL
Thomas, Isaiah 1749-1834 *WebBD*
Thomas, Jo *NF*
Thomas, John Jacobs 1810-1895 *Alli, DcAmA,*
DcNAA, HisAmM XR, WebBD
Thomas, Josephine D 1944?- *NF*
Thomas, Judy *NF*
Thomas, Katherine Elwes 1857?-1950 *BioIn 2*
Thomas, Leslie John 1931- *Au&Wr, ConAu 15R,*
Who 1974, WrDr 1976
Thomas, Lowell 1892- *AmAu&B, BioIn 1,*
BioIn 2, BioIn 3, BioIn 4, BioIn 5, BioIn 7,
BioIn 8, BioNews 1974, CelR 1973,
ConAu 45, CurBio XR, HisAmM XR,
IntMPA 1975, NewYTBE 1, OvPC, WebBD,
Who 1974, WhoAm 1974, WhJnl 1928
Thomas, Nick *NF*
Thomas, Norman Mattoon 1884-1968 *AmAu&B,*
AmJnl, AmRP, ConAu 25, CurBio XR,
EncAB, HisAmM XR, OhA&B, OxAm,
Pen Am, REn, REnAL, WebBD
Thomas, Norman S 1893- *WhJnl 1928*
Thomas, R H *HisAmM XR*
Thomas, Raymond A 1888- *WhJnl 1928*
Thomas, Richard G *NF*
Thomas, Robert Bailey 1766-1846 *Alli, AmAu&B,*
DcAmA, REnAL, WebBD
Thomas, Robert Joseph 1922- *AmAu&B,*
IntMPA 1975, WhoAm 1974, WhoWest 1974
Thomas, Robert McG, Jr. *NF*
Thomas, Rowland 1879- *HisAmM XR,*
WhJnl Sup, WhJnl 1928
Thomas, Ruth *AuBYP, BioIn 8*
Thomas, T I N *NF*
Thomas, W Herbert 1866?-1951 *BioIn 2*
Thomas, Walter L 1876- *WhJnl 1928*
Thomas, Will 1905- *BioIn 3, BlkAW*
Thomas, Sir William Beach 1868-1957 *BioIn 2,*
BioIn 4, Br&AmS, WhoLA
Thomas, William F, Jr. 1924- *BioIn 9, ConAu 69,*
WhoAm 1974
Thomas, William Hearn 1870- *BioIn 6*
Thomas, William Isaac 1863-1947 *DcNAA,*
HisAmM XR
Thomas, William J 1903?- *BioIn 1*
Thomason, Alan Mims 1910- *WhoAm 1974,*
WhoWor 1974
Thomason, Art *InvJ*
Thomason, Samuel Emory 1883-1944 *AmJnl*
Thomasson, Dan *InvJ*
Thomasson, H L 1903- *BioIn 10*
Thomey, Tedd 1920- *ConAu 5R, WhoWest 1974,*
WrDr 1976
Thompson, A L B 1917-1975 *ConAu 53,*
ConAu 61
Thompson, Albert B 1899- *WhJnl 1928*
Thompson, Albert E *NF*
Thompson, Alexander Mattock 1861-1948 *BioIn 1,*
WhoLA
Thompson, Alice 1910- *BioIn 1, BioIn 3*
Thompson, Carl *OvPC*
Thompson, Carol Lewis 1918- *DrAS 74H,*
HisAmM XR, WhoAm 1974,
WhoAmW 1974
Thompson, Cecil Vincent Raymond 1906-1951
BioIn 2
Thompson, Charles Hamilton 1872?-1950 *BioIn 2*
Thompson, Charles Miner 1864-1941 *AmAu&B,*
BiD&SB, DcAmA, DcNAA, HisAmM XR,
WebBD
Thompson, Charles T *AmJnl*
Thompson, Charles Willis 1871-1946 *AmAu&B,*
BioIn 1, CathA 1930, DcNAA, REnAL

Thompson, Claribel *BioIn 3*
Thompson, Clifford *HisAmM XR*
Thompson, Cyril C 1891- *WhJnl Sup*
Thompson, David Decamp 1852-1908 *DcAmA,*
   DcNAA, HisAmM XR, NatCAB 13,
   OhA&B
Thompson, Don 1935- *ConAu 53*
Thompson, Donald Hoyt 1899?-1949 *BioIn 2*
Thompson, Dorothy 1894-1961 *AmAu&B, AmJnl,*
   BioIn 1, BioIn 2, BioIn 4, BioIn 5, BioIn 6,
   BioIn 7, BioIn 8, BioIn 9, CurBio XR,
   EncAB, EvLB, ForP, HisAmM XR, OxAm,
   REn, REnAL, TwCA, TwCA Sup, WebBD
Thompson, E B *NF*
Thompson, Edward *HisAmM XR*
Thompson, Edward Kramer 1907- *BioIn 2,*
   BioIn 10, IntWW 1976, WhoAm 1974,
   WhoS&SW 1973
Thompson, Edward T *OvPC*
Thompson, Edward William *HisAmM XR*
Thompson, Era Bell *AmAu&B, ForWC 1970,*
   LivBAA, WhoAm 1974, WhoAmW 1974,
   WhoWor 1974
Thompson, Frank J *HisAmM XR*
Thompson, Fred Harris 1882- *WhJnl 1928*
Thompson, Frederick Ingate 1875-1952
   WhJnl 1928
Thompson, George 1840- *NatCAB 3*
Thompson, George F *HisAmM XR*
Thompson, Glenn 1904- *BioIn 4, WhoAm 1974*
Thompson, Harry Arthur 1867-1936 *HisAmM XR*
Thompson, Harry Charles 1921- *WhoAm 1974,*
   WhoE 1974
Thompson, Haynes *OvPC*
Thompson, Howard *FamWC*
Thompson, Hunter Stockton 1938?- *BioIn 9,*
   BioIn 10, ConAu 19R, NewMr, OvPC,
   WhoE 1974
Thompson, James H 1881- *WhJnl 1928*
Thompson, Jane *NF*
Thompson, John 1873-1958 *NF*
Thompson, John 1875- *WhJnl 1928*
Thompson, John H 1890- *WhNAA, WhJnl 1928*
Thompson, John H 1908- *WhoAm 1974*
Thompson, John Q *HisAmM XR*
Thompson, John Reuben 1823-1873 *Alli, AmAu,*
   AmAu&B, AmJnl, BiDSA, BioIn 3,
   BioIn 4, BioIn 8, CyAL 2, DcAmA,
   DcNAA, HisAmM XR, LiJA, OxAm,
   REnAL, WebBD
Thompson, John William, Jr. 1914- *WhoAm 1974,*
   WhoS&SW 1973
Thompson, Joseph Parrish 1819-1879 *Alli,*
   Alli Sup, AmAu&B, DcAmA, DcNAA,
   HisAmM XR, WebBD
Thompson, Leslie Stuart 1901-1959 *BioIn 7,*
   NatCAB 49
Thompson, Lydia *HisAmM XR*
Thompson, M Cordell *NF*
Thompson, Margaret C *NF*
Thompson, Maurice 1844-1901 *AmAu, AmAu&B,*
   BbD, BiD&SB, BiDSA, CarSB, CnDAL,
   DcAmA, DcLEL, DcNAA, OxAm, REnAL,
   WebBD
Thompson, Mel 1929- *NF*
Thompson, Milo M 1891- *WhJnl 1928*
Thompson, Mortimer Neal 1831-1875 *AmAu&B*
Thompson, Morton 1907?-1953 *AmAu&B,*
   BioIn 2, BioIn 3
Thompson, Myra M 1904-1953 *BioIn 3*
Thompson, Newton Wayland 1882- *BioIn 3*
Thompson, Noah Davis *WhJnl 1928*
Thompson, Oscar Lee 1887-1945 *AmAu&B,*
   CurBio XR, DcAmB S3

Thompson, Otis *HisAmM XR*
Thompson, Paul Jennings 1890- *TexWr,*
   WhJnl 1928
Thompson, Peggy *NF*
Thompson, Porter *HisAmM XR*
Thompson, Ralph 1904- *AmAu&B,*
   HisAmM XR, WhoAm 1974, WhoE 1974
Thompson, Reuben R 1882?-1952 *BioIn 2*
Thompson, Robert Elliott 1921- *AuNews 2,*
   BioIn 10, WhoAm 1974
Thompson, Robert Ellis 1844-1924 *Alli Sup,*
   AmAu, AmAu&B, DcAmA, DcNAA,
   HisAmM XR
Thompson, Robert W 1870- *WhJnl 1928*
Thompson, Roger Mark 1942- *DrAS 74F*
Thompson, Ruth *OvPC*
Thompson, S D *HisAmM XR*
Thompson, Samuel 1810-1886 *BioIn 1, DcNAA,*
   OxCan
Thompson, Samuel Emory *NF*
Thompson, Slason 1849-1935 *Alli Sup, AmAu&B,*
   AmJnl, DcAmA, DcAmB S1, DcNAA,
   HisAmM XR, WhNAA
Thompson, T Barney 1876?-1967 *BioIn 8*
Thompson, Thomas 1933- *ConAu 65*
Thompson, Thomas E 1860- *WhJnl 1928*
Thompson, Thomas Phillips 1843-1933 *BbtC,*
   DcNAA
Thompson, Thorwald E 1888- *WhJnl 1928*
Thompson, Toby *NF*
Thompson, William Leslie 1906- *WhJnl 1928*
Thompson, William Tappan 1812-1882 *AmAu,*
   AmAu&B, BiDSA, BioIn 2, BioIn 3,
   BioIn 8, CnDAL, DcAmA, DcLEL,
   DcNAA, LiJA, OhA&B, OxAm, REnAL
Thompson, Zan *NF*
Thoms, William M *HisAmM XR*
Thomson, Alexander McDonald 1822-1898 *BioIn 5,*
   DcNAA
Thomson, Bernard St. Dennis *NF*
Thomson, Clifford *HisAmM XR*
Thomson, David Coupar 1861?-1954 *BioIn 3*
Thomson, Edward 1810-1870 *Alli, Alli Sup,*
   DcAmA, DcNAA, HisAmM XR, OhA&B
Thomson, Edward William 1849-1924 *AmAu&B,*
   BiD&SB, CanWr, DcAmA, DcLEL,
   DcNAA, OxCan, REnAL, TwCA
Thomson, Estelle 1846- *DcNAA*
Thomson, George Malcolm 1899- *Au&Wr,*
   ConAu 9R, Who 1974, WrDr 1976
Thomson, George Morgan 1921- *IntWW 1976*
Thomson, Hugh Christopher 1791?-1834 *BbtC,*
   DcNAA
Thomson, James Campbell 1912- *WhoAm 1974*
Thomson, James McIlhany 1878-1959 *AmJnl,*
   BioIn 5
Thomson, John Robert 1914- *WhoAm 1974*
Thomson, Kenneth Roy 1923- *CanWW 1972,*
   ForP, IntWW 1976, WhoAm 1974,
   WhoCan 1973, WhoWor 1974
Thomson, Mortimer Neal 1831-1875 *AmAu,*
   AmAu&B, CnDAL, DcNAA, HisAmM XR,
   OxAm, REnAL, WebBD
Thomson, Mortimer Neal *see also* Doesticks, Q K
   Philander
Thomson, Paul Jones 1884- *WhJnl 1928*
Thomson, Ronald M 1876- *WhJnl 1928*
Thomson, Roy Herbert 1894-1976 *ConAu 69,*
   CurBio XR, ForP, WhoWor 1974
Thomson, Roy Herbert, Baron *see also* Thomson Of
   Fleet, R Herbert
Thomson, Thomas N 1867?-1954 *BioIn 3*
Thomson, Virgil 1896- *AmAu&B,*
   AmSCAP 1966, BiE&WWA, CelR 1973,

ConAu 41, CurBio XR, IntWW 1976,
NewYTBE 2, NewYTBE 3, REn, REnAL,
TwCA, TwCA Sup, WebBD, WhoAm 1974,
WhoE 1974, WhoMus 1972, WhoWor 1974
Thomson, William A 1879-1971 BioIn 9,
ConAu 33, NewYTBE 2, WhJnl 1928
Thomson Of Fleet, Roy Herbert, Baron 1894-1976
BioIn 3, BioIn 5, BioIn 6, BioIn 7, BioIn 8,
CanWW 1972, IntMPA 1975, IntWW 1976,
Lor&LP, Who 1974, WhoCan 1973
Thomson Of Fleet, Roy Herbert, Baron see also
Thomson, R Herbert
Thomson Of Fleet, 2nd Baron see Thomson, Kenneth
Roy
Thomson Of Monifieth, Baron see Thomson, George
Morgan
Thomy, Alfred Marshall 1925- ConAu 69
Thone, Frank 1891- WhJnl 1928
Thony, Wilhelm 1888-1949 BioIn 1, BioIn 2,
BioIn 4
Thoren, Arne 1927- ConAu 69
Thorild, Thomas 1759-1808 BiD&SB, CasWL,
DcEuL, EuAu, WebBD
Thorkelson, Willmar 1918- WhoAm 1974
Thorman, Donald Joseph 1924- ConAu 17R,
OvPC, WhoMW 1974
Thorn, Charles Seymour 1905- WhoAm 1974
Thornburg, Dick 1904- WhoAm 1974
Thornburgh, Richard A 1903- WhJnl 1928
Thornbury, George Walter 1828-1876 Alli,
Alli Sup, BbD, BiD&SB, BrAu 19, DcEnL,
NewC, WebBD
Thorndike, Charles Jesse 1897- AmAu&B,
WhoAm 1974, WhoAmA 1973,
WhoS&SW 1973
Thorndike, Joseph Jacobs, Jr. 1913- WhoAm 1974
Thorne, Bliss K 1916- ConAu 17R
Thorne, Harley HisAmM XR
Thorne, Homer NF
Thorne, John N, Jr. 1915?-1972 BioIn 9,
NewYTBE 3
Thorne, VanBuren 1870- WhJnl 1928
Thorne, William Henry 1839-1907 Alli Sup,
DcAmA, DcNAA, HisAmM XR
Thornell, Jack Randolph 1939- WhoAm 1974,
WhoS&SW 1973
Thornton, Francis Beauchesne 1898- BioIn 1,
BioIn 3, BkC 4, CathA 1952
Thornton, Francis G HisAmM XR
Thornton, Gene NF
Thornton, Jeannye BlkC
Thornton, Lee 1944- ConAu 73
Thornton, Robert F NF
Thornton, W B see Burgess, Thornton Waldo
Thornwell, James Henley 1812-1862 Alli, BiDSA,
CyAL 2, DcAmA, DcNAA, HisAmM XR
Thorold, Algar Labouchere 1866-1936 BioIn 1,
BioIn 3, CathA 1930, WhoLA
Thorpe, Day 1913- WhoAm 1974,
WhoS&SW 1973
Thorpe, Frederick HisAmM XR
Thorpe, Merle 1879-1955 AmAu&B, BioIn 4,
BioIn 5, WhNAA, WhJnl 1928
Thorpe, S L HisAmM XR
Thorpe, Thomas Bangs 1815-1878 Alli, AmAu,
AmAu&B, BiDSA, BioIn 4, BioIn 6,
BioIn 8, CnDAL, CyAL 2, DcAmA,
DcEnL, DcLEL, DcNAA, HisAmM XR,
LiJA, OxAm, REnAL, WebE&AL
Thorsen, Robert Mitchel 1914- WhoAm 1974
Thorson, Nelson Thor 1881-1951 BioIn 2
Thorsteinson, Axel 1895- BioIn 1
Thosteson, George C 1904?-1978 NF
Thrapp, Daniel Lincoln 1913- ConAu 11R,

WhoAm 1974
Thrasher, John S 1817-1879 Alli, BiDSA,
DcNAA
Thrasher, Max Bennett 1860-1903 DcAmA,
DcNAA
Threlkeld, Richard 1937- ConAu 65
Throm, Edward L NF
Throop, Frank Dwight 1878- WhJnl 1928
Thrope, Elsieliese NF
Thrower, Fred Mitchell 1910- IntMPA 1975,
WhoAm 1974, WhoE 1974
Thruelsen, Richard Delmar 1908- AmAu&B,
BioIn 1, HisAmM XR
Thrum, J F HisAmM XR
Thuan, Koh Han NF
Thuermer, Angus Maclean 1917- RpN,
WhoGov 1972
Thulstrup, Thure 1848-1930 HisAmM XR,
WebBD
Thum, Ernest Edgar 1884-1961 BioIn 2, BioIn 4
Thurber, Charles Herbert 1864-1938 Alli Sup,
DcAmA, DcNAA, HisAmM XR
Thurber, George 1821-1890 Alli, Alli Sup,
DcAmA, HisAmM XR
Thurber, James 1894-1961 AmAu&B, AnCL,
AtlBL, AuBYP, BioIn 1, BioIn 2, BioIn 3,
BioIn 4, BioIn 5, BioIn 6, BioIn 7, BioIn 8,
BioIn 9, BioIn 10, BkCL, CasWL, CnDAL,
CnMWL, ConAmA, ConAu 73, ConLC 5,
CurBio XR, CyWA, DcLEL, EncWL,
EvLB, LongC, McGWD, ModAL, MorJA,
OhA&B, OxAm, OxEng, Pen Am, RAdv 1,
REn, REnAL, TwCA, TwCA Sup, TwCW,
WebBD, WebE&AL, WhoGrA, WhoTwCL
Thureau-Dangin, Paul 1837-1913 WebBD
Thursfield, Sir James Richard 1840-1923 WebBD
Thursh, Joan NF
Thurson, James McIlhany WhJnl 1928
Thurston, Benjamin Franklin 1858-1939
NatCAB 30, WhJnl 1928
Thurston, Elliott Ladd 1895-1975 NatCAB 30,
WhoAm 1974
Thusgaard, Carl AmJnl
Thwaites, Norman Graham 1872-1956 BioIn 4
Thwaites, Reuben Gold 1853-1913 Alli Sup,
AmAu&B, BiD&SB, BiDSA, DcAmA,
DcAmB, DcNAA, OxAm, OxCan, REnAL,
TwCA, WebBD, WisWr
Thwing, Eugene 1866-1936 AmAu&B, DcNAA,
WhNAA
Tiajcliff, Y L NF
Tibbles, Thomas Henry 1838-1928 Alli Sup,
AmAu, DcAmB 18, DcNAA, OhA&B
Tibby, John Knox Milligan, Jr. 1913-
WhoAm 1974
Tichenor, Frank A HisAmM XR
Tichenor, George 1791-1871 BioIn 5
Tichenor, Henry Mulford 1858-1922 DcNAA,
NatCAB 20
Ticknor, Paul E NF
Ticknor, William Davis 1810-1864 AmAu&B,
OxAm, WebBD
Tidball, Harriet 1909-1969 BioIn 8
Tidball, W D HisAmM XR
Tidyman, Ernest 1928- BioIn 8, BioIn 9,
ConAu 73, WrDr 1976
Tiede, Tom Robert 1937- AmAu&B, BioIn 8,
ConAu 25, WhoAm 1974, WhoE 1974
Tiegel, Eliot NF
Tienken, Arthur 1890- WhJnl 1928
Tierkel, David B d1948 BioIn 1
Tiernan, Francis Fisher HisAmM XR
Tierney, Myles 1902- WhJnl 1928
Tierney, Richard Henry 1870-1928 AmLY,

BioIn 4, DcAmB 18, DcNAA
Tietjens, Eunice 1884-1944 *AmAu&B, ConAmL,*
DcLEL, DcNAA, HisAmM XR, JBA 1934,
OxAm, REn, REnAL, TwCA, TwCA Sup,
WebBD, WhNAA
Tietsort, Francis J 1877- *WhJnl 1928*
Tiffany, James Alfred 1875- *WhJnl 1928*
Tighe, Dixie 1905?-1946 *BioIn 1*
Tilden, George H *HisAmM XR*
Tilden, Linda Palmer Littlejohn 1888-1949 *BioIn 1*
Tilghman, Benjamin C *HisAmM XR*
Till, P J *NF*
Tilley, R H *HisAmM XR*
Tillier, Claude 1801-1844 *DcEuL, OxFr, WebBD*
Tillinger, Eugene 1908?-1966 *BioIn 7*
Tillman, Stephen Frederick 1900-1977 *ConAu 69,*
WhJnl 1928
Tillman, Vivian Lee 1906- *WhJnl 1928*
Tillotsen, Daniel *HisAmM XR*
Tiltman, Hessell 1897?-1976 *ConAu 69*
Tilton, Howard Winslow 1849-1902 *DcAmA,*
DcNAA
Tilton, Ralph 1869-1907 *HisAmM XR*
Tilton, Theodore 1835-1907 *Alli, Alli Sup,*
AmAu, AmAu&B, AmJnl, BbD, BiD&SB,
BioIn 3, DcAmA, DcNAA, HisAmM XR,
LiJA, OxAm, REnAL, WebBD
Tim 1920?- *BioIn 6, WhoGrA*
Timberlake, Josephine Baxter *BioIn 2*
Timerman, Jacobo *NF*
Timlin, Eileen C *NF*
Timmins, James P 1894?-1954 *BioIn 3*
Timmons, Bascom Nolley 1890- *BioIn 1,*
WhoAm 1974
Timothy, Ann 1727?-1792? *NF*
Timothy, Benjamin Franklin *AmJnl*
Timothy, Elizabeth *AmJnl*
Timothy, Lewis d1738 *AmJnl*
Timothy, Peter *AmJnl*
Timrod, Henry 1828-1867 *Alli, AmAu,*
AmAu&B, AmJnl, BiD&SB, BiDSA,
CasWL, CnDAL, CyAL 1, DcAmA,
DcLEL, DcNAA, EvLB, HisAmM XR,
OxAm, Pen Am, REn, REnAL, WebBD
Tims, John Frank, Jr. 1892-1969 *BioIn 8,*
WhJnl 1928
Tindall, Cordell Wayland 1914- *WhoAm 1974*
Tindall, R K 1892- *WhJnl 1928*
Tindiglia, Ron *NF*
Tinee, Mae *NF*
Tingley, Katherine 1852-1929 *HisAmM XR*
Tinker, Edward Larocque 1881-1968 *AmAu&B,*
ConAu 13, ConAu P-1, REnAL, TwCA,
TwCA Sup, WhNAA
Tinker, Frank 1920- *NF*
Tinkham, Kenneth Otis 1895- *WhJnl 1928*
Tinnin, David Bruce 1930- *ConAu 49,*
WhoAm 1974, WhoE 1974, WhoWor 1974
Tinniswood, Peter 1936- *Au&Wr, ConAu 25,*
ConNov 1976, WrDr 1976
Tipping, Edmond William 1915?-1970 *BioIn 8,*
RpN
Tippit, Jack *NF*
Titchener, Edward Bradford 1867-1927 *AmAu&B,*
DcAmA, DcNAA, HisAmM XR, REnAL,
WebBD
Titherington, Richard Handfield 1861-1935
DcAmA, DcNAA, HisAmM XR
Tittman, Edward D'Oench *NF*
Titzell, John M *HisAmM XR*
Titzell, Josiah Carlton 1905-1943 *DcNAA*
Toal, D C *HisAmM XR*
Tobenkin, Elias 1882-1963 *AmAu&B, BioIn 6,*
WhNAA

Tobey, Barney *NF*
Tobey, Charles H 1872-1949 *BioIn 1,*
WhJnl 1928
Tobey, Earle D 1883- *WhJnl 1928*
Tobin, Don 1915- *NF*
Tobin, James Edward 1905-1968 *BioIn 1, BioIn 8,*
CathA 1930, ConAu 23
Tobin, John R 1899- *WhJnl 1928*
Tobin, Richard Griswold 1882?-1953 *BioIn 3*
Tobin, Richard Lardner 1910- *AmAu&B,*
BioIn 1, BioIn 5, ConAu 2R, CurBio XR,
WhoAm 1974
Tobin, William Joseph 1927- *WhoWest 1974*
Toby, M P 1845-1924 *NewC, WebBD*
Toby, M P *see also* Lucy, Sir Henry
Toby, William C *AmJnl*
Todd, Alden 1918- *ConAu 1, OvPC,*
WhoE 1974
Todd, Burt Kerr *HisAmM XR*
Todd, Elmer Kenneth 1894- *WhJnl 1928*
Todd, F Dundas *HisAmM XR*
Todd, Frank M 1871-1940 *NatCAB 30*
Todd, Ian Menzies 1923- *ConAu 69*
Todd, Laurence 1882- *BioIn 2*
Todd, Mabel 1856-1932 *BioIn 4*
Todd, Marion 1841- *Alli Sup, AmAu&B,*
DcAmA, DcNAA
Todd, Richard *NF*
Todd, Ruth VanDorn 1889?-1976 *ConAu 65*
Todd, Sereno Edwards 1820-1898 *Alli, Alli Sup,*
DcAmA, DcAmB 18, DcNAA, NatCAB 9
Todd, William Burton 1919- *ConAu 41,*
DrAS 74E
Todd, William Kenneth 1916- *WhoAm 1974*
Todrin, Boris 1915- *AmAu&B, AmNov,*
ConAu 61, WhoAdv 1972
Toedtman, James Christian 1914- *WhoAdv 1972,*
WhoMW 1974
Toeplitz, Jerzy 1909- *ConAu 65, IntWW 1976*
Toffler, Alvin 1928- *AmAu&B, ConAu 15R,*
WhoAm 1974, WrDr 1976
Togliatti, Palmiro 1893-1964 *CurBio XR*
Tokoi, Oskari 1873-1963 *BioIn 4, BioIn 6*
Toksvig, *BioIn 1*
Toksvig, Claus B *OvPC*
Toksvig, Signe 1891- *Au&Wr, HisAmM XR*
Toland, John Willard 1912- *AmAu&B, Au&Wr,*
BioIn 4, ConAu 1, OvPC, WhoAm 1974,
WorAu, WrDr 1976
Tolbert, Francis Xavier 1912- *BioIn 2, ConAu 3R*
Tolbert, Francis Xavier *see also* Tolbert, Frank
Tolbert, Frank 1912- *AmAu&B, WhoAm 1974*
Tolbert, Frank *see also* Tolbert, Francis Xavier
Tolchin, Martin 1928- *WhoE 1974*
Tolchin, Sue *NF*
Toledano, Ralph De 1916- *AmAu&B, AuNews 1,*
ConAu 11R, CurBio XR, WhoAm 1974,
WrDr 1976
Toledano, Ralph De *see also* DeToledano, Ralph
Toler, Jon Thomas 1869- *WhJnl 1928*
Toler, Kenneth 1904?-1966 *BioIn 7*
Tolf, Robert W 1929- *ConAu 73*
Tolischus, Otto David 1890-1967 *AmJnl, BioIn 7,*
BioIn 8, CurBio XR
Tolkunov, Lev Nikolayevich 1919- *IntWW 1976,*
WhoWor 1974
Tollet, Axel Marcus 1883-1947 *BioIn 1*
Tolliver, Melba 1938- *BioIn 9, BlkC,*
ForWC 1970, NewYTBE 4
Tolman, Edgar Bronson 1859-1947 *BioIn 1*
Tolnay, Tom *NF*
Toluzzi, Henry *NF*
Tomalin, Nicholas 1931-1973 *Au&Wr, ConAu 45*
Tomalin, Ruth *Au&Wr, ConAu 15R,*

Townsend, Charles 1859-1917 *DcNAA*
Townsend, Charles E *WhJnl 1928*
Townsend, Clara Virginia 1858-1939 *DcNAA*
Townsend, Claudia *NF*
Townsend, Dallas *NF*
Townsend, Edward Thomas 1910- *WhoAm 1974*
Townsend, Edward Waterman 1855-1942
  *AmAu&B, BbD, BiD&SB, CurBio XR,
  DcAmA, DcNAA, HisAmM XR, OhA&B,
  OxAm, WebBD*
Townsend, George Alfred 1841-1914 *Alli,
  Alli Sup, AmAu, AmAu&B, BbD, BiD&SB,
  BioIn 1, BioIn 3, DcAmA, DcAmB 18,
  DcNAA, FamWC, OxAm, REnAL*
Townsend, Horace 1859-1922 *DcNAA*
Townsend, James Bliss 1855-1921 *AmAu&B,
  DcNAA, HisAmM XR*
Townsend, John Rowe 1922- *Au&Wr, ChlLR 2,
  ConAu 37, SmATA 4, WhoWor 1974,
  WrDr 1976*
Townsend, Meredith White 1831-1911 *WebBD*
Townsend, Morris D 1899- *WhJnl 1928*
Townsend, Ralph M 1901?-1976 *ConAu 65*
Townsend, Reginald Townsend 1890-1977
  *AmAu&B, WhNAA, WhoAm 1974,
  WhJnl 1928*
Townsend, Robert Donaldson 1854-1933
  HisAmM XR
Townsend, Sheperd Vincent 1901- *WhoAm 1974*
Townsend, Theodore H 1893- *WhJnl 1928*
Townsend, Virginia Frances 1836-1920 *Alli,
  Alli Sup, AmAu&B, BbD, BiD&SB,
  DcAmA, DcNAA, HisAmM XR*
Townsley, Charles *WhJnl 1928*
Townsley, Will *WhJnl 1928*
Towse, John Ranken 1845-1933 *HisAmM XR*
Toy, Crawford Howell 1836-1919 *Alli Sup,
  AmAu&B, BiD&SB, BiDSA, DcAmA,
  DcNAA, HisAmM XR, WebBD*
Toynbee, Theodore Philip 1916- *Au&Wr,
  ConAu 4R, DcLEL, EvLB*
Trachte, Don *NF*
Trachtenberg, Alexander *AmRP*
Trachtman, Paul *NF*
Tracy, Ebenezer Carter 1796-1862 *Alli, DcNAA*
Tracy, Frank Basil 1866-1912 *DcNAA,
  HisAmM XR*
Tracy, Honor Lilbush Wingfield 1913-
  *IntWW 1976, WhoAmW 1974,
  WhoWor 1974*
Tracy, Merle Elliott 1879-1945 *BioIn 1,
  HisAmM XR, NatCAB 33*
Tracy, Paul Aubrey *HisAmM XR*
Tracy, Phil *NF*
Trafford, E Channing *NF*
Trafford, F G 1832-1906 *Alli, Alli Sup, DcEnL,
  DcLEL, NewC*
Trafford, F G see also Riddell, Charlotte Eliza
  Lawson
Trafton, Alice *HisAmM XR*
Trafton, E H *HisAmM XR*
Trafton, Spalding 1866- *WhJnl 1928*
Trag, Walt *NF*
Traill, Henry Duff 1842-1900 *Alli Sup, BiD&SB,
  BrAu 19, DcEnA, DcEnA Ap, DcEuL,
  DcLEL, EvLB, NewC, OxEng, WebBD*
Traill, William Henry 1842?-1902 *BioIn 2*
Train, Susan *NF*
Trainor, Jim *NF*
Trammer, Monte I 1951- *NF*
Trancu, Theodore Constantine *OvPC*
Tranter, John H 1877-1948 *BioIn 1*
Trapp, William Oscar 1889-1964 *BioIn 7*
Traser, Lewis W *HisAmM XR*

Trask, Harry Albert 1928- *WhoAm 1974*
Trask, William Blake 1812-1906 *Alli, CyAL 2,
  DcNAA, HisAmM XR*
Trattner, John H 1930- *OvPC, USBiR 1974*
Traubel, Horace Logo 1858-1919 *AmAu&B,
  AmLY, CnDAL, DcNAA, HisAmM XR,
  OxAm, REn, REnAL, TwCA, TwCA Sup,
  WebBD*
Traunicek, Charles E 1899- *WhJnl 1928*
Trausch, Susan *NF*
Trautman, Robert G *NF*
Trautmann, Les 1918- *NF*
Travaglo, Eugene *AmRP*
Traver, G A *HisAmM XR*
Travers, James Wadsworth 1865-1949 *BioIn 5*
Travis, Neal *NF*
Traynor, W J H *HisAmM XR*
Treadgold, Mary 1910- *Au&Wr, BioIn 8,
  ConAu 13R, WhoChL, WrDr 1976*
Treadwell, Daniel 1791-1872 *Alli, AmAu&B,
  DcAmA, HisAmM XR*
Treanor, Arthur Ryan 1883-1956 *BioIn 4,
  WhJnl 1928*
Treanor, Tom 1908-1944 *AmJnl, BioIn 5,
  CurBio XR, DcNAA, NatCAB 42*
Treat, Roger L 1905- *AuBYP, BioIn 7*
Treat, Selah B *Alli, HisAmM XR*
Trebilcock, John Thomas 1914?-1955 *BioIn 3*
Trecker, Janice *NF*
Tredez, Alain 1929- *BioIn 8, BioIn 9, ThrBJA*
Tredway, Paul *NF*
Tree, Christina 1944- *ConAu 73*
Tree, Ronald 1897-1976 *ConAu 65, ConAu 69,
  Who 1974*
Trefethen, James Byron, Jr. 1916-1976 *ConAu 21,
  ConAu 69, WhoE 1974*
Treffinger, E J 1889- *WhJnl 1928*
Tregaskis, Richard William 1916-1973 *AmAu&B,
  AmJnl, Au&Wr, AuBYP, BioIn 9,
  ConAu 3R, ConAu 45, CurBio XR,
  SmATA 3, WhoAm 1974*
Trego, Charles B 1794-1874 *Alli, DcNAA,
  HisAmM XR*
Trego, Edward A 1859?-1946 *BioIn 1*
Treharne, Bryceson 1879-1948 *AmSCAP 1966,
  BioIn 1*
Trelford, Donald Gilchrist 1937- *IntWW 1976*
Treloar, James A 1933- *ConAu 45*
Treloar, Wilbert H *NF*
Tremaine, Frank 1914- *WhoAm 1974,
  WhoWor 1974*
Tremaine, Frederick Orlin 1889-1956 *AmAu&B,
  HisAmM XR*
Tremayne, Sydney 1912- *ConAu 7R*
Tremblay, Michael G *NF*
Tremblay, William C *NF*
Tremenheere, Hugh Seymour 1804-1893 *Alli,
  Alli Sup, BbtC, BioIn 4, BioIn 6, BioIn 7*
Trenchard, John *HisAmM XR*
Trendle, George Washington 1884-1972 *EncMys,
  NewYTBE 3*
Trenholm, Katherine *NF*
Trenholm, Lee 1899- *WhJnl 1928*
Treno, R 1910?-1969 *BioIn 8*
Trent, Harrison *HisAmM XR*
Trent, Madeline *WhoAmW 1974*
Trent, William 1919- *ConAu 3R*
Treon, William Cornelius 1936- *WhoAm 1974*
Trepanier, Leon *NF*
Tresca, Carlo 1879-1943 *AmRP, CurBio XR,
  DcAmB S3*
Tress, Irwin M *OvPC*
Trethowan, Ian 1922- *IntWW 1976, Who 1974*
Tretick, Stanley 1921- *AmJnl, WhoAm 1974*

Treves, Ralph 1906- *ConAu 13R, WrDr 1976*
Trevor, George S 1892?-1951 *BioIn 2*
Trewhitt, Henry L *RpN*
Trewin, Ion 1943- *ConAu 69*
Trewin, John Courtenay 1908- *Au&Wr, BioIn 1, BioIn 2, BioIn 3, Who 1974, WhoThe 1972*
Trexler, Fern B *WhJnl 1928*
Trexler, Pat *NF*
Trezevant, John Gray 1923- *WhoAm 1974*
Trezevant, Marye Beattie 1872-1930 *BioIn 2, NatCAB 34*
Tribble, Edwin 1907- *WhoAm 1974, WhoS&SW 1973*
Trier, Walter 1890-1951 *BioIn 2, BioIn 3, BioIn 5*
Trigg, Lindolph O 1879- *WhJnl 1928*
Triggs, Flloyd Willding 1870?-1919 *NF*
Triggs, Laurence F 1900- *WhJnl 1928*
Trill, Matthew 1887- *BioIn 1, CanNov*
Trilling, Ossia 1913- *WhoThe 1972*
Trillo Pays, Dionisio Martin Enrique 1909- *IntWW 1976*
Trim 1827-1900 *WebBD*
Trim *see also* Ratisbone, Louis Fortune Gustave
Trim, Hal *NF*
Trimble, Henry 1853-1898 *DcAmA, DcNAA, HisAmM XR*
Trimble, Jessie 1873?-1957 *BioIn 4*
Trimble, Joe *AuBYP, BioIn 7*
Trimble, Richard *OvPC*
Trimble, Vance Henry 1913- *BioIn 5, ConAu 49, ConAu 65, CurBio XR, WhoAm 1974*
Trimborn, Harry *NF*
Trinculo *see* Wheeler, Andrew Carpenter
Trinidad, Francisco D Flores, Jr. 1939- *ConAu 69, WhoAm 1974*
Tripp, Frank Elihu 1882-1964 *BioIn 1, BioIn 6, BioIn 7, WhJnl 1928*
Trippett, Frank 1926- *ConAu 21R*
Tristao, Carmen *OvPC*
Troan, Joan *NF*
Troan, John 1918- *WhoAm 1974*
Troelstra, Pieter Jelles 1860-1930 *CasWL, WebBD*
Troelstrup, Glenn C *OvPC*
Trohan, Walter 1903- *BioIn 1, WhoAm 1974*
Trommer, Lazarus 1888?-1957 *BioIn 4*
Trosley, G *NF*
Trotsky, Leon 1879-1940 *AmRP, CasWL, CurBio XR, LongC, REn, WebBD*
Trotta, Geri *NF*
Trotta, Liz 1937- *OvPC*
Trotter, James *NF*
Trotter, Thomas Fallon 1920- *WhoAm 1974*
Trotter, William Monroe 1872-1934 *EncAB*
Trottier, William 1899- *WhJnl 1928*
Troup, Alexander 1840-1908 *NatCAB 17*
Trousdale, Leonidas 1823-1897 *NatCAB 8*
Trousey, Maud *HisAmM XR*
Trout, Clement Eddy 1891-1960 *BioIn 3, BioIn 5*
Trout, Robert 1908- *BioIn 1, BioIn 7, CelR 1973, CurBio XR, OvPC, WhoAm 1974*
Troute, Dennis *NF*
Trowbridge, David *HisAmM XR*
Trowbridge, John Townsend 1827-1916 *Alli, Alli Sup, AmAu, AmAu&B, BbD, BiD&SB, CarSB, CyAL 2, CyWA, DcAmA, DcBiA, DcEnL, DcLEL, DcNAA, HisAmM XR, LiJA, OxAm, REnAL, WebBD*
Troxell, William S 1893?-1957 *BioIn 4*
Troy, Forrest 1933?- *BioIn 10, NewMr*
Troy, Frosty *see* Troy, Forrest
Troy, George F, Jr. 1909-1969 *BioIn 2, BioIn 8, ConAu 2R*

Troyer, Byron LeRoy 1909- *ConAu 65*
Truax, Virginia *NF*
Truby, J David 1938- *ConAu 53*
Truchan, Barbara *NF*
Trudeau, Garry B 1948- *BioIn 10, CurBio XR*
True, Frank 1893?-1974 *BioIn 10*
True, George *HisAmM XR*
Trueblood, Mark S 1900- *WhJnl 1928*
Trueblood, Ralph Waldo 1885-1954 *BioIn 3, BioIn 6, NatCAB 44*
Truesdell, John S *NF*
Truesdell, Seneca Ellis 1852-1899 *DcNAA*
Truitt, James McConnell 1921- *WhoAm 1974*
Trullinger, Earl Barton 1886- *WhJnl 1928*
Trullinger, James W *OvPC*
Truman, Benjamin Cummings 1835-1916 *Alli Sup, AmAu&B, DcAmA, DcAmB 19, DcNAA*
Truman, Lee *NF*
Trumble, Alfred 1861?- *Alli Sup, DcNAA, HisAmM XR*
Trumbo, Dalton 1905-1976 *AmAu&B, ConAu 21, ConDr, ConNov 1972, ConNov 1976, CurBio XR, IntMPA 1975, NewYTBE 1, REnAL, TwCA, TwCA Sup, WhoAm 1974, WrDr 1976*
Trumbull, Charles Gallaudet 1872-1941 *AmAu&B, AmLY, DcNAA, HisAmM XR, WhNAA*
Trumbull, Henry Clay 1830-1903 *Alli, Alli Sup, AmAu&B, BbD, BiD&SB, DcAmA, DcNAA, WebBD*
Trumbull, Levi R 1834-1918 *DcNAA*
Trumbull, Robert 1912- *AmAu&B, ConAu 11R, OvPC, WhoAm 1974, WhoWor 1974*
Trupp, Philip Z *NF*
Truscott, Alan 1925- *ConAu 25, OvPC*
Trussell, Charles Prescott 1892-1968 *BioIn 2, BioIn 8, CurBio XR, WhJnl 1928*
Trussell, Charles Tait 1925- *WhoAm 1974, WhoS&SW 1973*
Trussell, Percy Luman 1884?-1949 *BioIn 2*
Trussler, Simon 1942- *Au&Wr, ConAu 25, WrDr 1976*
Tryk, Sheila *NF*
Tryon, George Washington, Jr. 1838-1888 *Alli, Alli Sup, DcAmA, DcNAA, HisAmM XR*
Tryon, Virginia V 1903- *WhJnl 1928*
Ts'ai, Ting-Li 1910- *BioIn 2*
Tsuchida, Jataro *NF*
Tsutsumi, Teruo *NF*
Tu, Pei-Lin *NF*
Tubbs, Arthur Lewis 1867-1946 *AmAu&B, AmLY, DcNAA, WhNAA*
Tubby, Roger Wellington 1910- *BioIn 5, IntWW 1974, WhoAm 1974, WhoGov 1972*
Tucci, Nicolo *AmRP*
Tuchman, Barbara Wertheim 1912- *AmAu&B, Au&Wr, ConAu 1R, CurBio XR, DrAS 74H, IntWW 1976, OxAm, WhoAm 1974, WhoAmW 1974, WhoE 1974, WhoWor 1974, WhoWorJ 1972, WorAu, WrDr 1976*
Tucholsky, Kurt 1890-1935 *BioIn 3, BioIn 8, CasWL, EncWL, EvEuW, ModGL, OxGer, Pen Eur*
Tuck, Jay Nelson *AmRP*
Tucker, Benjamin Ricketson 1854-1939 *Alli Sup, AmRP, DcAmB S2, DcNAA, HisAmM XR, TwCA, TwCA Sup, WebBD*
Tucker, Carll *NF*
Tucker, Daniel Eugene 1925- *WhoAm 1974*
Tucker, Ernest Edward 1916-1969 *AuBYP, BioIn 7, BioIn 8, ConAu 61*
Tucker, George 1861- *WhJnl 1928*
Tucker, George C 1879- *WhJnl 1928*

Tucker, George H 1902-1952 *BioIn 3*
Tucker, Gideon John 1826-1899 *DcNAA*
Tucker, Gilbert Milligan 1847-1932 *AmAu&B,*
AmLY, DcAmA, DcNAA, HisAmM XR,
WebBD, WhNAA
Tucker, Glenn Irving 1892-1976 *AmAu&B,*
ConAu 5R, ConAu 69, IndAu 1917,
WhoAm 1974
Tucker, Henry Holcombe 1819-1889 *Alli,*
Alli Sup, BiDSA, DcAmA, DcNAA,
HisAmM XR
Tucker, Irwin St. John 1886- *AmRP, BioIn 1*
Tucker, James 1929- *Au&Wr, ConAu 21R,*
WrDr 1976
Tucker, Joshua Thomas 1812-1897 *Alli, DcAmA,*
DcNAA, HisAmM XR
Tucker, Lem *WhoE 1974*
Tucker, Luther 1802-1873 *Alli, AmAu&B,*
HisAmM XR, NatCAB 24, WebBD
Tucker, Luther H, Jr. *HisAmM XR*
Tucker, Mary Eliza 1838- *Alli, DcAmA,*
DcNAA, LivFWS
Tucker, Patricia 1912- *ConAu 65, ForWC 1970,*
OvPC, WhoAmW 1974
Tucker, Phyllis DeYoung 1892- *WhoAm 1974,*
WhoAmW 1974
Tucker, Pomeroy 1802-1870 *Alli, DcAmA,*
DcNAA
Tucker, Ray Thomas 1893-1963 *BioIn 6*
Tucker, Robert G 1873-1941 *NatCAB 30*
Tucker, Robin 1950- *ConAu 53*
Tucker, Samuel A 1894-1949 *BioIn 2,*
WhJnl 1928
Tucker, William Clifford 1898-1961 *BioIn 5*
Tucker, William Jewett 1839-1926 *BiD&SB,*
DcAmA, DcNAA, HisAmM XR, OhA&B
Tuckerman, Anne *NF*
Tuckerman, Henry Theodore 1813-1871 *Alli,*
Alli Sup, AmAu, AmAu&B, BbD, BiD&SB,
CasWL, CnDAL, CyAL 2, DcAmA,
DcLEL, DcNAA, EvLB, OxAm, REnAL,
WebBD
Tudor, William 1779-1830 *Alli, AmAu,*
AmAu&B, CyAL 2, DcAmA, DcNAA,
HisAmM XR, LiJA, OxAm, REnAL,
WebBD
Tueni, Ghassan 1926- *IntWW 1976*
Tues, C E *HisAmM XR*
Tuetsch, Hans E *NF*
Tuffli, Dave 1900- *WhJnl 1928*
Tufts, James Hayden 1862-1942 *AmAu&B,*
AmLY, CurBio XR, DcNAA, HisAmM XR,
WhNAA
Tufts, Warren 1923?- *BioIn 2*
Tufty, Esther VanWagoner 1896?- *BioIn 1,*
ForWC 1970, WhoAmW 1974
Tuller, W Lee 1884- *WhJnl 1928*
Tullidge, Edward Wheelock 1829-1894 *Alli Sup,*
DcNAA, HisAmM XR
Tully, Andrew Frederick, Jr. 1914- *AmAu&B,*
ConAu 19R, WhoAm 1974, WrDr 1976
Tumquist, Ralph A 1882-1926 *WhJnl 1928*
Tung, Theodore C M *NF*
Tunheim, Thorval 1896- *WhJnl 1928*
Tunis, Allyn Bernard 1888-1948 *BioIn 1*
Tunis, John Roberts 1889-1975 *AuBYP, BioIn 4,*
BioIn 6, BioIn 7, BioIn 8, ConAu 57,
ConAu 61, HisAmM XR, MorJA, REnAL,
TwCA, TwCA Sup
Tunison, Eileen Feretic 1949- *NF*
Tunison, Joseph Salathiel 1849-1916 *Alli Sup,*
AmAu&B, DcNAA, OhA&B
Tunley, Roul 1912- *AmAu&B, ConAu 13R,*
InvJ, WhoAm 1974, WrDr 1976

Tunstall, Ed *NF*
Tuohy, Ferdinand 1891- *WhJnl 1928*
Tuohy, James Mark 1859- *WhJnl 1928*
Tuohy, William Klaus 1926- *OvPC,*
WhoAm 1974, WhoWest 1974,
WhoWor 1974
Tuomey, Douglas *NF*
Turano, Anthony M *HisAmM XR*
Turati, Augusto 1888- *WebBD*
Turati, Filippo 1857-1932 *WebBD*
Turcott, Jack 1906?-1965 *BioIn 7*
Turing, Penelope *BioIn 8*
Turk, Peter B *NF*
Turkheimer, Nathan A 1921- *OvPC,*
WhoPubR 1972
Turkin, Hy 1915-1955 *BioIn 3*
Turnblad, Harold M 1900- *WhJnl 1928*
Turnbull, Andrew B 1884- *WhJnl 1928*
Turnbull, George Stanley 1882- *WhJnl 1928*
Turnbull, Lawrence *HisAmM XR*
Turnbull, Robert 1809-1877 *Alli, BiD&SB,*
DcAmA, DcNAA, HisAmM XR
Turnbull, Robert James 1775-1833 *Alli, BiDSA,*
DcAmA, DcNAA, HisAmM XR, WebBD
Turner, Alice K 1940- *ConAu 53, SmATA 10*
Turner, Andrew Jackson 1832-1905 *BioIn 5*
Turner, Arlin 1909- *ConAu 5, DrAS 74E,*
HisAmM XR, WrDr 1976
Turner, Dick 1909- *WhoAmA 1973*
Turner, Douglas L *NF*
Turner, Duane *NF*
Turner, Eardley d1929 *NF*
Turner, Edith L 1899?-1966 *BioIn 7*
Turner, Eugene Welford 1904?-1959 *BioIn 5*
Turner, George Kibbe 1869-1952 *AmAu&B,*
DcAmB S5, HisAmM XR, WhNAA
Turner, George W *AmJnl*
Turner, Graham 1932- *Au&Wr, ConAu 23R*
Turner, H L *HisAmM XR*
Turner, Harry B *WhJnl 1928*
Turner, Harry L *NF*
Turner, Henry E *Alli Sup, HisAmM XR*
Turner, John Frayn 1923- *Au&Wr, ConAu 9R,*
WrDr 1976
Turner, John Kenneth *HisAmM XR*
Turner, Joseph Addison 1826-1868 *AmAu,*
BioIn 6, HisAmM XR, LiJA, REnAL
Turner, Joseph S 1901- *WhJnl 1928*
Turner, Josiah 1821-1901 *WebBD*
Turner, Judith Axler *NF*
Turner, Kathleen *NF*
Turner, Leon L 1883- *WhJnl 1928*
Turner, Leslie *AmJnl*
Turner, Morris 1923- *BioIn 6, BioIn 7, BioIn 9,*
ConAu 29
Turner, Nancy Byrd 1880- *AmAu&B, BkCL,*
Str&VC, WhNAA
Turner, Nellie Wise d1950 *BioIn 2*
Turner, Ralph H 1895- *WhJnl 1928*
Turner, Robert E 1863- *WhJnl 1928*
Turner, Thomas Sloss 1860- *BiDSA, DcAmA.*
DcNAA
Turner, Tim *NF*
Turner, Timothy Gilman 1817-1904 *BioIn 2,*
IndAu 1816
Turner, Tom *NF*
Turner, Tom Jefferson 1887- *BioIn 2,*
WhJnl 1928
Turner, Wallace 1921- *BioIn 5, ConAu 19R,*
InvJ, RpN, WhoWest 1974
Turner, Walter James Redfern 1889-1946 *BioIn 1,*
BioIn 4, BioIn 5, BioIn 7, BioIn 9, CnMD,
DcLEL, EvLB, LongC, ModBL, NewC,
OxEng, REn, TwCA, TwCA Sup, TwCW,

U

Ubell, Earl 1926- *BioIn 5, BioIn 9, ConAu 37,*
  SmATA 4, WhoAm 1974
Uchida, Tadao 1939- *ConAu 65*
Udell, John 1880- *BioIn 1*
Udevitz, Norm *NF*
Udick, Robert E 1922- *WhoAm 1974,*
  WhoF&I 1974
Udwith, Jerry *NF*
Uebersax, P *NF*
Ueland, Brenda 1892- *BioIn 8*
Ueno, Riichi 1848-1919 *NF*
Ueno, Seiichi *ForP*
Ugboajah, Francis Okwuadigbo *NF*
Uhl, Alexander Herbert 1899-1976 *ConAu 69,*
  OvPC, WhoAm 1974
Uhl, Jacob *AmJnl*
Uhle, Charles P *HisAmM XR*
Uhlen, Axel *ForP*
Ujiie, Hisashi *NF*
Ukers, William Harrison 1873-1954 *AmAu&B,*
  WhNAA, WhJnl 1928
Ulanov, Barry 1918- *AmAu&B, Au&Wr,*
  ConAu 1R, DrAS 74E
Ulate, Otilio 1896-1973 *ForP*
Ulbach, Louis 1822-1889 *BbD, BiD&SB, WebBD*
Ulerich, William Keener 1910- *WhoAm 1974*
Ulevich, Neal *NF*
Ullman, Hermann 1884- *BioIn 3*
Ullmann, Bernard *NF*
Ulloa, Manuel *ForP*
Ullstein, Rudolf 1874-1964 *BioIn 2, BioIn 6*
Ulman, Neil *NF*
Ulrich, Charles Kenmore 1859?-1941 *AmAu&B,*
  DcNAA
Ulrich, John 1828-1894 *BioIn 5*
Ulrici, Hermann 1806-1884 *BbD, BiD&SB,*
  WebBD
Ultang, Don *NF*
Uluc, Dogan *NF*
Uluschak, E D *NF*
Ulvestam, Rolf *NF*
Ulyat, William Clarke 1823-1905 *Alli Sup,*
  DcNAA, HisAmM XR
Umbo 1902- *BioIn 10*
Umbstaetter, Herman Daniel 1851-1913 *DcNAA,*
  HisAmM XR, OhA&B
Uminski, Sigmund 1910- *BioIn 1, CathA 1930*
Umstead, William Lee 1921- *WhoAm 1974*
Uncle Ray *see* Coffman, Ramon Peyton
Underhill, John Garrett 1876-1946 *AmAu&B,*
  DcAmA, REnAL, WhNAA
Underhill, John Lispenard 1902?-1971 *BioIn 9*
Underwood, Agness May 1902- *BioIn 1, BioIn 2,*
  BioIn 6, BioIn 7
Underwood, Benjamin Franklin 1839-1914
  Alli Sup, BiD&SB, DcAmA, DcNAA,

HisAmM XR
Underwood, Bert Elias 1862-1943 *CurBio XR,*
  DcNAA
Underwood, Clarence F *HisAmM XR*
Underwood, Eric Gordon 1890-1952 *BioIn 2*
Underwood, Francis Henry 1825-1894 *Alli Sup,*
  AmAu, AmAu&B, BbD, BiD&SB, DcAmA,
  DcNAA, EvLB, HisAmM XR, LiJA, OxAm
Underwood, Paul S 1915- *OvPC*
Underwood, Thomas Rust 1898-1956 *BioIn 2,*
  BioIn 4, BioIn 5, NatCAB 42, WhJnl 1928
Underwood, William E *HisAmM XR*
Ungar, Arthur 1886?-1950 *BioIn 2*
Ungar, Sanford J 1945- *ConAu 37, WrDr 1976*
Ungaro, Joseph Michael 1930- *WhoAm 1974*
Unger, Arthur 1924- *ConAu 1*
Unger, James *NF*
Unger, Madeline *NF*
Ungerer, Tomi 1931- *AuBYP, BioIn 10,*
  ConAu XR, SmATA 5, ThrBJA, WhoGrA
Unna, Warren W 1923- *WhoAm 1974,*
  WhoWor 1974
Untermeyer, Louis 1885-1977 *AmAu&B, AmLY,*
  AnCL, AnMV 1926, Au&Wr, AuBYP,
  BioIn 7, BioIn 8, BioIn 9, CelR 1973,
  CnDAL, ConAmA, ConAmL, ConAu 5,
  ConAu 73, ConP 1970, ConP 1975,
  CurBio XR, DcLEL, EvLB, HisAmM XR,
  IntWW 1974, LongC, OxAm, REn, REnAL,
  SmATA 2, TwCA, TwCA Sup, TwCW,
  WebBD, WhNAA, Who 1974,
  WhoAm 1974, WrDr 1976
Unwin, James 1929- *NF*
Uobertson, Harrison 1856-1939 *WhJnl 1928*
Updegraff, Allan Eugene 1883-1965 *AmAu&B*
Updegraff, Laurence Vale 1884-1961 *BioIn 5*
UpDeGraff, T S *HisAmM XR*
Upton, Francis R *HisAmM XR*
Upton, George Putnam 1834-1919 *Alli Sup,*
  AmAu&B, BbD, BiD&SB, DcAmA,
  DcAmB 19, DcNAA, NatCAB 18, WebBD
Upton, Loren D 1898- *WhJnl 1928*
Upton, William Treat 1870- *AmAu&B, OhA&B,*
  WhNAA
Urban, Henry Zeller 1920- *WhoAm 1974*
Urdang, Barry 1915?- *BioIn 2*
Ure, George P d1860 *BbtC, DcNAA*
Uris, Michael 1902?-1967 *BioIn 8*
Urner, Mabel Herbert 1881-1957 *AmAu&B,*
  AmLY XR, OhA&B, WhNAA, WhJnl 1928
Urquhart, John *NF*
Urry, Donald Charles 1910- *WhoAm 1974,*
  WhoWest 1974
Urzidil, Johannes 1896-1970 *CasWL, ConAu 29,*
  ModGL, NewYTBE 1, OxGer
Usami, Shigeru *NF*

Usher, Ellis Baker 1852-1931 *BioIn 5, DcNAA*
Usher, Leonard Gray 1907- *WhoAm 1974*
Ushio, Shota *NF*
Uslar-Pietri, Arturo 1906- *IntWW 1974,*
WhoWor 1974
Usteri, Paul *ForP*
Ut, Nguyen Cong *NF*
Utley, Clifton Maxwell 1904-1978 *BioIn 5,*
Who 1974
Utley, Freda 1898-1978 *AmAu&B, BioIn 1,*
BioIn 2, BioIn 5, BioIn 8, CurBio XR,
WhoAm 1974, WhoS&SW 1973
Utley, Garrick 1939- *ConAu 69*
Utley, Henry Munson 1836-1917 *DcNAA*
Utley, William L 1814-1887 *BioIn 5*
Utter, Charles Wilbar 1917- *OvPC,*
WhoF&I 1974
Utter, George Benjamin 1881-1955 *BioIn 4,*
BioIn 6, NatCAB 46, WhJnl 1928
Uzanne, Louis Octave 1852-1931 *BbD, BiD&SB,*
WebBD
Uzzell, Thomas H 1884- *AmAu&B, WhNAA*

V

Vandenberg, Philipp 1941- *ConAu 61*
Vanderbilt, Amy 1908-1974 *AmAu&B, Au&Wr, CelR 1973, ConAu 4R, ConAu 53, CurBio XR, NewYTBS 5, WhoAm 1974, WhoAmW 1974, WhoE 1974*
Vanderbilt, Cornelius, Jr. 1898-1974 *AmAu&B, AmJnl, Au&Wr, AuNews 1, BioIn 5, BioNews 1974, ConAu 49, ConAu P-1, NewYTBS 5, WebBD, WhNAA, Who 1974, WhoAm 1974*
Vanderbilt, Sanderson 1909?-1967 *BioIn 7*
VanDerCook, Frank *AmJnl*
Vandercook, John Womack 1902-1963 *AmAu&B, BioIn 1, BioIn 6, CurBio XR, EncMys, REnAL, WebBD, WhNAA*
VanDeRepe, Abe C 1897- *WhJnl 1928*
VanDerHeuvel, Gerry Burch 1918- *BioIn 8, ForWC 1970, WhoAm 1974, WhoAmW 1974, WhoGov 1972*
VanDerHorst, Brian 1944- *ConAu 41*
VanDerLinden, Frank *NF*
VanDerLinden, Lyn *NF*
Vanderlip, Frank Arthur 1864-1937 *DcAmB S2, DcNAA, HisAmM XR, WebBD*
Vanderpoel, Robert P 1894- *BioIn 2*
Vanderschmidt, Frederick 1906-1956 *BioIn 4*
Vanderwalker, F N 1885- *WhJnl 1928*
VanDeventer, Fred 1903-1971 *BioIn 3, BioIn 9, ConAu 15, NewYTBE 2*
VanDeventer, J Hendrik 1941?- *NF*
VanDeventer, John Herbert 1881-1956 *WhJnl 1928*
Vandivier, Davis O 1903- *WhJnl 1928*
VanDoren, Carl Clinton 1885-1950 *AmAu&B, BioIn 1, BioIn 2, BioIn 4, BioIn 5, CnDAL, ConAmA, ConAmL, DcAmB S4, DcLEL, EvLB, HisAmM XR, LiJA, LongC, NatCAB 39, OxAm, REn, REnAL, TwCA, TwCA Sup, TwCW, WebBD*
VanDoren, Dorothy Graffe 1896- *AmAu&B, AmNov, ConAu 4R, ForWC 1970, HisAmM XR, REnAL, WebBD, WhoAm 1974, WhoAmW 1974*
VanDoren, Irita 1891-1966 *AmAu&B, BioIn 2, BioIn 6, BioIn 7, BioIn 8, CurBio XR, HisAmM XR, LongC, WebBD*
VanDoren, Mark 1894-1972 *AmAu&B, Au&Wr, BiE&WWA, CasWL, CnDAL, CnE&AP, ConAmA, ConAu 1, ConAu 37, ConLC 6, ConNov 1972, ConP 1970, CurBio XR, DcLEL, EvLB, HisAmM XR, LongC, ModAL, ModAL Sup, NewYTBE 3, OxAm, Pen Am, RAdv 1, REn, REnAL, SixAP, TwCA, TwCA Sup, TwCW, WebBD, WhNAA*
VanDrill, John *OvPC*
VanDusen, Bruce Buick 1930- *WhoAm 1974*
VanDusen, O L 1882- *WhJnl 1928*
VanDuzer, C D *HisAmM XR*
VanDuzer, Winifred d1951 *BioIn 2*
VanEes, Erik *NF*
Vanek, Edna *NF*
VanEvery, Edward 1878?-1952 *BioIn 2, BioIn 3*
VanEvrie, J H *HisAmM XR*
Vang, Eugene D *OvPC*
VanGelder, Robert 1904-1952 *AmAu&B, AmNov, BioIn 1, BioIn 2, REnAL*
VanGogh, Lucy *see* Sandwell, Bernard Keble
VanHafften, Madeleine *BioIn 3*
VanHamm, Caleb Marsh 1861-1919 *NF*
VanHerr, Edgar 1877- *WhJnl 1928*
VanHoek, Kees 1902-1954 *BioIn 3, CathA 1952*
VanHoesen, Walter H 1898?-1977 *ConAu 69*
VanHorn, Robert Thompson 1824-1916 *AmJnl, DcAmB 19, NatCAB 3*

VanHorne, Harriet 1920- *BioIn 3, BioIn 5, CelR 1973, CurBio XR, WhoAmW 1974*
VanKirk, Howard R 1897- *WhJnl 1928*
VanLaer, Ken *NF*
VanLaeys, L J 1887?-1950 *BioIn 2*
VanLiew, Charles Cecil 1862-1946 *BioIn 1*
VanLoan, Charles Emmet 1876-1919 *AmJnl, DcNAA, HisAmM XR, REnAL, TwCA*
VanLoan, Emory C 1884- *WhJnl 1928*
VanLoon, Hendrik Willem 1882-1944 *AmAu&B, AmRP, AnCL, AuBYP, ConAmA, ConAmL, CurBio XR, DcAmB S3, DcLEL, DcNAA, HisAmM XR, JBA 1934, LongC, NatCAB XR, OxAm, REn, REnAL, TwCA, TwCA Sup, WebBD, WhNAA*
VanMessel, Jim *NF*
VanMeter, Abraham Chenoweth 1842-1899 *BioIn 5*
VanMeter, Franc A R 1872-1942 *BioIn 5*
Vann, Jessie 1884?-1967 *BioIn 7*
Vann, Robert Lee 1887-1940 *BioIn 4, BioIn 6, BioIn 8, BioIn 9, BioIn 10, BlkC, CurBio XR*
VanNess, Fred 1884?-1959 *BioIn 5*
VanNess, Joseph 1849-1901 *NatCAB 18*
VanNorstrand, David 1811-1886 *HisAmM XR*
VanNuys, David Whitman 1940- *NF*
Vanocur, Sander 1928- *BioIn 6, BioIn 9, CurBio XR, WhoAm 1974, WhoS&SW 1973*
VanOost, John W *HisAmM XR*
VanPaassen, Pierre 1895-1968 *AmAu&B, CurBio XR, REnAL, TwCA, TwCA Sup*
VanPaassen, Pierre *see also* Paassen, Pierre Van
VanPelt, Henry *NF*
VanPelt, Sallie *NF*
VanPetten, Seward L 1901- *WhJnl 1928*
VanPrinsterer, Wilhelm Groen 1801-1876 *NF*
VanRaalte, Joseph 1880- *WhJnl 1928*
VanRensselaer, Alexander 1892-1962 *AuBYP, ConAu 73*
VanRiper, Frank Albert 1946- *ConAu 69*
VanSand, Albert 1881?-1973 *BioIn 10*
VanSchaick, John, Jr. 1873-1949 *AmAu&B, BioIn 1, BioIn 2, BioIn 3*
VanSchaick, S W *HisAmM XR*
VanSchoick, Emily C 1894- *BioIn 1*
VanSlyke, George Martin 1881-1961 *BioIn 5*
VanSmith, Howard 1910- *WhoAm 1974, WhoS&SW 1973*
VanSooy, Neal Edgar 1907- *WhoAm 1974*
VanValkenberg, Edwin Augustus 1869-1932 *AmJnl, BioIn 4, NatCAB 41*
VanVechten, Carl 1880-1964 *AmAu&B, CnDAL, ConAmA, ConAmL, CyWA, DcLEL, HisAmM XR, LongC, OxAm, Pen Am, REn, REnAL, TwCA, TwCA Sup, WebBD, WebE&AL*
VanVorst, Bessie 1873-1928 *AmAu&B, DcNAA, HisAmM XR*
VanWagoner, Lou *NF*
Vanwagoner, Robert E *OvPC*
VanWestrum, Adriaan Schade 1865-1917 *NF*
VanZandt, Lydia *WhoAm 1974*
VanZandt, Robert C *OvPC*
Vanzant, A C *NF*
VanZelm, Louis Franklin 1895-1961 *BioIn 5, BioIn 8, NatCAB 50*
Vanzi, Max *NF*
Vanzi, Victor *NF*
VanZile, Edward Sims 1863-1931 *Alli Sup, AmAu&B, AmLY, BbD, BiD&SB, DcAmA, DcNAA, HisAmM XR, WhNAA*
Varda, Agnes 1928- *CurBio XR, IntWW 1976, WhoWor 1974*
Varela, Carlos *NF*

Varenne, Alexandre Claude 1870-1947 *BioIn 1*
Vargas, Armando *NF*
Vargas Badillo, Pablo 1908-1971 *BioIn 9*
Vargas Llosa, Mario 1936- *CasWL, ConAu 73,*
ConLC 3, ConLC 6, DcCLAA, EncWL,
IntWW 1976, Pen Am, TwCW, WhoTwCL,
WhoWor 1974
Varn, William O *NF*
Varnas, Anthony J *NF*
Varney, Carleton *NF*
Varney, Harold Lord *HisAmM XR*
Vartan, Vartanig Garabed 1923- *BioIn 8,*
ConAu 61, WhoAm 1974
VasDias, A Arnold 1890-1966 *BioIn 7*
Vashedchenko, Vladimir *NF*
Vasili, Paul Comte *see* Adam, Madame
Vasili, Paul Comte *see* Adam, Juliette Lamber
Vasilyev, Vladimir V *NF*
Vasquez, Danilo *NF*
Vasquez DeAyllon, Lucas *HisAmM XR*
Vass, George 1927- *ConAu 37*
Vassiliev, Gennadi *NF*
Vathis, Paul *NF*
Vaudrin, Philip 1905?-1956 *BioIn 4*
Vaughan, Bill 1915-1977 *ConAu XR,*
WhoAm 1974, WhoMW 1974
Vaughan, Bill *see also* Vaughan, William Edward
Vaughan, Clifford 1911- *WhoAm 1974*
Vaughan, Robert 1795-1868 *Alli, BbD, BiD&SB,*
BrAu 19, DcEnL, EvLB, NewC, WebBD
Vaughan, William Edward 1915-1977 *BioIn 6,*
ConAu 5R, ConAu 69
Vaughan, William Edward *see also* Vaughan, Bill
Vaughn, Joe *NF*
Vaughn, Miles Walter 1891-1949 *BioIn 1*
Vautel, Clement 1876-1954 *BioIn 3*
Veber, Daniel 1876-1951 *BioIn 2*
Veblen, Paul *NF*
Vecsey, George 1939- *ConAu 61, SmATA 9*
Vedder, Byron Charles 1910- *WhoAm 1974*
Vedder, Henry Clay 1853-1935 *AmAu&B, AmLY,*
DcAmA, DcAmB S1, DcNAA
Veder, Slava *NF*
Veesey, George *NF*
Vega, Carlos Juan *OvPC*
Vega, Marylois Purdy *OvPC*
Veiller, Bayard 1869-1943 *AmAu&B,*
CurBio XR, DcNAA, REn, REnAL, TwCA,
TwCA Sup, WebBD
Veith, Harold B 1903- *WhJnl 1928*
Vela, David 1901- *BioIn 1, DcCLAA*
Velie, Lester 1907?- *BioIn 1, ConAu 17,*
WhoAm 1974
Vellela, Tony 1945- *ConAu 65*
Vellidis, Ioannis 1909?-1978 *NF*
Velogiannis, Costas *OvPC*
Veloz, Ruben *ForP*
Velvin, Ellen d1918 *DcNAA*
Venable, Richard Morton 1839-1910 *DcNAA,*
HisAmM XR
Venegas, Pascual *ForP*
Verbitsky, Gregorio 1910?-1978 *NF*
Verdon, Ida *HisAmM XR*
Verdumartins, Antonio 1889?-1950 *BioIn 2*
Verghese, Boobli George 1927- *IntWW 1976*
Verhaeren, Emile 1855-1916 *BbD, CasWL,*
CIDMEL, DcEuL, EncWL, EvEuW, LongC,
ModRL, ModWD, OxFr, Pen Eur, REn,
TwCA, TwCA Sup, WebBD, WhoTwCL
Verigan, Bill *NF*
Verissimo, Erico 1905- *BioIn 3, BioIn 5,*
CasWL, EncWL, Pen Am, REn, TwCW,
WebBD, WorAu
Vermeer, Al *NF*

Vermes, Hal G d1965 *AuBYP, BioIn 7*
Vermillion, Robert *NF*
Verner, Robert *NF*
Vernon, Charles Milo 1880- *WhJnl 1928*
Vernon, Grenville 1883-1941 *CathA 1930,*
CurBio XR, DcNAA
Vernon, Leroy Tudor 1878-1938 *NatCAB 28,*
WhJnl 1928
Veron, Docteur *see* Veron, Louis-Desire
Veron, Louis-Desire 1798-1867 *BioIn 7, BioIn 9,*
OxFr, WebBD
Verplanck, Gulian Crommelin 1786-1870 *Alli,*
AmAu, AmAu&B, BbD, BiD&SB, CyAL 1,
DcAmA, DcNAA, HisAmM XR, OxAm,
REnAL
Verran, William 1867- *WhJnl 1928*
Verran, William, Jr. 1894- *WhJnl 1928*
Verret, Alexandre 1914- *IntWW 1976*
Verrill, Addison Emory 1839-1926 *DcNAA,*
HisAmM XR
Vesey-FitzGerald, Brian Seymour 1900- *Au&Wr,*
BioIn 2, Br&AmS, IntWW 1974, Who 1974,
WhoWor 1974, WrDr 1976
Vesper, Will 1882-1962 *BioIn 1, CIDMEL,*
OxGer, WhoLA
Vesy, Barbara *NF*
Vetluguin, Voldemar 1897-1953 *BioIn 3*
Vette, Wilhelm 1821-1884 *BioIn 2*
Veuillot, Francis 1870-1952 *BioIn 2, BioIn 3*
Veuillot, Louis Francois 1813-1883 *WebBD*
Veysey, Arthur Ernest 1914- *WhoAm 1974,*
WhoWor 1974
Viardot, Louis 1800-1883 *BiD&SB, WebBD*
Vick, E C *HisAmM XR*
Vick, James 1818-1879 *HisAmM XR*
Vicker, Ray 1917- *ConAu 61, OvPC,*
WhoAm 1974, WhoWor 1974
Vickery, Howard F 1901?-1951 *BioIn 2,*
WhJnl 1928
Vickery, Marcia *NF*
Vickery, P O *HisAmM XR*
Vickroy, T R *HisAmM XR*
Vicky 1913-1966 *LongC*
Vicky *see also* Weisz, Victor
Victor, Metta Victoria Fuller 1831-1886 *Alli,*
Alli Sup, AmAu, AmAu&B, BiD&SB,
DcAmA, DcNAA, EncMys, HisAmM XR,
HsB&A, OhA&B, OxAm, REnAL
Victor, Orville James 1827-1910 *Alli, AmAu,*
AmAu&B, BiD&SB, DcAmA, DcNAA,
HisAmM XR, HsB&A, OhA&B, REnAL
Victor, William B *Alli, DcNAA*
Victory, Dick *NF*
Vidal, David *NF*
Vidmer, Dick *NF*
Viele, Herman Knickerbocker 1856-1908
AmAu&B, DcAmA, DcNAA, REnAL
Viereck, George Sylvester 1884-1962 *AmAu&B,*
AmLY, CasWL, CurBio XR, HisAmM XR,
OxAm, REnAL, TwCA Sup, WebBD,
WhNAA, WhJnl 1928
Vierge, Daniel 1851-1904 *WebBD*
Viernick, Peter d1926 *NF*
Vietor, Dean 1931- *NF*
Vietor, Wilhelm 1850-1918 *WebBD*
Viggiano, Nancy *NF*
Vigil, Constancio C 1876- *BioIn 4*
Vignaud, Henry 1830-1922 *AmLY, DcAmB 19*
Vigne, Paul 1859-1943 *WebBD*
Vigne D'Octon 1859-1943 *WebBD*
Vigouroux, George E 1878?-1964 *BioIn 6*
Vigouroux, Vincent J d1976 *NF*
Viguers, Ruth 1903-1971 *BioIn 8, BioIn 9*
Vikstein, Albert 1889- *BioIn 7*

VonWiegand, Karl Henry 1874-1961 *AmJnl,*
  BioIn 3, BioIn 5
Voorhees, Melvin Bernard 1904?-1977 *BioIn 3,*
  ConAu 69
Voorhies, Amos Earle *WhJnl 1928*
Vorpe, William Grant 1871-1953 *BioIn 3,*
  WhJnl 1928
Vorse, Albert White 1866-1910 *AmAu&B,*
  DcAmA, DcNAA
Vortriede, Heinrich Karl Julius 1820?-1899 *BioIn 2*
Vosburgh, Frederick George 1904- *HisAmM XR,*
  WhoAm 1974, WhoS&SW 1973
Vosburgh, William Wallace, Jr. 1900-1962 *BioIn 7,*
  NatCAB 49
Vose, Edward Neville 1870-1949 *AmAu&B,*
  AmLY
Vose, John Denison 1828-1881 *HisAmM XR,*
  HsB&A
Voss, Earl H 1922- *ConAu 9R*
Vreeland, Diana 1899?- *BioIn 6, BioIn 7,*
  BioIn 9, CelR 1973, WhoAm 1974,
  WhoAmW 1974
Vriesland, Victor Emanuel Van 1892- *CasWL,*
  IntWW 1976
Vroom, Lodewick 1884?-1950 *BioIn 2*
Vrooman, Carl 1872-1966 *AmLY, BioIn 7*
Vrooman, Frank Buffington *HisAmM XR*
Vuong, G Thuy 1938- *ConAu 69*
Vuur, W *NF*

W

Waagenaar, Sam 1908- *ConAu 57, OvPC, WrDr 1976*
Wachenhusen, Hans 1822?-1898 *BiD&SB, EvEuW, WebBD*
Wachs, Fred Bernard 1897- *WhoAm 1974, WhoF&I 1974, WhJnl 1928*
Wachs, Mark *OvPC*
Wachsman, Zvi H d1948 *BioIn 1, DcNAA*
Wack, Henry Wellington 1869-1954 *AmAu&B, BioIn 3, BioIn 10*
Wacker, Louis Henry Bud 1918- *WhoAm 1974*
Waddell, Charles Carey 1868-1930 *DcNAA, OhA&B*
Waddell, William S 1863-1952 *BioIn 3*
Waddingham, John Alfred 1915- *WhoAm 1974*
Wade, Allan 1881-1955 *BioIn 4*
Wade, Harry Vincent 1894-1973 *BioIn 1, WhJnl 1928*
Wade, Herbert Treadwell 1872-1955 *BioIn 3*
Wade, John Donald 1892-1963 *AmAu&B, HisAmM XR, WhNAA*
Wade, Nigel *NF*
Wade, Terry *NF*
Wadia, Sophia 1901- *IntWW 1976*
Wadley, Archie F *WhJnl 1928*
Wadley, James L 1855- *WhJnl 1928*
Wadley, James L, Jr. 1886- *WhJnl 1928*
Wadman, Florence 1900-1971 *BioIn 9*
Wadsworth, Alfred Powell 1891-1956 *BioIn 4*
Wadsworth, F L 1867-1936 *HisAmM XR*
Wadsworth, Harold *NF*
Wadsworth, Nelson Bingham 1930- *ConAu 65*
Waesche, James F *NF*
Waetherall, Ernest *NF*
Waffle, Arch L 1871- *WhJnl 1928*
Wager, Richard *NF*
Waggoman, R B 1895- *WhJnl 1928*
Waggoner, Clark 1820-1903 *DcNAA, NatCAB 14, OhA&B*
Waggoner, Glenn *NF*
Waggoner, J Fred *HisAmM XR*
Waggoner, Walter H *RpN*
Wagman, Robert J *NF*
Wagner, Alan Cyril 1931- *WhoAm 1974*
Wagner, Charles Abraham 1901- *AmAu&B, Au&Wr, ConAu 7R, DrAP 1975, RpN, WhNAA, WhoAm 1974, WhoWor 1974, WhoWorJ 1972, WrDr 1976*
Wagner, David F *NF*
Wagner, Fred *NF*
Wagner, Harr 1857-1936 *AmAu&B, DcNAA, HisAmM XR, WhNAA*
Wagner, Liecester 1904- *WhJnl 1928*
Wagner, Philip Marshall 1904- *IntWW 1976, WhoAm 1974*
Wagner, Richard *NF*

Wagner, Samuel 1842-1937 *HisAmM XR*
Wagner, Susan *ForWC 1970*
Wagner, Walter Frederick, Jr. 1926- *AmArch 1970, ConAu 69, WhoAm 1974*
Wagner, Wilhelm 1803?-1877 *BioIn 2*
Wagner, William *NF*
Wagnon, Hugh 1907?- *BioIn 3*
Wagoner, Clyde D d1964 *NF*
Wagoner, John L 1927- *ConAu 69*
Waha, Eric *NF*
Wahl, Richard *NF*
Wahl, William Henry 1848-1909 *Alli Sup, DcNAA, HisAmM XR*
Wahloo, Per 1926-1975 *ConAu 61, EncMys, NewYTBE 2*
Wainewright, Thomas Griffiths 1794-1852 *BrAu 19, DcLEL, OxEng, WebBD*
Wait, Thomas Baker 1762-1830 *BioIn 4, HisAmM XR*
Waite, B Franklin 1845- *WhJnl 1928*
Waite, C W *NF*
Waite, Clark F 1878- *WhJnl 1928*
Waite, Henry Randall 1845?-1909 *Alli Sup, DcAmA, DcNAA, HisAmM XR*
Waite, John L 1840- *NatCAB 16*
Waithman, Robert 1906-1956 *BioIn 4*
Wakabayashi, Jiro *NF*
Wakefield, Connie LaVon 1948- *ConAu 65*
Wakefield, Dan 1932- *AmAu&B, ConAu 21R, DrAF 1976, IndAu 1917, RpN, WhoAm 1974*
Wakefield, Robert, Jr. *NF*
Wakeman, Edgar L *HisAmM XR*
Wakeman, Thaddeus Burr 1834-1913 *DcAmA, HisAmM XR*
Wakenfield, Sherman Day 1894-1971 *BioIn 9*
Wakin, Edward 1927- *ConAu 5R, WhoE 1974*
Wakley, Thomas 1795-1862 *Alli, WebBD*
Wakley, Thomas Henry 1821-1907 *WebBD*
Wakley, Thomas 1851-1909 *WebBD*
Walbridge, Willard Eugene 1913- *WhoAm 1974, WhoF&I 1974, WhoS&SW 1973*
Walcott, Earle Ashley 1859-1931 *AmLY, DcNAA, NatCAB XR, WhNAA*
Walcott, John L 1949- *NF*
Wald, Richard C *IntMPA 1975, IntWW 1976, WhoAm 1974*
Walden, Alan *NF*
Walden, James H 1854-1942 *NatCAB 32*
Walden, John Reed d1963 *BioIn 6*
Waldman, Frank 1919- *AuBYP, BioIn 7*
Waldman, Jules Lloyd 1912- *OvPC, WhoAm 1974, WhoWor 1974*
Waldman, Lewis *AmRP*
Waldman, Milton 1895-1976 *AmAu&B, Au&Wr, ConAu 65, ConAu 69, OhA&B, Who 1974*

Waldman, Myron S *NF*
Waldmeir, Pete *NF*
Waidner, Francesco *NF*
Waldo, A Stone 1898- *WhJnl 1928*
Waldo, Fullerton Leonard 1877-1933 *AmAu&B,*
  DcNAA, OxCan, WhNAA, WhJnl 1928
Waldo, George C 1837-1921 *NatCAB 29*
Waldo, George Curtis 1888-1956 *BioIn 4*
Waldo, James E *HisAmM XR*
Waldo, Myra *ForWC 1970, OvPC*
Waldo, Richard H 1878-1943 *HisAmM XR,*
  NatCAB 32
Waldorf, John Taylor 1870-1932 *BioIn 8*
Waldron, Ann Wood 1924- *ConAu 13R,*
  WhoAm 1974
Waldron, Thomas F 1879-1953 *BioIn 3,*
  WhJnl 1928
Waldron, Webb 1882-1945 *AmAu&B, BioIn 2,*
  DcNAA, WhNAA
Waldrop, Arthur Gayle 1899- *WhJnl 1928*
Waldthausen, Peter Von 1924- *BioIn 9*
Wales, George E *HisAmM XR*
Wales, Henry C 1888-1960 *AmJnl, BioIn 5*
Wales, James Albert 1852-1886 *HisAmM XR*
Wales, Salem Howe 1825-1902 *HisAmM XR,*
  NatCAB 8
Wales, Wellington 1917?-1966 *BioIn 7, RpN*
Walesby, Stokes *NF*
Walewski, Alexandre F J, Duke De 1810-1868 *BbD,*
  BiD&SB, WebBD
Walford, L B *HisAmM XR*
Walker, Alexander Joseph 1818-1893 *AmAu&B,*
  BiD&SB, BiDSA, DcAmA, DcAmB 19,
  DcNAA, OhA&B
Walker, Andrew A, Jr. 1905- *NF*
Walker, Belle M 1869?-1953 *AmLY, BioIn 3*
Walker, C W *NF*
Walker, Charles Manning 1834-1920 *Alli,*
  Alli Sup, BioIn 2, DcAmA, DcNAA,
  IndAu 1816, OhA&B
Walker, Charles Rumford 1893-1974 *AmAu&B,*
  ConAu 17, ConAu 53, HisAmM XR,
  NewYTBS 5, WhNAA, WhoAm 1974
Walker, Clyde M *BioIn 9*
Walker, Danton MacIntyre 1899-1960 *AmAu&B,*
  BioIn 3, BioIn 5, REnAL
Walker, David Esdaile 1907-1968 *BioIn 3,*
  BioIn 8, CathA 1952
Walker, E C *HisAmM XR*
Walker, Edward Dwight 1859?-1890 *Alli Sup,*
  DcAmA, DcNAA, HisAmM XR
Walker, Edwin Anderson 1909- *HisAmM XR,*
  WhoAm 1974
Walker, Emily *NF*
Walker, Everett 1906- *OvPC, WhoAm 1974*
Walker, F B *WhoE 1974*
Walker, F D *NF*
Walker, Fred Allan 1867-1947 *AmAu&B, BioIn 1*
Walker, Gayle Courtney 1903- *WhJnl 1928*
Walker, George S 1862?-1954 *BioIn 3*
Walker, Gerald 1928- *ConAu 11R, DrAF 1976,*
  WhoE 1974
Walker, Gladys H *NF*
Walker, Gordon 1916?-1959 *BioIn 5*
Walker, Hal 1934?- *BlkC*
Walker, Harry Wilson 1859-1926 *HisAmM XR*
Walker, Helen D *HisAmM XR*
Walker, Herbert Elmer 1896- *WhJnl 1928*
Walker, Howell *HisAmM XR*
Walker, J Bernard *HisAmM XR*
Walker, J C *BioIn 1*
Walker, J Herbert 1891- *WhJnl 1928*
Walker, James 1794-1874 *Alli, Alli Sup,*
  AmAu&B, BiD&SB, DcAmA, DcNAA,

  HisAmM XR, WebBD
Walker, James C *OvPC*
Walker, Jerome Hopkins, Jr. 1904- *WhJnl 1928*
Walker, Jesse *BlkC*
Walker, John Brisben 1847-1931 *AmAu&B,*
  AmJnl, HisAmM XR, NatCAB 9, WebBD
Walker, John Hennessey 1911?-1960 *BioIn 5*
Walker, Joseph Henry 1891?-1949 *BioIn 2*
Walker, Lester A 1905- *WhJnl 1928*
Walker, Mrs. M L *HisAmM XR*
Walker, Martin *NF*
Walker, Mickey 1901- *BioIn 3, BioIn 4,*
  BioIn 5, BioIn 6, BioIn 8, BioIn 10
Walker, Mort 1923- *BioIn 2, BioIn 8,*
  ConAu 49, SmATA 8, WhoAm 1974,
  WhoAmA 1973, WhoE 1974, WhoWor 1974
Walker, P Wayne *NF*
Walker, Robert Alander 1912- *WhoAm 1974*
Walker, Robert J C *HisAmM XR*
Walker, Ronald R 1945- *NF*
Walker, Roy 1889-1939 *HisAmM XR,*
  NatCAB 30
Walker, Ryan 1870-1932 *HisAmM XR, WhNAA*
Walker, Samuel Sloan, Jr. 1926- *WhoAm 1974*
Walker, Stanley 1898-1962 *AmAu&B, BioIn 1,*
  BioIn 4, BioIn 6, CurBio XR, REnAL,
  TexWr
Walker, Susan *NF*
Walker, T Dart *HisAmM XR*
Walker, Thomas Jefferson 1877-1947 *BioIn 1*
Walker, Timothy 1802?-1856 *Alli, DcAmA,*
  DcNAA, HisAmM XR, OhA&B
Walker, Verna Widdoes 1878- *WhJnl 1928*
Walker, W D *HisAmM XR*
Walker, Walter 1883-1956 *BioIn 4*
Walker, Walter H *AmJnl*
Walker, Wareham *HisAmM XR*
Walker, William O 1896- *WhJnl 1928*
Walkley, Arthur Bingham 1855-1926 *LongC,*
  ModBL, TwCA, WebBD
Wall, Albert *OvPC*
Wall, Arthur E P *NF*
Wall, Asher *NF*
Wall, Bernard 1908- *Au&Wr, BioIn 3, BioIn 8,*
  CathA 1952
Wall, Dorothy M *NF*
Wall, Ethalmore Lamar 1894- *WhJnl 1928*
Wall, James McKendree 1928- *BioIn 9, BioIn 10,*
  WhoAm 1974, WhoAmP 1973
Wall, Marvin *RpN*
Wall, Oscar Garrett 1844-1911 *DcNAA,*
  IndAu 1917
Wall, Wendy Somerville 1942- *ConAu 49*
Wallace, Alfred Henry *HisAmM XR*
Wallace, Benjamin J *HisAmM XR*
Wallace, Bess *NF*
Wallace, Brian P *NF*
Wallace, Clarke *NF*
Wallace, Daniel Alden 1878-1954 *BioIn 3,*
  WhJnl 1928
Wallace, David 1888?-1955 *BioIn 3*
Wallace, DeWitt 1889- *AmAu&B, BioIn 1,*
  BioIn 2, BioIn 3, BioIn 4, BioIn 5, BioIn 6,
  BioIn 8, CelR 1973, CurBio XR, EncAB,
  IntWW 1976, WhoAm 1974, WhoWor 1974
Wallace, Edward Tatum 1906-1976 *ConAu 69*
Wallace, Frances Josephine 1889-1949 *BioIn 2*
Wallace, Francis 1894?-1977 *BioIn 3,*
  CathA 1952, ConAu 73, HisAmM XR,
  OhA&B
Wallace, Frank C 1867-1927 *NF*
Wallace, G David *NF*
Wallace, Grant 1867?-1954 *BioIn 3*
Wallace, Henry 1836-1916 *AmAu, AmAu&B,*

BioIn 1, BioIn 9, DcNAA, HisAmM XR,
REnAL, WebBD
Wallace, Henry Agard 1888-1965 AmAu&B,
BioIn 1, BioIn 2, BioIn 4, BioIn 5, BioIn 6,
BioIn 7, BioIn 8, BioIn 9, BioIn 10,
CurBio XR, EncAB, HisAmM XR, REnAL,
WhNAA, WhJnl 1928
Wallace, Henry Cantwell 1866-1924 BioIn 2,
BioIn 9, DcNAA, HisAmM XR
Wallace, J M Power HisAmM XR
Wallace, James N NF
Wallace, John Hankins 1822-1903 Alli Sup,
DcNAA, HisAmM XR
Wallace, John P WebBD
Wallace, John S HisAmM XR
Wallace, Kevin RpN
Wallace, Lila Bell Acheson 1889- AmAu&B,
BioIn 2, BioIn 4, BioIn 6, CanWW 1972,
CurBio XR, WhoAm 1974
Wallace, Michelle NF
Wallace, Mike 1918- BioIn 8, CelR 1973,
ConAu 65, CurBio XR, ForP, IntMPA 1975,
InvJ, WhoAm 1974, WhoE 1974,
WhoWorJ 1972
Wallace, Patrick NF
Wallace, Ray HisAmM XR
Wallace, Robert BioIn 6
Wallace, T C HisAmM XR
Wallace, Tom 1874-1961 BioIn 1, BioIn 2,
BioIn 5, BioIn 6, WhNAA, WhJnl 1928
Wallace, Walter W HisAmM XR
Wallace, Weldon 1912- WhoAm 1974
Wallace, William 1842-1891 HisAmM XR
Wallace, William N 1924- ConAu 15R
Wallace, William Stewart 1884-1970 DcLEL,
OxCan, WebBD, WhNAA
Wallach, Allan NF
Wallach, Edgar 1884?-1953 BioIn 3
Wallach, John P NF
Wallach, Rita Teresa HisAmM XR
Wallach, Sidney 1905- WhoAm 1974,
WhJnl 1928, WhoWorJ 1972
Wallack, W D NF
Wallenberg, Ernst 1879?-1948 BioIn 1
Waller, Helen 1913-1961 BioIn 6
Waller, Leslie 1923- AmAu&B, AmNov,
Au&Wr, ConAu 1
Wallgren, Abian Anders 1891?-1948 BioIn 1
Walling, Charles S WhJnl 1928
Walling, Robert Alfred John 1869-1949 BioIn 2,
BioIn 4, EncMys, LongC, NewC, TwCA,
TwCA Sup
Walling, William English 1877-1936 AmRP,
DcNAA, WebBD
Wallington, Nellie 1847-1933 DcNAA
Wallis, James Harold 1885-1958 BioIn 4
Wallis, Mary NF
Wallis, Severn Teackle 1816-1894 Alli, BiDSA,
DcAmA, DcNAA
Wallop, John Douglass, III 1920- AmAu&B,
ConAu 73, WhoAm 1974
Wallraff, Gunter NF
Walls, Arthur H 1894- WhJnl 1928
Walls, Carmage 1908- WhoAm 1974,
WhoS&SW 1973
Walmsley, Dorothy Hamilton 1894?-1968 BioIn 8
Waln, Nora 1895-1964 AmAu&B, BioIn 7,
CurBio XR, LongC, REnAL, TwCA,
TwCA Sup
Walpole, N H HisAmM XR
Walser, Frank Henry 1875-1957 BioIn 6
Walser, Frank Henry see also Walser, Henry
Walser, Henry 1875-1957 NatCAB 43
Walser, Henry see also Walser, Frank Henry

Walsh, Anna NF
Walsh, Christy 1891?-1955 BioIn 4, WhJnl 1928
Walsh, David C NF
Walsh, Denny Jay 1935- InvJ, NewMr,
WhoAm 1974
Walsh, Edward NewMr
Walsh, Francis, Jr. HisAmM XR
Walsh, George William 1931- WhoAm 1974
Walsh, Henry Collins 1863-1927, AmAu&B,
DcAmA, DcNAA, HisAmM XR, PoIre,
WebBD
Walsh, John K 1886- WhJnl 1928
Walsh, John Raymond 1901- BioIn 1, CurBio XR
Walsh, John Tomline 1816-1886 Alli Sup, BioIn 1
Walsh, Karin J 1914-1965 BioIn 7
Walsh, Patrick Walter 1891- WhJnl 1928
Walsh, Perry J 1901- WhJnl 1928
Walsh, Richard John 1886-1960 AmAu&B,
AuBYP, HisAmM XR
Walsh, Robert 1784-1859 Alli, AmAu,
AmAu&B, AmJnl, BiD&SB, BiDSA,
CyAL 1, DcAmA, DcAmB 19, DcNAA,
HisAmM XR, LiJA, OxAm, REnAL,
WebBD
Walsh, Robert Kevin 1903- BioIn 2
Walsh, Rodolfo d1977 NF
Walsh, Taylor 1947- ConAu 73
Walsh, Thomas 1875?-1928 AmAu&B, AmLY,
AnMV 1926, DcNAA, WhNAA
Walsh, Timothy 1876- WhJnl 1928
Walsh, Travis Walter 1924- WhoAm 1974
Walsh, William Shepard 1854-1919 Alli Sup,
AmAu&B, BbD, BiD&SB, DcAmA,
DcNAA, HisAmM XR
Walsh, William Shepherd HisAmM XR
Waltari, Mika 1908- ConAu 11R, CurBio XR,
IntWW 1976, Who 1974, WhoWor 1974
Walte, Juan Jorge 1940- NF
Walter, A F Paul, Jr. 1901- WhJnl 1928
Walter, Arthur Fraser 1846-1910 WebBD
Walter, Cornelia W Alli, AmJnl
Walter, Ellery 1906-1935 AmAu&B, DcNAA
Walter, Eugene 1874-1941 AmAu&B, CnDAL,
CurBio XR, DcNAA, McGWD, ModWD,
OhA&B, OxAm, REn, REnAL, WebBD
Walter, Eugene 1927- ConAu 11R
Walter, John 1739-1812 Alli, DcEnL, DcEuL,
ForP, REn, WebBD
Walter, John, II 1776-1847 WebBD
Walter, John, III 1818-1894 ForP, WebBD
Walter, John, IV 1873-1968 WebBD
Walter, Lynde M d1842 AmJnl
Walter, Martin Emmet 1894-1966 BioIn 9,
WhJnl 1928
Walter, Paul Alfred Francis 1873- AmAu&B,
WhNAA, WhJnl 1928
Walter, Ray G 1894- WhJnl 1928
Walters, Barbara 1931- AuNews 2, BioIn 7,
BioIn 8, BioIn 9, BioIn 10, BioNews 1974,
CelR 1973, ConAu 65, CurBio XR,
ForWC 1970, NewYTBE 3, WhoAm 1974,
WhoAmW 1974
Walters, Basil Leon 1896-1975 AmJnl, BioIn 3,
BioIn 4, BioIn 5, IntWW 1974,
WhoAm 1974
Walters, James E NF
Walters, John Beauchamp 1906- Au&Wr,
ConAu 7R, WrDr 1976
Walters, John Sherwood 1917- WhoAm 1974,
WhoS&SW 1973
Walters, Raymond, Jr. 1912- AmAu&B,
DrAS 74H, WhoAm 1974
Walters, Robert Mark 1938- ConAu 69, InvJ
Walthers, Bruce 1944- BioIn 10

Waltman, Franklyn, Jr. *NF*
Walton, Dale *NF*
Walton, Diane 1929?-1978 *NF*
Walton, Eliakim P 1812-1890 *NatCAB 20*
Walton, Ezekiel P 1789-1855 *NatCAB 16*
Walton, Francis *HisAmM XR*
Walton, Joseph 1817-1898 *HisAmM XR,*
  OhA&B
Walton, Lester Aglar 1882-1965 *BioIn 4, BioIn 7*
Walton, Leycester H *ForP*
Walton, Perry *NF*
Walton, W Robert 1902- *ConAu 69*
Walton, William 1909- *BioIn 5, BioIn 6,*
  WhoAm 1974, WhoGov 1972
Waltz, Elizabeth Cherry 1866-1903 *AmAu&B,*
  BiDSA, DcAmA, DcNAA, OhA&B
Waltz, Jean Jacques 1873-1951 *BioIn 2*
Walworth, John 1804-1895 *BioIn 5*
Walworth, Theodore Holton, Jr. 1924-
  WhoAm 1974
Walz, Jay 1907- *AmAu&B, ConAu 49,*
  IndAu 1917, WhoAm 1974
Wamsley, Janes S *NF*
Wanamaker, Thomas B 1861-1908 *AmJnl*
Wandel, Paul 1905- *IntWW 1976, WhoWor 1974*
Wanders, George 1895?-1961 *BioIn 5*
Wang, Brice S Y *NF*
Wang, Shou-Tao 1907- *IntWW 1976*
Wang, T'ao 1828-1897 *BioIn 8*
Wannamaker, William Hane 1873-1918
  HisAmM XR
Warburton, Barclay Harding 1866-1954 *BioIn 3*
Warburton, Charles E 1836-1896 *NatCAB 11*
Ward, Arch Burdette 1896-1955 *BioIn 1, BioIn 2,*
  BioIn 3, BioIn 4, DcAmB S5
Ward, Artemus 1834-1867 *Alli, AmAu,*
  AmAu&B, AmJnl, BiD&SB, CasWL,
  CnDAL, DcAmA, DcEnA Ap, DcEnL,
  DcLEL, DcNAA, EvLB, HisAmM XR,
  LiJA, OhA&B, OxAm, OxEng, Pen Am,
  REn, REnAL, WebBD, WebE&AL
Ward, Artemus see also Browne, Charles Farrar
Ward, Barbara 1914- *AmM&W 73S,*
  CathA 1930, ConAu 45, CurBio XR,
  IntWW 1976, TwCA Sup, WebBD,
  Who 1974, WhoAm 1974, WhoAmW 1974,
  WhoWor 1974
Ward, Betty Penson *NF*
Ward, C J *HisAmM XR*
Ward, Carl Small 1915- *WhoAm 1974*
Ward, Christopher Longstreet 1807-1870 *NF*
Ward, Clayton I 1885- *WhJnl 1928*
Ward, Edward Henry Harold 1905- *BioIn 1*
Ward, Fanny B *AmJnl*
Ward, Frank B 1885- *WhJnl 1928*
Ward, Fred H 1896- *WhJnl 1928*
Ward, Frederick William 1847-1934 *BioIn 2*
Ward, Grace M 1886- *WhJnl 1928*
Ward, Hiley Henry 1929- *Au&Wr, ConAu 2R,*
  IndAu 1917, WhoAm 1974, WhoMW 1974
Ward, James Myron 1919- *WhoAm 1974,*
  WhoS&SW 1973
Ward, Jonathan *NF*
Ward, Josiah M *NF*
Ward, Julius Hammond 1837-1897 *Alli, DcAmA,*
  DcNAA, HisAmM XR, LiJA
Ward, Kirk *HisAmM XR*
Ward, Lauriston *HisAmM XR*
Ward, Sir Leslie 1851-1922 *BioIn 8, LongC,*
  WebBD
Ward, Lester Frank 1841-1913 *Alli Sup, AmAu,*
  AmRP, DcAmA, DcNAA, HisAmM XR,
  OxAm, REnAL
Ward, Loren T 1893- *WhJnl 1928*

Ward, Maisie 1889-1975 *Au&Wr, BkC 4,*
  CathA 1930, ConAu 69, CurBio XR,
  NewYTBE 3
Ward, Norman 1918- *AmM&W 73S,*
  CanWW 1972, ConAu 41, OxCan Sup,
  WhoAm 1974, WrDr 1976
Ward, Paul W 1905-1976 *BioIn 2, ConAu 69,*
  WhoAm 1974
Ward, Peter *NF*
Ward, Russ *NF*
Ward, Ted *NF*
Ward, Ulysses *NF*
Ward, Wilfrid Philip 1856-1916 *Alli Sup, BioIn 2,*
  REn, TwCA, TwCA Sup, WebBD
Ward, William Gates 1929- *ConAu 21R,*
  WhoMW 1974
Ward, William George 1812-1882 *Alli, Alli Sup,*
  BrAu 19, DcEuL, DcLEL, EvLB, OxEng,
  WebBD
Ward, William Hayes 1835-1916 *AmAu&B,*
  BiD&SB, DcAmA, DcNAA, HisAmM XR,
  REnAL, WebBD
Ward, William J *NF*
Wardall, John *NF*
Warde, William F 1905- *AmRP, ConAu 49*
Warde, William F see also Novack, George
Wardell, John M 1895?-1978 *NF*
Wardell, Robert 1794-1834 *BioIn 2*
Warden, Albert Forman 1896- *BioIn 1,*
  WhJnl 1928
Warden, Oliver Sherman 1865-1951 *BioIn 2*
Warden, William *AmJnl*
Warder, Charles *NF*
Wardlaw, Frank Harper, Jr. 1913- *WhoAm 1974*
Wardle, Irving 1929- *WhoThe 1972*
Wardlow, Elwood M 1924- *WhoAm 1974*
Wardman, Ervin 1865-1923 *AmJnl, DcAmB 19,*
  DcNAA
Wardrop, G Douglas 1890- *WhJnl 1928*
Wardroper, John 1923- *ConAu 29*
Ware, Ashur 1782-1873 *Alli, WebBD*
Ware, Henry, Jr. 1794-1843 *Alli, AmAu,*
  AmAu&B, BiD&SB, CyAL 1, DcAmA,
  DcNAA, HisAmM XR, REnAL, WebBD
Ware, John 1795-1864 *Alli, CyAL 1, DcAmA,*
  DcNAA, HisAmM XR, REnAL, WebBD
Ware, Katherine Augusta 1797-1843 *Alli, DcAmA*
Ware, Leonard 1900-1976 *ConAu 69*
Ware, William Robert 1832-1915 *Alli Sup,*
  DcAmA, DcNAA, HisAmM XR, WebBD
Waren, Helen *BioIn 3*
Warfield, Benjamin Breckinridge 1851-1921
  Alli Sup, AmLY, BiDSA, DcAmA, DcNAA,
  HisAmM XR
Warfield, C Dorsey 1898-1947 *BioIn 1*
Warfield, Francis 1901- *WhJnl 1928*
Warfield, Mrs. Walter Wilson *WhJnl 1928*
Warhol, Andy 1931?- *AmAu&B, CelR 1973,*
  CurBio XR, DcCAA, IntWW 1974, WebBD,
  WhoAm 1974, WhoAmA 1973,
  WhoWor 1974
Waring, Houstoun *BioIn 2, RpN*
Waring, Thomas Richard 1907- *BioIn 5,*
  WhoAm 1974, WhoS&SW 1973
Wariship, Albert E 1845- *WhJnl Sup*
Wark, Tom *NF*
Warman, Cy 1855-1914 *AmAu, AmAu&B,*
  BiD&SB, DcAmA, DcAmB 19, DcNAA,
  HisAmM XR, REnAL, WebBD
Warn, W Axel 1867?-1947 *BioIn 1*
Warne, Colston Estey 1900- *AmM&W 73S,*
  HisAmM XR, NewYTBE 1, WhoAm 1974
Warne, William Elmo 1905- *AmM&W 73S,*
  ConAu 41, CurBio XR, IndAu 1917,

WhoAm 1974, WhoWest 1974
Warnecke, William F *AmJnl*
Warner, Charles Dudley 1829-1900 *Alli Sup,*
AmAu, AmAu&B, AmJnl, BbD, BiD&SB,
CasWL, CnDAL, CyAL 2, DcAmA, DcBiA,
DcEnA Ap, DcEnL, DcLEL, DcNAA,
HisAmM XR, OxAm, OxCan, Pen Am,
REn, REnAL, WebBD
Warner, Dean G 1891- *WhJnl 1928*
Warner, Denis Ashton 1917- *ConAu 5R, RpN,*
WhoWor 1974
Warner, Eltinge F 1880-1965 *HisAmM XR*
Warner, Francis Lester *HisAmM XR*
Warner, H J *HisAmM XR*
Warner, Henry Edward 1876-1941 *AmAu&B,*
DcNAA, OhA&B
Warner, Kenneth B 1894-1948 *NatCAB 37*
Warner, Kenneth Wilson, Jr. 1928- *ConAu 65*
Warner, William Bishop 1874-1946 *HisAmM XR*
Warnes, Carlos 1905?- *BioIn 5*
Warnock, Thomas H 1863- *BioIn 2*
Warren, A W *HisAmM XR*
Warren, Arthur 1860-1924 *AmAu&B, DcAmA,*
DcNAA
Warren, Austin 1899- *AmAu&B, ConAu 19,*
REnAL, TwCA Sup, WhoAm 1974
Warren, Billy *see* Warren, William Stephen
Warren, Burtt E 1874-1950 *NatCAB 40*
Warren, David M *WhJnl 1928*
Warren, Dorothy 1914?- *BioIn 1*
Warren, Doug 1935- *ConAu 61*
Warren, Elizabeth *NF*
Warren, Fitz Henry 1816-1878 *AmJnl, BioIn 7*
Warren, Forrest 1878?-1949 *BioIn 2*
Warren, Fred A *AmRP*
Warren, Fred D 1872-1959 *HisAmM XR*
Warren, Frederick B 1884?-1950 *BioIn 2*
Warren, George C *WhJnl 1928*
Warren, Gerald Lee 1930- *WhoAm 1974,*
WhoGov 1972, WhoS&SW 1973
Warren, Ina Russelle *AmAu&B*
Warren, Ina Russelle 1887?-1951 *BioIn 2*
Warren, J L L F *HisAmM XR*
Warren, James D 1823-1886 *NatCAB 27*
Warren, L D 1906- *WhoAm 1974,*
WhoAmA 1973
Warren, L E *NF*
Warren, Lucian Crissey 1913- *WhoAm 1974*
Warren, Maude Radford 1875-1934 *AmAu&B*
Warren, O G *Alli, HisAmM XR*
Warren, Orris H 1835- *NatCAB 3*
Warren, Richard Kearney 1920- *WhoAm 1974,*
WhoF&I 1974
Warren, Robert Penn 1905- *AmAu&B, AmNov,*
AmWr, Au&Wr, AuNews 1, CasWL,
CnDAL, CnE&AP, CnMD, ConAmA,
ConAu 13, ConLC 1, ConLC 4, ConLC 6,
ConNov 1972, ConNov 1976, ConP 1970,
ConP 1975, CurBio XR, CyWA, DcLEL,
DrAF 1976, DrAP 1975, EncWL, EvLB,
HisAmM XR, IntWW 1974, LongC,
ModAL, ModAL Sup, ModWD, OxAm,
Pen Am, RAdv 1, RComWL, REn, REnAL,
SixAP, TwCA, TwCA Sup, WebBD,
WebE&AL, WhNAA, Who 1974,
WhoAm 1974, WhoTwCL, WhoWor 1974,
WrDr 1976
Warren, Ross *NF*
Warren, William C 1859-1935 *NatCAB 27*
Warren, William Stephen 1882-1968 *AuBYP,*
BioIn 7, ConAu 21, SmATA 9
Warron, Clarence Walker 1855- *WhJnl 1928*
Warshaw, Jules J 1926- *WhoAm 1974*
Warshofsky, Fred 1931- *ConAu 11R,*

WhoE 1974
Warshow, Henry Wayne *OvPC*
Warshow, Robert S 1917-1955 *BioIn 3, BioIn 5*
Warwick, Charles Earl 1890- *WhJnl 1928*
Washburn, Alex Henry 1899- *WhJnl 1928*
Washburn, Charles Ames 1822-1889 *Alli Sup,*
AmAu&B, BiD&SB, DcAmA, DcNAA
Washburn, Edward Abiel 1819-1881 *Alli Sup,*
AmAu&B, DcAmA, DcNAA, HisAmM XR
Washburn, Harold Connett 1885?-1952 *BioIn 2*
Washburn, L K *HisAmM XR*
Washburn, Robert Morris 1868-1946 *AmAu&B,*
BioIn 1, DcNAA
Washburn, Stanley 1878-1950 *AmAu&B, BioIn 2,*
BioIn 6, NatCAB 43, WebBD, WhNAA
Washburne, George R 1860-1923 *NatCAB 40*
Washburne, Walter Avery 1876- *WhJnl 1928*
Washington, Betty *BlkC*
Wason, Betty 1912- *ConAu XR, CurBio XR,*
OvPC
Wason, Eugene *Lor&LP*
Wasserman, John 1938- *NF*
Wassersug, Joseph D 1912- *AuBYP, BioIn 7,*
ConAu 19, WhoWorJ 1972
Wasson, Robert Gordon 1898- *AmAu&B,*
WhJnl 1928
Wasson, William Dixon 1871-1962 *BioIn 8,*
NatCAB 50
Watai, Hiromi *NF*
Water, B *NF*
Waterbury, Edwin Morey 1884- *WhJnl 1928*
Waterbury, I Roy 1869- *WhJnl 1928*
Waterfield, Gordon 1903- *Au&Wr, ConAu 61,*
WrDr 1976
Waterfield, Lina 1874?- *BioIn 6, WhoLA*
Waterloo, Stanley 1846-1913 *Alli Sup, AmAu&B,*
BiD&SB, DcAmA, DcNAA
Waters, Arthur B 1896- *WhJnl 1928*
Waters, Arthur George 1888-1953 *BioIn 3*
Waters, Donald C *NF*
Waters, Frank Henry 1908-1954 *BioIn 3*
Waters, Harry F *NF*
Waters, Henry Jackson 1900- *WhJnl 1928*
Waters, Mark 1909-1966 *BioIn 7*
Waters, Mary-Alice 1942- *ConAu 61*
Waters, Michael J *NF*
Waters, Robert *NF*
Waters, Thomas F *NF*
Waters, William *NF*
Watkins, Ernest Shilston 1902- *BioIn 2,*
CanWW 1972
Watkins, George T *NF*
Watkins, John Chester Anderson 1912- *OvPC,*
WhoAm 1974, WhoE 1974
Watkins, John Elfreth 1875-1946 *AmAu&B,*
AmLY, WhNAA
Watkins, Mel *BlkC*
Watkins, Paul Ferguson 1895-1951 *BioIn 5,*
NatCAB 42, WhJnl 1928
Watkins, Roger *NF*
Watkins, Stephen Edward 1922- *WhoAm 1974*
Watkins, Tobias 1780-1855 *Alli, AmAu&B,*
BiDSA, DcNAA, HisAmM XR, REnAL
Watkins, William Turner 1895-1961 *BioIn 1,*
BioIn 5
Watling, Cyril *BioIn 7*
Waton, Harry *AmRP*
Watrous, A E *HisAmM XR*
Watrous, Jerome Anthony 1840-1922 *BioIn 5,*
DcNAA
Watrous, Louis E 1871-1962 *BioIn 6*
Watson, Alfred Edward Thomas 1849-1922
Alli Sup, BioIn 2, Br&AmS
Watson, Billy 1938- *NF*

Watson, Catherine Elaine 1944- *ForWC 1970,*
  WhoAm 1974, WhoAmW 1974
Watson, Charles Campbell 1900- *BioIn 9*
Watson, Dawson *HisAmM XR*
Watson, Douglas *NF*
Watson, E Y 1879?-1949 *NF*
Watson, Edmund Henry Lacon 1865-1948 *WebBD,*
  WhoLA
Watson, Egbert Pomeroy *Alli Sup, DcNAA,*
  HisAmM XR
Watson, Elizabeth *HisAmM XR*
Watson, Elmo Scott 1892-1951 *BioIn 2,*
  HisAmM XR, WhJnl 1928
Watson, Ernest William 1884-1969 *AmAu&B,*
  BioIn 8, BioIn 10, ConAu 5, ConAu 7R
Watson, Forbes 1880-1960 *NF*
Watson, George 1936- *OvPC*
Watson, Gloria *OvPC*
Watson, Harry Legare 1876- *WhJnl 1928*
Watson, Henry Brereton Marriott 1863-1921
  HisAmM XR, WebBD
Watson, Henry Clay 1831-1869 *Alli, AmAu&B,*
  BbD, BiD&SB, BiDSA, CarSB, DcAmA,
  DcNAA, HisAmM XR
Watson, Henry Cood 1818-1875 *AmAu&B,*
  HisAmM XR
Watson, J F *HisAmM XR*
Watson, James Murray 1888-1955 *BioIn 4*
Watson, James Sibley, Jr. 1894- *HisAmM XR,*
  WhoAm 1974
Watson, James V 1814-1856 *Alli, DcNAA,*
  HisAmM XR
Watson, Jane 1915- *BioIn 9*
Watson, Jerome R 1938- *InvJ*
Watson, John Fanning 1779-1860 *Alli, AmAu&B,*
  CyAL 1, DcAmA, DcNAA, WebBD
Watson, Joseph *NF*
Watson, Joseph H 1862- *WhJnl 1928*
Watson, Mark Skinner 1887-1966 *BioIn 1,*
  BioIn 2, BioIn 7, CurBio XR, WhJnl 1928
Watson, Morris 1901?-1972 *AmJnl, NewYTBE 3*
Watson, Murray *Lor&LP*
Watson, Russell 1939- *NF*
Watson, Stephen Marion *HisAmM XR*
Watson, Thomas C *NF*
Watson, Thomas Edward 1856-1922 *AmAu&B,*
  BiDSA, DcAmA, DcNAA, HisAmM XR,
  WebBD
Watson, Victor *NF*
Watson, W W *WhJnl 1928*
Watson, Warren *HisAmM XR*
Watson, William *HisAmM XR*
Watson, William Perry *HisAmM XR*
Watt, A P *OvPC*
Watt, David Laird *NF*
Watt, Douglas Benjamin 1914- *AmSCAP 1966,*
  ConAu 69, WhoAm 1974, WhoE 1974
Watt, J Millar *NF*
Wattenberg, Ben J 1933- *BioIn 8, ConAu 57*
Watters, James *HisAmM XR*
Watters, Pat 1927- *ConAu 23R*
Watters, Susan *NF*
Watterson, Harvey M 1811-1891 *NatCAB 1*
Watterson, Helen *AmJnl*
Watterson, Henry 1840-1921 *Alli Sup, AmAu&B,*
  AmJnl, BbD, BiD&SB, BiDSA, BioIn 2,
  BioIn 3, BioIn 4, BioIn 5, BioIn 9,
  BioIn 10, DcAmA, DcNAA, ForP,
  HisAmM XR, OxAm, REnAL, WebBD
Watterson, Joseph 1900-1972 *AmArch 1970,*
  BioIn 9, ConAu 25, ConAu 33,
  WhoAm 1974
Watterston, George 1783-1854 *Alli, AmAu&B,*
  DcNAA, REnAL

Wattles, John D *HisAmM XR*
Watts, Alaric Alexander 1797-1864 *Alli, BiD&SB,*
  BioIn 10, BrAu 19, CasWL, DcEnL, EvLB,
  NewC, WebBD
Watts, Daniel *NF*
Watts, Harvey Maitland 1864-1939 *DcNAA*
Watts, John T *NF*
Watts, Mary 1868- *NF*
Watts, Reginald *NF*
Watts, Richard, Jr. 1898- *AmAu&B,*
  BiE&WWA, WhoE 1974, WhoThe 1972
Watts, Roderick John 1904-1959 *BioIn 5*
Watts, Sarah Miles 1934- *ConAu 65*
Watts, Stephen 1910- *Au&Wr, ConAu 7R,*
  WhoThe 1972
Waud, Alfred R 1828-1891 *EarABI, EarABI Sup,*
  HisAmM XR
Waud, William d1878 *EarABI, EarABI Sup,*
  HisAmM XR
Waugh, Arthur 1866-1943 *Alli Sup,*
  HisAmM XR, LongC, TwCA,
  TwCA Sup, WebBD, WhoLA
Waugh, Auberon 1939- *Au&Wr, ConAu 45,*
  ConNov 1972, ConNov 1976, WrDr 1976
Waugh, Coulton 1896-1973 *BioIn 9, ConAu 41,*
  NewYTBE 4, WhoAmA 1973
Waugh, William W *HisAmM XR*
Wax, Melvin S *RpN*
Wax, Sheldon *NF*
Waxman, Chaim I *NF*
Waxman, Percy 1885-1948 *AmAu&B, BioIn 1,*
  DcNAA
Way, Norman *see* Norton, Roy
Wayland, Heman Lincoln 1830-1898 *Alli,*
  DcAmA, DcNAA, NatCAB 10
Wayland, Julius Augustus 1854-1912 *AmRP,*
  BioIn 2, DcNAA, HisAmM XR,
  IndAu 1917
Waymack, William Wesley 1888-1960 *BioIn 1,*
  BioIn 5, BioIn 6, CurBio XR
Wayman, Dorothy G 1893-1975 *AmAu&B,*
  BioIn 1, BioIn 3, CathA 1952, ConAu 61,
  ConAu 65, WhNAA, WhoAm 1974,
  WhoAmW 1974
Wayne, Donald 1913- *WhoAm 1974,*
  WhoWor 1974
Wayne, Frances *BioIn 1*
Wayne, Hamilton *HisAmM XR*
Waynick, Capus Miller 1889- *BioIn 2*
Ways, Max 1905- *WhoAm 1974*
Weadock, John Francis 1899- *WhJnl 1928*
Wear, James Smith 1914- *WhoAm 1974*
Weatherby, George W *HisAmM XR*
Weathercock, Janus *see* Wainewright, Thomas
  Griffiths
Weathers, Lee Beam 1886-1958 *BioIn 7,*
  NatCAB 48
Weaver, Audrey *NF*
Weaver, Ben J 1900?-1949 *BioIn 1*
Weaver, Denis *NF*
Weaver, Donald Emerson 1900- *WhJnl 1928*
Weaver, Earle W 1892- *WhJnl 1928*
Weaver, Harriet Shaw 1876-1961 *AmAu&B,*
  LongC
Weaver, Howard R *WhJnl 1928*
Weaver, Joe *NF*
Weaver, John Van Alstyn 1893-1938 *AmAu&B,*
  BioIn 3, CnDAL, ConAmL, DcNAA,
  HisAmM XR, OxAm, REn, REnAL,
  TwCA, WebBD
Weaver, Peter *NF*
Weaver, Richard M *HisAmM XR*
Weaver, Sylvester L, Jr. 1908- *AmJnl,*
  CurBio XR, IntMPA 1975

Weaver, Vic G 1901- *WhJnl 1928*
Weaver, Warren, Jr. 1923- *AmAu&B, ConAu 41, WhoAm 1974*
Weaver, William Dixon 1857-1919 *HisAmM XR*
Webb, Alfred *Alli Sup, HisAmM XR*
Webb, Alvin B *NF*
Webb, Arthur 1888?-1973 *BioIn 9*
Webb, Beatrice 1858-1943 *CurBio XR, DcLEL, EvLB, LongC, NewC, OxEng, TwCA, TwCA Sup, WebBD*
Webb, Benedict Joseph 1814-1897 *Alli Sup, DcNAA*
Webb, Catherine 1942?- *BioIn 9*
Webb, Charles Aurelius 1866-1949 *BioIn 2*
Webb, Charles Henry 1834-1905 *Alli, Alli Sup, AmAu, AmAu&B, AmJnl, BbD, BiD&SB, DcAmA, DcNAA, HisAmM XR, OxAm, REnAL, WebBD*
Webb, Duncan Thomas 1917- *BioIn 3*
Webb, Frank D 1897-1964 *NF*
Webb, George James 1803-1887 *Alli, DcNAA, HisAmM XR*
Webb, James Watson 1802-1884 *Alli, AmAu, AmAu&B, AmJnl, BiD&SB, BioIn 4, BioIn 8, DcAmA, DcAmB 19, DcNAA, HisAmM XR, NatCAB 3, REnAL, WebBD*
Webb, Kaye 1914- *Au&Wr, BioIn 9*
Webb, Maurice 1904-1956 *CurBio XR*
Webb, Mohammed Alex Russell *HisAmM XR*
Webb, Peter *NF*
Webb, Sam W, Jr. 1892- *WhJnl 1928*
Webb, Sidney James, Baron Passfield 1859-1947 *BbD, BiD&SB, DcLEL, EvLB, HisAmM XR, LongC, NewC, OxEng, TwCA, TwCA Sup, WebBD*
Webb, Thomas H *NF*
Webb, Wendell *NF*
Webbe, John *HisAmM XR*
Webber, Charles Wilkins 1819-1856 *Alli, AmAu, AmAu&B, BiDSA, CyAL 2, DcAmA, DcAmB 19, DcLEL, DcNAA, HisAmM XR, OxAm, REnAL*
Webber, Sir Robert John 1884-1962 *BioIn 6*
Weber, Arthur 1926- *WhoAm 1974*
Weber, Bob *NF*
Weber, Charles *HisAmM XR*
Weber, Karl *ForP*
Weber, Robert *NF*
Weber, Tommy *BioIn 8, OvPC*
Weber, Wolfgang 1902- *BioIn 10*
Weberman, Ben 1923- *NF*
Webster, C W 1896- *WhJnl Sup*
Webster, David *HisAmM XR*
Webster, Don *NF*
Webster, E B 1867- *WhJnl 1928*
Webster, Frank B *HisAmM XR*
Webster, Frank W 1892- *WhJnl 1928*
Webster, Franklin *HisAmM XR*
Webster, H Effa *NF*
Webster, Harold Tucker 1885-1952 *AmAu&B, AmJnl, BioIn 1, BioIn 2, BioIn 3, BioIn 5, CurBio XR, DcAmB S5, REnAL*
Webster, John White 1793-1850 *Alli, DcAmA, DcNAA, HisAmM XR*
Webster, Maurie 1916- *WhoAm 1974*
Webster, Noah 1758-1843 *Alli, AmAu, AmAu&B, BbD, BiD&SB, CasWL, CnDAL, CyAL 1, DcAmA, DcEnL, DcLEL, DcNAA, EvLB, ForP, HisAmM XR, MouLC 3, NatCAB 2, OxAm, OxEng, Pen Am, REn, REnAL, WebBD, WebE&AL*
Webster, R Howard 1909?- *BioIn 3*
Webster, Ray Archibald 1888?- *BioIn 3*

Webster, Tom 1890-1962 *BioIn 6, ForP*
Wechsberg, Joseph 1907- *AmAu&B, Au&Wr, BioIn 2, BioIn 3, BioIn 4, BioIn 9, CurBio XR, OxAm, REnAL, WhoAm 1974, WhoMus 1972, WhoWor 1974*
Wechsler, James Arthur 1915- *AmAu&B, AmRP, BioIn 1, BioIn 3, BioIn 6, BioIn 9, BioIn 10, IntWW 1976, WhoE 1974, WhoWor 1974, WhoWorJ 1972*
Weck, Phil *NF*
Wecksler, Sally *ForWC 1970, OvPC*
Wedda, John A 1886- *WhJnl 1928*
Wedekind, Franz *HisAmM XR*
Wedel, Mildred Mott *HisAmM XR*
Wedemar, Lou *NF*
Wedge, Will 1889?-1951 *BioIn 2*
Wedman, Les *NF*
Weed, Clarence Moores 1864-1947 *AmAu&B, DcAmA, DcNAA, HisAmM XR, OhA&B*
Weed, Clive 1884-1936 *NatCAB 27*
Weed, Thurlow 1797-1882 *Alli, Alli Sup, AmAu&B, AmJnl, BbD, BiD&SB, BioIn 8, BioIn 9, DcAmA, DcAmB 19, DcNAA, EncAB, HisAmM XR, NatCAB 3, REnAL, WebBD*
Weegar, Edwin Alexander, Jr. 1921- *WhoAm 1974, WhoWest 1974*
Weegar, Tom *NF*
Weegee *see* Fellig, Arthur
Weeghman, Richard B 1928- *NF*
Weekes, Hobart Godfrey 1901?-1978 *OvPC*
Weekes, W A *NF*
Weekley, John Martin 1872- *WhJnl 1928*
Weeks, Albert Loren 1888-1963 *WhJnl 1928*
Weeks, Edward Augustus, Jr. 1898- *AmAu&B, Au&Wr, BioIn 1, BioIn 2, BioIn 3, BioIn 4, BioIn 5, BioIn 10, CurBio XR, HisAmM XR, IntWW 1976, RAdv 1, REnAL, TwCA, TwCA Sup, Who 1974, WhoAm 1974*
Weeks, Jack 1907?-1971 *BioIn 9, NewYTBE 2*
Weeks, John Miran 1919?-1950 *BioIn 2*
Weeks, Joseph Dame 1840-1896 *Alli Sup, DcAmB 19, DcNAA, NatCAB 13, OhA&B*
Weeks, Ralph E 1878-1950 *NatCAB 39*
Weeks, Willet 1917- *WhoAm 1974*
Weel, Alexander B C 1889- *WhJnl Sup*
Weems, John Edward 1924- *ConAu 3R, WrDr 1976*
Weer, William *see* Kaufman, Isidor
Wehner, Herbert 1906- *IntWW 1976, WhoWor 1974*
Wehr, Elizabeth *NF*
Wehrwein, Austin Carl 1916- *WhoAm 1974*
Weidenfeld, Sir George, Lord 1919- *IntWW 1976, Who 1974, WhoF&I 1974*
Weidenthal, Bud *see* Weindenthal, Maurice David
Weidenthal, Maurice David 1925- *WhoAm 1974*
Weidling, Philip *NF*
Weigand, Paul D 1900- *WhJnl 1928*
Weighart, James *NF*
Weightman, Richard C 1844-1914 *NatCAB 16*
Weik, Mary Hays 1898- *BioIn 9, BioIn 10, ConAu 23, IndAu 1917, SmATA 3, WhoAm 1974*
Weil, Andrew Warren 1924- *OvPC, WhoCon 1973, WhoPubR 1972*
Weil, Louis A 1877- *BioIn 5, WhJnl 1928*
Weil, Louis Arthur, Jr. 1905- *WhoAm 1974, WhoMW 1974*
Weil, Ruth *NF*
Weiler, A H *NF*
Weiler, Fred Wilson 1902-1951 *BioIn 2, BioIn 5, NatCAB 42*

Weiler, Royal William 1880-1948 *BioIn 1,*
  WhJnl 1928
Weinbaum, Mark 1890-1973 *BioIn 9,*
  NewYTBE 4, WhJnl 1928
Weinberg, Arthur 1915- *ConAu 25,*
  WhoAm 1974
Weinberg, Joseph 1876?-1955 *BioIn 3*
Weinberg, Morris 1876?-1968 *BioIn 8*
Weinberger, Arthur G 1905- *WhJnl 1928*
Weiner, Margaret Milton 1902- *WhJnl 1928*
Weiner, Skip *NF*
Weingarten, Violet Brown 1915-1976 *BioIn 9,*
  ConAu 65, ForWC 1970
Weinraub, Bernard *NF*
Weinstein, Jerome *NF*
Weintal, Edward 1901-1973 *BioIn 9, ConAu 41,*
  NewYTBE 4
Weintraub, Joseph Heller 1900?-1953 *BioIn 3*
Weintraub, Louis 1922- *OvPC, WhoE 1974*
Weintraub, William H 1926- *ConAu 1R, OxCan*
Weintz, Jacob Frederick 1892- *WhJnl 1928*
Weir, David *InvJ*
Weir, Harold Leslie 1896- *WhJnl 1928*
Weir, James W *WhJnl 1928*
Weir, Martin J 1895- *WhJnl 1928*
Weir, Paul 1879-1952 *BioIn 3, WhJnl 1928*
Weir, William 1802-1858 *Alli, DcEnL*
Weirich, Frank *NF*
Weisberg, Harold 1913- *ConAu 41*
Weisberg, Joseph Gotland 1911- *LEduc 1974,*
  OvPC, WhoWorJ 1972
Weisbord, Albert *AmRP*
Weisbord, Marvin Ross 1931- *ConAu 65*
Weiser, Benjamin *NF*
Weisgal, Meyer Wolf 1894-1977 *CurBio XR,*
  IntWW 1976, WhoWor 1974,
  WhoWorJ 1972
Weisinger, Mortimer 1915-1978 *BioIn 7*
Weiskittel, Ralph Joseph 1924- *WhoAm 1974*
Weisman, Joel *InvJ*
Weisman, Marilee 1939- *ConAu 65*
Weisman, Russell 1890-1949 *BioIn 2, OhA&B*
Weisman, Steven R *NewMr*
Weiss, Anna M 1901- *WhJnl 1928*
Weiss, Anton C 1862- *NatCAB 16*
Weiss, Brian *NF*
Weiss, Ignazio *ForP*
Weiss, Jean Jacques 1827-1890 *BioIn 1,*
  CIDMEL, OxFr
Weiss, Kenneth A *NF*
Weiss, Lawrence Gerald 1920- *RpN,*
  WhoAm 1974
Weiss, Lewis Allen 1890- *WhJnl 1928*
Weiss, Louise *NF*
Weiss, Max *AmRP*
Weiss, Morris 1915- *NF*
Weiss, Murry *AmRP*
Weiss, Rubin T *NF*
Weiss-Rosmarin, Trude *BioIn 10,*
  WhoWorJ 1972
Weissblatt, Franz 1899?-1961 *BioIn 6*
Weissert, Charles Adam 1878-1948 *BioIn 1*
Weisskopf, Kurt 1907- *Au&Wr, ConAu 25*
Weissman, Harold *BioIn 4*
Weissman, Julia *NF*
Weissman, Paul 1932- *ConAu 45*
Weissman, Rozanne *NF*
Weisz, Victor 1913-1966 *BioIn 2, BioIn 4,*
  BioIn 6, BioIn 7, WhoGrA
Weisz, Victor *see also* Vicky
Weitzel, Edwin Anthony 1905- *WhoAm 1974*
Weitzenkorn, Louis 1893-1943 *AmAu&B,*
  CurBio XR, WebBD
Welbourne, Penny *NF*

Welch, Alden W 1888?-1961 *BioIn 6*
Welch, Anita *NF*
Welch, Charles Buckley 1883- *WhJnl 1928*
Welch, Charles Douglass 1906?-1968 *BioIn 4,*
  BioIn 8
Welch, Deshler 1854-1920 *Alli Sup, AmLY,*
  DcNAA
Welch, James S *BioIn 8*
Welch, Lewis Sheldon 1867-1940 *DcNAA*
Welch, Mary Scott Stewart *WhoAmW 1974*
Welch, Neal Byron 1894- *WhJnl 1928*
Welch, Ned 1882- *NF*
Welch, Philip Henry 1849-1889 *AmAu,*
  AmAu&B, BbD, BiD&SB, DcAmA,
  DcAmB 19, DcNAA
Welch, William *NF*
Weld, Carol *ForWC 1970, OvPC*
Weld, Ezra W *HisAmM XR*
Weld, Gardner Clarke 1891-1977 *WhoE 1974*
Weld, Horatio Hastings 1811-1888 *Alli,*
  AmAu&B, DcAmA, DcNAA, HisAmM XR
Weld, Mason Cogswell 1829-1887 *Alli Sup,*
  DcNAA, HisAmM XR
Weld, Philip Saltonstall 1914- *WhoAm 1974*
Weldon, Walter 1832-1885 *BioIn 5*
Welford, B R *HisAmM XR*
Weli, Carol *NF*
Welke, Elton 1941- *ConAu 65*
Welker, Harry L, Jr. *OvPC*
Well, Martin *NF*
Wellard, James 1909?- *ConAu 5R*
Weller, Bernard *NF*
Weller, Charles Heald 1870-1927 *DcNAA,*
  WhJnl 1928
Weller, Frank I d1951 *NF*
Weller, George Anthony 1907- *AmAu&B,*
  ConAu 65, OvPC, REnAL, RpN, WhNAA,
  WhoAm 1974, WrDr 1976
Weller, H Pierce 1880- *WhJnl 1928*
Weller, Samuel MacLeary 1876?-1957 *BioIn 4*
Welles, Chris *NF*
Welles, Gideon 1802-1878 *Alli Sup, AmAu&B,*
  AmJnl, DcAmA, DcNAA, EncAB,
  HisAmM XR, REn, REnAL, WebBD
Welles, Robin *NF*
Welles, Sara *NF*
Welling, James Clarke 1825-1894 *DcAmB 19,*
  DcNAA
Wellington, Arthur Mellen 1847-1895 *Alli Sup,*
  DcAmA, DcNAA
Wellington, Clarence George 1890-1959? *BioIn 5,*
  BioIn 7, NatCAB 48
Wellington, Elliot G 1890- *WhJnl 1928*
Welliver, Judson Churchill 1870-1943 *AmJnl,*
  HisAmM XR
Wellman, Paul Iselin 1898-1966 *AmAu&B,*
  AmNov, Au&Wr, AuBYP, ConAu 2R,
  ConAu 25, REn, REnAL, SmATA 3,
  TwCA Sup
Wellman, T V 1903- *WhJnl 1928*
Wellman, Walter 1858-1934 *AmJnl, BioIn 5,*
  BioIn 8, DcAmB 19, DcNAA,
  HisAmM XR, OhA&B, WebBD
Wellner, Charles J *OvPC*
Wells, Amos Russell 1862-1933 *AmAu&B,*
  AmLY, DcAmA, DcNAA, OhA&B
Wells, Benjamin Willis 1856-1923 *AmAu&B,*
  AmLY, DcAmA, DcNAA, HisAmM XR
Wells, Brian *NF*
Wells, Charles Arthur *WhoAm 1974*
Wells, Charles H *HisAmM XR*
Wells, David Ames 1828-1898 *Alli, Alli Sup,*
  AmAu, AmAu&B, BbD, BiD&SB, DcAmA,
  DcNAA, HisAmM XR, WebBD

Wells, Fay Gillis 1908- *ForWC 1970, OvPC, WhoAm 1974, WhoAmW 1974*
Wells, George S *NF*
Wells, George Young 1908?-1963 *BioIn 6*
Wells, Ida B 1862-1931 *BioIn 8, BioIn 9, BioIn 10*
Wells, James 1872- *WhJnl 1928*
Wells, James Ward 1879- *WhJnl Sup*
Wells, Joel Freeman 1930- *AmAu&B, ConAu 13R, WhoAm 1974*
Wells, John *AmJnl*
Wells, John Daniel 1878-1932 *DcNAA, WhNAA*
Wells, Linton 1893-1976 *AmAu&B, ConAu 61, OvPC, WebBD, WhNAA, WhoAm 1974*
Wells, Marion *NF*
Wells, Murray M *NF*
Wells, Reuben Field 1880-1938 *DcNAA*
Wells, Robert 1728?-1794 *Alli, AmJnl*
Wells, Robert W 1918- *ConAu 49*
Wells, Samuel Roberts 1820-1875 *Alli, DcAmA, DcNAA, HisAmM XR*
Wells, Thomas *NF*
Wells, Thomas Bucklin 1875-1941 *HisAmM XR*
Wells, William Benjamin 1809-1881 *BbtC, DcNAA*
Wells, William Bittle *HisAmM XR*
Wells, William Harvey 1812-1885 *Alli, Alli Sup, DcAmA, DcNAA*
Wells, William Vincent 1826-1876 *AmAu, CyAL 2, DcAmA, DcNAA, REnAL*
Wells-Barnett, Ida Bell 1862-1931 *EncAB*
Wellsford, C Mills, Jr. 1901- *WhJnl 1928*
Wellstood, William *HisAmM XR*
Welpott, Raymond William 1915- *WhoAm 1974*
Welsh, Deshler *HisAmM XR*
Welsh, George Wilson 1883-1974 *WhoMW 1974*
Welsh, Herbert 1851-1941 *BiD&SB, DcAmA, DcNAA, HisAmM XR, WhNAA*
Welsh, Thomas B *HisAmM XR*
Welsh, W Henry *HisAmM XR*
Welshimer, Helen Louise 1901-1954 *OhA&B*
Weltsch, Robert 1891- *BioIn 6, WhoWorJ 1972*
Welty, Newell G 1900- *WhJnl 1928*
Welty, Noble Desmond 1874- *WhJnl 1928*
Welty, Regnier Donald 1898- *WhJnl 1928*
Welz, Carl John 1913- *WhoAm 1974, WhoE 1974*
Wendland, Michael Fletcher 1946- *ConAu 65*
Wendt, Lloyd 1908- *WhoAm 1974, WhoMW 1974*
Weng, Will *BioIn 10*
Wenger, Martin D 1841-1901 *BioIn 2, IndAu 1816*
Wengert, James J 1900- *WhJnl 1928*
Wenner, Jann 1946- *BioIn 10*
Wentworth, E *HisAmM XR*
Wentworth, Eric *NF*
Wentworth, Franklin Harcourt 1866-1954 *AmAu&B, AmRP*
Wentworth, John 1815-1888 *Alli, Alli Sup, AmJnl, DcAmA, DcNAA, NatCAB 10*
Wentworth, Marion Craig 1872- *AmRP*
Werba, Hank *NF*
Wergeland, Henrik Arnold 1808-1845 *BbD, BiD&SB, CasWL, DcEuL, EuAu, EvEuW, Pen Eur, WebBD*
Werk, Emil *HisAmM XR*
Werkley, John Gerard 1913?-1949 *BioIn 2*
Wermiel, Stephen J *NF*
Wermuth, Burt 1879- *WhJnl 1928*
Werneke, Raymond A 1895?-1950 *BioIn 2*
Werner, Alfred 1911- *Au&Wr, WhoAm 1974, WhoAmA 1973, WhoWorJ 1972*
Werner, Anthony Matthias 1894- *BioIn 2*

Werner, Bruno Erich 1896- *BioIn 2*
Werner, Charles George 1909- *WhoAm 1974*
Werner, Edgar S *Alli Sup, HisAmM XR*
Werner, Eliot 1950- *NF*
Werner, Joe *NF*
Werner, Ludlow W 1907?-1967 *BioIn 7*
Werner, M R 1897- *AmAu&B, ConAmA, ConAmL, ForP, OxAm, WebBD, WhNAA*
Werner, Mary Lou *WhoAmW 1974*
Werner, Max 1901-1951 *BioIn 2, BioIn 3, CurBio XR*
Werner, Merle M *OvPC*
Werner, Mort 1916- *IntMPA 1975, WhoAm 1974*
Werner, Oscar Emil 1893-1953 *BioIn 3*
Werner, Ralph J *RpN*
Werntz, Carl N 1874-1944 *CurBio XR*
Wershba, Joseph 1920- *WhoAm 1974*
Werstein, Irving 1914?-1971 *AuBYP, ConAu 29, ConAu 73, NewYTBE 2*
Wertenbaker, Charles Christian 1901-1955 *BioIn 3, BioIn 4, BioIn 6, DcAmB S5*
Wertenbaker, Lael Tucker 1909- *Au&Wr, ConAu 5R, ForWC 1970, OvPC, WhoAmW 1974, WhoE 1974, WrDr 1976*
Wertenbaker, Thomas Jefferson 1879-1966 *AmAu&B, ConAu 7R, HisAmM XR, REnAL*
Werth, Alexander 1901-1969 *BioIn 8, BioIn 9, ConAu 25, ConAu P-1, CurBio XR, WebBD*
Wertheim, Maurice 1868-1950 *HisAmM XR*
Wertheimer, Rose M *HisAmM XR*
Wertman, Dan M 1915- *WhoAm 1974*
Wesley, Edward B *AmJnl*
Wespe, O S 1890- *WhJnl 1928*
Wessel, E L *HisAmM XR*
Wessel, Harry N *NF*
Wessertheil, Bruno *NF*
West, Alfred J 1886- *WhJnl 1928*
West, Anthony Panther 1914- *AmAu&B, WhoAm 1974, WhoWor 1974*
West, Carl *InvJ*
West, Clarence Jay 1886-1953 *BioIn 3*
West, Daniel F *NF*
West, Dick Sheppard 1920- *WhoAm 1974, WhoS&SW 1973*
West, Don 1928- *ConAu 57*
West, Dorothy Herbert 1902- *BioIn 3*
West, Eddie 1900?-1977 *NF*
West, Felton 1926- *WhoAm 1974*
West, Frederick 1895- *WhJnl 1928*
West, Henry Litchfield 1859-1940 *DcNAA*
West, Hollie I 1938?- *NF*
West, James *AmRP*
West, James Edward 1876-1948 *AmAu&B, DcAmB S4*
West, James Watt 1908- *WhoAm 1974, WhoS&SW 1973, WhoWor 1974*
West, John 1809-1873 *BioIn 2*
West, John B 1852-1922 *NatCAB 27*
West, Levon 1900-1968 *AmAu&B, CurBio XR*
West, Lillie 1860-1939 *AmAu&B, DcNAA, WhNAA*
West, Luther R 1943?- *NF*
West, Mary Allen 1837-1892 *Alli Sup, DcAmA, DcNAA*
West, Paul Clarendon 1871-1918 *AmAu&B, DcNAA*
West, Randolph 1890-1949 *BioIn 1, BioIn 2*
West, Ray Benedict, Jr. 1908- *AmAu&B, ConAu 1, DrAS 74E, REnAL, WhoAm 1974, WhoWest 1974*
West, Rebecca 1892- *Au&Wr, CasWL, ConAu 5, ConNov 1972, ConNov 1976,*

CurBio XR, CyWA, DcLEL, EncWL,
EvLB, IntWW 1976, LiJA, LongC, ModBL,
ModBL Sup, NewC, OxEng, Pen Eng,
RAdv 1, REn, TwCA, TwCA Sup, TwCW,
WebBD, Who 1974, WhoAmW 1974,
WhoLA, WhoTwCL, WhoWor 1974,
WrDr 1976

West, Robert Athow 1808-1865 Alli, DcNAA
West, Stuart Pullman 1876-1927 WhJnl Sup,
WhJnl 1928
West, Woody NF
Westberg, Frank Gustaf 1891- WhJnl 1928
Westcott, Linn Hanson 1913- WhoAm 1974
Westcott, Thompson 1820-1888 Alli, Alli Sup,
AmAu&B, DcAmA, DcAmB 20, DcNAA,
LiJA, WebBD
Westdal, Alvin T 1901- WhJnl 1928
Westdal, Stephen Th 1873- WhJnl 1928
Westell, Anthony 1926- CanWW 1972,
OxCan Sup
Westerfield, Putney 1930- IntWW 1974,
WhoAm 1974, WhoWor 1974
Westerkamp, Richard F 1917- NF
Westerman, Harry James 1876-1945 AmAu&B
Western, Maurice NF
Westfall, Alfred 1889- WhJnl 1928
Westfeldt, Wallace Ogden 1923- WhoAm 1974
Westgate, Robert D NF
Westheimer, David 1917- AmAu&B, AmNov,
Au&Wr, ConAu 1R, WrDr 1976
Westin, Avram Robert 1929- CurBio XR, InvJ,
NewMr, WhoAm 1974
Westin, Jeane NF
Westlake, William OvPC
Westler, Dudley F 1888- WhJnl 1928
Westley, Bruce Hutchinson 1915- AmM&W 73S,
ConAu 1R, WhoCon 1973
Westley, George Hembert 1865-1936 AmAu&B,
DcNAA
Westley, John J NF
Westmoreland, Reg 1926- ConAu 29
Weston, Bertine E HisAmM XR
Weston, Christine HisAmM XR
Weston, Edward Payson 1839-1929 Alli, AmJnl
Weston, George W NF
Weston, Henry Griggs 1820-1909 DcNAA,
HisAmM XR
Weston, John W HisAmM XR
Weston, Joseph H 1901?-1972 InvJ, NewYTBE 3
Weston, S E HisAmM XR
Weston, Samuel Burns 1855-1936 BioIn 2,
HisAmM XR
Weston, Theodore A 1911?-1964 BioIn 7
Westover, Russell 1886?-1966 AmJnl, BioIn 7
Westphal, Ken NF
Westrum, Adrian Schade Van HisAmM XR
Wetherell, William Thomas 1880- WhJnl 1928
Wetjen, Albert Richard 1900-1948 AmAu&B,
DcNAA, HisAmM XR, REnAL, WhNAA
Wetmore, Claude Hazeltine 1863?- AmAu&B,
DcAmA, DcNAA, HisAmM XR, OhA&B
Wetmore, Elizabeth Bisland 1862?-1929 BiDSA,
DcAmA, DcNAA, WhNAA
Wetmore, Elizabeth Bisland see also Bisland,
Elizabeth
Wetzler, Edward T 1862- WhJnl 1928
Wetzsteon, Ross NF
Wevill, George HisAmM XR
Weybright, Victor 1903-1978 AmAu&B, Au&Wr,
OvPC, REnAL, WhoAm 1974, WhoE 1974,
WhoF&I 1974, WhoWor 1974, WrDr 1976
Weyburn, Samuel Fletcher 1853-1941 DcNAA
Weydemeyer, Joseph HisAmM XR
Weyeneth, Eugene E OvPC

Weyher, Russell L 1900- WhJnl 1928
Weyl, Walter Edward 1873-1919 AmLY, DcAmA,
DcNAA, HisAmM XR
Weyman, William AmJnl, HisAmM XR
Weymuller, Frederick OvPC
Weyrauch, Martin Henry 1885-1958 BioIn 4
Wezell, Albert Beck HisAmM XR
Whalen, Richard James 1935- AmAu&B,
ConAu 15R, WhoAm 1974, WrDr 1976
Whalen, Robert G 1913-1969 BioIn 8
Whaley, Percival Huntington 1880-1963 BioIn 6
Wharf, Michael see Weller, George Anthony
Wharton, Charles Henry 1748-1833 Alli, BiDSA,
DcAmA, DcNAA
Wharton, Don 1905- HisAmM XR,
WhoAm 1974
Wharton, Elizabeth Austin 1920- WhoAm 1974,
WhoAmW 1974
Wharton, Francis 1820-1889 Alli, Alli Sup,
DcAmA, DcNAA, HisAmM XR, OhA&B,
WebBD
Wharton, George BioIn 1
Wharton, George Wilson 1875- WhJnl 1928
Wharton, Thomas 1735-1778 AmJnl
Wharton, Thomas Isaac 1791-1856 Alli, DcAmA,
DcNAA, HisAmM XR
Wharton, Thomas Isaac 1859-1896 Alli Sup,
AmAu&B, BiD&SB, DcAmA, DcNAA
Whatley, James NF
Whatley, William E WhJnl 1928
Whatmore, Marvin Clement 1908- WhoAm 1974,
WhoF&I 1974, WhoWor 1974
Whealan, J P RpN
Wheat, Carl Irving 1892-1966 AmAu&B, BioIn 8
Wheat, Harry V 1900- WhJnl 1928
Wheat, Patte NF
Wheat, Warren NF
Wheatley, Richard 1831-1909 Alli Sup, DcAmA,
DcNAA, HisAmM XR
Wheatley, William O, Jr. 1945?- NF
Wheaton, Anne 1892-1977 BioIn 4, BioIn 5,
ConAu 69, CurBio XR
Wheaton, Henry 1785-1848 Alli, AmAu,
AmAu&B, AmJnl, BiD&SB, CyAL 1,
DcAmA, DcNAA, HisAmM XR, OxAm
Whedon, Daniel Denison 1808-1885 Alli, Alli Sup,
DcAmA, DcNAA, HisAmM XR, WebBD
Whedon, Peggy WhoAmW 1974
Wheeler, Andrew Carpenter 1835-1903 Alli,
AmAu&B, AmJnl, BbD, BiD&SB, DcAmA,
DcAmB 20, DcNAA, HisAmM XR,
NatCAB 25
Wheeler, C W 1890- WhJnl 1928
Wheeler, Charles Newton 1874?-1949 BioIn 2
Wheeler, Cora Stuart HisAmM XR
Wheeler, Crawford 1895- WhJnl 1928
Wheeler, Daniel Edwin 1880- AmAu&B
Wheeler, Edward Jewitt 1859-1922 DcAmA,
DcNAA, HisAmM XR, NatCAB 18,
OhA&B
Wheeler, Edwin Kirk 1908- WhoAm 1974
Wheeler, George NF
Wheeler, Howard Duryee 1880-1958 AmAu&B,
BioIn 4, HisAmM XR
Wheeler, James Cooper 1849- DcNAA
Wheeler, John NF
Wheeler, John E NF
Wheeler, John Neville 1886- BioIn 6,
NewYTBE 4
Wheeler, Keith 1911- BioIn 6, ConAu 7R
Wheeler, Laura NF
Wheeler, Lawrence 1897?-1952 BioIn 3
Wheeler, Lloyd NF
Wheeler, Michael NF

White, Leander Mitchell 1883- *HisAmM XR,*
  WhJnl 1928
White, Lee A 1886-1971 *AmAu&B, WhJnl 1928*
White, Leigh *AmJnl, Bioln 2, RpN*
White, Leo 1918- *WhoAmA 1973*
White, Lillie D *NF*
White, Llewellyn Brooke 1899-1959 *Bioln 5*
White, Magner *NF*
White, Marjorie *NF*
White, Mary J 1933- *NF*
White, Matthew, Jr. 1857-1940 *AmAu&B,*
  DcAmA, DcNAA, HisAmM XR
White, Maunsell *HisAmM XR*
White, Nancy 1916- *AmAu&B, Bioln 5,*
  Bioln 9, ForWC 1970, WhoAm 1974,
  WhoAmW 1974, WhoE 1974, WhoGov 1972
White, Nancy Bean 1922- *AuBYP, ConAu 15R,*
  ForWC 1970
White, Owen Payne 1879-1946 *DcNAA,*
  HisAmM XR, TexWr, WhNAA
White, Paul Welrose 1902-1955 *Bioln 3, Bioln 4,*
  CurBio XR
White, Peter T *NF*
White, Philo 1796-1883 *Bioln 5*
White, Pliny Holton 1822-1869 *DcAmA, DcNAA*
White, Poppy Cannon 1906?-1975 *ConAu 57,*
  ConAu 65
White, Poppy Cannon *see also* Cannon, Poppy
White, Ralph Scoop *Bioln 4*
White, Raymond J 1936?- *NF*
White, Rex G *NF*
White, Richard d1910 *NF*
White, Richard Grant 1821-1885 *Alli, Alli Sup,*
  AmAu, AmAu&B, BbD, BiD&SB, CyAL 2,
  DcAmA, DcEnL, DcNAA, EvLB,
  HisAmM XR, OxAm, REnAL, WebBD
White, Richard Smeaton d1936 *NF*
White, Robert *OvPC*
White, Robert Mitchell, II 1915- *Bioln 5,*
  ConAu 73, CurBio XR, IntWW 1976,
  OvPC, WhoAm 1974
White, Robert Smeaton *NF*
White, Rosemary *NF*
White, Russell S 1896- *WhJnl 1928*
White, Ruth 1902?-1978 *NF*
White, Stoddard d1972 *NF*
White, Ten Eyck 1854-1942 *Alli Sup, DcNAA*
White, Ten Eyck *see also* White, Henry Ten Eyck
White, Theodore Harold 1915- *AmAu&B,*
  Au&Wr, Bioln 1, Bioln 2, Bioln 3,
  Bioln 4, Bioln 5, Bioln 7, Bioln 8, Bioln 9,
  ConAu 2R, CurBio XR, IntWW 1976,
  OxAm, REn, REnAL, WhoAm 1974,
  WhoWor 1974, WorAu, WrDr 1976
White, Thomas *NF*
White, Thomas Justin 1884-1948 *Bioln 1*
White, Thomas Willis 1788-1843 *Alli, AmAu&B,*
  HisAmM XR, LiJA
White, Tom *NF*
White, Trumbull 1868-1941 *AmAu&B, BiD&SB,*
  CurBio XR, DcAmA, DcNAA,
  HisAmM XR
White, W J 1920- *Bioln 8, ConAu 13*
White, Walter Francis 1893-1955 *AmAu&B,*
  Bioln 1, Bioln 3, Bioln 4, Bioln 6, Bioln 8,
  Bioln 9, BlkAW, REn, REnAL, TwCA,
  TwCA Sup, WebBD, WhNAA
White, Walter W 1900-1969 *WhJnl 1928*
White, Wilbur M 1890- *WhJnl 1928*
White, William 1910- *AmAu&B, ConAu 23R,*
  DrAS 74E, LiJA, WhoAm 1974, WrDr 1976
White, William Allen 1868-1944 *AmAu&B,*
  AmJnl, AmLY, Bioln 1, Bioln 2, Bioln 3,
  Bioln 4, Bioln 5, Bioln 7, Bioln 8, Bioln 9,

Bioln 10, CnDAL, CurBio XR, DcAmA,
  DcAmB S3, DcLEL, DcNAA, EncAB,
  HisAmM XR, LongC, OxAm, REn,
  REnAL, TwCA, TwCA Sup, WebBD,
  WhNAA, WhJnl 1928
White, William Alvin 1894- *WhJnl 1928*
White, William Anthony Parker 1911-1968
  AmAu&B, ConAu 25, ConAu P-1, EncMys,
  TwCA Sup
White, William Anthony Parker *see also* Boucher,
  Anthony
White, William Chapman 1903-1955 *Bioln 4,*
  HisAmM XR
White, William Henry 1924- *WhoAm 1974*
White, William Lindsay 1900-1973 *AmAu&B,*
  AmJnl, Bioln 1, Bioln 4, Bioln 10, CnDAL,
  ConAu 41, CurBio XR, NewYTBE 4,
  OxAm, REnAL, TwCA Sup, WebBD,
  WhoAm 1974
White, William Nathaniel 1819-1867? *Alli,*
  DcAmA, DcNAA, HisAmM XR
White, William Smith 1907- *AmAu&B, AmJnl,*
  Bioln 4, Bioln 5, Bioln 6, ConAu 5R,
  CurBio XR, IntWW 1976, OxAm,
  WhoAm 1974, WhoS&SW 1973
Whitebird, Joanie 1951- *ConAu 69*
Whited, Charles *NF*
Whitehead, Donald Ford 1908- *AmAu&B, AmJnl,*
  Bioln 3, Bioln 5, Bioln 9, ConAu 11R,
  CurBio XR, WhoAm 1974
Whitehead, E C *NF*
Whitehead, John 1850-1930 *DcNAA,*
  HisAmM XR
Whitehead, Ralph *NF*
Whitehead, Russell Fenimore 1884-1954 *Bioln 3*
Whitehead, Tom S 1900- *WhJnl 1928*
Whitehorn, Katharine Elizabeth 1928- *Au&Wr,*
  ConAu 5R, Who 1974, WrDr 1976
Whitehouse, Arch *see* Whitehouse, Arthur George
Whitehouse, Arthur George 1895- *AuBYP,*
  ConAu 5R
Whiteing, Richard 1840-1928 *Alli Sup, BbD,*
  DcEnA Ap, LongC, NewC, TwCA, WebBD
Whitelaw, Paul *NF*
Whiteleather, Melvin Kerr 1903- *OhA&B,*
  WhoAm 1974
Whiteley, Harry Huntington 1882-1957 *Bioln 6,*
  NatCAB 44, WhJnl 1928
Whiteley, L A *NF*
Whiteley, Lynne *NF*
Whitlock, Otto VonStockhausen 1903-
  WhoAm 1974
Whitelock, William Wallace 1869-1940 *AmAu&B,*
  BiDSA, DcNAA
Whitesell, J E *NF*
Whitesell, Naomi Adams *IndAu 1917*
Whitestone, Bruce 1922- *NF*
Whitford, James *OvPC*
Whiting, Charles Goodrich 1842-1922 *Alli Sup,*
  AmAu&B, BiD&SB, DcAmA, DcAmB 20,
  DcNAA, NatCAB 9
Whiting, Edward Elwell 1875-1956 *AmAu&B,*
  Bioln 4, WhJnl 1928
Whiting, Frances *HisAmM XR*
Whiting, John Randolph 1914- *WhoAm 1974*
Whiting, Kenneth *NF*
Whiting, Lilian 1859?-1942 *AmAu&B, AmLY,*
  BbD, BiD&SB, DcAmA, DcNAA,
  HisAmM XR, WhNAA
Whiting, Robert Rudd 1877-1918 *DcNAA*
Whitlock, Brand 1869-1934 *AmAu&B, DcAmA,*
  DcLEL, DcNAA, OhA&B, OxAm, REnAL,
  TwCA, WebBD
Whitlock, L L *HisAmM XR*

WhoPubR 1972
Wieniawski, Henri *HisAmM XR*
Wierzbianski, Boleslaw *OvPC*
Wierzynski, Gregory H 1939- *ConAu 73*
Wiese, Arthur E 1946- *ConAu 73*
Wiese, Otis Lee 1905-1972 *BioIn 1, BioIn 2,
   BioIn 9, HisAmM XR, NewYTBE 3,
   WhJnl 1928*
Wiesel, Elie 1928- *AmAu&B, Au&Wr,
   AuNews 1, BioIn 8, BioIn 9, ConAu 5,
   ConLC 3, ConLC 5, CurBio XR,
   DrAF 1976, EncWL, NewYTBE 4,
   WhoAm 1974, WhoE 1974, WhoWorJ 1972,
   WorAu*
Wiesner, Adolph 1815- *BioIn 2*
Wiessler, David A *NF*
Wiessler, Judy *NF*
Wigan, Anthony *NF*
Wigforss, Harald *ForP*
Wiggam, Albert Edward 1871-1957 *AmAu&B,
   BioIn 4, BioIn 6, CurBio XR, HisAmM XR,
   IndAu 1917*
Wiggin, Frank A *HisAmM XR*
Wiggin, James Henry 1836-1900 *DcNAA, WebBD*
Wiggin, Maurice 1912- *Au&Wr, BioIn 8,
   BioIn 9, ConAu 11R*
Wiggin, William H 1867-1951 *NatCAB 40*
Wiggins, Allen Frank 1939- *WhoAm 1974*
Wiggins, James Russell 1903- *AmJnl, AuNews 2,
   BioIn 8, CurBio XR, ForP, IntWW 1976,
   WhoAm 1974, WhoWor 1974*
Wiggins, Walt *OvPC*
Wigginton, Eliot 1943?- *AuNews 1, BioIn 10,
   BioNews 1974*
Wight, Frank C 1882-1927 *WhJnl 1928*
Wight, L J *NF*
Wightman, Richard *NF*
Wighton, Charles Ernest 1913- *Au&Wr,
   ConAu 7R, WrDr 1976*
Wiinblad, Emil 1854-1935 *ForP*
Wikoff, Henry 1813-1884 *Alli, Alli Sup,
   AmAu&B, DcAmA, DcNAA, HisAmM XR*
Wilamowitz-Moellendorff, Ulrich Von 1848-1931
   WebBD
Wilber, Carey 1916?- *BioIn 3*
Wilber, John *HisAmM XR*
Wilberforce, Henry William 1809?-1873 *Alli,
   Alli Sup, BioIn 7, BrAu 19*
Wilberforce, William 1759-1833 *Alli, BiD&SB,
   BiDLA, BrAu 19, DcEnL, DcEuL, DcLEL,
   EvLB, NewC, OxEng, WebBD*
Wilborn, Ed *BioIn 8*
Wilcock, John 1927- *ConAu 2R, NewMr,
   NewYTBE 4, WhoAm 1974*
Wilcox, Arthur Manigault 1922- *WhoAm 1974,
   WhoS&SW 1973*
Wilcox, Desmond 1931- *ConAu 69*
Wilcox, Ella Wheeler 1850-1919 *Alli Sup, AmAu,
   AmAu&B, AmLY, BbD, BiD&SB, CasWL,
   DcAmA, DcLEL, DcNAA, EvLB, LongC,
   OxAm, OxEng, Pen Am, REnAL, WebBD,
   WisWr*
Wilcox, Frank d1886 *NF*
Wilcox, Grafton Stiles 1879?-1964 *BioIn 6*
Wilcox, Herbert 1891- *ConAu 57*
Wilcox, Owen N 1880-1950 *NatCAB 39*
Wilcox, Richard L 1919?-1978 *NF*
Wilcox, Robert *NF*
Wilcox, Uthai Vincent 1890- *WhNAA,
   WhJnl 1928*
Wild, Glen *NF*
Wilde, James *NF*
Wilde, William Charles K 1852-1899? *BioIn 6,
   HisAmM XR, PoIre*

Wildeblood, Peter 1923- *Au&Wr, BioIn 4,
   ConAu 65, WrDr 1976*
Wilder, Amos Parker 1862-1936 *BioIn 5, BioIn 6,
   NatCAB 45*
Wilder, B F *HisAmM XR*
Wilder, Bruce 1918?-1951 *BioIn 2*
Wilder, C D *HisAmM XR*
Wilder, Daniel Webster 1832-1911 *Alli Sup,
   AmAu&B, DcAmA, DcNAA*
Wilder, George Warren 1866-1931 *HisAmM XR*
Wilder, Henry L 1883- *WhJnl 1928*
Wilder, Jones Warren *HisAmM XR*
Wilder, Marshall Pinckney 1859-1915 *AmJnl,
   DcAmA, DcNAA, HisAmM XR, WebBD*
Wilder, Robert Ingersoll 1901-1974 *AmAu&B,
   AmNov, Au&Wr, BioIn 2, BioIn 4,
   ConAu 13, ConAu 53, LongC, TwCA Sup,
   WhoAm 1974*
Wilder, Royal Gould 1816-1887 *DcNAA,
   HisAmM XR*
Wilder, Silas W *HisAmM XR*
Wilder, Stella *NF*
Wildes, Harry Emerson 1890- *AmAu&B,
   ConAu 57, WhoAm 1974*
Wildman, Edwin 1868?-1932 *AmLY, DcAmA,
   DcNAA, HisAmM XR, WhNAA*
Wildman, Rounsevelle 1864-1901 *DcNAA,
   HisAmM XR*
Wile, Frederic William 1873-1941 *AmAu&B,
   AmLY, BioIn 2, CurBio XR, DcNAA,
   IndAu 1816, WhJnl 1928*
Wile, Simeon *HisAmM XR*
Wile, William Conrad 1847-1913 *HisAmM XR*
Wiles, Cora Young 1864- *WhJnl 1928*
Wiley, Calvin Henderson 1819-1887 *Alli,
   AmAu&B, BiDSA, CnDAL, DcAmA,
   DcNAA*
Wiley, David 1768-1813 *HisAmM XR*
Wiley, Donald A 1900- *WhJnl 1928*
Wiley, Franklin Baldwin 1861-1930 *AmAu&B,
   DcNAA, NatCAB XR, WhJnl 1928*
Wiley, Harvey Washington 1844-1930 *AmLY,
   DcAmA, DcNAA, HisAmM XR,
   IndAu 1816, WebBD, WhNAA*
Wiley, John P, Jr. *NF*
Wiley, Karla H 1918- *AuBYP, BioIn 8,
   ConAu 61*
Wiley, Louis 1869-1935 *WhNAA, WhJnl 1928*
Wiley, Marcia *NF*
Wiley, Robert Hopkins 1886-1952 *BioIn 2*
Wiley, William Foust 1874?-1944 *CurBio XR*
Wilford, John Noble, Jr. 1933- *ConAu 29, OvPC,
   WhoE 1974*
Wilhelm, Donald George 1887-1945 *AmAu&B,
   DcNAA, OhA&B*
Wilhelm, John Remsen 1916- *ConAu 7R, OvPC,
   WhoAm 1974*
Wilhelm, Marion Bell 1925- *OvPC, USBiR 1974*
Wilk, Gerard Hermann 1902- *ConAu 69*
Wilke, L A 1897- *WhJnl 1928*
Wilken, Earl W *NF*
Wilken, Frank A 1885- *WhJnl 1928*
Wilken, Ray T 1891- *WhJnl 1928*
Wilkening, David *NF*
Wilkens, Emily 1918- *ForWC 1970,
   WhoAm 1974*
Wilkerson, Austin Coger 1890- *WhJnl 1928*
Wilkerson, Marcus Manley 1896-1953 *BioIn 3*
Wilkes, Eugene Peirce 1885- *WhJnl 1928,
   WhoS&SW 1973*
Wilkes, George 1817?-1885 *Alli, Alli Sup,
   AmAu, AmAu&B, BiD&SB, DcAmA,
   DcAmB 20, DcNAA, HisAmM XR, LiJA*
Wilkes, John 1727-1797 *Alli, BrAu, CasWL,*

DcEnA, DcEnL, EvLB, ForP, HisAmM XR,
NewC, OxEng, REn, WebBD, WebE&AL
Wilkes, Lillian Genn   *OvPC*
Wilkeson, Samuel   *FamWC*
Wilkie, David Julian 1888-1963   *BioIn 1, BioIn 5,*
BioIn 6
Wilkie, Franc Bangs 1832-1892   *AmAu&B,*
DcAmB 20, DcNAA, FamWC, NatCAB 1
Wilkin, Eugene Welch 1923-   *WhoAdv 1972,*
WhoAm 1974
Wilkins, Beriah 1846-1905   *AmJnl, NatCAB 6*
Wilkins, Ed   *NF*
Wilkins, Jack d1977   *NF*
Wilkins, Milan William 1856-   *HisAmM XR*
Wilkins, Roger Wood 1932-   *WhoAm 1974*
Wilkins, Roy 1901-   *CelR 1973, CurBio XR,*
IntWW 1974, WebBD, WhoAm 1974,
WhoAmP 1973, WhoWor 1974
Wilkins, W A   *NF*
Wilkins, William E   *HisAmM XR*
Wilkinson, Andrews d1921   *DcNAA*
Wilkinson, Charlotte Jefferson   *ConAu 69*
Wilkinson, Florence   *AmAu&B, DcAmA,*
HisAmM XR, WhNAA
Wilkinson, Fritz 1911?-1966   *BioIn 7*
Wilkinson, George W   *WhJnl 1928*
Wilkinson, Gerald T 1890-   *WhJnl 1928*
Wilkinson, Harold   *HisAmM XR*
Wilkinson, Marc A 1903-   *WhJnl 1928*
Wilkinson, R   *NF*
Wilkinson, Spenser 1853-1937   *BioIn 2*
Wilkinson, Stephan   *NF*
Wilkinson, W J   *NF*
Will, Allan Sinclair 1868-1934   *AmAu&B,*
DcAmB 20, WhJnl 1928
Will, George F 1941?-   *BioIn 10*
Will, Thomas Elmer 1861-   *HisAmM XR*
Willard, Charles Wesley 1827-1880   *NF*
Willard, Charlotte 1914-1977   *ConAu 73,*
WhoAm 1974, WhoAmA 1973,
WhoAmW 1974
Willard, Curvin David 1876-   *HisAmM XR,*
WhJnl 1928
Willard, Ernest R 1856-1937   *NatCAB 28*
Willard, Frank Henry 1893-1958   *AmJnl, BioIn 1,*
BioIn 3, BioIn 4, BioIn 5, BioIn 6,
NatCAB 46
Willard, James Herbert   *WhJnl 1928*
Willard, Mary B   *HisAmM XR*
Willard, Sidney 1780-1856   *Alli, AmAu&B,*
BioIn 3, DcAmA, DcNAA, HisAmM XR
Wille, Lois 1932-   *BioIn 7*
Wille, Wayne Martin 1930-   *WhoAm 1974*
Willets, Gilson 1869-   *AmAu&B, HisAmM XR*
Willett, John 1917-   *ConAu 9R*
Willette, Adolphe Leon 1857-1926   *WebBD*
Willey, John Douglas 1917-   *WhoAm 1974*
Willey, Keith 1930-   *ConAu 21R*
Williams, A J   *NF*
Williams, Al   *NF*
Williams, Albert Rhys 1883-1962   *AmAu&B,*
BioIn 6, HisAmM XR, OhA&B, WhNAA
Williams, Albert Ross 1891-   *IndAu 1917*
Williams, Alfred Mason 1840-1896   *Alli Sup,*
AmAu&B, BiD&SB, DcAmA, DcNAA
Williams, Alpheus Starkey 1810-1878   *NF*
Williams, Ariadna 1869-1962   *BioIn 6*
Williams, Arthur L 1902-1973   *BioIn 9*
Williams, Aubrey Willis 1890-1965   *BioIn 3,*
BioIn 7
Williams, B Lawton   *HisAmM XR*
Williams, Ben Ames 1889-1953   *AmAu&B,*
AmNov, CnDAL, DcAmB S5, OhA&B,
OxAm, TwCA, TwCA Sup, WhNAA

Williams, Ben H   *AmRP*
Williams, Bernard   *NF*
Williams, Betty Anne   *NF*
Williams, Brad 1918-   *ConAu 2R*
Williams, Burbank George 1873-   *WhJnl 1928*
Williams, Byron   *HisAmM XR*
Williams, C Herb   *NF*
Williams, Carl 1878-1953   *BioIn 3, IndAu 1917*
Williams, Charles Richard 1853-1927   *AmAu&B,*
BioIn 1, DcNAA
Williams, Chester S   *OvPC*
Williams, Churchill 1869-1945   *BioIn 3,*
HisAmM XR, NatCAB 38
Williams, Cranston 1895-   *BioIn 2, WhJnl 1928*
Williams, David   *WhJnl 1928*
Williams, David 1841-1927   *HisAmM XR,*
NatCAB 29
Williams, David, Jr.   *HisAmM XR*
Williams, Dean 1891-1955   *BioIn 1, BioIn 4*
Williams, Donald Ayres 1905?-1948   *BioIn 1*
Williams, Donald Cary 1899-   *WhJnl 1928*
Williams, Dorothy E   *NF*
Williams, Edgar   *AuBYP*
Williams, Edgar 1863?-1953   *BioIn 3*
Williams, Edward Francis 1903-1970   *ConAu 29*
Williams, Edwin 1797-1854   *Alli, AmAu&B,*
DcAmA, DcAmB 20, DcNAA
Williams, Edwin Moss 1903-   *BioIn 1*
Williams, Edwin N 1942-   *NF*
Williams, Ernest Eden 1916-   *WhoAm 1974*
Williams, Francis 1903-   *BioIn 1, CurBio XR,*
ForP
Williams, Francis Churchill 1869-1945   *AmAu&B,*
DcAmA, DcNAA
Williams, Frank L 1866-1943   *WhJnl 1928*
Williams, Fred Hart 1882-1961   *BioIn 6*
Williams, Gaar Campbell 1880-1935   *DcAmB S1*
Williams, George Forrester 1837?-1920   *Alli Sup,*
AmAu&B, BiD&SB, DcAmA, DcNAA,
FamWC
Williams, George Henry 1904-   *WhJnl 1928*
Williams, Gladstone 1898?-1968   *BioIn 8,*
WhNAA
Williams, Gluyas 1888-   *AmAu&B, AuNews 2,*
BioIn 1, BioIn 2, BioIn 3, BioIn 5,
CurBio XR, HisAmM XR, REnAL, WebBD,
WhoAmA 1973
Williams, Gordon 1895-   *WhJnl 1928*
Williams, Greer 1909-   *BioIn 1, ConAu 13*
Williams, Gurney 1906-1965   *BioIn 3, BioIn 7,*
HisAmM XR
Williams, Gurney, III 1941-   *ConAu 69*
Williams, H P   *NF*
Williams, Harold 1876-1928   *BioIn 8*
Williams, Harold Anthony, Jr. 1916-   *ConAu 37,*
WhoE 1974
Williams, Harry A 1879?-1953   *BioIn 3*
Williams, Harry E, Jr. 1870-   *WhJnl 1928*
Williams, Haynes Clark 1880-   *WhJnl 1928*
Williams, Henry T   *HisAmM XR*
Williams, Herbert Lee 1918-   *ConAu 1R,*
WhoAm 1974
Williams, Herbert Lloyd 1932-   *ConAu 29,*
ConP 1970, ConP 1975, WrDr 1976
Williams, Iolo Aneurin 1890-1962   *BioIn 6, LongC*
Williams, J H   *HisAmM XR*
Williams, Jack M 1886-   *WhJnl 1928*
Williams, James 1796-1869   *AmAu&B,*
DcAmB 20, DcNAA
Williams, James Cranston 1869-   *WhNAA,*
WhJnl 1928
Williams, James Robert 1888-1957   *BioIn 1,*
BioIn 2, BioIn 3, BioIn 4, BioIn 7,
NatCAB 47, WebBD

Williams, James Thomas 1881?-1969 *BioIn 8*
Williams, Jean 1924- *BioIn 3, BioIn 5*
Williams, Joe *NF*
Williams, John 1761-1818 *AmAu, AmAu&B,*
    AmJnl, BiD&SB, CnDAL, DcAmA,
    DcNAA, OxAm, OxEng, PoIre, REnAL,
    WebBD
Williams, John *see also* Pasquin, Anthony
Williams, John Alfred 1925- *AmAu&B, Au&Wr,*
    BlkAW, ConAu 53, ConLC 5,
    ConNov 1972, ConNov 1976, DrAF 1976,
    LivBAA, Pen Am, RAdv 1, WhoAm 1974,
    WorAu, WrDr 1976
Williams, John Francis 1887- *WhJnl 1928*
Williams, Sir John Francis 1901- *BioIn 4*
Williams, John L 1896?-1968 *BioIn 8*
Williams, John Lauris Blake 1893-1963 *BioIn 6*
Williams, John Shoebridge 1790-1878 *EarABI Sup,*
    HisAmM XR, OhA&B
Williams, John W d1837? *HisAmM XR*
Williams, Johnston 1879?-1957 *BioIn 4*
Williams, Joseph Peter 1893-1972 *BioIn 3,*
    BioIn 9, NewYTBE 3
Williams, June V *OvPC*
Williams, June Vanleer *OvPC*
Williams, Kathleen 1920?- *BioIn 9*
Williams, Kennard *WhJnl Sup*
Williams, Larry *NF*
Williams, Laurence Frederic Rushbrook 1890-
    IntWW 1976
Williams, Lillian 1901- *BioIn 7*
Williams, Logan H 1867- *WhJnl 1928*
Williams, Louise 1897- *WhJnl 1928*
Williams, Lyndell *NF*
Williams, Lynne 1931?- *BioIn 9*
Williams, Maynard Owen 1888-1963 *BioIn 9,*
    HisAmM XR, WhNAA
Williams, Michael 1877-1950 *AmAu&B, BioIn 1,*
    BioIn 2, BioIn 4, CathA 1930,
    HisAmM XR, REnAL, TwCA, TwCA Sup
Williams, Michaela *NF*
Williams, Miles Evans 1836- *HisAmM XR*
Williams, Minnie Olcott 1861- *WhJnl 1928*
Williams, Nick Boddie 1906- *IntWW 1976,*
    WhoAm 1974, WhoWest 1974
Williams, Paul *NF*
Williams, Paul F *OvPC*
Williams, Peter *Alli, BiDLA*
Williams, R B 1891- *WhJnl 1928*
Williams, Richard 1929- *BioIn 10*
Williams, Richard Lippincott 1910- *OvPC,*
    WhoAm 1974
Williams, Robert 1892-1953 *BioIn 3*
Williams, Robert H *NF*
Williams, Roger Lewis 1916- *WhoAm 1974,*
    WhoWest 1974
Williams, Roger M 1934- *ConAu 37*
Williams, Ross *NF*
Williams, Roy *BioIn 4*
Williams, Russel J 1944- *NF*
Williams, Samuel 1743-1817 *Alli, BioIn 5,*
    BioIn 8, CyAL 1, DcAmA, DcNAA,
    HisAmM XR
Williams, Samuel 1786-1859 *OhA&B*
Williams, Samuel 1788-1853 *Alli*
Williams, Samuel H *HisAmM XR*
Williams, Samuel M *NF*
Williams, Samuel Wells 1812-1884 *Alli, Alli Sup,*
    AmAu, AmAu&B, BiD&SB, DcAmA,
    DcNAA, WebBD
Williams, Sara Lawrence *BioIn 3*
Williams, Sara Lockwood *WhJnl 1928*
Williams, Sarah Langdon *HisAmM XR*
Williams, Shirley 1935- *WhoAm 1974*

Williams, Sidney Clark 1878-1949 *AmAu&B,*
    DcNAA, NatCAB 37, WhNAA
Williams, Spencer 1898?-1964 *BioIn 7*
Williams, Stephen 1949- *NF*
Williams, Steven Casey 1911?-1954 *BioIn 3*
Williams, Stuart 1936?- *BioIn 9*
Williams, T Walter d1942 *NF*
Williams, Talcott 1849-1928 *AmAu&B,*
    DcAmB 20, DcNAA, HisAmM XR,
    NatCAB 15, WebBD, WhJnl 1928
Williams, Thomas R 1878- *WhJnl 1928*
Williams, Valentine 1883-1946 *BioIn 1, BioIn 4,*
    CathA 1930, EncMys, HisAmM XR, LongC,
    NewC, TwCA, TwCA Sup, WhoLA
Williams, Vernon A 1881- *WhJnl Sup*
Williams, Walter 1864-1935 *AmAu&B, AmJnl,*
    BiDSA, BioIn 7, DcAmB S1, DcNAA,
    ForP, HisAmM XR, NatCAB 28, WhNAA,
    WhJnl 1928
Williams, Wilbur Herschel 1874-1935 *DcNAA,*
    IndAu 1816
Williams, Willard Wells 1870?-1948 *BioIn 1*
Williams, William 1787-1850 *BioIn 1, BioIn 2,*
    EarABI
Williams, William W *NF*
Williams, Wirt 1921- *BioIn 2, DrAS 74E*
Williams, Wythe 1881-1956 *AmAu&B, BioIn 4,*
    CurBio XR, HisAmM XR
Williamson, A J *BbtC*
Williamson, Al *NF*
Williamson, Amor J *HisAmM XR*
Williamson, Audrey 1913- *Au&Wr, ConAu 49,*
    WrDr 1976
Williamson, Bruce 1930- *AmSCAP 1966*
Williamson, Charles Clarence 1877-1965 *BioIn 7,*
    WhNAA
Williamson, George *OvPC*
Williamson, H L 1878- *WhJnl 1928*
Williamson, Lenora *NF*
Williamson, Merle 1880?-1961 *BioIn 6*
Williamson, Porter 1916- *NF*
Williamson, Samuel Thurston 1891-1962 *BioIn 6*
Williamson, Warren Pyatt, Jr. 1900-
    WhoAdv 1972, WhoAm 1974
Williamson, William *ForP*
Williamson, William J 1902?-1972 *BioIn 9,*
    NewYTBE 3
Willicombe, Joseph 1872?-1948 *BioIn 1*
Willicombe, Joseph, Jr. *OvPC*
Willing, Jennie F *HisAmM XR*
Willington, A S *AmJnl*
Willis, Anthony Armstrong 1897-1976 *ConAu 69,*
    Who 1974
Willis, Anthony Armstrong *see also* Armstrong,
    Anthony
Willis, C Delbert *RpN*
Willis, David K *NF*
Willis, Einfield *NF*
Willis, Ellen Jane 1941- *WhoAm 1974*
Willis, George Anthony Armstrong *see* Armstrong,
    Anthony
Willis, Henry Parker 1874-1937 *BiDSA,*
    DcAmB S2, DcNAA, WebBD, WhNAA,
    WhJnl 1928
Willis, John Alvin 1916- *ConAu 19R, WrDr 1976*
Willis, Julia *HisAmM XR*
Willis, L Clayton *OvPC*
Willis, Nathaniel 1780-1870 *AmAu&B, AmJnl,*
    BioIn 3, CyAL 2, DcAmB 20, HisAmM XR
Willis, Nathaniel Parker 1806-1867 *Alli, AmAu,*
    AmAu&B, BbD, BiD&SB, BioIn 1, BioIn 3,
    BioIn 4, BioIn 6, BioIn 7, BioIn 8, BioIn 9,
    BioIn 10, CasWL, CnDAL, CyAL 2,
    DcAmA, DcAmB 20, DcEnL, DcLEL,

HisAmM XR
Wilson, John Steuart 1913- *BiE&WWA,*
 WhoAm 1974
Wilson, Judith 1952- *NF*
Wilson, Keith Lewis 1912- *WhoAm 1974*
Wilson, Kenneth E *RpN*
Wilson, Kenneth Lee 1916- *ConAu 29,*
 WhoAm 1974
Wilson, Kenneth Ramsay 1903-1952 *BioIn 3*
Wilson, Kenneth W 1904- *WhJnl 1928*
Wilson, Lee *NF*
Wilson, Leo R 1888- *WhJnl 1928*
Wilson, Leslie Granville 1912- *ConAu 69*
Wilson, Louis Round 1876- *AmAu&B, AmLY,*
 BiDSA, BiDrLUS, WhNAA
Wilson, Lyle Campbell 1899-1967 *BioIn 6,*
 BioIn 7
Wilson, Margaret *NF*
Wilson, Mark 1888?-1950 *BioIn 2*
Wilson, Nancy *OvPC*
Wilson, Nelson Richard 1902- *WhJnl Sup*
Wilson, Noel Avon 1914- *ConAu 73, DrAS 74E,*
 WhoAdv 1972
Wilson, Philip Whitwell 1875-1956 *AmAu&B,*
 BioIn 4, LongC, TwCA Sup, WhNAA
Wilson, Phyllis Starr 1928- *WhoAmW 1974*
Wilson, R L 1889- *WhJnl 1928*
Wilson, Ray *NF*
Wilson, Richard C 1902?-1972 *BioIn 9*
Wilson, Richard Lawson 1905- *IntWW 1976,*
 WhoAm 1974
Wilson, Robert C 1870-1954 *NatCAB 41*
Wilson, Robert Forrest 1883-1942 *BioIn 4,*
 DcNAA, OhA&B
Wilson, Robert Forrest *see also* Wilson, Forrest
Wilson, Robert L 1900- *WhJnl 1928*
Wilson, Robert S 1905?-1967 *BioIn 8*
Wilson, Rowland Bragg 1930- *WhoAm 1974*
Wilson, Rudolph 1882- *WhJnl 1928*
Wilson, Russell 1876- *WhJnl 1928*
Wilson, Samuel Farmer 1805-1870 *Alli, BiDSA,*
 DcAmA, DcNAA
Wilson, Sloan 1920- *AmAu&B, ConAu 1,*
 ConNov 1972, ConNov 1976, CurBio XR,
 Pen Am, REnAL, WhoAm 1974, WorAu,
 WrDr 1976
Wilson, Steve *NF*
Wilson, Susan *NF*
Wilson, Theodora *OvPC*
Wilson, Thomas 1768?-1828? *DcAmA, DcNAA*
Wilson, Thomas B *NF*
Wilson, Thomas Williams, Jr. 1912- *ConAu 7R*
Wilson, Tom *NF*
Wilson, Upton Gwynn 1889-1945 *BioIn 1*
Wilson, Victor E *NF*
Wilson, William Grant 1864- *WhJnl 1928*
Wilson, Wood Levette 1865-1945 *BioIn 2,*
 IndAu 1816
Wilt, Matthew R *NF*
Wilton, Robert *NF*
Wimberly, Harrington 1901- *WhoAm 1974,*
 WhoS&SW 1973
Wimberly, Lowry Charles 1890-1959 *AmAu&B*
Wimbs, A D *WhJnl 1928*
Wimer, Arthur C 1904- *WhJnl 1928*
Wimmer, F *NF*
Wimpfen, Sheldon Phillip 1913- *AmM&W 73P,*
 BioIn 1, WhoGov 1972
Winans, Ione 1893- *WhJnl 1928*
Winans, Ray K 1894- *WhJnl 1928*
Winans, William H 1820?-1886 *DcNAA*
Winchell, Newton Horace 1839-1914 *Alli Sup,*
 DcAmA, DcNAA, HisAmM XR, WebBD
Winchell, Walter 1897-1972 *AmAu&B,*

AmSCAP 1966, BioIn 1, BioIn 2, BioIn 3,
 BioIn 4, BioIn 5, BioIn 8, BioIn 9,
 BioIn 10, ConAu 33, CurBio XR,
 NewYTBE 3, REnAL, WhJnl 1928
Winchester, Alice 1907- *AmAu&B, CurBio XR,*
 ForWC 1970, WhoAm 1974, WhoAmA 1973,
 WhoAmW 1974
Winchester, James Hugh 1917- *AmAu&B,*
 ConAu 17R, WhoAm 1974
Winchester, Jonas *HisAmM XR*
Winchester, Paul 1851-1932 *DcNAA*
Winchester, Simon 1944- *WrDr 1976*
Winchevsky, Morris 1856-1932 *AmAu&B,*
 DcNAA, REnAL, WebBD
Wind, Herbert Warren 1916- *ConAu 2R*
Windeler, Robert *NF*
Windham, Kathryn Tucker 1918- *ConAu 69*
Windle, Jerry 1942- *NF*
Windsor, Arthur Lloyd 1833?-1913 *BioIn 2*
Windsor, Garith *NF*
Windsor, Henry H 1859-1924 *NatCAB 15*
Windsor, Henry Haven, Jr. 1900- *WhNAA*
Winebrenner, D Kenneth 1908- *BioIn 3,*
 ConAu P-1
Winebrenner, David C 1897-1940 *NatCAB 30*
Winer, Jacob *HisAmM XR*
Wines, Frederick Howard 1838-1912 *Alli,*
 Alli Sup, DcNAA, HisAmM XR
Winfrey, Lee 1932- *ConAu 69*
Wing, Andrew S 1892- *WhJnl 1928*
Wing, Dewitt C *HisAmM XR*
Wing, Frank 1873- *AmAu&B*
Wing, Henry E 1840-1925 *BioIn 9, FamWC*
Wing, J M *HisAmM XR*
Wing, Joseph Elwyn 1861-1915 *BioIn 7, DcNAA,*
 HisAmM XR, OhA&B
Wing, Maurice J 1904- *WhoAm 1974*
Wingate, Charles Edgar Lewis 1861-1944 *Alli Sup,*
 AmAu&B, BioIn 1, DcAmA, DcNAA,
 HisAmM XR, NatCAB 33, WhNAA,
 WhJnl 1928
Wingate, Charles Frederick 1847-1909 *Alli Sup,*
 DcAmA, DcNAA, HisAmM XR
Wingate, Clara Blanche 1876- *WhJnl 1928*
Winger, Albert E 1883-1972 *HisAmM XR,*
 NewYTBE 2
Winger, C Glenn 1902?-1954 *BioIn 3*
Winget, Rader 1906?-1956 *BioIn 4*
Wingo, Hal *NF*
Wingo, Walter S 1931- *NF*
Winkleback, Sam H 1900- *WhJnl 1928*
Winkler, Herbert *NF*
Winkler, John Kennedy 1891-1958 *BioIn 5*
Winkler, Paul 1898- *IntWW 1976, OvPC*
Winkler, Wilbur Jennings 1896- *WhJnl 1928*
Winner, Charles H 1885-1956 *BioIn 4, BioIn 6,*
 NatCAB 43
Winner, Percy 1899-1974 *AmAu&B, AmNov,*
 BioIn 2, BioIn 10, ConAu 45, NewYTBS 5
Winnington, Alan 1915?- *BioIn 2, BioIn 3*
Winser, Henry Jacob 1833-1896 *Alli Sup,*
 DcAmA, DcNAA, NatCAB 10
Winsey, Val 1923- *NF*
Winship, Albert Edward 1845-1933 *AmAu&B,*
 AmLY, DcAmA, DcNAA, HisAmM XR,
 NatCAB 2, WhNAA, WhJnl 1928
Winship, Elizabeth 1921- *ConAu 41*
Winship, Frederick Moery 1924- *WhoAm 1974,*
 WhoWor 1974
Winship, Laurence Leathe 1890-1975 *BioIn 10,*
 WhoAm 1974
Winship, Thomas 1920- *BioIn 9, WhoAm 1974,*
 WhoE 1974, WhoWor 1974
Winslow, Dean Hendricks, Jr. 1934-1973

ConAu 37, ConAu 41

Winslow, Helen Maria 1851-1938 *AmAu&B,*
 AmLY, BiD&SB, DcAmA, DcNAA,
 HisAmM XR, WhNAA
Winslow, Horatio Gates 1882- *AmAu&B*
Winslow, John Seymour *WhJnl Sup*
Winslow, Ralph 1897- *WhJnl 1928*
Winslow, Sidney Wilmot, Jr. 1880-1963 *AmJnl,*
 BioIn 7, BioIn 8
Winslow, Thyra Samter 1893?-1961 *AmAu&B,*
 HisAmM XR, OxAm, REnAL, WhNAA
Winsmore, Robert 1876- *HisAmM XR, WhNAA*
Winsten, Archer 1904- *IntMPA 1975,*
 WhoAm 1974
Winster, Baron 1885- *CurBio XR*
Winston, Annie Steger d1927 *BiDSA, DcNAA*
Winston, Don C *NF*
Winston, Henry *AmRP*
Winter, Earl J 1904- *WhJnl 1928*
Winter, Ella 1898- *AmRP, BioIn 1, BioIn 6,*
 CurBio XR, HisAmM XR
Winter, James D 1893?- *WhJnl 1928*
Winter, Ruth *OvPC*
Winter, William 1836-1917 *Alli, Alli Sup,*
 AmAu, AmAu&B, AmJnl, BbD, BiD&SB,
 BioIn 7, CyAL 2, DcAmA, DcLEL,
 DcNAA, HisAmM XR, OxAm, REnAL,
 WebBD
Winterich, John Tracy 1891-1970 *AmAu&B,*
 AmJnl, BioIn 1, BioIn 4, BioIn 8, BioIn 9,
 ConAu 29, NewYTBE 1, OxAm, REnAL,
 TwCA, TwCA Sup
Winters, Ariel *NF*
Winters, Nancy *OvPC*
Winterton, Paul 1908- *ConAu 5R, EncMys,*
 WorAu
Wintour, Charles Vere 1917- *IntWW 1976,*
 Who 1974, WhoWor 1974
Wirges, Eugene H 1928?- *BioIn 7*
Wirsig, Woodrow 1916- *HisAmM XR, OvPC,*
 WhoAm 1974
Wirt, Sherwood Eliot 1911- *BioIn 9, ConAu 41,*
 WhoMW 1974
Wirth, Cliff *NF*
Wirth, Ed D d1970 *BioIn 9*
Wirth, Louis 1897-1952 *HisAmM XR*
Wisa, Louis 1876?-1953 *BioIn 3*
Wise, Alvin C 1895- *WhJnl 1928*
Wise, Daniel 1813-1898 *Alli, Alli Sup,*
 AmAu&B, BiD&SB, CarSB, DcAmA,
 DcNAA, HisAmM XR
Wise, David 1930- *AmAu&B, BioIn 5,*
 ConAu 2R, NewMr, WhoAm 1974,
 WrDr 1976
Wise, Erbon Wilbur 1920- *WhoAm 1974*
Wise, Hal M 1875- *WhJnl 1928*
Wise, Herbert C *HisAmM XR*
Wise, Herman J 1904- *WhJnl 1928*
Wise, Isaac Mayer 1819-1900 *Alli, Alli Sup,*
 AmAu&B, BiD&SB, DcAmA, DcNAA,
 EncAB, HisAmM XR, OhA&B, REnAL,
 WebBD
Wise, James Waterman 1901- *AmAu&B,*
 WhNAA
Wise, John Laing 1893- *WhJnl 1928*
Wise, Josh *see* Raper, John Wolfe
Wise, Lauress Lee 1919- *BioIn 8*
Wise, Stephen Samuel 1874-1949 *AmAu&B,*
 CurBio XR, REnAL, WebBD, WhNAA
Wiseman, Bernard 1922- *BioIn 9, ConAu 5,*
 SmATA 4, WrDr 1976
Wiseman, Rich *NF*
Wiseman, Thomas 1931- *Au&Wr, ConAu 25*
Wishengrad, Hyman 1903- *WhoAm 1974,*

WhoWorJ 1972

Wisherd, Edwin L *HisAmM XR*
Wisner, George W *AmJnl*
Wisner, Harry J 1875-1962 *NatCAB 50*
Wisner, William L *AuBYP, BioIn 8*
Wister, Emery *NF*
Witcover, Jules 1927- *AmAu&B, ConAu 25,*
 NewMr
Withers, Frank Caldwell 1870- *WhJnl 1928*
Withers, Hartley 1867-1950 *BioIn 2, BioIn 5,*
 WebBD, WhoLA
Witherstine, Horatio P *HisAmM XR*
Witt, Elder *NF*
Witte, George R 1895-1951 *BioIn 2, WhJnl 1928*
Witte, Mike *NF*
Witte, Sergius *HisAmM XR*
Wittenberg, Henri E 1931?- *BlkC*
Witter, James Clell *HisAmM XR*
Witze, Claude 1909?-1977 *ConAu 73*
Wiznitzer, Louis *NF*
Wjep-Olsen, Werner *NF*
Wodehouse, Sir Pelham Grenville 1881-1975
 AmAu&B, AmSCAP 1966, Au&Wr,
 AuNews 2, BiE&WWA, BioIn 1, BioIn 2,
 BioIn 3, BioIn 4, BioIn 5, BioIn 6, BioIn 7,
 BioIn 8, BioIn 9, BioIn 10, CasWL,
 CelR 1973, ConAu 45, ConAu 57, ConDr,
 ConLC 2, ConLC 5, ConNov 1972,
 ConNov 1976, CurBio XR, DcLEL, EncWL,
 EvLB, HisAmM XR, IntWW 1974, LongC,
 McGWD, ModBL, ModBL Sup, NewC,
 OxEng, Pen Eng, RAdv 1, REn, TwCA,
 TwCA Sup, TwCW, WebBD, WebE&AL,
 Who 1974, WhoAm 1974, WhoChL,
 WhoTwCL, WhoWor 1974
Woestendiek, Bill 1923?- *BioIn 8*
Woestendiek, Kay *BioIn 8*
Woestendiek, William J *RpN*
Wogan, Jere J *NF*
Wogan, Robert 1925- *WhoAm 1974*
Woggon, Elmer d1978 *NF*
Wohl, Jack *NF*
Wohl, Paul *OvPC*
Wojna, Ryszard 1920- *IntWW 1976*
Wolcott, Charles A 1896- *WhJnl 1928*
Wolcott, Frederick *HisAmM XR*
Wolcott, James *NF*
Wold, Erik *NF*
Wolf, Dan *NewMr*
Wolf, Frank G *NF*
Wolf, Lucien 1857-1930 *BioIn 3*
Wolf, Samuel A 1905- *WhJnl 1928*
Wolf, Thomas Howard 1916- *ConAu 69,*
 IntMPA 1975, WhoE 1974
Wolf, William *NF*
Wolf, William Almon 1885-1933 *HisAmM XR*
Wolf, William Almon *see also* Wolff, William Almon
Wolf, William Davis 1891- *WhJnl 1928*
Wolfard, Adolf d1951 *BioIn 2*
Wolfe, Edgar T 1925?-1975 *BioIn 4*
Wolfe, F I 1878- *WhJnl 1928*
Wolfe, George *NF*
Wolfe, Harry Preston 1872-1946 *BioIn 1, BioIn 2*
Wolfe, Henry Cutler 1898-1976 *AmAu&B,*
 ConAu 69, OhA&B, WhNAA,
 WhoAm 1974, WhoE 1974, WhoWor 1974
Wolfe, Laura 1884-1957 *BioIn 4*
Wolfe, Maynard Franks *OvPC*
Wolfe, Philip *WhJnl 1928*
Wolfe, Ralph Reed 1884?-1947 *BioIn 1*
Wolfe, Robert Huston 1899- *WhoMW 1974*
Wolfe, Thomas Kennerly, Jr. 1931- *AmAu&B,*
 ConAu 15R, WhoAm 1974, WhoWor 1974
Wolfe, Thomas Kennerly, Jr. *see also* Wolfe, Tom

CanWW 1972, CanWr, CasWL, ConAu 1,
ConP 1970, ConP 1975, ModBL, OxCan,
OxCan Sup, Who 1974, WhoAm 1974,
WrDr 1976
Woodcock, W H *HisAmM XR*
Woodfall, Henry Sampson 1739-1805 *Alli, WebBD*
Woodford, David 1906?-1948 *BioIn 1*
Woodford, Frank B 1903-1967 *ConAu 15,*
ConAu P-1
Woodhead, Henry George Wandesford 1883-1959
BioIn 5, WhoLA
Woodhouse, Henry 1884- *WebBD*
Woodhull, Victoria Claflin 1838-1927 *Alli Sup,*
AmAu, AmAu&B, DcNAA, OhA&B,
OxAm, REn, REnAL, WebBD
Woodhull, Zulu Maud *HisAmM XR*
Woodlief, Milton Wayne *NF*
Woodlock, Thomas Francis 1866-1945
CathA 1930, CurBio XR, DcNAA,
HisAmM XR, NatCAB 36
Woodman, C H *HisAmM XR*
Woodman, D K *NF*
Woodman, Dorothy d1970 *BioIn 9*
Woodridge, George L *HisAmM XR*
Woodrow, James 1828-1907 *AmAu&B, BbD,*
BiD&SB, BiDSA, HisAmM XR,
NatCAB 11
Woodruff, Douglas 1897-1978 *BioIn 1, BioIn 3,*
CathA 1930
Woodruff, Douglas *see also* Woodruff, John Douglas
Woodruff, Frank Edward 1855-1922 *DcNAA,*
HisAmM XR
Woodruff, Harvey T 1875- *WhNAA, WhJnl 1928*
Woodruff, John Douglas 1897-1978 *IntWW 1976,*
Who 1974
Woodruff, John Douglas *see also* Woodruff, Douglas
Woodruff, Judy 1946- *ConAu 73,*
WhoAmW 1974
Woodruff, Lee M 1899-1977 *WhJnl 1928*
Woodruff, Maurice 1916- *BioIn 7, BioIn 8*
Woodruff, William Edward 1795-1885 *BioIn 5,*
NatCAB 8
Woods, Charles Burton 1907-1965 *BioIn 7*
Woods, Donald *NF*
Woods, Frances Armstrong *HisAmM XR*
Woods, Frank E *HisAmM XR*
Woods, Franklin *HisAmM XR*
Woods, George A 1926- *ConAu 29*
Woods, Henry E 1857-1919 *HisAmM XR*
Woods, Howard B d1976 *NF*
Woods, J H *NF*
Woods, James B 1912- *WhoAm 1974*
Woods, Katherine Irvin 1886-1968 *AmAu&B,*
BioIn 8, WhNAA
Woods, Lawrence J *BioIn 9*
Woods, Leonard, Jr. 1807-1878 *Alli, CyAL 1,*
HisAmM XR
Woods, Rufus 1878-1950 *BioIn 2, WhJnl 1928*
Woods, Sherry *NF*
Woods, William Crawford 1944- *ConAu 29*
Woods, William Seaver 1872-1962 *AmAu&B,*
BioIn 6, BioIn 7, HisAmM XR,
NatCAB 47, WhNAA
Woodson, Carter Godwin 1875-1950 *AmAu&B,*
BioIn 1, BioIn 2, BioIn 3, BioIn 4, BioIn 5,
BioIn 6, BioIn 7, BioIn 8, BioIn 9,
BioIn 10, CurBio XR, REnAL
Woodson, Dorsey *NF*
Woodson, Marion Marle 1879-1933 *DcNAA*
Woodson, Urey 1859-1939 *DcNAA, NatCAB 29*
Woodstone, Arthur *ConAu 69*
Woodward, Bob 1943- *BioIn 9, InvJ, NewMr*
Woodward, Bob *see also* Woodward, Robert Upshur
Woodward, Carl Raymond 1890- *ConAu 41,*

DrAS 74H, LEduc 1974, WhJnl 1928
Woodward, Carol Helen 1898- *BioIn 2*
Woodward, Clement J 1850-1927 *NatCAB 22*
Woodward, Earl C 1889- *WhJnl 1928*
Woodward, Elizabeth *HisAmM XR*
Woodward, F W *Alli, HisAmM XR*
Woodward, Fred William 1888- *WhoAm 1974*
Woodward, George *HisAmM XR*
Woodward, George A 1835-1916 *HisAmM XR*
Woodward, George E *Alli, HisAmM XR*
Woodward, George Murgatroyd *HisAmM XR*
Woodward, Harold B 1892- *WhJnl 1928*
Woodward, J S *NF*
Woodward, James M *NF*
Woodward, John B *WhJnl 1928*
Woodward, John D *HisAmM XR*
Woodward, Joseph *HisAmM XR*
Woodward, Kenneth L *NF*
Woodward, Robert Upshur 1943- *AuNews 1,*
ConAu 69, WhoAm 1974
Woodward, Robert Upshur *see also* Woodward, Bob
Woodward, Stanley 1895-1965 *BioIn 1, BioIn 6,*
BioIn 7
Woodward, William *NF*
Woodward, William G 1883- *WhJnl Sup*
Woodworth, Frank D 1876- *WhJnl 1928*
Woodworth, Robert C 1902- *WhJnl 1928*
Woodworth, Samuel 1784?-1842 *Alli, AmAu,*
AmAu&B, AmJnl, BbD, BiD&SB, BioIn 5,
CyAL 1, DcAmA, DcLEL, DcNAA, EvLB,
HisAmM XR, McGWD, OxAm, Pen Am,
REnAL, WebBD
Woody, O H 1879- *WhJnl 1928*
Wool, Robert M *NF*
Wooldridge, Powhatan Jack, Jr. 1918-
WhoAdv 1972, WhoAm 1974
Woolf, Benjamin Edward 1836-1901 *DcAmA,*
HisAmM XR
Woolf, Bob *NF*
Woolf, Douglas G 1891- *WhJnl 1928*
Woolf, Leonard Sidney 1880-1969 *ConAu 7R,*
ConAu 25, DcLEL, EvLB, LongC, ModBL,
ModBL Sup, NewC, Pen Eng, RAdv 1,
REn, TwCA, TwCA Sup, TwCW, WebBD,
WhoLA
Woolf, Philip 1848-1903 *Alli Sup, DcAmA,*
DcNAA, HisAmM XR
Woolf, Samuel Johnson 1880-1948 *AmAu&B,*
BioIn 1, BioIn 2, BioIn 5, DcNAA,
HisAmM XR, REnAL, WhNAA
Woolfolk, E Joseph 1907-1969 *BioIn 9*
Woollcott, Alexander Humphreys 1887-1943
AmAu&B, AmJnl, BioIn 1, BioIn 2,
BioIn 3, BioIn 4, BioIn 6, BioIn 7, BioIn 8,
BioIn 9, CasWL, CnDAL, ConAmA,
CurBio XR, DcAmB S3, DcLEL, DcNAA,
EvLB, HisAmM XR, LongC, ModWD,
OxAm, REn, REnAL, TwCA, TwCA Sup,
WebBD
Woolley, Bryan 1937- *ConAu 49*
Woolley, Edward Mott 1867-1947 *DcNAA,*
HisAmM XR
Woolley, John *NF*
Woolman, David S 1916- *ConAu 29, WrDr 1976*
Woolsey, James J *HisAmM XR*
Woolson, F A 1883- *WhJnl 1928*
Wooster, Charles 1843-1922 *NatCAB 20*
Wooten, Terry *NF*
Wooton, Paul 1881-1961 *BioIn 5, WhJnl 1928*
Worcester, Noah 1758-1837 *Alli, BioIn 3,*
CyAL 1, DcAmA, DcNAA, HisAmM XR,
OxAm, WebBD
Worcester, Samuel 1770-1821 *Alli, DcAmA,*
DcNAA, HisAmM XR

Word, Lee B *NF*
Worden, Helen 1896- *AmAu&B, BioIn 1,*
  BioIn 5, WhoAm 1974, WhoAmW 1974
Worden, Herbert R 1891- *WhJnl 1928*
Worden, Wilbertine d1949 *BioIn 1*
Worden, William L 1910- *ConAu 15, ConAu P-1,*
  HisAmM XR
Wordham, Bill *NF*
Work, James A, Jr. 1904- *WhJnl 1928*
Workman, Frederick J 1886- *WhJnl 1928*
Workman, William Douglas, Jr. 1914- *ConAu 5R,*
  WhoAm 1974, WhoF&I 1974,
  WhoS&SW 1973, WrDr 1976
Worman, Ben James 1870- *HisAmM XR*
Worman, James Henry 1845?-1930 *Alli, DcAmA,*
  DcNAA, HisAmM XR, WhNAA
Wormser, Felix Edgar 1894- *AmEA 1974,*
  WhJnl 1928
Wormser, I Maurice 1887- *WhJnl Sup*
Wormser, Michael D *NF*
Wormwood, Robert S 1858- *WhJnl 1928*
Woron, Walter A *OvPC*
Worrall, John M *HisAmM XR*
Worsnop, Richard Laidlaw *NF*
Worster, J R *NF*
Worsthorne, Peregrine 1923- *ConAu 45*
Worth, C A 1877- *WhJnl 1928*
Worth, Gorham A 1783-1856 *Alli, DcNAA,*
  OhA&B
Worth, Patience *HisAmM XR*
Worth, Sol 1922?-1977 *NF*
Worth, Thomas 1834-1917 *Alli, EarABI,*
  EarABI Sup, HisAmM XR
Wortham, Hugh Evelyn 1884-1959 *BioIn 5*
Worthington, Alfred D *HisAmM XR*
Worthington, Helen *NF*
Worthington, James W 1891- *WhJnl 1928*
Worthington, Monroe 1904- *WhJnl 1928*
Worthington, Peter John 1927- *CanWW 1972*
Worthington, William C 1903- *WhJnl Sup*
Worthy, William *LivBAA*
Worthy, William, Jr. *RpN*
Wortis, Rose *AmRP*
Wortman, Denys 1887-1958 *BioIn 1, BioIn 3,*
  BioIn 5
Wortman, Helen Zene 1900- *WhJnl 1928*
Wostendiek, Jo *NF*
Wotherspoon, George 1861?-1949 *BioIn 2,*
  HisAmM XR
Wraga, Richard 1904?-1968 *BioIn 8*
Wragg, Joanne DiCarlo 1941- *WhoAm 1974*
Wragg, Otis *NF*
Wrangell, Baron George 1903?-1969 *BioIn 8*
Wray, Edwin Newton 1917- *WhoAdv 1972,*
  WhoAm 1974
Wray, F A *NF*
Wray, Laurence 1905- *BioIn 6*
Wreden, Nicholas 1901-1955 *AmAu&B,*
  NatCAB 48
Wren, Christopher S 1936- *ConAu 21R*
Wren, Percival Christopher 1885-1941 *CurBio XR,*
  DcLEL, EvLB, HisAmM XR, LongC,
  NewC, OxEng, Pen Eng, REn, TwCA,
  TwCW, WebBD
Wren, William Clinton 1891-1956 *BioIn 4,*
  BioIn 6, NatCAB 45
Wrench, Sir Evelyn 1882-1966 *BioIn 2, BioIn 7,*
  ConAu 7R, LongC
Wrenn, Charles Gilbert 1902- *AmM&W 73S,*
  BioIn 7
Wrensch, Frank Albert 1898- *WhJnl 1928*
Wright, Alfred, Jr. 1915?-1971 *BioIn 9,*
  NewYTBE 2
Wright, Arthur Justin 1889?-1954 *BioIn 3*

Wright, Arthur Walker 1855- *WhJnl 1928*
Wright, Ben G 1912- *OvPC, WhoAdv 1972,*
  WhoAm 1974, WhoF&I 1974
Wright, Benjamin Cooper 1834-1922 *DcNAA*
Wright, Boyd *NF*
Wright, Brooke Maynard 1877- *WhJnl 1928*
Wright, Clarence M 1905?-1967 *BioIn 8*
Wright, Cobina d1970 *BioIn 8, NewYTBE 1*
Wright, David McKee 1867?-1928 *BioIn 2,*
  DcLEL, PoIre
Wright, Dick *NF*
Wright, Don Conway 1934- *WhoAm 1974,*
  WhoS&SW 1973
Wright, Donald F *NF*
Wright, Donald T 1894-1965 *NatCAB 51*
Wright, Doug *NF*
Wright, Edan *BioIn 2, BioIn 5*
Wright, Ernest Hunter 1901-1968 *BioIn 8*
Wright, Fanny 1795-1852 *BiD&SB, DcAmA,*
  REnAL
Wright, Fanny *see also* Wright, Frances
Wright, Frances 1795-1852 *Alli, AmAu,*
  AmAu&B, AmJnl, HisAmM XR, OhA&B,
  OxAm, WebBD
Wright, Frances *see also* Wright, Fanny
Wright, Frank Gardner 1931- *InvJ, WhoAm 1974*
Wright, Frederick 1877-1952 *BbtC, BioIn 2,*
  PoIre
Wright, George Cable 1913?-1969 *BioIn 8*
Wright, George E 1851- *NatCAB 9*
Wright, George Frederick 1838-1921 *Alli Sup,*
  AmAu&B, AmLY, BiD&SB, DcAmA,
  DcNAA, HisAmM XR, OhA&B, WebBD,
  WhNAA
Wright, Guy *NF*
Wright, Guy W *HisAmM XR*
Wright, H C Seppings *FamWC*
Wright, Henry John 1866-1935 *AmJnl*
Wright, Hiram A 1823?-1855 *BioIn 5*
Wright, Holly *NF*
Wright, Horace 1891- *WhJnl 1928*
Wright, Hugh Elliott, Jr. 1937- *WhoAm 1974*
Wright, I B *HisAmM XR*
Wright, J T *HisAmM XR*
Wright, James Lloyd 1885-1952 *BioIn 3, WhNAA*
Wright, Jean *NF*
Wright, John E 1860-1924 *NatCAB 20*
Wright, John G *AmRP*
Wright, John R *HisAmM XR*
Wright, John Stephen 1815-1874 *Alli Sup, AmAu,*
  DcAmA, DcNAA
Wright, Joseph Franklin 1892- *WhJnl 1928*
Wright, Lawson M, Jr. *RpN*
Wright, Mary 1899?-1969 *BioIn 8*
Wright, Mitchell 1923?- *BioIn 1*
Wright, Muriel Hazel 1889?-1975 *BioIn 9,*
  ConAu 57, WhoAmW 1974,
  WhoS&SW 1973
Wright, Nathaniel C 1869-1923 *NatCAB 20*
Wright, Rawdon *HisAmM XR*
Wright, Richard A *NF*
Wright, Richard Robert, Jr. 1878-1967 *AmAu&B,*
  Au&Wr
Wright, Richardson Little 1887-1961 *AmAu&B,*
  BioIn 2, BioIn 3, BioIn 6, HisAmM XR,
  LiJA, REnAL, TwCA, TwCA Sup
Wright, Robert William 1816-1885 *Alli Sup,*
  AmAu&B, DcAmA, DcNAA
Wright, Robin *NF*
Wright, Rosalie Muller 1942- *NF*
Wright, Roy V 1876- *HisAmM XR, WhJnl 1928*
Wright, Rupert C *WhJnl 1928*
Wright, Theodore 1830-1924 *NF*
Wright, Theodore Francis 1845-1907 *Alli Sup,*

DcAmA, DcNAA, HisAmM XR
Wright, Virginia *NF*
Wright, W B *NF*
Wright, Wellington 1887- *WhJnl 1928*
Wright, Willard Huntington 1888-1939 *AmAu&B,
CnDAL, DcAmB S2, DcNAA, EncMys,
EvLB, HisAmM XR, LongC, OxAm,
Pen Am, REnAL, TwCA, TwCA Sup,
WebBD, WhNAA*
Wright, William 1824-1866 *Alli, DcAmA,
DcNAA*
Wright, William 1829-1898 *BioIn 1, DcAmB S1,
DcNAA, OhA&B, OxAm*
Wright, William 1930- *ConAu 53*
Wright, William Aldis 1836?-1914 *Alli, Alli Sup,
BbD, BiD&SB, BrAu 19, NewC, WebBD*
Wright, William Heermans 1900-1952 *OhA&B*
Wright, William Henry 1876-1951 *BioIn 2,
BioIn 3*
Wright, Winnifred *WhJnl 1928*
Wrightington, Sidney R *HisAmM XR*
Wrigley, Gladys Mary *BioIn 2, HisAmM XR*
Wronkow, George W *NF*
Wroth, Lawrence Counselman 1884-1970
*AmAu&B, ConAu 29, OxAm, REnAL,
WhNAA*
Wu, Edward K *NF*
Wulff, Louis Leopold Victor 1905- *Au&Wr,
BioIn 1, WrDr 1976*
Wulkotte, Bernard *NF*
Wunder, George 1912- *BioIn 1, BioIn 9*
Wunsch, William *NF*
Wurmbrand, Michael 1879-1952 *BioIn 4*
Wurts, William L 1857?-1948 *BioIn 1*
Wurz, John Francis 1885- *WhJnl 1928*
Wyant, G G *HisAmM XR*
Wyant, William K, Jr. *NF*
Wyatt, Edith 1873-1958 *HisAmM XR*
Wyatt, Edward Avery, IV 1910- *RpN,
WhoAm 1974, WhoS&SW 1973*
Wyatt, Eugene *NF*
Wyatt, Hugh *BlkC*
Wyatt, Joseph Paul 1942- *WhoAm 1974,
WhoS&SW 1973*
Wyatt, Susan *NF*
Wyatt, Virgil A 1899- *WhJnl 1928*
Wyatt, Woodrow 1918- *BioIn 3, BioIn 7*
Wyckoff, William Cornelius 1832-1888 *Alli Sup,
DcAmA, DcNAA, HisAmM XR*
Wyden, Peter H 1923- *AmAu&B, BioIn 8,
WhoAm 1974, WhoE 1974*
Wyder, Carl G *BioIn 8*
Wykert, John *NF*
Wylder, Robert Clay 1921- *ConAu 11R,
DrAS 74E*
Wylie, David 1811-1891 *BbtC, DcNAA*
Wylie, Francis E 1905- *ConAu 73*
Wylie, Jeff *ConAu XR*
Wylie, Joseph Caldwell, Jr. 1911- *WhoAm 1974*
Wylie, Josephine 1898- *WhJnl 1928*
Wyllie, Burnham *NF*
Wylly, W H *HisAmM XR*
Wyman, Julia E 1862?-1950 *BioIn 2*
Wyman, Walter Forestus 1881-1940 *DcNAA,
HisAmM XR, WhNAA*
Wyman, William W 1800?-1864 *BioIn 5*
Wyndham, Lee 1912- *AuBYP, ConAu 7R,
ForWC 1970, MorJA, SmATA 1,
WhoE 1974*
Wyngaard, Timothy J *NF*
Wynkoop, Rossman H 1897?-1958 *BioIn 4*
Wynn, Lloyd *NF*
Wynn, Octavia S 1891- *WhJnl 1928*
Wynn, Wilton *OvPC*

Wynn-Jones, Michael 1941- *ConAu 69*
Wynne, Arthur *NF*
Wynne, John Joseph 1859-1948 *BioIn 1, BkC 1,
CathA 1930, DcNAA, OxCan*
Wynne, Peter G *NF*
Wyrick, Bob *InvJ*
Wyrick, Charles R 1937?- *NF*

Y

Yaari, Ehud 1945- *ConAu 37*
Yablon, Leonard Harold 1929- *WhoAm 1974*
Yablonky, Ben 1911- *DrAS 74E, RpN*
Yaffe, Richard 1903- *ConAu 69, OvPC, WhoWorJ 1972*
Yahraes, Herbert C *RpN*
Yajima, Midori *NF*
Yakovitch, Linda *NF*
Yakstis, Ande *InvJ*
Yalcin, Huseyin Cahit 1875-1957 *BioIn 1, BioIn 4*
Yale, L P *NF*
Yale, Leroy Milton 1841-1906 *DcAmA, DcNAA, HisAmM XR*
Yalin-Mor, Nathan 1913- *BioIn 9, WhoWorJ 1972*
Yalman, Ahmet Emin 1888-1972 *BioIn 5, BioIn 9, BioIn 10, ConAu 37, NewYTBE 3*
Yalowitz, Gerson *NF*
Yamamoto, Kiyoshi *NF*
Yamashita, Stanley *NF*
Yancey, Ben C *HisAmM XR*
Yankelovich, Daniel 1924- *WhoAm 1974, WhoE 1974*
Yannopoulus, Yannis *NF*
Yao, Wen-Yuan 1924- *IntWW 1976*
Yarbrough, Charles *NF*
Yarbrough, William Thomas 1910- *WhoAm 1974*
Yard, Robert Sterling 1861-1945 *AmAu&B, AmLY, DcNAA, HisAmM XR, NatCAB 43, WhNAA, WhJnl 1928*
Yardley, Jonathan 1939- *ConAu 73, WhoS&SW 1973*
Yardley, Ralph 1880- *WhJnl 1928*
Yardley, Richard Quincy 1903- *BioIn 1, BioIn 5, WhoAm 1974, WhoE 1974, WhoWor 1974*
Yarman, Betty *NF*
Yarmon, Morton 1916- *ConAu 11R, WhoPubR 1972, WhoWorJ 1972*
Yarnell, Ray 1888- *WhJnl 1928*
Yaro, Boris *NF*
Yaroslavsky, Emelyan 1878-1943 *CurBio XR*
Yarros, Victor S 1865-1956 *BioIn 4, HisAmM XR*
Yates, Arthur B 1931?-1967 *BioIn 7*
Yates, Bill 1921- *BioIn 5*
Yates, Brock Wendel 1933- *AuBYP, BioIn 7, ConAu 11R*
Yates, Charles A *NF*
Yates, Edmund Hodgson 1831-1894 *Alli, Alli Sup, BbD, BiD&SB, BioIn 2, BrAu 19, DcEnA, DcEnL, DcEuL, DcLEL, EvLB, FamWC, HisAmM XR, HsB&A, NewC, REn, WebBD*
Yates, Emma Hayden Eames 1897?-1950 *BioIn 2, OhA&B*
Yates, Frederick Langdon 1931?-1967 *BioIn 7*

Yates, George W *NF*
Yates, John d1888 *NF*
Yates, Paul C 1892-1965 *BioIn 7*
Yates, Raymond Francis 1895-1966 *Au&Wr, AuBYP, MorJA, WhNAA*
Yates, Roberta M 1900- *WhJnl 1928*
Yates, Ronald *NF*
Yates, Ted 1930-1967 *NF*
Yates, Thomas L 1902- *WhJnl 1928*
Ybarra, Thomas Russell 1880- *BioIn 1, BioIn 4, CathA 1930, CurBio XR, HisAmM XR, REnAL, TwCA Sup, WebBD*
Yeadon, Clyde *BioIn 1*
Yeakley, Marjory Hall *see* Hall, Marjory
Yeats-Brown, Francis 1886-1944 *CurBio XR, DcLEL, EvLB, LongC, REn, TwCA, TwCA Sup, TwCW, WebBD*
Yee, Roger 1947- *NF*
Yeh, Francis 1907-1948 *BioIn 3*
Yeigh, Frank 1861-1935 *DcNAA, OxCan*
Yellin, Carol Lynn Gilmer 1920- *ConAu 19R, WhoAmW 1974*
Yerger, Roy *NF*
Yergin, Daniel *NF*
Yerkes, Charles Tyson 1837-1905 *AmJnl, HisAmM XR, WebBD*
Yerkes, Stephen *HisAmM XR*
Yerkes, Wally *NF*
Yermakov, Vladimir A 1924?-1978 *NF*
Yerrinton, J B *HisAmM XR*
Yerxa, Fendall Winston 1913- *BioIn 5*
Yette, Samuel F *BlkC, LivBAA*
Yglesias, Helen 1915- *ConAu 37*
Yindrech, Jan Holman *NF*
Ying, Diane *NF*
Yingling, Joseph 1893- *WhJnl 1928*
Yoakum, Robert 1922- *NF*
Yocom, Herbert Anderson 1907?-1957 *BioIn 4*
Yocum, David E *WhJnl 1928*
Yoder, Dorothy *NF*
Yoder, Edwin *NF*
Yoder, Jocelyn Paul 1884-1950 *BioIn 2*
Yoder, Robert McAyeal 1907-1959 *BioIn 5, HisAmM XR*
Yoes, Ralph *NF*
Yohe, Ralph Sandlin 1920- *WhoAm 1974*
Yohn, Frederick Coffay 1875-1933 *HisAmM XR*
Yolen, Steven H 1942- *ConAu 73, OvPC*
Yolen, Will Hyatt 1908- *ConAu 5R, OvPC, WhoAm 1974, WhoPubR 1972*
Yore, Clement 1875-1936 *AmAu&B, DcNAA, WhNAA*
York, H Boswell *NF*
York, Robert 1909-1975 *WhoAm 1974, WhoS&SW 1973*
Yorke, Henry Redhead 1772-1813 *Alli, BioIn 10*

Yorke, Ritchie 1944- NF
Yorston, Frederic 1871- WhJnl 1928
Yoshida, Kensei NF
Yoshimura, Shinsuke NF
Yoshizaki, Hirotaka NF
Yost, Casper Salathiel 1864-1941 AmAu&B,
    AmJnl, DcAmB S3, DcNAA, WhJnl 1928
Yost, Charles Woodruff 1907- ConAu 9,
    CurBio XR, IntWW 1974, WebBD,
    Who 1974, WhoAm 1974, WhoGov 1972,
    WhoWor 1974
Yost, Floyd H 1896- WhJnl 1928
Yost, Paul M 1902?-1968 BioIn 8
Yost, Robert M 1856-1916 NatCAB 16
Youle, Clint 1916- BioIn 2
Youman, Henry Mott 1851- WhJnl 1928
Youman, Roger Jacob 1932- ConAu 65
Youmans, Edward Livingston 1821-1887 Alli,
    AmAu, AmAu&B, BbD, BiD&SB, BioIn 1,
    BioIn 9, CyAL 2, DcAmA, DcNAA,
    HisAmM XR, WebBD
Youmans, Henry A 1894- WhJnl 1928
Youmans, Henry Mott 1851-1931 BioIn 5
Youmans, J W HisAmM XR
Youmans, Theodora 1863-1932 BioIn 5
Youmans, William Jay 1838-1901 Alli, AmAu&B,
    BiD&SB, CyAL 2, DcAmA, DcNAA,
    HisAmM XR, NatCAB 2, WebBD
Young, Alexander 1836-1891 Alli Sup, DcAmA,
    DcNAA, HisAmM XR
Young, Andrew White 1802-1877 Alli, BiD&SB,
    DcAmA, DcNAA
Young, Arthur Henry 1866-1943 AmAu&B,
    AmRP, DcAmB S3, DcNAA, HisAmM XR,
    OxAm, REnAL, WebBD, WhNAA
Young, Barbara NF
Young, Bertram Alfred 1912- ConDr, Who 1974,
    WhoThe 1972
Young, Charles Sommers 1873- WhJnl 1928
Young, Chic 1901-1973 BioIn 1, BioIn 3,
    BioIn 9, ConAu XR, NewYTBE 4,
    WhoAm 1974
Young, Chic see also Young, Murat Bernard
Young, Christopher NF
Young, Cortland H 1876-1930 HisAmM XR
Young, D Philip 1887- WhoAm 1974
Young, David NF
Young, Dean NF
Young, Desmond 1892?-1966 BioIn 6, BioIn 7
Young, Dick 1918?- BioIn 9
Young, Dwight Edwin 1884-1967 BioIn 2,
    BioIn 7, WhJnl 1928
Young, Edward C 1882- WhJnl 1928
Young, Edward S 1858-1914 NatCAB 16
Young, Edwin Parson 1908- WhoAm 1974,
    WhoF&I 1974
Young, Eugene Jared 1874-1939 DcNAA,
    WhJnl 1928
Young, Eugenie E 1874?-1950 BioIn 2
Young, Frank A WhJnl 1928
Young, George NF
Young, George Renny 1802-1853 Alli, BbtC,
    DcNAA
Young, Gordon NF
Young, Graham C OvPC
Young, H Walter 1890-1942 NatCAB 39
Young, Harry H 1825-1896 DcNAA
Young, Harvey R 1874- WhJnl 1928
Young, Hiram Walter 1890-1942 BioIn 4
Young, Hugo 1938- ConAu 25
Young, J F WhJnl 1928
Young, Jack 1882- WhJnl 1928
Young, James HisAmM XR
Young, James Capers 1888-1945 AmAu&B,

DcNAA
Young, James Lee NF
Young, James R NF
Young, James Rankin 1847-1924 AmJnl, DcNAA
Young, Jefferson 1921- BioIn 3
Young, John Frederick 1865-1947 BioIn 2,
    NatCAB 36
Young, John Philip 1849-1921 DcAmA, DcNAA,
    NatCAB 17
Young, John Russell 1840-1899 Alli Sup, AmAu,
    AmAu&B, AmJnl, BbD, BiD&SB, DcAmA,
    DcAmB 20, DcNAA, NatCAB 2, WebBD
Young, John Russell 1882-1966 BioIn 1, BioIn 7
Young, Joseph 1918- WhoS&SW 1973
Young, Julius R 1884- WhJnl 1928
Young, Kenneth 1916- Au&Wr, ConAu 9R,
    IntWW 1976, Who 1974, WhoWor 1974,
    WrDr 1976
Young, Lafayette 1848-1926 AmJnl, DcNAA,
    NatCAB 32
Young, Lafayette, Jr. 1878- WhJnl Sup
Young, Leah R 1942- NF
Young, Lewis Harold 1924- WhoAm 1974
Young, Lynn NF
Young, Marian 1909-1973 BioIn 2, BioIn 3,
    BioIn 10, CurBio XR
Young, Marjorie Willis ForWC 1970, OvPC,
    WhoAmW 1974, WhoS&SW 1973
Young, Mary Elizabeth Reardon BioIn 1,
    WhoAm 1974
Young, Murat Bernard 1901-1973 AmJnl,
    ConAu 41
Young, Murat Bernard see also Young, Chic
Young, N B BioIn 2
Young, Patrick 1937- AuBYP, BioIn 8,
    ConAu 69
Young, Perry Deane 1941- ConAu 57
Young, Peter NF
Young, Plummer Bernard 1884-1962 AmJnl,
    BioIn 7, NatCAB 49
Young, Plummer Bernard, Jr. 1909-1974 NF
Young, Ralph Harding WhJnl 1928
Young, Robert Cameron 1914- WhoAm 1974,
    WhoS&SW 1973
Young, Rose E 1869-1941 AmAu&B, DcAmA,
    DcNAA, WhNAA
Young, Samuel 1821-1891 AmAu&B, DcNAA
Young, Sarsfield HisAmM XR
Young, Scott Alexander 1918- ConAu 11R,
    OxCan, OxCan Sup, SmATA 5,
    WhoAm 1974
Young, Stanley Preston 1906-1975 AmAu&B,
    Au&Wr, ConAu 57, DrAS 74E, IndAu 1917
Young, Stark 1881-1963 AmAu&B, CasWL,
    CnDAL, ConAmA, ConAmL, CyWA,
    HisAmM XR, LongC, ModAL, OxAm,
    Pen Am, REnAL, TexWr, TwCA,
    TwCA Sup, WebBD, WhNAA
Young, Steve NF
Young, Thayne Harwood 1894- WhJnl 1928
Young, Thomas White 1908-1967 BioIn 8
Young, W W HisAmM XR
Young, Warren Richard 1926- ConAu 21R,
    OvPC, WhoE 1974
Young, Wayland 1923- ConAu 13R,
    IntWW 1974, Who 1974
Young, William HisAmM XR
Young, William 1809-1888 Alli, Alli Sup,
    DcNAA
Young, William Wesley 1868-1952 BioIn 3
Youngblood, Gene 1942- BioIn 10
Youngblood, Richard Neil 1936- WhoAm 1974
Younge, Shelia 1945?-1977 ConAu 73
Younger, J Kelley NF

Younghusband, Peter *NF*
Youngman, Elmer Haskell 1861-1948 *BioIn 1,*
    DcNAA, HisAmM XR, IndAu 1917
Youngman, Lawrence W 1905- *WhJnl 1928*
Youngs, Merwin W 1879- *WhJnl 1928*
Yu, Frederick T C 1921- *ConAu 11R, ForP*
Yu, Yu-Jen 1878-1964 *BioIn 7*
Yudain, Theodore 1907-1970 *NF*
Yui, David Z T 1882-1936 *WebBD*
Yun, Jong Min *NF*
Yuncker, Barbara *ForWC 1970, WhoAm 1974,*
    WhoAmW 1974
Yusof Bin Ishak 1910-1970 *BioIn 9*
Yust, Walter 1894-1960 *AmAu&B, BioIn 5,*
    CurBio XR, WebBD

Z

Zabel, Morton Dauwen 1901-1964 *AmAu&B,*
 HisAmM XR, TwCA Sup
Zabelka, John G 1902- *WhJnl 1928*
Zacharias, George J 1888?-1957 *BioIn 2, BioIn 4*
Zachary, Frank 1914- *WhoAm 1974*
Zagari, Mario 1913- *IntWW 1976*
Zagoria, Samuel D *RpN*
Zahn, Bob *NF*
Zahn, Leopold 1890-1965 *BioIn 7, BioIn 9*
Zahniser, Howard 1906-1964 *NatCAB 50*
Zaidan, Abe *NF*
Zaiser, Carol *NF*
Zakartan, John James 1938?- *NF*
Zakay, David 1886-1978 *WhoWorJ 1972*
Zakrzewski, Jan *NF*
Zalaznick, Sheldon 1928- *NF*
Zam, Herbert *AmRP*
Zamarripa Landi, Angel 1912- *BioIn 9*
Zamyatin, Leonid Mitrofanovich 1922-
 IntWW 1976, NewYTBE 1, WhoWor 1974
Zanger, Jack 1926?-1970 *BioIn 8*
Zangrandi, Ruggero 1915-1970 *BioIn 9, BioIn 10*
Zangwill, Israel 1864-1926 *BbD, BiD&SB,*
 CyWA, DcBiA, DcEnA Ap, DcEuL,
 DcLEL, EncMys, EncWL, EvLB,
 HisAmM XR, LongC, ModWD, NewC,
 OxEng, Pen Eng, TwCA, TwCW, WebBD
Zanker, Alfred *NF*
Zapp, Rudolphe De 1873- *WhJnl Sup*
Zarodov, Konstantin Ivanovich 1920- *IntWW 1976*
Zaslavskii, David Iosifovich 1879-1965 *BioIn 1,*
 BioIn 7
Zatt, Sol *OvPC*
Zavattini, Cesare 1902- *BioIn 2, CasWL,*
 CnMD, EvEuW
Zehrer, Hans 1899-1966 *BioIn 7*
Zeigler, Ron *NewMr*
Zeitlin, Arnodl *NF*
Zeitlin, Hillel 1870?-1942 *BioIn 9*
Zekman, Pamela Lois 1944- *InvJ, WhoAm 1974*
Zelditch, Morris, Jr. 1928- *AmM&W 73S,*
 ConAu 53, WhoAm 1974
Zelenka, Jan 1923- *IntWW 1976, WhoWor 1974*
Zelenka, Jerry M 1928- *NF*
Zellers, Margaret *NF*
Zelnick, C Robert 1940- *NF*
Zelnik, Joseph R 1933?- *NF*
Zeltner, Edward 1907?-1964 *BioIn 6*
Zemanek, Alexander 1921- *NF*
Zemer, Hanna *NF*
Zenger, Anna Catherine 1704?-1751 *AmJnl,*
 BioIn 1, BioIn 4, BioIn 5, BioIn 6
Zenger, John Peter 1697-1746 *Alli, AmAu,*
 AmAu&B, AmJnl, BioIn 1, BioIn 2,
 BioIn 3, BioIn 4, BioIn 5, BioIn 7, BioIn 8,
 BioIn 9, DcAmB 20, ForP, NatCAB 23,

 NewMr, OxAm, REn, REnAL, WebBD
Zenian, D *NF*
Zenier, Gene *OvPC*
Zenker, Arnold 1939?- *BioIn 8*
Zenkevich, Mikhail Aleksandrovich 1888- *BioIn 2*
Zenko, Franje *ForP*
Zerbe, Jerome 1904- *BioIn 9, CelR 1973,*
 ConAu 17, WhoAm 1974
Zerbey, Joseph Henry 1858-1933 *BioIn 2,*
 BioIn 4, NatCAB 39
Zerbey, Joseph Henry, Jr. 1888-1945 *NatCAB 34*
Zerner, Charles S 1897-1956 *BioIn 4*
Zevin, Israel Joseph 1872-1926 *WebBD*
Zhito, Lee *WhoAm 1974*
Zhukov, Iurii 1908?- *BioIn 8*
Zickler, James A 1865-1949 *BioIn 1, WhJnl 1928*
Ziebarth, Delores *NF*
Zieber, G B *HisAmM XR*
Ziedenberg, Leonard *NF*
Ziegfeld, William K, Jr. 1901- *WhJnl Sup*
Ziegler, Abraham *AmRP*
Ziegler, Edward 1870-1947 *AmAu&B*
Ziegler, Jack 1942- *NF*
Ziegler, P W *HisAmM XR*
Zielke, George Robert 1911- *WhoAm 1974,*
 WhoS&SW 1973
Ziemer, Gregor 1899- *ConAu 13, ConAu P-1,*
 CurBio XR, OvPC, WhoPubR 1972
Ziff, Howard M *NF*
Ziff, William Bernard 1898-1953 *AmAu&B,*
 BioIn 1, BioIn 3, CurBio XR, DcAmB S5
Ziff, William Bernard 1930- *AmAu&B*
Ziffren, Lester 1906- *OvPC, WhoF&I 1974,*
 WhoPubR 1972
Zigman, Joseph *OvPC*
Zilahy, Lajos 1891- *WebBD*
Zilboorg, Gregory 1890-1959 *AmAu&B, TwCA,*
 WebBD, WhNAA
Zilliacus, Konni 1894-1967 *BioIn 8*
Zillier, Carl 1838-1914 *BioIn 5*
Zilmer, Bertram G 1899?-1976 *ConAu 65*
Zimmerman, A Wallace 1898-1964 *BioIn 6,*
 NatCAB 51
Zimmerman, Eugene 1862-1935 *AmAu&B,*
 DcAmB S1, DcNAA, HisAmM XR
Zimmerman, Fred L *NF*
Zimmerman, M M 1889- *CurBio XR*
Zimmerman, Paul D *NF*
Zimmerman, Paul L 1932- *BioIn 9, ConAu 25*
Zimmerman, Richard G *NF*
Zimmerman, Thomas Cadwallader 1838-1914
 DcNAA
Zimmerman, William Dudley 1940- *ConAu 69,*
 ConAu 73
Zimyanin, Mikhail Vasilievich 1914- *IntWW 1976,*
 WhoWor 1974

Zinder, Harry NF
Zindler, Marvin 1921?- BioIn 10
Zingarelli, Italo 1891- IntWW 1976
Zingg, Charles J HisAmM XR
Zink, Lubor Jan 1920- ConAu 65, OxCan,
    OxCan Sup
Zinsser, William Knowlton 1922- BioIn 5,
    BioIn 6, ConAu 19, WhoAm 1974
Zion, Sidney NF
Zipser, Alfred R OvPC
Zismer, Gustave NF
Zito, Tom NF
Zittel, Theodore H 1902-1950 BioIn 2
Ziv-Av, Itzhak 1907- IntWW 1976,
    WhoWor 1974, WhoWorJ 1972
Zmaj, Jovan Jovanovic 1833-1904 BiD&SB,
    CasWL, Pen Eur
Zmaj, Jovan Jovanovic see also Jovanovic, Jovan
Zobeltitz, Hanns Von 1853-1918 WebBD
Zodac, Peter 1894-1967 BioIn 8
Zoercher, Philip 1866-1947 NatCAB 36
Zogbaum, Baird Leonard 1889?-1941 AmAu&B,
    DcNAA
Zogbaum, Baird Leonard see also Leonard, Baird
Zogbaum, Rufus Fairchild 1849-1925 Alli Sup,
    AmAu&B, AmJnl, BiD&SB, BiDSA,
    DcAmA, DcNAA, HisAmM XR
Zola, Emile 1840-1902 AtlBL, BbD, BiD&SB,
    CasWL, ClDMEL, CnThe, CyWA, DcBiA,
    DcEuL, EncWL, EuAu, EvEuW,
    HisAmM XR, McGWD, ModWD, NewC,
    OxEng, OxFr, Pen Eur, RComWL, REn,
    REnWD, WebBD, WhoTwCL
Zolciak, Kathleen NF
Zollicoffer, Felix Kirk 1812-1862 BioIn 5,
    DcAmB 20, NatCAB 11
Zollman, Joseph NF
Zolotow, Maurice 1913- AmAu&B, Au&Wr,
    BioIn 2, BioIn 4, ConAu 1, CurBio XR,
    REnAL, WhoAm 1974, WhoWorJ 1972,
    WrDr 1976
Zook, Nicholas NF
Zorek, Leon S 1902- WhJnl 1928
Zorthian, Barry 1920- WhoAm 1974,
    WhoF&I 1974
Zorza, Victor 1925?- BioIn 4
Zotos, Stephanos ConAu 23R
Zschiesche, Robert D NF
Zuber, J Osborn RpN
Zuccoli, Luciano 1870-1930 BioIn 1, ClDMEL
Zuckerman, Edward P NF
Zuckerman, George 1916- ConAu 53
Zuckerman, William 1885-1961 BioIn 6
Zuckoff, Murray NF
Zueblin, Charles 1866-1924 DcAmA, DcNAA,
    HisAmM XR, IndAu 1816, WebBD
Zukerman, Gloria OvPC
Zullen, Antoon Van OvPC
Zundelevich, Aaron NF
Zunser, Jesse 1898- BiE&WWA, IntMPA 1975
Zurawik, Dave NF
Zuver, John Henry 1873- BioIn 2, IndAu 1816
Zverina, Ivan NF
Zwart, Pieter 1938- ConAu 53
Zwasa, Charles A HisAmM XR
Zwerdling, Allen 1922- BiE&WWA
Zwerdling, Daniel NF
Zwick, Barry NF
Zwiedineck Von Sudenhorst, Hans 1845-1906
    WebBD
Zylstra, Donald L RpN